CREDIT MANUAL OF COMMERCIAL LAWS, 1986

CREDIT MANUAL OF COMMERCIAL LAWS, 1986

LESTER NELSON, J. D., LL.M., *Legal Editor*
Rabinovich, Nelson, Gordon & Burstein, *Counsel*

JAMES J. ANDOVER, *Editor*
National Association of Credit Management

Price $50

NATIONAL ASSOCIATION OF CREDIT MANAGEMENT

PUBLICATIONS DIVISION

520 EIGHTH AVENUE, NEW YORK, N.Y. 10018-6571

Pinpointed to pertinent chapters in this edition of the *Credit Manual of Commercial Laws* are summarizations of the past year's Federal and State legislation, and of 1984 measures passed after the 1985 issue went to press. Only statutory enactments by State legislatures are incorporated not local ordinances.

To be noted is the fact the contents of the publication must not be considered a substitute for the services of a competent attorney, nor does the National Association of Credit Management assume responsibility for any inadvertent misinformation or for omission of digests of legislation enacted after press time.

The editors have followed the Declaration of Principles adopted jointly by a Committee of the American Bar Association and a Committee of Publishers and Associations, as follows:

"This Publication is designed to provide accurate and authoritative information in regard to the subject matter covered. It is sold with the understanding that the publisher is not engaged in rendering legal, accounting or other professional service. If legal or other expert assistance is required, the services of a competent professional person should be sought."

ISSN: 0070-1467
ISBN: 0-934914-67-2
Library of Congress Catalog Card Number: 11-31760

Copyright 1986 by the National Association of Credit Management

All rights reserved
Printed in the United States of America
78th Edition

Table of Contents

TABLES AND STATUTORY SUM-
MARIES xiii

FEATURES

RECENT LEGISLATION OF
  INTEREST xix
WHEN REJECTION OF NON-
  CONFORMING GOODS COULD BE
  DEEMED AN ACCEPTANCE xxxi
WHEN "IN FULL PAYMENT" ISN'T
  ENOUGH xxxiv
THE BATTLE OF THE FORMS:
  VARIANCE WITH PURCHASE
  AND SALES TERMS xxxvi
RECENT CASES OF INTEREST xxxviii

Chapter 1
UNIFORM COMMERCIAL CODE

Background and Introduction 1-1
Main Subjects under Code:
  Article 1: General Provisions 1-2, 1-21
  Article 2: Sales 1-3, 1-28
    General Provisions 1-28
    Form, Formation, Readjustment .. 1-30
    General Obligation and Con-
      struction of Contract 1-33
    Title, Creditors, Good Faith
      Purchasers 1-43
    Performance 1-46
    Breach, Repudiation, Excuse 1-51
    Remedies 1-56
  Article 3: Commercial Paper 1-7, 1-62
  Article 4: Bank Deposits and Col-
    lections 1-9, 1-62
  Article 5: Documentary Letters
    of Credit 1-12, 1-63
  Article 6: Bulk Transfers 1-12, 1-69
  Article 7: Warehouse Receipts, Bills
    of Lading and Other Documents
    of Title 1-13, 1-69
  Article 8: Investment Securities . 1-14, 1-76
  Article 9: Secured Transactions . 1-15, 1-76
  Article 10: Effective Date and Re-
    pealer 1-76

Article 11: Effective Date and
  Transition Provisions 1-76

Chapter 2
THE LAW OF CONTRACTS—
LEGAL REQUIREMENTS

General 2-1
Essentials of a Valid Contract 2-1
OFFER AND ACCEPTANCE 2-1
  Communication of Offer 2-2
  Duration of Offer 2-2
  Termination of Offer 2-3
  Acceptance of Offer 2-3
  Unilateral and Bilateral Offers 2-4
  Orders Solicited By Salespersons 2-4
  Rejection of Offer 2-5
  Counteroffer 2-5
  Communication of Acceptance 2-6
  Acceptance by Telegraph 2-6
  Silence as Acceptance 2-7
COMPETENCY OF THE PARTIES 2-7
  Infants 2-7
  Competency of Infants—Table 2-8
  Married Women 2-11
  Insane Persons 2-11
  Corporations 2-11
  Agents 2-12
LEGALITY OF SUBJECT MATTER 2-12
CONSIDERATION 2-12
  Mutuality of Consideration 2-13
  Inadequacy of Consideration 2-13
  Composition of Creditors 2-14
  Statutes Affecting Consideration 2-14
  Special Statutes 2-15

Chapter 3
CONTRACTS—DISCHARGE AND
ENFORCEMENT

General 3-1
Interpretation of Contracts 3-1
How Contracts Are Discharged 3-2
Tender of Performance 3-3
Mistakes in Contracts 3-5
Fraudulent Contracts 3-5
Reality of Consent 3-5
Accord and Satisfaction 3-6
Assignments of Contracts 3-6

TABLE OF CONTENTS

Enforcement 3-6
Limitations for Suit 3-6

Chapter 4
CONTRACTS—FORMAL REQUIREMENTS

General 4-1
Classification of Contracts 4-1
The Statute of Frauds 4-1
Written Memorandum Required 4-2
STATUTORY REQUIREMENTS 4-2
  Sale of Land 4-3
  Not to Be Performed within a Year .. 4-3
  Promise by Executor or Administrator 4-3
  Special Promise 4-4
  Debt of Third Person 4-4
  Consideration of Marriage 4-4
  Sales of Goods or Personalty 4-4
  Uniform Commercial Code Provisions 4-5
  Representations as to Credit 4-5
  Promises to Pay Debts Contracted in Infancy 4-6
  Agreement Not to Be Performed During Life of Promisor 4-6
  Assignment of Wages 4-6
  Sale of Vessels 4-6
  Chattel Mortgages 4-7
SPECIAL STATUTORY PROVISIONS:
  In Louisiana 4-7
  In California 4-7
  Table of State Laws 4-8
Signatures on the Contract 4-15
Signature by Agents 4-16
Acknowledgments on Contracts 4-17
Contracts Under Seal 4-18

Chapter 5
TERMS OF PAYMENT IN COMMERCIAL CONTRACTS

General 5-1
Variance in Payment Terms 5-1
CASH TERMS 5-1
When Does Title Pass? 5-2
Two Legal Situations 5-2
Short Credit Terms 5-3
Offer of a Discount for "Cash" 5-3
Terms of Payment 5-3
Varieties of Cash Discounts 5-4
"Prox" and "Ult" Terms 5-4
"R.O.G." and "A.O.G." Terms 5-5
Ruling on Quantity Discounts 5-5
Validity of Cash Discounts 5-5

Chapter 6
SECURED TRANSACTIONS SUPERSEDED BY UNIFORM COMMERCIAL CODE ARTICLE 9

Bailments 6-1
CONSIGNMENTS 6-2
  May Require Return of Goods 6-3
  Obligations of Consignee 6-4
  UCC Provisions 6-4
LEASES 6-4
TRUST RECEIPTS 6-5
CONDITIONAL SALES CONTRACTS 6-5
  Form of Contract 6-6
  Sales of Fixtures 6-6
  Where Goods Are for Resale 6-7
CHATTEL MORTGAGES 6-7
  Louisiana 6-8
ASSIGNMENT OF ACCOUNTS RECEIVABLE 6-9
  Summary of Laws in Louisiana 6-10
FACTORS' LIEN LAWS 6-10

Chapter 7
SECURED TRANSACTIONS UNDER ARTICLE 9 UNIFORM COMMERCIAL CODE

INDEX TO SECURED TRANSACTIONS UNDER CODE 7-1
OUTLINE OF MECHANICS 7-2
  Creating the Security Interest 7-2
  Perfecting the Security Interest 7-2
  Financing Statement Form 7-5
  Financing Statement (Form) (Massachusetts, etc.) 7-6
  Financing Statement (Form) (Indiana, etc.) 7-7
  When Filing Is Required 7-4, 7-7
  When Interest Perfected 7-8
  Instruments or Documents 7-8, 7-19
  When Possession Perfects Interest 7-9
  Place of Filing and Fees 7-9, 7-30, 7-33
  Erroneous Filing 7-9
  Formal Requisites of Financing Statements 7-10
  Formal Requisites of Amendments ... 7-10
  Duration of Filing; Lapse 7-12
  Continuation Statement 7-12
  Filing Fee 7-13, 7-30
  Termination 7-13
  Assignment of Security Interest 7-14
  Release of Collateral 7-14
  Multiple State Transactions 7-15
  Property Brought into State 7-15
  Rights of Third Parties 7-17
  Rights of Buyer of Goods 7-18
  Rights of Purchaser of Chattel Paper and Instruments 7-18
  Rights of Purchasers of Instruments and Documents 7-19
  Priority of Certain Liens 7-19

TABLE OF CONTENTS

Priorities among Conflicting Security Interests in Same Collateral 7-19
Priorities of Security Interest in Fixtures 7-20
Priority When Goods Are Affixed to Other Goods 7-22
Priority When Goods Are Commingled or Processed 7-22
Priority Subject to Subordination 7-23
Security Interest Continues in Proceeds 7-23
Secured Party Not Obligated on Contract of Debtor 7-23
Defenses Against Assignee; Modification of Contract after Notification of Assignment; Term Prohibiting Assignment Ineffective; Identification and Proof of Assignment 7-23
When Security Interest Attaches 7-24
After-Acquired Property: Future Advances 7-25
Use or Disposition of Collateral Without Accounting Permissible ... 7-25
Agreement Not to Assert Defenses Against Assignee; Modification of Sales Warranties 7-25
Rights and Duties When Collateral Is in Secured Party's Possession 7-25
Request for Statement of Account or List of Collateral 7-26
Secured Party's Right upon Default 7-27
ARTICLE 9 UCC 1962 TEXT 7-27
INFORMATION FROM FILING OFFICER .. 7-30
FEES PAYABLE TO FILING OFFICER (by States) 7-30
FILING REQUIREMENTS ON FINANCING STATEMENTS (by States) 7-33

Chapter 8

RETAIL INSTALMENT SALES LAWS

State Statutes 8-1
Contract Requirements 8-1
Licensing Provisions 8-3
Insurance Provisions 8-4
Provisions Prohibited 8-4
Refinancing, Extensions and Rescheduling 8-5
Remedies of Seller 8-5
Penalties 8-7
Filing and Recording 8-7
State Laws 8-8

Chapter 9

FEDERAL AND STATE CONSUMER PROTECTION LEGISLATION

FEDERAL LAW 9-1
Fair Credit Reporting Act 9-4

Fair Credit Billing Act 9-7
Consumer Leasing Act 9-7
Consumer Products Safety Act 9-7
Equal Credit Opportunity Act 9-7
States' Truth in Lending Legislation 9-8
State Consumer Protection Legislation .. 9-20
General Consumer Protection Legislation 9-23
UNIFORM CONSUMER CREDIT CODE ... 9-24

Chapter 10

LEASING OF PERSONAL PROPERTY

Kinds of Leases Involved 10-1
Federal Consumer Leasing Act 10-1
Federal and State Laws 10-2–10-11

Chapter 11

COLLECTION AGENCY REQUIREMENTS AND PROHIBITED PRACTICES

General 11-1
Federal Trade Commission 11-1
Fair Debt Collection Practices Act 11-1
State Laws—Summary of Requirements, Exemptions, and Prohibited Practices 11-3–11-27

Chapter 12

THE CREDIT CARD— ITS LEGAL IMPLICATIONS

Forms of Credit Card Plans 12-1
Contractual or Civil Obligations 12-2
Lost, Stolen or Misused 12-3
Criminal Liability for Misuse 12-6
State Criminal Statutes 12-7
Federal Criminal Statutes 12-9

Chapter 13

ANTITRUST AND TRADE REGULATION LAWS

Sherman Act 13-1
Clayton Act 13-4
Robinson-Patman Act 13-5
Federal Trade Commission Act 13-12
Antitrust Procedures and Penalties Act 13-13
1976 Antitrust Act 13-14
State Antitrust Laws 13-14
Fair Trade Acts 13-15
Exchange of Credit Information 13-16
Court Decisions 13-18
Membership in Credit Groups 13-21

TABLE OF CONTENTS

Chapter 14
CORPORATIONS

Definition of a Corporation	14-1
Advantages of Incorporation	14-1
LIABILITY FOR CORPORATE DEBT	14-2
DOMESTIC CORPORATIONS	14-3
Constitutional Provision	14-4
FOREIGN CORPORATIONS	14-3
Constitutional Restrictions	14-5
Licensing Procedures	14-5
Penalties for Interstate Violations	14-6, 14-7
INTERSTATE BUSINESS, WHAT CONSTITUTES	14-7
Sales by Salesmen or by Mail	14-9
Isolated Transactions	14-9
Institution of Suit	14-10
Sales by Samples	14-10
Installations, Construction Work	14-10
When Interstate Business	14-11
When Not Interstate Business	14-11
Sale of Goods Stored in State	14-12
Free Port Laws	14-12
Consignment Sales	14-12
Office, Salesroom in Foreign State	14-13
Principal Place of Business	14-13
Jurisdiction Over Nonresidents—"Long-Arm Statutes"	14-14
Guaranties by Corporations	14-17
When Guaranty Is Authorized	14-17
Corporations as Guarantors	14-18
Between Parent and Subsidiary	14-19
COMMON LAW OR MASSACHUSETTS TRUSTS	14-19
Powers and Liabilities of Trustees	14-20
Business Trust as Partnership	14-20
Subject to Law of Foreign Corporations	14-21

Chapter 15
PARTNERSHIPS—JOINT VENTURES

Partnerships	15-1
How Partnerships Are Formed	15-1
Uniform Partnership Acts	15-2
State Statutes Apply	15-2
The Partnership Contract	15-3
Partners Jointly Liable	15-4
Dissolution of Partnerships	15-4
Continuation After Death of Partner	15-5
LIMITED PARTNERSHIPS	15-6
How Formed	15-7
Relationship to Third Persons	15-7
HUSBAND-WIFE PARTNERSHIPS	15-8
JOINT VENTURES	15-9

Chapter 16
PRINCIPAL AND AGENT

General Discussion of Agency	16-1
How Agents Are Appointed	16-1
Subagents	16-2
Liability of Agent Where Principal Is Undisclosed	16-2
Duties of Agent	16-2
Employees and Independent Contractors	16-3

Chapter 17
COMMUNITY PROPERTY LAWS

States Having Community Property Laws	17-1
Property Divided on 50-50 Basis	17-1
Questions of Interest to the Creditor	17-2
Property Presumed to Belong to Community	17-3
Husband's Dominion	17-3
Creditors and the Community Property	17-4
Upon Death of Spouse	17-4
Pitfalls for Creditors	17-5
General Remarks	17-5
Equitable Distribution	17-6

Chapter 18
LAWS GOVERNING NEGOTIABLE INSTRUMENTS

Uniform Commercial Code Governs Except in Louisiana	18-1
What Instruments Are Negotiable	18-1
Rules of Construction	18-2
Persons Liable	18-2
Who May Execute	18-2
Indorser Before Delivery	18-2
Consideration	18-2
Accommodation Party	18-2
Acceptance	18-2
Bearer Instrument	18-2
Liability of Indorsers	18-3
Negotiation	18-4
Warranties	18-4
Holder in Due Course	18-4
Collection	18-4
Discharge	18-6
Defenses	18-6
Checks	18-7
VALIDITY OF STIPULATION FOR ATTORNEYS' FEES OR COLLECTION COSTS	18-7
Interpretation by the Courts	18-8
JUDGMENT NOTES	18-9
Table, by States	18-10–18-14

TABLE OF CONTENTS

"Trade" and "Bank" Acceptances 18-14
Legal Nature and Incidents of Trade Acceptances 18-16
Effect on Lien 18-19
Letters of Credit 18-20
Checks, Special Provisions 18-21
Checks for Less Than One Dollar .. 18-21
Checks "In Full of Account" 18-21
Stopping Payment on Checks 18-22
Interest and Usury 18-23
Interest Table by States 18-26–18-36
Corporate Usury Defense by States 18-37–18-38
Interest on Past Due Accounts 18-39
Interest on Credit Sales 18-43
Finance or Service Charges 18-43
Calculation of Interest 18-44
Accommodation Paper 18-45

Chapter 19
MECHANIC'S LIEN LAWS AND FEDERAL TAX LIEN LAW

Federal Tax Liens 19-1
Objective of Tax Lien 19-1
Exceptions 19-1
Mechanic's Lien Laws 19-2
Who May File Lien 19-2
Subcontractor's Lien Rights 19-3
Effect of Provision in Contract Against Mechanic's Lien 19-4
Summary of State Laws 19-6–19-64

Chapter 20
PERSONAL PROPERTY LIENS

Statutory Liens vs Common Law Liens 20-1
Summary of State Laws:
Alabama ..... 20-1 Kansas 20-9
Alaska .... 20-2 Kentucky 20-9
Arizona ...... 20-3 Louisiana 20-10
Arkansas ..... 20-4 Maine 20-10
California .... 20-4 Maryland 20-11
Colorado ..... 20-4 Massachusetts . 20-11
Connecticut .. 20-5 Michigan 20-12
Delaware .... 20-5 Minnesota ... 20-12
District of   Mississippi ... 20-13
Columbia ... 20-5 Missouri 20-13
Florida .... 20-5 Montana 20-13
Georgia ...... 20-6 Nebraska 20-14
Hawaii .... 20-6 Nevada 20-15
Idaho .... 20-6 New
Illinois 20-7   Hampshire .. 20-15
Indiana ...... 20-7 New Jersey ... 20-16
Iowa .... 20-8 New Mexico .. 20-17
New York .... 20-18 South Dakota . 20-23
North   Tennessee..... 20-24
Carolina .... 20-19 Texas 20-24
North Dakota . 20-19 Utah 20-24
Ohio .... 20-20 Vermont 20-25
Oklahoma ... 20-20 Virginia 20-25
Oregon ...... 20-21 Washington ... 20-25
Pennsylvania .. 20-22 West Virginia . 20-27
Rhode Island .. 20-22 Wisconsin 20-27
South   Wyoming 20-28
Carolina 20-22
Landlords' Liens 20-29
Summary of State Laws 20-30–20-33

Chapter 21
BAD CHECK LAWS AND FALSE CREDIT INFORMATION

Nature of the Crime 21-1
Constitutionality 21-1
Time Within Which Check May Be Made Good 21-2
Limitations—By States 21-3
Checks in Payment of Preexisting Debts 21-3
Stopping Payment on Checks 21-4
Postdated Checks 21-4
Table of State Laws on Bad Checks 21-6–21-11
Necessity of Damage 21-12
Sufficiency of Notice............... 21-12
Rules of Evidence 21-12
To Whom Statutes Apply 21-13
Applying the Statute 21-13
Civil Penalties 21-13
Miscellaneous 21-14
Other Commercial Crimes 21-15
Use of Mails, Wire, Radio or Television to Defraud 21-15
Required Proof 21-17
False Financial Statements 21-19
Bankruptcy 21-19
Perjury........................ 21-20
Misappropriation of Security Interest......................... 21-20
Civil Liability for Issuing False Credit Information 21-20
Interpretation by the Courts 21-22

Chapter 22
ASSUMED OR FICTITIOUS NAMES

Forms of Statutes 22-1
Statutes Usually Penal 22-1
Effect of Noncompliance 22-1
In Case One Partner Retires 22-2
Corporations 22-2
Summary of State Laws 22-3–22-17

TABLE OF CONTENTS

Chapter 23
LEGAL PHASES OF COLLECTIONS

Importance of Collection to Every Business	23-1
COLLECTION METHODS	23-1
Extortion	23-2
Examples of Extortion	23-2
Don'ts for Collection Letters	23-3
Prohibited Collection Practices	23-3
Libel Per Se	23-4
Postal Laws	23-6
Privilege	23-6
Invasion of the Right of Privacy	23-6
State Statutes Penalizing Non-Payment	23-8
Prompt Payment Statutes	23-8
DEBT POOLING PLANS	23-8
Trade Association Practices	23-9
State Statutes Summarized	23-10–23-14
COLLECTION BY SUIT	23-15
Security for Costs	23-15
Collection Fees	23-15
Need for Full Information	23-15
STATES' LAWS ON CONFESSIONS OF JUDGMENT	23-17
STEPS IN SUITS	23-20
Attachment	23-20
Garnishment	23-21
State Statutes Differ	23-22
Wage Garnishments	23-22
Judgment, Execution and Levy	23-24
Supplementary Proceedings	23-25
Judgment Liens	23-25
Enforcement of Judgments	23-33
Replevin	23-34
LIMITATIONS OF ACTIONS	23-36
When Statute Begins to Run	23-37
What Law Governs	23-37
States' Laws on Tolling of Statute and Reviving of Barred Debt	23-38–23-40
Part Payment, Acknowledgment of Debt and New Promise	23-41
Limitations of Actions on Judgments	23-41
Lost Documents in Suits	23-41
Limitations for Civil Actions	23-42–23-45
EXEMPTIONS	23-46
Waivers of Exemptions, by States	23-46
Table of States Which Require Debtor to File Written Statement Claiming Personal Exemption and Household Exemption	28-48–23-49
Execution Exemptions	23-50–23-61
Exemptions on Insurance, by States	23-61
SOLDIERS' AND SAILORS' CIVIL RELIEF ACT	23-66
Protection Against Default Judgments	23-66
Stay of Proceedings	23-66
Stay of Foreclosure	23-67
Miscellaneous Provisions	23-67
ENFORCEABILITY OF ARBITRATION CLAUSE	23-69

Chapter 24
CLAIMS AGAINST DECEDENTS' ESTATES

How to File Claim Against Estates of Deceased Persons	24-1
When Claim Must Be Sworn to	24-1
Summary of State Laws	24-1–24-8

Chapter 25
SALES AND USE TAXES

Types of Sales Taxable	25-1
Use Taxes	25-2
State Taxation of Interstate Transactions	25-2
Court Decisions	25-2
Federal Legislation	25-8
SUMMARY OF STATE LAWS ON SALES AND USE TAXES	25-9–25-18

Chapter 26
FRAUDULENT CONVEYANCES—BULK TRANSFERS

Distinction in Intent	26-1
BULK TRANSFERS	26-2
UNIFORM COMMERCIAL CODE PROVISIONS	26-3
TRANSACTIONS WITHIN THE STATUTES	26-8
EFFECT OF NONCOMPLIANCE	26-8
CREDITORS' REMEDIES	26-8
SUBSEQUENT PURCHASES	26-9
ATTACKING SALES	26-9
LIST OF CREDITORS	26-9
PLACE OF FILING OR RECORDING IN STATES	26-10–26-11

Chapter 27
ASSIGNMENTS FOR BENEFIT OF CREDITORS—EQUITY RECEIVERSHIPS

General Discussion	27-1
Assignments and Bankruptcy	27-1
Duties of Assignee	27-2
Summary of State Laws	27-3–27-9
EQUITY RECEIVERSHIPS	27-9
STATE RECEIVERSHIPS	27-10

Chapter 28
BANKRUPTCY—SUMMARY OF PROCEDURE

Terminology	28-1
Who May File Petitions	28-2
By Whom and When an Involuntary Petition May Be Filed	28-3
Contested Petitions (Subpoena)	28-3
Automatic Stay	28-3
Adequate Protection	28-4
Duties of Debtor	28-5
Interim Trustees	28-5
Examination and Immunity of Debtor	28-6
Meetings of Creditors	28-6
Election of Trustee	28-6
Creditors' Committee	28-6
The Estate	28-7
The Trustee: Duties, Powers and Compensation	28-7
Duties	28-7
Sale, Use and Lease of Property	28-8
Obtaining Credit	28-8
Powers of Trustee	28-9
Executory Contacts	28-10
Compensation	28-10
Exemptions	28-10
Allowance of Claims	28-11
Proof of Claims	28-12
Secured Claimholders	28-12
Priority Claims	28-13
Fees	28-13
Dismissal	28-14
Discharge	28-14
Eligibility	28-14
Grounds for Denial of Discharge	28-14
Objections to Discharge	28-15
Revocation of Discharge	28-15
Scope of Discharge	28-15
Criminal Offenses	28-17
The Bankruptcy Court System and the Appeals Procedure	28-18
Notices	28-19
Turnover Proceedings	28-19
Distribution of Property of the Estate	28-20
Reclamation Proceedings	28-20
Liens	28-21
Setoff	28-22
Voidable Preferences	28-22
Fraudulent Transfers	28-23
Final Meeting of Creditors	28-24
REORGANIZATIONS—CHAPTER 11	28-24
Terminology	28-24
Jurisdiction and Function of the Court	28-25
Jurisdiction of Appellate Courts	28-26
How Proceedings Are Commenced	28-26
Court in Which Federal Proceedings May Be Commenced	28-26
Filing Fees	28-27
Procedure for Filing of Involuntary Petition	28-27
Filing of Petition	28-27
Conversion or Dismissal	28-27
Trustee or Debtor in Possession	28-27
Creditors and Creditors' Committees	28-28
Reorganization Plans	28-29
Who May Propose and File Reorganization Plan	28-29
Claims and Interest	28-29
Contents of the Plan	28-30
Impairment of Claims	28-31
Disclosure of the Plan	28-31
Acceptance of the Reorganization Plan	28-31
Modification of the Plan	28-32
Confirmation of the Plan	28-32
Cram-Down	28-33
Effect of Confirmation	28-34
Execution of the Plan	28-35
Revocation of a Confirmation Order	28-35
Exemption from Security Laws	28-35
Tax Consequences	28-36
ADJUSTMENT OF DEBTS OF AN INDIVIDUAL WITH REGULAR INCOME—CHAPTER 13	28-37

Chapter 29
INTERNATIONAL TRADE

Introduction	29-1
UNITED STATES AGENCIES	29-1
Export-Import Bank of United States	29-1
Agency for International Development	29-4
Overseas Private Investment Corporation	29-5
Commodity Credit Corporation	29-7
INTERNATIONAL AGENCIES	29-7
World Bank	29-7
International Development Assn.	29-9
International Finance Corp.	29-10
International Monetary Fund	29-10
Inter-American Development Bank	29-12
FOREIGN CREDIT INSURANCE ASSN.	29-17
INTERNATIONAL CREDIT INFORMATION	29-24
U.S. DEPARTMENT OF COMMERCE	29-27
CHAMBER OF COMMERCE OF U.S. INTERNATIONAL GROUP	29-32
DOMESTIC INTERNATIONAL SALES CORPORATION	29-33
UNIFORM CUSTOMS AND PRACTICES FOR DOCUMENTARY CREDITS	29-38
FOREIGN TRADE DEFINITIONS	29-50
Incoterms 1980	29-50

INTERNATIONAL CHAMBER OF COMMERCE	29-77
ARBITRATION BY INTERNATIONAL CHAMBER OF COMMERCE	29-78
AAA AND ICC COOPERATION	29-79
AMERICAN ARBITRATION ASSOCIATION	29-80
WEBB-POMERENE ACT	29-83

Chapter 30

BONDS ON PUBLIC WORKS

General	30-1
Heard Act	30-1
Miller Act	30-1, 30-7
FORMS FOR BONDS	30-2
Performance	30-2
Labor and Material Payment	30-4
SUMMARY OF FEDERAL BOND LAWS	30-7
Decisions under Miller Act	30-7
Other Projects	30-21
Necessary to Check on Bonds	30-23

Chapter 31

STATE BOND LAWS

Summaries by States	31-1
Puerto Rico	31-88

Chapter 32

U.S. DISTRICT COURTS	32-1

Chapter 33

SPECIMEN CREDIT AND OTHER INSTRUMENTS

In addition to the forms indexed here, there have been reproduced, throughout the text material in the various chapters, forms pertinent to the subject matter.

USE OF FORMS	33-1
SPECIMEN FORMS	33-1
Acknowledgment	33-1
Affidavit	33-2
Accord and Satisfaction	33-2
Arbitration Clause—Domestic	33-2
Arbitration Clause—Foreign	33-2
Assignment of Account	33-3
Assignment of Wages	33-3
Assignment Notice by Assignee	33-3
Assignment Notice by Creditor	33-3
Financing Statement (Standard Form) (UCC)	33-4
Assignment by Corporation	33-4
Agreement for Account Stated	33-4
Agreement to Revive Debt Discharged by Bankruptcy	33-4
Agreement to Pay Infancy Debt	33-5
Agreement to Revive Debt Barred by Statute of Limitations	33-5
Proof of Claim	33-5
Bill of Sale	33-5
General Form of Compromise Agreement	33-6
Guaranty of Indebtedness	33-6
Corporate Guarantee of Payment	33-7
Lease of Personal Property	33-7
Release of Lease of Personal Property	33-9
Power of Attorney	33-10
General Release	33-10
Waiver of Right to File Mechanic's Lien	33-10
Satisfaction of Mechanic's Lien	33-11
Letter of Credit	33-11
Negotiable Promissory Note	33-11
Instalment Note	33-11
Notes Series with Default Clauses	33-12
Judgment Note	33-12
Security Agreement under Article 9 of UCC	33-12
Subordination Agreement Form	33-13
Security Agreement for Accounts Receivable	33-14
Security Agreement for Equipment	33-16
Disclosure Statement	33-19
Retail Instalment Contract	33-20–33-22

Chapter 34

GLOSSARY OF LEGAL TERMS	34-1

Index

INDEX BY SUBJECTS AND STATES	I-1

Tables and Statutory Summaries

Competency of Infants	2-8
State Laws Controlling Assignment of Wages	4-8
Fees for Information on Filed Financing Statements	7-30
Filing Requirements with Respect to Financing Statements under Uniform Commercial Code	7-33
State Laws Controlling Retail Installment Sales	8-8
States' Truth in Lending Legislation	9-9
State Consumer Protection Legislation	9-20
Federal Consumer Leasing Act—Civil Penalties for Violations	10-2
State Laws Regulating Collection Practices for Collection Agencies	11-3
Penalties for Violations of Interstate Business Statutes	14-6
Validity of Judgment Notes and Stipulation for Attorney's Fee	18-10
Interest Table	18-26
Corporate Usury Defense—Table by States	18-37
State Laws Governing Mechanic's Liens	19-6
Personal Property Liens by State	20-1
State Laws Governing Landlord's Liens	20-30
Table of Bad Check Laws	21-6
Civil Penalties by State for Bad Checks	21-13
State Laws Governing Assumed Names	22-3
State Laws on Confessions of Judgment	23-17
How Lien Status Is Achieved—By State	23-27
States' Laws on Tolling of Statute and Reviving of Barred Debt	23-38
Limitations for Civil Actions	23-42
Waiver of Bankruptcy Exemptions	23-46
Table of States Which Require Debtor to File Written Statement Claiming Personal Exemption and Homestead Exemption	23-48
Property Exempt from Collection in Bankruptcy	23-50
State Laws Governing Exemptions on Insurance	23-61
State Laws on Arbitrating Agreements	23-69
State Laws Governing Claims Against Estates	24-1
State Statutes on Sales and Use Taxes	25-9
Place of Filing or Recording under Uniform Commercial Code	26-10
State Law Governing Assignments for Benefit of Creditors	27-3
Uniform Customs and Practice for Documentary Credits	29-38
Incoterms 1980	29-50
Summary of Federal Bond Laws	30-7
State Bond Laws	31-1
Locations of United States District Courts	32-1

Preface

Sound credit and financial decisions require up-to-date and factual information.

For 78 years NACM's Credit Manual of Commercial Laws has been an essential source of such information concerning the numerous state and federal statutes and regulations affecting commercial transactions and the credit and collection process.

This 1986 edition contains a compendium of such laws as well as a summary of changes adopted since the 1985 edition.

Other features include a treatment of the requirements of the Uniform Commercial Code dealing with rejection of non-conforming goods; preservation of creditor rights when accepting less than full payment; and variances in seller and customer terms as stated on their respective forms.

There are also several discussions of recent cases of particular interest to creditors.

Today more than ever this is the kind of concise, complete and factual information the commercial credit grantor needs at hand.

The National Association of Credit Management is proud to make it available in this volume.

Cooke O'Neal
Executive Vice-President

Features

Recent Legislation of Interest   xix
    A summary of Federal and State Legislation adopted during the year which affects subjects covered in the Credit Manual.

When Rejection of Non-Conforming Goods Could Be Deemed an Acceptance   xxxi
    A rejecting buyer must fulfill certain requirements of the Uniform Commercial Code. If he doesn't, his claim may be waived and he may have to accept the goods even though defective.

When "In Full Payment" Isn't Enough   xxxiv
    A creditor who wishes to preserve his rights by an endorsement such as "accepted under protest" should first determine whether controlling state law recognizes such rights.

The Battle of the Forms: Variance with Purchase and Sales Terms   xxxvi
    If the terms in the seller's forms are at variance with the buyer's, what are the terms of the contract?

Recent Cases of Interest   xxxviii
    A discussion of recent decisions in the following areas:
        (a) *Filing a Proof of Claim in Converted Chapter 11 Cases*
        (b) *Depending on State Law, A Mechanic's Lien May Be Filed after Debtor Files a Petition in Bankruptcy*
        (c) *What if the Filing Officer Makes a Mistake?*
        (d) *Repossession by Fraud and Trickery Is Unlawful*
        (e) *Timeliness of Payment under a Promissory Note*
        (f) *Guarantee: Limited or Not*
        (g) *Waiver of Security Interests*

Recent Legislation of Interest

FEDERAL

The Federal Trade Commission has issued rules regulating credit practices in consumer credit transactions. The rules designate certain practices as unfair credit practices. Such practices include the following:

1. A confession of judgment or warrant of attorney or other waiver of the right to notice and the opportunity to be heard;

2. An executory waiver or a limitation of exemption from attachment, execution or other process, on real or personal property, unless the waiver applies to property subject to a security interest executed in connection with the obligation;

3. An assignment of wages or other earnings, unless the assignment is revocable by debtor; the assignment is part of a payroll deduction plan or preauthorized payment plan; or the assignment applies only to wages or other earnings already earned at the time of the assignment;

4. A non-possessory security interest in household goods, other than a purchase money security interest.

Deceptive cosigner practices are proscribed. They include misrepresentation by lender or seller of the nature or extent of cosigner liability and a lender or a retail installment seller obligating a consigner without the consigner being informed prior to becoming obligated of the nature of his or her liability. A special notice prescribed by the rules is required to be given to a consigner to prevent unfair and deceptive cosigner practices.

In connection with collecting a debt arising out of the extension of credit to a consumer, it is an unfair act or practice to collect any delinquency charge on a payment which is otherwise a full payment for the applicable period and is paid on its due date, when the only delinquency is attributable to late fees or delinquency charges assessed on earlier installments.

If there is a state requirement which provides for a level of protection equal to the federal requirements, the state may obtain an exemption from application of these rules to it.

STATE

Chapter 6—Secured Transactions Superseded by Article 9 of the Uniform Commercial Code

LOUISIANA

Statute on Assignment of Accounts Receivable amended to redefine general assignment and place of business.

Chapter 7—Secured Transactions under Article 9 of the Uniform Commercial Code

CALIFORNIA

Technical changes to Section 9-102 of UCC are adopted. Section 9-403 is amended to clarify that a financing statement is effective from the day of filing until and for the entire day 5 years thereafter. If the last day is a Saturday, Sunday or holiday, the effectiveness continues until the next business day. Section 9-404 (2) is amended to instruct filing officer how to deal with termination statements.

California amends Section 9-504 to provide alternatives for publication of notices of public sale if no newspaper of general circulation is published in a county in which a sale is to be held.

ILLINOIS

A financial statement for crops must contain a metes and bounds description of the real estate.

MONTANA

Adopts act to establish with Secretary of State a centralized filing system for security interests covering agricultural products. Montana increases from 10 to 20 days time for filing purchase money security interest under the UCC. Legislation adopted to implement prior adoption of 1972 amendments to the UCC.

NEBRASKA

Nebraska adopts amendment to Sections 9-307, 9-401-406, 9-414, 9-415 and 9-417 of the UCC. Buyers may require that seller of farm products for a fee or commission declare and identify in writing the name of the holder of a first security interest or first lien on the farm products being sold. Good faith reliance by seller thereon permits him to take free of any security interest not disclosed if holder of lien authorizes negotiation of the check. This provision terminates on September 1, 1988.

After September 1, 1988, a person buying farm products from a person engaged in farming operations shall be subject to a security interest created by his or her seller only when the security interest is registered on the computer index established by the Secretary of State.

A buyer who wishes to protect himself shall post at his premises or deliver to a prospective seller the required statutory notice.

Filing fee increased from $5.00 to $6.00 on all filing statements.

Centralized computer systems for information on debtors will be available 24 hours a day starting June 30, 1987. Until June 30, 1987, telephone information is available 8:00 A.M. till 9:00 P.M.

Failure after demand to send termination statement to debtor subjects lienholder to fine of $100.00 and any losses.

Section 9-411 of UCC amended to provide for no fee for inspection on behalf of a single person of 10 names or less per day. For each inspection in excess of 10 names per day by a single person the fee is one dollar.

RECENT LEGISLATION OF INTEREST

NEW YORK

UCC Section 9-301(2) is amended to provide that a purchase money secured creditor must file a financing statement within 20 days after debtor receives possession in order to take priority over rights of transferee in bulk or of lien creditor. The time period in Subsection (4) is similarly amended from 10 to 20 days.

NORTH CAROLINA

New legislation provides that future obligations secured by security instrument need be evidenced by a written instrument only when the parties have agreed in writing that such obligation shall be evidenced by a written instrument.

NORTH DAKOTA

Owner of property cannot intentionally alter, conceal, destroy, damage or encumber it without prior consent of the secured party. New statute provides that one cannot destroy, remove or damage secured property to prevent collection of a debt.

OKLAHOMA

Technical change adopted to Article 9 of the UCC.

TENNESSEE

The 1972 amendments to the UCC are adopted.

TEXAS

A security interest in farm products may not be enforced against the purchaser of such farm products unless the secured party gives notice of the security interest to the buyer by certified mail not later than 90 days after the date of purchase.

A security interest in farm products has to be filed in the Office of the Secretary of State and not in the Office of the County Clerk.

A continuation statement filed to continue perfection of a security interest filed before September 1, 1985, relating to farm products, or such inventory, or general intangibles, must be filed in the Office of the Secretary of State.

Sale or disposition of secured property without authority is a misdemeanor or felony, depending on the amount of proceeds involved.

Chapter 8—Retail Instalment Sales

CONNECTICUT

Connecticut increases financing of charges on sale of motor vehicles and other goods to a maximum rate of 18% per annum on and after October 1, 1987. After October 1, 1985 and prior to October 1, 1987 it is 19% per annum. Open end credit plans for July 1, 1981 to October 1, 1987, interest rate is 1½% per annum. After October 1, 1987 it is 1¼% per annum.

FLORIDA

Delinquency charge limited to 5% of instalments due. $5.00 minimum has been eliminated.

HAWAII

Repayment of loan can be modified to effect amortization schedule of total amount refinanced, however term cannot be less than term of original contract.

KANSAS

Maximum rates are extended to March 24, 1988. Thereafter, they revert to rates in existence prior to March 25, 1982.

LOUISIANA

Adopts change to form of contract on instalment purchase sales.

NEVADA

Statutory amendment fixes prepayment charges on time balances prepaid.

Chapter 9—State Consumer Protection Legislation

ARIZONA

Legislation amends statute for closed end loans of $5,000 or less and revolving loans of $10,000 or less.

CALIFORNIA

Amendents and changes to Song-Berverly Consumer Warranty Act which deals with consumer credit loans to expand the definition of consumer credit contracts and to change the provisions for default or delinquency on late payment charges together with other technical changes. The law also revises the minimum charges which may be assessed for loans arranged by personal property brokers, and also includes other technical charges.

The Consumer Warranty Protection Act is amended to provide a new definition of consumer goods and establishes new rules for consumer leases.

COLORADO

Fair Debt Collection Practice Act revised and technical amendments to Consumer Credit Transactions Act adopted.

An out of state seller may not receive charges on consumer sales in Colorado in excess of those permitted by the UCCC.

A Fair Debt Collection Practice statute is adopted which applies to out of state collection agencies collecting debts in Colorado and which regulates communications between collection agencies and debtors and establishes unfair collection practices.

ILLINOIS

Compliance with the federal Truth in Lending Act is deemed compliance with the state Consumer Fraud and Deceptive Business Practices Act.

MAINE

Uniform Consumer Credit Code provisions amended with respect to default and late payments provisions and notice for credit insurance. Records of consumer transactions required to be maintained for specific time periods.

RECENT LEGISLATION OF INTEREST   xxiii

UCCC amended to require records of consumer debt transactions to be retained for at least 3 years and revised provisions for acceleration of unpaid balance of consumer credit obligations.

Copies of disclosure statements under the Fair Credit Reporting Act are to be retained for two years.

MARYLAND

Adopts new law authorizing consumer lenders to collect attorneys' fees and court costs on defaulted loans.

Statute regulating denial of credit has been amended to require that one who denies consumer credit must advise the applicant by a written statement of the reason for denial of such credit.

NEW JERSEY

Market Rate Consumer Loan Act regulates consumer credit transactions.

NORTH CAROLINA

Statute enacted which authorizes and regulates certain consumer credit transactions.

Instruments that contain no prepayment terms or terms that are not in accord with state law can be prepaid without penalty.

OREGON

Oregon adopts plain language statute for consumer contracts.

UTAH

Credit Service Organization Act adopted that regulates credit service organizations which obtain consumer credit for buyers.

The entire Uniform Consumer Credit Code has been restated.

Chapter 10—Leasing of Personal Property

Conversion of lease property occurs if lessee fails to return leased property in 10 days or 192 hours after notice from lessor demanding return of property.

LOUISIANA

Lease of movable statues is amended to provide that certain transactions are excluded, to regulate certain consumer leases, and to exclude consumer leases from Louisiana Consumer Credit Law.

Lease obligations may be assigned under Louisiana Assignment of Account Receivables Act.

MASSACHUSETTS

Every written lease of personal property used primarily for household or family purposes shall include a designation by the lessor, identifying the property as new or used.

Chapter 11—Collection Agency Requirements and Prohibited Practices

COLORADO

Colorado restricts certain communications between consumer collection agency and debtor, and provides that an agency cannot use false and misleading representations or unfair and unconscionable means to collect a debt. The statute is designated as the Colorado Fair Debt Collection Practices Act. For failure to comply, an agency is subject to civil liability and attorneys' fees and increased bond and license fees.

The Act applies to out of state collectors collecting debts in Colorado, and establishes fair collection practices.

ILLINOIS

A judgment against a collection agency cannot be maintained for more than one year after creditor obtains such judgment. Procedures are established by which a collection agency may assign an account for collection provided the requirements of the statute are met. Collection agencies must at all times maintain a separate bank account to which all money received shall be deposited in trust. Harassment of debtors by collection agencies is not permitted. Harassments include communicating with the debtor or his family without prior consent, publication of a list of consumers who refuse to pay debts (except to a consumer reporting agency), and annoying a debtor by certain actions involving use of the telephone.

MASSACHUSETTS

Massachusetts increases amount of renewal bond to $10,000 or two times the average monthly net collection received for proceeding year to a maximum of $25,000.

OREGON

Debt collection law amended to provide that collector is permitted to call debtor only during day or in evening from 6:00 to 9:00 P.M., and cannot call debtor at his place of employment, if he has reason to know that debtor's employer prohibits such communications.

Chapter 12—A Credit Card—Its Legal Implications

CALIFORNIA

Definition of a credit card is expanded to include an account number or code used to obtain money, goods, or services.

FLORIDA

Amends statute relating to credit card crimes in certain technical respects, and expands definition of credit card forgery to include possession of a counterfeit credit card.

MICHIGAN

Licenses issuers of credit cards. A licensee may collect interest not to exceed 1.5% a month.

MINNESOTA

Adopts technical amendments to its credit card statute.

NEVADA

Increases penalties for fraudulent or unauthorized use of credit card.

TEXAS

No surcharges are permitted for sales made by credit cards. In addition, technical changes defining credit card offense have been made. Credit card offense is made a felony of the third degree.

VIRGINIA

Adopts technical changes to credit card statute.

Chapter 13—Antitrust and Trade Regulation Laws

MICHIGAN

Michigan adopts a new statute which prohibits contracts, combinations and conspiracies in restraint of trade.

NEVADA

Nevada adopted a deceptive trade practices statute authorizing the Attorney General to bring criminal and civil actions against violators.

Chapter 15—Partnerships

DELAWARE

Adopts revised Limited Partnership Act.

MISSOURI

Adopts new law making substantial changes in Limited Partnership Law.

NEVADA

The Limited Partnership Act is amended.

OREGON

Oregon makes technical changes to its Limited Partnership Act.

RHODE ISLAND

Adopts new Limited Partnership Act.

Chapter 18—Law of Negotiable Instruments

ARKANSAS

Interest on judgment is 10% per annum or contract rate, whichever is greater.

CONNECTICUT

Bank cannot hold a check for more than four business days if drawn on bank in state and seven business days if drawn on out of state bank. Bank is required to notify depositor of such policy.

ILLINOIS

On revolving credit loans secured by interest in real estate it is lawful to collect any fees paid to a public officer.

MARYLAND

Statute provides that anyone who requires that a person submit an original check to prove discharge of a debt is required to return such check.

MINNESOTA

A contract for the loan or forbearance of money is determined by the law which exists when the contract was made, and the penalty as of such date shall apply.

NORTH CAROLINA

Interest on judgment on contracts is at contract rate.

Special statute adopted establishing interest rates on equity lines of credit.

Adopts statute authorizing variable rate of interest.

Authorizes a lender to charge a large charge as agreed, but not to exceed 4% of the amount of the payment due.

RHODE ISLAND

Banks must clear a check within the following times: if check drawn on same bank—1 business day; if drawn on local bank—2 business days; if drawn on bank in state—4 business days; if drawn on bank in Second Federal Reserve district—6 business days; if drawn on any other bank—8 business days.

Technical changes to interest and usury statute.

Chapter 19—Mechanic's Liens

FLORIDA

Mechanic's lien extended to include claims of interior designers.

Lessor can limit liability to a mechanic's lien as a result of tenant improvements by recording notice of no liability for such liens.

LOUISIANA

A party who files a bond is required to give notice thereof by certified mail to holders of liens, owners and contractors.

NEVADA

Lien extended to include claims of persons who seed plants, landscape or install systems of irrigation.

OHIO

Amendment to lien law establishes new time within which affidavit must be filed.

OREGON

A person who performs labor or assists in obtaining or handling timber or wood products has a lien.

TENNESSEE

Notice of completion cannot be registered before completion of improvement.

UTAH

New law simplifies filing of notice of mechanic's lien.

Chapter 20—Personal Property Liens

IOWA

Statute providing for a lien by an agricultural supply dealer is modified in various respects.

NEW MEXICO

Liens provided for repairs on aircraft.

TEXAS

Landlord lien statute amended to provide that landlord can seize non-exempt property only if no breach of the peace occurs and if seizure is authorized under lease. Sale of seized property can only occur if authorized by lease and prior notice is given to tenant.

WASHINGTON

Statute relating to agricultural liens has been amended to provide for a lien on behalf of one who processes agricultural products.

Chapter 21—Bad Check Laws

ALABAMA

Any lender of money or extender of credit who receives a dishonored check can charge not more than the greater of $10.00 or an amount equal to actual charges of the depository institution.

ARIZONA

Consumer Loan Law permits licensee to collect bad check charge for returned check in the amount of $10.00 or actual charge made by depository institution.

ARKANSAS

Drawer or third party holder has the right to initiate and maintain prosecution of criminal charges against maker of dishonored check. If more than one check is dishonored in a 90 day period and each check is less than $2,500.00, crime is a Class B felony unless total amount is in excess of $2,500.00.

Additional criminal offense is established for knowingly issuing a worthless check. Prosecuting attorney may demand a fee from person issuing a bad check; the amount of the fee depends on the amount of the check.

INDIANA

A person who issues a fraudulent check and does not pay within thirty days after receipt by certified mail of notice demanding payment is liable for triple the amount of the check, not to exceed $500.00 plus face amount of check.

IOWA

Imposes a civil penalty for issuance of worthless or fraudulent checks in triple amount of check but not to exceed amount of check plus $500.00, provided a written demand by certified mail is made therefor.

LOUISIANA

Owner of business premises 6 months after check has been dishonored can post on premises check or photo of maker of check, provided holder of check sends notice by registered mail to maker of check not more than 10 days before the lapse of 60 days that the check is unpaid.

MISSOURI

Civil penalty for issuing a bad check is amount of check or three times face amount owed to a maximum of $500.

Fraudulently stopping payment of a check is a class A misdemeanor unless face amount of check is $150 or more, in which case offense is a class D felony.

MONTANA

Eliminates from criminal offense of issuing a bad check requirement that it be done with the purpose of obtaining control over property.

NEVADA

A person who issues a bad check and does not pay within 30 days after demand by certified mail is liable for amount of check and damages equal to three times the amount of check but not less than $100.00 or more than $500.00.

NEW HAMPSHIRE

Civil penalty for bad checks is amount of check and all interest and collection costs. If the check is not paid within 10 days after notice by certified or registered mail and judgment entered, issuer of bad check shall pay to holder $10.00 per business day that the debt is outstanding up to a limit of $500.00. Payment of check within 14 days after notice is a sufficient defense to an action for issuance of a bad check.

NEW YORK

Holder of a dishonored check given in payment for a consumer transaction can charge the lesser of the amount agreed upon or $10.00.

NORTH CAROLINA

Civil penalty for issuing worthless check adopted. If check not paid 30 days after demand, issuer is liable for lesser of $500.00 or 3 times amount owing on check but not less than $100.00.

Holder of a dishonored check may advise issuer of check that legal action may be taken against him unless payment is made during prescribed time.

NORTH DAKOTA

Civil penalty permitted for dishonored check lesser of $100.00 or three times the amount of the check.

TENNESSEE

Fee of bad check restitution program increases from $6.00 to $10.00.

VIRGINIA

Civil penalty for issuing a bad check is lesser of $100.00 or three times the amount of check.

Chapter 22—Assumed or Fictitious Names

WASHINGTON

Each person who registered a trade name prior to October 1, 1984 is required to reregister before October, 1986.

RECENT LEGISLATION OF INTEREST   xxix

Chapter 23—Legal Phases of Collection

ARKANSAS

Judgment lien can be renewed for additional ten year period.

LOUISIANA

Statute provides for interest on arbitration awards.

Debtor who fails to pay open account within 15 days after written demand, is liable for attorney's fees of creditor for prosecution of past due claim.

NEVADA

Deletes requirement that head of family only may select homestead exemption and extends exemption to all relatives and co-owners.

Nevada increases statutory fees for debt adjusters.

Nevada adopts new procedures for renewal of judgments.

NORTH DAKOTA

Adopts prompt payment legislation requiring payment by state or its agencies within 45 days or interest must be paid at 1¾% per month on past due amounts.

North Dakota eliminates requirement to submit contract to arbitration from type of obligation that can be enforced specifically.

Account debtor may pay to assignor until he receives notice by certified mail that account has been assigned. Notice need not be given of intent to assign to identified assignee if intent to assign to an identified assignee is stated and acknowledged in account documents.

OHIO

Adopts prompt payment statute for state. Interest to be paid by state on unpaid accounts at an amount prescribed by statute.

RHODE ISLAND

Requires a surety bond by losing party in an arbitration. Eliminates from execution exemption farm animals, interest in church pew.

Adopts the Uniform Enforcement of Foreign Judgments Act.

TEXAS

Homestead exemption extended to burial lots. Homestead in city limited to 1 acre, in rural areas to 100 acres.

UTAH

When contractor receives payment he is required to make payment to subcontractor. If he fails to do so within 30 days, then contractor shall pay interest at 18% per annum.

Utah adopts revised procedure for enforcement of written arbitration awards.

VIRGINIA

Virginia adopts prompt payment legislation requiring state and its agencies to make payment after 45 days or else interest charged at business rate not to exceed 1% per month.

WASHINGTON

If arbitrator fails to make an award when required, court upon motion shall order arbitrator to enter an award, and court can fix sanctions. Other changes to statute on arbitration include power of court to direct arbitrator to modify award. Mandatory arbitration where money judgment is sought is increased from the amount of $15,000 to $25,000 if approved by two thirds or more of Superior Court judges.

Chapter 25—Sales and Use Tax

TENNESSEE

Creates an exemption from sales tax for persons selling tangible personal property on a semiannual or less frequent basis.

Chapter 26—Fraudulent Conveyances

HAWAII

Adopts the Uniform Fraudulent Transfer Act.

LOUISIANA

Deletes the requirement of notification to creditors as to terms of proposed bulk sale or consideration to be paid and requires advertisement in official journal of the parish as to date, time and place of bulk sale.

NEBRASKA

Nebraska amends notice Section 6-107 of UCC to provide notice by certified mail as well as by registered mail or by personal mailing.

OREGON

Adopts the Uniform Fraudulent Transfer Act.

Chapter 28—Bankruptcy

NEVADA

If corporation is under reorganization in federal court it may take any action necessary to carry out proceedings or perform any act directed by the federal court relating to the reorganization without further action by directors or stockholders; statute authorizes a class of persons to exercise such power. By filing a certified copy of a plan of reorganization with the Secretary of State, a corporation is authorized to perform certain acts such as amending the articles of incorporation and by-laws or filing certificate of dissolution. Within 30 days after filing petition of bankruptcy a corporation shall file a notice with the Secretary of State stating the name and address of court where petition is filed, the date of filing and number assigned thereto.

Chapter 32—U.S. District Courts

Federal judicial districts changed in following states: California, Georgia, Illinois, Louisiana, Texas, Vermont.

When Rejection of Non-Conforming Goods Could Be Deemed an Acceptance

BY LESTER NELSON *

The Uniform Commercial Code requires a buyer to complete his obligations under a contract (Sec. 2-302). If a seller does not perform as obligated, then Sec. 2-601 of the Code provides the buyer with three alternatives:
   (1) To reject all of the goods.
   (2) To accept all of the goods.
   (3) To accept any commercial unit of the goods and reject the rest.

Even if the buyer accepts all the goods he is still able to seek monetary adjustments for minor variations. However, if the buyer rejects the goods he must notify the seller of the non-conformity within a reasonable time or else the buyer will become responsible for the entire contract price. If the buyer chooses to accept only a part of the merchandise, the acceptance must be of a commercial unit. A "commercial unit" is defined by Sec. 2-105(6) as:

> "Such a unit of goods as by commercial usage is a single-whole for purposes of sale and division and which materially impairs its character or value on the market or in use."

Determination of what is a commercial unit is a question of fact to be decided by the courts. In one case, the buyer inspected a truck load of potatoes and attempted to accept part and reject the other part of the truck load.

The court held then that a truck load of potatoes was a commercial unit where the custom was that potatoes were sold in truck load quantities. The buyer could not reject part of the truck load. Consequently, the buyer was deemed to have accepted the delivery and was obligated to pay the purchase price for the entire load. *Dell v. Ball Potatoe Co.,* 430 A.2d 835 (Maine, 1981).

If a buyer seeks to reject the goods the following four requirements must be satisfied:
   (1) The buyer must not exercise ownership of the goods.
   (2) Notification must be given to the seller within a reasonable time.
   (3) The notice must reasonably inform seller that there is a rejection.
   (4) The rejecting party must fulfill his duty to hold the goods with reasonable care for a sufficient time to permit seller to remove them.

Unless the buyer is careful, his actions may be deemed to be an acceptance as defined by Sec. 2-606 of the Code. An acceptance of goods occurs when the buyer:

---
* Member of the Bar of the State of New York, General Counsel NACM.

"(a) after reasonable opportunity to inspect the goods signifies to the seller that the goods are conforming or that he will take or retain them in spite of their nonconformity; or

(b) fails to make an effective rejection, but such acceptance does not occur until the buyer has had a reasonable opportunity to inspect them; or

(c) does any act inconsistent with the seller's ownership; but if such act is wrongful as against the seller it is an acceptance only if ratified by him.

Acceptance of part of any commercial unit is acceptance of that entire unit."

Notice of the rejection of the goods by the buyer can be either oral or written but it must be communicated so that the seller understands that the goods are being rejected. Advising the seller that the buyer does not like the goods or that the goods are not of adequate quality is not sufficient to constitute rejection. It is of course advisable that a rejection be in writing.

Whether rejection is made within a reasonable time is a question of fact if the facts are in dispute, and is a question of law in cases of undisputed facts. The following are some cases which have considered the question:

(1) Rejection on November 18, 1974, of a load of potatoes was proper when the potatoes were inspected on November 7, 1974, and the report finding the potatoes defective was issued on November 15, 1974. *G. H. Land & Cattle Co. v. Heitzman & Nelson, Inc.,* 628 Pacific 2d. 1038 (1981).

(2) A buyer held cabinets in storage which were manufactured by a seller until such time as they were to be used. According to the contract the cabinets were to be carefully inspected at time of use. In the interim, however, the seller went out of business. The buyer inspected the cabinets when it intended to use them and rejected half of them as not meeting the contract specifications. The court held that the rejection was timely since the inspection contemplated by the contract and the dealing of the parties was not to occur until the cabinets were placed in production. *Bevel-Feld v. Rose Corporation,* 402 N.E. 2d 1104 (Mass, 1980).

(3) Seller agreed to accept rejected goods; however, buyer refused to return them because of fear of violence at his warehouse. Six months later buyer sent a notice of rejection which the court held not to be reasonable, since it was not sent within the time agreed or within reasonable time. U.C.C. 1-204(3). Sending a letter of rejection six weeks after delivery was held to be too long. *Robinson v. Jonathan Logan Financial* 277 A 2d. 115 (D.C., Ct. of Appeals, 1971).

(4) Waiting twenty-four hours to inspect a race horse and learn that it had a broken leg was deemed unreasonable since it is customary to have a veterinarian or trainer examine a horse on the day of sale. Trade usage and agreement of the parties may determine what is reasonable. *Miron v. Yonkers Raceway,* 400 F.2d. 112 (Second Circuit, 1968).

(5) A delay of four hours to reject delivery of pork roasts for excess fat content was deemed an unreasonable delay and the purchaser was deemed to have accepted the goods. What is a reasonable time for any action depends on the notice, purposes and circumstances of the transaction (U.C.C. 1-204 (2)). *Bauer Meatpacker, Inc. v. U.S.,* 458 F.2d. 88 (Court of Claims, 1972).

REJECTION OF NON-CONFORMING GOODS

A buyer who rightfully rejects goods has certain duties under Sec. 2-603 of the Code.

If the seller has no agent or place of business at the market of rejection, the rejecting buyer must follow any reasonable instructions received from the seller with respect to the goods and in the absence of such instructions make reasonable efforts to sell them for the seller's account if they are perishable or threaten to speedily decline in value.

What happens if the seller fails to give instructions within a reasonable time and the goods are not perishable? Sec. 2-604 of the Code assists the buyer. It provides that the buyer may store the rejected goods for the seller's account and the buyer may be reimbursed for any reasonable expenses incurred.

In *North America Steel Corp. v. Sideruis,* 75 Michigan App. 391 (1977), the buyer requested advice from the seller as to how to dispose of goods which had been rejected and such instructions were not received. The buyer then advised the seller that they would be sold for the seller's account. The seller still failed to answer and the buyer sold the goods. The court held that the sale did not constitute acceptance of the goods by the buyer and that the buyer was entitled to a sales commission which could be withheld from the proceeds of the sale.

There is a certain contradiction between Sec. 2-202 which prohibits a seller from exercising ownership of rejected goods and Sections 2-603 and 604 which authorizes sale of such goods. The answer lies in the requirement of good faith set forth in Section 2-603. The buyer is required to act in good faith, which is always a question of fact to be determined by the court.

A rejecting buyer is required by Section 2-605 to particularize his objections. The Code requires the buyer to set forth any particular defect which is ascertainable by reasonable inspection. If the buyer doesn't, he is precluded from relying on the defect to justify rejection, provided: (a) the seller could have cured the defect; or (b) the seller has requested a full and final written statement of all defects on which the buyer proposes to rely and the buyer has not submitted same. This section of the Code also provides that payment against documents made without reservation of rights precludes recovery of the payment for defects apparent on the face of the documents, so that if the defect appears on the face of the document itself and the buyer pays for such documents he is unable to recover for any such defects.

The buyer may also revoke his acceptance of accepted goods when they are non-conforming and their value is substantially impaired if acceptance was based on the assumption that the non-conformity could be cured and the acceptance was induced either by the difficulty of discovery or the seller's assurances (U.C.C. 2-608).

A buyer who has received goods which do not conform to the contract and desires to reject them must therefore act in good faith within a reasonable time and follow the requirements of the Code or else his claim against the seller for the defective goods may be waived and he will be deemed to have accepted the goods. On the other hand, a seller should be aware of the requirements imposed by the Code on a buyer who desires to reject goods as non-conforming to the contract. If those requirements are not fulfilled by the rejecting buyer, the seller may be able to insist that the buyer has accepted the goods.

When "In Full Payment" Isn't Enough

BY BERNARD S. GORDON *

The Supreme Court of Wisconsin recently considered the question of whether a check marked "in full payment" and accepted by a creditor constituted an accord and satisfaction discharging the debtor's claim in its entirety. *Flambeau Products v. Honeywell Info Systems,* 341 N.W. 2d 655 (Sup. Ct. Wisconsin, 1984).

Under the common law, a check offered by a debtor in full payment of a *disputed* claim that is cashed by the creditor is deemed to have been accepted in full payment as an accord and satisfaction. Any reservations that the creditor may have had or may have noted on the check are irrelevant. The common law rule, however, did not apply to liquidated and *undisputed* claims.

The basis of the rule is that it promotes fairness by protecting the *bona fide* expectations of the debtor who tenders payment on condition that it will be accepted as "payment in full." This common law rule also provides a method of settling disputes without litigation. Debtors would not be inclined to tender payment if the check would be accepted with the creditor still reserving the right to collect any balance due.

The issue in the *Flambeau* case was whether or not Section 1-207 of the Uniform Commercial Code changed the common law rule of accord and satisfaction. Section 1-207 provides:

> "A party who with explicit reservation of rights performs or promises performance or assents to performance in a manner demanded or offered by the other party does not thereby prejudice the rights reserved. Such words as 'without prejudice,' 'under protest' or the like are sufficient."

The question was whether Section 1-207 applies to checks marked "in full payment." This question has been considered by a number of courts and scholars which have come to contrary conclusions.

The express language of Section 1-207 does not answer the question of whether the section changes the common law rule of accord and satisfaction as it applies to "full payment" checks. Therefore, courts have looked to the legislative history of the Code for an answer. But that history is not conclusive. Experts in the field such as Professor Hawkland and Dean Rosenthal, after examination of the official commentaries to the Code, do not believe that Section 1-207 is applicable to "full payment" checks. See Hawkland, *The Effect of U.C.C., Section 1-207 on the Doctrine of Accord and Satisfaction by Conditional Check,* 74 Commercial Law Journal, 329, 331 (1969).

---

* Member, Rabinovich, Nelson, Gordon & Burstein, attorneys, New York City.

The *Flambeau* court, after a review of the Wisconsin legislative history, concluded that Section 1-207 should not be read to change the common law rule recognizing the effectiveness of the "full payment" check. In New York, however, the courts have come to a contrary conclusion. There, the New York Commission on Uniform State Laws, after reviewing Section 1-207 prior to its adoption by the state legislature, commented that it "permits a party involved in a Code covered transaction to accept whatever he can get by way of payment, performance, etc. without losing his rights to sue for the balance of the payment as long as he explicitly reserves his rights." Therefore, the New York courts have concluded that Section 1-207 applies to "full payment" checks and no accord and satisfaction results, if the Seller endorses the check with such words as "without prejudice" or "under protest."

The Wisconsin court in looking at the problem for the first time cited Section 1-102 of the Code which states that the underlying purposes and policies of the Code are: (a) to simplify, clarify and modernize the law governing commercial transactions; (b) to permit the continued expansion of commercial practices through the custom, usage and agreement of the parties; (c) to make uniform the law among the various jurisdictions.

The court in *Flambeau* held that to apply Section 1-207 to the "full payment" check would not serve to simplify or clarify and modernize the law, nor would it permit the continued expansion of commercial practice through agreement of the parties. Use of the "full payment" check by parties bargaining at arm's length is a convenient and valuable way of resolving disputes through mutual agreement. In the court's opinion fairness dictates that a creditor who cashes a check offered in "full payment" should be bound by the terms of the offer. The debtor's intent is known and allowing the creditor to keep the money and disregard the debtor's conditions seems unfair and violative of the obligation of good faith which the U.C.C. makes applicable to every contract or duty. Section 1-203 U.C.C.

Therefore, the court concluded that Section 1-207 is not applicable to "full payment" checks and that a valid accord and satisfaction had been created in the case before it.

A creditor who wishes to preserve its rights by an endorsement on the check such as "without prejudice" or "accepted under protest" should determine whether controlling state law recognizes such rights under U.C.C. Section 1-207. If not, such endorsement or notation on the check will be meaningless and an accord and satisfaction may result when the creditor deposits the check. Those jurisdictions which apply U.C.C. Section 1-207 to "full payment" checks hold that the section applies only to the sale of goods and not to service contracts.

The Battle of the Forms: Variance with Purchase and Sales Terms

One of the most difficult sections of the Uniform Commercial Code to apply is Section 2-207. This Section deals with sales transactions which are concluded by an exchange of documents. For example, the buyer sends a purchase order and the seller replies with an acknowledgement of the order and subsequently sends the goods. This is a routine transaction which occurs countless times and normally does not present any problem.

However, what if the terms in the seller's forms are at variance with the buyer's?

What then are the terms of the contract; what is the agreement between the parties?

Under common law, where there is no acceptance of an offer, no contract has resulted.

Section 2-207 of the Code seeks to deal with this problem specifically. The Section provides that an acceptance of a contract within a reasonable time is binding, even though it states terms additional to or different from those offered, unless such acceptance is *expressly* made conditional on the additional or different terms. The new terms are construed as proposals for additions to the contract. Between merchants such terms become part of the contract unless: (a) the offer expressly limits acceptance to the terms of the offer; (b) they materially alter it; or (c) a notification of objection to the terms has been given or is given within a reasonable time after notice is received. The Section, however, also provides that conduct by both parties which recognizes the existence of a contract is sufficient to establish a contract of sale, although the writings of the parties do not otherwise establish a contract. In such case, the contract consists of those terms in which the writings of the parties agree, together with any supplementary terms incorporated by provisions of the Code.

The effect of Section 2-207 is that an acceptance is legally binding despite the fact that there may be different terms or conditions contained therein. There has been much judicial and academic commentary on whether terms are additional or different and how they are to be handled under the Code. Substantial litigation has also resulted on the issue of whether particular terms materially alter the contract.

The official comments to the Code do not shed much light on the question. The comments provide that clauses which typically *materially alter* a contract include the following: (a) a clause negating standard warranties such as merchantability or fitness for a particular purpose; (b) a clause which will guarantee 90% or 100% delivery of a quantity of goods ordered where usage of the trade allows greater differences; (c) a clause reserving to the seller the power to cancel upon buyer's failure to pay any invoice when due; (d) a clause requiring that complaints be made in a time materially shorter than customary or reasonable.

The Code comments also provide examples of clauses which are *not deemed material* and involve no element of unreasonable surprise and which are to be incorporated into the contract unless notice of objection thereto is given; they include: (a) a clause setting forth and perhaps enlarging slightly upon the seller's exemption due to supervening causes beyond seller's control; (b) a clause fixing a reasonable time for complaints within customary limits or in the case of a purchase for resale, providing for inspection by the subsequent purchaser; (c) a clause providing for interest on overdue invoices or fixing the seller's standard credit terms, provided they are within the range of trade practice; or (d) a clause limiting the right of rejection for defects which fall within customary trade tolerances.

If the seller wishes to protect himself so that none of the terms of the acceptance are incorporated in the contract, general language such as the following should be included in the invoice or appropriate document: "Any statement in a purchase order or similar document which is not expressly approved or acknowledged in writing by seller will not be considered as part of the agreement between the parties." This language should be in bold and large type and be conspicuous so that it becomes immediately evident to the reader. Even better, if there is language in a purchase order that seller finds objectionable, it is of course best to specifically reject such objectionable language. It may not be possible or practicable to review each order for such objectionable language, and therefore a seller should provide the above-mentioned general provision in his invoice or appropriate acknowledgement of an order.

Some courts have taken the position that the contrary terms eliminate each other which is known as the "knockout rule." This was the holding in the case of *Daitom, Inc. v. Pennwalt Corp.*, 741 F.2d 1569, 39 U.C.C. Reporter 1203 (10th Cir., 1984). The case involved an offer by a seller that contained a one year statute of limitations on warranty claims. The acceptance was in direct conflict on this point since its terms contained an explicit reservation of the more usual four-year statute of limitation. The lower court opted to acknowledge the one-year limit in the initiating document. The Appellate Court, however, eliminated both the one- and the four-year rule. Use of the "knockout rule" in this instance worked well for the accepter since the court invoked the four-year statute which was the same as the provisions in the accepting offer. In other cases, application of the "knockout rule" may satisfy neither party.

Therefore, a seller who wishes to be certain that the terms of the purchase order do not vary from his selling terms should be careful to advise purchasers of the fact by including the statement mentioned above. The purchaser on the other hand who wishes to provide alternative terms in his purchase order should clearly state that the purchase order is conditioned and limited to the counter terms set forth in the purchase order. A party should clearly state its intention to be bound solely by the terms it provides. Parties who create their own agreements will avoid the expense and time of a court proceedings and what may be surprising results.

Recent Cases of Interest

Filing a Proof of Claim in Converted Chapter 11 Cases

Under Section 1111(a) of the Bankruptcy Code and Bankruptcy Rule 3003, a proof of claim is deemed filed under Chapter 11 if the claim or interest is scheduled by the debtor, unless the claim is scheduled as disputed, contingent or liquidated. That is very clear. However, what happens if the Chapter 11 case is converted to one in Chapter 7? Does the creditor have to then file a proof of claim in the Chapter 7 proceeding? The issue was considered in *Crouthamel Potato Chip Co.*, 11 C.B.C. 2d, 751 (E.D. Penn., 1984) and answered in the affirmative.

The creditor in *Crouthamel* had received a notice from the clerk of the Bankruptcy Court, stating that the case had been converted from Chapter 7 to Chapter 11 and advising the creditor that a Proof of Claim had to be filed pursuant to Bankruptcy Rule 3002. The creditor unfortunately either neglected or refused to file a Proof of Claim. It argued that Bankruptcy Rule 1019 provides that a claim filed in a superseded case is deemed filed in a Chapter 7 case. The Court responded, however, by saying that that rule applies only to claims actually filed and not to claims deemed to be filed. Therefore, it concluded that the creditor's failure to file the Proof of Claim required its disallowance.

A formal Proof of Claim is not always necessary. If the creditor has filed with the Court some documents in writing, containing a demand for payment from the estate and expressing an intent to hold the debtor liable for the debt, such document can be deemed the equivalent of a Proof of Claim. *McCoy Management Services, Inc.*, 44 B.R. 215 (W.D.KY, 1984).

It is, therefore, not advisable for a creditor to rely on the fact that a claim is deemed filed in a Chapter 11 proceeding. For safety, a creditor should always file a formal Proof of Claim and not rely on informal communication and telephone calls or letters to substantiate a claim.

Depending on State Law, A Mechanic's Lien May Be Filed After Debtor Files a Petition in Bankruptcy

A subcontractor sought to file a notice of a mechanic's lien against a debtor-in-possession after the filing of a petition seeking relief under Chapter 11 of the Bankruptcy Code. The debtor objected to the filing of such notice claiming that it violated the automatic stay provisions of the Code. This issue was decided in favor of the creditor in *In Re Yobe Electric, Inc.*, C.C.H. Bankr. Law Rep. Para. 70,112 (U.S.B.C., W.D. Penn., 1983).

The court held that the validity in bankruptcy of the filing of a notice of a mechanic's lien depended upon whether or not applicable Pennsylvania law related the filing back to the date materials were first furnished. On examination of the controlling state statute, the court concluded that under Pennsylvania law, on filing of the notice of mechanic's lien, the lien takes effect as of the date of the visible commencement of the improvement or the delivery of materials.

The court contrasted the Pennsylvania statute with the New Jersey one, in which filing of a notice of intention to file a mechanic's lien does not relate back to the time of delivery of materials; it is only effective against the owner as of the date of filing. Therefore, in the case before the court the subcontractor's filing of the notice of intention to file a mechanic's lien was not barred by the automatic stay provisions of the Code.

The lesson of the case is that the mere fact that the debtor has filed a petition in bankruptcy does not necessarily bar a filing of a mechanic's lien. The validity of filing such a lien will depend on the provisions of applicable state law.

What If the Filing Officer Makes a Mistake

Under Section 9-312(3) of the Code, a perfected purchase money security interest in inventory takes priority over a conflicting security interest in such inventory provided the purchase money security interest is perfected after the debtor receives possession of the inventory and the purchase money secured creditor gives notification in writing to the holder of the prior filed security interest. In *Borg Warner Acceptance Corp. v. ITT Diversified Credit Corp.*, 38 U.C.C. Rep. 1 (Minn., 1984), the issue considered was which of the secured parties had priority since the purchase money security inventory lender, ITT, did not give notice to Borg Warner as a prior filed secured creditor of the same collateral. It was acknowledged that the failure by ITT to give such notice to Borg Warner was the fault of the Minnesota Office of the Secretary of the State which failed to list Borg Warner as a secured party in response to a request for a UCC search by ITT.

The court held that the last to file should bear the risk of such mistake. Such policy was believed to promote the ease and certainty in the filing process. Therefore, Borg Warner did not have a perfected security interest in the collateral since it failed to give notice to ITT.

There is no way ITT or any second secured party could effectively protect itself against such a mistake. Borg Warner may, depending on state law, have a cause of action against the recording officer. But who wants a lawsuit?

Repossession by Fraud and Trickery Is Unlawful

Section 9-503 of the Uniform Commercial Code gives the secured party the right to repossess collateral upon the debtor's default. The Alabama Supreme Court in *Chrysler Credit Corp. v. McKinney* (38 U.C.C. Reporting Service 1409, 1984) held that such repossession may not be obtained by trick or fraud.

In the *McKinney* case, Jimmy McKinney bought a Dodge automobile from Countywide Dodge and financed the purchase through Chrysler Credit Corp. He made only two payments under the agreement because Countywide failed to repair the car to his satisfaction. Countywide repeatedly assured McKinney that the repairs, which included leaks in the roof, would be promptly made, but it never made the repairs. Thereafter a repossession agent of Chrysler Corp. contacted McKinney about the car and his failure to make payment on the note. The repossession agent assured McKinney that if he brought the car to a lot it would be repaired and after appropriate repairs were made he could bring the payments up to date. This was also confirmed to McKinney's attorney. McKinney then brought the car into the lot, only to be thereafter advised that the car had been repossessed by Chrysler Credit Corp. The jury returned a verdict against Chrysler Credit Corp. in the amount of $20,000 based on conversion.

The court held that the evidence supported that Chrysler Credit Corp. fraudulently permitted McKinney to believe that the car would not be repossessed unless McKinney failed to make the necessary payments after the car was repaired. The court held that Section 9-503 does not permit obtaining possession through trick or deception without knowledge of the debtor. To allow possession under such circumstances would encourage practices abhorrent to society such as fraud, trickery, chicanery or subterfuge.

Therefore, if you are seeking to repossess secured collateral on default of a debtor, be sure you do it in a legal and appropriate manner, and do not engage in subterfuge, fraud or trickery or else you may lose the benefits of a secured party.

Timeliness of Payment Under a Promissory Note

If a promissory note provides a thirty day grace period for payment of an interest instalment and if the thirtieth day falls on Saturday, which is a non-business day for both parties, can the creditor declare a default and accelerate the note to demand payment of the entire balance due? This issue was recently considered in *Reynolds Aluminum and Masonry Contractors, Inc., v. Alexander,* 38 U.C.C. Rep. 1315 (Fla.Dist.Ct. Appeals, 2nd Dist., 1984). The debtor there argued that it had until the following Monday which was the next business day to make timely payments. The court agreed, relying on a Florida statute that it admittedly said was ambiguous since it dealt primarily with presentment of negotiable instruments for payment in favor of the holder of a note and not with the obligor under a note. Nevertheless, based on legislative history the court concluded that the additional time provided in the statute should also be extended to benefit a maker of a note.

The debtor consistently made monthly interest payments after the first of the month, but before the end of the grace period; it ignored the holder's warnings that failure to make timely payments would be considered a violation of the terms of the note.

The holder of the note probably incurred substantial attorney's fees in seeking to accelerate the note and was unsuccessful. If you wish to avoid the problem of debtors taking advantage of holidays or non-business days, place a provision in the note or other document indicating that such additional days are not to be added to the time of payment.

Guarantee: Limited or Not

In the *First National Bank of Hastings v. McNamara,* 39 U.C.C. Reporting Service 1370 (Court of Appeals, Minn., 1984), Hastings loaned to McRaith, Inc. the sum of $30,821.59 which loan was guaranteed by McNamara. The guarantee read "will guarantee $32,300 refer McRaith Motor, M.D. McNamara."

Subsequently, McRaith filed in bankruptcy and Hastings sued McNamara on the guarantee. McNamara argued that the guarantee is conditional and is limited to $32,300 which was less than the principal, interest and attorney's fees due. The trial court concurred. Hastings claimed the guarantee to be unconditional and the guarantor's liability equal to that of the maker of the note. Therefore, he argued that McNamara was responsible for interest and any attorney fees incurred by the holder of the note in suing for collection. The appellate court agreed, and reversed the trial court holding that the term "$32,000" was not intended to serve as words of limitation but was merely identifying the note in question. Therefore, the guarantor was liable for the full amount due under the note, together with the costs of collection.

A guarantor who intends to limit his liability in a guarantee should expressly state so in precise language.

Waiver of Security Interests

A recent decision in Alabama considered the issue of whether a secured party had acted in such a manner as to waive its security agreement or to be estopped from asserting that the security agreement continued to exist. *General Electric Credit Corp. v. Strickland,* 437 So.2d. 1240 (Alabama, 1983).

Larry Terry operated a business in which he sold metal buildings and various other items, including trucks and appliances. Strickland furnished Terry on consignment with an inventory of metal buildings. Since Terry wished to increase the size of his inventory beyond the number of metal buildings which Strickland would deliver on a consignment basis, Strickland introduced Terry to representatives of GECC which agreed to supply Terry's inventory. Terry and GECC then entered into a financing agreement whereby GECC agreed to pay Strickland for all buildings Strickland shipped to Terry. Terry then repaid GECC as each building was sold for the full amount. Terry granted GECC a security interest "In all inventory, new and used, presently owned and hereafter acquired, together with all proceeds of the sale or other disposition thereof."

This procedure continued until Terry wrote GECC a bad check. As a result, GECC notified Strickland that it would not finance any further shipments to Terry. Strickland, however, informed GECC that it would resume shipments to Terry "on consignment." In addition, Smith agreed to supply inventory to Terry also on consignment. When Strickland resumed shipping buildings to Terry, it sent invoices for each shipment directly to Terry instead of GECC. Though the invoices suggested that they were purchase agreements and that the buildings were sold to Terry, Strickland and Terry entered into an oral consignment agreement by which Terry had the right to return unsold buildings to Strickland. Moreover, Terry was allowed to sell the buildings for whatever price he could get from the buyers and was permitted to keep as profit the difference between the amount he received and the wholesale price, plus 5%. Even if he was unable to sell a building and returned it to Strickland, he was still liable to Strickland for the 5% "up charge." Strickland began shipping buildings to Terry knowing that Terry owed GECC an outstanding balance which was secured by the inventory on the buildings purchased under the financing arrangements.

The issue that was presented in the case was whether GECC can claim a security interest in the buildings shipped to Terry "on consignment" by virtue of the after acquired property clause in the security agreement. The trial court determined that the security agreement was terminated by the actions of the parties and, consequently, no security interest attached thereafter to the inventory or any other property of debtor.

The Appellate Court held that the finding that the parties had mutually rescinded the security agreement was clearly erroneous, as nothing in their conduct justified such determination. The defendant urged on appeal that even if a valid security interest existed, GECC waived its rights to assert its lien in the property. Therefore, GECC was equitably estopped from claiming any rights in the inventory.

The essential elements of equitable estoppel are:
(1) The person against whom estoppel is asserted must communicate something in a misleading way with the intention that the communication will be acted on.
(2) The person seeking to assert the estoppel relies upon that communication.
(3) The person relying on the communication would be damaged materially if the other party is permitted to assert a claim inconsistent with its earlier conduct.

In the instant case there were no allegations that GECC ever made any misleading communications to the defendant with regard to its security interest. At most, it failed to inform Strickland of its interest in the after acquired property when Strickland informed GECC of its intent to supply goods to Terry on consignment, Strickland admitted at the trial that he knew about GECC's financing plan and was aware of Terry's outstanding balance to GECC when he shipped the buildings. Strickland's request of estoppel by GECC was rejected.

The Appellate Court held that estoppel should not be invoked against a creditor who in order to assist the debtor and enhance the likelihood of repayment fails to declare the debtor to be in default at the first available opportunity, nor does the creditor waive his lien on the debtor's property. The Court stated, "It is often in the best interest of all parties concerned to allow a financially unpaid debtor to continue in business in hopes that he will thereby have the opportunity to generate revenues in excess of the value of the collateral which may be used to satisfy obligations to secured and unsecured creditors."

The Court examined the so-called "consignment arrangement" between Strickland and Terry and concluded that it was not true consignment since Terry was able to keep whatever profit he made in excess of the wholesale price, and he was obligated to pay Strickland a 5% "up charge" even if he was unable to sell the buildings. Furthermore, the invoice prepared and delivered by Strickland of each shipment described the transaction as a purchase. Therefore, Strickland's assignment was an attempt to create a security interest and it was governed by Article 9. However, since no valid security agreement was created by Strickland, GECC's interest in the inventory prevailed over Stricklands. On the other hand, the agreement between Terry and Smith was a true consignment. But the buildings shipped by Smith, however, were subject to the claims of Terry's creditors unless Smith complied with the filing requirements of Article 9 or unless Terry was generally known by creditors to be engaged in selling goods of others or had such a sign posted (U.C.C. 2-326, 9-114).

The trial court found that Terry was generally known by creditors to be engaged in selling goods of others. Moreover, Terry had a flashing sign in front of his business advertising that he sold goods for other people and so advertised this fact on radio. Moreover, some creditors testified that it was commonly known that Terry had sold goods for others. Therefore, Smith was able to prevail and defeat GECC's interest in his property, whereas Strickland

RECENT CASES OF INTEREST xliii

was unsuccessful in warding off GECC's claim against the property delivered to Terry.

If goods are sent on consignment to a debtor, the consignor should be careful to comply with the consignment provisions of the Code which will either require filing or posting of a sign by the debtor or proof of debtor's reputation that he deals in goods of others.

Uniform Commercial Code

BACKGROUND AND INTRODUCTION

The movement toward uniform commercial laws began in the latter part of the last century with the principal impetus coming from the increased volume of interstate commerce that resulted from the industrial revolution. A manifestation of the need for uniformity of law in the several states was the creation of the National Conference of Commissioners on Uniform State Laws, whose first major project was the promulgation of the Negotiable Instruments Law in 1896. Thereafter the Conference commissioned the drafting of the Uniform Sales Act (1906), Uniform Warehouse Receipts Act (1906), Uniform Stock Transfer Act (1909), Uniform Conditional Sales Act (1918), and Uniform Trust Receipts Act (1933).

In the case of some acts, such as the Negotiable Instruments Law, the uniform law had been adopted by each of the states. Other uniform acts have been adopted in only a few states. Every state has adopted one or more of the uniform laws and each year the number of such enactments is increased. It should be kept in mind, however, that frequently in the adoption of a uniform law a state legislature may depart from the recommended provisions and adopt a statute with substantial variations or modifications. There are also occasions when it is necessary for the courts to interpret various uniform law provisions and such interpretations may vary among states.

In 1940, when the Conference met to consider amendments to the Uniform Sales Act in order to avoid conflict with a proposed Federal Sales Act, a proposal was made to abandon the piecemeal approach to codification of commercial law in favor of a single comprehensive statute. The suggestion was accepted and the Uniform Commercial Code (UCC or Code) was conceived.

In 1942 the American Law Institute and the Conference joined together in this undertaking and appointed an editorial board and numerous drafting committees composed of many nationally prominent judges, lawyers, and law professors. The Corporation, Banking, and Business Law sections of the American Bar Association worked with the editorial board and made numerous suggestions which were incorporated into the Code. In 1952 the official text was approved by the two sponsoring organizations and by the House of Delegates of the American Bar Association.

Pennsylvania was the first state to adopt the Code and Louisiana is the only state which has not adopted the Code in its entirety. In 1974 Louisiana adopted Article 1 (General Provisions); Article 3 (Commercial Paper); Article 4 (Bank Deposits and Collections); and Article 5 (Letters of Credit), and in 1978, it adopted Article 7 (Documents of Title).[1]

---

[1] In 1978, Louisiana enacted a chapter on Investment Securities which is similar to Article 8 of the Code. It has not, however, enacted Article 8 of the Code.

In an attempt to curtail the tendency to amend "parts" of the Code as it comes up for enactment in each state and to iron out defects as they appear in application, the Permanent Editorial Board was established to consider "uniform" amendments. This Board published its official recommendations in 1962 and its recommendations as amended in 1966. In 1972 the Editorial Board issued a revised version of the Code, which made substantial modifications to Article 9 and in 1977, the Board substantially modified Article 8. It is this 1977 edition of the Code which is deemed current. (See Chapter 7, *infra,* for discussion of the 1972 official Text of Revised Article 9.)

The basic premise on which the Uniform Commercial Code is based is that the personal property commercial transaction is a single subject of the law, notwithstanding its many facets, involving the sale of and payment for goods. There may be a contract for sale, the giving of a check for part of the purchase price which may be negotiated through the banking system for collection, and the acceptance of some form of security for the balance. The goods may be shipped or stored, requiring some form of document of title.

The basic objective of the Code is to bring all of these phases under one statute and to make the law simple, clear, modern, and uniform. The Code treats these various phases under eight separate articles. These consist of an article on sales, which replaces the Uniform Sales Act; an article on "commercial paper," which repeals the Negotiable Instrument Law; an article on bank deposits and collections, which repeals the Bank Collection Code; an article on letters of credit; an article on bulk transfers, which repeals the Bulks Sales Act; an article on documents of title, which repeals the Uniform Warehouse Receipts Act; and the Uniform Bill of Lading Act, an article on investment securities, which repeals the Uniform Stock Transfer Act; and finally, an article on all types of personal property security transactions, which repeals the Uniform Conditional Sales Act and the Uniform Trust Receipts Act as well as a number of statutes dealing with chattel mortgages and related matters. Article 1 is a general introductory article and Article 10 states the effective date of the Code and lists the existing statutes to be repealed.

The several predecessor statutes promulgated by the National Conference of Commissioners on Uniform State Laws were all drafted by various committees at different times. For the first time, the Code affords the opportunity of integrated coverage whereby the rules are written with regard to the interrelation between the many aspects of commercial transactions.

ARTICLE 1

GENERAL PROVISIONS

To be consistent with a major objective of flexibility in order to permit adaptability to change and expansion of commercial practice through custom, usage and agreement of the parties, Article 1 contains several general policy pronouncements as a guide to the construction of sections throughout the Code. The text of Article 1 is reproduced herein, commencing on page 1-21. Section 1-102 expresses a noncontroversial preference for freedom of contract. This general language is at once compromised by policy considerations which preclude enforcement of such contract terms which would relieve a party of the obligation of good faith, due care and other specific exceptions. For example, the invalidity of a clause in a security contract which deprives the debtor of certain rights in the collateral upon default is found in Section 9-501(3).

The preference for liberal administration of remedies (§ 1-106) is another policy contained in the Code. This is, no doubt, a reaction against the tendency to restrict damages for breach which is found in some court decisions. It is more specifically illustrated in the Code by Section 2-708, which permits a seller to include lost profits as part of his damages against a breaching party.

In interstate commercial transactions, the parties to the transaction are authorized to designate in their contract the application of the law of a state having some reasonable relation to the contract. Subsection (2) provides an index to other sections of the Code which specify the applicable law to govern a specific type of commercial transaction.

Section 1-201 contains definitions of 46 terms which are used throughout the Code. Some of these definitions were amended in 1977 to conform to Revised Article 8 of the Code. Some definitions were in familiar usage in the commercial field; others are new or are defined in a revised or modified way.

ARTICLE 2

SALES

Article 2 was designed to replace the Uniform Sales Act. It modified many of the provisions in order to meet modern commercial needs and fill gaps of coverage which could not have been anticipated when that uniform act was drafted in 1906. While there are about a dozen states which had never enacted the Uniform Sales Act, the Act was essentially a codification of the common law and, thus, most of the provisions had been followed by the case decisions in those states. Portions of the text of Article 2 have been reproduced herein, commencing on page 1-28.

A novelty of the sales article of the Code is the attempt to stratify sales law by enacting separate rules where the parties to a sale are merchants as opposed to the casual or inexperienced buyer or seller. This is more apparent than real, however, since the term "merchant" is defined in Section 2-104(1) as "a person who deals in goods of the kind . . . involved in the transacton" which would include the great bulk of all sales transactions. (Early drafts of this Article contained delineations for resale, industrial purchasers who buy for use, and sales to individual consumers. These distinctions have been deleted by subsequent drafts of the Code.)

Title Passing Concept

A much more significant aspect of Article 2 is the attempt to state the law without reference to what has been considered the central point in Anglo-American sales law for at least a century and a half—the location of title. Many of the controversies between buyer and seller have been answered by early common law decisions, and subsequently by the Uniform Sales Act, by a determination of the location of title to the goods which formed the subject matter of the sales transaction. It has been fictitiously supposed that the parties intended title to pass at some particular time. To compound the fiction, presumptions about when the parties intended the title to pass were invented; those presumptions now seem to approach the status of substantive rules of law. Having thus located title in either the buyer or seller, it appears to be a simple and certain matter to proceed from that point to resolve important questions such as the risk of loss, the right of the seller to maintain an action for the price (as distinguished from an action for damages), the buyer's right to have the goods, as well as matters not directly involved with sales law such as the tax upon the goods and the right of creditors and a trustee in bankruptcy of either the buyer or seller to reach the goods.

The drafters of Article 2 took the position that this "lump concept thinking" created many uncertain and unfair results since it is frequently difficult to predict when title passes or is even established. Furthermore, passing of title may have no logical relationship to the rights in question. The basic approach of "narrow-issue" thinking under the Code is generally stated in Section 2-401.

Each provision of this Article with regard to the rights, obligations and remedies of the seller, buyer, purchasers or other third parties applies irrespective of title to the goods except where the provisions refer to such title.

Having thus de-emphasized title, specific rules provide solutions to specific problems. Thus, for example, on the recurring risk of loss problem, possession of the goods is the controlling factor and replaces the test of when title passes. However, where either party is in breach, the loss falls on the breaching party (§§ 2-509, 2-510). Where the goods are to be shipped from the seller to buyer, possession, and thus risk of loss, passes to the buyer when the goods are delivered to the carrier, except in the case of a destination contract (e.g., "F.O.B., Columbia, South Carolina," where goods are to be shipped to the buyer in Columbia), where possession and risk of loss passes to the buyer when the goods are tendered at their destination.

Furthermore, the seller's rights, upon breach by the buyer, to recover the contract price (and hold the goods for the buyer—the seller's equivalent of the buyer's action for specific performance) would not turn on the passage of title under the Code but on the more functional basis of whether the seller may be able to resell the goods (§ 2-709).

Where there are no specific provisions dealing with an issue regarding who bears the risk of loss, and title passing remains relevant, such as in determining the tax incident or application of other public regulation, Section 2-401 prescribes the point in time when title passes. Generally, title passes when the seller completes his performance by delivery of the goods, or if there is to be no shipment of goods, when the documents of title are shipped, or if there is to be no delivery of goods, at the time and place of shipment; otherwise, title passes at the time of contracting. In no event, however, will title pass until the goods are identified to the contract, e.g., with respect to future goods, when they are designated by the seller as goods to which the contract refers (§ 2-501(b)).

Performance

While the Code seems to continue the standard of "perfect tender" for a seller's performance (under § 2-601, delivery is improper "if goods or the tender of delivery fail in any respect to conform to the contract"), as distinguished from "substantial performance" where delivery is to be made in installments (under § 2-612, the buyer may reject any nonconforming installment "if the nonconformity substantially impairs the value of that installment"), some of the sting has been removed by Section 2-508 which introduces the concept of "cure." A seller is permitted to remedy a defective tender if he can do so within the time set for performance. Furthermore, the seller may cure after the time for performance has passed, if the "buyer rejects a nonconforming tender which the seller had reasonable grounds to believe would be acceptable." This latter provision is designed to relieve the seller from the "forced breach" advantage enjoyed by the buyer who could wait until the eleventh hour and reject the goods (usually for the real reason that due to a change in market conditions the contract is no longer attractive) because of some minor defect.

Section 2-605 requires a buyer to state the grounds for rejection where a defect in the tender could have been ascertained by reasonable inspection and could have been cured by the seller if stated seasonably. Failure on the part of the buyer to so particularize will preclude him from relying on the unstated defect to justify his rejection. With respect to other grounds of rejection (those not readily apparent or not so minor as to be cured), the merchant buyer, upon request from a merchant seller, must make a written final statement of all the defects on which he proposes to rely. Thereafter, the buyer is limited to the objections so stated.

Remedies for Breach

Most of the remedy rules upon breach are continued from the Uniform Sales Act but with some modifications. The Code introduces the concept of "cover" which applies where the seller fails to perform; it gives the buyer an alternative right to purchase substitute goods and recover from the seller the difference between the contract price and the cost of cover as an absolute measure of damages, provided the buyer purchases in a reasonable manner (§ 2-712). Consistent with the right to cover, the buyer's alternative right to sue for damages is measured by the difference between the contract price and the market price at the time he learned of the breach (the time when he could have made a cover purchase), and not the market price at the time when the goods should have been delivered (§ 2-713). The buyer's right to specific performance is liberalized by Section 2-716. Thus, the buyer is entitled to specific performance not only when the goods are "unique" (the usual rule) but also "in other proper circumstances." This last phrase apparently permits the buyer to have the specific goods, for example, in an "output" or "requirements" contract where he is unable to cover even though the goods are not necessarily unique.

As in the case of the buyer's remedies, the seller's rights under the Code upon breach are similar to existing law but with some liberalizing modifications. The seller has the absolute right to resell the goods wrongfully refused by the buyer and to recover the difference between the resale price and the contract price, provided the resale is "commercially reasonable" (§ 2-706). Section 2-709 expressly permits the seller to recover any lost profits which he would have received had the buyer performed; the case law, on the other hand, has been reluctant to allow a recovery of profits.

Public policy restrictions are imposed on freedom of contract under Section 2-718; a liquidated damage clause upon breach is enforceable only where reasonable and is void if "unreasonably large." An interesting balance between freedom of contract and the policy limitations in the code is found in Section 2-725 which prescribes a four-year statute of limitations for actions on a sales contract which by agreement may be reduced to not less than one year, but which may not be extended.

The Court, under the provisions of Section 2-302, may refuse to enforce a contract which it finds to be unconscionable or may strike out any unconscionable clauses and enforce the contract as if the stricken clause had never existed. Consequential damages may be limited or excluded by contract unless the limitation is unconscionable. The Code provides, however, that limitation of consequential damages for injury to the person in the case of consumer goods is prima facie unconscionable, but limitation where the loss is commercial is not (§ 2-719(3)).

Formation of the Sales Contract

One area of sales law which was neither covered by the Uniform Sales Act nor treated separately from the general common law of contracts, is the formation of a sales contract. The application of the usual rules of offer, acceptance and consideration has resulted in some uncommercial and unexpected results—at least results which are not expected by the non-lawyer businessperson. The drafters of the Code took this opportunity to make sales contract law conform to commercial practice and understanding at least regarding when merchants are bound by their agreements. For example, under Section 2-205, a written firm offer to buy or to sell goods is not revocable for a limited time (not to exceed three months) even though no consideration has passed. Under Section 2-207, an offer to buy goods may be accepted and a contract formed, even though the acceptance contains some minor additional or different terms; such additional terms will become part of the contract unless acceptance is expressly conditioned on assent to those terms, the terms materially alter the contract, or notification of objection to the terms is sent within a reasonable time. Section 2-209 permits a good faith modification of an existing sales contract without additional consideration. In authorizing the commercially expedient open-price agreements and output and requirement contracts, Sections 2-305 and 2-306 deliver the final death blow to the common law objections of uncertainty and lack of mutuality.

Section 2-201 continues the application of the Statute of Frauds to sales contracts with some apparent reluctance, as evidenced by some liberalizing modifications. The amount of the purchase price creating the requirement of a writing is increased to $500. The language "some writing sufficient to indicate that a contract of sale has been made" rejects the strict early case law requirement of stating all material terms of the contract in a written memorandum. Where merchants make an oral contract and a confirmation of the conversation is sent by letter, the other party must object to the contents of the writing within ten days. Thereafter, the contract may be proved by oral evidence and is not subject to the Statute of Frauds defense. Partial performance of an oral contract satisfies the Statute of Frauds only to the extent that goods or payment have actually been received.

Warranties

In dealing with the frequently litigated problem of sales warranties, the Code makes some changes from the common law and the Uniform Sales Act. Under Section 2-314 there is an implied warranty not only for the sale of goods where "the seller is a merchant with respect to goods of that kind" but also for the "serving for value of food or drink to be consumed either on the premises or elsewhere."

Section 2-318 provides three alternatives (states are to select one) regarding third party beneficiaries of warranties. Under Alternative A, warranties, whether expressed or implied, are extended to any natural person who is in the family or household of the buyer, or who is a guest in the home of the buyer, if it is reasonable to expect that such person may use the goods and who is injured by breach of the warranty. The operation of this section cannot be limited by any action of the seller. Consequently, with respect to the class of persons covered by the section, no privity of contract is required before any action can be commenced for breach of warranty.

Disclaimer of warranties is still permitted as a matter of freedom of contract, but with the condition that if in a written contract, the disclaimer must be conspicuous; to disclaim the implied warranty of merchantability the writing must mention the word "merchantability" (§ 2-316).

Aside from the provisions mentioned here, the Code is silent on the question of privity between the seller and buyer as a prerequisite for a breach of warranty claim. This highly controversial issue, where a buyer seeks to hold the manufacturer of the goods liable for defects which constitute a breach of the "contractual" warranty obligation, is left to the courts.

Rights of Third Parties

A significant and substantial change is found in Section 2-403 with respect to the rights of third parties. Where a purchaser buys goods in the ordinary course of business from a merchant who deals in goods of that kind, the purchaser is protected against claims by the owner of the goods who had entrusted them to the merchant. Thus, recent case decisions have estopped the entrusting owner from asseting his title against a bona fide purchaser, based on the current tendency toward increasing the negotiability of goods. A transferor, therefore, is actually passing better title than he himself had.

Courts have held that, under various circumstances, a seller's creditors may treat a sale as fraudulent and thus void as to them. Section 2-402 modifies this general rule by finding "that retention of possession in good faith and current course of trade by merchant-seller for a commercially reasonable time after a sale or identification is not fraudulent."

When goods are sold and the seller remains in possession, court decisions have held under varying circumstances that the seller's creditors may treat the sale as fraudulent and thus void as to them. Section 2-402 modifies this rule by stating that retention of possession in good faith and current course of trade by a merchant-seller for a commercially reasonable time after a sale or identification is not fraudulent.

ARTICLE 3

COMMERCIAL PAPER

The scope of Article 3 is delineated by Section 3-103 which provides: "(1) This Article *does not apply* to money, documents of title or investment securities" (emphasis added). Included in the coverage of this Article are negotiable instruments, notes, checks, certificates of deposit, money orders and drafts. The predecessor of Article 3, the Uniform Negotiable Instrument Law, did not distinguish between securities and other forms of commercial paper [1] and this separation was one of the key innovations of the Code. The basic principle underlying Article 3 is ensuring that commercial paper is treated as a substitute for money; therefore, the "paper" must represent an unconditional promise to pay a definite amount at a definite time. To effectuate this goal, the Code, in effect, "protects the market for the paper."

Form and Negotiation

Part 1 of this Article deals with the forms of negotiable instruments; it is the form of the instrument that determines whether or not the instrument is within the scope of Article 3. The requirements of negotiable instruments are explicitly set out in Section 3-104. Subsequent sections define the terms contained in Section 3-104.

The essential element of commercial paper is that it can be transferred or negotiated. Negotiation is merely a type of transfer where the transferee becomes a holder. The negotiation of an order instrument is accomplished by an indorsement of the instrument while a bearer instrument is negotiated by mere delivery.

Part 2 outlines the requirements of negotiation (§ 3-202) and distinguishes between different types of indorsements which affect the negotiability of an instrument (§§ 3-204, 3-205 and 3-206). The policy of the Code, i.e., the facilitation of the use of commercial paper, is illustrated by Section 3-207 which provides that a negotiation is effective even if executed by an incompetent party or through fraud or illegality. Negotiations so obtained, however, may be rescinded. The implication is that commercial paper is equivalent to cash; the possession of the instrument enables it to be used for transactions.

Rights of a Holder

The basic rule of assignment is that the assignee takes the instrument subject to the same defenses and limited to the same rights as the assignor. When an instrument is negotiated, however, the transferee becomes a holder and, unlike the typical assignee, is not limited by the rights of the transferor (§ 3-301).

A "holder in due course" (§ 3-302) takes the instrument free from all claims and defenses which may be raised by a party to the instrument except for incompetence, fraud, or bankruptcy (§ 3-305). The importance of this concept is illustrated by the following example.

A buys goods from B and pays for them with a negotiable promissory note. B then negotiates the note to C. Subsequent to the negotiation of the note, A discovers that the goods are defective. If C is a holder in due course, A's valid defense against B is ineffective against him despite the fact that C took the note from B. Thus, C has acquired greater rights than B had.

---

[1] The UCC contains a specific section on securities, Article 8. See *supra* p. 1-14.

Liability of Parties

Liability can arise in two contexts, contractually or by a warranty. Contractually, the liability of an indorser is set out in Section 3-414 which essentially provides that the indorser guarantees to pay the instrument upon dishonor and presentment. The effect of an improper indorsement is covered by Sections 3-404 and 3-405. In most cases, an improper indorsement is effective, and the loss is borne by the drawer of the check, rather than the payee. Thus, in the situation where the name of a payee is improperly supplied and subsequently indorsed, the check will be paid and the bank (payee) will not be liable.

The second class of liability exists by virtue of a warranty. Section 3-417 provides that the transferor of the instrument grants an implied warranty that (1) he has good title, (2) that all signatures are genuine and authorized, (3) the instrument has not been materially altered, (4) no defense of any party is good against him, and (5) he has no knowledge of bankruptcy proceedings against the maker of the instrument. Violation of any of these warranties can impose liability upon the transferor.

The requirements of timely presentment to parties who are primarily liable (drawees, makers and acceptors) and notice of dishonor to parties who are secondary holders (indorsers) are condition precedents to any right of action (§ 3-501). Section 3-503 defines presumed reasonable periods within which checks are to be presented for payment. With respect to the liability of a drawee, the check must be presented within 30 days after date or issue, whichever is later; with respect to an indorser, presentment must be within seven days. The Code provides for the complete discharge of an indorser by a delay in presentment or notice of dishonor (§ 3-501) and limits the discharge of a drawer only to the extent of prejudice by such delay (usually as a result of insolvency of the drawee during the period of delay) (§ 3-502).

Discharge

Section 3-601 of the Code makes it clear that discharge from liability applies only to the parties to the instrument and not to the instrument itself and removes the implication that an act which constitutes a discharge may create a defense to a holder in due course. Section 3-603 permits the liability of any party to be discharged by payment to the holder, despite that party's knowledge of an adverse claim (thus preserving the payor's credit standing) unless the adverse claimant supplies indemnity. This does not apply, however, to a party who pays a holder who acquired the instrument by theft or who satisfies a holder where the instrument was "restrictively indorsed in a manner not consistent with the terms of such restrictive indorsement."

ARTICLE 4

BANK DEPOSITS AND COLLECTIONS

Attempts at codification of the law governing the bank collection process have been turbulent. The National Conference of Commissioners on Uniform State Laws made an effort to draft a uniform act, but it met with such opposition from bankers that it was never enacted into law in any jurisdiction. A Bank

Collection Code was drafted under the auspices of the American Bankers' Association (and, therefore, cannot be called a "Uniform Act" in the usual sense) and this "ABA Code" was passed in a number of states shortly after it was drafted. The enthusiasm for this legislation was slowed down by criticism that it was unfairly weighted in favor of banks and against their depositors, that it was poorly drafted (*see,* e.g., a series of articles in 8 Tulane L. Rev. 21, 236, 376 (1934)), and that one section was invalid as it applied to national banks. (The Court in *Jennings v. United States Fidelity & Guaranty Co.,* 294 U.S. 216 (1935), found the provision of the Bank Collection Code relating to bank collections where a bank fails or is closed inapplicable to national banks.)

After considerable vacillation and controversy, including an initial plan to include the bank collection material under Article 3, the drafters of the Code finally decided to include a separate article regarding bank collections and deposits. This decision was based on the need for uniform rules to govern the great volume of checks which continuously flow across state lines in the bank collection process. The scope of this Article encompasses practically every item, which is broadly defined as "any instrument for the payment of money," which passes through banks for the purpose of presentment, payment or collection (§ 4-104).

Final Payment of Checks

One of the most important problems in the bank collection process is the establishment of the precise time when a check is deemed to have been finally paid by the drawee bank. It is at that point that it is no longer possible for the drawer to stop payment; the drawer's account is charged with the amount of the check so that his creditors may not thereafter attach these funds on deposit. Additionally, the provisional credit to the account of the depositor of the check becomes irrevocable so that he may draw against that credit; drawers and indorsers of the check are discharged and the point of no return is reached so that the payor bank is accountable for the amount of the check.

Section 4-213 provides, obviously, that final payment occurs when the payor bank pays cash to the holder over the counter. This Section further fixes definite rules for time of payment in the more usual case when a check comes to the payor from a depository bank—either directly or through an intermediary bank or through a clearing house in the collection process. The usual practice in this case is for the payor bank to give provisional credit for the item at the time of receipt reserving the right to subsequently revoke that credit if it decides that the check should not be paid. Since time is of the essence, the payor bank will be deemed to have finally paid if it takes no action to revoke the provisional credit within the period prescribed by clearing house rules (in some instances, a matter of hours after receipt). When a check is sent through the mails to the payor bank, the Code requires a revocation of the provisional credit within the "midnight deadline." This is a new term which, in most cases, will extend the time within which a bank must act to avoid final payment; it is defined in Section 4-104 as "midnight on [the] next banking day following the banking day on which [the payor bank] receives the item." "Midnight deadline" is also the presumed period of time within which a collecting or intermediary bank receiving a check in the collection process must act in presenting a check for payment, sending notice of dishonor, etc. The Code recognizes the current banking practice of fixing an afternoon hour of 2 P.M. or later as a cutoff time after which items will be considered as being received on the next banking day for the purpose of computing the commencement of the "midnight deadline" (§ 4-107).

An alternative point of final payment, after which a check may not be returned, is the "posting" of the check by the payor, i.e., the mechanical act of debiting the drawer's account. The point of time after which a stop-payment order from the drawer or attachment of the account by the drawer's creditors is not effective is established as the time of "sight posting" the item to the account of the drawer (§ 4-303). The check does not actually have to be posted in order for there to be a final payment of a check. A bank may otherwise evidence its intention to pay the item. This is commonly referred to as "sight posting" (§ 4-303, Official Comment 3). In the collection process, this occurs when a clerk has placed the check in a stack to be sent to another office for final posting, and this alternative point is based on the practical difficulty of preventing the payment after this time.

Relationship Between Payor Bank and Its Customer

Article 4 contains a number of rules, some of which modify or directly change existing law or settle areas of present uncertainty, governing the relationship between a payor bank and its customers. Section 4-402 recognizes the generally understood rule that a drawee bank has a duty to pay a check which is a proper order to pay, but modifies the damage rule for breach of this duty by limiting recovery to actual damages proved. When two or more checks are presented for payment at the same time and the account is insufficient to pay them all, the bank may pay in any order with impunity until the deposit is no longer sufficient to pay any one (§ 4-303). Present uncertainty about what constitutes effective stop-payment orders is removed by Section 4-403, which makes an oral order binding upon the bank for 14 days and a written order effective for six months. A bank's duty to its depositor with respect to a stale check presented for payment is clarified by Section 4-404, which provides that the bank may, but need not, pay a check which is presented more than six months after its date. When the drawer of a check dies or is incompetent before the check is paid, the order to pay is still effective until the banks learn of the death or incompetence and may pay for ten days after knowledge of death (§ 4-405).

Section 4-406 incorporates the common law duty of a depositor to examine his bank statements and items paid and notify the bank with reasonable promptness of a forgery of his signature on a check that has been paid or any alteration; failure to do so will preclude the depositor from asserting such irregularities. This section gives the drawer 14 days after the return of an item and statement to discover and notify the bank of a forgery or alteration; thereafter, the drawer is estopped from asserting any subsequent forgery or alteration by the same wrongdoer which was paid in good faith prior to notification of the bank. In all other cases, without regard to negligence, the customer has one year from the time the statement and items are made available to him to discover and report to the bank a forgery of his signature or an alteration, and three years from such time to report a forged indorsement.

ARTICLE 5

LETTERS OF CREDIT

The commercial letter of credit has been employed principally in international trade where the foreign seller is willing to ship goods only on the credit of a known bank which promises to pay the purchase price upon the receipt of the bill of lading and other necessary documents. Prior to the enactment of the Code, the law concerning letters of credit came from common law decisions, principally of New York, Massachusetts and California, where the bulk of foreign commerce is financed. Thus, Article 5 of the Code breaks new ground in codifying the legal rules concerning this device. The text of Article 5 is reproduced herein commencing on page 1-63. The greater certainty and clarification afforded by statutory treatment may increase the use of letters of credit in domestic trade, where a distant seller may have the added protection of substituting the credit of a bank for that of a buyer, who may have already arranged for financing of the purchase price by the bank. The customary documentary sale, whereby the seller sends the bill of lading with a draft drawn on the buyer to a bank in the buyer's town for collection, unlike the letter of credit, does not shift the risk of nonpayment from the seller to the bank.

In order to serve this essential risk shifting function, the bank is legally divorced from matters relating to the underlying contract of sale, such as the quantity and quality of the goods. Thus, under the Code, the issuing bank's liability to pay and its entitlement to reimbursement from its customer becomes absolute upon the receipt of the documents required (§ 5-109). If the bank is notified prior to payment that the documents are forged or there is fraud in the transaction between the buyer and seller, the bank is given an option to honor the draft or demand for payment unless the customer has obtained a court injunction against the issuer's exercise of its option. (§ 5-114).

Normally, a bank will issue a straight letter of credit where the language "we engage with you" is used. In such form, the promise does not run to a purchaser of the draft as a holder in due course on the theory that the purchaser sees on the face that the promise runs only to the issuee. A letter of credit may, however, be made negotiable and negotiated to a holder in due course who may enforce it against the issuer regardless of any fraud in the transaction or forgery of the document (§ 5-114).

In order to properly examine the documents and make sure that they comply with the letter of credit, the bank is given until the close of the third banking day following receipt of the documents to honor the draft. Failure to act within that time constitutes dishonor (§ 5-112).

Upon wrongful dishonor under an irrevocable credit, the presentor may recover from the issuer the face amount of the draft, plus incidental damages recoverable by a seller under Article 2, less any amount realized from resale or other use of the subject matter of the transaction (§ 5-115).

ARTICLE 6

BULK TRANSFERS

Article 6 seeks to protect creditors of a merchant by voiding a bulk transfer of his merchandise out of the ordinary course of trade, unless the transferee gives notice of the contemplated transfer to all known creditors, at least ten days before he takes possession. A discussion of fraudulent conveyances, including the complete text of Article 6, is contained in Chapter 26.

Coverage is extended under Section 6-102 to include business equipment, if it is made in connection with a bulk transfer of inventory. Also, a bulk sale at an auction under Section 6-108 expands existing coverage so that the auctioneer is charged with the responsibility similar to that of a transferee of other bulk sales, i.e., where the auctioneer knows the auction constitutes a bulk transfer he is personally liable to the creditors of the transferor for uncollected debts. The rights of the purchasers, however, are not affected.

ARTICLE 7

DOCUMENTS OF TITLE

Article 7 repeals and modernizes the half-century old Uniform Warehouse Receipts Act (UWRA) and the Uniform Bills of Lading Act (UBLA) and integrates the statutory treatment of these documents. Some new coverage is included to cover modern shipping and the storage practices which were not contemplated by the original Uniform Acts, such as bonded storage required by federal or state statute and air bills and problems which arise under modern high-speed air or truck transportation. Of course, this state legislation would not affect federal legislation dealing with interstate shipments, such as the Federal Bills of Lading Act or the Federal Carriage of Goods by Sea Act. Portions of Article 7 are reproduced herein commencing on page 1-69.

As under the UWRA, a warehouse receipt, by definition, must be issued by a warehouse which does not include a person who stores his own goods (§ 7-201). An important exception to this is found in Section 7-201 (2) which treats a receipt as a warehouse receipt when issued by a non-warehouseman, including the owner of the goods, under a statute requiring a bond against withdrawal.

The essential terms of the warehouse receipts are similar to those under existing law, but the Code preserves the obligations of the issuer even though the document does not comply with the formal requirements (§ 7-202). Essential terms of a bill of lading provided by the UBLA are omitted from the Code, but federal regulation of the forms used in interstate commerce will continue to control.

An illustration of the Code's modernization of documents of title is the use of the "destination bill" which is designed to meet the problem of high-speed air transportation where the goods may arrive at the destination before the documents. This could be inconvenient where the carrier does not have storage facilities and could be even more serious where the goods are perishable. To meet this problem, Section 7-305 authorizes the carrier, upon receipt of the goods for shipment, to issue the bill at the destination point. (Of course, the carrier may not issue the bill until the goods are received.) Assuming the usual documentary sale, the bill would be issued to the buyer's bank, the seller would wire the bank a draft on the buyer, and the bank would indorse the bill to the buyer when he honors the draft.

Many of the familiar negotiable instruments rules apply where a document of title is negotiable and is taken by "due negotiation." A new requirement, however, is that negotiation must be in the "regular course of business or financing" in order for the transferee to take the instrument free of defenses and claims of ownership to which his transferor is subject. To qualify, the person making the transfer must be a person in the trade and the nature of the transaction must be a usual and ordinary transaction in which documents are transferred (§ 7-501).

A bona fide purchaser of an altered document of title may enforce it according to its original tenor. The same rule applies to the filling in of blanks in a bill of lading (§ 7-306) but a bona fide purchaser may treat as authorized the filling of a blank in a negotiable warehouse receipt (§ 7-208). This absolute liability imposed on a warehouseman for the unauthorized filling of blanks is in recognition of the dangerous practice of executing warehouse receipts in blank. It is often necessary for carriers to execute bills of lading in blank to be filled out by various employees, and thus the consequence of improper completion of bills carries no sanction.

ARTICLE 8

INVESTMENT SECURITIES

The Uniform Stock Transfer Act was the principal statutory law governing the transfer of certificates of stock as an investment security, prior to the Uniform Commercial Code. The Code repeals the Uniform Stock Transfer Act and replaces it with Article 8 which separates the law of investment securities from the short-term negotiable paper of Article 3. Article 8 extends new statutory coverage to registered bonds and other types of investment paper not covered by any other uniform act. The matter of regulation of securities under the federal and state "blue sky law" is not dealt with by this article.

The basic policies of free transferability and protection to a holder underlying the negotiable instruments law of securities, are similar to those of Article 3, but without the formal prerequisites of negotiability required by the Negotiable Instruments Law and Article 3 of the Code. Thus, a bona fide purchaser of securities is similar to a holder in due course in negotiable instrument law, in that he takes free of defenses and adverse claims of ownership. Similar to the rule of forged commercial paper, no holder has a right against an issuer of a counterfeit security or one on which the validating signature is unauthorized. Under Section 8-205, however, an unauthorized signature is valid in favor of a good faith purchaser for value when it is of a person entrusted by the issuer with signing the security or an employee entrusted with handling the security. Section 8-206 follows the change in the law of commercial paper under Article 3, and protects a purchaser for value without notice of incorrectness from the defense of improper completion where blanks are left upon the issue of a security.

The purchaser of commercial paper after maturity is automatically subject to all defenses under Article 3. His counterpart, i.e., a purchaser of security under Section 8-203, will be deprived of the bona fide purchaser status only where he purchases more than two years after a call for redemption or exchange, or one year after such call if the funds or securities are available for delivery when due.

Section 8-104 prescribes a forumula for adjusting the rights of a person entitled to issue against the issuer of an over-issue of securities, for example, where a stock transfer agent issues the new certificate without the surrender of a certificate for a corresponding number of shares, creating an excess of the issuer's chartered allowance. The Code resolves this problem by compelling the issuer to purchase shares on the market to replace the over-issue. If shares are not available from the market, the person entitled may obtain reimbursement at the price he or the last purchaser for value paid for the security with interest from the date of demand.

ARTICLE 9

SECURED TRANSACTIONS

Article 9 is probably the most important Article of the Code since its scope reaches transactions whose intended effect is to create security interests in personal property. In 1972, the Permanent Editorial Board published the Official Text and Comment thereby substantially revising Article 9. In 1977 a number of sections were again revised. All references and discussions in this Chapter are to the latest revisions.

Chapter 7, Secured Transactions under Article 9 of the Uniform Commercial Code, contains portions of the text of Article 9, tables giving filing information for each state, and a discussion of the creation and perfection of the security interest. Chapter 6, Secured Transactions Superseded by the Uniform Commercial Code Article 9, discusses Conditional Sales, Chattel Mortgages, Assignment of Accounts Receivable, and Factors' Liens.

In limiting the area of coverage to chattel financing, Article 9 divorces itself from its predecessor, the real property mortgage. Existing state statutory expressions of local public policy regulating credit (e.g., usury and small loan acts) and creating liens in favor of preferred creditors (e.g., landlords and materialmen) are unaffected by this Article. Also, existing federal legislation dealing with the recording of a security interest in certain types of collateral, such as airplanes and ships, and state automobile title laws, fit into the scheme of Article 9 without change. The remaining aspects of secured financing law, including the creation, attachment and perfection of a security interest, are treated for the first time in an integrated, comprehensive and uniform way by this Article.

In treating a security transaction as a single unity in which there is a conveyance of a security interest in personal property to secure the payment of a debt, Article 9 rejects any distinction based on the form or designation of the device employed, such as chattel mortgage, conditional sales agreement, trust receipt, etc. Different results are reached in some instances on functional grounds depending upon the nature of the collateral and its use. For this purpose, Section 9-109 divides all collateral into four classifications: consumer goods, used for personal purposes; equipment, used principally in business; farm products in possession of a person engaged in farming operations; and inventory held by a business enterprise for sale or materials used, consumed, or manufactured in a business.

Consistent with this functional, rather than formal and conceptual approach, Article 9 states substantive rules without regard to the ancient controversy over whether the secured party acquires "title" to collateral or a "mere lien." The rights, obligations and remedies provided for in Article 9 are applicable whether title to collateral is in the secured party or the debtor (§ 9-202). This approach is further reflected in the adoption in 1972 of Section 9-408 which authorizes consignors or lessors of goods to file a financing statement to protect their interest against the rights of creditors of the consignee or lessee.

Creation of the Security Interest

In order to create or convey a security interest which is valid between the parties, a minimum of formalities is prescribed by the Code. The pledge, a type of security interest, is recognized and requires nothing more than delivery of the collateral or documents of title which represent the goods pledged. For the creation of the more usual type of non-promissory security interest, the debtor must sign a simple security agreement containing a description of the collateral, give value, and have rights in the collateral; the security interest will then attach in favor of the secured party (§ 9-203). In many instances a financing statement, in addition to the security agreement, must be filed to perfect a security interest (§ 9-302). A financing statement must contain the names of the debtor and the secured party, must be signed by the debtor, and must include a statement indicating the types, or describing the items, of collateral (§ 9-402).

In a modern industrial economy there is frequently an urgent need for even the most successful and solvent business enterprise to acquire working capital in order to finance the acquisition of inventory and meet current operational expenses. A financier may be willing to supply these funds only when he can acquire a valid security interest in the commercial debtor's inventory or equipment which will stand up against claims of third parties. Since inventory is frequently in a state of motion in the resale or manufacturing cycle, what is needed is an effective "floating lien" which automatically feeds the security agreement as it is acquired by the debtor. Where the collateral is business equipment which may be replaced before the loan is repaid, it is also commercially desirable for the replacements to automatically attach to the security interest.

One of the most significant accomplishments of Article 9 is that it meets these needs by expressly validating the "after-acquired-property" clause in a security agreement whereby a lien on inventory or replacement equipment attaches as it is acquired by the debtor (§ 9-204). To complete the commercial objective of a continuing extension of credit secured by new inventory or equipment as acquired, Section 9-204 expressly validates the extension of the security interest to future advances.

The ability of this inventory financing arrangement to withstand the attack of unsecured creditors directly, or through their representative, e.g., the trustee in bankruptcy, has been in doubt ever since the 1925 United States Supreme Court decision of *Benedict v. Ratner*, 268 U.S. 353 (1925). The court held that the transaction was void where the debtor was given unfettered dominion or control over the inventory collateral. Section 9-205 removes any doubt regarding the effectiveness of this financing arrangement by rejecting the principle of *Benedict v. Ratner* as a matter of state law. (§ 9-205, 1972 official comment 1). The Code's acceptance of the "after-acquired-property" clause is not applicable in a bankruptcy setting. Under the new Bankruptcy Code, see Chapter 28, *infra*, property acquired by the estate or the debtor after the commencement of a bankruptcy proceeding is not subject to any lien resulting from a security agreement entered into by the debtor before the commencement of the case. 11 U.S.C. § 552(a) (Supp. v 1981). The Code does specify an exception to this general rule. If the security agreement extended to the proceeds, product, offspring, rents, or profits of property that the debtor had before the commencement of the case, then the proceeds, etc., are subject to the security interest. Id. § 552(b). The Bankruptcy Code also legislatively overrules *DuBay v. Williams*, 417 F.2d 1277 (9th Cir. 1969), in which the validity of assignments of future accounts receivables were upheld as against a trustee in bankruptcy in the face of an attack that such assignments constituted a preferential transfer. Under present bankruptcy law, a creditor with a security interest in a floating mass, such as inventory or accounts receivable, is subject to preference attack to the extent that he improves his position to the detriment of unsecured creditors during the ninety day period prior to the filing of the bankruptcy petition. Id. § 547.

The validation of the "after-acquired-property" clause, except as regards to the bankruptcy case, as the key to effective commercial financing, does not apply to consumer goods acquired by the debtor more than ten days after the secured party gives value. (§ 9-204). This is in recognition of the social and economic objection to tying up all the future acquisitions of an individual by a continuing blanket lien.

Perfection

The Code continues to recognize that for most types of collateral, perfection of the security interest against third parties—the real test of its effectiveness—may be accomplished alternatively by pledge or by record notice. The Code adopts what may be generally described as a "lien creditor race" approach. Prior to the 1972 change in Article 9, only creditors who had obtained a lien without knowledge of a security interest and before that interest was perfected could defeat a subsequent unperfected security interest (§ 9-301). The 1972 version of the Code, however, has eliminated the element of knowledge. As between conflicting perfected security interests in the same collateral, priority is accorded to the first to be perfected, regardless of knowledge, and regardless of the order of attachment. Furthermore, a bona fide purchaser of the collateral for value and without knowledge of the security interest has the right to rely on possession by the debtor and will usually take free of the unfiled security interest.

These generalizations are subject to some important exceptions and modifications which need to be outlined in order to present a clearer and more accurate picture of the Code's approach to perfection. It should be noted that perfection is a relative term since the security interest may be perfected as to one class of third parties but not as to another.

In the context of inventory financing, it is the usual understanding of the parties that the debtor will sell his inventory in the ordinary course of business and is usually so authorized. Section 9-307 recognizes this commercial understanding by providing that the buyer out of inventory in the ordinary course of business takes free of the inventory financer's security interest, even though he has knowledge of it. The proceeds received from such sale of inventory are subject to a continuing security interest in favor of the inventory financer if a financing statement is properly filed. In the event of insolvency proceedings by or against the debtor, the perfected security interest in proceeds which are commingled with other funds of the debtor is limited to an amount received by the debtor within ten days of the institution of the insolvency proceedings (§ 9-306). Thus, the inventory financer who properly perfects his security interest, will be protected against the honest insolvency of the debtor, to the extent of the value of the collateral. Despite the Code's rejection of the *Benedict* Rule, which compelled the security financer to exercise some control over the inventory collateral, some element of the policing and accounting doctrine of that case remains in order to avoid the loss of proceeds received by the debtor more than ten days prior to the institution of insolvency proceedings.

Where a purchaser, however, takes goods with knowledge that the sale is in violation of a security agreement, e.g., where a secured party did not authorize the sale of the collateral, such as in the case of business equipment, or where the purchaser takes farm products from a person engaged in farming, the purchaser takes the collateral subject to the perfected security interest (§ 9-307).

No filing is necessary in order to perfect a purchase money security interest in consumer goods (§ 9-302). Purchasers will take free of the perfected but unfiled security interest if they buy without knowledge of the security interest, for value, for their own personal purposes, and before a financing statement is filed. If a secured party does file a financing statement, however, all buyers take subject to the security interest (§ 9-307). This treatment of consumer goods does not apply to the financing of automobiles for private use where the state's certificate of title law governs (§ 9-302).

For the mechanics of perfecting a nonpossessory security interest in chattel by filing, the Code borrows the concept of "notice filing" from the Uniform Trust Receipts Act (enacted in 33 states) as an alternative to filing the security agreement itself. This is record or constructive notice as a result of the filing of an abbreviated statement which contains the addresses of the debtor and secured party, the signature of the debtor, and a general description of the types or items of the collateral (§ 9-402). This "financing statement" device is designed principally to facilitate the perfection of a security interest in inventory where there is a continuing change in the collateral and in the amount of indebtedness (§ 9-402, 1972 Official Comment 2). The record notice is effective for a period of five years from the time the statement is presented to the filing clerk with the fee, subject to renewal for a like term by filing a "continuation statement" (§ 9-403).

Since this noninformative notice filing does not reveal the amount of the secured debt nor the actual collateral secured at any given time, Section 9-208 makes provision for the debtor to obtain a statement of account or a list of collateral from the secured party which sets out this information; the statement may be then relied on by third parties who deal with the debtor. When there is no longer an outstanding obligation, Section 9-404 places the burden on the secured party of record to send a "termination statement" to the filing officer to remove the financing statement from the record. If the secured party fails to send such a termination statement within ten days after demand by the debtor, he is liable for $100 damages plus any loss caused to the debtor by such failure. In the case of consumer goods, no demand by the debtor is required.

Where the collateral remains at rest in the possession of the debtor, the secured party may continue the present practice of filing the security agreement as a "financing statement" rather than execute the separate abbreviated financing statement which will usually be limited to inventory financing. In that event, the Code eliminates most of the formal and technical prerequisites to filing such as acknowledgment or witnessing. Instead, the security agreement must merely comply with the information and signature requirements for financing statements (§ 9-402, 1972 Official Comment 1).

Priorities

It has been stated that priority among conflicting security interests in the same collateral is determined by the order of perfection. This is true regardless of the order in which the consideration passes—that is, the time when the secured loan is made—and regardless of actual knowledge. A most important application of this rule and the notice filing concept is the protection it affords to the inventory financer in granting maximum protection against the honest insolvency of his debtor. The financer, having determined that the debtor's property is not subject to a recorded security interest or creditor's lien, may execute and file the financing statement containing a general description of the collateral to be covered, an after-acquired property clause and claim of proceeds, if appropriate. Thereafter, the security agreement may be executed and the money advanced, at which time the security interest in the collateral attaches, but the effective date of perfection is the earlier time when the financing statement was filed. Even if a creditor of the debtor should acquire a lien or advance money and take a security interest in the same collateral, his interest would be subordinate to the security interest which was filed first, but which attached later. Assuming that the collateral is inventory and the secured party has authorized its sale, he may now look to the proceeds and any replacement of inventory which was covered by the after-acquired property clause, all of which were perfected as of time of initial filing. It is apparent that the drafters of Article 9 focused their attention on this chattel financing situation and set out to accomplish this result of giving maximum protection to the diligent secured party against losses resulting from the honest insolvency of the debtor. It is also apparent that the policy objective designed to lead to this result was to encourage the supplying of working capital to the debtor, which is a vital ingredient of the expanding industrial economy.

The "first-to-perfect" rule, as the basic formula for determining the order of priorities, is subject to an important qualification where one of the competing claimants holds a purchase money security interest to secure the purchase price of newly acquired goods and the other claimants claim the purchased collateral under an after-acquired property clause. In the context of equipment financing, if the purchase money financer perfects his security interest within ten days after the debtor receives possession of the collateral, he will have a priority claim in this collateral or its proceeds over the financer claiming under an after-acquired property clause (§ 9-312(4)). This preferred treatment of the purchase money security interest constitutes an exception to the usual rule that after-acquired property feeds a security interest when acquired and is deemed perfected as of the time of the filing of the financing statement containing an after-acquired property clause. Where the collateral is inventory, the purchase money security claimant has priority over a conflicting security interest, only when he perfects before the debtor receives possession of the collateral (without benefit of the ten-day grace period for filing) and only if he gives notice of his claim within five years before the debtor receives possession of the inventory to the inventory financer who has previously filed a financing statement claiming the same inventory under an after-acquired property clause (§ 9-312(3)). The reason for the additional requirement of notice in order for the purchase money financer of inventory to enjoy a priority position is to save the initial general inventory financer from the risk of continuing to make advances to the debtor under the belief that the subsequently acquired inventory continues to feed his security interest.

Several other special modifications of the first to perfect priority rule are provided for by the Code. Section 9-312(2) accords priority to a perfected security interest in crops to secure a loan given not more than three months before the crops are planted. The secured creditor will have priority even where he had knowledge of an earlier security interest where that earlier interest secured obligations due more than six months before the crops became growing crops. Section 9-310 gives priority to statutory liens for services or materials, unless the statute creating the lien provides otherwise.

A security interest in personal property, which thereafter becomes a fixture by attachment to real property, takes priority over all prior security claims in the realty (§ 9-313). Similarly, a security interest in goods which are affixed to other goods (typically a security interest in tires, subsequently installed on cars) takes priority over prior claims to the whole (§ 9-314).

Under Section 9-315, a perfected security interest in goods, which through processing become so commingled as to lose their identity in the product or mass (e.g., raw materials), continues in the product or mass. This section also covers the case where the collateral consists of components assembled into a machine and which do not lose their identity. In that case, the security interest may be continued in the product if expressly claimed in the filed financing statement; if not so claimed, the identifiable part will be treated as an accession under Section 9-314. When more than one security interest attaches to the product or mass, the secured parties share in proportion to their contribution.

Default

Part 5 of Article 9 is designed to afford greater flexibility and simplicity in the prescribed manner of liquidating the collateral on default in payment of the secured debt. This policy is balanced against the protection of both the debtor's interest and the interest of other creditors. As regards the debtor, the Code is designed so that the collateral will realize its fair value. This objective is expressed in Section 9-504 by the key standard for the liquidation sale that it be "commercially reasonable." Without an attempt at a specific definition of this term, certain guidelines and minimum standards are prescribed for the disposition of the collateral by the secured party. It may be by public or private sale, with or without processing, in bulk or in parcels. Reasonable notice of the time and place of the disposition must be given to the debtor and other secured parties of record, unless collateral is perishable, or threatens to decline speedily in value, or is of the type usually sold on recognized market.

Section 9-505 authorizes the secured party in the possession of the collateral after default to retain the collateral in satisfaction of the debt if the debtor, or any secured party of record, does not object to such written proposal within 30 days after receipt. Where the collateral is consumer goods and the debtor has paid 60% of the obligation, however, the collateral must be disposed of within 90 days after the secured party takes possession. If the secured party fails to comply with this requirement where the collateral is consumer goods, Section 9-507 gives the debtor the right to recover damages in an amount no less than the total credit charge plus 10% of the debt.

ARTICLE 1 [1]

GENERAL PROVISIONS

Part 1

Short Title, Construction, Application and Subject Matter of the Act

SECTION 1-101. *Short Title.*—This Act shall be known and may be cited as Uniform Commercial Code.

SECTION 1-102. *Purposes; Rules of Construction; Variation by Agreement.*—
(1) This Act shall be liberally construed and applied to promote its underlying purposes and policies.
(2) Underlying purposes and policies of this Act are
  (a) to simplify, clarify and modernize the law governing commercial transactions;
  (b) to permit the continued expansion of commercial practices through custom, usage and agreement of the parties;
  (c) to make uniform the law among the various jurisdictions.
(3) The effect of provisions of this Act may be varied by agreement, except as otherwise provided in this Act and except that the obligations of good faith, diligence, reasonableness and care prescribed by this Act may not be disclaimed by agreement but the parties may by agreement determine the standards by which the performance of such obligations is to be measured if such standards are not manifestly unreasonable.
(4) The presence in certain provisions of this Act of the words "unless otherwise agreed" or words of similar import does not imply that the effect of other provisions may not be varied by agreement under subsection (3).
(5) In this Act, unless the context otherwise requires
  (a) words in the singular number include the plural, and in the plural include the singular;
  (b) words of the masculine gender include the feminine and the neuter, and when the sense so indicates words of the neuter gender may refer to any gender.[2]

SECTION 1-103. *Supplementary General Principles of Law Applicable.*—Unless displaced by the particular provisions of this Act, the principles of law and equity, including the law merchant and the law relative to capacity to contract, principal and agent, estoppel fraud, misrepresentation, duress, coercion, mistake,

---

[1] Local variations of substantive importance are set forth in the text or in the footnotes, but for the complete text of the Code for any jurisdiction consult the local statute.

[2] Minnesota adds subsec. (6) which prohibits construction of this section to authorize branch offices for banks, trust companies, etc.

bankruptcy, or other validating or invalidating cause shall supplement its provisions.[1]

SECTION 1-104. *Construction Against Implicit Repeal.*—This Act being a general act intended as a unified coverage of its subject matter, no part of it shall be deemed to be impliedly repealed by subsequent legislation if such construction can reasonably be avoided.[2]

SECTION 1-105. *Territorial Application of the Act; Parties' Power to Choose Applicable Law.*—(1) Except as provided hereafter in this section, when a transaction bears a reasonable relation to this state and also to another state or nation the parties may agree that the law either of this state or of such other state or nation shall govern their rights and duties. Failing such agreement this Act applies to transactions bearing an appropriate relation to this state.

(2) Where one of the following provisions of this Act specifies the applicable law, that provision governs and a contrary agreement is effective only to the extent permitted by the law (including the conflict of law rules) so specified:

Rights of creditors against sold goods. Section 2-402.

Applicability of the Article on Bank Deposits and Collections. Section 4-102.

Bulk transfers subject to the Article on Bulk Transfers. Section 6-102.

Applicability of the Article on Investment Securities. Section 8-106.

Perfection provisions of the Article on Secured Transactions. Sections 9-103.[3]

SECTION 1-106. *Remedies to Be Liberally Administered.*—(1) The remedies provided by this Act shall be liberally administered to the end that the aggrieved party may be put in as good a position as if the other party had fully performed but neither consequential nor penal damages may be had except as specifically provided in this Act or by other rule of law.

(2) Any right or obligation declared by this Act is enforceable by action unless the provision declaring it specifies a different and limited effect.

SECTION 1-107. *Waiver or Renunciation of Claim or Right after Breach.*—Any claim or right arising out of an alleged breach can be discharged in whole or in part without consideration by a written waiver or renunciation signed and delivered by the aggrieved party.

SECTION 1-108. *Severability.*—If any provision or clause of this Act or application thereof to any person or circumstances is held invalid, such invalidity shall not affect other provisions or applications of the Act which can be given effect without the invalid provision or application, and to this end the provisions of this Act are declared to be severable.

SECTION 1-109. *Section Captions.*—Section captions are parts of this Act.

---

[1] Maryland and the District of Columbia provide that the age of majority as it pertains to the capacity to contract is eighteen years of age.

[2] Illinois gives preference to Section 40.23 of "The Civil Administrative Code of Illinois" in the event of a conflict. Section 40.23 deals with public warehousemen, grain dealers, etc.

[3] Mississippi provides that Mississippi law shall always govern with respect to disclaimers of implied warranties of merchantability and limitation of remedies for breach.

Part 2

General Definitions and Principles of Interpretation

SECTION 1-201. *General Definitions.*—Subject to additional definitions contained in the subsequent Articles of this Act which are applicable to specific Articles or Parts thereof, and unless the context otherwise requires, in this Act:

(1) "Action" in the sense of a judicial proceeding includes recoupment, counterclaim, setoff, suit in equity and any other proceedings in which rights are determined.

(2) "Aggrieved party" means a party entitled to resort to a remedy.

(3) "Agreement" means the bargain of the parties in fact as found in their language or by implication from other circumstances including course of dealing or usage of trade or course of performance as provided in this Act (Sections 1-205 and 2-208). Whether an agreement has legal consequences is determined by the provisions of this Act, if applicable; otherwise by the law of contracts (Section 1-103). (Compare "Contract.")

(4) "Bank" means any person engaged in the business of banking.[1]

(5) "Bearer" means the person in possession of an instrument, document of title, or certificated security payable to bearer or indorsed in blank.

(6) "Bill of lading" means a document evidencing the receipt of goods for shipment issued by a person engaged in the business of transporting or forwarding goods, and includes an airbill. "Airbill" means a document serving for air transportation as a bill of lading does for marine or rail transportation, and includes an air consignment note or air waybill.

(7) "Branch" includes a separately incorporated foreign branch of a bank.

(8) "Burden of establishing" a fact means the burden of persuading the triers of fact that the existence of the fact is more probable than its non-existence.

(9) "Buyer in ordinary course of business" means a person who in good faith and without knowledge that the sale to him is in violation of the ownership rights or security interest of a third party in the goods buys in ordinary course from a person in the business of selling goods of that kind but does not include a pawnbroker. All persons who sell minerals or the like (including oil and gas) at wellhead or minehead shall be deemed to be persons in the business of selling goods of that kind. "Buying" may be for cash or by exchange of other property or on secured or unsecured credit and includes receiving goods or documents of title under a preexisting contract for sale but does not include a transfer in bulk or as security for or in total or partial satisfaction of a money debt.[2]

(10) "Conspicuous": A term or clause is conspicuous when it is so written that a reasonable person against whom it is to operate ought to have noticed it. A printed heading in capitals (as: NONNEGOTIABLE BILL OF LADING) is conspicuous. Language in the body of a form is "conspicuous" if it is in larger or other contrasting type or color. But in a telegram any stated term is "conspicuous." Whether a term or clause is "conspicuous" or not is for decision by the court.

(11) "Contract" means the total obligation in law which results from the

---

[1] Idaho amends this section by defining "bank" with greater particularity.
[2] In New York the term "collateral loan broker" replaces the term "pawnbroker."

parties' agreement as affected by this Act and any other applicable rules of law. (Compare "Agreement.")

(12) "Creditor" includes a general creditor, a secured creditor, a lien creditor and any representative of creditors, including an assignee for the benefit of creditors, a trustee in bankruptcy, a receiver in equity and an executor or administrator of an insolvent debtor's or assignor's estate.

(13) "Defendant" includes a person in the position of defendant in a cross-action or counterclaim.

(14) "Delivery" with respect to instruments, documents of title, chattel paper or certificated securities means voluntary transfer of possession.

(15) "Document of the title" includes bill of lading, dock warrant, dock receipt, warehouse receipt or order for the delivery of goods, and also any other document which in the regular course of business or financing is treated as adequately evidencing that the person in possession of it is entitled to receive, hold and dispose of the document and the goods it covers. To be a document of title a document must purport to be issued by or addressed to a bailee and purport to cover goods in the bailee's possession which are either identified or are fungible portions of an identified mass.

(16) "Fault" means wrongful act, omission or breach.

(17) "Fungible" with respect to goods or securities means goods or securities of which any unit is, by nature or usage of trade, the equivalent of any other like unit. Goods which are not fungible shall be deemed fungible for the purposes of this Act to the extent that under a particular agreement or document unlike units are treated as equivalents.

(18) "Genuine" means free of forgery or counterfeiting.

(19) "Good faith" means honesty in fact in the conduct or transaction concerned.

(20) "Holder" means a person who is in possession of a document of title or an instrument or a certified investment security drawn, issued or indorsed to him or his order or to bearer or in blank.

(21) To "honor" is to pay or to accept and pay, or where a credit so engages to purchase or discount a draft complying with the terms of the credit.

(22) "Insolvency proceedings" includes any assignment for the benefit of creditors or other proceedings intended to liquidate or rehabilitate the estate of the person involved.

(23) A person is "insolvent" who either has ceased to pay his debts in the ordinary course of business or cannot pay his debts as they become due or is insolvent within the meaning of the federal bankruptcy law.

(24) "Money" means a medium of exchange authorized or adopted by a domestic or foreign government as a part of its currency.[1]

(25) A person has "notice" of a fact when
  (a) he has actual knowledge of it; or
  (b) he has received a notice or notification of it; or
  (c) from all the facts and circumstances known to him at the time in question he has reason to know that it exists.

A person "knows" or has "knowledge" of a fact when he has actual knowledge of it. "Discover" or "learn" or a word or phrase of similar import refers to

---

[1] New York amends this subsection to exclude rare or unusual coins used for numismatic purposes. Such rare or unusual coins are considered to be goods.

knowledge rather than to reason to know. The time and circumstances under which a notice or notification may cease to be effective are not determined by this Act.

(26) A person "notifies" or "gives" a notice or notification to another by taking such steps as may be reasonably required to inform the other in ordinary course whether or not such other actually comes to know of it. A person "receives" a notice or notification when
   (a) it comes to his attention; or
   (b) it is duly delivered at the place of business through which the contract was made or at any other place held out by him as the place for receipt of such communications.

(27) Notice, knowledge or a notice or notification received by an organization is effective for a particular transaction from the time when it is brought to the attention of the individual conducting that transaction, and in any event from the time when it would have been brought to his attention if the organization had exercised due diligence. An organization exercises due diligence if it maintains reasonable routines for communicating significant information to the person conducting the transaction and there is reasonable compliance with the routines. Due diligence does not require an individual acting for the organization to communicate information unless such communication is part of his regular duties or unless he has reason to know of the transaction and that the transaction would be materially affected by the information.

(28) "Organization" includes a corporation, government or governmental subdivision or agency, business trust, estate, trust, partnership or association, two or more persons having a joint or common interest, or any other legal or commercial entity.

(29) "Party," as distinct from "third party," means a person who has engaged in a transaction or made an agreement within this Act.

(30) "Person" includes an individual or an organization (see Section 1-102).

(31) "Presumption" or "presumed" means that the trier of fact must find the existence of the fact presumed unless and until evidence is introduced which would support a finding of its nonexistence.

(32) "Purchase" includes taking by sale, discount, negotiation, mortgage, pledge, lien, issue or reissue, gift or any other voluntary transaction creating an interest in property.

(33) "Purchaser" means a person who takes by purchase.

(34) "Remedy" means any remedial right to which an aggrieved party is entitled with or without resort to a tribunal.

(35) "Representative" includes an agent, an officer of a corporation or association, and a trustee, executor or administrator of an estate, or any other person empowered to act for another.

(36) "Rights" includes remedies.

(37) "Security interest" means an interest in personal property or fixtures which secures payment or performance of an obligation. The retention or reservation of title by a seller of goods notwithstanding shipment or delivery to the buyer (Section 2-401) is limited in effect to a reservation of a "security interest." The term also includes any interest of a buyer of accounts or chattel paper which is subject to Article 9. The special property interest of a buyer of goods on identification of such goods to a contract for sale under Section 2-401 is

not a "security interest," but a buyer may also acquire a "security interest" by complying with Article 9. Unless a lease or consignment is intended as security, reservation of title thereunder is not a "security interest" but a consignment is in any event subject to the provisions on consignment sales (Section 2-326). Whether a lease is intended as security is to be determined by the facts of each case; however, (a) the inclusion of an option to purchase does not of itself make the lease one intended for security, and (b) an agreement that upon compliance with the terms of the lease the lessee shall become or has the option to become the owner of the property for no additional consideration or for a nominal consideration does make the lease one intended for security.

(38) "Send" in connection with any writing or notice means to deposit in the mail or deliver for transmission by any other usual means of communication with postage or cost of transmission provided for and properly addressed and in the case of an instrument to an address specified thereon or otherwise agreed, or if there be none to any address reasonable under the circumstances. The receipt of any writing or notice within the time at which it would have arrived if properly sent has the effect of a proper sending.

(39) "Signed" includes any symbol executed or adopted by a party with present intention to authenticate a writing.

(40) "Surety" includes guarantor.

(41) "Telegram" includes a message transmitted by radio, teletype, cable, any mechanical method of transmission, or the like.

(42) "Term" means that portion of an agreement which relates to a particular matter.

(43) "Unauthorized" signature or indorsement means one made without actual, implied or apparent authority and includes a forgery.

(44) "Value." Except as otherwise provided with respect to negotiable instruments and bank collections (Sections 3-303, 4-208 and 4-209) a person gives "value" for rights if he acquires them
- (a) in return for a binding commitment to extend credit or for the extension of immediately available credit whether or not drawn upon and whether or not a charge back is provided for in the event of difficulties in collection; or
- (b) as security for or in total or partial satisfaction of a preexisting claim; or
- (c) by accepting delivery pursuant to a preexisting contract for purchase; or
- (d) generally, in return for any consideration sufficient to support a simple contract.

(45) "Warehouse receipt" means a receipt issued by a person engaged in the business of storing goods for hire.

(46) "Written" or "writing" includes printing, typewriting or any other intentional reduction to tangible form.

SECTION 1-202. *Prima Facie Evidence by Third Party Documents.*—A document in due form purporting to be a bill of lading, policy or certificate of insurance, official weigher's or inspector's certificate, consular invoice, or any other document authorized or required by the contract to be issued by a third party shall be prima facie evidence of its own authenticity and genuineness and of the fact stated in the document by the third party.

SECTION 1-203. *Obligation of Good Faith.*—Every contract or duty within this Act imposes an obligation of good faith in its performance or enforcement.

SECTION 1-204. *Time; Reasonable Time; "Seasonably."*—(1) Whenever this Act requires any action to be taken within a reasonable time, any time which is not manifestly unreasonable may be fixed by agreement.

(2) What is a reasonable time for taking any action depends on the nature, purpose and circumstances of such action.

(3) An action is taken "seasonably" when it is taken at or within the time agreed or if no time is agreed at or within a reasonable time.

SECTION 1-205. *Course of Dealing and Usage of Trade.*—(1) A course of dealing is a sequence of previous conduct between the parties to a particular transaction which is fairly to be regarded as establishing a common basis of understanding for interpreting their expressions and other conduct.

(2) A usage of trade is any practice or method of dealing having such regularity of observance in a place, vocation or trade as to justify an expectation that it will be observed with respect to the transaction in question. The existence and scope of such a usage are to be proved as facts. If it is established that such a usage is embodied in a written trade code or similar writing the interpretation of the writing is for the court.

(3) A course of dealing between parties and any usage of trade in the vocation or trade in which they are engaged or of which they are or should be aware give particular meaning to and supplement or qualify terms of an agreement.

(4) The express terms of an agreement and an applicable course of dealing or usage of trade shall be construed wherever reasonable as consistent with each other; but when such construction is unreasonable express terms control both course of dealing and usage of trade and course of dealing controls usage of trade.

(5) An applicable usage of trade in the place where any part of performance is to occur shall be used in interpreting the agreement as to that part of the performance.

(6) Evidence of a relevant usage of trade offered by one party is not admissible unless and until he has given the other party such notice as the court finds sufficient to prevent unfair surprise to the latter.

SECTION 1-206. *Statute of Frauds for Kinds of Personal Property Not Otherwise Covered.*—(1) Except in the cases described in subsection (2) of this section a contract for the sale of personal property is not enforceable by way of action or defense beyond five thousand dollars in amount or value of remedy unless there is some writing which indicates that a contract for sale has been made between the parties at a defined or stated price, reasonably identifies the subject matter, and is signed by the party against whom enforcement is sought or by his authorized agent.

(2) Subsection (1) of this section does not apply to contracts for the sale of goods (Section 2-201) nor of securities (Section 8-319) nor to security agreements (Section 9-203).

SECTION 1-207. *Performance or Acceptance Under Reservation of Rights.*— A party who with explicit reservation of rights performs or promises performance or assents to performance in a manner demanded or offered by the other party does not thereby prejudice the rights reserved. Such words as "without prejudice," "under protest" or the like are sufficient.

SECTION 1-208. *Option to Accelerate at Will.*—A term providing that one party or his successor in interest may accelerate payment or performance or require collateral or additional collateral "at will" or "when he deems himself insecure" or in words of similar import shall be construed to mean that he shall have power to do so only if he in good faith believes that the prospect of payment or performance is impaired. The burden of establishing lack of good faith is on the party against whom the power has been exercised.

SECTION 1-209. *Subordinated Obligations.*—An obligation may be issued as subordinated to payment of another obligation of the person obligated, or a creditor may subordinate his right to payment of an obligation by agreement with either the person obligated or another creditor of the person obligated. Such a subordination does not create a security interest as against either the common debtor or a subordinated creditor. This section shall be construed as declaring the law as it existed prior to the enactment of this section and not as modifying it.[1]

ARTICLE 2

SALES

Part 1

General Provisions

Part 1 consists of definitions of terms used in Article 2 and an index to terms defined in other sections of the Code. The text of four of the more significant sections of Part 1 is reprinted here.

SECTION 2-104. *Definitions: "Merchant"; "Between Merchants"; "Financing Agency."*—(1) "Merchant" means a person who deals in goods of the kind or otherwise by his occupation holds himself out as having knowledge or skill peculiar to the practices or goods involved in the transaction or to whom such knowledge or skill may be attributed by his employment of an agent or broker or other intermediary who by his occupation holds himself out as having such knowledge or skill.

(2) "Financing agency" means a bank, finance company or other person who in the ordinary course of business makes advances against goods or documents of title or who by arrangement with either the seller or the buyer intervenes in ordinary course to make or collect payment due or claimed under the contract for sale, as by purchasing or paying the seller's draft or making advances against it or by merely taking it for collection whether or not documents of title accompany the draft. "Financing agency" includes also a bank or other person who similarly intervenes between persons who are in the position of seller and buyer in respect to the goods (Section 2-707).

---

[1] Optional provision, adopted in the following states: Arizona, Arkansas, California, Illinois, Iowa, Kansas, Massachusetts, Michigan, Minnesota, New Jersey, New York, North Carolina, North Dakota, Oklahoma, Wisconsin, and Wyoming.

(3) "Between merchants" means in any transaction with respect to which both parties are chargeable with the knowledge or skill of merchants.

SECTION 2-105. *Definitions: Transferability; "Goods"; "Future" Goods; "Lot"; "Commercial Unit."*—(1) "Goods" means all things (including specially manufactured goods) which are movable at the time of identification to the contract for sale other than the money in which the price is to be paid, investment securities (Article 8) and things in action. "Goods" also includes the unborn young of animals and growing crops and other identified things attached to realty as described in the section on goods to be severed from realty (Section 2-107).

(2) Goods must be both existing and identified before any interest in them can pass. Goods which are not both existing and identified are "future" goods. A purported present sale of future goods or of any interest therein operates as a contract to sell.

(3) There may be a sale of a part interest in existing identified goods.

(4) An undivided share in an identified bulk of fungible goods is sufficiently identified to be sold although the quantity of the bulk is not determined. Any agreed proportion of such a bulk or any quantity thereof agreed upon by number, weight or other measure may to the extent of the seller's interest in the bulk be sold to the buyer who then becomes an owner in common.

(5) "Lot" means a parcel or a single article which is the subject matter of a separate sale or delivery, whether or not it is sufficient to perform the contract.

(6) "Commercial unit" means such a unit of goods as by commercial usage is a single whole for purposes of sale and division of which materially impairs its character or value on the market or in use. A commercial unit may be a single article (as a machine) or a set of articles (as a suite of furniture or an assortment of sizes) or a quantity (as a bale, gross, or carload) or any other unit treated in use or in the relevant market as a single whole.

SECTION 2-106. *Definitions: "Contract"; "Agreement"; "Contract for Sale"; "Sale"; "Present Sale"; "Conforming" to Contract; "Termination"; "Cancellation."*—(1) In this Article unless the context otherwise requires "contract" and "agreement" are limited to those relating to the present or future sale of goods. "Contract for sale" includes both a present sale of goods and a contract to sell goods at a future time. A "sale" consists in the passing of title from the seller to the buyer for a price (Section 2-401). A "present sale" means a sale which is accomplished by the making of the contract.

(2) Goods or conduct including any part of a performance are "conforming" or conform to the contract when they are in accordance with the obligations under the contract.

(3) "Termination" occurs when either party pursuant to a power created by agreement or law puts an end to the contract otherwise than for its breach. On "termination" all obligations which are still executory on both sides are discharged but any right based on prior breach or performance survives.

(4) "Cancellation" occurs when either party puts an end to the contract for breach by the other and its effect is the same as that of "termination" except that the cancelling party also retains any remedy for breach of the whole contract or any unperformed balance.[1]

---

[1] Alaska adds a subsection which provides a definition of a "door-to-door" sale.

SECTION 2-107. *Goods to Be Severed From Realty: Recording.*—(1) A contract for the sale of minerals or the like (including oil and gas) or a structure or its materials to be removed from realty is a contract for the sale of goods within this Article if they are to be severed by the seller but until severance a purported present sale thereof which is not effective as a transfer of an interest in land is effective only as a contract to sell.

(2) A contract for the sale apart from the land of growing crops or other things attached to realty and capable of severance without material harm thereto but not described in subsection (1) or of timber to be cut is a contract for the sale of goods within this Article whether the subject matter is to be severed by the buyer or by the seller even though it forms part of the realty at the time of contracting, and the parties can by identification effect a present sale before severance.[1]

(3) The provisions of this section are subject to any third party rights provided by the law relating to reality records, and the contract for sale may be executed and recorded as a document transferring an interest in land and shall then constitute notice to third parties of the buyer's rights under the contract for sale.

Part 2

Form, Formation and Readjustment of Contract

SECTION 2-201. *Formal Requirements; Statute of Frauds.*—(1) Except as otherwise provided in this section a contract for the sale of goods for the price of $500 or more is not enforceable by way of action or defense unless there is some writing sufficient to indicate that a contract for sale has been made between the parties and signed by the party against whom enforcement is sought or by his authorized agent or broker. A writing is not insufficient because it omits or incorrectly states a term agreed upon but the contract is not enforceable under this paragraph beyond the quantity of goods shown in such writing.

(2) Between merchants if within a reasonable time a writing in confirmation of the contract and sufficient against the sender is received and the party receiving it has reason to know its contents, it satisfies the requirements of subsection (1) against such party unless written notice of objection to its contents is given within 10 days after it is received.

(3) A contract which does not satisfy the requirements of subsection (1) but which is valid in other respects is enforceable

    (a) if the goods are to be specially manufactured for the buyer and are not suitable for sale to others in the ordinary course of the seller's business and the seller, before notice of repudiation is received and under circumstances which reasonably indicate that the goods are for the buyer, has made either a substantial beginning of their manufacture or commitments for their procurement; or

    (b) if the party against whom enforcement is sought admits in his pleading, testimony or otherwise in court that a contract for sale was made,

---

[1] Alabama and New Hampshire omit reference to timber.

UNIFORM COMMERCIAL CODE 1–31

but the contract is not enforceable under this provision beyond the quantity of goods admitted;[1] or

(c) with respect to goods for which payment has been made and accepted or which have been received and accepted (Section 2-606).

SECTION 2-202. *Final Written Expression: Parol or Extrinsic Evidence.*—Terms with respect to which the confirmatory memoranda of the parties agree or which are otherwise set forth in a writing intended by the parties as a final expression of their agreement with respect to such terms as are included therein may not be contradicted by evidence of any prior agreement or of a contemporaneous oral agreement but may be explained or supplemented

(a) by course of dealing or usage of trade (Section 1-205) or by course of performance (Section 2-208); and
(b) by evidence of consistent additional terms unless the court finds the writing to have been intended also as a complete and exclusive statement of the terms agreed upon.

SECTION 2-203. *Seals Inoperative.*—The affixing of a seal to a writing evidencing a contract for sale or an offer to buy or sell goods does not constitute the writing a sealed instrument and the law with respect to sealed instruments does not apply to such a contract or offer.[2]

SECTION 2-204. *Formation in General.*—(1) A contract for sale of goods may be made in any manner sufficient to show agreement, including conduct by both parties which recognizes the existence of such a contract.

(2) An agreement sufficient to constitute a contract for sale may be found even though the moment of its making is undetermined.

(3) Even though one or more terms are left open a contract for sale does not fail for indefiniteness if the parties have intended to make a contract and there is a reasonably certain basis for giving an appropriate remedy.

SECTION 2-205. *Firm Offers.*—An offer by a merchant to buy or sell goods in a signed writing which by its terms gives assurance that it will be held open is not revocable, for lack of consideration, during the time stated or if no time is stated for a reasonable time, but in no event may such period of irrevocability exceed three months; but any such term of assurance on a form supplied by the offeree must be separately signed by the offeror.[3]

SECTION 2-206. *Offer and Acceptance in Formation of Contract.*—(1) Unless otherwise unambiguously indicated by the language or circumstances

(a) an offer to make a contract shall be construed as inviting acceptance in any manner and by any medium reasonable in the circumstances;
(b) an order or other offer to buy goods for prompt or current shipment shall be construed as inviting acceptance either by a prompt promise to ship or by the prompt or current shipment of conforming or nonconforming goods, but such a shipment of nonconforming goods does

---

[1] California has omitted (3)(b) entirely.
[2] California has omitted Section 2-203 entirely.
[3] California adds subsec. (b) which provides different provisions where a merchant renders an offer to a contractor licensed under the state Business and Professions Code.

not constitute an acceptance if the seller seasonably notifies the buyer that the shipment is offered only as an accommodation to the buyer.

(2) Where the beginning of a requested performance is a reasonable mode of acceptance an offeror who is not notified of acceptance within a reasonable time may treat the offer as having lapsed before acceptance.

SECTION 2-207. *Additional Terms in Acceptance or Confirmation.*—(1) A definite and seasonable expression of acceptance or a written confirmation which is sent within a reasonable time operates as an acceptance even though it states terms additional to or different from those offered or agreed upon, unless acceptance is expressly made conditional on assent to the additional or different terms.

(2) The additional terms are to be construed as proposals for addition to the contract. Between merchants such terms become part of the contract unless: [1]

(a) the offer expressly limits acceptance to the terms of the offer;
(b) they materially alter it; or
(c) notification of objection to them has already been given or is given within a reasonable time after notice of them is received.

(3) Conduct by both parties which recognizes the existence of a contract is sufficient to establish a contract for sale although the writings of the parties do not otherwise establish a contract. In such case the terms of the particular contract consist of those terms on which the writings of the parties agree, together with any supplementary terms incorporated under any other provisions of this Act.

SECTION 2-208. *Course of Performance or Practical Construction.*—(1) Where the contract for sale involves repeated occasions for performance by either party with knowledge of the nature of the performance and opportunity for objection to it by the other, any course of performance accepted or acquiesced in without objection shall be relevant to determine the meaning of the agreement.

(2) The express terms of the agreement and any such course of performance, as well as any course of dealing and usage of trade, shall be construed whenever reasonable as consistent with each other; but when such construction is unreasonable, express terms shall control course of performance and course of performance shall control both course of dealing and usage of trade (Section 1-205).

(3) Subject to the provisions of the next section on modification and waiver, such course of performance shall be relevant to show a waiver or modification of any term inconsistent with such course of performance.

SECTION 2-209. *Modification, Rescission and Waiver.*—(1) An agreement modifying a contract within this Article needs no consideration to be binding.

(2) A signed agreement which excludes modification or rescission except by a signed writing cannot be otherwise modified or rescinded, but except as between merchants such a requirement on a form supplied by the merchant must be separately signed by the other party.

(3) The requirements of the statute of frauds section of this Article (Section 2-201) must be satisfied if the contract as modified is within its provisions.

---

[1] Montana inserts words "or different" following "additional."

(4) Although an attempt at modification or rescission does not satisfy the requirements of subsection (2) or (3) it can operate as a waiver.

(5) A party who has made a waiver affecting an executory portion of the contract may retract the waiver by reasonable notification received by the other party that strict performance will be required of any term waived, unless the retraction would be unjust in view of a material change of position in reliance on the waiver.

SECTION 2-210. *Delegation of Performance; Assignment of Rights.*—(This section authorizes delegation of performance unless otherwise agreed, or contrary to the intent of the parties, and also contains provisions relating to assignment of the contract or rights thereunder.)

Part 3

General Obligation and Construction of Contract

SECTION 2-301. *General Obligations of Parties.*—The obligation of the seller is to transfer and deliver and that of the buyer is to accept and pay in accordance with the contract.

SECTION 2-302. *Unconscionable Contract or Clause.*—(1) If the court as a matter of law finds the contract or any clause of the contract to have been unconscionable at the time it was made the court may refuse to enforce the contract, or it may enforce the remainder of the contract without the unconscionable clause, or it may so limit the application of any unconscionable clause as to avoid any unconscionable result.

(2) When it is claimed or appears to the court that the contract or any clause thereof may be unconscionable the parties shall be afforded a reasonable opportunity to present evidence as to its commercial setting, purpose and effect to aid the court in making the determination.[1]

* * * * * *

SECTION 2-305. *Open Price Term.*—(1) The parties if they so intend can conclude a contract for sale even though the price is not settled. In such a case the price is a reasonable price at the time for delivery if

(a) nothing is said as to price; or
(b) the price is left to be agreed by the parties and they fail to agree; or
(c) the price is to be fixed in terms of some agreed market or other standard as set or recorded by a third person or agency and it is not so set or recorded.

(2) A price to be fixed by the seller or by the buyer means a price for him to fix in good faith.

(3) When a price left to be fixed otherwise than by agreement of the parties fails to be fixed through fault of one party the other may at his option treat the contract as cancelled or himself fix a reasonable price.

(4) Where, however, the parties intend not to be bound unless the price be

---

[1] California omits Section 2-302 entirely.

fixed or agreed and it is not fixed or agreed there is no contract. In such a case the buyer must return any goods already received or if unable so to do must pay their reasonable value at the time of delivery and the seller must return any portion of the price paid on account.

SECTION 2-306. *Output, Requirements and Exclusive Dealings.*—(1) A term which measures the quantity by the output of the seller or the requirements of the buyer means such actual output or requirements as may occur in good faith, except that no quantity unreasonably disproportionate to any stated estimate or in the absence of a stated estimate to any normal or otherwise comparable prior output or requirements may be tendered or demanded.

(2) A lawful agreement by either the seller or the buyer for exclusive dealing in the kind of goods concerned imposes unless otherwise agreed an obligation by the seller to use best efforts to supply the goods and by the buyer to use best efforts to promote their sale.

SECTION 2-307. *Delivery in Single Lot or Several Lots.*—Unless otherwise agreed all goods called for by a contract for sale must be tendered in a single delivery and payment is due only on such tender but where the circumstances give either party the right to make or demand delivery in lots the price if it can be apportioned may be demanded for each lot.

SECTION 2-308. *Absence of Specified Place for Delivery.*—Unless otherwise agreed

(a) the place for delivery of goods is the seller's place of business or if he has none his residence; but
(b) in a contract for sale of identified goods which to the knowledge of the parties at the time of contracting are in some other place, that place is the place for their delivery; and
(c) documents of title may be delivered through customary banking channels.

SECTION 2-309. *Absence of Specific Time Provisions; Notice of Termination.*— (1) The time for shipment or delivery or any other action under a contract if not provided in this Article or agreed upon shall be a reasonable time.

(2) Where the contract provides for successive performances but is indefinite in duration it is valid for a reasonable time but unless otherwise agreed may be terminated at any time by either party.

(3) Termination of a contract by one party except on the happening of an agreed event requires that reasonable notification be received by the other party and an agreement dispensing with notification is invalid if its operation would be unconscionable.

SECTION 2-310. *Open Time for Payment or Running of Credit; Authority to Ship Under Reservation.*—Unless otherwise agreed

(a) payment is due at the time and place at which the buyer is to receive the goods even though the place of shipment is the place of delivery; and
(b) if the seller is authorized to send the goods he may ship them under

reservation, and may tender the documents of title, but the buyer may inspect the goods after their arrival before payment is due unless such inspection is inconsistent with the terms of the contract (Section 2-513); and

(c) if delivery is authorized and made by way of documents of title otherwise than by subsection (b) then payment is due at the time and place at which the buyer is to receive the documents regardless of where the goods are to be received; and

(d) Where the seller is required or authorized to ship the goods on credit the credit period runs from the time of shipment but postdating the invoice or [1] delaying its dispatch will correspondingly delay the starting of the credit period.

SECTION 2-311. *Options and Cooperation Respecting Performance.*—(1) An agreement for sale which is otherwise sufficiently definite (subsection (3) of Section 2-204) to be a contract is not made invalid by the fact that the agreement leaves particulars of performance to be specified by one of the parties. Any such specification must be made in good faith and within limits set by commercial reasonableness.

(2) Unless otherwise agreed specifications relating to assortment of the goods are at the buyer's option and except as otherwise provided in subsections (1) (c) and (3) of Section 2-319 specifications or arrangements relating to shipment are at the seller's option.

(3) Where such specification would materially affect the other party's performance but is not seasonably made or where one party's cooperation is necessary to the agreed performance of the other but is not seasonably forthcoming, the other party in addition to all other remedies

(a) is excused for any resulting delay in his own performance; and
(b) may also either proceed to perform in any reasonable manner or after the time for a material part of his own performance treat the failure to specify or to cooperate as a breach by failure to deliver or accept the goods.

SECTION 2-312. *Warranty of Title and Against Infringement; Buyer's Obligation Against Infringement.*—(1) Subject to subsection (2) there is in a contract for sale a warranty by the seller that

(a) the title conveyed shall be good, and its transfer rightful; and
(b) the goods shall be delivered free from any security interest or other lien or encumbrance of which the buyer at the time of contracting has no knowledge.

(2) A warranty under subsection (1) will be excluded or modified only by specific language or by circumstances which give the buyer reason to know that the person selling does not claim title in himself or that he is purporting to sell only such right or title as he or a third person may have.

(3) Unless otherwise agreed a seller who is a merchant regularly dealing in goods of the kind warrants that the goods shall be delivered free of the rightful

---

[1] North Carolina adds "intentionally."

claim of any third person by way of infringement or the like but a buyer who furnishes specifications to the seller must hold the seller harmless against any such claim which arises out of compliance with the specifications.[1]

SECTION 2-313. *Express Warranties by Affirmation, Promise, Description, Sample.*—(1) Express warranties by the seller are created as follows:

(a) Any affirmation of fact or promise made by the seller to the buyer which relates to the goods and becomes part of the basis of the bargain creates an express warranty that the goods shall conform to the affirmation or promise.

(b) Any description of the goods which is made part of the basis of the bargain creates an express warranty that the goods shall conform to the description.

(c) Any sample or model which is made part of the basis of the bargain creates an express warranty that the whole of the goods shall conform to the sample or model.

(2) It is not necessary to the creation of an express warranty that the seller use formal words such as "warrant" or "guarantee" or that he have a specific intention to make a warranty, but an affirmation merely of the value of the goods or a statement purporting to be merely the seller's opinion or commendation of the goods does not create a warranty.[2]

SECTION 2-314. *Implied Warranty: Merchantability; Usage of Trade.*— (1) Unless excluded or modified (Section 2-316), a warranty that the goods shall be merchantable is implied in a contract for their sale if the seller is a merchant with respect to goods of that kind.[3] Under this section the serving

---

[1] Massachusetts adds a subsec. (4) that provides that unless otherwise agreed, the warranty against infringement in subsec. (3) does not apply to any claim cognizable exclusively in the federal district courts or the Court of Claims.

[2] California has added Title 1.7 to its Civil Code dealing with consumer warranties. The statute requires a manufacturer, distributor, or retailer making express warranties of consumer goods to state the warranties in readily understood language and to clearly and conspicuously incorporate on the face of a work order or repair invoice, or on an attachment thereto, a statement informing the buyer of certain rights as specified concerning warranty repairs.

The statute further requires that the required statement shall be placed either on the face of a work order or repair invoice, or on the reverse side thereof, or on an attachment thereto. If the required statement is placed on the reverse side of a work order or repair invoice, the bill would require the face of the work order or repair invoice to give notice of that fact, as specified.

Michigan has a comprehensive statute regarding consumer sales which provides for the limitations on the servicing of warranties by the manufacturer.

[3] In Maryland paragraph (1) adds a definition of seller which includes manufacturers, distributors, dealers, wholesalers, or other middlemen and provides that any previous requirement of privity between buyer and seller is abolished.

In Maine, merchants selling consumer goods are held to warrant the goods "fit for the ordinary purposes for which such goods are used."

In Maryland, Massachusetts and the District of Columbia clauses which attempt to limit implied warranties of merchantability and fitness for a particular purpose or to exclude or modify a consumer's remedies in the case of sales of consumer goods is unenforceable. In Maryland, there are exceptions to the above regarding certain sales of motor vehicles.

South Dakota provides that there is no implied warranty on the sale of cattle, hogs, or sheep.

Alabama provides that there is no implied warranty that swine, cattle, sheep, goats, horses, mules and asses are free from disease.

for value of food or drink to be consumed either on the premises or elsewhere is a sale.

(2) Goods to be merchantable must at least be such as

   (a) pass without objection in the trade under the contract description; and
   (b) in the case of fungible goods, are of fair average quality within the description; and
   (c) are fit for the ordinary purposes for which such goods are used; and
   (d) run, within the variations permitted by the agreement, of even kind, quality and quantity within each unit and among all units involved; and
   (e) are adequately contained, packaged, and labeled as the agreement may require; and
   (f) conform to the promises or affirmations of fact made on the container or label if any.[1]

(3) Unless excluded or modified (Section 2-316) other implied warranties may arise from course of dealing or usage of trade.[2]

SECTION 2-315. *Implied Warranty: Fitness for Particular Purpose.*—Where the seller at the time of contracting has reason to know any particular purpose for which the goods are required and that the buyer is relying on the seller's skill or judgment to select or furnish suitable goods, there is unless excluded or modified under the next section an implied warranty that the goods shall be fit for such purpose.[3]

SECTION 2-316. *Exclusion or Modification of Warranties.*—(1) Words or conduct relevant to the creation of an express warranty and words or conduct tending to negate or limit warranty shall be construed wherever reasonable as consistent with each other; but subject to the provisions of this Article on parol or extrinsic evidence (Section 2-202) negation or limitation is inoperative to the extent that such construction is unreasonable.

(2) Subject to subsection (3), to exclude or modify the implied warranty of merchantability or any part of it the language must mention merchantability and in case of a writing must be conspicuous, and to exclude or modify any implied warranty of fitness the exclusion must be by a writing and conspicuous. Language to exclude all implied warranties of fitness is sufficient if it states, for example, that "There are no warranties which extend beyond the description on the face hereof."

---

[1] South Carolina omits this subsection.

[2] In Maryland paragraph (4) has been added which provides that subsections (1) and (2) apply to a lease of goods on a bailment for hire.

In Alabama, the donating, processing, or distribution of blood, plasma, etc., and of other human tissues is not considered a sale.

In Mississippi subsec. (4) provides that there shall be no implied warranty as regards cattle, hogs, or sheep.

[3] Rhode Island adds last sentence as follows: "As to foodstuffs or drinks sold for human consumption in sealed containers, there is an implied warranty that the goods shall be reasonably fit for such purpose, and such warranty shall extend from the seller and the manufacturer or packer of such goods to the person or persons described in section [Section 2-318] of this chapter."

In Maryland this section has been amended to apply to a lease of goods or a bailment for hire.

Mississippi and Tennessee provide that there shall be no implied warranty as to cattle, hogs, or sheep. Tennessee also finds no implied warranty as to horses.

South Dakota provides that implied warranties of merchantability and fitness are not applicable to a contract for blood or other human tissue.

(3) Notwithstanding subsection (2)

(a) unless the circumstances indicate otherwise, all implied warranties are excluded by expressions like "as is", "with all faults" or other language which is common understanding calls the buyer's attention to the exclusion of warranties and makes plain that there is no implied warranty; and

(b) when the buyer before entering into the contract has examined the goods or the sample or model as fully as he desired or has refused to examine the goods there is no implied warranty with regard to defects which an examination ought in the circumstances to have revealed to him; and

(c) an implied warranty can also be excluded or modified by course of dealing or course of performance or usage of trade.[1]

(4) Remedies for breach of warranty can be limited in accordance with the provisions of this Article on liquidation or limitation of damages and on contractual modifications of remedy (Sections 2-718 and 2-719).[2]

SECTION 2-317. *Cumulation and Conflict of Warranties Express or Implied.*— Warranties whether express or implied shall be construed as consistent with each other and as cumulative, but if such construction is unreasonable the intention of the parties shall determine which warranty is dominant. In ascertaining that intention the following rules apply:

(a) Exact or technical specifications displace an inconsistent sample or model or general language of description.

(b) A sample from an existing bulk displaces inconsistent general language of description.

(c) Express warranties displace inconsistent implied warranties other than an implied warranty of fitness for a particular purpose.

SECTION 2-318. *Third Party Beneficiaries of Warranties Express or Implied.*— A seller's warranty whether express or implied extends to any natural person who is in the family or household of his buyer or who is a guest in his home if it is reasonable to expect that such person may use, consume or be affected by the goods and who is injured in person by breach of the warranty. A seller may not exclude or limit the operation of this section.[3]

---

[1] Arkansas, Florida, Georgia, Illinois, Indiana, Kansas, Kentucky, Michigan, Missouri, Montana, Nebraska, New Hampshire, North Dakota, Ohio, Oklahoma, Oregon, South Dakota, Utah, Washington, Wisconsin and Wyoming add a subsection excluding the applicability of implied warranties from various livestock. The particular state code section should be consulted as the terms vary from state to state.

[2] Alabama, Connecticut, District of Columbia, Maine, Maryland, Massachusetts, Vermont, and Washington provide that sellers and/or manufacturers may not limit warranties and/or remedies for breach of warranties in the sale of consumer goods. The particular state code section should be consulted as the terms vary from state to state.

Mississippi omits Section 2-316 in its entirety.

South Carolina provides that language excluding the implied warranty of merchantability or fitness must be specific. If the language is ambiguous it is to be resolved against the seller.

[3] Section 2-318 has three alternatives regarding third party beneficiaries of warranties; each state is to select one alternative. California is the only state that has not adopted this action. The majority of the states have adopted Alternative A which is reprinted in the text, above.

(Footnote continued bottom next page)

UNIFORM COMMERCIAL CODE   1-39

SECTION 2-319. *F.O.B. and F.A.S. Terms.*—(1) Unless otherwise agreed the term F.O.B. (which means "free on board") at a named place, even though used only in connection with the stated price, is a delivery term under which

    (a) when the term is F.O.B. the place of shipment, the seller must at that place ship the goods in the manner provided in this Article (Section 2-504) and bear the expense and risk of putting them into the possession of the carrier; or

    (b) when the term is F.O.B. the place of destination, the seller must at his own expense and risk transport the goods to that place and there tender delivery of them in the manner provided in this Article (Section 2-503);

    (c) when under either (a) or (b) the term is also F.O.B. vessel, car or other vehicle, the seller must in addition at his own expense and risk load the goods on board. If the term is F.O.B. vessel the buyer must name the vessel and in an appropriate case the seller must comply with the provisions of this Article on the form of bill of lading (Section 2-323).

(2) Unless otherwise agreed, the term F.A.S. vessel (which means "free alongside") at a named port, even though used only in connection with the stated price, is a delivery term under which the seller must

    (a) at his own expense and risk deliver the goods alongside the vessel in the manner usual in that port or on a dock designated and provided by the buyer; and

    (b) obtain and tender a receipt for the goods in exchange for which the carrier is under a duty to issue a bill of lading.

(3) Unless otherwise agreed in any case falling within subsection (1) (a) or (c) or subsection (2) the buyer must seasonably give any needed instructions for making delivery, including when the term is F.A.S. or F.O.B. the loading berth of the vessel and in an appropriate case its name and sailing date. The seller may treat the failure of needed instructions as a failure of cooperation under this Article (Section 2-311). He may also at his option move the goods in any reasonable manner preparatory to delivery or shipment.

(4) Under the term F.O.B. vessel or F.A.S. unless otherwise agreed the buyer must make payment against tender of the required documents and the seller may not tender nor the buyer demand delivery of the goods in substitution for the documents.

    Maine, Massachusetts, and New Hampshire repealed their adoption of Alternative A and instead provide that a lack of privity shall not be a defense in an action brought against a manufacturer, seller or supplier of goods where the plaintiff was reasonably expected to use the goods.

    Arkansas adds a subsection which subjects a supplier to liability where the product supplied was defective; privity is not required. Rhode Island and Virginia amend the section so that it applies to manufacturers as well as sellers.

    Texas provides that the courts shall determine whether anyone other than the buyer can take advantage of an express or implied warranty or whether the buyer or anyone else who may take advantage of the warranty may sue a third party other than the immediate seller.

    In New York, the following phrase has been omitted from the section as adopted: "who is in the family or household of his buyer or who is a guest in his home." However, some persuasive authority exists for the notion that privity will be required in New York for breach of warranty actions despite the clear legislative intent to the contrary. *Martin v. Julius Dierck Equipment Co.,* 43 N.Y.2d 583, 589-90, 403 N.Y.S.2d 185, 188 (1978) (dictum).

SECTION 2-320. *C.I.F. and C. & F. Terms.*—(1) The term C.I.F. means that the price includes in a lump sum the cost of the goods and the insurance and freight to the named destination. The term C. & F. or C.F. means that the price so includes cost and freight to the named destination.

(2) Unless otherwise agreed and even though used only in connection with the stated price and destination, the term C.I.F. destination or its equivalent requires the seller at his own expense and risk to

   (a) put the goods into the possession of a carrier at the port for shipment and obtain a negotiable bill or bills of lading covering the entire transportation to the named destination; and
   (b) load the goods and obtain a receipt from the carrier (which may be contained in the bill of lading) showing that the freight has been paid or provided for; and
   (c) obtain a policy or certificate of insurance, including any war risk insurance, of a kind and on terms then current at the port of shipment in the usual amount, in the currency of the contract, shown to cover the same goods covered by the bill of lading and providing for payment of loss to the order of the buyer or for the account of whom it may concern; but the seller may add to the price the amount of the premium for any such war risk insurance; and
   (d) prepare an invoice of the goods and procure any other documents required to effect shipment or to comply with the contract; and
   (e) forward and tender with commercial promptness all the documents in due form and with any indorsement necessary to perfect the buyer's rights.

(3) Unless otherwise agreed the term C. & F. for its equivalent has the same effect and imposes upon the seller the same obligations and risks as a C.I.F. term except the obligation as to insurance.

(4) Under the term C.I.F. or C. & F. unless otherwise agreed the buyer must make payment against tender of the required documents and the seller may not tender nor the buyer demand delivery of the goods in substitution for the documents.

SECTION 2-321. *C.I.F. or C. & F.: "Net Landed Weights"; "Payment on Arrival"; Warranty of Condition on Arrival.*—Under a contract containing a term C.I.F., or C. & F.:

(1) Where the price is based on or is to be adjusted according to "net landed weights," "delivered weights," "out turn" quantity or quality or the like, unless otherwise agreed the seller must reasonably estimate the price. The payment due on tender of the documents called for by the contract is the amount so estimated, but after final adjustment of the price a settlement must be made with commercial promptness.

(2) An agreement described in subsection (1) or any warranty of quality or condition of the goods on arrival places upon the seller the risk of ordinary deterioration, shrinkage and the like in transportation but has no effect on the place or time of identification to the contract for sale or delivery or on the passing of the risk of loss.

(3) Unless otherwise agreed where the contract provides for payment on or after arrival of the goods the seller must before payment allow such preliminary

inspection as is feasible; but if the goods are lost delivery of the documents and payment are due when the goods should have arrived.

SECTION 2-322. *Delivery "Ex-Ship."*—(1) Unless otherwise agreed a term for delivery of goods "ex-ship" (which means from the carrying vessel) or in equivalent language is not restricted to a particular ship and requires delivery from a ship which has reached a place at the named port of destination where goods of the kind are usually discharged.

(2) Under such a term, unless otherwise agreed

   (a) the seller must discharge all liens arising out of the carriage and furnish the buyer with a direction which puts the carrier under a duty to deliver the goods; and
   (b) the risk of loss does not pass to the buyer until the goods leave the ship's tackle or are otherwise properly unloaded.

SECTION 2-323. *Form of Bill of Lading Required in Overseas Shipment; "Overseas."*—(1) Where the contract contemplates overseas shipment and contains a term C.I.F. or C. & F. or F.O.B. vessel, the seller unless otherwise agreed must obtain a negotiable bill of lading stating that the goods have been loaded on board or, in the case of a term C.I.F. or C. & F., received for shipment.

(2) Where in a case within subsection (1) a bill of lading has been issued in a set of parts, unless otherwise agreed if the documents are not to be sent from abroad the buyer may demand tender of the full set; otherwise only one part of the bill of lading need be tendered. Even if the agreement expressly requires a full set

   (a) due tender of a single part is acceptable within the provisions of this Article on cure of improper delivery (subsection (1) of Section 2-508); and
   (b) even though the full set is demanded, if the documents are sent from abroad the person tendering an incomplete set may nevertheless require payment upon furnishing and indemnity which the buyer in good faith deems adequate.

(3) A shipment by water or by air or a contract contemplating such shipment is "overseas" insofar as by usage of trade or agreement it is subject to the commercial, financing or shipping practices characteristic of international deep water commerce.

SECTION 2-324. *"No Arrival, No Sale" Term.*—Under a term "no arrival, no sale" or terms of like meaning, unless otherwise agreed,

   (a) the seller must properly ship conforming goods and if they arrive by any means he must tender them on arrival but he assumes no obligation that the goods will arrive unless he has caused the nonarrival; and
   (b) where without fault of the seller the goods are in part lost or have so deteriorated as no longer to conform to the contract or arrive after the contract time, the buyer may proceed as if there had been casualty to identified goods (Section 2-613).

SECTION 2-325. *"Letter of Credit" Term; "Confirmed Credit."*—(1) Failure of the buyer seasonably to furnish an agreed letter of credit is a breach of the contract for sale.

(2) The delivery to seller of a proper letter of credit suspends the buyer's obligation to pay. If the letter of credit is dishonored, the seller may on seasonable notification to the buyer require payment directly from him.

(3) Unless otherwise agreed the term "letter of credit" or "banker's credit" in a contract for sale means an irrevocable credit issued by a financing agency of good repute and, where the shipment is overseas, of good international repute. The term "confirmed credit" means that the credit must also carry the direct obligation of such an agency which does business in the seller's financial market.

SECTION 2-326. *Sale on Approval and Sale or Return; Consignment Sales and Rights of Creditors.*—(1) Unless otherwise agreed, if delivered goods may be returned by the buyer even though they conform to the contract, the transaction is

(a) a "sale on approval" if the goods are delivered primarily for use, and
(b) a "sale or return" if the goods are delivered primarily for resale.

(2) Except as provided in subsection (3), goods held on approval are not subject to the claims of the buyer's creditors until acceptance; goods held on sale or return are subject to such claims while in the buyer's possession.

(3) Where goods are delivered to a person for sale and such person maintains a place of business at which he deals in goods of the kind involved, under a name other than the name of the person making delivery, then with respect to claims of creditors of the person conducting the business the goods are deemed to be on sale or return. The provisions of this subsection are applicable even though an agreement purports to reserve title to the person making delivery until payment or resale or uses such words as "on consignment" or "on memorandum". However, this subsection is not applicable if the person making delivery

(a) complies with an applicable law providing for a consignor's interest or the like to be evidenced by a sign, or [1]
(b) establishes that the person conducting the business is generally known by his creditors to be substantially engaged in selling the goods of others, or
(c) complies with the filing provisions of the Article on Secured Transactions (Article 9).[2]

(4) Any "or return" term of a contract for sale is to be treated as a separate contract for sale within the statute of frauds section of this Article (Section 2-201) and as contradicting the sale aspect of the contract within the provisions of this Article on parol or extrinsic evidence (Section 2-202).[3]

SECTION 2-327. *Special Incidents of Sale on Approval and Sale or Return.*—(1) Under a sale on approval unless otherwise agreed

---

[1] California omits subsection (3) (a).
[2] New Mexico adds paragraph (d) which reads: "is delivering a work of art pursuant to the Artists' Consignment Act. . . ."
Alaska, Arkansas, Colorado and Michigan add a subsection which provides that a work of fine art delivered to an art dealer for sale to the public is not subject to claims of art dealer's creditors.
[3] Alaska adds a subsection which provides that an artist's work delivered to a dealer for sale or exhibition is not subject to the claims of the creditors of the art dealer. California adds a subsection that provides that sale goods used or bought for personal, family, or household purchases do not become property of the deliveree or cosignee unless the goods are fully paid for.

(a) although the goods are identified to the contract the risk of loss and the title do not pass to the buyer until acceptance; and
(b) use of the goods consistent with the purpose of trial is not acceptance but failure seasonably to notify the seller of election to return the goods is acceptance, and if the goods conform to the contract acceptance of any part is acceptance of the whole; and
(c) after due notification of election to return, the return is at the seller's risk and expense but a merchant buyer must follow any reasonable instructions.

(2) Under a sale or return unless otherwise agreed

(a) the option to return extends to the whole or any commercial unit of the goods while in substantially their original condition, but must be exercised seasonably; and
(b) the return is at the buyer's risk and expense.

SECTION 2-328. *Sale by Auction.*—(1) In a sale by auction if goods are put up in lots each lot is the subject of a separate sale.

(2) A sale by auction is complete when the auctioneer so announces by the fall of the hammer or in other customary manner. Where a bid is made while the hammer is falling in acceptance of a prior bid the auctioneer may in his discretion reopen the bidding or declare the goods sold under the bid on which the hammer was falling.[1]

(3) Such a sale is with reserve unless the goods are in explicit terms put up without reserve. In an auction with reserve the auctioneer may withdraw the goods at any time until he announces completion of the sale. In an auction without reserve, after the auctioneer calls for bids on an article or lot, that article or lot cannot be withdrawn unless no bid is made within a reasonable time. In either case a bidder may retract his bid until the auctioneer's announcement of completion of the sale, but a bidder's retraction does not revive any previous bid.

(4) If the auctioneer knowingly receives a bid on the seller's behalf or the seller makes or procures such a bid, and notice has not been given that liberty for such bids is reserved, the buyer may at his option avoid the sale or take the goods at the price of the last good faith bid prior to the completion of the sale. This subsection shall not apply to any bid at a forced sale.[2]

* * * * * *

Part 4

Title, Creditors and Good Faith Purchasers

SECTION 2-401. *Passing of Title; Reservation for Security; Limited Application of This Section.*—Each provision of this Article with regard to the rights, obligations and remedies of the seller, the buyer, purchasers or other third parties applies irrespective of title to the goods except where the provision refers to

---

[1] Georgia adds the following: "In sales by auction the auctioneer shall be considered agent for both parties so far as to dispense with further memorandum in writing other than his own entries."

[2] Alaska adds a [Section 2-329] which requires that a contract for sale for $10 or more by a door-to-door salesperson provide that the purchaser may revoke his offer to buy within five business days.

such title. Insofar as situations are not covered by the other provisions of this Article and matters concerning title become material the following rules apply:

(1) Title to goods cannot pass under a contract for sale prior to their identification to the contract (Section 2-501), and unless otherwise explicitly agreed the buyer acquires by their identification a special property as limited by this Act. Any retention or reservation by the seller of the title (property) in goods shipped or delivered to the buyer is limited in effect to a reservation of a security interest. Subject to these provisions and to the provisions of the Article on Secured Transactions (Article 9), title to goods passes from the seller to the buyer in any manner and on any conditions explicitly agreed on by the parties.

(2) Unless otherwise explicitly agreed title passes to the buyer at the time and place at which the seller completes his performance with reference to the physical delivery of the goods, despite any reservation of a security interest and even though a document of title is to be delivered at a different time or place; and in particular and despite any reservation of a security interest by the bill of lading

- (a) if the contract requires or authorizes the seller to send the goods to the buyer but does not require him to deliver them at destination, title passes to the buyer at the time and place of shipment; but
- (b) if the contract requires delivery at destination, title passes on tender there.

(3) Unless otherwise explicitly agreed where delivery is to be made without moving the goods,

- (a) if the seller is to deliver a document of title, title passes at the time when and the place where he delivers such documents; or
- (b) if the goods are at the time of contracting already identified and no documents are to be delivered, title passes at the time and place of contracting.

(4) A rejection or other refusal by the buyer to receive or retain the goods, whether or not justified, or a justified revocation of acceptance revests title to the goods in the seller. Such revesting occurs by operation of law and is not a "sale." [1]

SECTION 2-402. *Rights of Seller's Creditors Against Sold Goods.*—(1) Except as provided in subsections (2) and (3), rights of unsecured creditors of the seller with respect to goods which have been identified to a contract for sale are subject to the buyer's rights to recover the goods under this Article (Section 2-502 and 2-716).

(2) A creditor of the seller may treat a sale or an identification of goods to a contract for sale as void if as against him a retention of possession by the seller is fraudulent under any rule of law of the state where the goods are situated, except that retention of possession in good faith and current course of trade by a merchant-seller for a commercially reasonable time after a sale or identification is not fraudulent.

---

[1] Colorado, Montana, and Oregon add a subsection which provides that where livestock is delivered under a contract of sale, title does not pass until payment is made.

(3) Nothing in this Article shall be deemed to impair the rights of creditors of the seller

    (a) under the provisions of the Article on Secured Transactions (Article 9); or
    (b) where identification to the contract or delivery is made not in current course of trade but in satisfaction of or as security for a preexisting claim for money, security or the like and is made under circumstances which under any rule of law of the state where the goods are situated would apart from this Article constitute the transaction a fraudulent transfer or voidable preference.[1]

SECTION 2-403. *Power to Transfer; Good Faith Purchase of Goods; "Entrusting."*—(1) A purchaser of goods acquires all title which his transferor had or had power to transfer except that a purchaser of a limited interest acquires rights only to the extent of the interest purchased. A person with voidable title has power to transfer a good title to a good faith purchaser for value. When goods have been delivered under a transaction of purchase the purchaser has such power even though

    (a) the transferor was deceived as to the identity of the purchaser, or
    (b) the delivery was in exchange for a check which is later dishonored, or
    (c) it was agreed that the transaction was to be a "cash sale," or
    (d) the delivery was procured through fraud punishable as larcenous under the criminal law.[2]

(2) Any entrusting of possession of goods to a merchant who deals in goods of that kind gives him power to transfer all rights of the entruster to a buyer in ordinary course of business.

(3) "Entrusting" includes any delivery and any acquiescence in retention of possession regardless of any condition expressed between the parties to the delivery or acquiescence and regardless of whether the procurement of the entrusting or the possessor's disposition of the goods has been such as to be larcenous under the criminal law.

(4) The rights of other purchasers of goods and of lien creditors are governed by the Articles on Secured Transactions (Article 9), Bulk Transfers (Article 6) and Documents of Title (Article 7).[3]

---

[1] Connecticut a adds subsection as follows:
When a seller remains in possession of goods which have been sold or identified to a contract for sale or of goods which, after sale, have been leased back to him, the buyer or lessor of such goods may protect his interest by complying with the filing provisions of Article 9. On compliance the buyer or lessor has, against creditors of and purchasers from the seller, the rights of a secured party with a perfected security interest. Such filing does not, of itself, make the interest of the buyer or lessor a security interest, as defined by subsection (37) of section [1-201].

[2] Washington omits paragraph (d).

[3] Colorado and Oregon add a subsection that provides that where livestock is delivered, the buyer does not have power to transfer good title to a good faith purchaser for value until payment is made.

Part 5

Performance

SECTION 2-501. *Insurable Interest in Goods; Manner of Identification of Goods.*—(1) The buyer obtains a special property and an insurable interest in goods by identification of existing goods as goods to which the contract refers even though the goods so identified are nonconforming and he has an option to return or reject them. Such identification can be made at any time and in any manner explicity agreed to by the parties. In the absence of explicit agreement identification occurs

   (a) when the contract is made if it is for the sale of goods already existing and identified;
   (b) if the contract is for the sale of future goods other than those described in paragraph (c), when goods are shipped, marked or otherwise designated by the seller as goods to which the contract refers;
   (c) when the crops are planted or otherwise become growing crops or the young are conceived if the contract is for the sale of unborn young to be born within twelve months after contracting or for the sale of crops to be harvested within twelve months or the next normal harvest season after contracting whichever is longer.

(2) The seller retains an insurable interest in goods so long as title to or any security interest in the goods remains in him and where the identification is by the seller alone he may until default or insolvency or notification to the buyer that the identification is final substitute other goods for those identified.

(3) Nothing in this section impairs any insurable interest recognized under any other statute or rule of law.

SECTION 2-502. *Buyer's Rights to Goods on Seller's Insolvency.*—(1) Subject to subsection (2) and even though the goods have not been shipped a buyer who has paid a part or all of the price of goods in which he has a special property under the provisions of the immediately preceding section may on making and keeping good a tender of any unpaid portion of their price recover them from the seller if the seller becomes insolvent within ten days after receipt of the first installment on their price.

(2) If the identification creating his special property has been made by the buyer he acquires the right to recover the goods only if they conform to the contract for sale.

SECTION 2-503. *Manner of Seller's Tender of Delivery.*—(1) Tender of delivery requires that the seller put and hold comforming goods at the buyer's disposition and give the buyer any notification reasonably necessary to enable him to take delivery. The manner, time and place for tender are determined by the agreement and this Article, and in particular

   (a) tender must be at a reasonable hour, and if it is of goods they must be kept available for the period reasonably necessary to enable the buyer to take possession; but

(b) unless otherwise agreed the buyer must furnish facilities reasonably suited to the receipt of the goods.

(2) Where the case is within the next section respecting shipment tender requires that the seller comply with its provisions.

(3) Where the seller is required to deliver at a particular destination tender requires that he comply with subsection (1) and also in any appropriate case tender documents as described in subsections (4) and (5) of this section.

(4) Where goods are in the possession of a bailee and are to be delivered without being moved

- (a) tender requires that the seller either tender a negotiable document of title covering such goods or procure acknowledgment by the bailee of the buyer's right to possession of the goods; but
- (b) tender to the buyer of a nonnegotiable document of title or of a written direction to the bailee to deliver is sufficient tender unless the buyer seasonably objects, and receipt by the bailee of notification of the buyer's rights fixes those rights as against the bailee and all third persons; but risk of loss of the goods and of any failure by the bailee to honor the nonnegotiable document of title or to obey the direction remains on the seller until the buyer has had a reasonable time to present the document or direction, and a refusal by the bailee to honor the document or to obey the direction defeats the tender.

(5) Where the contract requires the seller to deliver documents

- (a) he must tender all such documents in correct form, except as provided in this Article with respect to bills of lading in a set (subsection (2) of Section 2-323); and
- (b) tender through customary banking channels is sufficient and dishonor of a draft accompanying the documents constitutes nonacceptance or rejection.

SECTION 2-504. *Shipment by Seller.*—Where the seller is required or authorized to send the goods to the buyer and the contract does not require him to deliver them at a particular destination, then unless otherwise agreed he must

- (a) put the goods in the possession of such a carrier and make such a contract for their transportation as may be reasonable having regard to the nature of the goods and other circumstances of the case; and
- (b) obtain and promptly deliver or tender in due form any document necessary to enable the buyer to obtain possession of the goods or otherwise required by the agreement or by usage of trade; and
- (c) promptly notify the buyer of the shipment.

Failure to notify the buyer under paragraph (c) or to make a proper contract under paragraph (a) is a ground for rejection only if material delay or loss ensues.

SECTION 2-505. *Seller's Shipment Under Reservation.*—(1) Where the seller has identified goods to the contract by or before shipment:

(a) his procurement of a negotiable bill of lading to his own order or otherwise reserves in him a security interest in the goods. His procurement of the bill to the order of a financing agency or of the buyer indicates in addition only the seller's expectation of transferring that interest to the person named.

(b) a nonnegotiable bill of lading to himself or his nominee reserves possession of the goods as security but except in a case of conditional delivery (subsection (2) of Section 2-507) a nonnegotiable bill of lading naming the buyer as consignee reserves no security interest even though the seller retains possession of the bill of lading.

(2) When shipment by the seller with reservation of a security interest is in violation of the contract for sale it constitutes an improper contract for transportation within the preceding section but impairs neither the rights given to the buyer by shipment and identification of the goods to the contract nor the seller's powers as a holder of a negotiable document.

SECTION 2-506. *Rights of Financing Agency.*—(1) A financing agency by paying or purchasing for value a draft which relates to a shipment of goods acquires to the extent of the payment or purchase and in addition to its own rights under the draft and any document of title securing it any rights of the shipper in the goods including the right to stop delivery and the shipper's right to have the draft honored by the buyer.

(2) The right to reimbursement of a financing agency which has in good faith honored or purchased the draft under commitment to or authority from the buyer is not impaired by subsequent discovery of defects with reference to any relevant document which was apparently regular on its face.

SECTION 2-507. *Effect of Seller's Tender; Delivery on Condition.*—(1) Tender of delivery is a condition to the buyer's duty to accept the goods and, unless otherwise agreed, to his duty to pay for them. Tender entitles the seller to acceptance of the goods and to payment according to the contract.

(2) Where payment is due and demanded on the delivery to the buyer of goods or documents of title, his right as against the seller to retain or dispose of them is conditional upon his making the payment due.

SECTION 2-508. *Cure by Seller of Improper Tender or Delivery; Replacement.*—(1) Where any tender or delivery by the seller is rejected because nonconforming and the time for performance has not yet expired, the seller may seasonably notify the buyer of his intention to cure and may then within the contract time make a conforming delivery.

(2) Where the buyer rejects a nonconforming tender which the seller had reasonable grounds to believe would be acceptable with or without money allowance the seller may if he reasonably notifies the buyer have a further reasonable time to substitute a conforming tender.

SECTION 2-509. *Risk of Loss in the Absence of Breach.*—(1) Where the contract requires or authorizes the seller to ship the goods by carrier

(a) if it does not require him to deliver them at a particular destination, the risk of loss passes to the buyer when the goods are duly delivered to the carrier even though the shipment is under reservation (Section 2-205); but

(b) if it does require him to deliver them at a particular destination and the goods are there duly tendered while in the possession of the carrier, the risk of loss passes to the buyer when the goods are there duly so tendered as to enable the buyer to take delivery.

(2) Where the goods are held by a bailee to be delivered without being moved, the risk of loss passes to the buyer

(a) on his receipt of a negotiable document of title covering the goods; or
(b) on acknowledgment by the bailee of the buyer's right to possession of the goods; or
(c) after his receipt of a nonnegotiable document of title or other written direction to deliver, as provided in subsection (4) (b) of Section 2-503.

(3) In any case not within subsection (1) or (2), the risk of loss passes to the buyer on his receipt of the goods if the seller is a merchant; otherwise the risk passes to the buyer on tender of delivery.

(4) The provisions of this section are subject to contrary agreement of the parties and to the provisions of this Article on sale on approval (Section 2-327) and on effect of breach on risk of loss (Section 2-510).

SECTION 2-510. *Effect of Breach on Risk of Loss.*—(1) Where a tender or delivery of goods so fails to conform to the contract as to give a right of rejection the risk of their loss remains on the seller until cure or acceptance.

(2) Where the buyer rightfully revokes acceptance he may to the extent of any deficiency in his effective insurance coverage treat the risk of loss as having rested on the seller from the beginning.

(3) Where the buyer as to conforming goods already identified to the contract for sale repudiates or is otherwise in breach before risk of their loss has passed to him, the seller may to the extent of any deficiency in his effective insurance coverage treat the risk of loss as resting on the buyer for a commercially reasonable time.

SECTION 2-511. *Tender of Payment by Buyer; Payment by Check.*—(1) Unless otherwise agreed tender of payment is a condition to the seller's duty to tender and complete any delivery.

(2) Tender of payment is sufficient when made by any means or in any manner current in the ordinary course of business unless the seller demands payment in legal tender and gives any extension of time reasonably necessary to procure it.

(3) Subject to the provisions of this Act on the effect of an instrument on an obligation (Section 3-802), payment by check is conditional and is defeated as between the parties by dishonor of the check on due presentment.[1]

---

[1] Colorado adds a subsection which provides that a seller, upon receipt of a brand inspection certificate for livestock which states that payment has not been received, must send a certificate of payment within 10 days after receipt of a check for payment, or within 3 days of payment in any other case.

SECTION 2-512. *Payment by Buyer Before Inspection.*—(1) Where the contract requires payment before inspection nonconformity of the goods does not excuse the buyer from so making payment unless

(a) the nonconformity appears without inspection; or
(b) despite tender of the required documents the circumstances would justify injunction against honor under the provisions of this Act (Section 5-114).[1]

(2) Payment pursuant to subsection (1) does not constitute an acceptance of the goods or impair the buyer's right to inspect or any of his remedies.

SECTION 2-513. *Buyer's Right to Inspection of Goods.*—(1) Unless otherwise agreed and subject to subsection (3), where goods are tendered or delivered or identified to the contract for sale, the buyer has a right before payment or acceptance to inspect them at any reasonable place and time and in any reasonable manner. When the seller is required or authorized to send the goods to the buyer, the inspection may be after their arrival.

(2) Expenses of inspection must be borne by the buyer but may be recovered from the seller if the goods do not conform and are rejected.

(3) Unless otherwise agreed and subject to the provisions of this Article on C.I.F. contracts (subsection (3) of Section 2-321), the buyer is not entitled to inspect the goods before payment of the price when the contract provides

(a) for delivery "C.O.D." or on like terms; or
(b) for payment against documents of title, except where such payment is due only after the goods are to become available for inspection.

(4) A place or method of inspection fixed by the parties is presumed to be exclusive but unless otherwise expressly agreed it does not postpone identification or shift the place for delivery or for passing the risk of loss. If compliance becomes impossible, inspection shall be as provided in this section unless the place or method fixed was clearly intended as an indispensable condition failure of which avoids the contract.

SECTION 2-514. *When Documents Deliverable on Acceptance; When on Payment.*—Unless otherwise agreed documents against which a draft is drawn are to be delivered to the drawee on acceptance of the draft if it is payable more than three days after presentment; otherwise, only on payment.

SECTION 2-515. *Preserving Evidence of Goods in Dispute.*—In furtherance of the adjustment of any claim or dispute

(a) either party on reasonable notification to the other and for the purpose of ascertaining the facts and preserving evidence has the right to inspect, test and sample the goods including such of them as may be in the possession or control of the other; and
(b) the parties may agree to a third party inspection or survey to determine the conformity or condition of the goods and may agree that the findings shall be binding upon them in any subsequent litigation or adjustment.

---

[1] California omits subsec. (1) (b).

Part 6

Breach, Repudiation and Excuse

SECTION 2-601. *Buyer's Rights on Improper Delivery.*—Subject to the provisions of this Article on breach in installment contracts (Section 2-612) and unless otherwise agreed under the sections on contractual limitation of remedy (Sections 2-718 and 2-719), if the goods or the tender of delivery fail in any respect to conform to the contract, the buyer may

    (a) reject the whole; or
    (b) accept the whole; or
    (c) accept any commercial unit or units and reject the rest.

SECTION 2-602. *Manner and Effect of Rightful Rejection.*—(1) Rejection of goods must be within a reasonable time after their delivery or tender. It is ineffective unless the buyer seasonably notifies the seller.

(2) Subject to the provisions of the two following sections on rejected goods (Sections 2-603 and 2-604),

    (a) after rejection any exercise of ownership by the buyer with respect to any commercial unit is wrongful as against the seller; and
    (b) if the buyer has before rejection taken physical possession of goods in which he does not have a security interest under the provisions of this Article (subsection (3) of Section 2-711), he is under a duty after rejection to hold them with reasonable care at the seller's disposition for a time sufficient to permit the seller to remove them; but
    (c) the buyer has no further obligations with regard to goods rightfully rejected.

(3) The seller's rights with respect to goods wrongfully rejected are governed by the provisions of this Article on seller's remedies in general (Section 2-703).

SECTION 2-603. *Merchant Buyer's Duties as to Rightfully Rejected Goods.*—(1) Subject to any security interest in the buyer (subsection (3) of Section 2-711), when the seller has no agent or place of business at the market of rejection a merchant buyer is under a duty after rejection of goods in his possession or control to follow any reasonable instructions received from the seller with respect to the goods and in the absence of such instructions to make reasonable efforts to sell them for the seller's account if they are perishable or threaten to decline in value speedily. Instructions are not reasonable if on demand indemnity for expenses is not forthcoming.

(2) When the buyer sells goods under subsection (1), he is entitled to reimbursement from the seller or out of the proceeds for reasonable expenses of caring for and selling them, and if the expenses include no selling commission then to such commission as is usual in the trade or if there is none to a reasonable sum not exceeding ten per cent on the gross proceeds.

(3) In complying with this section the buyer is held only to good faith and good faith conduct hereunder is neither acceptance nor conversion nor the basis of an action for damages.

SECTION 2-604. *Buyer's Options as to Salvage of Rightfully Rejected Goods.*—Subject to the provisions of the immediately preceding section on perishables if the seller gives no instructions within a reasonable time after notification of rejection the buyer may store the rejected goods for the seller's account or reship them to him or resell them for the seller's account with reimbursement as provided in the preceding section. Such action is not acceptance or conversion.[1]

SECTION 2-605.—*Waiver of Buyer's Objections by Failure to Particularize.*— (1) The buyer's failure to state in connection with rejection a particular defect which is ascertainable by reasonable inspection precludes him from relying on the unstated defect to justify rejection or to establish breach

(a) where the seller could have cured it if stated seasonably; or
(b) between merchants when the seller has after rejection made a request in writing for a full and final written statement of all defects on which the buyer proposes to rely.

(2) Payment against documents made without reservation of rights precludes recovery of the payment for defects apparent on the face of the documents.

SECTION 2-606. *What Constitutes Acceptance of Goods.*—(1) Acceptance of goods occurs when the buyer

(a) after a reasonable opportunity to inspect the goods signifies to the seller that the goods are conforming or that he will take or retain them in spite of their nonconformity; or
(b) fails to make an effective rejection (subsection (1) of Section 2-602), but such acceptance does not occur until the buyer has had a reasonable opportunity to inspect them; or
(c) does any act inconsistent with the seller's ownership; but if such act is wrongful as against the seller it is an acceptance only if ratified by him.[2]

(2) Acceptance of a part of any commercial unit is acceptance of that entire unit.[3]

SECTION 2-607. *Effect of Acceptance; Notice of Breach; Burden of Establishing Breach After Acceptance; Notice of Claim or Litigation to Person Answerable Over.*—(1) The buyer must pay at the contract rate for any goods accepted.

(2) Acceptance of goods by the buyer precludes rejection of the goods accepted and if made with knowledge of a nonconformity cannot be revoked because of it unless the acceptance was on the reasonable assumption that the nonconformity would be seasonably cured but acceptance does not of itself impair any other remedy provided by this Article for nonconformity.

(3) Where a tender has been accepted

---

[1] Ohio adds this section as the fourth subsection of Section 2-603.

[2] What constitutes acts inconsistent with the seller's ownership is determined on a case by case basis. In *Jorgensen v. Pressnall,* 274 Ore. 288, 545 P.2d 1382 (1976), the Oregon Supreme Court held that the continued use of a mobile home after a properly revoked acceptance is not a wrongful act that can be classified as an acceptance.

[3] South Carolina amends subsec. (2) which provides that, "Acceptance of a part of any commercial unit shall not be acceptable of the entire unit."

Arkansas adds a section which provides that unsolicited merchandise received by a person may be considered a gift and the recipient may use it as he choses without obligation.

(a) the buyer must within a reasonable time after he discovers or should have discovered any breach notify the seller of breach or be barred from any remedy;[1] and
(b) if the claim is one for infringement or the like (subsection (3) of Section 2-312) and the buyer is sued as a result of such breach he must so notify the seller within a reasonable time after he receives notice of the litigation or be barred from any remedy over for liability established by the litigation.

(4) The burden is on the buyer to establish any breach with respect to the goods accepted.

(5) Where the buyer is sued for breach of a warranty or other obligation for which his seller is answerable over

(a) he may give his seller written notice of the litigation. If the notice states that the seller may come in and defend and that if the seller does not do so he will be bound in any action against him by his buyer by any determination of fact common to the two litigations, then unless the seller after seasonable receipt of the notice does come in and defend he is so bound.
(b) if the claim is one for infringement or the like (subsection (3) of Section 2-312) the original seller may demand in writing that his buyer turn over to him control of the litigation including settlement or else be barred from any remedy over and if he also agrees to bear all expense and to satisfy any adverse judgment, then unless the buyer after seasonable receipt of the demand does turn over control the buyer is so barred.

(6) The provisions of subsections (3), (4) and (5) apply to any obligation of a buyer to hold a seller harmless against infringement or the like (subsection (3) of Section 2-312).[2]

SECTION 2-608. *Revocation of Acceptance in Whole or in Part.*—(1) The buyer may revoke his acceptance of a lot or commercial unit whose nonconformity substantially impairs its value to him if he has accepted it

(a) on the reasonable assumption that its nonconformity would be cured and it has not been seasonably cured; or
(b) without discovery of such nonconformity if his acceptance was reasonably induced either by the difficulty of discovery before acceptance or by the seller's assurances.

(2) Revocation of acceptance must occur within a reasonable time after the buyer discovers or should have discovered the ground for it and before any substantial change in condition of the goods which is not caused by their own defects. It is not effective until the buyer notifies the seller of it.

(3) A buyer who so revokes has the same rights and duties with regard to the goods involved as if he had rejected them.

---

[1] South Carolina in subsec. (3)(a) adds: "however, no notice of injury to the person in the case of consumer goods shall be required."
[2] Maine adds subsection (7) which provides that subsection (3)(a) "shall not apply where the remedy is for personal injury resulting from any breach."

SECTION 2-609. *Right to Adequate Assurance of Performance.*—(1) A contract for sale imposes an obligation on each party that the other's expectation of receiving due performance will not be impaired. When reasonable grounds for insecurity arise with respect to the performance of either party the other may in writing demand adequate assurance of due performance and until he receives such assurance may if commercially reasonable suspend any performance for which he has not already received the agreed return.

(2) Between merchants the reasonableness of grounds for insecurity and the adequacy of any assurance offered shall be determined according to commercial standards.

(3) Acceptance of any improper delivery or payment does not prejudice the aggrieved party's right to demand adequate assurance of future performance.

(4) After receipt of a justified demand failure to provide within a reasonable time not exceeding thirty days such assurance of due performance as is adequate under the circumstances of the particular case is a repudiation of the contract.

SECTION 2-610. *Anticipatory Repudiation.*—When either party repudiates the contract with respect to a performance not yet due the loss of which will substantially impair the value of the contract to the other, the aggrieved party may

(a) for a commercially reasonable time await performance by the repudiating party; or
(b) resort to any remedy for breach (Section 2-703 or Section 2-711), even though he has notified the repudiating party that he would await the latter's performance, and has urged retraction; and
(c) in either case suspend his own performance or proceed in accordance with the provisions of this Article on the seller's right to identify goods to the contract notwithstanding breach or to salvage unfinished goods (Section 2-704).

SECTION 2-611. *Retraction of Anticipatory Repudiation.*—(1) Until the repudiating party's next performance is due he can retract his repudiation unless the aggrieved party has since the repudiation cancelled or materially changed his position or otherwise indicated that he considers the repudiation final.

(2) Retraction may be by any method which clearly indicates to the aggrieved party that the repudiating party intends to perform, but must include any assurance justifiably demanded under the provisions of this Article (Section 2-609).

(3) Retraction reinstates the repudiating party's rights under the contract with due excuse and allowance to the aggrieved party for any delay occasioned by the repudiation.

SECTION 2-612. *"Installment Contract"; Breach.*—(1) An "installment contract" is one which requires or authorizes the delivery of goods in separate lots to be separately accepted, even though the contract contains a clause "each delivery is a separate contract" or its equivalent.

(2) The buyer may reject any installment which is nonconforming if the nonconformity substantially impairs the value of that installment and cannot be cured or if the nonconformity is a defect in the required documents; but if the nonconformity does not fall within subsection (3) and the seller gives adequate assurance of its cure the buyer must accept that installment.

(3) Whenever nonconformity or default with respect to one or more installments substantially impairs the value of the whole contract there is a breach

of the whole. But the aggrieved party reinstates the contract if he accepts a nonconforming installment without seasonably notifying of cancellation or if he brings an action with respect only to past installments or demands performance as to future installments.

SECTION 2-613. *Casualty to Identified Goods.*—Where the contract requires for its performance goods identified when the contract is made, and the goods suffer casualty without fault of either party before the risk of loss passes to the buyer, or in a proper case under a "no arrival, no sale" term (Section 2-324) then

- (a) if the loss is total the contract is avoided; and
- (b) if the loss is partial or the goods have so deteriorated as no longer to conform to the contract the buyer may nevertheless demand inspection and at his option either treat the contract as avoided or accept the goods with due allowance from the contract price for the deterioration or the deficiency in quantity but without further right against the seller.

SECTION 2-614. *Substituted Performance.*—(1) Where without fault of either party the agreed berthing, loading, or unloading facilities fail or an agreed type of carrier becomes unavailable or the agreed manner of delivery otherwise becomes commercially impracticable but a commercially reasonable substitute is available, such substitute performance must be tendered and accepted.

(2) If the agreed means or manner of payment fails because of domestic or foreign governmental regulation, the seller may withhold or stop delivery unless the buyer provides a means or manner of payment which is commercially a substantial equivalent. If delivery has already been taken, payment by the means in the manner provided by the regulation discharges the buyer's obligation unless the regulation is discriminatory, oppressive or predatory.

SECTION 2-615. *Excuse by Failure of Presupposed Conditions.*—Except so far as a seller may have assumed a greater obligation and subject to the preceding section on substituted performance:

- (a) Delay in delivery or nondelivery in whole or in part by a seller who complies with paragraphs (b) and (c) is not a breach of his duty under a contract for sale if performance as agreed has been made impracticable by the occurrence of a contingency the nonoccurrence of which was a basic assumption on which the contract was made or by compliance in good faith with any applicable foreign or domestic governmental regulation or order whether or not it later proves to be invalid.
- (b) Where the causes mentioned in paragraph (a) affect only a part of the seller's capacity to perform, he must allocate production and deliveries among his customers but may at his option include regular customers not then under contract as well as his own requirements for further manufacture. He may so allocate in any manner which is fair and reasonable.
- (c) The seller must notify the buyer seasonably that there will be delay or nondelivery and, when allocation is required under paragraph (b), of the estimated quota thus made available for the buyer.[1]

---

[1] Mississippi adds a subsec. (d) which provides that the buyer must seasonably notify the seller that there will be a delay or inability to take delivery and the cause thereof.

SECTION 2-616. *Procedure on Notice Claiming Excuse.*—(1) Where the buyer receives notification of a material or indefinite delay or an allocation justified under the preceding section he may by written notification to the seller as to any delivery concerned, and where the prospective deficiency substantially impairs the value of the whole contract under the provisions of this Article relating to breach of installment contracts (Section 2-612), then also as to the whole,

(a) terminate and thereby discharge any unexecuted portion of the contract; or
(b) modify the contract by agreeing to take his available quota in substitution.

(2) If after receipt of such notification from the seller the buyer fails so to modify the contract within a reasonable time not exceeding thirty days the contract lapses with respect to any deliveries affected.

(3) The provisions of this section may not be negated by agreement except insofar as seller has assumed greater obligation under preceding section.[1]

Part 7

Remedies

SECTION 2-701. *Remedies for Breach of Collateral Contracts Not Impaired.*— Remedies for breach of any obligation or promise collateral or ancillary to a contract for sale are not impaired by the provisions of this Article.

SECTION 2-702. *Seller's Remedies on Discovery of Buyer's Insolvency.*— (1) Where the seller discovers the buyer to be insolvent he may refuse delivery except for cash including payment for all goods theretofore delivered under the contract, and stop delivery under this Article (Section 2-705).

(2) Where the seller discovers that the buyer has received goods on credit while insolvent he may reclaim the goods upon demand made within ten days after the receipt, but if misrepresentation of solvency has been made to the particular seller in writing within three months before delivery the ten day limitation does not apply. Except as provided in this subsection the seller may not base a right to reclaim goods on the buyer's fraudulent or innocent misrepresentation of solvency or of intent to pay.

(3) The seller's right to reclaim under subsection (2) is subject to the rights of a buyer in ordinary course or other good faith purchase or lien creditor under this Article (Section 2-403). Successful reclamation of goods excludes all other remedies with respect to them.[2]

---

[1] Washington and Wisconsin omit subsec. (3). Connecticut amends subsec. (3) which provides that Section 2-616 may also be negated by a signed writing between merchants.

Indiana adds Sections 2-631, 2-632, and 2-633 (Sections 2-617 to 2-630 being reserved for future legislation) which provide that a contract for sale to a consumer at his residence must conspicuously provide that the purchaser has two days to cancel the contract and return the merchandise.

Mississippi adds Section 2-617 which provides for particular circumstances, e.g., Act of God, war, riots, inability to obtain fuel, under which the seller may suspend delivery without liability.

[2] The following states eliminate the phrase "or lien creditor" in subsec. (3): Arkansas, California, Connecticut, District of Columbia, Florida, Illinois, Iowa, Kansas, Maine, Maryland, Minnesota, Montana, New Jersey, New Mexico, New York, North Carolina, North Dakota, Oklahoma, Washington, Wisconsin and Wyoming.

SECTION 2-703. *Seller's Remedies in General.*—Where the buyer wrongfully rejects or revokes acceptance of goods or fails to make a payment due on or before delivery or repudiates with respect to a part or the whole, then with respect to any goods directly affected and, if the breach is of the whole contract (Section 2-612), then also with respect to the whole undelivered balance, the aggrieved seller may

    (a) withhold delivery of such goods;
    (b) stop delivery by any bailee as hereafter provided (Section 2-705);
    (c) proceed under the next section respecting goods still unidentified to the contract;
    (d) resell and recover damages as hereafter provided (Section 2-706);
    (e) recover damages for nonacceptance (Section 2-708) or in a proper case the price (Section 2-709);
    (f) cancel.

SECTION 2-704. *Seller's Right to Identify Goods to the Contract Notwithstanding Breach or to Salvage Unfinished Goods.*—(1) An aggrieved seller under the preceding section may

    (a) identify to the contract conforming goods not already identified if at the time he learned of the breach they are in his possession or control;
    (b) treat as the subject of resale goods which have demonstrably been intended for the particular contract even though those goods are unfinished.

(2) Where the goods are unfinished an aggrieved seller may in the exercise of reasonable commercial judgment for the purposes of avoiding loss and of effective realization either complete the manufacture and wholly identify the goods to the contract or cease manufacture and resell for scrap or salvage value or proceed in any other reasonable manner.

SECTION 2-705. *Seller's Stoppage of Delivery in Transit or Otherwise.*—(1) The seller may stop delivery of goods in the possession of a carrier or other bailee when he discovers the buyer to be insolvent (Section 2-702) and may stop delivery of carload, truckload, planeload or larger shipments of express or freight when the buyer repudiates or fails to make a payment due before delivery or if for any other reason the seller has a right to withhold or reclaim the goods.

(2) As against such buyer the seller may stop delivery until

    (a) receipt of the goods by the buyer; or
    (b) acknowledgment to the buyer by any bailee of the goods except a carrier that the bailee holds the goods for the buyer; or
    (c) such acknowledgment to the buyer by a carrier by reshipment or as warehouseman; or
    (d) negotiation to the buyer of any negotiable document of title covering the goods.

(3) (a) To stop delivery the seller must so notify as to enable the bailee by reasonable diligence to prevent delivery of the goods.

    (b) After such notification the bailee must hold and deliver the goods according to the directions of the seller but the seller is liable to the bailee for any ensuing charges or damages.

(c) If a negotiable document of title has been issued for goods the bailee is not obliged to obey a notification to stop until surrender of the document.

(d) A carrier who has issued a nonnegotiable bill of lading is not obliged to obey a notification to stop received from a person other than the consigner.

SECTION 2-706. *Seller's Resale Including Contract for Resale.*—(1) Under the conditions stated in Section 2-703 on seller's remedies, the seller may resell the goods concerned or the undelivered balance thereof. . . .

SECTION 2-708. *Seller's Damages for Nonacceptance or Repudiation.*— (1) Subject to subsection (2) and to the provisions of this Article with respect to proof of market price (Section 2-723), the measure of damages for nonacceptance or repudiation by the buyer is the difference between the market price at the time and place for tender and the unpaid contract price together with any incidental damages provided in this Article (Section 2-710), but less expenses saved in consequence of the buyer's breach.

(2) If the measure of damages provided in subsection (1) is inadequate to put the seller in as good a position as performance would have done then the measure of damages is the profit (including reasonable overhead) which the seller would have made from full performance by the buyer, together with any incidental damages provided in this Article (Section 2-710), due allowance for costs reasonably incurred and due credit for payments or proceeds of resale.

SECTION 2-709. *Action for the Price.*—(1) When the buyer fails to pay the price as it becomes due the seller may recover, together with any incidental damages under the next section, the price

(a) of goods accepted or of conforming goods lost or damaged within a commercially reasonable time after risk of their loss has passed to the buyer; and

(b) of goods identified to the contract if the seller is unable after reasonable effort to resell them at a reasonable price or the circumstances reasonably indicate that such effort will be unavailing.

(2) Where the seller sues for the price he must hold for the buyer any goods which have been identified to the contract and are still in his control except that if resale becomes possible he may resell them at any time prior to the collection of the judgment. The net proceeds of any such resale must be credited to the buyer and payment of the judgment entitles him to any goods not resold.

(3) After the buyer has wrongfully rejected or revoked acceptance of the goods or has failed to make a payment due or has repudiated (Section 2-610), a seller who is held not entitled to the price under this section shall nevertheless be awarded damages for nonacceptance under the preceding section.

SECTION 2-710. *Seller's Incidental Damages.*—Incidental damages to an aggrieved seller include any commercially reasonable charges, expenses or commissions incurred in stopping delivery, in the transportation, care and custody of goods after the buyer's breach, in connection with return or resale of the goods or otherwise resulting from the breach.

SECTION 2-711. *Buyer's Remedies in General; Buyer's Security Interest in Rejected Goods.*—(1) Where the seller fails to make delivery or repudiates or

UNIFORM COMMERCIAL CODE 1-59

the buyer rightfully rejects or justifiably revokes acceptance then with respect to any goods involved, and with respect to the whole if the breach goes to the whole contract (Section 2-612), the buyer may cancel and whether or not he has done so may in addition to recovering so much of the price as has been paid

(a) "cover" and have damages under the next section as to all the goods affected whether or not they have been identified to the contract; or
(b) recover damages for nondelivery as provided in this Article (Section 2-713).

(2) Where the seller fails to deliver or repudiates the buyer may also

(a) if the goods have been identified recover them as provided in this Article (Section 2-502); or
(b) in a proper case obtain specific performance or replevy the goods as provided in this Article (Section 2-716).

(3) On rightful rejection or justifiable revocation of acceptance a buyer has a security interest in goods in his possession or control for any payments made on their price and any expenses reasonably incurred in their inspection, receipt, transportation, care and custody and may hold such goods and resell them in like manner as an aggrieved seller (Section 2-706).

SECTION 2-712. *"Cover"; Buyer's Procurement of Substitute Goods.*—(1) After a breach within the preceding section the buyer may "cover" by making in good faith and without unreasonable delay any reasonable purchase of or contract to purchase goods in substitution for those due from seller.

(2) The buyer may recover from the seller as damages the difference between the cost of cover and the contract price together with any incidental or consequential damages as hereinafter defined (Section 2-715), but less expenses saved in consequence of the seller's breach.

(3) Failure of the buyer to effect cover within this section does not bar him from any other remedy.

SECTION 2-713. *Buyer's Damages for Nondelivery or Repudiation.*—(1) Subject to the provisions of this Article with respect to proof of market price (Section 2-723), the measure of damages for nondelivery or repudiation by the seller is the difference between the market price at the time the buyer learned of the breach and the contract price together with any incidental and consequential damages as provided in this Article (Section 2-715), but less expenses saved in consequence of the seller's breach.

(2) Market price is to be determined as of the place for tender or, in cases of rejection after arrival or revocation of acceptance, as of the place of arrival.

SECTION 2-714. *Buyer's Damages for Breach in Regard to Accepted Goods.*— (1) Where the buyer has accepted goods and given notification (subsection (3) of Section 2-607) he may recover as damages for any nonconformity of tender the loss resulting in the ordinary course of events from the seller's breach as determined in any manner which is reasonable.

(2) The measure of damages for breach of warranty is the difference at the time and place of acceptance between the value of the goods accepted and the

value they would have had if they had been as warranted, unless special circumstances show proximate damages of a different amount.[1]

(3) In a proper case any incidental and consequential damages under the next section may also be recovered.

SECTION 2-715. *Buyer's Incidental and Consequential Damages.*—(1) Incidental damages resulting from the seller's breach include expenses reasonably incurred in inspection, receipt, transportation and care and custody of goods rightfully rejected, any commercially reasonable charges, expenses or commissions in connection with effecting cover and any other reasonable expense incident to the delay or other breach.

(2) Consequential damages resulting from the seller's breach include

   (a) any loss resulting from general or particular requirements and needs of which the seller at the time of contracting had reason to know and which could not reasonably be prevented by cover or otherwise; and

   (b) injury to person or property proximately resulting from any breach of warranty.

SECTION 2-716. *Buyer's Right To Specific Performance or Replevin.*—(1) Specific performance may be decreed where the goods are unique or in other proper circumstances. . . .

SECTION 2-717. *Deduction of Damages from Price.*—The buyer on notifying the seller of his intention so to do may deduct all or any part of the damages resulting from any breach of the contract from any part of the price still due under the same contract.

SECTION 2-718. *Liquidation or Limitation of Damages; Deposits.*—(1) Damages for breach by either party may be liquidated in the agreement but only at an amount which is reasonable in the light of the anticipated or actual harm caused by the breach, the difficulties of proof of loss, and the inconvenience or nonfeasibility of otherwise obtaining an adequate remedy. A term fixing unreasonably large liquidated damages is void as a penalty.

(2) Where the seller justifiably withholds delivery of goods because of the buyer's breach, the buyer is entitled to restitution of any amount by which the sum of his payments exceeds

   (a) the amount to which the seller is entitled by virtue of terms liquidating the seller's damages in accordance with subsection (1), or

   (b) in the absence of such terms, twenty per cent of the value of the total performance for which the buyer is obligated under the contract or $500, whichever is smaller.

(3) The buyer's right to restitution under subsection (2) is subject to offset to the extent that the seller establishes

   (a) a right to recover damages under the provisions of this Article other than subsection (1), and

   (b) the amount or value of any benefits received by the buyer directly or indirectly by reason of the contract.

---

[1] Alabama amends subsec. (2) to add: "and nothing in this section shall be construed so as to limit the seller's liability for damages for injury to the person in the case of consumer goods. Damages in an action for injury to the person include those damages ordinarily allowable in such actions at law."

(4) Where a seller has received payment in goods their reasonable value or the proceeds of their resale shall be treated as payments for the purposes of subsection (2); but if the seller has notice of the buyer's breach before reselling goods received in part performance, his resale is subject to the conditions laid down in this Article on resale by an aggrieved seller (Section 2-706).

SECTION 2-719. *Contractual Modification or Limitation of Remedy.*—(1) Subject to the provisions of subsections (2) and (3) of this section and of the preceding section on liquidation and limitation of damages,

- (a) the agreement may provide for remedies in addition to or in substitution for those provided in this Article and may limit or alter the measure of damages recoverable under this Article, as by limiting the buyer's remedies to return of the goods and repayment of the price or to repair and replacement of nonconforming goods or parts; and
- (b) resort to a remedy as provided is optional unless the remedy is expressly agreed to be exclusive, in which case it is the sole remedy.

(2) Where circumstances cause an exclusive or limited remedy to fail of its essential purpose remedy may be had as provided in this Act.

(3) Consequential damages may be limited or excluded unless the limitation or exclusion is unconscionable. Limitation of consequential damages for injury to the person in the case of consumer goods is prima facie unconscionable but limitation of damages where the loss is commercial is not.[1]

SECTION 2-720. *Effect of "Cancellation" or "Rescission" on Claims for Antecedent Breach.*—Unless the contrary intention clearly appears, expressions of "cancellation" or "rescission" of the contract or the like shall not be construed as a renunciation or discharge of any claim in damages for an antecedent breach.

SECTION 2-721. *Remedies for Fraud.*—Remedies for material misrepresentation or fraud include all remedies available under this Article for nonfraudulent breach. Neither rescission nor a claim for rescission of the contract for sale

---

[1] California provides that "Limitation of consequential damages for injury to the person in the case of consumer goods is invalid unless it is proved that the limitation is not unconscionable. Limitation of consequential damages where the loss is commercial is valid unless it is proved that the limitation is not unconscionable."

Alabama adds subsection (4) as follows: "Nothing in this section or in the preceding section shall be construed so as to limit the seller's liability for damages for injury to the person in the case of consumer goods."

Washington amends subsec. (3) to provide that "Limitation of consequential damages for injury to the person in the case of goods purchased primarily for personal, family or household use or of any services related thereto is invalid unless it is proved that the limitation is not unconscionable. Limitation of remedy to repair or replacement of defective parts of nonconforming goods is invalid in sales of goods primarily for personal, family or household use unless the manufacturer or seller maintains or provides within this state facilities adequate to provide reasonable and expeditious performance of repair or replacement obligations.

Limitation of other consequential damages is valid unless it is established that the limitation is unconscionable."

Mississippi adds subsec. (4) which provides that, "Any limitation of remedies which would deprive the buyer of a remedy to which he may be entitled for breach of an implied warranty of merchantability or fitness for a particular purpose shall be prohibited."

Indiana permits recovery by the plaintiff, if he recovers judgment, of attorney fees in all actions based on fraud or material misrepresentation.

nor rejection or return of the goods shall bar or be deemed inconsistent with a claim for damages or other remedy.

* * * * * *

SECTION 2-725. *Statute of Limitations in Contracts for Sale.*—(1) An action for breach of any contract for sale must be commenced within four years after the cause of action has accrued. By the original agreement the parties may reduce the period of limitation to not less than one year but may not extend it.

(2) A cause of action accrues when the breach occurs, regardless of the aggrieved party's lack of knowledge of the breach. A breach of warranty occurs when tender of delivery is made, except that where a warranty explicitly extends to future performance of the goods and discovery of the breach must await the time of such performance the cause of action accrues when the breach is or should have been discovered.

(3) Where an action commenced within the time limited by subsection (1) is so terminated as to leave available a remedy by another action for the same breach such other action may be commenced after the expiration of the time limited and within six months after the termination of the first action unless the termination resulted from voluntary discontinuance or from dismissal for failure or neglect to prosecute.

(4) This section does not alter the law on tolling of the statute of limitations nor does it apply to causes of action which have accrued before this Act becomes effective.[1]

ARTICLE 3

COMMERCIAL PAPER

(This Article represents a complete revision and modernization of the Uniform Negotiable Instruments Law. The text of this Article is not reproduced in this volume. In Chapter 18, "Laws Governing Negotiable Instruments," the subject is discussed in detail.)

ARTICLE 4

BANK DEPOSITS AND COLLECTIONS

(This Article deals with matters relating to dealings between banks and their customers, other banks and third parties. It covers such matters as deposits and collection of negotiable instruments, the relationship between a bank and its customers, and the dealings between banks. The text of this Article is not reproduced in this volume.)

---

[1] Many states have adopted variations differing from the Official Text. The particular state code section should be consulted.

ARTICLE 5

DOCUMENTARY LETTERS OF CREDIT

Section 5-101. *Short Title.*—This Article shall be known and may be cited as Uniform Commercial Code—Letters of Credit.

Section 5-102. *Scope.*—(1) This Article applies
- (a) to a credit issued by a bank if the credit requires a documentary draft or a documentary demand for payment; and
- (b) to a credit issued by a person other than a bank if the credit requires that the draft or demand for payment be accompanied by a document of title; and
- (c) to a credit issued by a bank or other person if the credit is not within subparagraphs (a) or (b) but conspicuously states that it is a letter of credit or is conspicuously so entitled.

(2) Unless the engagement meets the requirements of subsection (1), this Article does not apply to engagements to make advances or to honor drafts or demands for payment, to authorities to pay or purchase, to guarantees or to general agreements.

(3) This Article deals with some but not all of the rules and concepts of letters of credit as such rules or concepts have developed prior to this Act or may hereafter develop. The fact that this Article states a rule does not by itself require, imply or negate application of the same or a converse rule to a situation not provided for or to a person not specified by this Article.[1]

Section 5-103. *Definitions.*—(1) In this Article, unless the context otherwise requires,
- (a) "Credit" or "letter of credit" means an engagement by a bank or other person made at the request of a customer and of a kind within the scope of this Article (Section 5-102) that the issuer will honor drafts or other demands for payment upon compliance with the conditions specified in the credit. A credit may be either revocable or irrevocable. The engagement may be either an agreement to honor or a statement that the bank or other person is authorized to honor.[2]
- (b) A "documentary draft" or a "documentary demand for payment" is one honor of which is conditioned upon the presentation of a document or documents. "Document" means any paper including document of title, security, invoice, certificate, notice of default and the like.
- (c) An "issuer" is a bank or other person issuing a credit.
- (d) A "beneficiary" of a credit is a person who is entitled under its terms to draw or demand payment.
- (e) An "advising bank" is a bank which gives notification of the issuance of credit by another bank.
- (f) A "confirming bank" is a bank which engages either that it will itself

---

[1] New York, Alabama, and Missouri add the following subsection: "(4) Unless otherwise agreed, this Article 5 does not apply to a letter of credit or a credit if by its terms or by an agreement, course of dealing or usage of trade such letter of credit or credit is subject in whole or in part to the Uniform Customs and Practice for Commercial Documentary Credits fixed by the Thirteenth or any subsequent Congress of the International Chamber of Commerce."

[2] Florida and Louisiana provide that where a credit does not state whether it is revocable or irrevocable, the credit is presumed to be irrevocable.

honor a credit already issued by another bank or that such a credit will be honored by the issuer or a third bank
  (g) A "customer" is a buyer or other person who causes an issuer to issue a credit. The term also includes a bank which procures issuance or confirmation on behalf of that bank's customer.
(2) Other definitions applying to this Article and the sections in which they appear are:

"Notation of Credit"	Section 5-108
"Presenter"	Section 5-112 (3)

(3) Definitions in other Articles applying to this Article and the sections in which they appear are:

"Accept" or "Acceptance"	Section 3-410
"Contract for sale"	Section 2-106
"Draft"	Section 3-104
"Holder in due course"	Section 3-302
"Midnight deadline"	Section 4-104
"Security"	Section 8-102

(4) In addition, Article 1 contains general definitions and principles of construction and interpretation applicable throughout this Article.

SECTION 5-104. *Formal Requirements; Signing.*—(1) Except as otherwise required in subsection (1) (c) of Section 5-102 on scope, no particular form of phrasing is required for a credit. A credit must be in writing and signed by the issuer and a confirmation must be in writing and signed by the confirming bank. A modification of the terms of a credit or confirmation must be signed by the issuer or confirming bank.

(2) A telegram may be a sufficient signed writing if it identifies its sender by an authorized authentication. The authentication may be in code and the authorized naming of the issuer in an advice of credit is a sufficient signing.

SECTION 5-105. *Consideration.*—No consideration is necessary to establish a credit or to enlarge or otherwise modify its terms.

SECTION 5-106. *Time and Effect of Establishment of Credit.*—(1) Unless otherwise agreed a credit is established
  (a) as regards the customer as soon as a letter of credit is sent to him or the letter of credit or an authorized written advice of its issuance is sent to the beneficiary; and
  (b) as regards the beneficiary when he receives a letter of credit or an authorized written advice of its issuance.

(2) Unless otherwise agreed once an irrevocable credit is established as regards the customer it can be modified or revoked only with the consent of the customer and once it is established as regards the beneficiary it can be modified or revoked only with his consent.

(3) Unless otherwise agreed after a revocable credit is established it may be modified or revoked by the issuer without notice to or consent from the customer or beneficiary.

(4) Notwithstanding any modification or revocation of a revocable credit any person authorized to honor or negotiate under the terms of the original credit is entitled to reimbursement for or honor of any draft or demand for payment

duly honored or negotiated before receipt of notice of the modification or revocation and the issuer in turn is entitled to reimbursement from its customer.

SECTION 5-107. *Advice of Credit; Confirmation; Error in Statement of Terms.*—(1) Unless otherwise specified an advising bank by advising a credit issued by another bank does not assume any obligation to honor drafts drawn or demands for payment made under the credit but it does assume obligation for the accuracy of its own statement.

(2) A confirming bank by confirming a credit becomes directly obligated on the credit to the extent of its confirmation as though it were its issuer and acquires the rights of an issuer.[1]

(3) Even though an advising bank incorrectly advises the terms of a credit it has been authorized to advise the credit is established as against the issuer to the extent of its original terms.

(4) Unless otherwise specified the customer bears as against the issuer all risks of transmission and reasonable translation or interpretation of any message relating to a credit.

SECTION 5-108. *"Notation Credit"; Exhaustion of Credit.*—(1) A credit which specifies that any person purchasing or paying drafts drawn or demands for payment made under it must note the amount of the draft or demand on the letter or advice of credit is a "notation of credit".

(2) Under a notation credit
   (a) a person paying the beneficiary or purchasing a draft or demand for payment from him acquires a right to honor only if the appropriate notation is made and by transferring or forwarding for honor the documents under the credit such a person warrants to the issuer that the notation has been made; and
   (b) unless the credit or a signed statement that an appropriate notation has been made accompanies the draft or demand for payment the issuer may delay honor until evidence of notation has been procured which is satisfactory to it but its obligation and that of its customer continue for a reasonable time not exceeding thirty days to obtain such evidence.

(3) If the credit is not a notation credit
   (a) the issuer may honor complying drafts or demands for payment presented to it in the order in which they are presented and is discharged pro tanto by honor of any such draft or demand;[2]
   (b) as between competing good faith purchasers of complying drafts or demands the person first purchasing has priority over a subsequent purchaser even though the later purchased draft or demand has been first honored.

SECTION 5-109. *Issuer's Obligation to Its Customer.*—(1) An issuer's obligation to its customer includes good faith and observance of any general banking usage but unless othewise agreed does not include liability or responsibility
   (a) for performance of the underlying contract for sale or other transaction between the customer and the beneficiary; or

---

[1] Massachusetts and New Hampshire omit the phrase "and acquires the rights of an issuer" from this subsection.

[2] Wisconsin replaces the words "pro tanto" with "to the extent of the draft or demand."

(b) for any act or omission of any person other than itself or its own branch or for loss or destruction of a draft, demand or document in transit or in the possession of others; or

(c) based on knowledge or lack of knowledge of any usage of any particular trade.

(2) An issuer must examine documents with care so as to ascertain that on their face they appear to comply with the terms of the credit, but unless otherwise agreed assumes no liability or responsibility for the genuineness, falsification or effect of any document which appears on such examination to be regular on its face.

(3) A non-bank issuer is not bound by any banking usage of which it has no knowledge.

SECTION 5-110. *Availability of Credit in Portions; Presenter's Reservation of Lien or Claim.*—(1) Unless otherwise specified a credit may be used in portions in the discretion of the beneficiary.

(2) Unless otherwise specified a person by presenting a documentary draft or demand for payment under a credit relinquishes upon its honor all claims to the documents and a person by transferring such draft or demand or causing such presentment authorizes such relinquishment. An explicit reservation of claim makes the draft or demand noncomplying.

SECTION 5-111. *Warranties on Transfer and Presentment.*—(1) Unless otherwise agreed the beneficiary by transferring or presenting a documentary draft or demand for payment warrants to all interested parties that the necessary conditions of the credit have been complied with. This is in addition to any warranties arising under Articles 3, 4, 7 and 8.

(2) Unless otherwise agreed a negotiating, advising, confirming, collecting or issuing bank presenting or transferring a draft or demand for payment under a credit warrants only the matters warranted by a collecting bank under Article 4 and any such bank transferring a document warrants only the matters warranted by an intermediary under Articles 7 and 8.

SECTION 5-112. *Time Allowed for Honor or Rejection; Withholding Honor or Rejection by Consent; "Presenter."*—(1) A bank to which a documentary draft or demand for payment is presented under a credit may without dishonor of the draft, demand or credit

(a) defer honor until the close of the third banking day following receipt of the documents; and

(b) further defer honor if the presenter has expressly or impliedly consented thereto.

Failure to honor within the time here specified constitutes dishonor of the draft or demand and of the credit [except as otherwise provided in subsection (4) of Section 5-114 on conditional payment].[1]

(2) Upon dishonor the bank may unless otherwise instructed fulfill its duty to return the draft or demand and the documents by holding them at the disposal of the presenter and sending him an advice to that effect.

(3) "Presenter" means any person presenting a draft or demand for payment

---

[1] Material in brackets appears only in Alabama, Alaska, Connecticut, Georgia, Hawaii, Idaho, Iowa, Michigan, Minnesota, New Mexico, Ohio, Oklahoma, Rhode Island, Texas, Utah, Virginia, Washington, West Virginia.

for honor under a credit even though that person is a confirming bank or other correspondent which is acting under an issuer's authorization.

SECTION 5-113. *Indemnities.*—(1) A bank seeking to obtain (whether for itself or another) honor, negotiation or reimbursement under a credit may give an indemnity to induce such honor, negotiation or reimbursement.
  (2) An indemnity agreement inducing honor, negotiation or reimbursement.

   (a) unless otherwise explicitly agreed applies to defects in the documents but not in the goods; and
   (b) unless a longer time is explicitly agreed expires at the end of ten business days following receipt of the documents by the ultimate customer unless notice of objection is sent before such expiration date. The ultimate customer may send notice of objection to the person from whom he received the documents and any bank receiving such notice is under a duty to send notice to its transferor before its midnight deadline.[1]

SECTION 5-114. *Issuer's Duty and Privilege to Honor; Right to Reimbursement.*—(1) An issuer must honor a draft or demand for payment which complies with the terms of the relevant credit regardless of whether the goods or documents conform to the underlying contract for sale or other contract between the customer and the beneficiary. The issuer is not excused from honor of such a draft or demand by reason of an additional general term that all documents must be satisfactory to the issuer, but an issuer may require that specified documents must be satisfactory to it.
  (2) Unless otherwise agreed when documents appear on their face to comply with the terms of a credit but a required document does not in fact conform to the warranties made on negotiation or transfer of a document of title (Section 7-507) or of a certificated security (Section 8-306) or is forged or fraudulent or there is fraud in the transaction,

   (a) the issuer must honor the draft on demand for payment if honor is demanded by a negotiating bank or other holder of the draft or demand which has taken the draft or demand under the credit and under circumstances which would make it a holder in due course (Section 3-302) and in an appropriate case would make it a person to whom a document of title has been duly negotiated (Section 7-502) or a bona fide purchaser of a certificated security (Section 8-302); and
   (b) in all other cases as against its customer, an issuer acting in good faith may honor the draft or demand for payment despite notification from the customer of fraud, forgery or other defect not apparent on the face of the documents but a court of appropriate jurisdiction may enjoin such honor.
  (3) Unless otherwise agreed an issuer which has duly honored a draft or demand for payment is entitled to immediate reimbursement of any payment made under the credit and to be put in effectively available funds not later than the day before maturity of any acceptance made under the credit.
  [(4) When a credit provides for payment by the issuer on receipt of notice that the required documents are in the possession of a correspondent or other agent of the issuer

---

[1] This subsection is omitted entirely in California, Maine, Massachusetts and Nevada.

(a) any payment made on receipt of such notice is conditional; and
(b) the issuer may reject documents which do not comply with the credit if it does so within three banking days following its receipt of the documents; and
(c) in the event of such rejection, the issuer is entitled by charge back or otherwise to return of the payment made.]

[(5) In the case covered by subsection (4) failure to reject documents within the time specified in subparagraph (b) constitutes acceptance of the documents and makes the payment final in favor of the beneficiary.] [1]

SECTION 5-115. *Remedy for Improper Dishonor or Anticipatory Repudiation.*—(1) When an issuer wrongfully dishonors a draft or demand for payment presented under a credit the person entitled to honor has with respect to any documents the rights of a person in the position of a seller (Section 2-707) and may recover from the issuer the face amount of the draft or demand together with incidental damages under Section 2-710 on seller's incidental damages and interest but less any amount realized by resale or other use or disposition of the subject matter of the transaction. In the event no resale or other utilization is made the documents, goods or other subject matter involved in the transaction must be turned over to the issuer on payment of judgment.

(2) When an issuer wrongfully cancels or otherwise repudiates a credit before presentment of a draft or demand for payment drawn under it the beneficiary has the rights of a seller after anticipatory repudiation by the buyer under Section 2-610 if he learns of the repudiation in time reasonably to avoid procurement of the required documents. Otherwise the beneficiary has an immediate right of action for wrongful dishonor.

SECTION 5-116. *Transfer and Assignment.*—(1) The right to draw under a credit can be transferred or assigned only when the credit is expressly designated as transferable or assignable.

(2) Even though the credit specifically states that it is nontransferable or nonassignable the beneficiary may before performance of the conditions of the credit assign his right to proceeds. Such an assignment is an assignment of an account right under Article 9 on Secured Transactions and is governed by that Article except that
(a) the assignment is ineffective until the letter of credit or advice of credit is delivered to the assignee which delivery constitutes perfection of the security interest under Article 9; and
(b) the issuer may honor drafts or demands for payment drawn under the credit until it receives a notification of the assignment signed by the beneficiary which reasonably identifies the credit involved in the assignment and contains a request to pay the assignee; and
(c) after what reasonably appears to be such a notification has been received, the issuer may without dishonor refuse to accept or pay even to a person otherwise entitled to honor until the letter of credit or advice of credit is exhibited to the issuer.

---

[1] Subsections (4) and (5) are optional and have been adopted by the states listed in the footnote on page 1-66, footnote 1.

(3) Except where the beneficiary has effectively assigned his right to draw or his right to proceeds, nothing in this section limits his right to transfer or negotiate drafts or demands drawn under the credit.[1]

SECTION 5-117. *Insolvency of Bank Holding Funds for Documentary Credit.*—
(1) Where an issuer or an advising or confirming bank or a bank which has for a customer procured issuance of a credit by another bank becomes insolvent before final payment under the credit and the credit is one to which this Article is made applicable by paragraph (a) or (b) of Section 5-102 (1) on scope, the receipt or allocation of funds or collateral to secure or meet obligations under the credit shall have the following results:

(a) to the extent of any funds or collateral turned over after or before the insolvency as indemnity against or specifically for the purpose of payment of drafts or demands for payment drawn under the designated credit, the drafts or demands are entitled to payment in preference over depositors or other general creditors of the issuer or bank; and

(b) on expiration of the credit or surrender of the beneficiary's rights under it unused any person who has given such funds or collateral is similarly entitled to return thereof; and

(c) a charge to a general or current account with a bank if specifically consented to for the purpose of indemnity against or payment of drafts or demands for payment drawn under the designated credit falls under the same rules as if the funds had been drawn out in cash and then turned over with specific instructions.

(2) After honor or reimbursement under this section the customer or other person for whose account the insolvent bank has acted is entitled to receive the documents involved.

ARTICLE 6

BULK TRANSFERS

(This Article is reproduced in Chapter 26 of this volume headed "Fraudulent Conveyances—Bulk Transfers.")

ARTICLE 7

WAREHOUSE RECEIPTS, BILLS OF LADING AND OTHER DOCUMENTS OF TITLE

(This Article is a consolidation and revision of the Uniform Warehouse Receipts Act and the Uniform Bill of Ladings Act and contains some provisions of the Uniform Sales Act relating to negotiation of documents of title. A portion of this Article, but not the complete text, is set forth below.)

---

[1] Section 5-116 was amended in 1972 to conform to Revised Article 9 of the Code. The following states have adopted this section as amended: Alabama, Arizona, Arkansas, California, Colorado, Connecticut, District of Columbia, Florida, Georgia, Hawaii, Idaho, Illinois, Iowa, Kansas, Maine, Maryland, Massachusetts, Michigan, Minnesota, Mississippi, Nebraska, Nevada, New Hampshire, New Jersey, New York, North Carolina, North Dakota, Ohio, Oklahoma, Oregon, Rhode Island, South Dakota, Texas, Utah, Virginia, Washington, West Virginia, Wisconsin.

South Dakota added a subsection requiring clearing corporations to furnish certain lists of depositors on payment of a fee.

Part 1

General

SECTION 7-102. *Definitions and Index of Definitions.*—(1) In this Article, unless the context otherwise requires:

(a) "Bailee" means the person who by a warehouse receipt, bill of lading or other document of title acknowledges possession of goods and contracts to deliver them.

(b) "Consignee" means the person named in a bill to whom or to whose order the bill promises delivery.

(c) "Consignor" means the person named in a bill as the person from whom the goods have been received for shipment.

(d) "Delivery order" means a written order to deliver goods directed to a warehouseman, carrier or other person who in the ordinary course of business issues warehouse receipts or bills of lading.[1]

(e) "Document" means document of title as defined in the general definitions in Article 1 (Section 1-201).

(f) "Goods" means all things which are treated as movable for the purposes of a contract of storage or transportation.

(g) "Issuer" means a bailee who issues a document except that in relation to an unaccepted delivery order it means the person who orders the possessor of goods to deliver. Issuer includes any person for whom an agent or employee purports to act in issuing a document if the agent or employee has real or apparent authority to issue documents, notwithstanding that the issuer received no goods or that the goods were misdescribed or that in any other respect the agent or employee violated his instructions.

(h) "Warehouseman" is a person engaged in the business of storing goods for hire.[2]

(2) Other definitions applying to this Article or to specified Parts thereof, and the sections in which they appear are:

"Duly negotiate". Section 7-501.
"Person entitled under the document". Section 7-403(4).

(3) Definitions in other Articles applying to this Article and the sections in which they appear are:

"Contract for sale". Section 2-106.
"Overseas". Section 2-323.
"Receipt" of goods. Section 2-103.[3]

(4) In addition Article 1 contains general definitions and principles of construction and interpretation applicable throughout this Article.

SECTION 7-104. *Negotiable and Nonnegotiable Warehouse Receipt, Bill of Lading or Other Document of Title.*—(1) A warehouse receipt, bill of lading or other document of title is negotiable

---

[1] California omits subsec. (1)(d).

[2] Illinois adds a sentence stating that owners of self storage service facilities are not warehousemen for the purposes of this article.

[3] Louisiana omits subsec. (3).

(a) if by its terms the goods are to be delivered to bearer or to the order of a named person; or
(b) where recognized in overseas trade, if it runs to a named person or assigns.

(2) Any other document is nonnegotiable. A bill of lading in which it is stated that the goods are consigned to a named person is not made negotiable by a provision that the goods are to be delivered only against a written order signed by the same or another named person.[1]

Part 2

Warehouse Receipts: Special Provisions

SECTION 7-201. *Who May Issue a Warehouse Receipt; Storage under Government Bond.*—(1) A warehouse receipt may be issued by any warehouseman.

(2) Where goods including distilled spirits and agricultural commodities are stored under a statute requiring a bond against withdrawal or a license for the issuance of receipts in the nature of warehouse receipts, a receipt issued for the goods has like effect as a warehouse receipt even though issued by a person who is the owner of the goods and is not a warehouseman.

SECTION 7-202. *Form of Warehouse Receipt; Essential Terms; Optional Terms.*—(1) A warehouse receipt need not be in any particular form.[2]

(2) Unless a warehouse receipt embodies within its written or printed terms each of the following, the warehouseman is liable for damages caused by the omission to a person injured thereby:
(a) the location of the warehouse where the goods are stored;
(b) the date of issue of the receipt;
(c) the consecutive number of the receipt;
(d) a statement whether the goods received will be delivered to the bearer, to a specified person, or to a specified person or his order;
(e) the rate of storage and handling charges, except that where goods are stored under a field warehousing arrangement a statement of that fact is sufficient on a nonnegotiable receipt;[3]
(f) a description of the goods or of the packages containing them;
(g) the signature of the warehouseman, which may be made by his authorized agent;
(h) if the receipt is issued for goods of which the warehouseman is owner, either solely or jointly or in common with others, the fact of such ownership; and
(i) a statement of the amount of advances made and of liabilities incurred for which the warehouseman claims a lien or security interest (Section

---

[1] California adds a subsection that requires nonnegotiable warehouse receipts and bills of lading to be conspicuously marked "nonnegotiable."

Louisiana adds a subsection that provides that a provision in a negotiable warehouse receipt or bill of lading that it is nonnegotiable is void.

[2] In Idaho all negotiable receipts are required to be issued on forms prepared by the Idaho Department of Agriculture.

[3] California amends subsec. (e) to add: "and except that where goods are stored in a public utility warehouse having a lawful tariff on file with the Public Utilities Commission, a statement that the rate of storage and handling charges are as provided in such tariff is sufficient."

7-209). If the precise amount of such advances made or of such liabilities incurred is, at the time of the issue of the receipt, unknown to the warehouseman or to his agent who issues it, a statement of the fact that advances have been made or liabilities incurred and the purpose thereof is sufficient.

(3) A warehouseman may insert in his receipt any other terms which are not contrary to the provisions of this Act and do not impair his obligation of delivery (Section 7-403) or his duty of care (Section 7-204). Any contrary provisions shall be ineffective.

SECTION 7-203. *Liability for Non-Receipt or Misdescription.*—A party to or purchaser for value in good faith of a document of title other than a bill of lading relying in either case upon the description therein of the goods may recover from the issuer damages caused by the non-receipt or misdescription of the goods, except to the extent that the document conspicuously indicates that the issuer does not know whether any part or all of the goods in fact were received or conform to the description, as where the description is in terms of marks or labels or kind, quantity or condition, or the receipt or description is qualified by "contents, condition and quality unknown", "said to contain" or the like, if such indication be true, or the party or purchaser otherwise has notice.

SECTION 7-204. *Duty of Care; Contractual Limitation of Warehouseman's Liability.*—(This section sets forth the liability for loss or injury to property which is in the possession of a warehouseman. There are many variations on this section so the state code should be checked.)

SECTION 7-205. *Title Under Warehouse Receipt Defeated in Certain Cases.*— A buyer in the ordinary course of business of fungible goods sold and delivered by a warehouseman who is also in the business of buying and selling such goods takes free of any claim under a warehouse receipt even though it has been duly negotiated.[1]

SECTION 7-209. *Lien of Warehouseman.*—(1) A warehouseman has a lien against the bailor on the goods covered by a warehouse receipt or on the proceeds thereof in his possession for charges for storage or transportation (including demurrage and terminal charges), insurance, labor, or charges present or future in relation to the goods, and for expenses necessary for preservation of the goods or reasonably incurred in their sale pursuant to law. If the person on whose account the goods are held is liable for like charges or expenses in relation to other goods whenever deposited and it is stated in the receipt that a lien is claimed for charges and expenses in relation to other goods, the warehouseman also has a lien against him for such charges and expenses whether or not the other goods have been delivered by the warehouseman. But against a person to whom a negotiable warehouse receipt is duly negotiated a warehouseman's lien is limited to charges in an amount or at a rate specified on the receipt or if no charges are so specified then to a reasonable charge for storage of the goods covered by the receipt subsequent to the date of the receipt.

---

[1] Arkansas provides that this section does not apply to rice, soybeans, wheat, corn, rye, oats, barley, flaxseed, sorghum, mixed grain or other food grains or oilseeds.

(2) The warehouseman may also reserve a security interest against the bailor for a maximum amount specified on the receipt for charges other than those specified in subsection (1), such as for money advanced and interest. Such a security interest is governed by the Article on Secured Transactions (Article 9).

(3) (a) A warehouseman's lien for charges and expenses under subsection (1) or a security interest under subsection (2) is also effective against any person who so entrusted the bailor with possession of the goods that a pledge of them by him to a good faith purchaser for value would have been valid but is not effective against a person as to whom the document confers no right in the goods covered by it under Section 7-503.

(b) A warehouseman's lien on household goods for charges and expenses in relation to the goods under subsection (1) is also effective against all persons if the depositor was the legal possessor of the goods at the time of deposit. "Household goods" means furniture, furnishings and personal effects used by the depositor in a dwelling.[1]

(4) A warehouseman loses his lien on any goods which he voluntarily delivers or which he unjustifiably refuses to deliver.

Part 3

Bills of Lading: Special Provisions

(The sections of this part of Article 7, with the exception of Section 7-307, are not reproduced.)

SECTION 7-307. *Lien of Carrier.*—(1) A carrier has a lien on the goods covered by a bill of lading for charges subsequent to the date of its receipt of the goods for storage or transportation (including demurrage and terminal charges) and for expenses necessary for preservation of the goods incident to their transportation or reasonably incurred in their sale pursuant to law. But against a purchaser for value of a negotiable bill of lading a carrier's lien is limited to charges stated in the bill or the applicable tariffs, or if no charges are stated then to reasonable charge.

(2) A lien for charges and expenses under subsection (1) on goods which the carrier was required by law to receive for transportation is effective against the consignor or any person entitled to the goods unless the carrier had notice that the consignor lacked authority to subject the goods to such charges and expenses. Any other lien under subsection (1) is effective against the consignor, and any person who permitted the bailor to have control or possession of the goods unless the carrier had notice that the bailor lacked such authority.

(3) A carrier loses his lien on any goods which he voluntarily delivers or which he unjustifiably refuses to deliver.

---

[1] The 1966 amended version of Section 7-209, as shown above, designated the then existing subsection (3) as (3) (a) and added paragraph (b). The following states have adopted the 1966 Official Text Amendments: Arkansas, California, District of Columbia, Georgia, Idaho, Kansas, Illinois, Iowa, Maryland, Minnesota, New Mexico, North Carolina, North Dakota, Oklahoma, Virginia, and Wyoming. The other states have adopted the former version which excludes subparagraph (b). California, Idaho, North Carolina, and Virginia have adopted the amendment with certain variations. Texas has adopted the former version with amendments.

Part 4

**Warehouse Receipts and Bills of Lading:
General Obligations**

(Sections 7-401 through 7-404, which are not reproduced, cover irregularities in issue of documents of title, obligations of warehouseman or carrier to deliver and nonliability for good faith delivery pursuant to document of title.)

Part 5

**Warehouse Receipts and Bills of Lading:
Negotiation and Transfer**

(Sections 7-501 and 7-502, which are not reproduced, cover form of negotiation of documents of title and the requirements of and rights acquired by "due negotiation." It accords to the payee who meets the necessary requirements, the rights of a holder in due course of a negotiable instrument.)

SECTION 7-503. *Document of Title to Goods Defeated in Certain Cases.*—(1) A document of title confers no right in goods against a person who before issuance of the document had a legal interest or a perfected security interest in them and who neither
  (a) delivered nor entrusted them or any document of title covering them to the bailor or his nominee with actual or apparent authority to ship, store or sell or with power to obtain delivery under this Article (Section 7-403) or with power of disposition under this Act (Sections 2-403 and 9-307) or other statute or rule of law; nor
  (b) acquiesced in the procurement by the bailor or his nominee of any document of title.

(2) Title to goods based upon an unaccepted delivery order is subject to the rights of anyone to whom a negotiable warehouse receipt or bill of lading covering the goods has been duly negotiated. Such a title may be defeated under the next section to the same extent as the rights of the issuer or a transferee from the issuer.[1]

(3) Title to goods based upon a bill of lading issued to a freight forwarder is subject to the rights of anyone to whom a bill issued by the freight forwarder is duly negotiated; but delivery by the carrier in accordance with Part 4 of this Article pursuant to its own bill of lading discharges the carrier's obligation to deliver.

SECTION 7-504. *Rights Acquired in the Absence of Due Negotiation; Effect of Diversion; Seller's Stoppage of Delivery.*—(1) A transferee of a document, whether negotiable or nonnegotiable, to whom the document has been delivered but not duly negotiated, acquires the title and rights which his transferor had or had actual authority to convey.

(2) In the case of a nonnegotiable document, until but not after the bailee receives notification of the transfer, the rights of the transferee may be defeated

---

[1] California omits subsec. (2).

(a) by those creditors of the transferor who could treat the sale as void under Section 2-402; or
(b) by a buyer from the transferor in ordinary course of business if the bailee has delivered the goods to the buyer or received notification of his rights; or
(c) as against the bailee by good faith dealings of the bailee with the transferor.[1]

(3) A diversion or other change of shipping instructions by the consignor in a nonnegotiable bill of lading which causes the bailee not to deliver to the consignee defeats the consignee's title to the goods if they have been delivered to a buyer in ordinary course of business and in any event defeats the consignee's rights against the bailee.[2]

(4) Delivery pursuant to a nonnegotiable document may be stopped by a seller under Section 2-705, and subject to the requirement of due notification there provided. A bailee honoring the seller's instructions is entitled to be indemnified by the seller against any resulting loss or expense.[3]

SECTION 7-505. *Indorser Not a Guarantor for Other Parties.*—The indorsement of a document of title issued by a bailee does not make the indorser liable for any default by the bailee or by previous indorsers.

SECTION 7-506. *Delivery Without Indorsement: Right to Compel Indorsement.*—The transferee of a negotiable document of title has a specifically enforceable right to have his transferor supply any necessary indorsement but the transfer becomes a negotiation only as of the time the indorsement is supplied.

SECTION 7-507. *Warranties on Negotiation or Transfer of Receipt or Bill.*—Where a person negotiates or transfers a document of title for value otherwise than as a mere intermediary under the next following section, then unless otherwise agreed he warrants to his immediate purchaser only in addition to any warranty made in selling the goods
   (a) that the document is genuine; and
   (b) that he has no knowledge of any fact which would impair its validity or worth; and
   (c) that this negotiation or transfer is rightful and fully effective with respect to the title to the document and the goods it represents.

Part 6

Warehouse Receipts and Bills of Lading: Miscellaneous Provisions

(Sections 7-601 through 7-603, which are not reproduced, cover lost and missing documents, attachment of goods and conflicting claims to goods.)

---

[1] Louisiana omits subsec. (2).
[2] Louisiana omits subsec. (3).
[3] Louisiana omits subsec. (4).

ARTICLE 8
INVESTMENT SECURITIES

(This Article, which is not reproduced, deals with bearer bonds, registered bonds and certificates of stock. Portions of this Article were formerly covered by provisions of the Uniform Negotiable Instruments Law and Uniform Stock Transfer Act.)

ARTICLE 9
SECURED TRANSACTIONS

(This Article is discussed in detail in Chapter 7, "Secured Transactions under Article 9 of the Uniform Commercial Code.")

ARTICLE 10
EFFECTIVE DATE AND REPEALER

(This Article, which of necessity varies in the several states which have enacted the Code, provides the date as of which it became effective and the repeal of various Uniform Laws and other statutes which it supersedes.)

ARTICLE 11
EFFECTIVE DATE AND TRANSITION PROVISIONS

(This Article includes provisions which cover the transition from the original version of the Code and the changes made by the 1972 edition.)

The Law of Contracts—
Legal Requirements

Although the term "contract" has been the subject of numerous and varied definitions, one that has found particular favor and has been frequently cited by the courts is that of Professor Williston. He states that "[a] contract is a promise, or set of promises, for breach of which the law gives a remedy, or the performance of which the law in some way recognizes as a duty."[1] A "promise" may be the expression of an intention to do something, or to refrain from doing something, communicated in a way so that a promisee may reasonably rely on performance.[2] Where the promise creates a legal duty, the promise constitutes a contract.

However, the full understanding of the nature of the legal concept of a contract and its implications cannot be derived from a definition. It is necessary to consider the basic requirements which the law imposes in order to constitute the enforceable promise referred to in the definition. The four basic requirements, each of which will be fully discussed, are as follows:
1. Offer and acceptance.
2. Competency of parties to contract.
3. Legality of subject matter.
4. Sufficient consideration.

OFFER AND ACCEPTANCE

In order to form a contract there must be assent to its terms by both parties. This manifestation of mutual assent must be objective; thus, intent to contract is not required, though it is usually present. One may be bound, irrespective of his subjective intent, by such actions as would reasonably justify the other party to understand that he assents to a certain contract or to specific terms. It is not necessary that the acting party realize a promise is being made or intend that a legal obligation shall be created. The law, not the parties, determines whether there is a contract.

In sharp contrast, however, the law carefully respects the parties' manifested mutual intent that their agreement, though otherwise fulfilling all the requisites, shall not become an enforceable contract. In these so-called "gentlemen's agreements" the parties prefer to rely on business, social or moral sanctions rather than legal ones; the law permits this, provided no illegality is involved.

Normally, manifested mutual assent is generally evidenced by an offer made by one party and its acceptance by the other. The party making the offer is known as the offeror; the party to whom it is made, the offeree. An offer is

---
[1] S. WILLISTON, A TREATISE ON THE LAW OF CONTRACTS § 1(3rd ed. 1957).
[2] A. Corbin, Corbin on Contract § 13 (1952).

"an expression by the offeror of his agreement that something over which he at least assumes to have control shall be done or happen or shall not be done or happen if the conditions stated in the offer are complied with." [1] An offer thus confers upon the offeree a conditional power of acceptance of the terms laid down by the offeror. The power must be exercised exactly as the offeror prescribes; if not, the purported acceptance is instead a rejection and, ordinarily, a counteroffer.

An offer comes into existence only when communicated to the offeree. The offeree should know that an offer has been made to him and it can be accepted only by him or his agent; he cannot assign it to another.

Communication of Offer

The offer may be made orally, in writing or by some act which may be interpreted as an offer. The offer may be made to one person or it may be made to a class of persons. Questions sometimes arise in connection with so-called public offers in the form of advertisements. It is generally held that when the person advertises merchandise for sale in a newspaper, such an advertisement is not an offer which will ripen into a contract by the acceptance of any person to whose attention the advertisement may come, but is merely an invitation to contract.

The same is true of trade circulars. In the case of *Montgomery Ward & Co. v. Johnson,* 209 Mass. 89, 95 N.E.290 (1911), the defendant sent out to the trade a circular stating the terms and conditions upon which its product would be supplied to the jobbing trade and that thereafter "no order would be filled except upon the terms set forth" in the circular. Of this circular and an accompanying letter the Court said, "[A] fair interpretation of the letter, and document, very plainly shows that it was not a general offer to sell to those addressed, but an announcement, or invitation, that the defendant would receive proposals for sales on the terms and conditions stated, which [the defendant] might accept or reject at her option."

Quotation of prices to the trade, or quotation of prices and furnishing other information in response to specific inquiries, generally is not considered as the making of an offer of sale. A response to an inquiry, however, may be couched in such terms that an offer of sale will be construed from it. Similarly, invitations to submit bids do not constitute offers. The bid submitted in response to such an invitation does constitute an offer on the part of the bidder but it creates no right until accepted. It has even been held that the fact that a contract is to be awarded to the lowest responsible bidder does not give such lowest bidder any contractual rights until his bid is actually accepted since there is no obligation to accept the offer.[2]

Duration of Offer

An offer that has been properly communicated continues until it is revoked, rejected or accepted within a specified period, or lapses after an unreasonable period of time. If the offeror stipulates the period of time during which it must

---

[1] S. Williston, *supra* note 1, at § 24A.
[2] See *Farrell v. Board of Education of West Orange,* 10 N.J. Misc. 88, 157 A. 656 (1932).

be accepted, the offer will lapse at the end of such period and an attempt to accept the offer after that date is considered as a new offer. If the offer contains no time limit for acceptance, the law presumes that it has been revoked after the expiration of a "reasonable" time. What is a reasonable time depends upon such facts as might indicate the intention of the parties; of particular weight in determining this intention is the nature of the transaction and the type of property involved. For example, an offer to sell merchandise whose value fluctuates rapidly would have to be accepted in a shorter period of time than would an offer for the sale of goods which maintain a relatively constant value.

Termination of Offer

At any time prior to the acceptance of the offer it may be withdrawn by the offeror.[1] Like the original offer, however, the revocation is only binding upon the offeree when it has been communicated prior to the acceptance by the offeree. It is sufficient, however, if the notice of revocation comes to the offeree even though not directly from the offeror. Thus, for example, an offer to sell specific merchandise is revoked when the offeree learns that the merchandise has been sold to a third party.

Where an offer has been made to the general public it may be revoked by the same medium by which it was made and in this case it is immaterial whether the offeree has actual knowledge of the revocation or not, for the law will presume that such revocation has come to his attention in the same manner as the offer did.[2]

The death of either the offeror or the offeree will cause an offer to lapse, regardless of whether the other party has notice of such occurrence. Where it is known to the other that one of the parties has become insane before the offer is accepted, it is generally recognized that the offer is terminated. However, where the insanity is not known, the question of whether the offer terminates will depend on whether the insane person has complete incapacity to contract. The destruction of the subject matter of the contract will also terminate the offer.

The only case in which an offer cannot be withdrawn by an offeror at his will is where the offeror and offeree have entered into an option contract. This is simply an agreement that the offeror will keep the offer open for a designated period of time. An agreement to keep an offer open for a definite period of time will not be binding on the offeror, however, unless there is some consideration for the agreement. Statutory changes with respect to consideration for option contracts are discussed below under *"Consideration."*

Acceptance of Offer

Upon the acceptance of the offer (if the other requisites are present) a contract is created, but the acceptance must be unequivocal and show a clear intention to accept, in every particular, the offer as presented.

---

[1] Under the Uniform Commercial Code a firm offer by a merchant to buy or sell goods is not revocable for lack of consideration if made in a signed writing. See UCC § 2-205.

[2] See *Shuey v. United States,* 92 U.S. 73 (1876).

An acknowledgment of the receipt of an offer is not equivalent to an acceptance. For example, it is customary with many firms to acknowledge receipt of orders, prior to passing upon the customer's credit, by dispatching a postcard or letter stating that the order has been received and will be given attention. There is no intent thereby, to accept the order, but the wording of the acknowledgment may frequently lead to serious difficulties.

The courts are not in accord as to the effect of the use of such terms as "your order will have our prompt attention." In *Manier v. Appling,* 112 Ala. 663, 20 S. 978 (1896), the plaintiff received from the defendants a post card acknowledging the receipt of the plaintiff's order, stating, "The same shall have prompt attention." The defendants subsequently refused to accept the order and the court held that the sending of the post card was not an acceptance of the order but, instead, a mere acknowledgment of its receipt and a promise to give the plaintiff's offer prompt attention.

The parties by their actions may evidence an intent to accept the order and such acts will be considered by the court in determining whether or not the parties are bound. In *Jordan v. Patterson,* 67 Conn. 473, 35A. 521 (1896), fourteen separate orders were sent. The seller acknowledged them, expressed thanks, and subsequently delivered a portion of the goods, but declined to deliver the remainder. The court held that the order was accepted, basing this finding not so much on the language of the parties as on their conduct.

Unilateral and Bilateral Offers

Offers are often classified as unilateral or bilateral. A unilateral offer is one which is accepted by the performance of the act called for by the offer. A bilateral offer is one which is accepted by the promise of the offeree to perform the act called for by the offer. The distinction between these two forms of offer is illustrated by common practices in making sales. A purchaser who writes to a seller requesting immediate shipment of designated merchandise makes a unilateral offer which is accepted by the seller's delivering the merchandise to the purchaser or placing the merchandise with a common carrier for shipment. Until this act is performed the offer is subject to revocation by the purchaser. The request from the purchaser to the seller for an agreement to sell designated merchandise, such as a purchase order solicited by the seller's salesperson which is subject to acceptance at the seller's home office, is a bilateral offer.

Orders Solicited By Salespersons

The question of acceptance or rejection of orders solicited by a salesperson without authority to bind his principal contractually is worthy of special consideration because of the large amount of business transacted by this method. It is important that the order form used by the seller clearly indicate that it is not binding upon the seller until acceptance by the seller's home office or by some designated representative. If this practice is not followed, a course of dealing between the seller and the purchaser may give rise to the implication of apparent authority on the part of the salesperson to accept orders binding upon the principal, even though the intention of the seller is that the purchase order is subject to acceptance at the seller's home office. In effect, the order constitutes an offer to purchase which is subject to the general rules relating to acceptance and rejection of offers. It is generally held that there is no obligation on the part of the seller until he has accepted the order.

A contrary view was expressed in the case of *Cole-McIntyre-Norfleet Co. v. Holloway*, 141 Tenn. 679, 214 S.W. 817 (1919). The court held that where the plaintiff's salesman solicited from the defendant an order for the purchase of goods which was subject to acceptance at the seller's office in Memphis, the failure of the seller to either accept or reject the order within a reasonable period of time was an acceptance of the order. While this case appears to be contrary to the weight of authority, the court's ruling was justified by the fact that the order specifically provided that it was not subject to countermand by the purchaser. Additionally, the course of dealing between the parties was such as to justify the assumption by the purchaser that his order was accepted in the absence of notice to the contrary. Note, however, that an order solicited by a salesperson does not constitute a contract until accepted by the seller; thus, in the absence of an agreement to the contrary, the purchaser may withdraw his order prior to the seller's acceptance.

While it is not essential that the seller confirm his acceptance of the order in writing (it has been held in numerous cases that the shipment of the goods or other acts indicating acceptance are sufficient), it is advisable that the seller do so to avoid the possibility of cancellation of the order or disputes which may arise in the absence of a clear indication of intent to accept.

Rejection of Offer

Upon the rejection of the offer by the offeree the offer will lapse. It cannot thereafter be revived if the offeree decides to accept the offer. Such an attempt will merely result in a new offer to the offeror who is free to accept or reject it as he will. A similar rejection will result when the offeree attempts to accept the offer by injecting into his acceptance terms which did not appear in the original offer. This is known as a counteroffer and the original offeror is free to accept or reject it. A counteroffer should be distinguished, however, from a request for further information. For example, an offer to sell a designated quantity of goods at a stipulated price is not rejected by a request for a quotation of a price on a different quantity.

Counteroffer

Uniform Commercial Code Section 2-207 determines, in those transactions governed by the Code, whether the response of the offeree is to be considered an acceptance or a counteroffer. This section was included in the Code to resolve the "battle of the forms" transactions where a buyer, using his own order blank, orders goods and stipulates in the order the terms and conditions thereof, and the seller acknowledges the order on a form setting out the seller's terms and conditions which differ from the buyer's proposals.

Under Section 2-207, an acceptance containing terms different from or in addition to terms of the offer operates as an acceptance of the original offer, unless the acceptance is expressly made conditional upon the offeror's assent to the variations. The terms are considered proposals for addition to the contract rather than proposals to alter it, and the offeror may accept or reject the terms without affecting the fundamental contractual obligations.

When both parties are merchants, the offeror is presumed, as a matter of law, to have adopted the offeree's counterproposals unless:

(a) He objects to them within a reasonable time;
(b) The offeror has expressly limited acceptance to the terms of the offer; or
(c) The counterproposals would materially alter the contract.

This last proviso is broadly drafted and litigation thereunder is frequent as to what is considered a material alteration of the contract.

Communication of Acceptance

The acceptance must be communicated to the offeror, prior to the withdrawal of the offer, by some act which is intended to communicate the acceptance. The Code permits "acceptance in any manner and by any medium reasonable in the circumstances." U.C.C. § 2-206(1)(a).

ACCEPTANCE BY MAIL

If the offer is made by means of the mail, it is not complete until the letter has actually been delivered. From the time of such delivery until the offer is accepted, the offeror is privileged to withdraw the same without liability. If the offeree wishes to accept the order and does so through the same medium (i.e., mail), in the absence of any request from the offeror for acceptance by other means of communication, the offer is deemed to be accepted as soon as the acceptance, properly stamped and addressed, is deposited in the post office or a post box. This is based upon the theory that by the use of the mails the offeror designated the postal authority as agent to receive an acceptance. If the offeree makes use of another medium to communicate his acceptance, the acceptance is not complete until its actual receipt by the offeror.

The offeror may withdraw his offer at any time by communicating the withdrawal to the other party before the offer has been accepted. If the acceptance is placed in the mail before the actual receipt of the withdrawal of the offer, the acceptance is complete, regardless of the fact that the acceptance was actually mailed subsequent to the mailing of the rejection.

It is important that parties negotiating a contract keep an accurate record of outgoing and incoming mail inasmuch as the law presumes the receipt of a letter which is properly stamped, addressed, and mailed. This record should include the exact time of mailing, name and address on the envelope, payment of postage, and the fact that the letter was deposited in the post office.

ACCEPTANCE BY TELEGRAPH

Where the offer is made by telegraph and the offeror does not specify some other medium for acceptance, the offer is deemed accepted as soon as the acceptance is placed in the hands of the telegraph company which transmitted the offer. As in the case of the use of the mails, it is assumed that the offeror has designated the telegraph company as his agent to receive the acceptance. However, where the offer has been communicated by mail, telephone, or in person, an acceptance by telegraph is not complete until it has actually been received by the offeror.

There is an irreconcilable conflict in the decisions of the courts of the various states concerning the liability of parties in the event of a mistake in the transmission of an offer or acceptance by telegraph. In some states parties making an offer by telegraph are held to be bound by the terms contained in the telegraphic message as delivered to the offeree. Other states hold that the acceptance of an erroneous offer, due to a mistake in transmission, does not bind the parties or create a contract.

SILENCE AS ACCEPTANCE

The failure of an offeree to advise the offeror whether he will accept or reject the offer will not be construed as an acceptance; silence will not be deemed an acceptance even though the offeror advises the offeree that if the offeree does not notify him to the contrary, he will consider the offer accepted. An exception to this rule is found where prior course of dealings between the parties requires the offeree to indicate his desire to reject the offer [1] or where the offeree takes the benefit of offered services with reasonable opportunity to reject them and reason to know that they were offered with the expectation of compensation. For example, in *Laredo National Bank v. Gordon*, 61 F.2d 906 (5th Cir. 1932), the court found that where the bank's attorney made an offer to the bank, the bank's silence amounted to an acceptance since "[i]t's silence amounted to conduct which misled its attorney to his detriment. . . ." Id. at 907.

It is common practice for many firms to send goods to prospective customers on approval with the request to return them within a designated period of time if the customer does not wish to purchase. While it is generally accepted that a party cannot thus force another into an agreement by a failure to respond in accordance with the offer made, where the other party uses or otherwise exercises dominion over the goods, his actions, coupled with his silence, may be interpreted as an acceptance.

COMPETENCY OF THE PARTIES

With the exception of the persons herewith enumerated below everyone is presumed to have the capacity to enter into contracts. The persons who have no capacity or a limited capacity to contract at common law or by statute, are (1) infants, (2) married women, (3) insane persons, (4) drunkards, (5) corporations, and (6) agents, fiduciaries and other legal representatives; each is discussed below.

Infants

Under the common law a person is an infant until the age of 21. In most states this has been changed so that a person becomes of age on his 18th birthday.

(Text continues on p. 2-10)

---

[1] See *Phelan v. Everlith*, 22 Conn. Supp. 377, 173 A.2d 601 (1961), where the Court found that "[a] single transaction [between the parties] does not establish a course of conduct or course of dealing," and, therefore, silence could not be considered acceptance of an insurance policy by the insured.

STATE SUMMARY OF MINOR'S CAPACITY TO CONTRACT

Set forth below is a table showing the age at which an infant attains majority in the various states. This summary also indicates those states in which an infant's disability to contract may be removed by appropriate court proceedings, and those states which have enacted special legislation to permit a minor veteran to contract to obtain rights and benefits under the Servicemen's Readjustment Act of 1944 and similar legislation. The table does not contain a reference to special statutory provisions which permit infants to borrow money for education or insurance, to contract for medical treatment, to donate blood or to contract for necessaries.

COMPETENCY OF INFANTS

STATE	AGE[1]	REMARKS	STATE	AGE	REMARKS
Ala.	19	(a) (d) Married persons emancipated; widow, widower at 18.	Idaho	18	(a) Married person is emancipated, mortgage, deed and convey.
Alaska	18	(a) Emancipation by marriage.	Ill.	18	(a) (b)
			Ind.	18	(a) (d, 16 or over)
Ariz.	18	(a)	Iowa	18	(a) Married person is emancipated.
Ark.	18	(a) (c)			
Calif.	18	(a) (d, minor under 16 must have written consent of parents.) Minors are emancipated when they are married, on active duty with armed forces.	Kan.	18	(b) Minor can be bound on insurance contracts; married persons of 16 are emancipated for contracts, property rights, liability, and capacity to sue.
Col.	18	(a) (d, 16 and over) Married women are emancipated.	Ky.	18	(a)
			La.	18	(a) (b) (d) Minor at 15 by declaration of parents.
Conn.	18	(a) (b) (d) or living apart from parent or guardian with their consent and managing own financial affairs.	Maine	18	(a) (d)
			Md.	18	(a) (d) Minors may join spouse of majority age to convey tenancy by entirety.
Del.	18				
D.C.	18	(a)			
Fla.	18	(a) Married persons are emancipated.	Mass.	18	(d, vehicle liability insurance at 16).
Ga.	18	Infant doing business by permission is bound. Married woman is emancipated.	Mich.	18	(a) (b) (d, 16 and over) Minor emancipated by marriage, active duty in military or parental conduct indicating release.
Hawaii	18	(a) (d) Married person is emancipated except for right to vote and criminal penalties.			
			Minn.	18	(a)

[1] In all of the states, the age requirement is the same for both males and females.

THE LAW OF CONTRACTS—LEGAL REQUIREMENTS 2-9

STATE	AGE	REMARKS	STATE	AGE	REMARKS
Miss.	21	(a) (b) (d, court permission in limited circumstances). All persons over 18 may contract regarding personal property. Married persons at 18 may contract, mortgage, deed, and convey residence.	N.Y.	18	(a) (d) Married persons may contract, deed, mortgage, and convey residence.
			N.C.	18	(a) (d) Married persons are emancipated.
			N.D.	18	(a) Parent may relinquish to minor right to control and receive earnings.
Mo.	18	(a) Married minor may join with adult spouse in conveying real estate.	Ohio	18	(a) (d)
			Okla.	18	(a) (b)
			Ore.	18	(a) Married person is emancipated.
Mont.	18	Abused, neglected or dependent minor if 16 or older for contracts and debts.	Penna.	18	(a)
			R.I.	18	(a)
			S.C.	18	(a) (b)
			S.D.	18	(a)
Neb.	19	(a) (d, 10 and over) Married persons are emancipated.	Tenn.	18	(a) (b)
			Texas	18	(b) (d, over 14 with parental consent).
Nevada	18	(a) (d, 16 or over or under 16 with parental consent).	Utah	18	(a) (d) Married person is emancipated.
			Vt.	18	(a)
N.H.	18	(a)	Va.	18	(a) (d, Parent must consent if minor resides with parent.)
N.J.	18	(a) (d)			
N.M.	18	(a) (b) Minor emancipated at 16 by marriage, military, or if living separate from parents, may contract, buy, and sell property.	Wash.	18	(d) Infants married to a person of majority age are emancipated.
			W.Va.	18	(a) (d)
			Wis.	18	(a)
			Wyo.	19	(a) (d)

(a) Servicemen's Readjustment Act in effect. Subject to local variations.
(b) Court may remove disability.
(c) Courts are granted special power to remove disability of male at age 18 and female at age 16 to permit transfer of a business and to permit minor to sell real estate.
(d) Infant, 15 or over, may contract for certain kinds of insurance. Generally, no right of rescission is permitted.

(Continued from p. 2-7)

Many states provide for the removal of an infant's disability to contract before the infant reaches the age stated for attaining majority. Some of these statutes provide that "married persons" (others "married females") attain majority on their marriage while others require that a person be over age eighteen before the fact of marriage will remove the disability to contract. The extent to which the disability is removed by this type of provision varies from state to state.

In several states an infant may obtain limited or complete majority rights by appropriate court proceedings. In such cases the minor cannot disaffirm contracts executed after obtaining such rights.

An infant has a limited capacity to contract. Generally his contracts are not void but, while the infant may enforce the contract against an adult, the adult may not enforce it against the infant if the latter elects not to perform the contract.

The common law provides that an infant may disaffirm his contract and recover his property, even from a subsequent bona fide purchaser for value. However, under Section 2-403 of the Uniform Commercial Code, a good faith purchaser for value can acquire good title from one who has a voidable title. An infant may still assert his infancy under a claim on a negotiable instrument in the hands of a holder in due course. U.C.C. § 3-305.

Under the common law, an infant upon reaching his majority, may ratify or disaffirm a contract made during his infancy. A failure to disaffirm the contract within a reasonable time after attaining a majority is deemed to be a ratification of the contract, and thereafter the contract is not subject to rescission on the grounds of disability of infancy.

It is the law of some states that if goods are sold to an infant, the infant may disaffirm the contract and refuse to pay the price, at any time before reaching the age of majority, or within a reasonable time thereafter. If the specific property sold to the infant remains in his possession at the time of disaffirmance, he is uniformly required to return it to the seller, but if he has squandered or otherwise disposed of the property, his inability to return the same to the seller and to put the seller *in status quo* in no way affects the infant's right to disaffirm the contract. Where it is impossible for the infant to restore the goods which he has purchased, it is held by some courts that he is liable for the benefit derived from whatever cannot be restored to the seller, but this rule is not followed in the majority of cases.

The one exception to the infant's right to disaffirm a contract is where the contract is one for necessaries, provided the infant's needs are not supplied by a parent or guardian. Even in this case, however, the infant is not responsible for the contract price but only for the reasonable value of the necessaries furnished. In general it may be stated that necessaries consist of food, clothing, shelter and education, but only such as are customary to a person in the infant's station.

Where the infant has induced the sale of goods to him, by falsely representing that he had attained the age of majority, he may, nevertheless, disaffirm the contract. Some states, in contrast to the common law, do not allow such infants to disaffirm. Furthermore the general rule is that an infant is not liable for his torts connected with and growing out of his contracts, although he may be liable if the tort is independent of or subsequent to the contract, i.e., not a mere breach of the contract, but a distinct, willful and positive wrong in itself. There is a conflict of authority regarding this rule about whether a false representation as to age in inducing a contract is a part of the contract and, therefore, cannot be the basis of an action in tort or whether such a false representation is not a part of or connected with the contract and, therefore, is the basis of a tort action.

The perpetration of fraud by infants, especially those close to the age of maturity, taking advantage of the broad protection given them under the common law rules discussed above, has resulted in statutory modifications of the law in some states.

Married Women

Under the common law married women were not permitted to make binding contracts and were given few rights in holding, possessing or enjoying their own property. At common law the property of a woman on marrying passed to her husband who had the right of disposition and control thereof.

Years ago, however, it was a distinct rarity to find a married woman carrying on business. This condition has changed considerably and states have found it necessary to enact laws giving broader rights to married women to hold their property.

Indeed the common law disability has been almost completely removed by statute and, in general, a married woman may now contract as freely as a single woman, though in some states a married woman cannot contract with her husband, enter into partnership with him, or act as his surety.

Insane Persons

Generally, contracts entered into by a person who has not been adjudicated insane, are valid where the contract was executed in good faith, for a fair consideration without notice of an infirmity, and where the parties cannot be restored to their original positions. It is the law in most jurisdictions that a contract made by an insane person may be voided if the insane person can restore to the other party to the contract the consideration with which he parted. The contract of a drunkard is treated the same as that of an insane person, provided he is in such a state of intoxication as not to understand the nature of his act in making the contract.

Corporations

The ability of a corporation to contract is limited by the terms of its charter and by various statutory enactments. These limitations are considered in Chapter 14, *supra,* on Corporations.

Agents, Fiduciaries and Other Legal Representatives

The powers of an agent are considered in Chapter 16, *infra,* on Principal and Agent. The capacity of administrators, executors, trustees, committees and other legal representatives to contract is strictly limited by the instruments or statutes from which their authority is derived and these must be thoroughly examined before entering into any agreement.

LEGALITY OF SUBJECT MATTER

A contract is illegal if either in its formation or its performance it is criminal, tortious or otherwise opposed to public policy. Since a contract creates rights for the breach of which courts of law give remedies, it is evident that any contract which has for its purpose illegal matters will not be enforced by any court and, therefore, fails as a valid contract. Contracts included within this class are usurious contracts, which in many states are absolutely void, gambling and wagering contracts, and agreements which are injurious to the peace, health, good order and morals of the people. Of recent years federal and state legislation to prevent restraint of trade, price fixing, and unfair trade practices have made many previously valid obligations illegal.

CONSIDERATION

The term "consideration" is frequently misunderstood by laypersons. It does not mean that the exchange of money is necessary to the formation of a valid contract. Consideration has a more varied meaning. Generally, it is doing something or promising to do something that one is not legally obliged to do in return for the promise of another. In effect it is the surrender of a legal right by a party for something he is to receive under a contract. Every contract in order to be enforceable (with certain exceptions, the principal one of which is a negotiable instrument in the hands of a holder in due course), must have a sufficient consideration; that is, there must be enough consideration, under the law, to enforce the promise.

In this regard it is important to note that a promise based upon a past consideration or a moral obligation is unenforceable. This principle is evident in promises to pay for services or things rendered gratuitously in the past. While the moral obligation to pay may be strong, a subsequent promise is of no validity; to give effect to such a promise, one must have been under a legal obligation to pay in order to enforce his promise to do so. There are certain important exceptions to this rule. In many states promises to pay, often if in writing, after a discharge in bankruptcy and after the running of the statute of limitations, are enforceable even though no new consideration passes. Similarly an adult may adopt contracts made during his infancy and an indorser of a note who has been discharged from liability for want of due notice of dishonor may waive his discharge.

The general rule is that the courts will not question the adequacy of the consideration. If the parties have contracted and a consideration within the above definition has passed, the contract will be enforced. But this rule also has exceptions. When a claim of fraud, mistake or duress is advanced, the question of the adequacy of the consideration becomes important in determining whether fraud, mistake or duress was a factor in the making of the contract.

Mutuality of Consideration

Consideration is most often found in mutual promises and the law does not concern itself, in the absence of gross inequality, with relative value of the consideration given by each party. However, where it appears that there does not exist a mutuality of consideration, no contract results. If both parties are not bound by the agreement neither party is bound thereby. Absence of mutual consideration is frequently found in contracts to supply the needs of a purchaser for a particular article. For example, an agreement by a seller to supply all the coal that the purchaser wants during the year is not a contract, for the purchaser has not agreed to buy anything from the seller.

This example is to be distinguished from a contract which measures the quantity purchased or sold by the output of the seller or the requirements of the buyer. Under the Uniform Commercial Code, such a contract is not deemed to be without consideration. UCC § 2-306(1). (See U.C.C. § 2-306, Official Comment 2.)

Section 2-306(2) provides that an exclusive dealing arrangement is also not deemed to be without consideration, even if the party who obtains the exclusive right makes no express promise in return. The law imposes on that party a duty to use its best efforts to supply the merchandise.

Inadequacy of Consideration

There is an exception to the general rule relating to the adequacy of consideration. If the consideration involves money, the consideration given must be the equivalent of the promise made. An existing debt which is presently due, therefore, cannot be discharged by merely paying or promising to pay less than the amount due and owing. The debtor, being under a legal obligation to pay the full amount, is giving no consideration by paying less than that, so the agreement is not binding on the parties and the creditor may accept the partial payment and thereafter enforce payment of the balance due.

In many states a person may agree in writing to accept a lesser sum than that actually due, and payment in accordance with the terms of such writing will discharge the debt; however, payment of the lesser sum must be accompanied by some additional consideration. This additional consideration may take almost any form. Payment in advance of the due date, change in the place of payment, giving of security or giving of any form of chattel will be sufficient.

Where there is a bona fide dispute between two parties over the amount of the indebtedness, a payment of any sum which is not less than that which both parties admit to be correct will discharge the claim. Thus, in a contract for the sale of goods, where the purchaser claims that by reason of defects the goods are not worth the amount charged, a payment of a sum not less than that which the purchaser claims the goods are worth will discharge his obligation to the seller on the contract.

The Uniform Commercial Code has made extensive changes in the traditional contract law requirements of consideration. Although the concept of consideration has by no means been eliminated from the Code, in certain situations the requirement of consideration has been dispensed with or replaced by the substitute of a signed writing.

Under U.C.C. § 2-209 an agreement modifying a contract for the sale of goods needs no consideration. No writing is required, but if the contract as modified is within the statute of frauds, then the statute's requirements must be satisfied. (U.C.C. § 2-201)

Consideration is not always required to keep an offer open. Section 2-205 provides that a written offer by a merchant to buy or sell goods is not revocable for a lack of consideration if the offer by its terms gives assurances that the offer will remain open. At the least, the offer is irrevocable for a reasonable period of time or the time stated in the offer, but in either case the period of irrevocability is not to exceed three months. Of course, an offer can remain open for longer periods if consideration is given.

Similarly, under Section 1-107, a claim arising out of a breach can be discharged without consideration by a written waiver or renunciation signed and delivered by the aggrieved party.

Composition of Creditors

When two or more creditors agree with each other and with their debtor to accept a certain percentage of their liquidated and undisputed claims in full satisfaction, the agreement is a valid contract binding on all the parties to it. The consideration consists of the agreement of each of the creditors with each of the other creditors to forego his legal rights for the enforcement of his claim against the debtor. The agreement is not invalidated by the fact that there are other creditors who are not party to it.

Statutes Affecting Consideration

Recent legislation in various states indicates a movement to abolish common law principles of consideration, especially where the contract is in writing and

THE LAW OF CONTRACTS—LEGAL REQUIREMENTS 2-15

signed. In New York, for example, no consideration is necessary for an option contract if it is written and signed.

Special Statutes

Some states have enacted statutes which provide that certain transactions and contracts must satisfy particular requirements. See Chapter 4, pp. 4-7–4-15, for "Special Statutes."

3
Contracts—Discharge and Enforcement

When the promises of the respective parties to a contract have been fulfilled, the contract has been discharged by performance and no further obligations remain on the part of either party. Most contracts are thus discharged or terminated in accordance with the terms thereof. A contract may also be discharged in various other ways including a breach by one or more parties. Except in the unusual situation where the nature of the contract might warrant a court to decree specific performance, the breach of a contract by any of the parties results in a discharge of the contract and relegates to the other party, or parties, the remedies afforded by law against the defaulting party. It may be presumed that parties enter into a contract with an intent to perform in accordance with their understanding of its terms. Although, in most cases, agreements are fulfilled in accordance with their terms and to the apparent satisfaction of the parties thereto, on numerous occasions questions will arise concerning the construction or interpretation of a contract or parts thereof.

Construction or Interpretation of Contracts

It has been said that a court will not resort to construction where the intent of the parties is expressed in clear and unambiguous language but will enforce and give effect to the contract according to its terms in the absence of fraud or other grounds affecting enforcement according to its terms. Ambiguity exists only when a contract is reasonably susceptible of different constructions. There have been many decisions in this field and, although each case must be decided on its own facts, an attempt has been made to lay down certain basic and fundamental rules.

A contract will be construed to carry out the intention of the parties as nearly as that may be determined, and in such manner as to make it lawful and enforceable if possible. Language will be considered in its ordinary and customary sense and technical terms will be construed as they are understood in the particular type of transaction involved. Where a contract is on a printed form furnished by one party, any ambiguous clauses will be construed against the party by whom the form was drawn and furnished.

The contract will be construed as a whole and effect given to all its parts, reconciling, if possible, apparent inconsistencies. An inconsistency in the provisions of a contract which is partly printed, typewritten and/or handwritten will be resolved favoring the handwritten over the typewritten and the typewritten over the printed provision. In the case of inconsistency between words and figures in a contract, the words will control. Where words, phrases—or even an entire contract—are susceptible of two meanings, the one which will uphold the contract as valid and enforceable will be favored.

Article 2 of the Uniform Commercial Code is devoted to the formation and interpretation of sales contracts and those provisions will govern any contract within its scope.

PRINTED CLAUSES ON LETTERHEADS AND BILLHEADS—Printed clauses appearing on letterheads and billheads do not become part of a contract unless referred to in the body of the agreement itself, or otherwise are brought to the attention of the other party. In *Haddaway v. Post,* 35 Mo. App. 278 (1889), it was held that terms printed on the back of the contract formed part of the agreement where a reference to such terms appeared beneath the signature. A statement on a letterhead that all quotations, orders and contracts are subject to car supply, strikes and causes beyond control, has been held in numerous cases to form part of a contract unless the letter written below was repugnant to the printed matter. However, in *Dale v. See,* 51 N.J.L. 378, 18 A.306 (1889), it was held that a printed notice on the defendant's bill that "All claims for deficiency or damage must be made within three days from date; otherwise not allowed" was not binding upon the plaintiff since notice of a condition after delivery of goods cannot amount to a contract.

Section 2-302 of the Uniform Commercial Code provides that if a court finds as a matter of law a contract or any clause thereof to be unconscionable, it may refuse to enforce the contract. This provision has been used to defeat printed contractual clauses deemed to be unconscionable.

How Contracts Are Discharged

A contract may be discharged in any of the following ways: (1) by performance; (2) by breach; (3) by agreement; (4) by alteration; (5) by operation of law.

DISCHARGE BY PERFORMANCE

Where discharge is by performance, the performance must be by both parties, and where a specific time is set for performance, performance must be within that time, if time is an essential element of the agreement. If no time is fixed, performance must be within a reasonable time. Where substantially performed, minor variations not strictly in accordance with the terms of the contract are immaterial.

DISCHARGE BY BREACH

Where one of the parties, without cause, fails to perform his obligations under the contract, the other party is generally excused from performing, the contract is considered terminated and a cause of action for damages accrues against the party who has breached the agreement. Under some instances, however, such as where one party has fully performed his part of the agreement, such party may elect to treat the contract as continuing and sue to recover the consideration or for specific performance.

There are certain situations, however, where a party's failure to perform his agreement will be excused and he will not be subjected to liability for damages. Such cases involve situations where, due to mistakes of both parties or fraud, coercion or duress on the part of one of the parties, it is held that there has been no agreement entered into between the parties.

DISCHARGE BY AGREEMENT

By the execution of a written agreement, or the exchange of releases, the parties to a contract may mutually agree to terminate and discharge the same. Also one party to a contract may by the delivery of a general release, duly executed, discharge the other.

Discharge by Alteration

If a party having a right under a contract makes a material change or alteration in the contract after the instrument becomes effective, the contract will be discharged if the alteration is made with fraudulent intention. If the alteration is assented to, excused, made to express more clearly the intent of the parties, or made to correct a real or supposed mistake, the contract has generally been held not discharged.

Discharge by Operation of Law

Bankruptcy or impossibility of performance may result in the discharge of a contract by operation of law. Bankruptcy results in such discharge only when, in the bankruptcy proceedings, the bankrupt receives a discharge from his debts.[1]

Impossibility of performance results in the discharge of the contract in the following cases:

(a) Where the contract deals with a specified article or piece of property which is destroyed before the contract is performed and for which an equivalent piece of property cannot be substituted, the contract is discharged.

(b) If, at the time the contract was made, the subject matter of the agreement was not in existence, and the agreement was executed in ignorance of that fact, the contract obviously cannot be performed and is void.

(c) If one party to the contract makes performance by the other impossible, that party will not be required to perform.

(d) If performance of a contract is rendered illegal by an act of the legislative authorities before performance, and the contract, therefore, cannot be carried out without a violation of law, the contract will be discharged.

(e) If the contract is for personal services and the person to perform the services dies or becomes physically incapacitated, the obligation to perform is discharged.

Acts of God, such as floods, earthquakes, or tornadoes, will not excuse performance unless the contracting party has expressly so stipulated in the agreement.

Tender of Performance

Where one party to a contract refuses to perform, the other party, in order to maintain his rights or establish his damages, may make a tender or offer of performance.

"Tender is attempted performance; and the word is applied to attempted performance of two kinds, dissimilar in their results. It is applied to a performance of a promise to do something and of a promise to pay something. In each case the performance is frustrated by the act of the party for whose benefit it is to take place."[2]

Tender implies not only a willingness to perform in accordance with the terms of the contract, but an actual production of the thing to be paid or delivered and an offer of it to the person to whom it is due. It implies also a refusal on the part of the other party to the contract.

Tender may be made when the debt to be paid or duty to be performed is definite and certain or capable of being made so by mere computation. Thus,

---

[1] See Chapter 28, *infra,* Discharge.
[2] W. Anson, Principles of the Law of Contract 518 (A. Corbin 4th Am. ed. 1924).

a tender may be made where by the terms of the agreement one party is to pay $100, or where the obligation is to deliver 100 bushels of wheat. In the first case the tender may be of the exact amount of money; in the second case the exact quantity of wheat. The effect of the tender in the two cases, however, is not the same. The requirement of a definite or liquidated obligation has been eliminated by statutes in many states and in those states an effective tender may be made in an action for unliquidated damages by tendering a sum sufficient to indemnify the other party for the injuries sustained.

TENDER OF MONEY—Where the obligation is the payment of money, tender before an action is begun does not discharge the debt. But if a tender is kept good by statutory tender after an action is begun, and if the plaintiff's judgment exclusive of costs is not in excess of the tender exclusive of the portion thereof deposited on account of costs, it discharges the debtor from liability for interest subsequent to the tender or from liability for damages for nonperformance and any costs that may ensue. Where a person holds a lien upon property, a valid tender of the amount of the lien by the owner of the property, while not affecting his personal liability for the debt, discharges the lien.

A tender is ordinarily an admission of an obligation equal to, but no more than, the sum tendered, and, if accepted, usually constitutes payment and discharges the debtor. But this is true only if expressly accepted, and the acceptance of less than is actually due on a liquidated or definite obligation may operate only as payment *pro tanto*. To preclude the creditor from later collecting the balance of a liquidated debt, the acceptance must be in full of all demands and supported by some additional consideration, or a signed release must be obtained, or protection must be sought under the terms of the statutes passed by a few states.

A tender of money must be of the precise amount of the debt or of a greater sum, and it must be made in legal tender. It must be unconditional and in such form that the other party is required to do nothing but accept it. If it is necessary to make a change, the tender is not good and the party making the tender may not demand a receipt. To prove effective as a defense in an action, the tenderer must be able to show that at all times his offer has been, and still is, kept good, and that the money actually has been paid into court for the benefit of the plaintiff. Money so paid in court becomes at once the property of the tenderee and cannot subsequently be reclaimed by the tenderer.

TENDER OF GOODS—Where the obligation is the delivery of merchandise, tender of the specific goods wholly discharges the seller from liability on the contract. He may thereafter sue for breach of contract or successfully defend an action brought against him by the buyer. A mere ability and readiness to perform is not sufficient; there must be an express offer of the thing to be delivered.

Tender of specific articles vests title to the property tendered in the other party and the tenderer thereafter holds the property as a bailee for the tenderee. The tenderer is, therefore, entitled to compensation.

The general rule is that money paid into court becomes at once the property of the tenderee and cannot subsequently be reclaimed by the tenderer, even after trial and judgment for the tenderer, but this rule has been changed by statutes in some states. In New York, for example, where if the tenderer recovers judgment after trial the money is to be paid back to him; and if the tenderee recovers judgment the money is to be applied on his judgment. The vendor, however, is not required to go through the idle ceremony of making a physical tender where the buyer has notified him that he will not accept the goods.

The vendor does all that he is obliged to do under such circumstances when he is ready and willing to deliver the goods at the time specified in the contract.

Mistakes in Contracts

Where a contract has been entered into between two parties, and one of them made a mistake about the quality or value of the subject matter of the contract, or about its legal effect, the mistaken party cannot evade liability by showing that the contract entered into was not what he intended. Nor can a party to a contract avoid liability thereon by showing that he misunderstood the law applicable to the transaction.

Where, however, there is a mutual mistake by the parties to an agreement concerning the subject matter, identity of the parties or terms or conditions of the agreement, there is no meeting of the minds and no contract results. The same is true where a mistake is made by one party which is induced by the fraud, misrepresentation or other wrongful act of the other party. But if the seller quotes a wrong price, which is innocently accepted by the other party, the person making the mistake about price will be bound. If the mistake, however, is obvious to the purchaser, no contract would result because it would be the duty of the buyer to see that the error was corrected in order not to take advantage of the seller.

Failure to read a written contract is no excuse, even though the contract contains terms and conditions of which the buyer was unaware. If one party to a contract, however, deliberately misrepresents the nature of the instrument, stating that it is not in fact a contract at all, and induces the other party by fraud and deceit to execute the instrument, the deceived party will not be bound.

Fraudulent Contracts

A person induced by fraud to enter into an agreement may refuse to perform, or, if the contract has been carried out, he may recover his property or its value, upon returning to the other party any consideration received therefor, unless the same was used up or destroyed prior to the discovery of the fraud, or he may affirm the fraudulent agreement and recover damages for any loss he may have sustained.

The elements that constitute a legal fraud are as follows:
1. There must be a false or fraudulent representation of a past or existing fact.
2. The representation must be known to be false, or must have been made recklessly, without any genuine belief or adequate knowledge as to its truth or authenticity.
3. The misstatement must be material.
4. The misstatement must be made seriously and with intent that it be relied upon.
5. The misstatement must be relied upon.
6. The misstatement must result in injury.

Reality of Consent

A party to a contract must consent to the contract and enter into the agreement voluntarily and without inducement by fraud or duress. If by the use of intimidation or threats a person is induced to sign an agreement, for example, where he is threatened with harm, or imprisonment, either to himself, his property, or to a relative, and under such circumstances that he might reasonably believe there was immediate danger of the threat being carried out, the agreement may be repudiated and is unenforceable, and any consideration paid thereunder may be recovered.

Accord and Satisfaction

Where the parties to a contract substitute a new contract, the new agreement is an accord, and when carried out results in a satisfaction.[1]

Assignments of Contracts

In the absence of a specific provision to the contrary, any party to a contract may assign his rights thereunder, but contract liabilities may not be assigned, nor may a contract involving a relation of personal competence, including a contract for personal services, be assigned without the consent of the other party thereto.

If the contract is in writing, the assignment should also be in writing; if oral, a written agreement of assignment is desirable.

Notice of the assignment should immediately be given by the assignee to the other party to the contract.

Enforcement

Failure or refusal by one party to perform a contract, which results in a breach, may entitle the other party thereto either to damages or to a judgment which requires the first party to carry out his agreement. Such a right and remedy is known as "specific performance."

Specific performance of a contract can be had only where an award of damages would not adequately compensate the other party for the breach of the agreement. A contract for the sale of land may always be enforced by an action for specific performance, but ordinarily an agreement to furnish goods, unless they are of a specific nature, such as a valuable painting or piece of sculpture which cannot be duplicated or replaced, will not be specifically enforced.

Limitations for Suit

All states prescribe statutory time limits, applicable to various types of contracts, within which an action to enforce contracts, or for the recovery of damages, must be commenced. These statutes are known as "statutes of limitations" and are set forth in Chapter 23, *infra,* in the table "Limitations for Civil Actions."

The period of limitations begins to run from the date of the happening of an event which would give rise to a right to institute suit. In the case of a contract this would be the date of the breach of the contract by nonpayment, nondelivery or other act of nonperformance. In the case of a tort the cause of action would accrue as of the date the injury was committed. The statute of

---

[1] See Chapter 18, *infra,* Checks Marked "In Full of Account."

limitations may be "tolled," that is, the period will be extended in the event that actions by the party in default prevent the commencement of an action against him, such as absenting himself from the jurisdiction. The same is true of a person under disability, such as a person who becomes insane or a person in the military service. Where the debtor acknowledges a debt or obligation the statute of limitations will run anew from the last date of such acknowledgment; such acknowledgment may be required, under applicable state law, to be in writing.

Contracts—Formal Requirements 4

In the absence of some specific rule of law, usually in the form of statutory requirements, no specific form or particular language or words are required to create a contract. Even in those cases where forms are provided by statute, in the absence of a specific prohibition against doing so, such terms may usually be modified or waived by agreement of the parties.

Classification of Contracts

There are numerous classifications used to distinguish types of contracts, such as written or oral, unilateral or bilateral, executed or executory, express or implied. The terms "written" and "oral" are self-explanatory. However, in many cases a contract may be partly in writing and partly oral. When a contract has been fully performed it is described as an "executed contract." When only one party has performed in full, it may be described as partly executed and partly executory. An "express contract" is one in which all the terms are expressed, or agreed upon, by the parties, either orally or in writing. The term "implied contract" is used to refer to an agreement which is inferred or implied by law from facts and circumstances which may be interpreted as an intent to contract. A "bilateral contract" is one in which there are mutual or reciprocal promises by both parties. The term "unilateral" (one-sided) is used to refer to an agreement the consideration for which is executed on the part of one party, but executory on the part of the other. The term has been subject to criticism and is often used to express the fact that a contract does not exist because of lack of mutuality of consideration.

A further classification applied to express contracts is "formal" or "informal," to distinguish the formal written agreement signed by both parties, often sealed and acknowledged before a notary public, from the oral agreement or agreements consisting of a series of letters, memoranda or other writings, or a combination of oral and written communications. The significance of formalism in the drawing and execution of contracts is gradually disappearing. Although at one time the courts would enforce only those contracts which were written, signed and sealed, courts today will enforce an agreement whether written or oral, or merely implied. The one major exception is the statutory requirements (generally referred to as The Statute of Frauds) of the various states which provide that certain contracts must be in writing to be enforceable.

The Statute of Frauds—Contracts Required to Be in Writing

After the courts at common law undertook to enforce oral agreements, it was determined that some agreements were so important that they ought not to rest in verbal promise only, because this might induce a witness to commit perjury. To remedy this the Statute of Frauds and Perjuries was enacted in England,[1]

---

[1] 29 Car. II, ch. 3 (1676).

requiring agreements of certain types to be in writing and signed by the party to be charged.

All of the states except Louisiana [1] have enacted "Statutes of Frauds" requiring certain contracts to be in writing. In the absence of a written agreement or memorandum evidencing the terms of the contract, signed by the party against whom action is brought, such contract is unenforceable.

Contracts required to be evidenced by a written memorandum are as follows:

(1) Contracts for the sale of land or any interest therein.

(2) Agreements not to be performed within a period of one year from the making thereof.

(3) Any special promise of an executor or administrator to answer for any debt or damages out of his own estate.

(4) Every special promise to answer for the debt, default or miscarriage of another.

(5) Agreements made upon the consideration of marriage.

(6) Contracts in relation to the sale of personal property where no part of the property has been delivered and no part of the price has been paid provided the value of the property involved in the transaction equals or exceeds a certain specified amount.

(7) A liability based upon, or by reason of, any representation or assurance made concerning the character, conduct, credit, ability, debt or dealings of any other person.

(8) An agreement to pay upon attaining legal majority a debt contracted during infancy.

(9) An agreement which by its terms is not to be performed during the lifetime of the promisor, or an agreement to devise or bequeath any property or to make any provision for any person by will.

(10) An assignment of wages to be earned in the future.

(11) An agreement for the sale or transfer of a vessel.

(12) A mortgage of personal property.

The Statute of Frauds is not uniform in the several states, and the variations in the statutory provisions are shown under similar headings below.

The written memorandum required by the statute need not be made or executed at the time the agreement is entered into, but may be signed by the "party to be charged, or his duly authorized agent," at any time before a suit involving the contract is commenced.

No particular form of language is necessary, and the memorandum may be formal or informal. It may consist of a single letter or a series of letters, documents or telegrams which taken together set forth all of the essential terms of the contract.

The important feature is that the memorandum so constituted must be complete and must be signed by the party against whom it is to be enforced, or by his duly authorized agent.

STATUTORY REQUIREMENTS

The following contracts or a memorandum thereof are required to be in writing:

---

[1] See "Louisiana Statute" under Special Statutes, *infra,* p. 4-7.

CONTRACTS—FORMAL REQUIREMENTS

1. Contracts for the Sale of Land or an Interest Therein.

All states require that an agreement for the sale of land or an interest therein be in writing. This section prevents the enforcement of oral mortgages, agreements to sell, leases or agreements to lease for a period longer than the time stipulated in the statute, and agreements to devise land by will, but it does not prevent the recovery of the price orally agreed to be paid for land where the land has actually been transferred.

Verbal leases not exceeding three years are valid in Indiana, New Jersey, New Mexico, North Carolina and Pennsylvania; however, in North Carolina a contract to convey a mining lease of any duration must be in writing. In Louisiana all oral leases are valid, and in Maine, New Hampshire and Ohio all leases must be in writing; however, in Ohio an oral lease for less than three years is valid where the tenant takes possession and pays rent. In all other states an oral lease for a term up to one year is valid.

Agreements authorizing or employing an agent or broker to sell or purchase real estate for compensation or commission must be in writing in all states except Alaska, Arkansas, Connecticut, District of Columbia, Florida, Indiana, Iowa, Kentucky, Maine, Maryland, Massachusetts, Nevada, New Mexico, North Carolina, Rhode Island, South Carolina, Tennessee, Vermont, Virginia, West Virginia, and Wyoming.

2. Agreements Not to Be Performed within One Year.

The wording of the statutes usually provides for a writing in the case of agreements not to be performed within one year from the making of the contract. This includes contracts which may not take a year to perform, but which are so drawn that it is contemplated that they will not be completed within a year after they are made. This section includes contracts of employment and instalment contracts. If the contract is such that it may be reasonably performed within a year, and no time is fixed, it is not within the statute though it may in fact take longer. Thus, a contract to perform continuing services or to do particular things, with no time being fixed during which the agreement is to remain in force, is not within the statute.

The statutes of Louisiana, North Carolina and Pennsylvania do not contain this provision. The Mississippi statute relates to contracts not to be performed within fifteen months. Georgia excepts contracts with overseers.

3. Promise by Executor or Administrator to Answer for Any Debt or Damages Out of His Own Property.

Any special promise by an executor or administrator to answer for any debt or damages out of his own property or estate is required to be in writing under the statutes of most of the states. This provision is omitted, however, in the statutes of Colorado, Louisiana, Minnesota, Nevada, New Mexico and Wisconsin.

The Iowa statute relates only to a promise by an executor to pay the debt of the decedent from his own estate. In Georgia, this section applies also to guardians, administrators and trustees and in Rhode Island it applies to trustees of express trusts.

4. SPECIAL PROMISE TO ANSWER FOR THE DEBT, DEFAULT, OR MISCARRIAGE OF ANOTHER.

This provision of the statute is intended to cover verbal promises to pay the debt of a third person. There are some very technical questions which arise in connection with it, for liability of the promisor turns largely upon the question of whether his promise is what is called an original one and the credit is in fact given to him, or whether it is a "collateral" promise which is in aid of an undertaking or liability of the third person. An original promise is not within this section, for if there is an original promise, it is in fact the liability of the promisor, and not that of the third person, which is to be enforced. For example, a promise made by one in his own name to pay for services rendered another need not be in writing while a promise to see that a person is paid if he renders such services must be in writing.

The Delaware statute applies only to promises to the value of $25 or over. Promises up to $5 are not within the statute and promises between $5 and $25 may be proved by the oath or affirmation of one witness. In Pennsylvania no person may be charged as acceptor of a bill of exchange, draft or order exceeding $20, unless the acceptance is written.

5. AGREEMENTS MADE UPON THE CONSIDERATION OF MARRIAGE.

Under this section a promise to marry need not be in writing, but a promise to transfer money or property in case of marriage must be.

This section is omitted in Pennsylvania and North Carolina. Marriage articles are excepted under the Georgia statute.

6. CONTRACTS FOR THE SALE OF GOODS OR PERSONALTY.

This section applies to contracts for the sale of all sorts of goods, wares, and merchandise for money or money's worth where the value of the goods is at least $500.[1] It does not apply where a part of the goods has been actually accepted and received, or where there has been a payment of something in earnest to bind the bargain, or where there has been a part payment. In any of these cases the giving of earnest money or the part payment must have been in good faith and not with the understanding that it is to be given back.

Under the Uniform Commercial Code, the Statute of Frauds does not apply to a contract for the sale of goods which are to be specially manufactured for the buyer and are not suitable for sale to others in the ordinary course of the seller's business if a substantial beginning of their manufacturing or commitments for their procurement have been made before a notice of repudiation is received. U.C.C. § 2-201.

In Mississippi, what is known as the "business sign statute" provides that if a person transacts business as a trader with the addition of the words "agent," "factor," "and Company" or "& Co" and fails to disclose the name of the principal or partner by signs easy to read, all of the property, stock and money used in the business is available to creditors of the business.

An auctioneer's memorandum in his sale book at the time of the sale regarding the kind of property sold, the terms of sale, the price and the names of the purchaser and the persons on whose account the sale was made is a sufficient memorandum under the statutes of Alabama, Arizona, California, Colorado,

---
[1] See Louisiana Statute, *infra,* p. 4-7.

Idaho, Minnesota, Montana, New York, North Dakota, and Wisconsin, and would probably be so held even in the absence of a statute.

Uniform Commercial Code Provisions.

(1) Section 1-206 provides that except in cases for sale of goods covered by Section 2-201 or for securities covered by Section 8-319 or security agreements covered by Section 9-203, a contract for the sale of personal property is not enforceable by way of action or defense beyond $5,000 in amount unless there is some writing which identifies that a contract for sale has been made between the parties at a defined or stated price, reasonably identifies the subject matter and is signed by the party against whom enforcement is sought or his authorized agent.

(2) Section 2-201 provides: A contract for the sale of goods for the price of $500 or more is not enforceable by way of action or defense unless there is some writing sufficient to indicate that a contract for sale has been made between the parties and signed by the party against whom enforcement is sought or by his authorized agent or broker. It is not necessary that all the terms be stated in writing but a contract cannot be enforced beyond the quantity shown in such writing if there is an error or omission.

(3) Between merchants, if within a reasonable time a written confirmation is sent and received, it satisfies the above requirement unless written notice of objection is given within 10 days after its receipt.

(4) The Code also excepts from the Statute of Frauds
    (a) under certain circumstances, goods to be specially manufactured for the buyer,
    (b) an agreement of sale to the extent that the same may be admitted in pleadings, testimony or other court proceedings,
    (c) sale of goods for which payment has been made and accepted or which have been received and accepted. See Section 2-606.

(5) Section 2-202 provides that terms which parties agree on in their confirmatory memoranda or other writings intended as a final expression of their agreement with respect to such terms, may not be contradicted by evidence of any prior agreement or of a contemporaneous oral agreement. Such terms may, however, be explained or supplemented by parol evidence of the course of dealing, usage of trade, or course of performance. Parol evidence of consistent additional terms will also be accepted unless the writing was intended to be a complete and exclusive statement of the terms of the agreement.

7. REPRESENTATIONS AS TO CREDIT.

No action may be brought and maintained, to charge any person upon or by reason of any representation or assurance made concerning the character, conduct, credit, ability, trade or dealings of any other person unless such representation or assurances is made in writing and signed by the party to be charged thereby, or by some lawfully authorized person.

This provision or one substantially the same is in force in Alabama, Alaska, California, Georgia, Hawaii, Idaho, Indiana, Kentucky, Maine, Massachusetts, Michigan, Missouri, Oregon, Utah, Vermont, Virginia, West Virginia and Wyoming.

In California, Idaho and Utah, it applies to any "representation as to the credit of a third person."

In Georgia, the statute provides that "no action shall be sustained for deceit in representation to obtain credit for another unless such misrepresentation be in writing signed by the party to be charged therewith."

In Oregon, the provision applies to representations as to the "credit, skill or character of a third person."

In West Virginia, the statute provides that no action shall be brought to charge "any person upon or by reason of a representation or assurance concerning the character, conduct, credit, ability, trade or dealings of another, to the intent or purpose that such other may obtain thereby credit, money or goods."

8. PROMISES TO PAY DEBTS CONTRACTED IN INFANCY.

A writing is necessary "to charge any person upon a promise made, after full age to pay a debt contracted during infancy; or upon a ratification after full age of a promise or simple contract made during infancy."

This is the wording of the West Virginia statute. Similar provisions exist in Arkansas, Kentucky, Maine, Mississippi, Missouri, New Jersey, South Carolina and Virginia.

9. AGREEMENT NOT TO BE PERFORMED DURING LIFE OF PROMISOR.

A writing is necessary to validate "an agreement which by its terms is not to be performed during the lifetime of the promisor, or an agreement to devise or bequeath any property, or to make any provision for any person by will."

This statute is in effect in Alabama, Alaska, Arizona, California and Hawaii. In Massachusetts and New York, an agreement to make a will of real or personal property or to give a legacy or make a devise must be in writing.

10. ASSIGNMENT OF WAGES.

In general, no assignment of, or order for, wages to be earned in the future is valid against a creditor of the person making it, until it has been accepted in writing and a copy of it, and of the acceptance, has been filed with the clerk of the town or city where the party making it resides. The clerks of towns and cities must keep for public inspection an alphabetical list of all such orders and assignments filed with them.

Most of the states have adopted legislation controlling assignment of wages in an effort to protect the wage earner. The table on pages 4-8–4-14 summarizes the law of the different states on such assignments.

The UCCC (see Chapter 9, *infra*) specifically prohibits assignment of wages in the states that have adopted the Act.

The Federal Trade Commission has adopted Consumer Credit Regulations which characterize as an unfair credit practice an assignment of wages unless: (i) the assignment is revocable; (ii) the assignment is a part of a payroll deduction plan; or (iii) the assignment applies to wages already earned.

11. SALE OF VESSELS.

Under the Alaska statute, a sale or transfer of a boat or vessel for a price of $500 or more is not valid unless it is in writing and signed by the party making the transfer.

12. Chattel Mortgages.

A mortgage of personal property is not valid unless made in writing and subscribed by the mortgagor. See Chapter 6, *infra,* under "Chattel Mortgages."

13. Miscellaneous additional provisions of the statute of frauds exist in various states. For example, the Michigan statute requires a writing for assignment of things in action and on agreements relating to medical care.

Special Statutes

Louisiana—In Louisiana the Statute of Frauds provides that all agreements relative to movable property and all contracts for the payment of money, where the value does not exceed five hundred dollars, which are not reduced to writing, may be proved by any other competent evidence; such contracts or agreements, above five hundred dollars in value, must be proved by at least one credible witness and other corroborative circumstances.

It further provides that parol evidence shall not be received:

"To prove any acknowledgment or promise to pay any judgment, sentence or decree of any court of competent jurisdiction, either in or out of this state, for the purpose or in order to take such judgment, sentence or decree out of prescription, or to revive the same after prescription has run or been completed.

"To prove acknowledgment or promise of a party deceased, to pay any debt or liability, in order to take such debt or liability out of prescription, or to revive the same after prescription has run or been completed.

"To prove any promise to pay the debt of a third person.

"To prove any acknowledgment or promise to pay any debt or liability evidenced by writing, when prescription has already run.

"But in all cases mentioned in this article, the acknowledgment or promise to pay shall be proved by written evidence signed by the party who is alleged to have made the acknowledgment or promise, or by his agent or attorney in fact specially authorized in writing so to do."

California—California has adopted a statute which requires persons engaged in trade or business who use the Spanish language orally or in writing in the course of entering into certain contracts or agreements to give notice of and to furnish on the request of any party to the contract, prior to its execution, an unexecuted Spanish language translation of the contract. The type of contracts covered by the statute are generally consumer contracts involving credit for personal, family and household purposes or leases. The statute also requires that the creditor supply notice both in English and Spanish to all persons who incur liability under such a consumer contract, without receiving the benefit of any property, money or services therefrom, that advises them of the liability undertaken.

A number of states have enacted a Plain Language Contracts Act which requires that all consumer contracts to buy or lease personal property or services be written in "plain language." Plain language consists of short sentences and paragraphs, everyday words, personal pronouns, and the actual names of the parties, simple and active verb forms, type of readable size, boldface captions

(Continued on p. 4-15)

STATE LAWS CONTROLLING ASSIGNMENT OF WAGES

	WHEN PERMITTED			LIMITATIONS		
State	Assignments Permitted for General Purposes	Assignments Permitted for Special Purposes Including Small Loans, Real Estate by Head of Family	Retail Installment Sales Assignments Prohibited	On Wages	Notice to Employer Required	Written Assignment Required	Other
Alabama	All assignments of future wages unenforceable.						
Alaska		X		50% of net disposable earnings.			
Arizona		X		10%		X	Employer cannot discharge employee because wages are subject to assignment for child support.
Arkansas		X		None	X[3]	X	Spouse's consent required; 48 months' duration. Child support and spousal maintenance.
California	X[5]	X[2]	X[5]	50%	X	X	Assignment filed with county recorder.[8] Consent of wife required.
Colorado	X[18,24]		X	Wages earned within 30 days from time of assignment.	X[29] (Within 5 days)	X	Spouse or parent's consent[12] (except for necessities). Must deny existence of other assignments. Spouse must sign.[4] Child support. Wage assignment notice and certified copy of assignment must be served upon the employer by certified mail.
Connecticut	Assignments void except for amounts due for support in public welfare cases.						
Delaware		X		None	X[3,29]		Assignments securing loans on "real estate or otherwise" need employer's written consent.
D.C.	All assignments of future wages unenforceable.[24]						
Florida	All assignments of wages, earned or to be earned are unenforceable;[29] child support assignments are controlled by statute.						

4–8

	There are no statutory provisions pertaining to assignment of wages except for child support.	Assignment of earnings for debt arising out of consumer credit transaction unenforceable by the assignee and revocable by the consumer. Also permitted for support and maintenance orders.		
Georgia			X	Signed by spouse; limited to 20 months' duration if repayable in equal monthly installments or 12 months if repayable in any other manner. Assignments in employment agency contract must be in form approved by director of labor. Child support.[29]
Hawaii	X			Special provisions for court-ordered wage assignments for the support of minor children.
Idaho	X[18]			
Illinois	X		X[29]	Wages of state and local government employees are not assignable. A court may, in its discretion, order assignment of wages to secure a support order. The words "Wage Assignment" must be boldly printed on the document. Wages of state and municipal government employees are not subject to collection under wage assignments.
Indiana	X[18,23]	None[6]	X	Spouse's consent. Assignment to wage broker void unless interest on loan not more than 8% per year.
Iowa	X	None	X[3]	Spouse's consent required. Creditor may not take an assignment to secure a consumer credit debt. Employer bound to honor court-ordered assignment for child support.
Kansas				
Kentucky		10% Loans under $200 limited to 90 days from execution.	X[3]	Wage assignments to banks and trust companies as security for installment loans prohibited; and assignment for less than $200 must meet technical requirements of obtaining signed written statement of assignor and statement of name, address of each assignee. Not binding on employer unless he accepts same.
Louisiana	X[28]	50% of disposable earnings.	X[3]	

4–9

STATE LAWS CONTROLLING ASSIGNMENT OF WAGES (Continued)

	WHEN PERMITTED			LIMITATIONS			
State	Assignments Permitted for General Purposes	Assignments Permitted for Special Purposes Including Small Loans, Real Estate by Head of Family	Retail Installment Sales Assignments Prohibited	On Wages	Notice to Employer Required	Written Assignment Required	Other
Maine	X[24]	X[9]		None	X	X	
Maryland	X[22]	X	X	6 month limitation.	X	X[4]	Must be signed and acknowledged by wage earner and recorded in clerk of district; spouse's consent and signature required; assignor must sign affidavit that interest limited to 6% per year.
Massachusetts	X[28]	X[28]	X	25% limited to 2 years on loans over $3,000; $10 per week for 1 year on loans under $3,000. Must comply with federal limitations.	X[3,29]	X	Signed by spouse.[4,10]
Michigan	X[28]	X[22]	X	Varies with assignment.	X	X	Filed in district or municipal court. Child support provisions.
Minnesota	X[28]	X[24,30]	X	10% on assignment for small loan.	X[29]	X	Limited to 60 days except on excess of $1,500 per month. Signed by spouse.[4] Child support provisions.
Mississippi		X[11]		None	X[3]	X	
Missouri	X[12,17]						Court order for family support.[27]

4–10

Montana	X	X		10%[7]	X	Signed and consented to by both spouses. Assignments of future wages to wage brokers invalid.[4] Court-ordered child support.
Nebraska	X	X		Amount of weekly earnings subject to assignments shall not exceed the lesser of 25% of disposable weekly earnings or the amount by which disposable weekly earnings exceed 30 times federal minimum hourly wage, or 15% of disposable weekly earnings if wage earner is a head of a family.	X[29]	Acknowledgment and consent of wage earner and spouse required.
Nevada	An assignment of wages is void if made at the time that an unsatisfied judgment exists against the maker.[25,27]					
New Hampshire	X[28]		X[13]	None	X[3]	See [4, 29]
New Jersey	Assignment of wages prohibited in most instances except by court order.[14, 29]					
New Mexico	X	X	X	Up to 25% or 10% for small loan.	X	Signed by spouse.[4]
New York	X[23, 28]	X	X	10% on indebtedness of under $1,000; no limit on excess amount provided wages exceed $85 per week.	X	Signature of spouse for small loan assignments; generally, void if to secure loan of over 18% interest per year.[4, 29]

4-11

STATE LAWS CONTROLLING ASSIGNMENT OF WAGES (Continued)

State	WHEN PERMITTED			LIMITATIONS			
	Assignments Permitted for General Purposes	Assignments Permitted for Special Purposes Including Small Loans, Real Estate by Head of Family	Retail Installment Sales Assignments Prohibited	On Wages	Notice to Employer Required	Written Assignment Required	Other
North Carolina	X [28]	X [22]			X [3]		Action for assignment of future wages must be commenced within 6 months of execution.
North Dakota		X [17]	X [17]	None			Assignment of future wages permitted only to satisfy judgment containing child support provisions. Court-ordered child support.
Ohio	Assignments invalid except for court-ordered support of spouse or minor child.						
Oklahoma	X [18]				X	X	
Oregon		X [17]	X				
Pennsylvania	X [12]		X	None			
Rhode Island	X [28]	X		One year from assignment; 10% for small loans.	X	X	Small loan assignment signed by spouse. [4]
South Carolina	X [24]	X			X [3]	X [2]	
South Dakota		X [4]		10% and time limits depending on amount of loan.	X [4]	X	Employer has option of accepting and honoring assignment. Court-ordered child support.
Tennessee	X [28]			None	X [3]	X	Court-ordered child support.

4-12

Texas	X		X	Court-ordered child support.
Utah	X [18]	X [17]		Court-ordered child support.
Vermont	X [2, 28]	X	X [26]	X	Small loan assignment signed by spouse.[4]
Virginia	X	X	25% or excess over 30 times federal minimum hourly wage; small loan limited to 10%.	X [3]	Small loan assignment signed by spouse.[4]
			10%	X	
Virginia	X	X	50% of net earnings per court-ordered child support.		
Washington		X [20]	50% of disposable income exempt for child support.	X [3]	Signed by spouse assignment and employer's acceptance filed with county auditor.
West Virginia	X [19, 28]		25% and limited to one year.	X [3]	Employee may revoke all assignments at will. Child support.
Wisconsin	X	X	6 month limitation.	X [27]	Signed by spouse.[4]
Wyoming	X [18]	X [20]	25% for child support only.	X [3]	Signed by spouse. Child support.

(Footnotes on following page)

STATE LAWS CONTROLLING ASSIGNMENT OF WAGES (Continued)

[1] 25% of wages necessary to support family.
[2] Necessities of life only.
[3] Assignment of future wages are not enforceable against the employer unless he has consented in writing.
[4] There are other technical limitations and requirements.
[5] Prohibited except for necessities of life.
[6] Assignments to wage brokers limited to part of wages to be earned within 30 days following date of assignment.
[7] Consumer loans only.
[8] Assignments of future wages given for less than $200 in money or goods and money.
[9] Prohibited in home repair contracts.
[10] Loans of over $3,000 limited to two years, assignments for loans under $3,000 limited to one year.
[11] To secure the purchases of goods.
[12] Assignment of future wages prohibited.
[13] Retail instalment sales of motor vehicles only.
[14] Employer who withholds or assigns wages as well as assignee of wages who violates this Act deemed a disorderly person.
[15] There are other limitations depending on the type of assignment.
[16] Assignments valid only pursuant to court order for support of wife or child.
[17] Assignments for small loans prohibited.
[18] Assignments arising out of a consumer credit transaction are unenforceable by assignee and revocable by buyer, lessee or debtor. These states have the UCCC in effect.
[19] No assignment of wages given to secure any loan is valid.
[20] Assignment of future wages given to secure loans of less than $300.
[21] Deductions under a collective bargaining agreement, pension plan, charitable contributions and certain other deductions allowed.
[22] Small loan licensee prohibited from taking an assignment of wages as payment or as security for a loan. Unenforceable by assignee and revocable by debtor.
[23] Employee must be given notice by certified mail twenty days before wage assignment filed with employer.
[24] Consumer Protection Law forbids assignment of consumer's earnings by creditor as payment of security for payment of consumer credit sale or direct instalment loan.
[25] Wage assignments may not be given to secure a loan under the Instalment Loan and Finance Act.
[26] Consumers cannot agree to assign wages by contract.
[27] For court-ordered support only. Employers who discharge or discipline their employees because of court-ordered support assignments are liable for a maximum fine of $200 plus damages.
[28] Only future earnings may be assigned.
[29] Employers may not fire employees because of assignment.

4–14

(Continued from p. 4-7)

for subdivisions, and a clear and coherent form. Connecticut, Hawaii, and West Virginia provide that the plain language requirement applies to consumer contracts that do not exceed $25,000 while Minnesota, New Jersey, and New York require plain language in contracts up to $50,000.

See Chapter 8, *infra* p. 8-1, regarding requirements under state Retail Instalment Sales Laws, and Chapter 10, *infra* p. 10-1, regarding requirements under state laws on leasing of personal property.

Signatures on the Contract

A signature may be made by a mark, sign, stamp, symbol or device if the intention of the party making the same is to thereby authenticate the writing to which it is attached. Often the term subscription is used in place of the word signature. A subscription is made by placing one's own signature (i.e., an autograph) at the end of a writing or at the bottom of an instrument. The signing of an instrument (as distinguished from a subscription) may be at the top or any other part of the instrument.

Where the contract is in writing, it is necessary to identify the parties with the writing. The signature is placed there to authenticate the writing and to indicate the intent that the signer be bound thereby. Should proof of the contract be necessary in litigation, it is effected by simply proving the signature of the party. To avoid the implication of the signature, the burden would be upon the party to show fraud, duress or such other facts to indicate that the signature was not placed on instrument with intent to be bound thereby. In *Metzger v. Aetna Insurance Co.*, 227 N.Y. 411, 416, 125 N.E. 814, 816 (1920), the court held: "He who signs or accepts a written contract, in the absence of fraud or other wrongful act on the part of another contracting party, is conclusively presumed to know its contents and to assent to them and there can be no evidence for the jury as to his understanding of its terms."

A valid signature may be made by use of initials or abbreviations of a name or by use of a given name or surname. A signature may also be made by the use of a fictitious name or a firm name or the name of another person, or by the use of any character, symbol, mark or other designation that a party wishes to adopt as his signature. It may be printed, stamped, typewritten, engraved, photographed or cut from one instrument and attached to another. It is imperative, of course, that it be placed on the instrument with the intent to authenticate it. There is no requirement that a signature be made in ink and if made by pencil it is equally valid.

Where the party is unable to write, his signature may be made by means of a mark in the manner prescribed by statute or by the common law. Almost all the states have a statutory provision for signing by means of a mark. In most of the states it will be sufficient if the contents are made known, in the presence of two witnesses, to the person who is to sign. Thereafter the party should place an "X" upon the instrument near which his name is subsequently to be written; the two witnesses should sign the instrument. It has been held in several cases that where a mark is not attested in accordance with the requirements of the statute, the signature is validated by reason of the fact that the signer acknowledged his signature (mark) before a notary public or other officer empowered to take acknowledgments.

A signature need not be made by the party himself but may be made by someone duly authorized by him. In *State v. Abernethy* 190 N.C. 768, 130 S.E. 619 (1925), the court held that a person may verbally authorize another to sign a note or other paper for him whether he can write his name or not. Not only may a party authorize another to make his signature, but he may also adopt a signature written by another in absence of authorization, and may even adopt a forged signature.

Signature by Agents

The law recognizes the right of an agent to sign for his principal and the principal is bound by the agent's signature, if the agent is duly authorized. It is sufficient that the agent merely signs the principal's name without indicating by whom the signature is made or the nature of the authorization. It is the more common practice, however, to have the agent make a signature for his principal by signing his own name with the words "on account of" or "on behalf of" or "for" the principal, or by the use of the principal's name "by" the agent.

Agents Signing Negotiable Instruments: Often an agent will sign a negotiable instrument and follow his signature with a designation such as "president," "agent" or "trustee" without any indication in the instrument as to who the principal might be. In innumerable cases the courts have held that such designations are merely descriptive terms and that the signer binds himself personally. It has even been held that where one signs his name and follows it with a designation "Agent for John Smith" or "President of ABC Corporation" the designation is merely descriptive matter and does not indicate an agency. In *Davis v. England* 141 Mass. 587, 6 N.E. 731 (1886), the signer was held to be personally liable in making such a signature. Where the corporate name is placed upon an instrument and this is followed by the signature, for example, "A B, President," the weight of authority holds that the corporation alone is bound thereby, but there are decisions holding both the corporation and officer liable. In other cases courts permit parol evidence to explain the intention of the parties in making the signature. It should be noted that because of the nature of negotiable instruments, courts are reluctant to permit any testimony which will vary the instrument. Section 3-403 of the Code provides that an authorized representative is personally obligated if the negotiable instrument contains neither the name of the person represented nor shows that the representative signed in a representative capacity. Parol evidence will not be allowed at trial to disestablish this obligation. Except as otherwise established between the original parties to the note, an authorized representative is personally obligated if the instrument names the person represented but does not show that the representative signed in a representative capacity, or if the instrument does not name the person represented but does show that the represented signed in a representative capacity. In such cases parol evidence is admitted in litigation between the immediate parties to the note to prove that the signature by the agent was made in a representative capacity.

It is also important in signing instruments other than negotiable instruments that the signature indicate the capacity in which the agent signs, although generally the courts will permit evidence to establish this. Even if the contract fails to disclose who the principal is, the principal is liable on and may enforce the contract unless it is a negotiable instrument or an instrument under seal. When this is true, the agent also becomes liable on the contract and acquires the right to enforce it in his own name whether or not the agent in signing indicates that he is acting in a representative capacity.

Section 3-403(3) provides that, unless established to the contrary, the name of an organization preceded or followed by the name and office of an authorized individual is a signature made in a representative capacity. Therefore all documents signed on behalf of a corporation should be signed as follows:

XYZ Corporation

by _____
Signature

as _____
Title

Acknowledgments on Contracts

An acknowledgment in its legal sense is a formal declaration before the authorized public officer by a person who has executed an instrument that such instrument is his act and deed. The word acknowledgment is also used to mean a certificate of acknowledgment often attached to formal documents.

In most of the states a particular form of acknowledgment is approved or required by statute and the acknowledgment should conform to the requirements of the particular state in which it is taken and in some cases to the requirements of the state where it is to be effective. In general the certificate of acknowledgment should contain the name of the state and county where the acknowledgment is made, the name of the person or persons making the acknowledgment, a statement to the effect that such persons were known to the officer, that they came before him, and that each acknowledged the signature on the instrument to be his own. This certificate must be subscribed by the public officer and should show his official designation and seal or such other identification as may be required by the law of the state. It should be noted that in most cases the public officer's authority to take acknowledgments is limited to a certain jurisdiction, such as a county or city.

The acknowledgment is seldom called for in the ordinary contract. It is required, however, in formal instruments such as deeds, leases and agreements; generally a statute will require the acknowledgment as a prerequisite to the filing or recording of an instrument. In the case of chattel mortgages and condition bills of sale most of the states require either a certificate of acknowledgment or attestation of the signatures of the parties.

The purpose of the certificate of acknowledgment is to make the instrument to which it is attached "self proving." Where a certificate of acknowledgment appears on an instrument, it may be introduced into evidence without further proof as to the signature of the parties. Although thereafter a party whose name appears upon the certificate of acknowledgment as having acknowledged the instrument may introduce evidence to show that he did not in fact sign and acknowledge it, he must overcome the strong presumption of validity.

A number of states have adopted the Uniform Acknowledgment Act which established standard forms of acknowledgments. See specimen forms reproduced in Chapter 33, *infra.*

Contracts Under Seal

The placing of a seal on a contract or legal instrument no longer has in most states the significance formerly attached to it.[1] The use of a seal on contracts of major importance is, however, still customary, and in some states required. For example, a seal may be required upon all deeds, mortgages and other conveyances of real estate. When a document is executed by a corporation, the presence of a seal is evidence of the authenticity of the signature. Under the laws of many of the states, the statute of limitations is longer as applied to sealed instruments than to instruments not under seal.[2] Uniform Commercial Code Section 2-203 states, in essence, that the affixing of a seal to a contract to buy or sell goods is of no effect.

---

[1] The requirement of placing a seal on a contract has been abolished in Alaska, Arizona, Arkansas, California, Colorado, Florida, Hawaii, Idaho, Illinois, Indiana, Iowa, Kansas, Kentucky, Louisiana, Michigan, Minnesota, Mississippi, Missouri, Montana, Nebraska, Nevada, New Mexico, New York, North Dakota, Ohio, Oklahoma, Tennessee, Texas, Utah, Washington, West Virginia, and Wyoming.

[2] In Alabama, Michigan, New Jersey, Oregon, and Wisconsin the law provides that sealed contracts are presumed, in the absence of evidence to the contrary, to have been made for sufficient consideration. This presumption does not apply to other written contracts.

Terms of Payment In Commercial Contracts

The expression "terms of sale" has frequently been applied by creditors and others who are engaged in commerce to only one of several terms in sales transactions, that is, the time for payment. A "term" in a contract, however, is any condition in a contract. Thus "terms" include the kind of goods, the time of delivery, the carrier to transport the goods, and, of course, the time for payment. To be more precise, the terms which deal with the time and method of payment should be called "terms of payment" instead of "terms of sale."

Variance in Payment Terms

There is a wide variance in the various "terms of sales." They may range from requiring the payment of cash to permitting a customer considerable time within which to pay for the goods after he has received them. From a practical standpoint there is a direct relation between the terms of sale and the seller's perception of the buyer's ability to pay. If the seller has little or no confidence in the buyer's paying ability, he may require immediate payment of cash. On the other hand, the period for payment may be extended if the seller believes the customer to be a good credit risk when there is no apprehension about the ability of the customer to pay.

Cash Terms

There are several types of "cash" terms. A seller may require cash with the order. Cash may consist of the customer's check which is subject to clearance, a certified check or a cashier's check. The symbol for such transaction is C. B. D.—"cash before delivery." No delivery is required of the seller until the buyer has first made the payment.

The most common "cash" transaction is the one known by the symbol C. O. D.—"cash on delivery." In this transaction the delivery of the goods and the payment therefor are concurrent conditions. The seller makes delivery (generally by agent) and the buyer makes payment simultaneously. If there is no payment, no delivery need be made; if there is no delivery, no payment need be made.

Another form of cash transaction is the sight draft attached to a bill of lading (S. D. B. L.). The seller usually issues an order bill of lading, to his own order, indorses and forwards it attached to a sight draft to a bank in the buyer's city. The buyer pays the draft and obtains the bill of lading; with the bill of lading he obtains the goods and the bank transmits the funds to the seller. This form of transaction is frequently employed in some industries without respect to the customer's paying ability.

In "documentary sales" the buyer is required to pay cash upon tender of the documents without first inspecting the goods. The symbol for this transaction is C.A.D.—"cash against documents." Payment under these circumstances, however, is not regarded as an acceptance. The buyer has the right to inspect after making payment, and he reserves all remedies for breach by the seller.

When Does Title Pass?

When title to goods passes is often a complex legal question frequently not resolved in the contract of sale. The Uniform Commercial Code does not focus on title passing as did the Uniform Sales Act, but in separate sections deals with specific problems arising from the relationship between buyer and seller. For example, if the problem is one involving the rights of a seller to sold goods, the specific provisions of Section 2-402 control. Where goods are injured or destroyed, the Code states directly whether the buyer or seller should bear the risk.

In the event that a problem is not solved by a particular section of the Code, then, pursuant to Section 2-401, the following rules are established to determine questions of title:

1. Title cannot be acquired until the goods under the contract are identified.

2. Any retention by the seller of title in goods shipped or delivered is as a security interest.

3. Unless otherwise agreed, title passes to the buyer at the time and place in which the seller completes performance with respect to physical delivery of the goods. This rule obtains even though a document of title is to be delivered at a different time or place. If a contract requires a seller to send the goods to the buyer but does not require him to deliver at destination, title passes at the time and place of shipment. However, should a contract require delivery at destination, title passes at that time. If delivery is to be made without moving the goods, if the seller is to deliver a document of title, unless explicitly agreed to otherwise, title passes when and at the place at which such delivery occurs. If goods at the time of contracting are already identified and no documents are to be delivered, title passes at the time and place of contracting.

4. If the buyer refuses goods, title reverts to the seller. The buyer's rejection of the goods need not be justified but, whether justified or unjustified, the rejection must be made within a reasonable time and the seller must be notified. In *Chrysler Corp. v. Adamatic, Inc.,* 59 Wis. 2d 219, 208 N.W. 2d 97 (1973), the Court held that where a buyer had retained goods for six months, and did not notify the seller of his rejection, the buyer, by his conduct, had accepted the goods and completed the sale; thus, the buyer acquired full title.

Two Legal Situations

It is in respect to the passing of title that sellers should also look over their sales transactions where the terms are stated to be "cash terms." This expression has two possible legal interpretations. It may mean, for instance, that title is to pass, but that the seller gives notice that he is not waiving a lien (at least as long as it is possible to hold the lien under rules of applicable state law until the price is paid). It may, on the other hand, mean that title is to remain in the seller until the price is paid.

The consequences are entirely different in the two situations. In the latter case (title not to pass until price is paid) all the risks of ownership remain with the seller. He has the risk of loss, destruction, etc.; he cannot sue for the price but can only take steps for repossession. In the former situation, the risk is on the buyer, and while the seller cannot repossess once the lien has been waived, he can sue for the price. Whether the seller prefers one form of transaction over the other is a matter for his own judgment, but he must make certain that the intention is expressed clearly in the bargain, whatever the choice may be. The expression "cash terms" can be used very loosely.

Short Credit Terms

Much that passes for "cash terms," or sales purportedly on a cash basis, does not measure up to the elements of actual cash terms. Sellers who state their terms to be "cash" often contemplate a short period of credit. Custom and usage develop frequently to the end that the cash payment is waived. In such instances, the word "cash" becomes virtually meaningless because it acquires, paradoxically, the meaning of *credit* for a brief period. For example, the term "Settlement in 10 days by cash" would be considered a credit transaction though the terms are clearly stated as "cash." The seller has acquiesced in receiving payment in 10 days.

Where a credit transaction is actually intended or where the cash payment is waived, the title passes to the buyer and the seller does not have the right of lien or the right of possession once delivery is made. The seller may, however, if he clearly stipulates, reserve title until payment is made, but in such a case, the transaction would still not be technically a "cash" transaction.

The most common form of "terms of sale" (or payment) in commerce is the delivery of both possession and title to goods to the buyer upon the express or implied agreement of the latter to pay within a certain specified period. Thus, "terms, 30 days" means technically that the buyer's performance under the contract (making payment of the price) is not due until 30 days after invoice date. The seller, under such terms, relinquishes all right and title to the goods (except the right of stopping the goods in transit upon learning of the buyer's insolvency); furthermore the seller has no right of repossession but must resort to legal action for the price if the buyer fails to pay.

Offer of a Discount for "Cash"

Many sellers dangle a bait before the buyer to induce payment in a shorter period. The buyer is offered a "cash discount." For example, the terms may be stated: "2% 10 days—net 30 days." If the buyer pays within 10 days he may deduct 2% from the amount of the invoice. Using an illustration, let us say that the buyer receives an invoice for $1000, dated June 10, terms 2% 10 days—net 30 days. If he pays by June 20th he needs to send only $980 and that amount pays the invoice in full. This is also known as "privilege" to buyers or as a "cash premium." If we calculate the benefit or the disadvantage (according to whether the buyer takes the discount or not) in terms of interest, the rate is, to say the least, enormous. For example, if the buyer does not take the discount, he pays $20 for the use of the $980 for 20 days. This is equal to about 37% per year.

Terms of Payment

Agreements whereby the buyer may become entitled to receive a discount are construed and given effect in accordance with the intent of the parties.

The buyer must strictly comply with the terms of the agreement in order to become entitled to the discount. In some cases, under an agreement providing for a sale "on credit" the buyer will anticipate a discount by payment prior to the expiration of the credit term. Under the general rules applicable to contracts it would appear that such a tender by the buyer of payment before it is due with an appropriate deduction for prepayment or "discount" would constitute an offer to modify the contract with respect to terms of payment and the acceptance of such tender of payment by the seller would fully discharge the buyer's obligation for payment. On the contrary, however, where the contract of sale contemplated a cash transaction, it would appear that the seller's acceptance of less than the full purchase price would not bar suit to recover the unauthorized discount.

Varieties of Cash Discounts

Some sellers use terms known as E. O. M. (end of the month). This does not mean that payment is due at the end of the month in which the purchases are made. E. O. M. means that the buyer can wait until the end of the month during which the purchases are made before the credit terms (or the discount terms) become effective. E. O. M. terms are thus simply longer than the ordinary stated period terms (such as 30 days) because the reckoning of the 30 days is suspended until the first day of the month following. For example: add to the usual terms, "2% 10 days—net 30 days" the letters "E. O. M."—the effect is that the buyer has *all* of the month following the month of the purchases to pay, and he has until the 10th of that month to take the cash discount.

A modified form of these E. O. M. terms are the M. O. M. (middle of the month) terms. Here all sales made between the 1st and the 15th of a month are considered dated as of the 15th of the month (instead of the first of the following month as in the case of E. O. M. terms). All sales made between the 15th and the end of the month are dated as of the 1st of the following month. There are therefore two dates in each month from which the conventional credit period runs and from which the discount period is reckoned when cash discounts are offered. With 30 day M. O. M. terms, therefore, the credit terms are longer than the usual 30 day terms but shorter than in the case of E. O. M. terms.

The E. O. M. and M. O. M. terms are undoubtedly expedient where in certain lines of trade, purchases are frequent and in small amounts during a month's time.

"Prox" and "Ult" Terms

"Prox" or *proximo* terms resemble the E. O. M. terms. A certain specified day of the month following the month of the sales is set as the date for discount. When these terms are used the net day is generally stated too. For example, where the terms are "2% 10th prox." there is usually added, "net 30th." Thus where an invoice is dated June 19th, the buyer may take the discount if he makes payment on July 10th. The net amount of the invoice is payable on the 30th of July. "Prox" is the shortened form of *proximo* which is the Latin word for next. When there is a "prox" discount date and a customer pays in *advance* of that discount date he is, under some contracts, allowed a previous or *ultimo* ("ult") discount in *addition* to the regular discount.

Sellers and buyers sometimes make use of longer credit terms than the foregoing. In certain lines (dry goods, ready to wear) sellers sometimes grant "long" or "season" datings. These extraordinary credit periods run from 60 days to several months. There are certain benefits to a buyer in being able to obtain the goods at a known price and take possession of them months before they are due for payment. The disadvantage of having to store the goods during the long period when they are not marketable may be overcome in some cases by permitting the seller to hold them for shipping instructions.

Sellers in the case of long datings encourage buyers to pay sooner by offering extra discount advantages. It is common in these cases to see terms stated: "3% 10 days—2% 70 days—60 days extra." Thus the buyer may take 3% discount if he pays within 10 days, or 2% if he pays in 70 days. Furthermore the buyer is generally allowed a certain rate of discount if he pays between the 10th day and the 70th, in addition to the 2%, according to a scale based on the number of days by which the discount is anticipated. While it has been asserted by some writers that the 2% is actually a trade discount and not a cash discount, manufacturers have contended that the carrying of an account for the extra period is a cost.

"R. O. G." and "A. O. G."

In cataloguing all the various credit terms we include another lesser-known one in connection with cash discounts. This is known as "R. O. G.," or "A. O. G.," meaning "Receipt of Goods" and "Arrival of Goods" respectively. Thus the discount period is calculated not from the date of the invoice but from the time the goods are received or have arrived at the customer's location. For example, a credit term may be stated as, "2% 10 days R. O. G.—net 30 days." In cases where goods are shipped to a buyer so far distant from the seller's location that normally they would not reach the buyer before the discount period had expired, this overcomes the disadvantage which would otherwise be imposed on the buyer of having to make the payment (to save the discount) before seeing the merchandise.

It becomes additionally a competitive measure where producers or sellers of the same type of goods are located in the same market community as the buyer.

Another term, "A.D.F.," means "After Deducting Freight."

Ruling on Quantity Discounts

As a general rule quantity discounts are lawful so long as they reflect an actual cost savings to the seller. However, if cost savings cannot be established, and the burden of proof to establish them is on the seller, such discounts may be unlawful as a violation of the Robinson-Patman Act, provided the effect thereof *may be* substantially to lessen competition in interstate commerce, even though there is no *actual* showing of competitive damage or harm. (See discussion of Robinson-Patman Act, in Chapter 13.)

Validity of Cash Discounts

To encourage payment of a bill within a brief stated period of time, many sellers offer a percentage discount from the price (e.g., 2% if payment is made in 10 days). Although this is an established business practice, the issue has not been adjudicated in reported cases on the question as to whether cash discounts are in any way in violation of the Robinson-Patman Act. There are some cases decided by the Federal Trade Commission in which cash discounts were held unlawful but only because they were offered to certain purchasers and not to others.

If such discounts are offered to all customers on an equal basis, it appears that the practice is lawful. Therefore, sellers who engage in the practice should review their policies to be certain that such terms are offered equally to all customers. Moreover, a seller should be careful that a discount is not given to a customer *after* the discount period has elapsed since this may be prejudicial to other customers and therefore possibly be in violation of the Robinson-Patman Act.

Secured Transactions Superseded by the Uniform Commercial Code Article 9

The Uniform Commercial Code has been adopted by 49 states,[1] the District of Columbia, and the Virgin Islands. Article 9 of the Code, which is entitled Secured Transactions, covers all forms of secured transactions and title retention contracts and supersedes the previous legislation relating to these forms of secured transactions. The provisions of Article 9 are reproduced or summarized in the next chapter and an explanation of the Article is found in Chapter 1. Because security rights which were created prior to the enactment of the Code are still governed by the superseded statutes, and because their concepts are still prevalent under the Code, these security devices are discussed in this chapter. Moreover, in many states these forms of agreement are still used provided they are adapted to meet the requirements of the Code.

Among the most common forms of secured transactions which are discussed are bailments, consignments, leases, trust receipts, chattel mortgages, conditional sales, assignment of accounts receivable and factor's liens. Current use of these varieties of secured transactions should meet the requirements of the UCC.

BAILMENTS

A "bailment" has been defined as a delivery of personal property (such as goods, wares and merchandise) for some particular purpose, upon the agreement that it shall be redelivered to the person who delivered it, or otherwise dealt with, according to his directions, or kept until he reclaims it, as the case may be.[2] The following are examples of bailments: delivery of textiles for processing, delivery of securities to an agent for transfer, checking of personal property, merchandise in possession of mechanic for repair, storage of automobile, and rental of equipment.

The person who delivers personal property or chattels under such circumstances is called the "bailor" and the person to whom such property is delivered is called the "bailee."

It is of the essence of such a contract that it contemplates the return of the property bailed, and in this respect is to be distinguished from a sale. If by the contract there is no obligation to restore the specific article, and the bailee may instead return either money or other goods of equal value, the relationship created is that of debtor and creditor and not that of bailor and bailee.

The fundamental distinction between a sale and a bailment, therefore, is determined by whether there is an obligation to restore the thing delivered in the same or in an altered form, and if title passes. Whether a transaction is a sale or bailment is to be determined from all the circumstances. The substance of

---

[1] Louisiana has adopted only portions of the Code. *See* Chapter 1, *supra* p. 2-1.
[2] Black's Law Dictionary 129 (5th ed.). See *Chickering v. Bastress,* 130 Ill. 206, 22 N.E. 542, 543 (1889).

the agreement and not its form or the particular expressions employed in it is controlling and the intention of the parties must be ascertained from the terms of their contract.

It is important to determine whether a transaction constitutes a true bailment or a form of secured interest. In the case of a bailment, the bailee receives possession of the goods for a particular purpose or under an agreement to redeliver them to the bailor after the purpose has been fulfilled. While in a secured transaction of a conditional sale variety, possession is delivered upon an agreement to sell and buy, title to the property remaining in the meantime in the seller until payment of the price. In the latter case, it will be necessary that filing under Article 9 of the UCC be accomplished to protect the security interest of the bailor. See Chapter 7, *infra.*

CONSIGNMENTS

A common method of selling merchandise is to deliver it to an agent, merchant, or commission merchant, for sale by him as the agent of the consignor, title to the merchandise remaining at all times in the consignor. This is known as a consignment.

Such a transaction is distinguished from a conditional sale or contract of sale in that there is no intention that title to the goods shall ever pass to the consignee. The feature which vitally distinguishes a conditional sale from a consignment is that in the former the purchaser undertakes an absolute obligation to pay for the property, whereas in the latter there is nothing more than a bailment for sale. If no binding obligation to buy or pay for the goods arises out of the agreement alone, or out of the agreement taken with the facts, but instead, only an obligation to account to the consignor for the proceeds of the goods when sold, the relationship between the parties must be held to be not one of buyer and seller, but one of consignor and consignee. If, however, intention to pass title to the consignee does appear from the contract, the transaction is likely to be construed as a contract of conditional sale regardless of what it may be denominated by the parties, and in such event unless the statutory requirements for filing or recording the contract are complied with, the attempted reservation of title will be void.

In determining whether a contract is one of consignment, sale or conditional sale, the following elements should be considered: reservation of title to proceeds of sale, obligation to pay for goods received, right to fix selling price, and right to return or compel return of goods. While the presence or absence of any of these elements has a bearing on a determination of the nature of the transaction, no one element is conclusive. The entire agreement must be considered to determine the intention of the parties, but the court will be guided by these elements in its interpretation of intent.

Often a contract purporting to be one of consignment will be held to be a conditional sale by reason of the fact that, although an intention to retain title to the chattels is evident, the contract does not reserve title to the proceeds of sale. In *In re United States Electrical Supply Co.,* 2 F.2d 378 (S.D. Ill. 1924), the court refused to sustain a purported consignment contract and said: "There is no provision in the contract, such as is found in all valid agency or bailment contracts, that the proceeds of the goods, when sold, should be kept separate and apart by the consignee and should be the property of the consignor and remitted to the consignor." Id. at 380.

Where the terms of a contract impose on the receiver of the goods for resale the obligation to pay for the goods not sold, it will generally be held to be a sale or conditional sale and not a consignment. In *In re Thomas,* 231 F. 513 (S.D. Ga. 1916) the court held:

> It is often quite difficult to determine whether a contract is one of agency or consignment, or whether it is one of conditional sale. In order to determine this question, it is always necessary to consider all the terms of the contract, so as to ascertain the intention of the parties. If it is intended and provided that the customer shall be absolutely bound in all events to pay for the goods, the title being reserved in the vendor, then the contract is one of conditional sale. However, if the vendor merely delivers the goods to the customer for sale by him as agent of the vendor, the customer not being absolutely bound by the contract to pay for the goods, then the contract is one of consignment for sale or an agency to sell; it is a mere bailment.

The importance that the question of liability for payment for unsold goods has in the determination of the nature of the contract is illustrated in *John Deere Plow Co. v. Mowry,* 222 F. 1 (6th Cir. 1915). In *Mowry,* although the contract provided for reservation of title to the goods, and to the proceeds of sale, the court held that the contract was not one of consignment since other provisions of the contract imposed upon the purchaser an absolute liability for payment for the goods whether he sold them or not.

The line of demarcation between contracts of sale and contracts of consignment or agency is, in many cases, shady and uncertain; thus, such an agreement should in all cases be drafted by competent attorneys and the terms of the contract itself should be strictly complied with if the object intended is to be accomplished.

May Require Return of Goods

A distinction should be made between a consignment contract (in which there is no obligation to pay for the goods unsold) and a contract of *sale or return.* In the latter case the purchaser buys the goods and acquires title to them but has the option of returning the goods within a designated time if unsold.

Although there are cases to the contrary, the weight of authority is to the effect that a provision in the contract permitting the consignee to fix the price at which the goods are resold and to retain the difference between the consignor's list price and the sales price, does not make the contract one of sale.

A provision frequently found in consignment contracts and distinguishing them from contracts of conditional sale is the right of the consignor to require the return of all the unsold goods. This express provision need not be included in the contract in order to make it a consignment contract for if it is apparent from the terms of the contract that a consignment is intended, the consignor will be entitled to a return of his goods on demand or at the termination of the contract. However, where the contract contains a provision to the contrary, such as where at the termination of the contract the buyer is to purchase the unsold goods at the market price, the agreement may be construed as a sale rather than a consignment.

Obligations of Consignee

No special form of consignment contract is required, nor must the contract contain any particular phraseology. A consignee is a special form of agent, and like other agents is required to exercise a reasonable degree of skill and care in the management of the consignor's property. He is not an insurer but is responsible for damage caused by his own negligence. Like other agents, he may not delegate his authority, nor may he pledge goods consigned to him as security for his own debts. He is bound by the instructions received from the consignor in regard to the manner of selling the property consigned to him, and is liable for any loss caused by disobedience of his instructions. It is not part of his duty to insure the goods in his possession unless he has contracted to do so.

A consignee has a lien on the goods consigned to him to the extent that he has made advances upon them or has otherwise incurred expense in their care. He also has a lien for commissions owed him by the consignor. The lien is valid only while the goods are in his possession but attaches both to the consigned merchandise and to the proceeds of goods sold for the consignor's account.

UCC Provisions

In a true consignment, the consignor does not reserve any security interest, and technically he does not have to comply with the provisions of the UCC. However, if a consignor wishes to protect his interest against other creditors of the consignee, he is well advised to follow the filing and notice requirements of the Code.

The question of consignment is dealt with in three places of the Code: Sections 2-326(3), 9-114 and 9-408. Under Section 2-326(3), goods which are consigned to a consignee are subject to the claims of creditors unless the consignor (1) complies with applicable law providing for the consignor's interest to be evidenced by a sign, or (2) establishes that the person conducting the business is generally known by his creditors to be substantially engaged in selling the goods of others, or (3) complies with the filing provisions of Article 9.

Under Section 9-144, a consignor is required to give notice in writing to the holder of a security interest if the holder has filed a financing statement covering the same type of goods before the date of the filing made by the consignor the notice must be received by the holder of the security interest within five years before consignee receives possession of the goods. The notification must characterize the delivery of the goods as a consignment and must describe them by item or type. This section provides that the notice provisions of Section 9-312(3) apply in cases of consignment.

Section 9-408 permits a financing statement to use the term "consignor" rather than "secured party" and expressly provides for filing under the Code even for consignments which are not security interests.

LEASES

According to the weight of authority, where possession of personal property or chattels is transferred under a contract in the form of a lease which reserves as rent a sum equivalent in the stated rental period to the price of the property and which provides that on compliance with lease terms or on the exercise of an option which it contains, title shall pass to the lessee, but that on noncompliance the lessor may retake possession, the transaction is generally considered to be a conditional sale and not a bailment or hiring.

A true lease of personal property, as distinguished from a lease which is in the nature of a security interest, does not need to be filed under the Uniform Commercial Code. Furthermore, a provision in a lease permitting filing is not itself a factor in determining whether or not a lease is a security agreement. In *Rollins Communications, Inc. v. Georgia Institute of Real Estate, Inc.*, 140 Ga. App. 448, 231 S.E. 2d 397 (1976), the Georgia Court of Appeals declared that the real purpose of the lease, not its wording, determines whether or not it is for security. Although the lease at issue contained provisions for filing and executing a financing statement, the court found these factors did not convert the lease into a security agreement. Since the lease created an option to purchase the leased equipment for more than nominal consideration, it was not a security agreement according to the court.

In order to avoid any problems about whether or not the lease constitutes a security interest or is a true lease, the lessor is advised to file under Article 9 of the Code. Section 9-408 specifically permits filing of financing statements in such situations.

TRUST RECEIPTS

Trust receipts were originally used in connection with the importation of merchandise and generally are still used in connection with such transactions. In recent years, however, the use of trust receipts in domestic trade has increased considerably. They are used principally in connection with the purchase of automobiles and household equipment from manufacturers by their dealers.

The trust receipt transaction, in principle, operates in this manner. The buyer places his order with the seller, and the goods thereafter are shipped to the buyer. The purchase price is paid by a bank or other lending agency and usually it receives the bill of lading or other document of title to the property. The seller then ceases his part in the transaction; the buyer is in possession of the goods, and the bank in possession of the documents of title. In the course of the transaction the buyer (trustee) issues a trust receipt to the bank (entruster) which permits the buyer to retain possession of the goods as trustee for the bank.

The law governing trust receipts had been codified by the National Conference of Commissioners on Uniform State Laws in the Uniform Trust Receipts Act. The Uniform Commercial Code covers trust receipts and supersedes the Uniform Trust Receipts Act in all the states where the Code is now in effect. Under the Code, trust receipts are a variety of secured transactions governed by Article 9, which are discussed in Chapter 7, *infra*.

CONDITIONAL SALES CONTRACTS

The Uniform Conditional Sales Act, which is no longer in effect in any jurisdiction, defines a conditional sales contract as "any contract for the sale of goods under which possession is delivered to the buyer and the property in the goods is to vest in the buyer at a subsequent time upon the payment of part or all of the price, . . . or any contract for the bailment or leasing of goods by which the bailee or lessee contracts to pay as compensation a sum substantially equivalent to the value of the goods, and by which it is agreed that the bailee or lessee is bound to become . . . the owner of such goods upon full compliance with the terms of contract." [1]

The basic concepts of conditional sales agreements are still used under the Code in arranging security agreements; therefore, an understanding of how conditional sales contracts operate is important.

Form of Contract

In some jurisdictions, a conditional sales contract is valid and effective against third parties, even if the contract was oral and neither filed nor recorded. In the majority of jurisdictions, however, the contract had to be in writing and filed or recorded by the seller in order to protect the interests of the seller against the rights of various third parties. In many states, the contract is also valid, though not filed or recorded, against those third parties who have actual knowledge of the reservation of title to the goods in the seller.

In those states which require the conditional sales contract to be in writing, it is also required that the contract be signed by one or both of the parties thereto. Some states require an acknowledgment by one or both of the parties or require that the signatures of one or two witnesses be affixed to the contract.

In preparing the conditional sales contract, it is important that the property to be sold is described in language that is clear enough to identify it.

Sales of Fixtures

One of the most troublesome problems in the law of conditional sales has been that regarding fixtures. Although in most states a conditional seller was permitted to sell fixtures under a title retention contract, often fixtures are of such nature that when they are attached to real property they take on the character of real property, and a reservation of title to the fixtures by the conditional seller was not valid against purchasers, encumbrancers or lienors acquiring an interest in such real property. The general rule is that a fixture retains its characteristic as personal property if it is so attached to the realty that it can be removed without material injury to the freehold. As between the buyer and seller it is generally held that, regardless of the nature of the affixation, the seller's retention of title is valid against the buyer and it is only subsequent purchasers of the realty, lienors, mortgagees and other encumbrancers who may dispute the seller's claims.

Generally, if the fixtures can be removed without impairing the usefulness of the property, the seller's retention of title will generally be upheld. In some cases the courts hold that where the chattels affixed to the realty are such that, even though their removal will not injure the realty, it will greatly affect the usefulness of the building, such reservation of title will not be upheld.

Under Article 9 of the Code, a secured party can remove collateral attached as fixtures but is obligated to reimburse the owner for any injury caused by such removal (§ 9-313 (8)).

---

[1] For a reprint of the Act, see I. Mariash, A Treatise on the Law of Sales 807 (1930).

Where Goods Are for Resale

In many states the law did not permit the seller to reserve title to conditional sold goods where such goods were to be resold by the buyer in the course of his business to third parties. In most cases it was held that such an attempted reservation of title was invalid as against a purchaser from the buyer. Subject to the limitations promulgated under Section 9-307, this principle of law has survived the enactment of the UCC. In many cases, the seller was permitted to sell to a buyer under a contract which provided that the buyer would account to the seller for the proceeds from the resale of such property. However, where no accounting was required of the conditional buyer, the sale was considered to be an absolute sale and not a conditional sale.

In most states it was permissible for either party to assign his rights under a conditional sales contract unless there was an express prohibition in the contract itself against such assignment.

Since the conditional seller retains title to the conditionally sold goods, the question arises as to who bears the loss in the event of the destruction of the property. Under the Uniform Act and in a majority of the states the rule was that the risk of loss was on the buyer unless the parties contracted otherwise.

CHATTEL MORTGAGES

The Uniform Commercial Code has superseded the laws relating to chattel mortgages in the states in which it has been adopted. Under the Code no distinction is made between chattel mortgages and conditional sales, both being secured transactions to which Article 9 is applicable. Our discussion of the Law of Chattel Mortgages in this chapter is limited to Louisiana, which has not adopted the Code, and to transactions concluded prior to the enactment of the Code. In some states, however, chattel mortgages are still used as a form of security agreement.

In those cases where the contract price is payable in instalments, the state law governing retail instalment sales, if any, may be applicable to the transaction. In such cases the transaction must comply with the provisions of the Retail Instalment Sales Law in addition to complying with the applicable provisions of the law governing chattel mortgages. See Chapter 8, *infra,* on Retail Instalment Sales Laws for the provisions governing instalment sales contracts.

Although in many respects chattel mortgages and conditional bills of sale may be similar, there are important differences which should not be overlooked in using the chattel mortgage form of title retention contract. In those states where the common law or title theory prevails, a chattel mortgage effects the transfer of title to the mortgagee; title reverts back to the mortgagor upon payment or performance of the obligations referred to in the mortgage. Under the title theory, the mortgagee's right of title to the property becomes absolute upon default by the mortgagor. In some states the so-called lien theory prevails. In these states the effect of the chattel mortgage is to give the mortgagee a lien upon the property to which the mortgagor retains title and in the event of a default by the mortgagor, the mortgagee is entitled to maintain foreclosure proceedings against the mortgaged property.

It is the general practice to use a contract of conditional sale in connection with the purchase and sale of goods and to use a chattel mortgage to cover property belonging to the mortgagor used to secure the repayment of loans. However, in some cases the seller will take back a purchase money chattel mortgage from the buyer which serves the same purpose as a conditional bill of sale. It is immaterial whether the parties describe the instrument as a chattel mortgage or a conditional bill of sale, if in fact the terms of the agreement effect a contrary result. The important distinction between the two is that in the case of a conditional bill of sale, title remains in the seller and does not pass to the buyer until fulfillment of the terms of the contract; whereas, in the case of a chattel mortgage, title is either originally in the mortgagor or passes from the seller to the buyer and thereafter the buyer executes an instrument conveying the title back to the seller or gives a lien upon the property in order to secure the purchase price or other payment.

The chattel mortgage is usually a more formal instrument than the conditional contract of sale. In most states the mortgage is required to be signed and acknowledged by the mortgagor and in some cases the attestation of witnesses is also required. In many states it is essential to the validity of a chattel mortgage that it be accompanied by a so-called affidavit of good faith which is filed or recorded with the mortgage. The contents of this affidavit and sometimes the required form are set forth in the statutes of the various states. Some states require an affidavit of good faith. In some cases this is to be made by the mortgagor, in others by the mortgagee and sometimes it must be made by both parties. Usually a failure to comply with this requirement will render the mortgage void except as between the immediate parties.

Many statutes require that the mortgage be acknowledged, witnessed or proved. Mortgages are witnessed by having one or more persons, as the statute requires, sign an instrument after having observed the signature of the mortgagor. An instrument is "proved" by having a witness sign the instrument and then having the witness go before a judicial officer, notary public or other authorized officer and testify to the execution of the instrument. An instrument is acknowledged by the signator appearing before a notary public and swearing under oath that he signed the document.

In order to be valid as against the rights of various third parties, the mortgage must be either filed or recorded as required by the UCC, unless the mortgagee has possession of the mortgaged property.

The following is a summary of the law of Louisiana where the law of chattel mortgages is still in effect:

LOUISIANA

1. AFFIDAVIT OF GOOD FAITH REQUIRED.—No.
2. ACKNOWLEDGE.—In order to affect third persons, mortgage must be by authentic act, i.e., executed before a notary in the presence of two competent witnesses, or private act duly authenticated in any manner provided by law.
3. WITNESSES.—Yes, two.
4. RECORD OR FILE.—Record multiple original or a certified copy.
5. WHERE RECORD OR FILE.—In parish where the mortgaged property is to be located according to the terms of the instrument, and if mortgagor is domiciled in the state, in the parish of his domicile.
6. RECORDING OR FILING OFFICE.—Office of the Recorder of Mortgages.
7. RECORDING OR FILING FEE.—$2; except for Parish of New Orleans, $1 first 100 words, 50¢ for each additional 100 words.
8. DURATION.—Five years from the date of execution or one year from the date of the last instalment payment, whichever is later.

SECURED TRANSACTIONS 6–9

9. FAILURE TO RECORD OR FILE.—If mortgage is not filed or recorded and possession of property not delivered to mortgage, void all third persons.

10. PROVISION FOR RENEWAL.—Yes, for two year periods. Fee, $2.

11. CLASSES OF PROPERTY WHICH MAY BE MORTGAGED.—Any and every kind of movable property and any of the following masses or assemblages of things: lumber, logs, staves, crossties, tiles, bricks, cotton seed and by-products, livestock and poultry.

12. MORTGAGES ON STOCKS OF MERCHANDISE.—Valid if provisions of Bulk Sales Law are complied with.

13. FIXTURES.—Where chattels subject to a mortgage are affixed to realty so as to be immovable the lien and remedies of the mortgage remain unimpaired. This is so even though the realty is subsequently sold or mortgaged.

14. CANCELLATION.—When mortgage is paid off or satisfied it may be cancelled in any manner provided by law for the cancellation of real property mortgages. The effect of a chattel mortgage shall cease if the inscription thereof has not been renewed in the same manner in which it was first made by the Recorder of Mortgages within five years from the date of the execution of the mortgage. Fee, $1.

15. REMARKS.—Mortgage must be in writing, even to be effective between the parties thereto, and must set out a full description of the property so that it may be identified. The obligation secured must also be described and the location of the property, exact sum and maturity date stated. A mortgage granted on any mass or assemblage of things, whether owned at the time of execution or to be acquired thereafter, and on such additions as may come from natural increase or otherwise, should be described as all of a particular class or classes or grade or kind or type or species or dimensions to be kept at a certain location. It is unlawful for the resident of any parish to purchase any mortgageable movable property from any nonresident of such parish without first obtaining an affidavit from the nonresident that there is no mortgage. Such a purchase without obtaining an affidavit renders the purchaser personally liable to the creditor for the debt secured by the property. It is unlawful for the mortgagor with intent to defeat the mortgage, and without the consent of the mortgagee, to sell, dispose of, conceal or injure the property or move it from the parish where it was located when the mortgage was executed. Such conduct besides rendering the mortgagor liable to fine and imprisonment matures and accelerates the mortgage and the obligation which it secures.

16. SPECIAL PROVISIONS FOR MORTGAGES ON HOME APPLIANCES AND/OR EQUIPMENT.—"Where any person, firm or corporation (including but not restricted to any bank, insurance company or other agency or institution) makes or has made a loan to any party, and said loan is secured by a vendor's lien and privilege and/or first mortgage on real estate, such loan or a new loan or a separate loan may be secured by a vendor's lien and privilege and/or mortgage on home appliances and/or equipment, including and restricted to heating, cooking, laundry, cooling, refrigerating, ventilating, airconditioning, washing, drying, or storage units, equipment or systems, provided such home appliances and/or unit, equipment or systems are located in, on or attached to the real estate to which the said vendor's lien and privilege and/or first mortgage applies and are owned by the owner of said real estate."

(a). REQUIREMENTS.—Mortgage or lien may be created by authentic act, either including the real estate or separately. Recordation of such authentic act in the same manner as a mortgage on real estate shall be binding on third persons.

(b). REMARKS.—The Act makes it a misdemeanor for any person to remove without written consent of the mortgagee, conceal, damage or destroy mortgaged home appliances or equipment until the debt has been paid in full.

17. MISCELLANEOUS.—Crops: No statutory provisions for mortgaging however farmer is given right to pledge or pawn crops to secure debts incurred in production for the current year; pledge must be in writing and be recorded in a book kept for that purpose in the office of the recorder of mortgages where the crop is to be produced. Fixtures: special provisions regarding tanks and buildings under U.S. Farm Storage Facility Loan Program. Motor Vehicles: Vehicle Certificate of Title Law governs. Watercraft: provisions regarding ships, steamboats, and other vessels.

ASSIGNMENT OF ACCOUNTS RECEIVABLE

The title acquired by an assignee of accounts receivable is valid as against the assignor upon the mere execution and delivery of the instrument of assignment.

The following is a summary of the laws governing assignment of accounts receivable in Louisiana, the only state in which the Code is not in effect. In all other states, accounts receivable transactions are governed by the Uniform Commercial Code.

LOUISIANA

1. *Statute Applicable:* Any assignment for valuable consideration of an account receivable. "Account receivable" or "Account" means and includes any indebtedness or part thereof due to, arising out of, or acquired in connection with any business, profession, occupation or undertaking of the assignor, carried on wholly or partly in the state, including but not limited to the sale of goods, performance of services, or the leasing of property. It does not include indebtedness due to, arising out of, or acquired in connection with claims in tort or indebtedness evidenced either by a promissory note or notes or by any other instrument creating a security right in the indebtedness.
2. *Requirements of Assignment:* Must be in writing.
3. *Notice to Debtor:* Not necessary.
4. *Filing:* Required.
5. *Where Filed:* Office of the Recorder of Conveyances of the parish in which the assignor's place of business is located. In Parish of Orleans record in "Sale of Movables Books."
6. *When Filed:* Anytime before or after the assignment but the assignment is not effective as to anyone other than the assignor and the assignee until it is filed.
7. *Filing Fee:* Usually $1—can vary locally by parish.
8. *What Notice of Assignment Must State:*

NOTICE OF ASSIGNMENT

Date . . . .
. . . . has made an assignment of accounts receivable to . . . .
in accordance with the Louisiana Assignment of Accounts Receivable Act.

The Assignor's place of business is . . . .
(Street Address
. . . .
City   Parish).
The principal place of business or business mailing address of the Assignee is . . . .
(Street Address
. . . .
City   Parish).
. . . .
Assignor
. . . .
Assignee

9. *When Assignment Perfected:* Within the effective period of a statement of assignment made and filed, the assignment is deemed to have been perfected when made. The statement becomes effective when filed.
10. *Payment by Debtor to Person Other Than Assignee:* If in good faith before notice from assignee, debtor may pay assignor or any other assignee or successor in interest.
11. *Effect of Assignments:* Enforceable against all other creditors or persons attaching, garnishing or levying except one who has through judicial proceedings perfected a superior lien on the account.
12. *Defenses of Debtor:* No provision.
13. *Duration of Effectiveness of Filed Statement:* Two years unless renewed in same manner as when first made.
14. *Cancellation:* May be cancelled by consent of assignee evidenced by any simple form of release. Filing fee: Usually 50¢—Can vary locally by parish.

FACTORS' LIEN LAWS

Until the beginning of the 1900's the term "factor" was generally understood to mean a selling agent, and as such the word was a commonplace one in the importing business, in textiles, and in commodities like cotton and other agricultural products. The factor not only sold merchandise for his principal, but in some cases made loans on the merchandise prior to sale. Since the merchandise was usually in the possession of the factor, this possession gave the factor a common law or nonstatutory lien on the merchandise as security for his commissions and for any loans that he might make.

In the textile industry, a short time prior to the First World War, the functions of a factor became divided. Some factors gave up the financial side of their business and restricted themselves to selling, although to a certain extent some still make loans against merchandise and discount sales. Such factors are now known as "commission merchants." The other factors discontinued selling and devoted themselves exclusively to credit checking and to making loans against inventory and accounts receivable. This latter type of business in the textile industry retained the old designation of "factoring." In addition to textiles this method of financing production and sales has now extended to furniture, shoes, floor coverings, heating equipment, and other industries.

Statutes enabling the factor to obtain a lien on goods pledged as security without taking possession were enacted by states which did not have the Code. While the statutes varied somewhat in their provisions, their general scope was as follows:

If provided by written agreement factors may have a continuing general lien upon all merchandise consigned or pledged to them and upon the proceeds of the sale of such merchandise, for all loans advanced and charges for the account of the owner, and providing that a notice of a lien setting forth certain required information, concerning the factor, the owner, or borrower and the merchandise, be filed or recorded with local authorities.

On the payment or satisfaction of the indebtedness secured by the lien, the factor on the request of anyone interested in the merchandise must sign and acknowledge a certificate setting forth such payment, on presentation of which the recording officer must note satisfaction.

Factors' lien laws have been superseded by the Uniform Commercial Code, and Louisiana, which has not adopted the Code in its entirety, does not have a Factors' Lien law.

Secured Transactions Under Article 9 of the Uniform Commercial Code

7

Article 9 of the Uniform Commercial Code governs all transactions in which a security interest in personal property is created. An explanation of this Article appears in Chapter 1, beginning on page 1-15. The provisions reproduced here are from the official 1972 version of the Uniform Commercial Code as approved by the American Law Institute and the National Conference of Commissioners on Uniform State Laws. Footnotes are supplied in the summary to denote some of the major differences among the codes of the jurisdictions which have enacted this uniform legislation. The following jurisdictions have not adopted the 1972 amendments: Indiana, Kentucky, Louisiana, Missouri, New Mexico, South Carolina, and Vermont.

INDEX TO SECURED TRANSACTIONS UNDER THE CODE

ACCOUNT, STATEMENT OF 7-26
AFTER-ACQUIRED PROPERTY .7-25
AGREEMENT (See Security
    Agreement) 7-2
APPLICATION OF ARTICLE 7-4
ASSIGNMENT OF RIGHTS IN
    SECURITY 7-14
    defenses 7-23
    filing 7-9
    fees ....7-9 et seq.
    identification 7-23
    modification of contract 7-23
    notification 7-23
    prohibition ineffective 7-23
    proof 7-23
BUYER 7-18
COLLATERAL
    brought into state..............7-10
    disposition 7-18, 7-19, 7-25
    list of 7-10, 7-26
    possession by secured party 7-9
        duties and rights 7-14, 7-25
        perfecting security interest 7-7
    release of....................7-14
    use 7-25
COMMINGLED GOODS 7-22

CONTINUATION STATEMENTS .7-12
CREATION OF SECURITY
    INTEREST 7-2
DEFAULT......................7-27
DEFENSES (See Assignment)
DEFINITION OF TERMS (used in
    Summary of Filing
    Requirements) 7-33
DURATION OF FILING (See
    Financing Statement)
FILING
    for requirements generally ..7-2 et seq.
    also see Financing Statements and
    other specific headings.
FINANCING STATEMENT
    amendments 7-10
    errors.......................7-9
    filing
        duration..................7-12
        error 7-11
        fees.....................7-13
        place ....7-34 et seq.
        requirement of ....7-33 et seq.
        time in which to file 7-4
        where to file ....7-34 et seq.
    forms 7-5–7-7
    requisites 7-10

FUTURE ADVANCES 7-25
INFORMATION FURNISHED BY
    AND OBTAINABLE FROM
    FILING OFFICER 7-30
JURISDICTION
    multiple state transactions 7-15
LAPSE OF FINANCING
    STATEMENT 7-12
OUTLINE 7-2
PERFECTION OF SECURITY
    INTEREST 7-2, 7-8
    instruments or documents 7-8
    when filing is required 7-7
    when perfected 7-8
PRIORITY
    commingled goods 7-22
    conflicting interest in same col-
        lateral 7-19
    fixtures 7-20
    goods affixed to other goods 7-22
installed property 7-20, 7-22
liens 7-17
    chattel paper 7-8, 7-17
    documents 7-19
    goods 7-18
    nonnegotiable instruments 7-18
    proceeds 7-23
    processed goods 7-22
    subordination 7-23
    unperfected security interest 7-17
PROPERTY BROUGHT INTO
    STATE 7-10, 7-15
RELEASE 7-14
SECURITY AGREEMENT 7-2
STATEMENT OF ACCOUNT 7-26
SUMMARY OF FILING
    REQUIREMENTS BY
    STATES ....7-33 et seq.
TERMINATION 7-13, 7-29
THE 1962 CODE 7-27

OUTLINE OF MECHANICS OF SECURED TRANSACTIONS

As discussed in Chapter 1 and the following sections this chapter, Article 9 of the Uniform Commercial Code consolidates all of the various devices previously used to create a security interest into a single form known as a Secured Transaction. The lender no longer need be concerned with which of the many security devices best suits his particular circumstance. Despite the fact that the Uniform Commercial Code has simplified the creation of security interest, confusion often arises over the mechanical aspects of creating and perfecting a security interest. The following is intended to be a practical guide to assist the secured lender in dealing with the mechanics of creating and perfecting a security interest.

Creating the Security Interest

The "Security Interest" is created by an agreement, called a "Security Agreement," between the secured party and the debtor. A general form for this agreement appears in Chapter 33, Specimen Credit and Other Instruments. The essential portion of the agreement is the statement "Debtor hereby creates a security interest in favor of *(secured party)* in the following property: *(insert description)*." After entering into such an agreement, the secured party is entitled to take possession of the identified personal property in the event of default by the debtor.

Perfecting the Security Interest

The Secured Party can protect his Security Interest against the claims of third parties by taking possession of the collateral or by filing notice that he has a Security Interest in the property covered by the Security Agreement with the appropriate filing officer. This is accomplished by filing a Financing Statement. Failure to file a financing statement does not invalidate the security agreement. It merely provides an opportunity for another secured creditor who files earlier to obtain priority.

The Uniform Commercial Code sets forth a form of a Financing Statement which is reproduced on page 7-5. The states of Massachusetts, New Hampshire and New Jersey have adopted a variation thereof set forth on page 7-6. The form of financing statement used by states which have not adopted the 1972 amendments to the UCC is set forth on page 7-7. In addition to the general requirements set forth by the Code, many states have given the Secretary of State or other filing officer the power to prescribe an official or approved form. Often the filing fees are greater if an unofficial form is used. We have not reproduced all of the official forms used in the various states because the Secured Party must obtain such a form and very often it can only be obtained in the state in which it is to be filed. It is suggested that when a Secured Transaction is first contemplated, the prospective secured party write to the Secretary of State of the state in which the Financing Statement is to be filed and request that he either forward copies of the Financing Statement or the address of the stationer from which the Financing Statement can be purchased. In this manner the prospective secured party can be assured that he is using the official Financing Statement form for the state in which he is filing. Once the Financing Statement has been obtained, completed and executed by both the Secured Party and the debtor, it must be filed. For details on how to complete and execute the Financing Statement see page 7-4. In most states the place or places in which the Financing Statement must be filed depend upon the type of property which is used as collateral. The classifications into which goods are placed for this purpose are as follows:

Accessions—Security interest in goods before they are installed in or affixed to other goods.

Accounts—Rights to payment for goods sold or leased or for services rendered not evidenced by an instrument of chattel paper, whether or not they have been earned by performance.

Chattel Paper—A writing which evidences both a monetary obligation and a security interest in or a lease of specific goods.

Consumer Goods—Goods which are used or bought for use primarily in personal, family or household purposes.

Documents—Documents of Title, including receipts issued in connection with the storage of goods under Government Bonds (§ 7-201).

Equipment—Goods which are used or brought for use primarily in business or by a debtor which is a nonprofit organization or a governmental subdivision or agency, or if the goods are not included in the definitions of inventory, farm products or consumer goods.

Farm Products—Goods which are crops or livestock of supplies used or produced in farming operations or goods which are products of crops or livestock in their unmanufactured states, and if they are in the possession of a debtor engaged in raising, fattening, grazing or other farm operations. If goods are "farm products" they are neither equipment nor inventory. [1]

Fixtures—Goods which have become so related to particular real estate that an interest in them arises under real estate law.

General Intangibles—Any personal property other than goods, accounts, contract rights, chattel paper, documents and instruments. Goodwill, literary rights, rights to performance, copyrights, trademarks and patents are all included.

Instrument—A negotiable instrument, or a security or any other writing which evidences a right to the payment of money and is not itself a security agreement or lease and is of a type which is in ordinary course of business transferred by delivery with any necessary indorsement or assignment.

Inventory—Goods which are held for sale or lease or furnished or to be authorized under contracts of service, or materials used or consumed for business purposes. Inventory is not to be classified as equipment.

---

[1] In Arkansas the definition includes fish.

Upon ascertaining which classification fits the collateral covered by the Security Agreement, the Financing Statement should be filed in the appropriate office set forth in the following state by state summary of filing requirements. The filing should be as soon as possible after Security Interest is created.

1. APPLICATION. This article applies to any transaction, regardless of its form, which is intended to create a security interest in personal property or fixtures including goods, documents, instruments, general intangibles, chattel paper, accounts or contract rights or any financing sale of accounts or chattel paper. It does not apply to a security interest subject to a statute of the United States regulating rights of parties to, and third parties affected by, transactions in particular types of property; or to a landlord's lien; or to a lien given by statute or other rule of law for services or material (except regarding priority rights); or to assignment of wages; or to a transfer by a government or governmental subdivision or Agency; or to a transfer of accounts as part of a sale of the business out of which they arose; or to a transfer of a right to payment under a contract to an assignee who is to perform the contract; or to a transfer of a single account to an assignee in whole or partial satisfaction of a preexisting indebtedness; or to a transfer of an interest or claim on a policy of insurance, except as provided with respect to proceeds (Section 9-306) and priorities in proceeds (Section 9-312); a right represented by a judgment (other than a judgment taken on a right to payment which was collateral); or to any right of setoff; or to a transfer of a tort claim; or of an interest in any deposit account except as provided with respect to proceeds and priorities in proceeds; or, except to the extent that provision is made for fixtures in Section 9-313 to the creation or transfer of an interest in or lien upon real estate, including a lease or rents thereunder. (Sections 9-102, 9-104) The Article does not strictly apply to true leases of personal property. In such instance, however, better practice suggests that a financing statement be filed to avoid the question as to whether a security interest was retained by the lessor.

2. CREATION OF SECURITY INTEREST—GENERAL VALIDITY OF SECURITY AGREEMENT. Except as otherwise provided by this Act a security agreement is effective according to its terms between the parties, against purchasers of the collateral and against creditors. Nothing in this Article validates any charge or practice illegal under any statute or regulation thereunder governing usury, small loans, retail instalment sales, or the like, or extends the application of any such statute or regulation to any transaction not otherwise subject thereto. (Sec. 9-201) [2]

3. INSTRUMENT TO BE FILED. A financing statement must be signed by the debtor [3] to perfect a security interest, except as set forth in 5 below. A

---

[2] In California, no nonpossessory security interest other than a purchase money security interest may be taken in the inventory of a retail merchant except in inventory comprised of durable goods with a minimum unit retail value of $500 or comprised of certain enumerated articles.

[3] In New York, the security agreement can authorize the secured party to sign the financing statement on behalf of the debtor.

NOTE: Consumer instalment sales and consumer loans present special problems of a nature which make special regulation of them inappropriate in a general commercial codification. Many states now regulate such loans and sales under small loan acts, retail instalment selling acts and

(Footnote continued bottom next page)

copy of the security agreement is sufficient for filing as a financing statement if it contains the requisite information and is signed by the debtor. A carbon photographic or other reproduction of a security agreement or a financing statement may qualify as a financing statement if the security agreement so provides or if the original has been filed in the same state. (Sec. 9-402)

4. FORM OF FINANCING STATEMENT. A statement substantially in the following form is sufficient to comply with the statute. (Sec. 9-402(3)):

FINANCING STATEMENT

Form [4] for states which have adopted the 1972 Code:

Name of debtor [5] (or assignor) ....
Address [6] ....
Name of secured party (or assignee) ....
Address ....

1. This financing statement covers the following types (or items) of property: (Describe) ....
2. (If collateral is crops) The above described crops are growing or are to be grown on: [7] (Describe Real Estate) ....
3. (If applicable) The above goods are to become fixtures on [8] (Describe Real Estate) .... and this financing statement is to be filed (for record) in the real estate records. (If the debtor does not have an interest of record) The name of a record owner is ....
4. (If products of collateral are claimed) Products of the collateral are also covered.

(use whichever   ....
is Signature of Debtor (or Assignor)
applicable) ....
Signature of Secured Party (or Assignee)

---

the like. While this Article applies generally to security interests in consumer goods, it is not designed to supersede such regulatory legislation. Nor is this Article designed as a substitute for small loan Acts or retail instalment selling Acts in any state which does not presently have such legislation. See Sec. 9-203(2) of the Code.

In those cases where the contract price is payable in instalments, the state law governing retail instalment sales, if any, is applicable to the transaction. In such cases the transaction must comply with the provisions of the Retail Instalment Sales Law in addition to complying with the provisions of this Article.

Item 3 does not appear on the California form.

[4] The reader is cautioned that slight deviations from the Uniform form exist in most states. Since these variations are for the most part cosmetic in nature, and since the official form in the relevant state is easy to obtain, the bulk of the variations were not reflected here.

[5] California has space for indication of trade names, although failure to do so will not damage an otherwise adequate financing statement. The statute provides that a financing statement covering timber, minerals or certain accounts, as specified, or filed as a fixture filing, is required to contain specified information in order to be effective.

[6] Utah urges that the debtor's social security number or the federal employer's identification number if the debtor is not an individual be indicated on the statement to facilitate indexing.

[7] Not in the form for Washington.

[8] Where appropriate substitute either "The above timber is standing on . . . ." or "The above minerals or the like (including oil and gas) or accounts will be financed at the wellhead or minehead of the well or mine located on . . . ."

FINANCING STATEMENT

Form in Massachusetts, New Hampshire, New Jersey statutes.

For Filing Officer Use
File No. ....
Date and Hour of Filing ....

Maturity Date (if any) ....
(Last Name First)
Name of Debtor [9] ....Address ....
Name(s) of Other Debtor(s) (if any)
................................Address ....
................................Address ....
Name of Secured Party ....Address ....
Name(s) of Other Secured Party or Parties (if any)
................................Address ....
................................Address ....

1. This financing statement covers the following types (or items) of property: (Describe) ....

CHECK (X) THE ITEMS WHICH APPLY

2. ( ) (If collateral is crops) The above described crops are growing or are to be grown on: (General description of real estate and name of record owner)
....

3. ( ) (If collateral is goods which are or are to become fixtures) The above described goods are affixed or are to be affixed to: (General description of real estate owner and name of record owner) [10]
....

4. ( ) Proceeds of collateral are also covered.
5. ( ) Products of collateral are also covered.

Signature(s) of Debtor(s)   Signature(s) of Security Party or Parties
....

---

[9] New Hampshire form adds "(or assignor)" after debtor and "(or assignee)" after secured party where those terms appear in form.

[10] Items 3, 4, 5 and 6 on the New Jersey form appear as follows:
  3. (If applicable) The above goods are to become fixtures on (Describe Real Estate) _____ and this financing statement is to be filed for record in the real estate records (If the debtor does not have an interest of record) The name of a record owner is _____
  4. (If applicable) The above timber is standing on (Describe Real Estate) _____ and this financing statement is to be filed for record in the real estate records. (If the debtor does not have an interest of record) The name of a record owner is _____
  5. (If applicable) The above minerals or the like (including oil and gas) or accounts will be financed at the wellhead or minehead, of the well or mine located on _____ (Describe Real Estate) _____ and this financing statement is to be filed for record in the real estate records. (If the debtor does not have an interest of record) The name of the record owner is _____
  6. Products of collateral are also covered. (Use whichever is applicable.)

New York requires a form similar to that in New Jersey as printed above.

FINANCING STATEMENT

Form for states which have not adopted the 1972 amendments to the UCC: Indiana, Kentucky, Louisiana, Missouri, New Mexico, South Carolina, Tennessee,[11] and Vermont.

Name of debtor (or assignor) ....

Address ....

Name of secured party (or assignee) ....

Address ....

(1) This financing statement covers the following types (or items) of property:
    (Describe) ....

(2) (If collateral is crops) The above described crops are growing or are to be grown on:
    (Describe Real Estate) ....

(3) (If collateral is goods which are or are to become fixtures) The above described goods are affixed or are to be affixed to: [12]
    (Describe Real Estate) [13]

(4) (If proceeds or products of collateral are claimed): [14]

(5) Proceed—Products of the collateral are also covered. Signature of Debtor (or Assignor) ....

Signature of Secured Party (or Assignee) ....

5. WHEN FILING IS REQUIRED TO PERFECT SECURITY INTEREST. (1) As set forth in Section 9-302, a financing statement must be filed to perfect all security interests except those covered in subsection (2) and the following: (a) A security interest in collateral in possession of the secured party. (b) A security interest in instruments or documents temporarily perfected without delivery under Section 9-304 or in proceeds for a 10-day period under Section 9-306. (c) A security interest arising upon transfer of a beneficial interest in the trust of decedent's estate.[15] (d) A purchase money security interest in consumer goods, but filing is required for a motor vehicle required to be registered; [16] and fixture filing is required for priority over conflicting interests in fixtures [17] to the extent provided in Section 9-313.[18] (e) An assignment of accounts which does not alone or in conjunction with other assignments to the same assignee transfer a significant part of the outstanding accounts of the assignor.[19] (f) A

---

[11] Must contain a statement showing who prepared the instrument.

[12] In Indiana if financing statement covers fixtures must state that "debtor's title to reality connected with title of ...."

[13] Oklahoma form provides, in addition, as follows:
(If the debtor does not have an interest of record) The name of a record owner is _____.

[14] This does not appear in the Oklahoma form.

[15] In Maryland and Wisconsin, a financing statement must be filed if the consumer goods have a purchase price in excess of $500; in Colorado, if the purchase price exceeds $250; in Maine, if the price is greater than $1,000. Kansas and Oklahoma do not provide for automatic perfection of purchase money security interests in consumer goods.

The 1962 code authorizes automatic perfection of purchase money security interests in farm equipment having a maximum purchase price of $2,500. In Indiana, Kentucky, Maine, Massachusetts, Missouri, New Hampshire, New Jersey, Tennessee and Vermont the amount is $500.

In California, filing is necessary for a boat required to be registered.

[16] This caveat does not appear in the codes of Maine, Massachusetts, Ohio or Wisconsin.

[17] Does not appear in the California code.

[18] Except in Kansas.

[19] Does not appear in the Washington code.

security interest of a collecting bank (Section 4-208) or arising under the Article on Sales (see Section 9-113) or covered in subsection (3) below. (g) An assignment for the benefit of all of the transferor's creditors, and subsequent transfers by the immediate assignee.[20]

(2) If a secured party assigns a perfected security interest, no filing under this Article is required in order to continue the perfected status of the security interest against creditors of and transferees from the original debtor.

(3) The filing of a financing statement otherwise required by Article 9 is not necessary or effective to perfect a security interest in property subject to (a) a federal statute or treaty which provides for a national or international registration or a national or international certificate of title or which specifies a place of filing different from that specified in this Article for filing of the security interest; or (b) various statutes of the appropriate state such as certificate of title statutes covering automobiles, trailers, mobile homes, boats, farm tractors, or the like or any central filing statute. However, during any period in which collateral is inventory held for sale by a person who is in the business of selling goods of that kind, the filing provisions of Part 4 of this Article apply to a security interest created by him as a debtor. A security interest in property subject to a certificate of title statute in one jurisdiction may be perfected without filing a financing statement in other relevant jurisdictions if the first jurisdiction mandates that indication of a security interest on the certificate of title is required as a condition of perfection.

(4) Since compliance with federal or state statutes described in subsection (3) is tantamount to filing a financing statement, strict adherence to the provisions of these statutes is necessary in order to perfect security interests in property falling within their scope. Duration and renewal of perfection of the security interest perfected by compliance with the statute or treaty are governed by the provisions of the statute or treaty; in other respects the security interest is subject to this Article. (Section 9-302) [21]

6. WHEN SECURITY INTEREST PERFECTED. (1) A security interest is perfected when it has attached and when all of the applicable steps required under Sections 9-302, 9-304, 9-305, and 9-306 have been taken. If such steps are taken before the security interest attaches, it is perfected at the time when it attaches.

(2) If a security interest is originally perfected in any way permitted under this Article and is subsequently perfected in some other way under this Article, without an intermediate period when it was unperfected, the security interest shall be deemed to be perfected continuously for the purposes of this Article. (Sec. 9-303)

7. PERFECTION OF SECURITY INTEREST IN INSTRUMENTS OR DOCUMENTS. (1) A security interest in chattel paper or negotiable documents may be perfected by filing. A security interest in money or instruments (other than instruments which constitute [22] part of chattel paper) can be perfected only by the secured

---

[20] In California, filing is not required to perfect a security interest in a deposit account. California has enacted a variation on subsection. (1). Oklahoma has enacted a variation on subsection (g) dealing with a security interest in a vehicle.

[21] Special provisions covering filing against utility companies or railroads or other transportation companies in Arizona, Connecticut, Georgia, Michigan, Minnesota, Montana, Nebraska, New Mexico, North Carolina, Oregon, South Carolina, Vermont, Virginia, West Virginia and Washington.

[22] Oklahoma adds words "certificated securities or."

party's taking possession, except as provided in subsections (4) and (5) of this section and subsections (2) and (3) of § 9-306 on proceeds.

(2) During the period that goods are in the possession of the issuer of a negotiable document therefor, a security interest in the goods is perfected by perfecting a security interest in the document, and any security interest in the goods otherwise perfected during such period is subject thereto.

(3) A security interest in goods in the possession of a bailee other than one who has issued a negotiable document therefor is perfected by issuance of a document in the name of the secured party or by the bailee's receipt of notification of the secured party's interest or by filing as to the goods.

(4) A security interest in instruments[23] or negotiable documents is perfected without filing or the taking of possession for a period of 21 days from the time it attaches to the extent that it arises for new value given under a written security agreement.

(5) A security interest remains perfected for a period of 21 days without filing where a secured party having a perfected security interest in an instrument,[23] a negotiable document or goods in possession of a bailee other than one who has issued a negotiable document therefor, (a) makes available to the debtor the goods or documents representing the goods for the purpose of ultimate sale or exchange or otherwise dealing with them in a manner preliminary to their sale or exchange, but priority between conflicting security interests in the goods is subject to subsection (3) of Section 9-312; or (b) delivers the instrument to the debtor for the purpose of ultimate sale or exchange or of presentation, collection, renewal or registration of transfer. After such 21 day period perfection depends upon compliance with applicable provisions of this Article. (Sec. 9-304)

(6) After the 21 day period in subsections (4) and (5), perfections depends upon compliance with applicable provisions of this Article.

8. WHEN POSSESSION PERFECTS SECURITY INTEREST WITHOUT FILING. A security interest in letters of credit and advices of credit, goods,[24] instruments (other than certificated securities),[24] money negotiable documents or chattel paper may be perfected by the secured party's taking possession of the collateral. If such collateral other than goods covered by a negotiable document is held by a bailee, the secured party is deemed to have possession from the time the bailee receives notification of the secured party's interest. A security interest is perfected by possession from the time possession is taken back without relation back and continues only so long as possession is retained, unless otherwise specified in this Article. The security interest may be otherwise perfected as provided in this Article before or after the period of possession by the secured party. (Sec. 9-305)

9. PLACE OF FILING AND FILING FEES: See pages 7-30 *et seq.,* and 7-33 *et seq.* (Secs. 9-401, 9-407)

10. ERRONEOUS FILING—(1) A filing which is made in good faith in an improper place or not in all of the places required by this Section is nevertheless effective with regard to any collateral as to which the filing complied with the

---

[23] Massachusetts and Oklahoma add "other than certificated securities."
[24] Most states omit this exception.

requirements of this Article and is also effective with regard to collateral covered by the financing statement against any person who has knowledge of the contents of such financing statement.

(2) A filing which is made in the proper place in the state continues effective even though the debtor's residence or place of business or the location of the collateral or its use, whichever controlled the original, is thereafter changed.

(3) The rules stated in Section 9-103 determine whether filing is necessary in a given state. (Sec. 9-401) [25]

11. FORMAL REQUISITES OF FINANCING STATEMENTS; AMENDMENTS. (1) A financing statement is sufficient if it gives the names of the debtor and the secured party, is signed by the debtor, gives an address of the secured party from which information concerning the security interest may be obtained, gives a mailing address of the debtor and contains a statement indicating the types, or describing the items, of collateral.[26] A financing statement may be filed before a security agreement is made or a security interest otherwise attaches. When the financing statement covers crops growing or to be grown the statement must also contain a general description of the real estate concerned and the name of the record owner thereof.[27] When the financing statement covers timber to be cut or covers minerals or the like (including oil and gas) or accounts resulting from the sale of interest in minerals, or the like (Section 9-103(5)) or when the financing statement is filed as a fixture filing (Section 9-313) and the collateral is goods which are or are to become fixtures and the debtor is not a transmitting utility, the statement must also show that it covers this type of collateral, must recite that it is to be filed in the real estate records and the financing statement must contain a description of the real estate. If the debtor does not have an interest of record in the real estate, the financing statement must show the name of a record owner. A copy of the security agreement is sufficient as a financing statement if it contains the above information and is signed by the debtor. A carbon, photographic or other reproduction of a security agreement or a financing statement is sufficient as a financing statement if the security agreement so provides or if the original has been filed. [California requires that such reproduction be certified.]

(2) A financing statement which otherwise complies with subsection (1) is sufficient when it is signed by the secured party instead of the debtor[28] if it is filed to perfect a security interest in

(a) a collateral already subject to a security interest in another jurisdiction when it is brought into the state or when the debtor's location is changed

---

[25] The Code provides for alternative subsections in Sec. 9-401. State statutes should be checked carefully to determine which alternative has been adopted.

[26] In Kansas, use of general classifications of collateral such as inventory, consumer goods, accounts, etc. is an adequate description of the collateral. Maine amended § 9-402 to provide that if the collateral is a mobile home, the financing statement must indicate the place where the mobile home is to be located.

[27] The name of the record owner of the real estate is required only in Alabama, Florida, Georgia, Hawaii, Idaho, Michigan, Minnesota, Mississippi, Nevada, New Jersey, New York, New Hampshire, North Carolina, Ohio, Rhode Island, Texas, Utah, Virginia and Wisconsin. In Missouri and Kansas the name of the record owner is required only when the collateral is a fixture. In Georgia, the financing statement need reflect the record owner or lessee of the realty only if the debtor does not have an interest of record in the real estate.

[28] New York permits filing of a financing statement not signed by the debtor, if the security agreement so provides.

to this state. Such a financing statement must state the collateral was brought into the state or that the debtor's location was changed to this state under such circumstances.

(b) proceeds under Section 9-306 if the security interest in the original collateral was perfected. Such a financing statement must describe the original collateral.

(c) collateral as to which the filing has elapsed or

(d) collateral acquired after a change of name, identity or corporate structure of the debtor.

(3) Each of the statutes sets forth an approved form. [See Item 4, page 7-5 (Form of Financing Statement), pages 7-5–7-7.]

(4) A financing statement may be amended by filing a writing signed by both the debtor, and the secured party. An amendment does not extend the period of effectiveness of a financing statement. If any amendment adds collateral, it is effective as to the added collateral only from the filing date of the amendment. Unless the context otherwise requires, the term "financing statement" means the original financing statement and any amendments.

(5) "A financing statement covering timber to be cut or covering minerals or the like (including oil and gas) or accounts subject to subsection (5) of 9-103, or a financing statement filed as a fixture filing (9-313), must show that it covers this type of collateral, must recite that it is to be filed for record in the real estate records, and the financing statement must contain a description of the real estate sufficient if it were contained in a mortgage of the real estate to give constructive notice of the mortgage under the law of this State. If the debtor does not have an interest of record in the real estate, the financing statement must show the name of a record owner."

(6) A mortgage is effective as a financing statement filed as a fixture filing from the date of its recording if (a) the goods are described in the mortgage by item or type, (b) the goods are or are to become fixtures related to the real estate described in the mortgage, (c) the mortgage complies with the requirements for a financing statement in this Section other than a recital that it is to be filed in the real estate records and (d) the mortgage is duly recorded. No fee with reference to the financing statement is required other than the regular recording and satisfaction fees with respect to the mortgage.

(7) A financing statement sufficiently shows the name of the debtor if it gives the individual, partnership or corporate name of the debtor, whether or not it adds other trade names or the names of partners. Where the debtor so changes his name or, in the case of an organization, its name, identity or corporate structure that a filed financing statement becomes seriously misleading, the filing is not effective to perfect a security interest in collateral acquired by the debtor more than four months after the change, unless a new appropriate financing statement is filed before the expiration of that time.[29] A filed financing statement remains effective with respect to collateral transferred by the debtor even though the secured party knows of or consents to the transfer.

(8) A financing statement substantially complying with the requirements of this Section is effective even though it contains minor errors which are not seriously misleading. (Sec. 9-402)

---

[29] California requires new filing before the acquisition of the collateral by debtor.

12. DURATION OF FILING; LAPSE. As a general proposition, a filed financing statement is effective for a period of five years from the date of filing.[30] The effectiveness of a filed financing statement lapses on the expiration of the five year period unless a continuation statement is filed prior to the lapse. If a security interest perfected by filing exists at the time insolvency proceedings are commenced by or against the debtor, the security interest remains perfected until termination of the insolvency proceedings and thereafter for a period of sixty days or until expiration of the five year period, whichever occurs later. Upon lapse, the security interest becomes unperfected, unless it is perfected without filing. If the security interest becomes unperfected upon lapse, it is deemed to have been unperfected as against a person who became a purchaser or a lien creditor before lapse.

If the debtor is a transmitting utility and a filed financing statement so states, it is effective until a termination statement is filed. A real estate mortgage which is effective as a fixture filing remains effective as a fixture filing until the mortgage is released or satisfied of record or its effectiveness otherwise terminates as to the real estate.[31] Presentation for filing of a financing statement and tender of the filing fee or acceptance of the statement by the filing office constitute filing. (Sec. 9-403)[32]

13. CONTINUATION STATEMENT. A continuation statement may be filed by the secured party within six months prior to the expiration of the five year period specified above. Any such continuation statement must be signed by the secured party, identify the original statement by file number and state that the original statement is still effective. A continuation statement signed by a person other than the secured party of record must be accompanied by a separate written statement of assignment signed by the secured party of record and complying with subsection (2) of Section 9-405, including payment of the required fee. Upon timely filing of the continuation statement, the effectiveness of the original statement is continued for five years [33] after the last date to which the filing was effective whereupon it lapses in the same manner as provided in Item 12 above unless another continuation statement is filed prior to such lapse. Succeeding continuation statements may be filed in the same manner to continue the effectiveness of the original statement. Unless a statute on disposition of public records provides otherwise, the filing officer may remove a lapsed statement from the files and destroy it immediately if he has retained a microfilm or other photographic record, or in other case after one year has elapsed. The filing officer shall arrange matters by physical annexation of financing statements to continuation statements or other related filings, or by other means. If he

---

[30] In Maryland, financing statements are effective for 12 years from the date of filing unless otherwise specified; in Arizona for 6 years.

In all of the 1962 code states save New Mexico, and Oklahoma a filed financing statement which states the obligation is payable on demand is effective for 5 years from the date of filing. When a filed financing statement designates that the maturity date of the secured obligation is five years or less, the period of filing is effective until the majority date plus 60 days.

[31] Alabama adds "A financing statement covering a mobile home, other than a mobile home constituting inventory, remains effective, if it so states, until a termination statement is filed."

[32] Oklahoma, Texas, and West Virginia have selected the Code alternative which requires filing of new financing statement in proper county, within four months of change in residence of debtor or location of collateral, or security interest becomes ineffective. See Sec. 9-401.

[33] 6 years in Arizona; 12 years in Maryland.

physically destroys the financing statements of a period more than five years past, those which have been continued by a continuation statement or which are otherwise still effective shall be retained. (Sec. 9-403)

14. FILING FEE. The fee for filing, indexing and furnishing filing data for an original or a continuation statement or any amendment of either is shown in listing below, *infra* p. 7-30. (No additional charge is made in most states for an assignment or statement of assignment if included in financing statement.) Also noted are those states which impose taxes on indebtedness upon the filing of instruments. (*See* Sec. 9-406)

15. TERMINATION. (1) If a financing statement covering consumer goods is filed on or after the effective date of the revised Article 9, then within one month or within ten days following a written demand by the debtor after there is no outstanding secured obligation and no commitment to make advances, incur obligations or otherwise give value, the secured party must file with each filing officer with whom the financing statement is filed, a termination statement to the effect that he no longer claims a security interest under the financing statement, which shall be identified by file number. In other cases whenever there is no outstanding secured obligation and no commitment to make advances, incur obligations or otherwise give value, the secured party must on written demand by the debtor send the debtor for each filing officer with whom the financing was filed, a termination statement to the effect that he no longer claims a security interest under the financing statement, which shall be identified by file number.[34] A termination statement signed by a person other than the secured party of record must be accompanied by a separate written statement of assignment signed by the secured party of record complying with subsection (2) of Section 9-405, including payment of the required fee. If the affected secured party fails to file such a termination statement as required by this subsection, or to send such a termination statement within ten days after proper demand therefor he shall be liable to the debtor for One Hundred ($100) Dollars, and in addition for any loss caused to the debtor by such failure.[35]

(2) On presentation to the filing officer of such a termination statement, he must note it in the index. If he has received the termination statement in duplicate, he shall return one copy of the termination statement to the secured party stamped to show the time of receipt thereof. If the filing officer has a microfilm or other photographic record of the filing statement, and of any related continuation statement, statement of assignment and statement of release, he may remove the originals from the files at any time after receipt of the termination statement, or if he has no such records, he may remove them from the files at any time after one year after receipt of the termination statement.

---

[34] In California the secured party only need send the debtor a termination statement within 10 days from receipt of a written demand, even if the collateral is consumer goods. If a financing statement was filed with the Secretary of State, Wisconsin mandates that a secured party file a termination statement with the Secretary within 1 month of discharge or 10 days from demand despite the character of the collateral.

[35] In Wisconsin, no termination statement need be filed if the financing statement lapses prior to the time when the termination statement is required to be filed, the financing statement states that the debtor and the secured party enjoy a continuing business relationship or the financing statement was filed prior to January 1, 1978.

(3) The fee for filing such a termination statement including sending the financing statement is set forth in the listing below, *infra* p. 7-30. (Sec. 9-404)

16. ASSIGNMENT OF SECURITY INTEREST. (1) A financing statement may disclose an assignment of a security interest in the collateral described in the statement by indication in the financing statement of the name and address of the assignee or by an assignment itself or a copy thereof on the face or back of the statement.[36] On presentation to the filing officer of such a financing statement the filing officer shall mark the same as provided in Section 9-403 (4). The uniform fee for filing, indexing and furnishing filing data for a financing statement so indicating an assignment is shown in the listing below.

(2) A secured party may assign of record all or a part of his rights under a financing statement in the place where the original financing statement was filed by the filing of a separate written statement of assignment signed by the secured party of record and setting forth the name of the secured party of record and the debtor, the file number and the date of filing of the financing statement and the name and address of the assignee and containing a description of the collateral assigned. A copy of the assignment is sufficient as a separate statement if it complies with the preceding sentence. On presentation to the filing officer of such a separate statement, the filing officer shall mark such separate statement with the date and hour of the filing. He shall note the assignment on the index of the financing statement, or in the case of a fixture filing, or a filing covering timber to cut, or covering minerals or the like (including oil and gas) or accounts subject to subsection (5) of Section 9-103, he shall index the assignment under the name of the assignor as grantor and, to the extent that the law of the state provides for indexing the assignment of a mortgage under the name of the assignee, he shall index the assignment of the financing statement under the name of the assignee. Notwithstanding the provisions of this subsection, an assignment of record of a security interest in a fixture contained in a mortgage effective as a fixture filing (Section 9-402 (6)) may be made only by an assignment of the mortgage in the manner provided by state law other than in the U.C.C.[37]

(3) After the disclosure or filing of an assignment under this section, the assignee is the secured party of record. (Sec. 9-405)

17. RELEASE OF COLLATERAL. A secured party of record may by his signed statement release all or a part of any collateral described in a filed financing statement. The statement of release is sufficient if it contains a description of the collateral being released, the name and address of the debtor, the name and address of the secured party, and the file number of the financing statement. A statement of release signed by a person other than the secured party of record must be accompanied by a separate written statement of assignment signed by the secured party of record and complying with subsection (2) of Section 9-405, including payment of the required fee. Upon presentation of such a statement to the filing officer he shall mark the statement with the hour and date of filing and shall note the same upon the margin of the index

---

[36] In the 1962 Code states and in Virginia, either the original secured party or the assignee may sign this statement as the assignee. In California, filing of a statement of assignment is mandatory when a secured party assigns a filed security interest.

[37] Fees for filing and assignment or statement thereof are set forth beginning page 7-30.

of filing of financing statement. The uniform fee for filing and noting such statement of release is shown in listing below, *infra* p. 7-30. (Sec. 9-406)

18. FINANCIAL STATEMENTS COVERING CONSIGNED OR LEASED GOODS.
A consignor or lessor of goods may file a financing statement using the terms "consignor," "consignee," "lessor," lessee" or the like instead of the terms specified in Section 9-402. The provisions of this subchapter shall apply as appropriate to such a financing statement but its filing shall not of itself be a factor in determining whether or not the consignment or lease is intended as security (Section 1-201(37)). However, if it is determined for other reasons that the consignment or lease is so intended, a security interest of the consignor or lessor which attaches to the consigned or leased goods is perfected by such filing. (Sec. 9-408)

19. PERFECTION OF SECURITY INTERESTS IN MULTIPLE STATE TRANSACTIONS. (1) Documents, instruments and ordinary goods.
    (a) This subsection applies to documents and instruments and to goods other than those covered by a certificate of title described in subsection (2), mobile goods described in subsection (3), and minerals described in subsection (5).
    (b) Except as otherwise provided, perfection and the effect of perfection or non-perfection of a security interest in collateral are governed by the law of the jurisdiction where the collateral is when the last event occurs on which is based the assertion that the security interest is perfected or unperfected.
    (c) If the parties to a transaction creating a purchase money security interest in goods in one jurisdiction understand at the time that the security interest attaches that the goods will be kept in another jurisdiction, then the law of the other jurisdiction governs the perfection, and the effect of perfection or non-perfection of the security interest from the time it attaches until thirty days after the debtor receives possession of the goods and thereafter if the goods are taken to the other jurisdiction before the end of the thirty-day period.[38]
    (d) When collateral is brought into and kept in the state while subject to a security interest perfected under the law of the jurisdiction from which the collateral was removed, the security interst remains perfected, but if action is required by Part 3 of Article 9 to perfect the security interest,
        (i) if the action is not taken before the expiration of the period of perfection in the other jurisdiction or the end of four months after the collateral is brought into the state, whichever period first expires, the security interest becomes unperfected at the end of that period and is thereafter deemed to have been unperfected as against a person who became a purchaser after removal;
        (ii) if the action is taken before the expiration of the period specified in subparagraph (i), the security interest continues perfected thereafter;
        (iii) for the purpose of priority over a buyer of consumer goods (subsection (2) of Section 9-307), the period of the effectiveness of a filing in the jurisdiction from which the collateral is removed is governed by the rules with respect to perfection in subparagraphs (i) and (ii).

---

[38] Iowa applies this subsection to all security interests.

(2) Certificate of title.

(a) This subsection applies to goods covered by a certificate of title issued under a statute of the state or of another jurisdiction under the law of which indication of a security interest on the certificate is required as a condition of perfection.

(b) Except as otherwise provided in this subsection, perfection and the effect of perfection or non-perfection of the security interest are governed by the law (including the conflict of laws rules) of the jurisdiction issuing the certificate until four months after the goods are removed from that jurisdiction and thereafter until the goods are registered in another jurisdiction, but in any event not beyond surrender of the certificate. After the expiration of that period, the goods are not covered by the certificate of title.

(c) Except with respect to the rights of a buyer described in the next paragraph, a security interest, perfected in another jurisdiction otherwise than by notation on a certificate of title, in goods brought into a state and thereafter covered by a certificate of title issued by a state is subject to the rules stated in paragraph (d) of subsection (1).

(d) If goods are brought into a state while a security interest therein is perfected in any manner under the law of the jurisdiction from which the goods are removed and a certificate of title issued by the state and the certificate does not show that the goods are subject to the security interest or that they may be subject to security interests not shown on the certificate, the security interest is subordinate to the rights of a buyer of the goods who is not in the business of selling goods of that kind to the extent that he gives value and receives delivery of the goods after issuance of the certificate and without knowledge of the security interest.

(3) Accounts, general intangibles and mobile goods.

(a) This subsection applies to accounts (other than an account described in subsection (5) on minerals) and general intangibles [39] and to goods which are mobile and which are of a type normally used in more than one jurisdiction, such as motor vehicles, trailers, rolling stock, airplanes, shipping containers, road building and construction machinery and commercial harvesting machinery and the like, if the goods are equipment or are inventory leased or held for lease by the debtor to others, and are not covered by a certificate of title described in subsection (2).

(b) The law (including the conflict of law rules) of the jurisdiction in which the debtor is located[40] governs the perfection and the effect of perfection or non-perfection of the security interest.

(c) If, however, the debtor is located in a jurisdiction which is not a part of the United States, and which does not provide for perfection of the security interest by filing or recording in that jurisdiction, the law of the jurisdiction in the United States in which the debtor has its major executive office in the United States governs the perfection and the effect of perfection or non-perfection of the security interest through filing. In the alternative, if the debtor is located in a jurisdiction which is not a part of the United States or Canada and the collateral is accounts or general

---

[39] Oklahoma adds directly after "intangibles" the phrase "other than uncertified securities."
[40] Maine adds, "when the last event occurs on which is based the assertion that the security interest is perfected or unperfected. . . ."

intangibles for money due or to become due, the security interest may be perfected by notification to the account debtor. As used in this paragraph, "United States" includes its territories and possessions and the Commonwealth of Puerto Rico.

(d) A debtor shall be deemed located at his place of business if he has one, at his chief executive office if he has more than one place of business, otherwise at his residence. If, however, the debtor is a foreign air carrier under the Federal Aviation Act of 1958, as amended, it shall be deemed located at the designated office of the agent upon whom service of process may be made on behalf of the foreign air carrier.

(e) A security interest perfected under the law of the jurisdiction of the location of the debtor is perfected until the expiration of four months after a change of the debtor's location to another jurisdiction, or until perfection would have ceased by the law of the first jurisdiction, whichever period first expires. Unless perfected in the new jurisdiction before the end of that period, it becomes unperfected thereafter and is deemed to have been unperfected as against a person who became a purchaser after the change.

(4) Chattel paper. The rules stated for goods in subsection (1) apply to a possessory security interest in chattel paper. The rules stated for accounts in subsection (3) apply to a nonpossessory security interest in chattel paper, but the security interest may not be perfected by notification to the account debtor.

(5) Minerals. Perfection and the effect of perfection or non-perfection of a security interest which is created by a debtor who has an interest in minerals or the like (including oil and gas) before extraction and which attaches thereto as extracted, or which attaches to an account resulting from the sale thereof at the wellhead or minehead are governed by the law (including the conflict of laws rules) of the jurisdiction wherein the wellhead or minehead is located. Section 9-103.

(6) Uncertificated securities. The law (including the conflict of laws rules) of the jurisdiction of organization of the issuer governs the perfection and the effect of perfection or non-perfection of a security interest in uncertificated securities. (Sec. 9-103)

20. RIGHTS OF THIRD PARTIES OVER UNPERFECTED SECURITY INTERESTS.

(1) Except as otherwise provided in subsection (2), an unperfected security interest is subordinate to the rights of:

(a) persons entitled to priority under Section 9-312;

(b) a person who becomes a lien creditor before the security interest is perfected;

(c) in the case of goods, instruments, documents, and chattel paper, a person who is not a secured party and who is a transferee in bulk or other buyer not in ordinary course of business or is a buyer of farm products in the ordinary course of business to the extent that he gives value and receives delivery of the collateral without knowledge of the security interest and before it is perfected;

(d) in the case of accounts and general intangibles, a person who is not a secured party and who is a transferee to the extent that he gives value without knowledge of the security interest and before it is perfected.

(2) If the secured party files with respect to a purchase money security interest

before or within ten days after the debtor receives possession of the collateral, he takes priority over the rights of a transferee in bulk or of a lien creditor which arise between the time the security interest attaches and the time of filing.[41]

(3) A "lien creditor" means a creditor who has acquired a lien on the property involved by attachment, levy or the like and includes an assignee for benefit of creditors from the time of assignment, and a trustee in bankruptcy from the date of the filing of the petition or a receiver in equity from the time of appointment.

(4) A person who becomes a lien creditor while a security interest is perfected takes subject to the security interest only to the extent that it secures advances made before he becomes a lien creditor or within 45 days thereafter or made without knowledge of the lien or pursuant to a commitment entered into without knowledge of the lien. (Sec. 9-301)

21. RIGHTS OF BUYER OF GOODS. (1) A buyer in ordinary course of business (subsection 9 of Section 1-201) other than a person buying farm products from a person engaged in farming operations, takes free of a security interest created by his seller even though the security interest is perfected and even though the buyer knows of its existence.

(2) In the case of consumer goods [42] a buyer takes free of a security interest even though perfected if he buys without knowledge of the security interest, for value and for his own personal, family or household purposes or his own farming operations unless prior to the purchase the secured party has filed a financing statement covering such goods.

(3) A buyer other than a buyer in the ordinary course of business (subsection (1) of this Section) takes free of a security interest to the extent that it secures future advances made after the secured party acquires knowledge of the purchase, or more than forty-five days after the purchase, whichever first occurs, unless made pursuant to a commitment entered into without knowledge of the purchase and before expiration of the forty-five day period. (Sec. 9-307) [43]

22. RIGHTS OF PURCHASER OF CHATTEL PAPER AND INSTRUMENTS. A purchaser of chattel paper or an instrument who gives new value and takes possession of it in the ordinary course of business has priority over a security interest in the chattel paper or instrument

(a) which is perfected under Section 9-304 (permissive filing and temporary perfection) or under 9-306 (perfection as to proceeds) if he acts without knowledge that the specific paper or instrument is subject to a security interest; or

---

[41] In Alabama, Arizona, Illinois, Iowa, Kansas, Maine, Maryland, Michigan, Montana, Nebraska, North Carolina, North Dakota, Texas, Washington, West Virginia, and Wisconsin, the filing deadline has been expanded to 20 days. In Florida and Georgia, expanded to 15 days.

Maryland adds a subsection that provides that the non-purchase-money security interest deadline is 10 days.

[42] Maryland and Wisconsin limit the reach of this subsection to consumer goods having a maximum price of $500; in Colorado, $250.

The states working with the 1962 version extend this subsection to farm equipment of $2,500 or less. In Indiana, Kentucky, Missouri, and Vermont, the amount is $500.

Subsection (2) is not found in the codes of California, Kansas, Maine and Oklahoma. Maryland omits subsec. (3).

[43] California and Washington omit the 45 day grace period.

(b) which is claimed merely as proceeds of inventory subject to a security interest (Section 9-306) even though he knows that the specific paper or instrument is subject to the security interest. (Sec. 9-308)

23. RIGHTS OF PURCHASERS OF INSTRUMENTS AND DOCUMENTS. Nothing in this Article limits the rights of a holder in due course of a negotiable instrument (Section 3-302) or a holder to whom a negotiable document of title has been duly negotiated (Section 7-501) or a bona fide purchaser of a security (Section 8-302) and such holders or purchasers take priority over an earlier security interest even though perfected. Filing under this Article does not constitute notice of the security interest to such holders or purchasers. (Sec. 9-309)

24. PRIORITY OF CERTAIN LIENS. When a person in the ordinary course of his business furnishes services or materials with respect to goods subject to a security interest, a lien upon goods in the possession of such person given by statute or rule of law for such materials or services takes priority over a perfected security interest unless the lien is statutory and the statute expressly provides otherwise. (Sec. 9-310) [44]

25. PRIORITIES AMONG CONFLICTING SECURITY INTERESTS IN THE SAME COLLATERAL. (1) The rules of priority stated in other sections of this Part and in the following sections shall govern when applicable: Section 4-208 with respect to the security interests of collecting banks in items being collected, accompanying documents and proceeds; Section 9-103 on security interests related to other jurisdictions; Section 9-114 on consignments.

(2) A perfected security interest in crops for new value given to enable the debtor to produce the crops during the production season and given not more than three months before the crops become growing crops by planting or otherwise takes priority over an earlier perfected security interest to the extent that such earlier interest secures obligations due more than six months before the crops become growing crops by planting or otherwise, even though the person giving new value had knowledge of the earlier security interest.[45]

(3) A perfected purchase money security interest in inventory has priority over a conflicting security interest in the same inventory and also has priority in identifiable cash proceeds received on or before the delivery of the inventory to a buyer if

(a) The purchase money security interest is perfected at the time the debtor receives possession of the inventory; and

(b) The purchase money secured party gives notification in writing to the holder of the conflicting security interest. If the holder had filed a financing statement covering the same types of inventory (i) before the date of the filing made by the purchase money secured party, or (ii) before the beginning of the 21 day period where the purchase money security interest is temporarily perfected without filing or possession (subsection 5 of Section 9-304); and

(c) The holder of the conflicting security interest receives the notification within five years [46] before the debtor received possession of the inventory; and

---

[44] In Colorado, this priority is not given. Alabama adds a subsection regarding priorities as to landlord's liens.
[45] Arizona, California, New Jersey and Nevada do not have subsection (2).
[46] Wisconsin omits the phrase "within 5 years" from this provision.

(d) The notification states that the person giving the notice has or expects to acquire a purchase money security interest in inventory of the debtor, describing such inventory by items or type.[47]

(4) A purchase money security interest in collateral other than inventory has priority over a conflicting security interest in the same collateral or its proceeds if the purchase money security interest is perfected at the time the debtor receives possession of the collateral or within ten days [48] thereafter.

(5) In all cases not governed by other rules stated in this Section (including cases of purchase money security interests which do not qualify for the special priorities set forth in subsections (3) and (4) of this Section), priority between conflicting security interests in the same collateral shall be determined according to the following rules:

(a) Conflicting security interests rank according to priority in time of filing or perfection. Priority dates from the time a filing is first made covering the collateral or the time the security interest is first perfected, whichever is earlier, provided that there is no period thereafter when there is neither filing nor perfection.

(b) So long as conflicting security interests are unperfected, the first to attach has priority.

(6) For the purposes of subsection (5), a date of filing or perfection as to collateral is also the date of filing or perfection as to proceeds.

(7) If future advances are made while a security interest is perfected by filing or the taking of possession, the security interest has the same priority for the purposes of subsection (5) to the future advances as it does with respect to the first advance. If a commitment is made before or while the security interest is so perfected, the security interest has the same priority with respect to advances made pursuant thereto. In other cases, a perfected security interest has priority from the date the advance is made. (Sec. 9-312)

26. PRIORITIES OF SECURITY INTERESTS IN FIXTURES.[49] (1) In this section and in the provisions of Part 4 of this Article referring to fixture filing, unless the context otherwise requires

(a) goods are "fixtures" when they become so related to particular real estate that an interest in them arises under real estate law [50]

(b) a "fixture filing" is the filing in the office where a mortgage on the real estate would be filed or recorded of a financing statement covering goods which are or are to become fixtures and conforming to the requirements of subsection (5) of Section 9-402

(c) a mortgage is a "construction mortgage" to the extent that it secures an obligation incurred for the construction of an improvement on land including the acquisition cost of the land, if the recorded writing so indicates.

(2) A security interest under this Article may be created in goods which are fixtures or may continue in goods which become fixtures, but no security

---

[47] The Florida statute provides that if any of the foregoing four requirements are not met, the priority of said purchase money security interest shall be determined under subsection (5).

[48] The 10 day grace period has been expanded to 20 days in Alabama, Arizona, Illinois, Iowa, Maine, Maryland, Michigan, Montana, Nebraska, North Carolina, North Dakota, Tennessee, Texas, Washington, West Virginia, and Wisconsin. In Florida and Georgia, the time limit is 15 days.

[49] Wisconsin has removed vehicles, for which certificates of title are required, from the operation of this section. Florida and Maryland have adopted a variation of this section.

[50] Slightly different definition in Kansas.

interest exists under this Article in ordinary building materials incorporated into an improvement on land.

(3) This Article does not prevent creation of an encumbrance upon fixtures pursuant to real estate law.

(4) A perfected security interest in fixtures has priority over the conflicting interest of an encumbrancer or owner of the real estate where

(a) [51] the security interest is a purchase money security interest, the interest of the encumbrancer or owner arises before the goods become fixtures, the security interest is perfected by a fixture filing before the goods become fixtures or within ten days therafter, and the debtor has an interest of record in the real estate or is in possession of the real estate; or

(b) the security interest is perfected by a fixture filing before the interest of the encumbrancer or owner is of record, the security interest has priority over any conflicting interest of a predecessor in title of the encumbrancer or owner, and the debtor has an interest of record in the real estate or is in possession of the real estate; or

(c) the fixtures are readily removable factory or office machines or readily removable replacements of domestic appliances which are consumer goods, and before the goods become fixtures the security interest is perfected by any method permitted by this Article; or

(d) the conflicting interest is a lien on the real estate obtained by legal or equitable proceedings after the security interest was perfected by any method permitted by this Article.

(5) A security interest in fixtures, whether or not perfected, has priority over the conflicting interest of an encumbrancer or owner of the real estate where

(a) the encumbrancer or owner has consented in writing to the security interest or has disclaimed an interest in the goods as fixtures; or

(b) the debtor has a right to remove the goods as against the encumbrancer or owner. If the debtor's right terminates, the priority of the security interest continues for a reasonable time.

(6) Notwithstanding paragraph (a) of subsection (4) but otherwise subject to subsections (4) and (5), a security interest in fixtures is subordinate to a construction mortgage recorded before the goods become fixtures if the goods become fixtures before the completion of the construction. To the extent that it is given to refinance a construction mortgage, a mortgage has this priority to the same extent as the construction mortgage.

(7) In cases not within the preceding subsections, a security interest in fixtures is subordinate to the conflicting interest of an encumbrancer or owner of the related real estate who is not the debtor.

(8) When the secured party has priority over all owners and encumbrancers of the real estate, he may, upon default, subject to the provisions of Part 5, remove his collateral from the real estate but he must reimburse any encumbrancer or owner of the real estate who is not the debtor and who has not otherwise agreed for the cost of repair of any physical injury, but not for any diminution in value of the real estate caused by the absence of the goods removed

---

[51] This subsection omitted in the Mississippi code. Section 9-313(9(a)) provides that a security interest in fixtures or goods that become fixtures shall not have priority over the conflicting interest of an encumberer or owner of real estate whose interest has been perfected under real estate law prior to a perfection of the security interest in the fixtures.

or by any necessity of replacing them. A person entitled to reimbursement may refuse permission to remove until the secured party gives adequate security for the performance of this obligation. (Sec. 9-313.) [52]

27. PRIORITY WHEN GOODS ARE AFFIXED TO OTHER GOODS. (1) A security interest in goods which attaches before they are installed in or affixed to other goods takes priority as to the goods installed or affixed (called in this Section "accessions") over the claims of all persons to the whole except as stated in subsection (3) and subject to Section 9-315 (1).

(2) A security interest which attaches to goods after they become part of a whole is valid against all persons subsequently acquiring interests in the whole except as stated in subsection (3) but is invalid against any person with an interest in the whole at the time the security interest attaches to the goods who has not in writing consented to the security interest or disclaimed an interest in the goods as part of the whole.

(3) The security interests described in subsections (1) and (2) do not take priority over

(a) a subsequent purchaser for value of any interest in the whole; or

(b) a creditor with a lien on the whole subsequently obtained by judicial proceedings; or

(c) a creditor with a prior perfected security interest in the whole to the extent that he makes subsequent advances; if the subsequent purchase is made, the lien by judicial proceedings is obtained or the subsequent advance under the prior perfected security interest is made or contracted for without knowledge of the security interest and before it is perfected. A purchaser of the whole at a foreclosure sale other than the holder of a perfected security interest purchasing at his own foreclosure sale is a subsequent purchaser within this section.

(4) When under subsections (1) or (2) and (3) a secured party has an interest in accessions which has priority over the claims of all persons who have interests in the whole, he may on default subject to the provisions of Part 5 remove his collateral from the whole but he must reimburse any encumbrancer or owner of the whole who is not the debtor and who has not otherwise agreed for the cost of repair of any physical injury but not for any diminution in value of the whole caused by the absence of the goods removed or by any necessity for replacing them. A person entitled to reimbursement may refuse permission to remove until the secured party gives adequate security for the performance of this obligation. (Sec. 9-314)

28. PRIORITY WHEN GOODS ARE COMMINGLED OR PROCESSED. (1) If a security interest in goods was perfected and subsequently the goods or a part thereof have become part of a product or mass, the security interest continues in the product or mass if

(a) the goods are so manufactured, processed, assembled or commingled that their identity is lost in the product or mass; or

(b) a financing statement covering the original goods also covers the product into which the goods have been manufactured, processed or assembled.

In a case to which paragraph (b) applies, no separate security interest in that

---

[52] Wisconsin adds subsection (9) exempting security interests in most kinds of motor vehicles from these priority provisions. Alabama adds subsection (9) exempting landlord's liens.

part of the original goods which has been manufactured, processed or assembled into the product may be claimed under Section 9-314.

(2) When under subsection (1) more than one security interest attaches to the product or mass, they rank equally according to the ratio that the cost of the goods to which each interest originally attached bears to the cost of the total product or mass. (Section 9-315)

29. PRIORITY SUBJECT TO SUBORDINATION. Nothing in this Article prevents subordination by agreement by any person entitled to priority. (Section 9-316)

30. SECURITY INTEREST CONTINUES IN PROCEEDS. A security interest continues in any identifiable proceeds from the sale of collateral including collections received by the debtor. The security interest continues to be perfected for only 10 days after receipt of the proceeds, but can be continuously perfected if the filed financing statement covers the original collateral and the proceeds are collateral in which a security interest may be perfected by filing in the office or officers where the financing statement has been filed and, if the proceeds are acquired with cash proceeds, the description of collateral in the financing statement indicates the types of property constituting the proceeds. Continuous perfection of the security interest in identifiable cash proceeds may also result if a filed financing statement covers the original collateral. In any event, perfection may be achieved before the expiration of the 10 day period. (Sec. 9-306)

As a general proposition, perfection of a security interest in proceeds must be done by the methods or under the circumstances permitted in this Article for original collateral of the same type. Sec. 9-306.

Unlike its earlier version, Section 9-104(g) as revised in 1972 provides that insurance proceeds are to be included in the definition of the proceeds of collateral subject to the security interest.

31. SECURED PARTY NOT OBLIGATED ON CONTRACT OF DEBTOR. The mere existence of a security interest or authority given to the debtor to dispose of or use collateral does not impose contract or tort liability upon the secured party for the debtor's acts or omissions. (Section 9-317)

32. DEFENSES AGAINST ASSIGNEE; MODIFICATION OF CONTRACT AFTER NOTIFICATION OF ASSIGNMENT; TERM PROHIBITING ASSIGNMENT INEFFECTIVE; IDENTIFICATION AND PROOF OF ASSIGNMENT. (1) Unless an account debtor has made an enforceable agreement not to assert defenses or claims arising out of a sale as provided in Section 9-206, the rights of an assignee are subject to
    (a) all the terms of the contract between the account debtor and assignor and any defense or claim arising therefrom; and
    (b) any other defense or claim of the account debtor against the assignor which accrues before the account debtor receives notification of the assignment.

(2) So far as the right payment or a part thereof [53] under an assigned contract has not been fully earned by performance, and notwithstanding notification of the assignment, any modification of or substitution for the contract made in good faith and in accordance with reasonable commercial standards is effective against an assignee unless the account debtor has otherwise agreed but the

---

[53] The phrase "or a part thereof" appears neither in the 1962 code nor in that of North Carolina.

assignee acquires corresponding rights under the modified or substituted contract.[54] The assignment may provide that such modification or substitution is a breach by the assignor.

(3) The account debtor is authorized to pay the assignor until the account debtor receives notification that the amount due or to become due has been assigned and that payment is to be made to the assignee. A notification which does not reasonably identify the rights assigned is ineffective. If requested by the account debtor, the assignee must seasonably furnish reasonable proof that the assignments has been made and unless he does so the account debtor may pay the assignor.

(4) A term in any contract between an account debtor and an assignor is ineffective if it prohibits assignment of an account or prohibits creation of a security interest in a general intangible for money due or to become due or requires the account debtor's consent to such assignment or security interest. (Sec. 9-318)

33. ATTACHMENT AND ENFORCEABILITY OF SECURITY INTEREST; PROCEEDS; FORMAL REQUISITES.[55] (1) Subject to the provisions of Section 4-208 on the security interest of a collecting bank and Section 9-113 on a security interest arising under the Article on sales, the security interest is not enforceable against the debtor or third parties with respect to the collateral and does not attach unless: (a) the collateral is in the possession of the secured party pursuant to agreement, or the debtor has signed a security agreement which contains a description of the collateral and in addition, when the security interest covers crops growing or to be grown or timber to be cut, a description of the land concerning; and (b) value has been given; and (c) the debtor has rights in the collateral.

(2) A security interest attaches when it becomes enforceable against the debtor with respect to the collateral. Attachment occurs as soon as all of the events specified in subsection (1) have taken place unless explicit agreement postpones the time of attaching.

(3) Unless otherwise agreed, a security agreement gives a secured party the rights to proceeds provided by Section 9-306.

It is not uncommon, particularly within the consumer field, for a transaction covered by Article 9 to also be subject to local statutes regulating small loans, retail installment sales and the like.[56] To the extent that they conflict with provisions of the Code with respect to such subjects as licensing, rates regulation and specific forms of contracts, the local statute should control. The framers of Code Section 9-203 suggested, however, that local statutes which antedate the enactment of the Code which provide for filing, rights on default, etc., should be repealed as inconsistent with this Article. On the other hand, inconsis-

---

[54] In New York it is further stipulated that to be effective the modification can not have a materially adverse effect upon the assignee's right or the assignor's ability to perform the contract.

[55] No security interest in consumer goods used primarily for family or household purposes and owned by a married debtor is enforceable in Colorado, unless the signature of both spouses appears on both the security agreement and the financing statement, provided the spouses were cohabitating at the time the security interest was created.

[56] In Kansas and Idaho subsection (4) includes the provision that transactions under this article may also be subject to the Uniform Consumer Credit Code and in the case of conflict the provisions of the UCC will control. A number of states provide that transactions are subject to various installment and finance statutes.

tent provisions as to deficiencies, penalties and the like, in the Uniform Consumer Credit Code and related legislation postdating the enactment of the Code, should remain since those statutes were intended to modify certain aspects of this Article. (Section 9-203)

34. AFTER-ACQUIRED PROPERTY: FUTURE ADVANCES (1) Except as provided in subsection (2), a security agreement may provide that any or all obligations covered by the security agreement are to be secured by after-acquired collateral.
(2) No security interest attaches under an after acquired property clause to consumer goods other than accessions (Section 9-314) when given as additional security unless the debtor acquires rights in them within ten days after the secured party gives value.[57]
3. Obligations covered by a security agreement may include future advances or other value whether or not the advances or value are given pursuant to commitment (subsection (1) of Section 9-105). (Sec. 9-204)
The after-acquired property provisions of the Code are regarded as one of its great advances since they permit creditors to make loans and obtain as security future inventory or accounts receivable.

35. USE OR DISPOSITION OF COLLATERAL WITHOUT ACCOUNTING PERMISSIBLE. A security interest is not invalid or fraudulent against creditors by reason of liberty in the debtor to use, commingle or dispose of all or part of the collateral (including returned or repossessed goods) or to collect or compromise accounts, or chattel paper, or to accept the return of goods or make repossessions, or to use, commingle or dispose of proceeds, or by reason of the failure of the secured party to require the debtor to account for proceeds or replace collateral. This section does not relax the requirements of possession where perfection of a security interest depends upon possession of the collateral by the secured party or by a bailee. (Section 9-205)

36. AGREEMENT NOT TO ASSERT DEFENSES AGAINST ASSIGNEE; MODIFICATION OF SALES WARRANTIES WHERE SECURITY AGREEMENT EXISTS. (1) Subject to any statute or decision which establishes a different rule for buyers of consumer goods, an agreement by a buyer that he will not assert against an assignee any claim or defense which he may have against the seller is enforceable by an assignee who takes his assignment for value, in good faith and without notice of a claim or defense, except as to defenses of a type which may be asserted against a holder in due course of a negotiable instrument under the Article on Commercial Paper (Article 3). A buyer who as part of one transaction signs both a negotiable instrument and a security agreement makes such an agreement.
(2) When a seller retains a purchase money security interest in goods the Article on Sales (Article 2) governs the sale and any disclaimer, limitation or modification of the seller's warranties. (Section 9-206)

37. RIGHTS AND DUTIES WHEN COLLATERAL IS IN SECURED PARTY'S POSSESSION. (1) A secured party must use reasonable care in the custody and preser-

---

[57] The 1962 Code generally prohibits the attachment of security interests, under after-acquired property clauses, to crops which become such more than 1 year from execution of the security agreement.

vation of collateral in his possession. In the case of an instrument or chattel paper reasonable care includes taking necessary steps to preserve rights against prior parties unless otherwise agreed.

(2) Unless otherwise agreed, when collateral is in the secured party's possession

(a) reasonable expenses (including the cost of any insurance and payment of taxes or other charges) incurred in the custody, preservation, use or operation of the collateral are chargeable to the debtor and are secured by the collateral;

(b) the risk of accidental loss or damage is on the debtor to the extent of any deficiency in any effective insurance coverage;

(c) the secured party may hold as additional security any increase or profits (except money) received from the collateral, but money so received, unless remitted to the debtor, shall be applied in reduction of the secured obligation;

(d) the secured party must keep the collateral identifiable, but fungible collateral may be commingled;

(e) the secured party may repledge the collateral upon terms which do not impair the debtor's right to redeem it.

(3) A secured party is liable for any loss caused by his failure to meet any obligation imposed by the preceding subsections but does not lose his security interest.

(4) A secured party may use or operate the collateral for the purpose of preserving the collateral or its value or pursuant to the order of a court of appropriate jurisdiction or, except in the case of consumer goods, in the manner and to the extent provided in the security agreement. (Section 9-207)

38. REQUEST FOR STATEMENT OF ACCOUNT OR LIST OF COLLATERAL. (1) A debtor may sign a statement indicating what he believes to be the aggregate amount of unpaid indebtedness as of a specified date and may send it to the secured party with a request that the statement be approved or corrected and returned to the debtor. When the security agreement or any other record kept by the secured party identifies the collateral, a debtor may similarly request the secured party to approve or correct a list of the collateral.

(2) The secured party must comply with such a request within two weeks after receipt by sending a written correction or approval. If the secured party claims a security interest in all of a particular type of collateral owned by the debtor, he may indicate that fact in his reply and need not approve or correct an itemized list of such collateral. If the secured party without reasonable excuse fails to comply he is liable for any loss caused to the debtor thereby; and if the debtor has properly included in his request a good faith statement of the obligation or a list of the collateral or both, the secured party may claim a security interest only as shown in the statement against persons misled by his failure to comply. If he no longer has an interest in the obligation or collateral at the time the request is received, he must disclose the name and address of any successor in interest known to him, and he is liable for any loss caused to the debtor as a result of failure to disclose. A successor in interest is not subject to this section until a request is received by him.

(3) A debtor is entitled to such a statement once every six months without charge. The secured party may require payment of a charge not exceeding $10 for each additional statement furnished. (Section 9-208)

39. SECURED PARTY'S RIGHT UPON DEFAULT. Unless otherwise agreed, secured party on default has the right to take possession of the collateral. He may proceed without judicial process if this can be done without breach of peace, or he may proceed by action. [But see discussion in chapters 11 and 23 below.] If the agreement so provides, the secured party may require the debtor to assemble the collateral and make it available to him at a reasonably convenient place. (Section 9-503) After default, secured party may also sell, lease, or otherwise dispose of the collateral in its then condition. Any sale is subject to Article 2 of the Code and must be made in a commercially reasonable manner and the proceeds must be used as prescribed in Section 9-504. In the event that the collateral is not sufficient to liquidate the indebtedness the creditor may be entitled to a deficiency judgment against the debtor. If the debtor has paid 60% of the cash price or loan of a purchase money security interest in consumer goods and not signed after default a statement renouncing his rights, a secured party who has possession of the collateral must dispose of it in accordance with the Code and if he fails to do so within 90 days after taking possession, the debtor may recover under conversion. In any other case involving consumer goods or other collateral, a secured party in possession may after default propose to retain the collateral in satisfaction of the obligation, provided written notice of such proposal has been sent to the debtor, if he has not signed after default a statement renouncing or modifying his rights to notice. In the case of consumer goods no other notice need be given. In other cases, the secured creditor must send notice of his proposal to retain the collateral to any other secured party from whom the proponent received written notice of a claim to the collateral. If written objection is not received within twenty-one days [58] the secured party may retain the collateral in satisfaction of the debtor's obligation. (Sec. 9-505)

ARTICLE 9 UNDER THE 1962 CODE

There remain 7 states which have not yet adopted the comprehensive 1972 amendments to Article 9. These states are as follows: Indiana, Kentucky, Louisiana, Missouri, New Mexico, South Carolina, and Vermont.

Summarized below are most sections of Article 9 as they appear in the 1962 Code prior to the 1972 revisions.

SECTION 9-102 includes "contract rights" within the scope of the Article. This Section also makes inapplicable the general choice of law provisions of Section 1-105.

SECTION 9-103 is more concerned with actual conflicts of law problems whereas the 1972 version makes clear where perfection of a security interest must occur.

SECTION 9-105 contains fewer definitions than does its 1972 counterpart. The changes add such terms as "encumbrance," "deposit accounts," "pursuant to commitment" and "transmitting utility."

SECTION 9-106 includes the term "contract rights."

SECTION 9-114 dealing with consignments does not appear in the 1962 Code.

---

[58] In Kansas, fifteen days. In Florida, Idaho, Maryland, and New Hampshire, 30 days.

SECTION 9-203 explains when a security interest becomes enforceable. The 1972 changes also explain when it attaches.

SECTION 9-204 details when a security interest attaches. There is also a prohibition against security interests in crops attaching under an after-acquired property clause more than one year after execution of the security agreement.

SECTION 9-205 includes the term "contract rights" within its context.

SECTION 9-301 includes the element of knowledge. A lien creditor can not prevail over a prior unperfected security interest of which he has actual knowledge.

SECTION 9-302 provides that filing is not required to perfect a purchase money security interest in farm equipment not in excess of $2,500 and omits reference to the non-filing rule for assignments of beneficial interests in trusts and estates. In addition, the provisions dealing with certificate of title laws and utilities security interests are worded differently.

SECTION 9-304 does not specifically state that security interests in cash may not be perfected by filing. This version does not make it clear that priority of security interests in instruments, negotiable documents and some stored goods rests upon filing.

SECTION 9-305 does not indicate that security interests in money may not be perfected by filing.

SECTION 9-306 excludes insurance proceeds from the definition of "proceeds" and states that a financing statement must include mention of proceeds in order to perfect security interests therein.

SECTION 9-307 refers to farm equipment with maximum value of $2,500 which reference is deleted by the amendments. The 1962 statute does not have the new subsection (3) dealing with the right of purchasers, other than those in the ordinary course of business, taking the purchase of collateral free of security interests due to future advances made by the secured party with knowlege of the purchase or made later than 45 days from the purchase.

SECTION 9-308 under the earlier Code did not apply to negotiable instruments.

SECTION 9-312 indicates only that a holder of a purchase money security interest in inventory collateral has to, among other things, send notification of his interest to holders of prior security interests who filed before the purchase money secured party filed. The amended section states that notification must be sent to holders of prior security interests who filed before either the purchase money secured party filed or before the beginning of the 21 day automatic perfection established by Section 9-304(5). Moreover, the 1962 Code only states that the notification must be given before the debtor takes possession of the inventory, whereas its amendments provide that notification must be within five (5) years before the debtor's possession.

Under the 1962 Code, a continuously perfected security interest is deemed to have been perfected at all times in the same manner by which it was originally perfected for purposes of the priority rules.

The 1972 amendments add a provision to the effect that the time of perfection as to collateral is the time of perfection as to proceeds, and also one stating that future advances are deemed perfected dating from the time of the original perfection.

SECTION 9-313 appears in totally different form in its 1962 version. The former Code still uses the "material injury to the freehold" concept as a means of defining fixtures. Such implements as "fixture filing" are not present in the unamended formula. The 1962 Code does not provide for subordination of security interests in fixtures to construction mortgages.

SECTION 9-318 reflects the inclusion of the phrase "contract rights" in the Code. It also does not specifically proscribe contract terms requiring the debtor's consent to assignments of security interests.

SECTION 9-401 is devoid of mention of timber or mineral collateral or of fixture filings. This Section does not contain the special provision concerning the place of filing of security interest in collateral belonging to transmitting utilities.

SECTION 9-402 [59] dictates that financing statements must be signed by both the debtor and the secured party. With respect to collateral other than proceeds, this Section only authorizes the secured party to sign the financing statement instead of the debtor when the collateral is already subject to a security interest in another jurisdiction when it is brought into this state. The 1962 Code does not include the special requisites visited upon financing statements covering timber, minerals, accounts subject to Section 9-103(5) or fixtures. A cause of much litigation under the 1962 Code was the failure to permit filing under the individual, partnership or corporate name of the debtor without need of inclusion of any trade names or the names of the partners. The 1972 amendment authorizes filing under the trade name of the debtor.

SECTION 9-403 provides that a financing statement shall extend until its stated maturity date or for a maximum of five (5) years and sixty (60) days, whichever is longer. A financing statement indicating that the secured transaction is payable on demand is effective for five (5) years.

This Section does not extend the life of a financing statement which was effective at the time insolvency proceedings were commenced against the debtor until the termination of the proceedings, despite lapse of the five (5) year period.

The statement of assignment requirement is absent in cases of a continuation statement being signed by a party other than the secured party.

The uniform filing fee section is less detailed. No mention is made of timber or mineral collateral, fixture filings or collateral of a transmitting utility.

SECTION 9-404 only requires a secured creditor to file a termination statement upon written demand of the debtor in the appropriate circumstances, even if the collateral is consumer goods.

SECTION 9-405 was amended in 1972 to conform to the mechanics of the Code.

SECTION 9-406 does not contemplate the statement of assignment necessary when a statement of release is signed by a person other than the secured party.

SECTION 9-408 does not exist in the 1962 Code.

SECTION 9-501 is substantially the same in both versions with a minor technical change.

SECTION 9-502 includes reference to contract rights.

SECTION 9-504 requires that notice be given to every person found in the records to have an interest in the collateral before the secured party may dispose of it upon default (e.g., a guarantor). It is not expressly mandated that only post-default waivers of a debtor's right to notice are effective.

SECTION 9-505 delineates more persons that are entitled to notice of the

---

[59] The standard financing statement forms differ according to whether a given state has adopted the 1972 revisions. Section 4 of this Chapter illustrates the typical forms using the 1972 Code.

secured party's election to retain the collateral rather than dispose of it than are so entitled under the 1972 Code.

INFORMATION TO BE FURNISHED BY FILING OFFICER PURSUANT TO SECTION 9-407

SECTION 9-407 of the UCC, which is set forth below, provides that for a fee a filing officer may furnish certain information to the public as to previously filed financing statements. Not all states, however, have adopted this section of the Code. Therefore, in the event a state has not adopted 9-407, it is necessary that the search of the records be conducted by an individual or some organization which engages in the business of conducting such searches. If 9-407 has been adopted, a search of the records will be made by the filing officer upon payment of his fee.

SECTION 9-407

(1) If the person filing any financing statement, termination statement, statement of assignment, or statement of release, furnishes the filing officer a copy thereof, the filing officer shall upon request note upon the copy the file number and date and hour of the filing of the original and deliver or send the copy to such person.

(2) Upon request of any person, the filing officer shall issue his certificate showing whether there is on file, on the date and hour stated therein, any presently effective financing statement naming a particular debtor and any statement of assignment thereof and if there is, giving the date and hour of filing of each such statement and the name and address of each secured party therein.

FEES PAYABLE TO FILING OFFICER * FOR FURNISHING INFORMATION PURSUANT TO SECTION 9-407 **

ALABAMA

For certificate $4, plus $1 for each statement reported therein; for a copy of an instrument $1 for each page. An additional fee of $2 for each request not made on a standard form.

ALASKA

Requests for information with copies are $15 per debtor and/or trade name listed, requests alone are $5 per name and individual copies are $2 per document, an additional fee of $1 for requests made on non-approved forms.

ARIZONA

For certificate from Secretary of State $6; Recorder, $10; for a copy of filed or certified documents from Secretary of State $1 per page. Recorder 50¢ per page.

ARKANSAS

For certificate $3; for copies of instruments $1 for the first three pages and 50¢ for each succeeding page.

CALIFORNIA

For certificate up to $15; copy of filed statement $1 plus 50¢ for each additional page over one. A combined certificate showing the information as to financing statements, state tax liens, attachment liens, and federal liens is available from the Secretary of State for $5.

---

* For title of Filing Officer see following summary of Filing Requirements.

** Includes only state charge; there may be additional county or local fees.

SECURED TRANSACTIONS UNDER ARTICLE 9

COLORADO
Certificate $5; plus $2 for each additional year searched. Copy of an instrument $1.25 per page plus 50¢ for certification.

CONNECTICUT
For certificate $6 (standard form), $11 (nonstandard form); for a copy of an instrument $3 for the first three pages and $3 for each page thereafter. $5 per debtor for inspecting Secretary of State's records.

DELAWARE
For certificate $5; for a copy of an instrument $2 per page.

DISTRICT OF COLUMBIA
For certificate showing effective statement, $15, copy of filed statement, $1 per page, also $1 for certification.

FLORIDA
For certificate $1; certified copy from Department of State $5 plus $1 per page over 1; Search of records for each year $1 per year. Department of State $7.50 for record search and $1 per page of copy; Clerk $5 per page of copy.

GEORGIA
No provision for a certificate; for a copy of an instrument 75¢ per page.

HAWAII
For certificate $1 plus 50¢ for each instrument reported therein; for a copy of an instrument 50¢ per page.

IDAHO
For certificate $6 ($7 if nonstandard form); for a copy of filed statements $6 ($1 per page if file number given.)

ILLINOIS
For certificate $5; plus 50¢ for each instrument reported therein; nonstandard form $10; for a copy of an instrument 50¢ per page.

INDIANA
For certificate $1; plus 50¢ for each instrument reported therein; for copy of an instrument 50¢ per page. Certification, $1 per certificate.

IOWA
Certificate $4 standard form; nonstandard form $5; certified copy $1 per page. Verbal requests $4 plus $1 for confirming certificate. Certified copy of any filed statement is $1 per page.

KANSAS
Certificate $5 plus 25¢ for each instrument in excess of 10 for Secretary of State; copy of an instrument $1 per page.

KENTUCKY
No provision.

LOUISIANA
UCC has not been adopted.

MAINE
For certificate $5 for the first page, 50¢ for each additional page; copy of an instrument $1 for the first three pages, 50¢ for each additional page.

MARYLAND
Reasonable fee plus $3 for certification.

MASSACHUSETTS
For certificate $5 ($10 for Secretary of State); for a copy of an instrument $2 for the first three pages and $1 for each additional page.

MICHIGAN
For certificate $3 standard form, $6 nonstandard form; plus $1 for each instrument reported therein; for a copy of an instrument $1 per page.

MINNESOTA
For certificate $5, nonstandard $10; plus 50¢ for each instrument reported therein over 5; copy of filed statement 50¢ per page over 5.

MISSISSIPPI
For certificate $2; $10 if nonstandard form used; $2 for each listing on the certificate; for a copy of an instrument $2 per page.

MISSOURI
Uniform fee—$4 for certificate and copies of financing statements and statements of assignment.

MONTANA
For certificate $3, nonstandard $5; for a copy of an instrument 50¢ per page.

NEBRASKA
$2 per debtor; $3 for attestation. All inquiries $1 per name.

NEVADA
For certificate $6; for copy of instrument $1 for the first page, 50¢ for each additional page thereafter.

NEW HAMPSHIRE
For certificate $3 ($4 if nonstandard form); for a copy of an instrument 50¢ for each page.

NEW JERSEY
For certificate $15; for a copy of an instrument $1 per page. Expedited service $5.

NEW MEXICO
For a copy of an instrument 75¢ a page; for certifying a copy of an instrument 50¢ with an additional fee of 75¢ for comparing each page so certified with the filed instrument.

NEW YORK
For certificate $4.50 if request for certificate is on standard form, if not, fee is $7.50; for copy of an instrument $1.50 a page.

NORTH CAROLINA
For certificate $5 plus $1 for financing statement or reported statement of assignment reported therein; copy of an instrument $1 per page. Computer printout $5.

NORTH DAKOTA
Certificate $3; plus $1 for each financing statement and assignment over 5 reported therein; copy of filed statement $1.

OHIO
For certificate $9, Secretary of State, $5 County Recorder; plus $1 for each instrument reported therein; for copy of an instrument $1 per page.

OKLAHOMA
For certificate $5 for copy of an instrument $1 a page.

OREGON
For certificate $3.75 if standard form; if nonstandard form $5; certificate $1.50 per page of a copied financing statement or statement of assignment.

SECURED TRANSACTIONS UNDER ARTICLE 9   7–33

PENNSYLVANIA
Counties of the 1st class—$30 for certified search for 5 year period; 2nd class—$20; all others—Search $5 per debtor named, plus $1 each statement found and for each statement of assignment reported. Copy of filed statement $1 per page.

RHODE ISLAND
For certificate $5; for copy of an instrument 50¢ a page.

SOUTH CAROLINA
For certificate $2 plus $1 for each instrument reported therein; for copy of an instrument $1 per page plus $2 for certification.

SOUTH DAKOTA
For certificate $4, for a copy of an instrument 50¢ per page; on nonstandard form $7.

TENNESSEE
For certificate $4; for copy of filed statement $1 per page.

TEXAS
Certificate $5 for standard form, nonstandard $10; for a copy of instruments $1 per page but not less than $5 per request.

UTAH
Certificate 50¢ per page; plus $1 for each financing statement and assignment reported therein; if standard form $3, plus $1 each statement reported if nonstandard form.

VERMONT
For certificate $5; plus 50¢ for each financing statement and assignment reported therein; for copy $2 per page unless the page is more than 5" × 8", in which case the fee is $5 per page.

VIRGINIA
Certificate $6; plus $1 per page; search $6, plus $1 for each number found.

WASHINGTON
For certificate $4; for a copy of instrument $8 for each statement requested.

WEST VIRGINIA
For certificate $2; plus 50¢ for each instrument reported therein; photocopies $1; certified copies $5.

WISCONSIN
For certificate $3 for standard form, nonstandard $4 plus $1 for each instrument reported therein; for copy of an instrument $1 per page plus 50¢ for certification. Fee for oral reply to oral request for filing information may not exceed $4, plus $1 for each financing statement or statement of assignment.

WYOMING
Certificate $5, plus 50¢ for each effective filing, copies 50¢ per page for first 10 pages, then 15¢ per page.

FILING REQUIREMENTS WITH RESPECT TO FINANCING STATEMENTS UNDER UNIFORM COMMERCIAL CODE

Definition of Terms used in the Summary of Filing Requirements

Accessions—Security interest in goods before they are installed in or affixed to other goods.

Accounts Receivable—Right to payment for goods sold or leased or for services rendered not evidenced by an instrument of chattel paper.

Chattel Paper—A writing which evidences both a monetary obligation and a security interest in or a lease of specific goods.

Consumer Goods—Goods which are used or bought for use primarily in personal, family or household purposes.

Contract Rights—Right to payment under a contract not yet earned by performance and not evidenced by an instrument or chattel paper.

Documents—Documents of Title.

Equipment—Goods which are used or bought for use primarily in business or by a debtor which is a non-profit organization or a governmental subdivision or agency, or if the goods are not included in the definitions of inventory, farm products or consumer goods.

Farm Products—Goods which are crops or livestock or supplies used or produced in farming operations or goods which are products of crops or livestock in their unmanufactured states, and if they are in the possession of a debtor engaged in raising, fattening, grazing or other farm operations. If goods are "farm products" they are neither equipment nor inventory.

Fixtures—Goods which are so annexed to realty as to become a part thereof.

General Intangibles—Any personal property other than goods, accounts, contract rights, chattel paper, documents and instruments.

Instrument—A negotiable instrument, or a security or any other writing which evidences a right to the payment of money and is not itself a security agreement or lease and is a type which is in ordinary course of business transferred by delivery with any necessary endorsement or assignment.

Inventory—Goods which are held for sale or lease or furnished or to be furnished, under contracts of service, or materials used or consumed for business purposes. Inventory is not to be classified as equipment.

ALABAMA

CENTRAL FILING—Secretary of State, UCC Division, State Office Building, Room 536, Montgomery, Alabama 36130 (205) 269-6185

LOCAL FILING—Judge of Probate (Refers to Probate Court)

PLACE OF FILING—

Accessions: Local or Central Filing—Varies according to kinds of goods attached: consumer goods, equipment, farm products or inventory.

Accounts Receivable: Central Filing—Except if accounts from sale of farm products by farmer, local filing.

Chattel Paper: Central Filing.

Consumer Goods: Local Filing—Place of debtor's residence; if nonresident, place of goods. However, for purchase money security interest, no filing except for fixtures and licensed motor vehicle.

Documents: Central Filing.

Equipment: Central Filing. No UCC filing when law requires indication of lien on certificate of will.

Farm Equipment: Local Filing—Place of debtor's residence; if nonresident, place of goods. However, for purchase money security interest of $2500 or less, no filing except for fixture or licensed motor vehicle.

Farm Products: Local Filing—Place of debtor's residence; if nonresident, place of goods. Additional filing where land is located, if crops. Single filing where located if products are timber.

Fixtures: Local Filing—Place where land is located.

General Intangibles: Central Filing—Except if intangibles from sale of farm products by farmer, local filing.

Instruments: No Filing: possession perfects.

Inventory: Central filing.

Timber: Central Filing. Local filing when collateral is timber to be cut, where land is.

FEES—All instruments, uniform fee of $5 for the first page plus $1 for each additional page; additional $2 for nonstandard form; additional $1 for additional names or statements concerning crops, timber to be cut or fixture filings. In Barbour, Jefferson, Limestone, Madison, Mobile, Montgomery, Shelby and Tuscaloosa counties, additional fee per instrument of $1; $1.50 in Bibb and Clay counties.

TAXES—15¢ per $100 for local filing; 50¢ per $500 of personalty conveyed.

ALASKA

CENTRAL FILING—UCC Central File System, Department of Natural Resources, Division of Technical Services, P.O. Box 3336, Anchorage, Alaska 99510

LOCAL FILING—Recorder of Recording District

PLACE OF FILING—
Accessions: Local or Central Filing—Varies according to kinds of goods being attached: consumer goods, equipment, farm products or inventory.
Accounts Receivable: Central Filing—Except if accounts from sale of farm products by farmer, local filing. No filing when assignment is not of a significant part of contract rights.
Chattel Paper: Central Filing.
Consumer Goods: Local Filing—Place of debtor's residence; if nonresident, place of goods. However, for purchase money security interest, no filing except for fixture and motor vehicle requiring licensing.
Contract Rights: Central Filing—Except if contract rights from sale of farm products by farmer, local filing. No filing necessary unless significant portion of contract assigned includes contract rights.
Documents: Central Filing.
Equipment: Central Filing. No filing necessary when law requires indication of lien on certificate of title.
Farm Equipment: Local Filing—Place of debtor's residence; if nonresident, place of goods. However, for purchase money security interest of $2500 or less, no filing except for fixture and motor vehicle requiring licensing.
Farm Products: Local Filing—Place of debtor's residence; if nonresident, place of goods. Also, additional filing in county where land is, if crops.
Fixtures: Local Filing—Place where land is located.
General Intangibles: Central Filing—Except if intangibles from sale of farm products by farmer, local filing.
Instruments: No Filing.
Inventory: Central Filing.
FEES—Financing statement $6; amendment of financing statement $6; assignment $6; termination statement $3; release $3; continuation statement $4. In addition there is a charge of 25¢ for indexing against name of each debtor in excess of four.

ARIZONA

CENTRAL FILING—Secretary of State, 1700 W. Washington, 7th Floor, Phoenix, Arizona 85007 (602) 271-4280
LOCAL FILING—County Recorder
PLACE OF FILING—
Accessions: Local or Central Filing—Varies according to kinds of goods attached: consumer goods, equipment, farm products or inventory.
Accounts Receivable: Central Filing—Except if accounts are from sale of farm products by farmer, local filing at debtor's place of residence, or location of goods if nonresident. If minerals, filing at same location where real estate mortgage would be recorded. No filing necessary unless significant portion of contract assigned includes accounts receivable. No filing when assignment is not a significant part of contract rights.
Chattel Paper: Central Filing.
Consumer Goods: Local Filing—Place of debtor's residence, or location of goods if nonresident. However, for purchase money security interest, no filing except for fixtures and motor vehicles requiring licensing.
Documents: Central Filing.
Equipment: Central Filing. No filing necessary when law requires indication of lien on certificate of title.
Farm Equipment: Local Filing—Place of debtor's residence, or location of goods if nonresident. However, for purchase money security interest, no filing except for fixtures or motor vehicles requiring licensing.
Farm Products: Local Filing—Place of debtor's residence, or location of goods if nonresident. Also, additional filing in county where land is, if crops. And, single filing where located if products are timber.
Fixtures: Local Filing—Place where land is located.
General Intangibles: Central Filing—Except if intangibles from sale of farm products by farmer, local filing.
Instruments: No Filing.
Inventory: Central Filing.
Minerals: Local Filing—Same place where real estate mortgage would be recorded.

Timber: Central Filing—But, if timber to be cut, local filing at same place where real estate mortgage would be recorded.

FEES—Secretary of State's fee is $3 for all filings except satisfaction, release or termination fee of $2. Recorder's fee is $5 for first 5 pages and $1 for each additional page and each additional name, except for satisfaction, release or termination fee of $3.

ARKANSAS

CENTRAL FILING—Secretary of State, State Capitol Building, Room 256, Little Rock, Arkansas 72201 Attn: UCC (501) 371-5078
LOCAL FILING—Clerk of Circuit Court and Ex-officio Recorder
PLACE OF FILING—

Accessions: Local or Central Filing—Varies according to kinds of goods attached: consumer goods, equipment, farm products or inventory.

Accounts Receivable: Central Filing—Also local filing if business of debtor located in only 1 county or, debtor's place of residence, if no business. And, if accounts from sale of farm products by farmer, local filing. No filing necessary unless significant portion of contract assigned includes accounts receivable.

Chattel Paper: Central Filing. Also local filing if debtor's business located in only one county.

Consumer Goods: Local Filing—Debtor's place of residence, or location of goods if nonresident. However, if purchase money security interest, no filing except for fixtures or motor vehicles requiring licensing.

Documents: Central Filing. Also local filing if business of debtor located in only one county or, debtor's place of residence, if no business.

Equipment: Central Filing—Also local filing if business of debtor located in only one county or, debtor's place of residence, if no business.

Farm Equipment: Local Filing—Place of debtor's residence, or location of goods if nonresident.

Farm Products: Local Filing—Place of debtor's residence, or location of goods if nonresident. Also, additional filing in county where land is, if crops.

Fixtures: Local Filing—Place where land is located.

General Intangibles: Central Filing—Also local filing if business of debtor located in only one county or, debtor's place of residence, if no business. If intangibles from sale of farm products by farmer, local filing.

Instruments: No Filing.

Inventory: Central Filing—Also local filing if business of debtor located in only one county or, debtor's place of residence, if no business.

Minerals: Local Filing—Same place where real estate mortgage would be recorded.

Timber: Central Filing—But, if timber to be cut, local filing at same place where real estate mortgage would be recorded.

FEES—Uniform fee of $3. Recording, indexing, cross indexing $3 for first page $1 for each additional page.

CALIFORNIA

CENTRAL FILING—Secretary of State, UCC Division, P. O. Box 1738, Sacramento, California 95808 (916) 445-8061
LOCAL FILING—County Clerk and Recorder
PLACE OF FILING—

Accessions: Local or Central Filing—Varies according to kinds of goods attached: consumer goods, equipment, farm products or inventory.

Accounts Receivable: Central Filing—Except if accounts derived from minerals, etc., local filing at same place where real estate mortgage recorded. No filing necessary unless significant portion of contract assigned includes accounts receivable.

Chattel Paper: Central Filing.

Consumer Goods: Local Filing—Place of debtor's residence, or location of goods if nonresident; county in which primary place of business is located, or organization. However, if purchase money security interest, no filing except for motor vehicles or boats requiring licensing.

Documents: Central Filing.

Equipment: Central Filing. No filing necessary when law requires indication of lien on certificate of title, or for vehicle or boat required to be registered under vehicle code.

Farm Equipment: Central Filing—However, if purchase money security interest, no filing except if for boats or motor vehicles requiring licensing.

SECURED TRANSACTIONS UNDER ARTICLE 9   7-37

Farm Products: Central Filing—Except if land is used or to be used for growing crops or for cutting timber, local filing.
Fixtures: Local Filing—Where real estate mortgage would be recorded.
General Intangibles: Central Filing.
Instruments: No Filing.
Inventory: Central Filing.
Minerals: Local Filing—Same place where real estate mortgage recorded.
Timber: Central Filing—But, if timber to be cut, local filing at same place where real estate mortgage would be recorded.
FEES—Uniform fee of $3; $4 if nonstandard form used.

COLORADO

CENTRAL FILING—Secretary of State, Uniform Commercial Code, Division, Room 200, 1575 Sherman Street, Denver, Colorado 80203 (303) 866-2563
LOCAL FILING—County Clerk and Recorder
PLACE OF FILING—
Accessions: Local or Central Filing—Varies according to goods attached: consumer goods, equipment, farm products or inventory.
Accounts Receivable: Central Filing—Except if accounts from sale of farm products by farmer, local filing. No filing necessary unless significant portion of contract assigned includes accounts receivable.
Chattel Paper: Central Filing.
Consumer Goods: Local Filing—Place of debtor's residence, or location of goods if nonresident. However, if purchase money security interest, no filing except of fixtures or motor vehicles requiring licensing.
Documents: Central Filing.
Equipment: Central Filing.
Farm Equipment: Local Filing—Place of debtor's residence or location of goods if nonresident. However, if purchase money security of $500 or less, no filing except for fixtures or motor vehicles requiring licensing.
Farm Products: Local Filing—Place of debtor's residence, or location of goods if nonresident. Also, additional filing in county where land is, if crops.
Fixtures: Local Filing—Place where land is located.
General Intangibles: Central Filing—Except if intangibles from sale of farm products by farmer, local filing.
Instruments: No Filing.
Inventory: Central Filing.
Minerals: Local Filing, where the real estate is located.
Timber: Central Filing—Local Filing when timber is to be cut, where the real estate is located.
FEES—The uniform fee is $3. If nonstandard form, additional $1 plus $1 per page for attachments.

CONNECTICUT

CENTRAL FILING—Secretary of State, UCC Division, 30 Trinity Street, P. O. Box 846, Hartford, Connecticut 06115 (203) 566-4070
LOCAL FILING—Town Clerk.
PLACE OF FILING—
Accessions: Central Filing.
Accounts Receivable: Central Filing. Local filing, where land lies, when accounts are of minerals or the like. No filing necessary unless significant portion of contract assigned includes accounts receivable.
Chattel Paper: Central Filing.
Consumer Goods: Central Filing. However, for purchase money security interest, no filing except for fixture or motor vehicle requiring licensing.
Documents: Central Filing.
Equipment: Central Filing. No filing necessary when law requires indication of lien on certificate of title.
Farm Equipment: Central Filing.
Farm Products: Central Filing. Local where land lies, when collateral is timber to be cut or is minerals or the like.
Fixtures: Local Filing—Town Clerk of town where land is.
General Intangibles: Central Filing.

Instruments: No Filing.
Inventory: Central Filing.
FEES—Financing statement $6, $11 if nonstandard form; assignment $5; termination $2 except $4 if on non-prescribed form additional $4 for financing statement covering timber, minerals or fixtures. Termination statement signed by other than secured party $5. Fixtures: $15 for first page.

DELAWARE

CENTRAL FILING—Department of State, Uniform Commercial Code, P.O. Box 793, Dover, Delaware 19901 (302) 678-4111
LOCAL FILING—Recorder of Deeds.
PLACE OF FILING—
Accessions: Central Filing.
Accounts Receivable: Central Filing.
Chattel Paper: Central Filing.
Consumer Goods: Central Filing. However, for purchase money security interest, no filing except for fixture or motor vehicle requiring licensing.
Contract Rights: Central Filing. No filing necessary unless significant portion of contract assigned includes contract rights.
Documents: Central Filing
Equipment: Central Filing.
Farm Equipment: Central Filing. However, for purchase money security interest of $2500 or less, no filing except for fixtures and motor vehicles requiring licensing.
Farm Products: Central Filing. Local filing where land lies, when collateral is timber to be cut or is minerals or the like.
Fixtures: Local Filing with Recorder of Deeds at place where land is located.
General Intangibles: Central Filing.
Instruments: No Filing.
Inventory: Central Filing.
FEES—Uniform fee of $5.

DISTRICT OF COLUMBIA

CENTRAL FILING—Recorder of Deeds, 6th and D Streets NW, Washington, D.C. 20001 (202) 655-4000
LOCAL FILING—None
PLACE OF FILING—
Accessions: No special provisions.
Accounts Receivable: Central Filing.
Chattel Paper: Filing may be used to perfect.
Consumer Goods: Central Filing—However, for purchase money security interest, no filing except for fixtures and motor vehicles requiring licensing.
Documents: Central Filing.
Equipment: Central Filing.
Farm Equipment: No special provisions.
Farm Products: No special provisions.
Fixtures: No special provisions.
General Intangibles: No special provisions.
Instruments: No Filing.
Inventory: Central Filing.
Minerals: No special provisions.
Timber: No special provisions.
FEES—Uniform fee of $6 for the first 2 pages, plus $2 for each additional page.

FLORIDA

CENTRAL FILING—Department of State, Bureau of Uniform Commercial Code, Division of Corporations, Tallahassee, Florida 32301 (904) 448-1018
LOCAL FILING—Clerk of the Circuit Court (Filing is complete and sufficient only if the writing is recorded)
PLACE OF FILING
Accessions: Local or Central Filing—Varies according to kinds of goods attached: consumer goods, equipment, farm products or inventory.
Accounts Receivable: Central Filing—Except if accounts from sale of farm products by farmer,

SECURED TRANSACTIONS UNDER ARTICLE 9 7-39

local filing. No filing necessary unless significant portion of contract assigned includes accounts receivable.
Chattel Paper: Central Filing.
Consumer Goods: Central Filing.
Documents: Central Filing.
Equipment: Central Filing.
Farm Equipment: Local Filing—Place of debtor's residence or location of goods if nonresident. However, for purchase money security interest of $2500 or less, no filing except for fixtures.
Farm Products: Local Filing—Place of debtor's residence, or location of goods if nonresident. Also, additional filing in county where land is, if crops.
Fixtures: Local Filing—Place where land is located.
General Intangibles: Central Filing—Except if intangibles from sale of farm products by farmer, local filing.
Instruments: No Filing.
Inventory: Central Filing.
Minerals: Local Filing: where a real estate mortgage would be recorded.
Timber: Central Filing.

FEES—Financing statement $5.25; assignment $5; termination statement $5; release $5; continuation statement $5. There is an additional charge of $2 per page for each page after the first for filing any instrument. There is an additional fee of $3 for filing a nonstandard form. Clerk of the Circuit Court $5 for first page, $4 for each page thereafter.

TAXES—15¢ per $100 of indebtedness must be paid before the financing statement covering such indebtedness will be accepted for filing.

GEORGIA

CENTRAL FILING—None
LOCAL FILING—Clerk of the Superior Court in county of debtor's residence, or if debtor is a nonresident or business entity, in county of debtor's principal place of business; or if no principal place of business, county where property is used or kept.
PLACE OF FILING—
Accessions: No special provisions.
Accounts Receivable: Local Filing—However, no filing when total assignment to the same party does not constitute a transfer of a significant amount of the debtor's receivables. No filing necessary unless significant portion of contract assigned includes accounts receivable.
Chattel Paper: Local Filing.
Consumer Goods: Local Filing—However, for purchase money security interest, no filing except for fixtures and motor vehicles requiring licensing.
Documents and Goods: Local filing (permissive).—Security interests in goods when security interests in correlative documents are perfected.
Equipment: Local Filing—However, no filing when indication of lien on a certificate of title is a requirement of Georgia law.
Farm Equipment: No special provisions.
Farm Products: No special provisions.
Fixtures: Local Filing—Place where land is situated.
General Intangibles: No special provisions.
Instruments: No Filing.
Inventory: Local Filing.

FEES—Financing statement $3.50 and 50¢ per additional page; DeKalb County, $5 for financing statement and continuation statements plus 50¢ for each page over one; assignment $2; termination statement $1 for financing statement filed before July 1, 1981, otherwise no fee; release $2; continuation statement $3.50; financing statement indicating assignment $3.50.

HAWAII

CENTRAL FILING—Registrar of Conveyances, Bureau of Conveyances, P. O. Box 2867, Honolulu, Hawaii 96803 (808) 548-2211
LOCAL FILING—None.
PLACE OF FILING—
Accessions: No special provisions.
Accounts Receivable: Central Filing—No filing when assignment is not a significant part of contract rights. No filing necessary unless significant portion of contract assigned includes accounts receivable.

Chattel Paper: Central Filing.
Consumer Goods: Central Filing—However, for purchase money security interest, no filing except for fixtures.
Documents: No filing necessary.
Equipment: Central Filing. No filing for a vehicle required to be registered, unless the vehicle is inventory.
Farm Equipment: No special provisions.
Farm Products: No special provisions.
Fixtures: No special provisions.
General Intangibles: No special provisions.
Instruments: No Filing.
Inventory: Central Filing.
Minerals: No special provisions.
Timber: No special provisions.
FEES—Uniform fee of $2 per page.

IDAHO

CENTRAL FILING—Secretary of State, Statehouse, Room 205, Boise, Idaho 83720 (208) 384-2300
LOCAL FILING—County Recorder
PLACE OF FILING—

Accessions: Local or Central Filing—Varies according to kinds of goods attached: consumer goods, equipment, farm products or inventory.
Accounts Receivable: Central Filing—Except if accounts from sale of farm products by farmers, local filing. Where accounts are of minerals or the like, where a real estate mortgage would be recorded. No filing necessary unless significant portion of contract assigned includes accounts receivable.
Chattel Paper: Central Filing.
Consumer Goods: Local Filing—Place of debtor's residence, or location of goods if nonresident. However, for purchase money security interest, no filing except for fixtures and motor vehicles requiring licensing.
Documents: Central Filing.
Equipment: Central Filing.
Farm Equipment: Local Filing—Place of debtor's residence, or location of goods if nonresident.
Farm Products: Local Filing—Place of debtor's residence, or location of goods if nonresident. Also, additional filing where land is, if products are crops.
Fixtures: Local Filing—Place where land is located.
General Intangibles: Central Filing—Except if intangibles from sale of farm products by farmer, local filing.
Instruments: No Filing.
Inventory: Central Filing.
Minerals: Local Filing, where a real estate mortgage would be recorded.
Timber: Central Filing, local filing when collateral is timber to be cut.
FEES—Financing statement $2; if nonstandard form $3; continuation and assignment $3 ($4 if nonstandard form); termination—no fee if standard form used, otherwise $1.

ILLINOIS

CENTRAL FILING—Secretary of State, UCC Division, Centennial Building, Springfield, Illinois 62756 (217) 782-7518
LOCAL FILING—Recorder of Deeds
PLACE OF FILING—

Accessions: Local or Central Filing—Varies according to kinds of goods attached: consumer goods, equipment, farm products or inventory.
Accounts Receivable: Central Filing—Except if accounts from sale of farm products by farmer, local filing. Also, if minerals, etc., filing at same place where real estate mortgage would be recorded. No filing necessary unless significant portion of contract assigned includes accounts receivable.
Chattel Paper: Central Filing.
Consumer Goods: Local Filing—Place of debtor's residence, or location of goods if nonresident. However, for purchase money security interest, no filing except for fixtures and motor vehicles requiring licensing.
Documents: Central Filing.

SECURED TRANSACTIONS UNDER ARTICLE 9   7-41

Equipment: Central Filing. No filing necessary where law requires indication of lien on certificate of title.
Farm Equipment: Local Filing—Place of debtor's residence, or location of goods if nonresident.
Farm Products: Local Filing—Place of debtor's residence, or location of goods if nonresident. Also, additional filing in county where land is, if crops.
Fixtures: Local Filing—Place where land located.
General Intangibles: Central Filing—Except if intangibles from sale of farm products by farmer, local filing.
Instruments: No Filing.
Inventory: Central Filing.
Minerals: Local Filing—Same place where real estate mortgage would be recorded.
Timber: Central Filing—But, if timber is to be cut, local filing at same place where real estate mortgage would be recorded.
FEES—Financing statement $4, if nonstandard form used, $8; assignment $4; termination statement $4; release $4; continuation statement $4. $4 per additional name except for that of a spouse when husband and wife are joint debtors.

INDIANA

CENTRAL FILING—Secretary of State, 201 Statehouse, Indianapolis, Indiana 46204 (317) 633-6531
LOCAL FILING—County Recorder
PLACE OF FILING—
Accessions: Local or Central Filing—Varies according to kinds of goods attached: consumer goods, equipment, farm products or inventory.
Accounts Receivable: Central Filing—Except if accounts are from sale of farm products by farmer, local filing. If debtor a corporation, also local filing at principal place of business.
Chattel Paper: Central Filing.
Consumer Goods: Local Filing—Place of debtor's residence, or place of goods if nonresident. However, for purchase money security interest, no filing except for fixtures and motor vehicles requiring licensing. If debtor or corporation, file with Secretary of State and where principal place of business is.
Contract Rights: Central Filing—Except if contract rights from sale of farm products by farmer, local filing. If debtor a corporation, also file where principal place of business is. No filing necessary unless significant portion of contract assigned includes contract rights.
Documents: Central Filing.
Equipment: Central Filing. No filing necessary where law requires indication of lien on certificate of title.
Farm Equipment: Local Filing—Place of debtor's residence, or location of goods if nonresident. If a corporation, file with Secretary of State and where principal place of business is. However, for purchase money security interest less than $500, no filing except for a fixture or motor vehicle requiring licensing.
Farm Products: Local Filing—Place of debtor's residence, or location of goods if nonresident; if a corporation, file with Secretary of State and where principal place of business is. Also, additional filing in county where land is, if crops.
Fixtures: Local Filing—Place where land is located.
General Intangibles: Central Filing—Except if intangibles from sale of farm products by farmer, local filing. If debtor is a corporation, also file where principal place of business is.
Instruments: No. Filing.
Inventory: Central Filing.
FEES—Uniform fee $4, except $8 where nonstandard form. Termination, releases of amendments thereof—no fee; statement on fixtures 50¢ additional.

IOWA

CENTRAL FILING—UCC Division, Secretary of State, Hoover Building, Des Moines, Iowa 50319 (515) 281-3326
LOCAL FILING—County Recorder
PLACE OF FILING—
Accessions: Local or Central Filing—Varies according to kinds of goods attached: consumer goods, equipment, farm products or inventory.
Accounts Receivable: Central Filing but if accounts are from minerals etc., local filing where

land is located. No filing necessary unless significant portion of contract assigned includes accounts receivable.

Chattel Paper: Central Filing.

Consumer Goods: Central Filing—Where debtor resides except if debtor resident, local filing at place of debtor's residence. However, for purchase money security interest, no filing except for fixtures and motor vehicles requiring licensing.

Documents: Central Filing.

Equipment: Central Filing. No filing necessary when lien may be indicated on vehicle certificate of title.

Farm Equipment: Central Filing.

Farm Products: Central Filing—Except if timber to be cut or a mineral, local filing a place where land located.

Fixtures: Local Filing—Place where land is located.

General Intangibles: Central Filing.

Instruments: No Filing.

Inventory: Central Filing.

Minerals: Local Filing—Where real estate mortgage would be recorded.

Timber: Central Filing—But if timber to be cut, local filing at place where real estate mortgage would be recorded.

FEES—Financing statement or statement of assignment $4; if nonstandard form is used $5. Continuation, release, separate statement of assignment accompanying financing or continuation statement $2; if nonstandard form is used $3. Termination fee no charge. The fee for recording a fixture filing is $3 per page; release of a fixture filing $3 per page.

KANSAS

CENTRAL FILING—Secretary of State, Attention: UCC, 2nd Floor, Capitol Bldg., Topeka, Kansas 66612 (913) 296-2236

LOCAL FILING—Register of Deeds

PLACE OF FILING—

Accessions: Local or Central Filing—Varies according to kinds of goods attached: consumer goods, equipment, farm products or inventory.

Accounts Receivable: Central Filing—Except if from sale of farm products by farmer, local filing. Also, if minerals etc., where a real estate mortgage would be recorded. No filing necessary unless significant portion of contract assigned includes accounts receivable.

Chattel Paper: Central Filing.

Consumer Goods: Local Filing—Place of debtor's residence, or location of goods if nonresident.

Documents: Central Filing.

Equipment: Central Filing.

Farm Equipment: Central Filing—Place of debtor's residence, or location of goods if nonresident. Also, additional filing where land is, if crops.

Farm Products: Central Filing—Place of debtor's residence, or location of goods if nonresident. Also, additional filing where land is, if crops.

Fixtures: Local Filing—Place where land is located.

General Intangibles: Central Filing—Except if intangibles from sale of farm products by farmer, local filing.

Instruments: No Filing.

Inventory: Central Filing.

Minerals: Local Filing—Where real estate mortgage would be recorded.

Timber: Central Filing—But if timber to be cut, local filing at place where real estate mortgage would be recorded.

FEES—The uniform fee is $3 for standard form if filed with Secretary of State and $5 for nonstandard form. For statements filed with other than the Secretary of State the fee is $3 for a standard form, $5 for nonstandard. No fee for termination statement.

KENTUCKY

CENTRAL FILING—Secretary of State, UCC Section, Capitol Building, Frankfort, Kentucky 40601 (502) 564-3490

LOCAL FILING—County Clerk

PLACE OF FILING—

Accessions: Local or Central Filing—Varies according to kinds of goods attached: consumer goods, equipment, farm products or inventory.

Accounts Receivable: Local or Central Filing—Resident debtor, county of place of residence; nonresident debtor, where principal place of business is; nonresident debtor without a place of business, with Secretary of State. If accounts are from sale of farm products by farmer, local filing. No filing when total assignment to the same party does not constitute a transfer of a significant part of the debtor's receivables.

Chattel Paper: Local or Central Filing (permissive) Resident debtor, county of place of residence; nonresident debtor, where principal place of business is; nonresident debtor without a place of business, with the Secretary of State.

Consumer Goods: Local Filing—Place of debtor's residence, or location of goods if nonresident. However, for purchase money security interest, no filing except for fixtures and motor vehicles requiring licensing.

Contract Rights: Local or Central Filing—Resident debtor, county of place of residence; nonresident debtor, where principal place of business is; nonresident debtor without a place of business, with Secretary of State. If accounts are from sale of farm products by farmer, local filing. No filing when assignment is of an insignificant portion of debtor's contract rights.

Documents and Goods: Local or Central Filing—Resident debtor, county of residence; nonresident debtor, where principal place of business is; nonresident debtor without a place of business, with the Secretary of State. When one perfects a security interest in a document of title, one effectively perfects a security interest in the goods represented by the document.

Equipment: Local or Central Filing—Resident debtor, county of residence; nonresident debtor, where principal place of business is; nonresident without a place of business, with the Secretary of State. No filing when indication of lien on a certificate of title is a requirement of Kentucky law.

Farm Equipment: Local Filing—Place of debtor's residence, or location of goods if nonresident. However, for purchase money security interest of $500 or less, no filing except for fixtures or motor vehicles requiring licensing.

Farm Products: Local Filing—Place of debtor's residence, or location of goods if nonresident. Also, additional filing in county where land is, if crops.

Fixtures: Local Filing—Place where land is located.

General Intangibles: Local or Central Filing—Resident debtor, county of residence; nonresident debtor, where principal place of business is; nonresident debtor without a place of business, with Secretary of State. If intangibles from sale of farm products by farmer, local filing.

Instruments: No Filing.

Inventory: Local or Central Filing—Resident debtor, county of residence; nonresident debtor, where principal place of business is; nonresident debtor without a place of business, with the Secretary of State.

FEES—Financing statement; continuation statement; termination statement; financing statement indicating assignment; separate assignment—$6. Central filing fee $3. Release $1.

TAXES—$1 levy on instruments over $200.

LOUISIANA

Louisiana has not adopted Article 9 of the UCC.

MAINE

CENTRAL FILING—Secretary of State, U.C.C. Bureau, State House Station 101, Augusta, Maine 04333 (207) 289-3676

LOCAL FILING—Clerk of Municipality

PLACE OF FILING—

Accessions: Local or Central Filing—varies according to kinds of goods attached: Consumer goods, equipment, farm products or inventory. Local filings, where land lies, when accounts are of mineral or the like.

Accounts Receivable: Central Filing—However, no filing when total assignment to the same party does not constitute a transfer of a significant part of the debtor's receivables. No filing necessary unless significant portion of contract assigned includes accounts receivable.

Chattel Paper: Central Filing (Permissive)

Consumer Goods: Central Filing—However, no filing for purchase money security interest unless interest is in fixtures.

Documents and Goods: Central Filing—Security interests in goods are perfected when security interests in correlative documents of title are perfected.

Equipment: Central Filing—However, no filing when indication of lien on certificates of title is a requirement of Maine law.

Farm Equipment: Central Filing—no special provisions.
Farm Products: Central Filing—Local filing at place land is located when collateral is timber to be cut, minerals or the like (including oil and gas), or crops (including oysters).
Fixtures: Local Filing—with Register of Deeds at place where land is located.
General Intangibles: Central Filing—No special provisions.
Instruments: No Filing.
Inventory: Central Filing.
Minerals: Local Filing—at the place or recordation of mortgages on realty when the collateral is minerals or the like (including oil and gas) or their accounts.
Timber: Central Filing—Local Filing at the place of recordation of mortgages on realty when collateral is timber to be cut.
FEES: Financing statement $5; continuation statement, separate assignment, an amendment of an original or continuation statement or a statement of release $3; termination statement for a financing statement filed prior to April 1, 1970 $2; no charge for filing a termination statement for financing statements filed after April 1, 1970.

MARYLAND

CENTRAL FILING—Department of Assessments and Taxation, 301 West Preston Street, Baltimore, Maryland 21201 (301) 267-5861
LOCAL FILING—Clerk of Circuit Court (Includes Clerk of Superior Court of Baltimore City)
PLACE OF FILING—
Accessions: Local or Central Filing—Varies according to kinds of goods attached: consumer goods, equipment, farm products or inventory.
Accounts Receivable: Central Filing—Also, local filing if business of debtor located in only one county or, place or residence, if no business. If accounts from sale of farm products by farmers, local filing: resident, place of residence; nonresident, place where goods located. No filing necessary unless significant portion of contract assigned includes accounts receivable.
Chattel Paper: Central Filing—Also local filing if business of debtor located in only one county or, place of residence, if no business.
Consumer Goods: Local Filing—Place of debtor's residence, or location of goods if nonresident. However, for purchase money security interest, no filing except for fixtures and motor vehicles requiring licensing. If value $500 or less, no filing.
Documents: Central Filing—Also local filing if business of debtor located in only one county or, place of residence, if no business.
Equipment: Central Filing—Also local filing if business of debtor located in only one county or, place of residence, if no business.
Farm Equipment: Local Filing—Place of debtor's residence, or location of goods if nonresident. However, for purchase money security interest of $500 or less, no filing except for a fixture or motor vehicle requiring licensing.
Farm Products: Local Filing—Place of debtor's residence, or location of goods if nonresident. Also, additional filing in county where land is, if crops.
Fixtures: Local Filing—Place where land is located.
General Intangibles: Central Filing—Also local filing if business of debtor located in only one county or, place of residence, if no business. If intangibles from sale of farm products by farmer, local filing: resident, place of business; nonresident, place where goods located.
Instruments: No Filing.
Inventory: Central Filing and also local filing if business of debtor located in only one county or, place of residence, if no business.
Minerals: Local Filing.
Timber: Central Filing; local filing where the collateral is timber to be cut.
FEES—Financing statement, assignment, termination statement, release, and continuation statement are all $4 per page (minimum $10) plus $1 for each name indexed for recording.
TAXES—Local filings are taxed at various rates from 55¢ to $3.50 per $500 in the different counties. Central filings are taxed at $1.65 per $500 of indebtedness.

MASSACHUSETTS

CENTRAL FILING—Office of the Secretary of State, Uniform Commercial Code Section, 1 Ashburton Place, Room 1711, Boston, Massachusetts 02108 (617) 727-2860
LOCAL FILING—Clerk of the Town
PLACE OF FILING—

SECURED TRANSACTIONS UNDER ARTICLE 9   7–45

Accessions: Local or Central Filing—Varies according to kinds of goods attached: consumer goods, equipment, farm products or inventory.

Accounts Receivable: Central Filing—In addition, local filing in town where debtor has only place of business, or town of residence if no place of business. If accounts from sale of farm products by farmer, local filing. No filing necessary unless significant portion of contract assigned includes accounts receivable.

Chattel Paper: Central Filing—In addition, local filing in town where debtor has only place of business, or in town of residence if no place of business.

Consumer Goods: Local Filing—Place of debtor's residence, or location of goods if nonresident. For purchase money security interest, no filing except for fixtures.

Documents: Central Filing—Also local filing in town where debtor has only place of business, or in town of residence if no place of business.

Equipment: Central Filing—Also local filing in town where debtor has only place of business, or in town of residence if no place of business.

Farm Equipment: Local Filing—Place of debtor's residence, or location of goods if nonresident. However, for purchase money security interest of $500 or less, no filing except for a fixture.

Farm Products: Local Filing—Place of debtor's residence, or location of goods if nonresident. Also, additional filing in county where land is, if crops.

Fixtures: Local Filing—Where land is located with Register of Deeds.

General Intangibles: Central Filing—Also local filing in town where debtor has only place of business, or in town of residence if no place of business. If intangibles from sale of farm products by farmer, local filing.

Instruments: No Filing.

Inventory: Central Filing—Also local filing in town where debtor has only place of business, or in town of residence if no place of business.

Minerals: Local Filing.

Timber: Central Filing, if collateral is timber to be cut, local filing.

FEES—Secretary of State and Clerk of the Town: Uniform fee $10, except for assignment or termination $5. Register of Deeds: Financing statement $5, continuation statement $5; other instruments $4, additional fee of $1 per page after first page and 75¢ to index each name over two.

MICHIGAN

CENTRAL FILING—Secretary of State, UCC Division, 300 East Michigan Avenue, Lansing, Michigan 48918 (517) 373-6610

LOCAL FILING—Register of Deeds

PLACE OF FILING—

Accessions: Local or Central Filing—Varies according to kinds of goods attached: consumer goods, equipment, farm products or inventory.

Accounts Receivable: Central Filing—Except if accounts from sale of farm products by farmer, local filing. No filing necessary unless significant portion of contract assigned includes accounts receivable.

Chattel Paper: Central Filing.

Consumer Goods: Local Filing—Place of debtor's residence, or location of goods if nonresident. However, for purchase money security interest, no filing except for fixtures and motor vehicles requiring licensing.

Documents: Central Filing.

Equipment: Central Filing.

Farm Equipment: Local Filing—Place of debtor's residence, or location of goods if nonresident.

Farm Products: Local Filing—Place of debtor's residence, or location of goods if nonresident. Also, additional filing in county where land is, if crops.

Fixtures: Local Filing in the office where a mortgage on the realty would be recorded.

General Intangibles: Central Filing—Except if intangibles from sale of farm products by farmer, local filing.

Instruments: No Filing.

Inventory: Central Filing.

Minerals: Local filing, where a real estate mortgage would be recorded.

Timber: Central Filing, if collateral is timber to be cut, local filing.

FEES—Uniform fee is $3 if standard form is used; otherwise, $6; local filing is $3; if statement indicates that it is to be recorded in the real estate records and standard form is used—$6; if standard form is not used—$6 plus $2 for each page over two. Additional names $3. Termination statement filed with respect to filing statement filed on or before June 30, 1976—$1; otherwise no fee.

MINNESOTA

CENTRAL FILING—Secretary of State, UCC Division, 180 State Office Building, St. Paul, Minnesota 55155 (612) 296-2434
LOCAL FILING—County Recorder
PLACE OF FILING—
Accessions: Local or Central Filing—Varies according to kinds of goods attached: consumer goods, equipment, farm products or inventory.
Accounts Receivable: Central Filing—If accounts are from a sale of farm products by farmer, filing at place of residence of individual debtor; otherwise file with Secretary of State. No filing necessary unless significant portion of contract assigned includes accounts receivable.
Chattel Paper: Central Filing.
Consumer Goods: Local Filing—If resident individual debtor, place of residence; otherwise file with the Secretary of State. However, for purchase money security interest, no filing except for fixtures and motor vehicles requiring licensing.
Documents: Central Filing.
Equipment: Central Filing. No filing necessary when law requires indication of lien on certificate of title.
Farm Equipment: Local Filing—If resident individual debtor, place of residence; otherwise with the Secretary of State.
Farm Products: Local Filing—If resident individual debtor, place of residence; otherwise with the Secretary of State. Also, additional filing in county where land is located, if crops.
Fixtures: Local Filing—Place where land is located.
General Intangibles: Central Filing—Except if general intangibles from sale of farm products by farmer, filing at place of residence of resident individual debtor, otherwise file with the Secretary of State.
Instruments: No Filing.
Inventory: Central Filing.
Minerals: Local Filing, where a real estate mortgage would be recorded.
Timber: Central Filing except where collateral is timber to be cut.
FEES—Uniform fee if $5, $10 if nonstandard form; no fee for standard termination, $5 for nonstandard; additional $5 fee for each name more than one or for statement covering timber, minerals or fixtures.

MISSISSIPPI

CENTRAL FILING—Secretary of State, UCC Division, P. O. Box 136, Jackson, Mississippi 39205 (601) 354-6545
LOCAL FILING—Clerk of the Chancery Court
PLACE OF FILING—
Accessions: Central or Local Filing—Varies according to the kinds of goods attached: consumer goods, equipment, farm products or inventory. When accounts are of minerals, local filing, where a real estate mortgage would be recorded.
Accounts Receivable: Central Filing—Also local filing if business of debtor located in only one county or, place of residence, if no business. If accounts from sale of farm products by farmer, local filing. No filing necessary unless significant portion of contract includes accounts receivable.
Chattel Paper: Central Filing—Also local filing if business of debtor located in only one county or, place of residence, if no business.
Consumer Goods: Local Filing—Place of debtor's residence, or location of goods if nonresident. However, for purchase money security interests, no filing except for fixtures and motor vehicles requiring licensing.
Documents: Central Filing—Also local filing if business of debtor in only one county or, place of residence, if no business.
Equipment: Central Filing—Also local filing if business of debtor in only one county or, place of residence, if no business. No filing necessary when law requires indication of lien on certificate of title.
Farm Equipment: Local Filing—Place of debtor's residence, or location of goods if nonresident.
Farm Products: Central Filing—Place of debtor's residence, or location of goods if nonresident. Also, additional filing in county where land is located.

SECURED TRANSACTIONS UNDER ARTICLE 9   7-47

Fixtures: Local Filing—Place where land is located.
General Intangibles: Central Filing. Also local filing if business of debtor in only one county or, place of residence, if no business. If intangibles from sale of farm products by farmer, local filing.
Instruments: No Filing.
Inventory: Central Filing—Also local filing if business of debtor in only one county or, place of residence, if no business.
Minerals: Local Filing.
Timber: Central Filing except where the collateral is timber to be cut.
FEES—Uniform fee is $5. Additional charge of $5 if nonstandard form used; $3 for a statement of release. Additional $5 plus $1 for pages 2 *et seq.* financing statement concerns timber or fixtures. Additional $1 for each name or trade name, plus $1 per entry, over one when statement concerns timber or fixtures; $2 for each additional name on financing statement.

MISSOURI

CENTRAL FILING—Secretary of State, Commercial Code Division, P. O. Box 1159, Jefferson City, Missouri 65102 (314) 751-4179
LOCAL FILING—Recorder of Deeds
PLACE OF FILING—
Accessions: Local or Central Filing—Varies according to kinds of goods attached: consumer goods, equipment, farm products or inventory.
Accounts Receivable: Central Filing—Also local filing if business of debtor in only one county or, place of residence, if no business. If accounts from sale of farm products by farmer, local filing.
Chattel Paper: Central Filing—Also local filing if business of debtor in only one county or, place of residence, if no business.
Consumer Goods: Local Filing—Place of debtor's residence, or location of goods if nonresident. However, for purchase money security interest, no filing except for fixtures and motor vehicles requiring licensing.
Contract Rights: Central Filing—Also local filing if business of debtor in only one county, or place of residence, if no business. If contract rights from sale of farm products by farmer, local filing. No filing necessary unless significant portion of contract assigned includes contract rights.
Documents: Central Filing—Also local filing if business of debtor in only one county, or place of residence, if no business.
Equipment: Central Filing—Also local filing if business of debtor in only one county, or place of residence, if no business.
Farm Equipment: Local Filing—Place of debtor's residence, or location of goods if nonresident. However, for purchase money security interest of $500 or less, no filing except for a fixture or motor vehicle requiring licensing.
Farm Products: Local Filing—Place of debtor's residence, or location of goods if nonresident. Also, additional filing in county where land is located, if crops.
Fixtures: Local Filing—Place where land is located.
General Intangibles: Central Filing—Also local filing if business of debtor in only one county, or place of residence, if no business. If intangibles from sale of farm products by farmer, local filing.
Instruments: No Filing.
Inventory: Central Filing—Also local filing if business of debtor in only one county, or place of residence, if no business.
FEES—Uniform fee is $2. If nonstandard form is used filing fee for all instruments is $4.

MONTANA

CENTRAL FILING—Secretary of State, UCC Division, The Capitol Post Office, Helena, Montana 59620 (406) 449-2034
LOCAL FILING—County Clerk and Recorder
PLACE OF FILING—
Accessions: Local or Central Filing—Varies according to kinds of goods attached: consumer goods, equipment, farm products or inventory.
Accounts Receivable: Central Filing—Except if accounts from sale of farm products by farmer, local filing.
Chattel Paper: Central Filing.
Consumer Goods: Local Filing—Place of debtor's residence, or location of goods if nonresident.

If purchase money security interest, no filing except for fixtures or motor vehicles requiring licensing.

Documents: Central Filing.

Equipment: Central Filing. No filing necessary when law requires indication of lien on certificate of title.

Farm Equipment: Central filing, also local filing where debtor resides.

Farm Products: Local Filing—Place of debtor's residence, or location of goods if nonresident. Also, additional filing in county where land is located, if crops.

Fixtures: Local Filing—Place where land is located.

General Intangibles: Central Filing—Except if intangibles from sale of farm products by farmer, local filing.

Instruments: No Filing.

Inventory: Central Filing.

FEES—Uniform fee is $2, $4 for nonstandard forms. There is an additional fee of $2 for each additional name. If collateral is equipment or rolling stock of a railroad, all fees are $15.

NEBRASKA

CENTRAL FILING—Secretary of State, UCC Division, Lower Level, State Office Building, Lincoln, Nebraska 68509

LOCAL FILING—County Clerk

PLACE OF FILING—

Accessions: Local or Central Filing—Depends upon whether goods being attached are consumer goods, equipment, farm products, or inventory.

Accounts Receivable: Central Filing—Local filing when accounts are from farmer's sale of farm products. When accounts are of minerals or the like (including oil and gas), where a real estate mortgage would be recorded.

Chattel Paper: Central Filing may be used to perfect—Without possession secured party loses to purchaser for new value without knowledge in ordinary course. Purchaser for new value with knowledge in ordinary course has priority over security interest claimed as proceeds of inventory subject to a security interest.

Consumer Goods: Local Filing—Where debtor resides; if nonresident, place of goods. No filing for purchase money security interest except for fixtures and motor vehicles required to licensed.

Documents and Goods: Central Filing—Security interest in negotiable documents includes goods in possession of issuer. Filing and possession are alternative means to perfect security interests in negotiable documents. Perfection for 21 days without filing or possession after giving new value under a written security agreement.

Equipment: Central Filing—No UCC filing when law requires indication of lien on certificate of title.

Farm Equipment: Local Filing—Where debtor resides; if nonresident, place of goods.

Farm Products: Local Filing—Where debtor resides; if nonresident, place of goods. In addition, central filing when collateral is crops growing or to be grown.

Fixtures: Local Filing with Register of Deeds where land is located.

General Intangibles: Central Filing—Local filing when intangibles arise from farmer's sale of farm products.

Instruments: No Filing. Possession Perfects—Perfection for 21 days without possession after giving new value under a written security agreement.

Inventory: Central Filing—Goods held for sale, lease, or materials used or consumed in a business. Vehicles held as inventory for sale must be filed under UCC.

Minerals: Local Filing—When collateral is minerals or the like (including oil and gas) or their accounts, where a real estate mortgage would be recorded.

Timber: Central Filing—Local filing when collateral is timber to be cut, where a real estate mortgage would be recorded.

FEES—The uniform fee is $6, plus 50¢ per page for the first five pages of attachments except for statements covering consumer goods; $6 all other statements. Nonstandard form—$3 additional to UCC filing fees. Fixture filing—$3 a page for recordings and $1.50 per page for a certified copy, plus 50¢ for certificate and seal. Extra names additional $4.

Federal identification number or social security number of debtor and secured party are required on each financing statement.

NEVADA

CENTRAL FILING—Secretary of State, UCC Division, Capitol Complex, Carson City, Nevada 89710 (702) 882-7439

LOCAL FILING—County Recorder
PLACE OF FILING—
Accessions: Local or Central Filing—Varies according to kinds of goods attached: consumer goods, equipment, farm products or inventory.
Accounts Receivable: Central Filing—Also local filing if business of debtor located in only one county, or place where debtor resides in state, if no business. If accounts from sale of farm products by farmer, local filing. When accounts are minerals etc., where a real estate mortgage would be recorded. No filing necessary unless significant portion of contract assigned includes accounts receivable.
Chattel Papers: Central Filing.
Consumer Goods: Local Filing—Place of debtor's residence, or location of goods if nonresident. However, for purchase money security interest, no filing except for fixtures and motor vehicles requiring licensing.
Documents: Central Filing.
Equipment: Central Filing—Also local filing if business of debtor located in only one county, or where debtor resides in state, if no business. No filing necessary when law requires indication of lien on certificate of title.
Farm Equipment: Central Filing—Place of debtor's residence, or location of goods if nonresident.
Farm Products: Central Filing—Place of debtor's residence, or location of goods if nonresident. Also, additional filing in county where land is located, if crops.
Fixtures: Local Filing—Place where land is located.
General Intangibles: Central Filing—Also local filing if business of debtor located in only one county, where debtor resides in state, if no business. If intangibles from sale of farm products by farmer, local filing.
Instruments: No Filing.
Inventory: Central Filing—Also, local filing if business of debtor in only one county, or where debtor resides in state, if no business.
Minerals: Local Filing—Where real estate mortgage would be recorded.
Timber: Central Filing—But if timber to be grown, local filing where real estate mortgage would be recorded.
FEES—Uniform fee is $5. If nonstandard forms used all fees are $6.

NEW HAMPSHIRE

CENTRAL FILING—Secretary of State, UCC—Records, 71 South Fruit Street, Concord, New Hampshire 03301 (603) 271-1110
LOCAL FILING—Clerk of the Town
PLACE OF FILING—
Accessions: Local or Central Filing—Varies according to kinds of goods attached: consumer goods, equipment, farm products or inventory.
Accounts Receivable: Central Filing—Also local filing if business of debtor located in only one town, or in town or residence, if no business. If accounts from sale of farm products by farmer, local filing. No filing necessary unless significant portion of contract assigned includes accounts receivable.
Chattel Paper: Central Filing—Also local filing if business of debtor in only one town, or in town of residence, if no business.
Consumer Goods: Local filing—Place of debtor's residence, or if nonresident, location of goods. However, for purchase money security interest, no filing except for fixtures and motor vehicles requiring licensing.
Documents: Central Filing—Also local filing if business of debtor located in only one town, or in town of residence, if no business.
Equipment: Central Filing—Also local filing if business of debtor located in only one town, or in town of residence, if no business. No filing necessary where law requires indication of lien on certificate of title.
Farm Equipment: Local Filing—Place of debtor's residence or location of goods if nonresident. However, for purchase money security interest of $500 or less, no filing except for a fixture or motor vehicle requiring licensing.
Farm Products: Local Filing—Place of debtor's residence, or location of goods if nonresident. Also, additional filing in county where land is located, if crops.
Fixtures: Local Filing—With Register of Deeds where land is located.
General Intangibles: Central Filing—Also local filing if business of debtor located in only

one town, or in town of residence, if no business. If intangibles from sale of farm products by farmer, local filing.
Instruments: No Filing.
Inventory: Central Filing—Also local filing if business of debtor located in only one town, or in town or residence, if no business.
Minerals: Local Filing.
Timber: Central Filing except where the collateral is timber to be cut.
FEES—Uniform fee $8.

NEW JERSEY

CENTRAL FILING—Secretary of State, UCC Division, State House, Trenton, New Jersey 08625 (609) 292-2121
LOCAL FILING—Register of Deeds and Mortgages (Counties of Camden, Essex, Hudson, Passaic and Union) or County Clerk
PLACE OF FILING—
Accessions: Local or Central Filing—Varies according to kinds of goods attached: consumer goods, equipment, farm products or inventory.
Accounts Receivable: Central Filing—Except if accounts from sale of farm products by farmer, local filing. No filing necessary unless significant portion of contract assigned includes accounts receivable.
Chattel Paper: Central Filing.
Consumer Goods: Local Filing—Place of debtor's residence or location of goods if nonresident. However, for purchase money security interest, no filing except for fixtures and motor vehicles requiring licensing.
Documents: Central Filing.
Equipment: Central Filing. No filing necessary where law requires indication of lien on certificate of title.
Farm Equipment: Local Filing—Place of debtor's residence, or location of goods if nonresident. However, for purchase money security interest of $500 or less, no filing except for a fixture or motor vehicle requiring licensing.
Farm Products: Local Filing—Place of debtor's residence, or location of goods if nonresident. Also, additional filing in county where land is located, if crops.
Fixtures: Local Filing—Place where land is located.
General Intangibles: Central Filing—Except if intangibles from sale of farm products by farmer, local filing.
Instruments: No Filing.
Inventory: Central Filing.
Minerals: Local Filing.
Timber: Central Filing.
FEES—Uniform filing fee $10. Expedited service additional $5.

NEW MEXICO

CENTRAL FILING—Secretary of State, UCC Division, Legislative Executive Bldg., Santa Fe, New Mexico 87503 (505) 827-2717
LOCAL FILING—County Clerk
PLACE OF FILING—
Accessions: Local or Central Filing—Depends whether or not goods being attached and whether or not the debtor is a resident.
Accounts Receivable: Local or Central Filing—Local: Place of residence of debtor. Central: Nonresident debtor.
Chattel Paper: Local or Central Filing—Local: Place of residence of debtor. Central: Nonresident debtor.
Consumer Goods: Local Filing—Place of debtor's residence, or location of goods if nonresident. However, for purchase money security interest, no filing except for fixtures and motor vehicles.
Contract Rights: Local or Central Filing—Local: Place of residence of debtor. Central: Nonresident debtor. No filing necessary unless significant portion of contract assigned includes contract rights.
Documents: Local or Central Filing—Local: Place of residence of debtor. Central: Nonresident debtor.

SECURED TRANSACTIONS UNDER ARTICLE 9   7-51

Equipment: Local or Central Filing—Local: Place of residence of debtor, if nonresident, where goods located. Central: Nonresident debtor where collateral is not goods.

Farm Equipment: Local Filing—Place of debtor's residence, or location of goods if nonresident. However, for purchase money security interest of $2500 or less, no filing except for a fixture or motor vehicle requiring licensing.

Farm Products: Local Filing—Place of debtor's residence, or location of goods if nonresident. Also, additional filing in county where land is located, if crops.

Fixtures: Local Filing—Place where land is located.

General Intangibles: Local or Central Filing—Local: Place of residence of debtor. Central: Nonresident debtor.

Instruments: No Filing.

Inventory: Local or Central Filing—Local: Place of residence of debtor, if nonresident, location of goods. Central: Nonresident debtor where collateral is not goods.

FEES—Financing statement $3; assignment $2; termination statement $3; release $3; continuation statement $3. Termination accompanied by assignment $5.

NEW YORK

CENTRAL FILING—Department of State, UCC Division, 162 Washington Avenue, Albany, New York 12231 (518) 474-4763

LOCAL FILING—Clerk of County (City Register in Bronx, Kings, Queens and New York Counties)

PLACE OF FILING—

Accessions: Local or Central Filing—Varies according to kinds of goods attached: consumer goods, equipment, farm products or inventory.

Accounts Receivable: Central Filing—Except if accounts from sale of farm products by farmer, local filing. Also, local filing if business of debtor located in only one county. No filing necessary unless significant portion of contract assigned includes accounts receivable.

Chattel Paper: Central Filing—Also local filing if business of debtor located in only one county. When accounts are of minerals or the like, where a real estate mortgage would be recorded.

Consumer Goods: Local or Central Filing—Place of debtor's residence, or if nonresident, Secretary of State. Also, local filing if business of debtor located in only one county. However, for purchase money security interest, no filing except for fixtures and motor vehicles requiring licensing.

Documents: Central Filing—Also, local filing if business of debtor located in only one county.

Equipment: Central Filing—Also, local filing if business of debtor located in only one county. No filing necessary where law requires indication of lien on certificate of title.

Farm Equipment: Local Filing—Place of debtor's residence, if nonresident, with Secretary of State. Also, local filing if business of debtor located in only one county.

Farm Products: Local Filing—Place of debtor's residence, if nonresident, Secretary of State. Also, local filing if business of debtor located in only one county. Also, if crops, additional filing required in county where land is located.

Fixture: Local Filing—Place where land is located.

General Intangibles: Central Filing—Also, local filing if business of debtor located in only one county. If intangibles from sale of farm products by farmer, local filing.

Instruments: No Filing.

Inventory: Central Filing—Also, local filing if business for debtor located in only one county.

Minerals: Local Filing.

Timber: Central Filing—Local when collateral is timber to be cut, where a real estate mortgage would be recorded.

FEES—Uniform fee is $3 for standard forms; $4.50 if nonstandard form used or additional sheets attached. $1.50 for termination; $2 for release; termination accompanied by assignment $2. Each debtor over one 75¢.

(a) if statement covers crops or fixtures and is not filed in the office of the Secretary of State, an additional 50¢, and in addition

(b) if the real estate is in the City of New York or in the County of Nassau any block fees which are allowed,

(c) for each additional person, firm or organization beyond the first named as a debtor 75¢.

NORTH CAROLINA

CENTRAL FILING—Secretary of State, UCC Division, Raleigh, North Carolina 27611 (919) 829-3433

LOCAL FILING—Register of Deeds
PLACE OF FILING—
Accessions: Local or Central Filing—Varies according to kinds of goods attached: consumer goods, equipment, farm products or inventory.
Accounts Receivable: Central Filing—Also, local filing if business of debtor located in only one county, or where he resides, if no business. If accounts from sale of farm products by farmer, or if accounts are minerals, etc., local filing. No filing necessary unless significant portion of contract includes accounts receivable.
Chattel Paper: Central Filing—Also, local filing if business of debtor located in only one county, or where he resides, if no business.
Consumer Goods: Local Filing—Place of debtor's residence, or location of goods if nonresident. However, for purchase money security interest, no filing except for fixtures and motor vehicles requiring licensing.
Documents: Central Filing—Also, local filing if business of debtor located in only one county or, if none, where he resides.
Equipment: Central Filing—Also, local filing if business of debtor located in only one county, or where he resides, if no business.
Farm Equipment: Local Filing—Place of debtor's residence, or location of goods if nonresident.
Farm Products: Local Filing—Place of debtor's residence, or location of goods if nonresident. Also, additional filing in county where land is located, if crops.
Fixtures: Local Filing—Place where land is located.
General Intangibles: Central Filing—Also, local filing if business of debtor located in only one county, or where he resides, if no business. If intangibles arise from sale of farm products by farmer, local filing.
Instruments: No Filing.
Inventory: Central Filing—Also, local filing if business of debtor located in only one county, or where he resides, if no business.
Minerals: Local Filing—In county where land is located
Timber: Central Filing—But if timber to be cut, local filing in county where land is located.
FEES—Fee of $5 or unapproved form $10 and additional $2 if instrument about timber, minerals or fixture. No fee for termination statement.

NORTH DAKOTA

CENTRAL FILING—Secretary of State, Capitol Building, Bismarck, North Dakota 58505 (701) 224-2900
LOCAL FILING—Register of Deeds.
PLACE OF FILING—
Accessions: Local or Central Filing—Varies according to kinds of goods attached: consumer goods, equipment, farm products or inventory.
Accounts Receivable: Central Filing—Except accounts from sale of farm products by farmer, local filing. If minerals, etc., where a real estate mortgage would be recorded. No filing necessary unless significant portion of contract assigned includes accounts receivable.
Chattel Paper: Central Filing.
Consumer Goods: Local Filing—Place of debtor's residence, or location of goods if nonresident. However, for purchase money security interest, no filing except for fixtures and motor vehicles requiring licensing.
Documents: Central Filing.
Equipment: Central Filing.
Farm Equipment: Local Filing—Place of debtor's residence, or location of goods if nonresident. However, for motor vehicles requiring licensing, no filing.
Farm Products: Local Filing—Place of debtor's residence, or location of goods if nonresident. Also, additional filing in county where land is located, if crops.
Fixtures: Local Filing—Place where land is located.
General Intangibles: Central Filing—Except if intangibles from sale of farm products by farmer, local filing.
Instruments: No Filing.
Inventory: Central Filing.
Minerals: Local Filing—Place where real estate mortgage would be recorded.
Timber: Central Filing—But if timber to be cut, place where a real estate mortgage would be recorded.
FEES—Uniform fee $3 with an additional $2 for a nonstandard form. Termination statement $3.

SECURED TRANSACTIONS UNDER ARTICLE 9 7-53

OHIO

CENTRAL FILING—Secretary of State, UCC Division, State Office Tower, Columbus, Ohio 43216 (614) 466-3126.
LOCAL FILING—County Recorder
PLACE OF FILING—

Accessions: Local or Central Filing—Varies according to kinds of goods attached: consumer goods, equipment, farm products or inventory.

Accounts Receivable: Central Filing—Also, local filing if business of debtor located in only one county, or if none, where he resides. Local filing when accounts are from farmer's sale of farm products or from minerals or the like. No filing necessary unless significant portion of contract assigned includes accounts receivable.

Chattel Paper: Central Filing—Also, local filing if business of debtor located in only one county, or where he resides, if no business.

Consumer Goods: Local Filing—Place of debtor's residence, or location of goods if nonresident. However, for purchase money security interest, no filing except for fixtures.

Documents: Central Filing—Also, local filing if business of debtor located in only one county, or where he resides, if no business.

Equipment: Central Filing—Also, local filing if business of debtor located in only one county, or where he resides, if no business. No filing necessary where law requires indication of lien on certificate of title.

Farm Equipment: Local Filing—Place of debtor's residence, or location of goods if nonresident.

Farm Products: Local Filing—Place of debtor's residence, or location of goods if nonresident. Also, additional filing in county where land is located, if crops.

Fixtures: Local Filing—Place where land is located.

General Intangibles: Central Filing—Also, local filing if business of debtor located in only one county, or where he resides, if no business. If intangibles from sale of farm products by farmer, local filing.

Instruments: No Filing.

Inventory: Central Filing—Also, local filing if business of debtor located in only one county, or where he resides, if no business.

Minerals: Local Filing—in county where land is located.

Timber: Central Filing—local when collateral is timber to be cut.

FEES—Financing statement $9; indicating assignment $9; unapproved form $11; assignment $5. No charge for termination statement.

OKLAHOMA

CENTRAL FILING—Central Filing Office for UCC, Oklahoma County Clerk's Office, Room 141, County Office Building, Oklahoma City, Oklahoma 73102 (405) 236-2727
LOCAL FILING—County Clerk
PLACE OF FILING—

Accessions: Local or Central Filing—Varies according to kinds of goods attached: consumer goods, equipment, farm products or inventory.

Accounts Receivable: Central Filing—Except if accounts from sale of farm products by farmer, local filing. No filing necessary unless significant portion of contract assigned includes accounts receivable.

Chattel Paper: Central Filing.

Consumer Goods: Local Filing—Place of debtor's residence, or location of goods if nonresident.

Documents: Central Filing.

Equipment: Central Filing. No filing when law requires indication of lien on certificate of title.

Farm Equipment: Local Filing—Place of debtor's residence, or location of goods if nonresident.

Farm Products: Local Filing—Place of debtor's residence, or location of goods if nonresident. Also, additional filing in county where land is located, if crops.

Fixtures: Local Filing—Place where land is located.

General Intangibles: Central Filing—Except if intangibles from sale of farm products by farmers, local filing.

Instruments: No Filing.

Inventory: Central Filing.

Minerals: Local Filing—Place where mortgage would be recorded.

Timber: Central Filing—Local filing if timber is to be cut.

FEES—Financing statement $10; assignment $10; termination statement none; release none; continuation statement $10.

OREGON

CENTRAL FILING—Secretary of State, UCC Division, Room 122, State Capitol, Salem, Oregon 97310 (503) 378-4139

LOCAL FILING—County Clerk if a Recorder of Conveyances, otherwise County Recorder (Linn, Marion and Umatilla counties).

PLACE OF FILING—

Accessions: Central Filing—No special provision.

Accounts Receivable: Central Filing—In addition, local filing if business of debtor located in only one county, or in county of residence, if no business. If minerals etc., local filing where real estate mortgage would be recorded. No filing necessary unless significant portion of contract assigned includes accounts receivable.

Chattel Paper: Central Filing.

Consumer Goods: Central Filing—However, for purchase money security interest, no filing except for motor vehicles or fixtures.

Documents: Central Filing—Also, local filing if business of debtor located in only one county, or in county of residence, if no business.

Equipment: Central Filing—Also, local filing if business of debtor located in only one county, or in county of residence, if no business.

Farm Equipment: Central Filing.

Farm Products: Central Filing, but if collateral is timber to be cut or is minerals or the like, local filing where land lies.

Fixtures: Local Filing—Place where land is located.

General Intangibles: Central Filing—Also, local filing if business of debtor located in only one county, or in county of residence, if no business. If intangibles from sale of farm products by farmer, no filing.

Instruments: No Filing.

Inventory: Central Filing—Also, local filing if business of debtor located in only one county, or in county of residence, if no business.

Minerals: Local Filing—where a real estate mortgage would be recorded.

Timber: Central Filing—But if timber to be cut, local filing where a real estate mortgage would be recorded.

FEES—Uniform fee $3.75. $5 if nonstandard form used. Additional fee of $3.75 for each name more than one against which instrument must be indexed. County Clerk—75¢ per page, minimum fee of $5.50 for five pages or less.

PENNSYLVANIA

CENTRAL FILING—Secretary of Commonwealth, UCC Division, Harrisburg, Pennsylvania 17120 (717) 787-7630

LOCAL FILING—County Prothonotary

PLACE OF FILING—

Accessions: Local or Central Filing—Varies according to kinds of goods attached: consumer goods, equipment, farm products or inventory.

Accounts Receivable: Central Filing—Also, local filing if business of debtor located in only one county, or in county of residence, if no business. If accounts from sale of farm products by farmer, local filing.

Chattel Paper: Central Filing—Also, local filing if business of debtor located in only one county, or in county of residence, if no business.

Consumer Goods: Local Filing—Place of debtor's residence, or location of goods if nonresident. However, for purchase money security interest, no filing except for fixtures and motor vehicles requiring licensing.

Documents: Central Filing—Also, local filing if business of debtor located in only one county, or in county of residence, if no business.

Equipment: Central Filing—Also, local filing if business of debtor located in only one county, or in county of residence, if no business. No filing necessary when lien may be indicated on certificate of title.

Farm Equipment: Local Filing—Place of debtor's residence, or location of goods if nonresident. However, for purchase money security interest of $2,500 or less, except for a fixture or motor vehicle requiring licensing.

SECURED TRANSACTIONS UNDER ARTICLE 9 7-55

Farm Products: Local Filing—Place of debtor's residence, or location of goods if nonresident. Also, additional filing in county where land is located, if crops.

Fixtures: Local Filing—With Recorder of Deeds where land located.

General Intangibles: Central Filing—Also, local filing if business of debtor located in only one county, or county of residence, if no business. If intangibles from sale of farm products by farmer, local filing.

Instruments: No Filing.

Inventory: Central Filing—Also, local filing if business of debtor located in only one county, or county of residence, if no business.

Minerals: Local Filing.

Timber: Central Filing.

FEES—The uniform fee is $5, no fee for standard size supplementary pages; for first page of nonstandard size $2; for each additional page $1. In addition, special provisions authorize fee for recording according to the size of the respective county.*

RHODE ISLAND

CENTRAL FILING—Division of Uniform Commercial Code, Office of the Secretary of State, State House—Room 18, Providence, Rhode Island 02903 (401) 277-2521

LOCAL FILING—Recorder of Deeds

PLACE OF FILING—

Accessions: Local or Central Filing—Varies according to kinds of goods attached: consumer goods, equipment, farm products or inventory.

Accounts Receivable: Central Filing—Except if accounts from sale of farm products by farmer, local filing. No filing necessary unless significant portion of contract assigned includes accounts receivable.

Chattel Paper: Central Filing.

Consumer Goods: Central Filing—However, for purchase money security interest, no filing except for fixtures and motor vehicles requiring licensing. No filing when the price is less than $300, exclusive of interest, insurance and finance charges.

Documents: Central Filing.

Equipment: Central Filing.

Farm Equipment: Local Filing—Place of debtor's residence, or location of goods if nonresident. However, for purchase money security interest of $500 or less, no filing except for a fixture or motor vehicle requiring licensing.

Farm Products: Local Filing—Place of debtor's residence, or location of goods if nonresident. Also, additional filing in county where land is located, if crops.

Fixtures: Local Filing—With Town Clerk or Recorder of Deeds at place where land is located.

General Intangibles: Central Filing—Except intangibles from sale of farm products by farmer, local filing.

Instruments: No Filing.

Inventory: Central Filing.

Minerals: Local Filing.

Timber: Central Filing, local filing when the collateral is timber to be cut, where a real estate mortgage would be recorded.

FEES—Financing statement $4; assignment $4; termination statement $2, if nonstandard form, $3; release $4; continuation statement $4.

SOUTH CAROLINA

CENTRAL FILING—Secretary of State, UCC Section, P.O. Box 11350, Columbia, South Carolina 29211 (803) 758-2744

LOCAL FILING—Register of Mesne Conveyances, (Aiken, Charleston, Greenville, Lexington, Richland and Spartanburg Counties) or Clerk of Court

PLACE OF FILING—

Accessions: Local or Central Filing—Varies according to kinds of goods attached: consumer goods, equipment, farm products or inventory.

Accounts Receivable: Central Filing—Except if accounts from sale of farm products by farmer, local filing.

Chattel Paper: Central Filing.

---

* The Uniform Commercial Code Division of the Bureau of Corporation is prohibited to accept nonstandard forms for filing.

Consumer Goods: Local Filing—Place of debtor's residence, or location of goods if nonresident. However, for purchase money security interest, no filing except for fixtures and motor vehicles requiring licensing.

Contract Rights: Central Filing—Except if contract rights from sale of farm products by farmer, local filing. No filing necessary unless significant portion of contract assigned includes contract rights.

Documents: Central Filing.

Equipment: Central Filing. No filing necessary when law requires indication of lien on certificate of title.

Farm Equipment: Local Filing—Place of debtor's residence, or location of goods if nonresident. However, for purchase money security interest of $2,500 or less, no filing except for a fixture or motor vehicle requiring licensing.

Farm Products: Local Filing—Place of debtor's residence, or location of goods if nonresident. Also, additional filing in county where land is located, if crops.

Fixtures: Local Filing—Place where land is located.

General Intangibles: Central Filing—Except if intangibles from sale of farm products by farmer, local filing.

Instruments: No Filing.

Inventory: Central Filing.

FEES—Financing statement $4, if unapproved form $6; assignment $2; termination statement $2, if unapproved form $4; release $1; continuation statement $4.

TAXES—Documentary Stamp Tax 2¢ per $100 of indebtedness.

SOUTH DAKOTA

CENTRAL FILING—Secretary of State, 500 East Capitol, Pierre, South Dakota 57501 (604) 224-3537

LOCAL FILING—Register of Deeds

PLACE OF FILING—

Accessions: Local or Central Filing—Varies according to kinds of goods attached: consumer goods, equipment, farm products or inventory.

Accounts Receivable: Central Filing—Except if accounts from sale of farm products by farmer, local filing.

Chattel Paper: Central Filing.

Consumer Goods: Local Filing—Place of debtor's residence, or location of goods if nonresident. However, for purchase money security interest, no filing except for fixtures and motor vehicles requiring licensing.

Documents: Central Filing.

Equipment: Central Filing.

Farm Equipment: Local Filing—Place of debtor's residence, or location of goods if nonresident. However, for purchase money security interest of $2,500 or less, no filing except for a fixture or motor vehicle requiring licensing.

Farm Products: Central Filing—Place of debtor's residence, or location of goods if nonresident. Also, additional filing in county where land is located, if crops.

Fixtures: Local Filing—In county where land is located.

General Intangibles: Central Filing—Except if intangibles from sale of farm products by farmer, local filing.

Instruments: No Filing.

Inventory: Central Filing.

Minerals: Local Filing.

Timber: Central Filing.

FEES—Uniform fee is $3 for filing and indexing an original statement, continuation statement; $4 for statement of assignment. When a nonstandard form is used, an additional charge of $4 is made. Fee for filing a statement of release is $1, $2 for additional names. Additional fee of $2 for financing statement concerning timber, minerals or fixtures. $1 for financing statement noting an assignment.

TENNESSEE

CENTRAL FILING—Secretary of State, Commercial Code Division, C1-100 Central Services Building, Nashville, Tennessee 37219 (615) 741-3276

LOCAL FILING—County Register

PLACE OF FILING—
Accessions: Local or Central Filing—Varies according to kinds of goods attached: consumer goods, equipment, farm products or inventory.
Accounts Receivable: Central Filing—Except if accounts from sale of farm products by farmer, local filing.
Chattel Paper: Central Filing.
Consumer Goods: Local Filing—Place of debtor's residence, or location of goods if nonresident. However, for purchase security interest, no filing except for fixtures and motor vehicles requiring licensing.
Contract Rights: Central Filing—Except if contract rights from sale of farm products by farmer, local filing. No filing necessary unless significant portion of contract assigned includes contract rights.
Documents: Central Filing.
Equipment: Central Filing.
Farm Equipment: Local Filing—Place of debtor's residence, or location of goods if nonresident. However, for purchase money security of $500 or less, no filing except for a fixture or motor vehicle requiring licensing.
Farm Products: Local Filing—Place of debtor's residence, or location of goods if nonresident. Also, additional filing in county where land is located, if crops.
Fixtures: Local Filing—Place where land is located.
General Intangibles: Central Filing—Except if intangibles from sale of farm products by farmer, local filing.
Instruments: No Filing.
Inventory: Central Filing.
FEES—Financing statement and continuation statement the greater of $5 or $1 for each full year statement in effect; plus 50¢ per page for each page over two; assignment $5; termination statement $2; release $2; continuation statement $5; plus 50¢ per page for each page over one. Termination accompanied by assignment $4.
TAXES—10¢ per $100 of indebtedness over $2,000.

TEXAS

CENTRAL FILING—Secretary of State, UCC Division, P.O. Box 13193, Austin, Texas 78711 (512) 475-2015
LOCAL FILING—County Clerk
PLACE OF FILING—
Accessions: Local or Central Filing—Varies according to kinds of goods attached: consumer goods, equipment, farm products or inventory.
Accounts Receivable: Central Filing—Except if accounts from sale of farm products by farmer, local filing. If minerals, etc., where a real estate mortgage would be recorded. No filing necessary unless significant portion of contract assigned includes accounts receivable.
Chattel Paper: Central Filing.
Consumer Goods: Local Filing—Place of debtor's residence, or location of goods if nonresident. However, for purchase money security interest, no filing except for fixtures and motor vehicles requiring registration.
Documents: Central Filing.
Equipment: Central Filing. No filing necessary when law requires indication of lien on certificate of title.
Farm Equipment: Local Filing—Place of debtor's residence, or location of goods if nonresident. However, for a fixture or vehicle requiring registration, no filing.
Farm Products: Local Filing—Place of debtor's residence, or location of goods if nonresident. Also, additional filing in county where land is located, if crops.
Fixtures: Local Filing—where land is located.
General Intangibles: Central Filing—Except if intangibles from sale of farm products by farmer, local filing.
Instruments: No Filing.
Inventory: Central Filing.
Minerals: Local Filing—Where a real estate mortgage would be recorded.
Timber: Central Filing—But, if timber to be cut, local filing at place where a real estate mortgage would be recorded.
FEES—Uniform fee is $5. $15 if nonstandard forms are used or additional sheets filed. Additional fee of $3 for instruments relating to minerals or timber to be cut.

UTAH

CENTRAL FILING—Division of Corporations and Commercial Code, UCC Division, P.O. Box 5801, Salt Lake City, Utah 84110 (801) 328-5111
LOCAL FILING—County Recorder
PLACE OF FILING—
Accessions: Local or Central Filing—Varies according to kinds of goods attached: consumer goods, equipment, farm products or inventory.
Accounts Receivable: Central Filing. Local filing, where land lies, when accounts are of minerals or the like. No filing necessary unless significant portion of contract assigned includes accounts receivable.
Chattel Paper: Central Filing.
Consumer Goods: Central Filing—However, for purchase money security interest, no filing except for fixtures and motor vehicles requiring licensing.
Documents and Goods: Central Filing.
Equipment: Central Filing.
Farm Equipment: Central Filing.
Farm Products: Central Filing.
Fixtures: Local Filing—With Recorder of Deeds at place where land is located.
General Intangibles: Central Filing.
Instruments: No Filing.
Inventory: Central Filing.
Minerals: Local Filing.
Timber: Central Filing, local filing when the collateral is timber to be cut.
FEES—Financing statement $2; assignment $2; release $2; continuation statement $2; $10 for documents on nonstandard forms. $5 for first page and $1 for each additional page for County Recorder. If nonstandard size then $7 for first page and $2 for additional pages.

VERMONT

CENTRAL FILING—Secretary of State, UCC Division, Montpelier, Vermont 05602 (802) 828-2363
LOCAL FILING—Town Clerk
PLACE OF FILING—
Accessions: Local or Central Filing—Varies according to kinds of goods attached: consumer goods, equipment, farm products or inventory.
Accounts Receivable: Central Filing—Also, local filing if business of debtor located in only one town, or in town of residence, if no business. If accounts from sale of farm products by farmer, local filing.
Chattel Paper: Central Filing—Also, local filing if business or debtor located in only one town, or in town of residence, if no business.
Consumer Goods: Local Filing—Place of debtor's residence, or location of goods if nonresident. However, for purchase money security interest, no filing except for fixtures and licensed motor vehicles.
Contract Rights: Central Filing—Also, local filing if business of debtor located in only one town, or in town of residence, if no business. No filing when assignment is not a significant part of contract rights. No filing necessary unless significant portion of contract assigned includes contract rights.
Documents: Central Filing—Also, local filing if business of debtor located in only one town, or in town of residence, if no business.
Equipment: Central Filing—Also, local filing if business of debtor located in only one town, or in town of residence, if no business. No filing necessary when lien may be indicated on the certificate of title.
Farm Equipment: Local Filing—Place of debtor's residence, or location of goods if nonresident. However, for purchase money security interest of $500 or less, no filing except for a fixture or licensed motor vehicle requiring license.
Farm Products: Local Filing—Place of debtor's residence, or location of goods if nonresident. Also, additional filing in county where land is located, if crops.
Fixtures: Local Filing—Place where land is located.
General Intangibles: Central Filing—Also, local filing if business of debtor located in only one town, or in town of residence, if no business.
Instruments: No Filing.

SECURED TRANSACTIONS UNDER ARTICLE 9 7-59

Inventory: Central Filing—Also, local filing if business of debtor located in only one town, or in town of residence, if no business.
FEES—$5 for UCC statements filed; assignment $5; no fee for termination statement; $10 fee for nonstandard financing.

VIRGINIA

CENTRAL FILING—State Corporation Commission, Uniform Commercial Code Division, P. O. Box 1197, Richmond, Virginia 23209 (703) 770-3689
LOCAL FILING—Clerk of the Court of the County or Corporation
PLACE OF FILING—
Accessions: Local or Central Filing—Varies according to kinds of goods attached: consumer goods, equipment, farm products or inventory.
Accounts Receivable: Central Filing—Also, local filing if business of debtor located in only one county, or in county of residence, if no business. If accounts from sale of farm products by farmer, local filing. When minerals, etc., file where real estate mortgage would be recorded. No filing necessary unless significant portion of contract assigned includes accounts receivable.
Chattel Paper: Central Filing—Also, local filing if business of debtor located in only one county, or in county of residence, if no business.
Consumer Goods: Local Filing—Place of debtor's residence, or location of goods if nonresident. However, for purchase money security interest, no filing except for fixtures or motor vehicles.
Documents: Central Filing—Also, local filing if business of debtor located in only one county, or in county of residence, if no business.
Equipment: Central Filing—Also, local filing if business of debtor located in only one county, or in county of residence, if no business.
Farm Equipment: Local Filing—Place of debtor's residence, or location of goods if nonresident.
Farm Products: Local Filing—Place of debtor's residence, or location of goods if nonresident. Also, additional filing in county where land is located, if crops.
Fixtures: Local Filing—Place where land is located.
General Intangibles: Central Filing—Also, local filing if business of debtor located in only one county, or in county of residence, if no business. If tangibles from sale of farm products by farmer, local filing.
Instruments: No Filing.
Inventory: Central Filing—Also, local filing if business of debtor located in only one county, or in county of residence, if no business.
Minerals: Local Filing—Where real estate mortage would be filed.
Timber: Central Filing—But, if timber to be cut, local filing at same place where a real estate mortgage would be recorded.
FEES—Uniform fee $10 for central filing; $5 for local filing; nonstandard form $10.

WASHINGTON

CENTRAL FILING—The Department of Licensing, UCC Division, P.O. Box 9660, Olympia, Washington 98504 (206) 753-2523
LOCAL FILING—County Recording Officer
PLACE OF FILING—
Accessions: Central Filing
Accounts Receivable: Central Filing—Except if accounts from sale of farm products by farmer, local filing. No filing necessary unless significant portion of contract assigned includes accounts receivable.
Chattel Paper: Central Filing.
Consumer Goods: Central Filing—Place of debtor's residence, or location of goods if nonresident. However, for purchase money security interest, no filing except for fixtures and motor vehicles requiring licensing.
Documents: Central Filing.
Equipment: Central Filing. No filing necessary when law requires indication of lien on certificate of title.
Farm Equipment: Central Filing.
Farm Products: Central Filing.
Fixtures: Local Filing—Recording officer where land is located.
General Intangibles: Central Filing—Except if intangibles from sale of farm products by farmer, local filing.
Instruments: No Filing.

Inventory: Central Filing.
Minerals: Local Filing.
Timber: Central Filing.
FEES—Financing statement $4; assignment $4; termination statement no fee; release $4; continuation statement $4; nonstandard form financing statement or continuation statement $7; $7 for nonstandard form assignment or release.

WEST VIRGINIA

CENTRAL FILING—Office of Secretary of State, Capitol Bldg., Charleston, West Virginia 25305 (304) 348-2112
LOCAL FILING—County Clerk
PLACE OF FILING—

Accessions: Local or Central Filing—Varies according to kinds of goods attached: consumer goods, equipment, farm products or inventory.

Accounts Receivable: Central Filing—Also, local filing if business of debtor located in only one county, or in county of residence, if no business. If accounts from sale of farm products by farmer, local filing. When accounts are minerals, file at place where a real estate mortgage would be recorded. No filing necessary unless significant portion of contract assigned includes accounts receivable.

Chattel Paper: Central Filing—Also, local filing if business of debtor located in only one county, or in county of residence, if no business.

Consumer Goods: Local Filing—Place of debtor's residence, or location of goods if nonresident. However, for purchase money security interest, no filing except for fixtures and motor vehicles requiring licensing.

Documents: Central Filing—Also, local filing if business of debtor located in only one county, or in county of residence, if no business.

Equipment: Central Filing—Also, local filing if business of debtor located in only one county, or county of residence, if no business.

Farm Equipment: Local Filing—Place of debtor's residence, or location of goods if nonresident.

Farm Products: Local Filing—Place of debtor's residence, or location of goods if nonresident. Also, additional filing in county where land is located, if crops.

Fixtures: Local Filing—Place where land is located.

General Intangibles: Central Filing—Also, local filing if business of debtor located in only one county, or in county of residence, if no business. If intangibles from sale of farm products by farmer, local filing.

Instruments: No Filing.

Inventory: Central Filing—Also, local filing if business of debtor located in only one county, or in county of residence, if no business.

Minerals: Local Filing—Where real estate mortgage would be recorded.

Timber: Central Filing—But if timber to be cut, local filing at same place where real estate mortgage would be recorded.

FEES—Uniform fee $1; if nonstandard form is used $5. If the financing statement covers timber to be cut or minerals or their accounts an additional $1 is charged. A $1 charge is additionally made for each name more than one indexed. The secured party may show a trade name for any person for an additional $1.

WISCONSIN

CENTRAL FILING—Secretary of State, Commercial Code Division, P. O. Box 7847, Madison, Wisconsin 53707 (608) 266-3087
LOCAL FILING—Register of Deeds
PLACE OF FILING—

Accessions: Local or Central Filing—Varies according to kinds of goods attached: consumer goods, equipment, farm products or inventory.

Accounts Receivable: Central Filing—Except if accounts are from sale of farm products by farmer, local filing. If accounts are minerals, etc., at place where real estate mortgage would be recorded. No filing necessary unless significant portion of contract assigned includes accounts receivable.

Chattel Paper: Central Filing.

Consumer Goods: Local Filing—Place of debtor's residence, or location of goods if nonresident. However, for purchase money security interest of $500 or less, no filing except for fixtures.

Documents: Central Filing.

Equipment: Central Filing—But, if equipment used in farming operations in county of the debtor's residence, also local filing, or if nonresident, place where goods located. No filing necessary when applicable title law requires notation of lien on certificate of title.
Farm Equipment: Local Filing—Place of debtor's residence, or location of goods if nonresident.
Farm Products: Local Filing—Place of debtor's residence, or location of goods if nonresident. Also, additional filing in county where land is located, if crops.
Fixtures: Local Filing—Place where land is located.
General Intangibles: Central Filing—Also, if intangibles from sale of farm products by farmer, local filing in county of debtor's residence, or if nonresident, place where goods located.
Instruments: No Filing.
Inventory: Central Filing.
Minerals: Local Filing—Where real estate mortgage would be recorded.
Timber: Central Filing—But if timber to be cut, local filing where real estate mortgage would be recorded.
FEES—Secretary of State: Financing $4 if standard form, additional $2 if nonstandard; termination no fee unless financing statement filed before 1/1/78 where fee is $2, $4 if nonstandard; additional name $2 for financing statement, others $2; continuations $2, additional $1 per page if nonstandard.
Register of Deeds: $2 if standard form, $4 if nonstandard, plus an additional fee of $1 for each name against which the statement must be indexed.

WYOMING

CENTRAL FILING—Secretary of State, State Capitol, Cheyenne, Wyoming 82002 (307) 777-7378
LOCAL FILING—County Clerk
PLACE OF FILING—
Accessions: Local or Central Filing—Local filing at principal place of business of debtor, or debtor's county of residence, if no business. Central filing if nonresident.
Accounts Receivable: Local and Central Filing—If accounts from sale of farm products by farmer, local filing. Local when assignor's business place in state.
Chattel Paper: Local or Central Filing—Local filing at principal place of business of debtor, or debtor's county of residence, if not business. Central filing if nonresident.
Consumer Goods: Local or Central Filing—Local filing at principal place of business of debtor, or debtor's county of residence, if no business. Central filing if nonresident. However, for purchase money security interest, no filing except for fixtures and motor vehicles requiring licensing.
Contract Rights: Local or Central Filing—Local filing at principal place of business of debtor, or debtor's county of residence, if no business. Central filing if nonresident. No filing necessary unless significant portion of contract assigned includes contract rights.
Documents: Local or Central Filing—Local filing at principal place of business of debtor, or debtor's county of residence, if no business. Central filing if nonresident.
Equipment: Local or Central Filing—Local filing at principal place of business of debtor, or debtor's county of residence, if no business. Central filing if nonresident.
Farm Equipment: Local or Central Filing—Local filing at principal place of business of debtor, or debtor's county of residence, if no business. Central filing if nonresident. However, for purchase money security interest of $2,500 or less, no filing except for fixtures and motor vehicles requiring licensing.
Farm Products: Local or Central Filing—Local filing at principal place of business of debtor, or debtor's county of residence, if no business. Central Filing if nonresident.
Fixtures: Local Filing—With Register of Deeds of place where land is located.
General Intangibles: Local or Central Deeds—Local filing at principal place of business of debtor, or debtor's county of residence, if no business. Central filing if nonresident.
Instruments: No Filing.
Inventory: Local or Central Filing—Local filing at principal place of business of debtor, or debtor's county of residence, if no business. Central filing if nonresident.
FEES—Uniform fee—$3. 50¢ each additional name; 10¢ per page for attachments, $1 extra for statements not 5 x 8.

Retail Instalment Sales Laws

Most states have enacted laws regulating retail instalment sales. Retail instalment sales are sales of goods or services where the price is payable in periodic instalments. An analogue of the retail instalment sale is the open-end credit plan. The open-end credit plan allows the buyer to purchase goods or services and have the unpaid balance debited to an account, e.g., credit cards. The balance is then paid off in instalments. The application of retail instalment sales laws is often limited to certain kinds of goods; in some states they apply to all retail sales payable in instalments; in others they apply to only specific types of goods such as automobiles and in still others they apply only to personal and household goods.

A common feature of these laws is a disclosure requirement, by which interest charges must be separately stated. In addition, many statutes specify a particular form of contract, regulate interest rates and require that sales finance companies be licensed. Civil or criminal penalties may be provided for violations of statutory provisions.

Other state and federal statutes may have application to retail instalment sales. A seller is advised to consider the requirements of Article 9 of the Uniform Commercial Code which deals with Secured Transactions, even though filing may not be required to perfect a security interest.

There are a number of federal statutes which may apply to retail instalment sales transactions. The Truth in Lending Act, 15 U.S.C. §§ 1601 et. seq. (1976 & Supp. V 1981), and the Equal Credit Opportunity Act, 15 U.S.C. §§ 1691-1691f (1976 & Supp. V 1981), (which prohibits the denial of credit to an individual because of sex or marital status) are two examples. In addition, the following states have also adopted legislation which prohibits discrimination in granting credit based on sex or marital status (and in some cases race, religion, creed, physical disability or age): Alaska, Arkansas, California, Colorado, Connecticut, Florida, Georgia, Hawaii, Illinois, Indiana, Iowa, Kentucky, Louisiana, Maine, Maryland, Massachusetts, Michigan, Minnesota, Missouri, Montana, Nevada, New Jersey, New Mexico, New York, North Carolina, North Dakota, Ohio, Oklahoma, Rhode Island, Tennessee, Texas, Utah, Vermont, Virginia, Washington, West Virginia, and Wisconsin.

Contract Requirements

Most of the state statutes contain specific requirements as to the form and contents of a retail instalment sales contract. These include such items as: the contract shall be dated and in writing; the printed portion thereof shall be in at least 8 point type; it shall contain the names of the seller and the buyer, the place of business of the seller, the residence or place of business of the buyer (in some cases, post office addresses), as specified by the buyer; and an adequate description of the goods (including make and model, if any), or services to be rendered. With minor exceptions, the document can contain no blank spaces at the time it is signed by the purchaser. The contract must contain the entire agreement between the parties. The contract must be signed by the buyer and the seller and a copy must be delivered to the buyer at the time of execution or delivery of the goods, or within another specified period of time.

Provisions with respect to price and time payment. Most of the statutes require specifically that the contract set forth the following items:

1. The cash sale price of goods (and/or services).
2. The amount of the buyer's down payment, indicating the amount paid in cash and in goods, and briefly describing the goods traded in.
3. The difference between items one and two.
4. The amount, if any, included for insurance, specifying the insurance coverage and the cost of each type of coverage.
5. The amount, if any, of official fees (filing fees).
6. The principal balance, which is the sum of items three, four and five, above.
7. The amount of the credit service charge.
8. The time balance, which is the sum of items six and seven, payable by the buyer to the seller, the number of each instalment required, the amount of each instalment expressed in dollars and the due date or period thereof.
9. The time sale price.
10. If the instalments are not in substantially equal amounts, in some states it is required that the contract contain a statutory statement to this effect in bold type of a stated size.

Many of the states require that the contract contain an acknowledgment of receipt of a copy thereof by the buyer, in 10 point bold type, or larger. In most cases this is required to appear immediately above the buyer's signature. In Maryland and California, this acknowledgment must be signed specifically by the buyer besides his signature at end of contract.

In most of the states, there is also a requirement that a special notice addressed to the buyer be printed in bold type ranging from at least 8 to 12 point. The most common form of notice is as follows: NOTICE TO THE BUYER: 1. Do not sign this agreement before you read it, or if it contains any blank space. 2. You are entitled to a completely filled-in copy of this agreement. 3. Under the law, you have the right to pay off in advance the full amount due and under certain conditions to obtain a partial refund of the credit service charge.

Some states provide that their disclosure requirements must conform to federal requirements. For example, in Connecticut, disclosure requirements under the state sales act must conform to those requirements in the Truth in Lending Act. See Chapter 9, *infra*.

The contract requirements vary from state to state. The following are offered as examples only. Creditors must be certain to check the applicable law.

Many states permit the buyer in a retail instalment sales contract to cancel the contract on written notice mailed to the seller within two or three days after execution of the contract, especially in cases involving house-to-house sales or home improvements.

Many states require periodic statements to be mailed out within a reasonable time at the end of the billing cycle.

In Illinois, a retail instalment contract cannot be accelerated unless the buyer

RETAIL INSTALMENT SALES LAWS

has been in default at least 30 days or has abandoned or destroyed the property or the holder believes the buyer is leaving state. A cosigner, except for a parent or spouse, is liable only if he actually receives the goods sold and the seller must compute the total amount of the finance charges paid by the buyer during the year and furnish such information to the buyer, on request, within 30 days after the end of the year. If a creditor, within 30 days from receipt of a written letter from the debtor concerning an alleged account error sent within 60 days of receipt of the statement containing the alleged error, fails to resolve the allegation, the debtor is excused from paying any service charge on the disputed amount.

In Massachusetts, a statute has been adopted which provides that the default provisions of a retail instalment contract are enforceable only to the extent that the default is material and consists of the buyer's failure to make one or more instalment payments as required.

Delinquency charges—Attorney's fees. Most of the statutes contain provisions authorizing the seller, or holder of the contract, to impose a delinquency charge for late payment of any instalment. Generally, the instalment must be overdue by at least ten days, and only one delinquency charge can be made with respect to any one instalment. While the charges are based upon the percentage of the instalment due, most of the statutes fix a maximum, usually $5. Where the buyer defaults under the contract, and it is necessary to procure the services of an attorney, most of the statutes permit the judgment against the buyer of a reasonable attorney's fee, and costs. In many cases, the statute limits the amount of such fees to approximately 15 per cent of the amount then due on the contract. If the terms of the statute are not adhered to, seller may forfeit delinquency charge, fees or time price differential.

In New Hampshire, if a contract provides for attorneys fees to be awarded to the retail seller in any action against the buyer involving a credit transaction, the contract must also provide for reasonable attorneys fees to be awarded to the buyer. The waiver by a buyer of any such rights is unenforceable and void.

The Federal government and a number of states have adopted the Fair Credit Billing Act, discussed in Chapters 9 and 12.

Licensing Provisions

In Alabama, Alaska, Arizona, Connecticut, Delaware, the District of Columbia, Florida, Illinois, Iowa, Kentucky, Louisiana, Maine, Maryland, Massachusetts, Michigan, Minnesota, Mississippi, Missouri, Montana, Nebraska, New Hampshire, New Jersey, New Mexico, New York, North Carolina, Pennsylvania, Rhode Island, South Dakota, Tennessee, Texas, Vermont, West Virginia, and Wisconsin, a "sales finance company" (which is defined as a person or firm engaged in the business of purchasing retail instalment contracts from one or more retail sellers) is required to be licensed with an annual license fee frequently required. These statutes also make provision for examination of the books and records of the licensees. Alabama, Florida, Louisiana, and Vermont also require annual license fees of retail instalment sellers. Under most statutes, banks and other financial institutions are exempted from the licensing provisions.

Most states have separate licensing requirements for sales financing companies purchasing sales contracts from retail sellers of motor vehicles.

The Uniform Consumer Credit Code provides for licensing of certain persons engaged in the business of extending supervised loans. Colorado, Idaho, Indiana, Iowa, Kansas, Maine, Oklahoma, South Carolina, Utah and Wyoming have enacted the UCCC.

Insurance Provisions

The statutes of the several states vary as to the contract provisions and requirements or limitations relating to insurance coverage. However, in general, the statutes contain the following requirements:

Contract Provisions. If the cost of insurance is included in the total price, it must be stated as a separate item in the contract together with a description of the coverage. In some states, the contract must indicate whether the insurance is to be procured by the buyer or the seller.

Cost of Insurance. Under most statutes it is provided that the cost of insurance included in the contract cannot exceed the actual cost to the seller, or the usual charges made by the insurance carrier, or charges based upon the carrier's rates filed with the appropriate state agency having jurisdiction.

Copies of Policies. Most statutes provide that within a designated number of days following the making of the contract or delivery of the merchandise, the seller must deliver to the buyer a certificate of insurance, or copy of the insurance policy, or other statement which will be sufficient to advise the buyer concerning the insurance coverage, and his rights under the policy.

Miscellaneous. Under some statutes it is specifically required that the insurance carrier be licensed to do business in the state, and a number of the statutes provide that the buyer has the right to have the insurance placed with a company of his own choosing, usually subject to the seller's approval. Where the contract is prepaid, or for any other reason there is a refund or rebate in insurance charges, the statutes usually require that they be refunded to the buyer.

Provisions Prohibited

The statutes not only make special provisions as to what the contract shall contain, but also specify that which is prohibited. Although the prohibitions vary in the several states, the following are some of the prohibited provisions found:

(a) waiver by the buyer of claims or defenses against the seller of rights under the statute;

(b) acceleration of the maturity of any amount owing under the contract other than for a default on the part of the buyer;

(c) power of attorney to confess judgment or an assignment of wages;

(d) authorization to enter upon the buyer's premises unlawfully and to commit any breach of the peace in repossession of goods;

(e) waiver by the buyer of rights against an assignee of the seller; (However, some of the statutes contain a provision that a notice be sent by the assignee to the buyer informing him of the assignment and notifying him that unless he advises the assignee of any right of action or defense against the seller arising out of the sale, if the buyer does not respond within a limited period of time to this demand, such claims or defenses may not be raised against the assignee.) Many statutes even provide that the assignee of an instalment sales contract is not a holder in due course. See table in Chapter 9, *infra.*

(f) power of attorney appointing the seller, or holder of a contract, or other person, as agent of the buyer, in collection of payments under the contract or repossession of the goods;

(g) execution of notes separate from an instalment contract which would cut off the buyer's rights or defenses against the seller.

States may prohibit other clauses in a contract. For example, in California, a seller is prohibited from acquiring a lien on goods; in New York, there is a prohibition against liens on goods other than the subject of the sale; in Maryland a seller may not have the buyer open two accounts in order to impose a higher interest rate; in Virginia the maximum late charge is 5%; in Massachusetts a person is prohibited from being obligated to any seller under more than one retail instalment contract.

Under some of the statutes the inclusion of such prohibitive provisions is made ineffectual, or void, by the statute. In other cases, penalties may be imposed for failure to comply with the statutory restrictions.

While, as previously noted, some statutes require special contractual provisions and notice with respect to unequal instalments, in other states such provisions for irregular or uneven payments or instalments, such as "balloon payments" at the maturity date, are prohibited.

Prior to the advent of specific legislation on instalment sales, the question was raised as to whether a finance charge which exceeded the legal rate of interest permitted under state statute constituted usury. This question has been litigated over the years in numerous states, and it has invariably been held that the usury statutes are not applicable since the "time price differential" does not constitute interest and the parties could fix, by agreement, such prices as they determined appropriate for a purchase on either a cash or time sale basis. With the advent of legislative controls on instalment selling, the states began to impose limits on finance charges. With a few exceptions all of the state statutes regulating instalment selling fix the amounts of the legally permissible "time price differential" or "finance charge."

Refinancing, Extensions and Rescheduling

Many of the state statutes contain provisions with respect to refinancing of instalment contracts, extension of the period for repayment, or rescheduling of instalment payments. In some of the states the basic rates set forth above are applicable to such extension periods. In other cases, the statutes make specific provision for either straight interest charges or combinations of flat charges and specified rates on the extended balances.

Many of the statutes also contain provisions with respect to the inclusion of additional provisions. In New York and some other states, for example there are provisions for retail instalment obligations to cover future purchases of goods or services with or without the use of merchandise certificates.

Buyer's Default—Remedies of Seller

In the event of a default by the buyer in payment of the instalments or other breach of the contract, the seller or holder of the contract is afforded certain remedies. In some states these remedies are set forth in the Retail Instalment Sales Statute, and in others the statutes relating to conditional sales or secured transactions (under Uniform Commercial Code) will be applicable.

While the statutes vary in the several states, in general the remedies are as follows: (a) suit against the buyer for the unpaid instalment or balance due under the contract; (b) repossess the goods without process if it can be done peaceably, otherwise repossess by appropriate legal process; (c) sell the goods, after repossession, and hold the buyer for any deficiency in the event that the proceeds of sale are insufficient to cover the costs of repossession, storage, reconditioning, sale, etc.; (d) institute foreclosure, or other special proceeding, as authorized by state statute, in which the rights of the parties will be determined and fixed by court order or decree; (e) after repossession, under some statutes, the seller or the holder of the contract may treat the repossessed property as his own, free of any claim by the buyer, and may dispose of it accordingly.

Under most of the state statutes there are provisions requiring a sale of the goods in cases where the buyer has paid a substantial part of the purchase price (usually more than 50 per cent); notice of sale must be given to the buyer and after all costs and expenses and the balance due on the contract have been paid, any proceeds still remaining from the sale are payable to the buyer.

In most states, the buyer has the right to make good his default by paying past-due instalments and reasonable expenses incurred in retaking, storing, etc., although the buyer usually has the right of redemption until the property has been disposed of. Some of the statutes make provision for a notice to be given to the buyer prior to repossession or resale, and in the event that the buyer does not make good his default within a prescribed time limit his right of redemption will be lost.

Under some statutes the giving of a notice prior to retaking is also a prerequisite to the recovery of the costs of retaking, storing, etc.

While the rights of the seller, or holder of the contract, are generally cumulative where the property is retaken and it is not resold within the time limited by statute, it is usually considered that the seller has elected to accept the goods in full satisfaction of the buyer's obligation, and he is barred from resorting to other remedies.

In many states the assignee of a retail instalment sales contract is subject to all claims and defenses that the buyer could have asserted against the original seller.

On March 1, 1985 The Federal Trade Commission's Trade Regulation Rule entitled "The Credit Practices Rule" became effective. This rule specifies remedies that may not be used by lenders and retail installment sellers in consumer credit contracts for use against defaulting buyers. The rule covers contracts offered by finance companies and retail sellers and is designed to protect consumers from unfair or deceptive collection practices by creditors.

The FTC's Credit Practices Rule restricts the use of the following remedies in the consumer credit contracts: confessions of judgment, waivers of exemption, wage assignments, security interests in household goods, and certain late charges. The rule further prohibits misrepresentations of cosigner liability and provides that potential cosigners be furnished a "Notice of Cosigner" which explains in general terms their obligations and liabilities.

The rule is applicable industry wide in all states unless a particular state has requirements which are substantially equivalent to the FTC rule, in which case, that state can apply to the FTC for an exemption from the rule.

Penalties

Most of the state statutes contain provisions imposing penalties upon the seller or holder of a Retail Instalment Contract for failure to comply with statutory requirements. These penalties vary in the several states and range from rendering void any provision contrary to the statute, to the imposition of fines and imprisonment. It is usually provided that the inclusion in the contract of prohibited provisions renders such provision void and unenforceable, but does not otherwise affect the contract.

Where the violations relate to the amount of finance charges and other costs and charges, penalties include the loss of the right to recover such charges, civil action by the buyer to recover overcharges, and prohibitions against enforcement of the contract. In Illinois, creditor's violations of the state retail instalment sales act is an affirmative defense to an action for default on the sales contract.

While the most severe penalties of fines and imprisonment are imposed for violations with respect to licensing provisions, under a number of statutes such penalties are also imposed for willful violations of other provisions. Under the Code, however, no filing is generally required for consumer transactions.

Filing and Recording—General Considerations

Retail Instalment Sales laws do not provide for the filing or recording of the agreements. However, as previously noted, in those cases where the contract provides for the retention of title or a security interest by the seller there must be compliance with the filing or recording statute, generally the Uniform Commercial Code, in order to afford to the seller, or holder of the contract, protection against the rights of creditors of the buyer, or other third parties.

The foregoing review of the Retail Instalment Sales laws of the various states is not intended to give detailed information for the preparation of agreements or carrying on instalment selling under any specific statute. The statutes are highly technical and it is recommended that competent counsel be consulted in preparing instruments which conform to the various state statutes, as well as to advise on practices and procedures. In some states, operations under the statute are subject to control and regulation by governmental agencies. The state statutes are also subject to periodic revision, and additional states have legislation in this field under consideration.

The following chart illustrates the maximum rates applicable to Retail Instalment Sales as well as the scope of coverage of the Retail Instalment Sales laws.

STATE LAWS CONTROLLING RETAIL INSTALMENT SALES

State	Coverage	Interest Rate Regulation
Alabama	Statute covers property or services for personal, family, household or agricultural purpose, bailments or leases with rentals substantially equal to value of property or services and with nominal or no-cost option to become owner; open-end credit plans, and credit sales.	Greater of (A) total of (i) $15 per $100 per year to $750, (ii) $10 per $100 per year on over $750 and not over $2,000 and (iii) $8 per $100 per year on over $2,000; or (B) $8 per $100 per year on entire amount financed if originally over $2,000. Alternative variable rate fixed by statute is also permitted. Open-end credit plan: 1½% per month on unpaid balances.
Alaska	Sale (including catalog sale) of goods and services primarily for personal, family, or household use; also includes revolving credit.	On retail instalment contract ⅚ of 1% per month on balances not over $1,000; ⅔ of 1% per month on amounts in excess of $1,000; on retail charge agreements or revolving charge agreements, 1½% per month on balances up to $1,000; 1% per month on amounts in excess of $1,000.
Arizona	Statute covers tangible chattels, including fixtures and merchandise certificates; also includes revolving credit. Separate statute covering motor vehicles.	Maximum rate set by contract applies to retail instalment sales, revolving charge agreements and motor vehicle sales in excess of $1,500, based on a time price differential calculated from date of transaction to date last instalment becomes due. Separate rates for motor vehicles.
Arkansas	No statutory enactment.	No statutory enactment.
California	Sale of goods for personal, family, or household use excluding resale; property and services, other than for commercial or business use; also covers revolving credit. Separate statute covers automobiles for personal use.	Greater of 11/12 of 1% per mo. not over $3,000; ⅔ of 1% per mo. over $3,000, or $12; $10 on contract of 8 mo. or less if precomputed; if simple-interest basis, $10 for first $500, $25 if unpaid balance of $500 to $1,000, $50 if over $1,000 up to $2,000, or $75 if over $2,000. For instalment accounts, 1.6% on $3,000 or less, 1% on excess.
Colorado	Uniform Consumer Credit Code is in effect.	U.C.C.C. finance service charges: Consumer credit sales—greater of 21% on all unpaid balances or total of 25% of unpaid balance of $630 or less; 20% on amounts over $630 to $2,100, and 15% on amounts over $2,100; revolving credit: 1¾% on average daily balance.

8–8

State	Coverage	Interest Rate Regulation
Connecticut	Consumer goods for personal, family or household use, motor vehicles, up to $25,000.	14% on sales made after October 1, 1985 and prior to October 1, 1987 and 18% on sales after October 1, 1987. Open-end credit: after July 1, 1981 and prior to October 1, 1987, 1½% per month, after October 1, 1987, 1¼% per month.
Delaware	Retail instalment sale of goods for personal, family or household use, including services or goods for improvement to real property, and services for other than a commercial or business use; also includes revolving credit. Does not apply to goods of which the cash sale price is $75 or less, or where no security interest is retained. Sales of motor vehicles are covered by Motor Vehicle Sales Finance Act.	Rate as specified in contract. Separate rate for motor vehicles.
District of Columbia	Statute covers tangible chattels used for personal, family or household use, merchandise certificates and revolving credit, not over $25,000. There is a separate statute which covers motor vehicles.	No statute governing retail instalment sales except for motor vehicles; revolving credit cannot exceed 1½% per month on balance.
Florida	Retail instalment sale of goods and services for personal, family or household use excluding resale; also includes revolving credit. Motor vehicles are covered by the Motor Vehicle Sales Finance Act.	12% per $100 per year. Revolving credit, 1.5% per month. Separate rates for motor vehicles. 1½% on $5,000 maximum for bank loans and credit cards.
Georgia	Retail instalment sale of goods and services purchased for personal, family, or household use; also includes revolving credit. Motor vehicles are covered by the Motor Vehicle Sales Finance Act.	13% per year on principal balance. Revolving credit, 1.75% per $10 per month on unpaid amounts. Separate rate for motor vehicles.
Hawaii	Sale of personal chattels not for resale and services for family, household, commercial or business use on goods or realty.	12% per year for not over 18 months; 9% per year for next 12 months; 6% per year for next 12 months; 3% per year for next 6 months. There are no open end consumer credit provisions.

8–9

STATE LAWS CONTROLLING RETAIL INSTALMENT SALES (*Continued*)

State	Coverage	Interest Rate Regulation
Idaho	Uniform Consumer Credit Code is in effect.	U.C.C.C. finance service charges: Consumer credit sales—No charge limit. Revolving credit: No charge limit.
Illinois	Instalment sale of goods for personal, family or household use and services for use other than in business; also includes revolving credit. Motor vehicles covered by separate statute.	No limit or consumer credit sales or revolving credit.
Indiana	Uniform Consumer Credit Code is in effect.	U.C.C.C. finance service charges: Consumer credit sales—greater of 21% on all unpaid balances or total of 36% on all unpaid balances not in excess of $660, 21% on amounts of $660 to $2,200, and 15% on amounts over $2,200; revolving credit: 1¾% on monthly balance.
Iowa	The State Consumer Credit Code covers goods, services, or interest in land for personal, family or household up to $25,000. Motor vehicles covered by separate statute.	21% per year. Separate rate for motor vehicles. Open-end credit sale 1½% on $500 or less, 1¼% on excess.
Kansas	Kansas Uniform Consumer Credit Code in effect.	21% on first $300, 18% on $300 to $1,000, 14.45% on balance over $1,000. Revolving consumer credit sales; 1¾% on first $300, 1½% on $300 to $1,000, 1½% on excess over $1,000.
Kentucky	Goods and services for personal, family or household use, and revolving credit. Separate statute covers motor vehicles.	No provisions except for motor vehicles.
Louisiana	Goods and services for personal, family, household or agricultural use; also covers revolving credit. Motor vehicles are covered by Motor Vehicle Sales Finance Act.	On consumer credit sales: greater of (1) 24% per year on balances not over $1,750; 18% on balances over $1,750 but not over $5,000; 12% on balances over $5,000 or (2) 18% per year on amount deferred. Revolving credit: 1½% permitted on average daily balance.
Maine	Consumer Credit Code is in effect. There is a separate Home Repair Financing Act.	Credit Sales: 30% per year on unpaid balance of $660 or less, 21% per year on $660 to $2,200, 15% on over $2,200, or 18% per year on total unpaid balance. Revolving credit: charge may not exceed 1½% per month.

State	Coverage	Interest Rate Regulation
Maryland	Instalment sales of personal chattels for use or consumption of buyer having a cash price of $25,000 or less. Includes revolving credit.	After July 1, 1982 and before July 1, 1985, 24% or balance. Separate rates for motor vehicles.
Massachusetts	Retail instalment sale of movable goods or services for personal, family or household use. Agreement must provide finance charge and more than one payment or no finance charge and five or more payments. Exclusion if three or less payments, finance charge under $1 and no security. Includes revolving credit. Separate statute covers motor vehicles.	12% per year.
Michigan	Retail instalment sales of chattels for personal, family or household use; includes revolving credit, but not for commercial or business use. Separate statute covers home improvements for sales in excess of $300 and motor vehicle sale.	12% per year on principal balance not in excess of $500; 10% per year on the principal balance in excess of $500. Revolving credit, 1.7% of unpaid balance per month. Separate rates for motor vehicles and home improvement sales.
Minnesota	Statute covers motor vehicles not for resale only.	On open-end consumer credit sales, a finance charge not to exceed 1½% per month; 1⅓% per month for sellers with gross annual sales over $25 million. Separate rates for motor vehicles.
Mississippi	Retail instalment of tangible property or services other than pursuant to a revolving charge agreement, closed end credit sales of goods. Motor vehicles not for resale.	$2,500 or less—24%; on accounts more than $2,500—21%. None until one month after initial billing statement. Separate rates for motor vehicles.
Missouri	Retail instalment sales of goods and services. Statute includes revolving credit. Motor vehicles with a maximum cash price of $7,500 or less are covered by the Motor Vehicle Time Sales Act.	15% per year on $750 or less; 12% on $750 to $1,000; 10% on $1,000 to $7,500; by agreement on over $7,500. Charge agreement: 1.5% on unpaid balance.
Montana	Retail instalment sale of personal chattels, including motor vehicles and the furnishing of services. Includes revolving credit.	Rate agreed by seller and buyer.
Nebraska	Personal property and services.	18% per year. Revolving charge agreements 1¾% on $500 or less and 1½% on portion over $500.

8–11

STATE LAWS CONTROLLING RETAIL INSTALMENT SALES (Continued)

State	Coverage	Interest Rate Regulation
Nevada	Retail instalment sale of goods and services for personal or household use; also covers merchandise certificates and revolving credit including credit cards.	Any amount agreed upon. Revolving credit, 1.8% per month on deferred balance.
New Hampshire	Motor vehicles not for resale only with a $7,500 maximum price.	Statutory limitations apply to motor vehicles only.
New Jersey	Retail instalment sale of goods and services having a cash price of $10,000 or less, other than for a commercial or business use, including motor vehicles; also covers most services to consumers including professional services; includes retail charge accounts. Separate statute covers home improvements with minimum cash price of $300.	As agreed by buyer and seller; contract may provide for increase or decrease in rate up to 6% over life of loan, but no more than 3% in only 12 month period. Separate rates for motor vehicles and home improvement sales. Charge account, 1½% per month on $700 or less, 1% per month on excess.
New Mexico	Retail instalment use of tangible goods and services other than for a commercial or business use or resale; also covers merchandise certificates and retail charge agreements. Retail instalment sales of motor vehicles are covered by separate statute.	No special provision. Usury laws control.
New York	Retail instalment sale of goods and services other than for a commercial or business use; also covers revolving credit. Retail instalment sales of motor vehicles are covered by separate statute.	Rate agreed to by buyer. Revolving credit, Rate agreed to by partners. Separate rates for motor vehicles.
North Carolina	Retail consumers instalment sale of movable goods including merchandise certificates, services for personal, family, household or agricultural purpose and goods for improvement of real property, in amount less than $25,000. Separate statute covers motor vehicles.	On regular instalment sales maximum 24% per year where amount financed is less than $1,500; 22% per year where the amount financed is between $1,500 and $2,000; 20% per year where the amount financed is between $2,000 and $3,000; 18% per year where the amount financed is $3,000 or greater. Motor vehicles have separate rates as do sales secured by interest in real property. Revolving credit charges: 1½% per month.

State	Coverage	Interest Rate Regulation
North Dakota	Retail instalment sale of personal property, including motor vehicles, for personal, family or agricultural purposes, up to a value of $25,000 except for purpose of resale.	No provisions. Revolving credit, 1½% per month on balance.
Ohio	Retail instalment sale of personal goods not for resale, motor vehicles and mobile homes, and revolving credit if the base finance and service charge exceed $15.	8% per year plus service charge of 50¢ per month for the first $50 unit of the principal balance for each month, and 25¢ per month for each of the next five $50 units. Alternatively, any amount agreed upon not exceeding 25%. Revolving credit, same as retail instalment sales but not to exceed 1½% per month.
Oklahoma	Uniform Commercial Code in effect.	U.C.C.C. finance-service charges: Consumer credit sales—greater of 21% on all unpaid balances or total of 30% on unpaid balance of $600 or less. 21% on over $600 and less than $2,000, and 15% on over $2,000; Revolving credit: 1¾% on monthly balance if monthly billing cycles.
Oregon	Retail instalment sales of goods and services for personal, family or household use, and revolving credit. Separate statute covers motor vehicles.	No statutory limitation.
Pennsylvania	Retail instalment sale of goods and services bought primarily for personal, family or household purposes, merchandise certificates, and revolving credit. Motor vehicles, and home improvements costing over $300, are covered by separate statutes.	18% per year, 15% for gasoline credit card issuers. Retail instalment account, 1½% per month. Separate statutes for motor vehicles and home improvement rates.
Rhode Island	Merchandise and services involving credit.	21% simple interest per year; revolving credit: 18%. 30 day free period after purchase.
South Carolina	Goods, services or interest in land for personal, family or household purpose whose value does not exceed $25,000. Includes open-end credit plans. Separate statute covers motor vehicles.	Greater of any rate filed and posted as provided by law or 18% per year on unpaid balances. Revolving credit: same.

STATE LAWS CONTROLLING RETAIL INSTALMENT SALES (*Continued*)

State	Coverage	Interest Rate Regulation
South Dakota	Tangible personal chattels including things which are at time of sale to be affixed to real property. Statute also covers work, labor and other personal services. Separate statute covers motor vehicles.	Interest rate set by agreement. Revolving charge accounts: as agreed.
Tennessee	Retail instalment sales of personalty not for resale and services for goods or realty, excluding commercial and industrial use and motor vehicles. Revolving credit is also covered.	11.75% per year on principal balance of each transaction. Revolving credit: 1.5% per month on balance.
Texas	Personal property and services for personal, family or household use and not for commercial or business use. Also covers revolving credit and merchandise certificates. Motor vehicles covered by separate statute.	12% per year on principal balance not in excess of $1,450; 10% per year on an amount over $1,450 but not over $2,900; 8% per year on an amount over $2,900. Charge agreement: 1.5% per month on $1,400 or less, 1% on excess. Alternatively, parties may agree to rate not exceeding rate authorized by statute: Separate rates for motor vehicles.
Utah	Uniform Consumer Credit Code in effect.	U.C.C.C. finance-service charges: Consumer credit sales—greater of 19.6% on all unpaid balances or total of 36% on unpaid balances of $840 or less, 21% on over $840 but less than $2,800, 15% on over $2,800. Revolving credit, if billing is monthly, the charge may equal any amount agreed to.
Vermont	Sale of goods and services purchased for personal, family or household use and not for commercial, industrial or agricultural use; also includes merchandise certificates. Includes revolving credit. Motor vehicles covered by separate statute.	18% per year on amounts of $500 or less; 15% per year on amounts in excess of $500. Revolving credit, $500 and under, 1½% per month; 1¼% per month on excess. Separate rates for motor vehicles.
Virginia	Consumer goods. Separate statute covers motor vehicles.	As agreed by the parties. Revolving credit: Any amount agreed on, free period 25 days from billing, no charge if bill not mailed within 8 days of the billing date.

8–14

State	Coverage	Interest Rate Regulation
Washington	Retail instalment sales of goods and services for goods for personal, family or household use and not for commercial or business use, including merchandise certificates. Includes revolving credit.	Higher of either rate on outstanding balance that exceeds 6% above the average coupon yield for 26-week treasury bills or $10.
West Virginia	Goods, services or interest in land for personal family or household use; value not to exceed $25,000. Includes open-end credit plans. Separate statute covers motor vehicles.	18% if $1,500 or less, 12% for excess over $1,500; revolving credit: 1.5% on first $750, 1% for excess over $750. Alternative rate set by Lending and Credit Rate Board (18% as of July 1, 1983). Separate rates for motor vehicles.
Wisconsin	Goods, services, or an interest in land for personal, family, household, or agricultural purpose; value not to exceed $25,000. Also covers consumer leases and open-end credit plans. Separate statute covers motor vehicles for personal use only.	Till November 1, 1984, greater of 18% per year or 6% in excess of rate applicable to 6-month U.S. treasury bills. Revolving charge: Till November 1, 1984, 18% per year or parties may agree to any rate after notice when yield on most recently auctioned 2-year U.S. treasury notes for 5 successive Thursdays exceeds 15% per year. A consumer credit transaction entered into after Oct. 31, 1984, and before Nov. 1, 1987, is not subject to any maximum limit on finance charges.
Wyoming	Uniform Consumer Credit Code in effect.	U.C.C.C. finance-service charges: Consumer credit sales—greater of 21% on all unpaid balances or total of 36% on unpaid balances of $300 or less, 21% on over $300 but less than $1,000 and 15% on over $1,000; revolving credit: 1¾% on average monthly balance.

Federal and State Consumer Protection Legislation

FEDERAL LAW

In 1968, Congress enacted the Consumer Credit Protection Act 15 U.S.C. §§ 1601 *et seq.*, which includes the popularly known Truth in Lending Act. Id. §§ 1601-1614, 1631-1646, 1661-1665a, 1666-1666j, 1667-1667b. The Act, which had been pending in Congress since 1960, was a major advance in the law of consumer protection. The most significant aspect of the Act is the requirement of written disclosure to the borrower of the true cost of credit. The following is a brief summary of the law:

Title I deals with consumer credit costs and disclosure and declares the following as its declaration of purpose:

> The Congress finds that economic stabilization would be enhanced and the competition among the various financial institutions and other firms engaged in the extension of consumer credit would be strengthened by the informed use of credit. The informed use of credit results from an awareness of the cost thereof by consumers. It is the purpose of this subchapter to assure a meaningful disclosure of credit terms so that the consumer will be able to compare more readily the various credit terms available to him and avoid the uninformed use of credit, and to protect the consumer against inaccurate and unfair credit billing and credit card practices. Id. § 1601(a)

The Act exempts the following transactions from its scope, Id. § 1603:

1. Credit transactions involving extensions of credit for business, commercial or agricultural purposes or to governmental agencies, instrumentalities or to organizations, such as cooperatives, partnerships or trusts.

2. Transactions in securities or commodities accounts by a broker-dealer registered with the Securities and Exchange Commission.

3. Credit transactions, other than real property transactions, in which the total amount to be financed exceeds $25,000.

4. Transactions under public utility tariffs if it is determined that a state regulatory body regulates the charges for public service.

The amount of the finance charge in connection with any consumer credit transaction, determined by Section 1605, is to be the sum of all charges, payable directly or indirectly by the borrower or imposed on him by the creditor, including: interest charges, service or carrying charges, finders' fees, fees for investigation of credit reports, insurance guaranty charges, premiums for credit life, accident or health insurance (unless the issuance of such insurance is not a factor in obtaining the credit, and the borrower is so advised in writing, but nevertheless specifically requests such insurance in writing after disclosure of the cost). Charges or premiums for insurance against loss or damage to property or liability for its use shall be included in the finance charge unless the borrower is advised in writing of the cost of such insurance and the fact that it can be obtained from any person the borrower chooses.

Excluded from the finance charge are the following items, provided a separate disclosure is made: Fees prescribed by law that actually are or will be paid to public officials, and premiums for insurance obtained in lieu of perfecting any security interest, provided the cost of such insurance is not in excess thereof.

In connection with real estate loans, the finance charge excludes title examinations and title insurance fees, appraisal fees, credit reports, escrows for future payment of taxes and insurance and fees for preparation of documents.

Section 1606 of the Act requires that the finance charge for credit sales and loans must be disclosed and expressed as an annual percentage rate, and defines how that rate is computed.

Section 1635 deals with abuses arising from sales on credit for home improvements. It provides that, in the case of any credit transactions in which a security interest is retained or required in any real property which the borrower uses as his residence, except for first liens created to finance the acquisition of such property, the borrower shall have the right to rescind the transaction until midnight of the third business day following the consummation of the transaction or the delivery of the making of the disclosures required by the Act, whichever is later. Upon rescission, the borrower is not liable for any finance or any other charge; any security interest becomes void and the creditor is obligated to return down payment. The creditor has 20 days within which to call for his merchandise to be delivered to the borrower or forfeit his claim to it.[1]

Before any creditor permits a borrower to open an open end consumer credit plan, he is obligated to advise the borrower of any of the following applicable items:

1. The conditions under which a finance charge may be imposed; the time period, if any, when credit extended may be repaid without incurring a finance charge.

2. The method of determining the balance upon which the finance charge is imposed.

3. The method of determining the amount of the finance charge.

4. Identification of any other charges.

5. Whether any security interest is acquired by the creditor.

The creditor is also obligated at the end of each billing cycle to submit a statement setting forth the following, as well as other information: The outstanding balance at the beginning and end of the period, the credit charges during the period together with a brief identification of the goods or services purchased, the finance charge and the total amount credited to the account during the period.

In credit sales which are not under an open end credit plan the creditor is obligated to disclose:

1. The identity of the creditor.

2. The "amount financed," which is to be determined pursuant to 15 U.S.C. § 1632(a)(2)(A), and a written itemization of amount financed if requested by the consumer.

3. The "finance charge."

---

[1] The FTC has issued regulations which permit a consumer to cancel home solicitation sales in excess of $25 within three days after the date of sale.

4. The finance charge expressed as an "annual percentage rate" except if amount financed does not exceed $75 and the service charge does not exceed $5 or if amount financed exceeds $75 and finance charge does not exceed $7.50.

5. The "total of payments."

6. The number, amount, and due dates scheduled to repay the total of payments.

7. In a sale of property, the "total sale price."

8. Descriptive explanations of above terms.

9. A statement that a security interest has been taken, where appropriate.

10. A charge which may be imposed due to a late payment.

11. A statement indicating whether consumer entitled to rebate of any finance charge upon prepayment or refinancing.

12. A statement referring consumer to appropriate contract document for information.

13. In a residential mortgage transaction, a statement whether the debt is assumable on original terms and conditions.

If a consumer makes an order or a creditor receives a loan request by mail or telephone without personal solicitation, disclosures must be made not later than date first payment is due.

Regulation Z, 12 C.F.R. §§ 226.1-226.1503 (1983), which implements the provisions of the Truth in Lending Act, provides that a seller who regularly arranges for his customers to obtain outside financing is also required to make Truth in Lending disclosures if he is compensated by the bank for his services or participates in the preparation of the contract documents required in procuring a loan. This does not include assisting customers in filling out bank loan applications.

Written acknowledgment by the borrower of receipt of a statement containing the disclosures required to be made under the Act is conclusive proof of compliance as to the assignee of a creditor, without knowledge to the contrary. Therefore, such acknowledgments should be obtained in all transactions covered by the Act. 15 U.S.C. § 1641(b).

Sections 1661 through 1665 of the Act establish controls over credit advertising and set forth certain requirements for different types of advertising.

The Act charges various Federal agencies with the responsibility of enforcing different parts of the Act, and the Board of Governors of the Federal Reserve System is authorized to prescribe regulations to carry out the purpose of Title I.

Criminal penalties for willful and knowing violation of the Title I are a fine of not more than $5,000 or imprisonment of not more than one year, or both. Id. § 1611.

A creditor who fails to properly disclose information as required under the Act is liable for an amount equal to twice the finance charges or $100, whichever is greater, with a maximum penalty of $1,000. Id. § 1640.

Any person engaged in the business of making loans or sales on credit or advertising credit loans is advised to review the specific provisions of the Act to be certain that his practices are in compliance on the effective dates.

Title II of the Act is intended to control and regulate the prevalence of organized crime in the extension of credit, and makes it a federal offense to make, finance or collect extortionate extensions of credit. 18 U.S.C. § 892 (1976).

Title III of the Act restricts garnishments of wages. 15 U.S.C. §§ 1671-1677. Congress found that the unrestricted garnishment of compensation encourages the predatory making of credit and results in the loss of employment by borrowers. The amount of weekly wages subject to garnishment is limited to the lesser of 25% of disposable earnings of the debtor *or* the amount by which the weekly disposable earnings exceed thirty times the federal minimum hourly wage, except that these restrictions do not apply to court orders for support of a person, payments of state or federal taxes or payment pursuant to a bankruptcy court order. An employer is also prohibited from discharging any employee because of a garnishment for one indebtedness.

The Act authorizes the Secretary of Labor to enforce this title and further authorizes him to exempt the garnishments of certain states if it is determined that the laws of such states provide restrictions on garnishments substantially similar to those provided for by the Act.

The Act was amended in 1970 to control issuance and misuse of credit cards. See Chapter 12, *infra.* Regulation Z, which implements the Truth in Lending Act, has added a provision allowing merchants to give discounts to customers who pay by check or cash rather than by credit card.

FAIR CREDIT REPORTING ACT

Title VI of the Consumer Credit Protection Act was enacted on October 26, 1970, and became effective on April 25, 1971. It is known as the Fair Credit Reporting Act. 15 U.S.C. §§ 1681-1681t (1976). The purpose of the Act is to require that consumer reporting agencies adopt reasonable procedures for meeting the needs of consumer credit, personnel insurance and other information in an accurate, fair and equitable manner. The Act is intended to apply only to *consumer* credit transactions and not to *commercial* credit transactions.

The following are the three most important concepts defined by the Act:

1. A CONSUMER REPORT is any written, oral or other communication of any information by a consumer reporting agency bearing on a consumer's credit worthiness, credit standing, credit capacity or reputation which is used or expected to be used in establishing the consumer's eligibility for (1) credit or insurance primarily for personal, family or household purposes, (2) employment purposes, or (3) other specific purposes authorized by the Act. The term, however, does not include (a) any report containing information solely as to transactions or experience between the consumer and the person making the report, (b) any authorization or approval for a specific extension of credit by the issuance of a credit card, (c) any report made by a person who has been requested by a third party to extend credit to a consumer, provided the third party advised the consumer of the name and address of the person to whom the request is made and such person makes the disclosures to the consumer required by the Act.[1] Id. § 1681a(d).

Credit guides or delinquent creditor's lists including bad check blacklists, are alphabetical listings rating consumers according to certain criteria which are assembled into a book and are distributed to credit grantors. Such lists are "consumer reports" according to FTC rulings, and are subject to the Act. No permissible purpose for obtaining the information exists at the time they are distributed to credit grantors since no credit grantor could possibly be consid-

---

[1] A credit report used in connection with a lease application for business purposes, in other words, an application for commercial credit, is not considered a consumer report. *Sizemore v. Bambi Leasing Corp.,* 360 F.Supp. 252 (N.D. Ga. 1973).

ering advancing credit to every consumer listed. Thus, in order to be in compliance with the Fair Credit Reporting Act, these credit guides and bad check blacklists must be coded so that the consumer's identity is not disclosed until decoded. Appropriate identifiers would include social security numbers, driver's license, and bank account numbers which a credit grantor could use to decode information concerning specific consumers in whom it was interested.

2. An INVESTIGATIVE CONSUMER REPORT is a report in which information about a consumer's character, general reputation, personal characteristics or mode of living is obtained through personal interviews. However, such information may not include factual data obtained directly from a creditor of the consumer. Id. § 1681a(e).

3. A CONSUMER REPORTING AGENCY is any person which for compensation or on a cooperative nonprofit basis regularly engages in whole or in part in the practice of assembling or evaluating consumer information or other information on consumers for the purpose of furnishing consumer reports to third parties, and for using any facility of interstate commerce for this purpose. Id. § 1681a(f).

The Act provides that a consumer reporting agency may furnish a consumer report for the following purposes only:

1. In response to a court order.
2. At the written request of a consumer who is the subject of the report.
3. To a person which it has reason to believe intends to use the information on the consumer's behalf in connection with (a) a credit transaction; (b) for employment purposes; or (c) insurance purposes; or (d) a license granted by a branch of the government; or (e) some other business purpose. Id. § 1681b.

An investigative consumer report may not be prepared unless there is disclosed in writing to the consumer, within three days after the date on which the report was first requested, that such a report is being prepared, and the consumer is advised that he has a right to certain information. However, such disclosure need not be given to the consumer if the report is to be used for employment purposes for which the consumer has *not* specifically applied. Any person who prepares an investigative consumer report must upon a written request made by the consumer make a complete and accurate disclosure of the nature and scope of the investigation requested. The disclosure must be made in writing not later than five days after the date of the request from the consumer. Id. § 1681d.

No consumer reporting agency may issue any consumer report containing any of the following items of information which are deemed obsolete:

1. Bankruptcies older than 10 years.
2. Suits and judgments older than seven years or until the governing statute of limitation has expired, whichever is the longer period.
3. Paid tax liens older than seven years.
4. Accounts placed for collection older than seven years.
5. Records of arrests, indictments or convictions of a crime older than seven years.
6. Any other adverse information older than seven years.

These prohibitions, however, do not apply to credit or insurance transactions involving more than $50,000 or employment for a salary in excess of $20,000. Id. § 1681c.

Every consumer reporting agency shall, upon the request of and the proper identification of the consumer, disclose to him:

1. The nature and substance of all information in its files on the consumer (except medical information).
2. The source of the information (except the sources of an investigative consumer report and used solely for that purpose).
3. The recipients of any consumer report which it has furnished for employment (a) within two years, (b) for any other purpose within six months.

The disclosures must be made upon reasonable notice and during normal business hours. They can be made to the consumer in person, by telephone or by mail upon proper identification. A consumer may be accompanied by one other person of his choice who can furnish reasonable identification. Id. § 1681h.

A consumer reporting agency must make the disclosures required by the Act without charge to the consumer if, within 30 days after receipt by the consumer of notice that his credit rating has been or may be adversely affected, a request for such disclosure is made by the consumer. Otherwise, the consumer reporting agency may impose a reasonable charge on the consumer for making the disclosures of which the consumer shall be advised prior to the furnishing of such information. Id. § 1681j.

If the completeness or accuracy of any information is disputed by a consumer, the consumer reporting agency must within a reasonable time reinvestigate and record the current status of such information unless it has reasonable grounds to believe that the dispute by the consumer is frivolous or irrelevant. If the agency cannot resolve the dispute by reinvestigation, it must make such an entry in the report. If the information is found to be inaccurate or not capable of being verified, the consumer reporting agency must at the request of the consumer notify the recipient of any report which contained the disputed information received within two years prior thereto for employment purposes, or within six months prior thereto for other purposes. Id. § 1681i.

Whenever credit or insurance for personal, family or household purposes or employment of a consumer is denied or the charge for such insurance or credit is increased, because of information contained in a consumer report issued by a consumer reporting agency, the user of the consumer report must advise the consumer of the name and address of the consumer reporting agency making the report. If such credit is denied or if the charges are increased because of information obtained from a person other than a consumer reporting agency, the user of such information must within a reasonable period of time, upon the consumer's written request for the reasons for such adverse action, received within 60 days thereafter, disclose the nature of such information. In addition, the user of such information must clearly and accurately disclose to the consumer his right to make such written request at the time such adverse action is communicated to the consumer. Id. § 1681m.

The Act imposes civil liability for noncompliance in the amount of any damages sustained plus punitive damages. Id. § 1681n. Liability is also imposed for negligent failure to comply with the Act. Id. § 1681o. Penalties in the nature of a fine or imprisonment may be imposed on any person who obtained information on a consumer from a consumer reporting agency under false pretenses, id. § 1681q, or upon any officer or employee of a consumer reporting agency who knowingly and willingly provides information to an unauthorized person. Id. § 1681r.

Compliance with the Act is enforced by the Federal Trade Commission and other federal agencies. Id. § 1681s.

Fair Credit Billing Act

This Act requires creditors to respond to inquiries by consumers on credit card accounts and other charge accounts in which an allegedly improper or incorrect charge is made on a bill. 15 U.S.C. §§ 1601, 1602, 1610, 1631, 1632, 1637, 1666-1666j. The Act authorizes creditors to inquire into an applicant's sex, marital status, race, national origin and age, but the applicant is not required to answer these questions. It sets 62 at the age to which the term "elderly" applies and describes the working of a nondiscriminatory credit-scoring system. The Act is further discussed in Chapter 12, *infra* p. 12-10.

Consumer Leasing Act

The Consumer Leasing Act of 1976 added six new sections to the Truth in Lending Act, and became effective March 23, 1977. Id. §§ 1601, 1640, 1667-1667e. The new law:

1. Requires lessors to disclose information affecting the cost of consumer leases defined as leases of personal property, primarily for personal, family or household use for a term greater than four months where the consumer's total contractual obligation is less than $25,000.

2. Limits the amount of the final balloon payment required by open-end leases at the end of the term.

3. Seeks to insure meaningful and accurate disclosure in advertising of leasing terms.

Consumer Products Safety Act

In late 1972 Congress enacted the Consumer Products Safety Act, 15 U.S.C. § 2501, et seq., which is intended to protect the public against unreasonable risks of injury associated with consumer products, to assist consumers in evaluating the comparative safety of consumer products, to develop uniform safety standards, and to promote research and investigation into product-related deaths, illnesses, and injuries.

The Act creates a commission which collects, analyzes, and investigates information of injuries associated with consumer products. It may also conduct research studies and investigations and test consumer products. The commission is authorized to make rules with respect to consumer product safety standards and requirements. The Act contains punitive measures for failure to comply with any rules or standards promulgated by the commission and also provides for civil penalties and private enforcement.

Equal Credit Opportunity Act

Since March 23, 1977, federal law has not only prohibited creditors from discriminating against a person because of sex or marital status, but it has also been unlawful to discriminate because of race, color, religion, national origin, age, welfare assistance or the exercise of debtor's rights assured by the Consumer Credit Protection Act. 15 U.S.C. §§ 1601, 1691-1691f. The law and Regulation B, which implements it, 12 C.F.R. 202.1-202.114 (1983), is not limited to consumer transactions, but applies to credit extended to any individual, partnership or corporation for any purpose. It also applies to consumer leases even though the Equal Credit Opportunity Act does not specify that consumer leases are covered by its provisions. When viewed in light of the Consumer Credit Protection Act, it is clear that the ECOA applies to all transactions covered by Truth in Lending. Under Regulation B, to the Act, grantors of business credit are not required to notify an applicant of the reasons for the denial of credit unless the applicant within thirty (30) days after oral or written notification that adverse action has been taken requests the reasons for such action. Such request must be responded to by a credit grantor by advising the inquirer as to the reasons for such denial which can be expressed in a brief statement such as "insufficient credit references" or "unable to verify credit references." If information on the debtor is obtained from a consumer reporting agency, the name and address of such agency must be set forth. The source of such information other than from a consumer reporting agency need not be revealed.

Fair Debt Collection Practices Act

See Chapter 11 *infra.*

Federal Trade Commission Regulation of Credit Practices

The Federal Trade Commission has issued rules regulating credit practices in consumer credit transactions. The rules designate certain practices as unfair credit practices. Such practices include the following:

1. A confession of judgment or warrant of attorney or other waiver of the right to notice and the opportunity to be heard;

2. An executory waiver or a limitation of exemption from attachment, execution or other process, on real or personal property, unless the waiver applies to property subject to a security interest executed in connection with the obligation;

3. An assignment of wages or other earnings, unless the assignment is revocable by debtor; the assignment is part of a payroll deduction plan or preauthorized payment plan; or the assignment applies only to wages or other earnings already earned at the time of the assignment;

4. A non-possessory security interest in household goods, other than a purchase money security interest.

Deceptive cosigner practices are proscribed. They include misrepresentation by lender or seller of the nature or extent of cosigner liability and a lender or a retail installment seller obligating a cosigner without the cosigner being informed prior to becoming obligated of the nature of his or her liability. A special notice prescribed by the rules is required to be given to a cosigner to prevent unfair and deceptive cosigner practices.

In connection with collecting a debt arising out of the extension of credit to a consumer, it is an unfair act or practice to collect any delinquency charge on a payment which is otherwise a full payment for the applicable period and is paid on its due date, when the only delinquency is attributable to late fees or delinquency charges assessed on earlier installments.

If there is a state requirement which provides for a level of protection equal to the federal requirements, the state may obtain an exemption from application of these rules to it.

STATE LEGISLATION

Truth in Lending Acts

Twenty-seven states and the District of Columbia have truth in lending legislation in effect.[1] Their common requirement is that disclosure of the cost of credit

(Continued on page 9-19.)

---

[1] See chart, *supra* p. 9-9.

STATES' TRUTH IN LENDING LEGISLATION*

JURISDICTION	EXEMPTIONS & EXCEPTIONS	TRANSACTIONS SUBJECT TO DISCLOSURE PROVISIONS	ADMINISTRATION	ANNUAL RATE CALCULATION	PENALTIES CIVIL	PENALTIES CRIMINAL	TYPE SIZE
CALIFORNIA Retail Instalment Sales Law, Motor Vehicle Sales and Finance Act	Disclosures made in any retail instalment contract, conditional sale contract, or other document may be set forth in terminology required or permitted under Federal Reserve Board Regulation Z. Nothing in the state laws is deemed prohibitive of the disclosure in such contracts or documents of additional information required or permitted under Regulation Z at the time the disclosure is made. Compliance with FRB interpretations of Regulation Z is deemed full compliance with that Regulation with respect to the subject matter of the interpretations.						
COLORADO U.C.C.C.	Credit to governmental bodies. Insurance sales by insurers.[1] Regulated public and municipal utilities and common carriers. Licensed pawnbrokers. Rates and charges of credit unions under state or federal law.	Sales Loans Revolving credit	Assistant attorney general. District attorney's with administrator's consent.	Actuarial method or other rule prescribed by administrator. Exemptions: charge under $5, debt under $75. Charge $7.50, debt over $75 but less than $500, and $15 if amount financed is more than $500	Twice the finance charge Minimum $100 Maximum $1,000	$5,000 maximum; 1 year, or both	Clear and conspicuous
CONNECTICUT Truth in Lending Act	Creditors and lessors are required to comply with the Federal Truth in Lending Act and Regulations Z and M by reference.						

* States not listed do not have truth-in-lending provisions.
[1] Insurance sales to insurers (except those under UCCC Article 4)

STATES' TRUTH IN LENDING LEGISLATION (Continued)

JURISDICTION	EXEMPTIONS & EXCEPTIONS	TRANSACTIONS SUBJECT TO DISCLOSURE PROVISIONS	ADMINISTRATION	ANNUAL RATE CALCULATION	PENALTIES CIVIL	PENALTIES CRIMINAL	TYPE SIZE
DELAWARE Retail Instalment Sales Act and Motor Vehicle Sales Finance Act	Disclosures made under the Federal Truth in Lending Act are compliance with comparable, but literally inconsistent, disclosures under state laws.						
DISTRICT OF COLUMBIA Consumer Retail Credit Regulation	Business credit; credit over $25,000. Motor vehicles; 90-day credit if no finance charge. Prices, tariffs regulated by govt.	Sales Revolving credit	Com. of Dist. of Col.	Actuarial or US Rule Exemptions: charge under $5, debt under $75; charge under $7.50 debt over $75.	No provisions	Loss or suspension of license; $300 max. fine; 10 days	Same as federal Truth in Lending Act
FLORIDA Retail Instalment Sales Act	A creditor who discloses all information required by the Federal Truth in Lending Act will be deemed in compliance with state contract requirements, except that a separate written itemization of the amount financed must be provided in accordance with state law, and state requirements for revolving accounts.						
HAWAII Industrial Loan Companies Act, Retail Instalment Sales Act, Small Loan Act, Disclosure of Finance Charges Law	Under the Hawaii Industrial Loan Companies Act, Retail Instalment Sales Act, Small Loan Act, any transaction governed by the Federal Truth in Lending Act is not required to have any disclosure which is inconsistent with the Federal Law. The Disclosure of Finance Charges Law does not apply to transactions governed by Federal Law.						

IDAHO Credit Code, effective March 31, 1983		Creditors covered by the Federal Truth in Lending Act and the regulations issued pursuant thereto are required to comply with the provisions of the law and regulations administered by the Director of the Dept. of Finance.			
ILLINOIS Retail Installment Sales Act—RISA Motor Vehicle Retail Installment Sales Act—MVRISA Consumer Installment Loan Act—CILA Revolving Credit Act Revolving Charge Act Consumer Finance Act—CFA Premium Finance Companies Act—PFC	RISA: Business credit and motor vehicles. MVRISA: Business credit not including farm or professional CILA and Revolving Charge Acts have no exemptions. Revolving Credit Act: Accounts without unpaid balances. CFA: Business loans by state licensed entities PFC: Financial institutions, insurance companies, consumer finance agencies.	RISA: Sales and Revolving Credit. MVRISA: Sales CILA: Loans Revolving Credit and Revolving Charge Acts: Revolving Credit. CFA: Loans PFC: Loans	CILA: Director of Financial Institutions. CFA—Department of Financial Institutions The other statutes have no provisions	Actuarial or US Rule for both RISA, CFA, and MVRISA. Other statutes have no provisions. Exemptions: RISA: charge under $5, debt under $75. Charge under $7.50, debt over $75 CFA—same as RISA	Revolving credit: contract unenforceable. Revolving Charge: only balance of cash price collectible. CFA: Balance of cash price minus atty's fees and court costs only collectible. PFC: Revocation of license. The other statutes have no provisions.	RISA and MVRISA $1,000 maximum 1 year or both. The other statutes have no provisions. CFA: $100-1000 fine; Class A misdemeanor.	RISA, MVRISA AND CILA: Clear and conspicuous in 8-point type. Revolving charge: equal prominence. Revolving credit: no provision. CFA and MVRISA: in English. PFC: 8-pt. type.
INDIANA UCCC	Credit to governmental bodies. Insurance sales by insurers.[2] Regulated public and municipal utilities and common carriers. Licensed pawnbrokers.	Sales Loans Revolving credit [3]	Dept. of Financial Institutions, Division of Consumer Credit.	Actuarial method or other prescribed by administrator. Exemptions: charge under $5, debt under $75. Charge under $7.50, debt over $75	Twice the finance charge Minimum $100 Maximum $1,000	$5,000 maximum; 1 year or both	Clear and conspicuous

[1] The liability of a creditor under the Truth in Lending Act is in lieu of, not in addition to liability, under the Uniform Commercial Code. No action with respect to the same violation may be maintained under both acts.
[2] Insurance sales to insurers (except those under UCCC Article 4).
[3] Effective July 1, 1983, sellers, lessors, and lenders are required to provide disclosure information pursuant to the Federal Consumer Credit Protection Act.

STATES' TRUTH IN LENDING LEGISLATION *(Continued)*

JURISDICTION	EXEMPTIONS & EXCEPTIONS	TRANSACTIONS SUBJECT TO DISCLOSURE PROVISIONS	ADMINISTRATION	ANNUAL RATE CALCULATION	PENALTIES		TYPE SIZE
					CIVIL	CRIMINAL	
IOWA Consumer credit code	A creditor must comply with the Federal Truth in Lending Act and disclose to the consumer all information required by the Act. Exemptions and exclusions include business or governmental credit, insurance sales by insurers, regulated public utilities and common carriers, and nonrealty credit over $35,000. Administration is by the Attorney General.				Twice the finance charge: Min.: $100 Max.: $1,000	$5,000 max., 1 year, or both	
KANSAS UCCC, Insurance Premium Financing Act—IPFCA	UCCC: Business or governmental credit, nonrealty credit over $25,000, regulated public utilities and common carriers. Insurance sales by insurers.[1] IPFCA: no provision.	A creditor must comply with the Federal Truth in Lending Act and disclose to the consumer all information required by the Act.	UCCC: Consumer Credit Commissioner and enforcement agencies IPFCA: Commissioner of Insurance	UCCC: A creditor must comply with the Federal Truth in Lending Act IPFCA: No provisions.	UCCC: Twice the finance charge Min: $100 Max: $1,000 $5000 for repeated violations IPFCA: No provision	UCCC: Class A misdemeanor or Federal Truth in Lending penalties IPFCA: No provisions	UCCC: A creditor must comply with the Federal Truth in Lending Act IPFCA: 8-pt. type.
KENTUCKY Credit Disclosure Law, Banking Commission Regulations	Sales under the Instalment Sales Law; Motor Vehicle Sales; Pawnbrokers; Credit over $25,000. No finance charge. Compliance with Federal Truth in Lending Act constitutes compliance with the Kentucky Credit Disclosure Law.	Loans Revolving credit Sales	Com. Dept. of Banking and Securities	Constant ratio method. Exemptions: No provisions.	Forfeiture of finance charge	$500 max., 6 mos. or both	Annual Rate 12 point bold

[1] Except those under UCCC Article 4.

MAINE Truth in Lending Law	Business or commercial credit; agricultural transactions; transactions not secured by realty where amount financed exceeds $25,000; securities or commodities transactions; public utilities; leases of personal property incident to lease of real property where there is no option to purchase	Sales, loans, revolving credit	Supt. Consumer Protection	Actuarial or US Rule; in unusual circumstances constant ratio method; Exemptions for charge under $5, debt under $75; charge under $7.50, debt over $75.	Actual damages or twice the finance charge; min $100, max $1,000.	Organizations: $5,000 max or 1 yr. or both; Natural Persons: $1,000 or 1 year or both	Clear and conspicuous
MARYLAND Interest and Usury Law, Credit Grantor Revolving Credit and Closed End Credit Provisions	Transactions subject to the Credit Grantor Revolving Credit and Closed End Credit Provisions are subject to the disclosures and requirements of that law and the Federal Truth in Lending Act.	Loans	No provs.	Annual effective rate Exemptions: No provs.	No provs.	$1,000 max., 1 year or both	No provs.

STATES' TRUTH IN LENDING LEGISLATION (Continued)

JURISDICTION	EXEMPTIONS & EXCEPTIONS	TRANSACTIONS SUBJECT TO DISCLOSURE PROVISIONS	ADMINISTRATION	ANNUAL RATE CALCULATION	PENALTIES CIVIL	PENALTIES CRIMINAL	TYPE SIZE
MASSACHUSETTS Truth in Lending Act—TILA; Retail Instalment Sales and Service—RISS; Motor Vehicle Retail Instalment Sales—MVRIS; Insurance Premium Financing Act—IPFA; Bank Commission Regulations	TILA: Business or commercial credit, agricultural transactions, transactions not secured by real property, dwellings where amount financed exceeds $25,000, securities or commodities transactions, public utilities, home fuel budget plans; RISS: loans, sales with less than 3 payments, charge of $1 or less and no collateral; MVRIS: no provisions. IPFA premiums financed at not more than 6% per year; Life endowment, retirement income insurance.	TILA: sales, loans, revolving credit, RISS: sales, revolving credit; MVRIS and IPFA: sales.	TILA, RISS, MVRIS, IPFA: Commissioner of Banks	TILA, RISS, MVRIS, IPFA: Actuarial method or US rule; Exemptions: charges under $5, debt under $75. Charge under $7.50, debt over $75.	TILA: Actual damages; Twice the finance charge, min. $100, max. $1,000. RISS, MVRIS: Forfeiture of finance charge; IPFCA: No provisions	TILA: $5,000, max. 1 yr. or both; RISS, MVRIS: $500 max. or 6 mos. or both; IPFCA: No provision	TILA, RISS, MVRIS, IPFCA: Clear and conspicuous. RISS: No provision.

9–14

MICHIGAN Retail Instalment Sales Act, Home Improvement Finance Act, Motor Vehicle Retail Instalment Sales Act, Retail Charge Accounts	Michigan creditor compliance with the Federal Truth in Lending Act constitutes compliance with the disclosure provision of the listed State Acts.
MINNESOTA Regulated Loan Act	Open-end loans made by licensed regulated lenders must comply with the disclosure requirements of the Federal Truth in Lending Act and Regulation Z.
NEW JERSEY Designated Consumer Credit Law; Retail Charge Accounts	To the extent that N.J. laws are inconsistent with disclosure, advertising, terminology, type size, method of computation of finance charges, form, content or time of delivery provisions and requirements of the Federal Truth in Lending Act and Regulation Z, compliance with the Federal Rules is deemed compliance with the N.J. laws. Retail charge accounts are subject to the requirements of the Federal Truth in Lending Act and Regulation Z applicable to open end credit.
NEW MEXICO Retail Instalment Sales	Compliance with the Federal Truth in Lending Act and Regulation Z is deemed compliance with the Retail Instalment Sales Law.

STATES' TRUTH IN LENDING LEGISLATION *(Continued)*

JURISDICTION	EXEMPTIONS & EXCEPTIONS	TRANSACTIONS SUBJECT TO DISCLOSURE PROVISIONS	ADMINISTRATION	ANNUAL RATE CALCULATION	PENALTIES CIVIL	PENALTIES CRIMINAL	TYPE SIZE
NEW YORK Retail Instalment Sales Act; Motor Vehicle Retail Instalment Sales Act; Sales Finance Companies Law; Insurance Premium Financing Law; Small Loan Law, Penal Law and Banking Law	Credit transactions are subject to the Federal Truth in Lending Act and the regulations thereunder.						
NORTH DAKOTA Retail Instalment Sales Act; Revolving Charge Accounts	Sale of personal property for $25,000 or above; property used primarily for business, commercial, or agricultural purposes.	Revolving credit [1]	No provs.	Annual simple interest Exemptions: no provs.	RISA: No provision RCA: Forfeiture of finance charge	RISA: No provision RCA: Class A misdemeanor	No provs.
OKLAHOMA Uniform Consumer Credit Code, Department of Consumer Affairs, Rules of the Administrator.	Business, government, credit insurance, sales by issuers,[2] licensed pawnbrokers, margin accounts, regulated public utilities, common carriers, non-realty credit over $45,000	Sales Loans Revolving credit	Administrator of Consumer Credit	Actuarial or US Rule. In certain circumstances, constant ratio method. Exemptions: charge under $5, debt under $75; charge under $7.50, debt over $75.	Actual damages and twice the finance charge Min: $100 Max: $1,000	$5,000 max., 1 year or both	Clear and conspicuous

[1] Sellers may comply with the Federal Truth in Lending Act instead of the disclosure provisions of the RISA.
[2] Except those under UCCC Article 4.

9–16

OREGON Retail Instalment Sales and Motor Vehicle Retail Instalment Sales Act		Any compliance with the disclosure requirements of the Federal Truth in Lending Act is deemed compliance with disclosure provisions of the Retail Instalment Sales Law and the Motor Vehicle Retail Instalment Sales Act. Administered by the Administrator of Consumer Affairs.			
SO. CAROLINA Consumer Protection Code		A creditor must disclose to the consumer all the information required by the Federal Truth in Lending Act and otherwise comply with the entire Act.		Twice the finance charge: Min: $100 Max.: $1,000	$5,000 max., 1 year, or both.
TENNESSEE		Compliance with Federal Truth-in-Lending Act is compliance with state disclosure requirements.			
TEXAS Insurance Premium Finance Law		Compliance with federal Truth in Lending Act and Regulation Z is deemed compliance with IPFA.			
UTAH UCCC; Department of Financial Institutions	Business or government credit, sales of insurance by insurers,[1] regulated public utilities and common carriers, licensed pawnbrokers, margin accounts, credit for agricultural purposes, transactions in securities.	Sales Loan Revolving credit [2]	Comm. of Financial Institutions	Actuarial, US Rule, under unusual circumstances, constant ratio method. Exemptions: charge under $5, debt under $75; charge under $7.50, debt over $75	Twice the finance charge Min: $100 Max: $1,000 Class action: Min: none Max: lesser of $500,000 or 1% of net worth	$5,000 max. or 1 year or both
WASHINGTON Credit Disclosure Act	Home improvement retail sales transactions under FHA Service contracts subject to governmental price control and margin accounts	Sales	State Attorney General	Actuarial Exemptions: No provisions	Fine up to $1,000 for violation of injunction or order	$1,000 max, 6 mos. or both	10 pt. Bold

[1] Except under UCCC Article 4.
[2] The provisions on disclosure of the Federal Truth in Lending Act and Regulations Z and M have been adopted by reference.

9–17

STATES' TRUTH IN LENDING LEGISLATION (Continued)

JURISDICTION	EXEMPTIONS & EXCEPTIONS	TRANSACTIONS SUBJECT TO DISCLOSURE PROVISIONS	ADMINISTRATION	ANNUAL RATE CALCULATION	PENALTIES CIVIL	PENALTIES CRIMINAL	TYPE SIZE
WISCONSIN Consumer Act	Creditors are required to comply with disclosure provisions of the Federal Truth in Lending Act in addition to those of the Consumer Act.						
WYOMING UCCC, Installment Loan Law	UCCC: Credit to governmental bodies; Insurance sales by insurers;[1] Regulated public utilities and common carriers; Licensed pawnbrokers; Rates and charges of credit unions under state or federal law; nonrealty credit over $25,000 ILL: no provisions	Sales Loans Revolving credit ILL: Loans	State Examiner ILL: No provisions	UCCC: Actuarial or US Rule, under unusual circumstances. Constant Ratio Method. Exemptions: charge under $5, debt under $75. Charge under $7.50, debt over $75 ILL: No provisions	Twice the finance charge Minimum $100 Maximum $1,000 ILL: No provisions	$5,000 maximum; 1 year or both ILL: No provisions	No provisions.

[1] Except under UCCC Article 4.

9–18

CONSUMER PROTECTION LEGISLATION

(Continued from page 9-8.)

be in the form of an annual percentage rate, thus simplifying the task of the consumer as he shops for the best credit purchase.

The majority of these states have adopted the federal bill, or a modified version thereof, and most of these states have made the disclosure requirement applicable to the types of transactions normally entered into by consumers: sales, loans and revolving credit transactions.

All such states require the creditor to disclose detailed credit information to the debtor, at or before the time when credit is extended. The information required is essentially the same as that in the Federal Act. In some states, creditors need not disclose finance charges on transactions to a certain maximum limit, as in the Federal Act. Other states have no such exceptions. (See chart, *infra*.)

Section 111(a) of the Federal Truth in Lending Act specifies that it is not intended to preempt state creditor disclosure legislation unless the state provision is inconsistent with federal rules, and then only to the extent of the inconsistency. 15 U.S.C. § 1610. The Act does not preempt the entire body of state law if an inconsistency arises in one case. The intent of this federal legislation, in fact, is "to encourage as much state legislation in this area as is possible so that the Federal law will no longer be necessary." (Senate Committee on Banking and Currency, Report 392 (§5), 90th Congress, 1st Session, June 29 1967, p. 8)

The annual percentage rate to be disclosed under local law is not a simple interest rate, but, similar to the Federal Act, is a complex "finance charge" which includes all costs of credit, including legal interest and other charges incident to the extension of credit.

The Federal Reserve Board of Governors is authorized to exempt any class of credit transactions in any state if it finds that the state requires essentially the same information as the Federal Act, and has made adequate provision for enforcement of the state law. Id. § 1633.

Methods of Determining Annual Percentage Rate:

Constant Ratio Method

The constant ratio method for determining the annual percentage rate is useful for highly irregular contracts. The constant ratio formula assumes that (a) all scheduled instalments of a credit transaction are equal in amount, payable at equal intervals, and fall on due dates which are the same day of each month or other payment period as that on which the agreement is entered into, and (b) the debtor makes all payments at the times and in the amounts scheduled. The formula is:

$$R = \frac{2\,P\,C}{A\,(N+1)}$$

R equals the percentage rate; P equals the number of payment periods in a year; C equals the finance charge; A equals the principal balance to be paid by the debtor; and N equals the number of instalments.

Actuarial Method (United States Rule)

This is a method for computing the simple annual rate on the declining balance and assumes that a uniform periodic rate is applied to a schedule of

(Continued on page 9-23.)

STATE CONSUMER PROTECTION LEGISLATION

States	1 Credit Reporting Act	2 Small Loan Act	3 Consumer or Installment Loan Act	4 Revolving Sales Credit Act *	5 Home Solicitation Act	6 Home Improvement Loan Act	7 Unfair Trade or Consumer Protection Act	8 Insurance Premium Financing Act *	9 Unsolicited Merchandise Act	10 Consumer Defenses against Assignee *	Creditor Billings Error
ALA.		X	X	X	X	X		X		X	
ALASKA		X	X	X	X	X	X	X	X	X	
ARIZ.	X	X	X	X	X	X	X			X	
ARK.					X		X				
CALIF.	X	X	X	X	X	X	X	X		X	
COLO.**		X	X	X	X	X	X			X	,
CONN.	X	X	X	X	X		X	X	X	X	X
DEL.		X	X	X	X		X	X		X	
D. OF COL.		X	X	X	X	X	X	X	X	X	
FLA.	X	X	X	X	X	X	X	X	X	X	
GA.		X		X	X		X	X	X	X	
HAWAII		X	X	X	X	X	X		X	X	
IDAHO**		X	X	X	X	X	X	X	X	X	
ILL.		X	X	X	X	X	X	X	X	X	X
IND.**		X	X	X	X	X	X	X	X	X	
IOWA**		X	X	X	X		X	*	X	X	
KANS.		X	X	X	X		X	X	X	X	

9–20

States	1 Credit Reporting Act	2 Small Loan Act	3 Consumer or Instalment Loan Act	4 Revolving Sales Credit Act*	5 Home Solicitation Act	6 Home Improvement Loan Act	7 Unfair Trade or Consumer Protection Act	8 Insurance Premium Financing Act*	9 Unsolicited Merchandise Act	10 Consumer Defenses against Assignee*	Creditor Billings Error
KY.	X	X	X	X	X		X	X		X	
LA.		X	X	X	X				X	X	
ME.	X	X	X	X	X	X	X	X	X	X	
MD.	X	X	X	X	X	X	X	X	X	X	X
MASS.	X	X	X	X	X		X	X	X	X	X
MICH.		X	X	X	X	X	X	X	X	X	
MINN.		X	X	X	X		X	X	X	X	
MISS.		X	X	X	X		X	X			
MO.		X	X	X	X		X		X	X	
MONT.	X	X	X	X	X		X	X		X	
NEB.	X	X	X	X	X	*	X	X			
NEV.		X		X	X	*	X		X	X	
N.H.	X	X			X	X	X	X	X	X	
N.J.		X	X	X	X	X	X	X	X	X	X
NEW MEX.	X	X	X	X			X	X		X	
N.Y.	X	X	X	X	X	X	X	X	X	X	X
N.C.		X	X	X	X	X	X	X	X	X	
N.D.		X		X	X		X	X		X	
OHIO		X	X	X	X		X	X		X	

9–21

STATE CONSUMER PROTECTION LEGISLATION (Continued)

States	1 Credit Reporting Act	2 Small Loan Act	3 Consumer or Instalment Loan Act	4 Revolving Sales Credit Act *	5 Home Solicitation Act	6 Home Improvement Loan Act	7 Unfair Trade or Consumer Protection Act	8 Insurance Premium Financing Act *	9 Unsolicited Merchandise Act	10 Consumer Defenses against Assignee *	Creditor Billings Error
OKLA.**	X	X	X	X	X	X	X	X	X	X	
ORE.		X	X	X	X	X	X	X	X	X	
PA.	X	X	X	X	X	X	X		X	X	
R.I.		X	X	X	X		X		X	X	
S.C.		X	X	X	X	X	X	X	X		
SD.		X	X	X	X		X		X	X	
TENN.		X	X	X	X	*	X	X	X	X	
TEX.	X	X	X	X	X		X	X	X	X	
UTAH **		X	X	X	X	X	X	X		X	X
VT.		X	X	X	X		X	X	X	X	
VA.		X		X	X	X	X	X			
WASH.		X	X	X	X		X	X		X	
W. VA.		X	X		X		X				
WIS.		X	X	X	X	X	X	X	X	X	
WYO.**		X	X	X	X	X	X	X	X	X	

* Many states include revolving credit legislation, insurance premium financing, legislations, home improvement loan legislation and legislation on consumer defense as part of Retail Instalment Act or other laws.

** The UCCC has, for the most part, supplanted the Acts listed in the Chart, but the reader is cautioned to check both the UCCC and the statute in question in the specific states. Some of the states adopting the UCCC have not repealed a number of the statutes under consideration, but, rather, have maintained them to be interpreted and applied along with the UCCC.

CONSUMER PROTECTION LEGISLATION 9–23

(Continued from page 9-19.)

instalment payments such that the principal is reduced to zero upon completion of the payments. The actuarial rate is the periodic rate multiplied by the number of periods in a year.

Many states which have adopted Retail Instalment Sales Acts have a provision in such acts requiring disclosure of the amount of finance charges to a retail buyer on the purchase of consumer goods. However, such statutes do not provide that the disclosure take the form of an annual percentage rate which is required under the federal law or under the state laws set forth in the above chart. See *supra* p. 9-9. For a more detailed discussion of the disclosure requirements under the Retail Instalment Sales Acts see Chapter 8.

Those states which require some form of disclosure of finance charges but not an annual percentage rate are Florida, Georgia, Montana, Missouri, Nebraska, Nevada, Ohio, Tennessee, and Vermont.

Alaska and New Hampshire have in effect a Retail Instalment Sales Act which allows disclosure either in the form of an annual percentage rate or as a dollar amount. Minnesota and Mississippi, have some form of disclosure requirement (although not an annual percentage rate) on sales of vehicles only.

In New York use of the previous balance method to compute finance charges on retail charge accounts is illegal under the Personal Property Law; sellers are required to use the adjusted balance method.

General Consumer Protection Legislation

In addition to statutes governing disclosures of rates of interest on sales or instalment sales, every state in the country has adopted some legislation which can be characterized as "consumer protection." The major types of such legislation are:

Fair Credit Reporting Act—Controls issuance and accuracy of credit reports.

Small Loan Acts—Governs the rates and terms of loans in amounts usually less than $3,000.

Instalment, Personal or Consumer Loan Act—Governs the rates and terms of loans for personal or consumer use in amounts usually $5,000 or less.

Revolving Sales Credit Act—Governs the rates and terms of consumer credit sales in which charge accounts are used.

Home Solicitation Act—Governs sales made at home, usually permitting cancellation of such contract within a short period of time (2-3 days).

Home Improvement Loan Act—Governs the terms of contracts for home improvements which are financed, and usually provides for cancellation of such contracts within a short period of time (2-3 days).

Unfair Trade or Consumer Protection Act—Comprehensive state legislation which protects the consumer against unfair or deceptive advertising or business practices.

Insurance Premium Financing Act—Governs the rates and terms of financing of insurance premiums.

Unsolicited Merchandise Act—Provides that unsolicited merchandise may be retained by recipient as a gift.

Consumer Defense—The right of a purchaser to assert against the obligee or his assignee any rights or defenses he might have against the original seller of the goods or services.

Creditor Billing Errors Act—Requires a creditor to rectify any error in billing within a specified period of time upon a consumer complaint.

Set forth below are examples of some state consumer protection legislation.

Oregon has a statute which abolishes deficiency judgments on consumer goods after repossession if the unpaid balance at the time of default is less than $1,250.

California's consumer warranty act requires manufacturers of consumer goods to maintain sufficient service and repair facilities in the state, and provides remedies for retailers and consumers. California and Illinois require persons conducting or negotiating a retail transaction in a language other than English to provide an unexecuted copy of the agreement to the consumer in that language.

Maryland has a statute which declares the use of a consumer contract which contains a confession of judgment clause that waives the consumer's legal defenses to be an unfair or deceptive trade practice and is subject to certain applicable penalties.

New Hampshire has a Distributorship Disclosure Act which requires those offering distributorships within the state to file certain disclosures to the consumer protection division of the Attorney General's office, and to provide prospective distributors with the same information at least seven days prior to entering into any distributorship agreement. The Act also forbids fraud in advertising or contracting and provides remedies for violations.

Washington has a Financial Institutions Disclosure Act requiring lending institutions with more than $10 million in assets to file information annually with the Secretary of State concerning loans and mortgages rejected and granted. Each financial institution and the Secretary of State is required to make this information available to any interested party. Penalties are provided for failure to file or for furnishing false information.

THE UNIFORM CONSUMER CREDIT CODE

The Uniform Consumer Credit Code (UCCC) is a comprehensive consumer protection law prepared by the National Conference of Commissioners on Uniform State Laws. It seeks to codify various state statutes dealing with consumer protection, such as Small Loan Acts, Personal Loan Acts, Instalment Loan and Sales Acts, Truth In Lending Acts, Consumer Unfair Trade Practices Acts, and Home Solicitation Sales Acts.

The Act, to mention a few of its provisions, establishes maximum rates of interest on loans and credit sales, requires disclosure of finance charges and other information, and prohibits deceptive advertising and unconscionable contract provisions.

To date, only the 10 states of Colorado, Idaho,[1] Indiana, Iowa, Kansas, Maine, Oklahoma, South Carolina,[2] Utah and Wyoming[3] have adopted the UCCC, and in consequence have repealed the numerous local laws that previously dealt with consumer protection. In this respect, the situation is comparable to the adoption by a state of the Uniform Commercial Code which similarly necessitated the repeal of a number of statutes encompassed within the scope of the Code.

There is no inherent conflict between the UCCC and the Uniform Commercial

---

[1] In 1983 Idaho replaced its original enactment of the 1969 UCCC with the Idaho Credit Code. It is similar to the 1974 UCCC but with a few variations.

[2] The South Carolina Consumer Protection Code does not conform precisely to the UCCC, but covers essentially the same subjects.

[3] Louisiana has adopted a similar statute called the Louisiana Consumer Credit Law which has the same objectives but is not the Uniform Act.

CONSUMER PROTECTION LEGISLATION

Code, and consumer credit transactions may be subject to both statutes. However, in the event of any conflict between the two, the UCCC provides that it controls.

The UCCC conforms to the requirements of the Federal Truth in Lending Act; therefore, any state which adopts it will meet the minimum standards of the Federal Act, and be eligible for the exemptions provided by it.

The Code applies to consumer credit transactions, including sales, leases and loans, and not to regular business or commercial transactions, and only to individuals and not to business organizations, except for sole proprietors or governmental units. Consumer credit is defined as that which is for personal, family, household or agricultural purposes [1] where the amount of the transactions involved is not in excess of $25,000. Real estate transactions are included irrespective of the $25,000 limit, but only if a rate of interest in excess of 10% per year is charged.[2] Consequently, the standard first mortgage is not within the scope of the law, but the second mortgage, which is usually at a higher rate of interest, may be covered by it.

The following is a brief summary of the Code:

ARTICLE 1—GENERAL PROVISIONS AND DEFINITIONS. The statute states that the Code is to be liberally construed and applied to promote its underlying purposes. This article contains provisions for adjustment of dollar amounts in the Code, depending upon changes in the Consumer Price Index For Urban Wage Earners and Clerical Workers. In addition, it states that a buyer or lessee cannot waive the benefits of the Code.

ARTICLE 2—CREDIT SALES. Provides for maximum rates of interest on regular consumer credit sales and on consumer sales on revolving charge accounts. With respect to regular credit sales, the service charge may not exceed the greatest of the following:
1. The total of
   A. 36% per year on that part of the unpaid balance of the amount financed which is $300 or less;
   B. 21% per year on that part of the unpaid balance of the amount financed which is more than $300 and less than $1,000;
   C. 15% per year on that part of the unpaid balance of the amount financed which is more than $1,000; [3] *or*
2. 18% per year of the amount of the unpaid balance financed.[4]

These are maximum rates and the parties to the transaction can of course agree on lesser rates or charges. A seller may also receive a minimum credit service charge of not more than $5 when the amount financed does not exceed

---

[1] In Colorado, Indiana, Kansas, Maine, Oklahoma, and Wyoming, credit transactions entered into primarily for an agricultural purpose are excluded from the coverage of the Code.

[2] In Oklahoma and Idaho the rate of interest is 13% per year and in Colorado and Kansas the rate is 12% per year. In Maine, the rate is 12¼% per year. Colorado, however, exempts from the UCCC debts secured by a mobile home or an interest in land where the rate of interest is less than 12% which does not include sales and loans involving a residence or where the mobile home is note used as a residence and amount financed does not exceed $55,000. There is a $55,000 limit in Idaho, a $45,000 limit in Utah and Oklahoma and a $37,500 limit in Indiana.

[3] Only Iowa and Wyoming have retained these original parameters. Check particular state statutes for variations.

[4] Only Maine and South Carolina have retained the 18% limitation. Other states have opted for 21%. Utah's rate is 19.6%.

$75, or $7.50 when the amount financed exceeds $75.[1] In addition to the credit service charge, a seller may receive additional charges for official fees and taxes, insurance and charges for other benefits conferred on the buyer if such benefits are of value and if the charges are reasonable to the benefits conferred.[2] This article also fixes the amount of the maximum delinquency charges on any instalments not paid within 10 days after the due date.

For revolving charge accounts, the maximum rate of interest that may be charged for a monthly billing cycle is 2% of that amount which is $500 or less, and 1½% of that part of the amount which is more than $500.[3] In addition, if there is any unpaid balance on the account, there may be a credit service charge of $.50 per month or a pro rata portion thereof.

This section also provides that the buyer shall have the right to prepay, without penalty, any amounts due and any unearned credit service charge must be rebated.

Part 3 of Article 2 deals with disclosure and advertising. The disclosure requirements are those of the Federal Truth in Lending Law or as established under the Code. The information must be clearly and conspicuously made in writing to the buyer or lessee.

For all consumer credit sales not made pursuant to a revolving charge account, the seller is required to disclose to the buyer certain information, including a description of the goods, cash prices, amount of down-payment, amount financed, amount of the credit service charge, rate of the credit service charge, default charges, number of payments and security interest. For revolving charge account sales, the seller is required to provide the buyer with certain information before making a sale, including the conditions under which credit service charge is to be made, method of determining balance upon which service charge will be made, method of determining amount of the service charge, and security interest retained. The following information is required to be given to buyer if at the end of any billing cycle there is a balance due: the outstanding balance at the beginning of the billing cycle, price and date of each sale during the cycle, amount credited to the account, amount of credit service charge, balance upon which credit service charge is computed, balance at the end of the billing cycle, and date by which payment must be made to avoid additional credit service charges.

Specific information is also required to be given to a buyer in the event a loan is refinanced or consolidated.

The Code also contains a prohibition against a seller engaging in false or misleading advertising concerning the terms and conditions of credit with respect to a consumer credit sale or consumer lease.

The seller or lessor in consumer credit sales or leases, other than those primarily for agricultural purposes, is prohibited from taking a negotiable instrument other than a check, as evidence of an obligation of the buyer or lessee.

---

[1] In Colorado a minimum charge of $15 is permitted when the amount financed is $500 or more; in Maine a minimum charge of $25 is permitted for sales of $250 or more; in Utah a minimum finance charge of $35 is permitted.

[2] Including closing costs in connection with a real estate transaction in Colorado. Utah has repealed this section.

[3] In Maine flat service charge of 1½%; Colorado, Indiana, Oklahoma, and Wyoming 1¾%. In Iowa the rate is 1½% for the first $500, 1¼% on the balance. In Kansas the interest rate is 1¾% for $300, 1½% for $300 to $1,000 and 1⅕% for over $1,000; in South Carolina the greater of any rate provided by law or 18%. In Idaho and Utah the amount contracted for is controlling.

The Code provides two alternative sections with respect to the liability of an assignee of a seller to the claims and defenses of the buyer. One alternative proposes that the assignee is subject to all claims and defenses of the buyer, and the other alternative provides that assignee is not subject to such claims and defenses if he advises buyer of assignment, and within three months thereafter is not informed in writing by buyer of any claim or defense.

A buyer in a consumer credit sale, is given, under the Code, the right to refinance the loan in the event there is any balloon payment required.

A security interest in the property sold is specifically permitted in consumer credit sales, but no assignment of earnings of a buyer or lessee is permitted as security for payment of a debt. Confessions of judgment are also not permitted.

The Code provides alternatives with respect to attorneys fees. Alternative A prohibits payment of the seller's attorneys fees by the buyer or lessee. Alternative B provides that the buyer or lessee may pay reasonable attorneys fees not in excess of 15% of the unpaid debt after default.[1]

Home solicitation sales are controlled by Part 5 of this Article of the Code, and the buyer is given the right to cancel any home solicitation sale until midnight of the third business day after the day on which he signs the agreement to purchase. In such event, the seller must return the downpayment within 10 days except for retention of 5% of the cash price.

Part 6 deals with consumer related sales where an effort is made to extend the protection of the Code to nonconsumer credit transactions involving individuals in amounts under $25,000.

ARTICLE 3—CONSUMER LOANS. Establishes maximum finance charges for consumer loans, other than supervised loans as defined in the Code. The interest charged on loans may not exceed 18%[2] per year, except for supervised loans made by banks or licensed lenders, together with certain additional charges for official fees and insurance, delinquency charges and deferral charges. All loans may be prepaid without penalty or interest, and in the event of any prepayment, any previously paid finance charge must be rebated.

The Code provides for clear and conspicuous disclosure requirements with respect to all loans by which the buyer is to be advised in writing of the annual percentage rate. In addition, the lender is required to so advise the debtor of other information such as net amount to be paid, amount of fees and taxes, description of insurance to be provided, amount of any additional charges, number of payments required, and delinquency charges.

On a revolving loan account, lender must advise buyer of specified information, also to be disclosed on credit card transactions.

A lender is prohibited from engaging in false or misleading advertising concerning the terms and conditions of a consumer loan.

The restrictions against balloon payments and the prohibitions of assignment of earnings, and alternatives with respect to attorneys fees, cited above with respect to consumer sales, also apply to consumer loans.

Part 5 controls regulated loans, which are consumer loans in which the finance

---

[1] Colorado, Idaho, Indiana, Iowa, Maine (but not permitted in consumer credit sales or leases or supervised loans), Utah, and Wyoming adopted alternative B with modifications.

[2] In Colorado and Kansas 12% per year; in Indiana 21%; Wyoming and Oklahoma 10%; Maine 12.25%; Utah 19.6%. Idaho and Iowa have no provisions.

charge is in excess of 10% per year, and supervised loans in which the finance charge exceeds 18% [1] per year.

Part 6 controls consumer related loans which are nonconsumer loans of under $25,000 [2] to individuals.

ARTICLE 4—This section regulates sales of insurance on credit.

ARTICLE 5—This deals with limitations on creditor's remedies. It limits the rights available to a creditor in the event of a default, and imposes limitations on permissible wage garnishments more severe than those of the Federal Truth in Lending Act. Garnishments before judgment are proscribed and an employer cannot discharge an employee because his wages have been subject to one or more garnishments. The Federal Act restricts the employer from discharging an employee only in the instance of one garnishment.

In the event a court finds, as a matter of law, any provision in a credit sale, lease or loan unconscionable, the court may refuse to enforce the agreement or the unconscionable provision.

Part 2 of Article 5 provides remedies available to debtors for violations of the Code, including the right to rescind certain transactions, right to demand a refund, and penalties for violations of the disclosure provisions of the Code.

Part 3 establishes criminal penalties for violations of the Code.

ARTICLE 6 deals with administration of the Code.

ARTICLES 7 and 8 are reserved for future use.

ARTICLE 9 covers Code's effective date and laws to repeal.

---

[1] In Colorado, Indiana, Iowa, Oklahoma and Wyoming 21%; and in Utah 19.6%.

[2] In Colorado the limit is $3,000; in Indiana $55,000. Oklahoma and Utah have repealed this section.

Leasing of Personal Property

10

The leasing of personal property is governed by both federal and state law. The federal law, which is contained in a 1976 amendment to the Truth in Lending Act, 15 U.S.C. §§ 1601-1614, 1631-1646, 1661-1665a, 1666-1666j, 1667-1667e (1976 & Supp. V 1981), and known as the Consumer Leasing Act of 1976, 15 U.S.C. §§ 1601, 1640, 1667-1667e (1976 & Supp. V 1981), is primarily concerned with protection of the consumer lessee, while the state law for the most part deals with remedies available to the lessor whose personal property has been damaged or wrongfully converted.

In addition to the state statutes governing the rights, duties and remedies involved in the leasing of general personal property, most states have some legislation dealing with the specific leasing of motor vehicles, aircraft and watercraft.

Ten states [1] have adopted the Uniform Consumer Credit Code (UCCC) which governs all aspects of consumer credit sales transactions, including certain types of leases of personal property, and provides protection to consumers against unfair practices. Louisiana and Wisconsin have adopted their own consumer credit codes very similar to the Uniform Consumer Credit Code.

This chapter deals only with leases (whether or not combined with an option to buy), in which title remains in the lessor. It does not cover those leases in which the lessee contracts to pay a sum essentially equal to or in excess of the value of the property and will become, or for no further or minimum consideration has the option to become, the owner of the property upon termination of the lease. Such a transaction is considered a sale for purposes of this chapter. Nor does the chapter deal with leases which are in reality secured transactions which fall within the ambit of Article 9 of the Uniform Commercial Code. (See Chapter 7) The chapter contains a summary of the federal and state law on the subject of personal property leasing so that the reader will be aware of the legal requirements. Recourse to the specific state statutes should be made to ensure proper procedure under local variations.

Federal Consumer Leasing Act

Federal law concerning the leasing of personal property is contained in the Consumer Leasing Act of 1976 and in Regulation Z, issued by the Federal Reserve Board. 12 C.F.R. §§ 226.1-226.29 (1983). The Consumer Leasing Act governs all "consumer leases," defined as leases of personal property to a natural person (not an organization, government or governmental agency or instrumen-

---

[1] Colorado, Idaho, Indiana, Iowa, Kansas, Maine, Oklahoma, South Carolina, Utah and Wyoming. Utah repealed its disclosure requirements under the UCCC. Instead, creditors and lenders must follow the disclosure requirements of the federal Truth in Lending Act. Utah has made other changes in the UCCC relating to refinancing of consumer credit sales, loans, and revolving charge and loan accounts.

tality) primarily for personal, family or household purposes. The lease must be for a term exceeding four months, and total payments thereunder may not exceed $25,000. The definition does not include leases for agricultural, commercial, or business purposes. 15 U.S.C. § 1667.

The Act requires all consumer leases to disclose certain information, whether or not the lessee has the option to purchase the leased property, including an identification of the lessor and lessee, a description of the property to be leased, all expenses which will foreseeably be incurred by the lessee at the inception of the lease, during its term and upon its expiration, express warranties, the number, amount due dates or periods of payment, insurance provided or paid for by the lessor or required of the lessee, and the respective rights of both lessor and lessee concerning termination of the lease and any liquidated damages. Id. § 1667a.

If upon termination of the lease the lessee is liable for charges based upon the difference in anticipated and actual fair market value of the property, the Act prescribes reasonable standards and presumptions to limit the lessee's liability. Id. § 1667b.

Advertising of consumer leases that includes information about the amount and number of payments or down payments must also include other information for the benefit of the consumer. Id. § 1667c.

The Act provides civil penalties for violations of the lease contract and advertisement disclosure requirements. Id. § 1667d.

The federal act has no effect on state legislation concerning consumer leases. However, in the case of inconsistencies, federal law will prevail unless state law provides the consumer with greater benefits and protection, in which case state law will prevail. Id. § 1667e.

SUMMARY OF STATE LAWS

ALABAMA

LESSOR'S STATUTORY OBLIGATIONS—None.

CRIMINAL ACTIONS AND FRAUD—Lessee's sale or conversion of leased property is considered embezzlement. Failure of lessee to return property within seven days after lessor's notice of demand is prima facie evidence of intent to sell or convert leased property. Use of false or noncurrent identification to obtain lease of property subjects property to return on lessor's demand whether or not lease term has expired.

SPECIFIC LEASE LEGISLATION—Motor vehicles.

MISCELLANEOUS—Third party trespass gives both lessor and lessee a cause of action. Lessor may terminate the lease when lessee permits a use contrary to agreement or does not make repairs within a reasonable time after request.

ALASKA

LESSOR'S STATUTORY OBLIGATIONS—None.

CRIMINAL ACTIONS AND FRAUD—Lessee's refusal to return leased property, or sale or conversion of leased property subjects lessee to fines and/or imprisonment. Leasing property with intent to defraud gives rise to criminal action. Misrepresentation or impersonation in obtaining property is prima facie evidence of intent to defraud.

SPECIFIC LEASE LEGISLATION—Motor vehicles.

MISCELLANEOUS—Banks under certain conditions are permitted to lease personal property.

ARIZONA

LESSOR'S STATUTORY OBLIGATIONS—None.

CRIMINAL ACTIONS AND FRAUD—Lessee's failure to return leased property within 72 hours of the time provided in lease agreement without notice to and permission of lessor subjects lessee to fines and/or imprisonment.

LEASING OF PERSONAL PROPERTY 10-3

SPECIFIC LEASE LEGISLATION—Motor vehicles, motorcycles, boats.

ARKANSAS

No general statutory provisions.
SPECIFIC LEASE LEGISLATION—Aircraft, motor vehicles.
MISCELLANEOUS—Banks under certain conditions are permitted to lease personal property.

CALIFORNIA

LESSOR'S STATUTORY OBLIGATIONS—Lessor must secure the lessee's quiet enjoyment of leased property, put the property into condition for the purpose leased and repair all deterioration not lessee's fault or the result of natural use. Failure to comply with above requirements imposes liability on lessor for lessee's reasonable expenditures. Lessee bears reasonably foreseeable expenses of use.

CRIMINAL ACTIONS AND FRAUD—Lessee's failure to return property within twenty days of written demand after lease's expiration creates a presumption of intent to commit theft by fraud. If lessor fails to make a written demand of return within thirty days of the lease's expiration, no such presumption will arise. Lessee's use of false identification creates presumption of intent to commit theft by fraud.

SPECIFIC LEASE LEGISLATION—Charter parties, boats, motor vehicles. Leases of motor vehicles for over four months for primarily personal, family or household purposes are covered by the California Vehicle Leasing Act.

COLORADO

LESSOR'S STATUTORY OBLIGATIONS—None.

CRIMINAL ACTIONS AND FRAUD—Lessee subject to criminal action for obtaining property by threat or deception, or without consent of owner. Also liable for failure to return leased property within 72 hours of expiration of lease.

SPECIFIC LEASE LEGISLATION—Motor vehicles.

U.C.C.C. CONSUMER LEASES—Colorado has adopted the Uniform Consumer Credit Code which contains provisions concerning the leasing of personal property. The Code governs all consumer leases, which are defined as leases of goods which a lessor regularly engaged in the business of leasing makes to a person, other than an organization, who takes under the lease primarily for a personal, family, household, or agricultural purpose and in which the amount payable under the lease does not exceed $25,000, and which is for a term exceeding four months. The definition does not include a lease made pursuant to a lender credit card or similar arrangement.

The Code affords the lessee protection by requiring the consumer lessor to disclose with respect to all consumer leases the following information: (a) a description of goods, (b) the amount of the down payment required, (c) the official fees, (d) taxes and other charges, (e) the types and amounts of insurance provided by the lessor, (f) the number, amount and due dates of periodic payments including the total amount payable by lessee, (g) the conditions for premature termination by the lessee, and (h) the extent of lessee's liability at the end of the term. In addition to the disclosure requirements, the Code forbids all false or misleading advertising concerning the terms or conditions of credit with respect to consumer leases.

Other significant provisions of the Code are:

(1) In all consumer leases except those primarily for agricultural purposes, the assignee of the rights of the lessor is subject to all claims and defenses of the lessee against the lessor arising from the lease of goods. The claim or defense may be asserted against the assignee only to the extent of the amount owing to the assignee with respect to the lease of the goods as to which the claim or defense arose at the time the assignee has written notice of the claim or defense.

(2) At the expiration of a consumer lease, other than one primarily for agricultural purposes, the lessee's liability is limited to twice the average monthly periodic payment, but this limitation does not apply to charges for damages to leased property or for other default.

(3) The lessor may not take a security interest (other than a security deposit) in the lessee's property to secure the debt arising from the lease. Nor may the lessor obtain an assignment of the lessee's earnings for payment of the debt.

(4) The lessor is prohibited from offering a rebate or other arrangements of value in consideration of lessee giving names of prospective buyers or lessees if the rebate or arrangement is contingent upon events subsequent to the time lessee agrees to lease. An agreement in violation of this provision renders the lease unenforceable, or the lessee has the option of keeping the goods already delivered without any obligation to pay for them.

(5) The lessee must continue to pay the lessor directly until adequate notice of an assignment is given.

(6) The lease may provide that the lessee pay reasonable attorney's fees not in excess of 15% of the unpaid debt after default and referral to an attorney not in the employ of lessor. The court may also prescribe an additional fee.

(7) The lessee cannot authorize anyone to confess a judgment arising from the lease.

(8) Rights or benefits under the Code may not be waived, but any claim arising from the Code which is disputed in good faith may be settled by agreement.

(9) Discrimination by a consumer lessor in consumer leases solely because of race, creed, religion, color, sex, marital status, national origin or ancestry is prohibited in cases in which the aggregate of the original unpaid balances arising from all consumer leases from such consumer lessor for the previous calendar year is greater than or equal to one million dollars.

CONNECTICUT

LESSOR'S STATUTORY OBLIGATIONS—None.

CRIMINAL ACTIONS AND FRAUD—Any lessee under written agreement who places property beyond the control of the lessor, conceals it or aids in its concealment, refuses to return it, sells or encumbers it without the written consent of the lessor and without notifying the transferee of the lease is subject to fine and/or imprisonment. Use of a false name or failure to return leased property within ten days of expiration of the lease or within five days after lessor's written demand, whichever is later, is prima facie evidence of a violation. Lessee is guilty of conversion on failure to return leased property within 10 days after lease terminates or 192 hours after notice from lessor demanding return of property.

SPECIFIC LEASE LEGISLATION—Motor vehicles, watercraft.

DELAWARE

No general statutory provisions

SPECIFIC LEASE LEGISLATION—Aircraft, motor vehicles.

MISCELLANEOUS—A lessor's license is required annually of all those engaged in business as a lessor of tangible personal property, unless otherwise licensed as a retailer. According to *Collier v. Leedom Construction Co.,* 84 F. Supp. 348 (D.C. Del. 1949), a lessor has a duty to mitigate damages. When a lessee gives notice of discontinuation of use of the leased property before expiration of the term of the lease, the lessor is only entitled to damages if he can show that he could not use the property or find a user for it.

DISTRICT OF COLUMBIA

No general statutory provisions

SPECIFIC LEASE LEGISLATION—Motor vehicles.

FLORIDA

LESSOR'S STATUTORY OBLIGATIONS—None.

CRIMINAL ACTIONS AND FRAUD—If lessee with intent to deprive or defraud lessor takes possession of property, converts it, obtains it through false representation, forgery or threat, he is guilty of larceny. Failure to return or make arrangements to return property within ten days of lessor's proper written notice following expiration of lease, or use of false or noncurrent identification is prima facie evidence of intent to commit larceny. Failure to return leased motor vehicle, aircraft, boat or boat motor within 72 hours of agreed return time and date is prima facie evidence of intent to commit larceny.

SPECIFIC LEASE LEGISLATION—Motor vehicles.

GEORGIA

LESSOR'S STATUTORY OBLIGATIONS—Lessor may not interfere with lessee's enjoyment of leased property, must keep leased property fit for the use for which it was leased, and warrant right of possession and freedom from secret fault. Risk of death or inevitable accident to the leased property resulting from leased property is with lessor. Lessor may take immediate possession or hold lessee to extraordinary care if lessee sublets without permission from lessor.

CRIMINAL ACTIONS AND FRAUD—Lessee liable to criminal penalties for selling or converting property without lessor's consent, or for wrongfully neglecting or refusing to surrender property upon expiration of lease. Conversion by the lessee is presumed when he violates his agreement by disposing of any part of the property without the consent of the lessor, permits its concealment or removal, or refuses to surrender at end of lease.

LEASING OF PERSONAL PROPERTY

SPECIFIC LEASE LEGISLATION—Boats.

MISCELLANEOUS—In the case of third party trespass, if the trespass interferes with possession, lessee has cause of action; if trespass injures property or interferes with property rights, lessor also has cause of action. Under certain conditions, banks are permitted to lease personal property. In foreclosure actions, the owner of the leased property in a consumer rental transaction may obtain a writ of possession in order to regain possession of leased property. When the writ is obtained, the leased property must be delivered to the owner and need not be levied upon.

HAWAII

LESSOR'S STATUTORY OBLIGATIONS—None.

CRIMINAL ACTIONS AND FRAUD—Lessee of personal property, other than a rental motor vehicle, who knowingly or intentionally fails to return property within 14 days after return date is guilty of a petty misdemeanor unless he gives notice that he will be unable to return property by that date and the owner gives permission to extend that date.

SPECIFIC LEASE LEGISLATION—Aircraft, motor vehicles.

IDAHO

LESSOR'S STATUTORY OBLIGATIONS—None.

CRIMINAL ACTIONS AND FRAUD—Prima facie evidence of lessee's intent to embezzle exists if lessee fails to return property within ten days of lease expiration and within 48 hours after written notice by lessor. Use of false or noncurrent identification is also prima facie evidence of intent to embezzle.

SPECIFIC LEASE LEGISLATION—Aircraft, livestock.

U.C.C.C. CONSUMER LEASES—Follows general pattern set for above for Colorado with the following changes: A consumer lease includes all such leases for amounts payable not over $45,000, which amount is subject to adjustment. Idaho has no clause concerning discrimination. Payment by lessee of reasonable attorney's fees upon default is not limited to 15% of the unpaid debt upon default.

ILLINOIS

LESSOR'S STATUTORY OBLIGATIONS—None.

CRIMINAL ACTIONS AND FRAUD—Lessee's failure to return leased property within thirty days of lessor's demand after expiration of the lease is prima facie evidence of knowingly exerting of unauthorized control over property.

SPECIFIC LEASE LEGISLATION—Motor vehicles.

MISCELLANEOUS—If money advanced for security on payment of rentals, such money shall be deposited in a separate bank account along with a copy of the agreement. Banks have the power to lease personal property.

INDIANA

LESSOR'S STATUTORY OBLIGATIONS—None.

CRIMINAL ACTIONS AND FRAUD—Lessee is guilty of theft for obtaining possession of property by deception or threat with the purpose of avoiding payment of rent. Purpose of avoiding rent payments is inferred from refusal to pay or absconding without payment or offer to pay.

MISCELLANEOUS—Personal property of an estate may be leased in accordance with provisions of a will, or under court order. A bank may become lessor of personal property at the request of a customer.

SPECIFIC LEASE LEGISLATION—Motor vehicles, snowmobiles and off-road vehicles.

U.C.C.C. CONSUMER LEASES—Follows general pattern set forth above for Colorado with the following changes: Indiana has no provisions concerning false or misleading advertising. An agreement by lessee not to assert claims or defenses against assignee is enforceable if assignment was in good faith for value, notice of assignment was given lessee, assignee is not related to assignor, and notice of any claims or defenses of lessee is not given to assignee within 60 days after receiving notice of the assignment. A rebate arrangement in consideration of lessee giving names of prospective buyers or lessees is allowed if only contingent upon prospective buyers or lessees submitting to an interview or demonstration. Payment by lessee of reasonable attorney's fees upon default is not limited to 15% of the unpaid debt upon default.

MISCELLANEOUS—Banks or trust companies may be lessors of personal property under certain circumstances.

IOWA

No general statutory provisions.

SPECIFIC LEASE LEGISLATION—Boats, motor vehicles.

MISCELLANEOUS—There is a Louisiana Consumer Credit Law which does not cover consumer lease transactions.

U.C.C.C. CONSUMER LEASES—Follows the general pattern set forth above for Colorado with the following changes: A consumer lease includes credit card transactions. An agreement by lessee not to assert claims or defenses against assignee is enforceable if assignment was in good faith for value, notice of assignment was given lessee, assignee is not related to assignor, and any claims or defenses of lessee are not provided to assignee within thirty days after receiving notice of the assignment. No attorney's fees awarded lessor upon lessee's default.

KANSAS

LESSOR'S STATUTORY OBLIGATIONS—None.

CRIMINAL ACTIONS AND FRAUD—Use of false identification or failure to return property within ten days of expiration, unless the property is returned within seven days of lessor's notice, is prima facie evidence of lessee's intent to deprive lessor of property.

SPECIFIC LEASE LEGISLATION—Motor vehicles.

MISCELLANEOUS—Banks under certain circumstances are permitted to lease personal property.

U.C.C.C. CONSUMER LEASES—Follows general pattern set forth above for Colorado with the following changes: No attorney's fees awarded lessor upon lessee's default. Lessee may assert claims and defenses against lessor's assignee only if he gives notice when requested to do so by lessor or assignee.

KENTUCKY

LESSOR'S STATUTORY OBLIGATIONS—None.

CRIMINAL ACTIONS AND FRAUD—Lessee cannot remove personal property to another location or relinquish custody without giving ten day's written notice to lessor. To do so is prima facie evidence of intent to defraud and lessee is liable for fine and/or imprisonment.

SPECIFIC LEASE LEGISLATION—Motor vehicles, watercrafts.

MISCELLANEOUS—Banks may under certain circumstances lease personal property. Assignee of lease in all but credit card transactions is subject to same defenses of lessee against lessor except in cases defined by any federal agency having jurisdiction.

LOUISIANA

LESSOR'S STATUTORY OBLIGATIONS—Lessor must maintain property in condition for use for which it was leased and must guarantee the lessee's peaceable possession. Lessor must make repair for all unforeseen events or lessee can make them and credit them to rent. Lessor cannot alter property during term of lease and must pay all charges in connection with property. License based upon gross annual receipts required for those carrying on business of leasing personal property. If lessor has reserved right to take possession, he must give 10 day's notice before the end of the month already begun.

CRIMINAL ACTIONS AND FRAUD—Upon lessee's default, lessor has the option either to cancel the lease and exercise rights granted him thereunder, including recovery of liquidated damages and/or other damages, or to enforce his claim for all rentals and other amounts due before property is leased out again. Lessor has the right to a speedy hearing to obtain a judgment ordering the lessee to surrender possession of the leased property and to obtain a writ of possession ordering surrender and sequestration of possession of the leased property. Lessor may also cancel lease for unauthorized use by lessee.

SPECIFIC LEASE LEGISLATION—Motor vehicles, musical instruments.

MISCELLANEOUS—There is a Louisiana Consumer Credit Code governing consumer transactions.

MAINE

LESSOR'S STATUTORY OBLIGATIONS—None.

CRIMINAL ACTIONS AND FRAUD—Lessee is guilty of misdemeanor for fraudulent conversion of leased property. Failure to return or account for property is prima facie evidence of intent to convert, but prosecution may be brought only if lessee fails to return goods within ten days after lessor's written demand.

SPECIFIC LEASE LEGISLATION—Motor vehicles.

U.C.C.C. CONSUMER LEASES—There is a Maine Consumer Credit Code governing consumer leases. See Colorado above for general provisions. In Maine, however, amount payable under lease cannot exceed $55,000 and there is no exception for consumer leases for agricultural purposes.

MARYLAND

LESSOR'S STATUTORY OBLIGATIONS—None.

CRIMINAL ACTIONS AND FRAUD—Failure to redeliver is prima facie evidence of conversion.

LEASING OF PERSONAL PROPERTY 10-7

Fines and/or imprisonment may be levied against lessee for secretion or sale of property with intent to defraud or for removal of property from location without lessor's consent with intent to defraud. A Maryland resident will not be prosecuted if he restores the property or accounts for it within 10 days of written demand.

SPECIFIC LEASE LEGISLATION—Aircraft, batteries, motor vehicles.

MISCELLANEOUS—Banks under certain circumstances may lease personal property. Lease of personal property is covered under the Maryland Consumer Protection Act, protecting consumers against false or misleading advertising or representations.

MASSACHUSETTS

LESSOR'S STATUTORY OBLIGATIONS—None.

CRIMINAL ACTIONS AND FRAUD—Lessee criminally liable for conversion of leased personal property without consent of and notice to lessor. Lessee guilty of larceny if with intent to conceal property lessee fails to return property within 10 days of the expiration of the lease or rental agreement. Use of false identification or failure to return the leased or rented property within 30 days of notice shall be *prima facie* evidence of intent not to return.

SPECIFIC LEASE LEGISLATION—Motor vehicles and aircraft.

MISCELLANEOUS—Trust companies operating banking departments may lease personal property under certain conditions. The use of leased personal property in connection with illegal sale of liquor is subject to criminal penalties. Leases are among the transactions covered by the Massachusetts Retail Instalment Sales & Service Law. Lessee may cancel a lease with notice within three days of its consummation if not executed at lessor's place of business.

MICHIGAN

LESSOR'S STATUTORY OBLIGATIONS—None.

CRIMINAL ACTIONS AND FRAUD—Lessee is guilty of larceny if after lessor's notice he refuses or willfully neglects to return property with intent to defraud. If property is worth less than $100, lessee is guilty of a misdemeanor.

SPECIFIC LEASE LEGISLATION—Motor vehicles, motorcycles, snowmobiles.

MISCELLANEOUS—Banks may under certain circumstances lease personal property.

MINNESOTA

LESSOR'S STATUTORY OBLIGATIONS—None.

CRIMINAL ACTIONS AND FRAUD—Lessee is liable for theft for conversion of leased property and subject to fine and/or imprisonment. Use of fictitious identification or failure to return property within five days of personal service or certified or registered mailing of the lessor's written demand is evidence to commit theft.

SPECIFIC LEASE LEGISLATION—Motor bicycles, aircraft, motor vehicles.

MISCELLANEOUS—Banks under certain circumstances may lease personal property.

MISSISSIPPI

LESSOR'S STATUTORY OBLIGATIONS—None.

CRIMINAL ACTIONS AND FRAUD—Fraudulent appropriations of leased property past expiration date of lease is embezzlement by lessee.

SPECIFIC LEASE LEGISLATION—Motor vehicles.

MISCELLANEOUS—Permit required for leasing dealers.[1]

MISSOURI

LESSOR'S STATUTORY OBLIGATIONS—None.

CRIMINAL ACTIONS AND FRAUD—If lessee, with intent to steal, fails to return leased personal property, he shall be deemed guilty of stealing. It is prima facie evidence of intent to steal if lessee fails to return property within ten days of lessor's demand following expiration of the lease.

SPECIFIC LEASE LEGISLATION—Watercraft.

MONTANA

LESSOR'S STATUTORY OBLIGATIONS—Lessor must secure lessee's quiet enjoyment, put property in condition for use and repair all deterioration not the natural result of use. If he fails to do so,

---

[1] When a lessee is injured due to a defect in the leased property of which he is aware, the lessor, even if negligent in duty of inspection, is relieved of liability. *Runnels v. Dixie Drive-It-Yourself System Jackson Co.,* 71 So.2d 453, 220 Miss. 678 (1954).

lessee may make the repairs and recover from lessor. Lessor bears all costs not naturally foreseeable from use.

CRIMINAL ACTIONS AND FRAUD—Lessee who converts property, removes it without lessor's consent, or purposely or knowingly fails to return it after lessor's demand shall be guilty of larceny if done with intent to deprive lessor of his interest in the property. Lessee must repair all deteriorations resulting from his negligence or due to forseeable use.

SPECIFIC LEASE LEGISLATION—Motor vehicles, watercraft.

NEBRASKA

LESSOR'S STATUTORY OBLIGATIONS—For tax purposes, leased property shall be reported by lessor as owner, or lessee as agent of lessor.

CRIMINAL ACTIONS AND FRAUD—If lessee converts, fails or refuses to return or removes leased personal property, other than a motor vehicle outside of the state without permission of the lessor, he is guilty of theft. Prima facie evidence of theft exists if lessee uses false identification or refuses to return the leased property within 10 days of receipt of notice that lease has expired. This last sentence must be included in the lease to preserve a cause of action. Any person destroying or changing the serial numbers on leased manufactured goods is guilty of a misdemeanor.

SPECIFIC LEASE LEGISLATION—Motor vehicles, watercrafts.

MISCELLANEOUS—Mayor and city council of first or second class cities may lease personal property for purposes for which they could buy personal property. Banks under certain circumstances may lease personal property.

NEVADA

LESSOR'S STATUTORY OBLIGATIONS—None.

CRIMINAL ACTIONS AND FRAUD—Obtaining or retaining possession of leased property through misrepresentation or artifice is larceny. Failure to return property within 72 hours of lessor's demand following expiration of lease with intent to defraud is larceny. Failure to return property to place specified is prima facie evidence of intent to defraud or retain possession.

SPECIFIC LEASE LEGISLATION—Gaming equipment, railroads, motor vehicles, watercrafts, aircrafts.

NEW HAMPSHIRE

LESSOR'S STATUTORY OBLIGATIONS—None.

CRIMINAL ACTIONS AND FRAUD—If lessee fails to return property upon expiration of lease and refuses or wilfully neglects to return the property on lessor's written demand, he is guilty of larceny. False identification and failure to return on written demand is prima facie evidence of intent to commit larceny. A person is guilty of theft if he intentionally fails to comply with the terms of a rental or lease agreement concerning the return of property, if such noncompliance constitutes a gross deviation from the agreement.

SPECIFIC LEASE LEGISLATION—Aircraft, motor vehicles, criminal provision regarding all propelled vehicles.

NEW JERSEY

LESSOR'S STATUTORY OBLIGATIONS—None.

CRIMINAL ACTIONS AND FRAUD—Using false or fraudulent misrepresentation to lease personal property is theft.

SPECIFIC LEASE LEGISLATION—Aircraft, motor vehicles, sanitation supplies.

NEW MEXICO

LESSOR'S STATUTORY OBLIGATIONS—None.

CRIMINAL ACTIONS AND FRAUD—Procuring lease with false identification subjects lessee to criminal penalties. Failure to return, according to specific written arrangements, with intent to defraud is a criminal violation. Failure to return within 72 hours after written demand creates presumption of intent to defraud.

SPECIFIC LEASE LEGISLATION—Motor vehicles, watercraft.

NEW YORK

LESSOR'S STATUTORY OBLIGATIONS—None.

SPECIFIC LEASE LEGISLATION—Aircraft, motor vehicles.

MISCELLANEOUS—Under certain circumstances, banks and trust companies may lease personal property.

LEASING OF PERSONAL PROPERTY 10–9

NORTH CAROLINA

LESSOR'S STATUTORY OBLIGATIONS—None.

CRIMINAL ACTIONS AND FRAUD—Willful or malicious damage, fraudulent conversion, subletting without lessor's consent, failure to return property at expiration of lease and misrepresentation with intent to defraud are misdemeanors punishable by fine and/or imprisonment. But if the value of the property fraudulently converted exceeds $400, the lessee is guilty of a felony. Intent to convert leased property is shown prima facie if lessee fails to return property within ten days after expiration of lease and within 48 hours of lessor's written demand, or if lease was procured with false identification.

SPECIFIC LEASE LEGISLATION—Aircraft, batteries, livestock, motor vehicles.

NORTH DAKOTA

LESSOR'S STATUTORY OBLIGATIONS—Lessor must secure lessee's quiet enjoyment, put property into condition fit for use for which it was let, and repair deteriorations not lessee's fault and not the result of normal use. If he fails to do this, lessee can expend and recover the necessary amounts. Lessor responsible for all expenses not natural or foreseeable.

CRIMINAL ACTION AND FRAUD—Lessee must use ordinary care for preservation of property and may be held absolutely liable for safety of property or lessor may rescind lease. Lessee must bear all natural and foreseeable expenses.

SPECIFIC LEASE LEGISLATION—Aircraft, motor vehicles.

MISCELLANEOUS—Banks under certain circumstances may lease personal property.

OHIO

LESSOR'S STATUTORY OBLIGATIONS—None.

CRIMINAL ACTIONS AND FRAUD—Lessee cannot lease any aircraft, motor vehicle, motorcycle, motorboat, sailboat, camper, trailer, horse or buggy with intent to defraud. Prima facie evidence of intent to defraud exists if lessee uses deception to hire one of above-mentioned properties, hires them knowing he cannot pay, absconds without payment, knowingly fails to pay or return property without a reasonable excuse or knowingly fails to return the hired property without reasonable excuse. Violation is a misdemeanor, or felony for recidivism.

SPECIFIC LEASE LEGISLATION—Watercraft.

MISCELLANEOUS—Banks under certain circumstances may lease personal property. "Consumer transactions" include leases whose purpose is primarily personal, family, or household and are governed by the Ohio retail instalment sales law.

OKLAHOMA

LESSOR'S STATUTORY OBLIGATIONS—Lessor must secure lessee's quiet possession, put the property into condition fit for the purpose for which it was let, and repair all deteriorations not lessee's fault and not occasioned by normal use. Failure to make required expenditures entitles lessee to provide repairs himself and recover from lessor.

CRIMINAL ACTIONS AND FRAUD—Lessee's fraudulent failure to return leased property within ten days of lease's expiration or fraudulent secretion or appropriation of the property is embezzlement.

SPECIFIC LEASE LEGISLATION—Motor vehicles, oil and gas well equipment, watercraft.

MISCELLANEOUS—Banks under certain circumstances may lease personal property.

U.C.C.C. CONSUMER LEASES—Follows general pattern set forth above for Colorado with the following changes: A consumer lease includes such lease for amounts payable not over $45,000. Oklahoma forbids discrimination in leasing based upon sex or marital status. An agreement by lessee not to assert claims or defenses against assignee is enforceable if assignment was in good faith for value, notice of assignment given lessee, assignee not related to assignor, and notice of any claims or defenses of lessee is not given to assignee within thirty days after receiving notice of the assignment.

OREGON

No general statutory provisions.[1]

SPECIFIC LEASE LEGISLATION—Aircraft, motor vehicles, watercraft.

---

[1] Oregon case law provides that the lessor, in an action to recover for damage to or loss of leased chattel, need only "allege the bailment and failure of the bailee to return the property." At that point a presumption of negligence on the part of the lessee arises. *National Fire Insurance Co. v. Mogan,* 206 P.2d 963, 965, 186 Or. 285 (1949).

PENNSYLVANIA

LESSOR'S STATUTORY OBLIGATIONS—None.

CRIMINAL ACTIONS AND FRAUD—A lessee of personal property is guilty of theft if he intentionally sells, secretes, destroys, converts to his own use or otherwise disposes of the property. There is a presumption of theft if the person uses a false name and fails to return the property on time or fails to return the property within seven days after written demand is delivered by registered or certified mail to the lessee's last known address.

SPECIFIC LEASE LEGISLATION—Aircraft.

MISCELLANEOUS—Savings banks are permitted under certain circumstances to lease personal property.

RHODE ISLAND

No general statutory provisions.

SPECIFIC LEASE LEGISLATION—Horse and carriages, motor vehicles, watercraft.

SOUTH CAROLINA

LESSOR'S STATUTORY OBLIGATIONS—None.

CRIMINAL ACTIONS AND FRAUD—Lessee's wilful and fraudulent failure to return leased property within 72 hours after lease's expiration or secretion or unauthorized use is larceny.

SPECIFIC LEASE LEGISLATION—Aircraft, watercraft.

MISCELLANEOUS—Lease qualifying as a "consumer lease" is covered by South Carolina's Consumer Protection Code. See Colorado consumer credit code for general provisions.

SOUTH DAKOTA

LESSOR'S STATUTORY OBLIGATIONS—Lessor must secure lessee's quiet enjoyment, put property into condition fit for use for which property was leased, and repair all deterioration not lessee's fault or the result of normal use. Lessor bears all but naturally foreseeable expenses or else lessee can make expenditures and recover from lessor.

CRIMINAL ACTIONS AND FRAUD—Any person who knowingly converts leased or rented personal property after having received a written demand sent by certified or registered mail to the lessee is guilty of theft. The defenses available to the lessee are: (1) at the time of the lease, lessee accurately stated name and address, (2) the failure to return was lawful, (3) the lessee failed to receive the written demand personally, and (4) the lessee returned the property and paid any added charges or damages to the leased property.

SPECIFIC LEASE LEGISLATION—Aircraft, watercraft.

MISCELLANEOUS—Banks under certain conditions may lease personal property.

TENNESSEE

LESSOR'S STATUTORY OBLIGATIONS—None.

CRIMINAL ACTIONS AND FRAUD—Appropriation by lessee of lessor's property is larceny. Failure to return property with fraudulent intent within ten days after lessor's written demand or use of false identification and failure to return property upon expiration of lease are both counts of larceny. Failure to return property within such time or use of false identification is prima facie evidence of intent to defraud.

SPECIFIC LEASE LEGISLATION—Aircraft, livestock and livery vehicles, watercraft.

MISCELLANEOUS—Banks under certain conditions may lease personal property.

TEXAS

No general statutory provisions.

SPECIFIC LEASE LEGISLATION—Motor vehicles.

MISCELLANEOUS—Banks under certain conditions may lease personal property.

UTAH

No general statutory provisions.

SPECIFIC LEASE LEGISLATION—Motor vehicles, watercraft.

U.C.C.C. CONSUMER LEASES—The U.C.C.C. is not applicable to consumer leases; it is only applicable to consumer credit sales and consumer loans.

VERMONT

LESSOR'S STATUTORY OBLIGATIONS—None.

CRIMINAL ACTIONS AND FRAUD—Lessee's conversion of rental property, removal from state

LEASING OF PERSONAL PROPERTY   10-11

or failure to return as agreed subjects lessee to fine and/or imprisonment. Failure to return property within 72 hours of lessor's demand or within fifteen days of expiration of lease or use of false identification is evidence of intent to commit larceny.

SPECIFIC LEASE LEGISLATION—Aircraft, watercraft.

VIRGINIA

LESSOR'S STATUTORY OBLIGATIONS—None.

CRIMINAL ACTIONS AND FRAUD—Wilful injury to or unauthorized subletting of leased property is a misdemeanor. Lessee's conversion of leased property with intent to defraud, fraudulent removal of property from the state without lessor's permission, or failure to return property within ten days of lease's expiration subjects lessee to penalties for larceny. Failure to return property within five or 10 days, depending on the property leased, of lessor's demand following expiration of lease is prima facie evidence of intent to defraud. Procuring rental property by use of false identification or misrepresentation with intent to defraud is a misdemeanor. Failure to pay rent, or absconding without payment is prima facie evidence of intent to defraud at time of leasing.

SPECIFIC LEASE LEGISLATION—Motor vehicles, aircraft, livestock, watercraft.

MISCELLANEOUS—Banks under certain conditions may lease personal property.

WASHINGTON

LESSOR'S STATUTORY OBLIGATIONS—As a prerequisite to prosecution for lessee's failure to return leased personal property, lease must state that failure to return may result in criminal prosecution and written demand must state that lessee will be criminally liable if property not returned within ten days.

CRIMINAL ACTIONS AND FRAUD—Conversion or destruction and failure to return leased property within ten days of lessor's notice of expiration of lease is a gross misdemeanor. Wilful failure to return a leased motor vehicle worth more than $1,500 within five business days from receipt of the lessor's written demand therefor is a class C felony.

SPECIFIC LEASE LEGISLATION—Motor vehicles, motorcycles, and dune buggies.

MISCELLANEOUS—Lease transactions are regulated under a separate consumer leasing law.

WEST VIRGINIA

LESSOR'S STATUTORY OBLIGATIONS—Lessor must place any security deposit in trust for lessee at bank or trust company.

SPECIFIC LEASE LEGISLATION—Motor vehicles, watercraft.

MISCELLANEOUS—Banks may under certain circumstances lease personal property. A lease qualifying as a "consumer lease" is governed by West Virginia's Consumer Credit Act.

WISCONSIN

LESSOR'S STATUTORY OBLIGATIONS—None.

CRIMINAL ACTIONS AND FRAUD—Failure to return lease property within ten days of expiration of lease is a misdemeanor if property is valued under $500 and a felony if valued above $500.

SPECIFIC LEASE LEGISLATION—Motor vehicles, livestock.

MISCELLANEOUS—Leases qualifying as "consumer leases" are governed by Wisconsin Consumer Act.

WYOMING

No general statutory provisions.

SPECIFIC LEASE LEGISLATION—Watercraft.

U.C.C.C. CONSUMER LEASES—Follows general pattern set forth for Colorado with the following changes: A consumer lease includes all such leases payable in five or more instalments. Wyoming has no provisions concerning discrimination in leases. An agreement by lessee not to assert claims or defenses against assignee is enforceable if assignment was in good faith for value, notice of assignment was given lessee, assignee is not related to assignor, and notice of any claims or defenses of lessee is not given to assignee within 45 days after receiving notice of the assignment. Wyoming allows an assignment of commissions or accounts receivable payable to lessee for payment of debts arising from consumer leases. Award of attorney's fees is not limited to 15% of the unpaid debt.

Collection Agency Requirements and Prohibited Practices

11

With the rapid increase in the extension of credit, especially consumer credit, credit grantors are relying more and more upon collection agencies as a tool for collecting past-due debts. Many states and the federal government, therefore, have adopted legislation which either controls and licenses collection agencies or regulates and prohibits certain practices of collection agencies, especially as applied to consumers.

FEDERAL LAW

Fair Debt Collection Practices Act

In 1977 Congress enacted the Fair Debt Collection Practices Act, 15 U.S.C. §§ 1692-1692o (Supp. V 1981), which prohibits debt collectors from engaging in certain practices in the collections of *consumer debts,* which are defined as debts arising out of a transaction "primarily for personal, family or household purposes." Id. § 1692a(5)

Any person who regularly collects debts owed to a third party is also subject to the provisions of the Act. The Act does not apply, however, to a person to the extent that he receives an assignment or transfer of a debt in default solely for the purpose of facilitating the collection of the debt for another. As a general rule, therefore, a creditor who in its own name collects debts due it in such a manner as to not affect interstate commerce is exempt from the purview of this legislation. Id. § 1692a(6).

The Federal Trade Commission has been empowered to enforce the statute. Id. § 1692l. It has issued a Guide Against Debt Collection Deceptions which establishes improper debt collection practices.

The federal act will on occasion overlap state collection practices legislation. To the extent that the laws are consistent, they coexist. To the extent that they conflict, the federal statute controls unless the relevant state law provides greater protection for the consumer. Id. § 1692n.

The following is a summary of the major provisions of the statute:

1. The statute establishes certain procedures to be followed in the acquisitions of location information about a debtor, and prohibits use of postal cards or language on an envelope or in the communications that indicate that the debt collector is in the debt collection business.

2. Communications by debt collectors concerning debt collection tactics are regulated as follows:

   (a) No communications with a debtor can be made at any unusual time or place which is known or should be known to be inconvenient. In the absence of special circumstances, convenient time is assumed to be between 8:00 A.M. and 9:00 P.M.

(b) If a debt collector knows a debtor is represented by an attorney, has knowledge of or can obtain the name of such attorney, the debt collector must communicate with such attorney unless the attorney fails to respond within a reasonable time or unless the attorney consents to direct communications with the debtor.

(c) Communications at the debtor's place of employment are prohibited if the debt collector knows or has reason to know the debtor's employer does not permit such communications.

(d) Communications with third parties are prohibited except for the attorney of the debtor, or a consumer reporting agency, or the creditor or as is necessary to effectuate a post judgment judicial remedy. This restriction does not apply to acquisition of information on the location of the debtor.

(e) A debt collector may not communicate with a debtor, except in limited circumstances, who has in writing advised that he refuses to pay a debt and that the debtor wishes the debt collector to cease further communications with him.

3. A debt collector may not engage in any conduct the consequence of which is to harass, oppress or abuse any person in connection with a collection of a debt, such as the use of or threat of use of violence, use of obscene or profane language, publication of a list of consumers who allegedly refuse to pay debts, except to a consumer reporting agency as defined by the Fair Credit Reporting Act, or the advertisement for sale of any debt.

4. A debt collector may also not use any false, deceptive or misleading representation or means in connection with the collection of any debt, which includes the false representation that any individual is an attorney, or representation or implication that nonpayment of a debt will result in the arrest or imprisonment of any person or a false representation that action will be taken that cannot be taken.

5. The debt collector may not use any unfair or unconscionable means to collect or attempt to collect any debt such as collection of interest, fees, or expenses unless the amount therefor is expressly authorized by the agreement creating the debt. The following practices are deemed to be in violation of this section:

(a) The acceptance by a debt collector of a postdated check by more than five days unless the person is notified in writing of the debt collector's intent to deposit the check not more than ten nor less than three business days prior to such deposit;

(b) solicitation of a postdated check for the purpose of threatening or instituting criminal prosecution;

(c) depositing or threatening to deposit a postdated check prior to the date on the check;

(d) taking or threatening to take any nonjudicial action with respect to the property of the debtor;

(e) communicating with a consumer regarding a debt by postcard;

(f) using language or symbols on an envelope, other than the debt collector's address;

(g) taking or threatening to take any nonjudicial action with respect to a debtor's property;

(h) falsely representing himself as vouched for, bonded by, or affiliated with, the United States or any state.

COLLECTION AGENCY REQUIREMENTS 11-3

6. The debt collector is required to advise the debtor within five days after initial communication with him of the following information:
   (a) the amount of the debt;
   (b) the name of the creditor;
   (c) a notice that unless the consumer within thirty days after receipt of the notice disputes the validity of the debt, the debt will be assumed to be valid;
   (d) a statement that if the consumer notifies the debt collector in writing within a thirty day period that the debt or a portion thereof is disputed, the debt collector will obtain verification of the debt or a copy of the judgment against the consumer.
   (e) a statement that upon the consumer's written request within a thirty day period, the debt collector will provide the debtor with the name and address of the original creditor, if different than the present creditor;
   (f) if the debtor notifies the debt collector within a thirty day period that the debt or any portion thereof is disputed or the consumer requests the name and address of the original creditor, the debt collector shall cease collection until he obtains a verification of the debt and a copy of the judgment, if any.

7. It is also unlawful to design, compile and furnish any deceptive debt collecting forms.

8. The Act establishes civil liability on the part of a debt collector who violates the statute for the actual damages sustained by a debtor or such additional damages as a court may allow, but not exceeding $1,000. In a class action, liability may be up to $1,000 for each named plaintiff, plus an amount set by the court for all other class members not to exceed the lesser of $5,000 or 1% of the net worth of the debt collector. In the case of any successful action, the cost of the action together with reasonable attorneys' fees as determined by the court may also be recovered by the debtor.

State Law

Set forth below is a summary of the laws of each state which licenses collection agencies and/or regulates collection practices. This summary does not consider any rules or regulations which may be promulgated by any collection service board, agency, or department.

ALABAMA

A. Requirements:

1. LICENSE: Yes.
   (a) WHERE OBTAINED: County judge of probate or license commissioner.
   (b) DURATION: One year, expiring Sept. 30.
   (c) FILING FEES: In cities with a population of 20,000 or more—$100; in cities with a population of less than 20,000—$25.
   (d) EXAMINATION: None.
   (e) BRANCH OFFICES: No separate provisions.
2. BOND: No.

B. Exemptions:

None.

C. Prohibited Practices:

It is illegal for a collection agency to give legal advice or engage in the practice of law.

ALASKA

A. Requirements:

1. LICENSE: Yes.
    (a) WHERE OBTAINED: Department of Commerce.
    (b) DURATION: Two years, expiring June 30 of each second year.
    (c) FILING FEES: Application fee of $100; biennial collection agency license fee of $200.
    (d) EXAMINATION: None.
    (e) BRANCH OFFICES: $200 biennial license fee for each branch office.
    (f) MISC.: Agency must file a verified annual statement for the preceding calendar year by Jan. 31.
2. BOND: $5,000 and a semiannual statement of employees listing their names and addresses on June 1 and Dec. 1 of every year.

B. Exemptions:

The above requirements do not apply to the following persons and businesses: practicing attorneys, banks, common carriers, title insurers and abstract companies while doing an escrow business, licensed real estate brokers, regular employees of a creditor, and substation payment offices of public utilities.

C. Prohibited Practices:

None.

D. Remarks:

Each office of a licensed agency must be under the management of a licensed operator. Application fee for an operator's license is $40; an operator's license is renewable on or before July 1 of each second year, and the biennial fee is $100.

Applicant for operator's license must be:
   (a) a resident of the state for one year;
   (b) a high school graduate;
   (c) of good moral character;
   (d) free from any conviction of certain crimes or of a violation of statutes regulating collection agencies;
   (e) 19 years of age or older;
   (f) neither a disbarred attorney nor bankrupt.

Some of these requirements may be waived.

ARIZONA

A. Requirements:

1. LICENSE: Yes.
    (a) WHERE OBTAINED: State Banking Department.
    (b) DURATION: One year, expiring Jan. 1.
    (c) FILING FEES: Initial investigation fee of $50 and yearly license fee of $100.
    (d) EXAMINATION: None.
    (e) BRANCH OFFICES: No separate licensing provisions.
2. BOND: $3,000 for each office in Arizona.

B. Exemptions:

The statute does not apply to practicing attorneys, banks, common carriers, title insurers and abstract companies while doing an escrow business, licensed real estate brokers, regular employees of a creditor and substation payment offices of public utilities.

C. Prohibited Practices:

1. It is unlawful to use forms that simulate any legal process or give the impression that the collection agency is a law firm or an instrumentality of the state, and thereafter to sell the obligation of the debtor.
2. A collection agency shall not advertise or threaten to advertise a claim as a means of enforcing payment thereof or for the purposes of soliciting claims. This provision does not affect agencies acting as assignees for the benefit of creditors, or acting pursuant to court order.

D. Remarks:

The term "collection agency" includes in part all persons who, in the course of collecting debts arising from their own business, use false names to suggest that a third person is effecting the collection.

ARKANSAS

A. Requirements:

1. LICENSE: Yes.
    (a) WHERE OBTAINED: State Board of Collection Agencies.
    (b) DURATION: Expires annually on June 30.
    (c) FILING FEES: Annual license fee of $100 for collection agency license.
    (d) EXAMINATION: None.
    (e) BRANCH OFFICES: Receive a branch office certificate upon payment of the fee for the original license.
    (f) MISC.: Each employee of the collection agency who collects delinquent accounts must be licensed at an annual fee of $10 payable on or before Jan. 1.
2. BOND: The amount of the bond is determined by the population of the city in which the collection agency has its principal place of business. The latest United States Census is used. The amounts of the required fees are as follows:

Up to 25,000 population	$1,500
Up to 75,000 population	$2,000
Over 75,000 population	$5,000

B. Exemptions:

The statute does not apply to the following: regular employees of a single creditor, banks, trust companies, savings and loan associations, abstract companies doing an escrow business, licensed real estate brokers, express and telegraph companies subject to public regulation, practicing attorneys, and persons handling collections under a court order.

C. Prohibited Practices:

Collection agencies are prohibited from engaging in the following acts:
1. Publishing or posting any list of debtors, commonly known as "deadbeat" lists.
2. Attempting to collect by the use of any methods contrary to U.S. postal regulations.
3. Possessing a badge, using a uniform of any law enforcement agency, or making statements which might be construed as indicating an official connection with any governmental law enforcement agency.
4. Distributing any printed matter which is made to resemble government forms or documents, or legal forms used in civil or criminal proceedings.
5. Advertising for sale or threatening to advertise a claim in order to enforce payment, except where the collection agency has acquired a claim as an assignee for the benefit of creditors or where it is acting under court order.
6. Engaging in any unethical practices or resorting to any illegal means of collection.
7. Using profanity, obscenity, or vulgarity.
8. Calling or writing to any debtor at his or her place of employment without first making a good-faith effort to contact him or her at home.
9. Using violence or threats of physical violence.

CALIFORNIA

A. Requirements:

1. LICENSE: Yes.
    (a) WHERE OBTAINED: Chief of Bureau of Collection and Investigative Services, Dept. of Consumer Affairs.
    (b) DURATION: One year, expiring June 30.
    (c) FILING FEES: Original license fee of $500, renewable yearly for $390.
    (d) EXAMINATION: Each applicant must pass an examination, for which the examination fee is $100, and obtain a qualification certificate for an annual fee of $100.
    (e) BRANCH OFFICES: Each location must apply for its own license and bond.
    (f) MISC.: All employees must be registered, except those engaged exclusively in secretarial or clerical activities. The fee is $25 per employee each year.
2. BOND: $10,000 or a deposit with the state of cash, evidence of deposit, investment certificates or share accounts in the sum of $10,000.

B. Exemptions:

Members of the California Bar, persons collecting accounts for one employer, common carriers, licensed real estate brokers, personal property brokers, banks, savings and loan associations, industrial loan companies, title insurance companies, and underwritten title companies are exempt.

C. Prohibited Practices:

Any collection agency [1] is prohibited from engaging in the following acts:
1. Publishing or posting any list of debtors, commonly known as "deadbeat" lists.
2. Attempting to collect by the use of any methods contrary to U.S. postal regulations.
3. Possessing a badge, using a uniform of any law enforcement agency, or making statements which might be construed as indicating an official connection with any governmental law enforcement agency.
4. Distributing any printed matter which is made to resemble government forms or documents, or legal forms used in civil or criminal proceedings.
5. Advertising for sale or threatening to advertise a claim in order to enforce payment, except where the collection agency has acquired a claim, as an assignee for the benefit of creditors or where it is acting under court order.
6. Engaging in any unethical practices or resorting to any illegal means of collection.
7. Using profanity, obscenity, or vulgarity.
8. Using any name while engaged in the collection of claims other than its true name except as prescribed by rules and regulations.
9. Using violence or threats of physical violence.
10. Commingling the money of its customers with its own.
11. Printing, publishing or selling collection letters, etc. upon which the licensee's name appears in such manner as to indicate that the demand is being made by the licensee to be used by a person having an address different from that of the address of the licensee.
12. Violating any of the provisions of title 1.6c § 1788 et seq. of the Civil Code.

D. Remarks:

To be licensed, a collection agency must have a net worth of not less than $15,000 of which not less than $5,000 must be deposited in a bank.

COLORADO

A. Requirements:

1. LICENSE: Yes.
    (a) WHERE OBTAINED: Administrator of the U.C.C.C., Department of Law
    (b) DURATION: One year, expiring June 30.

---

[1] Not limited to licensed collection agencies but includes persons engaging in debt collection on behalf of themselves or others, in the ordinary course of business.

COLLECTION AGENCY REQUIREMENTS   11-7

    (c) FILING FEES: Determined by Collection Agency Board.
    (d) EXAMINATION: None.
    (e) MISC.: Every employee who solicits claims must register as a debt collector.
2. BOND: $8,000 for each office plus $2,000 for each $10,000 or part thereof by which average monthly sums remitted exceed $15,000.

B. Exemptions:

Salaried employees working for a firm not engaged in the collection business, banks, abstract companies doing an escrow business, licensed real estate broker, railway express companies, public officers and persons acting under a court order, sales finance companies with respect to purchased accounts or any company with respect to commercial accounts receivable financing, and licensed attorneys are exempt.

C. Prohibited Practices:

No collection agency shall:
1. Advertise or threaten to advertise for sale any claim as a means of enforcing payment unless it is acting as assignee for the benefit of creditors, or acting under a court order.
2. Threaten, coerce, intimidate, infer consequences which are untrue, simulate legal process, use innuendoes or misleading phraseology, or engage in unethical or unfair tactics.
3. Invoke any cognivit clause without notice to the debtor.
4. Harass the employer of a debtor.
5. Publish "deadbeat" lists.
6. Restrictions on certain communications between collection agency and consumer.

CONNECTICUT

A. Requirements:

1. LICENSE: Yes.
    (a) WHERE OBTAINED: Bank Commissioner.
    (b) DURATION: One year, expiring annually on May 1.
    (c) FILING FEES: Original license fee of $200 and investigation fee of $50; annual renewal fee of $200.
    (d) EXAMINATION: None.
    (e) BRANCH OFFICES: Each branch office must be licensed separately.
2. BOND: $5,000 for each place of business in Connecticut.

B. Exemptions:

The statute does not apply to regular employees of a creditor, banks, lenders licensed by the Banking Commission under Chapter 647, abstract companies doing an escrow business, real estate brokers, companies or railway express business subject to the supervision of the public utilities commission, any public officer or person acting under court order, and any attorney licensed to practice in Connecticut.

C. Prohibited Practices:

It is unlawful for a collection agency to perform legal services, solicit claims for collection under an ambiguous or deceptive contract, or advertise any claim for sale. Under the Connecticut Act to regulate Collection Practices of Creditors (defined as any person who in the ordinary course of business extends credit to a consumer debtor residing in this state) creditors are prohibited from using any abusive, harassing, fraudulent, deceptive or misleading representation, devise or practice to collect any debt. A licensee may not communicate or threaten to communicate information about the alleged debt either to a debtor's employer, or others not bound by the debt, with the exception of a credit rating bureau, an attorney, or the debtor's spouse. A licensee shall not receive a collection fee in excess of 15% of the amount collected.

DELAWARE

A. Requirements:

1. LICENSE: Yes.
   (a) WHERE OBTAINED: Division of Revenue, Department of Finance.
   (b) DURATION: One year.
   (c) FILING FEES: $50 annually.
   (d) EXAMINATION: None.
   (e) BRANCH OFFICES: $10 annual license fee for each branch office.
2. BOND: None.

B. Exemptions:

The statute does not apply to attorneys licensed to practice in Delaware.

C. Prohibited Practices:

None.

DISTRICT OF COLUMBIA

A. Requirements:

1. LICENSE: No.
2. BOND: No.

B. Exemptions:

None.

C. Prohibited Practices:

It is unlawful for a debt collector to:
1. Create the impression that he or she represents the District of Columbia.
2. Use or threaten violence.
3. Threaten that nonpayment will result in arrest.
4. Threaten to sell or assign the obligation so that the debtor will lose any defense to the claim.
5. Use profanity.
6. Harass the debtor.
7. Place telephone calls without disclosing the caller's identity.
8. Cause expense in the form of long-distance telephone tolls, telegram fees, or other communication charges.
9. Unreasonably publicize information relating to the indebtedness or debtor.
10. Use any fraudulent, deceptive, or misleading representation or means to collect claims or obtain information about the debtor.
11. Use any written communication that violates or fails to conform to U.S. postal laws and regulations.

FLORIDA

A. Requirements:

1. LICENSE: None.
2. BOND: None.

B. Exemptions: None.

C. Prohibited Practices:

It is unlawful for a collection agency to:
1. Simulate an attorney, law enforcement officer, or representative of any governmental agency.

COLLECTION AGENCY REQUIREMENTS

2. Use or threaten force or violence.
3. Communicate or threaten to communicate with a debtor's employer without the debtor's consent prior to obtaining final judgment.
4. Disclose information affecting the debtor's reputation.
5. Harass the debtor or his or her family.
6. Use profanity.
7. Use a communication which simulates a legal form.
8. Advertise or threaten to advertise for sale any claim as a means to enforce payment except under court order.
9. Publish "deadbeat" lists.
10. Refuse to provide adequate identification as a collection agent.
11. Mail any communication to a debtor in an envelope or postcard with words on the outside of the envelope or postcard calculated to embarrass the debtor.

GEORGIA

A. Requirements:

1. LICENSE: No.
2. BOND: $50,000 bond filed with the Clerk of the Superior Court in the county in which the collection agency's principal place of business is located.

B. Exemptions:

Any collection agency which handles or administers fewer than twenty payments per month or has received written authorization from a third party to act as agent for the third party is exempt.

C. Prohibited Practices:

No debt collector shall collect or attempt to collect any money alleged to be due through:
1. coercion;
2. the threat of physical violence;
3. false statements that the debtor is willfully refusing to pay just debts;
4. the threat to assign the obligation with an attending representation that the result of such an assignment will be the loss of all the debtor's defenses;
5. the use of profane language;
6. the placement of telephone calls intended to harass;
7. unreasonable publication of calumnious information;
8. any false representation concerning the purpose of or position of the debt collector.

HAWAII

A. Requirements:

1. LICENSE: Yes.
   (a) WHERE OBTAINED: Collection Agency Board.
   (b) DURATION: One year, expiring June 30.
   (c) FILING FEES: If the initial license is obtained between July 1 and Dec. 31, the fee is $60, but if it is obtained between Jan. 1 and July 1, the fee is $30. Annual renewal fee is $60.
   (d) EXAMINATION: None.
   (e) BRANCH OFFICES: A license for each place of business other than the principal one is obtained by paying an additional annual fee of $30.
2. BOND: A $25,000 bond is required for the first or only office, and a $15,000 bond for each additional office to be filed with the director of commerce and consumer affairs. An irrevocable letter of credit for amount of bond may be substituted in lieu of the bond.

B. Exemptions:

Practicing attorneys, licensed real estate brokers, banks, trust companies, building and loan associations, companies doing an escrow business, individuals regularly employed in the capacity of credit persons for a single employer who is not a collection agency, persons doing business subject to public supervision and regulation, and public officers or persons acting under a court order are exempt.

C. Prohibited Practices:

It is unlawful for a collection agency to:
1. Use violence or threats of physical violence.
2. Threaten arrest.
3. Threaten to sell or assign the obligation of a debtor so that the debtor would lose any defense to the claim.
4. Use profanity.
5. Place telephone calls without disclosing caller's identity.
6. Harass the debtor.
7. Cause expense to the debtor in the form of long-distance telephone tolls, telegram fees, or other communication charge by concealing the true purpose of the communication.
8. Unreasonably publish information relating to the indebtedness.
9. Simulate a governmental agency or affiliation.
10. Distribute any printed matter which is made to resemble legal forms.
11. Use unfair or unconscionable means to collect any claim.
12. A collection agency may collect a fee or commission not in excess of 25% of the unpaid principal balance after filing of a suit against debtor.

IDAHO

A. Requirements:

1. LICENSE: Yes.
   (a) WHERE OBTAINED: Director of the Department of Finance.
   (b) DURATION: One year, expiring Dec. 31.
   (c) FILING FEES: Initial examination fee of $100; initial permit fee of $100; annual renewal fee of $50.
   (d) EXAMINATION: Yes; no office may be operated by a collection agency unless the person who is actively in charge of its operation passes an examination.
   (e) BRANCH OFFICES: Each place of business requires a separate license.
   (f) MISC.: Each office of a collection agency must have a financial net worth of at least $2,500.
2. BOND: Two bonds are required: (a) $5,000 bond for failure to account for and pay over the proceeds of any collection made; (b) $2,000 bond to indemnify the Dept. of Finance for expenses incurred as a result of investigations, administrative proceedings and prosecutions.

B. Exemptions

The above requirements do not apply to practicing attorneys, national banks, real estate brokers, building and loan associations, savings and loan associations, abstract and title companies doing an escrow business, and court appointed trustees or receivers.

C. Prohibited Practices:

It is illegal to sell, distribute or make use of collection letters or demand forms which resemble governmental forms or documents or legal forms used in civil or criminal proceedings. Similarly, it is illegal to use any trade name, address, insignia, picture or emblem which creates an impression that a person is connected with or is an agency of the government.

D. Remarks:

Any employee of a collection agency whose primary function is to engage in collection or receiving payment must obtain a license in the form of an identification card. The fee is $20, renewable annually.

A foreign corporation may be licensed to do business as a collection agency on filing application with the Department of Finance if such corporation: (i) is qualified to do business in the State of Idaho, and (ii) is the holder of a valid permit or license engaged in the collection agency business in the state where it has its principal place of business, and (iii) directs debtors to pay accounts directly to the debtor's creditor, and (iv) initiates collection activity with debtors solely through the use of written communication, and (v) is paid its collection commissions directly by its customer pursuant to periodic bills sent to its customers. Such an agency, designated as a limited permitee, must designate an office in the state through which it may be contacted during normal business hours and maintain books and records in accordance with generally accepted accounting principles. It can, however, maintain its books and records at its principal place of business outside Idaho.

ILLINOIS

A. Requirements:

1. LICENSE: Yes.
   (a) WHERE OBTAINED: Department of Registration and Education.
   (b) DURATION: One year.
   (c) FILING FEES: Application fee of $50; renewal fee of $40.
   (d) EXAMINATION: None.
   (e) BRANCH OFFICES: No separate provisions.
2. BOND: $25,000.

B. Exemptions:

The law does not apply to persons whose collection activities are confined to the operation of a business other than that of a collection agency and specifically excludes banks, financing and lending institutions, abstract companies doing an escrow business, real estate brokers, public officers acting under a court order, attorneys, insurance companies, credit unions, loan and finance companies, and retail stores collecting their own accounts.

C. Prohibited Practices:

It is unlawful for collection agencies to:
1. Use or threaten physical violence.
2. Threaten arrest.
3. Threaten the seizure, attachment or sale of a debtor's property where such action can only be taken pursuant to court order without disclosing that prior court proceedings are required.
4. Disclose false information to affect credit worthiness.
5. Communicate with debtor's employer unless there has been a default of payment of the obligation for at least 30 days and at least five days' written notice is given.
6. Harass debtor or his or her family.
7. Use profanity.
8. Disclose debtor's indebtedness to persons without a legitimate business need.
9. Engage in any conduct causing mental or physical illness to the debtor or his or her family.
10. Fail to disclose debt collector's identity.
11. Simulate legal process or governmental appearance.

INDIANA

A. Requirements:

1. LICENSE: Yes.
   (a) WHERE OBTAINED: Secretary of State.
   (b) DURATION: One year, expiring Dec. 31.
   (c) FILING FEES: Original application fee is $100 plus an additional fee of $15 for each branch office. Renewal fee is $15 and an additional $15 for each branch office.
   (d) EXAMINATION: None.
   (e) BRANCH OFFICES: There are no separate requirements for branch office registration other than an additional $15 fee. However, each office must have its own bond.
2. BOND: $5,000 for each office in Indiana.

B. Exemptions:

Attorneys, persons employed on a regular wage or salary in the capacity of credit persons except as an independent contractor, banks and financial institutions, licensed real estate brokers, public utilities, and express companies subject to the regulation of the Indiana Public Service Commission are exempt.

C. Prohibited Practices:

It is unlawful for collection agencies, to print, circulate, sell, send or deliver simulated legal documents where the intention is to lead the debtor to believe the same to be a genuine court or legal process.

IOWA

A. Requirements:

1. LICENSE: None.
2. BOND: None.

B. Exemptions:

None.

C. Prohibited Practices.

A debt collector shall not collect or attempt to collect a debt by:
1. the use, or threat of use, of force;
2. the false accusation of fraud or any other crime;
3. the threat to assign to another the debtor's obligation with the implication that such an assignment will extinguish the debtor's defenses;
4. the false threat of arrest;
5. harassment of the debtor;
6. the use of profane or obscene language;
7. the dissemination of false or slanderous information about the debtor.

KANSAS

A. Requirements:

1. LICENSE: None.
2. BOND: None.

B. Exemptions:

None.

C. Prohibited Practices:

None.

KENTUCKY

A. Requirements:

1. LICENSE: None.
2. BOND: None.

B. Exemptions:

The following are not considered debt adjusters: attorneys, employees of the debtor, creditors, agents of creditors, charitable, religious or educational organizations and persons acting pursuant to a court order or judgment or statute.

COLLECTION AGENCY REQUIREMENTS   11-13

C. Prohibited Practices:

None.

LOUISIANA

A. Requirements:

1. LICENSE: Yes.
    (a) WHERE OBTAINED: Commissioner of Financial Institutions.
    (b) DURATION: One year, expiring April 1.
    (c) FILING FEES: $25 per year.
    (d) EXAMINATION: None.
    (e) BRANCH OFFICES: Each branch office is considered a separate entity.
2. BOND: None.

B. Exemptions:

See Remarks.

C. Prohibited Practices:

A creditor may not contact any person outside of the debtor's household without the debtor's consent, except to ascertain the whereabouts of the debtor if there is reason to believe the debtor was moved or to discover property belonging to the debtor that may be seized to satisfy a debt that has been reduced to judgment.

If the debtor has defaulted on his promise to pay and he has given specific notice in writing instructing the creditor to cease further contacts regarding the debt, the creditor is then limited to one notice per month by mail, and four personal contacts with the debtor for the purpose of settling the obligation.

D. Remarks:

This statute applies only to collection agencies who undertake direct collection of payments from or enforcement of rights against debtors arising from consumer credit sales, consumer leases, or consumer loans.

MAINE

A. Requirements:

1. LICENSE: Yes.
    (a) WHERE OBTAINED: Superintendent of the Bureau of Consumer Protection.
    (b) DURATION: Two years, expiring July 31.
    (c) FILING FEES: $200 per year annual license fee.
    (d) EXAMINATION: None.
    (e) BRANCH OFFICES: Each branch office must procure a separate license.
2. BOND: A bond is required but the amount is at the Superintendent's discretion.

B. Exemptions:

Persons whose collection activities are confined to and directly related to the operation of a business such as banks, savings banks, credit unions, credit union leagues, real estate brokers, public officers or persons acting under a court order, lawyers, trust companies, building and loan associations, and savings and loan associations.

C. Prohibited Practices:

It is unlawful for a collection agency to:
1. Threaten to bring legal action in its name or list the name of a lawyer.
2. Use justice of the peace, constable, sheriff, or any other officer authorized to serve legal papers in connection with the collection of a claim.

3. Use or threaten to use physical violence.
4. Engage in the practice of law.
5. Use instruments which simulate legal or judicial process.
6. Demand a share of the compensation for services performed by a lawyer in collecting a claim.
7. Publish a list of debtors except for credit reporting purposes.
8. Use "shame cards," "shame automobiles," or similar devices.
9. Use any methods of collection contrary to postal regulations.
10. Advertise or threaten to advertise for sale any claim as a means of forcing payment.
11. Operate under a name or in a manner which implies association with a governmental agency.
12. Commingle money collected for a customer with the agency's own funds.
13. Share offices or have a common waiting room with a practicing lawyer.
14. Make repeated or harassing communications to employers.
15. Make collect telephone calls by subterfuge.
16. Engage in the business of lending money to any person.
17. Collect or attempt to collect an amount in excess of the amount submitted by the creditor for collection.

MARYLAND

A. Requirements:

1. LICENSE: Yes.
   (a) WHERE OBTAINED: Collection Agency Licensing Board of the Office of the Commissioner of Consumer Credit.
   (b) DURATION: One year, expiring Dec. 31.
   (c) FILING FEES: $100 for each place of business.
   (d) EXAMINATION: None.
   (e) BRANCH OFFICES: Each branch office must be licensed separately.
2. BOND: $5,000 for each office.

B. Exemptions:

Regular employees of a creditor acting under the general direction and control of that creditor in the collection of a claim owed to that creditor, any bank, trust company, savings and loan association, building and loan association, mortgage banker, abstract company doing an escrow business, attorney at law, or any person acting under court order are exempt.

C. Prohibited Practices:

It is unlawful for collection agencies to:
1. Use or threaten physical violence.
2. Threaten arrest.
3. Disclose false information to affect credit worthiness.
4. Communicate with debtor's employer before obtaining final judgment against the debtor.
5. Harass debtor or his or her family.
6. Use profanity.
7. Disclose debtor's indebtedness to persons without a legitimate business need.
8. Claim to enforce a right with knowledge that the right does not exist.
9. Simulate legal process or governmental appearance.
10. Harass the debtor by communicating with him frequently or at inconvenient hours.

MASSACHUSETTS

A. Requirements:

1. LICENSE: Yes.
   (a) WHERE OBTAINED: Commissioner of Banks.
   (b) DURATION: One year, expiring Oct. 1.
   (c) FILING FEES: $100 annual license fee.

COLLECTION AGENCY REQUIREMENTS 11-15

(d) EXAMINATION: None.
(e) BRANCH OFFICES: Each branch office must procure its own license.
2. BOND: $10,000 for initial bond; renewal bond $10,000 or 2 times average monthly net collections received for preceding year to a maximum of $25,000.

B. Exemptions:

The following persons and businesses are exempt: practicing attorneys, national banking associations, an agent or independent contractor employed for the purpose of collecting bills owed by a tenant to a landlord or owed by a customer to a corporation subject to the supervision of the Department of Public Utilities or the Division of Insurance.

C. Prohibited Practices:

It is unlawful for collection agencies to:
1. Use documents simulating judicial process.
2. Communicate, threaten to communicate or imply the fact of a debt to a person other than the debtor except with the written permission of the debtor.
3. Harass or embarrass the debtor by doing such things as calling at an unreasonable hour, with unreasonable frequency, using threats of violence and offensive language.
4. Communicate directly with the alleged debtor after notification from an attorney representing such debtor that all further communications should be addressed to him.

D. Remarks:

Prohibited practices described in paragraph C above apply to attorneys as well as collection agencies.

MICHIGAN

A. Requirements:

1. LICENSE: Yes.
   (a) WHERE OBTAINED: Director of Licensing and Regulation.
   (b) DURATION: One year, expiring June 30.
   (c) FILING FEES: Investigation fee $150; annual license fee is $100 but if application is made after December 31, the initial annual license fee shall be $50.
   (d) EXAMINATION: Every manager must pass an examination for which there is a $50 examination fee and a $25 annual license fee.
   (e) BRANCH OFFICES: Each branch office must obtain its own license.
   (f) MISC.: Each collection agency office must be under the personal supervision of a qualified manager. A manager may not be in charge of more than one office. An out of state collection agency which initiates any collection activity from within the state must be under the personal supervision of a licensed manager.
2. BOND: Amount in the discretion of the Director, but can be no less than $5,000 or more than $50,000.
3. SEPARATE ACCOUNTS: Collection agencies must keep all money collected in a separate account designated "trust account."

B. Exemptions:

Persons whose collection activities are confined and directly related to the operation of a business other than that of a collection agency are exempt. These include regular employees when collecting accounts for one employer if all collection efforts are carried on in the name of the employer, banks, trust companies, savings and loan associations, any business licensed by the state under a regulatory act, abstract companies doing an escrow business, licensed real estate brokers, public officers acting under court order, and attorneys. The Act only applies to collection agencies which handle consumer accounts.

C. Prohibited Practices:

Collection agencies cannot:
1. Communicate with a debtor between the hours of 9 P.M. and 8 A.M.
2. Conceal the collection agent's identity.

3. Cause expenses to the debtor for long-distance phone calls, telegrams, or other charges.
4. Disclose information relating to a debtor's indebtedness to an employer unless specifically authorized in writing by the debtor.
5. Use or threaten to use physical violence.
6. Publish lists of debtors.
7. Harass a debtor.
8. Use profanity.
9. Use a collection method contrary to U.S. postal laws.
10. Share office space or have a common waiting room with a practicing attorney or any lender.
11. Advertise or threaten to advertise for sale a claim as a means of forcing payment unless the agency is acting as the assignee for the benefit of creditors or acting under a court order.
12. Receive an assignment for the sole purpose of instituting an action.
13. Furnish legal advice or represent competence to do so.
14. Identify the collection agency other than by name appearing on license.
15. Represent that nonpayment of the debt will result in the debtor's arrest, or mislead or deceive the debtor in any manner such as simulating judicial or governmental forms in the course of collection.

MINNESOTA

A. Requirements:

1. LICENSE: Yes.
   (a) WHERE OBTAINED: Consumer Services Section, Dept. of Commerce.
   (b) DURATION: One year, expiring June 30.
   (c) FILING FEES: $100 initial license fee; $100 annual renewal fee.
   (d) EXAMINATION: None.
   (e) BRANCH OFFICES: Each branch office must procure its own license.
   (f) MISC.: An investigation, at the expense of the applicant, may be required at a fee not to exceed $100.
2. BOND: $20,000, but applicant may file for a reduction.

B. Exemptions:

Any person whose collection activities are confined to and directly related to the operation of a business other than that of a collection agency is exempt. This includes banks, abstract companies doing an escrow business, real estate brokers, public officers, persons acting under a court order, lawyers, trust companies, insurance companies, credit unions, building and loan associations, savings and loan associations, and loan or finance companies.

C. Prohibited Practices:

It is unlawful for a collection agency to:
1. Furnish legal advice.
2. Communicate with debtors in a misleading or deceptive manner by using the stationery of a lawyer, simulating judicial forms, or appearing to be a governmental agency.
3. Publish any list of debtors except for credit reporting purposes.
4. Use shame cards or shame automobiles.
5. Advertise or threaten to advertise for sale any claim as a means of forcing payment.
6. Commingle money collected for a customer with the agency's operating funds.

MISSISSIPPI

A. Requirements:

1. LICENSE: Yes.
   (a) WHERE OBTAINED: City or County Tax Collector.
   (b) DURATION: One year from date of issue.
   (c) FILING FEES: An annual fee for each place of business is based on the population of the municipality in which the office is located. The rates are as follows:

COLLECTION AGENCY REQUIREMENTS   11-17

      Municipalities having a population of 25,000 inhabitants or more—$50.
      Municipalities having a population between 15,000 and 25,000—$35.
      Municipalities having a population between 10,000 and 15,000—$25.
      Municipalities having a population under 10,000—$15.
   (d) EXAMINATION: None.
   (e) BRANCH OFFICES: Each office must pay a separate license tax.
2. BOND: None.

B. Exemptions:

Mutual associations or organizations formed for the purpose of collecting indebtedness for its members without profit are exempt.

C. Prohibited Practices:

It is unlawful for any person to use printed matter which simulates legal or judicial process.

MISSOURI

A. Requirements:

1. LICENSE: None.
2. BOND: None.

B. Exemptions:

None.

C. Prohibited Practices:

None.

MONTANA

A. Requirements:

1. LICENSE: None.
2. BOND: None.

B. Exemptions:

None.

C. Prohibited Practices:

None.

NEBRASKA

A. Requirements:

1. LICENSE: Yes.
   (a) WHERE OBTAINED: Secretary of State.
   (b) DURATION: One year, expiring Dec. 31.
   (c) FILING FEES: Investigation fee of $50; initial license fee of $50; renewal of license fee of $25; branch office certificate and branch office renewal fee of $25.
   (d) EXAMINATION: None.
   (e) BRANCH OFFICES: Branch offices must obtain a branch office certificate by submitting a $25 fee annually.
   (f) MISC.: Each solicitor of claims must obtain a solicitor's certificate at an annual fee of $1.
2. BOND: $2,000.

B. Exemptions:

Regular employees of a single creditor, banks, trust companies, savings and loan associations, abstract companies doing an escrow business, licensed real estate brokers, express and telegraph companies subject to public regulation, attorneys, and a person acting under a court order are exempt.

C. Prohibited Practices:

It is unlawful for a collection agency to engage in the practice of law.

NEVADA

A. Requirements:

1. LICENSE: Yes.
   (a) WHERE OBTAINED: Superintendent of Banks.
   (b) DURATION: One year, expiring June 30.
   (c) FILING FEES: For license—investigation fee of $100; initial license fee of $100; renewal license fee of $50. For manager—$75 investigation fee; $20 for manager's annual certification and registration fee of $10 for each employee.
   (d) EXAMINATION: An examination must be taken by each manager. The examination is given twice a year at a cost of $7.50 per hour.
   (e) BRANCH OFFICES: None.
   (f) MISC.: Each manager must obtain a manager's certificate and all employees who handle money or make contact with the public must be registered.
2. BOND: $10,000; may be substituted by an obligation of a bank, savings and loan association and the like provided for by statute.

B. Exemptions:

Regular employees of a single creditor, banks, non-profit cooperative associations, abstract companies doing an escrow business, licensed real estate agents, and attorneys licensed to practice in Nevada are exempt.

C. Prohibited Practices:

It is unlawful for a collection agency to:
1. Use any deceptive means or representations to collect a debt, such as simulating legal process or purporting to be from a governmental agency.
2. Operate its business or solicit claims for collection from any location other than that listed on its license.
3. Harass the debtor or his or her employer.
4. Advertise or threaten to advertise for sale any claim as a means to enforce payment unless under a court order.
5. Publish or post any list of debtors.
6. Conduct or operate, in conjunction with its collection agency business, a debt counselling or prorater service.

NEW HAMPSHIRE

A. Requirements:

1. LICENSE: None.
2. BOND: None.

B. Exemptions:

None.

COLLECTION AGENCY REQUIREMENTS

C. Prohibited Practices:

It is unlawful for a debt collector to:
1. Communicate with the debtor by calling repeatedly or at unusual hours.
2. Use profanity.
3. Communicate with the debtor at his or her place of employment without first trying to contact the debtor at his or her residence.
4. Use any written communication or place a phone call which fails to clearly identify the name of the debt collector or the person for whom the debt collector is attempting to collect the debt.
5. Cause any expense to the debtor in the form of long-distance telephone calls, telegram fees or other charges by concealing the true purposes of the communication.
6. Use or threaten to use violence.
7. Threaten to take any unlawful action or action which the debt collector in the regular course of business does not take.
8. Communicate, except by proper judicial process, the fact of such debt to a person other than the person who might reasonably be expected to be liable.
9. Use forms which simulate legal or judicial process.
10. Threaten that nonpayment of a debt will result in arrest, attachment, or garnishment when a court order is a legal prerequisite to any such action.
11. Threaten to assign or sell the claim against the debtor as a means of enforcing payment.

NEW JERSEY

A. Requirements:

1. LICENSE: None.
2. BOND: $5,000, and a $25 filing fee to the Secretary of State for the filing of the bond.

B. Exemptions:

Attorneys authorized to practice in New Jersey, national banks, and banks and trust companies incorporated in New Jersey are exempt.

C. Prohibited Practices:

It is unlawful for a debt collector to send, mail or deliver a notice, document or other instrument which simulates a summons, court order, etc., or is otherwise calculated to induce a belief that such notice or document has an official sanction.

D. Remarks:

Notice of discontinuance must be filed with the Secretary of State.

NEW MEXICO

A. Requirements:

1. LICENSE: Yes.
   (a) WHERE OBTAINED: Commissioner of Banking.
   (b) DURATION: One year, expiring July 1.
   (c) FILING FEES: Original license fee and renewal fee of $100; examination fee of $25.
   (d) EXAMINATION: Each application (e.g., manager) must pass an examination given at least twice a year.
   (e) BRANCH OFFICES: Each branch office is treated as a separate entity.
   (f) MISC.: Each office must be under the active charge of a person who possesses a manager's license at a fee of $25 annually, and each solicitor must possess a solicitor's certificate at a cost of $2.50.
2. BOND: $2,000.

B. Exemptions:

Attorneys, regularly employed persons of a creditor, banks, licensed loan companies, finance companies, automobile dealers, common carriers, title insurers and abstract companies doing an escrow business, licensed real estate brokers and licensed personal property brokers are exempt.

C. Prohibited Practices:

It is unlawful for a collection agency to:
1. Advertise or threaten to advertise for sale any claim as a means of endeavoring to enforce payment.
2. Publish or post any list of debtors, commonly known as "deadbeat" lists.
3. Collect or attempt to collect by the use of any methods contrary to U.S. postal laws and regulations.
4. Commingle the money of his or her customers with the agency's.

D. Remarks:

Each collection agency must have a net worth of not less than $3,000 of which not less than $1,000 is in liquid assets.

NEW YORK

A. Requirements:

1. LICENSE: None.
2. BOND: None.

B. Exemptions:

None.

C. Prohibited Practices:

It is unlawful for a debt collector to:
1. Simulate a law enforcement officer, a governmental agent, or legal or judicial process.
2. Disclose information affecting the debtor's reputation for credit worthiness knowing that the information is false.
3. Communicate or threaten to communicate the nature of a consumer claim to the debtor's employer prior to obtaining final judgment.
4. Abuse or harass the debtor or any member of his household.
5. Threaten any action which the principal creditor in the usual course of his business does not in fact take.
6. Claim or threaten to enforce a right with knowledge or reason to know that the right does not exist.

D. Remarks:

Issuance of a document which appears or simulates a summons, complaint or court order or improperly suggests that it is judicially or officially sanctioned or is issued by a governmental agency is an unlawful collection practice and is a misdemeanor.

NORTH CAROLINA

A. Requirements:

1. LICENSE: Yes.
   (a) WHERE OBTAINED: Commissioner of Insurance.
   (b) DURATION: One year, expiring June 30.
   (c) FILING FEES: $500 annually.
   (d) EXAMINATION: None.
   (e) BRANCH OFFICES: Each location is treated as a separate entity.
2. BOND: $5,000 initially, it varies thereafter.

COLLECTION AGENCY REQUIREMENTS

B. Exemptions:

Regular employees of a single creditor, banks, trust companies, corporations engaged in accounting, bookkeeping or data processing services where a primary component of such services is the rendering of statements of accounts and bookkeeping services for creditors, mortgage banking companies, savings and loan associations, building and loan associations, licensed real estate brokers, express and telegraph companies, subject to public regulation, attorneys, and persons acting under a court order are exempt.

C. Prohibited Practices:

North Carolina has detailed provisions concerning prohibited practices for debt collection agencies, forbidding various types of threats and coercion, harassment, unreasonable publication, deceptive representation, and other unconscionable means.

D. Remarks:

Every collection agency must obtain a state license from the Secretary of Revenue for the privilege of engaging in the collection agency business. It must pay a tax of $50 for such license.

NORTH DAKOTA

A. Requirements:

1. LICENSE: Yes.
   (a) WHERE OBTAINED: Dept. of Banking and Financial Institutions.
   (b) DURATION: One year, expiring June 30.
   (c) FILING FEES: $100 annual license fee.
   (d) EXAMINATION: None.
   (e) BRANCH OFFICES: No separate provisions.
2. BOND: $5,000.

B. Exemptions:

Attorneys, licensed real estate brokers, banks, trust companies, building and loan associations, abstract companies doing an escrow business, creditors collecting their own debts, persons who purchase or take accounts renewable for collateral purposes, regular employees of a single creditor, public officers, receivers or trustees acting under court order are exempt.

C. Prohibited Practices:

None.

OHIO

A. Requirements:

1. LICENSE: None.
2. BOND: None.

B. Exemptions:

None.

C. Prohibited Practices:

It is unlawful for a collection agency to engage in activities which constitute the practice of law.

OKLAHOMA

A. Requirements:

1. LICENSE: None.
2. BOND: None.

B. Exemptions:

None.

C. Prohibited Practices:

None.

OREGON

A. Requirements:

1. LICENSE: Yes.
    (a) WHERE OBTAINED: Credit Agencies Board of the Dept. of Commerce.
    (b) DURATION: One year, expiring June 30.
    (c) FILING FEES: Application fee of $200, annual license fee of $175 for the principal place of business and $175 for each branch office.
    (d) EXAMINATION: To qualify for an operator's license, an applicant must pass an examination. Examination fee is $25.
    (e) BRANCH OFFICES: Each branch office is licensed individually.
    (f) MISC.: Each office must be under the management of a licensed operator. Annual operator's license fee is $50. Each solicitor must obtain a solicitor's certificate at an annual fee of $15.
2. BOND: $10,000 for each business location.

B. Exemptions:

Any attorney or licensed certified public accountant not specializing in collection agency business, banks, consumer finance companies, trust companies, savings and loan associations, real estate or escrow agents, any individual employed as a credit man by one person not engaged in the collection business, public officers or any person acting under court order, any person acting as a property manager in collecting rent due landlords, any person collecting directly from the obligor any account purchased from the owner thereof if the purchase is without recourse of any kind against such owner, requires no guarantee by such owner of the payment by the obligor of such account and requires no reserve account be established by such owner, or if the purchase is with recourse or requires a guarantee of payment or requires a reserve and the account arose out of other than a consumer transaction.

C. Prohibited Practices:

It is unlawful for a collection agency to:
1. Use or threaten to use force or violence.
2. Threaten arrest or criminal prosecution.
3. Threaten legal action on the debtor's property without disclosing that prior court proceedings are required.
4. Use profanity.
5. Harass the debtor or his family.
6. Communicate or threaten to communicate with a debtor's employer.
7. Communicate with the debtor at his place of employment without his permission, unless collection agency does not identify itself as such and agency has been unable to reach debtor at his residence. Debt collector cannot telephone debtor at his place of employment if advised not to by debtor or if he knows debtor's employer prohibits such calls.
8. Communicate with the debtor without identifying itself and for whom it is collecting the debt.
9. Threaten to enforce a right or remedy that it knows does not exist.

COLLECTION AGENCY REQUIREMENTS

11-23

10. Attempt to collect additional unauthorized fees.
11. Threaten to assign or sell debtor's account with an implication that debtor would lose any defense or be subjected to abusive collection practices.
12. Misrepresent the source of any communication.
13. Cause expense to the debtor by concealing the true purpose of the debt collector's communication.

PENNSYLVANIA

A. Requirements:

1. LICENSE: None.
2. BOND: None.

B. Exemptions:

None.

C. Prohibited Practices:

It is unlawful for a collection agency to:
1. Appear for or represent a creditor or other person in any proceeding.
2. Buy or take an assignment of any claim for the purpose of enforcing payment.
3. Furnish legal services.
4. Act for any debtor with regard to the proposed settlement or adjustment of the affairs of the debtor.
5. Solicit employment for any attorney.
6. Coerce or intimidate any debtor by using documents which simulate legal or judicial process.
7. Abuse or harass by telephone, calls at place of employment, or household visits.
8. Falsely represent that a debtor has committed a crime.

RHODE ISLAND

A. Requirements:

1. LICENSE: None.
2. BOND: None.

B. Exemptions:

None.

C. Prohibited Practices:

None.

SOUTH CAROLINA

A. Requirements:

1. LICENSE: None.
2. BOND: None.

B. Exemptions:

None.

C. Prohibited Practices:

None.

SOUTH DAKOTA

A. Requirements:

1. LICENSE: None.
2. BOND: None.

B. Exemptions:

None.

C. Prohibited Practices:

None.

D. Remarks:

A collection agency cannot be operated in conjunction with a licensed lending business where any loan results from the collection business.

TENNESSEE

A. Requirements:

1. LICENSE: Yes.
    (a) WHERE OBTAINED: Tennessee Collection Service Board.
    (b) DURATION: One year, expiring Dec. 31.
    (c) FILING FEES: Initial investigation fee—$50; annual licensing fee—$150, $75 if issued after June 30; solicitor's identification card—$10.
    (d) EXAMINATION: Each office manager must pass an examination, for which there will be a $50 fee for each reexamination.
    (e) BRANCH OFFICES: No separate requirements.
    (f) MISC.: Private tax must also be paid. Each solicitor must be certified annually at a cost of $10.
2. BOND: $15,000.
3. SEPARATE ACCOUNTS: Each licensee shall maintain a separate fiduciary or trust account with the money collected.

B. Exemptions:

Regular employees of a single creditor, lawyers, any person engaged in the collection of debts incurred in the normal course of business, and any person handling claims under a court order are exempt.

C. Prohibited Practices:

It is unlawful for a collection agency to simulate legal forms. All collection agencies must comply with the guides against debt collection deception of the FTC and to the use of the telephone for debt collection purposes as defined by the FCC. A collector may not collect from the debtor the fees owed the collector by his creditor client.

TEXAS

A. Requirements:

1. LICENSE: None.
2. BOND: None.

B. Exemptions:

None.

COLLECTION AGENCY REQUIREMENTS

C. Prohibited Practices:

It is unlawful for a debt collector to:
1. Use or threaten to use violence.
2. Threaten to sell or assign the obligation.
3. Threaten that the debtor will be arrested for nonpayment without proper court proceedings.
4. Threaten to file charges, complaints, or criminal action against a debtor when in fact the debtor has not violated any criminal laws.
5. Threaten that nonpayment will result in the seizure, repossession, or sale of any property with proper court proceedings.
6. Oppress, harass, or abuse a debtor.
7. Use any fraudulent, deceptive, or misleading representations.

UTAH

A. Requirements:

1. LICENSE: None.
2. BOND: $5,000 filed with the Secretary of State.

B. Exceptions:

Attorneys licensed in Utah, national banks, and banks and trust companies incorporated in Utah are exempt.

C. Prohibited Practices:

None.

VERMONT

A. Requirements:

1. LICENSE: Yes.
   (a) WHERE OBTAINED: State Tax Commissioner.
   (b) DURATION: One year, expiring Dec. 20.
   (c) FILING FEES: Application fee of $50; investigation fee of $50; renewal fee of $50.
   (d) EXAMINATION: Without notice at least once a year.
   (e) BRANCH OFFICES: No provisions.
2. BOND: $10,000.

B. Exemptions:

Attorneys, banks or financing institutions which perform debt adjustment in the regular course of business, persons acting under law or order of court, any *bona fide* nonprofit or fraternal organization offering debt services exclusively, employees of licensee working in regular course of business.

C. Prohibited Practices:

None.

VIRGINIA

A. Requirements:

1. LICENSE: None.
2. BOND: $5,000.

B. Exemptions:

None.

C. Prohibited Practices:

No collection agency shall purchase any debt or other cause of action for the purpose of collecting it by legal proceedings.

WASHINGTON

A. Requirements:

1. LICENSE: Yes.
   (a) WHERE OBTAINED: Director of the Dept. of Motor Vehicles.
   (b) DURATION: One year, expiring Dec. 31.
   (c) FILING FEES: Licensing fee of $100; investigation fee of $100; annual renewal fee of $100.
   (d) EXAMINATION: None.
   (e) BRANCH OFFICES: A branch office certificate will be issued annually for a fee of $50.
2. BOND: $5,000.

B. Exemptions:

Any employee collecting for his or her employer, trust companies, savings and loan associations, building and loan associations, abstract companies doing an escrow business, real estate brokers, public officers, lawyers, insurance companies, credit unions, loan or finance companies, and banks are exempt.

C. Prohibited Practices:

Harassment, which is defined as communicating with the debtor more than three times a week or more than once a week at his or her job, or communicating with him or her between 9:00 P.M. and 7:30 A.M; publishing a "bad debt list," sending forms that simulate judicial practice; practicing law; use of unauthorized name; use of unclear illegible type in notice; threatening debtor with impairment of credit rating; use of forms that simulate the form or appearance of judicial process.

WEST VIRGINIA

A. Requirements:

1. LICENSE: Yes (known as a business franchise registration certificate).
   (a) WHERE OBTAINED: State Tax Commissioner.
   (b) DURATION: One year, expiring June 30.
   (c) FILING FEES: $15 annually.
   (d) EXAMINATION: None.
   (e) BRANCH OFFICES: A separate license and bond are required for each branch office.
2. BOND: $5,000.

B. Exemptions:

Regular employees of a single creditor, banks, trust companies, savings and loan associations, building and loan associations, industrial loan companies, small loan companies, abstract companies doing an escrow business, licensed real estate brokers, express and telegraph companies subject to public regulation, attorneys, and any person acting under a court order are exempt.

C. Prohibited Practices:

It is unlawful for a debt collector to:
1. Engage in the practice of law.
2. Attempt to collect any money by means of any threat or coercion.
3. Unreasonably oppress or abuse any person in connection with the collection of any claim.
4. Unreasonably publicize information relating to the debt.
5. Use any fraudulent, deceptive or misleading representation or means to collect claims.
6. Use unfair or unconscionable means to collect.
7. Use, distribute, sell or prepare for use any written communication which violates or fails to conform to U.S. postal laws and regulations.

WISCONSIN

A. Requirements:

1. LICENSE: Yes.
    (a) WHERE OBTAINED: Commissioner of Banking.
    (b) DURATION: One year, expiring June 30.
    (c) FILING FEES: Investigation fee of $100; annual license fee of $100.
    (d) EXAMINATION: None.
    (e) BRANCH OFFICES: Each location must obtain its own license.
    (f) MISC: Each collector or solicitor must obtain a license for an annual fee of $2.
2. BOND: Required at the discretion of the Commissioner of Banking.

B. Exemptions:

Attorneys licensed in Wisconsin, banks, express companies, savings and loan associations, insurance companies, trust companies, professional men's associations collecting accounts for its members on a nonprofit basis where such members are required by law to have a license, diploma or permit to practice or follow their profession, and real estate brokers are exempt.

C. Prohibited Practices:

In attempting to collect a debt arising from a consumer credit transaction, it is unlawful for a debt collector to:
1. Use or threaten force or violence.
2. Threaten criminal prosecution.
3. Disclose or threaten to disclose information adversely affecting the customer's reputation for credit worthiness with knowledge or reason to know that the information is false.
4. Communicate or threaten to communicate with the customer's employer prior to obtaining final judgment against the customer.
5. Disclose or threaten to disclose to a person other than the customer or his or her spouse information affecting the customer's reputation, with knowledge or reason to know that the other person does not have a legitimate business need for the information.
6. Communicate with the customer or a relative with such frequency or at such unusual hours as can reasonably be expected to threaten or harass the customer.
7. Use profanity.
8. Threaten to enforce a right with knowledge or reason to know that the right does not exist.
9. Use a communication which stimulates legal or judicial process.
10. Threaten action against the customer that is not taken in the regular course of business or not intended with respect to the particular debt.

WYOMING

A. Requirements:

1. LICENSE: Yes.
    (a) WHERE OBTAINED: Secretary of State.
    (b) DURATION: One year from the date of issuance.
    (c) FILING FEES: $100 for each original license; $50 for each renewal license.
    (d) EXAMINATION: None.
    (e) BRANCH OFFICES: A branch office license is obtained for a $25 annual fee.
2. BOND: $2,000.

B. Exemptions:

Regular employees of a single creditor engaged in interstate transportation, corporation, labor unions, or voluntary association not engaged in the collection business, banks, abstract companies doing an escrow business, licensed real estate brokers, public officers or persons acting under court order, and licensed attorneys are exempt.

C. Prohibited Practices:

None.

The Credit Card—
Its Legal Implications

One of the most significant commercial developments since World War II is the emergence of the credit card as a substitute for cash. The rapid growth in the use of credit cards is indicative of the fact that they serve a useful purpose to both the user and creditor. From available information it appears that losses due to improper or fraudulent use of credit cards is negligible compared to overall volume of use. However, there have been some startling examples of individuals who have stolen thousands of dollars through fraudulent use of credit cards, and in a number of locations and over a period of time losses have increased due to the inability of users to meet their financial obligations. The general criminal statutes of the various states relating to larceny and forgery seem to cover most of the more flagrant misuses of credit cards. In addition, many states have enacted statutes imposing criminal penalties for specified improper uses. Our purpose will be to consider the various civil and criminal aspects relating to the use or misuse of credit cards including recent statutory enactments.

Forms of the Credit Card Plans

There are many different systems presently in use but most fall within three general categories known as the two-party, three-party or four-party plans.

The two-party plan is the simple arrangement (typical of which is the department store charge-plate plan) between the customer, who will be described as the "holder" of the credit card, and the merchant, who may be described as both the "issuer" and "creditor" under this plan. The holder applies to the issuer for the credit card on a prescribed form giving references and other pertinent credit information. The issuer makes a credit investigation and if satisfied issues a credit card, coin, plate or other device to the holder, usually subject to certain conditions which the holder agrees to in writing or impliedly by acceptance and use of the credit card. Some of the more common conditions are the following:

(1) It will be used only by the holder or other designated persons;

(2) Purchases may be limited to special types of products or a maximum dollar amount;

(3) The holder will assume responsibility for all charges against the card;

(4) The holder will notify the issuer immediately if the card is lost;

(5) The issuer has the right to cancel the card at any time;

(6) The use of the card is limited to the period specified on its face.

The three-party plan brings in a separate issuer and creditor or creditors. Typical of this type is the credit card issued by the oil companies for use at service stations selling their products and by organizations offering credit privileges at designated restaurants, hotels and other establishments. Under this plan the application, credit investigation and issuance of the credit card are handled by the issuer, and the agreement between the issuer and holder follows the same general form as those described in the two-party plan. In many of these plans an annual fee is also paid by the holder to the issuer. The holder in making his purchase presents his credit card and invariably is required to sign an invoice for his purchase. The creditor sends his invoices to the issuer periodically and is paid the amount of the invoices, less any service charge provided for under the plan. The issuer then bills the holder for the purchases against his credit card, usually monthly.

The so-called four-party plan, as its name implies, introduces another party to the "holder," "creditor" and "issuer" previously described. This fourth party (usually a bank), under an agreement with the issuer, attends to servicing the plan by paying the creditors, and by billing and receiving payments from the holders. There are numerous forms which these four-party plans may take; the above description is intended merely as a generalization for our further discussion.

Contractual or Civil Obligations of Parties

Under the various types of plans described a contractual relationship exists between the holder and issuer, between creditor and issuer, and between issuer and "fourth party." In general, the provisions of these various agreements will determine the contractual rights and obligations of the parties. There are some areas, however, which may not be covered by a written contract, or the language of the contract may be restricted by judicial construction.

Many analogies have been made between the credit card and other legal instruments, and various legal principles have been applied to the relationships between the various parties to the several types of plans. In the simplest form these relationships may be described as follows:

Two-party system.—The holder and issuer stand in the relationship of debtor and creditor and the transactions between the parties are subject to the general rules applicable to sales of goods on credit.

Three-party system.—The holder and creditor relationship is substantially the same as in the two-party system. The issuer has a contractual relationship with both the holder and the creditor. In effect, the contract with the creditor provides that the issuer will purchase the creditor's accounts (i.e., credit card invoices) and collect the same from the holders. The holders in turn agree to pay the issuer in accordance with terms of the credit card plan.

Four-party system.—The relationship of holder, creditor and issuer is substantially the same as in the three-party plan. Under this system, however, the invoices signed by the holder are discounted by the fourth party (bank) within a few days after the purchase, and the issuer is obligated to honor or discharge the draft covering such invoices regardless of possible claims which might exist among the other three parties.

What are the rights and liabilities of the respective parties under these plans if the holder is financially unable to meet his obligations? Obviously under the two-party system the issuer has whatever remedies are available to a creditor to enforce the obligations of his debtor. Under the three-party system, in the usual course of events, the creditor will have been paid by the issuer and the issuer will have his only recourse against the holder either under the contract between the parties or as the assignee of the creditor's account with the holder. The inability of the holder to pay does not affect the issuer's obligation to pay the creditor and accept the account, since he has so obligated himself under the provisions in the contract with the creditor. Under the four-party system the ultimate loss also falls upon the issuer if the creditor does not pay.

In *Franklin National Bank v. Kass,* 19 Misc. 2d 280, 184 N.Y.S. 2d 783 (Sup. Ct. 1959), the court considered the rights and liabilities of parties under a four-party plan. The defendant was an employee of a corporation which subsequently failed. His employer was a "company member" of the Esquire Credit Club and designated the defendant as a "designated card holder" under this credit plan. The plan provided that the company agreed to pay the charges of all its designated card holders and that each card holder agreed to pay the charges incurred by him. Defendant made various purchases for company purposes and signed his name on the invoices with his card number. The creditors signed "Esquire Club Drafts" for these purchases and sent them to the Esquire Club, which in turn discounted them with the plaintiff bank. The bank transmitted the "drafts" to defendant with this statement: "If incorrect, please return within ten days. Otherwise retention constitutes acceptance." In holding the defendant liable for charges incurred through his use of this credit card plan, the court found that the "drafts" constituted negotiable instruments; although it would be questionable whether the manner of presentment of the drafts for acceptance were in compliance with the Negotiable Instruments Law, any objection is overcome by the holder's agreement that he would accept all drafts drawn by him; the holder of a credit card is charged with notice of conditions printed on the reverse side and by his retention and use of the card he assented to them; the holder of the credit card, having assumed responsibility for payment, cannot escape personal liability because the purchases were made on behalf of his employer.

Another New York case, *American Express v. Geller,* 74 Misc. 2d 284, 343 N.Y.S. 2d 644 (Civ. Ct. N.Y. 1973), considered the question as to the personal liability of an employee for charges incurred under a credit card which he was required to obtain as a condition of employment. The court held that the employee had no liability since he was not a principal of the employer corporation, which was now bankrupt, and all charges incurred were for business purposes. Despite the language of the contract with American Express by which the employee became obligated for charges under the account, it was the court's view that to impose liability on the employee would be unconscionable.

Connecticut has adopted a statute applicable in consumer sales conducted by use of a credit card by which all claims and defenses which the buyer may have against the seller arising out of a transaction involving $50 or more may be asserted against the issuer of the card.

The Lost, Stolen or Misused Credit Card

Under the Federal Truth In Lending Law, no credit cardholder can be held responsible for more than $50 of unauthorized purchases provided the cardholder has received prior written notice from issuer of such potential liability. 15 U.S.C. 1643. The statute has been held applicable to limit liabilities of corporations on credit cards issued to employees. In addition, all cards must permit identification of the cardholder.

Of particular concern to the credit executive is the corporate liability for unauthorized use of credit cards issued to a corporation for the business use of officers and employees. As the cardholder, the corporation has normally agreed to be primarily liable for the obligations arising from the issuance and use of the card. Where the card is actually used for transactions of a personal nature, however, it is arguable that the transaction may be treated as though the card were stolen. Such an "unauthorized use" of the card will limit the corporation's liability to the $50 provision discussed above. Two requirements must be met for the transaction to be considered an "unauthorized use" of the card. First, there must be a total lack of authority—actual, implied or apparent—from the cardholder for use of the card. As a matter of proof, where an officer or employee has broad responsibilities, it may be difficult to avoid the implication of authority for the particular use in question. The second requirement is that the corporation must not receive any benefit from the use of the card. This is true even if there is a total lack of authority for the purchase. Thus, if an employee purchases materials for which he clearly has no authority, but which nevertheless are used in the business of the corporation, the corporate cardholder will be liable on its underlying obligation to the issuer of the card for the full purchase price of the materials.

Many states have enacted legislation limiting liability of credit card holders. In 1961, New York State enacted a statute limiting liability for use of lost or stolen credit cards. This statute, N.Y. Gen. Bus. Law § 512 (McKinney Supp. 1982), provides in part:

> A provision which imposes liability upon a holder for a cash advance or loan or for the purchase or lease of property or services obtained by the unauthorized use of a credit card shall not be enforceable to the extent that it imposes a greater liability upon the holder than is imposed under the provisions of the act of congress entitled "Truth in Lending Act" and the regulations thereunder, as such act and regulations may from time to time be amended.

North Dakota and Vermont have enacted statutes which limit liability of the owner of a credit card for unauthorized use to $100 provided adequate notice of loss is given to the issuer of the card, the unauthorized use occurs prior to the notice, and the user of the card can be identified by signature or photograph. California, Kansas, Maine, Massachusetts, Minnesota, New Mexico, and Wyoming have similar statutes except the amount is limited to $50. In Illinois maximum liability for card without signature panel is $25; with signature panel, $50. While in Maryland, the holder is not liable for any unauthorized use.

A large number of states have enacted statutes which provide that a person who receives an unsolicited credit card which he does not accept by use or authorization of use is not responsible for any liability resulting from its loss or theft; failure to return or destroy an unsolicited card does not constitute acceptance. Included in these states are Alaska, California, Connecticut, Florida, Hawaii, Illinois, Kansas, Maryland, Massachusetts, Minnesota, Mississippi, New Mexico, New York, North Dakota, Ohio, Rhode Island, South Dakota, Tennessee, Vermont, Virginia, Wisconsin and Wyoming. In Connecticut, Delaware, Florida, Hawaii, New York, Rhode Island and South Dakota, the unauthorized issuance of credit cards is in itself a crime; in Illinois, it is a business offense resulting in a maximum fine of $500. Delaware law requires that an issuer of an unsolicited credit card must send the recipient 14 days' notice before the card is mailed to him. The notice must be accompanied by a conspicuous statement that the recipient has a right of refusal. Additionally, a prepaid return envelope must be included. However, use of the card will constitute acceptance.

It appears fairly well established by general legal principles as well as reported decisions that, where the holder permits another to use his credit card, the holder is responsible for the purchases made therewith, notwithstanding the fact that the authorized user exceeds the authority given. See *Jones Store v. Kelly*, 225 Mo. App. 833, 36 S.W. 2d 681 (1931); *Sinclair Refining Co. v. Consolidated Van & Storage Co.*, 192 F. Supp. 87 (N.D. Ga. 1960).

While the agreement between the parties will control their rights and liabilities, subject to any statutory limitations, it appears that a provision imposing absolute liability on the holder of a credit card for purchases thereon will not be enforceable if the issuer or creditor bears a major responsibility for the card's misuse by another. In *Gulf Refining Co. v. Williams Roofing Co.*, 208 Ark. 362, 186 S.W. 2d 790 (1945), the defendant had procured from the plaintiff eight credit cards for use by its truck drivers. The card provided that the holder (defendant) assumed full responsibility for all purchases through its use and that its loss be immediately reported to the issuer. The defendant wrote across the face of each card "Good for Truck Only," and then turned them over to its drivers. An employee of one of the issuer's authorized dealers misappropriated one of the cards from the holder's driver and went on a "90-day orgy of buying from Gulf dealers" gas and oil for his own passenger car, home and car radios, tires and other merchandise. He forged the name of the holder's driver on invoices and there appeared to be evidence that some of the dealers involved knew of and abetted his larcenous activities. In upholding the dismissal of the issuer's suit to recover the cost of these purchases from the holder, the Arkansas Supreme Court made the following determinations:

(1) The collusion of creditors (the retail dealers), in honoring a credit card known to be wrongfully used, is a defense to an action by the issuer (the oil company) against the holder, irrespective of whether the dealers are agents of the issuer or independent contractors, since the issuer is an assignee of the invoices with no greater rights than its assignor;

(2) Even though the contract provides that the holder assumes responsibility for all purchases made through use of the credit card, it necessarily implies that the person extending credit must do so in good faith in accordance with the provisions of the card and any limitations appearing on its face;

(3) A limitation as to the use of a credit card ("Good for truck only") placed thereon by the holder without the concurrence of the issuer is nonetheless effective since it protects both holder and issuer against wrongful acts of the creditor;

(4) Where the facts indicate that the creditors by their collusion or negligence have been the proximate cause of the wrongful obtaining of goods through misuse of a credit card, they must bear responsibility for the loss;

(5) In circumstances of the type presented by this case the court will not impose liability on the holder in favor of the issuer on the theory that of the two innocent parties (holder and issuer) the loss must fall on the one bearing the initial or major responsibility for the loss. It is suggested that

since the thief is apparently solvent, recourse may be had against him or that the issuer might hold the creditors responsible by reason of their collusion or negligence.

This decision makes it clear that the holder of a credit card will be bound by the conditions printed on the card or appearing on the application or in other contractual arrangements between the parties. If one of the conditions is that the holder guarantees the payment, or assumes the liability for payment, of all purchases through use of the card until the issuer is notified of its loss, theft or misappropriation, this condition will be enforced.[1] It would appear that in most jurisdictions the fact that the holder used due care in the use and custody of his credit card or did not know that it was lost, stolen or misappropriated would not constitute a valid defense.

Criminal Liability for Misuse of Credit Cards

Under most state larceny statutes, there can be little question that one who by theft or otherwise acquires possession of a credit card issued to another and thereafter makes credit purchases thereon commits a larceny in some form which can be punished under the general criminal statutes of the various states. Under most credit plans, the holder is required to sign a check, invoice or other document for the merchandise or services received. If one other than the legitimate holder signs the holder's name to such a document without the holder's authority the crime of forgery is also committed.

Many different problems may be presented in connection with the procuring of credit cards by misrepresentation or misuse of a card by a holder to whom it has been properly issued. It would clearly appear that a person who obtains a credit card by misrepresentation and thereafter uses the card to purchase goods or services on credit commits larceny the same as one who directly obtains property from the owner by false pretenses. There would also appear to be reasonable grounds for prosecution of one who obtains a credit card by false pretenses even though he does not use it. By analogy to other forms of documents, there also appears to be little doubt that the material alteration of a credit card such as by change of name, number of expiration date and subsequent use would constitute a criminal offense in the areas of forgery or larceny.

A more difficult problem is presented by the holder who uses his credit card after the expiration date or who is financially unable to pay for his credit purchases on a valid card. As will be noted later, many states have passed statutes making it a criminal offense to use a credit card after it has expired or has been revoked. It is questionable whether in the absence of such a statute a holder could be successfully prosecuted under general larceny statutes, and certainly not in the absence of a strong showing of criminal intent to defraud.

We have progressed from the days of the "debtor's prison" and surely no one would urge that the inability of a debtor to pay for credit purchases when due should constitute a criminal offense. A strong argument can be made, however, that a person who uses a credit card to obtain goods or services with

---

[1] Some courts have required that if the contract makes the holder a guarantor or indemnitor for all purchases, the issuer has a duty to act carefully in protecting the holder from unauthorized purchases. In *Union Oil Co. of Calif. v. Lull,* 220 Ore. 412, 349 P.2d 243 (1960), the court refused to recognize the contract establishing the holder as an indemnitor until the issuer had proved that the dealers from whom the purchases had been made had exercised reasonable care in checking the identity of the purchaser.

the intent not to pay for them is not different from the person who obtains property by issuing a "bad check." While the intent not to pay may be difficult to establish, it is possible to do so and has been done in those few jurisdictions where this rule obtains. In the absence of a special statutory enactment, it would be held that no crime is committed by obtaining goods or services under a valid credit card even though with intent not to pay when payment is due.

State Criminal Statutes

All states have enacted statutes which make the misuse, misappropriation or fraudulent use of a credit card a criminal offense. In some states, the statute also makes it a crime to obtain a credit card by misrepresentation.

Many of the statutes define the term "credit card." In Kansas the law governs "financial cards," and the Tennessee and Virginia statutes concern "debit cards," which include devices allowing the account of the cardholder with a bank or other person to be charged even though no credit is thereby extended. The Alabama and Kentucky statutes include debit cards as well as credit cards within their purview. The Georgia, Idaho, North Carolina, South Carolina, and Utah statutes use the term "financial transaction cards" which includes any instrument or device known as credit card, credit plate, bank service card, banking card, debit card or by any other name issued by the issuer for the use of the card holder in obtaining money, goods, services, etc. A typical definition of a credit card is contained in the Florida law, which provides that it is "any instrument or device, whether known as a credit card, credit plate or by any other name, issued with or without fee by an issuer for use of the cardholder in obtaining money, goods, services or anything else of value on credit." Fla. § 817.58(a) (1976) Other statutes merely refer to credit cards, credit numbers, or credit devices without definition of the terms.

Most states make it unlawful to use the credit card of another for the purpose of obtaining credit without the consent of the person to whom the card was issued. Knowing use of an expired or revoked credit card to obtain goods or services on credit where notice of the revocation has been given to the person to whom the card was issued is also prohibited; however, in some states the violation is restricted to knowing use with intent to defraud.

Where the statute provides that notice of revocation be given to the person to whom the card was issued, a provision is usually included that notice can be in person or by a writing sent by registered or certified mail in the United States mail addressed to such person at his last known address. The following states require notice of revocation in writing: Alabama, Arkansas, Colorado, Florida, Georgia, Hawaii, Idaho, Iowa, Indiana, Kansas, Kentucky, Louisiana, Maine, Nevada, New Jersey, Pennsylvania, Rhode Island, South Carolina, Tennessee, Wisconsin, Wyoming. In Alabama and California such notice can be either oral or written.

A few states provide that the presentation of an expired or revoked card is *prima facie* evidence of knowledge that the card is expired or revoked unless the purchaser within ten days after receipt of notice that the card has expired or been revoked at the time of the purchase, makes payment in full of the amount due on such purchase.[1] The notice of revocation or expiration in that case must also state the amount due on such purchase.

---

[1] Georgia requires payment within 30 days; Texas presumes that user had knowledge if he received notice.

Some states have included in their statutes relating to credit cards a prohibition against obtaining telephone, telegraph or other message service by fraudulent scheme, devise, means or method with intent to avoid payment of lawful charges for such services. Intent to avoid the payment of the charges is an element of the offense in such a situation, and apparently a credit card need not be involved.

In most states misuse by a consumer of a credit card is a misdemeanor. Kansas makes the violation a felony where the value of the service, purchase, credit or benefit procured is $50 or more; in Arizona, Kentucky, Michigan, Nevada, and Tennessee, it is $100 or more; in Idaho it is $150 or more; in Oregon and Virginia it is $200; in Utah it is $250 or more; in Delaware, Illinois, Maryland, Nebraska, New Mexico, and Ohio it is $300 or more; in California it is $400 or more; in Connecticut, Hawaii, New Hampshire, North Dakota, Pennsylvania, and Wisconsin it is $500 or more; while in Colorado and Wyoming it is $2,000 or more.

California provides that one who, with intent to defraud, either forges, materially alters or counterfeits a credit card is guilty of a felony. Indiana makes felonious the procurement of property of any value through fraudulent misuse of credit cards. The Texas statute also makes a third offense a felony regardless of the amount involved. Utah provides that improper use of a credit card to obtain goods or services for a value of $2,500 is a felony of the second degree.

The usual penalty provided by the statutes when the amount involved is under $50 is a fine of not more than $100 or 30 days' imprisonment, or both; when the amount is more than $50, a fine of not less than $100, or imprisonment for not more than one year, or both. Where the violation of the act is a felony, the penalty is, of course, more severe. In Virginia, for example, confinement in a penitentiary can be for as long as three years where the amount involved is $200, or more. The Florida law defines credit card forgery to include possession of a counterfeit credit card.

Many states have enacted statutes regulating frauds and misuses in connection with credit cards and providing penalties therefor. For example, in Colorado, it is a crime to purchase goods or services on credit under an assumed or fictitious name with an intent to cheat or defraud. The statute applies to the fraudulent use of credit cards as well as other means of illegally obtaining goods and services. In Utah, provisions dealing with fraudulent use of credit cards have been amended to include both forged and expired credit cards. In Virginia, the credit card law dealing with credit cards has been amended to encompass use of cards to obtain money, goods or services that debit the account of the cardholder with his bank even though no credit was actually extended.

Illinois has adopted a credit card act which regulates frauds and misuses in connection with the issuance of credit cards. The law details and sets out penalties for specified acts done with intent to make fraudulent use of a credit card. Among the violations regulated are the fraudulent use, sale, possession or transfer of any credit card without the knowledge or permission of the cardholder or issuer as well as the fraudulent use, sale, possession or transfer of forged, counterfeited, altered, revoked or expired credit cards.

Nevada law provides that any person who has in his possession or under his control two or more credit cards issued in the name or names of another person or persons is presumed to have obtained and to possess such credit cards with the knowledge that they have been stolen and with the intent to circulate, use, sell or transfer them with intent to defraud. Kentucky has a similar statute. The penalty for conviction of such a crime is imprisonment in the state prison for not less than one year nor more than six years.

Under the new Montana Criminal Code, it is a deceptive practice to obtain property, labor, or services by the unauthorized use of a credit card of another or by use of revoked, cancelled, forged, altered or expired credit card. In addition, persons convicted of defrauding secured creditors are subject to punishment; Texas also has adopted a similar statute.

North Carolina has a Financial Transaction Card Theft Statute which subjects to criminal penalties anyone who takes, keeps, or uses a credit card without the proper owner's consent or who retains possession with intent to use a card that he knows to be lost, mislaid, or delivered to him by mistake. Possession of a card not in the name of the possessor, or in the name of a family member of the possessor, is a *prima facie* evidence of theft.

Many credit card plans provide for payment of fixed interest in the event that such payments are not received within a specified period of time and the maximum amount of such interest is frequently determined by state statute.

New York has enacted at law which prohibits surcharges on holders of credit cards who elect to use a credit card in lieu of payment by cash or check. Violation of this provision is a misdemeanor.

Maryland has enacted the Credit Card Number Protection Act which is intended to prohibit the unauthorized use or disclosure of credit card and payment device numbers unless the use or disclosure is made to a particular person or agency for a specific permitted purpose. Violation of this law is a felony.

Federal Statutes

In addition to the possibilities of prosecution under the state statutes referred to above, the misuse of a credit card under certain circumstances may give rise to a prosecution under various federal criminal statutes. Section 1341 of title 18 of the United States Code, makes it a criminal offense to use the United States mails to defraud. 18 U.S.C. § 1341 (1976). It would appear that the statute is broad enough to cover the procurement of a credit card by misrepresentation in order to perpetrate a fraud, or to carry out a fraud through the use of a stolen or forged credit card, provided that the use of the mails was a significant step in the execution of the fraudulent scheme. When the postal service is only used by the defrauded merchant to secure payment, there has not been a violation of the mail fraud statute. It is necessary to constitute this offense that the mails be used as an instrumentality in perpetration of the fraud. Additionally, Section 2314 of Title 18 makes it a criminal offense to transport in interstate or foreign commerce stolen goods, securities, monies or articles used in counterfeiting. In part, this statute is applicable to one who:

> [W]ith unlawful or fraudulent intent, transports in interstate or foreign commerce any falsely made, forged, altered, or counterfeited securities or tax stamps, knowing the same to have been falsely made, forged, altered, or counterfeited; or
>
> . . . With unlawful or fraudulent intent, transports in interstate or foreign commerce, any tool, implement, or thing used or fitted to be used in falsely making, forging, altering, or counterfeiting any security, or tax stamps, or any part thereof.

18 U.S.C. § 2314 (1976).

In *Williams v. United States,* 192 F. Supp. 97 (S.D. Cal. 1961), the court upheld a conviction under the 18 U.S.C. § 2314. The defendant had obtained property through use of another's credit card and carried the charge slip, on which he had forged the name of the rightful owner of the credit card, from Vancouver, Washington, to Los Angeles, California. The Court determined that the credit card in and of itself is not a security within the section pertaining to the transportation of securities, but that the charge slip constituted a security within the meaning of the statute. A similar determination with regard to the charge slip was made in *United States v. Rhea,* 199 F. Supp. 301 (W.D. Ark. 1961). As opposed to *Williams,* however, the Court found the credit card was "a thing" embraced within Section 2314 and that the transportation of the credit card itself in interstate commerce with unlawful and fraudulent intent to use it in "falsely making, forging, altering or counterfeiting" was "evidence of indebtedness . . . or document or writing evidencing ownership of goods, wares, and merchandise or transferring or assigning of any right, title, or interest" therein, 18 U.S.C. § 2311 (1976), constitutes a violation of Section 2314.

However, other cases have held that neither a credit card nor a charge voucher is within the meaning of Section 2314. See *United States v. Fordyce,* 192 F. Supp. 93 (S.D. Cal. 1961), *Merrill v. United States,* 338 F.2d 763 (5th Cir. 1964).

The Federal Truth in Lending Law also imposes criminal liability for the wrongful use of credit cards. Section 1644 of Title 15 makes a felony the knowing misuse of a credit card to procure property or services which have a minimum aggregate value of $1,000 within one year. 15 U.S.C. § 1644 (1976). If the Government can prove unlawful or fraudulent intent, then the defendant can be convicted under this provision regardless of the value of the goods or services obtained. However, the transaction must be one which can be said to have affected interstate commerce. Upon conviction, the defendant could face maximum imprisonment of ten years, a fine of up to $10,000, or both.

The unsolicited issuance of credit cards is prohibited by 15 U.S.C. § 1642 (1976).

The Fair Credit Billing Act was enacted in 1974. 15 U.S.C. § 1601-1602, 1610, 1631-1632, 1666-1666j (1976 & Supp. V 1981). It seeks to protect consumers against inaccurate and unfair credit billing practices. The act requires a grantor of credit through credit cards or other types of charge accounts to respond to inquiries by a consumer that allege a billing error. A billing error is defined to be (1) a charge which the consumer alleges he did not incur, (2) an error in the amount of the charge or, (3) a charge for which additional clarification is required, (4) a charge for goods for which the consumer refused to accept delivery of goods or services that were not delivered in accordance with the agreement or, (5) one in which the creditor did not properly post a credit or payment or, (6) some other type of error. The consumer has to notify the creditor, specifying the error, within 60 days of the date of the bill. The creditor is required to take corrective action within two complete billing cycles, but not later than 90 days, after receipt of the consumer's notice, and unless corrective action is made within 30 days after receipt of the notice. Id. § 1666. Notification of a resolution of a billing error may be made on a periodic statement if the statement is mailed promptly after the error is resolved. While a creditor is verifying the alleged billing error, the creditor may not make any adverse credit report on the consumer. Id. § 1666a. If the creditor fails to comply with the statute, it forfeits the right to collect the lesser of the amount in dispute or $50. Id. § 1666.

The Act also confers upon consumers rights against third-party card issuers which the consumer would have against the person who honored the card provided (1) the consumer has made a good faith effort to resolve the problem with the person who honored the card, (2) the amount of the transaction is over $50 and the transaction was local in nature, which is defined as to be within the same state as the cardholder's home address or within a hundred miles of that address. Id. § 1666i.

The Act further provides that a creditor must mail a bill at least 14 days prior to the date payment is due, Id. § 1666b, and promptly post payments by consumers to their accounts. Id. § 1666c.

A number of states have adopted similar statutes.

Antitrust and Trade Regulation Laws

Distasteful as the antitrust laws are to most businessmen, it is, nevertheless, largely due to their existence and enforcement that the American system of private enterprise has been so successful. Without these restraints our economic system might indeed have become one of "monopoly capitalism."

It was because of the growth of vast so-called "trusts" and the resulting concentration of economic powers that Congress enacted the Sherman Act, which became law on July 2, 1890. Congress extended federal control and regulation of business by enactment of the following additional legislation: the Clayton Act, which became law on October 15, 1914; the Robinson-Patman Act, enacted as an amendment to the Clayton Act in 1936; and the Federal Trade Commission Act, which became law on September 26, 1914.

The power of Congress to regulate trade or business practices through the antitrust and trade regulation laws is derived from its constitutional power to regulate interstate and foreign trade and commerce. Therefore, all acts which are in violation of the antitrust laws must involve, relate to, or affect interstate commerce.

The Sherman Act

The Sherman Antitrust Act, 15 U.S.C. §§ 1-7 (1976), prohibits contracts, combinations and conspiracies in restraint of trade in interstate commerce, and declares that any person who monopolizes or attempts to monopolize, or who combines with another or others to monopolize trade or commerce, shall be guilty of a felony, punishable by a maximum $100,000 fine or $1,000,000 fine for corporate defendants and/or imprisonment for three years.

To constitute an offense under the Sherman Act, there must be a contract, combination or conspiracy between two or more persons or companies which has the effect of restraining or monopolizing trade or commerce among the several states or with foreign nations. The district courts of the United States are vested with jurisdiction to restrain violations of the Act. In addition to the criminal penalties provided by the Act, any property owned under any contract, or by any combination, or pursuant to any conspiracy, which is in the course of transportation from one state to another, or to a foreign country, may be declared forfeited to the United States, and may be seized and condemned.

To constitute an offense under the Sherman Act, it is not necessary that the offending person or corporation be actually engaged in interstate commerce; it is sufficient that the practice complained of *involves* interstate commerce. However, in the absence of any purpose to create or maintain a monopoly, a trader or manufacturer may freely choose the parties with whom he will deal. In *United States v. Colgate & Co.*, 250 U.S. 300 (1919), the Supreme Court held:

The purpose of the Sherman Act is to prohibit monopolies, contracts, and combinations which probably would unduly interfere with the free exercise of their rights by those engaged, or who wish to engage, in trade and commerce—in a word, to preserve the right of freedom to trade. In the absence of any purpose to create or maintain a monopoly, the act does not restrict the long-recognized right of trader or manufacturer engaged in an entirely private business, freely to exercise his own independent discretion as to parties with whom he will deal. And, of course, he may announce in advance the circumstances under which he will refuse to sell. (p. 13-19)

A trader does not violate the Sherman Antitrust Act by refusing to sell to others, and he may withhold his goods from those who will not sell them at the prices which he fixes for their resale. But he may not, consistent with the Act, go beyond the exercise of this right and by contracts or combinations, express or implied, unduly hinder or obstruct the free and natural flow of commerce in the channels of interstate trade. So, in the absence of an agreement sanctioned by the so-called "Fair Trade Acts," see *infra* p. 13-15, an agreement may not be made which undertakes to obligate vendees to observe specified resale prices, and any system of policing purchasers to see that they maintain suggested resale prices may constitute a violation of the Sherman Act or Federal Trade Commission Act. See *infra* p. 13-12.

It was originally held in some cases that any restraint of commerce, whether reasonable or unreasonable, was prohibited, but in 1911, in the case of *Standard Oil Co. v. United States,* 221 U.S. 1 (1911), the Supreme Court held that only unreasonable restraints of trade or commerce are within the prohibition of the statute. Although this decision had been followed for a number of years, the Court, in *United States v. Socony-Vacuum Oil Co.,* 310 U.S. 150 (1940), modified this rule of reason to the extent of characterizing certain activities as illegal *per se* whether reasonable or unreasonable, provided that such activities operate to the prejudice of the public interest. In that case, price fixing was deemed to be illegal *per se* and no justification or reason would excuse such activity. Where a price fixing agreement, or an agreement that causes a stabilization of prices through a stifling of competitive forces, is shown to exist the court need not inquire into the reasonableness of the agreement. An agreement to fix minimum, as well as maximum, prices is a *per se* violation. *Kiefer-Stewart Co. v. Seagram & Sons, Inc.,* 340 U.S. 211 (1951). Other actions which are deemed to be illegal *per se* are division of markets, group boycotts and tying arrangements.

The Court in *United States* v. *Topco Associates,* 405 U.S. 596 (1972), held that it was a *per se* violation of the Sherman Act for a cooperative association of small and medium-sized regional supermarket chains to allocate territories for private label products distributed by the Association among the chain members. The Court characterized this behavior as a "horizontal" conspiracy which— although it allowed the smaller chains to compete more effectively against the larger chains—had the deleterious effect of stifling competition among the smaller stores.

In 1967, the Supreme Court announced in *United States v. Arnold, Schwinn & Co.,* 388 U.S. 365 (1967), that vertical resale restrictions are absolutely barred as being *per se* illegal. However, this case was overruled by *Continental*

T.V., Inc. v. *GTE Sylvania Inc.,* 433 U.S. 36 (1977) and vertical restrictions are now to be judged by the "rule of reason" that governed these restrictions prior to *Schwinn,* rather than by the *per se* rule.

Credit executives' most frequent contacts with the restrictions of the Sherman Act are in connection with Credit Group activities. Readers are referred to the discussion, later in this chapter, headed "Antitrust Laws and the Exchange of Credit Information." See *infra* p. 13-16.

The Sherman Act creates both civil rights for damages against antitrust violators as well as criminal sanctions for violations of the Act. Until 1978 no significant distinction had been judicially drawn between the elements necessary to establish a criminal and a civil violation of the Sherman Act. Such a distinction, however, was made by the U.S. Supreme Court in *United States* v. *United States Gypsum Co.,* 438 U.S. 422 (1978).

In *Gypsum,* the Supreme Court was confronted with a criminal proceeding, brought under Section 1 of the Sherman Act, against defendants, leading members of the gypsum board industry, who it was alleged had violated the Sherman Act by engaging in interseller price verification. The defendants interposed a defense under Section 2(b) of the Robinson-Patman Act that such activity was lawful as a good faith effort to verify prices of a competitor before attempting to meet such prices.

The District Court had instructed the jury that if the exchange of price information had the effect of raising, fixing, maintaining or stabilizing the price of gypsum board, then the parties are presumed, *as a matter of law* to have intended that result. The Supreme Court rejected the legal presumption approach and held that a defendant's state of mind or intent is an essential element of a criminal antitrust case which *must* be established by evidence and inferences drawn therefrom; such criminal intent cannot be based upon a legal presumption of wrongful intent from proof of an effect on prices. See *infra* p. 13-9 for a further discussion of *Gypsum.*

Since the Sherman Act is addressed to "conspiracies" in restraint of trade, it is often ineffective in combating such anti-competitive practices as price leadership, where contact between parties is minimal and therefore evidence of conspiracy is difficult to obtain. A solution to this problem was developed by the courts by use of the theory of "conscious parallelism." The leading case to make use of this theory was *Interstate Circuit, Inc.* v. *United States,* 306 U.S. 208 (1939). In *Interstate* a movie exhibitor which controlled first-run movie theaters in six southern cities wrote letters to eight branch managers of major film distributors demanding that they distribute second-run films only to theaters in those cities charging at least $.25 or they would lose the exhibitor's first-run business. There was no evidence that the branch managers of the film distributors ever met or conspired together, but in fact all the distributors changed their policies towards second-run movie theaters in accordance with Interstate's request. The Supreme Court declared that in order to establish an agreement, the government is compelled to rely on inferences drawn from the course of conduct of the alleged conspirators. The Court felt that a mere coincidence could not explain how such a severe departure from standard business practice could be simultaneously undertaken by eight distributors. Noting that each letter from Interstate had the names of all eight distributors on its title, that the plan required uniformity of action, and that the action of the distributors was unanimous, the Court declared that there was a conspiracy and a Sherman Act violation because, knowing that concerted action had been invited, the distributors gave their adherence to and participated in the scheme. The three major elements of the doctrine of "conscious parallelism" according to *Interstate Circuit* are: shared knowledge of a proposed plan, a motive for concerted action, and substantial unanimity of action. Actual agreement is not necessary. Subsequent Supreme Court cases have clarified and narrowed the use of the theory of "conscious parallelism." In *Theater Enterprises v. Paramount Distributors Corp.,* 346 U.S. 537 (1954), the Court noted that "this Court has never held that proof of parallel business behavior conclusively establishes agreement or, phrased differently, that such behavior itself constitutes a Sherman Act offense. . . . '[C]onscious parellism' has not yet read conspiracy out of the Sherman Act entirely." Id. at 541.

Of particular concern to credit executives is the Supreme Court decision in *Catalano, Inc. v. Target Sales, Inc.,* 446 U.S. 643 (1980), which held that agreements between competitors to fix credit terms are *per se* violations of the Sherman Act.

The Clayton Act

The Clayton Act, 15 U.S.C. §§ 12, 13, 14-19, 20, 21, 22-27 (1976), was designed to correct defects which had appeared in the Sherman Act, as well as to supplement the Sherman Act by conferring upon certain administrative agencies power to stop violations of the law in their incipience and before a threatened conspiracy has ripened into actuality.

The Clayton Act declares unlawful the following acts where the effect is to substantially lessen competition or to tend to create a monopoly:

(a) Leases and sales on condition that the lessee or purchaser shall not use or deal in the commodities of a competitor of the lessor or seller (tie-in sales, exclusive dealing arrangements, and requirements contracts);
(b) Acquisitions of stock of other corporations;
(c) Interlocking directorates.

A person injured in his business or property as the result of a violation of the Clayton Act may recover treble damages in a civil action. The Supreme Court in *Illinois Brick Co. v. Illinois,* 431 U.S. 720 (1977), interpreted Section 4 of the Clayton Act to allow only those customers who buy directly from proven price fixers to maintain an action for treble damages. The Court found that the purpose of the law was better served by holding direct purchasers to be injured to the full extent of the overcharge paid by them, and thus allowing them to recover treble damages, than by attempting to apportion the overcharge among all those that may have indirectly absorbed a part of it.

Violations of the Act may be enjoined either by the government or by private individuals if loss or damage by reason thereof results or is threatened. The Act vests jurisdiction in the Interstate Commerce Commission to enforce its prohibitions in the case of common carriers, the Federal Communications Commission in the case of common carriers engaged in wire or radio communication or radio transmission of energy, the Federal Reserve Board in the case of banks, and the Federal Trade Commission in all other cases. Such administrative boards or commissions, upon finding a violation or threatened violation, and after hearings on notice to the defendants, may issue an order to cease and desist from the

ANTITRUST AND TRADE REGULATION LAWS 13-5

act complained of, and such order may be enforced by decree of a United States circuit court of appeals.

Labor organizations, agricultural associations and certain nonprofit organizations are exempt from the Act's provisions.

In 1955 the Clayton Act was amended to add new subdivisions 4(a) and 4(b). 15 U.S.C. §§ 15a, 15b. Subdivision (a) gives to the United States a right of action for actual damages sustained by reason of any violation of any antitrust law, and subdivision (b) imposes a four-year statute of limitations on actions by private persons or by the United States to recover damages under the Act.

The Robinson-Patman Act

The Robinson-Patman Act, 15 U.S.C. §§ 13-13b, 21a (1976), (which was enacted as an amendment to the Clayton Act) provides in substance that it shall be unlawful for any person engaged in commerce, or in the course of such commerce, either directly or indirectly, to discriminate in price between different purchasers of commodities [1] of like grade and quality when (a) either or any of the purchasers involved in such discrimination are engaged in interstate commerce, and where the commodities are sold for use, consumption or resale within the United States or any other place within the jurisdiction of the United States, and (b) where the effect of such discrimination may be substantially to lessen competition or tend to create a monopoly in any line of commerce, or to injure, destroy, or prevent competition with any person who either grants or knowingly receives the benefit of such discrimination or with customers of either of them.

Unlike the Sherman Act, the Robinson-Patman Act is designed to afford protection against acts of *individual* competitors, with a view to prevent discriminatory practices injuriously affecting free competitive enterprise, to preserve competition generally, and to protect small businesses against their larger competitors.

The Act is in four sections or subsections as follows: Section 2(a) is an amendment and extension of the prohibitions formerly contained in Section 2 of the Clayton Act prohibiting direct and indirect discrimination in price having the proscribed adverse effect on competition. The section is qualified by two provisos: (1) excepting price differentials which make due allowances for differences in cost of manufacture, sale or delivery resulting from the differing methods or quantities in which the commodities are sold or delivered, and (2) permitting the Federal Trade Commission, after investigation and hearing, to fix and establish quantity limits as to particular classes of commodities where it finds that available purchasers in greater quantities are so few as to render differentials on account thereof unjustly discriminatory or promotive of a monopoly in any line of commerce. The section contains further provisos preserving the right of persons engaged in selling goods, wares, or merchandise in commerce to select their own customers in *bona fide* transactions and not in restraint of trade, and the right to effect price changes from time to time where in response

---

[1] The term "commodities" has been consistently interpreted by the courts as encompassing only tangible products. *See, e.g., Freeman v. Chicago Title & Trust Co.*, 505 F.2d 527 (7th Cir. 1974). However, the Federal Trade Commission took the position that newspaper advertising space is a "commodity" within the meaning of the Act without involving itself in a metaphysical discussion of the tangible or intangible properties of the product concerned. *See The Times-Mirror Co.* [1976-1979 Transfer Binder] Trade Reg. Rep. (CCH) ¶ 21, 448(1978).

to changing conditions affecting the market for, or the marketability of, the goods concerned, such as actual or imminent deterioration of perishable goods, obsolescence of seasonable goods, distress sales, or sales in good faith in discontinuance of business in the goods concerned.

Subdivision (b) of Section 2 provides that upon proof that there has been discrimination in price or services or facilities furnished, the burden of rebuttal by showing justification shall be upon the person charged with the violation, provided, however, that nothing shall prevent a seller from rebutting the *prima facie* case by showing that his lower price for the furnishing of services or facilities to any purchaser or purchasers was made in good faith to meet an equally low price by a competitor.

Subdivision (c) makes the following unlawful: Paying, granting, receiving or accepting a commission, brokerage or other compensation, or an allowance of a discount in lieu thereof, except for services rendered in connection with the sale or purchase of goods, wares or merchandise, either to the other party to such transaction or to an intermediary acting on his behalf.

Subdivision (d) prohibits payments or other transfers of benefit to a customer as compensation for any consideration of services or facilities furnished by or through such customer in connection with the processing, handling, sale or offering for sale, of any products or commodities manufactured, sold or offered for sale by such person, unless such payment or consideration is available on proportionally equal terms to all competing customers.

Subdivision (e) prohibits discrimination in favor of one purchaser as against another of a commodity bought for resale by contracting to furnish, or furnishing, any services or facilities not accorded to all purchasers on proportionally equal terms.

Subdivision (f) provides that it shall be unlawful for any person engaged in commerce, in the course of such commerce, knowingly to induce or receive a discrimination in price which is prohibited by the Act.

The provisions of Section 2 of the Clayton Act, as amended by the Robinson-Patman Act, are enforceable, as are violations of other provisions of the Clayton Act, in the following manner:

1. By a proceeding before the Federal Trade Commission resulting, if a violation is proved, in the issuance of an order to cease and desist. Such order may be enforced by decree of the United States court of appeals, which decree in turn is enforceable by proceedings as for a contempt of court.

2. By an action for an injunction either by the federal government or by a private person in the United States district court.

3. By a suit for treble damages by any person injured in his business or property by reason of a violation of the section.

Section 3 of the Act declares it unlawful for any person engaged in commerce, in the course of such commerce, to be a party to, or assist in, any transaction or sale or contract to sell which discriminates, to his knowledge, against competitors of the purchaser in that any discount, rebate, allowance, or advertising service charge is granted to a purchaser over and above those which are at the same time available to competitors of the buyer with respect to goods of like grade, quality and quantity, to sell or contract to sell goods in any part of the United States at prices lower than those charged by the seller elsewhere in the United States with the purpose of destroying competition or eliminating a competitor, or to sell or contract to sell goods at unreasonably low prices for the purpose of destroying competition or eliminating a competitor. Violation of this section is a criminal offense subject to a fine of $5,000 or imprisonment for not more than one year, or both.

It is to be noted that to constitute a discrimination in price, within the meaning of the Robinson-Patman Act, there must be actual sales at different prices to at least two different purchasers, and that a prohibited price discrimination must be as between purchasers of commodities of *like grade and quality,* and the effect of the discrimination must be to lessen competition or tend to create a monopoly in any line of commerce, or to injure, destroy, or prevent competition with any person who either grants or knowingly receives the benefits of such discrimination or with customers of either of them. These prohibitions, which were never before included in the antitrust statutes, reach discriminatory practices resulting in injuries to a *single individual, as well as to competition generally.* Proof that there is a *reasonable probability* that the effect of a prohibited discrimination will be to substantially lessen competition, or tend to create a monopoly, is not necessary; rather, the test is whether there is a *"reasonable possibility"* of injury to competition.

It is common for sellers to establish price differentials based upon the *distributional function* of the purchasers. Thus, there is usually one price to customers engaged in manufacturing or processing, a different price to wholesalers, another to retailers, and another to consumers. These are known as *"functional discounts,"* which are neither prohibited nor expressly permitted by the statute, and are, therefore, subject to the same tests as any other price difference in determining whether they amount to unlawful discrimination. If injury to competition results, the fact that the differential was made in good faith on functional grounds is no defense.

Where a purchaser is engaged in business both as a wholesaler and as a retailer and he receives a wholesale price differential, he obviously has a competitive advantage when selling at retail. Therefore, a supplier selling to this type of customer must keep informed as to the true nature and scope of his customer's business activities, or he may run afoul of the Robinson-Patman Act.

One means of protection in any such case is to bill all goods at the retailer price subject to rebate upon satisfactory proof that the goods were actually resold at wholesale. Functional differentials, if based upon a *bona fide* classification of customers at noncompetitive levels, will not result in unlawful discrimination unless used by recipients of the lower price to create competitive advantage at a lower level of competition, either for themselves or for their customers.

As noted in the foregoing, Section 2 (b) of the Act provides that it shall be a defense to an alleged violation of the Act to show that a lower price granted to a customer was made in good faith to meet an equally low price of a competitor. This provision has been the subject of directly opposite opinions by the United States Courts of Appeals for the Second and the Seventh Circuits.

The issue in both cases was whether such defense is limited to cases where the discrimination in price was made in self-defense against competitive price attacks upon the seller's *existing customers,* or whether the defense may also be asserted to meet competitive prices offered to *new customers.*

Thus, in *Standard Motor Products, Inc. v. FTC,* 265 F.2d 674 (2d Cir. 1959), the Second Circuit held that the defense is available only when used defensively to hold customers rather than to gain new ones. The Court cited as its authority *Standard Oil Co. v. FTC,* 340 U.S. 231 (1951).

In Standard Oil the Supreme Court stated that the core of the Section 2 (b) defense "consists of the provision that wherever a lawful lower price of a competitor threatens to deprive a seller of a customer, the seller, to retain that customer, may in good faith meet that lower price." Id. at 242.

On the other hand, in *Sunshine Biscuits, Inc. v. FTC,* 306 F.2d 48 (7th Cir. 1962), the Seventh Circuit, disagreeing with both the Federal Trade Commission and the Court of Appeals for the Second Circuit, said with respect to the *Standard Oil* case: "As we read the opinion, the issue was whether 'it is a complete defense to a charge of price discrimination for the seller to show that its price differential has been made in good faith to meet a lawful and equally low price of a competitor.' " Id. at 51.

The Court continued: "Since the Standard Oil Company had made the lower price in question only to retain its customers and had not acquired new customers thereby, the question presented in the instant case was not before the Supreme Court." Id.

The Seventh Circuit, therefore, found that the *Standard Oil* case was not persuasive authority for the Second Circuit Court's decision.

Furthermore, the court held that the language of the statute "is clear and unambiguous. The plain meaning of the term 'purchaser' is one who buys, and no connotation of the term is justified that would limit its meaning to those purchasers who had been customers of the seller before his lowering of prices to meet those of a competitor." Id.

The court further pointed out that the distinction made by the Commission and the Second Circuit Court between allowable and unallowable price differentials is unworkable as a practicality and is economically unsound; the distinction between old and new customers would defeat the purposes of the Robinson-Patman Act. The court said:

> If, in situations where the Section 2 (b) proviso is applicable, sellers could grant good faith competitive price reductions only to old customers in order to retain them, competition for new customers would be stifled and monopoly would be fostered. In such situations an established seller would have the monopoly of *his* customers and the seller entering the market would not be permitted to reduce his prices to compete with his established rivals unless he could do so on a basis such as cost justification. Moreover, the distinction would create a forced price discrimination between a seller's existing customers to whom he had lawfully lowered his prices under Section 2 (b) and a prospective new customer.

Id. at 52.

The reasoning of the Seventh Circuit was followed in *Hanson v. Pittsburgh Glass Industries Inc.,* 482 F.2d 220 (5th Cir. 1973) and *Cadigan v. Texaco,* 492 F.2d 383 (9th Cir. 1974).

These conflicting opinions confronted the Federal Trade Commission with the necessity of determining whether or not it would seek a review of the decision of the Seventh Circuit Court. It decided not to, but pointed out that its decision in this respect was not to be construed as an abandonment of its position as sustained by the Second Circuit Court.

Not all price discriminations may be protected under the guise of an effort to meet a competitor's price. In order to invoke the Section 2(b) exemption of the Robinson-Patman Act, the businessman must establish that his effort was made in good faith.

It was thought by many courts that interseller price verification (i.e., the practice of communicating with a competitor to verify the price at which merchandise is sold to a customer) was often a useful if not necessary means of corroborating otherwise unreliable information concerning competitors' prices. Based upon this premise, federal courts have held that exchanges of price information when made part of a good faith effort to comply with Section 2(b) of the Robinson-Patman Act were "controlling circumstances" insulating the exchanges from a violation of the Sherman Act. *See, e.g., Belliston v. Texaco,* 455 F.2d 175, 182 (10th Cir. 1972); *Wall Products Co., v. National Gypsum Co.,* 326 F.Supp. 295, 312-15 (N.D. Cal. 1971).

The reasoning of these cases has been rejected by the United States Supreme Court in *United States* v. *United States Gypsum Co.,* 438 U.S. 422 (1978).

The thesis of the *Gypsum* majority is that interseller price verification is neither necessary nor desirable to establish the success of a Robinson-Patman, Section 2(b), defense. The Court doubted the need or the efficacy of interseller verification and recognized the tendency for price discussions between competitors to contribute to the stability of prices and growth of anti-competitive activity. It therefore refused to recognize even a limited "controlling circumstance" exception for interseller verification which it held subject to "close scrutiny" under the Sherman Act. See *supra* p. 13-6 for a further discussion of *Gypsum.*

Therefore, sellers who desire to avail themselves of the Section 2(b) defense under the Robinson-Patman Act are advised to use means of verifying or corroborating the alleged lower prices of competitors other than direct contact with competitors.

All that the Robinson-Patman Act requires is a good faith belief rather than an absolute certainty that a price concession is being offered to meet an equally low price offered by a competitor. Although casual reliance on uncorroborated reports of buyers or sales representatives without further investigation may not be sufficient to make the requisite showing of good faith, a direct discussion of prices between competitors is likely to be deemed illegal.

The defenses available to a seller charged with violation of Section 2(a) of the Act are based upon the theory that while a seller may not use discrimination in price to grant an unearned competitive advantage as between his customers; nevertheless, if a purchaser, by virtue of the method or quantities in which he buys, creates savings to the seller in the cost of the goods sold, the seller may reflect such savings in the prices which he charges.

A seller has the option to either pass along the cost savings so arising to the purchaser responsible for them, or he may sell to all customers at the same price.

It is to be noted, however, that not all differences in a seller's cost of manufacture, sale or delivery in selling goods of like grade and quality to different purchasers may be used to justify a discrimination in price, but cost savings may be reflected in prices *only to the extent that they result from differing methods or quantities of sale or delivery.* Thus differences in manufacturing costs resulting from seasonal fluctuations in costs of raw materials, or from varying labor costs, would not in themselves justify the sale of the lower cost goods at a lower price, because such differences in cost do not result from differing methods or quantities of sale or delivery. Nor does the fact that large orders from a single customer may reduce the seller's unit cost of production *of all goods sold* permit a differential in favor of a large purchaser, except to the extent that additional savings may result from such purchaser's method of buying or result in reduced costs of shipment attributable to him alone.

Thus some purchasers order during rush periods and demand immediate delivery while others place their orders well in advance, thereby permitting the manufacturer to produce the goods during off seasons, and resulting cost savings may be treated as resulting from different methods of purchase and may be reflected in the prices charged.

Differences in costs of sale and delivery also result where one customer's order calls for periodic deliveries over a long period of time while another customer places a number of small orders requiring more frequent calls by salesmen. Again, one customer may buy from traveling salesmen, while other customers buy across the counter, and others by mail.

Differences in *cost of production* are infrequent as between separate customers or classes of customers served, because goods and commodities of like grade and quality are usually manufactured to stock and orders are filled from stock. It is, therefore, in the manner of distribution and delivery that cost differences are most likely to arise.

Advertising costs do not justify price differences between purchasers of the goods advertised, since each sale presumably is benefited equally.

The cost proviso of Section 2(a) does not by its terms permit differences in transportation costs resulting from delivey at different points to be used as justification of price differences. Such cost differences do not result from differing methods or quantity of deliveries. However, the omission from the statute appears to have been inadvertent and the Federal Trade Commission treats such differences as differences in cost of delivery which may be reflected in prices charged.

Other types of delivery-cost differences which may be reflected by different prices are as follows:

(a) Differences in costs of packing or crating due to shipping in different quantities or meeting the special requirements of particular customers.

(b) Differences in cost of shipment by different methods or carriers due to the different locations of purchasers, different quantities shipped, or different specifications in terms of sale as to time or method of delivery.

(c) Differences in cost of delivery as between purchasers, packing, multiple store-delivery, and those taking single warehouse delivery resulting in savings in trucking and other delivery costs.

In two related decisions *Corn Products Refining Co. v. FTC,* 324 U.S. 726 (1945), and *FTC v. A. E. Staley Mfg. Co.,* 324 U.S. 746 (1945), the Supreme Court had occasion to pass upon the legality of a system of pricing whereby the seller adopted an arbitrary basing point in Chicago and sold only at delivered prices computed by adding to a base price at Chicago the published freight tariff to point of delivery even though deliveries were made from factories both at Kansas City and Chicago. The effect was that where shipments were made from Kansas City there was included in the delivered price an amount of "phantom freight" which usually did not correspond to the actual freight. It was contended by the Federal Trade Commission that the basing point system resulted in discrimination in prices between different purchasers which were not measured by differences in the cost of manufacture, sale or delivery resulting

ANTITRUST AND TRADE REGULATION LAWS

from the differing methods or quantities in which the commodities were sold and delivered.

The Supreme Court found that purchasers in all places other than Chicago paid a higher price than did Chicago purchasers; in the case of all shipments from Kansas City to purchasers in cities having a lower freight rate from Kansas City than from Chicago, the delivered price included unearned freight to the extent of the difference in freight rates and, conversely, when the freight from Kansas City to the point of delivery was more than from Chicago, the sellers absorbed freight from shipments from Kansas City to the extent of the differences in freight.

The Court found that the systematic inclusion of the freight differential in computing the delivered price resulted in systematic discrimination, and that this was so even though the purchasers were in different parts of the United States, since the prohibition against price discrimination extends to all competing purchasers. *Corn Products Refining Co.*

Similarly in the *Staley* case, the Court struck down the use of basing point for determining delivered prices. It was contended, however, that the discriminations were made in good faith to meet equally low prices of competitors and that the sellers were thus within the exception contained in Section 2(b) of the Act in adopting and following the basing point prices of their competitors.

The Court rejected this argument and held that it is no defense that a person charged with unlawful discrimination was merely meeting another's low price, where the latter was itself unlawful.

The Court pointed out, however, that "it does not follow that respondents may never absorb freight when their factory price plus actual freight is higher than their competitors' price, or that sellers, by doing, may not maintain a uniform delivered price at all points of delivery, for in that event there is no discrimination in price." 324 U.S. at 757.

Another case, *FTC v. Cement Institute*, 333 U.S. 683 (1948), involved the question of the legality of the use of a multiple basing point delivered price system. Cement manufacturers sold cement at uniform delivered prices at various basing points throughout the United States, such basing points in many cases being distant from the place where the cement was actually manufactured.

The Federal Trade Commission contended that the varying "mill nets" thus received by the respondents on sales to customers in different localities constituted illegal price discrimination within the meaning of the Robinson-Patman Act. This position was sustained by the Supreme Court, which pointed out that the Robinson-Patman Act permits a single company to sell to one customer at a lower price than it sells to another only if the price is made in good faith to meet an equally low price of a competitor, i.e., as a good faith effort to meet individual competitive situations, but that a seller may not use a sales system which constantly results in his getting more money for like goods from some customers than he does from others. Thus, where the country is divided into zones and uniform prices are charged within each zone, discrimination within the meaning of the Robinson-Patman Act, as construed in *Cement Institute* is almost certain to exist.

Quantity discounts are a violation of the Act if they result in injury to competition, unless the discounts can be wholly justified by cost differences, and the differences must be supported by proof. They must be available to all customers and should be granted only when the buyer purchases a required amount.

Sellers can rarely justify cumulative or volume discounts granted on the basis of a customer's total purchases over a period of time because the difference in the unit cost of serving different customers depends upon the average cost of single purchases and single deliveries, not upon the quantities purchased over a given period. Where, for example, a chain store qualifies for a quantity discount on the basis of total purchases but requires deliveries to its individual stores, there may be no provable cost savings as against independent stores who purchase in quantities as large as the chain store does.

The question is sometimes asked whether or not it is an unlawful discrimination under the Robinson-Patman Act to deny credit to certain customers while granting credit to others. The answer seems clearly to be that if a seller applies substantially uniform criteria in determining whether a customer is worthy of credit, there will be no unlawful discrimination.

A price change made in the regular course of business must apply at the same time to all competing purchasers and *customers must be given an equal opportunity* to place orders in advance for future delivery at the old and lower price.

The Federal Trade Commission Act

In addition to the Sherman Act, the Clayton Act, and the specific provisions of the Robinson-Patman Act affecting price discrimination, there is another antitrust law which is all-inclusive, namely, the Federal Trade Commission Act. 15 U.S.C. §§ 41-77. This statute declares unlawful unfair methods of competition and unfair or deceptive acts or practices in commerce. Its prohibitions include false advertising of foods, drugs, devices and cosmetics, and any other practice which is designed to deceive the public.

The FTC Act is the broadest of all of the antitrust and trade regulation laws. Any practice which constitutes a violation of the Sherman Act, the Clayton Act, or the Robinson-Patman Act, or even if it falls short of a violation of such laws but is related to the type of practice which they prohibit, may constitute an unfair method of competition in violation of the Federal Trade Commission Act.

The FTC Act also applies to practices which are outside the express prohibitions of the Sherman Act, the Clayton Act, and the Robinson-Patman Act, such as false representations, disparagement of competitors or their products, and various other unfair competitive tactics. The Federal Trade Commission has exclusive authority to enforce the FTC Act; private individuals cannot sue to enjoin violations of the FTC Act, or seek damages for such violations.

With respect to the prohibition of "unfair methods of competition" the Supreme Court has said that these words "are clearly inapplicable to practices never heretofore regarded as opposed to good morals because characterized by deception, bad faith, fraud or oppression, or as against public policy because of their dangerous tendency unduly to hinder competition or create monopoly. The act was certainly not intended to fetter free and fair competition as commonly understood and practiced by honorable opponents in trade." *FTC v. Gratz,* 253 U.S. 421, 427-28 (1920).

The Commission is called upon first to determine, as a necessary prerequisite to the issuance of a complaint charging the use of an unfair method of competition, whether there is reason to believe that a given person, partnership or corporation has been, or is, using such unfair method of competition, and, that being determined in the affirmative, the Commission still may not proceed unless it further appears that the proceeding would be in the interest of the public and that such interest is specific and substantial.

The Supreme Court has said,

> In a case arising under the Trade Commission Act, the fundamental questions are, whether the methods complained of are 'unfair,' and whether, as in cases under the Sherman Act, they tend to the substantial injury of the public by restricting competition in interstate trade and 'the common liberty to engage therein.' The paramount aim of the Act is the protection of the public from the evils likely to result from the destruction of competition or the restriction of it in a substantial degree, and this presupposes the existence of some substantial competition to be affected, since the public is not concerned in the maintenance of competition which itself is without real substance.

FTC v. Raladam Co., 283 U.S. 643, 647-48 (1931).

In addition to restraining incipient combinations or conspiracies in restraint of trade, the Commission, under its mandate to prevent unfair and deceptive acts or practices in commerce, has authority to inquire into such matters as false advertising, deceptive brands, and similar other matters, and the great majority of the cases coming before the Commission involve practices of this type.

Antitrust Procedures and Penalties Act

In 1974, the Antitrust Procedures and Penalties Act was adopted. It was codified in 1976. 15 U.S.C. §§ 1-13, 16, 28, 29, 47 U.S.C. § 401 (1976), 49 U.S.C. § 43 (repealed 1978). The Act increased penalties for violation of the Sherman Act, changed consent decree procedures and revised the provisions for appellate review of antitrust cases.

Since approximately 80% of antitrust complaints filed by the United States are settled by consent decree, the Act seeks to reform this procedure. The Act requires that the Justice Department file a "competitive impact statement" concerning the proposed settlement and provide the public with an opportunity to comment on its own. The statute also enables district court judges to determine as a matter of law whether a proposed consent judgment is in the public interest. The Act requires disclosure by the settling defendant of any lobbying with government officials concerning the terms of the consent decree. Previously, judges were required to accept proposed consent decrees.

Neither the judicial determination of public interest nor the statement of competitive impact that the Justice Department must file in consent decrees as required by this statute may be used as evidence against defendants in private antitrust litigation.

The law also raises the maximum fine for violation of the Sherman Act from $50,000 for individuals and corporations to $500,000 for individuals and noncorporate businesses and to $1,000,000 for corporations. A number of technical amendments are also made with respect to appellate procedure in public civil antitrust cases.

The penalties for violation of antitrust laws are severe, including fine, imprisonment, and liability for triple damages. The conviction and imprisonment of officers of some of our largest electrical manufacturing concerns for violation of the price-fixing provisions of the Sherman Act should serve as a warning to businessmen that these laws are not to be taken lightly.

1976 Antitrust Act

The Act has three main sections: (1) It grants the federal government new disclosure powers in antitrust litigation, (2) It requires companies of a certain size to file pre-merger notices, (3) It permits a state Attorney General to sue for damages on behalf of the state's citizens. Under the Act State Attorneys General are given the right to appoint private attorneys to bring suits on the state's behalf. The legal fees for such suits must be approved by the court as reasonable. The Act permits Attorneys General in *parens patriae* suits to establish damages not based on individual claims but based on general economic statistics.

Antitrust Laws and Foreign Activities

The application of U.S. antitrust laws to foreign activities raises some difficult questions about which activities are within the laws' sanctions. Normally, the acts of a U.S. citizen are governed by the law of the country where they take place. The antitrust laws are, however, not limited in application to those transactions that take place within the United States—they can also be applied to foreign acts. Basically, the entry into a foreign market by a U.S. corporation subjects the enterprise to dual antitrust regulations—the U.S. laws and the antitrust laws, if any, of the foreign country.

The application of the U.S. laws extends to those transactions that will have a substantial and foreseeable effect on U.S. commerce.[1] This principle of law applies regardless of the citizenship of the participants to the agreement or acts. Where the participants are foreign corporations, a problem arises about whether a United States court can exert jurisdiction over them.

Any transaction conducted by a U.S. businessman or corporation that affects imports into the United States or the ability of U.S. companies to compete in foreign countries or any other aspect of U.S. commerce, must comply with the antitrust laws and the fact that the illegal activity occurred out of the United States will not be a defense to any suit. The tests used to determine the lawfulness of foreign transactions are the same as that used in domestic transactions, either the *per se* doctrine or the rule of reason test. See *supra* pp. 13-2–13-3.

State Antitrust Laws

Although the federal legislation in the antitrust field is basically directed toward activities in interstate commerce, it is difficult these days to draw a line between what constitute intra-state and interstate activities. Even in a situation where a firm's activities are confined wholly to a single state, those activities may come within the control of the federal antitrust laws. Such laws include prohibitions against contracts, combinations and conspiracies in restraint of trade, fair trade or resale price maintenance laws, and prohibitions against price discrimination and sales below cost.

---

[1] *United States v. Aluminum Co. of America,* 148 F.2d 416, 443-44 (2d. Cir. 1945).

Although the statutes vary in form, almost all of the states have statutes prohibiting monopolies, contracts, conspiracies and combinations in restraint of trade. Among the few states which do not have a comprehensive antitrust statute are Pennsylvania and Vermont. Some of these states do, however, have restraint of trade statutes dealing with specific industries, e.g., the insurance business or the dairy industry.

Arizona has adopted the Uniform State Antitrust Act which is a uniform law regulating antitrust activities; other states such as Minnesota and Illinois have enacted statutes that are substantially similar.

Fair Trade Acts

As a general rule it is unlawful for a person to fix the price at which his product must be resold to others. No federal antitrust statute directly permits resale price maintenance agreements. The legality of a fair trade pricing system, therefore, has depended upon the provisions of applicable state law for local transactions, and on federal law for interstate transactions.

State laws generally have exempted from the prohibitions of the common law and the antitrust laws contracts relating to the resale of a commodity which bears the trademark, brand or name of the producer of such commodity and which is in free and open competition with commodities of the same general class produced or distributed by others. While the exact language of the state laws differ, the substance is usually similar.

Where the commodity in question is sold in interstate commerce, however, the fact that the price maintenance agreement is valid in a particular jurisdiction would be of no avail as to its validity under federal law.

Originally, state antitrust laws made it unlawful for a person to fix resale prices, but with the enactment of the California Fair Trade Act in 1931, laws permitting resale price maintenance agreements were enacted in many states. At one time, all states except Alaska, Arizona, Missouri, Texas and Vermont had such legislation known as fair trade statutes. State laws permitting fair trade prices apply only between persons who are not in competition with each other and are not permitted between producers, wholesalers or retailers.

The fair trade acts of Alabama, Montana, Utah and Wyoming were held unconstitutional by the highest courts of those states. In Arkansas, Colorado, Florida, Georgia, Indiana, Iowa, Kentucky, Louisiana, Massachusetts, Michigan, Minnesota, New Mexico, Ohio, Oklahoma, Oregon, Pennsylvania, South Carolina, South Dakota, Washington and West Virginia, though the constitutionality of the fair trade acts as to the contracting parties has either been affirmed or undisputed, the application of these statutes to those persons who have not contracted to maintain fair trade prices (non-signers), has been held unconstitutional. Many of the state statutes require that where a valid resale price maintenance agreement has been entered into by one party and notice given to others, non-signing parties are required to observe the fair trade prices.

In August, 1937, Congress enacted the Miller-Tydings Fair Trade Act. August 17, 1937, Ch. 690, 50 Stat. 673. This statute provided an exemption from the prohibitions of the Sherman Act and the Federal Trade Commission Act to state fair trade legislation and had no effect unless there was an applicable state law which authorized fair trade pricing in intra-state commerce.

After the enactment of the Miller-Tydings Act, and until May 21, 1951, the exercise of the rights granted by state fair trade laws to enforce fair trade prices against non-signers was not questioned. But on that date the United States Supreme Court in *Schwegmann Bros. v. Calvert Distillers Corp.,* 341 U.S. 384 (1951), held that the exemption contained in the Miller-Tydings Act extended only to the persons who entered into fair trade contracts and such contracts were applicable to persons who had not entered into them.

The result of this decision was to undermine the effectiveness of the Miller-Tydings Act and the fair trade laws which by then had been enacted by 45 states. A little over a year thereafter, Congress remedied the situation created by the *Schwegmann* case by enacting the McGuire Act, July 14, 1952, Ch. 745, §§ 1, 2, 66 Stat. 632, as an amendment to the Federal Trade Commission Act. Under this law non-signers of fair trade agreements may be compelled, if the state law so provides, to maintain the resale prices established by the seller. Like the Miller-Tydings Act, the McGuire Act did not legalize resale price maintenance agreements between manufacturers, producers, wholesalers or other persons who are in competition with each other.

Almost every state has repealed its version of the Fair Trade Act. In those states where the state fair trade laws have not been repealed, they have been held unconstitutional.

Congress repealed the federal fair trade authorization law so that state legislation no longer can insulate resale price maintenance contracts from federal antitrust scrutiny. Pub. L. No. 94-145, 89 Stat. 801.

Antitrust Laws and the Exchange of Credit Information

Of particular interest and concern to the credit executive is the relationship of the antitrust laws, referred to above, to the activities of credit groups, and the applicability of the laws to concerted action by business firms in connection with the extension of credit.

An examination of the decisions and study of the Sherman Act and Federal Trade Commission Act lead to the following conclusions:

1. Any agreement, express or implied, between members of a credit group or other competitors to establish and maintain uniform prices, discounts, terms or conditions of sale, is illegal.

2. Any agreement, express or implied, between members of a credit group or other competitors to concertedly refuse to sell merchandise to a person listed as delinquent in the payment of his accounts to other members of the group, is illegal.

3. Any agreement, express or implied, between members of a credit group or other competitors to concertedly refuse to extend credit to accounts listed as delinquent and to place all such accounts on a C.O.D. or cash basis, while perhaps unobjectionable where there is a showing of exceptionally hazardous credit conditions in the industry, has never been approved by an appellate court and should be avoided.

4. Membership in a credit group must be open to all qualified applicants upon nondiscriminatory terms and conditions. Companies meeting the general qualifications for membership cannot be arbitrarily excluded and denied the benefits of membership, and particularly the privilege of receiving the credit information gathered and disseminated by the group. However, it would appear that if the credit group establishes reasonable standard qualifications for member-

ship, it can legally limit its membership and the use of its facilities to companies which meet such qualifications, as for example:

(a) That the applicant shall be a member of a designated credit association or affiliated association;

(b) That the applicant be engaged in the business of selling its products to customers within a certain territory or classification;

(c) That the applicant have good standing in the community, financially and morally;

(d) That the applicant shall have been engaged in business over a stated number of years, and shall have gross sales of not less than a stated amount per annum.

5. Lists of delinquent accounts identifying the name of the debtor and stating the amount owed, accounts in hands of attorneys for collection, and similar data, are unobjectionable if proper care is taken to exclude the names of persons who have an honest and legitimate reason for not paying their accounts, and names are promptly removed when the accounts are paid. It is preferable that the names of the creditors to whom the delinquent accounts are owing should not be revealed. Coded references on confidential reports are, however, permissible provided such codes are known only to the offices or agencies issuing such reports. There must be no agreement or understanding among creditors to adopt any uniform or concerted action with respect to such delinquent accounts. It is advisable to include in any such list a statement to the following effect:

> The inclusion on this list of the name of any debtor is not to be understood as implying any recommendation on the part of the XYZ Credit Group, or of the XYZ Association of Credit Management, that further credit should be denied to any of the concerns listed. The extension of further credit is a question to be determined by individual sellers in accordance with their own judgment after appropriate investigation.

6. Credit reports issued to a subscriber upon request are privileged communications and unobjectionable, but if given general circulation are not privileged and any defamatory information contained therein should be verified before the reports are issued.

7. Discussions of delinquent accounts at meetings of group members are unobjectionable provided the discussion is limited to past transactions and there is no agreement, express or implied, for uniform action with respect to such accounts. Discussions of price, discounts and terms of sale with respect to future transactions must be avoided. Minutes should be taken of all group meetings.

8. It should be remembered that proof that concerted action *has resulted* from the dissemination of information, orally or in writing, may justify an inference that an agreement actually existed although in fact there was no formal agreement or understanding. Suits against concerted action are usually pursued under Section 5 of the Federal Trade Commission Act which, unlike the Sherman Act, has no conspiracy requirement. See *supra* p. 13-12.

9. A bylaw provision for expulsion from membership in a credit group, or other penalty for violation of its rules, is not illegal. See *supra* p. 13-12. However, such provision should be uniformly enforced.

10. An act, harmless when done by one, may become a public wrong when done by many acting in concert.

Court Decisions

As early as 1925, the question of the legality of issuing lists of delinquent debtors came before the Supreme Court in *Cement Manufacturers' Protective Association v. United States,* 268 U.S. 588 (1925). The Court was called upon to review a judgment and decree which, among other things, had held illegal under the Sherman Act the circulation of such lists by the Credit Bureau of the Cement Manufacturers' Protective Association.

It appeared from the evidence that the Association had set up a reporting system to combat certain fraudulent practices of cement purchasers. Thereafter, a credit reporting system was set up and maintained whereby the members of the Association furnished to the Secretary a monthly alphabetical list of all accounts two months or more overdue, consisting of the name and address of the delinquent debtor, the amount of the overdue account, the ledger balance, bills receivable, accounts in the hands of attorneys for collection, and any explanation as, for example, that the debtor claims an offset where an account is disputed. There was also compiled and circulated a comparison of the general totals of delinquencies with those for the past twelve months. The rules of the Association provided for immediate notification of the payment of an account in the hands of an attorney for collection. The reports did not contain the names of the sellers nor any information regarding terms, discounts, rebates, etc.

The Supreme Court found no violation of the Sherman Act and held:

> There were never any comments concerning names appearing on the list of delinquent debtors. The government neither charged nor proved that there was any agreement with respect to the use of this information, or with respect to the persons to whom or conditions under which credit should be extended. The evidence falls far short of establishing any understanding on the basis of which credit was to be extended to customers, or that any cooperation resulted from the distribution of this information, or that there were any consequences from it other than such as would naturally ensue from the exercise of the individual judgment of the manufacturers in determining, on the basis of available information, whether to extend credit or to require cash or security from any given customer.

Id. at 599.

With respect to the industry reports on specific job contracts, the Court stated:

> [I]n our view, the gathering and dissemination of information which will enable sellers to prevent the perpetration of fraud upon them, which information they are free to act upon or not, as they choose, cannot be held to be an unlawful restraint upon commerce even though, in the ordinary course of business, most sellers would act on the information and refuse to make deliveries for which they were not legally bound.

Id. at 603-04.

Quoting from its earlier opinion in *Swift & Co. vs. United States,* 196 U.S. 375, 395 (1905), to the effect that "defendants should not be restrained 'from establishing and maintaining rules for the giving of credit to dealers where such rules in good faith are calculated solely to protect the defendants against dishonest or irresponsible dealers,'" the Court also held that:

> Distribution of information as to credit and responsibility of buyers undoubtedly prevents fraud and cuts down to some degree commercial transactions which would otherwise be induced by fraud. . . . [W]e cannot regard the procuring and dissemination of information which tends to prevent the procuring of fraudulent contracts, or to prevent the fraudulent securing of deliveries of merchandise on the pretense that the seller is bound to deliver by his contract, as an unlawful restraint of trade, even though such information be gathered and disseminated by those who are engaged in the trade or business principally concerned.

Id. at 604.

Where information was distributed, however, by and among members of an association, not as a measure of protection against fraud but with a view to coercing members to refrain from dealing with third persons regarded by the members as "unfair," the Court adjudged the scheme an illegal conspiracy. *Eastern States Retail Lumber Dealers' Association vs. United States*, 234 U.S. 600 (1914). The Court noted,

> These lists were quite commonly spoken of as blacklists, and when the attention of a retailer was brought to the name of a wholesaler who had acted in this wise it was with the evident purpose that he should know of such conduct and act accordingly. True it is that there is no agreement among the retailers to refrain from dealing with listed wholesalers, nor is there any penalty annexed for the failure so to do; but he is blind indeed who does not see the purpose in the predetermined and periodical circulation of this report to put the ban upon wholesale dealers whose names appear in the list of unfair dealers trying by methods obnoxious to the retail dealers to supply the trade which they regard as their own.

Id. at 608-09.

> A retail dealer has the unquestioned right to stop dealing with a wholesaler for reasons sufficient to himself, and may do so because he thinks such dealer is acting unfairly in trying to undermine his trade. 'But,' as was said by Mr. Justice Lurton, speaking for the Court in Grenada Lumber Co. vs. Mississippi, 217 U.S. 433 (1910), . . . 'when the plaintiffs in error combine and agree that no one of them will trade with any producer or wholesaler who shall sell to a consumer within the trade range of any of them, quite another case is presented. An act harmless when done by one may become a public wrong when done by many acting in concert, for it then takes on the form of a conspiracy, and may be prohibited or punished, if the result be hurtful to the public or individual against whom the concerted action is directed.'
> When the retailer goes beyond his personal right, and, conspiring and combining with others of like purpose, seeks to obstruct the free course of interstate trade and commerce and to unduly suppress competition by placing obnoxious wholesale dealers under the coercive influence of a condemnatory report circulated among others, actual or possible customers of the offenders, he exceeds his lawful rights, and such action brings him and those acting with him

within the condemnation of the act of Congress, and the District Court was right in so holding.

Id. at 614.

The question of the legality of an express or implied agreement among members of a credit group not to extend credit to delinquent or financially irresponsible debtors has not been passed upon by the Supreme Court. However, some lower courts have ruled that such agreements are valid. Better practice would be to avoid such lists as they too easily may be construed as a conspiracy on the part of the members of an association to refuse to sell to a particular customer.

In *United States v. Fur Dressers' & Fur Dyers' Assn.,* 5 F.2d 869 (S.D.N.Y. 1925) case the court said,

> The provisions that lists of customers who have failed to pay their overdue accounts to members of the association shall be distributed to members of the association for their information, and that no delivery of dressed or dyed skins shall be made to any person by any member so long as the name of that person appears upon the list, except upon payment of cash or by check upon the delivery of skins, do not go beyond the reasonable requirement to correct the abuses which have crept into the trade. The provisions discriminate against none other than those who do not pay agreed prices for services rendered to them. . . . The rules only require that the dressing and dyeing for customers who have failed to pay bills should be for cash. . . .
>
> Not every agreement which suppresses competition or restrains trade is illegal. Only such agreements and combinations as unreasonably suppress competition or restrain trade are illegal. . . . Only such contracts and combinations are within the act as, by reason of intent or the inherent nature of the contemplated acts, prejudice the public interests by unduly restricting competition or unduly obstructing the course of trade.

Id. at 870-71 (citations omitted).

The Supreme Court has ruled, however, that, where the refusal to extend credit was not based upon financial irresponsibility, a group agreement violated the Sherman Act. In *United States v. First National Pictures,* 282 U.S. 44 (1930), an association of distributors of motion picture films, controlling 98% of the business, had established a rule which forbade any member from entering into a contract for the exhibition of motion pictures at any theatre listed on a credit information list containing the names of persons to whom theatres had been sold or transferred, unless the transferee of such theatre arranged security for the performance of the contracts. No member of the association was permitted to contract for the exhibition of pictures at such theatre unless the new owner or lessee paid in cash to member the amount of security specified on the credit information list.

The Court found that the rules were unlawful in that their obvious purpose was to restrict the liberty of those who were represented in the organization and to secure their concerted action for the purpose of coercing purchasers of theatres by excluding them from dealing in a free market.

It is significant that upon remand by the Supreme Court to the District Court for the Southern District of New York for further proceedings, the final decree provided that it should not be construed "as prohibiting any defendants, . . . from exchanging, either directly or indirectly through a committee or other agency, information concerning the financial or moral responsibility of any exhibitor of motion pictures in the United States; always provided that there shall not be made in connection with or in supplement of such exchange of information any comment in the nature of a recommendation as to any action to be taken thereon."

In 1969 the Supreme Court issued two decisions in the antitrust field that are of significance to credit groups. *United States* v. *Container Corp. of America,* 393 U.S. 333 (1969), held that corrugated box manufacturers violated Section 1 of the Sherman Act by exchanging price information as to specific sales to identified customers, since the effect of such exchange was to stabilize prices, albeit at a downward level. The case reaffirmed the well-established rule that any effort to control prices will be deemed to be a *per se* violation of the Sherman Act. The Court distinguished this case from others in which the exchange of information was held legal by the fact that on the facts before it the information exchanged related to identified customers and was not merely statistical reportage. Furthermore, the Court expressly distinguished the case from the *Cement Manufacturers' Protective Association,* see *supra* p. 13-18, by noting that in that case the exchange of information related to the desire of the Cement Manufacturers' Protective Association to protect themselves from fraudulent inducements in making sales.

In *Fortner Enterprises Inc.* v. *United States Steel Corp.,* 394 U.S. 495 (1969), the plaintiff borrowed money from the United States Steel Homes Credit Corp., a subsidiary of United States Steel Corp., for the purpose of purchasing and developing land, and was required to erect prefabricated houses manufactured by and purchased from United States Steel on the lands acquired with the loan proceeds. The loans were made at relatively low interest rates and were in amounts sufficient to enable the plaintiff to obtain 100% financing.

Plaintiff alleged that this constituted an illegal tie-in sale, and further that the materials supplied by United States Steel were defective and high priced. The Court reversed the decision of the district court and court of appeals, which had granted a motion for summary judgment made by the defendants, and held that the plaintiff was entitled to its day in court to establish that the arrangements described constituted either a *per se* violation of the Sherman Act, or a conventional tie-in sale, or otherwise constituted an unreasonable restraint of trade. The Court distinguished the transaction from the ordinary sale of a single product on credit. Although the defendants did not have a dominant share of the market, the Court deemed that by virtue of the unique lending terms offered they had sufficient power to act so as to have an adverse effect on competition.

Membership in Credit Groups

As previously noted, membership in a credit group must be open to all applicants upon nondiscriminatory terms and conditions to avoid violation of the antitrust laws. See *supra* p. 13-16.

In *United States vs. National Electric Sign Association,* 1954 Trade Case ¶ 67,724, the District Court for the Northern District of Illinois, Eastern Division, entered a final judgment in which it ordered the defendant association "to grant equal, uniform and nondiscriminatory membership in said Association, upon application therefor, to any parts manufacturer, parts jobber or sign manufacturer."

In *United States v. Allied Florists Association of Illinois,* 1953 Trade Case ¶ 67,433, the defendant Allied Florists Association of Illinois, was ordered to admit to membership any retail florist, grower or wholesaler on nondiscriminatory terms and conditions, and the Chicago Association of Credit Men's Service Corporation was directed to admit to membership in the Florists Wholesaler Credit Group "any wholesaler making a written request therefor and to make available its services and facilities to all wholesalers upon nondiscriminatory terms and conditions."

The right of a trade association or credit group to impose penalties, including expulsion, for violation of its rules has been held permissible where the activities of the association or group are otherwise lawful.

In *Anderson v. United States,* 171 U.S. 604 (1898), the Supreme Court had before it the question about whether an agreement among persons engaged in the business of buying cattle at a city stockyard violated the Sherman Act where it provided that the members would not transact business with any other traders who are not members of the Association or buy cattle from those who also sell to nonmember traders. The Court held that a rule that the members would not recognize nonmember traders was not in restraint of trade or otherwise in violation of the Sherman Act, there being nothing to prevent all traders from being members of the exchange; the Court expressly held that the rules of the Association calling for the disciplining and expulsion of members who violated the Association's rules and regulations by failing to transact business in the honest and straightforward manner provided for by the rules, were not in violation of the Sherman Act.

The *Anderson* case was followed by the Court of Appeals for the First Circuit in *Wm. Filene's Sons Co. v. Fashion Originators' Guild,* 90 F.2d 556 (1937), where the court held that "[t]he imposition of reasonable fines and the penalty of expulsion in the event of repeated violation as a means of making effective the rules of a trade association is permissible." Id. at 562.

Where the activities of a trade association constitute conduct which is in violation of the antitrust laws, such conduct can be expected to be censored and the association penalized. In *Hollow Metal Door & Buck Association, Inc.,* 82 F.T.C. 1404 (1973), a consent decree was entered into by the Hollow Metal Door & Buck Association by which it was restrained from engaging in unfair credit-reporting activities, engaging in customer boycotts, or the submission of bids after any price or term of sale had been subject to competitive discussions. The Association was also directed to maintain minutes of all discussions and to permit resignation of members at any time.

A divided Court of Appeals for the Third Circuit held, *interalia,* that a complaint is sufficient to state a cause of action in alleging a conspiracy or combination in violation of the Sherman Act based on a course of interdependent consciously parallel action which imposed unlawful tying agreements upon lessees of oil companies. *Bogosian* v. *Gulf Oil Corp.,* 561 F.2d 434 (1977). The significance of this case for credit groups is that it confirms that not only can explicit agreements be in violation of the Sherman Act but any actions which constitute intentional and conscious efforts at concerted action are illegal. Proof of consciously parallel business behavior is circumstantial evidence from which an agreement can be inferred.

Corporations

"A corporation is an artificial being, invisible, intangible, and existing only in contemplation of law. Being the mere creature of law, it possesses only those properties which the charter of its creation confers upon it . . . . By these means, a perpetual succession of individuals are capable of acting for the promotion of the particular object, like one immortal being." *Trustees of Dartmouth College v. Woodward,* 17 U.S. (4 Wheat) 518, 636 (1819).

In addition to having perpetual life, a corporation is a legal entity or artificial person, entirely separate and apart from the persons who compose its members. A corporation has the power to receive, hold and convey property, enter into contracts, sue and be sued, and otherwise exercise those rights and privileges which may be accorded by the laws under which it was created, in the same manner as a natural person.

A corporation, being a creature of the state, has no inherent rights or powers except within the framework of the law of its creation. Thus, the corporation must be organized in strict accordance with the legal requirements of the state of its domicile. While it is afforded protection as a "person" by our Federal Constitution, including its right to engage in interstate commerce, it cannot step beyond the bounds of its domicile into another state without having that state confer upon it the "right to exist" within its borders. Its powers and purposes are fixed by charter and cannot be changed at will as in the case of an individual or partnership. Such a change as entering into a new type of business or increasing its capitalization, in fact any variation from the rights or powers conferred by its charter, can be effected only by amending that charter in accordance with the laws of the state which issued the charter.

Advantages of Incorporation

To the stockholders of a corporation this form of business organization affords two prime advantages we have not previously considered—limited liability and potentially unlimited capital. The individual in business for himself must risk everything he owns in his venture, his capital being what he owns plus what he can borrow on his personal credit. Broadly speaking, the partnership does little more than increase the potential capital by the means of one or more additional individuals while at the same time spreading the risk or liabilities among the several individuals. See Chapter 15, *infra*. A stockholder of a corporation, however, who holds fully paid and nonassessable shares of stock, generally has no potential liability other than the loss of the money paid for the shares. An exception is the holder of banking corporation stock who in some states may be subject to a so-called "double liability" if the bank becomes insolvent. In general a stockholder is not liable for the debts of the corporation in the absence of special circumstances. (See discussion *infra*.) Liability may exist in the event of defective incorporation, irregularity in issuance of stock or under special statutory enactments such as those which in some states impose a liability on stockholders of an insolvent corporation unable to pay wage claims.

With the advantage of this limited liability as well as the relative simplicity with which the shareholder can purchase or dispose of his interest in the corporation, this form of business organization has attracted investment of funds running into billions of dollars from millions of individuals.

Under the federal tax laws, however, a corporation may enjoy the tax advantages of a partnership if it meets the special requirements of the Internal Revenue Code, 26 U.S.C. §§ 1371-1377 (1976 & Supp. V 1981).

LIABILITY FOR CORPORATE DEBTS BY OFFICERS, DIRECTORS OR STOCKHOLDERS

Incorporation serves to insulate directors, officers and shareholders of a corporation from personal liability. However, there are a number of exceptions both statutory and at common law to this general rule.

Liability of Directors or Officers

Directors are in a position analogous to that of trustees; they have a fiduciary responsibility to stockholders and creditors. At common law directors are liable to creditors and to the corporation for distribution of improper dividends provided such distribution resulted from willfulness, negligence, bad faith or fraud. If the directors act in good faith and with due care, no liability results unless imposed by statute.

Directors and officers are not liable for corporate debts unless the director or officer specifically agrees to become liable and they are not bound for corporate contracts. See, for example, *MJZ Corp. v. Gulfstream First Bank & Trust,* 420 So.2d 396 (Fla. Dist. Ct. App. 1982). The court held that though an individual must indicate he is signing a check in his corporate capacity to avoid personal liability under statutory law, that capacity can otherwise be established between the parties, e.g., the bank account upon which the check was drawn can be in the corporate name. Individuals must be careful, however, to avoid personal liability. See *James G. Smith & Associates, Inc. v. Everett,* 1 Ohio App. 3d 118, 439 N.E.2d 932 (1981). The court found that an individual could be personally liable for corporate debts if he fails to make it clear that he is an agent of the corporation and is not acting in his personal capacity.

Aside from common law causes of action, there are a number of statutes that can subject a director or officer to personal liability.

Many jurisdictions have a minimum capitalization requirement for incorporation. Often the threshold capitalization is very small compared to the potential liabilities. Therefore, it is important for a creditor to consider the integrity of management before extending credit. Failure to meet the minimum capitalization requirement can make the director, officer or shareholder personally liable for acts done prior to acquiring the minimum required capital.

Every jurisdiction imposes personal liability on directors who participate in the declaration and payment of illegal dividends or other distributions to shareholders. The liability may be enforced, depending on the state, by the corporation, or creditors or shareholders who did not benefit from the illegal dividends. A number of states have statutes that permit creditors to hold directors liable for the distribution of illegal dividends.

Shareholder Liability

In the absence of any specific statutory provisions, shareholders are generally not liable for the debts or obligations of a corporation. Persons dealing with the corporation must look to it and not to the individual stockholders for payment of claims. This is true despite the fact that an individual stockholder may own all or practically all of the shares of stock, except as noted below.

Many states provide for statutory liability of shareholders for the receipt of illegal dividends. Most of the statutes make the shareholder liable to the corporation. Louisiana explicitly allows creditors to enforce liability against shareholders; however, as a practical matter creditors are more likely to sue the directors or the corporation. A number of statutes condition shareholder liability upon the shareholder having knowledge that the dividend was illegal, or that the corporation has become insolvent.

Disregard of Corporate Entity

Although a corporation is a legal entity existing separate and apart from the persons composing it, the courts will not permit this concept to be used for purposes of fraud and injustice. In appropriate cases the corporate entity will be disregarded (frequently referred to as "piercing the corporate veil") and the corporation and the individual or individuals owning all or substantially all of its stock and assets will be treated as one. In order to impose corporate liability on a shareholder, a strong showing of fraud, illegality, manipulation, injustice or wrongdoing by the shareholder must be clearly demonstrated. This matter is controlled by local law which varies from state to state.

UCC 3-403(2)(a) contains an important provision that should be noted by those signing checks on behalf of a corporation. It provides that "An authorized representative who signs his own name to an instrument is personally obligated if the instrument neither names the person represented nor shows that the representative signed in a representative capacity." Problems under this provision can be avoided if the signer will follow three simple steps. First, the signer should have authority to sign. Second, the name of the corporation should be on the check. Third, the signer should always clearly indicate that he or she is signing in a representative capacity. Omission of any step, especially the third, may lead to the signer being held personally liable for the check.

DOMESTIC AND FOREIGN CORPORATIONS

A corporation is known as a domestic corporation within the state in which it is organized. As to all other states and countries, it is a foreign corporation. Foreign corporations are subject to statutory regulation by every state in which they do business. The broad subject of rights and liabilities is treated below.

A foreign corporation may be broadly defined as one created by or organized and existing under the laws of another state or territory or of a foreign government. Some states, such as Montana and Delaware, include within the definition of foreign corporations those organized under the laws of the United States, while New York provides that corporations organized under the laws of the

United States shall be considered "domestic." Likewise a business, or Massachusetts trust, see *infra* p. 14-19, is a "corporation" within the meaning of the laws discussed below.

Ever since the decision of the Supreme Court in the case of *Paul v. Virginia* 75 U.S. (8 Wall.) 168 (1869), it has been the settled law of this country that a corporation is not entitled to "all the privileges and immunities of citizens in the several States," but that each state has the power and privilege of prescribing the terms upon which it will allow foreign corporations to transact business within its borders.

No state may deny to a corporation "the equal protection of the laws" or pass any law "impairing the obligation of contract," but this proscription by the fourteenth amendment to the Federal Constitution does not prohibit a state "from discriminating in the privileges it may grant to foreign corporations as a condition of their doing business or hiring offices within its limits, provided always such discrimination does not interfere with any transactions by such corporations of interstate or foreign commerce. . . . The States may, therefore, require for the admission within their limits of the corporations of other States, or of any number of them, such conditions as they may choose. . . ." *Pembina Consolidated Silver Mining Co. v. Pennsylvania*, 125 U.S. 181, 189 (1888).[1]

U.S. Constitutional Provision

Article I, section 8 of the Constitution of the United States, the power to regulate commerce with foreign nations and among the several states, is given exclusively to the federal government. This power has been reviewed frequently by the United States Supreme Court, and state statutes which have attempted to place burdens upon interstate commerce have been found unconstitutional and void.

The question which most frequently arises today, under this section of the Constitution, is whether or not a state may legally impose a tax upon foreign corporations, and whether or not the conditions which it imposes, or attempts to impose, upon foreign corporations for the privilege of doing business interfere with the constitutional right of the corporation to transact interstate business free from local interference. When the State of South Dakota attempted by statute to restrict the use of the state courts by foreign corporations transacting strictly interstate business, the United States Supreme Court held the statute an unreasonable burden on interstate commerce. *Sioux Remedy Co. v. Cope*, 235 U.S. 197 (1914). Additionally, when the State of Kansas attempted to levy a tax upon the entire authorized capital stock of the Western Union Telegraph Company, a foreign corporation, it was found that the tax was an attempt to place a burden upon interstate commerce and, therefore, was unconstitutional. *Western Union Telegraph Co. v. Kansas*, 216 U.S. 1 (1910).

In later decisions of the United States Supreme Court, however, the restriction on the states' rights to tax interstate transactions has been relaxed. For example, the imposition of a net income tax on income derived from interstate sales

---

[1] No state may provide, as a condition to permitting a foreign corporation to do business within the state, that creditors who are residents of the state shall have priority over nonresidents. But, in *People v. Granite State Provident Assn.*, 161 N.Y. 492 (1900), it was held that a statute requiring a foreign banking corporation, as a condition of doing business within the state, to deposit a special fund which would be applied to the claims of domestic creditors only in the event of insolvency, was not unconstitutional.

solicited by local salesmen was upheld in *Northwestern States Portland Cement Co. v. Minnesota,* 358 U.S. 450 (1959). (A federal statute was subsequently enacted, 15 U.S.C.A. §381-384 (1976), which prohibited the imposition of such a tax where the seller is not engaged in business in the taxing state and his only activity there consists of soliciting orders which are accepted and filled outside the state.) In *Scripto, Inc. v. Carson,* 362 U.S. 207 (1960), the Court upheld the state's right to collect use taxes from an out-of-state seller when it had agents in the taxing state soliciting orders for interstate shipment.

Restrictions Imposed on Foreign Corporations

The distinction between interstate business and intrastate business is not easily defined, and the decisions of the courts are conflicting in many instances as to whether a given course of procedure is properly defined as an *interstate* transaction, or amounts to *intrastate* business. It is of the highest importance that businessmen be familiar with the restrictions imposed by the states upon the transaction of intrastate business by foreign corporations because the penalties imposed by the statutes are usually severe.

By the comity of nations, foreign corporations may make such contracts and transact business not contrary to the laws of the place where such contracts are made or such business is transacted, and there is a presumption of law in favor of the power of a foreign corporation to exercise all of the powers conferred by its charter; but the limitations contained in its charter follow it into every state in which it may do business. Discrimination against foreign corporations, however, is unlawful insofar as such discrimination does not violate constitutional provisions relating to interstate commerce and equal protection of the laws.

In *Columbia Gas Transmission Corp. v. Pennsylvania,* 468 Pa. 145, 360 A.2d 592 (1976), a higher excise tax rate for foreign corporations than for domestic corporations was held to violate the state constitution's uniformity clause and was a denial of equal protection of laws under the United States Constitution. The court found that different tax rates may be acceptable but that arbitrary distinctions were discriminatory; therefore, it held that the Pennsylvania law was unconstitutional.

Licensing of Foreign Corporations

The requirements with which a foreign corporation must comply to obtain a license or right to do business in any particular state, the fees incident thereto, and the initial or annual franchise tax imposed upon such corporation by the state for a license or certificate of authority to do business within its borders, are too varied to be susceptible to concise summary, and resort in each case must be made to the statutes themselves. Insurance and banking corporations are usually subject to special laws and the limitations upon their powers are more severe than those which are placed upon ordinary business corporations. Indeed, insurance has been held not to be "commerce," which a foreign corporation has a right to engage in under federal laws. *Paul v. Virginia,* 75 U.S. (8 Wall.) 168 (1869).

The tables on pp. 14-6 and 14-7 indicate the penalties imposed by the various states for failure of a foreign corporation to qualify to do business in another state.

In all states except Arkansas, Mississippi, and Vermont, a corporation may

(Continued on page 14–7 following table)

PENALTIES FOR VIOLATIONS OF INTERSTATE BUSINESS STATUTES

Consequences which can be imposed on foreign corporations transacting interstate business in violation of applicable statutes

	Penalties Imposed on Corporation, Its Agents or Officers	Injunction to Enjoin Corporation from Transacting Business in State	Contracts Void, Voidable,[1] or Valid	Liability of Officers, Directors, Stockholders or Agents for Debts or on Contracts
Alabama [7]	Yes		Void [4]	Yes
Alaska	Yes		Valid	
Arizona	Yes	Yes	Valid	
Arkansas [3,7]	Yes		Void	Yes
California [8]	Yes	Yes	Valid	Yes
Colorado	Yes		Valid	
Connecticut	Yes		Valid	
Delaware [2]	Yes	Yes	Valid	
D.C.	Yes		Valid	
Florida	Yes		Valid	
Georgia	Yes		Voidable	
Hawaii	Yes		Valid	
Idaho [5]	Yes		Valid [6]	Yes
Illinois	Yes		Valid	
Indiana [8]	Yes		Voidable	
Iowa [3,7,8]	Yes		Valid	
Kansas	Yes	Yes	Valid	
Kentucky	Yes		Valid	Yes
Louisiana [8]	Yes		Valid	
Maine	Yes	Yes	Valid	
Maryland [8]	Yes		Valid	
Massachusetts	Yes		Valid	
Michigan	Yes		Valid	
Minnesota	Yes		Valid	
Mississippi [3]	Yes		Valid	
Missouri	Yes		Valid	
Montana	Yes		Valid	
Nebraska	Yes		Valid	
Nevada	Yes		Valid	
New Hampshire	Yes		Valid	
New Jersey	Yes	Yes	Valid	
New Mexico [7]	Yes		Valid	
New York	Yes	Yes	Valid	
North Carolina	Yes		Valid	
North Dakota	Yes		Valid	
Ohio	Yes		Valid	
Oklahoma [8]	Yes		Valid	
Oregon	Yes		Valid	
Pennsylvania	No		Valid	
Rhode Island	Yes		Valid	
South Carolina	Yes	Yes	Valid	
South Dakota	Yes		Valid	
Tennessee	Yes		Valid	

PENALTIES FOR VIOLATIONS OF INTERSTATE BUSINESS STATUTES *(Continued)*

Consequences which can be imposed on foreign corporations transacting interstate business in violation of applicable statutes

	Penalties Imposed on Corporation, Its Agents or Officers	Injunction to Enjoin Corporation from Transacting Business in State	Contracts Void, Voidable,[1] or Valid	Liability of Officers, Directors, Stockholders or Agents for Debts or on Contracts
Texas	Yes		Valid	
Utah	Yes		Valid	
Vermont [3,7]	Yes	Yes	Voidable	
Virginia	No		Valid	Yes
Washington	Yes		Valid	
West Virginia	Yes		Valid	
Wisconsin	Yes		Valid	
Wyoming	Yes		Valid	

[1] A contract otherwise void or voidable may frequently be cured by obtaining a certificate of qualification and the payment of any applicable fines.

[2] Delaware has a reciprocal penalties provision whereby penalties imposed upon Delaware corporations doing business in other states which are greater than those imposed by Delaware law under similar conditions are imposed on foreign corporations doing business in Delaware.

[3] If corporation is unqualified at time of making of contract, no suit may thereafter be maintained.

[4] This does not include mortgages insured by the Federal Housing Administration or Veterans Administration.

[5] The Supreme Court of Idaho has held that a foreign corporation which is qualified at time of trial is able to maintain a suit. *Spokane Merchants' Association v. Olmstead,* 80 Idaho 166, 327 P.2d 385 (1958).

[6] In Idaho, real estate deeds of unlicensed foreign corporations are voidable.

[7] Statutes regulating contract enforcement by unlicensed foreign corporation are limited to contracts executed within the state.

[8] Violation is a misdemeanor.

(Continued from page 14-5)

maintain an action on a contract made when unqualified to do business in state by thereafter qualifying under the state law. In Alabama, an unqualified foreign corporation may not maintain a law suit even after qualifying under state law unless the contract involves a mortgage insured by the Federal Housing Administration or the Veterans Administration.

In Massachusetts, a foreign corporation which is doing business in the Commonwealth, which has not complied with the statutory requirements and obtained authorization to do business there, is deemed to have appointed the State Secretary as its true attorney upon whom all lawful process may be served in any litigation for liability incurred while doing business in the Commonwealth.

WHAT CONSTITUTES INTERSTATE BUSINESS?

It is impossible to formulate from the many decisions of the various states a comprehensive definition of the phrase "doing business" within the foreign state to such an extent, or in such a manner, that the business becomes *intra*state as opposed to *inter*state, and renders the corporation liable to the restrictions and the penalties imposed by state laws.

All states except Arkansas, South Dakota, and Wyoming have attempted to define "doing business." The majority of those states defining the term have done so negatively by enumerating activities which do *not* constitute the transaction of business, e.g., maintaining bank accounts or borrowing money, creating evidences of debts, transacting business in interstate commerce, and conducting isolated transactions completed within 30 days. See ABA Model Bus. Corp. Act Annotated 2d Ed. (1970 & Supp. 1977).

Only two states, Kansas and Vermont, have attempted to affirmatively define what constitutes doing business. These activities include owning property, commiting a tort, maintaining a distribution point or performing a corporate function within the state.

The United States Supreme Court considered this question in the case of *Allenberg Cotton Co., Inc. v. Pittman,* 419 U.S. 20 (1974). The issue in this case was whether or not the activities of Allenberg constituted intrastate business of sufficient magnitude to permit the State of Mississippi to apply its qualification statute without violating the commerce clause of the United States Constitution. The Allenberg Cotton Co. was a cotton merchant with its principal office in Memphis, Tennessee. It had arranged with a Mississippi resident to act for it to purchase cotton produced by cotton farmers in Mississippi. The agent would contact the farmers and relay the purchase terms to Allenberg's office in Tennessee, where, if acceptable, a contract would be prepared and signed by Allenberg. Thereafter, a copy would be sent to the agent in Mississippi to be executed by the farmer. The agent negotiated a contract with one Pittman who was to plant, cultivate and harvest a crop of cotton for Allenberg. Pittman, however, refused to deliver the cotton to Allenberg who then commenced suit in Mississippi demanding injunctive relief and damages.

Pittman responded by claiming that Allenberg was a foreign corporation doing business in Mississippi and that it had not qualified to do so by securing a certificate of authority as required. Pittman alleged that Allenberg was not entitled to maintain its suit under the Mississippi statute which provided that: "No foreign corporation transacting business in this state without a certificate of authority shall be permitted to maintain any action, suit or proceeding in any court of this state." Id. at 21 n.l.

The local court in Mississippi held that Allenberg was not doing business in that state within the meaning of the statute. The Supreme Court of Mississippi reversed that decision and held that Allenberg was doing business within the state. The United States Supreme Court in turn reversed. In an opinion by Mr. Justice Douglas, holding that Allenberg's local activities were inseparable from the overall interstate aspects of its transactions, the Court stated that: "The cotton in this Mississippi sale . . . though temporarily in a warehouse [in Mississippi] was still in the stream of interstate commerce." Id. at 30.

The case is not a departure from prior law. It rests on the factual determination that Allenberg did not have a sufficient corporate presence in Mississippi to require qualification. Generally, when a domestic corporation is being sued by an unqualified foreign corporation, the burden is on the domestic corporation to prove by competent evidence: (1) that the suer's activities are of a kind that constitute "doing business" in the state and require authorization; and

CORPORATIONS

(2) that the suer had not received authority to do business in the state. In a Georgia case, *Unilease No. 16, Inc. v. Dunrite Sales Corp.*, 147 Ga. App. 728, 250 S.E.2d 179 (1978), the domestic corporation testified that it had been informed that the foreign corporation had not procured a certificate of authority to do business in Georgia. The court excluded this testimony as hearsay and determined that the domestic corporation had neither proved that the foreign corporation needed a certificate nor produced proper evidence of the lack of one.

Sales by Traveling Salesmen or by Mail

It is well settled that where traveling salesmen solicit orders in one state which are approved at the home office of a corporation in another state and filled by the shipment of goods from the home state direct to customers in the other state, the foreign corporation is engaged in interstate commerce, and such business cannot be interfered with nor can burdens be imposed thereon by the local authorities. While there are numerous authorities to support this proposition, it should be qualified insofar as use taxes are concerned by reason of the Supreme Court decision in *Scripto, Inc. v. Carson*, 362 U.S. 207 (1960).

Where a Minnesota corporation, operating flour mills in that state and selling its products to wholesale dealers throughout the country, maintained an office in Massachusetts where it employed salesmen for the purpose of inducing local tradesmen to carry and deal in its flour, and these salesmen solicited and took orders from retail dealers and turned them over to the nearest wholesale dealer, by whom the orders were filled and to whom the retailers paid the purchase price, the United States Supreme Court held that the transactions were domestic business, inducing one local merchant to buy a particular class of goods from another, and that the foreign corporation was subject to taxation by the state of Massachusetts regardless of the motive with which the business was conducted.

Where a corporation maintains an office or salesroom within the foreign state, and such office is merely for the convenience of the salesmen securing orders which are filled by shipments made from another state, and no stock of goods is carried within the state, but merely samples are kept for the purpose of exhibition, and no bank account, and no books of account are kept in the foreign state, the decisions are practically unanimous that the business is interstate commerce and not subject to local regulation or income taxation.

One must however distinguish between "doing business" for purposes of taxation or corporate law qualification and "transacting business" as defined in many of the state statutes which permit courts of a state to acquire jurisdiction over a corporation that transacts business in the state by means of substituted service of legal process or by some other method other than personal service. See discussion *infra* p. 14-12.

Isolated Transactions

The great weight of authority supports the proposition that a single transaction of business within a foreign state is not "doing business" therein within the meaning of the statutes prescribing conditions upon which foreign corporations may enter the state.

It is well to note, however, that where a single transaction involves the activities of employees of a foreign corporation within a state for a considerable period, or where the activities necessarily imply that there will be further operations carried on by the foreign corporation, the corporation is required to be authorized to do business within the state. See *infra* p. 14-13.

Institution of Suit

The mere institution and prosecution of a suit does not, by itself, constitute doing business within the meaning of constitutional and statutory provisions against doing business without obtaining a certificate of authority.

An important distinction is made between actions on contract and actions for tort. Where a statute expressly prohibits a foreign corporation from suing on any contract made within the state, an unlicensed foreign corporation has nevertheless been permitted to bring an action of replevin for the recovery of property sold on conditional sale, though the corporation was denied the use of the courts for the purpose of suing to recover the money due under the contract.

The federal courts are always open to a foreign corporation even when the corporation is barred from the use of the state courts because it has failed to comply with the state requirements (this, of course, providing there is at least $10,000 involved and the controversy is between citizens of different states. 28 U.S.C. § 1332 (1976)). The states have frequently attempted to deny the right of a foreign corporation to do business within their borders unless the corporation would stipulate in advance that it would not remove to a federal court any suit brought against it by a citizen of the state, but such statutes have been held repugnant to the Constitution and laws of the United States.

There are no specific state statutes which deal with the right of an unlicensed foreign corporation to interpose a counterclaim in an action. The courts that have considered this question appear to be divided into two groups. Those such as New York, Idaho, Minnesota and Texas, which regard a counterclaim as tantamount to defense, hold that the defendant corporation is not barred from asserting the counterclaim. In contrast, New Jersey, Colorado, Maryland, and Wisconsin hold that counterclaims are the equivalent of a new action and do not permit them to be asserted.

Sales by Samples

Analogous to the principle set forth as regards the sale of goods by traveling salesmen is the matter of selling by sample within a foreign state. A sale by sample of goods not yet brought into a state, and owned by a nonresident, cannot be subjected to a tax or license fee, since that would constitute a regulation of interstate commerce. This is true even though the goods are later delivered by the agents of the seller within the foreign state, for "[t]he right to sell implies the obligation and right to deliver. It is as much interstate commerce to do the one as the other." *In Re Spain,* 47 F. 208 (C. C. E. D. N.C. 1891) (construing a statute of North Carolina).

Installations and Construction Work

Whenever a foreign corporation enters a state for the purpose of erecting or installing machinery or apparatus of any sort, the question is immediately

CORPORATIONS

raised as to whether or not the corporation has engaged in interstate business and made itself subject to the restrictions imposed by the state statutes. It is only in rare instances that an unlicensed foreign corporation can safely engage in construction work in a foreign state. In *Browning v. City of Waycross,* 233 U.S. 16 (1914), the Supreme Court reaffirmed the doctrine "that a state may not burden by taxation or otherwise the taking of orders in one state for goods to be shipped from another, or the shipment of such goods in the channels of interstate commerce up to and including the consummation by delivery of the goods at the point of destination . . . ." Id. at 19-20. It was held, however, that the business of erecting in one state lightning rods shipped from another state "was within the regulating power of the state [of Georgia], and not the subject of interstate commerce, for the following reasons: (a) Because the affixing of lightning rods to houses was the carrying on of a business of a strictly local character, peculiarly within the exclusive control of state authority. (b) Because, besides, such business was wholly separate from interstate commerce, involved no question of the delivery of property shipped in interstate commerce, or of the right to complete an interstate commerce transaction, but concerned merely the doing of a local act after interstate commerce had completely terminated." Id. at 22-23. The court went on to point out that while it was true that, under the contract according to the terms of which the rods were shipped, the seller was bound to attach the rods to the houses of the citizens who ordered the rods, the mere act of the parties in joining the sale of the goods to the erection thereof could not change the nature of the act involved in erecting the rods from one of intrastate commerce to interstate commerce.

a. Held as Interstate Business

The Supreme Court of Michigan has handed down several decisions which exemplify the lengths to which the doctrine of *Browning v. Waycross* has been carried. In *Decorators' Supply Co. v. Chaussee,* 211 Mich. 302, 178 N.W. 665 (1920), the contract for certain ornamental plaster work in a building under construction in Michigan contained a stipulation that the material to be used was to be "furnished, delivered, and set in place by us." In a suit to recover the price of the material and work, the court held that the plaintiff could not collect because it was an unregistered foreign corporation engaged in interstate business. The court said in part:
> The record discloses that there are concerns in at least two or three cities of Michigan furnishing ornamental plaster work in competition with the plaintiff, and it is apparent that there are mechanics in the state entirely competent to erect such material. We think it is equally apparent that there is no such "intrinsic or peculiar quality or inherent complexity" in the article sold in the case at bar as would prevent its sale unless erected by the vendor.

An examination of the cases cited by the court shows that the test applied to contracts of this sort is whether or not the installation or construction of the article sold is such an essential requisite to the sale that it can be said that but for the installation by the seller, the sale could not take place.

b. When Not Interstate Business

It is difficult to find a case in which the sale of an article will necessarily fail unless the manufacturer agrees to install, erect or construct the material or apparatus within a foreign state. It is even more difficult to think of a case in which the plaintiff can offer proof that there are no mechanics within the state in question, who are capable of erecting, installing or constructing material or apparatus. Yet in the absence of proof that such is the case, it would seem that the unregistered foreign corporation will be held to have entered into an interstate contract and will be denied the use of the courts of the foreign state to enforce payment.

A leading decision of the United States Supreme Court on the subject of the installation contract is the case of *York Mfg. Co. v. Colley,* 247 U.S. 21 (1910), which was an appeal from the Texas Court of Civil Appeals. The York Mfg. Co. was not qualified to do business in the state of Texas where it contracted to install certain ice machinery. The contract contained a stipulation to the effect that the York Mfg. Co. would send an engineer to supervise the installation of the machine, but his services were to be paid for by the purchaser, and all labor, material, etc., in connection therewith, were to be performed and furnished by the purchaser. The Supreme Court, reversing the Texas court, held that the services of the engineer in assembling and erecting the machinery were relevant and appropriate to the interstate sale of the ice machinery and, because of its complexity, formed a part of the interstate transaction. Therefore, the interstate sale was entitled to the "protection" of the Constitution.

Sale of Goods Stored in State as Interstate Business

Where it appears that a foreign corporation is maintaining an agency for the sale of goods within another state, the authorities hold uniformly that the corporation is engaging in interstate commerce and is subject to taxation and regulation. But the mere storing of goods in a foreign state for some other purpose than that of sale does not amount to the transaction of interstate commerce and the goods do not lose their character as articles of interstate commerce.

Free Port Laws

Thirty-seven states and the District of Columbia have adopted "free port laws." These laws, intended to reduce the incidence of multiple taxation, exempt goods stored in the state while awaiting shipment to points outside the state from *ad valorem* property taxation. The specific rules vary from state to state; e.g., some states require that the goods remain in their original packages, whereas others do not. The reader is therefore advised to consult the statutes of those states with which he is concerned. The following jurisdictions now have "free port" legislation; Alabama, Arizona, Arkansas, California, Colorado, Connecticut, District of Columbia, Florida, Georgia, Idaho, Illinois, Indiana, Iowa, Kansas, Kentucky, Louisiana, Maine, Massachusetts, Michigan, Minnesota, Mississippi, Missouri, Montana, Nebraska, Nevada, New Jersey, New Mexico, North Carolina, Ohio, Oklahoma, Oregon, South Carolina, South Dakota, Tennessee, Texas, Utah, Wisconsin and Wyoming.

Consignment Sales

The question whether a foreign corporation is engaged in business within a given state is largely determined by whether it is in the actual ownership and possession of goods within the state for the purpose of barter and sale. A foreign corporation is doing business within the state when it consigns goods to a merchant to be sold *for the corporation* and not for himself, where the merchant does not purchase the goods, and the corporation does not actually part with the possession thereof.

The shipment of goods to a factor for sale by the factor on commission is ordinarily not doing business within the state. Nor is shipping goods in the state for sale in the name of the seller, although on commission, considered doing business within the states; nor is a foreign corporation doing business in the state by selling its products in the state by a factor in his own name, who is to make the sale, receive the consideration in his own name, and guarantee the collection of any credit extended to purchasers.

Where a foreign corporation consigns goods to a factor for sale, but does maintain a warehouse, office or a place of business, and does not pay any of the expense of receiving, handling, storing or selling its goods in a foreign state, and it is the factor who transacts local business, and bears the expense of receiving, selling, handling and storing the goods, it is the factor who is doing business in the foreign state and *not the corporation.*

Office or Salesroom in Foreign State

Corporations which maintain foreign offices or salesrooms must be careful to avoid adding other factors which may lead to the characterization of their business as interstate. These factors include the maintenance of a bank account, the carrying of a stock of goods for sale, the keeping of books of accounts, the hiring of employees, the making of collections by local agents within the state, the consummation of contracts in the foreign state or other acts which show an intention to carry on a local or interstate business. Isolated transactions are not interstate commerce within the meaning of the law, see *supra* p. 14-9, but even these should be guarded against for the reason that a suit on an isolated transaction, in a foreign state, of an unlicensed corporation is more than likely to be met with the defense that the corporation is engaged in interstate business and has no standing in the state courts. Even though the defense may be overruled, the corporation will be put to the expense of proving that it is not engaged in interstate business or that its transaction was an isolated one.

Principal Place of Business

The "principal place of business" of a corporation is of important significance. That phrase is one of the standards used in 28 U.S.C. § 1332 to determine if federal courts can acquire jurisdiction of a matter based on diversity of jurisdiction. The statute provides: "A corporation shall be deemed a citizen of any state by which it has been incorporated and of the state where it has its principal place of business." The courts are therefore frequently called upon to determine the location of a corporation's principal place of business in an effort to decide if the requirements of diversity jurisdiction have been fulfilled.

Where a corporation has its principal place of business is a question of fact to be determined in each particular case by taking into consideration such factors as the character of the corporation, its purposes, the kind of business in which it is engaged and the situs of its operations. But the weight to apply to each of these particular facts is a question of law. The federal courts have not developed one test by which a place of business can be ascertained. Instead, three general theories have developed:

1. The "home office" or "nerve center" tests used for corporations engaged in far-flung and varied activities which are carried on in different states. The principal place of business is the location of the nerve center from which information and decisions radiate to constituent parts, and from which the nerve center office has direct control and coordinates all activities. *Scot Typewriter Co. v. Underwood Corp.,* 170 F. Supp. 862 (S. D. N.Y. 1959).

2. The "place of operations" test holds that a corporation's principal place of business for purposes of diversity jurisdiction is where the actual physical operations of the company are carried on and directed rather than where occasional high-level policy decisions are made. *Leve v. General Motors Corp.,* 246 F. Supp. 761 (1965). Under this test, the courts select the state in which the operations predominate in accordance with such factors as the location of real property, equipment, inventory and other tangible assets, distribution of employees, payroll, production and other physical activities.

3. The "center of corporate activity" is the third test and it is similar to the place of operations test except that it stresses the site of the daily operational control of the corporation rather than the location of its actual physical operations. *Kelly v. United States Steel Corp.,* 284 F.2d 850 (1960). In that case, although the president and top executive officers had offices in New York where they spent substantial time, the board of directors met regularly in New York and the general counsel, secretary and treasurer had their offices in New York, high-level decisions were made in that state, the operation policy committee of the corporation conducted its affairs in Pennsylvania and the day-to-day business of the corporation was conducted in that state. The court concluded that Pennsylvania was the corporation's principal place of business.

Jurisdiction Over Nonresidents—"Long-Arm Statutes"

The preceding discussion concerns itself with the taxation and regulation by a foreign state of a corporation which is doing business within its territory. The criteria used for the purpose of doing business are different from those used by the courts of a state to determine whether it can acquire jurisdiction over a foreign corporation without personal service of a summons based on its "transacting business" in such state.

With the rise in interstate business transactions as a result of increased use of rapid communication and transportation, a creditor frequently was in a situation in which he desired to sue the defaulting party on a contract but was unable to obtain jurisdiction over it since its place of business was in another state. The cost and expense of commencing suit in the foreign jurisdiction and his unfamiliarity with the law were perhaps sufficient to deter the creditor from pursuing his rights.

In a response to this problem a number of states have enacted legislation by which a foreign corporation, if it engages in certain acts, becomes subject to the jurisdiction of the state's courts without the necessity of obtaining personal service of process. The New York Long-Arm Law, Civ. Prac. § 302 (McKinney 1971 & Supp. 1982), is typical of this type of statute. It provides:

CORPORATIONS 14–15

(a) *Acts which are the basis of jurisdiction.* As to a cause of action arising from any of the acts enumerated in this section, a court may exercise personal jurisdiction over any non-domiciliary, or his executor or administrator, who in person or through an agent:
    1. transacts any business within the state or contracts anywhere to supply goods or services in the state; or
    2. commits a tortious act within the state, except as to a cause of action for defamation of character arising from the act; or
    3. commits a tortious act without the state causing injury to person or property within the state, except as to a cause of action for defamation of character arising from the act, if he
        (i) regularly does or solicits business, or engages in any other persistent course of conduct, or derives substantial revenue from goods used or consumed or services rendered, in the state, or
        (ii) expects or should reasonably expect the act to have consequences in the state and derives substantial revenue from interstate or international commerce; or
    4. owns, uses or possesses any real property situated within the state.

The requirements necessary to "transact any business" within a state under the statute are substantially less than those required for "doing business" within a state. It would be impossible to enumerate all the possible circumstances which would satisfy the phrase "transacting business." In *Longines-Wittnauer Watch Co., Inc. v. Barnes & Reinecke, Inc.,* 15 N.Y.2d 443, 261 N.Y.S.2d 8, 209 N.E.2d 68 (1965), the defendant, a Delaware corporation which conducted its business in Illinois, manufactured special machinery for the plaintiff. Extensive negotiations were held in New York and in Illinois with principal officers of the defendant visiting New York in connection with the performance of the contract. The contract was executed in Illinois, although it stated that New York law was to govern. The Court of Appeals of New York sustained jurisdiction in New York because of the totality of the defendant's voluntary activities within the state. The court stated that the defendant had engaged in "purposeful acts" in New York thereby invoking the benefits of New York law; correspondingly, it must assume the liabilities as well.

Generally, the negotiation, execution or performance of a contract within a state is activity which would meet the requirements of the "long-arm" statute. Certain acts, however, standing by themselves will not be deemed sufficient contact with a state to invoke the statute, e.g., the mere shipment of goods into the state. However, the solicitation of business by means of catalogues, advertisements, promotional material or salesmen, when coupled with the shipment of goods into the state, may result in a transaction subjecting a foreign corporation to jurisdiction. *Singer v. Walker,* 15 N.Y.2d 443, 261 N.Y.S.2d 8, 209 N.E.2d 68 (1965).

Most of these "long-arm" statutes specifically provide that the business can be transacted in person or through an agent as provided by the New York statute. Therefore, even though an officer or employee of the foreign corporation does not appear in the state, the corporation can be subject to jurisdiction as a result of the acts of its representatives or exclusive sales agents. In *Schneider v. J & C Carpet Co.,* 23 A.D.2d 103, 258 N.Y.S.2d 717 (1st Dept. 1965), the plaintiff, a New York resident, sued a Georgia corporation for breach of an employment contract. Plaintiff was national sales director for defendant and performed his services out of New York. The court held that the employment of plaintiff in New York by the defendant was sufficient conduct to constitute the transaction of business within the state.

Hardy v. Pioneer Parachute Co., 531 F.2d 193 (4th Cir. 1976) involved an out-of-state manufacturer that sold its goods through a local distributor. The manufacturer also advertised in a national magazine and took telephone orders for the sale of parachutes. The court held that the manufacturer had sufficient contact with the state of South Carolina so that plaintiff, after purchasing a defective parachute, was able to use the South Carolina long-arm statute to obtain jurisdiction. In New York, a Dutch corporation was subject to a patent antitrust action because it was doing business through an owned subsidiary and agent, and satisfied the New York long-arm statute. *Meat Systems Corp. v. Ben Langel-Mol, Inc.,* 410 F.Supp. 231 (S.D.N.Y. 1976).

The debate over what activities constitute sufficient contact to trigger the jurisdiction of a state court over a nonresident has been stimulated by the landmark Supreme Court decisions, *Shaffer v. Heitner,* 433 U.S. 186 (1977), and *World-Wide Volkswagen Corp. v. Woodson,* 444 U.S. 286 (1980). In *Shaffer,* the Court held that a Delaware statute which allowed a court to take jurisdiction over a lawsuit by sequestering property in Delaware belonging to a nonresident violated that nonresident's due process rights. Justice Marshall, writing for the majority, declared that the "presence" of property belonging to a nonresident within a state's borders was not sufficient to establish that the nonresident had sufficient "minimum contact" with the state to subject him to the jurisdictional "long arm" reach of the state's courts. This is especially true when the property which the state has attached is unrelated to the cause of action in the lawsuit. To assert jurisdiction the court must involve itself in a broader inquiry of the nonresident's activities in the state.

In *World-Wide Volkswagen,* however, the Court held that an Oklahoma "minimum contacts" statute, which permitted the exercise of jurisdiction over any defendant deriving "substantial revenues from goods used or consumed" in the state, 444 U.S. at 290 n.7, could not be applied to a New York auto dealer and a northeastern distributor of a car involved in an accident within Oklahoma. The Court observed that to uphold Oklahoma jurisdiction in this case would mean that sellers of products would be subject to the jurisdiction of every state where the product happens to be used. The Court concluded that "whatever marginal revenues petitioners may receive by virtue of the fact that their products are capable of use in Oklahoma is far too attenuated a contact" to justify the exertion of jurisdiction. Id. at 299.

The ramifications of *Shaffer* and *World-Wide Volkswagen* will be worked out in the courts over the next few years. Whether the shift in emphasis from "presence" of property to "minimum contacts" will have a significant effect on jurisdictional decisions will be revealed over time. Many decisions will hinge on the issue of what the relationship is between the property attached as the basis for jurisdiction, and the cause of action. In a New York case, *Feder v. Turkish Airlines,* 441 F.Supp. 1273 (S.D.N.Y. 1977), New York residents brought a wrongful death action in New York against a foreign corporation. Plaintiffs attached a bank account in a New York bank which the defendants had used for payment of replacement parts for its aircraft. After the *Shaffer* decision, defendants moved to dismiss the case for lack of jurisdiction. The District Court for the Southern District of New York, although noting that the property in question was completely unrelated to the cause of action, concluded that the defendants had opened the bank account in New York to facilitate the conduct of their business and therefore the "minimum contacts" standard was satisfied.

Guaranties by Corporations

The general rule is that no corporation has power by any form of contract or endorsement to become a guarantor or surety or otherwise lend its credit to another person or corporation. Power to so act will not be implied from a provision in the charter of a corporation authorizing it to engage in a particular kind of business and such other business as may not be inconsistent therewith nor from a charter provision that the corporation may make contracts, possessing the same powers in such respects as private individuals now enjoy. The reasons for the rule are that such a contract risks the capital and funds of the corporation in an enterprise not contemplated by the stockholders in subscribing for or purchasing its stock, prejudices the rights of its creditors, and exceeds the authority conferred by its charter. This power has been denied to banking, loan, and trust companies, to insurance companies, to railroad, plank road, and other transportation companies, to land and irrigation companies and to manufacturing and merchandising companies.

So the courts have held that a corporation cannot issue accommodation paper for the payment of, or as security for, an individual debt of another person in which it has no interest, and for which it is not responsible, that it cannot assume liability for the individual debt of a stockholder, that it cannot execute a guaranty for the purpose of promoting a sale by another corporation, and that it has no power to guarantee the payment of other person's notes in which it has no interest.

Where a corporation is without power to become a surety on the note of another corporation, the fact that such contract of suretyship is based upon independent consideration does not render the corporation liable thereon. Nor does the fact that the corporation acting as surety has the same stockholders and officers as the corporation whose note it guarantees have any effect to validate the contract of suretyship.

When Guaranty Is Authorized

Sometimes a corporation is expressly authorized by charter or statute to make contracts of guaranty or suretyship, and frequently corporations are created for that express purpose. Such a company cannot, however, escape the general rule of law that a corporation cannot guarantee the liability of others, except insofar as it becomes a guarantor in the ordinary course of its business, or unless it receives the proceeds of the paper which it guarantees. Nor has a corporation authorized by statute to guarantee contracts any authority thereunder to enter into contracts of indemnity, not even on the theory that the making of indemnity contracts falls within the implied powers of such a corporation.

A corporation has, however, implied power to enter into a contract of guaranty or suretyship whenever the transaction can reasonably be said to be incidental to the conduct of the business authorized by its charter. But it must appear that the giving of the guaranty or the making of the contract of suretyship is reasonably necessary to enable the corporation to accomplish the object for which it was created, or that the particular transaction is reasonably necessary or proper in the conduct of its business. The mere fact that a contract of suretyship or guaranty may or will result in gain or benefit to the corporation, by increasing its business or otherwise, is not alone sufficient to authorize the same.

Cases Where Corporations May Be Guarantors

A corporation, to enable its customer to continue business and to pay the whole account due to the corporation, has been held to have power to guarantee such customer's payment for goods purchased from another corporation. Where a corporation sells a large quantity of goods on credit to a customer, whose only means of payment is derived from the profit in his business, it has implied power to pledge its credit to assist such debtor to borrow money to enable him to continue his business and thereby pay for such goods. A corporation, in order to collect an indebtedness which has arisen from the conduct of its business, may take over all the property of the debtor, and agree to guarantee the debtor's indebtedness to a third party and on the sale of the property to apply the proceeds of the goods to the guaranteed debt. The guarantor's securing to itself by means of the guaranty the payment of its own claim against the guarantee, however, must enter into the transaction as the real consideration for it. If the guaranty is solely for the accommodation of another, the guaranty will be unenforceable, even though the guarantee is a customer of the guarantor, and that fact influenced the guarantor to sign the guaranty.

A corporation may guarantee the payment of another's debt where such guaranty is accepted as payment of the guarantor's own debt. Additionally, a corporation may guarantee the payment of another's debt where it is shown that, while in form the debt of another, it is in substance the corporation's own debt. Thus, when a partnership is incorporated and the corporation takes the property of the firm, it has power to assume or guarantee the liabilities of the firm.

The general principle of law underlying decisions as to the validity of corporate guaranties which result in an increase of the business of the corporation is that no authority in a corporation to lend credit to another is to be implied simply from the fact that it may be beneficial to the corporation. Applying this principle to these decisions, the rule is that a guaranty or contract of suretyship by a corporation is not within its powers merely because it will result in an increase of trade or business. If, however, the contract of guaranty is within the scope of the legitimate business of the corporation and is made for the purpose of increasing the guarantor's business and can reasonably be expected to have that effect, it is a contract within the powers of the corporation.

In some states there are statutory provisions permitting a corporation, for a valuable consideration, to guarantee or assume the debt of another corporation. Such statutory authority should be consulted before accepting a corporate guaranty or extending credit upon it.

Unless there is specific authority contained in its charter, a bank has no implied power to lend its credit and cannot become an accommodation indorser or a guarantor. There are exceptions to this rule; when it is necessary for the bank to protect its own rights, where the guaranty relates to commercial paper and is incidental to the purchase and sale thereof, or where such guaranty is specially authorized by law, the bank can lend its credit.

It was held that where a bank directed a letter to a person stating that it would guarantee fulfillment of the obligations of another party for a certain amount of goods for a certain time and it did not appear that the party purchased the letter or deposited securities therefor or that the bank had any interest in the transaction, the letter, considered either as a guaranty or a letter of credit, was void and the bank was not liable thereon. *Tilmany v. Iowa Paper-Bag Co.,* 108 Iowa 333, 79 N.W. 68 (1899).

It should be noted, however, that the accommodation indorsement or guaranty of a bank becomes binding in favor of a bona fide holder of the instrument so indorsed or guaranteed for the reason that there is no obligation on the holder to inquire whether the bank owned the paper at the time of its indorsement. *Mechanics' Banking Association v. New York & Saugerties White Lead Co.,* 35 N.Y. 505 (1866).

Guaranties Between Parent and Subsidiary Corporations

Problems frequently arise with respect to the right of a parent corporation to guarantee the obligations of its subsidiary and conversely the subsidiary's power to act as guarantor for the parent. There is ample authority to support the proposition that a parent corporation may make a valid guaranty for the benefit of its subsidiary. It should be noted, however, that the various cases in which this question has been considered point up the fact that the guaranty is in furtherance of the parent's authorized business, whether from the point of view of protecting its investment in the subsidiary or in support of its customary business activities.

It is obvious that a guaranty by a subsidiary for the benefit of its parent does not present a comparable basis for authorization, and no authority can be found which will support such a guaranty solely by reason of the relationship. The subsidiary ordinarily has no investment in the parent to protect, and as previously noted a corporation has no authority to guarantee obligations of its stockholders. There appears, however, to be no reason why the relationship between the two corporations would prevent a valid and enforceable guaranty if the act can be justified by business considerations previously discussed in the case of unrelated corporations.

COMMON LAW OR MASSACHUSETTS TRUSTS

The business trust, more commonly referred to as a common law or Massachusetts trust, is a form of business organization which is in some respects related to corporations. It is not a corporation, however, and is to be distinguished from the corporate form in many respects. This form of organization has been recognized for centuries in England and came to be known as a Massachusetts trust as a result of its extensive use in that state. It has since been recognized and used throughout the United States. For example, Ohio recently amended its Code to authorize and govern the creation and operation of business trusts. "A business trust is hereby declared to be a permitted form of association for the conduct of business in this state. A business trust is a separate unincorporated legal entity, not a partnership, joint venture, joint-stock association, agency, or any other form of entity." Ohio Rev. Code Ann. § 1746.02 (Page 1983). However, in some states, notably Texas, it has been treated more as a partnership or joint-stock company than as a business trust.

In its simplest form a Massachusetts trust is created by the transfer of property to a trustee or trustees under an appropriate agreement whereby the trustees operate the property or business for the benefit of the beneficiaries. Certificates are issued to the beneficiaries according to their proportionate interests, and the certificate holders, or stockholders, as they are commonly referred to, participate in the income of the trust and, upon its termination, the principal. Generally, as in the case of stockholders of a corporation, the shareholders of the trust are not subject to liability for the debts and obligations of the trust. Although some states have statutes regulating business trusts, basically the trust derives no power, rights or privileges from statutory law as does a corporation. These powers, rights or privileges come from the trust agreement, subject to the rules governing trusts generally. In many states the statutes relating to corporations are applicable in many respects to business trusts.

Depending upon the agreement creating it, a business trust may continue for a fixed duration of time or may have perpetual existence. The death of a certificate holder does not effect a dissolution of the trust any more than would the death of a stockholder affect the corporation. The certificates of the shareholder in either case would pass through his estate in the same manner as a certificate of corporate stock.

Powers and Liabilities of the Trustees

The business of the trust is managed by the trustees who hold legal title to all its property. The extent of their rights and authority with regard to the management of the trust property and the incurring of obligations for which the trust property will be bound must be determined from the instrument creating the trust and the applicable law in the jurisdiction of its creation. While there may be some delegation of powers by the trustees to one or more of the trustees, or even to administrative personnel, as a general rule the business trust must act through its trustees functioning as a unit.

There is imposed upon the trustees in their relation to the certificate holders substantially the same fiduciary relationship and obligations as in the case of any trustee and beneficiary. They are held to the strictest accountability in their dealings with or on behalf of the trust and are accountable to the shareholders for the property entrusted to them and any loss sustained as a result of misconduct or mismanagement. In their dealings with third persons the trustees act as principals and are personally liable for obligations arising out of the operation of the business of the trust unless they have been absolved from this responsibility by agreement with the party with whom they contract. As in the case of any trustee, the trustees of the business trust are entitled to reimbursement from the trust fund for all obligations properly incurred on its behalf. They are not relieved of liability, however, if the obligation cannot be discharged by the trust due to insufficient assets.

Business Trust Considered a Partnership

We have previously indicated that in some states the business trust has been treated as a partnership. What we have said heretofore with respect to business trusts relates solely to those trusts which are properly organized and conform to the requirements of what is sometimes known as a "pure trust." There have been many instances where, because of the nature of the trust agreement and the control exercised by the shareholders over the trustees in the conduct of the business, the organization has been held to constitute a partnership. The mere fact that the trust instrument provides that the certificate holders are exempt from personal liability for debts will not be effective if in fact the organization is a partnership.

On the other hand, many cases have held that where the beneficiaries retain no control over the trustees and are not, in fact, associated in the actual carrying on of the business, but are limited in interest to having the trust administered in their interest, the organization should be regarded as a strict trust rather than a partnership. It is frequently a difficult problem to determine whether a common law business trust is of partnership character or is to be regarded as a pure trust.

Subject to Law of Foreign Corporations

In *Hemphill v. Orloff,* 277 U.S. 537 (1928), the plaintiff, a common law or Massachusetts trust, brought an action in Michigan on a note executed in that state. The defense was interposed that the plaintiff was a foreign corporation not entitled to do business in the state of Michigan.

The court held that the trust sufficiently partook of the nature of a corporation to be amenable to the Foreign Corporation Law, saying:

> Obviously the Trust here involved is a creature of local law which demands the privilege of carrying on business in Michigan as an association—an entity—clothed with peculiar rights and privileges under a deed of settlement, undertaking to exempt all of the associates from personal liability. . . .
>
> Whether a given association is called a corporation, partnership, or trust, is not the essential factor in determining the powers of a state concerning it. The real nature of the organization must be considered. If clothed with the ordinary functions and attributes of a corporation it is subject to similar treatment.

Id. at 550

The importance of the distinction as to the form of organization arises particularly in connection with questions of taxation, it being held that where the members are found to be partners, the partnership property may be taxed at the place where the business is conducted; whereas, if the certificate holders are merely *cestuis que trustent,* the interest of each beneficiary in the trust estate is taxable in the city or town of his residence and the business itself escapes direct taxation.

The purposes for which such trusts may be formed are subject to no limitations in jurisdictions where common law business trusts are permitted. Instances of the objects of such organizations embrace the holding, managing, improving, selling, and leasing of real estate, the operating of factories and power plants, disposing of patent rights, carrying on of express business, dealing in stocks, bonds, and securities, operating trading companies, and working mines. In short, practically any business of any nature may be organized in this form unless prohibited by statute.

The most important question from the standpoint of the credit grantor is the validity of the provisions limiting liability. There seems to be no question that the trustees may lawfully be limited by agreement as to incurring indebtedness so as not to bind the certificate holders personally. Thus, in *Bank of Topeka v. Eaton,* 100 F. 8 (C.C.D. Mass. 1900), where the articles of association of a joint-stock company provided that any debt incurred by the trustees for the association should be a lien upon the trust property, but that they had no power to bind the shareholders personally, it was held that one who took a note from the trustees containing an express statement that it was given under the articles of association, and not otherwise, would be limited to a proceeding against the trust property so that he could not maintain an action against the shareholders individually. The fact that the liability of each member is expressly limited to his share has been held not enough to make illegal a joint-stock which in its nature is a business trust.

Partnerships—Joint Ventures

15

The advent of the corporate form of business organization, and the growth of commercial enterprises requiring substantially greater capital, have been accompanied by a decrease in the use of the partnership. While the partnership form afforded many advantages over the operation of a business by a single entrepreneur, by uniting the capital and skills of its members and spreading the risks of loss, it cannot match the advantage of limitation of personal liability provided by incorporation. Notwithstanding the corporate advantages, a substantial volume of the nation's business continues to be carried on by partnerships.

Where activities of a business extend beyond one state or into foreign countries it is often found that the restrictions imposed on foreign corporations, as well as tax considerations, make the partnership a preferable vehicle of operation. It is also found that many of the risks inherent in commercial transactions can be adequately covered by insurance and thus the advantages offered by incorporation are of less significance. The problems of taxation are another important consideration in determining whether incorporation is preferable to partnership operation. In many jurisdictions corporations pay taxes which are not levied against partnerships. In the past there were statutory prohibitions regarding the conduct of certain businesses in the corporate form, especially the professions, but these restrictions now have been removed by most states.

The tax advantage of the partnership permits the partners to deduct losses from their personal tax returns while shareholders in a corporation ordinarily cannot do so. This advantage has been minimized by the addition of Sub-Chapter S to the Internal Revenue Code which permits corporations of no more than thirty-five shareholders to be taxed as a partnership upon the consent of all shareholders. I.R.C. §§ 1371-1379.

A partnership results from an agreement, express or implied, between two or more competent parties to unite their property, money, skill or labor, for the entering into of a lawful business for profit. No particular form of contract is necessary to create a partnership. It need only be in writing if it comes within the provisions of the Statute of Frauds. See Chapter 4, *supra* p. 4-1. Like other contracts the general rules regarding the creation, validity and discharge of the contract are applicable. The partnership may be formed for the purpose of carrying out a single transaction or it may be formed for the operation of a general business over a period of time. Of course, the partnership must contemplate a legal purpose.

It should be noted that there must be mutual assent by all the parties to form a partnership agreement and that each person must give his consent; he cannot be made a partner by the act of another. A person may act, however, in such a manner with another that the law will not permit him to deny that a partnership relationship exists. For example, where a person permits his name to be employed by a partnership, so that persons doing business with the partnership will rely upon his ostensible membership in extending credit, such person will not be permitted thereafter to deny the existence of his membership in the partnership.[1] Where there is an actual partnership, third parties are entitled to rights against the partnership in dealing with it even though the existence of the partnership is unknown to them.

Uniform Partnership Acts

Today every state, except Louisiana, has adopted the Uniform Partnership Act which has defined to a great extent the powers and liabilities of partners. The Act defines a partnership to be "an association of two or more persons to carry on as co-owners a business for profit." Uniform Partnership Act § 6(1). Within the purview of this Act, in order to have a partnership it is necessary that the elements of this definition be found in all relationships. One element without the other cannot create a partnership liability. For example, the mere fact that one shares profits in an enterprise is not a conclusive test of a partnership for it is frequent that profits are paid as compensation for services, in other than partnership transactions. The Uniform Partnership Law recognizes this distinction and makes provision for it.

There are three possible kinds of partners in a partnership: general, limited, and silent (also known as a dormant or secret partner). A general partner, as the term suggests, is one who is liable for the firm's obligations without limitation as to amount. Before such a partner may relieve himself of liability to creditors, in the event that he wishes to sever his relation with the partnership, he must give notice of his withdrawal to all those with whom the partnership has dealt. Limited partners are those who contribute capital to the partnership and who are liable only to the extent of their contribution. Full partnership liability may not be fastened upon them. A silent partner is one who, although not publicly acknowledging the relationship, has either by act or deed placed himself in such position that he is regarded in law as a general partner and, consequently, is liable for all the firm's obligations.

Frequently an individual engages in business under a firm name; such practice is lawful unless contrary to the provisions of some statute. However, such person stands in the same position with respect to creditors and others as he would be if he conducted his business under his individual name. In many jurisdictions statutory provisions have been enacted which prohibit the doing of business under an assumed or fictitious name without complying with certain statutory requirements. These requirements will be found in Chapter 22, *supra*, "Summary of State Laws." The statute usually provides that a failure to conform to its provisions constitutes a misdemeanor and subjects the violator to a fine. In such cases the contracts of such persons are not affected as to their validity. In some states the violation of statutory provisions of this type will affect the validity of the contract.

State Statutes Apply

When a partnership is formed, in the absence of statutory restrictions, it may do business under any name that it wishes to assume. Here again there are

---

[1] The filing of a certificate of doing business under an assumed name by two or more persons may constitute *prima facie* evidence of partnership.

many statutory provisions regarding the use of partnership names, such as the use of the name of one who is not a partner, the use of fictitious names, and the use of the designation "& Company" or "& Co." where such designation does not represent an actual partner. In many states there are statutes requiring the filing of partnership certificates which must set forth the names of individual partners, the firm name, place of business and similar information. This subject is discussed in Chapter 21, *supra,* "Other Commercial Crimes."

The property of the partnership consists of such property as is contributed to the firm by the individual partners and which thereafter may be acquired in the course of partnership transactions. Profits received from the partnership business become the partnership's property as do goods manufactured or other types of capital produced or acquired by the partnership in its operations.

At common law a partnership could not, as such, hold title to real estate, but by statute, such as the Uniform Partnership Act, a partnership is in many states permitted to own real property. See, for example, Uniform Partnership Act § 8(3); N.Y. Partnership Law § 12(3) (McKinney 1948). If a partnership is not permitted to own real estate, property must be acquired in the individual names of all the partners or in the name of one partner who is deemed to hold the property in trust for the partnership. When the partnership acquires real estate it is deemed to be converted into personalty and is subject to partnership debts.

The Partnership Contract

The partnership contract usually sets forth the partners' rights and duties and the extent of their liability. See generally Uniform Partnership Act §§ 15, 18-22. The partners in some jurisdictions are expressly declared to be trustees for each other with respect to partnership property, and in all jurisdictions the partners are required to deal in partnership affairs with the utmost good faith; each partner is entitled to full knowledge of all partnership affairs. Every partner is entitled to take part in the conduct and management of the firm's business in the absence of a contrary agreement of the parties which may assign certain duties to each of the partners. In the event that the partners differ about the management or conduct of the business, the will of the majority is controlling.

Upon each of the partners rests the duty of seeing that proper books are kept of the firm's affairs and that each partner is entitled to statements of account of partnership transactions. The partners are entitled to share equally in the profits of the business in the absence of an agreement which apportions the profits. Likewise, the partners must share equal liability for expenses and losses in the absence of a contrary agreement. If a partner contributes personal service to the partnership business, in the absence of a contrary agreement, he is entitled to compensation for such service in addition to his share of the profits. The law does not permit suit against a partnership by a partner or by the partnership against a partner. The proper course is to secure an accounting.

Each partner is deemed the agent for all the other partners and such agent is empowered to contract and bind the partnership. In this respect the principles of the law of agency are applicable to partnership transactions. Ordinarily third parties are entitled to rely upon the general power of a partner to contract on behalf of the partnership, except where the character of the transaction is such that the person may have reason to believe that the partner is not acting within the scope of the partnership business or is exceeding his authority. Within the scope of partnership business are such matters as making contracts in ordinary course of business, sales, purchases, payments and receipts of money, borrowing money, including mortgaging or pledging firm assets, signing negotiable instruments and hiring or discharging employees or agents. Where the partner attempts to do some act such as to dispose of the entire assets of the business, assign for the benefit of creditors, sell furniture and fixtures, or confess judgment he is probably acting beyond the scope of his authority and one dealing with him acts at his own risk if the partner is actually exceeding his authority. A partner cannot bind his copartners by a contract of guaranty or suretyship for some third person. In *First National Bank v. Farson,* 226 N.Y. 218 (1919) the court held: "When a party takes a guaranty, to which the partnership name is signed, the burden of proof is on him to show that the partner who signed such name had authority, from one of the legitimate sources, so to do." Id. at 225.

The partnership is liable for all acts done or representations made by each partner in the course of partnership business. This liability is, in general, the same as the liability of a principal for acts and representations of his agent.

Partners Jointly Liable

Partners are generally held to be jointly liable for partnership obligations, although in a few jurisdictions they are held to be liable jointly and severally and such liability may be altered by agreement. In general it may be stated that each partner is personally liable to the full extent of the partnership debts. See, for example, Uniform Partnership Act § 15. Creditors of the firm, who are generally required to proceed first to satisfy judgment and liens against firm property, may resort to the property of the individual partners. With respect to the rights of creditors of an individual partner it may be stated that such creditors' rights are limited to the personal property of the partner and his proportionate interest in the partnership.

Dissolution of Partnerships

The dissolution of the partnership may be effected by agreement of the parties or through court proceedings or by reason of some occurrence which effects a dissolution.

Under the Uniform Partnership Law, dissolution of a partnership is defined to be a change in relationship of the partners caused by any partner's ceasing to be associated in the carrying on, as distinguished from the winding up, of the business. Id. § 29.

The causes of dissolution are as follows:

1. Without violation of the agreement between the partners: (a) by the termination of the definite term or particular undertaking specified in the agreement; (b) by the express will of any partner when no definite term or particular undertaking is specified; (c) by the express will of all the partners who have not assigned their interests or suffered them to be charged for their separate debts, either before or after the termination of any specified term or particular undertaking (d) by the bona fide expulsion of any partner from the business in accordance with such a power conferred by the agreement between the partners.

2. In contravention of the agreement between the partners, where the circum-

stances do not permit a dissolution under any other provision of this section, by the express will of any partner at any time.[1]

3. By any event which makes it unlawful for the business of the partnership to be carried on or for the members to carry it on in partnership.

4. By the death of any partner.

5. By the bankruptcy of any partner or the partnership.[2]

Id. § 31.

In addition to the foregoing causes of dissolution, a judicial dissolution may be decreed under the following circumstances:

1. On application by or for a partner the court shall decree a dissolution whenever (a) a partner has been declared mentally incompetent in any judicial proceeding or is shown to be of unsound mind; (b) a partner becomes in any other way incapable of performing his part of the partnership contract; (c) a partner has been guilty of such conduct as tends to affect prejudicially the carrying on of the business; (d) a partner wilfully or persistently commits a breach of the partnership agreement, or otherwise so conducts himself in matters relating to the partnership business that it is not reasonably practicable to carry on the business in partnership with him; (e) the business of the partnership can only be carried on at a loss; (f) other circumstances render a dissolution equitable.

2. On the application of a purchaser of a partner's interest: (a) after the termination of the specified term or particular undertaking; (b) at any time if the partnership was a partnership at will when the interest was assigned or when the charging order was issued.

Id. § 32.

It is important to note that dissolution does not effect a complete termination of the partnership, but that the partnership continues until the winding up of partnership affairs is completed. Id. § 30.

Continuation of Business After Death of Partner

Although the death of a partner terminates the partnership, it continues for some purposes long enough to enable the surviving partners to settle the partnership affairs and wind up the business. However, the partners may agree prior thereto that the death of one will not terminate the partnership or the will of a deceased partner may sanction the continuation of the partnership business.

In the absence of agreement or will to the contrary, the partnership is dissolved and the partnership assets vest in the surviving partners as "trustees" for the purpose of settling the partnership affairs. After payment of all the firm's debts, the deceased partner's estate is entitled to a pro-rata share of the partnership assets depending upon the proportionate interest of the decedent in the partnership. If the partnership is continued, the estate of the deceased partner is liable to the extent of its interest in the partnership assets but not beyond this.[3]

---

[1] The statutes of Georgia and Louisiana do not provide for unilateral dissolution of a partnership in contravention of the partnership agreement.

[2] Although the bankruptcy of one or more general partners effects a dissolution of the partnership, it does not follow that the partnership itself is bankrupt.

[3] *Continued use of firm name.* Where a partner dies, the right of the surviving partners to conduct business under a name including the name of the deceased partner varies in the several states. Some hold the name is a firm asset inseparable from good will and as such can be sold with other assets. In some states the consent of the legal representative of the deceased partner is required.

The death of a partner does not generally terminate existing contracts to which the firm is a party. However, in special cases, such as where the performance of personal services by the deceased partner was an essential part of the contract, his death may terminate it. The surviving partners take possession of the assets, have the sole right to collect and sue upon claims, and may make new contracts for the winding up of the partnership business. Except where it is essential to winding up the business, the surviving partners cannot make new contracts or incur obligations binding on the firm or deceased partner's estate unless authorized by the decedent's will or prior agreement. The partnership business may be continued for a short time in order to dispose of stock on hand and small purchases of additional stock may be made to render that on hand more saleable; existing contracts of the firm, in most cases, may be completed. Contracts beyond the scope of the surviving partners' authority as above bind the surviving partners personally but not the estate of deceased partner. After dissolution a partner can bind the partnership by any act appropriate to the winding up of partnership affairs. Furthermore, the partnership is bound by any post-dissolution transaction which would have bound the partnership if dissolution had not taken place, if the other party to the post-dissolution transaction had been a creditor prior to the dissolution and had no knowledge of the dissolution *or,* had not previously extended credit but knew of the partnership before its dissolution, had no knowledge or notice of the dissolution, and the dissolution had not been advertised in a local general circulation newspaper. No definite rule can be laid down about how long a period of time the business may be continued, as this will depend on the nature of the business and the work necessary to settle its affairs and wind up the partnership. The surviving partners may sell, mortgage or pledge the firm's assets for the purpose of raising money to pay firm debts or to secure the payment thereof.

Where the partnership assets are insufficient to pay its obligations, the creditors may have recourse to the property of the surviving partners and the estate of the deceased partner. There is conflict of authority about whether a creditor of an insolvent partnership is precluded from asserting a claim against the deceased partner's estate after the time for filing claims against the estate has expired. No general rule can be laid down about the terms on which creditors of the partnership and creditors of the deceased partner may share in assets of the deceased partner's estate if the assets of the firm are insufficient to pay all partnership creditors. There are conflicting decisions in the various states and in many states this subject is covered by statute.

LIMITED PARTNERSHIPS

A limited partnership is defined in the Uniform Limited Partnership Act as a partnership "having as members one or more general partners and one or more limited partners." Id. § 1. A limited partner is one who contributes to the partnership capital and shares in its profits but who has no powers in the control of the business of the partnership and no personal liability for its debts. The extent of such partner's liability is the amount of his capital investment in the partnership which, like all partnership property, is subject to claims of creditors. In all respects, except the relationship of the limited partner to the other members and to third persons, the limited partnership is substantially the same as a general partnership. The general partners retain the same powers and are subject to the same liabilities to creditors as in a general partnership. This relationship must not be confused with statutory partnership associations, such as are authorized in Michigan, which have the word "limited" following their names and which have the character of quasi-corporations.

The Uniform Limited Partnership Act has been adopted in most states.

How Formed

Most states require the filing of a limited partnership certificate signed by all partners containing (1) firm name and principal place of business; (2) nature of business partnership will engage in; (3) names and addresses of partners, specifying which are general and which limited partners; (4) amount of capital contributed by each limited partner; (5) duration of partnership. See, e.g., Uniform Limited Partnership Act § 2; Del. Code Ann. tit. 6, § 17-201 (1982). The contribution of capital by limited partners is usually required to be wholly in cash and prior to the formation of the partnership. This requirement, however, varies from state to state. For example, in New York a limited partner may contribute "cash or other property, but not services." N.Y. Partnership Law § 93 (McKinney 1948). In Delaware the limited partner may contribute or give a promissory note to contribute, cash, property, or services. Del. Code Ann. tit. 6, § 17-201 (a) (5) (1982). In many states a general partner must file an affidavit stating that such contributions have been made. All the required papers are usually filed or recorded with recording officer of the county in which the business is to be conducted and the certificate of partnership published for a specified number of times in a newspaper of general circulation in the locality.

Various state statutes contain provisions as to use of firm name and partners' names so as to advise the public of the nature of the partnership. Usually the name of at least one general partner must appear in the firm name. In some states the partnership is required to display a sign in front of its place of business designating which of its partners are general and which special partners.

There are a number of distinctions between limited and general partnerships, including the following: The limited partnership continues only for the period of time mentioned in its certificate; the limited partner may not usually engage in management of the business of the firm; his interest in the partnership assets is limited to his capital investment; the limited partner's compensation is in the form of interest on his contribution and a proportion of the profits; he is not permitted to withdraw any part of his capital contribution to the firm during the partnership's existence; under most statutes the death of a limited partner does not terminate the partnership.

Relationship to Third Persons

The general partners in a limited partnership are subject to all the liabilities of partners in a general partnership, and are jointly and severally liable for the partnership debts and obligations. The limited partners are not liable beyond the capital contributed to the firm. Dealings between the firm and third parties are to be carried on by the general partners. Although a limited partner cannot usually bind the partnership by his contract, such contract may be ratified by the general partners. The general participation of a limited partner in conduct of the firm business can subject him to liability as a general partner. For example, in Tennessee a limited partner may be liable for the obligations of the limited partnership if "he takes part in the control of the business." Tenn. Code Ann. § 61-2-107 (1983). The limited partner will also be subjected to personal liability for obligations incurred after the firm has altered its capital, membership or business. The withdrawal of his capital contribution, or part thereof, from the firm may subject the limited partner to liability of a general partner and to restoration of the capital so withdrawn, depending on the statutory provisions of each state. A limited partner is not liable for torts of general partners and agents of the firm to which he is not a party. A limited partner is personally liable as a general partner to any person whom he has induced to deal with the partnership on the representation that he is a general partner. A limited partner is ordinarily not a proper party to a suit against the partnership.

Upon insolvency the partnership's assets become a trust fund for payment of claims of creditors. The partnership may make an assignment for the benefit of creditors or file a petition in bankruptcy. After all the general creditors are paid a limited partner may share in the firm assets on his claim for capital contribution and loans. In some states he is permitted to share in assets along with general creditors for loans made to the partnership above his capital contribution. An individual creditor of a limited partner can assert no claim against the partnership. Nor can his interest be the subject of attachment or execution. In other respects the insolvency of limited partnerships is substantially the same as that of a general partnership.

As with corporations, most states require that a foreign limited partnership shall register in the state before it conducts business there.

A limited partnership may be dissolved upon death or bankruptcy of a general partner, misconduct of a general partner, fraud practiced upon a limited partner or by expiration of the term for which partnership was organized. Dissolution may also be by the consent of all partners. The general partners are obliged to distribute assets and settle the partnership affairs.

HUSBAND-WIFE PARTNERSHIPS

At common law a partnership agreement between husband and wife was on its face invalid because the identity of the husband and wife was regarded as so closely merged that one could not contract with the other. The tendency in most states to greatly enlarge the rights of married women in contracting and dealing with their property has led to the recognition of the validity of such partnership agreements in the majority of the states. The District of Columbia, Maine, Michigan, and Washington are the only jurisdictions in the United States which do not recognize the validity of partnership agreements between husbands and wives.

Where a husband and wife purport to enter into a partnership in a state which does not recognize the validity of such agreements, the agreement is invalid for all purposes. The property of the married woman cannot be subjected to liability for partnership debts and neither the husband nor the wife can impose any liability upon the other by any action taken in the name of the partnership.

JOINT VENTURES

Joint ventures, or joint adventures, as they are sometimes called, may be defined as contracts in which two or more persons (together constituting one party thereto), as contractors, jointly and severally bind themselves, for their mutual benefit, to perform definite promises or obligations in a certain special transaction, their interests being separate and apart from and not joined with any other interests. As more briefly defined in the decision in *Forman v. Lumm*, 214 A.D. 579, 212 N.Y.S. 487 (1st Dept. 1925), a joint venture "is an association of two or more persons to carry out a single business enterprise for profit, for which purpose they combine their property, money, effects, skill, and knowledge." 212 N.Y.S. at 490-91.

As the relationship is now understood, it is almost purely American although it is also used in England. The authorities report that during the remote Roman period some such relationship was recognized, but, like the ancient mortgage transaction, it was not always practiced in a manner equitable to all. It took years of experience and American ingenuity to develop the relationship into an instrument which is really helpful in conducting business affairs.

The relationship of the joined parties in such contracts verges on partnership, and very little difference actually exists. In fact, as the decisions reveal, it is quite apparent that the theory of the law of partnership is being applied in joint venture situations. For example, in *Hardin v. Robinson* 178 A.D. 724, 162 N.Y.S. 531 (1st Dept. 1916), the court stated that the joint venture is subject to the same rules as a partnership so far as concerns questions of duration and the exclusion of a member from participation in the profits; the intention of the joined parties is controlling.

A slight difference does exist, however, when one coadventurer attempts to bind the other in his dealings with third persons. Also, the joint venture covers but one particular transaction while a partnership may continue indefinitely for various kinds of transactions.

The difference between a joint venture and an ordinary contract is marked. The usual contract may be made between a buyer and seller, the latter of whom agrees and is able to deliver merchandise or to perform certain specified services. Joint contractors or adventurers, on the other hand, agree to perform the contract as one collective party to the transaction by exercising their respective combined resources, often quite different in nature, while depending upon each on the other for the completion of the enterprise. Joint venturers are mutual fiduciaries.

Often the joint contractors do not realize the status of their relationship when they enter into the agreement and do not know that they are operating under and are controlled by the law relating to joint ventures, which is gradually being placed in a special category. Consequently, a contract, which is believed to be just an ordinary written statement of mutual promises, or an agreement of employment, or even a partnership, may be held to be a joint venture.

As a result, the status of the relationship of the promisors and their liabilities and obligations which each assumes jointly as well as severally, becomes more important. A properly drawn contract of joint venture, therefore, will set forth the intent and will use appropriate words to bind the promisors to complete the whole of the obligations either together, or separately if one or the other fails to perform. In connection with these requirements a credit statement evidencing the ability of both parties to perform is a wise preliminary.

In most jurisdictions the words "we jointly and severally," "we, or either of us," or, "I promise" (followed by the signatures of two or more promisors), mean what they say, but in other jurisdictions, where the influence of the Roman Laws still prevails, these expressions are not always so interpreted. It follows, therefore, that such expressions should be supported by additional words of explanation so that the joint and several obligations may be enforced and the contract fully completed regardless of subsequent events, including the insolvency or the death of one of the parties.

Such expressions as "we will undertake," "the directors promise," or "we promise" import only a joint liability, and do not carry the joint and several feature which is so necessary in joint ventures, as above mentioned.

Releasing one adventurer from his obligations discharges all from liability, in some jurisdictions, and a well-drawn joint contract provides for this contingency.

The status of the joint adventurers, as between themselves, is one of the most important features of the agreement. Is there in fact a joint venture, or is there merely a contract of employment between the parties, or is there a partnership relation?

Another element worthy of mention is the right of another person who deals with the joint adventurer in good faith and without knowledge of any limitations upon his authority. There is a presumption that the adventurer has been given the power to bind his associates by such contracts as are reasonably necessary to carry on the business in which they are presently engaged, and this is so even though they may have expressly agreed among themselves that they should not be so liable.

This is not the law, however, if commitments are made covering transactions outside the scope of the business of the adventurers. A third person, under such conditions, deals with a joint adventurer at his peril. While this feature resembles a partnership, and is one of the similarities referred to above, there still exists a fine distinction between them because the contract covering joint ventures will (or should) define the scope of an explicit enterprise.

Principal and Agent

An agent is a person who represents, or is authorized to represent, another person in a transaction or transactions with third parties. The person represented is known as the "principal" and the person appointed is designated as "agent," "attorney," "broker," "proxy," "factor," or by some other similar term.

Any competent person may appoint an agent to represent him, and any qualified and competent person may be appointed agent of another. Agents may be either general, in which case they are authorized to assume entire charge of their principal's business, or special, in which event they are authorized to act only in a specific transaction or a limited amount of business.

An agent who guarantees the payment of the accounts that he sells is a *"del credere* agent." Under the laws of most states such an agent may be held primarily liable for his principal's debt, but in a few jurisdictions he is regarded only as surety for the debt.

The power and authority of an agent are limited by the terms of his employment. A person dealing with an agent, in the absence of specific information as to the limitations of the agent's authority, or because charged with notice of such limitations by virtue of past transactions with the agent, may rely upon the agent's authority to bind his principal in all matters coming within the usual scope of such an agent's employment.

A traveling salesman, in the absence of special circumstances, cannot be presumed to have authority to bind his company by the acceptance of an order for its product. His usual function is merely to solicit orders and forward them to the office of his employer, where they are subject to acceptance or rejection. The limit of a salesperson's usual authority has been consistently recognized by the courts, and the acts of the salesperson's employer subsequent to the receipt of the order usually determine whether or not the order has been so accepted as to bind the seller to deliver.

Ordinarily a traveling salesman has no authority to accept and receipt for payment on behalf of his principal, and in the absence of evidence about the extent of the salesman's authority, a payment made to the agent will not discharge the debt unless the moneys are actually received by the principal.

How Agents Are Appointed

While the agent's appointment does not have to be evidenced by writing, it is prudent to insist upon proof of the agent's authority in all transactions involving substantial amounts. A special agent is often appointed by means of a written power of attorney which specifically delineates the scope of the agent's authority.

A person may, however, without authorization, act on behalf of a principal, and the acceptance by the principal of the fruits of such person's performance ratifies such person's agency. If a duly appointed agent performs an unauthorized act, the principal on learning of it may either refuse to be bound by it, or may expressly or impliedly ratify it.

Even if an agent has no express authority from his principal, the principal's conduct may be such as to indicate that the agent has apparent authority. A third person dealing with the agent and relying on such apparent authority may hold the principal liable. For example, if A stands by and permits B, an unauthorized agent, to sell A's goods, and makes no protest, but acquiesces in the transaction, A will be held to have appointed B his agent and will be bound by the transaction.

A wife has implied authority to represent her husband in the purchase of all household supplies and clothing for the use of herself and her children within the limits of the parties' accustomed station in life. But a wife may not go beyond this point in binding her husband without express authority. Likewise minor children have implied authority to purchase the necessaries of life on the credit of their father.

Subagents

The authority of an agent is delegated and is subject to the principle that a delegated power may not be further delegated. Therefore, an agent may not, without express authority from the principal, delegate to subagents authority to make contracts on behalf of the principal.

Liability of Agent Where Principal Is Undisclosed

If the person who is in fact an agent for another conceals the fact of his agency, and makes a contract in his own name, he renders himself personally liable. But if he acted within his authority as agent, the third party, upon discovering the identity of the principal, may elect to hold the principal liable instead of the agent. This rule is, however, subject to the following exceptions: 1. An undisclosed principal cannot be held if the contract made by the agent is in the form of a negotiable instrument or a sealed contract; 2. If the principal, before his identity was disclosed, furnished the agent with the money due on the contract the principal cannot be held; 3. If the third party elects to hold the agent, he cannot thereafter proceed against the principal; 4. If the contract expressly recites that there are no other parties to the agreement, then the principal is not liable.

Duties of Agent

An agent must, in dealing with his principal, act within the scope of his authority, and exercise good faith as well as the requisite prudence, skill and diligence.

Information received by the agent in the course of his employment is confidential and may not be used by the agent for his own benefit. He must at all times act in the highest good faith, with complete loyalty to his employer, and may not, without the permission of his principal, act for either a conflicting interest or for himself. If he enters into a contract without real or apparent authority from his principal or in excess of an existing authority, he is personally liable unless the principal is estopped to deny his authority or subsequently

PRINCIPAL AND AGENT 16-3

ratifies the contract. The agent is also personally liable for any tortious conduct resulting in damages to a third party, whether within or without the scope of his authority; the principal joins in this liability when the conduct is within the scope of authority of the agent.

Employees and Independent Contractors

There are no uniform criteria by which one can easily differentiate between an employee—who is an agent of an employer, and an independent contractor—who is generally not an agent. However, the theory adopted by most jurisdictions to differentiate between an employee and an independent contractor is based upon whether the person is subject to, or free from, the control of the employer with respect to the details of the work. An employee is subject to the employer who has the right to control his conduct with respect to the details of the matters entrusted to him. On the other hand, an independent contractor is a person who, in exercising an independent employment, contracts to do certain work according to his own methods, without being subject to the control of his employer, except as to the product of his work. Accordingly, where an employer may prescribe what shall be done, but not how it shall be done or who shall do it, the person employed is an independent contractor and not an agent.

While the existence of the relation of independent contractor and employer usually excludes the relation of principal and agent, there are occasions when both relations exist at the same time with regard to different portions or phases of the work. A person may be an independent contractor as to certain work, and a mere agent as to other work for the same employer not embraced within the independent contract. It should also be noted that a person may be both an agent and an independent contractor by virtue of being an attorney, a broker or an auctioneer. These persons are agents, although as to their physical activities they are independent contractors, because they have the power to act for and bind the principal in business negotiations within the scope of their agency.

Community Property Laws 17

The Law of Community Property is still effective in a number of states, and although repealed in some others, some few vestiges thereof still remain. These laws present special problems of credit extension and collection in dealing with customers in such states. The eight states in which the law of community property still exists are:

>   Arizona   Idaho   Nevada   Texas
>   California   Louisiana   New Mexico   Washington

In the following states community property laws are no longer in effect although rights acquired during the period in which such laws were in force are still extant in some.

Hawaii—Enacted 1945, repealed effective June 30, 1949. Rights acquired during effective period continue in force.

Michigan—Enacted 1947, repealed effective May 10, 1948. Very limited rights continue.

Nebraska—Enacted 1947, repealed 1949.

Pennsylvania—Enacted 1947 and declared unconstitutional in 1947. No rights continue.

Oklahoma—Enacted 1945, repealed effective June 2, 1949. By action taken prior to June 2, 1952, law authorized establishment of community property rights. All rights terminated if not recorded prior to June 2, 1950, or established by court action.

Oregon—Enacted 1947, repealed effective April 11, 1949. On death of either spouse after April 11, 1951, separate property is treated as though the 1947 law had not been enacted.

The change in the federal income tax law which provides for a joint return and division of income by a husband and wife and similar amendments to the estate and gift tax laws have eliminated the pressure to adopt community property laws.

Property Divided on 50-50 Basis

The term "Community Property" is applied to a husband-wife ownership of property and to the gains from such property during marriage. In some respects it resembles a partnership though it is not much like a partnership in respect to the allocations of gains and profits. In a partnership gains are usually divided in proportion to the contributions by way of capital or services. In the community the division is 50-50 between husband and wife regardless of the disparity in contribution of capital, property, energy, services and ingenuity. The division is based on law and is an incident of marriage and it does not arise out of a contract between the parties.

The main purpose of the community is to provide for an equal division of the marital gains between husband and wife or their heirs, on the dissolution of the marriage by divorce, death, etc. In the interpretation of the status of the community according to the courts of the respective states mentioned above, and by way of statutes in the same states, there are wide differences as to the respective rights of the spouses and their heirs, as well as the rights of creditors. Frequent changes result, almost from year to year, in statutory enactments, and what may be true this year in a certain situation may not be so next year.

In a sense the marriage community may be considered as a distinct legal entity although as such *it* cannot hold property, *it* cannot make contracts and *it* cannot sue or be sued. The husband is recognized by the law as the legal representative of the community and he transacts the business for it in his name. Consequently, contracts can be made with him and title can be taken by him to property owned by the community; he can be sued and he can sue for the community.

Although generally property acquired by the spouses during marriage becomes community property, either spouse may hold separate property. A husband or a wife may acquire separate property as by a bequest or devise under a will. Most states define separate and community property. Property owned by either husband or wife before marriage is considered separate property. Other factors (for example, statutory provisions for the administration of community property upon death of spouse) render the distinction between separate property and community property quite different at times.

Questions of Interest to the Creditman

Any property bought by either spouse on credit becomes part of the community, except that if credit is definitely and expressly based on a wife's separate property, and she intends to pay out of her separate property, such property does not become community property. Where a wife is buying for her separate business, the creditor should, of course, determine from investigation whether the community or the wife's separate estate has the greater financial responsibility.

If one of the spouses pledges or mortgages separate property for credit, the property thus acquired on the extension of credit becomes separate property of the spouse.

Generally (but the statutes and the law of any given state should always be checked), a wife may arrange to have credit issued to her personally and separately if the credit is predicated on her separate property and is to be satisfied out of her separate property. In Louisiana there is a statute permitting a married woman to carry on a business as a public merchant, but the business must be separate from the husband's business.

Even though property comes to a spouse during marriage it may have simply been the completion or perfection of a title already held equitably by one of the spouses before marriage. In such case it is considered the separate property of such spouse. For example, a contract of life insurance may have been made by a man while still unmarried. If the policy becomes payable to him after marriage the proceeds do not belong to the community even if the community has paid some of the premiums. The community in such case has, of course, the right of reimbursement out of the husband's separate estate for such premiums.

Difficult questions arise when there has been a dissolution of the marriage. In contrast to the proposition above, if an equitable title is held by the community and death intervenes before the title is perfected, the title enures to the benefit of the community when it is perfected. For example, a conveyance to a husband during marriage omitted a parcel of land by mistake. A conveyance of the omitted parcel after the death of the husband will enure to the benefit of the community.

Profits, gains, rents, etc., of separate property belong, in some states, to the community, but according to statutes in other states, to the separate estate. The profits of a business into which the toil and energy of both spouses entered belong to the community.

Property Presumed to Belong to Community

Ordinarily, property acquired by either spouse after marriage belongs to the community *by presumption*. Proof must be adduced to overcome the presumption. Each case must be considered on its own facts.

A husband and wife must exercise due care and caution when they desire to acquire separate property either by exchange of property already owned, or by money. In the case of money particular care is necessary because money is not ordinarily earmarked.

Often in those states recognizing the community, husbands and wives make antenuptial contracts relative to the fixing of their right in property.

Conveyance to a married woman can of course recite that the property is transferred as separate property but even this can be contraverted by proof to the contrary. In some states if there is no fraud, such a recital is generally binding. In some states the recital is only *prima facie* evidence that the conveyance is in fact separate property.

Husband's Dominion over Community Property

In many states, a husband may dispose of or encumber community real estate and deal with it as if it were his own. A conveyance of the property, however, is subject to attack from the wife if the husband intends to defraud her. This is not because his right is superior to his wife's but because the law contemplates that there must be someone to act as agent for the community and for the sake of expediency and convenience the husband seems to have been the selection for such purpose. In some states this right has been limited to personal property. The tendency in many states has been to require a husband to obtain his wife's signature to deeds, mortgages and leases. For example, the Louisiana Community Property Law has been reworded to spell out the equality of the spouses in the control over community property. In California, a spouse may not encumber community personal property which is used as the family residence without the written consent of the other spouse. Statutes in community states should always be checked to find whether the wife must join in deeds, mortgages or leases.

The wife could not in any of the states transfer the community property herself. Her interest has been traditionally considered an inchoate one, like that of a wife's right to dower which does not ripen until the husband's death. In some states a wife has the right to convey community property if her husband abandons her.

Though the husband in many states has a right to dispose of community property, he cannot do anything to prevent the wife from exercising her interest upon dissolution of the marriage for any cause.

Creditors and the Community Property

The community property is liable for community debts and, consistent with the doctrine that the husband has dominion over the community property, he alone can be sued on a community debt. Therefore an execution on the judgment secured against him can be enforced against the community property.

Of course it follows that if the husband can contract for the community, he can incur debts for it.

In some states the community property may even be taken for the husband's debts created before marriage and for his separate debts. In some of the states, however, the wife's earnings are exempt from attachment or levy by creditors of the husband. Likewise, in many states the community property may be taken for the wife's debts which were created before marriage.

Although some debts created during the existence of the community may be considered noncommunity when contracted by the husband, it may be said that nearly all debts so contracted are community debts. However the following may be declared noncommunity by the courts: a judgment rendered on a tort committed by the husband; a surety undertaking for a corporation in which the husband held stock and which stock in no way enured to the benefit of the community; a debt of the husband contracted in a noncommunity state before removing to a state recognizing the community.

In some states it is unlawful for a husband to contract debts on account of the community or to dispose of the community real estate after an action for divorce is brought. This is because divorce dissolves the community (as does death) and dissolution of marriage brings about the need for division or administration of the property. This brings us to another point of interest to creditors. What happens to community property when the husband or wife dies?

Community Property upon Death of a Spouse

The law regarding the effect of death on community property differs according to the jurisdiction. In some states upon the death of the wife the husband retains control of the estate but only for the purpose of settling it. In the settlement the community debts have a right to be paid first. Creditors may sue the husband; and the property, under this rule, will be subject to such judgments even as against the claims of the wife's heirs. In these states the creditors fare satisfactorily.

In these states the wife, if she is survivor, may renounce the community, and if she does, she will not be liable at all for the community debts. If, on the contrary, she accepts, her liability is limited to 50% of the property.

In some other states the rule is somewhat similar except that the surviving husband stands on a footing somewhat like that of a surviving partner in a business partnership. He is in a sense a trustee for the community and may convey community property to pay debts. The existence of community obligations becomes a condition of his right to sell. The surviving wife has the same powers although a remarriage on her part revokes that authority.

Law May Hold Pitfalls for Creditors

In a few states the surviving spouse takes the entire community title as his or her own; recent statutes have qualified the absolute rule of survivorship of title. Thus a spouse may make a disposition of his or her interest by will and therefore prevent automatic vesting of title in the other spouse. Furthermore, in some states it makes a difference whether or not there are children. If the husband has abandoned his wife and lived apart from her without justifiable cause, it also may prevent operation of the survivorship rule. In the states recognizing the vesting of the whole title in the survivor upon death, creditors may be at some disadvantage. If they have not completed legal proceedings against the community property, through levy of execution and sale before death of the spouse, the law places the title in the survivor at the death. Nevertheless, in some states the separate property of the husband is liable for community debts and in such cases the creditors are not deprived of their remedies. Furthermore, by statute in some states the survivorship is subject to community debts.

In other states the survivor takes only the half interest upon death of the spouse. Some states allow the survivor the choice of the half interest or accepting the terms of the will.

A spouse may devise his or her half by will to others and such interest will vest in the devisee or devisees. A testator cannot devise more than his or her half and thus a husband cannot defeat his wife's right to her one-half of the community property.

If there is no will the community property (except in those states where the spouse takes the whole property by survivorship) descends to the heirs, but subject to the debts of the community and the debts of each spouse.

General Remarks

In states recognizing the community some confusion and doubt arise as to the right of ownership. This is true especially as to the wife. The seriousness of this is evidenced in cases of titles to real estate. If real estate stands in a wife's name she may have difficulty giving a marketable title because of the presumption that it is community property. In some states proof is permitted to overcome this presumption and in some places a recital in the deed to the effect that the property was transferred to the wife as her separate property may help. Nonetheless, in some community states, one who buys real estate from a married woman does so at his peril.

In those states recognizing the dominion over the property in the husband, proof may be shown of the wife's separate ownership and therefore there exists some peril here, too.

It would seem a practical rule for those who acquire or who attempt to acquire property from a married party to have both husband and wife join in the conveyance. Creditors might follow the rule to require the undertaking of both husband and wife in credit transactions in these states. In such event the undertaking ought to be in the nature of a joint and several one, as for example: "We jointly and severally," or "We and each of us," etc. Thus redress on default could be had against either the community property or separate property, whichever the property turns out to be later.

Married persons residing in community property states had a tax advantage as against married persons residing in other jurisdictions, because only a husband and wife residing in a community property state were permitted to divide their earnings and the income derived from community property between themselves and thus take advantage of graduated surtax rates.

The federal tax laws, however, were amended in 1948 to permit spouses in noncommunity property states similarly to divide their income between themselves for *federal income tax purposes only*. The 1948 amendment does not affect state income taxes in any way, unless it is so expressly provided for by state statute.

Equitable Distribution

Nearly all common-law states have equitable distribution statutes which provide for what will happen to a married couple's property, however title is held, upon divorce or dissolution.

MARITAL PROPERTY:

Marital property in such states is not the same as community property where each spouse has a present, vested, undivided one-half interest in the earnings and assets acquired by either spouse. Instead, the states in marital property states define what is considered marital property upon divorce or dissolution. For example, nearly half the noncommunity property states expressly or impliedly indicate that all property owned by one or both spouses, including property acquired before the marriage, is to be considered marital property. Other states, however, apply a presumption that all property acquired by either or both spouses after marriage, regardless of how title is held, is marital property for purposes of divorce. Still other states specifically define what is marital property and what is separate property.

EQUITABLE DISTRIBUTION AND THE CREDITOR:

It is important that the creditor be aware of how a state defines marital property upon dissolution or divorce. Since the court may consider many factors, which are generally specified by statute, in equitably dividing the marital property, the creditor must know what property may be divided and what factors the court will consider in its decision. For example, it is important that a creditor know whether property inherited by one spouse after the marriage is considered marital property; whether a court will consider antenuptual agreements in dividing the property and if so, whether the couple have made such an agreement. The creditor must know as much as he can about the law and the facts in order to fully protect himself.

Laws Governing Negotiable Instruments

Article 3 of The Uniform Commercial Code is the statutory law governing checks, promissory notes, bills of exchange, trade acceptances, and similar instruments. In this chapter the general provisions of this law relating to negotiable instruments are summarized; trade and bank acceptances, judgment notes, attorneys' fees, and negotiable instruments, checks for less than one dollar, checks marked in full of account, and interest and usury are treated and discussed.

The Uniform Commercial Code has been adopted and is effective in the District of Columbia, the Virgin Islands and in every state except Louisiana, which has adopted only Articles 1, 3, 4, 5, and 7. The statute as enacted in the different states varies in minor details to some extent, but the principal provisions are practically identical in all of the states. See *supra* Chapter 2 for a general discussion of the provisions of the Code. See also *supra* Chapter 7 for a summary of Article 9 of the UCC.

What Instruments Are Negotiable

The importance to those interested in a transaction of determining whether an instrument is negotiable is based principally on the fact that the rights of transferees of negotiable paper are much more protected against defenses where the paper is in the hands of a bona fide holder in due course than the rights of transferees of nonnegotiable instruments who ordinarily are subject to the same defenses as may be interposed against the payee. In order to be negotiable the instrument must be in writing, signed by the maker or drawer, contain an unconditional promise or order to pay a sum certain in money,[1] be payable on demand or at a fixed or determinable future time, be payable to order or to bearer, and where addressed to a drawee, the drawee must be named or otherwise indicated therein with reasonable certainty. Negotiability is not affected by the want of a date, the failure to specify a consideration, the failure to specify the place where it is drawn or is payable, the fact that it has a seal, or the fact that it designates a particular kind of current money in which payment is to be made. The Code also expressly defines when an instrument is payable on demand, when payable to order, and when payable to bearer.

DATE—The instrument need not be dated to be negotiable, but where dated, the date is *prima facie* the true date. Antedating or postdating does not invalidate the instrument unless done for an illegal or fraudulent purpose. If the date is omitted, any holder may insert the true date.

BLANKS in an instrument may be filled by the person in possession thereof, and even where not filled in accordance with the authority given, a bona fide holder in due course may recover.

---

[1] Negotiability is generally not destroyed by a promissory note containing a variable rate of interest which is legal and readily ascertainable by an objective standard.

DELIVERY is necessary to make a binding contract, but a valid delivery will be presumed where the instrument is in the hands of a holder in due course.

Rules of Construction

Words govern figures. Interest runs from the date where not otherwise specified. Where undated, the instrument is considered as dated as at the time issued. Written provisions control printed ones. If the instrument is ambiguous about whether it is a bill or note, the holder may treat it as either. If it is not clear in what capacity a person intended to sign, the signer is deemed an indorser. The words "I promise to pay," where the instrument is signed by two or more, make them jointly and severally liable.

PERSONS LIABLE—No person is liable on the instrument whose signature does not appear thereon.[1]

WHO MAY EXECUTE—An agent may execute. The agent is personally liable if the principal is not disclosed or if the instrument does not indicate that his signature was made in a representative capacity, but not otherwise.

INDORSER BEFORE DELIVERY—A person placing his signature upon an instrument otherwise than a maker, drawer or acceptor is deemed an indorser and liable as such unless a contrary intention is clearly indicated by appropriate words. This settles a point about which there was great conflict, with many of the states holding such an indorser liable as a maker.

CONSIDERATION—A valuable consideration is presumed. An antecedent or preexisting debt is a sufficient consideration, and one having a lien on the instrument is deemed a holder for value.

ACCOMMODATION PARTY—A person who signs, with or without receiving any consideration for the purpose of lending his name to some other party, is liable to a holder for value, although such holder knew him to be only an accommodation party.

ACCEPTANCE—Acceptance is necessary to charge the drawee of a bill of exchange. Presentment for acceptance, unless excused, is necessary in case of sight bills to fix their maturity; where it is stipulated for in the bills; and where the bill is payable elsewhere than at the residence or place of business of the drawee. Acceptance must be in writing and signed by the drawee. Certification of a check is acceptance. Drawee is allowed twenty-four hours to decide whether he will accept. The presentment must be at a reasonable hour and may be on any day on which presentment for payment may be made. If made at a bank, presentment must be made during its banking day. If presentment is due on a day which is not a full business day, either because it is an official holiday or merely because of a practice to close for a full or a half day, the time for presentment is extended and presentment is due on the next and following full business day.

BEARER INSTRUMENT—Section 3-204 of the Uniform Commercial Code provides that a special indorsement on a bearer instrument will change it from a bearer instrument to one payable to the indorsee and then negotiable by further indorsement.

---

[1] In Nevada a person must report to the bank an unauthorized signature or any alteration of a check within one year from receipt of his bank statement, and failure to do so precludes him from asserting liability against the bank for such unauthorized signature or alteration.

Liability of Indorsers of Negotiable Instruments

Each indorsement of a negotiable instrument is a separate contract, standing apart from that of the maker or any other indorser.

Indorsements may be classified generally into two distinct kinds: "general" and "qualified." A "general indorsement" is one without reservation or qualification of any sort, while a "qualified indorsement" has, accompanying the name of the indorser, written words which qualify the general liability which would otherwise be implied from the written name alone. The words "without recourse" are those which are most generally employed to indicate such qualification. By adding "without recourse" to his signature, the indorser disclaims liability on the instrument and cuts off his obligation to future indorsers and holders to pay on the instrument.

Even the use of the words "without recourse," or words of similar import, however, does not wholly relieve the indorser from liability. Under the Uniform Commercial Code, § 3-417, it is provided that every person who signs his name as a qualified indorser of a negotiable instrument warrants, by his signature, that:

(a) he has a good title to the instrument or is authorized to obtain payment or acceptance on behalf of one who has a good title and the transfer is otherwise rightful; and

(b) all signatures are genuine or authorized; and

(c) the instrument has not been materially altered; and

(d) he has no knowledge of any defense of any party that is good against him; and

(e) he has no knowledge of any insolvency proceeding instituted with respect to the maker or acceptor or the drawer of an unaccepted instrument.

A "general indorser" warrants not only everything mentioned in (a), (b), (c) and (e) above, but also that he has good title, there is no defense of any party good against him, and that he has no knowledge that the signature of the maker or drawer is unauthorized and that the instrument has not been materially altered. He engages, by his signature, that the paper will be honored, or that, if dishonored, and the proper steps thereafter are taken (protest, etc.), he will himself pay the amount of the instrument to the holder or to any subsequent indorser.

As stated, an indorser impliedly warrants the genuineness of the instrument and if it is a forgery, he is liable. Even if the indorser's signature be obtained by fraud, he will still be liable on the paper if it has passed into the hands of one who has no actual knowledge of a defect and who has accepted the paper in good faith, for value, and without notice that it is overdue, or has been dishonored, or of any defense against it.

That a negotiable instrument is usurious as between the original parties (i.e., the maker and the payee) is not a defense which an indorser can successfully urge as against a person to or for whom he has indorsed the instrument.

A bank on which a check is drawn is not bound, as against an indorser cashing the same, to detect the fact that the check has been "raised," because, as stated above, the indorser warrants the genuineness of the paper and, upon discovery of the fraud, the bank can recover the amount of the fraudulent increase from the indorser.

However, it has been held that, if the fact that the check had been tampered with was evident or should have been discovered upon inspection, the bank may be held liable.

It should be noted, however, that the warranty of genuineness applies only if the paper is in the precise form in which it left the hands of the indorser, and if it is subsequently altered, the warranty does not apply to the instrument in its altered form.

As stated above, each indorsement is a separate contract and in an action by a trustee in liquiduation of a bank against an indorser of a note held by the bank at the time of its insolvency, the indorsee may set off, as against the bank's claim, the amount of money which he had on deposit in the bank at the time of its failure.

An "accommodation indorser" is one who puts his name on a negotiable instrument with or without consideration, for the purpose of lending his credit to some other person who is to pay the paper when it falls due. It represents and is a loan of credit to the party accommodated.

An ordinary indorser of commercial paper is liable to all parties to the instrument, including the payee, but this is not so in the case of an accommodation indorser. However, it is no defense to the enforcement of the liability of an accommodation indorser, where the paper is in the hands of one other than the party accommodated, and the paper was taken for value, before maturity, and in good faith, that it was without consideration, and this is so, although the holder may have had knowledge, before the paper was transferred to him, that it was accommodation paper.[1]

NEGOTIATION—The instrument may be negotiated by delivery if payable to bearer or by indorsement and delivery if payable to order. The indorsement must be written on the instrument or on a paper attached thereto, and may be either the mere signature of the indorser without additional words, or it may be an indorsement to a particular person, or it may be qualified, as by adding the words "without recourse," or it may be conditional. All payees must indorse unless partners of one has authority to act for the other. If the name of the payee is wrongly designated or spelled, he may indorse by that name and then add his proper signature. The indorsement is presumed, where not dated, to have been made before the instrument was due and to have been made at the place where the instrument was dated. The holder may strike out unnecessary indorsements.

WARRANTIES—Persons negotiating an instrument by delivery where payable to bearer, or by indorsement, warrant the genuineness of the instrument, a good title to it, that prior parties had capacity to contract and that the instrument has not been materially altered.

HOLDER IN DUE COURSE—By this is meant a bona fide holder for value without notice of possible defenses and before maturity.

Collection

PRESENTATION AND DEMAND FOR PAYMENT—In accordance with terms unless waived, presentation and demand for payment are necessary to charge the drawer (except where he has no right to expect the drawer or acceptor to

---

[1] In New York, an accommodation party warrants to all subsequent good faith holders except the accommodated party that all signatures are genuine, that the instrument has not been materially altered, that all prior parties had capacity to contract, and that he had no knowledge of any insolvency proceeding against the maker, drawer, or acceptor of the instrument.

pay), and indorsers (except in case of accommodation paper). It must be made on the day the instrument falls due, except where the instrument is payable on demand, in which case presentment must be made within a reasonable time after its issue, except in case of a bill of exchange, in which case presentation made within a reasonable time after the last negotiation of the instrument is sufficient. An uncertified check, not drawn by a bank, is presented within a reasonable time—with respect to the liability of the drawer—in the thirty days after the later of its date or issue; with respect to the liability of an indorser, within seven days of his indorsement. The presentment must be made at a reasonable hour on a business day, and if payable at a bank, must be made during banking hours unless there are no funds there to pay it, in which case presentment before the bank is closed is sufficient. Presentment must be made to all primarily liable, except where they are partners. Delay in presentment is excused when caused by circumstances beyond the control of the holder.

Under the UCC, a bank is under no obligation to a customer with a checking account to pay an uncertified check presented more than six months after its date. (Section 4-404) However, in *Advanced Alloys, Inc. v. Sergeant Steel Corp.,* 72 Misc.2d 614, 340 N.Y.S.2d 266 (Civ. Ct. Queens County), rev'd, 79 Misc.2d 149, 360 N.Y.S.2d 142 (Sup. Ct. 1973), a New York court held that a bank which makes payment of a stale check is not liable to the drawer. In this case payment on the check had been stopped, but the stop order was only good for six months (Section 4-403) and the depositor failed to renew it. On appeal, the Supreme Court reversed the summary judgment for the bank identifying as the factual issue whether the bank had acted with reasonable care, as well as in good faith.

PROTEST—Under the Code the requirement of formal protest is limited to a draft drawn in a foreign country upon a drawee located in the United States.

NOTICE OF DISHONOR—Unless waived, notice of dishonor must ordinarily be given to each drawer and indorser. Notice must be given *by a bank* before its midnight deadline—midnight of the next banking day after receipt of the item to be dishonored. By any other person notice must be given by midnight after the third business day after the dishonor. It may be either written or oral, and delivered personally or by mail. Joint parties not partners must all be notified. If the person giving and the person to receive notice reside in the same place, notice must be given so that it will be received not later than the day following the day of maturity; if they reside in different places, it must be mailed in time to go by mail the day following the date of maturity, or if otherwise sent must reach its destination as soon as if so mailed. A party receiving notice of dishonor need not forward it to antecedent parties before the next day. Deposit in an official mailbox is sufficient, and the sender is not responsible for any miscarriage of the mail. Waiver of "protest" includes waiver of notice of dishonor.

THE TIME OF PAYMENT—Time of payment is thirty days with respect to the liability of the drawer and seven days after endorsement with respect to the liability of an indorser.[1]

---

[1] Connecticut has adopted a statute that states that the maximum time limit permitted by a bank before it clears a check is four days if it is a check drawn on a bank within the state, and seven days if a check is drawn on an out-of-state bank. Rhode Island has a similar statute with the following time periods: items drawn on the same bank, one business day; items drawn on a local bank, two business days; items drawn on a bank in the state, four business days; items drawn on a bank in the Second Federal Reserve District, six business days; items drawn on any other bank in the United States, eight business days.

Discharge

NEGOTIABLE—The instrument is discharged by payment, intentional cancelation, by the principal debtor becoming the holder, or by any other act sufficient to discharge a simple contract for the payment of money. Persons secondarily liable, such as indorsers, are also discharged by the discharge of a prior party, by a valid tender of payment by prior party, by a release of the principal debtor unless the right of recourse is expressly reserved, or by extending the time of payment without their consent. No discharge of any party is effective against a holder in due course unless he has notice of the discharge when he takes the instrument.

DEMAND BEFORE SUING THE MAKER—On a note payable on demand, demand before suing the maker is generally not necessary. It is necessary, however, in some states, but only on demand notes payable in property other than money.

Defenses

A "holder in due course" stands in a superior posture with respect to defenses and claims to negotiable instruments than do mere holders or transferees. A holder in due course takes free from legal or equitable claims,[1] other parties do not. In discussing defenses available against a holder in due course, it is necessary to distinguish between real and personal defenses. Whereas both personal and real defenses may be asserted against mere holders and transferees, only real defenses are available as against holders in due course. UCC Section 3-305(2) describes real defenses as follows:

(a) contractual incapacity by reason of infancy whether the instrument is voidable or void;

(b) other types of incapacity, duress or illegality to the extent that in the relevant jurisdiction these defenses render the instrument void and not simply voidable;

(c) misrepresentation or fraud in the factum, described as tricking the issuer into signing the instrument while he was "excusably ignorant" of its contents;

(d) discharge in insolvency proceedings;

(e) any other discharge of which the holder in due course had notice when he took the instrument.

Personal defenses include all other defenses such as lack of consideration, fraud in the inducement, unconscionability, and breach of warranty and such defenses cannot be effectively asserted against a holder in due course, unless the defendant was in privity with him.[2]

In addition to the real defenses, a holder in due course may not enforce an instrument against a party whose signature was unauthorized (i.e., forged or made by an agent acting *ultra vires*), unless the party has ratified the signature or was negligent. However, a forged indorsement in the name of a payee is effective when an imposter has induced the maker or drawer to issue the instrument to him in the name of the payee; a person signing on behalf of

---

[1] A legal claim would be one based upon ownership; an equitable claim would be one in the nature of a lien.

[2] Many states now provide that the holder in due course of a consumer's promissory note or other evidence of indebtedness delivered in connection with the sale of consumer goods is subject to all the defenses and claims of the consumer which would be available to the consumer in a simple contract action.

the maker or drawer intends the payee to have no interest in the instrument; or an employer of the maker or drawer has supplied the name of a payee, intending the payee to have no such interest. In all cases, a person who in good faith pays the instrument or takes it for value, may enforce it against the unauthorized signer. A material alteration is a defense except as against a bona fide holder who may enforce payment according to the original tenor of the instrument. Alterations are material when they change the date, sum payable, time or place of payment, number of relations of the parties, medium of payment, or add a place of payment, as well as any other change which alters the effect of the instrument. (But see earlier paragraph headed "Blanks.")

GENERAL PROVISIONS AS TO TIME—When the day or the last day for an act required or permitted to be done by the statute falls on Sunday or a holiday, the act may be done on the next succeeding secular or business day. Where an act is required to be done in a reasonable length of time, regard is to be had to the nature of the instrument, the usage of the trade or business (if any) with respect to the instrument and the facts of the particular case.

CHECKS—Provisions applicable to bills of exchange apply to checks except where otherwise provided. Checks must be presented for payment within a reasonable time (construed as not later than next day after receipt) to prevent loss to drawer. Certification discharges drawer and all indorsers from liability. A bank is not liable until it accepts or certifies the check.

VALIDITY OF STIPULATION FOR ATTORNEYS' FEES OR COLLECTION COSTS

There are four questions that are raised by the inclusion in a negotiable instrument of a stipulation for the payment of the costs of collection or of attorney's fee, if the instrument is not paid at maturity. They are:
1. Does such a stipulation affect the validity of the instrument itself?
2. Does such a stipulation destroy the negotiability of the instrument?
3. Is such a provision valid and enforceable?
4. What law governs the validity and enforceability of such a stipulation?

1. EFFECT UPON THE INSTRUMENT ITSELF—It seems to be universally conceded that such a stipulation does not destroy the validity of the instrument.

2. EFFECT UPON NEGOTIABILITY OF THE INSTRUMENT—It is specifically provided by the Uniform Commercial Code that a note is negotiable though it provides for payment of attorney's fee, or the costs of collection, in case payment shall not be made at maturity (Section 3-106).

3. VALIDITY AND ENFORCEABILITY OF STIPULATION—Upon the question of the *validity* of such stipulations, the Uniform Commercial Code expressly provides that nothing within it validates any term which is otherwise illegal. The presence of the stipulation itself does not impair *negotiability*. The different states are in hopeless conflict with respect to the validity of stipulations in negotiable instruments for attorneys' fees, although the decided preponderance of opinion favors their validity. Where the question has been raised it has generally been the opinion of the courts that there is no valid reason for distinguishing between such stipulations in mortgages, and the same stipulations in negotiable instruments.

A study of the cases would indicate that those states which have held valid stipulations for the payment of a specific percentage for attorneys' fees will likewise hold valid stipulations for the payment of a "reasonable fee" or of "the cost of collection." But it does not follow that where stipulations for "reasonable fees" or "the cost of collection" have been upheld, any given state will sustain a stipulation for the payment of a "specific percentage" for attorney's fees. The question has not been decided in all states, and where the courts have not passed upon it, it is impossible to predict what the decision will be.

In *Citizens Nat'l Bank of Orange v. Waugh,* 78 F.2d 325 (4th Cir. 1935), the validity of a note containing a provision for the payment of a 10% attorney's fee for collection in case of default was sustained. The court, after holding that such a provision is not to be condemned as contrary to public policy, said:

> "Of course, if it should appear that a particular provision were used as a mere cloak for usury or that the provision were for so large an amount or were of such a character as to show an intention to provide a mere penalty for nonpayment, a different question would be presented, and it might well be condemned as in conflict with the well-settled policy of the law. But, where the provision is reasonable in amount and legal services are required and are actually rendered in the collection of the instrument, we can think of no consideration of public policy which should condemn it. In such case, it is properly viewed, not as a provision for additional interest exacted of the borrower for the use of the money, or as a provision for a penalty imposed upon him for breach of his contract, but as a provision for indemnifying the lender for the expense to which he may be put by reason of the borrower's default. . . . The question is not a new one, but has been repeatedly before the courts; and the overwhelming weight of authority is in accordance with the view herein expressed. . . ." Id. at 329.

A stipulation for the payment of attorneys' fees, being in the nature of an indemnity agreement, has been interpreted so that the holder of the instrument can recover only such sums as have been reasonably expended. See *Citizens Nat'l Bank of Orange v. Waugh; Taylor v. Continental Supply Co.,* 16 F.2d 578 (8th Cir. 1926); *Sarasota Publishing Co. v. E. C. Palmer & Co.,* 102 Fla. 303; *First Nat'l Bank of Eagle Lake v. Robinson,* 104 Texas 166; *Conway v. American Nat'l Bank of Danville,* 146 Va. 357.

For a summary of the law of each of the states on the question of attorneys' fees, see the table below.

4. WHAT LAW GOVERNS THE VALIDITY AND ENFORCEABILITY OF SUCH A STIPULATION—It should be noted that the states which refuse to give effect to stipulations in negotiable instruments for the payment of attorneys' fees hold that such provisions render the contract usurious, or that they are attempts to enforce a penalty for breach of contract, or that they are contrary to public policy. Such being the case, these states will usually not enforce such stipulations whether the contracts were made within their borders or elsewhere, even though such stipulation was valid at the place where the contract was made or at the place where the instrument was to be paid.

It has been held, however, in New York and Virginia that a stipulation for attorneys' fees valid in the state where the instrument is executed may be enforced in other states. The general rule, however, is that if such a provision is invalid in the state where suit is brought, such fees are not recoverable.

LAWS GOVERNING NEGOTIABLE INSTRUMENTS 18–9

JUDGMENT NOTES

Judgment notes have been defined as promissory notes which contain a power or warrant of attorney whereby the holder of the note, or an attorney or any other person, named or unnamed, is authorized, after maturity of the note, to appear in a court having jurisdiction of the subject matter and confess judgment on the note against the maker for such amount as may be due thereon. They are sometimes known as *"cognovit"* notes.

Provision in a promissory note for a post-maturity confession of judgment does not affect negotiability. (See UCC § 3-112(1)(d).) A Pennsylvania court held in *Cheltenham Nat'l Bank v. Snelling,* 326 A.2d 557 (Pa. Sup. 1974), held that a note which contained a clause authorizing a confession judgment "anytime before or after maturity" invalidated the negotiability of the note since it was not in accord with the requirements of the UCC which authorizes a confession only after default. (Section 3-112)

A confession of judgment is not valid unless it meets the requirements of the Code concerning negotiability. The hostility toward clauses authorizing confession judgments *prior* to maturity probably stems from the Code requirement that the instrument contain an unconditional promise to pay at one definite time. Furthermore, the Code provides that an instrument cannot contain any promise or grant any power not authorized by the Code. (Section 3-104(1)(b).) The power to confess judgment before maturity is not authorized by the Code and therefore the granting of such power invalidates negotiability. For proper form see *infra,* p. 33-12.

In *Broadway Management Corp. v. Briggs,* 30 Ill. App. 3d 403, 332 N.E. 2d 131 (1975), the court stated that the Code required that the power to confess judgment on a negotiable instrument must be clearly given and strictly construed. In that case, the warrant of attorney to confess judgment against the maker was on a note payable to order, but the note did not contain the name of a payee. The court held that the power to confess judgment on order paper could not be extended to "bearer" and, therefore, could not be exercised by the holder of the note. The negotiability of the note was destroyed because the confession was not limited to the period when the note was due.

The constitutionality of such notes in certain consumer transactions is open to question. In *Swarb v. Lennox,* 405 U.S. 191 (1972), the Supreme Court declared that the Pennsylvania confession of a judgment process was unconstitutional as to a class of debtors with annual incomes of less than $10,000. See also *Jamerson and Wright v. Lennox,* 356 F. Supp. 1164 (1972) (where the court held that the plaintiffs were barred from asserting the general invalidity of confession of judgment clauses), aff'd, 414 U.S. 802 (1974). In *D. H. Overmeyer Co. v. Frick Co.,* 405 U.S. 174 (1972), the Supreme Court sustained a confession of judgment which had been willingly, knowingly and intelligently bargained for in a commercial situation.

A form of judgment notes will be found in Chapter 34, *infra,* "Specimen Instruments." Judgment notes frequently provide for the payment of costs and attorneys' fees as in the form referred to. It should be noted that the Retail Instalment Sales Laws of many of the states contain provisions restricting the use of judgment notes and limiting attorneys' fees which may be imposed upon the debtor. See *supra,* Chapter 8. A judgment note should be distinguished

(Continued on page 18-14.)

VALIDITY OF JUDGMENT NOTES AND STIPULATION FOR ATTORNEY'S FEE

	VALIDITY OF JUDGMENT NOTES	PROVISION FOR ATTORNEY'S FEE
ALABAMA	Judgment notes are void. Foreign judgment notes if they are valid in that state will be enforced.	Enforceable.
ALASKA	Judgment notes not authorized by statute.	No statutory provisions.
ARIZONA	No provision.	Enforceable.
ARKANSAS	No provision. Will give full faith and credit to foreign note executed in a state where such notes are valid.	Enforceable, not to exceed 10% of principal due, plus accrued interest.
CALIFORNIA	No provision. Foreign judgment on a judgment note made in California but payable in the foreign jurisdiction where such notes are valid is enforceable.	Enforceable.
COLORADO	Judgment notes are recognized but strictly construed against parties in whose favor they are made. Foreign judgment note enforceable if recognized in that state.	Enforceable; provision in consumer credit sales (including installment sale of a motor vehicle) consumer leases and consumer loans valid up to 15% of amount due.
CONNECTICUT	Judgment notes are authorized.	Enforceable to the extent of reasonable compensation determined by court; installment contract provision valid up to 15% of amount due.
DELAWARE	Judgment notes are authorized.	No statutory provisions.
DISTRICT OF COLUMBIA	Judgment notes not recognized.	Enforceable for reasonable amount.
FLORIDA	Judgment notes not recognized. Foreign notes are enforceable if they are recognized in that state.	Enforceable where note is turned over to attorney for collection after maturity. Reasonableness of amount within discretion of court.

VALIDITY OF JUDGMENT NOTES AND STIPULATION FOR ATTORNEY'S FEE *(Continued)*

	VALIDITY OF JUDGMENT NOTES	PROVISION FOR ATTORNEY'S FEE
GEORGIA	No provision.	Void and unenforceable unless defendant is given written notice of intention to bring suit 10 days prior thereto and defendant fails to pay obligation on or before return day of the court in which the suit is filed.
HAWAII	No statutory provision.	In district or circuit court, where 25% fee or more is specified, 25% fee is enforceable; less than 25%, then specified fee is allowable; however, fee is not to exceed $250 in district court nor what is deemed reasonable by court.
IDAHO	No provision.	No provision.
ILLINOIS	Judgment notes are recognized by statute.	Enforceable.
INDIANA	Void.	If payment is contingent upon condition set forth in a note the provision is void; otherwise enforceable.
IOWA	No provision.	Enforceable but limited to 10% on first $200; 5% on $200 to $500; 3% on $500 to $1,000; 1% on excess.
KANSAS	No statutory provisions.	Void in notes, bills of exchange bonds or mortgages. Unenforceable in consumer credit transactions.
KENTUCKY	Judgment notes are void.	Invalid and unenforceable except in a motor vehicle retail instalment contract where an attorney's fee of 15% of amount due is valid.

VALIDITY OF JUDGMENT NOTES AND STIPULATION FOR ATTORNEY'S FEE *(Continued)*

	VALIDITY OF JUDGMENT NOTES	PROVISION FOR ATTORNEY'S FEE
LOUISIANA	Judgment notes are not recognized.	Enforceable.
MAINE	No statutory provisions.	Valid.
MARYLAND	Judgment notes are recognized.	Enforceable.
MASSACHUSETTS	Judgment notes are not recognized by statute.	Enforceable.
MICHIGAN	No provision.	Invalid.
MINNESOTA	Judgment notes are not recognized.	Enforceable. A motor vehicle retail instalment contract may provide for payment of attorney's fees not to exceed 15%.
MISSISSIPPI	Judgment notes are void.	Enforceable. A motor vehicle retail instalment contract may provide for payment of attorney's fees not to exceed 15%.
MISSOURI	Judgment notes are against public policy.	Enforceable.
MONTANA	Judgment notes are void.	Enforceable.
NEBRASKA	No provision.	Void.
NEVADA	No statutory provisions.	Enforceable only in retail instalment sales contract and only for reasonable costs in the event of delinquency.
NEW HAMPSHIRE	Judgment notes are recognized.	Valid in motor vehicle time sales contract only if provision is for a reasonable fee.
NEW JERSEY	Judgment notes are not recognized unless in a separate instrument.	Valid. Also, the Retail Instalment Statute permits a retail instalment contract, or a retail charge account to provide for attorney's fee not to exceed 20% of the first $500 and 10% on any excess.

LAWS GOVERNING NEGOTIABLE INSTRUMENTS   18–13

VALIDITY OF JUDGMENT NOTES AND STIPULATION
FOR ATTORNEY'S FEE *(Continued)*

	VALIDITY OF JUDGMENT NOTES	PROVISION FOR ATTORNEY'S FEE
NEW MEXICO	Judgment notes are prohibited by statute. It is a misdemeanor to procure another to make, indorse or assign a cognovit note or to accept such note.	Enforceable.
NEW YORK	Judgment may be conferred on the debtor's affidavit but it is invalid before default on instalment contents for $1,500 or less if goods are not for commercial use. Note must comply with confession of judgment requirements.	Enforceable. On retail instalment contract on a motor vehicle may provide up to a 15% attorney's fee on the amount due; for other goods, up to 20%.
NORTH CAROLINA	No provision.	No provision.
NORTH DAKOTA	No provision.	Not enforceable.
OHIO	Judgment notes are recognized. On a consumer transaction or loan after Jan. 1, 1974 judgment notes are not enforceable. On all other instruments judgment notes are enforceable only if they provide notice of loss of rights by a conspicuous warning on the document.	Void.
OKLAHOMA	No provision.	Enforceable.
OREGON	No provision.	Enforceable by either party to contract.
PENNSYLVANIA	Judgment notes are recognized by statute. Unless the debtor voluntarily and knowingly consents to the confession procedure when he signs the note his due process rights have been violated. No judgment note enforceable on a consumer debt against resident with less than $10,000 income.	Enforceable.
RHODE ISLAND	No statutory provision for judgment notes.	Enforceable.
SOUTH CAROLINA	No provision.	Reasonable fees enforceable.
SOUTH DAKOTA	No provision.	Void.
TENNESSEE	Judgment notes are forbidden.	Enforceable.

VALIDITY OF JUDGMENT NOTES AND STIPULATION FOR ATTORNEY'S FEE *(Continued)*

	VALIDITY OF JUDGMENT NOTES	PROVISION FOR ATTORNEY'S FEE
TEXAS	Judgment notes are forbidden.	Enforceable.
UTAH	Judgment notes are recognized.	Enforceable.
VERMONT	Judgment notes are not recognized.	Enforceable, however, enforcement has been refused by Vermont Supreme Court in a case involving a note with a 10% attorney's fee provision. The court concluded that "something must more be shown than the mere agreement."
VIRGINIA	Judgment notes are recognized if the warrant to confess judgment in the note names the attorney who will confess judgment in the court in which it will be made and debtor is notified of the confession of judgment against him.	Enforceable.
WASHINGTON	There are no statutory provisions.	Enforceable.
WEST VIRGINIA	No provision.	Unenforceable.
WISCONSIN	Judgment notes are void and unenforceable.	Enforceable.
WYOMING	Judgment notes are recognized by implication.	Permitted on foreclosure of real or chattel mortgages provided instrument provides for same and required affidavit of attorney is submitted.

(Continued from page 18-9.)

from a confession of judgment. The former is part of a promissory note and relates only thereto; the latter is a separate document applicable to any indebtedness. See discussion on confession of judgments, *infra,* Chapter 23.

"TRADE" AND "BANK" ACCEPTANCES

A *trade acceptance* is a draft, order, or bill of exchange drawn by the seller of merchandise upon the purchaser and accepted by the purchaser as payable at a certain definite time and place without qualifying conditions.

A *bank acceptance* is a written agreement on the part of a bank that it will pay at a certain definite time and place a certain amount to the seller of goods for and on behalf of the purchaser of such goods.

LAWS GOVERNING NEGOTIABLE INSTRUMENTS 18-15

A trade acceptance is to be filled out in accordance with the terms of sale—it is to be made for the amount of the invoice or statement, and the due date is the maturity of the account. If an invoice amounts to $100 on thirty-day terms, the trade acceptance is made out for $100 due in 30 days. If the terms are 2 per cent, ten days, net 30 days, the customer has the option of discounting the invoice in ten days or signing the thirty-day acceptance.

The trade acceptance can be made to run for any length of time. To obtain the most liquid instrument possible and to make an acceptance that will conform with the requirements of eligibility for rediscount at a Federal Reserve Bank, the acceptance should have a maturity not exceeding ninety days from its date. But upon the indorsement of any of its member banks, any Federal Reserve Bank may discount or purchase bills of exchange payable at sight or on demand which grow out of the domestic shipment or the exportation of nonperishable, readily marketable, agricultural or other staples and are secured by bills of lading or other shipping documents conveying or securing title to such staples.

The trade acceptance is created by the seller drawing on the buyer. The bank acceptance is created by the seller drawing on a bank with which the buyer has previously made arrangements to accept such bills as the seller might draw upon it.

Let it be supposed that A in New York purchases hemp from B in Manila, the invoice amounting to $5,000 and payment to be made in four months. B does not know A, so he suggests to A that an arrangement be made with A's bank by which the bank will accept bills drawn on it to the amount of $5,000. A makes this arrangement with his bank, notifies B, and B then forwards documents covering the shipment to A's bank and draws on the bank for the amount of the invoice. The bank, on receipt of the draft accompanied by bills of lading, insurance papers, etc., accepts A's draft, payable in four months, thus giving to B a piece of negotiable paper bearing the acceptance of a well-known financial institution and readily convertible into cash. If the foreign seller had an acceptance bearing the name of A as acceptor he might find difficulty in disposing of it because A's name was not known to the foreign banks.

The bank now holds title to the goods shipped by B. It allows A to have the use of these goods, taking a trust receipt for the goods as assurance that A will reimburse it for the amount of the acceptance and charging A a commission for its services in accepting B's bills. Before the maturity date of the acceptance, A will have made arrangements to have funds on hand to meet the acceptance.

This example illustrates how, through the use of the acceptance, a transaction can be financed from its beginning to its end. B has the cash obtained from discounting the bank's acceptance long before the end of the four-month credit period. A has the goods for which the acceptance was given and has had an opportunity to dispose of them and thus obtain the funds necessary to liquidate the acceptance at its maturity date. The bank has financed the transaction by lending its credit to A for a period of four months, thus enabling A to make his profit on the original goods. This is placing the burden of financing business where it rightly belongs—with the banks.

In the above transaction it will be noted that neither A nor B had the sum of $5,000 tied up for the four-month credit period, as would have been the case under the open-account system. Under the open account B would have had a charge against A on his books for four months—and he could not use the money represented by this charge until the maturity of the account. Or, if A were required to pay in advance for the goods, then A would have had the $5,000 tied up in merchandise until he had disposed of the goods.

The trade acceptance works in a similar manner. Let it be supposed that A in New York sells an invoice amounting to $5,000 to B in Chicago, terms 2 percent ten days, net sixty days. Under the open-account system, if B did not discount the bill in ten days, the entire amount ($5,000) would remain on A's books for sixty days. It would represent an asset of A's—but a frozen nonusable asset. And if there were many such accounts on A's books, regardless of the credit standing of the buyers, a considerable portion of A's capital would soon be tied up in open accounts receivable. But if a trade acceptance were issued by A and accepted by B, payable in sixty days, A would have available a negotiable instrument of the best type, which he could present for discount at his bank and obtain cash forthwith instead of awaiting the expiration of the period of credit.

The Federal Reserve Board early laid down certain requirements to distinguish the trade acceptance from any other commercial paper. The first and most important rule is that the acceptance bear on its face the statement that it arises out of the purchase and sale of goods; the second, that the acceptance be a clear, definite order to pay, free from any qualifying conditions; the third, that the acceptance be accepted in writing across the face of the instrument; and fourth that it bear conspicuously the label—"Trade Acceptance."

National banks have been authorized to rediscount such paper regardless of the limitations imposed by the National Bank Act on the amount of paper that may be discounted for any one concern. Under the old laws, a national bank might not discount for any one concern in excess of 10 percent of its capital and surplus. But under the trade acceptance system, such bank may discount practically any amount of acceptances brought to it by any concern.

In using a trade acceptance, the creditor will do well to keep in mind the following points:

1. DON'T use an acceptance to cover a past-due account;
2. DON'T use an acceptance where you would not grant an open-account credit;
3. DON'T sell to a customer merely because he is willing to sign an acceptance. When you indorse an acceptance, you guarantee that it will be met at its maturity. Your bank will watch such paper—let it be good;
4. DON'T use an acceptance form which bears qualifying phrases. The use of such phrases as "as per invoice of" or "as per invoice No." may render the acceptance ineligible for rediscount;
5. DON'T use an acceptance form which bears a provision for discount if paid on or before a certain date (see following discussion of this subject).

Legal Nature and Incidents of Trade Acceptances

1. NATURE OF INSTRUMENT: A trade acceptance is a special form of bill of exchange or draft drawn by the seller of goods on the purchaser and accepted by the purchaser. If drawn and executed in the form recommended by the National Association of Credit Management, it is negotiable, and is governed by the law with respect to negotiable instruments as set forth elsewhere in this chapter.

LAWS GOVERNING NEGOTIABLE INSTRUMENTS

A trade acceptance differs from a promissory note in that *a trade acceptance is a draft drawn on a merchant by a merchant,* while a note is an instrument drawn *by a person to the order of another person.* Merely stamping on a promissory note such words as "This is a trade acceptance" will not change the nature of the instrument.

2. NEGOTIABILITY: The Uniform Commercial Code provides that the negotiability of an instrument is not affected by the fact that it contains on its face a statement of the transaction "which gave rise to the instrument." (Section 3-105(1)(b)). So, therefore, an acceptance containing the words: "The transaction which gives rise to this instrument is the purchase of goods by the acceptor from the drawer," is a negotiable instrument.

This phrase should not, however, be altered in any respect, for so slight a variation as "the obligation of the acceptor of this bill arises out of the purchase of goods from the drawer" has been held to make the instrument nonnegotiable. *Citizens' State Bank of Marianna v. Hinson,* 90 Fla. 517 (1925). While this decision is against the weight of authority, it is, nevertheless, inadvisable to use an acceptance in this form.

Section 3-105 provides that two types of clauses will render an instrument conditional and, therefore, non-negotiable: (1) when an instrument recites that it is subject to another instrument, or (2) when payment is to be made from a particular fund or source.

A title retention clause in a trade acceptance has been held to render it nonnegotiable. *Pierce, Butler & Pierce Mfg. Corp. v. Russell Boiler Works, Inc.,* 159 N.E. 625 (Mass. 1928). The Uniform Commercial Code provides that a statement that the instrument is secured, whether by mortgage, reservation of title or otherwise, does not affect negotiability. (Section 3-105(1)(e)). In *Holly Hill Acres, Ltd. v. Charter Bank,* 314 So. 2d 209 (Fla. Ct. of App. 1975) a promissory note secured by a mortgage which contained the provision that "the terms of said mortgage are by this reference made a part thereof," was declared nonnegotiable because the instrument failed to satisfy the requirement that an instrument on its face contain an unconditional promise to pay. The court explained in dictum that where a note merely refers to a separate agreement, negotiability is not impaired. However, if the instrument itself states, or it is clear from reading the instrument, that it is "subject to or governed by" another agreement it is not negotiable.

The insertion of the following clauses does not affect negotiability:

Waiver of exemption and attorneys' fees.
Provision for costs of collection.
Provision for payment of interest after maturity.

3. RIGHT OF A BANK TO CHARGE ACCEPTANCE AGAINST MAKER'S ACCOUNT: When an instrument is made "payable at a bank," this phrase has a double meaning within the United States. In some states it constitutes an order to the bank to make payment thereof and is the equivalent of a draft on the bank. In other states, the phrase merely designates the place of payment. The Code therefore, in order not to upset this variance in meaning among the states, proposed the following two alternative definitions of the phrase (Section 3-121):

Alternative A

A note or acceptance which states that it is payable at a bank is the equivalent of a draft drawn on the bank payable when it falls due out of any funds of the maker or acceptor in current account or otherwise available for such payment.

Alternative B

A note or acceptance which states that it is payable at a bank is not of itself an order or authorization to the bank to pay it.

The following is a summary of the states that have adopted either Alternative A or B:

Alternative A		*Alternative B*	
Alaska	New Hampshire	Alabama	Mississippi
Connecticut	New Jersey	Arizona	Missouri
Delaware	New York	Arkansas	Montana
District of	North Dakota	California [1]	Nebraska
Columbia	Ohio	Colorado	New Mexico
Hawaii	Pennsylvania	Florida	North Carolina
Kentucky	Rhode Island	Georgia	Oklahoma
Maine	Texas	Idaho	Oregon
Massachusetts	Vermont	Illinois	South Carolina
Nevada	Wyoming	Indiana	South Dakota
		Iowa	Tennessee
		Kansas	Utah
		Louisiana	Virginia [2]
		Maryland	Washington
		Michigan	West Virginia
		Minnesota	Wisconsin

The Uniform Commercial Code also contains a provision with respect to instruments "Payable Through" a bank which does not appear in the Negotiable Instruments Law. Section 3-120 provides:

An instrument which states that it is "payable through" a bank or the like designates that bank as a collecting bank to make presentment but does not of itself authorize the bank to pay the instrument.

The following is the wording of the Trade Acceptance Form as adopted by the National Association of Credit Management:

"The transaction which gives rise to this instrument is the purchase of goods by the acceptor from the drawer. The drawee may accept this bill payable at any bank, banker or trust company in the United States which such drawee may designate. Such bank, banker, or trust company is directed to pay this acceptance and charge it to the account of the acceptor upon presentation at maturity or within one year thereafter."

---

[1] California provides that, "An instrument which states that it is payable at a bank is not of itself an order or authorization to the bank to pay unless the bank is the drawee."

[2] Virginia provides that, "A note or acceptance which states that it is payable at a bank is not of itself an order to the bank to pay it, but the bank may consider it an authorization to pay."

LAWS GOVERNING NEGOTIABLE INSTRUMENTS   18–19

4. NECESSITY FOR PROTEST: Protest is not strictly necessary except where the instrument is a "foreign bill of exchange." In no case is it necessary unless there are indorsers on the instrument. The acceptor is a primary obligor and is absolutely liable to pay whether the instrument be protested or not.

5. STOPPING PAYMENT: The acceptor has the same right to stop payment of a trade acceptance as the maker of a check has to order payment stopped on a check.

6. EFFECT ON MECHANIC'S LIEN RIGHTS: It may be stated, as a general rule, subject to the important exceptions hereinafter noted, that a mechanic's lien claimant does not waive or forfeit his right to a lien by taking a trade acceptance of the owner or the contractor for what is due to him unless the parties have agreed that the acceptance shall have the effect of extinguishing the lien, or such intention can be otherwise established. The cases so holding are too numerous to cite and it has been so held in the courts of a majority of states and the United States.

The law is stated in *Hopkins v. Forrester,* 39 Conn. 351, 354 (1872), as follows:

"The lien . . . remains until the *debt* is *paid* or until it is satisfied or discharged or extinguished. The mere giving of promissory notes by the debtor is no payment. Such notes are evidence of debt and are securities for its payment, but surely a promise to pay, whether verbal or in writing, is not in itself payment. If, indeed, the plaintiff expressly agreed to receive the notes in satisfaction and discharge of his lien, he ought to be held to his agreement, but no such contract appears, express or implied, verbal or written."

In the case of *Paddock v. Stout,* 121 Ill. 571 (1887), it was contended that the claimant had accepted notes in absolute payment of the debt and that the right to a mechanic's lien was therefore discharged. The court said:

"By taking the note of the owner of the premises, who incurred the debt, the petitioner does not waive his lien. Such a note merely serves to liquidate the demand."

The courts are in accord upon the proposition that if there is an agreement to accept a note in absolute payment of the indebtedness, the right to a lien is waived, but it is not to be presumed that a note taken by a person entitled to a lien was taken as payment; even in those states where the acceptance of a negotiable promissory note is presumed, in the absence of any testimony or circumstance to the contrary, to be a payment of the indebtedness for which it was given, this presumption is overcome by the fact that the acceptance of a note in payment would deprive the creditor taking the note of the substantial benefit of some security.

Effect on Lien of Acceptance of a Promissory Note

Where, however, a trade acceptance or other negotiable instrument is accepted and the time of payment of such instrument extends beyond the period allowed by statute for enforcing the right to a mechanic's lien, it is held that the taking of such a note evidences the intention of the claimant to rely upon the general credit of the maker and to waive his claim to a lien. It was held by the Supreme Court of Minnesota in *Flenniken v. Liscoe,* 64 Minn. 269, 279 (1896), that:

"A special agreement inconsistent with the right to lien waives or destroys the lien. Plaintiff's lien was not destroyed because a promissory note was taken, but because the credit was extended to the defendant beyond the period within which an action to enforce a lien must be brought. If parties enter into a special contract, inconsistent with the existence of a lien, the statute was never intended so as to create or preserve the lien and thereby destroy the special contract."

The Supreme Court of Wisconsin passing upon the same question held:

"The preponderance of authority doubtless is to the effect that a mechanic's lien will be deemed waived either by taking therefor a promissory note maturing not until after the statutory time fixed for enforcing the lien, or by taking independent security." *Phoenix Mfg. Co. v. McCormick Harvesting Company,* 111 Wis. 570, 87 N.W. 458 (1901).

But in Wisconsin, there is a statute which changes the rule just stated so far as the effect of taking a new note or other evidence of indebtedness is concerned, regardless of the time of maturity of the note. Similar statutes will be found in other jurisdictions.

It is a condition precedent to the enforcement of a mechanic's lien, however, that a negotiable promissory note taken for the same indebtedness must be surrendered or otherwise accounted for before an action to foreclose the lien can be maintained. This was held in *Kankakee Coal Co. v. Crane Brothers Mfg. Co.,* 128 Ill. 627 (1889), where the Court pointed out the injustice of permitting the mechanic's lien claimant, under such circumstances, to enforce his lien when the negotiable notes might, at the same time, be outstanding in the hands of a third person.

LETTERS OF CREDIT

Although not truly a negotiable instrument, letters of credit represent a useful and popular form of payment, particularly for international transactions. A letter of credit is essentially a guarantee by a buyer's bank to pay the seller upon the presentation of specified documents. The crucial element of the transaction is that the bank's credit-worthiness is substituted for the buyer's. The bank's obligation to honor the letter is independent of any defense to payment the buyer may have.

A basic letter of credit transaction involves three parties: The buyer, the seller, and the buyer's bank. The buyer contracts with his bank to issue a letter of credit in favor of a seller. The bank charges a small fee, usually a fraction of one percent of the sale price, for issuing the letter and it may also acquire a security interest in the buyer. The bank then informs the seller that a letter has been "established," meaning that the seller's drafts will be honored against the letter when accompanied by the documents listed in the letter. After a seller ships the goods, he presents the bank with the required documents, usually a bill of lading or some other document evidencing seller's performance of the contract, and payment is made.

In the last few years, some letters of credit have been utilized in a different way. Known as "standby" letters of credit, these instruments are drawn on only if the buyer fails to pay; in effect, they are used as guarantees. Standby letters are used in many transactions; in sales, as backing for commercial paper or as quasi-performance bonds.

In addition to the UCC provisions that govern letters of credit, the International Chamber of Commerce also has adopted provisions governing letters of credit. Since the time that the International Chamber of Commerce (ICC) published its provisions regarding documentary credit documents in 1974, there have been a number of changes with respect to letters of credit. In response to these new developments, ICC has adopted a Uniform Customs and Practice for documentary credits (UCP), ICC publication No. 400. In reviewing the effect of the UCP, it is important to note that the UCP does not have the force of law. Rather, it becomes effective only by explicit reference in a contract dealing with letter of credit documentation.

The differences between the provisions of the UCC and the UCP are significant enough to merit close attention. For example, under the UCC an issuer has three days to examine draw documents while under the UCP the issuer has a "reasonable" time; under the UCP transferable letters of credit may be transferred only once, while under the UCC they may be transferred an unlimited number of times. Parties that are interested in providing that the UCP should be incorporated in their letter of credit dealings should examine carefully the provisions of the ICC publication No. 400.

CHECKS—SPECIAL PROVISIONS

Checks for Less Than One Dollar

The Act of Congress of July 17, 1862, §2 (12 Stat. 592; Rev. Stat. 711, §3583) (repealed) declares that:

"No private corporation, banking association, firm or individual shall make, issue, circulate or pay out any note, check, memorandum, token or other obligation, for a less sum than one dollar, intended to circulate as money, or to be received or used in lieu of lawful money of the United States."

The penalty for the offense was fine or imprisonment or both.

In a case entitled *United States v. Van Auken,* 96 U.S. (6 Otto) 366 (1878), the Supreme Court held that the offense under the statute must consist of two ingredients: (1) the token or obligation must be for a less sum than one dollar, and (2) it must be intended to circulate as money or in lieu of money of the United States.

It would seem clear from this decision that a check used in the ordinary course of business is not within the meaning or intent of the law since such a check would not be in lieu of money but, instead, would actually be a note for goods.

Checks Marked "In Full of Account"

Does a check given in payment of an account, marked "In full of account," which does not as a matter of fact pay the entire account, constitute payment in full, and is the payee who holds the check estopped from moving for the uncovered balance? The general rule is as follows: If the claim is liquidated and there is no dispute as to the amount due, a check for a lesser amount than the claim, even though marked "In full of account," does not settle the account and the creditor may keep the check and sue for the balance. If, however, there is a bona fide dispute as to the amount of the claim, and the same is not liquidated, a check sent and marked "In full payment of account" is payment in full and the creditor must either return the check and sue for the amount claimed or accept the check in complete payment. Whether a bona fide dispute exists can be a matter of dispute in itself and obviously a debtor wishing to pay a lesser sum can very easily make such a claim.

The retention and use of the check by the creditor will constitute an accord and satisfaction even though the creditor notifies the debtor that it is received only as a partial payment on account. The creditor is therefore placed in a difficult position, either he must reject such a check and demand payment of the full amount or accept the check and possibly be deemed to have made an accord and satisfaction. One possible solution to this problem is to stamp all collection checks with a legend which states that "The check is accepted without prejudice and with full preservation of all rights pursuant to Section 1-207 of the Uniform Commercial Code." Under this section of the Code, a party who explicitly so reserves his rights does not prejudice the rights reserved. However, some courts have held that this section of the Code applies only to Code-covered transactions such as sale of goods, and does not apply to service contracts; other courts have entirely rejected application of the Code to checks marked "in full payment."

In some instances, however, the courts have held that where a creditor gave a release under seal the acceptance of a smaller amount than the amount due, even in a liquidated claim, releases the debt.

This raises a question in regard to checks that are sent in after the discount period has passed, with the discount deducted, such checks being marked "In full of account." Can such checks be properly deposited and claim made for cash discount? The answer is that they obviously fall under the above-mentioned rule, and claim can be made for the cash discount so deducted in cases where there is no dispute about the terms. The practical effect of the matter is, however, that each single transaction represents, in most instances of this character, a comparatively small sum, for which it would be impractical, either on account of expense or distance, to sue, and the chances are that a debtor accustomed to stealing discounts would be even less likely to pay such discount after he had in his possession a cancelled check voucher marked "In full of account."

Stopping Payment on Checks

It is frequently necessary to stop payments on checks lost in transmittal to the payee or for other reasons. The drawer of a check may revoke or countermand the payment thereof but the order must be received by the bank at such time and in such manner as to afford the bank a reasonable opportunity to act. Failure of a bank to comply with the order subjects it to liability, but the burden of establishing the amount of loss is on the customer.

The notice to stop payment must be positive and unqualified. *Shude v. American State Bank,* 263 Mich. 519 (1933). The notice must be explicit and describe the check with reasonable accuracy. *Mitchell v. Security Bank,* 85 Misc. 360, 147 N.Y.S. 470 (Sup. Ct. 1914). It is advisable to include in the notice the date of check, number, amount, name of payee, and any further information which may be necessary for an accurate description. Care should be exercised that this information is accurate as inaccuracies may render the notice ineffective. See *Mitchell v. Security Bank,* where it was held that a notice to stop payment on a check No. 4028, dated December 21 payable to "Helfand and Abel" in the amount of $196.76 was ineffectual to stop payment on the check No. 4028 dated December 23, 1910, payable to "bearer" in the amount of $196.75. It has been held however that minor inaccuracies, such as a wrong date, would not alone render the notice ineffective where the bank's failure to comply with the order was not a result of such inaccuracy. *Shude v. American State Bank.*

There is no required form for the notice to stop payment in the absence of a statute or special agreement between the bank and drawer. In *Hiroshima v. Bank of Italy,* 78 Cal. App. 362 (1926) the Court held "there is nothing in the law which requires a stop notice to be in writing; and a verbal or oral notice, given by plaintiff to the defendant prior to the signing of the stop notice, was sufficient to require the defendant to observe such directions, and the writing only aided in identifying the check on which the stop notice was given." The Michigan statute providing that a stop payment order shall remain in effect for not more than six months, unless the same be renewed in writing, was held not to require the original notice to be in writing. *Shude v. American State Bank.* The better practice would appear to be to give notice in writing signed by the drawer even where by necessity of immediate notification the order is first given orally. A stop order in the form of a typewritten letter and *signed with a typewritten signature* has been held to be sufficient notice. It has been held that an order to stop payment may be communicated to the bank by telegram. *Ozhunn v. Corn Exchange National Bank,* 208 Ill. App. 155 (1917); *Western Union Tel. Co. v. Louissell,* 11 Ala. App. 563 (1915).

The Uniform Commercial Code, Section 4-403, provides that an oral order is binding on the bank for only 14 days unless confirmed in writing within that period. A written order is effective for only six months unless renewed in writing. In Arizona, California, Florida, Nevada and Utah, the statute provides that an order may be disregarded by a bank six months after receipt, unless in writing. The District of Columbia, Texas and Utah require the order to be in writing.

Stopping the payment on a check has collateral consequences as sadly discovered by a defendant in a New York decision. A plaintiff was granted a motion for summary judgment on a liquidated damages claim after the defendant purchaser stopped payment on a $250,000 personal check. The plaintiff contended that defendant's stopping payment on the check which was the initial payment on a $10,500,000 sale of real property was an anticipatory breach which gave the seller an immediate right to $250,000 liquidated damages. The court agreed and judgment for liquidated damages in that amount was awarded to plaintiff. *Hanson Properties v. Kotowski* (N.Y.L.J., August 11, 1975, Supreme Court of N.Y. County, Special Term).

INTEREST AND USURY

The law of usury is an important and complicated aspect of the legitimate extension of commercial credit. Although the great bulk of usury limitations are contained in the various state laws, important exceptions have been recently created at the federal level. The Monetary Control Act of 1980 sets forth federal preemptions of state usury laws with regard to certain transactions and lenders. PL 96-221, 94 Stat 132. These preemptions may be summarized as follows:

Mortgage Usury Laws—A separate title of the Act provides permanent federal preemption of state usury laws relating to loans, mortgages, credit sales or advances which are secured by first liens on residential real property, by first liens on stock in residential cooperative housing corporation, or by first liens on residential manufactured homes. The preemption applies to any such transaction made after March 31, 1980. Although the preemption is permanent, any state could have, between April 1, 1980, and April 1, 1983, adopted a law or certified that the voters of the state had voted in favor of any provision, constitutional or otherwise, which explicitly and by its terms states that the federal preemption is not desired in that state (Colorado, Georgia, Hawaii, Idaho, Iowa, Kansas, Massachusetts, Minnesota, Nebraska, Nevada, North Carolina, South Carolina, South Dakota, and Wisconsin have enacted such legislation. Maine has specifically overriden the preemption of state usury ceilings on home consumer credit transactions and first lien mortgages on real estate granted by supervised lenders.) After a state has overriden the preemption, any loan that is based on a loan commitment made between April 1, 1980, and the date the state acted to override the preemption will still be subject to interest limits set on the basis of the federal preemption. (Massachusetts has overridden the prohibition against set loan fees and points and mortgages.)

Other Loans—State-chartered insured banks, including insured savings banks, insured mutual savings banks and insured branches of foreign banks subject to the Federal Deposit Insurance Act, insured institutions under the National Housing Act and insured credit unions under the Federal Credit Union Act, are also protected from state interest limits by federal preemption on a limited basis. The federal limitation permits interest under these laws to be charged at the greater of one percent above the discount rate, or the applicable state limit. Small business investment companies may make small loans under the Small Business Investment Act at the lowest of the following rates: (a) the maximum rate prescribed by regulation of the Small Business Administration, (b) the maximum rate under applicable state law which has not been preempted, or (c) the higher of one percent above the discount rate or the maximum rate authorized under applicable state law without regard to preemption.

On or after April 1, 1980, a state may act to override the federal preemption with regard to all insured loans described above and small business loans in the same manner in which it would override the federal preemption of mortgage loan and business and agricultural loan rates.

In addition to the complexity of the relationship between the federal and state usury laws, the credit manager must also be concerned with the diverse limitations of the state laws themselves. There are severe penalties for charging more than the legal rate of interest. For example, a creditor in one state might prepare a promissory note which is perfectly valid in his own state, send it to a debtor in another state for execution, only to find upon suit that the debtor might successfully set up usury as a complete defense; in some jurisdictions, if more than the rate of interest fixed by the statute is exacted, both principal and interest are forfeited. Moreover, a contract may provide for the maximum lawful rate yet, because of other provisions be usurious. Thus, in *Cochran v. American Savings & Loan Assoc. of Houston,* 568 S.W.2d 672 (Tex. Ct. App. 1978), the court found a contract for the maximum interest usurious because interest was based on the 360, rather than the 365 day year. However, in *Libowsky v. Lakeshore Commercial Finance Corp.,* 110 Wis.2d 748, 331 N.W.2d

391 (1983), the court found that though the interest was calculated on a 360-day basis through a computer error, the lender was not liable since he lacked intent.

In some states the creditor loses the excess or usurious interest, while in others he loses the entire interest. So abhorrent to the lawmakers in some jurisdictions is usury that they have provided that when usurious interest is taken or received, lender forfeits double or triple such amount of interest.

The New York Court of Appeals held that if a corporation is formed merely to avoid the usury rates for individuals, and the loan is in fact given for the benefit of an individual and not for corporate purposes, the usury defense may be available. *Schneider v. Phelps,* 41 N.Y.2d 238, 391 N.Y.S.2d 568, 359 N.E.2d 1361 (1977).

Service charges and interest charges after an obligation is due, if bona fide and not in violation of any specific statutory prohibition (cf. Table on Maximum Finance Charges, *supra,* Chapter 8) have generally been held not to violate the usury laws, although the loan payments, when coupled with the amount charged for interest, may be in excess of the statutory rate. See further discussion on pages 18-39–18-40.

The California state usury law is limited to loan transactions. The law was held inapplicable to the legitimate sale of a going business where the monthly instalments included interest in excess of the permissible maximum rate under usury legislation. *Lenes v. Dean,* 64 Cal. App. 3d 845, 135 Cal. Rptr. 14 (1976).

Since then, the California Superior Court for Los Angeles County held the law violative of the Commerce Clause and the fourteenth amendment of the Federal Constitution. See *Committee Against Unfair Interest Limitations v. State of California,* 95 Cal. App. 3d 801, 157 Cal. Rptr. 543 (1979).

In some states a debtor having paid usurious interest may recover the interest even if he has paid it in settlement of a judgment; in other states, statutes have been enacted expressly giving a right to recover usurious interest, and some states have made the exacting of illegal interest a crime.

In some states the parties may agree on any rate of interest, and in many they may agree on a rate above the legal rate, but within certain statutory limits. In states where the parties are permitted to agree on higher than the legal rate, it is not sufficient to print on the invoice such words as "Interest at rate of one per cent a month charged on past due accounts," for the courts in some states have held that there must be a definite agreement in order to validate a rate of interest higher than the legal rate.

Statutes in several states expressly provide that the defense of usury cannot be raised against negotiable paper in the hands of one who takes it as a bona fide holder, for value before maturity. In many jurisdictions paper tainted with usury is declared void even in the hands of a bona fide purchaser.

Under laws of Connecticut, Hawaii, Kentucky, New Mexico, North Dakota, and Vermont the charging of usurious interest is a misdemeanor. In Texas habitual offenders against the usury laws may be enjoined in the court.

Those, such as variable-rate lenders, who wish to avoid the usury laws have several alternatives: conduct transactions in a state which exempts from the usury laws that type of transaction desired; add a provision subjecting the transaction to the law of another jurisdiction more favorable to the transaction; or

(Continued on page 18-38.)

INTEREST TABLE

The following table sets forth the legal rate of interest and the rate which may be charged by special agreement. Usually such agreements must be in writing. Many of the statutes contain special provisions with reference to call loans and in favor of banks, trust companies, pawnbrokers, etc., and with respect to interest on small loans, usually of $5,000 or less, instalment loans, student loans or credit card loans. These provisions are not summarized. Illinois has special provisions with respect to demand loans of not less than $5,000 on certain types of negotiable instruments pledged as collateral security and with respect to business loans to associations, sole proprietors, joint ventures, partnerships, etc. See footnote references (a) through (u) at end of chart. Many states have special legislation limiting the maximum interest rate which can be charged on consumer transactions. *See* Chapter 9 *supra*.

Interest rates have been increasing rapidly and it is advisable to verify, during the course of the year, the maximum rate in effect in any state.

Attention is also called to the federal law, outlined above, which preempts state usury laws with regard to certain transactions and lenders.

State	Legal Rate (a)	Contract Rate (b)	Corporate Rate (c)	Judgment Rate	Civil Penalty (d)
Ala. (u)	6%	8% or 1% above discount rate; alternative rate 2% above prime rate plus 2% surcharge up to $20 (e)	any rate if over $2,000	12% (f)	forfeit all interest, payments applied on principal (i)
Alaska	10.5%	5% above the annual rate charged member banks for advances to the 12th Federal Reserve District that prevailed on the 25th day of the month preceding the commencement of the calendar quarter during which the contract or loan was made; no limit on loans in excess of $25,000	no special rate	10.5% or as provided in contract, but not above 10%	forfeit all interest; recover double all interest paid within 2 years of payment
Ariz.	10%	Rate agreed to in writing	no special rate	20% or as set forth in instrument	forfeit all interest; interest paid applied to principal, may be set off or recovered
Ark.	6%	5% above discount rate on 90-day commercial paper in Federal Reserve District containing Arkansas. 17% limit on consumer loans and credit sales	no special rate	10% (r) or as provided in contract up to contract rate, whichever is greater	contract is void; recover twice interest paid
Calif.	7%	5% plus the discount rate of the Federal Reserve Board; *plus* applicable surcharge; 10% on loans for personal, family or household use (real property excluded)	no special rate	10%	forfeit all interest; recover 3 times amount within 1 year of payment

LAWS GOVERNING NEGOTIABLE INSTRUMENTS   18–27

State	Legal Rate (a)	Contract Rate (b)	Corporate Rate (c)	Judgment Rate	Civil Penalty (d)
Colo.	8%	as set out in instrument except that if the contract or instrument provides for a variable rate, at the rate in effect under the contract or instrument on the date judgment enters; also limited by UCCC.	no special rate	8% or at rate specified in contract (v)	no statutory provision except with reference to UCCC transactions
Conn.	8%	12% (h)	any rate if over $10,000 or revolving charge agreement with debt over $10,000	10%; 10% on negligence judgments; on out-of-state secured or executed contracts as agreed up to legal rate in that state	forfeit all principal and interest; no recovery of interest paid (i)
Del.	12.5%	12.5% plus applicable surcharge if any; any rate if over $100,000 and not secured by principal residence mortgage	no special rate	12.5% unless otherwise specified in contract sued upon	all excess forfeited or applied to principal; recover greater of treble excess interest paid or $500, within 1 year after payment
D.C.	6%	24%; loans over $1,000 any rate; secured mortgage loans 24%	any rate	70% of the interest rate set by the Secretary of the Treasury for overpayment and underpayment of taxes to IRS	forfeit all interest, recover double unlawful interest actually collected or paid within three years
Fla.	12%	18% (j) 25% if amount over $500,000	no special rate	12% or rate contracted, if less	forfeit all interest; corporations recover interest paid; individuals recover double interest. No penalty if refund is made before suit instituted
Ga.	7%	any rate if over $3,000; where $3,000 or less, any rate not in excess of 16%	no special rate up to $3,000; no limit on excess	12% (f)	forfeit all interest; interest paid can be recovered within 1 year
Hawaii	10%	1% per month; no limit where principal exceeds $750,000	no special rate	10% (f)	all interest forfeited; interest paid applied to reduce principal; borrower recovers costs (i)

State	Legal Rate (a)	Contract Rate (b)	Corporate Rate (c)	Judgment Rate	Civil Penalty (d)
Idaho	12%	no limit, except if a consumer transaction then as limited by the UCCC; 13% on loans secured by personal residence	no special rate	18%; 6% if debtor is local government or school district	all interest forfeited; recover interest paid plus twice that amount
Ill.	5%	9%; any rate on residential mortgage loans, state bank loans and business loans	no limit	9%, 6% on judgments against governmental entities	contract is void; forfeit all interest; recover twice total interest on contract or payment whichever is greater, within 2 years of last payment
Ind.	8%	UCCC limits apply	no special rate	12%	UCCC penalties which provide for greater of finance charge or 10 times excess charge if refund is refused
Iowa	5%	maximum written contract rate equals 4% above the monthly average 10 year constant maturity rate of U.S. Government bonds and notes for the second month preceding the first month of each quarter. The rate is published by the Federal Reserve Board. Any rate agreed upon for: persons buying real estate, obtaining credit for over $25,000 for home improvements, or for personal, family or household purposes, and obtaining credit for business or agricultural purposes	any rate	10% (f)	all interest and 8% of all unpaid principal forfeited to the state for the county school fund
Kan.	10%	15% unless U.C.C.C. provides otherwise; on residential mortgage loans, an amount equal to 1½% above the yield of 30-year fixed rate conventional home mortgages committed for delivery within 61 to 90 days accepted under federal home loan mortgage corporation's daily offerings	no special rate	15%	forfeit all interest in excess of maximum equivalent amount deductible from principal and lawful interest

LAWS GOVERNING NEGOTIABLE INSTRUMENTS 18–29

State	Legal Rate (a)	Contract Rate (b)	Corporate Rate (c)	Judgment Rate	Civil Penalty (d)
Ky.	8%	13%; 11.5% on loans of $15,000 or less, 8.5% on bank and trust company loans of $15,000 or less; $10 minimum bank loans permitted; others, any rate	no special rate	15%	forfeit all interest; recover twice interest paid within 2 years of transaction (i)
La.	12%	12%; 12% if secured by immovable property; any rate for business or commercial purpose loans except for adjustable rate loans (t)	no limit	12%	forfeit all interest; recover interest within 2 years of payment
Me.	6%	no maximum if in writing	no special rate	8% from filing of complaint to rendering of judgment (f); 15% thereafter	no provisions
Md.	6%	8%; unlimited for business loans over $15,000 and residential mortgages	no special rate	contract rate or 10%	forfeit 3 times excess collected, or $500, whichever is greater
Mass.	6%	unlimited	no special rate	contract rate or 12%	court may void a criminally usurious loan contract
Mich.	5%	7%; any rate on business loans by state or national banks, insurance carrier or finance subsidiary of manufacturing corp.; business loans by other entities 15%; until 4/1/85 any rate on realty-secured loans, federal or state regulated loans, land leases with tenant-owned improvements, loans or land contracts of $100,000 or over and secured by non-single family residence realty; other mortgage loans and land contracts at 11% calculated as Fed. Truth in Lending "finance charge"	no limit	12% from date of complaint to date of judgment; 13% after judgment date	forfeit interest, pay court fees, costs, attorneys' fees

State	Legal Rate (a)	Contract Rate (b)	Corporate Rate (c)	Judgment Rate	Civil Penalty (d)
Minn.	6%	8%; no limit on loans in excess of $100,000; 12% business and agricultural loans; loans by bank or savings bank; 4½% above discount rate on 90-day commercial paper at Federal Reserve Bank for district of Minnesota	no special rate	rate based on the weighted average discount yield for U.S. Treasury Bills with one year maturity; rate may not be less than 8% per year	contract void except as to bona fide purchaser; recover interest within 2 years; ½ amount recovered to school fund
Miss.	8% until 7/1/84	5% above discount rate on commercial paper at Federal Reserve District where lender is located	no limit on loan to $2,500; 5% over the federal discount rate for loans over $2,500	8% (f)	forfeit all interest; forfeit all interest, principal and finance charges if the finance charge received exceeds the maximum amount authorized by law by more than 100%
Mo.	9%	the greater of 10% or the "market rate" (monthly index of long term United States government bond yields plus 3%) except that parties may agree to any rate of interest in connection with business loan of $5,000 or more (excluding loans for agricultural activity, real estate loans other than residential real estate loans and real estate for agriculture purposes) loans of $5,000 or more secured soley by negotiable instruments	no limit	9% (f)	liable for excess interest, together with cost of the suit including reasonable attorneys' fees applied on principal
Mont.	6%	not more than 6% above prime rate of major New York banks as published in Wall Street Journal edition dated 3 days prior to execution of agreement	no special rate	10% (f)	forfeit double interest charged, recoverable within 2 years after payment

LAWS GOVERNING NEGOTIABLE INSTRUMENTS 18–31

State	Legal Rate (a)	Contract Rate (b)	Corporate Rate (c)	Judgment Rate	Civil Penalty (d)
Neb.	6%	16% per annum; maximum does not apply to loans made to any corporation, partnership or trust, guarantor or surety of corporate loans, loans of $25,000 or more, federal and state insured loans, loans repayable on demand made solely with securities as collateral, with loan used only for the purchase of securities	no limit	14% (f)	forfeit all interest and costs
Nev.	12%	any rate agreed on; secured mortgage 12% except if lowest daily prime rate at three largest United States banking institutions is 9% or more, maximum rate of interest shall not exceed such lowest daily prime rate plus 3½%	no special rate	12%	no statutory provision
N.H.	10%	unlimited	no special rate	10% (f)	no statutory provisions
N.J.	no statutory provision	16%; based on monthly index of long term U.S. bond yield plus 8%; 17% on loans sec. by realty with 1 to 6 dwelling units; no limit for loans purchased by governmental organizations	no special rate	no statutory provision	forfeit all interest and costs
N. Mex.	15%	as agreed by parties in writing if disclosure requirements satisfied	no special rate	15% (f)	forfeit all interest; recover double interest within 2 years of time of transaction (i)
N.Y.	16%	16% (generally same as legal rate); no limit on loans over $2.5 million	no special rate	9%	contract void and unenforceable, recover excess over lawful rate

State	Legal Rate (a)	Contract Rate (b)	Corporate Rate (c)	Judgment Rate	Civil Penalty (d)
N.C.	8%	16.5% on less than $25,000; any rate agreed by parties where greater than $25,000	no limit if agreed to in writing by a for-profit corporation	8%; interest on judgments on contracts at contract rate	forfeit all interest; recover double interest paid
N.D.	6%	5½% over average rate for 6-month U.S. treasury bills but not less than 7%; any rate on business loans over $35,000	no special rate	12% (f)	forfeit all interest and 25% of principal or double interest paid applied on principal; recover double plus 25% of principal within 4 years or offset against any indebtedness (i)
Ohio	10%	8%; any rate for securities pledged as collateral; any rate on business loans over $100,000; interest on real estate mortgages may be charged at a rate not in excess of 3% above the discount rate on 90-day commercial paper in force in the fourth federal reserve district at the time of execution of the mortgage	no special rate	10%	excess applied to principal
Okla.	6%	special rates as determined by UCCC; generally no limit on non-consumer or consumer related loans (e.g., loans in excess of $25,000 are non-consumer loans)	no special rate	15% (f); personal injury damages 15% added for period of suit	greater of excess interest charged or 10 times excess of refund refused within reasonable time after demand
Ore.	9%	rate agreed to by the parties; business, agricultural and other loans up to $50,000 based on Federal Reserve Bank discount rate (k)	no special rate	9% (f)	forfeiture of interest on loans subject to discount rate

LAWS GOVERNING NEGOTIABLE INSTRUMENTS

State	Legal Rate (a)	Contract Rate (b)	Corporate Rate (c)	Judgment Rate	Civil Penalty (d)
Pa.	6% to $50,000	6% to $50,000; residential mortgages-rate of interest on mortgages changes monthly as determined by Secretary of Banking and is equal to 2½% over the monthly index of long-term U.S. bonds; also excepted from maximum rate are unsecured loans in excess of $35,000 or business loans in excess of $10,000; principal obligation over $50,000 or any loan secured by real property (other than residential), no limit	no special rate	6%	forfeit excess over lawful rate; recover 3 times excess of lawful rate in action brought within 4 years; excess applied to principal
R.I.	12%	21% or alternate rate of 9% above index on Treasury Bills of less than one year maturity	no special rate	12% (f)	recover payments; contract void (i)
S.C.	6%; 8¾% when term "legal rate" or "lawful rate" used in contract	any rate provided for by UCCC	no special rate	14% (f)	forfeit all interest plus costs; recover double interest paid
S.D.	18%	any rate unless specifically limited by Code	any rate specifically limited by code	15%	no statutory provision
Tenn.	10%	for loans of $100 or more, 4% above average prime loan rate, whichever is less; state banks, based on Federal Reserve Bank surcharge; for home loans, two percentage points above accepted offers to Federal National Mortgage Association for commitments to purchase home mortgages	no special rate	10%	forfeit excess over lawful rate within 3 years (i)

State	Legal Rate (a)	Contract Rate (b)	Corporate Rate (c)	Judgment Rate	Civil Penalty (d)
Tex.	6%	any rate of interest agreed to in writing up to a 24% ceiling based on the following computation: the auction rate for the preceding week for 26-week U.S. treasury bills, multiplied by two, rounded to the nearest quarter percent; or, in the alternative, an annualized or quarterly rate based upon averages of auction rates of 26-week U.S. treasury bills, as calculated and published by the consumer credit commissioner; if the computation results in a rate less than 18%, the ceiling is 18%, if more than 24%, the ceiling is 24% per year	1½% per month on debt over $5,000; alternative contract rate, interest must not exceed contract rate	18% or rate specified in contract, whichever is less; if no contract then rate is based on discount rate for 52-week treasury bills but not less than 10% nor more than 20%	forfeit triple amount of interest charges plus attorneys' fees; amount forfeited may not be less than $2,000 or 20% of the principal whichever is less
Utah	10%	special rates as determined by UCCC; generally no limit on non-consumer loans (e.g., loans in excess of $25,000 are non-consumer loans)	no special rate	12% (f)	greater of excess interest charged or 10 times excess of refund refused within reasonable time after demand
Vt.	12%	12%; loans or credit secured by first lien against real estate—interest same as permitted by federal usury preemption law to financial institutions or residential real estate sellers	no limit	no statutory provision	forfeit all interest and 50% of principal; recover excess paid with interest from date of payment plus costs and fees (i)

State	Legal Rate (a)	Contract Rate (b)	Corporate Rate (c)	Judgment Rate	Civil Penalty (d)
Va.	6%	8%; any rate on nonagricultural loans secured by first mortgage on realty including leaseholds over 25 years; special provisions for other real estate loans by banks and other special institutions	no special rate	12% or rate entered into by contract, up to contract rate	forfeit all interest; recover 2 times total interest paid within 2 years of transaction
Wash.	12%	higher of 12% or 4% above equivalent coupon issue yield of 26-week treasury bill	no special rate	12% or 4% above yield for 26-week treasury bills, whichever is higher; unless contract provides otherwise	forfeit all interest and deduct from principal; deduct twice interest where paid plus all accrued and unpaid interest, costs, fees, and amount by which contract exceeds adjusted liability
W. Va.	6%	8%; the Commissioner of Banking may promulgate, on a monthly basis, maximum interest rates. The rates shall not exceed 1½% above the monthly index of long-term U.S. government bond yields for the preceding month; alternative rate set semiannually by Lending on Credit Rate Board; separate rate for state banks	no special rate	10%	all interest void; recover 4 times all interest agreed to be paid, minimum $100; recover payment over unlawful rate
Wis.	5%	no limit	no limit	12%	no statutory provision
Wyo.	7%	special rates as determined by UCCC; generally no limit on nonconsumer related loans (e.g., loans in excess of $25,000)	no special rate	as contract specifies, if rate less than 10%, otherwise 10% per year	greater of excess interest charged or 10 times excess of refund refused within reasonable time after demand

(a) Maximum rate permitted by state law absent any agreement to the contrary.

(b) Maximum rate that can be charged individuals by agreement.

(c) Rate which may be charged to corporations. "No special rate" means that corporation is controlled by contract rate. "No limit" means that corporations can be charged any rate of interest.

(d) Excludes criminal penalties and multiple damages.

(e) Special statute controls consumer transactions.

(f) Unless otherwise provided up to maximum contract rate permitted by law and provided for in contract.

(g) Special statutory provisions concerning maximum interest on loans by personal property brokers and industrial lenders, and premiums for mortgage loans.

(h) Maximum rate does not apply to loans by Conn. banks, trust companies or private bankers, nor to any real estate mortgage loan in excess of $5,000 nor to any loan carrying an interest rate of not more than 18% made to any corp. engaged primarily in commercial, manufacturing or industrial pursuits provided original indebtedness is in excess of $10,000 or to any one advance of less than $10,000 made pursuant to revolving loan agreement, provided all loans to borrower are in excess of $10,000.

(i) Violator deemed guilty of misdemeanor.

(j) Florida's contract and corporate rates do not apply to loans or other advances of credit insured by FHA, guaranteed by VA or made by a financial institution at the time of originating loan to FNMA, GNMA, or FHLMC or its successor, pursuant to act of Congress or federal regulation.

(k) Does not include loans by state and national banks, or such chartered savings and loans, credit unions, pawnbrokers and interest charges by reg. brk.-dlrs. and lenders approved by the NHA. Loans sec. by a first lien on real property, or insured by FHA, VA or Farmers Home Administration are also not subject to these rates.

(l) Vermont statute provides that lender shall make no charges to the borrower for the use or forbearance of money other than reasonable cost of credit investigation and appraisal fees, cost of title evidence, cost of protection against insurable hazards, cost of creditor life or disability insurance, filing fees, reasonable value of services rendered in connection with loans of $2,000 or less subject to limitations as determined by the Commissioner of Banking, reasonable cost of private mortgage guarantee insurance subject to limitations of the Commissioner of Banking.

(m) Judgment bears interest at contract rate not in excess of 12%; if not founded on contract then interest is 10%.

(n) All interest void; in addition, from original lender or creditor, amount equal to four times all interest or minimum of $100.

(o) Wisconsin law requires certain contract provisions and disclosure relating to use of interest adjustment clauses and variable rate contracts in connection with certain first lien residential mortgage loans. Penalty for intentional violation is liability to borrower for all excess interest collected, plus interest thereon at 5%. Borrower may also recover damages.

(p) Defense of usury not available for loans of $5,000 and more for business purposes secured by second mortgages.

(q) New York permits a variable interest rate not in excess of the maximum rate permitted at the time the loan of forebearance is made on loans which have an initial principal of more than $5,000 and which the borrower has the right to repay at any time without penalty.

(r) A judgment on a contract for the loan of money shall earn the contract rate of interest upon the unpaid principal until maturity.

(s) A financial institution may, on a loan secured by a savings or time account, charge interest 2% above the interest payable on the account.

(t) No limit on mortgages on immovable property which are guaranteed by the VA or insured by the FHA. It is sufficient if the mortgage was eligible to be so guaranteed or insured but the application was denied for reasons other than the rate of interest.

(u) Alternative rate on loans, lease or sales—2% above prime rate.

(v) If a judgment in a civil case is appealed by judgment debtor and judgment affirmed, rate of interest is 2% above discount rate. As of 1/1/83, rate is 11%.

CORPORATE USURY DEFENSE—TABLE BY STATES

State	Corporate Usury Defense
Alabama	No defense on contracts over $2,000
Alaska	No statutory provisions
Arizona	No statutory provision
Arkansas	No statutory provisions
California	Defense allowed
Colorado	No statutory provisions
Connecticutt	No statutory provisions
Delaware	No defense
District of Columbia	No defense
Florida	No statutory provisions
Georgia	Defense subject to corporate rate. No defense on loans over $3,000
Hawaii	No defense on contracts or notes over $750,000
Idaho	No statutory provision
Illinois	No statutory provision
Indiana	No statutory provisions
Iowa	No defense
Kansas	No defense
Kentucky	No defense except if principal asset involved is one or two family dwelling
Louisiana	No defense
Maine	No statutory provisions
Maryland	No statutory provisions
Massachusetts	No statutory provisions
Michigan	No defense
Minnesota	No defense
Mississippi	Defense subject to corporate rate
Missouri	No defense
Montana	No statutory provisions
Nebraska	No statutory provisions
Nevada	No statutory provisions
New Hampshire	No statutory provisions
New Jersey	No defense
New Mexico	No defense
New York	No defense unless principal asset is one or two family dwelling and corporation formed or controlled within 6 months before loan creating lien on such dwelling; defense of criminal usury may be asserted for rates over 25%.
North Carolina	No defense for for-profit corporations
North Dakota	No statutory provisions
Ohio	No defense
Oklahoma	No defense
Oregon	No statutory provisions
Pennsylvania	No defense
Rhode Island	No statutory provisions
South Carolina	No statutory provision
South Dakota	No statutory provisions
Tennessee	Defense available
Texas	Defense subject to corporate rate
Utah	No statutory provisions
Vermont	No statutory provisions

CORPORATE USURY DEFENSE—TABLE BY STATES (Continued)

State	Corporate Usury Defense
Virginia	No defense for certain business loans
Washington	No usury defense for profit and nonprofit corporations, Mass. trusts, associations, general or limited partnerships, joint ventures, governmental agencies, or for trade or business loans
West Virginia	No defense
Wisconsin	No statutory provisions
Wyoming	No statutory provisions

(Continued from page 18-25.)

add a savings clause limiting the interest to a rate no higher than the law allows. The validity of the latter two provisions in a loan transaction will vary from state to state. The effect of such provisions in exempting loans from the usury laws must be determined before their use in each jurisdiction.[1]

A bill of exchange or other form of negotiable instrument, valid in its inception and which has been once negotiated, may be sold at any discount that the holder sees fit. Where the sale of a bill of exchange is a mere loan, a rate of discount higher than the legal rate effects usury. The usury statutes, it will be remembered, forbid only the loan or forebearance of money at more than the established rate of interest. The bill of exchange, having once been negotiated becomes a chattel in the hands of the holder and may be sold for as low a price as the holder is willing to accept. Thus it is that a trade acceptance drawn by A and accepted by B may be taken to the bank by C and sold by or discounted at whatever price the bank will pay.

Where, however, a bill of exchange has been indorsed or otherwise guranteed by the seller, the seller becomes contingently liable to pay to the purchaser at a future day, a sum greater than that received with legal interest. "As to the character and effect of such a transaction, the authorities present some four different views: (1) Some courts have held such a transaction clearly usurious, and that the usurious indorsee takes no rights against any of the parties to the instrument. (2) Others have held that while the transaction between the indorser and indorsee is usurious, the defense of usury is personal to the indorser and is not available to the prior parties. (3) A third view, while holding the transfer not usurious, limits the right of recovery against the vendor-indorser to the amount received by him with lawful interest, and gives the purchaser recourse against prior parties to the full amount of the obligation. (4) In other jurisdictions such a transaction is regarded as a valid sale of a chattel with a warranty of its soundness, and the purchaser is allowed to enforce the obligation to its full extent against his own indorser and all prior indorsers." (91 C.J.S. pages 594-595.)

Were A to make his promissory note to B's order, and were B to obtain possession of the note by theft, or in any other manner other than by delivery from A, or if A were to give his promissory note to B, without consideration, and B were to discount the note at more than the legal rate, the transac-

---

[1] *See* Raymond J. Werner, "Usury and the Variable-Rate Mortgage," 5 Real Estate Law Journal 155 (Fall 1976) for discussion of approaches to the special usury problems of variable-rate mortgages.

tion in either event would have no valid inception and would constitute not a sale but a usurious loan. In all cases where the taker knows that the paper had no valid inception, the courts are in agreement in declaring the transaction usurious; but where the taker does not know that the paper had no prior inception, a different question arises, some states holding the loan usurious and the ignorance of the taker immaterial, while others have held to the contrary.

Interest on Past Due Accounts

As the cost of doing business mounts, businesses become increasingly more anxious to find ways of reducing expenses. An economy used by some is to defer making payments to trade creditors, which enables cash resources to be used to pay more pressing obligations or avoids the need to borrow. Creditors consequently are often squeezed by the pressures of their own demanding creditors which they are unable to meet because of slow-paying debtors. In response to these problems, more firms have begun to impose interest charges on past due accounts.

The purpose of such charges is generally not to produce additional revenue, but to encourage customers to make timely payments of their bills. Sellers, therefore generally charge a rate of interest on past due accounts which is in excess of the prevalent commercial rate of interest so as to discourage purchasers from delaying payment. But in doing so, however, sellers must be mindful of the requirements of the law of usury and not charge a rate of interest in excess of that permitted under applicable state law, which generally is the law of the state in which the contract is made.[1]

A majority of the states that have considered the question of interest on past due accounts have held that a provision in a promissory note or contract by which a debtor agrees to pay after maturity interest at a higher rate than permitted by the usury laws is not deemed usurious, provided that the parties have no intent that the basic contractual obligation not be paid at maturity and have not established the higher interest rate as a pretext to avoid the usury laws. Restatement of Contracts, §536:45; 45 Am. Jur. 2d 144; 28 ALR 3rd 449. This doctrine is ancient, some authorities attributing it to the time of James I in England (1603-1625). The reason for the rule is that the debtor has it within his control to avoid the higher interest rate by making payment on the due date.

Most of the reported cases on this question involve promissory notes in which a fixed interest is agreed upon until maturity and thereafter the rate of interest is increased. The issue of the legality of a service charge on sales contracts has arisen less frequently. Presumably, however, the same principles would apply.

For example, in *Hayes v. First National Bank of Memphis,* 507 S.W.2d 701 (Ark. 1974), it was held that delinquency charges collected on an installment sales contract did not render the contract usurious. The court stated that since delinquency charges are avoidable by the borrower, they do not render a contract usurious unless the form is a sham. Similarly, in *Scientific Products v. Cyto Medical Laboratory, Inc.,* 457 F. Supp. 1373 (D. Conn. 1978), the defense of

---

[1] See Lobell & Gelb, "Late Charges On Overdue Accounts," N.Y.L.J., April 28, 1983, at 1, col. 1, for a discussion of the New York state statute and the federal law which would apply if the seller extends consumer credit.

usury was held not applicable to interest charged after default in payment of a debt which arose out of a credit sale.

A minority of jurisdictions have declined to follow the majority rule and several states have modified it through statutory enactment.

Jurisdictions which remove the maximum rate of interest on past due accounts from the coverage of the usury laws by following the majority rule or by way of legislation permit charging interest at any rate agreed to by the parties, unless such rate is deemed unconscionably high. For example, a New Jersey court, in *Feller v. Architects Display Buildings,* 54 N.J. Supp. 205 (1959), held unenforceable as a penalty a contract clause that provided for an interest charge after maturity of 1/23 of 1% per day. The Court deemed such rate to be unconscionably high and therefore unenforceable. With respect to another loan adjudicated in that case in which interest at 19% per annum was charged, such interest was not deemed to be objectionable.

If the majority viewpoint does not obtain in any state, then the applicability of the usury law should be considered. Although many of the statutes speak of loans this language has often been interpreted to apply to a transaction in which forebearance of collection of a debt is involved. Therefore, one cannot rely solely on the express language of the statute, but of course it always should be consulted first. See 91 ALR 1105.

In considering this question one should also be aware of the substantial body of law in many of the states that holds there is no violation of the usury law if a higher price is charged in a credit sale than in a cash sale.

To determine whether a transaction is a true cash sale or credit sale (frequently called a time-price sale because a higher price is charged since payment is to be made at a later date)—the following questions must be answered: On what amount is the sales tax charged? Is disclosure of the two different prices available made to the customer? Is there an express agreement by seller to finance the sale? Basically there must be a bona fide difference in price between the cash and credit sale. The effort to transform a cash sale into a credit sale by merely adding thereon a service or interest charge has been unsuccessful in the courts. The problem was discussed in *State v. J. C. Penney & Co.,* 179 N.W.2d 641 (Wis. 1970), a case which involved revolving retail credit. For purposes of commercial financing the distinction between credit sales and cash sales is not of great significance since most commercial sales are with terms permitting delayed payment.

The following is a summary of the laws of each state as it relates to maximum permissible interest rate on past due accounts arising out of credit sales. The discussion of maximum interest rates in the various states deal only with commercial transactions. It does not deal with consumer sales which are often governed by special statutes.

In Arkansas, Connecticut, Idaho, Michigan,[1,2] New Jersey, New York, Tennessee, Washington and Wisconsin, creditors can charge interest on past due accounts at a rate higher than permitted by the respective usury laws. The courts in these states have ruled that a provision *in a contract* by which a debtor agrees after maturity to pay interest at a higher rate than permitted

---

[1] Based on old case law.
[2] These states have adopted time/price differential theory. Consequently, if a creditor decides to rely upon this doctrine, he may charge as high a service charge as the market will permit. In relying on this doctrine, however, it is necessary that the merchandise be available on cash terms if the purchaser so desires.

by the usury laws is not deemed usurious, provided that the parties have no intent that the basic contractual obligation not be paid at maturity and have not established the higher interest rate as a pretext to avoid the usury law.

Similarly, in Pennsylvania and Vermont, it is possible to charge interest on past due accounts at a higher rate than permitted by the usury laws. The attorneys general of those states have each rendered an opinion to the effect that default charges are not subject to the usury laws as long as there has been no agreement to forbear collection of the overdue amounts in consideration of the additional payments.

On the other hand, courts in the states of Hawaii and Texas [2] have held that damages due for delay in the performance of a debtor to pay money are called interest and subject to usury laws. It must be noted, in addition, that the federal preemption law is not applicable in Hawaii. Courts in Kentucky [3] and Missouri [2,3] also took the minority position, although the cases are very old. California [2] courts have held that interest on past due accounts is not subject to usury laws. The authority of such cases are, however, currently in doubt. Accordingly, creditors are advised to abide by the usury limitations of those states.

In Alaska,[4] Delaware,[3] Florida,[5] Minnesota,[2,3] Montana,[4] North Carolina,[2,5] Ohio [3] and Rhode Island,[4] the issue has not been specifically decided by courts nor by legislators. Hence, creditors are advised to abide by the usury limitations in those states. For state usury limitations on contracts, please refer to the table contained in this book.

The statutes of Colorado, Indiana, Maine, Oklahoma, Utah and Wyoming provide that the parties may contract for payment by the buyer of any credit service charge for sales transactions that are not consumer credit sales or consumer related sales.

In Arizona,[6] Massachusetts,[6] Nevada, New Hampshire, New Mexico, Oregon and South Dakota [6] parties may agree to interest at any rate. In the foregoing states, therefore, it is advisable for evidentiary purposes that a creditor obtain a written request from a customer specifying the rate at which late payments will be charged, even though a written agreement is not actually required.

The following is a summary of the governing law for the other states.

Alabama—Until June 1, 1983 a vendor in credit sales may charge a maximum of 2% above the prime rate at the time the sales contract is executed. The prime rate is the average prime rate at the three largest New York City banks at close of business three days immediately preceding the date of the rate (maximum of 1¾% per month on first $750 or less, and 1½% per month on the excess).

District of Columbia—A corporation formed under the laws of the District of Columbia can agree to any interest rate.

Georgia—The late charge of not more than 1½% per month is permissible only if the account is overdue for 30 days or longer. This applies to all commercial customers, corporate or not.

Illinois—The statute provides that it is lawful to charge any rate of interest

---

[2] See footnote 2, page 18-40.
[3] Corporations can be charged any interest rate.
[4] No law on corporate usury defense.
[5] Corporation organized for profit may be charged interest at any rate provided that the obligation is secured by personalty.
[6] If agreed to in writing.

with respect to any credit transactions between a merchandise wholesaler and retailer. For business loans and loans to corporations, parties can agree to any interest rate.

Iowa—The parties may contract for payments by the buyer of any credit service charge for sales transactions that are not consumer credit sales or consumer related sales.

Kansas—Under the Kansas statute rate of interest for credit sales is not subject to the usury laws.

Louisiana [2,7]—The damages due for delay in the performance of a debtor to pay money are called interest and subject to usury laws.

Maryland—In Maryland, a delinquency charge of up to 5% of the total amount owed is permissible for all customers, provided that the amount is at least 15 calendar days overdue. If the amount owed is greater than $5,000, or customer is a corporation, seller may charge interest at any rate.

Mississippi—Late payment charge, not exceeding $5 or 4% of the amount of any delinquency whichever is greater, if contracted for in writing shall not be considered a finance charge but no such charge shall be made unless such delinquency is more than 15 days past due.

Nebraska—Corporations and partnerships can be charged interest at any rate. For individuals as opposed to partnerships and corporations, a service charge of $1\frac{1}{3}\%$ per month is permissible provided the account is unpaid for 30 days following rendition of account.

North Dakota—Late charge of not more than 18% per year on all money due can be imposed from thirty days after the obligation of the debtor to pay has been incurred, provided that the creditor supplies the debtor with a monthly disclosure statement.

South Carolina [2]—Corporations may be charged interest at any rate regardless of the amount of the account, so long as they have issued capital stock in an amount greater than $40,000.

Texas—Interest on past due open accounts can only be charged 30 days after the due date at the maximum rate of 6% when no specified rate of interest is agreed upon in writing. Notice of interest in excess of 6% on invoices to debtor does not constitute an agreement in writing. Any attempt to collect interest in excess thereof results in forfeiture of principle and twice the interest charged, plus debtor's attorneys' fees.

Virginia—Late charges may be imposed at a rate not exceeding 5% of the overdue amount provided that the charge is specified in the contract between the lender or seller and debtor.

West Virginia [3]—The interest rate limitations do not apply to loans or credit sales evidenced by notes. Usury limitations are not applicable to a debt that is incurred by a loan, installment sale, or other similar transaction, and is incurred for a business purpose.

---

[2] See footnote 2, page 18-40.

[7] Charges assessed because of the nonpayment of the loan or any installment or part thereof after said loan or any installment of principal or interest thereof has become delinquent and is not timely paid, including cost of collecting and a reasonable attorney's fees are not considered interest provided that such charges or the methods of fixing same are provided in writing in either the note or the mortgage securing same.

[3] See footnote 3, page 18-41.

Interest on Credit Sales

The question has also been raised about whether there is any violation of the usury laws if a seller quotes one price for a cash sale, and a higher price for a sale on credit. Prior to the widespread use of instalment sales, early cases rejected the application of the usury laws to this factual situation. However, more recently, judicial thinking has changed and sales on credit have been subject to greater scrutiny. In some jurisdictions, such as Arkansas, Minnesota and Nebraska, the usury rule has been applied to these facts, whereas in other jurisdictions such as California, Illinois, New York, Texas, and Pennsylvania the doctrine still obtains which holds that no usury exists. Often, the indicia used to determine whether usury applies are whether the buyer was told of the two distinct prices, one for the sale on credit and the other for a cash sale, the existence of any relationship between the seller and a finance company, and the use of terms such as finance charts, interest rates, etc., in the sale.

In *State of Wisconsin v. J. C. Penney Co.,* 179 N.W.2d 641, the court held that a service charge of 1½% per month on retail charge accounts constituted a violation of the state's usury law. It rejected the defense, offered by J. C. Penney, that the credit transaction constituted a time-price sale in which a higher price was charged for the right to pay on credit. The imposition of a finance charge was held to be received for "forebearance" of money within the meaning of the usury statute. A similar decision was arrived at in *Rathbun v. W. T. Grant Company,* 300 Minn. 223, 219 N.W.2d 641 (1973), which involved the sale by W. T. Grant of a merchants retail instalment credit coupon book.

Finance or Service Charges

In lieu of the term "interest" or "finance charge," the term "service charge" is often used. If the term is intended to apply to the charge for the extension of credit or forebearance for collection, then it has the same meaning as interest or finance charge and is subject to the same laws and regulations of usury and maximum interest rates. Otherwise the term "service charge" may refer to charges for particular services rendered by a seller to the buyer such as alteration of the product to fit the customer's requirements; delivery of merchandise; storage of merchandise; or charge for return of merchandise. For this type of charge, the usury laws would not apply. See, *Cohen v. District of Columbia National Bank,* 382 F. Supp. 270 (D.D.C. 1974).

A finance charge as a result of the regular discount of consumer contracts may be deemed an interest charge to the consumer in excess of the maximum legal rate of interest permitted by state law. This was the holding of a California court in *Glaire v. LaLanne-Paris Health Spas, Inc.,* 12 C.3d 915, 117 Cal. Rptr. 541, 528 P.2d 357 (1974).

The United States Court of Appeals for the Seventh Circuit has held that regulations promulgated under the Wisconsin Consumer Act which impose maximum finance charges on Wisconsin residents by out-of-state companies do not violate the U.S. Constitution. A Chicago, Illinois mail order firm contended that Wisconsin should not determine the maximum rate the firm could charge under its revolving charge account plan for purchases by Wisconsin residents. The Court, however, agreed that Wisconsin's interest in determining the maximum charges its residents had to pay was sufficient to avoid violation of due process. *Aldens, Inc. v. LaFollette,* 552 F.2d 745 (7th Cir. 1977).

Late charges imposed by an electric utility company were not deemed usurious under Tennessee law. *Ferguson v. Electric Power Bd. of Chattanooga, Tenn.,* 378 F. Supp. 787 (E.D. Tenn. 1974). In a recent case involving sale of fuel to a consumer in which a 1¼% monthly finance charge was made by the seller, the contention of the consumer that the finance charge was in excess of the maximum rate of the usury statute of Pennsylvania was rejected by the court. The restrictions under the usury statute, the court held, applied to loans or use of money, but not to sale of goods or furnishing of services. *Kressley v. Atlantic Richfield Company,* 230 Pa. Super. 710, 326 A.2d 418 (1974).

The following is a list of how various states have resolved the issue of whether a creditor won compound interest on revolving credit accounts:

(1) *Compounding of Interest Authroized:* Michigan, Missouri, New Jersey, New York, Ohio, So. Dakota and Wisconsin.
(2) *Compounding of Interest Probably Authorized:* Colorado, District of Columbia, Idaho, Indiana, Iowa, Kansas, Kentucky, Maine, Maryland, Oklahoma, So. Carolina, Texas, Utah, Virginia, Washington, and Wyoming.
(3) *Compounding of Interest Prohibited:* Arkansas, California, Georgia, Hawaii, Louisiana, Mississippi, No. Dakota and Pennsylvania.
(4) *Compounding of Interest Probably Not Authorized:* Alabama, Florida, Illinois, Oregon and Rhode Island.
(5) *No Provision or Judicial Decisions with Respect to Compounding of Interest:* Alaska, Arizona, Connecticut, Delaware, Massachusetts, Minnesota, Montana, Nebraska, New Hampshire, Nevada, New Mexico, No. Carolina, Puerto Rico, Tennessee, Vermont and W. Virginia.

Calculation of Interest

There are a number of alternative ways of calculating interest. These include the simple interest, add-on, and discount methods. Unless the parties agree to a different method, or such other method is the established custom, a reference to interest would be simple interest. The following is a brief description of the various methods:

(1) Under the simple interest method, interest is charged only on the unpaid balance. For example, in calculating the monthly payment for a loan of $1,000 made at 6% for one year, the monthly payment could be 1/12th of $1,000, plus interest of ½ of 1% on the remaining unpaid balance.
(2) Under the discount method the interest charge on the loan is deducted in advance from the proceeds at the time the loan is made. The borrower, however, repays the full face amount. For example, an individual borrowing $1,000 for one year at 6% has the interest charge of $60 deducted from the proceeds of the loan at the time that the loan is made. The borrower gets only $940 and pays back $1,000 through the end of the year
(3) Under the add-on method, the interest charge on the loan is added to the face amount of the loan and the borrower pays back this larger amount rather than the principal. For example, if the borrower pays 6% on a $1,000 loan for one year, $60 is added to the principal. The borrower receives $1,000 initially, but repays $1,060.

In *American Timber & Trading Co. v. First Nat'l Bank of Oregon,* 511 F.2d 980 (9th Cir. 1973), an Oregon bank's method of computing interest by calculating the daily rate on the basis of a 360-day year and then applying that rate each day of a 365-day calendar year was held to violate the state's maximum interest rate statute.

In New Jersey, time periods are determined by statute; for purposes of interest: a day is determined to be 1/360 part of a year, and a month to be 1/12 of a year.

Under a New York decision, a plaintiff's loan to a defendant was evidenced by a promissory note stating interest at 7½% per annum, compounded quarterly. The court in *Giventer v. Arnow,* 44 A.D.2d 160, 354 N.Y.S.2d 162 (3rd Dept. 1974), held that the provision for compounded interest could not be enforced since it was contrary to the usury law of New York which had at that time a maximum rate of 7½% per annum.

A national bank in California has been held guilty of false and misleading advertising in quoting as a "per annum" rate, interest computed on the basis of a 360 day year. By using the 360 day calculation, the bank is actually collecting an annual interest rate greater than the advertised rate. 127 Cal. Rptr. 110, 544 P.2d 1310 (Calif. Sup. Ct. 1976).

Accommodation Paper

Where paper has been indorsed by A for the accommodation of B, there has been no valid negotiation of the paper and it falls into the class of paper which has had no legal inception; until it is negotiated for value, it cannot be discounted for more than the legal rate. Where the discounter is ignorant that the paper is accommodation paper, the conflict noted above occurs again; Alabama, Maryland, Massachusetts, New York, North Carolina, Ohio, South Carolina and Texas hold that the transaction is usurious and Connecticut, Illinois, Iowa, Kansas, Louisiana, Minnesota, Pennsylvania, Tennessee, Virginia and Wisconsin among others holding the contrary.

In *Holmes v. State Bank,* 53 Minn. 350, the court said:

"We are aware of the doctrine of the courts of New York and some other states, that accommodation paper in the hands of the payee cannot be the subject of a sale; 'that, to be the subject of a sale, the paper must have a pre-existing vitality'; that an accommodation note having, in fact, as against the maker, no validity and no legal inception, anyone who buys it of the payee takes the precise place of the payee in respect to the defense of usury, although he purchases in ignorance of its true character, and supposing it to be, as it appears on its face, business paper, and given for value; and hence when such a note is sold, even to a bona fide purchaser, at a discount greater than the legal rate of interest, the transaction is usurious. The same courts hold, as do all courts, that if a party buys of the payee an accommodation note for its face, he can recover on it, and that the fact that the maker received no consideration will be no defense; also, that after paper has had an inception, and has become live business paper, a person may buy at any discount he can get for it, without rendering the transaction usurious. We confess that these distinctions are altogether too refined to commend themselves to our judgment."

Mechanic's Lien Laws and Federal Tax Lien Law

FEDERAL TAX LIENS

The federal government by statute may impose a lien on the property or right to property of any taxpayer who refuses or neglects to pay any tax due, in the amount of tax, including interest and penalties. 26 U.S.C. § 6321 (1976). This lien may be imposed on any form of property, including insurance proceeds, real estate, assignments of accounts receivable, and other types of deposits and monies due.

In 1966, Congress adopted the Federal Tax Lien Act which was intended to eliminate the former problems of priority of creditors arising from concepts as to whether a lien was choate or inchoate. 26 U.S.C. §§ 6322 et. seq., 28 U.S.C. §§ 1346, 1401, 2410, 40 U.S.C. § 270a (1976).

Under the Act, the assessment of the tax constitutes a lien in favor of the United States on all property of the taxpayer subject to the priority rights of persons who hold a security interest, mechanic's lien or are purchasers or judgment creditors. Once the tax lien is recorded, however, it takes priority over all other rights to the taxpayer's property except for the priority given to the class of persons mentioned above and for the super priority status created by the statute for the following persons (26 U.S.C. § 6323):

1. Purchasers of motor vehicles provided possession is obtained prior to notice or knowledge of tax lien.
2. Purchasers of securities who did not have notice or knowledge of the existence of the tax lien.
3. Purchasers of personal property purchased at retail who had no knowledge or notice of the lien.
4. Purchasers of personal property purchased in a casual sale for an amount less than $250.
5. Persons holding a possessory lien on tangible personal property for repairs or improvements thereto.
6. Holders of a lien on real property subject to a lien for local real property tax and special assessment or charges for utilities on public services.
7. Holder of a mechanic's lien on residential property for certain repairs or improvements thereto to a maximum amount of $1,000.
8. Attorneys holding an attorney's lien.
9. Savings banks which have made loans secured by a passbook account.
10. Insurers of certain insurance contracts.
11. Persons involved in the following transactions:
    (a) Certain commercial financing agreements if the loan is made before the 46th day after the date of filing of the tax lien.
    (b) Certain real property, construction or improvement financing agreements.

(c) Obligatory disbursement agreements if the disbursement is made before the 46th day after the date of the filing of the tax lien.

The statute provides that in enumerated circumstances notice of the Government's claim will destroy the super priority status created.

Notice of the federal tax lien is to be filed in the office of the state or county in which the property is situated, and the statute authorizes each state to designate such office. Personal property is deemed to be situated in the state in which the taxpayer resides.

MECHANIC'S LIEN LAWS

A mechanic's lien is a special statutory lien on buildings and other improvements upon realty and, in most jurisdictions, upon the land on which they are situated, in favor of certain designated classes of persons, in order to secure to them compensation for the work and labor which they have performed in, or the material which they have furnished for, the construction, and in many jurisdictions, the repair or alteration of such building or improvements.

The interest of creditors in the laws governing mechanic's liens is manifest. The ability of a materialman to obtain a lien which will afford him ample protection may be an essential consideration in extending credit.

The statutory requirements in the various states differ so widely in so many particulars that space is not available in which to print the procedure in sufficient detail to make it safe for creditors to prepare and file their own liens in reliance thereon. Many of the states have prepared statutory forms and many others set out in detail numerous provisions which are required to be included in the notice of lien to be filed, or served upon the owner, and while there is a tendency in many of the states to be satisfied with less than a strict compliance with the statute, it is usually safer to protect rights involving a recourse to the mechanic's lien statute by retaining a local attorney.

For liens on personal property see the state law summary in Chapter 20, *infra*.

Contractors on public works are frequently required by federal and state statutes to provide bonds for the protection of laborers and materialmen in lieu of mechanic's lien rights. These statutes are summarized in Chapters 30 and 31 *infra*.

Who May File Lien

The statutes usually provide that any person who furnishes material or does work shall have a lien, and such lien may be acquired by an individual, partnership or corporation, whether a resident or nonresident of the state where the lien is claimed. There are three types of claimants to whom the benefits of the mechanics' liens statutes apply, the original or principal contractor, the subcontractors, or all persons supplying labor or materials. The statute will provide to whom the benefit of the lien will run.

Generally, all property is subject to the lien, except public property and property of quasi-public corporations, such as railway property devoted to strictly public uses.

The basis of a mechanic's or materialman's lien is that labor or material has gone into and added to the value of the property and become part of the

MECHANIC'S LIEN LAWS AND FEDERAL TAX LIEN LAW   19–3

realty. The lien may be claimed either for services performed or for material furnished in the erection, repair, or alteration of a building, usually also for transportation of the material to be used in the construction of the building, in each case as the statute provides.

The right to a lien for material furnished extends to all materials used in the construction of a building or which are within the express or implied terms of the building contract. In the absence of statutory provisions to the contrary, materials used for construction of, but not incorporated into, the building, such as lumber for scaffolding, do not give rise to a right of lien. Where material was furnished for use in a given building, and was subsequently diverted by the owner of the building before such use, however, the lien still attaches.

The mere sale of material, without reference to the building in which it is to be used, however, does not create a lien upon the building in which it is, in fact, afterwards used. The labor must have been performed or the materials furnished upon the credit of the building and not merely upon the general credit of the owner or contractor.

Whether or not a lien may be claimed depends upon the nature of the contract and whether or not it conforms to the requirements of the statute of the state where the property is situated. Some jurisdictions permit the contract to be oral, but others require a written contract embodying a description of the land on which the building is to be erected or work done, and usually a description of the building or improvement in contemplation, and a specification of the work to be done or materials furnished. The statutes of certain states allow a lien to attach only when the amount due or to become due is fixed in the contract. Similarly, some states require that the terms of payment be set forth in the contract.

Many states have a provision for the filing or recording of the contract, and the statutory requirements must be strictly complied with.

Subcontractor's Lien Rights

Subcontractors and materialmen are allowed liens in the several states under two distinct and essentially different concepts.

One concept, which is used in New York and other states that follow it, limits the lien of a subcontractor to the amount due to the general contractor by the owner. In order to recover his claim in full, the subcontractor must show that the amount due to the general contractor by the owner is as much as or greater than the amount of his claim.

Under the other concept, the right of subcontractors to a lien is not limited by the amount due the contractor from the owner. State statutes under this system give a direct lien to the subcontractor. Even if payments have been made by the owner under the contract, his liability is not reduced. The states that follow this system thus give the subcontractor a lien on the owner's property for the entire amount of his claim whether or not payment has been made to the contractor.

Set forth below is a chart distinguishing those states which would give the subcontractor a direct lien for the value of the services rendered or materials supplied on property from those states which would restrict the subcontractor's lien to reflect only the unpaid amount of the principal contract price.

LIEN LIMITED BY UNPAID PORTION OF GENERAL CONTRACT	DIRECT LIEN
Alabama	Arizona
Alaska	California
Arkansas	Colorado
Connecticut	Hawaii
Delaware	Idaho
District of Columbia	Indiana
Florida	Louisiana
Georgia	Maryland
Illinois	Minnesota
Iowa	Missouri
Kansas	Montana
Kentucky	Nevada
Maine	New Hampshire
Massachusetts	New Jersey
Michigan	New Mexico
Minnesota	North Dakota
Mississippi	Oregon
Nebraska	Pennsylvania
New York	Rhode Island
North Carolina	South Dakota
Ohio	Texas
Oklahoma	Vermont
South Carolina	Washington
Tennessee	Wisconsin
Utah	Wyoming
Virginia	
West Virginia	

Effect of Provision in Contract Against Filing of Mechanic's Lien

Where the principal contract for improvements on real estate contains a direct and positive covenant that no liens shall attach to the property because of the work, questions at once are raised as to whether such a provision is effective to prevent the contractor, subcontractors, and materialmen from filing liens. An example of a lien waiver follows:

"No contractor, subcontractor, materialman, or other person furnishing labor or materials for the work herein provided for, or for any alterations or additions thereto, shall have any right to file any mechanic's lien, or claim of any sort or kind, against the premises or any part thereof."

1. THE CONTRACTOR—Generally, a clear and unambiguous waiver of a right to a mechanics lien in a contract will bind the principal contractor, even if the event of default of payment by the owner. However, where the waiver clause promises only to deliver the property "free from mechanics liens" the following states have held that such a clause does not preclude the principal contractor from claiming a lien but applies only to subcontractors and materialmen.

Arkansas—*Plunkett v. Winchester,* 98 Ark. 160, 135 S.W. 860 (1911).
Idaho—*Smith v. Faris-Kesl Const. Co.,* 27 Idaho 407, 150 P. 25 (1915).
Illinois—*Concord Apartment House Co. v. O'Brien,* 128 Ill. App. 437, (1896); *Davis v. Willmore,* 186 Ill. App. 510. (1914). But see *Herman H. Hettler*

Lumber Co. v. Hodge, 227 Ill. App. 383, in which *Concord* is distinguished.
Massachusetts—*Poirier v. Desmond,* 177 Mass. 201, 58 N.E. 684 (1900).
New York—*Kertscher & Co. v. Green,* 205 N.Y. 522, 99 N.E. 146 (1912).
Washington—*Gray v. Hickey,* 94 Wash. 370, 162 P. 564 (1917).

2. SUBCONTRACTORS AND MATERIALMEN PRECLUDED—In the absence of a statute to the contrary, it has been held in some jurisdictions that a provision similar to that quoted above precludes subcontractors, laborers and materialmen from claiming liens against the premises. Cases so holding are:

California—*Bowen v. Aubrey,* 22 Cal. 566. Compare *Whittier v. Wilbur,* 48 Cal. 175.
Illinois—*W. W. Brown Const. Co. v. Central Illinois Const. Co.,* 234 Ill. 397, 84 N.E. 1038 (1908); *Kelly v. Johnson,* 251 Ill. 135, 98 N.E. 1068 (1911); *Rittenhouse & Embree Co. v. William Wrigley, Jr., Co.,* 264 Ill. 40, 105 N.E. 743 (1914).
Indiana—*Baldwin Locomotive Works v. Edward Hines Lumber Co.,* 189 Ind. 189, 125 N.E. 400, 401 (1919).

In this case, the Court said:

The better rule seems to be that, where there is a direct and positive covenant in the principal contract against liens, it precludes all who work under, or furnish material to, the principal contractor.... The cases which seem to be at variance to this, and are so cited, sometimes, when examined, disclose that there was not a direct and positive covenant against liens, but some stipulation by which the contractor agreed to indemnify the owner against liens....

Missouri—*Early v. Atchison, T. & S. F. R. Co.,* 167 Mo. App. 252.

3. SUBCONTRACTORS AND MATERIALMEN NOT PRECLUDED—In some states it has been held that a clause such as that quoted above does not deprive subcontractors, laborers and materialmen of their right to file liens against the property, especially where the subcontractor, laborer or materialman was unaware of the stipulation in the principal contract at the time of entering into the subcontract. The following are decisions to this effect:

Alabama—*Baker Sand & Gravel Co. v. Rogers Plumbing & Heating Co.,* 228 Ala. 612, 154 So. 591 (1934).
Arizona—*Arizona Easton Ry. Co. v. Globe Hardware Co.,* 14 Ariz. 397, 129 P. 1104 (1913).
Arkansas—*Cost v. Newport Builders' Supply & Hardware Co.,* 85 Ark. 407, 108 S.W. 509 (1908). *Peoples Building & Loan Assn. v. Leslie Lumber Co.,* 183 Ark. 800, 38 S.W. 2d 759 (1931).
Colorado—*Jarvis v. State Bank,* 22 Colo. 309, 45 P. 505 (1896); *Aste v. Wilson,* 14 Colo. App. 323, 59 P. 846 (1900).
Indiana—*Kokomo F. & W. Traction Co. v. Kokomo Trust Co.,* 193 Ind. 219, 137 N.E. 763 (1923).
Maine—*Norton v. Clark,* 85 Me. 357.
Michigan—*Smalley v. Gearing,* 121 Mich. 190, 79 N.W. 1114 (1899).
Montana—*Miles v. Coutts,* 20 Mont. 47, 49 P. 393 (1897).
Nebraska—*Coates Lumber & Coal Co. v. Klaas,* 102 Neb. 660, 168 N.W.

647 (1918); *Walker v. Collins Const. Co.,* 121 Neb. 157, 236 N.W. 334 (1931).

New Jersey—*Bates Mach. Co. v. Trenton & N.B.R. Co.,* 70 N.J.L. 684 (1904), 58 A 935 (1904).

New York—*Miller v. Mead,* 127 N.Y. 544, 28 N.E. 387 (1891).

Oregon—*G. Zanello & Son v. Portland Central Heating Co.,* 70 Or. 69, 139 P. 572 (1914); *St. Johns Lumber Co. v. Pritz,* 75 Or. 286, 146 P. 483 (1915); *Myers v. Strowbridge Estate Co.,* 82 Or. 29, 160 P. 135 (1916) .

Washington—*Pacific Lumber & Timber Co. v. Dailey,* 60 Wash. 566, 111 P. 869 (1910).

Wisconsin—*Seeman v. Biemann,* 108 Wis. 365, 84 N.W. 490 (1900).

4. CONTRACT BETWEEN PRINCIPAL CONTRACTOR AND SUBCONTRACTOR—But where the contract between the principal contractor and the subcontractor contains an agreement to the effect that no lien shall be filed by the subcontractor, the cases appear to be unanimous to the effect that the subcontractor is bound by this provision, and in a number of states where a subcontract by its express terms adopts the terms of the principal contract, a provision against the filing of liens in the principal contract is carried over into the subcontract and is binding as against the subcontractor.

SUMMARY OF STATE LAWS GOVERNING MECHANIC'S LEINS

ALABAMA

1. WHO MAY CLAIM.—Every mechanic, person, firm or corporation who does or performs any work or labor upon, or furnish any material, fixture, engine, boiler, or machinery for any building or improvement on land, or for repairing, altering or beautifying the same, under or by virtue of any contract with the owner or proprietor thereof, or his agent, architect, trustee, contractor, or subcontractor, upon complying with the provisions of this statute, shall have a lien therefor on such building or improvements, and on the land on which the same is situated. A lien is also granted to persons, firms or corporations who perform work on, or furnish material for paving, gutter, or other improvements in or on any public street or other public way under or by virtue of any contract with the abutting land owner or proprietor, and if the amount involved exceeds $100.

2. HOW CLAIMED.—It shall be the duty of every original contractor and of every journeyman and day laborer and of every other person entitled to such lien to file a statement in writing, verified by the oath of the person claiming the lien, or of some other person having knowledge of the facts.

3. WHERE FILED.—Office of the judge of probate of the county in which the property upon which the lien is sought to be established is situated.

4. WHEN TO BE FILED.—Every general contractor within six months, every journeyman and day laborer within thirty days and every other person entitled to such a lien within four months after the last item of work has been performed or the last item of material has been furnished.

5. SERVICE OF COPY OF NOTICE.—Every person, except the original contractor, who may wish to avail himself of the provisions of this article, shall, before filing his statement in the Office of the Judge of Probate, give notice in writing to the owner or proprietor, or his agent, that he claims a lien on such building or improvement. But the provisions of this section shall not apply to the case of any material furnished for such building or improvement, of which the owner was notified in advance, as provided in Number 9 below.

6. DURATION OF LIEN.—Generally, all liens arising under this article shall be deemed lost, unless suit for the enforcement thereof is commenced within six months after the maturity of the entire indebtedness secured thereby.

7. FILING FEE.—Fifteen cents per one hundred words.

8. CONTENTS OF NOTICE OF LIEN.—The verified statement must contain the amount of the demand secured by the lien, after all just credits have been given, a description of the property on which the lien is claimed, and the name of the owner. No error in amount or name of the owner shall effect the lien. Anyone other than the original contractor must first give written notice

MECHANIC'S LIEN LAWS AND FEDERAL TAX LIEN LAW 19-7

to the owner or proprietor or his agent that he claims a lien and shall state the amount, for what and from whom it is going.

9. EXTENT OF LIEN.—The contractor's lien extends to all the right, title and interest of the owner or proprietor. The subcontractor's lien extends only to the amount of any unpaid balance due the contractor by the owner or proprietor unless he notifies the owner or proprietor that he will furnish the contractor with certain materials. If the owner does not disclaim responsibility for the price before the materials are used, the subcontractor shall have a lien for the full price regardless of whether the amount exceeds the unpaid balance.

10. PRIORITY.—Such lien as to the land and buildings or improvements thereon, shall have priority over all other liens, mortgages or incumbrances created subsequent to the commencement of work on the building or improvement; and as to liens, mortgages or incumbrances created prior to the commencement of the work, the lien for such work shall have priority only against the building or improvement, the product of such work which is an entirely, separable from the land, building or improvement subject to the prior lien, mortgage or incumbrance, and which can be removed therefrom without impairing the value or security of any prior lien, mortgage or incumbrance; and the person entitled to such lien may have it enforced by a sale of such buildings or improvement under the provisions of this article and the purchaser may, within a reasonable time thereafter, remove the same.

11. PUBLIC IMPROVEMENTS.—See Chapter 30, *infra*, Bonds on Public Works.

ALASKA

1. WHO MAY CLAIM—A person is entitled to a lien if he (1) performs labor upon real property at the request of the owner or his agent for the construction, alteration, or repair of a building or improvement; (2) is a trustee of an employee benefit trust for the benefit of individuals performing labor on the building or improvement and has a direct contract with the owner or his agent for direct payments into the trust; (3) furnishes materials that are delivered to real property under a contract with the owner or his agent which are incorporated into the construction, alteration or repair of a building or improvement; (4) furnishes equipment that is delivered to and used upon real property under a contract with the owner or his agent or the construction, alteration or repair of a building or improvement; (5) performs services under a contract with the owner or his agent in connection with the preparation of plans, surveys, or architectural or engineering plans or drawings for the construction, alteration or repair of a building or improvement, whether or not actually implemented on that property; or (6) is a general contractor.

2. HOW CLAIMED.—A claimant must provide the owner with a written notice of right to lien. The notice must contain a legal description sufficient for identification of the real property upon which the building or other improvement is located, the name of the owner, the name and address of the claimant, the name and address of the person with whom the claimant contracted, a general description of the labor, materials, services or equipment provided or to be provided, and a statement that the claimant may be entitled to record a claim of lien. In addition, the notice must contain the following statement in type no smaller than that used for the preceding information: "WARNING: Unless provision has been made for payment of this claim you may be liable for payment directly to this claimant notwithstanding the fact that payment has been made to a prime contractor or other party."

In all cases, the claim of lien must be verified and contain the following information:
1. Sufficient legal description of the real estate concerned.
2. Name of the owner.
3. Name and address of the lien claimant.
4. Name and address of the party with whom the claimant contracted.
5. General description of the contribution.
6. The amount due the claimant for his contribution.
7. The date of the contribution.

A subcontractor other than an individual must also record an authenticated copy of an acknowledgment of right to lien received from the owner. Acknowledgment must be recorded at the time claimant records a claim of lien or a notice of right to lien.

3. WHERE FILED—Recorder of the district where building or improvement is situated.

4. WHEN FILED—Claim of lien must be filed within 10 days after notice of completion is filed. Certain claimants have up to 15 days after notice of completion is recorded. If notice of completion is not recorded by owner, lien claim must be recorded within 90 days after the contract is completed or persons cease to furnish labor, material, services or equipment.

5. DURATION OF LIEN—A lien is lost unless suit is brought within six months after the claim has been filed. If an extension notice is recorded during the original six month period, then suit

must be brought within six months after the recording. However, no lien continues in force for a longer period than one year from the date of the filing of the original lien notice.

6. FILING FEE—First page $3; each additional page $2; indexing each name over four—25¢.

7. EXTENT OF LIEN—Any building or improvement constructed with the knowledge of the owner, unless the owner objects by the means prescribed by the Alaska Code. The lien extends to the land upon which the building rests as well as to the area necessary for the use and occupancy of the building. No claimant may collect more than the amount due under the general contract.

8. PRIORITY OF LIEN—A lien which is recorded before all subsequent encumbrances are recorded has priority. If the lien is for work actually performed or for an employee benefit trust, then the lien is preferred to prior encumbrances. The building or other improvement may be sold separately from the land to satisfy the lien and the purchaser may remove the same within 30 days.

9. PUBLIC IMPROVEMENTS—See Chapter 30, *infra,* Bonds on Public Works.

10. LIENS FOR IMPROVEMENTS OF OIL AND GAS WELLS—Work done at the instance of the owner gives rise to a lien upon a mine or mining claim, oil, gas or other well, so long as the property is in one mass and can be identified as being produced by the labor of the lienor.

ARIZONA

1. WHO MAY CLAIM.—Every person who labors or furnishes materials, machinery, fixtures or tools to be used in the construction, alteration, or repair of any building or other structure or improvement whatever, shall have a lien thereon for the work or labor done or materials, machinery, fixture, or tools furnished, whether said work was done, or article furnished, at the instance of the owner of the building, structure or improvement, or his agent. Every contractor, subcontractor, architect, builder or other person having charge or control of the construction, alteration or repair, either in whole or in part, of any building, structure or improvement, shall be held to be the agent of the owner and the owner shall be liable for the reasonable value of labor or materials furnished to his agent. A person furnishing material or labor on a lot in an incorporated city or town, or on any parcel of land not exceeding 160 acres in the aggregate, or fills in or otherwise improves the lot or such parcel of land, or an alley or street, or proposed alley or street, within, in front of or adjoining such lot or parcel of land shall have a lien for the material and labor. Right of lien is also given for labor or materials used in construction or repair of canals, ditches, aqueducts, bridges, fences, roads, excavations, railroads, etc., and in connection with mines and mining claims.

2. HOW CLAIMED.—Make two copies of a notice and claim of lien and record one copy and serve the other copy on the owner. In addition, every person other than the original contractor must give the owner, contractor and construction lender, if any, a written preliminary notice within 20 days of the first furnishing labor, materials, machinery, fixtures or tools to the jobsite.

3. WHERE FILED.—With the County Recorder of the county in which the property or some part thereof is located.

4. WHEN TO BE FILED.—Original contractor must file within 90 days and every other person but original contractor within 60 days after completion, alteration or repair of building, structure or improvement, if notice of completion has been recorded and copy sent by certified or registered mail to person from whom owner received preliminary 20-day notice.

5. SERVICE OF COPY OF NOTICE.—Upon the owner or owners of said building, structure or improvement, if he can be found within the county, within a reasonable time after recording.

6. DURATION OF LIEN.—Six months after the recording thereof in the County Recorder's office, unless suit is brought within such period action to foreclose the same is commenced.

7. FILING FEE.—$5 for the first 5 pages, $1 for each additional page, not to exceed $250.

8. CONTENTS OF NOTICE OF LIEN.—Description of the lands and improvements to be charged with the lien.

The name of the owner or reputed owner of the property, if known, and also the name of the person by whom the lienor was employed or to whom he furnished materials.

A statement of the terms, time given and conditions of his contract, if the same be oral, or a copy of the contract, if written.

A statement of the lienor's demand, after deducting all just credits and offsets.

A statement of date of completion of the building structure, or improvement. Completion is deemed to be cessation of work on property for period of 60 days, except for strike or shortage of labor.

(Claim of lien must be made under oath by the claimant or by someone in his behalf who has knowledge of the facts.)

The subcontractor's 20-day preliminary notice must contain:

A general description of the labor, materials, machinery, fixtures, or tools furnished or to be furnished, and an estimate of the total price thereof. The name and address of the person furnishing such labor, materials, machinery, fixtures, or tools. The name of the person who contracted for purchase of such labor, materials, machinery, fixtures, or tools. The legal description subdivision plat, street address or other landmarks in the area, or any other description of the job site sufficient for identification; the validity of the notice will not be affected by omission of the street address or an erroneous address. The following statement in bold-face type:

"**In accordance with Arizona Revised Statutes section 33-992.01, this is not a lien, this is not a reflection on the integrity of any contractor or subcontractor.**

NOTICE TO PROPERTY OWNER

If bills are not paid in full for the labor, materials, machinery, fixtures or tools furnished or to be furnished, a mechanic's lien leading to the loss, through court foreclosure proceedings, of all or part of your property being improved may be placed against the property. You may wish to protect yourself against the consequence by either:

1. Requiring your contractor to furnish a release signed by the person or firm giving you this notice before you make payments to your contractor.

2. Using any other method or device which is appropriate under the circumstances."

If the notice is given later than 20 days, any lien cannot apply to labor, materials, machinery, fixtures, or tools furnished beyond 20 days prior to the giving of notice. The notice may be served by delivering it personally, by leaving it at the residence or place of business of the person to be served with some person of suitable age and discretion residing or working there, or by first class, registered or certified mail, postage prepaid, addressed to the person to whom notice is to given at his residence or business address.

9. EXTENT OF LIEN.—If land lies outside the limits of the recorded map or plot of a townsite, an incorporated city or town, or a subdivision, the lien extends to and includes not exceeding 10 acres of land upon which the improvement is made and the labor performed. If land lies within said limits the lien extends to and includes only the particular lot or lots upon which the improvement is made and the labor performed. The lien upon a mining claim extends to the whole of the claim and to the group of which said claim is a part, if the group is operated as one property.

10. PRIORITIES.—These liens are preferred to all liens, mortgages or other encumbrances which shall have attached upon the property subsequent to the time the labor was commenced or the materials commenced to be furnished, also to all liens, mortgages and other encumbrances of which the lienholder had no actual or constructive notice at the time he commenced the labor or the furnishing of the materials. All liens of this character shall attach upon an equal footing, without reference to date of recording the notice and claim of lien and without reference to time of performing such work and labor or furnishing the material. If a lien is foreclosed and the proceeds are insufficient to discharge all liens against the property without reference to the date of recording, the proceeds shall be prorated over the respective liens.

11. PUBLIC IMPROVEMENTS.—See Chapter 30, *infra*, Bonds on Public Works.

12. LIENS FOR IMPROVEMENTS OF OIL AND GAS WELLS.—When separately owned property is embraced within one established drilling unit, and a pooling of interests is established, the owner drilling and operating for the benefit of others has a lien on the share of production from the unit accruing to the interest of each of the owners for the payment of his share of the expenses.

ARKANSAS

1. WHO MAY CLAIM.—Mechanics, builders, artisans, workmen, laborers, engineers, surveyors, or other persons who shall work upon buildings, erections, improvements upon land, or clear or excavate land, or boats or vessels of any kind, and those who furnish any materials, fixtures, engines, boilers, or machinery for same or for repairing same. Persons who perform labor or furnish fuel, material, machinery, or supplies used in digging, drilling, torpedoing, operating, completing, equipping, maintaining or repairing oil or gas wells, water wells, mines or quarries, or oil or gas pipe lines. Laborers and repairmen shall have an absolute lien on work performed and materials furnished for the repair of any vehicle or airplane.

2. HOW CLAIMED.—By filing verified account, showing balance due after allowing all credits, and describing the property upon which the lien is claimed and the labor performed or material furnished.

3. WHERE FILED.—Office of Clerk of the Circuit Court of county where property is situated.

4. WHEN TO BE FILED.—Within 120 days after work performed or material furnished.

5. SERVICE OF COPY OF NOTICE.—Act requires ten days' notice to owner or his agent by person wishing to avail himself of lien, excepting the original contractor. Notice must state the amount and from whom the same is due.

The notice may be served by any officer authorized by law to serve process in civil actions or by any person who would be a competent witness. When served by an officer, his official returned endorsement thereon is proof thereof, and by other person fact of service verified by affidavit of serving person.

Notice in cases where owner is nonresident of county or state, has no agent in the county where property is situated, or conceals or absents himself, should be filed with the Recorder of Deeds of the county where the property is situated.

6. DURATION OF LIEN.—Suit must be filed within 15 months from filing of lien.

7. FILING FEE.—$3.

8. CONTENTS OF NOTICE OF LIEN.—Notice should state that claimant (naming him) holds a claim against such building, erection, or improvement (describing same), the amount thereof and from whom it is due.

The act requires that the following warning be given to the owner or his agent on a separate sheet of paper prior to the furnishing of material, etc. except where the principal contractor has supplied a performance or payment bond or where the transaction involved a direct sale to the property owner. The signature of the owner or his authorized agent is not required where such notice is delivered by certified mail.

IMPORTANT NOTICE

I UNDERSTAND THAT PERSONS SUPPLYING MATERIAL ARE ENTITLED TO A LIEN AGAINST PROPERTY IF THEY ARE NOT PAID IN FULL FOR MATERIALS USED TO IMPROVE THE PROPERTY EVEN THOUGH THE FULL CONTRACT PRICE MAY HAVE BEEN PAID TO THE CONTRACTOR. I REALIZE THAT THIS LIEN CAN BE ENFORCED BY THE SALE OF THE PROPERTY IF NECESSARY. I AM ALSO AWARE THAT PAYMENT MAY BE WITHHELD TO THE CONTRACTOR IN THE AMOUNT OF THE COST OF ANY MATERIALS OR LABOR NOT PAID FOR. I KNOW THAT IT IS ADVISABLE TO AND I MAY REQUIRE THE CONTRACTORS TO FURNISH TO ME A TRUE AND CORRECT FULL LIST OF ALL OF HIS SUPPLIERS UNDER THE CONTRACT, AND I MAY CHECK WITH THEM TO DETERMINE IF ALL MATERIALS FURNISHED FOR THE PROPERTY HAVE BEEN PAID FOR. I MAY ALSO REQUIRE THE CONTRACTOR TO PRESENT LIEN WAIVERS BY ALL SUPPLIERS STATING THAT THEY HAVE BEEN PAID IN FULL FOR SUPPLIES PROVIDED UNDER THE CONTRACT, BEFORE I PAY THE CONTRACTOR IN FULL.

9. EXTENT OF LIEN.—The lien extends to all the right, title and interest of the owner for whose benefit the work was done. It includes the entire lot in any town, city or village, as well as the building or improvement made upon same. If not within a city, the lien extends to those areas on which work has been done or improvements erected. Where the improvement is on leased premises, the lien attaches to the improvement and to the leasehold term. Liens attach to the boats or vessels upon which work was done or material furnished.

10. PRIORITIES.—The lien shall be preferred to all other encumbrances which may be attached to or upon such buildings, erections, improvements, or boats, or the land, or either of them prior or subsequent to the commencement of such buildings or improvements, except where such prior lien, mortgage or other encumbrance was given to raise money for such buildings, erections or improvements. Any person enforcing such lien may have the building or improvement sold under execution. Lien for work performed or materials furnished to improve oil, gas and water wells, mines or quarries or oil or gas pipe lines is superior and paramount to any and all other liens or claims of any kind.

11. LIENS FOR IMPROVEMENTS OF OIL AND GAS WELLS.—Lien arises for performing labor or furnishing materials, machinery or supplies for the construction, maintenance and repair of any oil, gas or water well, mine or quarry, or pipeline. Lien extends to the land, plant, building and appurtenances and is established in the same manner and the same time as a mechanic's lien. If labor or material is supplied to a leaseholder, the lien does not attach to the underlying fee title to the land.

12. PUBLIC IMPROVEMENTS.—See Chapter 30, *infra,* Bonds on Public Works.

CALIFORNIA

1. WHO MAY CLAIM.—Mechanics, materialmen, contractors, subcontractors, lessors of equipment, artisans, architects, machinists, builders, miners, teamsters, draymen, registered engineers, licensed land surveyors, plastic fabricators, and all persons and laborers rendering service or furnishing material, labor, appliances, teams and power contributing to construction, alteration, repair of any building, wharf, bridge, ditch, flume, aqueduct, well, tunnel, fence machinery, railroad, wagon road or other structure. Express trust fund established under a collective bargaining agreement to

MECHANIC'S LIEN LAWS AND FEDERAL TAX LIEN LAW 19-11

which payments are made on fringe benefits to one entitled to lien a particular realty will have lien for amount of fringe benefit. Any claimant who, at the instance of the owner of any lot or tract of land, has made any site improvement has a lien upon such lot.

2. HOW CLAIMED.—Claimant other than one under direct contract with owner is entitled to enforce lien only if he has given preliminary 20-day notice for private work. Each claimant, in order to enforce lien, must record his claim of lien within 90 days after completion of work of improvement if no such notice of completion or cessation was recorded, or within 60 days after filing of such notice in case of original contractor, and within 30 day after such date in case of other claimants. Where improvement is made under two or more original contractors, owner may, within ten days after completion of any such contract, record notice of completion containing specified data. Upon such filing, original contractor under contract covered by notice must, within 60 days after filing, and other claimant must, within 30 days after filing, record his claim of lien.

Owner of, or in certain cases contractor or subcontractor upon, property sought to be charged with claim of lien may free property from such claim by recording bond in penal sum one and one-half times amount of claim.

3. WHERE RECORDED.—County Recorder of county or city and county in which such property or some part is situated.

4. WHEN TO BE RECORDED.—(a) Every original contractor must file after completion of his contract and within sixty days after date owner files for record a notice of completion, or, if notice of completion is not filed by owner within 10 days after completion, the original contractor must file within ninety days after completion of contract. (b) Every person other than an original contractor shall file his claim after he has ceased to perform labor or furnish material, or both, and within thirty days after the date of filing of the owner's notice of completion or, if such notice of completion is not filed within 10 days after completion, the notice of claim must be filed within ninety days after the completion of such work of improvement. (c) Every person, except one under direct contract with the owner or one performing actual labor of wages, must, as a necessary prerequisite to the validity of any claim of lien subsequently filed cause to be given not later than 20 days after the claimant has first furnished labor, etc. a written preliminary notice to the owner and to the original contractor and to the reported construction lender. (d) Where the work of improvement is pursuant to two or more original contracts, original contractor must file claim within 60 days after owner files notice of completion; all other persons within 30 days after date of filing notice of completion. If said notice not filed, time for filing is 90 days after completion. (e) If, after the commencement of a work of improvement, there shall be a cessation of labor for a continuous period of sixty days, all persons claiming lien rights shall within ninety days from the expiration of such sixty-day period file for record their claims of lien, provided that if, after there shall be a cessation of labor thereon for a continuous period of thirty days or more, the owner files for record a notice of cessation, every original contractor must file within sixty days and every other person within thirty days after the date of filing of such notice of cessation.

5. SERVICE OF COPY OF NOTICE.—Service of notice by every person, other than one under direct contract with owner or one performing actual labor for wages, is prerequisite to filing claim of lien. See 4 (c).

6. DURATION OF LIEN.—No lien binds any property for a period of time longer than 90 days after the recording of the claim of lien, unless within that time, an action to foreclose the lien is commenced in a proper court.

7. RECORDING FEE.—$1 for recording notice for record and making necessary entries, plus $2 for recording the first page and $1 for each additional or fractional page; $1 per page additional for nonstandard size.

8. CONTENTS OF PRELIMINARY NOTICE OF LIEN.—(1) General description of the labor, service, equipment or materials furnished or to be furnished, and if there is a construction lender, he must be furnished with an estimate of the total price; (2) the name and address of the person furnishing such labor, etc.; (3) the name of the person who contracted for purchase of such labor, etc.; (4) a description of the jobsite sufficient for identification; and (5) a statement in boldface type that if bills are not paid in full for labor, etc., furnished, or to be furnished, the improved property may be subject to mechanic's liens. If an invoice for such materials contains the information required, a copy of such invoice shall be sufficient notice if properly served.

9. CONTENTS OF CLAIM.—Statement signed and verified by claimant or agent containing the following:

(a) Statement of demand after deducting credit and offsets.
(b) Name of owner or reputed owner.
(c) Statement of kind of labor, service or equipment or materials furnished.

(d) Name of person by whom employed or to whom furnished labor, service, equipment or materials.

(e) Description of the site sufficient for identification.

10. EXTENT OF LIEN.—The building, improvement, or structure upon which labor is bestowed or materials furnished is subject to the lien, as is also the land upon which such building, etc., stand and as much ground around the same as is required for its use and occupation. Lien attaches to land improved by filling, grading or adding sidewalks, sewers and other improvements. The liens of subcontractors are direct liens and are not limited as to amount by contract price agreed upon between contractor and owner, but shall not exceed a reasonable value of the labor or materials furnished nor the price agreed upon between the claimant and the person by whom employed, and shall not extend to labor or materials not covered by the original contract, provided claimant had notice thereof. A filing of the contract with the County Recorder is equivalent to actual notice. The owner may limit his liability to subcontractors, etc., by procuring the filing of a bond for not less than 50% of the contract price conditioned by the payment of claims of all persons furnishing labor or materials. The owner's liability shall then be limited to the amount found to be due from the owner to the contractor, and the subcontractors shall look to the contractor and the sureties on his bond for any deficiency. The owner, however, must record the release bond and provide notice to the lienholder.

11. PRIORITIES.—Liens (other than mechanic's liens with respect to site improvement) take priority over any lien, mortgage, or other encumbrance which attached subsequent to time when the building, improvement, or structure was commenced, work done, or materials were commenced to be furnished; also to any lien, mortgage, deed of trust or other encumbrance of which the lienholder had no notice and which was unrecorded at the time building, improvement, or structure was commenced, work done, or the matierals were commenced to be furnished.

12. PUBLIC IMPROVEMENTS.—See Chapter 30, *infra*, Bonds on Public Works.

13. STOP NOTICES.—Any lien holder and those performing work or furnishing materials upon any public improvement, except original contractors, may serve stop notice upon public entity responsible for such public work. Stop notice must be served before expiration of: 30 days after recording notice of completion or notice of cessation, or if neither notice is recorded, 90 days after completion or cessation. To enforce stop notice, claimant having no direct contractual relationship with prime contractor must give preliminary 20-day notice and file stop notice. Upon giving of such notice it is duty of entity so notified to withhold from contractor sufficient money or bonds to answer such claim and to provide for cost of any litigation thereunder.

14. LIENS FOR IMPROVEMENTS OF OIL AND GAS WELLS.—Labor or materials for the drilling or operating of oil or gas wells give rise to liens on the leasehold and appurtenances, all materials and fixtures owned by the lessee, all oil and gas produced and the proceeds thereof. Lien is claimed by filing verified statement in the office of the county recorder for the county where property is located within 6 months after the date on which labor was performed or material furnished and extends for six months after recording.

COLORADO

1. WHO MAY CLAIM.—All persons performing any labor upon or furnishing any materials to be used in the construction, alteration, addition to or repair of any building, mill, bridge, ditch, flume, aqueduct, reservoir, tunnel, fence, railroad, wagon road, tramway or any other structure or improvement upon land, including architects, civil and mining engineers, surveyors and draftsmen.

No one is entitled to a mechanic's lien if a performance bond and a labor and materials payment bond, each equal to 150% of the contract price, have been executed by the principal contractor.

2. HOW CLAIMED.—By recording verified statement of claim and by filing *lis pendens* when suit is started.

When a lien statement covering one transaction is filed within four months after completion of entire work it has priority over a chattel mortgagee's claim, even though the latter accrued prior to the filing of the lien statement.

A contract with a contractor which exceeds $500 must be in writing and a copy or memorandum thereof containing a description of the property and of the character of the work to be done, the amount to be paid and a schedule of payments shall be filed by the owner in the office of the County Recorder where the property is located before the work is commenced. If not so filed, the labor and materials furnished by all persons shall be deemed to have been done and furnished at the instance of the owner and such persons shall have a lien for the value thereof.

In addition, every contractor who enters into a contract with the owner or his agent for the improvement, repair, restoration, or remodeling of, or for construction of additions to, any residential property, and who has contracted or will contract with any subcontractor, equipment supplier, materialman, or other person to provide labor or materials for the improvement must give the owner or his agent the following notice before he can claim a lien in connection with the work. The notice must be delivered in person or by certified mail within five days after the contract is entered into. The notice must be in at least ten-point bold type, if printed, or in capital letters, if typewritten. It must identify the contractor by name and address and state substantially as follows:

IMPORTANT NOTICE TO OWNER

Persons furnishing labor or materials for the improvement of your residential property may collect their money from you by a lien pursuant to Article 22 of Title 38, Colorado Revised Statutes 1973, on your property if they are not paid by the contractor for their labor or materials, even though you have paid your contractor for those items. You may wish to discuss with your contractor possible means of avoiding double payment. These means include a bond guaranteeing payment for this specific job, the use of lien waivers, holding an adequate amount of the contract price in escrow until you are satisfied that all claims for labor or materials have been paid, or joining as payees on every check issued by or on behalf of the property owner to such potential lienholders as the said owner feels necessary for his protection.

The notice requirement does not apply to any person who only furnishes materials or supplies, or to a contract for construction of a new residence.

3. NOTICE OF LIEN.—Notice should identify the property, name the person with whom contracted and list name, address and telephone number of the claimant. The notice must be filed with the Clerk and Recorder where the property is located. The filing of this notice will serve as notice that the claimant may thereafter file a lien statement within four months after the completion of the structure or other improvement or six months after the date of filing of the notice, whichever occurs first. The notice will automatically terminate in six months; if the structure or improvements are not completed, the claimant may file a new or amended notice. Upon termination of the agreement to supply labor or materials, the owner or someone in his behalf may demand a termination of notice, which will identify the properties upon which labor has not been performed or materials have not been furnished and as to which properties the notice is terminated.

4. WHERE FILED.—Office of County Clerk and Recorder in county where principal part of property is located.

5. WHEN TO BE FILED.—Four months after the last labor was performed or the last labor or material furnished. Abandonment of labor for 3 months is deemed completion.

6. SERVICE OF COPY OF LIEN STATEMENT.—To preserve lien of subcontractor, on owner, reputed owner, or agent, if he can be located, otherwise by recording affidavit.

7. DURATION OF LIEN.—Unless suit is begun within six months after completion of structure, lien is void. No lien shall hold the property longer than one year from date of filing unless within 30 days of each anniversary of such filing the lien claimant files affidavit stating that the improvements have not been completed.

8. FILING FEE.—Fee for lien depends on number of claimants named; average fee is $1.

9. CONTENTS OF LIEN.—(1). Name of owner or reputed owner (2). Name of person claiming lien. (3). Name of principal contractor if lien claim by subcontractor. (4). Description of property to be charged. (5). Statement of total indebtedness, total credits, and balances. (6). Statement must be signed and sworn to by claimant or his agent.

10. EXTENT OF LIEN.—The right or interest of the owner or person claiming an interest in the land, including landlord or vendor, is subject to liens for labor or material. Lien extends to the interest of the owner for the entire contract price and attaches to the property, structure, or improvement.

11. PRIORITIES.—Claimant's lien takes effect as of date when work was commenced on the structure on a contract between the owner and first contractor and has priority over any encumbrances thereafter recorded, and unrecorded encumbrances of which claimant had no actual notice. No lien except those claimed by laborers or mechanics filed more than two (2) months after completion will encumber interest of any bona fide purchaser of real property the principle improvement on which is a single double family dwelling, except if purchaser had knowledge, lien is filed prior to conveyance or notice is filed. As between lien claimants liens extend for the benefit first, of day laborers; second, subcontractors and materialmen; third, other principal contractors.

12. TRUST FUNDS.—All funds disbursed to any contractor or subcontractor under any building construction, remodeling contract or construction project, shall be held in trust for payment of subcontractors, materials, suppliers or laborers who have a lien or may have a lien. Contractors and subcontractors are required to maintain separate records for each project, but not separate bank accounts.

13. PUBLIC IMPROVEMENTS.—See Chapter 30, *infra*, Bonds on Public Works.

14. LIENS FOR IMPROVEMENTS OF OIL AND GAS WELLS.—Liens for improvements arise by virtue

of contracts—express or implied—with the owner or lessee. Lienor must file verified statement claiming lien with the county clerk and recorded within six months after the material is furnished or labor performed and suit must be commenced within six months after filing.

CONNECTICUT

1. WHO MAY CLAIM.—Any person having a claim for more than $10 for materials furnished or services rendered in the construction, raising, removal, or repair of any building, or any of its appurtenances or improvement of any lot or plot of land, by virtue of an agreement with or by consent of the owner of the land upon which the building is erected or has been moved, or his agent.

2. HOW CLAIMED.—(a) *Contractors.* Person performing services or furnishing materials within 60 days after he has ceased so to do must lodge with the town clerk of the town in which the building, lot or plot of land is situated a certificate in writing, subscribed and sworn to by the claimant, describing the premises, the amount claimed, the name of the person against whom the lien is being filed, the date of commencement of the work or furnishing of the materials, and stating that the amount claimed is justly due.

(b) *Subcontractors.* All persons, except the original contractor and a subcontractor, whose contract with the original contractor is in writing, must within sixty days after ceasing to furnish materials or render services, give written notice to the owner of the building that they have furnished materials or rendered services or commenced to do so and that they intend to claim a lien therefor on the building, lot or plot of land. This notice must be served on the owner by leaving at his residence a copy thereof. Where the owner resides out of town, the notice may be served on his agent or may be mailed by registered or certified mail to the owner. If the copy is returned unclaimed, notice must be given by publication. When there are two or more owners, such notice must be served upon each owner. No lien is valid, unless within sixty days after he has ceased to furnish materials or render services, the person claiming the lien lodges with the town clerk of the town in which the building, lot or plot of land is situated a certificate in writing, subscribed and sworn to by the claimant, describing the premises, the amount claimed, the name of the person against whom the lien is being filed, the date of the commencement of the performance of services or furnishing materials, and stating that the amount claimed is justly due.

3. WHERE RECORDED.—Town Clerk of town in which building is situated.

4. WHEN TO BE RECORDED.—Within 60 days after ceasing to perform services or to furnish materials. Within 60 days after the contractor shall have ceased to perform services or furnish materials, he shall lodge with the town clerk of the town in which the building, lot or plot of land was situated, a certificate in writing in accordance with the statute, which certificate shall be recorded by the town clerk with deeds of land, and within the same time or prior to the lodging of such certificate but not later than thirty days after lodging such certificate, serve a true and attested copy of such certificate upon the owner of such building, lot or plot of land.

5. DURATION OF LIEN.—No lien shall continue in force for longer than one year after such lien has been perfected, unless the party claiming such lien commences an action to foreclose the same by complaint, crossclaim or counterclaim and files a notice of *lis pendens* on the land records of the town in which the lien is recorded within one year from date such lien was filed, or within 60 days of any final disposition of an appeal.

6. RECORDING FEE.—$5 for each page, additional $1 for illegible type, etc.

7. CONTENTS OF LIEN CERTIFICATE.—1. Description of premises. 2. Amount claimed as a lien thereon. 3. Date of commencement of performance of services or furnishing of materials. 4. Statement that amount claimed is justly due, as nearly as the same can be ascertained. 5. The name of the person against whom the lien is being filed, and subscribed and sworn to by the claimant.

8. EXTENT OF LIEN.—The lien attaches to the building or the appurtenances to the extent of the amount which the owner agreed to pay. It includes and attaches to the land upon which such building or appurtenances or any lot or plot of land are located.

9. PRIORITIES.—Mechanics' lien take precedence of any other encumbrance originating after the commencement of the services or the furnishing of any materials. If a lien exists in favor of two or more persons on the same building for the same work, no one person has precedence over the other. Where the united claims of several claimants exceed the price agreed upon to be paid by the owner, then the claimants other than the original contractor are paid in full first, if the price is sufficient, or if not, the amount is apportioned between them. If an encumbrance other than a mechanic's lien be filed for record during the time of construction, all mechanic's liens originating prior to the filing of such encumbrance for record shall take precedence over such encumbrance, but mechanic's liens for materials or services, originating after the filing of said other encumbrance shall be subject thereto.

10. PUBLIC IMPROVEMENTS.—See Chapter 30, *infra,* Bonds on Public Works.

DELAWARE

1. WHO MAY CLAIM.—Any person having performed work and labor or furnished material to an amount exceeding $25 in or for the erection, alteration, or repair of any house, building, or structure, in pursuance of any contract, express or implied, with the owners of such house, building or structure, or with his agent. Where work or labor is performed on a house, building, bridge or structure in any amount less than $100, person performing work may obtain lien. Liens cover work and materials performed and furnished in gas fitting, plumbing, paving, paperhanging, placing iron works and machinery of every kind in mills and factories. Liens also extend to architects and corporations. Work or materials for a building, house or structure may be furnished under oral contract but for improvement to land alone, must be written contract. No lien can be obtained on residential property if the owner has made full payment to the contractor with whom he contracted and received verified and notarized statement from contractor that all claims have been paid, or received a waiver of mechanic's lien; if owner has not made full payment, lien can only be obtained for balance due to be paid pro rata on any claimants who perfect lien.

2. HOW CLAIMED.—By filing statement of claim in writing. No contractor shall be allowed to file any statement of his claim until after the expiration of ninety days from the completion of such building, house, etc.—and he must file his statement within thirty days after the expiration of the ninety days, and all other persons shall file a statement within ninety days from the completion of the work and labor performed or from the last delivery of materials furnished by them respectively.

3. WHERE FILED.—An amount exceeding $25 must be filed in the office of the Prothonotary in county where such structure is located. Statement of claim for labor in any amount less than $100 may be filed with the Justice of the Peace of the county where the property is situated.

4. WHEN TO BE FILED.—A contractor (i.e., a contractor who has made his contract with the owner or reputed owner of the building, and who has furnished both work and labor and material, in and for the building), must file his statement within 30 days after the expiration of ninety days from the completion of such building. No claim can be filed prior to such 90 day period. All other persons must file within ninety days from the completion of the work or labor, or delivery of material where the claim exceeds $25. Where amount claimed is under $100 and is for work or labor, a lien may be filed before any Justice of the Peace of the county wherein the building, etc. is situated, within 10 days after the expiration of 20 days from the time of the last work or services performed.

5. DURATION OF LIEN.—No statement of claim can be filed after the expiration of 90 days from the completion of the structure; but the statement of claim must be filed within 30 days after the expiration of such 90-day period.

6. RECORDING FEE.—$10 for issuing a mechanic's lien; this includes $6.50 for issuing writ of *scire facias.*

7. CONTENTS OF LIEN CERTIFICATE.—1. Names of the party, claimant and owner, or reputed owner, and also of the contractor, and whether the contract of the claimant was made with such owner or his agent or with such contractor. 2. Amount or sum claimed, with particulars, of work done or material furnished. 3. Time when the work and labor or furnishing of materials was commenced and finished. 4. Locality of the property, with description to identify it. 5. That the work and labor were performed on the credit of the property. 6. That the amount of claim exceeds $25, and has not been paid.

8. EXTENT OF THE LIEN.—The lien attaches to the building and the land upon which the work was rendered or material furnished.

9. PRIORITIES.—Any judgment obtained upon such claims becomes a lien on such property and upon the ground upon which same is situated and relates back to the day when such work and labor was begun or furnishing of material was commenced. If proceeds of state are not sufficient to pay all liens in full, proceeds are divided ratably without priority to preference.

10. PUBLIC IMPROVEMENTS.—See Chapter 30, *infra,* Bonds on Public Works.

DISTRICT OF COLUMBIA

1. WHO MAY CLAIM.—Contractor, subcontractor or laborer for work or materials.

2. HOW CLAIMED.—By filing notice of intention to hold lien on property, with amount claimed, etc.

3. WHERE FILED AND FEE.—Recorder of Deeds, D.C. Filing fee is $1.

4. WHEN TO BE FILED.—During construction or within 3 months after completion of building whether the claim is due or not.

5. SERVICE OF COPY OF NOTICE.—Subcontractor must serve notice upon the owner of the property on which lien is claimed.

6. CONTENTS OF NOTICE OF LIEN.—1. Description of premises. 2. Amount claimed. 3. Name of party against whose interest a lien is claimed.

7. EXTENT OF LIEN.—Lien attaches to building erected, improved, added to or repaired, and the lot of ground used in connection therewith to the extent of the right, title and interest at the time existing of the owner.

8. DURATION OF LIEN.—Any person entitled to a lien may commence suit at any time within a year from and after the filing of the notice or within six months from the completion of the building or repairs.

9. SUBCONTRACTORS, MATERIALMEN, ETC.—All liens in favor of parties employed by the contractor are subject to the terms and conditions of the original contract except such as shall relate to the waiver of liens and are limited to the amount to become due to the original contractor and may be satisfied, in whole or in part, out of said amount only; and if said original contractor for any reason shall be entitled to recover less than the amount agreed upon in his contract, the liens of said parties so employed by him are enforceable only for said reduced amount, and if said original contractor be entitled to recover nothing said liens are not enforceable at all.

10. PRIORITIES.—Lien preferred to all judgments, mortgages, deeds of trusts, liens, and encumbrances, attached to building or ground subsequently to the commencement of work, as well as to the conveyances executed but not recorded before that time, except mortgages or deeds of trust given to secure purchases of land recorded within 10 days from date of acknowledgment. The lien of subcontractor preferred to that of contractor.

11. PUBLIC IMPROVEMENTS.—See Chapter 30, *infra,* Bonds on Public Works.

FLORIDA

1. WHO MAY CLAIM.—Liens upon real property for the value of labor, services or materials furnished to improve the property are authorized for the following: architect, engineer, interior designer or land surveyor, and when done with a direct contract a lien may be imposed regardless of whether really actually improved; persons grading, levelling, excavating and filling land, grading and paving streets, curbs and sidewalks, laying pipes; material man or laborer in privity with owner or contractor in accordance with direct contract; and material man or laborer not in privity with owner or subcontractor; in accordance with his contract and with direct contract.

2. HOW CLAIMED.—By recording claim of lien. In addition to recording, all lienors, except laborers and persons contracting directly with the owner, shall serve a notice on the owner setting forth the lienor's name and address, a description sufficient for identification of the real property and the nature of the services or materials furnished or to be furnished. This notice must be served before commencing or not later than 45 days from commencing to furnish his services or materials. The serving of this notice shall not dispense with recording the claim of lien.

In addition to the requirement of the above paragraph, for the purpose of perfecting his lien, every lienor, including laborers and persons in privity, shall record a claim of lien which shall state; (a) the name and address of the lienor, (b) the name of the person with whom the lienor contracted or by whom he was employed, (c) the labor, services or materials furnished and the contract price or value thereof, (d) a description of the real property sufficient for identification, (e) the name of the owner, (f) the time when the first and the last item of labor or services or materials were furnished, (g) the amount unpaid the lienor for such labor or services or materials, (h) if the lien is claimed by a person not in privity with owner, the date and method of service to owner. If the lien is claimed by a person not in privity with the contractor or subcontractor, the date and method of service of the copy of notice on the contractor or subcontractor.

The authority issuing building permits shall print, on the face of each permit, a summary of the mechanics' lien law, among other things.

The owner shall not pay any money on account of a direct contract prior to recording of the notice, and any amount so paid, shall be held improperly paid. If the description of the property in the notice is incorrect and the error adversely affects any lienor, payments made on the direct contract shall be held improperly paid to that lienor but this does not apply to clerical errors when the description listed covers the property where the improvements are.

3. WHERE FILED.—Office of the Clerk of the County in which the real property is situated. If property is situated in two or more counties, record in each county.

4. WHEN TO BE FILED.—During the progress of the work or thereafter but not later than 90 days after the final furnishing of the labor or services or materials by the lienor, provided, if the original contractor defaults or contract is terminated or abandoned, no claim for a lien attaching prior to such default shall be recorded after 90 days from the date of such' default or 90 days after the final performance of labor or services or furnishing of materials, whichever occurs first.

5. DURATION OF LIEN.—No lien shall continue for a longer period than one year after the

claim of lien has been recorded, unless an action to enforce the lien is commenced within that time. The continuation of the lien effected by the commencement of the action shall not be good against creditors or subsequent purchasers for a valuable consideration and without notice unless a notice of *lis pendens* is recorded. Owner can shorten to 60 days by filing notice of contest of lien.

6. FEE FOR RECORDING.—The fee for recording, indexing, and filing any instrument not more than 14 inches by 8½ inches is $5 for the first page and $4 for each additional page. For indexing instruments with more than four names, there is a fee of $1 for each additional name. For indexing each entry not recorded there is a fee of $1.

7. EXTENT OF LIEN.—Liens shall extend to, and only to, the right, title and interest of the person who contracts for the improvement, as such right, title and interest exist at the commencement of the improvement or are thereafter acquired in the real property.

8. PRIORITY OF LIENS.—All such liens shall have priority over any conveyance, encumbrance or demand not recorded against the real property prior to the time such lien attached. Such liens shall have preference in the following order: (1). Liens of all laborers; (2). Liens of all persons other than the contractor, and (3). Liens of the contractor. Should total amount be less than all claims, all liens in a class must be allowed their full amounts before any liens of a subsequent class are allowed; if amount insufficient for class, pro rata share will be paid.

9. REMARKS.—If a husband and wife, who are not separated and not living apart from each other, own property individually or together, the husband or wife who contracts shall be deemed to be the agent of the other to the extent of subjecting the right, title or interest of the other in said property to liens, unless such other shall within ten (10) days after learning of such contract notify the contractor and file with the Circuit Court of the County in which the property is situated, written notice of his or her objection thereto. Any lienee may release his property from a lien thereon by filing a bond in the amount of the final bill with the clerk of the Circuit Court.

10. LIMITATIONS ON LESSORS.—If a lease expressly provides that interest of lessor shall not be subject to liens for improvements, Lessee shall notify contractor making the improvements, and the failure of lessee to provide such notice to contractor shall render contract voidable at option of contractor.

Interest of lessor shall not be subject to lien for improvements made by lessee if lease prohibits such liability and:

1. Lease or short form is recorded; or
2. All leases of lessor prohibit liabilities for improvements and a notice is recorded in office of public records where property is located which notice states name of lessor and legal description of property or contains specific language in lease prohibiting such liability and a statement that all leases for that property contain such a clause.

11. IMPROVEMENTS ON OIL AND GAS WELLS.—Extends to the leasehold interest held for oil or gas purposes or for any oil or gas pipeline except that neither the land itself, apart from the rights granted under an oil and gas lease, nor any mineral interest, nor any royalty interest is subject to such liens. Lien also extends to materials and fixtures owned by the interest holder and any oil or gas produced. Lien is prefected in the same manner as a mechanic's lien and exists for one year.

12. PUBLIC IMPROVEMENTS.—See Chapter 30, *infra,* Bonds on Public Works.

GEORGIA

1. WHO MAY CLAIM.—All mechanics of every sort, who have taken no personal security therefor, shall, for work done and material furnished in building, repairing, or improving any real estate of their employers; all contractors and all subcontractors and all materialmen furnishing material to subcontractors and all laborers furnishing labor to subcontractors, materialmen, and persons furnishing material for the improvement of real estate; all registered architects furnishing drawings, designs, or other architectural services with respect to any real estate; all registered land surveyors and registered professional engineers performing or furnishing services as such on or with respect to real estate; all contractors and subcontractors and materialmen furnishing material, including the reasonable rental value of tools, appliances, machinery and equipment used in the improvement of real estate, to subcontractors and all laborers furnishing labor for subcontractors, for building factories, furnishing material for the same, or furnishing machinery for the same; and all machinists and manufacturers of machinery, including corporations engaged in such business, who may furnish or put up in any county any steam mill or other machinery, or who may repair the same; and all contractors to build railroads, shall each have a special lien on such real estate, factories or railroads.

2. HOW CLAIMED.—To validate such liens, they must be created and declared in accordance with the provisions of the statute. Substantial compliance by the claimant of the lien with the

contract is necessary. He must file for record his claim of lien within three months after the completion of the work or furnishing of architectural services, or furnishing or performance of surveying or engineering services, or within three months after such material or machinery is furnished in the office of the clerk of the superior court in the county in which the property is situated.

3. WHERE RECORDED.—In office of Clerk of Superior Court where property is located.

4. WHEN TO BE RECORDED.—Within 3 months after completion of work or furnishing machinery or materials. Preliminary notice within 30 days.

5. SERVICE OF COPY OF NOTICE.—Not required.

6. DURATION OF LIENS.—Lien lost unless action to recover claim commenced within 12 months from the time claim becomes due and payable. If the action is not filed in the superior court of the county in which the claim of lien was filed, then within such 12 months' period, the party claiming the lien shall also file under oath with the clerk of the superior court of the county wherein the subject lien was filed, a notice identifying the court wherein the action is brought, the style and number of the action, including the names of all parties thereto, the date of the filing of the action, and the book and page number of the records of the county wherein the subject lien is recorded. Failure to bring action and to file such notice within the time required shall extinguish the subject claim of lien and render the same unenforceable. Before a subcontractor, laborer or materialman can obtain a judgment, a judgment establishing a lien against a property owner, he must first obtain judgment against the contractor for the amount of the claim. If contractor or subcontractor absconds, dies or removes from state during this 12 month period so that personal service cannot be made, or he is in bankruptcy, or no final judgment can be obtained by reason of death or bankruptcy, then the lienor need not obtain a judgment as a prerequisite to enforcing a lien against the property improved by the contractor.

7. RECORDING FEE.—$1.50 per page; in counties of 350,000 or more, the fee is $5 per page.

8. CONTENTS OF NOTICE OF LIEN.—Statute provides for claim to be in substance as follows:

"A.B., a mechanic, contractor, subcontractor, materialman, machinist, manufacturer, or other person (as the case may be), claims a lien in the amount of (specify the amount claimed) on the house, factory, steam mill, machinery, or railroad (as the case may be), and the premises or real estate on which it is erected or built, of C. D. (describing the house, premises, real estate, or railroad) for satisfaction of a claim which became due on (specify the date the claim was due) for building, repairing, improving, or furnishing material (or whatever the claim may be)."

9. EXTENT OF LIEN.—Liens attach to the real estate, factories, buildings, etc., erected, improved, or repaired, for the amount of work done or material furnished or value of services performed but in no event shall the aggregate amount of liens exceed the contract price for the improvements made or services performed.

10. PRIORITIES.—As among themselves, mechanics' liens rank according to date of filing, within 3 months after the work is done, but are inferior to liens for taxes, to the general and special liens of laborers, to the general lien of landlords for rent when a distress warrant is issued out and levied, to claims for purchase money due persons who have only given bonds for titles, and to other general liens, when actual notice of such materials or services were furnished; but the lien shall be superior to other liens not here excepted.

11. PUBLIC IMPROVEMENTS.—See Chapter 30, *infra,* Bonds on Public Works.

HAWAII

1. WHO MAY CLAIM.—Any person or association furnishing labor or material to be used in the improvement of real property, including persons rendering professional services of planning or supervision. A person advancing cash only is not entitled to lien.

2. HOW CLAIMED.—Any person claiming a lien shall apply in a special proceeding to the Circuit Court of the circuit where the property is situated. Such application shall be accompanied by a written notice of lien setting forth the alleged facts upon which the lien is claimed. A copy of the application and notice shall be served in the manner prescribed by law for service of summons upon the owner of the property and any person with an interest therein or who contracted for the improvements. If any such persons intended in the notice can not be served, notice may be given to such person by posting same on the improvement. The application shall set forth the amount of the claim, the labor or material furnished, a description of the property sufficient to identify the same and any other matter necessary to a clear understanding of the claim. If the claim has been assigned, the name of the assignor shall be stated. The application shall contain the names of the parties who contract for the improvement, the name of the general contractor, the names of the owners of the property and any person with an interest therein. The application may specify the name of the mortgagee or other encumbrancers of the property and the name of

the surety or general contractor. The application and notice shall be returnable not less than three nor more than ten days after service on the return day. On the return day a hearing shall be held by the Court to determine if probable cause exists to attach a lien to the property. Any person to whom notice is required to be given shall be permitted to offer testimony and documentary evidence on the issue of whether probable cause exists to permit the lien to attach. If the person who contracted for the improvement from which the requested lien arises claims a setoff against the lienor or if any person to whom notice is required to be given otherwise disputes the amount of the requested lien, the court shall hear and receive all admissible evidence offered and shall only permit the attachment of a lien in the net amount which the court determines is the reasonably probable outcome of any such dispute. The return day hearing may be continued at the order of the court so that the entire controversy need not be determined on the originally scheduled return day. The lien shall not attach to the property until the court finds probable cause exists and so orders. No such order shall be entered before the Application and Notice have been served on the party contracting for the improvement, the general contractor and the owner of the property, and they were given an opportunity to appear at the hearing.

3. WHERE FILED.—With the Clerk of the Circuit Court where the property is located.

4. WHEN FILED.—The Application and Notice shall be filed not later than forty-five days after the date of completion of the improvement against which it is filed. Where title to the property involved, or any portion thereof, is registered in the land court it shall be incumbent upon the lienor to file a certified copy of the Order Directing Lien To Attach in the office of the assistant registrar of the land court within seven days after the entry thereof in order to preserve his rights against subsequent encumbrancers and purchasers of the property.

5. SERVICE OF COPY OF APPLICATION AND NOTICE.—Must be served upon owner of property and any person with an interest and persons who contracted for the improvements.

6. DURATION OF LIEN.—Lien continues for three months after the entry of order directing the lien to attach unless suit is commenced within that time.

7. FILING FEE.—$2.50.

8. CONTENTS OF APPLICATION AND NOTICE OF LIEN.—Names of the parties, amount of the claim, the labor and material furnished, a description of the property and any other matter necessary to a clear understanding of the claim.

9. EXTENT OF THE LIEN.—Lien for the price agreed to be paid (if the price does not exceed the value of the labor and materials) for the fair and reasonable value thereof, upon the improvement as well as upon the interest of the owner of the improvement and the real property on which the same is situated.

10. PRIORITIES.—Mechanics' liens have priority over all other liens except liens in favor of the government and mortgages or judgments recorded or filed prior to the time of the visible commencement of operation. Mortgages recorded subsequent to the visible commencement of operations and before the date of completion have priority over mechanics' liens provided such mortgages secure advances made for the purpose of paying for the improvement. Mechanics' liens rank equally in priority with all other such liens.

11. EXCEPTIONS.—(a) In connection with the repair or improvements on property which prior to such repair and improvements was used primarily for dwelling purposes no lien shall exist either for the furnishing of materials to a general contractor or his subcontractor either of whom is required to be licensed but is not, or if unreasonable advancement of credit was given by the furnisher or the materials to the general contractor or subcontractor. Whether there is reasonable advancement of credit is to be determined by the Circuit Judge at a hearing on the matter. If the furnisher of materials has secured a credit application form from the general contractor or subcontractor to whom the materials were furnished or has reasonably inquired into the credit status of the general contractor or subcontractor the advancement of credit by the furnisher of materials shall be prima facie reasonable. The credit application shall be current and updated every three months and shall include at least the following information: name, address, type of business, date business started, contractor's license numbers, bonding companies generally used, banks used, list of current creditors, balance sheet, total of outstanding construction contracts, uncompleted portion of all contracts, names of partners, co-venturers. Corporation should also include names of officers, authorized capital and paid in capital.

(b) No general contractor or his subcontractor or the subcontractor's subcontractor shall have lien rights unless such contractor or subcontractor was licensed under Chapter 444 when the improvements to the real property were made or performed.

(c) All real property owned or held by the Hawaii Housing Authority are exempt from mechanics' liens.

12. PUBLIC IMPROVEMENTS.—See Chapter 30, *infra,* Bonds on Public Works.

IDAHO

1. WHO MAY CLAIM.—Any person performing labor upon, or furnishing materials to be used in the construction, alteration or repair of any mining claim, building, wharf, bridge, ditch, dike, flume, tunnel, fence, machinery, railroad, wagon road, aqueduct to create hydraulic power, or any other structure, or who grades in, fills in, levels, surfaces or otherwise improves any land, or who performs labor in any mine or mining claim, has a lien upon the same for the work or labor done or materials furnished, at the instance of the owner of the building or other improvement or his agent. For the purposes of the statute, every contractor, subcontractor, architect, builder or any other person having charge of any mining claim or of the construction, alteration or repair, in whole or in part, of any building or other improvement, shall be held to be the agent of the owner.

2. HOW CLAIMED.—Every original contractor, professional engineer or licensed surveyor claiming the benefit of this chapter must, within 90 days, and every other person must, within 60 days, after the completion of any building, improvement, or structure, or after the completion of the alteration or repair thereof, or in case he ceases to labor thereon before the completion thereof, then after he so ceases to labor or after he has ceased to labor thereon for any cause, or after he has ceased to furnish materials therefor, or after the performance of any labor in a mine or mining claim, must file a lien certificate.

3. WHERE RECORDED.—In the office of the County Recorder of the County where the structure is situated.

4. WHEN TO BE RECORDED.—By original contractors within 90 days, and all other persons 60 days after ceasing to furnish labor or material.

5. SERVICE OF COPY OF NOTICE.—A copy of the claim of lien must be served on the owner of the property within 24 hours of the filing of the claim.

6. DURATION OF THE LIEN.—For six months after claim has been filed, unless proceedings commenced within said time to enforce lien.

7. RECORDING FEE.—$2 per page.

8. CONTENTS OF LIEN CERTIFICATE.—Must state the amount of demand after deducting all just credits and offsets, with the name of the owner, or reputed owner, if known, and also the name of the person by whom he was employed or to whom he furnished the materials, and also a description of the property to be charged with the lien, sufficient for identification, which claim must be verified by the oath of the claimant, his agent or attorney, to the effect that the affiant believes the same to be just.

9. EXTENT OF LIEN.—Lien attaches to building or structure together with land on which same is situated or so much as may be required for the convenient use and occupation thereof, if at the commencement of the work the land belonged to the person causing the construction or improvement. If such person owns less than a fee simple, only his interest therein is subject to such lien.

10. PRIORITIES.—Mechanics' liens take precedence over any other encumbrance which attached after work or materials commenced to be furnished, or any other encumbrance of which lienholder had no actual notice and which was unrecorded at commencement of work. Rank of the liens as follows: (1) all laborers, other than contractors or subcontractors; (2) all materialmen, other than contractors or subcontractors; (3) subcontractors; (4) original contractor; (5) all professional engineers and licensed surveyors.

11. PUBLIC IMPROVEMENTS.—See Chapter 30, *infra,* Bonds on Public Works.

ILLINOIS

1. WHO MAY CLAIM.—Any person who contracts with the owner of a lot or tract of land or his agent for the improving, altering, repairing or ornamenting of any house, building, walk, fence or improvement, or filling, sodding, excavating or landscaping, raising, lowering or removing house, or to perform services as architect, professional and structural engineer or land surveyor or to drill a water well or to furnish labor or services as superintendent, timekeeper, mechanic, laborer or otherwise or furnish material, fixtures, apparatus or machinery, is entitled to a lien for the same. Every mechanic, workman or other person who furnishes materials, apparatus, machinery or fixtures or performs labor for the contractor is also entitled to a lien for the value thereof. Laborers and miners working and developing coal mines also may be lienholders.

2. HOW CLAIMED.—(a) *Contractors.* The contractor must give to the owner and owner must require, before any money is paid to the contractor, a statement in writing, under oath or verified by affidavit of the names and addresses of all parties furnishing materials and labor and the amount due to each. Failure of contractor to furnish statement has been held not to preclude him from enforcing his lien by suit.

(b) *Subcontractors.* Subcontractor (including mechanics, laborers, materialmen, etc.) must within

90 days after completion of work or final delivery of materials serve a written notice of his claim and the amount due on the owner, his agent, architect or superintendent. Where Torrens System of registration is in use notice must also be filed in the office of the Registrar of Titles in the county in which the land or lot is situated. This notice is not required where a contractor has given the sworn statement to the owner as set forth in (a) above. If owner, architect, superintendent, or agent cannot be found in the county where improvement is located, or does not reside therein, the subcontractor may file notice with Recorder of Deeds or the Registrar of Titles of the County.

Subcontractors who furnish materials or labor for existing owner-occupied single family residence must notify occupant or his agent at the residence within 14 days from first furnishing labor or materials, that he is supplying labor or materials. Notice given after 14 days will preserve the lien only to the extent that the owner has not been prejudiced by payments made prior to receipt of the notice. Notice must contain the following warning:

NOTICE TO OWNER

DO NOT PAY THE CONTRACTOR FOR THIS WORK OR MATERIAL DELIVERED UNLESS YOU HAVE RECEIVED FROM THE CONTRACTOR A WAIVER OF LIEN BY, OR OTHER SATISFACTORY EVIDENCE OF PAYMENT TO, THE SUBCONTRACTOR OR MATERIAL MAN.

3. WHERE FILED.—In the office of the Recorder of Deeds or the Register of Titles in the county in which the property is situated. Where the land is registered under the Torrens system the notice of the subcontractor must be filed in the office of the Registrar of Titles of the county in which the property is situated. For contractors, a claim of lien must be filed with the office of the Recorder in the county in which the property is situated. For subcontractors, claim is filed with the clerk of the circuit court.

4. WHEN TO BE FILED.—As against third persons the contractor must file within 4 months after completion of his contract either bring suit to enforce lien or file a claim of lien. Subcontractors must serve notice upon the owner within 90 days after completion of extra work and if filing of notice is necessary, filing must be effected within the same period. A contractor's lien as against the owner is valid if filed at any time after the contract is made and within 2 years after the completion of the contract or extra work or furnishing extra materials. Upon written demand of the owner, a person claiming a lien can, within 30 days after such demand is served, be required to commence suit to enforce lien or else lien is forfeited.

5. SERVICE OF COPY OF NOTICE.—Subcontractor must give written notice by registered or certified mail, return receipt requested, with delivery limited to addressee only or by delivering the written notice to the officials of the county, municipality, or township whose duty it is to pay the contractor. Copy of the notice may be sent to the contractor in a like manner.

6. DURATION OF LIEN.—Suit to enforce the lien must be commenced within 2 years after completion of contract or extra work or furnishing of extra material.

7. FILING FEE.—$5.

8. CONTENTS OF NOTICE OF LIEN.—If by a contract the suit or notice shall show the following: (a) Name of owner. (b) Brief statement of contract. (c) Balance due after deducting credits. (d) Description of property subject to lien. (e) Verification of claimant or his agent or employee.

Where notice is served by a subcontractor or owner, it shall show the following:

(a) Name of owner. (b) Name of contractor. (c) Brief statement of subcontract. (d) Description of property subject to lien. (e) Amount due or to become due. If service cannot be made upon owner, then notice must be filed with Clerk of the Circuit Court, and it must be verified.

9. EXTENT OF LIEN.—The lien attaches to the whole of the lot or tract of land upon which the property is situated and to the adjoining lots used in connection with the same. It extends to an estate in fee for life, for years, or any other estate, right of redemption or other interests which the owner may have at the time of contract or subsequently arise. Subcontractors' liens are limited to the value of service rendered and materials furnished on the same property, as contractor, material, fixtures, apparatus, machinery and on money due or to become due from the owner under the original contract. The owner cannot be compelled to pay a greater amount than the price fixed in the original contract, in the absence of fraud or a violation of the right of subcontractors.

10. PRIORITIES.—No encumbrance upon land created before or after the making of the contract under the Mechanics' Lien Act shall operate upon the building erected or materials furnished until a lien in favor of persons having done work or furnished material is satisfied. All previous encumbrances are preferred to the extent of the value of the land at the time of making of the contract, and the lien creditor is preferred to the value of the improvements. As between different contractors no preference is given to the one whose contract was made first, except the claim of any person for wages by him personally performed is a preferred lien. The contractor's lien is superior to any right of dower if the owner of the dower interest had knowledge of the improvement

and gave no written notice of his or her objection. A subcontractor has no right to bring a civil action against either owner or contractor until he furnishes a statement of the persons furnishing material and labor, and the lien of such sub-contractor shall be subject to the liens of all other creditors.

11. PUBLIC IMPROVEMENTS.—See Chapter 30, *infra,* Bonds on Public Works.

12. LIENS FOR IMPROVEMENTS OF OIL AND GAS WELLS.—Such lien is created, perfected and enforced in the same manner as mechanic's liens. Any lien which extends to oil or gas or the proceeds of the sale of oil or gas is ineffective against any purchaser or pipe line carrier until written notice of the claim is given.

13. IMPROVEMENTS ON OIL AND GAS WELLS.—Liens exist for any person who perform labor or furnishes material under contract with owner of land. Lien also exists for any persons who perform for a subcontractor. Lien extends to the whole of the land or leasehold, appurtenances, materials furnished, all oil and gas wells, and oil and gas produced and their proceeds; it does not extend to underlying fee or royalty interest. If the claim under contract with owner, must file a lien within 4 months; if claim under subcontract, within 3 months.

INDIANA

1. WHO MAY CLAIM.—Contractors, subcontractors, mechanics, journeymen, laborers, materialmen and all persons performing labor or furnishing materials for certain improvements to real property. Registered engineers, land surveyors and architects may also secure and enforce the same lien.

2. HOW CLAIMED.—By filing a sworn statement in duplicate of intention to hold a lien upon the property for the amount claimed. The recorder may charge $1.50 for mailing a copy of such statement to the owner.

3. WHERE FILED.—In the office of the Recorder of the County where the land is situated.

4. WHEN TO BE FILED.—Within 60 days after performing the labor or furnishing the material.

5. SERVICE OF COPY OF NOTICE.—A duplicate copy of the notice of intention to hold a lien is forwarded to the owner by the recording office.

6. DURATION OF LIEN.—One year from receipt of the notice by the county recorder office or, if credit was given, one year from the expiration of such credit.

7. FILING FEE.—$2.50 for the first page, $1 for each additional page and $1 for mailing duplicate to owner. Documents larger than 9 × 15 cost $5 for the first page and $2 for each additional page.

8. CONTENTS OF NOTICE.—Statement must set forth the amount claimed, name and address of claimant, name of owner and a legal description of the lot of land where the improvement may stand.

9. EXTENT OF LIEN.—The lien extends to the building, erection or improvement, including the land where it is situated, to the extent of all the right, title and interest of the owner. The lien extends to and includes leasehold interest and mortgaged lands.

10. PRIORITIES.—Mechanic's liens take precedence over all other subsequent encumbrances. Claims of several lien claimants are paid in proportion to the amount due each, where proceeds are insufficient.

11. PUBLIC IMPROVEMENTS.—See Chapter 30, *infra,* Bonds on Public Works.

12. REMARKS.—No lien can be acquired for labor, machinery or materials supplied to a contractor, subcontractor or mechanic for the *alteration or repair of a single or double family dwelling* unless notice of such delivery or work and of the existence of lien rights is submitted to the owner within thirty days of the first delivery to or labor performed for the owner of the land where the material, labor or machinery was delivered. Similarly, a person intending to claim a lien for material, labor and machinery sold to a contractor, subcontractor and mechanic for the *original construction of a single or double family dwelling* must furnish the owner a written notice of such delivery or labor and of the existence of lien rights within sixty days after the date of the first delivery or labor performed. The furnishing of such notice is a condition precedent to the right of acquiring a lien upon such property. A lien for material or labor in original construction shall not be valid without notice against an innocent purchaser for value of a single or double family dwelling for occupancy by the purchaser, unless notice of intention to hold such lien be recorded prior to the recording of the deed by which the purchaser takes title.

IOWA

1. WHO MAY CLAIM.—Any person who shall furnish any materials, machinery or fixtures or labor for, or perform any labor upon, any building or land for improvement, alteration or repair thereof, including those engaged in the construction or repair of any work of internal or external

improvement, and those engaged in improving any land by virtue of any contract with the owner, his agent, trustee, contractor, or subcontractor.

2. HOW CLAIMED.—By filing verified statement or account showing time, materials furnished or labor performed and when completed with a correct description of the property charged with lien and the name and last known address of the owner of the property.

3. WHERE FILED.—With the Clerk of the District Court of the county in which property is situated.

4. WHEN TO BE FILED.—By principal contractor within 90 days and by subcontractor within 60 days from the date the last labor was performed or the last material furnished. If a subcontractor's lien is filed after this period, written notice must be immediately served upon the owner, agent or trustee upon the filing of the lien.

5. DURATION OF LIEN.—Two years from expiration of 90 days or 60 days from filing of lien, as case may be.

6. FILING FEE.—$3 per page.

7. CONTENTS OF NOTICE OF LIEN.—Name of claimant, name of party charged with lien, the amount, the description of property charged, itemized statement of account showing dates furnished and when completed. Must be verified.

8. EXTENT OF LIEN.—Lien attaches to the building or improvement and includes entire land upon which situated to the extent of the interest of the person for whose benefit work performed or material furnished. Liens also attach to leasehold interests. Where the lien is for work or material furnished in the construction, repair or equipment of any railroad, canal, viaduct or other similar improvement, it attaches to the erections, excavations, embankments, bridges, road beds, rolling stock and other equipment and to all land upon which such improvements may be situated, except an easement or right of way. Subcontractor liens perfected after the lapse of the 60 day period may be enforced only to the extent of the balance due from the owner to the contractor at time of service of notice of claim. The lien of a subcontractor is not enforceable against an owner-occupied dwelling, except to the extent of the amount owed to the principal contractor at the time the subcontractor serves a written notice of the claim on the owner.

9. PRIORITIES.—Mechanic's liens have priority over each other according to the order of filing. They take priority over garnishments of the owner without regard to date of filing of lien claim. Mechanics' liens shall be preferred to all others which may attach to or upon any building or improvement and to the land upon which it is situated, except liens of record prior to the time of original commencement of work or improvements. However, construction mortgage liens shall be preferred to all mechanics' liens of claimants who commenced their particular work or improvement subsequent to the date of the recording of the construction mortgage lien.

10. PUBLIC IMPROVEMENTS.—See Chapter 30, *infra,* Bonds on Public Works.

See Bonds on Public Improvements.

11. LIENS FOR IMPROVEMENT OF GAS AND OIL WELLS.—The mechanic's lien statute is applicable to labor or materials furnished in connection with gas and oil wells or pipe liens. Liens do not attach to realty, but only to lease, wells, buildings, appurtenances and pipe lines.

KANSAS

1. WHO MAY CLAIM.—Persons furnishing labor, equipment, material or supplies used or consumed for the improvement of realty, under a contract with the owner, trustee, agent or spouse of the owner, shall have a lien upon the property for all services and material, and for the transportation of same.

2. HOW CLAIMED.—The contractor shall file with the Clerk of the District Court of the county in which the land is situated within 4 months after the date of furnishing or performance; a statement setting forth the amount claimed and the items thereof as nearly as practicable, the names respectively of the owner, the contractor, and the claimant, and a description of the property subject to lien, verified by affidavit.

A subcontractor must give a written warning statement to the owner of residential property containing substantially the following:

"Notice to owner: (name of supplier or subcontractor) is a supplier or subcontractor providing materials or labor on Job No. _____ at (residence address) under an agreement with (name of contractor). Kansas law will allow this supplier or subcontractor to file a lien against your property for materials or labor not paid for by your contractor unless you have a waiver of lien signed by this supplier or subcontractor. If you receive a notice of filing of a lien statement by this supplier or subcontractor, you may withhold from your contractor the amount claimed until the dispute is settled."

The subcontractor must file with said Clerk within 3 months from the last material furnished or labor performed by him a verified statement as contractor filed and must state name of contractor and thereafter serve a written notice of such filing upon the owner of the land.

3. WHERE FILED.—Office of Clerk of District Court of the county in which the land is located.

4. WHEN TO BE FILED.—Contractor's statement shall be filed within four months after the last material furnished or labor performed.

Subcontractor must file three months from last material furnished or last labor performed.

5. SERVICE OF COPY OF NOTICE.—Only subcontractor (furnishing labor or material) need serve on owner written notice of filing aforesaid statement.

6. DURATION OF LIEN.—One year from filing lien, but where promissory note given one year from maturity.

7. FILING FEE.—$5 for entering statement of lien of principal contractor. $5 for entering statement of lien of subcontractor.

8. CONTENTS OF NOTICE OF LIEN.—See 2 above.

9. EXTENT OF LIEN.—A mechanic's lien attaches to the property improved for labor, equipment, material or supplies furnished.

The owner of any land affected by such lien shall not thereby become liable to any subcontractor for any greater amount than he contracted to pay the original contractor; except for payments to the contractor made prior to the expiration of the 3 month period for filing lien claims.

10. PRIORITIES.—Liens (for labor and material under contract) shall be preferred to all other encumbrances attaching to such property subsequent to the commencement of the furnishing of labor, equipment, material or supplies at the site of the property. When two or more liens attach to the same improvement, priority is accorded to the earliest unsatisfied lien.

11. PUBLIC IMPROVEMENTS.—See Chapter 30, *infra*, Bonds on Public Works.

12. LIENS FOR IMPROVEMENTS OF OIL AND GAS WELLS.—Lien claimed must be filed with the clerk of the district court of the county where the land is located within six months after the material or labor was furnished or performed. Such liens are preferred to all other liens and suit shall be brought within 6 months from filing.

13. ASSIGNMENTS.—All claims for mechanics' liens and rights of action to recover are assignable.

KENTUCKY

1. WHO MAY CLAIM.—Any person performing labor or furnishing material for erecting, altering, or repairing any house, building or other structure, or for any fixture or machinery therein or for excavating or in any manner for improving real estate, by contract with or the written consent of owner, contractor, subcontractor, architect, or authorized agent. A person who performs labor or furnishes materials to a lessee relating to oil, gas, or other minerals shall have a lien on the leasehold for the entire interest of the lessee.

Special statutory provision is also made for the filing of liens in favor of any person engaged in the business of selling, repairing or furnishing accessories or supplies for any kind of equipment and machinery, including motors.

2. HOW CLAIMED.—(a) Contractor:—The claimant must file a statement of lien in the office of the County Clerk of the county in which the building is situated, within six months after he ceases to perform labor or furnish materials.

(b) Subcontractor:—Such person must notify the owner, or his authorized agent, in writing within seventy-five (75) days for claims less than $1,000 and one hundred and twenty (120) days for claims more than $1,000 after the last time of the material or labor is furnished, of his intention to hold his property liable, and the amount for which he will claim a lien for owner occupied single or double family dwellings. No lien can be obtained if such owner occupant has prior to receipt of the notice paid contractor, subcontractor, or architect. In order that such lien shall take precedence of a mortgage, lease or bona fide conveyance for value with notice duly recorded, the person claiming the lien must, before the recording of such other instruments, have filed in the Clerk's office of the County Court of the county wherein he shall have performed or furnished, or expects to perform or furnish, labor and materials, a statement that he furnished the same or expects to do so, and the amount thereof in full. Such notice may be mailed to the last known address of the owner, or his agent. Unless the claimant files a statement in the office of the Clerk of the County Court of the county in which the property is situated within six months after he ceases to perform labor, or furnish materials, the lien is deemed dissolved.

3. WHERE FILED.—In County Clerk's office.

4. WHEN TO BE FILED.—Within six months after the claimant ceases to perform labor or furnish materials.

5. SERVICE OF COPY OF NOTICE.—Not required where the claimant has contracted directly with the owner or his agent. Subcontractors must notify owner of claim in writing.

6. DURATION OF LIEN.—Expires in one year if no suit brought to enforce lien; where debtor dies within year, period extended another six months after qualification of personal representative.
7. FILING FEE.—$5.
8. CONTENTS OF NOTICE OF LIEN.—Statement of amount due, with all just credits and setoffs known to him, description of property sufficiently accurate to identify, name of owner, if known, and whether the labor was performed or materials were furnished by contract with owner, contractor, or subcontractor and subscribed and sworn to.
9. EXTENT OF LIEN.—The lien of a principal contractor attaches to the extent of the interest of the owner in the house, building or other structure and the land upon which the same is situated; the lien of a subcontractor, materialman or laborer attaches to the same extent, but in no case may the liens be for a greater amount in the aggregate than the contract price under the original contract. Lienor entitled to interest at legal rate.
10. PRIORITIES.—The liens are superior to any mortgage or encumbrance created subsequent to the beginning of the labor or the furnishing of materials, and relate back and take effect from the time of the commencement of the labor or the furnishing of materials.
11. REMARKS.—Where the owner of real property upon which a lien attaches, sells or mortgages the property without applying the proceeds thereof to the payment of sums owing for labor or material used in the erection or repair of any structure thereon, he is deemed guilty of a misdemeanor, is subject to a fine of not less than $50 nor more than $1,000, or to imprisonment for not less than one nor more than twelve months, or both. A similar penalty applies for failure of contractors or other persons receiving money from the owner to apply it to payment of bills for labor or material.
12. PUBLIC IMPROVEMENTS.—See Chapter 30, *infra,* Bonds on Public Works.

LOUISIANA

1. WHO MAY CLAIM.—The following persons have a privilege on an immovable to secure the following obligations of the owner arising out of work on the immovable: (1) contractors for the price of their work; (2) laborers or employees of the owner for the price of work performed at the site of the immovable; (3) sellers for the price of movables sold to the owner that become component parts of the immovable or are consumed at the site of the immovable or are consumed in machinery or equipment used at the site of the immovable; (4) lessors for the rent of movables used at the site of the immovable and leased to the owner by written contract; (5) registered or certified surveyors or engineers or licensed architects employed by the owner for the price of professional services rendered in connection with a work that is undertaken by the owner. The following persons have a claim against the owner and a claim against the contractor to secure payment: (1) subcontractors, for the price of their work; (2) laborers or employees of the contractor or a subcontractor for the price of work performed at the site of the immovable: (3) sellers for the price of movables sold to the contractor or a subcontractor that become component parts of the immovable or are consumed at the site of the immovable or are consumed in machinery or equipment used at the site of the immovable; (4) lessors for the rent of movables used at the site of the immovable and leased to the contractor or a subcontractor by written contract.

The contract must be reduced to writing and signed by the parties, and must be recorded in the office of the Clerk or the Recorder of Mortgages of the parish where the work is to be executed before the date on which the work is to commence, and not more than 30 days after the date of the contract. The owner must require the contractor to give a bond with good and sufficient surety. The amount of the bond must be the amount of the contract, if the contract does not exceed $10,000, between $10,000 and $100,000 not less than 50% of the contract, and in no event less than $10,000. For contracts over $100,000, but not in excess of $1,000,000, the bond must be 33⅓% of the contract, and for contracts exceeding $1,000,000 the bond must be not less than 25% of the amount of the contract but not less than $333,333. The bond must be attached to and recorded with the contract.

2. HOW CLAIMED.—A. CONTRACTORS. Contract must be recorded before the date fixed on which the work is to commence. Where no contract was entered into or contract not recorded and owner or agent has filed an affidavit that work has been completed, an affidavit of claim must be recorded in the office of the Recorder of Mortgages in the parish where the work was done within 60 days after the date of the affidavit of completion or if no affidavit of completion was filed, within 60 days after the date of the last delivery of material or performance of labor. Architects, engineers and surveyors must record lien no later than 60 days after registry of notice, acceptance of notice or substantial completion of work. Affidavit in lieu of contract must set forth the amount due and must be sworn to and recorded in the office of the Recorder of the parish in which the property is located.

B. SUBCONTRACTORS. Subcontractors, materialmen, and laborers must serve personally on the owner, or by certified or registered mail, a sworn detailed statement of claim, and must file same for record in office of the Recorder of Mortgages in the parish in which the work was done, all within 30 days after registry in the office of the Recorder of notice of termination. If no contract has been entered into, or the contract has not been recorded, claimant must record a copy of his estimate, or an affidavit of his claim within 60 days after the date of the last delivery of materials or last performance of services or after filing of the affidavit of completion of owner in the office of the Recorder of Mortgages.

3. WHERE RECORDED.—In the office of the Recorder of the parish in which the property is located.

4. RECORDING FEE.—$2 except in Calcasieu Parish where $1.50.

5. EXTENT OF LIEN.—The lien attaches to the land and improvements in the amount of the claim and interest and the cost of recording the lien. Single lien may be filed against adjacent parcels concurrently under improvement and commonly owned.

6. DURATION OF LIEN.—One year from date of filing, unless proceedings are begun. If contractor does not join with owner to cancel lien after 1 year, claimant has an additional 60 days.

7. PERSONAL LIABILITY OF OWNERS.—If bond furnished by contractor is insufficient in amount or has not a proper and solvent surety, or if no bond has been furnished or recorded, but the contract has been timely recorded, the owner is personally liable to subcontractors, laborers and materialmen who recorded and served their claims as above provided.

8. PRIORITY OF LIENS.—The privileges rank among themselves and as to other mortgages and privileges in the following order of priority: (1) privileges for *ad valorem* taxes or local assessments for public improvements against the property are first in rank; (2) privileges granted to laborers and employees rank next and equally with each other; (3) bona fide mortgages or vendor's privileges that are effective as to third persons before the privileges here discussed are effective rank next and in accordance with their respective rank as to each other; (4) privileges granted to sellers, lessors, and subcontractors rank next and equally with each other; (5) privileges granted to contractors, surveyors, engineers, and architects rank next and equally with each other; (6) other mortgages or privileges rank next and in accordance with their respective rank as to each other.

9. PUBLIC IMPROVEMENTS.—See Chapter 30, *infra,* Bonds on Public Works.

10. LIENS FOR IMPROVEMENTS OF OIL AND GAS WELLS.—Persons performing labor or services in connection with the drilling or operation of any oil, gas or water will acquire liens on the oil or gas produced from the well, proceeds, the wells, lease rigs, machinery and other structures on the property by filing a notice of claim in the mortgage records of the parish where the property is located within 90 days from the last day of performance. Lien is for the amounts due for work performed plus costs of recording and 10% of attorney's fees if necessary to enforce collection.

11. BONDS.—Any interested party may file a bond for a maximum of 125% of the principal amount of the claim asserted. If the recorder of mortgage finds the bond adequate, he may then cancel the statement of claim or privilege. Any party who files a bond or other security to guarantee payment shall give notice by certified mail of the posting of such bond to the owner of the immovable, the holder of the lien and the contractor.

MAINE

1. WHO MAY CLAIM.—Whoever performs labor or furnishes labor or materials or performs services as an architect or engineer, in erecting, altering, moving, or repairing a house or building or appurtenances including any public building erected or owned by any city, town, county school district or other municipal corporations, or in constructing, altering, repairing a wharf or pier or any building thereon, by contract with or by consent of owner, or in repairing or leasing equipment used in the work, has a lien thereon and on the land on which it stands. (Liens on logs, lumber, wood and bark are given to those who work in lumber camps.)

2. HOW CLAIMED.—By filing proper notice, no notice need be filed if labor or materials are furnished under a contract with the owner of the property affected. However, a bona fide purchaser for value will take free of lien unless before taking title the lien claimant files the notice described in 8 below, or files notice that claimant will perform, is performing or, has performed, and may claim lien. This notice is effective relative to a bona fide purchaser for value for a period of 120 days from the date of recording. Where the labor, materials, or services are furnished by a contract with the owner of the property affected, the contractor may preserve and enforce his lien by action against the debtor and owner of the property affected and all other parties interested therein, filed with the Superior Court or District Court Clerk in the county where the house or building on which the lien is claimed is situated, within 120 days after the last of the labor is performed or the labor or materials are so furnished. The lien may also be enforced by attachment in actions

commenced within 180 days in any court having jurisdiction where the property on which the lien is claimed is situated. Where labor or materials not furnished by contract with owner, subcontractor must file in office of register of deeds.

3. WHERE FILED.—Subcontractor, materialman or laborer must file in office of the Register of Deeds in the county or registry district in which the building or other improvement is situated, a statement of his claim. Contractor must file with the Clerk of the District or Superior Court in the County where the building is situated.

4. WHEN TO BE FILED.—Contractor must file within 120 days after he ceases to labor or furnish material. Subcontractor must file within 90 days.

5. SERVICE OF COPY OF NOTICE.—If labor, material or service was not performed or furnished by contract with the owner, this lien is enforceable against the property only to the extent of the balance due from the owner to the person with whom he contracted; however, this defense is available only with respect to sums paid by the owner prior to commencement of action to enforce the lien or written notice from the claimant to the owner including a warning that if owner fails to assure that claimant is paid before further payment to the contractor the owner may be required to pay twice.

6. DURATION OF LIEN.—Action to enforce must be brought within 120 days after the last of the labor is performed or materials furnished. Where owner dies or is adjudicated bankrupt within said 120 days, action may be commenced within 90 days after adjudication or after notice is given of appointment of an executor or administrator.

7. FILING FEE.—Between $5 and $10. Fee for subcontractor is 75¢.

8. CONTENTS OF NOTICE OF LIEN.—A true statement of amount due lienor with all just credits with description of property, names of owners if known and supported by oath of lienor or some one in his behalf.

9. EXTENT OF LIEN.—Owner's right, title and interest in building or improvement covered and the land upon which it stands. Where owner has no legal interest in the land, then lien attaches to the building or other structure. A bona fide purchaser for value of the property takes free and clear of any liens which have not yet been filed.

10. PRIORITIES.—Lien for labor and materials furnished under contract takes precedence over encumbrance subsequent to making of contract, though labor and materials actually furnished after encumbrance given. If not under contract, priority determined by date work performed.

11. PUBLIC IMPROVEMENTS.—See Chapter 30, *infra,* Bonds on Public Works.

MARYLAND

1. WHO MAY CLAIM.—Any person may claim a lien for work done and material furnished without regard to the amount of the claim.

2. HOW CLAIMED.—By filing statement of claim including petition, affidavit of facts on which claim is based, photostatic copies of material papers. Subcontractor must give written notice to owner of intention to claim a lien.

3. CONTENTS OF STATEMENT OF LIEN—Name and address of claimant, name and address of owner, nature or kind of work done or the kind and amount of materials furnished, name of person for whom work was done or materials furnished, amount or sum claimed to be due less any credit recognized by the claimant, a description of the land, a description adequate to identify the building, and the amounts claimed on each building if lien is sought against several buildings or separate parcels.

4. WHERE FILED.—The Clerk of Circuit Court of the county in which the building is situated.

5. WHEN TO BE FILED.—Within 180 days of completion of work or delivery of material. A subcontractor must give notice to owner within 90 days and then file claim with clerk.

6. SERVICE OF COPY OF NOTICE.—If contract is with any person other than owner, notice must be served upon owner within ninety days after completion of labor or furnishing material. Where property is owned by more than one person, then the notice is sufficient if received by any owner. Owner is authorized to withhold from contractor the amount ascertained to be due to party giving such notice.

7. DURATION OF LIEN.—One year from date of filing. Enforcement proceedings may be commenced within the one-year period.

8. FILING FEE.—There are no provisions for fees.

9. CONTENTS OF NOTICE OF LIEN.—Name and address of petitioner and owner of building, and also of the contractor, architect, or builder, when the contract was made with such contractor, architect, or builder; the amount claimed to be due and the nature of the work or materials furnished and the time when furnished; the locality of the property whether any part is in another county and a description of the building. Where one claim for materials is filed by one person against

two or more buildings owned by the same person, claimant must designate amounts due on each. Subcontractor must include facts showing notice given.

10. EXTENT OF LIEN.—Every building erected and every building repaired, rebuilt or improved to the extent of one-fourth its value is subject to a lien for the payment of all debts contracted for work done and for materials furnished for or about the same, including the drilling and installation of water wells, the construction or installation of any swimming pools, the sodding, seeding or planting in or about the premises and the grading, filling, landscaping and paving thereon. If the owner of the land or the owner's agent contracts for the installation of water lines, sanitary sewers, storm drains, or streets to service all lots in a development of the land, each lot and its improvements are subject on a basis pro rata to the number of lots being developed to any lien for work and material. Any machine, wharf, or bridge erected, constructed, or repaired within Maryland may also be subject to a lien. However, a building or the land on which it is erected may not be subjected to a lien if, prior to the establishment of a lien, legal title has been granted to a bona fide purchaser for value. The lien extends to the land covered by the building and so much adjacent thereto as may be necessary for the ordinary and useful purposes of the building. Where a building is commenced and not finished, the lien attaches to the extent of the work done or materials furnished. A lien may attach to a leashold to the extent of the interest of the lessee. "Building" includes any unit of a nonresidential building that is leased or separately sold as a unit.

11. PUBLIC IMPROVEMENTS.—See Chapter 30, *infra*, Bonds on Public Works.

MASSACHUSETTS

1. WHO MAY CLAIM.—A person entering into a written contract with the owner for the erection of a building or structure upon land or for furnishing material has a lien therefor. Any person to whom a debt is due for personal labor performed in the erection, alteration, removal or repair of a building or structure upon land by virtue of an agreement with, or by consent of the owner or person acting for him, has a lien thereon and on the owner's interest in the lot of land on which it is situated for not more than 18 days work actually performed. Stipulation of owner and contractor does not bar right of subcontractor or laborer to establish his lien.

A person who has a written contract with the owner of the land for the whole or any part of the erection, alteration, repair or removal of a building or structure upon land, or for furnishing material therefore also has lien. Lien is also given on vessels for labor and materials, and on vessels not more than 40 feet in length for storage.

2. HOW CLAIMED.—(a) Contractor: Person obtaining lien by written contract must file or record notice of contract. This notice which must be signed and sworn to should be in substantially the following form:

> "Notice is hereby given that by virtue of a written contract date . . . . between . . . ., owner, and . . . ., contractor, said contractor is to furnish labor and material for the erection, alteration, repair or removal of a building on a lot of land described as follows:
> Said contract is to be completed on or before . . . ."

If the contract does not contain a completion date the person filing the notice of contract shall set forth a date of completion which shall be subject to objection by the owner if such date is later than the time for performance under the original contract for any extension thereof. After the filing of such notice any person may have a lien for labor and material supplied under the contract with the contractor or any subcontractor. Lien invalid as against a mortgage actually existing and recorded prior to the filing of the notice of the contract.

(b) Subcontractor: Where notice of a written contract between owner and contractor is filed or recorded in the Registry of Deeds any person subsequently furnishing labor or material under a written contract with the contractor or subcontractor may enforce a lien on the premises. The lien is enforced by filing a notice of his contract in the following form:

> "Notice is hereby given that by virtue of a written contract dated . . . . between . . . . contractor (or subcontractor), and . . . . said . . . . is to furnish labor or material, or both labor and material or perform labor in the erectional duration, repair or removal of a building or structure by . . . ., contractor, for . . . ., owner, on a lot of land described as follows: . . . . Said contract to be completed on or before . . . ."

Upon filing such notice actual notice to the owner must be given of such filing. If the contract does not contain a completion date, the person filing the notice of a contract must set forth a date of completion which is subject to objection by the owner.

3. WHERE RECORDED.—Registry of Deeds for the county or district where land is located.

4. WHEN TO BE RECORDED.—Within 30 days after date on which principal contract and contract of the subcontract is to be performed or within 40 days in the case of claim for personal labor.

5. SERVICE OF COPY OF NOTICE.—Notice of contract by party furnishing labor or material to

contractor or subcontractor must be served on owner together with notice that subcontractor intends to file a lien.

6. DURATION OF LIEN.—For the lien to endure beyond 60 days from the date of the filing of the statement, it is necessary that a bill in equity be brought to enforce said lien.

7. RECORDING FEES.—$10 plus $1 for each page over 4.

8. CONTENTS OF STATEMENT OF LIEN.—(a) A just and true account of the amount due to the claimant, with all just credits. (b) A brief description of the property. (c) The name of the owner or owners as set forth in the notice of contract. (d) Must be signed and sworn to by the claimant or by some person in his behalf.

9. EXTENT OF LIEN.—Where the owner for whom the work was done or material furnished has an estate less than a fee simple in the land or if the property is subject to a mortgage or other encumbrance, the lien binds the owner's whole estate and interest in the property. The lien attaches to the building or structure and upon the interest of the owner of the land as appears of record at the time the notice of the contract is perfected. A person to whom money is due for personal labor has a lien for not more than 18 days' work actually performed during the 40 days next prior to his filing a statement. The liens do not attach to any land, building or structure thereon owned by the commonwealth, or by a county, city, town, water or fire district.

10. PRIORITIES.—A mortgage existing and recorded prior to the recording of the notice of the contract shall have priority except over a lien for labor actually begun before the recording of the mortgage. The rights of an attaching creditor do not prevail against a lien for personal labor nor against a lienor when notice of the contract has been recorded. In the construction of vessels, liens for labor and materials actually used in the construction of such vessels have priority even over prior mortgages.

11. RIGHTS AGAINST BANKRUPT CONTRACTORS AND SUBCONTRACTORS.—If general contractor or subcontractor is adjudged a bankrupt, makes a general assignment for creditors or has a receiver appointed, each person furnishing labor and materials has a lien in proportion to the amount of his claim on all sums due or to become due in connection with the particular construction, provided that a lien on any of the sums arising out of the recording or filing of an instrument or notice under the Mechanic's Lien Law or other application, provision of the general law has priority over any lien for labor and materials under this section. (Section 31 added by laws of 1961.)

12. PUBLIC IMPROVEMENTS.—See Chapter 30, *infra*, Bonds on Public Works.

MICHIGAN

1. WHO MAY CLAIM.—Each contractor, subcontractor, supplier, or laborer who provides an improvement to real property has a construction lien upon the interest of the owner or lessee who contracted for the improvement to the real property.

2. HOW CLAIMED.—By recording a claim of lien in the office of the register of deeds for each county where the real property to which the improvement was made is located within 90 days after the lien claimant's last furnishing of labor or material for the improvement. A claim of lien shall be valid only as to the real property described in the claim of lien and located within the county where the claim of lien has been recorded. A subcontractor who contracts to provide an improvement must provide notice of furnishing to the owner within 20 days after furnishing first labor or material; contracting laborers must give the notice within 30 days after wages were contractually due but not paid; other laborers must give the notice by the fifth day of second month following month wages withheld.

A contractor is not entitled to any payment and may not file any claim to enforce the lien unless he provides the owner with a sworn statement on demand or when payment is due to the contractor or when the contractor requests payment.

A claim of lien shall be in substantially the following form:

CLAIM OF LIEN

Notice is hereby given that on the .... day of ....,
19............,.................... first
(name) (address)
provided labor or material for an improvement to ....,
(legal description of real property from
notice of commencement)
the (owner) (lessee) of which property is ....
(name of owner or lessee from notice
of commencement)
The last day of providing the labor or material was the ...... day of ...., 19........

TO BE COMPLETED BY A LIEN CLAIMANT WHO IS A CONTRACTOR, SUBCONTRACTOR, OR SUPPLIER:

The lien claimant's contract amount, including extras, is $......... The lien claimant has received payment thereon in the total amount of $........, and therefor claims a construction lien upon the above-described real property in the amount of $..........

TO BE COMPLETED BY A LIEN CLAIMANT WHO IS A LABORER:

The lien claimant's hourly rate, including fringe benefits and withholdings, is $.......

There is due and owing to or on behalf of the laborer the sum of $.............. for which the laborer claims a construction lien upon the above-described real property.

....
(lien claimant)
by ....
(signature of lien claimant, agent, or attorney)
....
(address of party signing claim of lien)

Date:....................
State of Michigan)
) ss.
County of ......)
Subscribed and sworn to before me this .... day of ...., 19......
....
Signature of Notary Public
My commission expires: ....

Prepared by:..............................
(name and address of party)

3. WHERE RECORDED. Office of the Register of Deeds for each county where the real property to which the improvement was made is located.

4. WHEN FILED.—Contractor must file within 90 days after last furnishing of labor or material. Subcontractor must also file within 90 days but does not have to give a sworn statement regarding payment.

5. DURATION OF LIEN.—One year after recording unless action to foreclose is begun.

6. RECORDING FEE.—The Register of Deeds is entitled to receive for recording the lien and all subsequent papers affecting the lien the same fee as for recording real estate mortgages, which is $5 for the first page and $2 for each additional and succeeding page. A page is one side of single sheet of 8½ by 14 inches containing no smaller than 8-point type.

7. EXTENT OF LIEN.—The lien attaches to the entire interest of the owner or lessee who contracted for the improvement, including any subsequently acquired legal or equitable interest. The sum of the construction liens cannot exceed the amount which the owner or lessee agreed to pay the person with whom he or she contracted for the improvement, as modified by any and all additions, deletions, and any other amendments, and less payments made by or on behalf of the owner or lessee.

8. PRIORITIES.—As between lien claimants themselves, valid liens are deemed simultaneous mortgages. The liens take priority to all garnishments made after commencement of the first actual physical improvement. They take priority over all other liens or encumbrances given or recorded, subsequent to the commencement of said building or buildings, erection, structure or improvement. However, such liens are subject to prior recorded encumbrances.

9. PUBLIC IMPROVEMENTS.—See Chapter 30, *infra,* Bonds on Public Works.

10. LIENS FOR IMPROVEMENTS OF OIL AND GAS WELLS.—Lien extends to the oil and gas leasehold, oil or gas well, lease, pipeline, buildings, fixtures and any things of value furnished. Lien must be recorded in the Register of Deeds in the county where the property is located within 6 months from the date on which the last material was furnished or labor performed. Must be enforced within one year or lien will expire.

MINNESOTA

1. WHO MAY CLAIM.—Anyone contributing to the improvement of real estate by performing labor or furnishing skill, material or machinery including the erection, alteration, repair or removal of any building, fixture, bridge, wharf, fence or other structure thereon or for grading, filling in or excavating, clearing, grubbing, first breaking, furnishing and placing soil or sod, or digging or repairing any mine, ditch, drain, or etc., or performs engineering or land surveying services; whether under a contract with the owner thereof, or agent, contractor, or subcontractor. Separate provisions for liens on logs and timber.

2. HOW CLAIMED.—By recording statement of claim and serving on or mailing to owner copy of the notice of claim.

3. WHERE FILED.—County Recorder of county where real estate is situated or if made upon railway, telephone, telegraph or electric line with the Secretary of State.

4. WHEN CLAIM OF LIEN TO BE FILED.—Within 120 days from furnishing of last item of work, labor or materials.

5. CONTRACTORS' NOTICE.—Every person who enters into a contract with the owner for the improvement of real property and who has contracted or will contract with subcontractors or materialmen to provide labor, skill or materials for the improvement must give the owner notice of lien personally or by certified mail within ten (10) days after the date of the contract for the work. The notice shall be in at least ten point bold type and shall state as follows:

(a) Persons or companies furnishing labor or materials for the improvement of real property may enforce a lien upon the improved land if they are not paid for their contributions, even if such parties have no direct contractual relationship with the owner;

(b) Minnesota law permits the owner to withhold from contractor so much of the contract price as may be necessary to meet the demands of all other lien claimants, pay directly such liens and deduct the cost thereof from the contract price, or withhold amounts from contractor until the expiration of 120 days from the completion of such improvement unless the contractor furnishes to the owner waivers of claims for mechanics' liens signed by persons who furnished any labor or material for the improvement and who provided the owner with timely notice. If a contractor fails to provide the notice, it shall not have a lien on the property.

6. NOTICE BY SUBCONTRACTORS.—Every subcontractor must, as a prerequisite to the validity of any claim or lien, give the owner or his authorized agent, by personal delivery or by certified mail not later than 45 days after the lien claimant has furnished labor, skills or materials for the improvement a written notice in at least ten point bold type which shall state:

"Please take NOTICE that persons or companies furnishing labor or materials for the improvement of real property may enforce a lien upon the improved land if they are not paid for their contributions, even if such parties have no direct contractual relationship with the owner.

We (name and address of subcontractor) have been hired by your contractor (name and address of contractor) to provide (type and service) or (material) for use in improving your property. We estimate our charges will be (value of service or material).

If we are not paid by your contractor, we can file a claim against your property for the price of our services unless, prior to your receipt of this notice, you have paid to your contractor the full amount of all improvements furnished.

To protect yourself, Minnesota law permits you, as the owner, to withhold from your contractor so much of the contract price as may be necessary to meet our demands, pay us directly and deduct the cost thereof from the contract price, or withhold the amount of our claim from your contractor until the expiration of 120 days from the completion of the improvement unless your contractor furnishes to you a waiver of claim for mechanics' liens signed by me (us)."

7. REQUEST FOR INFORMATION.—A subcontractor or materialman may request a contractor for the name and address of the owner of real estate for which it has provided labor, skill and materials.

8. DURATION OF LIEN.—The lien shall cease at the end of 120 days after the doing of the last of the work of furnishing of materials unless the statement of claim is filed within that time. No lien shall be enforced unless the holder shall assert it within one year after the date of the last item of his claim as set forth in the recorded lien statement.

9. FILING FEE.—$1 for each page with minimum fee of $5.

10. CONTENTS OF NOTICE OF LIEN.—(1) Notice of intention to claim a lien and amount thereof. (2) Nature of claim. (3) Name of claimant and person for whom work, labor or materials were performed or furnished. (4) Dates of first and last items of furnishing or performing work, labor etc. (5) Description of premises to be charged. (6) Name of owner of property to best of lien claimant's information and belief at time of making statement. (7) Post office address of claimant. (8) That copy of statement of notice was mailed. (9) Verification.

11. EXTENT OF LIEN.—The lien shall extend to all the interest and title of the owner in and to the premises improved not exceeding 80 acres or in the case of agricultural land, 40 acres.

With respect to any contract or improvement for which notice is not required to be given the amount of the lien shall be as follows:

(a) If the contribution is made under a contract with the owner and for an agreed price, the lien as against him shall be for the sum so agreed upon.

(b) In all other cases it shall be for the reasonable value of the work done and of the skill, material and machinery furnished.

With respect to any contract or improvement as to which notice is required, the amount of the lien shall be as follows:

If the contribution is made under a contract with the owner and for an agreed price, the lien against him shall be for the agreed upon sum. In all other cases it shall be for the reasonable value of the work done and of the skill, material and machinery furnished provided, however, the total sum of all items shall not exceed the total of the contract price plus the contract price or reasonable value of any additional contract or contracts between the owner and the contractor less the total of the following:

A. Payments made by the owner or his agent to the contractor prior to receiving any notice.

B. Payment authorized by law made by the owner or his agent to discharge any liens or claims.

C. Payments made by the owner or his agent pursuant to presentation of valid lien waivers from persons or companies contributing to the improvement where previously given the required notice.

12. OWNER MAY WITHHOLD PAYMENT.—Owner may withhold from his contractor so much of the contract price as may be necessary to meet the demands of all persons other than the contractor having a lien upon the premises for labor, skill or material furnished for the improvement and in which the contractor is liable and he may pay and discharge all such liens and deduct the cost thereof from the contract price. No owner is required to pay his contractor until the expiration of 90 days from the completion of the improvement except to the extent that the contractor shall furnish to the owner waivers of claims for mechanics' liens signed by persons who furnished labor, skill or material for the improvement and given the notice required by statute.

13. PRIORITIES.—All liens attach and take effect from the time the first item of material or labor is furnished upon the premises from the beginning of the improvement and shall be preferred to any mortgage or other encumbrance not then of record unless the lien holder had actual notice thereof.

14. PUBLIC IMPROVEMENTS.—See Chapter 30, *infra,* Bonds on Public Works.

MISSISSIPPI

1. WHO MAY CLAIM.—Architects, engineers, surveyors, laborers, water well drillers, and materialmen and/or the contractors who rendered services and constructed improvements shall have a lien therefor. The operator of an oil or gas well has a lien on the proportionate share of a non-operator owner's interest in the mineral leasehold. The lien for all contractors and subcontractors exists only in favor of the person employed, or with whom the contract is made, to perform such labor or funish such materials, or render such architectural service, and his assigns, when the contract or employment is made by the owner, his authorized agent, representative, guardian, or tenant.

2. HOW CLAIMED.—As to real property and fixtures, by filing suit, or by filing contract for record in the office of the Chancery Clerk of the county in which the land is situated. As to personal property, by retaining possession, or, if possession has been parted with, by filing suit, in same manner as if for purchase price, under vendor's lien statute. If by subcontractor, materialman, architect or laborer, by notice to the owner, in writing and filing same in lis pendens record in office of Clerk of Chancery Court, or by suit.

3. WHERE FILED.—In the office of Clerk of the Chancery Court in county where property is situated.

4. WHEN TO BE FILED.—There is no specified time for filing contract or notice but subsequent purchasers and encumbrancers are bound by the lien only if filing is prior to the purchases or encumbrances. Suits to enforce as to real property, and when by subcontractors or laborers, within twelve months from the time the debt became due.

5. SERVICE OF COPY OF NOTICE.—Necessary only in case of subcontractors or laborers; must serve written notice and affidavit. If served, owner is bound to make payment to subcontractor or laborer. In suits, service as in other cases.

6. DURATION OF LIEN.—If the amount of the lien exceeds $200, suit must be commenced within 12 months from the time when the money became due and payable.

7. FILING FEE.—$2 for the first page, $1 for each additional page.

8. CONTENTS OF NOTICE OF LIEN.—The contractor files a copy of the contract. The subcontractor (including materialmen and architects) and laborer must serve and file a notice of his claim in writing: (a) amount of claim (b) basis of claim (c) all parties thereto or to be affected thereby (d) description of property sought to be bound (e) rights claimed therein. This must be signed and sworn to by claimant.

9. EXTENT OF LIEN.—If such house, building, structure, or fixture be in a city, town or village, the lien shall extend to and cover the entire lot of land on which it stands and the entire curtilage thereto belonging; or, if not in a city, town or village, the lien shall extend to and cover one acre of land on which the same may stand, if there be so much, to be selected by the holder of the lien. If structure be a railroad or railroad embankment, lien extends to entire roadway and right of way, depots, and other buildings used or connected therewith. If the structure be a water well, the lien extends only to all pumps, pipes, equipment thereon and all water well appurtenances.

A subcontractor's lien may not exceed the amount owed the general contractor by the owner.

10. PRIORITIES.—As to real property, liens arising out of the same transaction are concurrent; if arising out of different transactions, they take precedence in order of filing contract or commencing suit.

As between such liens, and other liens, the mechanic's or materialman's lien takes precedence over all liens of which he has no notice, actual or constructive, except taxes, and assessments in the nature thereof.

The lien shall take effect as to purchasers for a valuable consideration without notice thereof only from the time of commencement of suit to enforce the lien, or from the time of filing the contract under which the lien arose.

11. PUBLIC IMPROVEMENTS.—See Chapter 30, *infra*, Bonds on Public Works.

MISSOURI

1. WHO MAY CLAIM.—Every mechanic or other person, who shall do or perform any work or labor upon, or furnish any material, fixtures, engine, boiler or machinery for any building, erection or improvements upon land, or for repairing the same, or for construction of any street, curb, sidewalk, other pipe line in front of or alongside of any lot or land, under or by virtue of any contract with the owner or proprietor thereof, or his agent, trustee, contractor or subcontractor, including architect, engineer and land surveyor, shall have for his work or labor done, or material, fixtures, engine, boiler or machinery furnished, a lien.

Any person who furnishes and plants trees, shrubs, bushes or other plants or who does any type of landscape planting shall have a lien on the trees, shrubs, bushes or other plants so planted and upon the land on which they are situated to the same extent and enforceable in the same manner as are mechanics' liens, except that there shall be no enforceable lien if the trees, shrubs, bushes or other plants have been delivered to the land on which they are situated and are planted by a person other than the person furnishing them; such lien shall be enforceable only against the property of the original purchaser of such plants unless the lien is filed against the property to the conveyance of such property to a third person.

2. HOW CLAIMED.—By filing a just and true account of demand. Every person except original contractor must give 10 days notice before filing lien, to the owner.

3. WHERE FILED.—Office of Clerk of Circuit Court in County where property is situated.

4. WHEN TO BE FILED.—By original contractors within six months after indebtedness shall have accrued; day laborer, or journeyman, within sixty days; others within four months after indebtedness shall have accrued.

5. SERVICE OF COPY OF NOTICE.—All persons, other than original contractor, shall give ten day's notice before filing lien to owner, owners, or agents, or either, that they hold claim against such building or improvement, setting forth amount of claim and from whom due. Notice to be served by an officer or person who would be a competent witness.

6. DURATION OF LIEN.—For 6 months after filing of lien. Lien lapses unless suit is filed within that time.

7. FILING FEE.—$1. For filing notice of lien upon nonresident or an owner who cannot be found 25¢.

8. CONTENTS OF LIEN.—Just and true account of demand, description of the property upon which lien is intended to apply, name of owner and contractor, verified under oath.

9. EXTENT OF LIEN.—Upon the building, erection or improvement and upon the land to the extent of 3 acres, unless improvement is for manufacturing, industrial or commercial purposes, and not within any city, town or village, then not limited to 3 acres, plus a 40-foot right of ingress and egress.

10. PRIORITIES.—Lien attaches in preference to any prior lien, encumbrance or mortgage upon the land upon which such building, erections, improvements, or machinery have been erected, or put. Liens have precedence over all encumbrances subsequent to commencement of such building or improvements.

11. PUBLIC IMPROVEMENTS.—The law of Missouri does not provide for the filing of mechanics' liens on public improvements. See Chapter 30, *infra*, Bonds on Public Works.

12. LIENS FOR IMPROVEMENT OF WELLS.—Person to whom another is indebted for expenses incurred in drilling and operating a well or a drilling unit with pooled interests by recording an affidavit setting forth amount due and interest of debtor in production in office of Recorder of Deeds in county where property is located.

13. NOTICE TO OWNER—Every original contractor shall provide to the person with whom the contract is made prior to receiving payment in any form of any kind from such person either (a) at the time of the execution of the contract, (b) when the materials are delivered, (c) when the work is commenced or (d) delivered with the first invoice a written notice which shall include the following disclosure language in ten point bold type.

NOTICE TO OWNER

FAILURE OF THIS CONTRACTOR TO PAY THOSE PERSONS SUPPLYING MATERIAL OR SERVICES TO COMPLETE THIS CONTRACT CAN RESULT IN THE FILING OF A MECHANIC'S LIEN ON THE PROPERTY WHICH IS THE SUBJECT OF THIS CONTRACT PURSUANT TO CHAPTER 429, RSMo. TO AVOID THIS RESULT YOU MAY ASK THIS CONTRACTOR FOR "LIEN WAIVERS" FROM ALL PERSONS SUPPLYING MATERIAL OR SERVICES FOR THE WORK DESCRIBED IN THIS CONTRACT. FAILURE TO SECURE LIEN WAIVERS MAY RESULT IN YOUR PAYING FOR LABOR AND MATERIAL TWICE.

Service of notice is a condition precedent to the creation and valid existence of any mechanic's lien. Any original contractor who fails to provide the notice is guilty of a misdemeanor and can be fined.

MONTANA

1. WHO MAY CLAIM.—Every mechanic, miner, machinist, architect, foreman, engineer, builder, lumberman, artisan, workman, laborer, and any other person performing any work and labor upon, or furnishing any material, machinery or fixture for any building, structure, bridge, canal, ditch, aqueduct, mining claim, coal mine, quartz lode, tunnel, city or town lot, farm, ranch, fence, railroad, telephone, telegraph, electric light, gas or water works, or plant.

2. HOW CLAIMED.—By filing claim in writing, verified.

3. WHERE FILED.—County Clerk of county where property is situated.

4. WHEN TO BE FILED.—Within 90 days from the date of last work performed or material furnished. The time for filing the claim of lien is reduced to 60 days if a notice of completion together with an affidavit of publication is filed in the office of the County Recorder where the property is situated. The notice of completion and affidavit must set forth the name and address of the owner; a description of the property sufficient for identification; the nature of the title, if any, of the person signing the notice, and the name of the contractor, if any. The notice must be verified by the owner or his agent and a copy published once each week for 3 successive weeks in a newspaper of general circulation in the county where the land on which the work or improvement was performed is situated. A lien must then be filed within 60 days immediately following the first publication of the notice of completion. For the purpose of filing a notice of completion, "completion of any work or improvement" constitutes the following: (1) The written acceptance by the owner, his agent or his representative of the building, improvement or structure. (2) The cessation from labor for 30 days upon any building, improvement or structure, or the alteration, addition to or repair thereof.

5. SERVICE OF COPY OF NOTICE.—Service shall be made by personal service on each owner or by mailing a copy of the lien by certified or registered mail with return receipt requested to each owner's last known address.

6. DURATION OF LIEN.—Two years from date of filing of lien.

7. FILING FEE.—$2. Where recording of lien is done by photographic or similar process, fee is $2.50.

8. CONTENTS OF NOTICE OF LIEN.—A just and true account of the amount due after allowing all credits, containing a correct description of the property to be charged, verified by affidavit.

9. EXTENT OF LIEN.—Lien extends to the lot or land upon which building, structure or improvement is situated, to the extent of one acre if outside of town or city, or if within town or city to lot or lots on which situated, in either case to the extent of the interest of the owner.

10. PRIORITIES.—All liens filed for work done or material furnished, within 30 days after filing of the first lien shall share pro rata in the proceeds from foreclosure; all liens thereafter filed within 60 days shall share, as liens of the second class, pro rata, in the fund remaining after payment of liens of the first class. Precedence over any and all prior encumbrances made subsequent to commencement of work.

11. PUBLIC IMPROVEMENTS.—See Chapter 30, *infra*, Bonds on Public Works.

MECHANIC'S LIEN LAWS AND FEDERAL TAX LIEN LAW   19-35

12. LIENS FOR IMPROVEMENTS OF OIL AND GAS WELLS.—Liens are created and perfected in the same manner as mechanic's liens except that filing affidavit must be within 6 months of completion of work. Where materials and services are furnished to a part owner of the acreage, lien extends to that interest.

NEBRASKA

Nebraska has adopted the Comprehensive Construction Lien Act.

1. WHO MAY CLAIM.—Any person who furnishes services or materials pursuant to a real estate improvement contract. This includes: (1) Altering the surface by excavating, filling, grading or changing a bank or flood plain of a body of water; (2) Construction or installation on, above or below the surface of the land; (3) Demolition, renovation, repair or removal of an existing structure or installation; (4) Seeding, sodding or other landscaping; (5) Surface or subsurface testing, boring or analyzing; and (6) Architectural or engineering plans, drawings, surveys or preparation thereof regardless if actually used incident to producing a change in the real estate.

2. HOW CLAIMED.—A claimant may record a lien which shall be signed by the claimant and state:

(a) The real estate subject to the lien, with a description thereof sufficient for identification;

(b) The name of the person against whose interest in the real estate a lien is claimed;

(c) The name and address of the claimant;

(d) The name and address of the person with whom the claimant contracted;

(e) A general description of the services performed or to be performed or materials furnished or to be furnished for the improvement and the contract price thereof;

(f) The amount unpaid, whether or not due, to the claimant for the services or materials or if no amount is fixed by the contract a good faith estimate of the amount designated as an estimate; and

(g) The time the last services or materials were furnished or if that time has not yet occurred, an estimate of the time.

3. WHERE RECORDED.—Register of Deeds of county where land is situated.

4. WHEN TO BE RECORDED.—Not later than 120 days after materials or services are last furnished.

5. SERVICE OF COPY OF NOTICE.—A party claiming a lien or his attorney shall within five days after the last day of filing send by mail, postage prepaid, notice of such filing to the owners of record of the property. Proof by affidavit of such mailing shall be filed with the Register of Deeds no later than 10 days after mailing of the notice. Failure to serve the notice of lien shall make the lien void and unenforceable unless such party has waived notice in writing or has actual knowledge of the filing of the lien.

6. DURATION OF LIEN.—Lien is enforceable for 2 years from date of filing. If owner demands that lienor commence suit within 30 days, lien will lapse unless leinor does so.

7. FILING FEE.—$5 per page.

8. EXTENT OF LIEN.—(1) If at the time a construction lien is recorded there is a recorded notice of commencement covering the improvement pursuant to which the lien arises, the lien is on the contracting owner's real estate described in the notice of commencement.

(2) If at the time a construction lien is recorded there is no recorded notice of commencement covering the improvement pursuant to which the lien arises, the lien is on the contracting owner's real estate being improved or directly benefited.

For a subcontractor a lien is for the amount unpaid under claimant's contract.

9. PRIORITIES.—A mechanic's lien has equal priority except where there is an intervening lien. Liens attaching at the same time have equal priority. Liens attaching at different times have priority in order of attachment. A claimant who records a notice of commencement after he or she has recorded a lien has only equal priority with claimants who recorded a lien while the notice of commencement is effective.

10. LIENS FOR IMPROVEMENT OF GAS AND OIL WELLS.—Lien is accorded to any person furnishing material or services under contract of the owner of any leasehold interest or owner of any pipe line for digging, drilling, operating or repairing of wells, or the construction of any pipe line. The lien extends to the leasehold interest on materials and fixtures of the owner, oil and gas wells located on the leasehold interest, and oil or gas produced therefrom and the proceeds thereof and the pipe line. Lien is not effective against the oil or gas until written notice of claim is given to the purchaser. Verified lien statement must be filed within four months after date of furnishing last material or services in office of Clerk of County in which land is situated. Action to enforce lien must be brought within two years after date of filing.

11. PUBLIC IMPROVEMENTS.—See Chapter 30, *infra*, Bonds on Public Works.

NEVADA

1. WHO MAY CLAIM.—Every person performing labor upon or furnishing material of the value of fifty dollars or more, to be used in the construction, alteration or repair of any building or other superstructure, railroad, tramway, toll road, canal water ditch, flume, aqueduct or reservoir, building, bridge, fence or other structure, has a lien upon the same for the work or labor done or material furnished by each, respectively, whether done or furnished at the instance of the owner of the building or other improvement, or his agent (contractors, subcontractors, architects, etc. are deemed agents of owner); and all miners, laborers and others who work or labor to the amount of fifty dollars or more in or upon any mine or upon any shaft, tunnel, adit or other excavation, designed or used for the purpose of prospecting, draining or working any such mine, and all persons who shall furnish any timber or other material to the value of fifty dollars or more to be used in or about any such mine, whether done or furnished at the instance of the owner of such mine or his agent, shall have, and may each respectively claim and hold, a lien upon such mine for the amount and value of the work or labor so performed, or material furnished; foundry men, boiler makers and all persons performing labor or furnishing machinery or boilers or castings, or other materials for the construction or repairing or carrying on of any mill, manufactory or hoisting works shall have a lien on such mill, manufactory or hoisting works; every contractor, subcontractor, architect, builder, or other person, having charge or control of any mining claim, or any part thereof, or the construction, alteration or repair, either in whole or in part, or any building or other improvement, as aforesaid, shall be held to be the agent of the owner. Any person who at request of owner grades, plants, seeds, landscapes, installs system of irrigation or improves lot, has a lien for work done and materials furnished.

In any case where a mechanic's lien attaches to any of the foregoing buildings or structures it also attaches to the land on which the building or structure stands provided at the commencement of the work or the furnishing of the materials for the same, the land belonged to the person who caused the building or structure to be constructed, altered or repaired. If the owner's interest is less than a fee simple the lien attaches to whatever interest the owner has.

Any person who at the request of the owner of any lot in any incorporated town, grades, fills or improves it or the street in front of or adjoining it, has a lien on the lot for the value of his labor and materials.

Prior to execution of a construction contract, a contractor must inform the owner that he may receive notices of materials supplied or services performed.

2. NOTICE OF INTENTION TO CLAIM A LIEN.—Anyone other than a person who performs only labor, in order to claim a lien in addition to recording the lien claim must within 31 days after the first delivery of material or performance of work deliver in person or by certified mail to the owner or person whose name appears as owner on the building permit a notice of intention to claim a lien. A general contractor, or other person who contracts directly with the owner or sells material directly to the owner is not required to give such notice.

3. HOW CLAIMED.—By filing a notice of lien. In addition, a subcontractor must send a copy of notice to the general contractor by certified mail.

4. WHERE FILED.—County Recorder of the county where the property or some part of it is situated.

5. WHEN FILED.—Every person claiming a lien shall record his notice of lien not later than 90 days after the completion of the work or improvement; or 90 days after the last delivery of material; or 90 days after last performance of labor, whichever is last to expire. However, if owner files a notice of completion, lienor must record within 40 days after the owner's recording.

6. SERVICE OF NOTICE.—In addition to the recording, a copy of the lien claim shall be served upon the record owner of the property within 30 days.

7. DURATION OF LIENS.—Foreclosure proceedings must be commenced within six months after filing.

8. RECORDING FEE.—First page $3, each additional page $1.

9. CONTENTS OF LIEN CLAIM.—(1) A statement of his demand after deducting all just credits and offsets. (2) The name of the owner or reputed owner, if known. (3) The name of the person by whom he was employed or to whom he furnished the material. (4) A statement of the terms, time given, and conditions of his contract. (5) A description of the property to be charged sufficient for identification.

10. PRIORITIES.—(a) Liens against property rank in priority as between themselves as follows: (1) Labor; (2) All persons other than original contractors and subcontractors; (3) The subcontractors; (4) The original contractors;

(b) Priorities as between mechanics' and other liens: Mechanics' liens are preferred to any lien, mortgage or other encumbrance which may have attached subsequent to the time when the building,

MECHANIC'S LIEN LAWS AND FEDERAL TAX LIEN LAW   19-37

improvement or structure was commenced, or of which the lienholder had no notice and was not recorded at the time when the building, improvement or structure was commenced.

11. PUBLIC IMPROVEMENTS.—See Chapter 30, *infra,* Bonds on Public Works.

NEW HAMPSHIRE

1. WHO MAY CLAIM.—Any person performing labor or furnishing materials, by himself or others, to the amount of $15 or more for erecting, repairing a house or other building or appurtenance, or for building any dam, canal, bridge, sluice way or well, other than for a municipality. Special statute covering shipbuilding, logging and work on railroad properties.

2. HOW CLAIMED.—Where mechanic dealing directly with the owner, by attachment within 90 days of finishing work. Where subcontractor, by giving notice to owner before starting the work and by furnishing a statement of work done or material furnished every thirty days thereafter, to the owner. If prior notice has not been given, lien for the amount due from the owner to contractor may be acquired on the property by the subcontractor by giving notice at any time.

3. NOTICE OF LIEN.—Principal contractor, no notice of lien is required; subcontractor, notice must be given to owner before starting work, and a statement furnished to him every 30 days.

4. DURATION OF LIEN.—Ninety days after services are performed, or material furnished. When lien is perfected by attachment, lien is permanent.

5. FILING FEE.—No recording required.

6. CONTENTS OF NOTICE OF LIEN.—Notice in writing that subcontractor shall claim a lien for services to be performed.

7. EXTENT OF LIEN.—Covers land and buildings. Subcontractors lien is limited to the sum due contractor by the owner at the time notice of lien is given to the owner.

8. PRIORITIES.—Perfected lien has priority over all claims except liens on account of taxes. Among lienholders, liens take precedence in the order of their perfecting except for liens acquired in performance of a contract existing when the attachment was made, or was necessary to preserve the property, in which case they share pro rata. A "perfected lien" is one in which an attachment has been made claiming a lien, within 90 days of finishing the work.

9. PUBLIC IMPROVEMENTS.—See Chapter 30, *infra,* Bonds on Public Works.

NEW JERSEY

1. WHO MAY CLAIM.—Those furnishing labor or material in erecting, constructing, completing, or altering any building or for the erection or filling in of any docks, wharves, piers, bulkheads, returns, jetties, piling and boardwalks and the lots of land in front of which or upon which the same may be erected and the interests of the owners of such land in the soil or waters of such navigable waters in front of such lands; and including labor or material furnished in or about sinking, driving, digging or drilling well, or for improving land by sodding, seeding or planting any shrubs, trees, etc., or by landscaping, have a right to file a lien. No lien may attach if debt does not exceed $200. Material delivered on the ground, although not actually used in building, is sufficient to support a right to lien. Where the debtor for the labor or material does not own the real estate, no lien can be claimed unless there has been a written consent by the owner of the land to the performance of the work, except in the case of husband and wife. Absent such written consent, only the interest, if any, of the debtor in the real estate can be subjected to a lien.

2. NOTICE OF INTENTION.—Before performance of such labor or furnishing of such materials, the prospective lienor shall file in the office of the County Clerk of the county wherein the land or building to be affected by the lien is situated, a mechanic's notice of intention to perform such labor or furnish such materials, which notice shall be signed by or on behalf of the one for whose benefit the same is filed, and shall contain:

(a) The name of anyone who shall, within ten days prior to the filing of the notice, have been the owner of record in the lands to which the lien is to attach.

(b) A description of the land sufficient to identify it.

(c) The name of the one for whom the labor is to be performed or to whom the materials are to be furnished.

(d) The full name and address of the one for whose benefit the notice is filed, and the name of the person or persons whose signature shall be binding on the one for whose benefit the notice is filed when affixed to any instrument relating to such right of lien.

A written notice of the filing of the notice of intention must be given within five days of such filing to the owner of the premises described in the notice of intention, personally or by registered mail, to the last known address, and unless such notice is given to the owner, the filing of the notice of intention has no effect.

The foregoing provisions do not apply to anyone performing labor which is to be paid for within two weeks from the date of performance when the amount due for such labor does not exceed the sum of $200.

When there is a written contract for the improvement signed by the owner, the contractor is entitled to a lien for labor performed or materials furnished if a copy of the contract is filed with the County Clerk in the county where the property is located. This filing is in lieu of filing the notice of intention described above.

If a notice of intention shall have been filed by someone other than a contractor prior to filing of the contract the property shall be first liable to the lien resulting from such notice previously filed, notwithstanding that any labor was performed or materials furnished subsequent to the filing of the contract; and the owner of the property whenever he pays anyone for whose benefit the notice filed shall be entitled to an allowance therefore in settlement of his account with the contractor. But if written notice is given by the owner or by the contractor or other person, served personally or by registered mail, to the one for whose benefit the notice of intention was filed of the time and place of the filing of the contract, then the owner shall thereafter be liable to the contractor alone for labor performed or materials furnished pursuant to the contract.

3. HOW CLAIMED.—By signed and verified written claim.

4. WHERE FILED.—Office of the Clerk of the county wherein the real estate is situated.

5. WHEN TO BE FILED.—Within 2 years of filing a copy of the contract or of the notice of intent, unless the right of lien is extended by the filing of a further notice before expiration of the 2 year period. In addition lien claim must be filed within four months after the last labor or material has been performed or furnished.

6. DURATION OF LIEN.—A mechanic's notice of intention protects the right to claim a lien for two years from the filing thereof and may be renewed, for an additional two year period. Suit to enforce the lien claim notice must be instituted within 4 months after the last labor and material has been performed or furnished except that time to commence such suit may be extended for a period not exceeding 4 months by written agreement of all parties affected, filed with the original claim prior to the expiration of said first four-month period. Such suit must be prosecuted diligently within one year from date of issuing summons unless further time allowed by court, or time extended by written agreement of all parties whose interest may be affected, for not to exceed four months. A mechanic's notice of intention protects the right to claim a lien for two years from the filing thereof and may be renewed. Owner by serving written notice on lien claimant can require him to commence action within 30 days of notice.

7. CLAIM OF SUBCONTRACTORS AGAINST CONTRACTORS.—When a contractor refuses to pay any subcontractor, materialman or laborer the amount of wages or money due, the latter may file a written notice of such refusal with the Clerk of the county in which shall be stated the owner's name, claimant's name, where property is located and amount due. After such notice is filed the owner is authorized to retain from the monies due the contractor the amount claimed, provided copy of notice is given to the subcontractor. The notice can be served personally or by mail.

Five days after receipt of notice from the owner, if contractor should desire to contest the claim he shall notify the owner in writing that he has notified the subcontractor or materialmen of the dispute and the owner shall not make any payment on the claim. Action to establish the claim must thereafter be brought after 60 days after the notice.

8. FILING FEE.—Filing and recording mechanic's lien claim—$6. Recording, filing and noting on the record the discharge, release or satisfaction of mechanic's lien claim—$6. Filing satisfaction, discharge or release of mechanic's lien, $6. Recording judgment in mechanic's lien proceeding—$6. Filing, indexing and recording mechanic's notice of intention—$3.

9. CONTENTS OF NOTICE OF LIEN CLAIMED.—(1) a description of the building and land so that it may be identified; (2) the name of the owner; (3) the name of the person who contracted the debt or requested the labor or materials; (4) particulars giving the details as to labor performed or materials furnished, deductions made, and balance due.

10. EXTENT OF LIEN.—When a lot on which a building is erected is not separated from the adjoining lands of the same owner by an enclosure, then the lien on the lot shall extend to the track as it is usually known, and designated as a building lot, and bounded by lines laid down on any map made for its sale or on file in the proper public office. In the absence of a map, the lot may be designated, but shall not exceed half an acre nor extend to any building not used in connection with the building in which the lien is claimed. When work is done on behalf of one holding an interest, other than that of the owner, the lien shall extend only to such interests in the absence of the owner's written consent to such work. When a building or part thereof is removed from

its situs, by a person other than the owner of the land to which it is removed, the lien shall attach only to the estate of the person removing the building, in the absence of the landowner's written consent.

11. PRIORITIES.—Lien claimants, as among themselves, share pro rata, regardless of the date of accrual of the debt or filing of the lien, except that wage claims are entitled to priority over all other claimants. They take precedence over judgments, transfers and mortgages, made after date of furnishing of labor and material. Journeymen and laborers shall have preference for the payment of their wages over employers of labor, contractors or materialmen within reference to the date of the filing of their liens.

(A) Mortgages on land shall have priority over liens when at the time of the recording or registration thereof (1) the buildings upon the lands covered thereby shall have been fully or substantially completed, and no mechanic's notice of intention shall have been filed, recorded and indexed as in this Act provided, or (2) there shall be no building upon the lands, nor any excavation, footing or foundation construction, evidencing an intention to erect a building thereon, or (3) there shall be upon the lands covered thereby any excavation, footing, or any foundation construction, evidencing an intention to erect a building thereon or any partially completed building, or any unfinished addition, alteration or repair, upon any of which labor shall not have been performed nor materials furnished within four months next prior to the time of registering or recording.

(B) Priority shall also exist where the mortgage funds have been applied:

(1) To the payment or the securing of payment of all or part of the purchase price of the lands covered thereby, or

(2) To the payment of any valid lien or encumbrance which is, or can be established as, prior to any lien given under this Act.

(3) To the payment of any tax, assessment or other State or municipal lien or charge due or payable at the time of such payment, or

(4) To the payment of any premium, counsel fees, and/or other financing charges and costs the total of which shall not be in excess of five per centum of the principal of the mortgage securing the loan upon which they are based, or

(5) To the payment of everyone who shall have furnished labor or materials for said building and to whom any moneys are due therefor at the time of any advance, and who shall have filed or in whose behalf there shall have been filed a mechanic's notice of intention or the legal representative, receiver, or trustee of such a one. All such claimants shall be entitled to participate in each advance made under any mortgage, except when made for payments under subdivisions No. 1 to No. 4, inclusive, unless such person shall have:

(a) Subordinated, released, partially released or postponed his rights of payment or lien to the lien of the mortgage; no postponement, however, to be effective, for the purpose of this Act except for the first payment made in reliance thereon, and any preceding payments which may have been made, or shall

(b) Neglect or refuse after a demand in writing deposited in the United States registered mail, with proper postage prepaid, addressed for delivery to the address given in the mechanic's notice of intention, or personally served upon the person to be bound thereby or upon the person duly authorized by the mechanic's notice of intention to represent the one on whose behalf such notice was filed, to advise in writing any mortgagee or the owner of any interest in said mortgage, within five days from the date of mailing or service of such demand, of the amount due at the date of the reply to the demand; such neglect or refusal to be effective only as to first advance made after giving of such notice.

If the amount being advanced be not sufficient to pay in full all claimants having a right to participate therein, the mortgagee may pay to each of said claimants such proportionate amount of his claim as the total amount being advanced bears to the total amount of the claims of all persons entitled to participate, and all liens or rights of liens given under this Act or any Act amendatory hereof or supplementary hereto shall be subordinate to the said mortgage to the extent of the payment so made.

(6) To the payment, out of funds remaining after payment of claimants as aforesaid, to person or persons named by the owner of the mortgaged lands or the mortgagor in a written statement, declaration or affidavit, duly sworn to or affirmed before a person who may administer or take oaths and affidavits, as the person or persons who have supplied material or furnished labor actually used in the erection, construction, completion, addition to, alteration or repair of any building upon the mortgaged premises to whom money is due for such labor or materials, and presented to the mortgagee or the agent of the mortgagee, of the amounts of money due to each such person as the same shall be slated opposite the name of such person in such written statement, declaration or affidavit; and to the payment to the owner of the mortgaged lands or the mortgagor of the

amount which such owner of the mortgaged lands or mortgagor shall state in a written statement, declaration or affidavit, sworn to or affirmed as aforesaid, to have been paid by such owner of the mortgaged lands or mortgagor to persons therein listed as having been paid stated sums of money set opposite their respective names for labor or materials actually used in and about the erection, construction, completion, addition to, alteration or repair of a building upon the lands covered by such mortgage, for which there has been no reimbursement; provided, however, that the mortgage funds or any part thereof advanced or paid by the mortgagee under this Subsection shall be applied first to payment in full or payment proportionately of the moneys due to the person or persons listed in the written statement, declaration or affidavit of the owner or the mortgaged lands or the mortgagor as persons not theretofore paid by him; or

(7) To the payment to the mortgagor or owner of the mortgaged premises of any balance out of any advance made on account of such mortgage after the substantial completion of the building on the mortgaged premises and the payment or barring in the manner provided by this article of everyone by, or on whose behalf, a "mechanic's notice of intention" shall have been filed, recorded and indexed.

12. PUBLIC IMPROVEMENTS.—See Chapter 30, *infra,* Bonds on Public Works.

NEW MEXICO

1. WHO MAY CLAIM.—Every person performing labor upon, providing or hauling equipment, tools or machinery for, or furnishing materials for the construction, alteration or repair of any mining claim, building, wharf, bridge, ditch, flume, tunnel, fence, machinery, railroad, road or aqueduct to create hydraulic power or any other structure, or who performs labor in any mining claim, has a lien upon the same for the work or labor done or materials furnished by each respectively, whether done or furnished at the instance of the owner of the building or improvement, or his agent, and every contractor, subcontractor, architect, builder, or other person having charge in whole or in part shall be held to be the agent of the owner. A contractor may not file a mechanic's lien, if not licensed under the construction industries licensing law.

2. HOW CLAIMED.—By filing verified lien claim.

3. WHERE FILED.—County Clerk of the county where property or some part thereof is situated.

4. WHEN TO BE FILED.—At any time during progress of work and furnishing of materials. An original contractor is given 120 days after the completion of his contract to file said lien. Every other person must file his notice of lien within 90 days after the completion of any building or completion of any alteration or repair thereof, or the performance of any labor in a mining claim.

When an original contractor entitled to payment presents his bill for final payment, or an agreement for the sale of the premises, he must notify the owner, his successor (including a prospective purchaser, if known), or his agent in writing that liens may be filed within the next 20 working days. On the same day, he must notify in writing all persons with whom he had contracted for materials or labor and whom he has not paid in full that the 20-day period has commenced and the day upon which it will expire. He must furnish the owner or successor an affidavit of mailing or delivery of such notices. Within five days or receipt of the notice, a subcontractor must certify to the general contractor in writing that his material and labor supplies have been notified. The notice to those furnishing materials or labor must contain the name and street address of the owner or successor and the legal description of the premises at which the work was performed and must be sent by certified mail, return receipt requested.

5. DURATION OF LIEN.—One year after notice has been filed, unless proceedings in a proper court be instituted with one year to enforce same, or if a credit be given, then six months after expiration of such credit, but no lien continues in force for a longer time than two years from the time the work is completed by any agreement to give credit.

6. FILING FEE.—$1.75. Where instrument contains more than 200 words in description of property an additional charge of 25 cents is made for each 100 words. If instrument is photocopied, fee is $3 for first page and $1 for each additional page.

7. CONTENTS OF NOTICE.—(1) Statement of demands after deducting all just credits and offsets. (2) Name of owner or reputed owner, if known. (3) Name of persons by whom he was employed or to whom he furnished materials. (4) Statement of terms, time given and condition of contract. (5) Description of property to be charged with the lien sufficient for identification. (6) Claim must be verified by oath of claimant or of some other person on his behalf.

8. EXTENT OF LIEN.—Lien extends to building, structure or improvement and the land on which situated, together with a convenient space about the same or so much as may be required for the convenient use and occupation of the same. To the extent of the right, title and interest of the person who caused such building, structure or improvement to be enacted, repaired etc. Liability is limited to the amount contracted to be paid to the original contractor.

MECHANIC'S LIEN LAWS AND FEDERAL TAX LIEN LAW   19-41

9. CONTRACTOR LIABLE FOR LIENS OF SUBCONTRACTOR.—The contractor shall be entitled to recover upon a lien filed by him only such amount as is due pursuant to the terms of the contract, less the amount of claims of subcontractors who have filed liens.

Upon notice of the pendency of any action on the lien of a subcontractor, the owner may withhold the amount due principal contractor. If a judgment be obtained against the owner including costs, such total sum may be charged against the amount due the contractor, or he may be sued for difference, if he has already been paid.

10. PRIORITIES.—Lien takes preference over any lien, mortgage or other encumbrance which attaches subsequent to the time when the building, improvement, or structure was commenced, work done or materials were commenced to be furnished; also to any lien, mortgage or other encumbrance of which the lienholder has no notice, and which was unrecorded at the time the building, improvement, or structure was commenced, work done or materials were commenced to be furnished.

Where different liens are asserted against the same property, the rank of preference is as follows: (1) All persons other than contractor or subcontractor. (2) Subcontractor. (3) Original Contractors.

11. PUBLIC IMPROVEMENTS.—See Chapter 30, *infra*, Bonds on Public Works.

12. LIENS FOR IMPROVEMENT OF GAS AND OIL WELLS.—Every person who performs labor or furnishes or hauls material, equipment, tools, etc., in digging, drilling, completing, maintaining, operating and repairing oil or gas well, or pipe line, or equipment in connection therewith shall have a lien upon the land, leasehold, pipe line, buildings and equipment thereon, and the materials, tools, etc., so furnished, and the oil and gas well. Lien does not extend to the underlying fee or royalty interest unless expressly provided by contract. Verified claim must be filed by original contractor within 120 days, and by other lien claimant within 90 days after furnishing last material or last labor with the Clerk of the county in which property is located. Proceedings to enforce lien must be instituted within 1 year from date of filing.

NOTE.—A contractor is required to file a bond with the contractor's license board which, among other things, provides for materials, labor and supplies.

NEW YORK

1. WHO MAY CLAIM.—Contractor, subcontractor, laborer, materialman, landscape gardener, nurseryman or person or corporation selling fruit or ornamental trees, roses, shrubbery, vines and small fruit, who performs labor or furnishes materials for the improvement of real property, with the consent, or at the request, of the owner thereof, or of his agent, contractor, or subcontractor. Where the contract for an improvement is made with a husband or wife and the property belongs to the other or both, the husband or wife contracting shall also be presumed to be the agent of the other, unless such other having knowledge of the improvement shall, within ten days after learning of the contract, give the contractor written notice of his or her refusal to consent to the improvement. Materials actually manufactured for but not delivered to the real property, shall also be deemed to be materials furnished. Lien also for person who performs labor for a railroad corporation for value of such labor upon the railroad track, rolling stock, and appurtenances and upon the land upon which they are situated.

The term "improvement" includes the demolition, erection, alteration or repair of any structure upon, connected with or beneath the surface of any real property and any work done upon such property or materials furnished for its permanent improvement, including work done or materials furnished in equipping any such structure with chandeliers, brackets or other fixtures or apparatus for supplying gas or electric light; the drawing by an architect or engineer or surveyor of plans or specifications or survey which are prepared for or used in connection with such improvement; the value of materials actually manufactured for but not delivered to the real property; the reasonable rental value for the period of actual use of machinery, tools and equipment and the value of compressed gases furnished for welding or cutting; the value of fuel and lubricants consumed by machinery operating on the improvement, or by motor vehicles owned, operated or controlled by the owner, or a contractor or subcontractor while engaged exclusively in the transportation of materials to or from the improvement for the purposes thereof; and the performance of real estate brokerage services in obtaining a lessee for a term of more than 3 years where property not to be used for residential purposes.

2. HOW CLAIMED.—By filing notice of lien.

3. WHERE FILED.—County Clerk of county where property is situated. Where property is situated in more than one county, file in each county where part of property is situated. If the Clerk maintains a block index, the notice filed shall contain the number of every block on the land map of the county which is affected.

4. WHEN TO BE FILED.—At any time during progress of work and furnishing of materials, or within eight months after completion of contract, or final performance of work, or final furnishing of materials, dating from last item of work or materials furnished (four months for single family dwelling) except where lien by real estate broker, notice may be filed only after performance of brokerage services. Notice of lien on railroad property filed in any county where railroad is situated.

5. SERVICE OF COPY OF NOTICE.—A copy of the notice must be sent by certified mail within 10 days to the owner, contractor, or subcontractor, but failure to provide the copy does not affect the validity of the lien. Any lienor who fails to serve such copy is liable for the attorney's fees, costs, and expenses incurred in obtaining the copy.

6. DURATION OF LIEN.—One year after notice has been filed, unless within that time an action is commenced to foreclose the lien, or unless order be granted within one year by court of record or a judge or justice thereof, continuing lien for not more than one additional year, and lien be redocketed pursuant to such order. Lien may be continued from year to year by successive orders.

7. FILING FEE.—$15 for filing a notice of mechanic's lien or for filing a notice of pendency of action.

8. CONTENTS OF NOTICE OF LIENS.—(1) Name and residence of lienor; and if lienor is a partnership or corporation, business address of such firm, or corporation, names of partners and principal place of business, and if a foreign corporation, its principal place of business within the state. (2) Name and address of lienor's attorney, if any. (3) Name of owner of property and owner's interest therein. (4) Name of person by whom lienor was employed, or to whom he furnished or is to furnish materials, or if lienor is a contractor or subcontractor, person with whom contract was made. (5) The labor performed or materials furnished and agreed price or value thereof, or materials actually manufactured for but not delivered to the real property and the agreed price or value thereof. (6) Amount unpaid to lienor for such labor or materials. (7) Time when first and last items of work were performed and materials were furnished. (8) Property subject to the lien, with a description and, if in a city or village, its location by street and number, if known. (9) Verify by lienor or his agent to effect that statements therein contained are true to his knowledge, except as to the matters therein stated to be alleged on information and belief, and as to those matters on which he believes them to be true.

9. EXTENT OF LIEN.—Owner's right, title or interest in the real property and improvements existing at or after the time of filing notice of lien. Extends to an interest assigned for the benefit of creditors where the the assignment was within 30 days prior to the filing. Lien cannot exceed amount earned and unpaid on contract at time of filing notice or any sum subsequently earned thereon. Owner's liability may not exceed, by reason of all liens filed, a sum greater than the value or agreed price of the labor and materials remaining unpaid at the time of filing notices.

10. INSURANCE PROCEEDS LIABLE FOR DEMANDS.—In the event that an improvement on which a lien is claimed is destroyed by fire or other casualty and insurance proceeds paid to the owner for such loss or casualty, the owner must retain an amount equal to the premiums paid and balance is subject to the lien as realty would have been. If insurance is payable to contractor after he reimburses himself for premiums paid, contractor must pay balance to laborers and materialmen to whom he is liable as if payments made to him under the contract.

11. PRIORITIES.—(1) A lien for material furnished or labor performed in the improvement of real property has priority over a conveyance, mortgage, judgment or other claim against such property not recorded, docketed or filed at the time of the filing of the notice of lien; over advances made upon any mortgage or other encumbrance thereon after such filing; and over the claim of a creditor who has not furnished materials or performed labor upon such property, if such property has been assigned by the owner by a general assignment for the benefit of creditors, within thirty days before the filing of either of such notices; and also over an attachment issued or a money judgment recovered upon a claim, which, in whole or in part, was not for material furnished, labor performed or moneys advanced for the improvement of such real property; and over any claim or lien acquired in any proceedings upon such judgment. Such liens also have priority over advances made upon a contract by an owner for an improvement of real property which contains an option of purchase to the contractor, his successor or assigns to purchase the property, if such advances were made after the time when the labor began or the first item of material was furnished, as stated in the notice of lien. If several buildings are erected, altered or repaired, or several pieces or parcels of real property are improved, under one contract, and there are conflicting liens thereon, each lienor has priority upon the particular building or premises where his labor is performed or his materials are used. Persons have no priority on account of the time of filing their respective notices of liens, but all liens are on a parity except that laborers, subcontractors and materialmen are preferred over contractors.

(2) When a building loan mortgage is delivered and recorded, the lien has priority over advances

made on the building loan mortgage after the filing of the notice of lien; but such building loan mortgage, whenever recorded, to the extent of advances made before the filing of such notice of lien, has priority over the lien, provided it or the building loan contract contains a covenant by the mortgagee to receive and hold advances thereunder as trust funds for payment of the costs of the improvement, and provided the building loan contract is filed. No mortgage recorded subsequent to the commencement of the improvement and before the expiration of four months after the completion thereof shall have priority over liens thereafter filed unless it contains such covenant.

(3) Every such building loan mortgage and every mortgage recorded subsequent to the commencement of the improvement and before the expiration of four months after the completion of the improvement shall contain a similar covenant by the mortgagor that he will receive the advances secured thereby as a trust fund to be applied first for the purpose of paying the cost of improvement, and that he will apply the same first to the payment of the cost of improvement before using any part of the total of the same for any other purpose, provided, however, that if the party executing the building loan contract is not the owner of the fee but is the party to whom such advances are to be made, a building loan contract executed and filed pursuant to this chapter shall contain the said covenant by such party executing such building loan contract, in place of the covenant by the mortgagor in the building loan mortgage. Nothing in the statute is to be considered as imposing upon the lender any obligation to see to the proper application of such advances by the owner.

(4) No instrument of conveyance recorded subsequent to the commencement of the improvement, and before the expiration of four months after the completion thereof, is valid as against liens filed within four months from the recording of such conveyance, unless the instrument contains a covenant by the grantor that he will receive the consideration for such conveyance as a trust fund to be applied first for the purpose of paying the cost of the improvement and that he will apply the same first to the payment of the cost of the improvement and that he will apply the same first to the payment of the cost of the improvement and that he will apply the same first to the payment of the cost of the improvement before using any part of the total of the same for any other purpose. Nothing in the statute is to be construed as imposing upon the grantee any obligation to see to the proper application of such consideration by the grantor. Does not apply to a deed given by a referee or other person appointed by the court for the sole purpose of a selling real property, or to the consideration received by a grantor who, pursuant to a written agreement entered into and duly recorded prior to the commencement of the improvement, conveys to the person making such improvement, the land upon which such improvement is made. However, such a conveyance is subject to liens filed prior thereto. Section does not apply to mortgages taken by Home Owners Loan Corp.

12. WAIVER OF LIEN.—Notwithstanding the provisions of any other general, specific or local law, any contract, agreement or understanding whereby the right to file or enforce any lien is waived, shall be void as against public policy and wholly unenforceable. This shall not preclude a requirement for a written waiver of the right to file a mechanic's lien executed and delivered by a contractor, subcontractor, material supplier or laborer simultaneously with or after payment for the labor performed or the materials furnished has been made to such contractor, subcontractor, material man or laborer. Nor shall this section be applicable to a written agreement to subordinate, release or satisfy all or part of such a lien made after a notice of lien has been filed.

13. BOOKS AND STATEMENT THEREOF AND DEPOSIT OF FUNDS.—(1) An owner, contractor or subcontractor shall keep blocks or records showing the allocation to each improvement of real property or a public improvement of the funds received and disbursed on account thereof.

(2) The funds received by an owner under any and all advances made pursuant to a building loan contract and secured by a building loan mortgage and the funds received by an owner under every mortgage containing such covenant and the funds received by an owner under every instrument of conveyance containing the covenant and the funds received by a contractor from an owner or assignee or by a subcontractor from a contractor, subcontractor or assignee on account of an improvement of real property, if deposited in a bank or other depository, shall be deposited in the name of such owner, contractor or subcontractor, as the case may be.

(3) Such books or records shall contain the following entries: the names and addresses of all persons from whom such and other funds have been received on account of each improvement, the dates when such funds have been received, the name and address of the bank or depository wherein such funds have been deposited, the names and addresses of the persons to whom payments have been made on account of each improvement, the amounts paid to each of such persons, the dates when such payments were made, and a description of the items of the improvement on account of which such payments have been made.

(4) A person entitled to a payment on account of an improvement of real property or a public improvement, as provided, from such owner, contractor or subcontractor, shall, after the expiration of 60 days from the due date of such payment, be entitled to a statement under oath, as herein provided.

(5) Within ten days after a written request for such statement, served personally or by registered mail, by or on behalf of a person entitled thereto, specifying the improvement on account of which such payment is due, such owner, contractor or subcontractor, as the case may be, shall furnish to such person or his agent designated in such written request, a statement setting forth the entries contained in such books and/or records relating to such specified improvement. Such statement shall be verified by the oath of the owner, contractor or subcontractor, as the case may be, or by an officer of the owner, contractor or subcontractor, as the case may be, or by an officer of the owner, contractor or subcontractor that he has read such statement subscribed by him and knows the contents thereof and that the same is true of his own knowledge.

(6) The failure to keep such books or records and/or the failure of an owner, contractor or subcontractor, or of an officer, director or agent of such owner, contractor or subcontractor, to furnish such statement shall be presumptive evidence that such owner, contractor or subcontractor, as the case may be, has applied and/or consented to the application of trust funds for purposes other than those specified.

14. EXAMINATION OF BOOKS AND COPY THEREON.—(1) After the expiration of sixty days from the date of the docketing of a judgment based upon a cause of action for material furnished and/or labor performed on account of an improvement of real property or a public improvement against an owner, contractor or subcontractor, as the case may be, the judgment creditor whose judgment has not been satisfied shall be entitled to an examination of the books and/or records of such owner, contractor or subcontractor and to make copies of any part or parts thereof relating to the improvement for which such material has been furnished and/or such labor has been performed.

(2) Within ten days after request for such examination and copy made by such judgment creditor or his agent, personally or by registered mail, such owner, contractor or subcontractor, as the case may be, shall produce his books and/or records and shall permit such judgment creditor or his agent duly accredited in writing to examine such books and/or records and to make copies of any part or parts thereof. The request shall specify the improvement relating to which the examination is desired. Unless otherwise agreed upon in writing, the examination and copy shall be made during the usual business hours, in the county in which the improvement is situated, at a place designated in writing, within such ten days, by such owner, contractor or subcontractor.

(3) The failure of an owner, contractor or subcontractor, or of an officer, director, or agent of such owner, contractor or subcontractor, to produce and to permit an examination and copy of such books and/or records shall be presumptive evidence that such owner, contractor or subcontractor, and/or the officer, director or agent of such owner, contractor or subcontractor, as the case may be, has applied and/or consented to the application of trust funds for purposes other than those specified in the statute.

15. LIABILITY OF LIENOR WHERE LIEN HAS BEEN DECLARED VOID ON ACCOUNT OF WILFUL EXAGGERATION.—Where in any action or proceedings to enforce a mechanic's lien upon a private or public improvement the Court shall have declared said lien to be void on account of wilful exaggeration the person filing such notice of lien shall be liable in damages to the owner or contractor. The damages which said owner or contractor shall be entitled to recover shall include the amount of any premium for a bond given to obtain the discharge of the lien or the interest on any money deposited for the purpose of discharging the lien, reasonable attorney's fees for services in securing the discharge of the lien, and an amount equal to the difference by which the amount claimed to be due or to become due as stated in notice of lien exceeded the amount actually due or to become due.

16. ASSIGNMENTS OF CONTRACTS AND ORDERS TO BE FILED.—Assignments of contracts the improvement of real property; orders drawn by contractors upon owners of real property for the payment of money; orders drawn by subcontractors upon contractors or subcontractors for such payments; orders drawn by an owner upon the maker of a building loan; and assignments of money due and to grow due on a building loan contract, must be filed within 10 days after the date of such assignment of contract, or such assignment of moneys or such order in the office of the County Clerk of the county where the realty is situated. Unfiled assignments and orders are absolutely void as against subsequent assignees in good faith and for a valuable consideration whose assignments and orders are first duly recorded.

17. LIENS ON PUBLIC IMPROVEMENTS.—See Chapter 30, *infra,* Bonds on Public Works.

18. LIENS FOR IMPROVEMENT OF WELLS.—Under lien law real property includes all oil or gas

wells and structures and fixtures connected therewith, and any lease of oil lands or other right to operate for the production of oil or gas upon such lands.

NORTH CAROLINA

1. WHO MAY CLAIM.—Any person who performs or furnishes labor, furnishes materials, professional design or surveying services pursuant to a contract either express or implied with the owner of real property for the making of improvement thereon. "Improvement" means all or any part of any building, structure, erection, alternation, demolition, excavation, clearing, grading, filling, or landscaping, or real property. Waiver of right to file or claim a lien is against public policy and is unenforceable.

2. WHERE FILED.—Office of the clerk of the superior court in each county wherein the real property subject to the claim is located. A subcontractor perfects a lien upon the giving of notice in writing to obligor; effective upon receipt.

3. WHEN NOTICE FILED.—Notice of lien shall be filed at any time after maturity of the obligation but not later than 120 days after the last furnishing of labor or materials by persons claiming them.

4. CLAIM OF LIEN.—The contents of a lien claim must be in substantially the following form:
(a) Name and address of the person claiming the lien.
(b) Name and address of the record owner of the real property claimed to be subject to the lien at the time the claim of lien is filed.
(c) Description of the real property upon which the lien is claimed: (Street address, tax lot and block number, reference to recorded instrument, or any other description of real property is sufficient, whether or not it is specific, it is reasonably identifies what is described.)
(d) Name and address of the person with whom the claimant contracted for the furnishing of labor or materials
(e) Date upon which labor or materials were first furnished upon said property by the claimant.
(f) General description of the labor performed or materials furnished and the amount claimed therefor.
(g) Date upon which labor or materials were last furnished upon said property by the claimant.

5. FILING FEE.—$4 per page or fraction thereof.

6. NOTICE OF LIEN.—Notice of lien must be sent by subcontractor for labor or materials to the obligor and sending of such notice perfects the lien. Upon receipt of such notice, the obligor is under a duty to retain the funds subject to the lien. If, after receipt of notice, the obligor makes any payment to a contractor or subcontractor against whom the lien is claimed, the lien shall continue on the funds in the hands of the contractor or subcontractor who receives the payment and in addition the obligor shall be personally liable. A subcontractor can enforce any contractor's lien against owner. Upon the filing of the notice, a claim of lien and commencement of an action by subcontractor, no action of the contractor shall be effective to prejudice the rights of the subcontractor without his written consent.

Before holding a public sale of property, a lienor must publish a notice of the sale in a newspaper not less than five days prior to the sale.

7. CONTENTS OF NOTICE OF CLAIM OF LIEN.—The notice must contain the following: (1) the name and address of person claiming the lien; (2) a general description of the real property improved; (3) the name and address of the person with whom the lien claimant contracted to improve real property; (4) the name and address of each person against or through whom subrogation rights are claimed (5) a general description of the contract and the person against whose interest the lien is claimed; and (6) the amount claimed by the lien claimant under his contract.

8. EXTENT OF LIEN.—Lien extends to the improvement and to the lot or tract on which improvement situated and to extent of interest of owner. Lien secures payment of all debts owing for labor done or material furnished pursuant to the contract. Lien extends to the improvement and to the lot or tract on which it stands and to extent of the owner's interest therein. A subcontractor's lien extends to the funds owed its contractor or to the person with whom it dealt.

9. DURATION OF LIEN.—An action to enforce the lien may be instituted in any county in which the lien is filed. Such action may not be commenced later than 180 days after the last furnishing of labor or materials at the site of the improvement.

10. PRIORITIES.—Liens of general contractors are entitled to priority in accordance with time of the filing of notice. Liens of subcontractors or laborers employed to furnish or who do furnish material for the building, repairing or altering of any house, or other improvement on real estate, are preferred to the liens of general contractors. Exemptions of personal and real property shall

not be construed as to prevent a laborer's lien for work done and performed for the person claiming such exemption, or a mechanic's lien for work done on the premises. Subcontractor's liens perfected by notice to the obligor have priority over all interest including garnishment, attachment, levy, and judgment. If the amount due the contractor by the owner is not sufficient to pay in full the laborer, mechanic or artisan for his labor and the person furnishing materials, owner must distribute amount pro rata among several claimants.

11. PUBLIC IMPROVEMENTS.—See Chapter 30, *infra,* Bonds on Public Works.

NORTH DAKOTA

1. WHO MAY CLAIM.—Any person who improves real estate by the contribution of labor, skill or materials, whether under contract with the owner of such real estate, or at the instance of any agent, trustee, contractor or subcontractor of such owner, shall have a lien upon the improvement, and upon the land on which it is situated or to which it may be removed, for the price or value of such contribution. Liens also upon railroad property and in favor of miners.

2. HOW CLAIMED.—A contractor for materials must keep an itemized account thereof separate and apart from all other items of account against the purchaser; serve a written notice by registered or certified mail upon owner demanding payment of such account and notify him that unless payment is made within 15 days of mailing a lien will be perfected; and, record a verified notice of intention to claim a lien. The notice of intention to claim lien shall contain the following:

(1) Name of the person in possession of the land;
(2) The description of the property to be charged with the lien;
(3) The date of the contract; and
(4) That a mechanic's lien against the building, improvement, or premises will be perfected according to law unless the account has been paid.

A claimant other than a contractor, may serve upon the owner at any time, a notice of his claim. The owner, within 15 days after completion of the contract, may require the claimant to furnish an itemized and verified account, the amount due, and his name and address.

3. WHERE FILED.—Register of Deeds in county where land, building or improvement is situated.

4. WHEN TO BE FILED.—Every person desiring to perfect his lien shall file with the Register of Deeds of the county in which the property is situated, within 90 days after all his contribution is done, a true account of the demand due him after allowing all credits and containing a correct description of the property to be charged with a lien, which account shall be verified by affidavit. Failure to file within 90 days shall not defeat lien except as to purchasers or encumbrancers in good faith and for value whose rights accrue after the 90 days and before any claim for lien is filed, and as against the owner to the extent of the amount paid to a contractor after the expiration of the 90 days and before filing of the account.

5. DURATION OF LIEN.—Suit to enforce lien must be commenced within 30 days after written demand of the owner, his agent or contractor if debt is then due, or, if not yet due, within 30 days after it becomes due. In any event action must be instituted within 3 years after last item of claim becomes due.

6. FILING FEE.—The fee for recording the notice of intention to claim a lien is $5 for the first page and $2 for each additional page.

7. EXTENT OF LIEN.—The lien attaches from the time the first item of material or labor is furnished. It covers the agreed contract price, otherwise, the reasonable value of the work done. The entire land upon which the building or improvement situated is subject to the lien to the extent of the landowner's right, title and interest. When the interest owned in land by the owner of the building or other improvement for which the lien is claimed is only a leasehold interest, the forfeiture of the lease will not impair the lien so far as it applies to the buildings or improvements, but the improvements may be sold to satisfy the lien and may be removed by the purchaser within 30 days after the sale.

8. PAYMENT TO CONTRACTORS WITHHELD.—The owner may withhold from his contractor so much of the contract price as may be necessary to meet the demands of all persons, other than such contractor, having a lien upon the premises for labor, skill, or material furnished for the improvement, and for which the contractor is liable, and he may pay and discharge all such liens and deduct the cost thereof from such contract price. Any such person having a lien under the contractor may serve upon the owner at any time a notice of his claim. The owner, within fifteen days after the completion of the contract, may require any person having a lien hereunder, by written request therefor, to furnish to him an itemized and verified account of his claim, the amount thereof, and his name and address, and no action or other proceeding shall be commenced for the enforcement of such lien until ten days after such statement is so furnished. The word "owner,"

as used in this Section, includes any person interested in the premises otherwise than as a lienor thereunder.

9. PRIORITIES.—Liens shall have priority in the following order: (1) for manual labor; (2) for materials; (3) subcontractors other than manual laborers; and (4) original contractors. Liens for manual labor filed within 90-day period share pro rata; those filed thereafter shall have priority in order of filing; liens for materials have priority in order of the filing of notices of intention.

10. IMPROVEMENTS NOT AUTHORIZED BY OWNER.—Any person who has not authorized the same may protect his interest from such liens by serving upon person doing work, etc., within 5 days after he has knowledge thereof, a written notice that the improvement is not being made at his instance, or by posting like notice and keeping the same posted, in a conspicuous place on the premises. As against a lessor no lien is given for repairs made by or at the instance of his lessee, unless the lessor shall have actual or constructive notice thereof and not object thereto.

11. SUITS BY SUBCONTRACTORS.—No person may have a lien for improving real property which lien resulted from extending credit to or making a contract with an agent, contractor, or subcontractor of the owner, unless that person notifies the owner in writing of the relevant provisions and obtains a copy of the instrument authorizing the agent contractor or subcontractor to procure credit or make contracts in the owners' name.

Such person claiming a lien for improving real estate shall first proceed by judicial action against the agent, contractor or subcontractor and exhaust his remedies of collection before he shall have a lien upon the improvement or the land on which it is situated.

12. PUBLIC IMPROVEMENTS.—See Chapter 30, *infra*, Bonds on Public Works.

13. LIENS FOR IMPROVEMENTS OF OIL AND GAS WELLS.—Such liens are created, perfected and enforced in the same manner as mechanic's liens, except that filing must be made within 6 months of performing labor or furnishing materials and the filing fee is $1. Notice must also be given to any purchaser of the oil or gas before the lien extending to the proceeds becomes effective.

OHIO

1. WHO MAY CLAIM.—Every person who does work or labor upon, or furnishes machinery, material, or fuel for constructing, altering, or repairing a boat, vessel, or other water craft, or for erecting, altering, repairing, or removing a house, mill, manufactory, or any furnace or furnace material therein, or other building, appurtenance, fixture, bridge or other structure, or for digging, drilling, boring, operating, completing, or repairing of any gas well, oil well, or other well, or for altering, repairing, or constructing any oil derrick, oil tank, oil or gas pipe line, or furnishes tile for the drainage of any lot or land or who does work or labor or furnishes material for the improvement of real property by seeding, sodding, or the planting thereon of shrubs, trees, flowers, etc., or nursery stock of any kind or by grading or filling to establish a grade by virtue of a contract, express or implied, with the owner, part owner, or lessee, of any interest in real estate, or the authorized agent of the owner, part owner, or lessee, of any interest in real estate, and every person who shall as subcontractor, laborer or materialman, perform any labor, or furnish machinery, materials, or fuel to each original or principal contractor, or any subcontractor in carrying forward, performing, or completing any such contract shall have a lien.

Any person who performs labor or furnishes machinery, material or fuel for the construction, alteration or repair of any street, turnpike, road, sidewalk, way, drain, ditch, or sewer by virtue of a private contract between him and the owner, part owner or lessee of lands upon which the same may be constructed, altered or repaired, or of lands abutting thereon, or any person who shall as subcontractor, laborer, or materialman, perform labor or furnish machinery, material or fuel to such original or principal contractor or to any subcontractor in carrying forward or completing such contract, shall have a lien.

Any person, firm, partnership or corporation furnishing any of the following materials or services is deemed a materialman: Gasoline, lubricating oils and other petroleum products, explosives, powder, dynamite, blasting supplies, tools, use of machinery and equipment and repairs thereto furnished to contractors, subcontractors and others and used in delivering or hauling materials to, or otherwise used for, in, in connection with or in preparation for the construction, erection, alteration, or repair of any highway, road, sewer, street or other public improvement, public building or public works, or in preparing ground therefor, whether or not said products enter into and become component parts of or are substantially consumed, in connection with or in preparation for the construction, erection, alteration, or repair of said highway, road, sewer, street or other public improvement, public building or public works, or in preparing ground therefor.

2. HOW CLAIMED.—Whenever money is due to the original contractor or he desires to draw some on his contract he must give the owner a statement under oath showing the name and address of every laborer in his employ who has not been paid, and of his subcontractors and

materialmen and giving the amount owing to any of them. This statement must be accompanied by a certificate under oath signed by every person furnishing material, machinery or fuel to such contractor. A similar statement must be furnished by each subcontractor. A materialman who furnishes materials only is not required to furnish this preliminary affidavit unless demanded. If he does more than furnish materials he is a subcontractor and must furnish the affidavit.

If owner or agent fails to make payments due a subcontractor for a period of 10 days, a subcontractor shall within four months thereafter file with the Recorder of the county where property is situated an affidavit containing an itemized statement and description of the amount due him, together with the affidavit of lien referred to above.

3. WHERE FILED.—Office of the Recorder of the county where the land, building or improvement is situated.

4. WHEN TO BE FILED.—The affidavit shall be filed within one of the following periods:
   (1) If lien arises in connection with a 1, 2 or 3 family dwelling or in connection with condominium property or in connection with home purchase contract, within 60 days from the date the last machinery, material, equipment or labor was furnished.
   (2) If the lien arises in connection with furnishing machinery, equipment, material or supplies to oil wells, derricks, or tanks, within 120 days from the date on which last machinery, equipment or supplies were furnished.
   (3) If lien is not within (1) or (2) above, then within 90 days from the date in which last machinery, materials, fuel or labor was furnished, except that the affidavit shall not be filed later than 60 days after the date on which the last machinery, material or fuel is furnished by any person or after last work is performed pursuant to the general contract at the property to be charged.

5. SERVICE OF COPY OF AFFIDAVIT FOR LIEN.—On owner within thirty (30) days after filing of affidavit for lien with recorder. If owner cannot be found, posted in a conspicuous place on the premises within 10 days after the expiration of the 30 days.

6. DURATION OF LIEN.—6 years after affidavit for lien is filed with Recorder. Where the lien attached to adjacent lots on which separate dwelling units are being constructed to be separately sold, the lien rights on any lot on which all construction has been completed and which has been conveyed to purchaser for value shall terminate either 60 days from the date on which the last labor and materials, machinery or fuel was furnished, or 60 days after the instrument of conveyance to such purchaser separating such lot from the contiguous or adjacent lots, shall be filed for recording, whichever is earlier, unless and except for lien rights which are evidenced by an affidavit filed for record in accordance with the statute before the expiration of said 60 day period.

7. FILING FEE.—$1 per 100 words, 20 cents for each name indexed.

8. CONTENTS OF AFFIDAVIT FOR LIEN.—1. Amount due over and above all setoffs. 2. Description of property to be charged. 3. Name and address of person to whom material or labor was furnished or performed and name of owner, part owner or lessee if known. 4. Date on which last of material was furnished or labor performed. 5. Subscribed and sworn to by claimant, his agent or attorney.

9. EXTENT OF LIEN.—The lien shall extend to the property upon which the work was done or for which the materials were furnished and upon the materials furnished and upon the interest, leasehold, or otherwise of the owner, part owner or lessee in the lot or land upon which the property stands or to which it may be removed, to the extent of the right, title and interest of the owner, part owner, or lessee, at the time the work was commenced, or materials were begun to be furnished by the contractor, under the original contract, and also to the extent of any subsequently acquired interest of any such owner, part owner or lessee. Where the improvement consists of two or more buildings, situated on contiguous or adjacent lots, the lien attaches to all improvements, together with the land, as in the case of a single improvement. Where the person owning the improvement has no legal title to the land the mechanic shall have a lien upon the building or structure and the forfeiture or surrender of any title or claim of lien, or equitable interest by such contracting person to such land shall not defeat the lien upon such building. Any lien claimant may pay off any prior recorded lien, and be subrogated to the rights of that lienor.

10. PRIORITIES.—No priority among several liens obtained upon the same job except for liens for manual labor performed during 30 days immediately preceding date of performance of last labor. Loans made for construction purposes or to pay off prior encumbrances, the proceeds of which are actually used in the improvement, are prior to all liens which are filed subsequent to the filing of the improvement mortgage. Mechanics' liens have priority over other liens, titles and encumbrances arising after commencement of the construction or repairs.

11. PUBLIC IMPROVEMENTS.—See Chapter 30, *infra,* Bonds on Public Works.

NOTE.—There are some special provisions relating to condominiums.

12. LIENS FOR IMPROVEMENTS OF OIL AND GAS WELLS.—Created and perfected in same manner

MECHANIC'S LIEN LAWS AND FEDERAL TAX LIEN LAW

as mechanics' liens except that such liens must be filed within 120 days from last date services performed or materials supplied.

OKLAHOMA

1. WHO MAY CLAIM.—Any person who shall perform labor or furnish material for the erection, alteration or repair of any building (or who shall furnish material and perform labor in putting up any fixtures, or who shall plant any trees, vines, plants or hedges, or who shall furnish labor, or material for buildings, or repairs any fence, footwalk or sidewalk), shall have lien upon the land upon which such buildings or improvements are made and upon such buildings and appurtenances. Miners and other employees in or about mines have lien on machinery, equipment, income, leases, etc., for payment for work done.

2. HOW CLAIMED.—By filing statement and verified affidavit in county in which the land is situated. In addition, a mechanic's lien cannot attach to an owner-occupied dwelling unless the contractor gives the owner notice of his rights before the first performance of labor or furnishing materials. The owner of equipment leased or rented must give written notice to the owner of the property that the equipment used was leased or rented.

3. WHERE RECORDED.—In the office of the County Clerk in the county where the land is situated.

4. WHEN TO BE RECORDED.—Original contractor has four months after the date upon which the material was last furnished or labor last performed, within which to file his statement for a lien; subcontractors, 90 days. Subcontractors must serve notice of filing on the owner.

5. DURATION OF LIEN.—Claim for laborer's lien lapses unless suit commenced within 8 months after work completed; all other liens action commenced within one year from date of filing lien claim, provided where note attached, one year from maturity of note.

6. FILING FEE.—$10 for the recording and filing of mechanics' or materialmen's liens and the release thereof.

7. NOTICE OF LIEN.—County Clerk shall charge notice of lien to owner of property on which lien attaches. The clerk may charge a maximum fee of $5 for mailing of such notice. The notice shall contain date of filing, name and address of party claiming lien, a legal description of the property and the amount claimed.

8. CONTENTS OF NOTICE OF LIEN.—Statement setting forth amount claimed and items thereof, name of the owner, the contractor and claimant, and description of the property subject to the lien, verified by affidavit. In addition, a lien cannot attach to an owner-occupied dwelling unless prior to first performance the contractor, subcontractor, laborer, or materialman provides a written notice with the following language:

NOTICE TO OWNER

YOU ARE HEREBY NOTIFIED THAT THE UNDERSIGNED PERSONS PERFORMING LABOR ON YOUR PROPERTY OR FURNISHING MATERIALS FOR THE CONSTRUCTION, REPAIR OR IMPROVEMENT OF YOUR PROPERTY WILL BE ENTITLED TO A LIEN AGAINST YOUR PROPERTY IF THEY ARE NOT PAID IN FULL, EVEN THOUGH YOU MAY HAVE PAID THE FULL CONTRACT PRICE TO YOUR CONTRACTOR. THIS COULD RESULT IN YOUR PAYING FOR LABOR AND MATERIALS TWICE. THIS LIEN CAN BE ENFORCED BY THE SALE OF YOUR PROPERTY. TO AVOID THIS RESULT, YOU MAY DEMAND FROM YOUR CONTRACTOR LIEN WAIVERS FROM ALL PERSONS PERFORMING LABOR OR FURNISHING MATERIALS FOR THE WORK ON YOUR PROPERTY. YOU MAY WITHHOLD PAYMENT TO THE CONTRACTOR IN THE AMOUNT OF ANY UNPAID CLAIMS FOR LABOR OR MATERIALS. YOU ALSO HAVE THE RIGHT TO DEMAND FROM YOUR CONTRACTOR A COMPLETE LIST OF ALL LABORERS AND MATERIAL SUPPLIERS UNDER YOUR CONTRACT, AND THE RIGHT TO DETERMINE FROM THEM IF THEY HAVE BEEN PAID FOR LABOR PERFORMED AND MATERIALS FURNISHED.

9. EXTENT OF LIEN.—Lien is upon the whole of the tract or piece of land, the buildings and appurtenances. If the title to the land is not in the person with whom contract was made, lien shall be allowed on the buildings and improvements separate from the real estate. The owner shall not be liable for a subcontractor's lien for an amount greater than he contracted to pay the original contractor.

10. PRIORITIES.—Such lien shall be preferred to all other liens or encumbrances which may attach to or upon such land, building or improvements subsequent to the commencement of such building or furnishing or putting up fixtures or machinery.

11. PUBLIC IMPROVEMENTS.—See Chapter 30, *infra*, Bonds on Public Works.

12. LIENS FOR IMPROVEMENT OF OIL OR GAS WELLS.—A lien exists for anyone contracting to perform labor or services, or furnish material, machinery and oil well supplies used in the digging,

drilling, torpedoing, operating, completing or repairing of any oil or gas well. The lien extends to the whole leasehold including the proceeds from sale of the oil or gas. The lien has priority as to all other encumbrances obtained subsequent to the commencement of the furnishing or putting up of the material or supplies. The lien will follow the property and be enforceable against the property wherever it may be found. Filing of a lien statement will constitute constructive notice of the lien to third parties. No lien on the proceeds from the sale of oil or gas produced shall be effective against any purchaser of such oil or gas until a copy of the statement of lien has been delivered to such purchaser by registered or certified mail. Notice of such lien is given and filed in same manner as mechanics' liens. Liens for oil and gas wells are limited to the leasehold estate; they do not affect any other interest in the real property involved. However, if the owner also owns a working interest in a well located thereon, the lien attaches the working interest.

OREGON

1. WHO MAY CLAIM.—(1) Any person performing labor upon, transporting or furnishing any material to be used in, or renting equipment used in the construction of any improvement, which includes any building, wharf, bridge, ditch, flume, reservoir, well, tunnel, fence, street, sidewalk, machinery, aqueduct and all other structures and superstructures, whenever it can be made applicable thereto, shall have a lien upon the improvement for the labor, transportation or material furnished or equipment rented at the instance of the owner of the improvement or his construction agent. (2) Any person who engages in or rents equipment for the preparation of a lot or parcel of land, or improves or rents equipment for the improvement of a street or road adjoining a lot or parcel of land at the request of the owner of the lot or parcel, shall have a lien upon the land for work done and materials furnished or equipment rented. (3) The lien for rented equipment is limited to the reasonable rental value of the equipment notwithstanding the terms of the underlying rental agreement. (4) Trustees of an employee benefit plan shall have a lien upon the improvement for the amount of contributions, due to labor performed on that improvement, required to be paid by agreement or otherwise into a fund of the employee benefit plan. (5) An architect, landscape architect, land surveyor, or registered engineer who, at the request of the owner or an agent of the owner, prepares plans, drawings, or specifications that are intended for use in or to facilitate the construction of an improvement or who supervises the construction shall have a lien upon the land and structures necessary for the use of the plans, drawings, or specifications so provided or supervision performed. (6) A landscape architect, land surveyor, or other person who prepares plans, drawings, surveys, or specifications that are used for the landscaping or preparation of a lot or parcel of land or who supervises the landscaping or preparation shall have a lien upon the land for the plans, drawings, surveys, or specifications used or supervision performed. (7) A person who performs labor on or assists in obtaining and handling timber or wood products.

2. HOW CLAIMED.—Except when material or labor described in (1) to (3), (5) and (6) above is furnished at the request of the owner, a person furnishing any materials or labor for which a lien may be claimed shall give a notice of the right to lien to the owner of the site. The notice may be given at any time during the progress of the improvement, but it only protects the right to claim a lien on those materials and that labor provided after a date which is 8 days not including Saturday, Sunday or holidays before the notice is delivered or mailed. No right to claim a lien under (5) or (6) above exists for any services provided for an owner-occupied residence at the request of an agent of the owner. The notice must include the following information and must be in substantially the following form:

NOTICE OF THE RIGHT TO LIEN

WARNING: READ THIS NOTICE. PROTECT YOURSELF FROM PAYING ANY CONTRACTOR OR SUPPLIER TWICE FOR THE SAME SERVICE.

To: _____   Date of mailing: _____
    Owner
    Owner's address

This is to inform you that _____ has begun to provide _____ (description of materials, labor or services) ordered by _____ for improvements to property you own. The property is located at _____.

A lien may be claimed for all materials, labor and services furnished after a date that is 10 days before this notice was mailed to you.

Even if you or your mortgage lender have made full payment to the contractor who ordered these materials or services, your property may still be subject to a lien unless the supplier providing

MECHANIC'S LIEN LAWS AND FEDERAL TAX LIEN LAW   19–51

this notice is paid. THIS IS NOT A LIEN. It is a notice sent to you for your protection in compliance with the construction lien laws of the State of Oregon.

This notice has been sent to you by:

NAME: _____
ADDRESS: _____
TELEPHONE: _____

IF YOU HAVE ANY QUESTIONS ABOUT THIS NOTICE, FEEL FREE TO CALL US.

IMPORTANT INFORMATION ON REVERSE SIDE

IMPORTANT INFORMATION FOR YOUR PROTECTION

Under Oregon's laws, those who work on your property or provide materials and are not paid have a right to enforce their claim for payment against your property. This claim is known as a construction lien.

If your contractor fails to pay subcontractors, material suppliers or laborers or neglects to make other legally required payments, the people who are owed money can look to your property for payment, *even if you have paid your contractor in full.*

The law states that all people hired by a contractor to provide you with materials, labor or services must give you a notice of the right to lien to let you know what they have provided.

WAYS TO PROTECT YOURSELF ARE:

—RECOGNIZE that this notice of delivery of materials, labor or services may result in a lien against your property unless all those supplying a notice of the right to lien have been paid.

—LEARN more about the lien laws and the meaning of this notice by contracting the Builders Board, an attorney or the firm sending this notice.

—WHEN PAYING your contractor for materials, labor or services, you may make checks payable jointly to the contractor and the firm furnishing materials, labor or services for which you have received a notice of the right to lien.

—GET EVIDENCE that all firms from whom you have received a notice of the right to lien have been paid or have waived the right to claim a lien against your property.

—CONSULT an attorney, a professional escrow company or your mortgage lender.

3. WHERE FILED.—County Clerk in county or counties where such property is located.

4. WHEN TO BE FILED.—Every person claiming a lien as a contractor or subcontractor excluding persons renting equipment, trustees of employment benefit plans, architects and landscape architects, shall file a claim not later than 90 days after ceasing to provide labor, rent, equipment or furnished materials or 60 days after completion of construction, whichever is earlier. Every other person claiming a lien shall file the claim not later than 60 days after the completion of construction. The person filing a claim for lien shall deliver to owner not later than 20 days after the date of filing a notice in writing that the claim has been filed.

5. DURATION OF LIEN.—Six months unless suit commenced; or if a credit be given within 6 months after expiration of credit term but no longer than 2 years from date claim for lien is filed.

6. FILING FEE.—Minimum fee is $5.50 for filings in the county clerk. Fee dependent upon number of folios lien recorded in.

7. CONTENTS OF LIEN CLAIM.—Lien claim must contain: (1) true statement of demand, after credit and deductions; (2) name of owner; (3) name of person by whom claimant employed or to whom he furnished materials; (4) description of property, including address. The claim must be verified by the claimant or another person having a knowledge of the facts.

8. EXTENT OF LIEN.—Lien applies to land upon which any improvement is constructed together with any such space as may be required for the convenient use and occupation thereof to be determined by the court at the time of the foreclosure of the lien. If the owner has less than absolute ownership then only his interest in the land shall be subject to the lien.

9. PRIORITIES.—Lien takes priority over any lien, mortgage (except purchase money mortgages or duly perfected security interest and purchase money security interest), or other encumbrance not recorded, or filed at time the improvement was commenced, or materials were commenced to be furnished and all prior liens, mortgages or other encumbrances upon the land on which such improvement is situated when altered or repaired. To enforce lien improvement may be sold separately from the land. If proceeds of sale are insufficient to pay all claimants the payments shall be made to each class pro rata. A lien for materials and supplies shall have priority over any recorded mortgage on land or buildings if the person supplying the materials, not later than 8 days not including Saturdays, Sundays or holidays after date of delivery, delivers a notice of the supply to the mortgagee. Unless the mortgage or trust deed is given to secure a loan made to finance an

alteration or repair, a lien for the alteration or repair of an improvement commenced and made subsequent to the date of record of a mortgage or trust deed on the improvement or on the site shall not take precedence over the mortgage or trust deed. Suits to enforce a lien shall have preference over any other civil suit, except suits to which the state is a party and shall be tried without unnecessary delay.

10. PUBLIC IMPROVEMENTS.—See Chapter 30, *infra,* Bonds on Public Works.

PENNSYLVANIA

1. WHO MAY CLAIM.—Contractors and subcontractors are entitled to a lien for all debts due for labor or materials furnished in the erection or construction, or the alteration or repair of an improvement, provided, that the amount of the claim exceeds $500. Persons not entitled to liens include persons who are not contractors or subcontractors, even though such persons furnished labor or material to an improvement; contractors or subcontractors furnishing labor or materials for a purely public purpose; and persons furnishing material subject to a security interest under the Uniform Commercial Code. Persons who furnish labor or material to subcontractors do not have a right of lien.

2. HOW CLAIMED.—Every claimant must file a claim with the prothonotary of the county where improvement located and serve notice of filing upon the owner within one month after filing.

3. WHERE FILED.—The claim must be filed with the prothonotary of the county where the improvement is located. Where the improvement is located in more than one county, the claim may be filed in any one or more said counties but shall be effective only as to the part of the property in the county in which it has been filed.

4. WHEN FILED.—Claim must be filed within 4 months after the completion of the work.

5. NOTICE TO OWNER.—Notice of intention to file a claim must only be given by a subcontractor.

a. Preliminary Notice.—The subcontractor for alterations and repairs must give to the owner on or before the date of completion of his work a written preliminary notice of his intention to file a claim after the amount due or to become due is not paid. This notice must include the name of the subcontractor, a general description of the property against which the claim is to be filed, the amount then due or to become due and a statement of intention to file a claim.

b. Formal Notice.—In all cases a subcontractor must give notice to the owner at least thirty days before he files his intention to file a claim except if proceeding in response to a rule as discussed in (d) below.

c. Notice of Fact of Filing Claim.—Notice must be given by all claimants whether contractors or subcontractors. Notice must be served upon the owner within one month after filing, giving the court term and number of date of filing of the claim.

An affidavit of service or notice or the acceptance of service must be filed within twenty days after such service setting forth the date and manner of service. Failure to serve such notice or file the affidavit within the time specified shall be sufficient ground for striking off the claim.

d. Rule by Owner.—After completion of the work by a subcontractor any owner or contractor may file a rule or rules in the court in which the claim may be filed requiring the party named to file his claim within 30 days after notice of the rule. Failure to file the claim within such period shall defeat the right to do so. If subcontractor files as a result of the rule, no notice of intention to file is required. Where a claim is filed by a subcontractor, owner may give written notice thereof to a subcontractor.

6. CONTENTS OF THE CLAIM.—The claim of lien must state:

(1) the name of the party claimant and whether he files as contractor of subcontractor;

(2) the name and address of the owner or reputed owner;

(3) the date of completion of the claimant's work;

(4) if filed by subcontractor the name of the person with whom he contracted and the dates on which preliminary notice if required and of formal notice of intention to file a claim were given;

(5) if filed by a contractor under a contract or contracts for an agreed sum an identification of the contract and a general statement of the kind and character of the labor or materials furnished;

(6) in all other cases than that set forth in clause (5) of this section a detailed statement of the kind and character of the labor or materials furnished or both and the prices charged for each thereof;

(7) the amount or sum claimed to be due;

(8) such description of the improvement and of the property claimed to be subject to the lien as may be reasonably necessary to identify them.

7. DURATION OF LIEN.—An action to obtain a judgment must be commenced within 2 years from date of filing of lien unless time extended in writing by owner. A verdict may be recovered or judgment entered within 5 years from date of filing claim.

8. FILING FEES.—$10; $9 in home rule counties and in smaller counties.

9. EXTENT OF LIEN.—Every improvement and the estate or title of the owner in the property is subject to the lien. Claimant may maintain a lien against the owner in fee or any other person having any estate or interest in the property who by agreement, express or implied, contracts for the erection or alteration of the property. If the subcontractor has actual knowledge of the total contract price between the owner and contractor before he began work, his lien will be limited to the unpaid balance to the contractor or a pro rata portion thereof.

10. PRIORITIES.—Liens filed take effect and have priority: (1) in the case of an improvement, as of the date of the visible commencement of the improvement, and (2) in the case of alteration or repair of an improvement, as of the date of filing of the claim.

11. WAIVER OF LIENS.—The contractor may enter into an agreement with the owner waiving the right of the contractor and of all persons under him to file or maintain a mechanic's lien claim. Such an agreement is binding upon a subcontractor, provided such subcontractor has had actual notice thereof before he has furnished any labor or material, or a signed copy of said waiver has been filed in the office of the Prothonotary of the Court of Common Pleas of the county or counties where the structure or other improvement is situated prior to the commencement of the work upon the ground, or within ten days after the execution of the principal contract, or in less than ten days prior to the contract with the claimant. Such a waiver of lien is indexed by the prothonotary.

Although an agreement waiving liens has been filed, the owner may, by an appropriate agreement, restore the right of lien either to the contractor or to any one or more subcontractors. Such a waiver of the waiver will not restore the right of lien to persons other than those to whom the right is restored by the owner.

A waiver appearing in a contract between the contractor and one not intended in good faith to be the owner does not defeat the right of one who furnishes labor and material to such a contractor to file a lien.

12. PUBLIC IMPROVEMENTS.—See Chapter 30, *infra*, Bonds on Public Works.

RHODE ISLAND

1. WHO MAY CLAIM.—Any person who constructs, erects, alters or repairs any building, canal, turnpike, railroad or other improvement with the consent of the owner, tenant or lessee (but not of the state) for all work done and for materials furnished.

A covenent, promise, agreement of understanding in, or in connection with or collateral to, a contract or agreement relative to the construction, alteration, repair or maintenance of a building, structure, appurtenance and appliance, including moving, demolition and excavating connected therewith, purporting to bar the filing of a notice of contract or the taking of any steps to enforce a lien is against public policy and is void and unenforceable.

2. HOW CLAIMED.—By serving and filing a notice of intention to claim a lien.

3. WHERE FILED.—In the records of land evidence in the city or town in which the land is located.

4. WHEN TO FILE.—Within 150 days after the notice is mailed.

5. SERVICE OF COPY OF NOTICE.—A copy of the notice must be served not later than 120 days after furnishing work or materials by certified or registered mail with return receipt requested, addressed to the last known address of the owner or lessee or, if not known to the address of the land. If the notice is returned undelivered it must be filed with its envelope within 30 days after the return and in no event more than 120 days after the mailing. Claimant must also mail a copy of notice by certified mail to inspector of buildings of the city or town. An hourly paid employee has an enforceable lien without regard to service and filing of notice. Architects and engineers must serve notice within 10 days after visible commencement of construction.

6. CONTENTS OF NOTICE OF INTENTION.—The notice of intention shall contain the name of the owner of record of the land or if the lien is claimed against the interest of the lessee, the name of the lessee, general description of the land, a general description of the work to be done or of the materials to be furnished, the name and address of the person for whom directly the work has been done or the materials furnished, the name and address of the person mailing such notice, and a statement that the sender may perfect his lien by filing the notice of intention within 120 days. The filing of the notice perfects the lien of work done 120 days before the notice and thereafter, but not for work done before the 120-day period.

7. DURATION OF LIEN.—Unless renewed, the notice of intention to claim a lien expires one year from the date of filing.
8. FILING FEE.—$1 for filing notice of intention to claim a lien and renewals.
9. PRIORITY OF LIEN.—All liens receive distribution equally. Liens are senior to any subsequently recorded encumbrances, but junior to prior recorded encumbrances.
10. EXTENT OF LIEN.—Lien improvement and land on which situated; when contract with husband of owner consent in writing of both husband and wife required.
11. PUBLIC IMPROVEMENTS.—See Chapter 30, *infra*, Bonds on Public Works.

SOUTH CAROLINA

1. WHO MAY CLAIM.—Any contractor, subcontractor, laborer, or materialman who furnishes materials used in the erection or repair of any building upon real estate with the consent or at the request of the owner thereof, or of his agent, contractor, or subcontractor. A surveyor of real estate acting pursuant to an agreement with the owner of the property. Liens are also upon vessels, railroads and for the boring and equipping of wells. The term laborer includes persons providing private security guard services at the site.
2. HOW CLAIMED.—By serving upon the owner or the person in possession and filing sworn statement of account describing property covered and naming the owner or owners thereof.
3. WHERE FILED.—In the office of the Register of Mesne Conveyances or Clerk of the Court of the county where property is situated.
4. WHEN TO BE FILED.—At any time during the progress of work and furnishing of materials or within ninety days after the party claiming the lien ceases to labor or to furnish labor or materials for such building or structure.
5. SERVICE OF COPY OF NOTICE.—Copy of notice must be served upon owner or, if owner cannot be found, upon person in possession.
6. DURATION OF LIEN.—Unless a suit for enforcing the lien is commenced and a notice of pendency of the action is filed, within six months after person desiring to avail himself thereof ceases to labor on or to furnish labor or material for such building or structure, the lien shall be dissolved.
7. FILING FEE.—$4 plus $1 per page over 3.
8. CONTENTS OF NOTICE OF LIEN.—A statement of a just and true account of the amount due with all just credits given, together with a description of the property intended to be covered by the lien, sufficiently accurate for identification, with the name of the owner or owners of the property, if known, which certificate shall be subscribed and sworn to by the person claiming the lien, or by someone in his behalf. Lien can include amount of reasonable attorney's fees.
9. EXTENT OF LIEN.—The lien shall extend to the building or structure and the interest of the owner thereof and the land or place upon which the same is situated. A subcontractor's lien shall in no event exceed the amount due by the owner under the original contract.
10. PRIORITIES.—Lien of laborer, mechanic, subcontractor or materialman is subject to existing liens of which he had actual or constructive notice. The liens of laborer, materialman and subcontractor take precedence over the lien of the principal contractor. Mortgage recorded at date of contract is prior to lien but attachment subsequent to recording statement of lien is inferior.
11. PUBLIC IMPROVEMENTS.—See Chapter 30, *infra*, Bonds on Public Works.

SOUTH DAKOTA

1. WHO MAY CLAIM.—Whoever furnishes skill, labor, services, or materials for the improvement, development or operation of building, fixture, bridge, or fence, or other structure or public utility or mine or well. Liens also to persons furnishing services, skills, labor, parts, materials, etc., for the alteration, repair, storage, etc., of personal property.
An owner may protect his property against liens for unauthorized improvements by serving upon persons doing the work, within 5 days after knowledge thereof, written notice that improvement not made at his instance, or by posting such notice in a conspicuous place on the premises.
2. HOW CLAIMED.—By filing verified statement of some person shown by such verification to have knowledge of facts stated. Contractor files a brief statement of the nature of his contract, which statement constitutes his notice of lien. In addition, subcontractor must serve notice of his claim on the owner.
3. WHERE FILED.—With the Register of Deeds of the county in which improved premises are situated. With Secretary of State if filing against a public utility.
4. WHEN TO BE FILED.—Subcontractors, materialmen and laborers must file within 120 days after doing the last of such work or furnishing the last item of such skill, material or machinery.

Persons other than original contractor may serve upon owner at any time notice of claim. Owner within 15 days after completion of the contract may require person having such lien to furnish him with an itemized and verified account of the claim, the amount thereof and his name and address. No action shall be commenced or enforcement of the lien until 10 days after this statement is furnished. Before filing lien with Register of Deeds claimant must mail to the property owner, at his last known address by registered or certified mail, a copy of the lien statement, and receipt for mailing must be attached to the lien statement and filed in the Office of the Register of Deeds.

5. SERVICE OF COPY OF NOTICE.—Notice must be served by registered or certified mail prior to filing. Filed statement must be accompanied by Post Office receipt. Owner may demand written itemized account within 15 days after the contract is completed. Owner may then pay claim or claimant may proceed to enforce his lien upon the expiration of 10 days after furnishing such statement.

6. DURATION OF LIEN.—Action to establish the same must be instituted within six years after the date of the last item of the claim as set forth in the filed lien statement; provided that upon written demand of the owner, his agent or contractor served on the person holding the lien, requiring him to commence suit to enforce such lien, suit shall be commenced within thirty days thereafter or the lien shall be forfeited.

7. FILING FEE.—$3.

8. CONTENTS OF STATEMENT OF LIEN.—(a) A notice of intention to claim and hold a lien and the amount thereof. (b) That such amount is due and owing to the claimant for labor performed or for skill, material or machinery furnished and for what improvement the same was done or supplied. (c) The names and addresses of the claimant and of the person for or to whom performed or furnished. (d) The dates when the first and last items of the claimant's contribution to the improvement were made. (e) The name of the owner thereof at the time of making such statement according to the best information then had. (f) A description of the premises to be charged, identifying same with reasonable certainty. (g) An itemized statement of account upon which lien is claimed.

9. EXTENT OF LIEN.—If work or materials made under contract with owner for an agreed price, lien shall be for the sum agreed on plus cost of any additional material or work agreed on, otherwise for the reasonable value of work done. Lien shall not extend or affect any right in any homestead otherwise except by law.

10. PRIORITIES.—The liens shall, as against the owner of the land, attach and take effect from the time the first item of material or labor is furnished upon the premises by the lien claimant, and shall be preferred to any mortgage or other encumbrance not then of record, unless the lienholder had actual notice thereof. As against the owner of the land it is preferred to any mortgage or other encumbrance not on record unless lienholder had actual notice thereof. As against a bona fide purchaser, mortgagor, or encumbrancer without notice, however, no lien shall be attached prior to the actual and visible beginning of the improvement of the grounds, but a person having a contract for such improvement may file with the Register of Deeds of the county within which the premises are situated, a brief statement of the nature of such contract, which statement shall be notice of his lien for the contract price or value of the contribution of such improvement thereafter made by him or at his instance.

11. PUBLIC IMPROVEMENTS.—See Chapter 30, *infra*, Bonds on Public Works.

12. LIENS FOR IMPROVEMENTS OF OIL AND GAS WELLS.—The mechanic's lien laws are equally applicable to oil and gas wells.

TENNESSEE

1. WHO MAY CLAIM.—The mechanic, contractor, laborer, founder, or machinist who does the work or furnishes the materials or any part of them, or puts thereon any fixtures, machinery by special contract with the owner or his agent. Any land surveyor who has, by special contract with the owner or his agent, performed upon any lot of ground or tract of land the practice of land surveying. Licensed architects and engineers have liens on the land or building for which they have performed services under special contracts with the owner or his agent. Every journeyman or other person employed by such mechanic to work on the building, or fixtures, machinery, etc.

2. HOW CLAIMED.—Original contractor and furnisher must bring suit within one year after completion of the work. No statutory provision for filing of claim. Subcontractor, furnisher or laborer employed by original contractor, must serve on owner written notice of lien within 90 days after structure is completed, setting forth amount due, by registering statement of amount due for work or material furnished with County Register. Suit must be brought within ninety days to enforce lien of subcontractor, laborer and materialman.

3. WHERE FILED.—A copy of the subcontractor's notice of lien must be filed with County Register in the county where the premises, or any part, are situated.

4. WHEN TO BE FILED.—The subcontractor, furnisher, or laborer employed by original contractor may file claim for lien at any time within ninety days after notice to owner.

5. SERVICE OF COPY OF NOTICE.—Tennessee's Truth in Construction and Consumer Protection Act of 1975 requires any contractor who is about to enter into a contract, either written or oral, for improving real property with the owner or owners thereof, prior to commencing the improvement of said real property or making of the contract, to deliver by register mail or otherwise, to the owner or owners of the real property to be improved written notice.

6. TIME OF ATTACHMENT OF LIEN.—Such lien shall relate to and take effect from the time of the visible commencement of operations, excluding however, demolition, surveying, excavating, clearing, filling or grading and the delivery of materials therefor. If there be a cessation of all operations at the site of the improvement for more than 90 days, any lien for labor of any nature performed or for materials of any nature furnished after the visible resumption of operations shall relate to and take effect only from said visible resumption of operations.

7. DURATION OF LIEN.—The mechanic, founder or machinist under contract with owner has lien for one year after the work is finished or materials are furnished and until the decision of any suit brought within that time. The lien in favor of the subcontractor, laborer, or furnisher employed by original contract extends for period of ninety days after notice to the owner. If suit is brought in a Justice's court, after judgment is obtained and within 20 days an abstract thereof must be registered to constitute a lien. Owner of property against which lien has been filed can, before entry of judgement enforcing the lien, discharge the lien by posting a bond for double the amount thereof.

8. FILING FEE.—$6 plus $3 per page for each additional page over 2.

9. CONTENTS OF NOTICE OF LIEN.—1. Statement of the labor performed or materials furnished and value thereof. 2. Description of the premises and by whom employed.

10. EXTENT OF LIEN.—The claims secured by lien for work and labor done and materials furnished shall in no case exceed the amount agreed to be paid by the owner or proprietor in his original contract with the undertaker. Lien attaches to building, fixture or improvements as well as land upon which same is situated.

11. PRIORITIES.—Take precedence over all other encumbrances originated after commencement of services or furnishing of materials. Lien of principal contractor is inferior to other mechanic's liens. Prior mortgagee may consent to liens' taking priority, either expressly or by failure to object thereto, within 10 days after receiving a notice of the same.

12. PUBLIC IMPROVEMENTS.—See Chapter 30, *infra,* Bonds on Public Works.

13. LIENS FOR IMPROVEMENT OF WELLS OR EQUIPMENT.—Lien to persons who have drilled a well by contract with owner or authorized agent against tract of land for all labor, materials and equipment used or furnished by driller. Lien is effective for 2 years after completion of well or after furnishing pump or other apparatus unless sooner discharged by payment in full.

14. MISCELLANEOUS.—Requires a contractor who is about to enter into a contract involving real property to deliver to the owner written notice to be signed by the owner which contains information that includes the address of the property, and by which the owner acknowledges that a lien may be imposed against the property. Upon completion of the contract or improvement and upon the receipt of the contract price, the contractor shall deliver to the owner a notice providing that the contractor agrees to pay all subcontractors for services, labor or materials no later than ten (10) days from the date a bill is rendered for such services, labor or materials; that the owner has accepted the work and paid for it in full and that the contractor agrees to hold the owner harmless against any liens, claims or suits by others in connection with the work. In the event the contractors fails to comply with the act, he shall be guilty of a misdemeanor, and subject to fine of not less than $5,000 nor more than $20,000 or confinement in the county workhouse, not to exceed 11 months and 29 days. Notice of completion cannot be registered before completion of the improvement.

TEXAS

1. WHO MAY CLAIM.—Any person or firm, lumber dealer, or corporation, artisan, laborer, mechanic or subcontractor who may perform labor or furnish specially fabricated material, machinery, fixtures or tools, (a) to erect or repair any house, building or improvement whatever, (b) for the construction or repair of levees or embankments, for the reclamation of overflow lands, (c) or who may furnish any material for the construction or repair of any railroad within this State. The word "improvement" shall include clearing, grubbing, draining or fencing of land and shall

MECHANIC'S LIEN LAWS AND FEDERAL TAX LIEN LAW

include wells, cisterns, tanks, reservoirs or artificial lakes or pools and all pumps, siphons and windmills or other machinery used for raising water.

2. HOW CLAIMED.—Original contractor must execute an affidavit claiming a lien and send two copies thereof by certified or registered mail to the owner. Every subcontractor, materialman, or laborer must execute an affidavit claiming a lien and send two copies by certified or registered mail to the owner.

3. WHERE FILED.—With County Clerk of the county in which such property is located.

4. WHEN TO BE FILED.—Must file affidavit and send two copies to owner within 120 days after accrual of indebtedness if original contractor, within 90 days if other than original contractor.

The indebtedness accrues immediately upon any material breach or termination of the original contract by the owner on the 10th day of the month next following the month in which the original contract was completed, finally settled, or abandoned. In the case of an artisan, laborer or mechanic, at the end of the calendar week during which the labor was performed; in the case of a subcontractor on the 10th day of the month next following the last month in which labor was performed or material furnished; in the case of specially fabricated material on the 10th day of the month next following the last month in which delivery was made, or in which delivery would normally have been required at the job site, or immediately upon any material breach or termination of the original contract.

5. SERVICE OF COPY OF NOTICE.—Notices are required as a condition precedent to the validity of their liens in the case of subcontractors, materialmen and laborers as follows:

(A) If an agreement providing for retainage exists, written notice must be given to the owner not later than 36 days after the 10th day of the month next following the making of the agreement, and a copy to the original contractor where the agreement is between a claimant and a subcontractor. Notice must be sent by certified or registered mail, state the sum to be retained, the due dates if known, and generally indicate the nature of the agreement. Lien for retainage may not be in greater amount than amount specified to be retained in contract between claimant and contractor.

(B) The claimant may elect to give the following notices. Where claim arises from debt incurred by a subcontractor: notice of the unpaid balance due the original contractor not later than 36 days after the 10th day of the month next following each month in which claimant's labor or material was furnished; and a like notice to owner not later than 90 days after such 10th day. Where claim arises from a debt incurred from the original contractor, no notice need be given to the contractor, but notice must be given to the owner. A copy of the statement or billing is sufficient notice, and if it is to authorize owner to retain funds for payment, it must contain or be accompanied by a statement that owner may be personally liable and his property subject to lien unless he withholds payment or the bill is paid.

(C) If claim is based on items specially fabricated, notice to owner must be given not later than 36 days after the 10th day of the month next following receipt and acceptance of order for material, stating that the order was received and accepted together with the price; in cases where indebtedness was incurred by one other than an original contractor a copy must also be given to the original contractor.

An owner withholding payments from the original contractor must pay a claim, which is not disputed by the contractor, within 30 days after receiving copy of the demand sent to the owner.

6. DURATION OF LIEN.—In general the lien is valid until the indebtedness secured thereby is barred by the statute of limitations. Where surety bonds are filed indemnifying against liens on private improvements, the claimant has 30 days after notice is given of the filing of such bond in which suit may be brought.

7. FILING FEE.—The filing fee depends upon the length of the contract or statement of the account to be recorded.

8. CONTENTS OF STATEMENT OF LIEN.—The affidavit claiming a lien must be signed by the claimant or his agent and contain in substance:

(1) a sworn statement of his claim including amount, the copy of agreement or contract, if any, may be attached;

(2) the name of owner;

(3) a general statement of the kind of work done or materials furnished;

(4) name of the person by whom claimant was employed or to whom the materials or labor were furnished, and name of original contractor;

(5) a description of the property sought to be charged with the lien, sufficient for identification.

9. EXTENT OF LIEN.—If work performed for or material furnished to owner direct, the lien extends to the extent of the price due; if furnished to a contractor, the owner cannot be made liable for more than the contract price of the improvement. Lien attaches to building or improvement

and lot or lots of land on which same situated; if land is in the county the lien will attach to land to the extent of 50 acres.

10. PRIORITIES.—The lien upon the improvement shall be preferred to any prior lien or encumbrance upon the land on which the structure was put, or labor performed, but liens upon the structure and land existing at the time of the inception of the lien are not affected. The time of the inception of the lien refers to the occurrence of the earliest of any of the following events: (1) the actual commencement of work; or (2) if the construction agreement is in writing, recording it in the mechanic's lien records of the county wherein the land is located; or (3) if the construction agreement is oral, recording of an affidavit containing a description of the land, the name and address of the lien claimant and the name and address of the person with whom he has contracted for the work, and a general description of the improvements contracted for. The liens of the subcontractor, laborers and materialmen shall be preferred to the creditors of the principal contractor. Except as is otherwise provided, the liens for work performed or materials furnished shall be equal without reference to date of filing account or lien. If the proceeds are insufficient to pay all in full, they shall share *pro rata*. Whenever work is done whereby a lien may be claimed, it is the duty of the owner to retain, during the progress of such work and for 30 days after the work is completed, 10% of the contract price. All persons sending notices or filing affidavits claiming a lien no later than 30 days after the work is completed shall have a lien upon the fund so retained by the owner with preference to artisans, mechanics, who share ratably to the extent of their claims, with the balance to be shared ratably among all other participating claimants. If the owner fails to retain the fund, the claimants have liens at least to the extent of the fund which should have been retained against the improvement, lands, etc.

11. PUBLIC IMPROVEMENTS.—See Chapter 30, *infra*, Bonds on Public Works.

12. LIENS FOR IMPROVEMENT OF GAS AND OIL WELLS.—A lien is accorded to any person furnishing labor, material or services under contract with the owner of any land, mine, or quarry, gas, oil, or mineral leasehold interest, or pipe line for digging, drilling, operating, completing, maintaining or repairing. The lien extends to the supplies and materials furnished and to the property or goods for or upon which furnished. Verified lien statement must be filed within six months after indebtedness accrues in the Office of the Clerk of the county where the property is located. In the case of a subcontractor, a notice of claim must be served on the owner at least 10 days prior to filing lien statement.

UTAH

1. WHO MAY CLAIM.—Contractors, subcontractors and all persons performing any services or furnishing or renting any materials or equipment used in the construction, alteration or improvement of any building or structure or improvement to any premises in any manner, or persons who shall do work or furnish materials for prospecting, development, preservation or working of any mining claim, mine, quarry, oil or gas well or deposit. Licensed architects and engineers and artisans may all have lien for value of service or labor performed or materials furnished for the value thereof.

2. HOW CLAIMED.—By filing a claim containing a notice of intention to hold and claim a lien.

3. WHERE FILED.—With County Recorder in county in which property or some part is located.

4. WHEN TO BE FILED.—By original contractor within 100 days and every other person within 80 days after the completion of his contract, except that a subcontractor or anyone who supplies labor or materials at the instance of request of the original contractor may file within 80 days after the original contractor has completed the contract.

5. SERVICE OF COPY OF NOTICE.—Within 30 days after filing notice of lien, the lien claimant shall deliver or mail by certified mail to either the reputed owner or record owner of the real property a copy of the said notice of lien. Where the record owner's current address is not readily available, the copy of the claim may be mailed to the last known address of the record owner using for such purpose the names and addresses appearing on the last completed real property assessment rolls of the county where the affected property is located. Failure to deliver or mail the notice of lien to the reputed owner or record owner shall prevent the lien claimant from collection of interest or costs and attorney's fees against the reputed owner or record owner in an action to enforce the lien.

6. DURATION OF LIEN.—Must be enforced within 12 months after completion of original contract or suspension of work thereunder for 30 days.

7. FILING FEE.—$5. If more than one description, 50¢ for each.

8. CONTENTS OF NOTICE OF LIEN.—A statement of the demand, after deducting all just credits and offsets, with the name of the owner of the property, if known, and also the name of the person by whom the claimant was employed, or to whom he furnished the material, with a statement

of the terms, time given, and conditions of his contract, specifying the time when the first and last labor was performed, or the first and last material furnished, and also a description of the property to be charged with the lien, sufficient for identification, which claim must be verified by oath of claimant or other person.

9. EXTENT OF LIEN.—Lien shall extend only to such interests as the owner or lessee may have in the real estate. Subcontractors' liens shall extend to the full contract price. But if at the time of commencement to do work or furnish materials, owner has paid upon the contract any portion of the contract price either in money or property the lien of the contractor shall extend only to such unpaid balance and the lien of any subcontractor having notice of such payment shall be limited to the unpaid balance of the contract price. No part of the contract price shall by the terms of any contract be made payable nor shall the same nor any part thereof be paid in advance of the commencement of the work for the purpose of defeating the lien law. Lien shall extend to so much of the land on which the improvement is situated as may be necessary for its convenience and use and if the improvement shall occupy two or more lots or other subdivisions of land they shall be deemed as one lot and lien shall attach all machinery and other fixtures used in connection with such improvement.

10. PRIORITIES.—Such a lien is prior to an attachment, levy or garnishment by the original contractor and is preferred to encumbrance which may have attached to the land subsequent to the commencement of the building—or any unrecorded encumbrance. Lien of principal contractor is inferior to the other mechanic's liens; among the latter there is no priority.

11. PUBLIC IMPROVEMENTS.—See Chapter 30, *infra,* Bonds on Public Works.

12. REMARKS.—In the case of a building contract involving more than $2,000 the owner must require from the contractor a bond equal to the contract price running to the owner and conditioned for the payment of the accounts contracted. An owner, failing to demand and receive such bond, is held personally liable to materialmen and subcontractors for debts of contractor.

VERMONT

1. WHO MAY CLAIM.—A person who proceeds in pursuance of a contract for erecting, repairing, moving or altering a building, steam engine or water wheel attached to real estate, or for furnishing materials or labor therefor has a lien; and a person who performs labor or furnishes material to the amount of $15 or more, in the above named works, under an agreement with the contractor or subcontractor of the owner shall have a lien.

2. HOW CLAIMED.—Claimant must file signed written memorandum. Notice of such memorandum must be given by materialmen and laborers to the owner or his agent that the mechanic will claim a lien for labor to be performed or materials to be furnished. Materialmen, laborers, and contractors file for record a written memorandum asserting claim.

3. WHERE FILED.—Town Clerk of town in which real estate is situated.

4. WHEN TO BE FILED.—Within 60 days from time payment becomes due.

5. SERVICE OF COPY OF NOTICE.—Required of materialmen and laborers.

6. DURATION OF LIEN.—Three months from time of filing of the memorandum if payment was then due or within three months after payment is due action may be instituted. If no filing is made, the lien shall continue in force for sixty days from the time when payment becomes due for such labor or materials, and the judgment may be recorded in the office of the Clerk of the town where the property is situated.

7. FILING FEE.—60¢ per folio, minimum fee is $1.

8. CONTENTS OF STATEMENT OF LIEN.—Statements of contract and statements of items of claim signed by the party claiming the lien.

9. EXTENT OF LIEN.—Not to exceed the amount due at the time when lien is asserted or to become due by virtue of such contract or agreement. Lien attaches to project and lot of land on which situated.

10. PRIORITIES.—Does not take precedence over a mortgage given by the owner upon such building, etc., as security for the payment of money loaned and to be used by said owner in payment of the expenses of the same. No priority among claimant with mechanic's liens.

11. PUBLIC IMPROVEMENTS.—See Chapter 30, *infra,* Bonds on Public Works.

VIRGINIA

1. WHO MAY CLAIM.—All persons performing labor or furnishing materials, including surveying, of the value of $50 for the construction, removal, repair or improvement of any building or structure permanently annexed to the freehold and all persons performing labor or furnishing materials for the construction of any railroad. The statute includes the furnishing of labor or materials in connection with wells, excavations, sidewalks, driveways, pavements, parking lots, retaining walls, curb

and/or gutter, breakwater, water system, drainage structure, filtering system (including septic or waste disposal systems) or swimming pools and grading, clearing or earth moving and furnishing of shrubbery, sod, sand, gravel, brick and other materials. Every mechanic who shall alter or repair any request of any person legally in possession thereof under a reservation of title contract, chattel mortgage, deed or trust, or other instrument securing money, mechanic shall have a lien thereon for reasonable charges to the extent of $75, plus lien against proceeds, if any, remaining after satisfaction of all prior security interests or liens, and may retain possession of such property until such charges are paid. Any person providing labor or materials for the installation of streets, sanitary sewers or water lines for the purpose of providing access of service to the individual lots in a development shall have a lien from each individual lot in the development for that fractional part of the total cost of such labor or material as is obtained by using one as the numerator and the number of lots as the denominator; provided, however, no such lien shall be valid as to any such lot unless the person providing such labor or material shall, prior to the sale of such lot, file with the Clerk of the Circuit Court of the jurisdiction in which such land lies a document setting forth the full disclosure of the nature of the lien to be claimed, the amount claimed against each lot and a description of the development.

2. HOW CLAIMED.—By filing memorandum under oath. Subcontractor must also give notice of contract and probable amount of claim to owner or original contractor, and file such notice in order to hold owner or general contractor personally liable.

3. WHERE FILED.—In Clerk's office of county or city in which property is located. In the City of Richmond—file in Clerk's office of Chancery Court if property is located north of James River; and in Clerk's office of the Circuit Court, Division II if south of James River.

4. WHEN TO BE FILED.—General Contractors—Any time after work is commenced, but not later than 90 days after the last day of the month in which he last performed or furnished material, and in no event later than 90 days after the improvement is completed.

5. SERVICE OF COPY OF NOTICE.—Subcontractor must give notice in writing to owner of property of the amount and character of his claim in addition to the filing of the memorandum.

6. DURATION OF LIEN.—No suit to enforce any lien may be brought after six months from time memorandum of lien was recorded, or after 60 days from the time the building, structure or railroad was completed or work terminated, whichever time shall last occur.

7. FILING FEE.—Minimum of $9 for up to 3½ pages and $1 for each additional page.

8. CONTENTS OF STATEMENT OF LIEN.—Memorandum showing the names and addresses of the owner of the property, and of the claimant of the lien, amount and consideration of his claim, the time or times when the same is or will become due and type of materials or services and type of structure on which work or services performed. Statutory forms are provided for. Any number of such memoranda may be filed, but no memorandum may include sums due for labor or materials furnished more than 150 days prior to the last day on which labor was performed or material furnished to the job preceding the filing. Retainages of up to ten percent of the contract price may be included in any memorandum. Any person who, with intent to mislead, includes in the memorandum work not performed upon, or materials not furnished for the property described in the memorandum forfeits any right to this lien.

9. EXTENT OF LIEN.—Upon the buildings or structures, and so much land therewith as shall be necessary for the convenient use and enjoyment thereof to the extent of the interest of the owner therein and upon such railroad and franchises for work done and materials furnished. A subcontractor may not perfect a lien for an amount greater than the amount in which the owner is, or shall thereafter become, indebted to the general contractor. If a purchaser of real estate causes a building or structure to be erected or repaired on the land being purchased, and the current owner has actual knowledge of this, the interest of the owner is subject to any liens arising out of the work.

10. PRIORITIES.—Subcontractors have priority over their general contractors, and the lien of a person performing labor or furnishing materials for a subcontractor shall be preferred to that of such subcontractor. Manual laborers are preferred to other lienors for labor performed during last 30 days of work. If owner is compelled to finish his own structure the amount so expended shall have priority over all mechanics' liens. No lien upon land created after work commenced or materials were furnished shall operate on the land or the new building until the mechanic's lien is satisfied.

11. PUBLIC IMPROVEMENTS.—See Chapter 30, *infra,* Bonds on Public Works.

NOTE.—Special provisions exist for liens on condominiums.

13. WAIVER.—The right to file or enforce a mechanic's lien may be waived at any time by the person entitled to the lien.

MECHANIC'S LIEN LAWS AND FEDERAL TAX LIEN LAW

WASHINGTON

1. WHO MAY CLAIM.—Laborer, materialman, contractor and subcontractor, or one renting, leasing, or otherwise supplying equipment to be used in the construction, alteration or repair of any mining claim, building, wharf, bridge, dyke, flume, tunnel, well, fence, machinery, railroad, street railway, wagon road, aqueduct to create hydraulic power or any other structure. Liens also for improving property with nursery stock.
2. HOW CLAIMED.—By giving notice to owner that claim may be filed and by filing notice of claim of lien.
3. WHERE FILED.—County Auditor's office of county where property is situated.
4. WHEN TO BE FILED.—Within 90 days from the date of cessation of performance of labor, furnishing material, or supplying equipment. However, the owner may, within 10 days after there has been a cessation of performance of labor or furnishing materials for a period of 30 days, file for record in the office of the County Auditor a verified notice setting forth the date such cessation occurred, together with his name, address and the nature of his title, a legal description of the property and a statement that a copy of said notice was delivered or mailed to the general contractor, if any. Such notice shall be conclusive evidence of such cessation on or before the date of cessation as stated in said notice, unless controverted by claimant's claim of lien which must be recorded within 60 days from the date of recording of such notice by the owner. This provision shall not extend the time for filing lien claims within the ninety-day period as set forth above. Liens for supply of agricultural materials must be filed after commencement of delivery of materials and products, but before commencement of the harvest of the crops.
5. SERVICE OF COPY OF NOTICE.—Materialman furnishing material to contractor or agent or directly to owner must mail by registered or certified mail to the owner or reputed owner or by personal service evidenced by obtaining a receipt or other acknowledgment signed by such owner or reputed owner a notice in writing, which notice shall cover materials, supplies or equipment furnished during 60 days prior thereto, as well as subsequent materials, etc., stating that he has commenced to deliver material for use on the property with the name of the contractor or agent ordering the same and that a lien may be claimed for all material furnished by such person. However, in the case of providing material for a single family residence or garage, the notice must be given not later than 10 days after the date of the first delivery of materials. Where the notice for a claim of a mechanic's lien is not given within the time specified by law, the lien is enforceable only for materials delivered subsequent to the notice being given and is secondary to any lien for which notice was properly given. Contractors or subcontractors required to be licensed or registered shall be deemed agents for the owner only if so registered or licensed.
6. DURATION OF LIEN.—No lien shall exist longer than eight months after the filing of the lien (or expiration of credit if credit be given) unless suit be started within that time. The action is to be prosecuted to judgment within two years after the commencement thereof. If the suit is not prosecuted within the two-year period, the court, in is discretion, may dismiss the action for want of prosecution, and the dismissal of such action or a judgment rendered therein, that no lien exists, shall constitute a cancellation of the lien. An action to enforce a lien is not considered timely commenced unless the filing of summons and complaint in a court of competent jurisdiction is made prior to the expiration of the eight-month period, and service of the summons and complaint is made upon all necessary parties personally, or by commencement of service by publication, not later than ninety days after filing of the summons and complaint.
7. FILING FEE.—$3.
8. CONTENTS OF STATEMENT OF LIEN.—Notice shall state time of commencement and cessation of performance of labor or furnishing material; name and address of person performing labor or furnishing material; name of person employing laborer or to whom material is furnished; legal description of property to be charged sufficient to identify same; name of owner or reputed owner, and if not known fact should be mentioned; amount for which lien is claimed; must be signed by claimant or some person on his behalf and verified by oath of claimant or some person on his behalf.
9. EXTENT OF LIEN.—Owner's right, title or interest in the property or so much thereof as may be necessary to satisfy the lien. Contractor may recover from the owner only so much as is due under contract. If judgment claims of other lienors in excess of amount due from owner to contractor, excess may be recovered by owner from contractor.
10. PRIORITIES.—(1) All persons performing labor. (2) Contributions owed to employee benefit plans. (3) All persons furnishing material or supplying equipment. (4) Subcontractors. (5) Contractors. Prior to all mortgages and encumbrances attaching subsequent to commencement of labor, furnishing material, or the supplying of equipment, and that may have attached prior to that

date but which have not been filed for record prior to that time and of which the lien claimant had no notice.

11. PUBLIC IMPROVEMENTS.—See Chapter 30, *infra*, Bonds on Public Works.

12. REMARKS.—Where there is not a payment bond of at least 50% of the amount of construction financing, potential lien claimants who have not received payment within 20 days after such is due may file notice the lender must withhold from subsequent draws a percentage thereof equal to the percentage of completion which is attributable to the lien claimant. Sums withheld may not be disbursed by owner and general contractor, or by order of court of competent jurisdiction.

WEST VIRGINIA

1. WHO MAY CLAIM.—Every person, workman, artisan, mechanic, laborer or other person who shall erect, build, construct, alter, remove or repair any building or other structure or other improvement appurtenant to any such building or other structure under and by virtue of a contract with the owner or his authorized agent.

2. HOW CLAIMED.—If contract made with owner by recording notice in the office of the Clerk of the County Court of the county wherein such property is situated; if contract made with subcontractor by serving notice on the owner and recording in County Clerk's office.

3. WHERE FILED.—In the office of the Clerk of the County Court where the property is situated.

4. WHEN TO BE FILED.—At any time during the progress of the work or during the time in which the material is furnished. If the work is done for the owner, the laborer or materialman has 90 days in which to file; if the work is done or material furnished to subcontractor the same must be filed within 60 days; original contractor—90 days and subcontractor 60 days after completion of contract.

5. SERVICE OF COPY OF NOTICE.—On the owner, when the material or labor was furnished to the subcontractor within 60 days after completion of subcontract.

6. DURATION OF LIEN.—Liens must be perfected within the following time from the completion of the contract or furnishing of materials: the original contract, for the erection of an improvement—90 days; subcontractor furnishing materials—60 days; original contractors, for materials—90 days; materialmen furnishing materials to contractors or subcontractor—60 days; workmen, etc., performing labor by virtue of contract with owner—90 days; workmen, etc., performing labor under employment of a contractor—60 days; unless within the said respective periods, the claimant of any such lien shall have perfected and preserved the same, as hereinafter provided. Unless suit in chancery is brought within six months after the filing of the notice such lien shall be discharged, but a suit commenced by any person having such lien shall for the purpose of preserving the same, inure to the benefit of all other persons having a lien under this chapter on the same property, and such persons may intervene in such suit for the purpose of enforcing their liens, in the same manner as in other chancery suits.

7. FILING FEE.—$1, and 50¢ per page in excess of two.

8. CONTENTS OF STATEMENT OF LIEN.—Description of property. Amount of the claim. Date of commencement to furnish material or labor, date last material was furnished or last work done.

9. EXTENT OF LIEN.—Lien extends to interest of owner in the improvement and the land on which same is situated.

10. PRIORITIES.—Deeds of trust made subsequent to commencement of work or furnishing material are inferior to mechanic's lien. There are no priorities among lienors except that the lien of the contractor and subcontractor is inferior to mechanics' liens for labor and materials.

11. PUBLIC IMPROVEMENTS.—See Chapter 30, *infra*, Bonds on Public Works.

WISCONSIN

1. WHO MAY CLAIM.—Every person who performs any work or labor or furnishes any material, plans or specifications for the improvement of land, including any building, structure, fixture, demolition, erection, alteration, excavation, filling, grading, tiling, planting, clearing or landscaping. Prime contractor is a person, other than laborer, including a surveyor, architect, professional engineer or surveyor employed by the owner, who enters into a contract with an owner or an owner acting as his own general contractor. Despite owner's payment bond, unless contract between owner and contractor contains a provision for payment by prime contractor of all claims for labor and materials a subcontractor's lien rights are effective except as to plans furnished by the architect, professional engineer, or surveyor employed by the owner.

2. HOW CLAIMED.—A construction lien does not exist and no action to enforce it can be maintained unless (1) a claim for lien is properly filed; (2) a written notice of intent to file a lien claim is served on the owner; and (3) for prime contractors only, a written notice about the lien law, either as part of the contract or separately stated is given to the owner.

MECHANIC'S LIEN LAWS AND FEDERAL TAX LIEN LAW   19-63

(a) Claim for Lien.—The claim for lien must have attached a copy of the notice of intent to file a lien claim and a copy of any prime contractor's notice about the lien law. The claim must contain a statement of the contract or demand upon which it is founded, the name of the person against whom the demand is claimed, the name of the claimant, and any assignee, the last date of the performance of any labor or the furnishing of any materials, a legal description of the property against which the lien is claimed, a statement of the amount claimed and all other material facts. Claim must be signed by claimant or attorney.

(b) Notice of Intent to File.—The notice of intent to file must be served on the owner personally or by registered mail, return receipt requested, at least 30 days before filing of the liened claim. The written notice is required whether or not the claimant has given the written notice about the lien law. The notice of intent to file must briefly describe the nature of the claim, its amounts and the land and improvements to which it relates.

(c) Notice About Lien Law.—Every prime contractor who has contracted or will contract with any subcontractors or material men for the improvement must include in any written contract with the owner or if an oral contract, prepared separately and serve personally or by registered mail within ten days after the first labor or materials are furnished the following notice printed in at least eight-point bold-face type or in capital letters if typewritten in substantially the following form:

"As required by the Wisconsin construction lien law, builder hereby notified owner that persons or companies furnishing labor or materials for the construction on owner's land may have lien rights on owner's land and buildings if not paid. Those entitled to lien rights, in addition to the undersigned builder, are those who contract directly with the owner or those who give the owner notice within 60 days after they first furnish labor or materials for the construction. Accordingly, owner probably will receive notices from those who furnish labor or materials for the construction, and should give a copy of each notice received to his mortgage lender, if any. Builder agrees to cooperate with the owner and his lender, if any, to see that all potential lien claimants are duly paid."

In the following instances the notice need not be given.

(1) By any laborer or mechanic employer by any prime contractor or subcontractor. (2) By any lien claimant who has contracted directly with the owner for the work or materials furnished, unless the claimant is a prime contractor. (3) By any lien claimant furnishing labor or materials for an improvement in any case where more than four-family living units are to be provided or added by such work of improvement which is wholly residential in character, or in any case where more than 10,000 total usable square feet of floor space is to be provided or added by such work of improvement which is partly or wholly nonresidential. (4) By any prime contractor who is himself an owner of the land to be improved, by any corporate prime contractor of which an owner of the land is an officer or controlling shareholder, by any prime contractor who is an officer or controlling shareholder of a corporation which is an owner of the land, or by any corporate prime contractor managed or controlled by substantially the same persons who manage or control a corporation which is an owner of the land. (5) By any lien claimant, other than a prime contractor, who furnishes labor or materials for an improvement on a project on which the prime contractor is not required to give notice under this section.

(d) Notice by Subcontractor, Materialmen or Laborers.—Every person other than a prime contractor must, within 60 days after furnishing the first labor or materials, serve two signed copies on the owner either by personal service or by registered mail, return receipt requested. The owner must provide a copy of the notice within 10 days after receipt to any mortgage lender providing funds for the construction of the improvement. The notice must be in substantially the following language:

"As part of your construction contract, your contractor or builder has already advised you that those who furnish labor or materials for the work will be notifying you. The undersigned first furnished labor or materials on .... (give date) for the improvement now under construction on your real estate at .... (give legal description, street address or other clear description). Please give your mortgage lender an extra copy of this notice within 10 days after you receive this, so your lender, too, will know that the undersigned is included in the job."

The failure to give this notice prohibits the acquisition of a lien.

3. WHERE FILED.—In office of Clerk of the Circuit Court for the county in which the real estate is situated.

4. WHEN TO BE FILED.—Lien claim recorded within six months from date last labor or materials performed or furnished.

5. DURATION OF LIEN.—Action to foreclose must be commenced within two years from date of filing such claim for lien.

6. FILING FEE.—$3.

7. EXTENT OF LIEN.—Lien attaches upon the interest of the owner, in and to the land. Lien extends to all contiguous land of the owner, but if improvement is located wholly on one or more plotted lots belonging to the owner, the lien applies only to the lots on which the improvement is located.

8. PRIORITIES.—Take precedence over any other encumbrances originated after commencement of service or furnishing materials. Also prior to any unrecorded mortgage given before commencement of such services, etc., of which mortgage person claiming lien has no notice. An exception to general priority rules is that recorded mortgages of state savings and loan associations and federal savings and loan associations have priority over all liens filed subsequent to the recording, except tax and special assessment liens. Among merchanics' liens no priority.

9. PUBLIC IMPROVEMENTS.—See Chapter 30, *infra,* Bonds on Public Works.

WYOMING

1. WHO MAY CLAIM.—Every person performing any work on or furnishing any materials or plans for any building or any improvement upon land shall have a lien upon the building or improvements and upon the land of the owner on which they are situated.

2. HOW CLAIMED.—A lien claimant must file a lien statement with the county clerk, sworn to before a notary public. The statement must contain the following information, as appropriate: (1) the name and address of the person seeking to enforce the lien; (2) the amount claimed to be due and owing; (3) the name and address of the person against whose property the lien is filed; (4) an itemized list setting forth and describing materials delivered or work performed; (5) the name of the person against whom the lien claim is made; (6) the date when labor was last performed or services were last rendered or the date when the project was substantially completed; (7) the legal description of the premises where the materials were furnished or upon which the work was performed; and (8) a copy of the contract, if available. Notice must be given of the lien to the last known owner by certified mail.

3. WHERE FILED.—Office of County Clerk of proper county.

4. WHEN TO BE FILED.—Every contractor shall file his lien statement within 120 days, and every other person within 90 days: (1) after the last day when work was performed or materials furnished under contract; (2) from the date the work was substantially completed or substantial completion of the contract to furnish materials, whichever is earlier; or (3) with respect to an employee or subcontractor, after the last day he performed work at the direction of his employer or contractor. The parties may agree to extend the time for filing for up to twice the otherwise applicable time limit. The agreement must be acknowledged before a notary public and signed by the owner, the contractor, and any other parties to the contract.

5. SERVICE OF COPY OF NOTICE.—Subcontractors must give notice of claim to owner, 10 days before filing.

6. DURATION OF LIEN.—Duration 180 days after filing lien, unless action commenced.

7. FILING FEE.—$3.

8. CONTENTS OF STATEMENT OF LIEN.—A just and true account of demand and all credits given, a true description of property, or so near as to identify same, upon which it is intended to apply, with name of owner, contractor, or both, if known to person filing lien, which shall be verified by lienor or by some reliable person for him.

9. EXTENT OF LIEN.—Upon improvements and the land belonging to owner upon which same is erected to the extent of one acre, or if such building, erection or improvement be upon any lot in town, city or village, then lien shall be upon said building, erection, or improvement and lot upon which situated.

10. PRIORITIES.—Liens are on equal footing without reference to date of filing. Lien has preference over any subsequent lien, security interest, or mortgage, but they are subordinated to liens perfected prior to the commencement of any construction work or repairs.

11 PUBLIC IMPROVEMENTS.—See Chapter 30, *infra,* Bonds on Public Works.

12. LIENS FOR IMPROVEMENTS OF OIL OR GAS WELLS.—Such liens are created, perfected and enforced in the same manner as mechanic's liens except that filing must be made within 180 days and amount due must exceed $750. Written notice of the claim must be personally delivered, or by registered or certified mail, to a purchaser of the oil or gas to be effective as against him.

Personal Property Liens

At common law, although the lienor was entitled to retain possession of chattel upon which he had a personal property lien, he was not permitted to enforce the lien by any court proceeding. For example, the common law provided a lien to an artisan who retained possession of property on which he performed services for the value of the services rendered; similarly, one who permitted animals to graze on his property had a lien on the animals for the value of the debt due. Neither lienor, however, could satisfy the lien by a court proceeding.

Although common law liens may still exist in many jurisdictions, they have in large measure been either superseded or supplemented by statutory liens on personal property of various sorts depending generally on the primary industries and economy of the state.

Set forth below is a summary of the most significant statutory liens on personal property which would be of interest to commercial credit grantors. In that liens for the improvement of oil and gas wells are in the nature of mechanic liens and often constitute a lien on the real property of the owner, these liens have therefore been summarized in Chapter 19, *supra,* "Mechanic's Lien Laws and Federal Tax Lien Law." In general, artisan's liens and liens for animals, hospital and innkeeper's liens, attorney's liens, liens for performing services and other species of liens which do not involve extension of commercial credit have been eliminated from this summary. For information on liens based on such types of services, it will be necessary to consult the state statutes directly.

Many of these statutes have not been modernized in a substantial number of years and consequently are vague. Others are highly technical, and the assertion of rights thereunder will usually require the services of an attorney.

Uniform Commercial Code Section 9-310 determines the priority applicable with respect to certain personal property liens which are in conflict with security interests in the same collateral. If the lien arises by operation of statutory or decisional law (i.e., noncontractual liens) and if the lien secures payment due for the furnishing of services or materials in the ordinary course of business with respect to goods in the lienor's possession, then the lien will be superior to a prior security interest, *whether perfected or not,* unless the lien is created by statute, and that statute provides otherwise.

ALABAMA

1. WHO MAY CLAIM.—Owners of timber land or their assignees; operators of a public sawmill; keeper, owner, or proprietor of a livery stable; owners of a cotton gin, peanut machine or pickler, or hay bailing machine or press, or plant for drying or processing planting seeds (hereinafter agricultural commodities processors).

2. PROPERTY COVERED.—Timber sold for the purposes of rafting, shipping, or manufacture; all lumber sawed by a sawmill under any contract with the owner; agricultural commodities processed under any contract with the owner of such commodities.

3. EXTENT OF THE LIEN.—Timber liens are for the stipulated price or value thereof. A sawmill

operator's lien is for the amount agreed upon, or if none, for the reasonable or customary price of the sawing, as long as the lumber remains at the sawmill or in the sawmill owner's possession, and if removed without the knowledge and consent of that owner, the lien will follow the lumber.

An agricultural commodities processor's lien is for the toll or charge under any contract with the owner of the commodity whether the charge is expressed or implied. Livery stable keeper has lien on all stock kept and fed by him for payment of charges; he has right to keep stock for six months after notice of lien.

4. DURATION OF LIEN.—Where the process of attachment is authorized (see 7 below), suit must be commenced within six months after the demand becomes due.

5. ENFORCEMENT OF LIEN BY SALE.—Liens on lumber or agricultural commodities, if the charges due are not paid within ten days after demand therefor, may be enforced, upon notice as described below, by sale of the lumber or commodity to the highest bidder, for the payment of the expense of such sale and the charges due, and the residue paid to the owner of the property sold.

6. NOTICE OF SALE.—Ten days' notice of the time and place of sale must be given by advertisement in a newspaper published in the county in which the sawmill is located or the agricultural commodity processed, once a week for two successive weeks, or if there is no such paper, by posting the notice in two or more public places in the county; three places are required in the case of agricultural commodities liens.

7. ENFORCEMENT OF LIEN BY ATTACHMENT.—Available if lumber or agricultural commodity has been removed without the knowledge and consent of the lienor.

Available on liens for timber removed without consent of the lienor and without payment, or when the claimant has good cause to believe that the timber is about to be removed.

8. ENFORCEMENT OF LIEN BY GARNISHMENT.—Available for the enforcement of agricultural commodity liens.

9. PRIORITY.—A sawmill operator's lien is paramount to all others; an agricultural commodity processor's lien has priority over all other liens, mortgages, or encumbrances whether existing or not at the time of commencement of the processing or work.

ALASKA

1. WHO MAY CLAIM.—Common carriers or persons who, at the request of the owner or lawful possessor of personal property, carry, convey, or transport properties;

Persons who safely keep or store grain, wares, merchandise and personal property at the request of the owner or lawful possessor;

Persons who perform, labor on, or assist in obtaining or securing timber, the owner of a tugboat or towboat which assists in towing lumber, the owner of a team or machine which hauls or assists in hauling lumber, the owner of a logging road over which timber is transported and delivered;

Persons who contribute to the preparation of fish or aquatic animals for food, fish, meal, fertilizer, oil, or other article of commerce by furnishing material or labor for it.

Persons employed as watchman has a lien upon the property for wages earned by him.

Persons who pasture or feed livestock or bestow labor, care, or attention thereupon.

2. PROPERTY COVERED.—Property transported by carrier or stored; timber and the product of a cannery, saltery, or other plant or establishment, and the plant or establishment itself.

3. HOW CLAIMED.—Claims for timber liens must be filed and follow substantially the following form:

CLAIM OF LIEN

_____ Claimant v. _____, Defendant.
Notice is given by this claim that _____, residing at _____, State of Alaska, claims a lien upon a _____ of _____, being about _____ in quantity, which were cut in _____ recording district, State of Alaska, and are now lying or being at _____, for labor performed and assistance provided in said _____; that the name of the owner or reputed owner is _____; that _____ employed said _____ to perform the labor and provide the assistance upon the following terms and conditions, to wit: —
Thai _____ agreed to pay the _____ for labor and assistance _____; that the contract has been faithfully performed and fully complied with on the part of _____, who performed labor and assisted in _____ for the period of _____; that the labor and assistance were

PERSONAL PROPERTY LIENS 20–3

so performed and provided upon _____ between the day of _____, and 45 days have not elapsed since that time; that the amount of the claimant's demand for the service is _____; that no part of the claim has been paid except _____; and there is now due and remaining unpaid on the claim, after deducting all just credits and offsets, the sum of _____, and he claims a lien in this upon the _____ also claims a lien on all the _____ now owned by _____ in the recording district to secure payment for the work and labor in obtaining or securing the saw logs, spars, piles, cordwood, fuel-wood, shingle bolts or other timber herein in this claim.

_____
(Signature)

State of Alaska }
_____ Judicial District } ss.:
_____, being first duly sworn on oath says that he is _____ named in the foregoing claim of liens, has heard the claim read, knows the contents of the claim and believes the claim to be true.

_____
(Signature)

Subscribed and sworn to
before me this _____ day
of _____

_____
(Signature)

4. WHERE FILED.—The recorder's office of the recording district where the property is located, where the cannery, saltery, or other plant is located, or where the timber is cut.

5. WHEN TO BE FILED.—Within 90 days of the completion of the work or furnishing of material for fishpacker and processor's lien;

Within 60 days after completion of service or close of work for a timber lien.

6. EXTENT OF LIEN.—Carrier and storage liens are for the just reasonable charges.

Timber liens are for the value of the work and services performed.

Fishpacker and processor's lien is for the value of service, work or material furnished for the six months, or a shorter period, preceding the filing of a claim.

7. DURATION OF LIEN.—Six months after notice of the lien is filed for record, unless suit is brought within that time, or if credit is given, within six months after the expiration of the credit; no lien may be carried in force for more than one year from the stopping of the work by an agreement to give credit.

8. ENFORCEMENT OF LIEN BY SALE.—If the just and reasonable charges of a carrier or person engaged in storage, are not paid within three months after the service or food is furnished, the lienor may proceed to sell, at public auction, property sufficient to pay the charges and the expense of the sale, with the balance paid to the owner. A warehouseman is not authorized to sell more of the wool, wheat, oats, or other grain than is sufficient to pay charges due the warehouseman on the wool, wheat, oats, or other grain.

9. NOTICE OF SALE.—Before the sale is made, notice of the sale shall be given to the debtor by registered letter directed to him at his last-known place of residence, if his residence is known, and also by posting notice of the sale in three public places in the recording district, one of which shall be at or near the front door of the post office nearest the place of sale, for 10 days before the day of sale. The notice shall contain a particular description of the article to be sold, the name of the owner or reputed owner, the amount due on the lien, and the time and place of said sale.

ARIZONA

1. WHO MAY CLAIM.—Person laboring or furnishing labor, machinery or equipment in improving and preparing agricultural lands for planting crops, and to whom wages or moneys are due and owing. Person fabricating from patterns, molds, tools for work accepted by the customer.

2. PROPERTY COVERED.—Crops produced on such land.

3. HOW CLAIMED.—In the same manner as a mechanic's lien, described in the previous chapter.

4. WHERE FILED.—The office of the county recorder of the county in which the land is located.
5. WHEN TO BE FILED.—Within 10 days after the labor is performed or the use of the machinery and equipment is terminated.
6. DURATION OF LIEN.—Six months after claim is filed, unless civil action is commenced with that time.
7. ENFORCEMENT BY SALE.—When possession of property has continued for 20 days after charges accrue and remain unpaid, the person holding the property may notify the owner to pay charges. Upon failure to pay within 10 days, the holder may sell it at public auction and apply proceeds to payment of the charges.

ARKANSAS

1. WHO MAY CLAIM.—The owner of a cotton gin or plant engaged in processing rice or other similar farm products.
2. PROPERTY COVERED.—Cotton seed and baled cotton produced by cotton ginner; Agricultural products of a rice processor or other similar farm products processor.
3. DURATION OF LIEN.—A cotton ginner's lien must be enforced within six months after the cotton is ginned; a rice (or other similar farm product) processor's lien must be enforced within eight months after the agricultural product is processed.
4. ENFORCEMENT.—Cotton, seed, rice and other similar farm products may be held for thirty days unless the claim is sooner paid, and after that time may sell the same at the market price, at private sale, and from the proceeds pay his just debt, turning any residue over to the owner. Where the cotton, seed, rice or other similar farm product is not in the ginner or processor's possession, he may enforce his claim in court.
5. PRIORITY.—Cotton ginner, or rice or other similar farm product processor's lien is an absolute lien superior to all other prior liens.

CALIFORNIA

1. WHO MAY CLAIM.—Producers and transporters of farm products that sell such products grown and harvested by them to processors under contract, express or implied; carriers; sellers of livestock to meat packers in California.
2. PROPERTY COVERED.—Agricultural producer's lien is on the farm product sold and all processed or manufactured forms of such farm product.
Carrier's lien is on the property transported, cared for, or preserved.
Livestock lien is on livestock sold and identifiable proceeds.
3. EXTENT OF LIEN.—Agricultural producer's lien is for the agreed price, or if none, for the value of the product as of the date of the delivery.
Carrier's lien is for freightage and for services rendered at the request of the shipper or consignee, and for money advanced at the request of shipper or consignee to discharge a prior lien.
4. DURATION OF LIEN.—Agricultural producer's liens continue in effect for 60 days after delivery. After filing of notice, livestock lien is valid for 5 years.
5. PRIORITY.—Agricultural producer's lien is preferred to all other liens, claims or encumbrances except labor claims for wages and salaries for personal services rendered to the processor after delivery, or a warehouseman's lien as provided in the Uniform Commercial Code.
Livestock lien is superior to all other liens.
6. LIMITATIONS.—No agricultural producer may have a lien on any farm product, or any manufactured or processed product derived from any farm product, that is hypothecated or pledged to a lender that advances new value to the processor and that has filed a statement in writing with the director.
California sellers of livestock to meat packers now have a lien on the livestock and the identifiable proceeds for the purchase price or the unpaid value of the livestock. The lien is superior to all other liens but expires in 21 days unless a notice is filed with the Secretary of State.

COLORADO

While Colorado provides statutory liens for artisans, agisters, common carriers and garagemen, it does not provide any statutory liens of special relevance to commercial credit grantors.

CONNECTICUT

1. WHO MAY CLAIM.—Persons in the business of manufacturing, spinning, throwing, bleaching, mercerizing, printing or finishing yarn or other goods made of cotton, wool, silk, linen, rayon, nylon, synthetic fibers or artificial silk or goods of which such materials form a component part.

Any person with a claim of at least $50 for work done, materials furnished or expenses incurred in connection with the building, repairing, mooring, dockage or storage of any vessel.

Owners of self-storage facilities will have a lien upon personal property located at the facilities for the amounts of any rent, labor, or charges incurred in relation to the property. Such liens will not have priority over other liens or security interests which attached or are perfected prior to default.

2. PROPERTY COVERED.—The goods and property of others which come into the possession of such a person for the purpose of being so processed.

3. EXTENT OF LIEN.—This lien is for the amount of any debt due the lienor from the owner of the material by reason of any work performed or materials furnished in or about the processing of such goods or property, or other goods of such owner of which the lienor's possession has terminated.

4. ENFORCEMENT BY SALE.—This lien may be enforced by public sale of the property after proper notice. The proceeds are applied to the payment of the amount of the lien and expenses of the sale, the balance to be paid to the owner.

5. NOTICE OF SALE.—Notice of sale must be published at least once each week for two weeks preceding the date of the sale in a newspaper published in the county in which the goods or property is located, and by mailing, postage prepaid, a copy of such notice, at least 5 days before the date of the sale, to the owner of the property, addressed to his last-known residence or place of business.

DELAWARE

1. WHO MAY CLAIM.—Owners of a threshing machine, corn picker, or hay baler.

2. PROPERTY COVERED.—Wheat, corn, hay or other grain threshed, picked or baled by him with such machine.

3. HOW CLAIMED.—No statutory claim requirements.

4. PRIORITY.—Threshing machine owners have first lien. Where property subject to lien is sold upon any claim whatsoever, this claim shall be paid out of the proceeds of any such sale before any part of those proceeds are applied to any other claim.

DISTRICT OF COLUMBIA

While the District of Columbia provides statutory liens for artisans, hotels, garagekeepers, and deliverymen, it does not provide any statutory liens of special relevance to commercial credit grantors.

FLORIDA

1. WHO MAY CLAIM.—Persons who furnish any locomotive or stationary engine, water engine, windmill, car or other machine, parts or instrument for any railroad, telegraph or telephone line, mill, distilling or other manufactory. The owner of a self-service storage facility has a lien upon all personal property located at the facility for rent, labor or other charges incurred in relation to the property. The lien attaches as of the date the property is brought into the facility.

2. PROPERTY COVERED.—Material supplier's lien is on the articles furnished and the articles manufactured therefrom.

Engine and machinery suppliers lien is on the articles furnished.

3. HOW CLAIMED.—Supplier's liens on personal property are acquired by persons in privity against the owner by the furnishing of the materials and against purchasers and creditors without notice only while lienor remains in possession. Lien may be acquired by person not in privity with the owner only by delivery of notice to the owner, in writing, that the person to whom material has been furnished is indebted to the lienor by the sum stated.

4. DURATION OF LIEN.—Supplier's liens against purchasers and creditors without notice continue as long as possession continues, not to exceed 3 months after furnishing of the material.

5. PRIORITY.—As among supplier's liens, priority is established chronologically when liens attach to the property.

GEORGIA

1. WHO MAY CLAIM.—All those furnishing sawmills with timber, logs, provisions or other things necessary to carry on the work of the sawmill, and all those who haul stocks, logs or lumber. The lien is for the amount of indebtedness and, if the price is not agreed on, the value of services. Owner of self-storage facility has a lien for all personal property stored in the facility for rent, labor or other charges incurred in relation to the property. Such liens will not have priority over liens perfected and recorded prior to the date of the rental agreement, tax liens or liens and security interests disclosed in the rental agreement.

2. PROPERTY COVERED.—Sawmills and their products; material hauled.

3. HOW CLAIMED.—By affidavit showing all facts necessary to constitute a lien, and the amount claimed due.

4. WHERE FILED.—Clerk of the Superior Court or, if the claim is under $100, the Justice of the Peace.

5. DURATION OF LIENS.—Liens must be prosecuted within one year after the debt comes due.

6. PRIORITIES.—Sawmill liens are superior to all liens except those for taxes, labor, and those of which the lienor had actual notice before their debts were created. Among themselves these liens are ranked by the date on which the debts were created.

7. ENFORCEMENT.—By foreclosure.

HAWAII

Hawaii has statutory liens for dentists, bailees, hotels, laundries, and repairmen and warehousemen under the UCC. There are no other statutory liens of special relevance to commercial credit grantors.

IDAHO

1. WHO MAY CLAIM.—Persons who perform labor on a farm, till land, or cultivate, harvest, thresh or house crops.

Persons performing labor upon, or assisting in obtaining or securing saw logs, spars, piles, core wood or other timber; manufacturing such into lumber or permitting another upon their timberland to cut such timber.

Persons rendering service for the protection, improvement, safekeeping, or carriage of personal property.

Agricultural commodity producer or dealer who sells an agricultural product, e.g., wheat, corn, oats, etc.

2. PROPERTY COVERED.—Crops; saw logs, spars, piles, core wood or other timber or lumber; agricultural products; personal property protected, improved, stored or carried.

3. HOW CLAIMED.—Agricultural and timber liens are claimed by filing a claim in substantially the following form:

_____ Claimant v. _____

Notice is hereby given that _____ of _____ county, State of Idaho, claims a lien upon a _____ of _____ being about _____ in quantity, which were cut in _____ county, State of Idaho, are marked thus _____, and are now lying in _____ for labor performed upon and assistance rendered in _____ said _____; that the name of the owner or reputed owner is _____; that _____ employed said _____ to perform such labor and render such assistance upon the following terms, to wit: The _____ agreed to pay the said _____ for such labor and assistance _____; that said contract has been faithfully performed and fully complied with on the part of said _____, who performed labor upon and assisted in _____ said _____ for the period of _____ that said labor and assistance were so performed and rendered upon said _____ between the _____ day of _____ and the _____ day of _____, and the rendition of said services was closed on the _____ day of _____ and _____ days have not elapsed

PERSONAL PROPERTY LIENS

since that time; that the amount of claimant's demand for said services is _____; that no part thereof has been paid except _____, and there is now due and unpaid thereon, after deducting all just credits and offsets, the sum of _____, in which amount he claims a lien upon said _____.

State of Idaho, _____ County, ss.: _____, being first duly sworn, on oath says that he is _____ named in the foregoing claim, has heard the same read and knows the contents thereof, and believes the same to be true _____.

Subscribed and sworn to before me this _____ day of _____, 19 _____.

4. WHERE FILED.—With the county recorder of the county in which the agricultural work is performed, the timber cut or the lumber manufactured.

5. WHEN TO BE FILED.—Within 60 days after the close of the rendition of services or the close of work and labor. For agricultural commodity dealer lien, within 90 days after date of product sold or delivered, whichever occurs last.

6. EXTENT OF LIEN.—Liens for labor or service related to timber or lumber are for work, labor, or purchase price for eight months preceding filing of claim.

7. DURATION OF LIEN.—Agricultural and timber liens are valid for six months.

8. ENFORCEMENT BY SALE.—Liens on personal property cared for by the lienor may, if not paid within 60 days after the work is done or service supplied, be enforced by sale of the property at public auction. The proceeds of the sale are applied to the discharge of the lien, and the remainder, if any, is paid over to the owner.

9. NOTICE OF SALE.—Ten days' public notice by advertising in a newspaper published in the county where the property is situated, or if there is no such paper, by posting notices in three of the most public places in the county, for ten days previous to such sale.

10. PRIORITY.—Liens on crops are perferred prior to any security interest therein. However, any interest in crops of a lessor of land for a share in the crop is not subject to such lien.

Timber liens are prior to any other liens. No sale or transfer shall divest such lien and the lien will follow the property into any county in the state where notice is filed.

ILLINOIS

1. WHO MAY CLAIM.—All persons who furnish to a railroad fuel, ties, material, supplies or labor by contract; and subcontractors, materialmen and laborers who furnish such items to a contractor with a railroad;

2. PROPERTY COVERED.—All property of a railroad.

3. HOW CLAIMED.—Liens on railroads are claimed by serving notice on the president or secretary of such railroad corporation, substantially as follows:

To _____ president (or secretary, as the case may be) of the _____: You are hereby notified that I am (or have been) employed by _____ as a laborer (or have furnished supplies, as the case may be) on or for the _____ and that I shall hold all the property of said railroad (or railway, as the case may be) company to secure my pay.

A copy of the contract between the original contractor and subcontractor, materialman or laborer, if any, should be attached to the notice. If neither the president nor the secretary of such railroad corporation reside or can be found in the county in which the subcontract was made or labor performed, lienor must file the notice in the office of the clerk of the circuit court.

4. WHEN CLAIMED.—Notice of claim of a railroad lien must be made within 20 days after the completion of the subcontract or labor.

5. DURATION OF LIEN.—A suit to enforce a railroad lien must be brought within six months after the contractor or laborer has completed the contract, or after the labor is performed or material furnished (three months for subcontractors).

6. PRIORITY.—Railroad lien is preferred to all other subsequent liens.

INDIANA

1. WHO MAY CLAIM.—Persons engaged in repairing, storing, servicing or furnishing supplies or accessories for motor vehicles, airplanes, construction, machinery and equipment, and farm machinery;

Transfermen, draymen and all others involved in packing for shipment or storage, hauling or conveying articles of value, or erecting machinery and equipment;

Owners or operators of machinery or tools used in threshing or hauling grain or seed, plowing, disking or cultivating the land, or combining, picking or baling of crops.

Pawnbrokers for loan, interest, and charges.

2. PROPERTY COVERED.—Motor vehicles, airplanes or construction and farm equipment stored, serviced or maintained.

Property transferred or packed and machinery and equipment erected.

Grain or seed so threshed or welled, crops produced or prepared for market or storage by such plowing, disking, cultivating, combining, picking or baling.

3. HOW CLAIMED.—By filing notice in writing of the intention to hold the lien which sets forth the amount claimed and gives a substantial description of the property in question. In addition a lien on grain or crops must designate the person for whom such work was done, the location of such crops and the date on which the work was done.

4. WHERE FILED.—The recorder's office of the county where the work or service was performed, or the material furnished.

5. WHEN TO BE FILED.—Notice of liens on motor vehicles, airplanes and machinery, and those on property transferred or packed and machinery erected must be filed within 60 days after labor is performed, or service or material furnished.

Notice of liens on grain and crops must be filed within 30 days after the completion of plowing, disking or cultivating and within 10 days after the completion of combining, picking or baling.

6. DURATION OF LIEN.—One year after filing of notice of intention to hold lien.

7. PRIORITY.—A lien on property transferred or packed, or machinery and equipment erected has priority over all subsequent liens.

8. COMMENTS.—Where crops subject to lien are sold by the party for whom the work was done, such party must notify the purchaser that the account has not been paid, and the lien will shift from the crops to the purchase price thereof in the hands of the purchaser. Where such crops are sold with the consent and knowledge of the lienor, such lien will not attach to the crops or the purchase price unless the lienor personally notifies the purchaser of the lien.

IOWA

1. WHO MAY CLAIM.—Operator of a machine for threshing, baling or combining any kind of grain or seed, baling hay, straw or other farm product, or mechanical husking and shelling of corn;

Livery and feed stablekeepers, herders, feeders, keepers of stock and of places for the storage of motor vehicles, boats and boat motors and engines;

A lessor owning or operating a refrigerated locker plant.

2. PROPERTY COVERED.—Grain and seed threshed, farm product baled, or corn shelled or husked;

All property stored by livery and feed stablekeepers, herders, feeders and keepers of stock, motor vehicles, boats, boat motors and engines;

All property of every kind in the possession of a refrigerator locker plant owner or operator.

3. HOW CLAIMED.—A thresherman, baler or corn sheller's lien is preserved by filing an itemized and verified statement setting forth the services rendered, the number of bushels of grain threshed or corn shelled, the value of the services, the person for whom such services were rendered, and where such services were rendered.

4. WHERE FILED.—In the office of the clerk of the district court of the county in which the services were rendered.

5. WHEN TO BE FILED.—Within ten days from the completion of the work for which the lien is claimed.

6. ENFORCEMENT BY SALE.—When charges for care of stock and storage of motor vehicles and boats are not paid, the lien-holder may sell the stock and property at public auction after giving proper notice. The proceeds go to satisfy the charges and expenses of keeping the property, and the cost and expenses of the sale; the balance to be paid to the owner.

7. NOTICE OF SALE.—Proper notice consists of ten days written notice to the owner of the time and place of the sale if such owner is found within the county, and the posting of written notices in three public places in the township where the stock or property was kept or received.

8. DURATION OF LIEN.—Proceedings to enforce a thresherman's, baler's, or cornsheller's lien must be brought within 30 days after the filing of the verified statement.

9. PRIORITY.—A thresherman's, baler's, or cornsheller's lien is prior and superior to any landlord's lien or mortgage lien.

PERSONAL PROPERTY LIENS

A lien for the care of stock and storage of motor vehicles, boats, boat motors and engines, is subject to all prior liens of record.

KANSAS

1. WHO MAY CLAIM.—Any person at, or with the owner's request or consent performs work, makes repairs or improvements on any goods, personal property, chattels, horses, mules, wagons, buggies, automobiles, trucks, trailers, locomotives, railroad rolling stock, barges, aircrafts, equipment of all kinds including but not limited to construction equipment, vehicles of all kinds, and farm implements of whatsoever kind. Operators of threshing machines or persons engaged in the business of threshing and harvesting grain or grain crops. Shucking, husking, or gathering corn for others under contract with the owners or mortgagees thereof.

Operators of broom corn seeders and balers, or hay balers or persons engaged in the business of seeding and baling broom corn and baling hay under contract with the owners or mortgagees thereof.

2. PROPERTY COVERED.—All personal property worked on, repaired or improved by lien claimant. Grain and crops threshed and harvested and corn shucked, husked or gathered.

Broom corn or hay seeded or baled.

The lien extends to the full contract amount and the reasonable value of the services rendered, and includes the reasonable value of all material used in the performance of the service.

3. HOW TO CLAIM.—Agricultural liens are claimed by filing a verified statement setting forth the name of the owner, kind of agricultural product, description of the land upon which such product was raised, the contract price, the date on which the work was done, the amount due and the name of the claimant.

Liens on other goods are claimed by filing under oath a statement of the items of the account and a description of the property on which the lien is claimed, with the name of the owner thereof.

4. WHERE FILED.—Agricultural liens are filed in the office of the register of deeds of the county in which the work was done.

Liens on other goods are filed in the office of the register of deeds of the county in which the work was done, and in the county of the residence of the owner, if such is known to the claimant.

5. WHEN TO BE FILED.—Agricultural liens must be filed within 15 days after completion of the work. In the case of threshing or harvesting, which has begun and been interrupted for more than five days, the statement must be filed within 15 days after the beginning of the interruption.

Liens on other goods in claimant's possession do not require filing. After parting with possession of said property, claimant may retain the lien by filing within 45 days. If lien claimant was never in possession of said property, he may retain said lien by filing within 45 days after the date upon which work was last performed or materials last furnished.

6. DURATION OF LIEN.—For agricultural liens, 90 days after the filing of the statement. All other liens are valid as long as the lienor retains possession.

7. PRIORITY.—Agricultural liens are preferred to those of any prior security interest or encumbrance.

KENTUCKY

1. WHO MAY CLAIM.—Any person engaged in the business of selling, repairing, or furnishing accessories or supplies for any kind of equipment or machinery—including motors.

2. PROPERTY COVERED.—Equipment, machinery and motors.

3. HOW CLAIMED.—Filing sworn statement showing the amount and cost of materials furnished or labor performed. Lien is not dependent on possession.

4. WHERE FILED.—Office of the county clerk in the county where the owner resides or if a nonresident, in the county where the equipment is located.

5. WHEN TO BE FILED.—Within 3 months of furnishing material or performing labor.

6. EXTENT OF LIEN.—For the reasonable or agreed charges for repairs, work done, accessories, parts and supplies furnished. As against a holder of a mortgage or purchaser for value the lien shall not exceed the amount claimed in the statement.

7. CONTENTS OF LIEN STATEMENT.—Amount due the claimant, with all just credits and set-offs known to him, description of the property intended to be covered by the lien, subscribed and sworn to by the person claiming the lien.

8. PRIORITY.—Such lien is preferred to all subsequent mortgages or liens.

LOUISIANA

1. WHO MAY CLAIM.—Persons who furnish water to another for the purpose of assisting in growing or maturing a crop:

Threshermen, combinemen, and grain dryers;

Persons engaged in the business of hauling;

Persons providing money or supplies to enable another to deaden, cut, load or transport any logs or to manufacture poles or cross ties;

Persons performing labor or services in deadening, cutting, loading or transporting any logs, staves, poles or cross ties, or in manufacturing poles, cross ties, lumber, staves, hoops, boxes, shingles, doors, blinds or window sashes;

Any person operating a garage or other place where automobiles or other machinery are repaired.

2. PROPERTY COVERED.—Crops to which water is furnished except where by agreement water is supplied for a share of the crop, in which case that share is unaffected by the lien; Crops threshed, combined or dried; Property hauled; Logs and products manufactured therefrom.

3. EXTENT OF LIEN.—Lien for water supplied to crops is to secure the agreed compensation. Threshermen's, combinemen's, and grain dryer's lien is for services rendered.

Carrier's lien is for the charges or labor performed in connection with hauling.

Log liens are for the debt due for money advanced, or labor and services.

Garage keeper's liens are for the amount of the cost of repairs made, parts made or furnished, and labor performed. If estimate was given, then in order for amount of privilege to exceed the amount of estimate, authorization from owner must be secured.

4. DURATION OF LIEN.—A carrier's lien continues for a period of 90 days from the last day of hauling or performing labor.

Log liens are effective for a period of 90 days from maturity of the debt.

Garage keeper's liens are effective for a period of 90 days from the last day on which repairs were made, parts made or furnished or labor performed.

5. PRIORITY.—Threshermen's, combinemen's and grain drier's lien is ranked as equal with the lien of a laborer and overseer, and above that of a lessor, a furnisher of supplies and money, a furnisher of water and a physician (not discussed herein), and pledges.

A lien for water supplied to crops is ranked equal to that of a furnisher of supplies and money, and a physician, and below that of a laborer, thresherman, combineman, grain drier, overseer, lessor, and pledges.

Log liens are of concurrent rank.

MAINE

1. WHO MAY CLAIM.—Persons who perform or furnish labor or wood manufacturing and burning bricks;

Persons who furnish corn or other grain or fruit for canning or preservation;

Persons who drive logs or lumber or a person who cooks for those doing that kind of work under contract with the owner or other person;

Owners of steamboats employed in towing logs or lumber on inland waters of the state;

Persons making advances of money or merchandise to the owner or person entitled to possession of any logs, lumber, or pulpwood to finance or furnish supplies for the cutting, hauling, rafting, booming, driving or towing of the same.

2. PROPERTY COVERED.—Brick lien is on bricks manufactured or burned. Canned goods lien is on the preserved article and everything with which it may have been mingled, including the cans or other vessels and the cases.

Log driver's lien is on the logs or lumber driven.

Steamboat owner's lien is on the logs or lumber towed.

Lien of person making advances for logging is on all of the logs, lumber and pulpwood for which the advance was made and on which he has at any time caused his registered mark to be placed.

3. EXTENT OF LIEN.—Brick lien is for the labor. Canned goods lien is for the value of the preserved article when delivered.

Log driver's lien is for the amount payable under the contract.

Steamboat owner's lien is for the amounts due for such towing.

Lien of person making advances is for the amount of all such advances made.

4. DURATION OF LIEN.—Brick liens and canned goods liens continue for 30 days after such

bricks are burned (provided they remain in the yard where stored) or such canned or preserved articles are delivered (and until shipped on board a vessel or laden in a car).

Log driver's liens and steamboat owner's liens continue for 60 days after the logs or lumber arrive at the place of destination for sale or manufacture.

Lien of person making advances for logging with respect to each advance or series of advances, continue for 2 years after the making of the last such advance or series of advances.

5. ENFORCEMENT.—These liens may be enforced by attachment or by suit in the superior court of the county where claimant resides for a court ordered sale of the property.

6. PRIORITY.—Brick liens take precedence over all other claims except attachments and encumbrances made to secure a similar lien.

Log driver's liens take precedence over all other claims except liens for labor, stumpage, or towing.

Steamboat owner's liens take precedence over all other claims except liens reserved to the state, and liens for labor and stumpage.

Liens of person making advances for logging take precedence over all other claims except liens for labor stumpage, towing, or driving whenever acquired and all other liens legally acquired prior to the placing of the claimants registered mark on the logs or lumber.

7. LIMITATION.—Whenever a log driving contract is made with anyone other than the owner of the logs or lumber, actual notice in writing must be given to the owner before work is begun, stating the terms of the contract. If the owner, at the time of notice or immediately thereafter, notifies the contractor that he will not be responsible for the amount payable under that contract, then the contractor will not have a lien on the logs or lumber driven.

MARYLAND

1. WHO MAY CLAIM.—All persons having custody of and providing service or material for an aircraft, boat or motor vehicle, and any airport operator.

2. PROPERTY COVERED.—Aircraft, boats, and motor vehicles.

3. EXTENT OF LIEN.—Aircraft liens are for inspection, maintenance, repair, servicing, rebuilding, storage, parking, handling or tiedown; or parts, accessories, materials, or supplies. Airport owners have liens for landing fees, flight or similar charge.

Boat and motor vehicle liens are for repair or rebuilding; storage; or parts and accessories.

4. ENFORCEMENT BY SALE.—If charges remain due and unpaid for 30 days, lienor in possession of the property subject to the lien may sell such property at public sale. The sale must be in a location convenient and accessible to the public between the hours of 10 a.m. and 6 p.m. The proceeds of the sale are applied first to the costs of holding the sale, second to the amount of the lien, and finally the remainder to the owner.

5. NOTICE OF SALE.—Notice of the time, place and terms of the sale and a full description of the property must be published by the lienor once a week for the two weeks immediately preceding the sale, in one or more newspapers of general circulation in the county where the sale is to be held. In addition, the lienor must send the notice by registered or certified mail at least 10 days before the sale to the owner of the property, if the owner's address is known, or to General Delivery at the post office of the city or county where the business of the lienor is located if the addresses of both the owner and the person who incurred the charges are unknown.

6. COMMENT.—If the owner of the property disputes the charges he may institute appropriate judicial proceedings, which stays execution of the lien until final determination of the dispute. The owner may also, if he disputes the charges, gain immediate repossession of the property by filing a corporate bond for double the amount of the charges claimed.

7. PRIORITY.—An aircraft lien is subject only to the rights of the holder of the bill of sale, contract of conditional sale, conveyance, a mortgage or assignment of mortgage, executed and recorded with the Federal Aviation Administration before the time the lien becomes effective.

Boat and motor vehicles liens are subordinate only to a security interest perfected as required by law.

MASSACHUSETTS

1. WHO MAY CLAIM.—Persons furnishing work, labor, and materials in the spinning, throwing, manufacturing, bleaching, mercerizing, dyeing, printing, finishing or otherwise processing of cotton, wool, silk, artificial silk or synthetic fibers, leather goods or hides, or goods of which such materials form a component part; and in the processing of wood, metal, paper, paperboard, plastic, and

plastic compounds, including the addition of materials and labor furnished in printing, cutting, milling, extruding, combining and serving.

2. PROPERTY COVERED.—Goods in the lienor's possession.

3. EXTENT OF LIEN.—This lien extends to any unpaid balance of account for work, labor, and materials including that furnished in the course of such process in respect of any other such goods of the same owner whereof the lienor's possession has terminated.

4. ENFORCEMENT BY SALE.—If any part of the amount due remains unpaid for 10 days after the earliest item becomes due and payable, the lienor may sell the goods at public auction. If goods are readily divisible, no more may be sold than is necessary to discharge the underlying indebtedness and cover the expenses of the sale, any balance of proceeds being paid to the owner or person entitled thereto.

5. NOTICE OF SALE.—Notice of the time and place of the sale must be published once in each of two successive weeks in a newspaper published in the town, if any, otherwise in the county in which the goods are situated, the last publication not less than 5 days prior to the sale. If the residence or business address of the owner can be ascertained, a copy of such notice must be sent by registered mail at least 5 days before the day of sale.

MICHIGAN

1. WHO MAY CLAIM.—Garage keepers who furnish labor, material or supplies to vehicles under contract, express or implied.

Any owner, part owner or lessee of a hay press, threshing machine, huller, or similar machine, used for another person.

Any person who labors or provides any service in manufacturing lumber or shingles in or about any lumber or shingle mill.

2. PROPERTY COVERED.—Vehicles stored, maintained, supplied or repaired.

Hay, grain or other vegetable product pressed, threshed or hulled.

3. HOW CLAIMED.—Liens for pressing, threshing, or hulling by filing a verified statement setting forth the name of the lienor, the amount, quantity, and kind of hay or grain, seed or vegetable product, the amount due over and above all legal setoffs, the name of the person for whom the work was done, and a description of the land upon which the hay, grain, seed or product was grown and processed.

4. WHERE FILED.—The office of the register of deeds of the county where the hay, grain, seed or other product was pressed, threshed, or hulled.

5. WHEN TO BE FILED.—Pressing, threshing, or hulling liens must be claimed within 20 days after the work is completed.

6. EXTENT OF LIEN.—A garage keeper's lien is for the proper charges due.

A pressing, threshing, or hulling lien is for the agreed price, or if none, the value of services rendered, but the lien will not attach where the hay, grain or product has passed into the hands of an innocent purchaser or dealer in the usual course of trade.

7. ENFORCEMENT BY SALE.—A garage keeper's liens may be enforced by sale of the vehicle at public auction if the charges are not paid within 45 days after personal serving upon the owner of a claim of lien together with an itemized statement of the account. The sale must be held not less than 20 days nor more than 60 days after the expiration of the 45-day period.

8. NOTICE OF SALE.—Not less than 10 days' written notice of the time and place of the sale must be provided to the department of state and any lien holders shown on department records. Notice to the department and lienholders may be given by first-class mail. Notice to the owner must be certified mail to the last-known address of the owner.

9. PRIORITY.—A garage keeper's lien, insofar as it is for labor and materials furnished in making repairs, has priority over all other liens upon the vehicle. The lien becomes of no effect as against the holder of a chattel mortgage, conditional sales agreement, or other prior lien, by payment by the prior lien holder to the garage keeper of the amount of the lien, not exceeding $600 in the case of a ground vehicle, $200 in the case of watercraft. Such payment may then be added to the amount of the prior lien.

The lumberman's lien has precedence over all other liens and claims.

MINNESOTA

1. WHO MAY CLAIM.—Performers of manual labor or other personal service for hire in or in aid of cutting, saving, loading, peeling, hauling, rafting, etc. any logs or timber;

Owners and operators of threshing machines, harvesters, clover hullers, corn picking machines, shellers, shredders, ensilage cutters or hay bailers.

2. PROPERTY COVERED.—Logs and timber cut, loaded, hauled etc.

Grain, clover, corn, ensilage and hay processed as described above.

3. HOW CLAIMED.—By filing a verified statement setting forth the lienor's address, the dates when service was begun and ended, the agreed compensation, amounts paid if any, amount due, and a description of the timber or crop.

4. WHERE FILED.—Timber lien statements are filed with the surveyor general or, if no mark or description of such timber is filed with that office, then with the clerk of the district court of the county in which the labor or service was performed.

Threshing and harvesting liens are filed with the register of deeds of the county in which the work was done.

5. WHEN TO BE FILED.—Timber lien statements must be filed not less than 5 days after demand is made or more than 30 days after termination of the work, except that if such termination is by the employer the lien may be filed at once. If labor or service is wholly performed between October 1 and April 1 following, the statement may be filed on or before the last day of that April.

Threshing and harvesting liens must be filed within 15 days after the work is completed.

6. DURATION OF LIEN.—A timber lien continues for 90 days after filing.

A threshing or harvesting lien continues for 6 months after filing.

7. ENFORCEMENT.—A timber lien may be enforced through process of attachment in a civil action in a district court of any county or judicial district in which labor or service was performed or in which the surveyor general's office (wherein the marks of the property are recorded) is located.

A threshing or harvesting lien may be enforced by seizure and sale, authorized by a certified copy of the statement of so much grain, clover, corn or hay covered by the lien as may be necessary to satisfy the claim; and reasonable costs and expenses.

8. PRIORITY.—Timber liens are preferred to all other claims except those of the state and of the owner of the land from which the timber may have been unlawfully removed.

Threshing or harvesting liens are preferred to all other liens or encumbrances except those given for the seed from which the grain was grown.

MISSISSIPPI

Mississippi provides statutory liens for hotel keepers, artisans, and employees. Liens for farm labor are provided on crops. There are, however, no specific statutory liens on personal property which have special relevance to commercial credit.

MISSOURI

Missouri provides statutory liens for artisans, garagemen, locker plant operators and common carriers of logs and timber. Statutory lien for storing and repairing vehicles include boats and other water transport crafts. There are, however, no specific statutory liens on personal property which have special relevance to commercial credit.

MONTANA

1. WHO MAY CLAIM.—Persons performing labor upon, or assisting in obtaining or securing, sawlogs, pilings, ties, cordwood or other timber, or assisting in the manufacture of timber into lumber or shingles;

Persons who furnish seed to be sown or planted, or funds or means with which to purchase such seed, to another for use on lands owned, used, or occupied by that person;

Threshermen or swathers owning or operating threshing or swathing machines, and all owners of combine harvesters and threshers.

2. PROPERTY COVERED.—Timber and lumber liens are on the timber for which labor or assistance was furnished and upon all other timber which, at the time of filing the lien, belonged to the person for whom labor or assistance was provided; and upon lumber for which labor or assistance was furnished while it remains at the mill where manufactured, or in the possession or under the control of the manufacturer.

Seed lien is on the crop produced from the seed furnished, and upon the seed or grain threshed therefrom.

Threshermen's, swather's, and combiner's liens are on the grain or other crops swathed, threshed or cut.

3. HOW CLAIMED.—Timber and lumber liens are claimed by filing for record a claim containing a statement in substantially the following form:

Seed liens are claimed by filing a verified written statement stating the kind and quantity of seed and grain furnished, its value, or the amount advanced therefor, the name of the person to whom furnished, and a description of the land.

Threshermen's, swather's, and combiner's liens are claimed by filing a notice that within 20 days a lien will be claimed, and within those 20 days filing a just and true account of the amount due containing a description of the grain or crop, the agreed price for services, the name of the person for whom services were performed, a description of the land where the crop was raised, a description of the legal subdivision of land upon which grain is stored, and a description of the elevator. If the grain or crop is being hauled directly from the machine to the elevator or other purchaser, notice of claim must be served on the elevatorman as other purchaser.

4. WHERE FILED.—Timber and lumber lien claims are filed with the county in which the timber was cut or lumber manufactured.

Seed liens claims are filed in the office of the county clerk and recorder of the county in which the seed or grain is to be planted or used.

Notice of intention to claim a threshermen's, swather's or combiner's lien is filed with the county clerk of the county in which the grain or crops were grown. The account claiming such lien is filed with the county clerk and recorder of that county.

5. WHEN TO BE FILED.—Timber and lumber liens, and seed liens must be filed within 30 days after the close of work or rendition of services, or after the seed, grain, or funds are furnished. Seed liens must be filed within 90 days.

Notice of intention to claim a threshermen's, swather's or combiner's lien must be filed within 10 days after the last service was rendered or labor performed. Actual claim of lien must be filed within 20 days thereafter.

6. EXTENT OF LIEN.—Timber and lumber liens are for services and work rendered within the period of 3 months preceding the filing of the claim.

Seed liens are for the payment of the amount or value of the seed grain or funds furnished, but may not exceed the purchase price of 700 bushels of the crop.

Threshermen's, swather's, and combiner's lien is an account of the services rendered, and is charged for at the prevailing price for the particular locality in which the grain or crop is threshed, harvested, or combined.

7. DURATION OF LIEN.—Timber and lumber liens continue for 8 months after the claim is filed.

Action to enforce threshermen's, swather's, and combiner's lien must be brought within 6 months after filing of the lien.

8. PRIORITY.—Timber and lumber liens are preferred and prior to any other liens, and no sale will divest such liens. As between timber and lumber liens, liens for work and labor are preferred, and liens on logs which can be identified are preferred over general claims.

Seed liens have priority over all other liens and encumbrances on the crops.

Threshermen's, swather's, and combiner's liens are prior to and take precedence over any mortgage, encumbrance or other lien, except the lien for the seed furnished to produce the crop.

NEBRASKA

1. WHO MAY CLAIM.—Owner or operator of any threshing machine or combine used to combine or hull grain or seed, any corn picker or husker, or any corn sheller;

Any person who furnishes fuel, oil, grease, or other petroleum product to another to be used in farm machinery in the production of any agricultural crop;

Frozen-food locker plant owners.

2. PROPERTY COVERED.—Grain seed or corn threshed, combined, hulled, picked, husked, or shelled;

All crops produced by such machinery and owned by the person to whom petroleum products were furnished;

The contents of each locker or space in the frozen-food locker plant.

3. HOW CLAIMED.—Threshing and petroleum products liens may be claimed by filing notice of lien setting forth the name of the person for whom work was done or petroleum products supplied, the amount of grain covered or petroleum furnished, the location of the grain or the land on which crops were grown, the amount due or claimed, the name of the person for whom

PERSONAL PROPERTY LIENS

the threshing was done and when, or the name of the claimant of a petroleum products lien.

4. WHERE CLAIMED.—The office of the county clerk where the threshing was done, the crop produced.

5. WHEN TO BE FILED.—Within 30 days after the threshing, combining, hulling, picking, husking, or shelling is done.

Within six months after the fuel or lubricant is furnished.

6. DURATION.—Threshing and petroleum products liens must be enforced within 30 days after filing.

7. ENFORCEMENT BY SALE.—Frozen-food locker plant liens may be enforced by sale of the contents of the locker at public or private sale for its reasonable value. Proceeds in excess of the amount of the lien are paid to the locker-space renter.

8. NOTICE OF SALE.—Ten days' written notice by registered mail to the renter of the locker.

NEVADA

1. WHO MAY CLAIM.—Any person engaged in the business of buying and selling automobiles or airplanes, keeping a garage, airport or place for the storage, repair, or maintenance of motor vehicles, airplanes, and trailers; keeping a trailer park; and in connection therewith stores, repairs, or furnishes service or supplies to any motor vehicle, airplane, or trailer, at the request or with the consent of the owner or at the direction of a place officer who orders towing or storage; goods in storage.

Persons selling ore to custom mills or reduction works.

2. PROPERTY COVERED.—Motor vehicles, aircraft and trailers, and parts thereof; bullion product of mill or reduction works.

3. EXTENT OF LIEN.—Lien on motor vehicles, aircraft, and trailers are for the sum due and all costs incurred in enforcing such lien. The lien of trailer park keeper may not exceed $300 or the amount due and unpaid for four months for rental and utilities, whichever is less. The lien is subordinate when the vehicle or aircraft is the subject of a secured transaction.

4. ENFORCEMENT BY SALE.—A motor vehicle, airplane or trailer lien may be enforced by sale at auction of the property subject to the lien. The sale must be held where the lien was acquired, or if unsuitable, at the nearest suitable place.

Proceeds of the sale go first to the satisfaction of the lien, including the reasonable charges of notice, advertisement and sale; and the balance goes to the person to whom the lien would have delivered the vehicle, airplane, or trailer.

5. NOTICE OF SALE.—Written notice of sale must be given to the person on whose account service was rendered, to any other person known to have an interest in the property to be sold, and to the motor vehicle registration division of the Department of Motor Vehicles.

In case of enforcement of a lien for storage charges, the notice must include a statement of the claim, a description of the goods, a demand for full payment and a statement that the goods will be advertised for sale and sold at public auction unless payment is made in full before the time and date of the sale specified in the notice.

Notice must be given by delivery in person or by registered or certified letter addressed to the last known place of business or abode of the person to be notified, and if no address is known, then addressed to that person at the place where the lien claimant has his place of business.

NEW HAMPSHIRE

1. WHO MAY CLAIM.—Persons who perform labor or furnish material or fuel to the amount of $15 or more for the making of brick under contract with the owner thereof or a contractor;

Persons furnishing labor or supplies to the amount of $15 or more for rafting, driving, cutting, hauling, sawing, or drawing wood, bark, lumber or logs, or hauling supplies for such labor, under contract with the owner of the wood or a contractor;

Persons who maintain a public garage, public or private airport or hangar, or trailer court, for the parking, storage, or care of motor vehicles, aircraft or house trailers, by or with consent of the owners;

Persons making advances of money to the owner or lawful possessor of logs, lumber or pulpwood to finance cutting, hauling, yarding, piling, trucking, rafting, booming, driving or towing.

Any person furnishing storage, labor, hauling or transportation for any vessel; boat or vessel or boat motor.

2. PROPERTY COVERED.—Brick, the materials and fuel supplies to make same, and the kiln containing the brick;
Wood, bark, lumber, or logs transported or cut;
Motor vehicles, aircraft, or house trailers in the lienor's possession;
Logs, lumber, or pulpwood for which an advance was made and upon which lienor has caused his registered mark to be placed.
Boats, vessels and boat and vessel motors stored, worked on, hauled or transported.

3. HOW CLAIMED.—Brick and lumber subcontractors must give written notice to the owner, or a person in charge of the property, that he will claim the lien before furnishing the labor and material.

4. EXTENT OF LIEN.—Brick and lumber liens are for labor and materials.
Motor vehicle, aircraft, and trailer liens are for proper charges due.
Lumber advance liens are for the advance and for all advances for two years after the date of making the advance.

5. DURATION OF LIEN.—Brick and lumber liens exist for 90 days after services are performed or supplies furnished.
Boat and vessel liens exist during lienor's possession, and once possession is relinquished, two years from the time the indebtedness became due and payable.

6. ENFORCEMENT BY SALE.—Persons having liens on personal property, where no time limit is limited for the payment of the debt or redemption of the property, may sell the property at auction. Before the sale the lienor must send a written inquiry to the Secretary of State and town clerk to ascertain if there is another lien on the property. If there is not, or if there is no response for 14 days, the lienor may proceed with the sale. If there is a lien, notice to that lienor must be provided. From the proceeds the lienor may reimburse himself for his debt and the expenses incident to the sale. The balance, if any, must be paid to the owner on demand. When time is limited for payment or redemption of property, the property may be sold at any time after the expiration of the limited time. In the case of liens on motor vehicles, aircraft, boats, vessels, boat and vessel motors and trailers, for care and storage, sale may be held after charges remain unpaid for 60 days.

7. NOTICE OF SALE.—Notice must be provided at least 14 days prior to the sale, by posting such notice in two or more public places in the town in which the property is located by serving such notice upon the owner, if a county resident, and, if the value of the property exceeds $100 by publishing the notice. The lienholder must also provide 14-day notice to other lienholders of record by certified mail return receipt requested. Any such lienholder of record shall be entitled to redeem the property prior to the sale by payment of the amount demanded by the claimant. In the case of boat and vessel liens, notice must be served on any holder of a security interest in such property stating time and place of sale, property to be sold and amount of lien.

8. ENFORCEMENT BY ATTACHMENT.—Brick and lumber liens, and liens for lumber advances made, may be enforced by attachment.

9. PRIORITY.—Brick and lumber liens take precedence over all other claims except tax liens.
Liens for lumber advances take precedence over all claims except taxes, the lumber lien discussed above, and prior liens.
Boat and vessel liens are subordinate to all prior and subsequent perfected security interests and to the rights of subsequent purchasers for value without actual notice of such lien.

NEW JERSEY

1. WHO MAY CLAIM.—Persons operating hangers for the storage, maintenance, keeping; or repair of aircraft and who perform such services or supply materials for such aircraft;
Garage keepers who store, maintain, keep, repair, or furnish gasoline, accessories or other supplies to motor vehicles;
A processor who spins, manufactures, bleaches, dyes, finishes, dresses, or otherwise treats or processes linen, cotton, wool, real and artifical silk, yarn or goods, skins, pelts, furs or hides, or products of which they form a part;
Film processors who furnish any work, supplies, or materials in connection with any motion picture film, or loan money in connection with such film or the production or distribution thereof.
Self-service storage facility owner who stores personal property.

2. PROPERTY COVERED.—Aircraft or any part thereof.
Motor vehicle or any part thereof;
Any property of others coming into the hands of a cloth or fur processor;

PERSONAL PROPERTY LIENS 20-17

All motion picture films, belonging to the owner of the film for which services or advance were furnished, and to all parties authorized with respect to such film; and the negatives and prints in the possession of the processor.

3. DETENTION AND DEMAND OF PROPERTY.—Owner or person entitled to possession of any aircraft or motor vehicle upon learning of the detention of same by the lienor, may demand a statement of the amount due and owing. If such owner considers the amount excessive, he may offer what he considers reasonable and demand possession. If possession is refused, he may obtain possession by depositing the amount claimed with the clerk of any court of competent jurisdiction in the county where the aircraft or motor vehicle is situated, together with $12 to cover costs at county district court, or $60 in any other court. Lienor must then assert his claim in court, and if he fails to do so may be liable for damages to the owner of the aircraft or motor vehicle. Lienor of aircraft must file within 90 days after work performed or materials furnished. Statement must include the name of the person entitled to the lien, the owner of the aircraft, description of the aircraft, the amount for which a lien is claimed and date of work, etc.

4. ENFORCEMENT BY SALE.—If no proceedings are taken for the repossession of aircraft detained, lienor may sell such aircraft at public auction after the expiration of 30 days from the date of detention.

A cloth or fur processor's lien may be enforced by sale of the property at public auction after amount due has remained due and unpaid, in whole or in part, for two months.

A film processor's lien may be enforced by sale of the film at public auction, at any time after the date on which the indebtedness became due and payable.

Storage owner's lien may be satisfied by sale if amount due remains unpaid after demand.

5. NOTICE OF SALE.—Notice of sale of aircraft or motor vehicle must be published for at least 2 weeks at least once each week, in a newspaper circulating in the municipality in which the aircraft or garage is located. Not less than 5 days notice must be given by posting the notice in five public places in the municipality.

Notice of a cloth or fur processor's lien must comply with the above, and in addition a copy must be mailed to the owner, if known, at least 5 days before the sale, at his last known post-office address. Posted notice must be within 15 days before the sale.

Notice of a film processor's lien must comply with the requirements for aircraft and motor vehicle liens, and in addition 10 days' written notice must be provided to the owner or authorized party either by personal service or registered mail using the last-known address of such owner or authorized party.

Notice of self-storage owner's lien must be published once a week for 2 consecutive weeks where facility located. Sale no sooner than 15 days after final publication.

6. PRIORITY.—Aircraft liens are superior to all other liens, except tax liens.

Garage keeper's liens are not superior to, nor affect a lien, title, or interest held by virtue of a prior conditional sale or prior chattel mortgage properly recorded.

Cloth and fur processors' liens are paramount to the title lien interest or encumbrance of the owner where the owner or representative consented or authorized the acquiring of possession by the lienor.

NEW MEXICO

1. WHO MAY CLAIM.—Common carriers, including all persons carrying goods for another for hire or pay;

Garage owners and persons engaged in the business of towing automobiles, storing automobiles, or furnishing wrecker service;

Owners or lessees of threshing machines who thresh grain for another.

2. PROPERTY COVERED.—Anything carried by a common carrier;

Automobiles towed, stored or upon which wrecker service is performed at the request or with the consent of one in lawful possession;

Grain threshed.

3. HOW CLAIMED.—Threshing liens may be claimed by filing written, verified statement showing the amount and quantity of grain threshed, the agreed price, the name of the person for whom the work was done, and a description of the land.

4. WHERE FILED.—In the office of the county clerk of the county in which the grain was grown.

5. WHEN TO BE FILED.—Within 10 days after threshing is completed.

6. ENFORCEMENT.—Liens of common carriers and garage owners may be enforced in the same manner as the foreclosure of a chattel mortgage. When the property is under the control or in

the possession of the lienor, he may, upon proper notice and demand, sell the property at public auction to the highest bidder for cash. Proceeds are applied to the cost of the sale, the satisfaction of the lien; and the residue, if any, is refunded to the debtor. Reasonable attorneys fees may be awarded to prevailing party in suit relating to possession of and indebtedness on motor vehicle.

7. NOTICE OF SALE.—Lienor may serve the lien debtor with a written notice, or forward by certified or registered mail, return receipt requested, a written statement setting forth the indebtedness. If the lien is not paid within 10 days after such notice, the lienor may advertise the sale, giving at least 20 days notice, by at least 6 handbills posted in public places in the county in which the sale is to be held, or by publishing once each week for at least two successive weeks in a newspaper of general circulation in the county. Where the property is a motor vehicle subject to a towing, storage, or wrecker lien, in addition to the 10-day notice period, the vehicle must be held for 30 days if registered in a foreign jurisdiction or if registration cannot be found in the records of New Mexico.

8. PRIORITY.—A thresher's lien has priority over all other liens and encumbrances on the grain.

Artisan or mechanic with possessory lien or motor vehicle has priority over other liens, including recorded liens on motor vehicles. If vehicle released on payment of a check or other money order which proves insufficient, possessory lien shall continue 30 days past date actual possession was relinquished. After such time, lien shall become subordinate to prior recorded liens.

NEW YORK

1. WHO MAY CLAIM.—Persons keeping a garage, hangar, a place for the storage, maintenance, keeping, or repair of motor vehicles, motor boats, or aircraft, and who in connection therewith performs such services or furnishes gasoline or supplies, at the request or with the consent of the owner;

Persons who manufacture, spin or throw silk into yarn or other goods;

Persons engaged in carting or trucking property;

Persons operating motion picture film laboratories or in the business of developing, titling, storing, assembling, or reproducing such film.

A person employed in a quarry, mine, yard or dock may have a lien on the stone for the amount due.

Any person who shall perform any labor for a railroad corporation shall have a lien for the value of such labor.

2. PROPERTY COVERED.—Motor vehicles, motorboats, or aircraft;

Goods and property of others in the possession of silk good manufacturers and throwsters;

Property carted or trucked by truckman or drayman;

Positive prints printed or in any way prepared at the request or with the consent of the owner or his agent, and the negative film from which such print was prepared, including distribution and exhibition rights; and any other mortgagee or conditional vendee.

Railroad track, rolling stock, appurtenances and land on which such property is situated.

NOTE.—Liens for labor for railroad companies are claimed by filing a notice of such lien in the clerk of any county where such property is located.

3. EXTENT OF LIEN.—A garage keeper's lien is for the sum due.

4. ENFORCEMENT BY SALE.—Liens against personal property may, upon proper notice, be enforced by sale of the property at public auction to the highest bidder.[1] The sale is held in the town where the lien was acquired. Proceeds of such sale are first used to satisfy the lien and expenses of advertisement and sale; the balance to be held by the lienor subject to the demands of the owner; and notice of such balance must be served on such owner. If balance is not claimed by the owner within 30 days from the day of the sale, it is deposited with the treasurer, financial administrator or supervisor of the village, city, or town in which the sale was held.

5. NOTICE OF SALE.—The lienor must serve notice on the owner, if not found in the county where the lien arose, then to the person for whose account the lien is held. If neither can be found in the county, or if the property is of a value under $100, notice may be served by mail to the owner's last-known residence or address, or if not known, to the last-known residence or address of the person for whose account the lien is held. Similar notice is required for persons who have

---

[1] In *Sharrock* v. *Dell Buick-Cadillac, Inc.*, 45 N.Y. 2d 155, 408 N.Y.S.2d 39, 379 N.E.2d 1169 (1978), the New York Court of Appeals declared unconstitutional a provision of the lien law which permitted a garageman to conduct an ex parte sale of a bailed vehicle. (See "Recent Cases of Interest.")

notified the lienor of an interest in the property. Such notice must state the nature of the debt, an itemized statement of claim, the time due, a description of the property, and its estimated value, the amount of the lien, and must require payment by a date not less than 10 days after service of notice, stating the time and place of the sale. After such time, notice of sale of property valued at $100 or more must be published once a week for two consecutive weeks, in a newspaper published in the town or city where the sale is to be held. The sale may not be less than 15 days from the first publication. If there is no such newspaper, notice must be posted at least 10 days before the sale in at least 6 conspicuous places. Property of a value under $100 may be sold at bona fide private sale upon 20 days posted notice.

NORTH CAROLINA

1. WHO MAY CLAIM.—Any person who tows, alters, repairs, stores, services, treats, or improves personal property, other than a motor vehicle, in the course of business under contract with the owner or legal possessor;

Any person who repairs, services, tows, or stores motor vehicles in the ordinary course of business under contract with the owner or legal possessor;

Any person who improves any textile goods in the ordinary course of business under contract with the owner or legal possessor.

2. PROPERTY COVERED.—The property towed, altered, repaired, stored, serviced, treated, or improved;

The motor vehicle repaired, serviced, towed or stored;

All textile goods of the owner in the claimant's possession for improvement.

3. EXTENT OF LIEN.—Liens on personal property other than motor vehicles are for the lesser of (1) the reasonable charges for services and materials, or (2) contract price, or (3) $100 if the lienor has dealt with a legal possessor not an owner.

Motor vehicle liens are for reasonable charges.

Textile liens are for the contract charges for improvement and any amount owed for improvement of goods relinquished.

4. DURATION OF LIEN.—Liens arise when lienor acquires possession and become unenforceable when the lienor voluntarily relinquishes possession. Reacquisition of the property voluntarily relinquished does not reinstate the lien. Action to enforce lien for storage charge must be taken within 180 days following the commencement of storage; a lien for storage pursuant to an express contract may be enforced within 120 days of default.

5. ENFORCEMENT BY SALE.—If the charges remain unpaid for 30 days after maturity of the obligation, the lien may be enforced by public or private sale. If an owner, secured party, or other person claiming an interest in the property notifies the lienor, before the date of the private sale, that public sale is requested, enforcement must be by public sale. Proceeds of the sale are applied to payment of the expenses of the sale, satisfaction of the lien, and the surplus, if any, to the person entitled thereto.

6. NOTICE OF SALE.—At least 20 days prior to the date of the sale, notice of private or public sale must be made to the person holding legal title to the property if ascertainable, and to the person with whom the lienor dealt, if different, and to each secured party or person claiming interest in the property who is actually known to the lienor, by registered or certified mail. Notice must include the name and address of the lienor; the name of the title holder, if not ascertainable, the person with whom lienor dealt, a description of the property, the amount due, the place and time of sale, and a statement that recipient has 10 days to request a hearing. If the property is a motor vehicle that is required to be registered, notice must also be sent to the Commissioner of Motor Vehicles.

In addition, public sale must be advertised by posting a copy of the notice of sale at the courthouse door in the county in which the sale is to be held, and by publishing the notice of sale once per week for two consecutive weeks in a newspaper in general circulation in the same county.

7. PRIORITY.—Liens have priority over perfected and unperfected security interests.

NORTH DAKOTA

1. WHO MAY CLAIM.—Owner or lessee of a threshing machine or combine;

Persons furnishing or applying fertilizer, farm chemicals or seed to another to be spread, sown, or planted;

Persons furnishing sugar beet seed for planting, supplying insecticide or fertilizer, labor, materials, cash advances, or services necessary to the production, harvesting or hauling of sugar beet crops;

Garage keeper or keeper of a place for the storage of motor vehicle who so stores or keeps motor vehicles at the request or with the consent of the owner or lawful possessor.

2. PROPERTY COVERED.—Grain threshed or dried; crops produced from the fertilizer, chemicals or seed furnished;

Sugar crop produced;

Motor vehicles stored or kept.

3. HOW CLAIMED.—By filing a written verified statement of lien, or in the case of a sugar beet lien, a verified copy of the contract. Filing a statement of a garage keeper's lien is necessary only where possession is relinquished. On a repairman's lien, or a lien by a farm equipment dealer, garage keeper, or aviation operator, if the cost of repair would exceed one thousand dollars or twenty-five percent of the value of the property in its repaired condition, whichever is greater, and the repairman, etc., intends to have the entire bill constitute a lien, the repairman, etc., shall give notice by registered mail to the owner of the estimated cost of repair, and the estimated value of the property in its repaired condition. If notice is not provided the lien is not valid in any amount in excess of $1,000 or 25%, whichever is greater.

4. WHERE FILED.—Statements of the thresher's liens, fertilizer, chemical and seed liens, and garage owner's liens, and sugar beet contracts are filed in the office of the register of deeds of the county in which the grain is threshed, the seed sown, crops raised, or in which the motor vehicle owner resides or, if he is not a resident of the state, where the motor vehicle is stored.

5. WHEN TO BE FILED.—Thresher's lien statement must be filed 30 days after threshing is completed.

Fertilizer, farm chemical, and seed lien statements must be filed within 90 days after fertilizer, chemical, or seed is furnished or applied.

Sugar beet contracts must be filed within 60 days after contract is entered into.

6. EXTENT OF LIEN.—A thresher's lien is for the value of his services.

A fertilizer, chemical, or seed lien is for the purchase price.

A sugar beet lien is for the full amount due under the contract.

A garage keeper's lien is for the reasonable charges for storage.

7. PRIORITY.—A thresher's lien has priority over all other liens and encumbrances upon the grain threshed. Grain threshing or drying liens have equal priority.

A seed lien has priority over all other liens and encumbrances except threshing liens and crop production liens in favor of the federal or county government.

A fertilizer or farm chemical lien has priority over all other liens and encumbrances except a seed lien, thresher's lien, and the crop production lien in favor of the federal or county government.

A sugar beet lien has priority over all other liens and encumbrances except crop production liens in favor of the federal or county government.

A garage keeper's lien is subject and inferior only to mortgages and conditional sales contracts properly filed on or before the time when the property covered came into the possession of the lienor.

OHIO

Although Ohio provides statutory liens for repairmen, bailees and liverymen, it does not provide specific liens of special relevance to the commercial creditor.

OKLAHOMA

1. WHO MAY CLAIM.—Persons who, while in lawful possession of personal property, render service to the owner by furnishing material labor or skill for the protection, improvement, safekeeping, towing, storage, or carriage thereof;

Persons who thresh or combine grain or seed for another;

2. PROPERTY COVERED.—Property protected, improved, kept, towed, stored, or carried;

Grain or seed threshed or combined.

3. HOW CLAIMED.—A thresher's lien may be claimed by filing verified written statement showing the amount, quantity, and kind of grain, the price agreed to for threshing or combining, the name

PERSONAL PROPERTY LIENS

of the person for whom work was done, and a description of the land. A verified account must be filed with the clerk of the district court of the county in which the debtor resides within 30 days of the completion of work.

4. ENFORCEMENT BY SALE.—Liens of persons rendering service to personal property may be enforced by sale of the property upon proper notice. Proceedings for foreclosure by sale may not be commenced until 30 days after lien has occurred.

5. NOTICE OF SALE.—Notice of sale must include the name of the owner and other parties claiming interest in the property, a description of the property, nature of the services rendered, the time and place of the sale, and the name of the lienor. This notice must be posted in 3 public places in the county where the property is to be sold at least 10 days prior to the time of sale, and a copy must be mailed to the owner and other interested parties.

6. PRIORITY.—Thresher's lien is subject to prior mortgage liens, unless the holder receives notice of the intention of threshing or combining the grain or seed and consented in writing, after which the mortgagee becomes jointly liable with the owner for the expenses of threshing or combining.

OREGON

1. WHO MAY CLAIM.—Persons performing labor upon or assisting in obtaining, securing, handling or transporting sawlogs, spars, piles, cordwood or other timber, or in manufacturing timber into lumber or other wood products.

Common carrier's or persons who, at the owner's request, transport personal property from one place to another, and persons who store grain, merchandise, or personal property at the request of the owner or lawful possessor.

2. PROPERTY COVERED.—Timber lien is on the timber lumber or other wood product for which labor or assistance is furnished.

Transportation and storage lien is on the property transported or stored.

3. HOW CLAIMED.—A timber lien is claimed by filing a verified claim in substantially the following form.

_____, Claimant, v. _____, Defendant.

Notice is hereby given that _____ claims a lien upon (describing property), being about _____ more or less, which were (cut or manufactured) in _____ County, State of Oregon, are marked thus _____, are now lying in _____, for labor performed upon and assistance rendered in (cutting or manufacturing logs or lumber). That the name of the owner, or reputed owner, is _____; that _____ employed said _____ to perform such labor and render such assistance upon the following terms and conditions (state contract, if any, or reasonable value); that the contract has been faithfully performed and fully complied with on the part of _____, who performed labor upon and assisted in (cutting or manufacturing) for the period of _____; that said labor and assistance were so performed and rendered upon the property between the _____ day of _____, and the _____ day of _____, and the rendition of such services was closed on the _____ day of _____, and 30 days have not elapsed since that time; that the amount of the claimant's demand for the services is _____; that no part thereof has been paid (except _____), and there is now due and remaining unpaid thereon, after deducting all just credits and offsets, the sum of _____, in which amount he claims a lien upon such property.

State of Oregon,
County of _____ } ss.

I, _____, being first duly sworn, on oath say that I am the _____ named in the foregoing claim; that I have heard the same read, know the contents thereof, and believe the same to be true.

Subscribed and sworn to before me this _____ day of _____.

Transportation and storage liens are claimed by filing a verified notice of intention to so claim. This notice must state the name of the claimant, the name of the property owner, and a description of the property. A copy of the notice must be sent to the owner.

4. WHERE FILED.—With the recording officer of the county in which the timber was cut or lumber manufactured, or where the property transported or stored is located.

5. WHEN TO BE FILED.—Within 60 days after the close of rendition of services for timber or lumber or after the accrual of the transportation or storage claim.

6. EXTENT OF LIEN.—Timber and lumber liens are for services, work or labor done during the 6 months preceding the filing of notice of claim of lien.

Transportation or storage lien may not extend to charges covering a period exceeding 5 months from the date the claim first began to accrue.

7. ENFORCEMENT.—Transportation or storage liens are enforceable by suit, or by sale at public auction if the reasonable value of the property does not exceed $100.

8. PRIORITY.—Transportation and storage liens have preference over all other liens or encumbrances except a lien for herding animals.

PENNSYLVANIA

1. WHO MAY CLAIM.—Persons engaged in the business of manufacturing, spinning or throwing cotton, wool or silk into yarn or other goods, or dying cotton, wool or silk yarns.

2. PROPERTY COVERED.—Goods and property of others coming in the possession of such spinners, throwsters and dyers for the purpose of being so manufactured, spun, thrown or dyed.

3. EXTENT OF LIEN.—The amount of the account due from the owner of the cotton, wool or silk.

4. ENFORCEMENT.—Lien may be enforced by levy and sale, upon ten days notice, if the lien has not been satisfied within 30 days, and the owner has not instituted a replevin suit.

RHODE ISLAND

1. WHO MAY CLAIM.—Processors in the business of spinning, manufacturing, dying, or otherwise treating or processing linen, cotton, wool, silk, artificial silk, yarn or goods, skins, pelts, furs or hides, or goods of which any of these form a component part.

2. PROPERTY COVERED.—Property of others coming into the possession of processors.

3. EXTENT OF LIEN.—The entire indebtedness of the person for whose account work was performed or materials furnished for the property in question or other property of such debtor.

4. ENFORCEMENT BY SALE.—When amount due remains unpaid, in whole or part, for two months after it becomes due and payable, lienor may sell the property subject to the lien at public auction. No more of the property may be sold, if easily separated, than is necessary to pay the lien and expenses of sale, and the balance, if any, is paid to those entitled thereto.

5. NOTICE OF SALE.—Notice of sale must be published for two weeks prior to the day of sale, at least once each week, in a newspaper published in the county where the property is located, and a copy of the printed notice must be mailed to the owner, if known, at least 5 days before the day of sale if his address can be ascertained.

6. PRIORITY.—Lien is paramount to the title, lien, interest, or encumbrance of any owner unless such owner notifies the processor by registered or certified mail of such interest prior to the commencement of work and the creation of the lien.

SOUTH CAROLINA

1. WHO MAY CLAIM.—Persons performing work and furnishing materials in manufacturing, bleaching, dyeing, or otherwise processing natural or man-made fibers, or goods of which such fibers form a component part.

Persons who service or furnish supplies or accesories for aircraft.

2. PROPERTY COVERED.—Goods in the lienor's possession.

3. EXTENT OF LIEN.—Lien extends to any unpaid balance of account for work, labor, and materials furnished in the course of the processing described above, in respect of any other property of the same owner no longer in the lienor's possession.

4. FILING NOTICE.—The lien on aircraft property or service is dissolved in 90 days unless the lienor files in the office of the Register of mesne conveyances for the clerk of county in which the aircraft was located at the time the services were rendered.

PERSONAL PROPERTY LIENS

5. ENFORCEMENT BY SALE.—If any amount due remains unpaid for two months after it becomes due and payable, the lienor may sell the property at public auction. If the property is readily divisible, no more may be sold than is necessary to discharge the indebtedness and cover the expense of the sale. The balance of the proceeds, if any, is paid to the owner or person entitled thereto.

6. NOTICE OF SALE.—Notice of the time and place of the sale must be published once in each of two consecutive weeks in a newspaper published in the city or town, or if none, in the county, in which the property is situated, the last publication to be not less than 5 days before the sale; 5 days before the sale, notice must also be given by posting in 5 or more public places in the county, one of which must be in the town or city ward in which the property is situated, and sending by registered mail a copy of such notice to the owner, if his address can be ascertained.

SOUTH DAKOTA

1. WHO MAY CLAIM.—Persons furnishing wheat, oat, barley, rye, corn, flax or potatoes (seedgrain) to be sown or planted on another's land;

Persons owning and operating threshing machines, combines, cornshellers, cornhuskers, cornshredders, silage cutters, seed hullers, balers, mowers, grinders, rakes on agricultural pulverizing machines;

Persons who, at the request or consent of the owner or lawful possessor, furnish services, materials or facilities for the repair, storage or maintenance of any personal property;

Persons who, while in lawful possession of personal property, render service to the owner by carriage.

2. PROPERTY COVERED.—A seedgrain lien is on the crop produced from the kind of seed furnished. Thresher's and processor's liens are on all grain or agricultural products threshed or processed. Persons furnishing service or material to personal property have a lien on such property.

A carrier has a lien on the property carried.

3. HOW CLAIMED.—Seedgrain liens, thresher's and processor's liens may be claimed by filing a written account of the claim. If the person furnishing services or material to personal property loses possession thereof, he may preserve his lien by filing notice of such lien in the same manner as the carrier's lien below.

Carriers may give public record notice of lien by filing a sworn, written statement of such lien. Before filing, a copy must be sent by registered or certified mail to the owner at his last-known post office address, and the post office receipt of such mailing is filed with the statement.

4. WHERE FILED.—Seedgrain lien accounts are filed in the office of the register of deeds in the county where the crop was produced and in the county of residence of the person who produced the crop, if he is a state resident.

Notice of lien on personal property by person furnishing service on material thereto is filed in the office of the register of deeds of the county where the property is located.

Carrier's lien statement is filed in the office of the register of deeds of the county where the property is located.

5. WHEN TO BE FILED.—Notice of a lien on personal property by a person furnishing services or material thereto must be filed within 60 days after loss of possession.

6. EXTENT OF LIEN.—Seedgrain lien is for payment for the seed furnished.

Thresher's and processor's lien is for the value of services rendered.

Lien of person rendering services or material for property is for the agreed price, if none, for the reasonable charge, dependent on possession or notice.

Carrier's lien is for the compensation due him for his service, dependent on possession.

7. ENFORCEMENT BY SALE.—Subject to the right of adversely interested parties to require foreclosure by court action (except in the case of a carrier's lien), these liens may be satisfied by sale of the property at public auction.

8. PRIORITY.—Seedgrain lien, if filed within 30 days after the seedgrain is furnished, shall have preference in the order of filing, and shall have priority over all other liens and encumbrances except thresher's liens.

Thresher's and processor's lien, if filed within 10 days after the threshing or processing is completed, have priority over all other liens and encumbrances.

Liens of persons furnishing services or material to personal property are subject only to liens, mortgages, and conditional sales contracts properly filed on or before the time the property comes into the possession of the lien claimant.

9. NOTICE OF SALE.—A signed notice of sale including the names and addresses of the owner

and all lien claimants, a description of the property and its location, the grounds on which lien is claimed, and the nature of default, the amount claimed and the time and place of the sale, must be mailed to the property owner and all other lien claimants, and published for at least one issue in a legal newspaper published in the county nearest the sale, or if none, by mailing and posting one copy on the bulletin board at the front of the courthouse, or if none, at the place where the circuit court was held in the county. This notice must be made at least 10 days before the date of sale.

10. LIMITATIONS ON SALE.—Lien of person furnishing services or material to personal property may be foreclosed any time after 60 days from the date of furnishing the last item.

Sworn statement must be filed with register of deeds before foreclosure of lien.

TENNESSEE

1. WHO MAY CLAIM.—Cotton ginners;

Persons in the business of manufacturing, bleaching, mercerizing, dying, printing or furnishing cotton, silk or artificial silk, or goods of which they form a component part;

Typographers, printers, lithographers, photoengravers, electrotypers, stereotypers, book binders, and book manufacturers.

One furnishing material or labor in any transportation industry has a lien on the property.

2. PROPERTY COVERED.—Cotton ginned and baled by cotton ginner;

Goods and property of others coming into the possession of textile processors;

All plates, dies, engravings, and or materials of any sort prepared or supplied by the manufacturer or furnished by the customer to facilitate production; which remain in the custody of the manufacturer.

3. HOW CLAIMED.—Printers' and binders' wishing to enforce a lien must give notice of intention to claim lien, to the person for whom the work was done, by registered mail.

4. EXTENT OF LIEN.—Cotton ginner's lien covers all ginning and baling charges.

Textile processor's lien is for amounts due from the owners for freight advanced, processing performed, or materials furnished with respect to the same or other goods of the owner.

Printer's and binder's lien is for amounts owing from the customer.

5. DURATION OF LIEN.—A cotton ginner's lien continues for 6 months after tolls and charges become due and payable.

A textile processor's lien does not continue after the property has been transferred from the lienor.

Printer's and binder's liens continue for 90 days from the giving of notice.

The transportation, labor or services lien is effective for 12 months.

6. ENFORCEMENT BY SALE.—Textile processor's liens may be enforced by sale at public auction when the amount due, in whole or part, remains unpaid for two months after the time it became due. Proceeds of the sale are applied to the payment of the lien and the expenses of the sale, and no more may be sold, if easily divided, than is necessary to pay such lien and expenses. The balance, if any, is paid to the owner entitled thereto.

7. NOTICE OF SALE.—Notice of the sale must be published for two preceding weeks, at least once in each week, in the county where the goods are located, and upon 5 days notice of the sale set up in three or more public places in the same county one of which places is the town or the city, if any, in which the goods are located. A copy of the notice must be mailed to the owner, if his residence can be ascertained, at least 5 days before the day of the sale.

8. PRIORITY.—Cotton ginner's lien is second only to the landlord and furnisher's lien. Printer's and binder's liens are subject to prior liens.

TEXAS

Although Texas provides statutory liens for artisans, garagemen and liverymen, it does not provide specific statutory liens of special relevance to the commercial creditor.

UTAH

Although Utah provides statutory liens for livestock, hotels and laundries, it does not provide specific statutory liens of special relevance to the commercial creditor.

VERMONT

1. WHO MAY CLAIM.—Persons who advance money to owners of, or persons entitled to possession of, logs or pulpwood for the purpose of financing the cutting, yarding, piling, trucking, rafting, booming, driving, or towing of such logs or pulpwood.
2. PROPERTY COVERED.—All such logs and pulpwood on which it has caused its registered mark to be placed.
3. HOW CLAIMED.—Lien is not valid, except as against the person to whom the advances were made, until written notice of advances made or to be made is recorded.
4. WHERE CLAIMED.—The town clerk of the town where such logs or pulpwood are situated.
5. EXTENT OF LIEN.—For the amount of all advances made.
6. DURATION OF LIEN.—Two years after the date of making the last advance.
7. ENFORCEMENT.—The lien may be enforced by attachment.
8. PRIORITY.—Lien takes precedence over all claims except taxes and liens for wages of persons cutting or drawing logs, and all other liens legally acquired and filed or recorded prior to the placing of the lienor's registered mark on the property.

VIRGINIA

1. WHO MAY CLAIM.—Persons furnishing railroad iron, engine, cars, fuel, and other supplies necessary to the operation of a railway, canal, or other transportation company; any person storing or repairing a motor vehicle.
2. PROPERTY COVERED.—The franchises, gross earnings, and all real and personal property, used in the operation of the company to whom supplies were furnished.
3. HOW CLAIMED.—By filing a memorandum certified by affidavit of the amount and consideration of the claim and when due and payable.
4. WHERE FILED.—In the clerk's office of the circuit court of the county or corporation court of the city in which the chief office in Virginia of the company against which the claim is located, or when that office is in Richmond, in the office of the chancery court of Richmond, or with the receiver, trustee, or assignee of such company.
5. WHEN TO BE FILED.—Within 90 days after the last item of the bill becomes due and payable.
6. EXTENT OF LIEN.—For the moneys due. Lien for storing motor vehicles limited to extent of $150; lien for repairing motor vehicles limited to $300.
7. ENFORCEMENT.—Lien may be enforced in a court of equity. The owner may give a bond and receive possession of the property.
8. PRIORITY.—Lien is superior to, and has priority over, any amount due by the company for rents or royalties. No mortgage, deed of trust, sale, hypothecation, or conveyance executed since May 1, 1888, may defeat or take precedence over this lien. Supply lien is subordinate to that allowed clerks, mechanics, foremen, superintendents and laborers for services furnished to such company. Lien for repairing motor vehicle given priority with mechanics' liens over all other liens in the vehicle.

WASHINGTON

1. WHO MAY CLAIM.—Persons who at the request of the owner or tenant of any farm or land, do or cause to be done any work, in tilling, or preparing for growing, crops, or in cultivating, harvesting, gathering or hauling any crop or grain to any warehouse, or threshing grain;
Persons who, under contract, furnish service or materials in crop dusting or spraying for weed, disease, or insect control, or promoting crop growth;
Persons who furnish commercial fertilizer and/or pesticide, and/or weed killer to others for use on their lands.
Persons who perform labor or assist in obtaining or securing saw logs, or other timber, and manufacturing lumber, owners of tow boats used to tow logs and timber, and owners of logging teams or engines who haul logs and timber;
Persons, who, as warehousemen, commission merchants, carriers, or wharfingers, make advances for freight, transportation, wharfage, and storage of personal property.
Persons who prepare livestock products for market or who feed livestock.
2. PROPERTY COVERED.—Agricultural lien is on the crops produced.
Crop dusting lien is on the crops dusted or sprayed.
Fertilizer, pesticide and weed-killer lien is on the crops on which such product is used.

Timber lien is on the logs and timber for which service was performed, and on lumber still under the control of the manufacturer.

Transportation and storage lien is for the personal property for which service was performed, still in the lienor's possession.

Preparer or processor lien is for agricultural products delivered, products delivered, to the inventory, and to accounts receivable.

3. HOW CLAIMED.—Agricultural liens must be claimed by filing a claim of lien, subscribed and verified under oath, to the effect that it is believed to be just.

Crop dusting liens, and fertilizer, pesticide and weed-killer liens are claimed by filing a claim of lien in substance in accordance with requirements of a claim for a mechanic's lien (See Chapter 19, *supra* p. 19-61).

Preparer or processor lien must be claimed by filing a statement, signed and verified with description of lien, that amount claimed is *bona fide* and date payment was due.

Timber liens are claimed by filing a claim statement in substantially the following form:

_____ Claimant v. _____

Notice is hereby given that _____ of _____ of _____, being about _____ in quantity, which were cut or manufactured in _____ county, state of Washington, are marked thus _____, and are now lying in _____, for labor performed upon and assistance rendered in _____ said _____; that _____ employed said _____ to perform such labor and render such assistance upon the following terms and conditions, to wit:

The said _____ agreed to pay the said _____ for such labor and assistance _____; that said contract has been faithfully performed and fully complied with on the part of said _____, who performed labor upon and assisted in _____ said _____ for the period of _____; that said labor and assistance were so performed and rendered upon said _____ between the _____ day of _____ and the _____ day of _____; and the rendition of said service was closed on the _____ day of _____ and thirty days have not elapsed since that time; that the amount of claimant's demand for said service is _____; that no part thereof has been paid except _____, and there is now due and remaining unpaid thereon, after deducting all just credits and offsets, the sum of _____, in which amount he claims a lien upon said _____.

The said _____ also claims a lien on all said _____ now owned by said _____ of said county to secure payment for the work and labor performed in obtaining or securing the said logs, spars, piles, or other timber, lumber, or shingles herein described.

State of Washington, county of _____ ss. _____ being first duly sworn, on oath says that he is _____ named in the foregoing claim, has heard the same read, knows the contents thereof, and believes the same to be true.

_____

Subscribed and sworn to before me this _____ day of _____

_____

4. WHERE FILED.—Lien claims are filed with the county auditor of the county in which the crops were raised, or timber cut or lumber manufactured.

Preparer or processor lien must be filed with the department of licensing.

5. WHEN TO BE FILED.—Agricultural liens must be filed within 20 days after the cessation of work.

Crop dusting liens, fertilizer, pesticide and weed-killer liens, and timber liens must be filed within 30 days after the dusting is completed, after commencement of delivery of fertilizer, pesticide or weed-killer, or after timber is cut or lumber manufactured.

Processor lien must be filed within 20 days of date payment due and remains unpaid.

6. EXTENT OF LIEN.—Agricultural liens extend to all crops grown during the calendar year in which the work was done, for the contract price, or reasonable value of the services rendered, except that where service is rendered in preparing a crop to be grown and harvested in the following calendar year, the lien is on the crop so grown or harvested.

Crop dusting lien is for and on account of services and material.
Fertilizer, pesticide and weed-killer liens are for the purchase price.
Timber liens are for services rendered.
Transportation and storage liens are for charges for advances, freight, transportation, wharfage or storage.
Preparer or processor lien is for the contract price, if any, or the fair market value of the products delivered.

7. DURATION OF LIEN.—Agricultural liens may not bind a crop for longer than a period of 8 months after claim was filed, except that if the lien is on a crop to be harvested in the following calendar year, the lien shall extend for 12 months after it is filed.
Crop dusting liens and timber liens extend for 8 months after filing.
Fertilizer, pesticide and weed-killer liens extend for 12 months after filing.
The processor lien extends for 6 months; the preparer lien 50 days after, unless suit to foreclose has been filed.

8. ENFORCEMENT BY SALE.—Lien on personal property transported or stored may be enforced by sale if the property subject to lien is in store and uncalled for with charges unpaid and due, for a period of 30 days after such charges became due.

9. NOTICE OF SALE.—Ten days must be given by posting written notice of the time and place of sale in three public places in the county where the sale is to take place.

10. PRIORITY.—Agricultural liens are preferred to any other encumbrances on the crops to which they attach.
Fertilizer, pesticide and weed-killer liens are subordinate to any crop lien, or crop mortgage filed for record prior to the furnishing of the product.
Timber liens are preferred and prior to any other liens.
Processor or preparer lien has priority over all other liens, except for taxes or labor perfected before filing of the processor or preparer lien, if such lien is filed within 20 days.

WEST VIRGINIA

1. WHO MAY CLAIM.—Persons who, while in possession, make, alter, repair, store, or transport or in any way enhance the value of personal property.

2. PROPERTY COVERED.—The property for which service is rendered.

3. EXTENT OF LIEN.—This lien is for the charges agreed upon, or if not agreed, for just and reasonable charges.

4. ENFORCEMENT BY SALE.—This lien may be enforced by sale at auction in the county where lien was acquired, or, if unsuitable, at the nearest suitable place. Proceeds go to satisfy the lien, including seasonable charges for notice, advertisement, and sale; and the balance, if any, is to be delivered on demand to the person to whom the lienor would have been bound or justified to deliver the goods.

5. NOTICE OF SALE.—The lienor must personally or by registered mail give notice to the person on whose account the goods are held to any other persons known to the lienor who claim an interest in the property. The notice should include an itemized statement of the claim, a description of the property, a demand for payment by a certain date, not less than 10 days from delivery of the notice, a statement that, unless paid, the property will be advertised and sold at a certain time and place. After the time specified for payment, advertisement of the sale must be published once a week for two consecutive weeks in a newspaper published in the place where the sale is to be held. The sale may not be less than 15 days after the first publication. If no such newspaper is published, the advertisement may be posted at least 10 days before the sale in not less than three conspicuous places including the premises where the property is held under lien.
Where the value of the property is less than $500, newspaper advertisement is not required, and the posting in these places is sufficient.

WISCONSIN

1. WHO MAY CLAIM.—Persons performing services in cutting, hauling, running, felling, piling, driving, rafting, booming, cutting, towing, sawing, peeling, or manufacturing, logs, timber, staves, pulpwood, cordwood, firewood, railroad ties, pilings, telegraph poles, telephone poles, fence posts, paving timber, tan or other barks, or in preparing wood for manufacturing charcoal;
Persons who thresh grain, cut, shred, husk or shell corn, or bale hay and straw by machine for another.

2. PROPERTY COVERED.—Log liens are on the material to which labor or service is furnished. Agricultural liens are on the grain threshed, the corn processed, or the straw or hay baled.

3. HOW CLAIMED.—Log liens are claimed by filing a signed and verified petition setting forth the nature of the demand, the amount claimed, and a description of the property.

To apply to an innocent purchaser for value, an agricultural lien must be filed.

4. WHERE FILED.—Log liens are claimed in the office of the clerk of the circuit court of the county in which the services or some part thereof were performed.

Agricultural liens may be filed in the office of the register of deeds of the county where the services were performed.

5. WHEN TO BE FILED.—Log liens must be filed within 20 days after last day of performing continuous services.

Agricultural liens may be claimed within 15 days from the date of completion of service.

6. EXTENT OF LIEN.—Log liens are for the amount owing for services.

Agricultural liens are for the value of services to extent that the person contracting for such services has an interest in the property subject to the lien.

7. DURATION OF LIEN.—Action to enforce a log lien must be taken within 4 months after filing of petition.

Agricultural liens may be foreclosed at any time within 6 months from the date of the last charge for services.

8. ENFORCEMENT BY SALE.—Agricultural liens may be enforced by sale at public auction. Proceeds are applied to the payment of services and the expense of seizure and sale, the residue being returned to the party entitled thereto.

9. NOTICE OF SALE.—Notice of sale must be not less than 10 nor more than 15 days from the date of taking possession of such grain, corn, straw or hay. Notice is to be given personally and by posting in at least three public places in the town where the debtor resides or in the town where the sale is to be made and, if the debtor is a nonresident of the State, in the town where the grain, corn, straw or hay, or part thereof, was threshed, processed or baled.

WYOMING

1. WHO MAY CLAIM.—Persons who work upon, or furnish, or rest material or services for constructing, altering, digging, drilling, boring, operating, completing or repairing any mine or quarry, under contract express or implied.

Persons performing work upon, or furnishing any material for the construction or repair of any ditch, canal, or reservoir under contract.

Threshermen, haybalers, and combiners operating such machines.

2. PROPERTY COVERED.—Mines, quarries, materials furnished, the land or leasehold, all other wells, buildings and appurtenances located on the land or leasehold where the improvement is located.

Ditches, canals, reservoirs, right-of-way and water rights, and the land owned by the owner or proprietor for the reclamation of which the ditch, canal or reservoir was constructed.

Grain, hay or other crops threshed, baled or combined.

3. HOW CLAIMED.—Mine and quarry liens are claimed by filing notice setting forth the fact that claimant furnished the material, services or labor, the name of the party to whom furnished, the dates of such furnishing, the amount claimed, claimant's name and address, and a description of the premise to which the material, service or labor was furnished.

Ditch, canal, or reservoir liens are claimed by filing an account of the demand due in conformance with that required for a mechanic's lien to the extent possible.

Threshermen's, haybailers' and combiners' liens are claimed by filing an account of the amount due, containing a description of hay, grain or other crop, the agreed price, a description of the land upon which crops, hay or grain were raised, a description of the legal subdivision of land upon which grain or hay is stored, and, if stored in an elevator, the location of the elevator. Notice must be served on purchasers of grain, hay, or crops being hauled from the machine direct to the elevator or any purchaser.

4. WHERE CLAIMED.—Mine and quarry liens, and threshermen's, haybailers' and combiners' liens are filed with the county clerk of the county in which the land, leasehold or part thereof, is situated, or where the grain, hay, or crops were grown.

Ditch, canal, or reservoir liens are filed in the same manner as mechanic's liens.

5. WHEN TO BE CLAIMED.—Mine and quarry liens must be filed within 6 months after the last day when material or service was delivered or work done.

PERSONAL PROPERTY LIENS

Ditch, canal, or reservoir liens are filed in the same manner as mechanic's liens.

Threshermen's, haybalers', and combiners' liens must be filed within 60 days after the last service was rendered or work done.

6. EXTENT OF LIEN.—Quarry and mine liens are for payment for services and material, including transporation and mileage charges, and interest from the date due.

7. DURATION OF LIEN.—Enforcement of mine and quarry liens must be commenced within 6 months after filing notice.

Duration of ditch, canal or reservoir liens is 6 months.

Enforcement of the threshermen's, haybalers' and combiners' liens must be commenced within 60 days from the filing of the lien.

8. PRIORITY.—Mine and quarry liens attaching to materials, machinery and supplies and specific improvements are in preference to any prior lien or encumbrance or mortgage on the land or leasehold, provided that such liens, mortgages, encumbrances on the land, or leasehold existing at the inception of the lien are not affected.

Threshermen's, haybalers' and combiners' liens are prior to and have precedence over any mortgages, encumbrance, or other crops, except the lien for the seed furnished to grow the specific crop, if filed or of record.

LANDLORDS' LIENS

At common law, before the enactment of modern statutes, the landlord had a right to seize or distrain the property of his tenant, and sell it for payment of accrued rent. In many states, this common law right of distraint has been abolished and in most jurisdictions a landlord has no lien on his tenant's chattels in the absence of a judgment for unpaid rent.

In the states enumerated in the summaries a landlord may obtain a lien for unpaid rent which, under certain circumstances, may entitle the landlord to priority of payment as against all other claims against the tenant.

It may not always be easy, however, to identify those "circumstances." For example, in cases concerning conflict between the landlords' lien and a security interest perfected under Article 9 of the Uniform Commercial Code, it may be difficult to identify which priority rules to apply. The problem arises because Section 9-104(b) specifically excludes the landlords' lien from the scope of Article 9.

Some courts resolve the problem by applying the pre-code law of the pertinent jurisdiction. *See e.g., Bates & Springer of Arizona, Inc. v. Friermood*, 109 Ariz. 203, 507 P.2d 668 (1973). A typical pre-code priority formula tends to give preference to the landlords' lien provided it attached before perfection of the security interest. *See Associate Financial Services of Texas, Inc. v. Solomon*, 523 S.W.2d 722 (Tex. Civ. Ct. App. (1975)).

Other courts approach the issue by distinguishing between statutory and contractual landlords' liens. *See e.g., In Re King Furniture City, Inc.*, 240 F.Supp. 453 (E.D. Ark. 1965). *See also*, R. Anderson, *Uniform Commercial Code*, Section 9-104:4 (2d ed. 1971 & Supp. 1982). Under this approach, Section 9-104(b) is read to exclude only statutory and not contractual liens. Priority between a contractual landlords' lien and a conflicting security interest would therefore be resolved by reference to Section 9-301.

The summaries do not cover the special statutory liens that exist in almost all states in favor of innkeepers, or boardinghouse keepers, or tillers of crops on leased premises. The latter exist in practically all the agricultural states, but are not regarded as of sufficient interest to credit grantors to justify extensive discussion of them in this Manual.

Summary of State Laws Governing Landlords' Liens [1]

ALABAMA
The landlord of any storehouse, dwelling house or other building has a lien on the goods, furniture and effects belonging to the tenant or subtenant for his rent, which is superior to all other liens except for taxes and crops bought on leased premises.

ALASKA
No statutory provisions.

ARIZONA
Every landlord has a lien on all of the property of his tenant, except the property of any other person or property exempt by law, placed upon or used on the leased premises until his rent shall be paid, with the proviso that the lien does not secure the payment of rent for any period of the lease ensuing after the death or bankruptcy of the lessee or after an assignment for the benefit of lessee's creditors. He may seize for rent any personal property of his tenant found on the premises.

ARKANSAS
No statutory provisions.

CALIFORNIA
California dies not exclude a landlord's lien from the secured transactions provisions of the U.C.C.

COLORADO
A person renting to transients has a lien upon their personal property upon the premises for lodging and boarding services and all costs incurred in enforcing the lien. Any persons who rent furnished or unfurnished rooms have a lien upon any personal property of the tenant on the premises for rent, boarding, or lodging. The lien does not include necessaries.

CONNECTICUT
No statutory provisions.

DELAWARE
Distress for rent has been abolished except pursuant to a rental agreement for a commercial unit.

DISTRICT OF COLUMBIA
A landlord has a lien for his rent upon the tenant's personal chattels, on the premises, subject to execution for the debt. Lien to commence with the tenancy and continue for three months after the rent is due and until the termination of any action for the rent brought within said three months. Lien may be enforced by attachment, by judgment, by judgment execution or by action against any purchaser of the chattels with notice of the liens.

FLORIDA
A landlord has a lien on all property found on or off the premises; attaches to agricultural products and has priority over all other liens; against all other property tenant usually keeps on premises and is superior to other liens obtained subsequent to bringing the property on the premises. Lien may be enforced against all other property of tenant.

GEORGIA
A landlord has a general lien upon the property of his debtor and a special lien for rent on crops grown on land rented from him. The special lien is superior to all liens except tax liens. The general lien is inferior to tax liens, but ranks with other liens and other general liens according to date, the date being from the time of levying a distress warrant.

HAWAII
No statutory provisions.

IDAHO
No statutory provisions.

---

[1] Self-service facilities are considered in the previous section covering personal property liens.

PERSONAL PROPERTY LIENS

ILLINOIS

In all cases of distress for rent, the landlord may seize for rent any personal property of his tenant that may be found in the county where tenant resides. In no case shall property of any other person, although found on the premises, be liable to seizure for rent due from tenant. Distress and copy of property levied upon must be filed immediately with a justice of the peace.

Such lien is good for six months after expiration of the term. Lessor may enforce lien rights against sublessee or assignee.

INDIANA

The landlord has a lien on a tenant's household goods of the same effect as a chattel mortgage under the common law; by statute, a lien on crops for payment of rent which may be enforced by sale of crops.

IOWA

The landlord has a lien for his rent on all personal property of the tenant kept on the leased premises, and not exempt from execution, for one year after rent falls due, but the lien continues only for six months after expiration of term.

KANSAS

The lessor of space for a mobile home site has a lien upon the mobile home for unpaid rent. Written notice of the lien must be posted on the home. The lien has priority to all other liens except prior perfected security interests. At any time following 30 days of the notice, the lessor may remove the mobile home, provided that it is unoccupied by the lessee. Any rent due for farming land shall be a lien on the crop growing or made on the premises.

KENTUCKY

Landlords are given a lien on the fixtures, household furniture and other personal property for 4 months rent due. If property subject to the lien is openly removed without fraudulent intent, the lien is good for 15 days from date of removal and can be enforced wherever property is found. Landlord renting property for farming or coal mining given lien on tenant's personal property.

LOUISIANA

Lessor has a right of pledge of the lessee's movables which are found on the property for payment of his rent and other obligations of the lease. This includes the furniture of the lessee and the merchandise in the house or apartment. A privilege for rents of immovables exists on the crops of the year.

MAINE

No statutory provisions.

MARYLAND

Prior recorded security interest in al! chattels in which tenant has an interest is exempt from distress for rent by the landlord. Upon paying the amount owing on the goods, however, the landlord may then seize them for rent owing. Property exempt from distress when the property of the tenant includes tools used by a tenant in his occupation and books and files of an attorney or physician.

MASSACHUSETTS

Statutes only provide for liens on crops produced on leased premises.

MICHIGAN

No statutory provisions.

MINNESOTA

No statutory provisions.

MISSISSIPPI

A landlord has a lien upon lessee's personal property located on leased land, except for stock of merchandise sold in the normal course of business, for payment of rent and may not be removed from land until rent is paid. Every landlord has a lien on the agricultural product of the leased premises. The lien on personal property is subordinate to prior perfected security interests; the agricultural lien is superior.

MISSOURI
Missouri has no landlord's lien except as to growing crops. Statute authorizes attachment of lessee's property for nonpayment of rent in cases where lessee is about to remove from the premises. The lien continues for 8 months after rent becomes due and payable.

MONTANA
No statutory provisions.

NEBRASKA
No statutory provisions.

NEVADA
Lien is given to keeper of trailer parks on trailers for unpaid rent and utilities.

NEW HAMPSHIRE
No statutory provisions.

NEW JERSEY
Landlord has preferred claim for rent for not exceeding one year on goods of tenant located on the premises. May seize tenant's goods, including goods, chattels, livestock, and crops, for unpaid rent. A renter has a lien on the machinery and other chattel of the tenant.

NEW MEXICO
Landlord has lien on property in leased premises for rent due or to become due. Lien on money, and value of tools, animals, provisions, supplies furnished by landlord where landlord of agricultural land. If landlord has taken collateral for amount due before debt accrued, he is not entitled to a lien.

NEW YORK
Apartment-hotel keeper has lien on property of guest on premises.

NORTH CAROLINA
A landlord has a lien upon crops; preferred against all other liens. A landlord has a lien for the amount of rent due him on tenant's personal property, trade fixtures and equipment remaining on the premises 21 or more days after the tenant having title to the property has vacated the premises.

NORTH DAKOTA
No statutory provisions.

OHIO
No statutory provisions.

OKLAHOMA
Landlord owed rent for farming land has lien on crops growing or made on premises; may recover from purchaser of crops with notice.

OREGON
Landlord has a lien upon all personal property owned by a tenant, or occupant legally responsible for rent, brought upon the premises except for wearing apparel. Such lien is inferior to the lien of duly perfected security interests and purchase money security interests existing before personal property is brought upon the lease premises; lien on chattels owned by the tenant or occupant legally responsible for the rent includes instances of rental or lease of space in storage facilities to a person who has access to the space in order to store chattels for which no warehouse receipt, bill of lading or other document of title is issued. The general exemption of wearing apparel from a landlord's lien does not apply in the case of such rentals or leases of storage space.

PERSONAL PROPERTY LIENS

PENNSYLVANIA
The landlord may seize any personal property on the premises for rent due. In general, the property of strangers brought by tenant on the premises may be seized for rent. A landlord cannot levy or sell on distress for rent personal property which is leased or sold in any transaction in which a purchase money security interest is retained and written notice describing the property is placed upon the demised premises or within 10 days thereafter.

RHODE ISLAND
No statutory provisions.

SOUTH CAROLINA
A landlord may enforce the collection of rent by distress, except for certain household articles. Distress lien is inferior to a recorded chattel mortgage, but the landlord may pay balance owing chattel mortgage and claim the property.

SOUTH DAKOTA
No statutory provisions.

TENNESSEE
Statutes only provide for liens on crops produced on leased premises.

TEXAS
Landlord leasing residential or commercial property has lien on all non-exempt property of tenant on premises for rents due and to become due provided that in order to secure the lien for rents that are more than six months due the landlord files a verified statement with Clerk of County where building is located. Property can only be seized by landlord if authorized by lease and no breach of peace occurs. A lien arises on property of tenant stored in a bonded warehouse for storage and moving charges.

UTAH
Landlord has a lien for rent due on all the property of the tenant not exempt from execution while in the building and for thirty days thereafter. Such lien has priority over all other liens except taxes, mortgages for purchase money and labor liens. In case of assignment for benefit of creditors, bankruptcy, or receivership, lien is limited to ninety days rent prior thereto.

VERMONT
No statutory provisions.

VIRGINIA
The landlord has a lien for six months' rent on tenant's or subtenant's property found on the premises in a city or town, and not more than 12 months' rent if land or premises are used for farming, or property which may have been removed from the property not more than thirty days, unless another recorded lien is on the property.

WASHINGTON
Landlord has lien upon personal property of tenant used or kept upon premises. Conditional bill of sale or a mortgage has preference over landlords' liens. Landlords' liens on crops have priority over other encumbrances on such crops.

WEST VIRGINIA
Landlord has a lien upon any goods of tenant found on premises or removed within 30 days.

WISCONSIN
No statutory provisions.

WYOMING
No statutory provisions.

Bad Check Laws and False Credit Information

All states have so-called "Bad Check Laws," enacted in one form or another. While the statutes differ in details, they are essentially the same in principle. Under them, a maker who issues, and the holder (whether he be maker or not) who negotiates a check knowing that there are insufficient funds or credit behind it, are guilty of a crime. Most of the statutes contain a provision to the effect that in any prosecution, proof that a check, draft or order was made, drawn, uttered or delivered and that payment of the same was refused by the drawee because of lack of funds or credit, establishes a *prima facie* case of intent to defraud and of knowledge of insufficient funds in, or credit with, the bank.

THE NATURE OF THE CRIME—In a majority of the states the offense is described or treated as a misdemeanor. In many, the amount of the check determines whether it is a misdemeanor or felony. In other states the law provides for fines and/or imprisonment without specifically labelling the crime as a misdemeanor or felony. This subject is summarized in the "Table of Bad Check Laws" which is set forth in this chapter.

CONSTITUTIONALITY—There has been much discussion as to the constitutionality of bad check laws, but very few cases have passed directly upon the question. The decisions generally uphold such statutes against state constitutional objections. Thus it has been held that statutes of the kind under consideration do not violate a constitutional provision against imprisonment for debt. *Hollis v. State,* 152 Ga. 182, 108 S.E. 783 (1921); *State v. Avery,* 111 Kan. 588, 207 p. 838 (1922). On the other hand, a South Dakota statute which provided that the giving of a postdated check with insufficient funds to cover it was a criminal offense, was held unconstitutional since it resulted in imprisonment for debt. *State v. Nelson,* 237 N. W. 766 (1931). In *Neidlinger v. State,* 17 Ga. App. 811, 88 S.E. 687 (1916), it was expressly held that unless the statute required fraudulent intent as an element of the crime, it would be invalid since it would be but an instrument for the collection of debt by the criminal law process in contravention of sound public policy and of the constitutional provision against imprisonment for debt. In order to sustain the constitutionality of the statute, the court construed it to require a fraudulent intent. See also *Seaboard Oil Co. v. Cunningham,* 51 F.2d 321 (5th Cir. 1931). The presumption of fraudulent intent from issuing a check without sufficient funds has been held not to be a violation of the due process clause of the Federal Constitution. *Carter v. Lowry,* 169 Ga. 515, 151 S.E. 23 (1929).

INTENT TO DEFRAUD AND KNOWLEDGE OF INSUFFICIENT FUNDS AS NECESSARY ELEMENTS—Most of the bad check laws expressly provide that intent to defraud is a necessary element of the offense, and where not required by statute it is so required by judicial decision. The means of effecting this intent to defraud is the making, drawing, uttering, or delivering of any check, draft or order for the payment of money upon any bank or other depository, knowing at the time of such making, drawing, uttering or delivering that the maker or drawer has not sufficient funds in or credit with such bank or other depository, for the payment of such check, draft, or order in full upon its presentation. The making, drawing, uttering or delivering of such check, draft or order is, under most of the statutes, *prima facie* evidence of intent to defraud. The word "credit" as used in the bad check laws means an arrangement or understanding with the bank or depository for the payment of such check, draft or order.

The words "with intent to defraud" as used in the statutes do not mean that the payee need have been actually defrauded. The intention to defraud is sufficient. The majority of the statutes provide in effect that failure to pay the check, draft or order within a specified number of days after demand, shall be presumptive evidence of intent to defraud and of knowledge of insufficient funds in, or credit with, the bank for the payment of the same. These presumptions of fraudulent intent and of knowledge of insufficient funds are not conclusive, but are rebuttable. Where the evidence introduced by the state in prosecuting an alleged offender against the statute makes it appear that the maker of the check was not actuated by an intent to defraud in making, drawing, uttering or delivering the instrument, the presumption is overcome. Of course, the presumption is overcome where the maker pays the check within the statutory grace period. See *Berry v. State,* 153 Georgia 169, 115 S.E. 669 (1922). Not all states presume intent. In California, intent to defraud must be affirmatively proved by the prosecution; it can be proved by circumstantial evidence. The presumption of law is held insufficient. *People v. Becker,* 137 Cal. App. 349, 30 P.2d 562 (1934). The drawer must also have knowledge of insufficient funds or credit. *Ex parte Leuschen,* 134 Cal. App. 246, 25 P.2d 243 (1933).

In those states where an intent to defraud is presumed, knowledge of insufficient funds, which is a necessary element in proving the intent to defraud, is also presumed. The presumption may arise at the time of the making of the check, although it usually arises upon the notice of nonpayment.[1]

A number of states provide that the presumption of intent to defraud is rebutted upon the payment, after receipt of notice by the maker, of the amount of the check plus a service charge within the grace period as provided by statute. See, e.g., Florida law which provides that the *prima facie* evidence of intent is rebutted upon payment by the maker of the amount of the check plus a service charge of $10 or 5% of the face amount of the check, whichever is greater, within seven days after notice; Georgia provides for a service charge of $5 or 5%, whichever is greater, within 10 days; Indiana provides for payment of $15 or 5% (but not more than $250) within 10 days; Mississippi and South Carolina provide for payment of $10 within 15 days; North Dakota provides for $10 within 10 days; and Texas provides for payment of $15 within 10 days.

TIME WITHIN WHICH CHECK MAY BE MADE GOOD—In many of the states the person who makes, draws, utters or delivers a bad check, is given a period of time specified in the statute within which to "make good" after receiving notice that the check has been dishonored. Under some of the statutes, prosecution cannot be commenced until the expiration of the time allowed; in other states, the statute provides that the prosecution shall be abated in the event

---

[1] When the payee has agreed to hold the check for a period of time there is a question of fact as to whether the check was issued with the required intent to defraud. See *People v. Will,* 289 N.Y. 413, 46 N.E.2d 498 (1943).

BAD CHECK LAWS AND FALSE CREDIT INFORMATION 21-3

that the check is made good within the time specified; and in other states, if the check is made good within the time specified, the presumption that the check was given with fraudulent intent and with knowledge of insufficient funds does not attach.

In Louisiana if issuer of check has not paid in 6 months, holder of check, after prior notice to issuer, may post a copy of check or photograph of maker on its business premises.

The table below specifies the time limitations within which a check may be made good. Unless otherwise indicated, the grace periods noted begin upon receipt of notice, by the maker or drawer of the dishonored check. The notice in most states is effected by written notice delivered by certified or registered mail or receipt of the unpaid check by its maker.

State	Number of Days	State	Number of Days
Alabama	10	Montana	5
Alaska	5	Nebraska	10
Arizona	12	Nevada	10
Arkansas	10	New Hampshire	14
California	No provision	New Jersey	10
Colorado	15	New Mexico	3
Connecticut	8	New York	10
Delaware	10	North Carolina	No provision
District of Columbia	5	North Dakota	10
Florida	7	Ohio	10
Georgia	10 [1]	Oklahoma	5
Hawaii	5	Oregon	10
Idaho	No provision	Pennsylvania	10
Illinois	No provision	Rhode Island	7
Indiana	10	South Carolina	15
Iowa	10	South Dakota	5
Kansas	7	Tennessee	10 [1]
Kentucky	10	Texas	10
Louisiana	10	Utah	14
Maine	5	Vermont	8
Maryland	10	Virginia	5
Massachusetts	2	Washington	15
Michigan	5	West Virginia	10
Minnesota	5	Wisconsin	5
Mississippi	15	Wyoming	5
Missouri	10		

[1] Notice by mail to residents of state. No notice to nonresidents or a resident who has left the state. No notice if situs of drawee is outside the state. Tennessee provides that where a maker tenders a bad check for the payment of taxes there will be a presumption of intent to defraud unless the holder receives the amount due within 15 days of receipt of notice.

CHECKS IN PAYMENT OF PREEXISTING DEBTS—Generally, the giving of a check in payment of an antecedent debt due by the maker to the payee, even when accompanied by a false statement by the maker that he had the money in the bank to meet the same, whereby this statement the maker did not deprive the payee of any right, procure anything of value from the payee when making such statement, or wrongfully appropriate anything belonging to the payee, is usually not a violation of the statute. Bank checks are not payment in most cases until they are paid. For example, in Alabama and Utah the offense consists of inducing the person to whom the check is given to part with money or something of value in exchange. Payment of a past due indebtedness is, therefore, held not to be within the purview of the statute. *Phillips v. State,* 24 Alabama App. 456, 136 So. 480 (1931). The Florida statute refers to a person who secures services, goods, wares or other things of value for the check. The Georgia and Virginia statutes specifically include checks in payment of obligations for wages. The Maryland statute applies to obtaining "property or services." Massachusetts also specifically includes obtaining "services" thereby. The phrase "to apply on account or otherwise" was added by an amendment to the Michigan Bad Check Law in 1923. The Missouri statute expressly includes checks in payment of past due obligations, as does Arizona's. See *State v. Meeks,* 30 Ariz. 436, 247 P. 1099 (1926).

In New York it has been held that whether the check is given for past due indebtedness or otherwise is immaterial. *People v. Nibur,* 238 App. Div. 233, 264 N.Y.S. 148 (1st Dept. 1933). In Texas the new statute is applicable to past due obligations and also to giving a check for purpose of retaining or securing possession of any personal property to which a lien has attached or in payment of rental of a house or apartment. In Ohio when a bad check is given in payment of a preexisting debt or for any other past consideration, it is a question of fact for the jury to determine whether or not there existed an intent to defraud sufficient to justify a conviction. *State v. Lowenstein,* 142 N.E. 897 (S.C. Ohio 1924).

STOPPING PAYMENT ON CHECKS—It has been held that, one who gives a check for the purchase of property, drawn on a bank in which he has sufficient funds to meet the check, but with the intent to and subsequently does stop payment thereon, is guilty of the statutory crime of cheating and swindling. *Garner v. State,* 100 Ga. 257, 28 S.E. 24 (1897). However, it has also been held that a person who obtains property under similar circumstances is not guilty of obtaining money under false pretenses, within provisions of a statute making it an offense for any person, by any false pretense, to obtain from any other person anything of value, with intent to cheat or defraud. *People v. Orris,* 52 Colo. 244, 121 P. 163 (1912).

Georgia provides that the payee of any check written for goods or for services rendered has a lien on such goods perfected in the same manner as a mechanic's lien in the event the payor has subsequently issued a stop payment order.

POSTDATED CHECKS—The Uniform Commercial Code, Section 3-104(2) (b) defines a check as "a draft drawn on a bank and payable on demand." A postdated check, since it is not payable on demand, does not satisfy this definition. Consequently, it has generally been held that the giving of a postdated check does not constitute a present fraud nor is it within the scope of the "bad check laws."

Under the decision of the Supreme Court of Ohio in *State v. Lowenstein,* cited above, it would seem that it makes no difference if the check is postdated or not if intent to defraud existed at the time the check was delivered. The same was held by the Supreme Court of Illinois in *People v. Westerdahl,* 316 Ill. 86, 146 N.E. 737 (1925), where value was given for the check, and the payee relied upon the check and not upon the personal credit of the maker.

In *State v. Taylor*, 335 Mo. 460, 73 S.W.2d 378 (1934), a postdated check was held to come within the purview of Missouri's bad check law. *But see State v. Humphrey*, 74 S.W.2d 86 (Mo. Ct. App. 1934) where statute not applicable to an undated check. In *State v. Barone*, 98 N.J.L. 9, 118 A. 779 780 (1922), under a statute defining the crime as a misdemeanor, the court held:

> The giving of a check presently payable is an implied representation by the drawer that he then has funds on deposit in the bank upon which it is drawn sufficient to meet it upon its presentation for payment.
>
> The giving of a postdated check carries with it no such implication, but rather the contrary. It is a mere promise to discharge a present obligation on a future day. And the fact of its nonpayment when the due date arrives—without more—is no more evidence that it was given with fraudulent intent than is the permitting of a promissory note to go to protest proof of such intent or the failure to pay the purchase price of goods sold on credit, standing alone, evidence of fraud in the making of the contract. Fraud is never presumed, but must always be proved, and an intent to defraud cannot be predicated solely upon the mere nonperformance of a future promise. The citation of authority in support of such proposition is unnecessary.

The same has been held in Arkansas, Georgia, Iowa, New Jersey, North Carolina and South Carolina. A postdated check, however, is within the operation of a statute providing punishment to a person who willfully, with intent to defraud, draws a check or draft on a bank for payment of money, knowing that he has no funds or credit with which to meet it on presentation. *People v. Berkovitz*, 163 Cal. 636, 126 P. 479 (1912).

In North Carolina it is held that the giving of a postdated check merely implies that the maker will have or expects to have sufficient funds on hand to cover the same when presented. Therefore, it is not within intent of statutory prescriptions. *State v. Crawford* 198 N.C. 522, 152 S.E. 504 (1930). Florida, although not passing on the question directly in *Anderson v. Bryson* 94 Fla. 1165, 115 So. 505 (1927), holds that where a payee accepts a check with knowledge of maker's insufficient funds and relies on maker's promise to secure funds by the due date, the offense contemplated by the statute is not committed. A statute providing that it is a misdemeanor to fraudulently make a check knowing at the time that there are insufficient funds to cover the check, and providing further that the making itself shall be *prima facie* evidence of intent to defraud, was held not to cover a postdated check accepted by the payee with the knowledge that the paper represented nothing more than a promise that on a future date there would be sufficient funds to cover the check. *Strickland v. State*, 27 Ga. 772, 110 S.E. 39, (App. Ct. 1921). The Kansas, Minnesota and New Mexico statutes specifically except postdated checks from the coverage of their statutes.

The Indiana statute provides that the giving of a bad check in Indiana, whether antedated or not, and whether for an antecedent debt or otherwise, is probably an offense. The Michigan statute would seem to make the giving of a postdated check a crime since the statute refers to "no account" or "insufficient funds" for payment of check at the time of "its presentation." The Utah statute contains a similar provision. The Maryland statute makes it an offense if payment is not provided for and the check is not paid at time of its presentation.

(Continued following table)

TABLE OF BAD CHECK LAWS

STATES	MISDEMEANORS	FELONY	PENALTIES	EVIDENCE RULES
ALABAMA	All Amounts	....	Check of $500 or more, fine of not less than $500 nor more than $5,000, or imprisonment up to 3 years, or both; under $500 check, fine depends on amount and offense. Court shall also order restitution to plaintiff; defendant shall pay court costs if convicted.	Nonpayment within 10 days of receiving notice from holder is *prima facie* evidence of intent to defraud and knowledge of insufficient funds.
ALASKA	Less than $500	$500 or more	Issuing check for $25,000 or more, maximum fine of $50,000, imprisonment up to 10 years, or both. Issuing check for $500 or more, up to $25,000, maximum fine of $50,000, imprisonment up to 5 years, or both. Issuing check for $50 or more, up to $500, maximum of $5,000, imprisonment up to 1 year, or both. Issuing check under $50, maximum fine of $1,000, imprisonment up to 90 days, or both.	It is *prima facie* evidence of intent to defraud if drawer fails to pay check within 12 days of first-class mailing of notice of dishonor, provided dishonor occurred within 30 days of issuance of the check, or if drawer had no account with drawee at the time the check was issued.
ARIZONA	Less than $25	$25 or more or no account	Up to 6 months in jail or up to $300 or both if under $25; up to 5 years in state prison or up to 1 year in county jail or up to $500 fine or both if between $25 and $100; up to 5 years in state prison if over $100 or if no account.	An issuer's knowledge is presumed if payment refused and issuer fails to pay full amount of check and reasonable costs within 12 days of notice.
ARKANSAS	Less than $200	One or more checks totaling over $200	Checks of $200 or less for 1st conviction fine of not less than $50 nor more than $500 or imprisonment up to 30 days or both, 2nd offense fine of not less than $100 nor more than $1,000 or imprisonment up to 90 days or both; 3rd and subsequent offenses fine of not less than $200 nor more than $2,000 or imprisonment up to one year or both. When more than one check is involved and such checks were drawn within 90 days of each other and each is an amount less than $200, the amount of such separate checks may be added together to arrive at and be punishable under the $200 or more amount to which this category refers. Checks for $500 involve a fine not exceeding $10,000 or imprisonment up to 10 years or both. Prosecuting attorney can collect fee depending on amount of check dishonored.	Nonpayment within 10 days of receiving notice from holder of the amount due and the service fee not exceeding $10 is *prima facie* evidence of intent to defraud if issuer had no account or payment refused for lack of funds.
CALIFORNIA	Discretion of Court	On any amount	Where amount is less than $200 and is first offense, up to one year in county jail.	Making, drawing, uttering or delivering with intent to defraud and knowledge of insufficient funds is the crime. Notice of protest is presumptive evidence of knowledge of insufficiency of funds, but intent to defraud must be affirmatively proved by the prosecution.

COLORADO	From $50 up to $200	Misdemeanor—imprisonment in county jail for not less than 3 months nor more than 12 months or by fine of not less than $250 nor more than $1,000 or both. Felony—imprisonment in state penitentiary for not less than 1 year nor more than 5 years or by fine of not less than $1,000 nor more than $15,000 or both. If twice previously convicted, punishment is imprisonment in state penitentiary for not less than 1 year and not more than 10 years or fine of not less than $2,000 nor more than $30,000 or both.	Except as to a postdated check, if the person has no account with the bank at the time he issues the check, or if there are insufficient funds, it is presumptive evidence of intent. Full satisfaction of check with 15 days after dishonor is a defense. Person instituting prosecution who fails to cooperate in the full prosecution of alleged offender may be liable for costs of prosecution.
	$200 or more or conviction involving 2 or more bad checks within 60 days totaling $200		
CONNECTICUT	Less than $1,000	Up to $1,000 fine or 1 yr. in jail or both.	Issuer is presumed to know that check other than a postdated check would not be paid if no payment made within 8 days after receiving notice of dishonor. Notice of dishonor is presumed if mailed by certified mail, return receipt requested, to the issuer at his last known address. Presumption also raised if drawee had no account at time check was issued.
	$1000 or more		
DELAWARE	Less than $300	Misdemeanor—up to 2 years in jail, $1,000 fine, or both. Person who issued check must make restitution to person to whom check was issued. Felony—up to 7 years and such fine as court may order.	Nonpayment in 10 days is *prima facie* evidence of knowledge of insufficient funds. Having no account at time of drawing is also a *prima facie* case.
	$300 or more		
DISTRICT OF COLUMBIA	Less than $100	Up to 3 years imprisonment and $3,000 fine or both.	Making, drawing, uttering, or delivering is *prima facie* evidence of intent to defraud and knowledge of insufficient funds if payment and fees not paid within 7 days of receiving notice.
	$100 or more		
FLORIDA	Less than $50	Felony—up to 5 years in prison or $1,000 fine. Misdemeanor—up to $300 or 6 mos. in jail.	Making, drawing or delivery of check, payment of which is refused, shall be *prima facie* evidence of intent to defraud, or of knowledge of insufficient funds.
	$50 or over		
GEORGIA	Less than $500	Check for less than $100, for 1st offense: a fine of not less than $50 nor more than $100; or imprisonment up to 30 days, or both; for 2nd offense: a fine of not less than $100 nor more than $200 or imprisonment up to 60 days, or both; and for 3rd and subsequent offenses: a fine of not less than $200 nor more than $400 or imprisonment up to 12 months, or both. Check for $100 or more but less than $500, for 1st offense: a fine of not less than $100 nor more than $200; or imprisonment up to 60 days, or both; for 2nd offense: a fine of not less than $200 nor more than $800 or imprisonment not to exceed 3 months, or both; for 3rd offense: a fine of not less than $400 nor more than $800 or imprisonment of up to 12 months, or both. When more than one check is involved and such checks were drawn within 90 days of one another and each is in an amount less than $100, the amounts of such separate checks may be added together to arrive at and be punishable as above. Check for $500 or more; a fine of not less than $500 nor more than $5,000 or by imprisonment for up to three years, or both.	Drawing, uttering or delivery is *prima facie* evidence of knowledge of insufficient funds if maker has not paid amount due within 10 days after notice by certified mail. It is also *prima facie* evidence of intent if the accused had no account with the drawee at the time the instrument was made.
	$500 or over		

TABLE OF BAD CHECK LAWS *(Continued)*

STATES	MISDEMEANORS	FELONY	PENALTIES	EVIDENCE RULES
HAWAII	All Amounts	....	Up to 1 year in jail or $1,000 fine or both.	Insufficient funds or credit is *prima facie* evidence of intent provided check not paid within 5 days.
IDAHO	All Amounts	....	Fine or imprisonment or both as follows: If under $25, 1st offense—$300 and 6 months; 2nd offense—$1,000 and 1 year; 3rd offense, or if amount in excess of $25—$5,000 and 3 years.	Making, drawing, uttering or delivering is *prima facie* evidence of intent.
ILLINOIS	All Amounts	Subsequent offenses over $150	Up to $500 fine or up to 1 year in jail, or both.	Failure to have sufficient funds is *prima facie* evidence of intent.
INDIANA	All Amounts	....	Up to $5,000 fine or up to 1 year in jail, or both.	Failure to have sufficient funds in or an account with the drawee institution constitutes *prima facie* evidence that drawer knew it would not be paid.
IOWA	Under $20	Over $20 or no account	Up to $100 fine or 30 days in jail for misdemeanor. Up to 7 yrs. in penitentiary, or (1 yr. in jail or up to $500 fine, or both) for felony.	Nonpayment is *prima facie* evidence of intent providing maker shall not have paid the amount due within 10 days.
KANSAS	Under $50	Over $50	Up to $2500 fine or up to 1 year in jail or both. Up to $5000 fine or 1 to 5 years in jail or both.	No payment 7 days after notice.
KENTUCKY	Under $100	Over $100	Up to $500 fine. 1 year in penitentiary for a misdemeanor. Felony punishable by imprisonment from one to five years and a fine of not more than $10,000, or double the offender's gain from commission of the crime, whichever is greater.	Making or delivering is *prima facie* evidence of intent. Withdrawal to prevent payment is crime.
LOUISIANA	Under $100	Over $100. When two or more worthless checks have been issued within a 180 day period the aggregate amount of all the worthless checks issued within that period shall determine the grade of offense	Check for under $100, imprisonment for not more than 6 months or fine of not more than $500 or both. A third or more such conviction, fine of not more than $1,000 or imprisonment for not more than 2 years or both. Check for $100 or more and less than $500, imprisonment for not more than 2 years or fine of not more than $2,000 or both. Check for $500 or more, imprisonment for not more than 10 years or fine of not more than $3,000 or both. In addition, the court may order as part of the sentence restitution of the amount of the bad check plus reasonable attorney's fees.	Failure to pay within 10 days of written notice is presumptive evidence of intent to defraud.
MAINE	All Amounts	....	Up to $1,000 fine or 11 months in jail, or both.	Nonpayment in 5 days after notice is *prima facie* evidence of intent.
MARYLAND	Obtaining property under $300	Obtaining property over $300	Misdemeanor—maximum fine of $100, imprisonment up to 18 months, or both. Felony—maximum fine of $1,000, imprisonment up to 15 years, or both.	When a check is drawn on an account having funds insufficient to cover it, the drawer is presumed to know of the insufficiency.

21–8

State			
MICHIGAN	Less than $50	..... Over $100	Up to $600 fine and up to 2 yrs. in jail or up to 5 yrs. in penitentiary.	Nonpayment in 2 days after notice is *prima facie* evidence of intent.
MINNESOTA	All Amounts	Over $50	Up to $250 fine or 6 mos. in jail. Up to $500 fine or 1 year in jail.	Nonpayment within 5 days after notice is *prima facie* evidence of intent.
MISSISSIPPI	Less than $100		Up to $100 fine, 90 days in jail or both.	Nonpayment within 5 days, no account with drawee at time of issuance, insufficient funds when check presented within reasonable time are *prima facie* evidence of intent.
		Over $100 or less than $100 if third or subsequent offense	Checks under $100—a fine of not less than $25 nor more than $500 or imprisonment in the county jail for not less than 5 days nor more than 6 months or both. Upon conviction of second offense for check less than $100 a fine of not less than $50 nor more than $1,000 or imprisonment of not less than 30 days nor more than 1 year. For the third offense a felony regardless of amount involved, imprisonment in the state penitentiary for a term of not less than 1 year nor more than 5 years. For a check of more than $100, deemed a felony, punishment of fine of not less than $100 nor more than $1,000 or by imprisonment for a term of not more than 3 years or both.	Nonpayment of check and service charges within 15 days is *prima facie* evidence of knowledge.
MISSOURI	Less than $150	$150 or over	Up to $500 fine or 6 mos. in jail, or both. Up to $1,000 fine or 1 yr. in jail. or both.	Nonpayment of check and costs in 10 days after notice is *prima facie* evidence of intent.
MONTANA	Insufficient funds under $300	Insufficient funds over $300 or ..... No account	Up to $500 fine or 6 mos. in jail, or both. Up to $50,000 fine or 10 yrs. in penitentiary or both.	Nonpayment in 5 days after notice is *prima facie* evidence of knowledge.
NEBRASKA	Issuing or passing check of any amount; using bad check to acquire property, etc., worth less than $300.	Using bad check to acquire property worth $300 or more; second conviction for acquiring property worth less than $300	Obtaining property worth: More than $1,000—Class III felony. More than $300—Class IV felony. More than $75—Class I misdemeanor; 2nd offense—Class IV felony. Less than $75—Class II misdemeanor; 2nd offense—Class IV felony. Issuing or passing a check of any amount—Class II misdemeanor.	Nonpayment in 10 days after notice of dishonor is *prima facie* evidence of intent.
NEVADA	Less than $100	Over $100	Up to 6 mos. in county jail or $500 fine, or both. State prison of one to 10 years or $10,000 fine or both.	Nonpayment within 10 days after notice is *prima facie* evidence of intent to defraud and knowledge of insufficient funds.
NEW HAMPSHIRE	Less than $500	Over $500	Up to $200 fine or up to 1 yr. in jail, or both.	Making and drawing is *prima facie* evidence of intent, if the issuer has no account with the drawee at the time made or check not paid within 10 days are prima facie evidence of intent.
NEW JERSEY	$200 or more ..... Issuance or passing of check with knowledge that it will be dishonored is a "disorderly persons offense."		Up to $1,000 fine or up to 1 yr. in jail or both.	If maker has no account with the drawee or if maker fails to pay check within 10 days of dishonor, which dishonor occurred within 30 days from issuance of the check, then there is a presumption of knowledge
NEW MEXICO	More than $1, less than $25.	$25 or over	Up to $100 fine or 30 days in jail, or both. 1 to 3 years in jail, or up to $1,000, or both.	Prima facie evidence of intent from fact that the maker had no account at the bank the check was drawn on or that the maker failed to pay check and costs within 3 days of notice.

21–9

TABLE OF BAD CHECK LAWS (Continued)

STATES	MISDEMEANORS	FELONY	PENALTIES	EVIDENCE RULES
NEW YORK	All Amounts Class B misdemeanor	....	Up to 3 months in jail, or up to $500, or up to double the amount of the drawer's gain from the commission of the offense.	Nonpayment is *prima facie* evidence of intent. Notice of Protest Certificate or officer of bank under oath to prove nonpayment. Full payment within 10 days after dishonor is an affirmative defense.
NO. CAROLINA	All Amounts	....	$50–$500 or up to 6 months in jail. If check is less than $50—$50 fine or up to 30 days in jail. Over 3 convictions, up to 1 year. If check drawn on nonexistent account, fine not to exceed $1,000 or imprisonment for not more than 2 years or both. If check drawn on account closed by drawer prior to time check drawn, fine not to exceed $400 or imprisonment for not more than 5 months or both.	The making of a worthless check, draft, or order shall be *prima facie* evidence of an intent to cheat and defraud.
NORTH DAKOTA	All Amounts	Second offense All amounts	$25–$250 fine, or up to 3 months in county jail, or both. If no account—fine up to $500 and one year in jail.	The fact that payment has been refused by a drawee because of insufficient funds or because the drawer has no account with the drawee shall constitute *prima facie* evidence of intent to defraud.
OHIO	Less than $150	Over $150, subsequent offenses	Misdemeanor: Up to 6 months in jail, $1,000 fine, or both. Felony: Up to 5 years, $2,500 fine, or both.	Refusal of drawee to pay within 10 days is *prima facie* evidence of intent.
OKLAHOMA	$20 or less	More than $20 or one of a series of checks whose total exceeds $20.	Up to one yr. imprisonment or up to $1,000 fine or both. 1 to 10 yrs. imprisonment or up to $5,000 fine.	Refusal of payment by bank is *prima facie* evidence of intent provided not paid within 5 days after presentation.
OREGON	Up to $75	Over $75	Misdemeanor: Up to $1,000 fine or up to 1 year in jail, or both. Felony: Imprisonment for not more than 5 years.	Refusal of drawee to pay within 10 days is *prima facie* evidence of intent. Notice of protest is proof of presumptive intent.
PENNSYLVANIA	Over $200	....	Up to $1,000 fine or up to 2 yrs. in penitentiary, or both.	Making is *prima facie* evidence of intent if not paid in 10 days after notice.
RHODE ISLAND	Not exceeding $100.	Over $100	Up to $500 fine, or up to 1 yr. imprisonment, or both. Up to $1,000 fine, or up to 1 yr. imprisonment, or both.	As against maker or drawer the making, drawing, uttering or delivering payment of which is refused due to insufficient funds is *prima facie* evidence of intent to defraud unless paid within 7 days.
SO. CAROLINA	All Amounts	....	Up to $2,000 fine or up to 10 years in jail, or both.	If not paid in 15 days after notice, *prima facie* evidence of intent. When maker or drawer did not have account with bank on which check is drawn, prima facie evidence of intent to defraud.
SOUTH DAKOTA	All Amounts	Agent or Officer of business issues check or checks totalling $1,000 or more within 30 days.	First offense: a fine of not more than $100 or imprisonment for not more than 30 days or both. Second offense: a fine of not more than $300 nor less than $100 and imprisonment of not more than 6 months or less than 30 days. Third and subsequent offenses: a fine of not more than $500 nor less than $300 and imprisonment for not more than 1 year nor less than 6 months. Felony: Up to 3 years and not more than $1,000 fine.	Making, drawing, uttering and delivering is *prima facie* evidence of intent.

21-10

State	Amount	Penalty	Evidence of Intent
TENNESSEE	Less than $100	Not over $100—not over 11 months 29 days in jail, not over $500 fine, or both. Over $100—from 3 to 10 years in jail.	Nonpayment within 10 days after receiving notice is *prima facie* evidence of intent.
TEXAS	1st offense under $50 2nd offense under $50	Up to 2 yrs. in county jail or up to $1,000 or both. 30 days to 2 yrs. in jail and up to $2,000.	Nonpayment within 10 days after notice is *prima facie* evidence of intent and knowledge.
	3rd offense or over $50	2 to 10 years.	
UTAH	Less than $300	Less than $200-up to 6 months or $299 or both; more than $200 but less than $300-up to 1 year or $1,000 or both.	Making, drawing, uttering, or delivering check is *prima facie* evidence of intent. Presumption of knowledge if issuer had no account with drawee at time of issue.
	Over $300	More than $300 but less than $1,000-up to 5 years or $5,000 or both; more than $1,000-up to 15 years or $10,000 or both.	

VERMONT	All Amounts	Up to 1 year in jail and $1000 fine or both.	Courts can infer that the issuer knew that the check would not be paid, if:
			1. the issuer had no account with the drawee at the time the check or order was issued; or
			2. the issuer had insufficient funds with the drawee at the time the check or order was issued or presented for payment, and
			  a. the check or order was presented to the drawee for payment not more than 30 days after the date of issuance, and
			  b. payment was refused by the drawee for reasons other than seizure or attachment of the issuer's funds by order of a court or authorized governmental agency, and
			  c. the issuer or a person acting in his behalf failed to make full satisfaction of the amount of the check or order within 10 days after receiving notice of its dishonor by the drawee.

VIRGINIA	$200 or less	$200 or less fine or 10 days to 12 months in jail, or both. 1-5 yrs. in the penitentiary or fine and jail, or 1-10 yrs. penitentiary in discretion of court.	Nonpayment in 5 days is *prima facie* evidence of intent.
	Over $200		
WASHINGTON	Less than $250	Misdemeanor—Full restitution; the defendant need not be imprisoned, but the court shall impose a minimum fine of five hundred dollars. Of the fine imposed, at least fifty dollars shall not be suspended or deferred. Upon conviction for a second offense within any twelve-month period, the court may suspend or defer only that portion of the fine which is in excess of five hundred dollars.	Giving of check is *prima facie* evidence of intent.
	$250 or over	Felony—Up to 1 yr. in jail or up to $1,000 fine, or both.	
WEST VIRGINIA	For issuing worthless check of any amount; for obtaining property worth $200 or less using such worthless check	Issuance of worthless check—maximum fine of $100, up to 10 days in jail, or both; For obtaining property under $200—maximum fine of $200, imprisonment up to 6 months, or both; For obtaining property over $200—maximum fine of $500, imprisonment from 1-5 years, or both.	Making check is *prima facie* evidence of intent. If paid before trial or examination by Justice of the Peace, no presumption of knowledge shall arise.
	For obtaining property over $200 with such worthless check.		
WISCONSIN	All Amounts	Up to $1,000 fine or 1 yr. in jail.	Nonpayment within 5 days after notice is *prima facie* evidence of intent. Issuer liable for costs and expenses of collection.
WYOMING	$200 or less	Misdemeanor—Fine of not more than $750 or imprisonment for not more than 6 months, or both.	Proof that the accused did not have an account with the drawee at the time of issuance of the check, or failure to pay within 5 days of notice of nonpayment is *prima facie* evidence of intent.
	$200 or more, or if involving 2 or more checks within any 60 day period aggregating $500 or more	Felony—Fine of not more than $10,000 or imprisonment for a maximum of 10 years, or both.	

21–11

(Continued from page 21-6.)

NECESSITY OF DAMAGE—Under a statute making it a misdemeanor to draw a worthless check with intent to defraud, it is held that the payee need not have been actually defrauded,—the intention to defraud is sufficient, *People v. Bullock,* 123 Cal. App. 299, 11 P.2d 441 (1932), and even though a person defrauded through the giving of a bad check with intent to defraud subsequently obtains the money on the check from an indorser, the maker of the check is nevertheless guilty of the crime. *People v. Kawano,* 38 Cal. App. 612, 177 P. 174 (1918). See also *People v. Walker,* 15 Cal. App. 400, 114 P. 1009 (1911).

SUFFICIENCY OF NOTICE OF NONPAYMENT—Most of the statutes provide that failure to make the worthless check good within a certain number of days after receipt of written notice of nonpayment shall be *prima facie* evidence of intent to defraud and of knowledge of insufficient funds in, or credit with, the bank to pay the same. (See "Table of Bad Check Laws" on preceding pages.)

The written notice to the maker of the presentation and nonpayment of the worthless check required by the statutes, is held to have been complied with by a letter sent by the payee to the maker, where the letter sufficiently identified the check by reference to the names of the maker and payee and the amount and date of the check, and demanded payment of the check, since the purpose of the notice is simply to give the maker an opportunity to make payment or to restore the property received in exchange for the check. *Grantham v. State,* 83 Fla. 16, 90 So. 697 (1922).

In Tennessee failure to pay a check *after notice* is an essential element of the crime. *State v. Crockett,* 137 Tenn. 679, 195 S.W. 583 (1917). In Arkansas, the defendant has the burden of showing that he was not notified of the nonpayment. *Collier v. State,* 183 Ark. 1057, 40 S.W.2d 455 (1931). Where written notice is required, the defendant cannot be convicted by showing an oral notice was given. *Cooper v. State,* 157 Miss. 1, 127 So. 684 (1930); *Payne v. State,* 158 Tenn. 209, 12 S.W.2d 528 (1928).

RULES OF EVIDENCE—In most states intent to defraud and knowledge of insufficient funds are presumed (see chart, *supra,* or for rules of evidence for particular state).

In California, Maryland, Minnesota, New Jersey and New York, protest notice is evidence of presentation, nonpayment and protest of a check. In New York and Maryland, where such check, draft or order has not been protested, a certificate under oath of any officer of such bank or other depository that there was a lack of funds in or with such a bank or other depository is admissible as proof and is presumptive evidence of such lack of funds.

In New Jersey it is provided that notice of protest is not only presumptive evidence of lack of funds in or with the bank but also of lack of *credit* with the bank as well as evidence of the maker's knowledge of the insufficiency. California's statute is similar to that of New Jersey on this point.

Florida law requires the drawee to write, print or stamp on the check the reason for nonpayment or dishonor. The check then becomes *prima facie* evidence of the making or uttering of the check, presentation for payment and dishonor thereof, and that it was properly dishonored for the reasons stated thereon. Additionally, the Florida statute also expressly provides not only that the making of the check, when there are not sufficient funds in the drawee's hands to meet it, is punishable, but also that the maker is subject to a fine and imprisonment if he withdraws the funds between the time of delivering the check and its presentation for payment, if presented "within a reasonable me after negotiation." Refusal of payment by the drawee is *prima facie* evidence of intent to defraud, and of knowledge of insufficient funds or credit with the drawee. If the payee at the time of accepting the check had knowledge or reason to believe that the drawee did not have sufficient funds on deposit, then the payee shall be assessed all court costs in connection with the prosecution. Payment for goods or services by check and stopping payment on the check with intent to defraud is also a crime.

TO WHOM STATUTES APPLY—The statutes expressly apply to "any person who shall make, or draw, or utter, or deliver any check, etc.," so therefore they apply not only to the maker, but to anyone who passes a bad check with fraudulent intent, even though the check be that of a third person. It also applies to one who, with intent to defraud, indorses and transfers a worthless check. *Siegel v. Commonwealth,* 176 Ky. 772, 197 S.W. 467 (1917). See also *Dawson v. State,* 79 Tex. Crim. Rep. 371, 185 S.W. 875 (1916).

In many states one instigating or abetting the issuance of a bad check can also be liable to prosecution. See, e.g., *State v. Johnson,* 116 Kan. 390, 226 P. 758 (1924). However, in New York a treasurer of a corporation who signed a check for the corporation in such capacity was held not to be liable to prosecution for drawing, uttering or delivering a check with intent to defraud since the corporate officers are not the "maker" within the statute. *People v. Fleishman,* 133 Misc. 288 232 N.Y.S. 187 (Magis. Ct. 1928). The Utah statute refers to one who for himself or as agent of another, or as an officer of a corporation makes, draws or delivers a check.

HOW TO TAKE ADVANTAGE OF THE STATUTE—As a practical matter, if a bad check is received, a written notice to the maker and a demand that the check be made good within the number of days specified in the statute, or if none are specified, within five days, will generally produce results. Such notice is required in most states, and where required should be served personally upon the maker of the check. If the check is not made good after demand, it is advisable to consult with the District Attorney of the city or town in which the check was made and delivered and a request that he direct the holder as to the proper course to pursue.

Because of the uncertainty as to the application of the statutes to postdated checks or checks given in payment of an existing indebtedness, it is suggested that in no event should the holder of such a check have the maker arrested without an indictment by a Grand Jury. To do so is to court a dismissal of the prosecution and an action for false imprisonment or malicious prosecution.

Civil Penalties

Many states impose civil penalties on a person who issues a bad check requiring such person to honor the check and be responsible for attendant costs. The following is a summary of such state legislation:

STATE	CIVIL PENALTIES
Arizona	Twice the amount of the check or $50, whichever is greater, costs of suit, reasonable attorney's fees.
Alabama	Greater of $10 or actual bank charges.
Arkansas	Amount due, service charge not to exceed $10.
California	Amount due, damages of treble the amount so owing, but in no case less than $100 or more than $500.
Colorado	Treble the amount of such check and in no case less than $100 including reasonable fees.
Connecticut	Amount due, costs of suit, protest fees.

STATE	CIVIL PENALTIES
Delaware	Amount due, costs of suit, protest fees.
District of Columbia	Amount due, protest fees.
Florida	Amount due, costs of suit, protest fees.
Hawaii	Amount due, costs of suit, protest fees.
Idaho	$100 or triple the amount of the check, whichever is greater, but not more than $500 greater than the amount of the check.
Indiana	Treble amount of check not to exceed $500 plus amount of check, attorney's fees of not less than $100 and interest at 18% per annum.
Iowa	Triple amount of dishonored check but not to exceed amount of check plus $500.
Maine	Amount due, costs of suit and protest fees for corporations and partnerships.
Maryland	Amount due, costs of suit, interest from date of dishonor, and $10 fee.
Massachusetts	Amount due, costs of suit, protest fees.
Minnesota	Amount due, $100 penalty, interest (at judgment rate), reasonable attorney's fees if amount of check over $1,250, $15 service charge.
Mississippi	Amount due plus additional damages of 100% on checks up to $25,000, 50% (not to exceed $50 or fall below $25) on checks of $25 to $200, and 25% on checks over $200.
Missouri	Greater of amount of check or 3 times face amount owed or $100.
Nebraska	Amount due, costs, protest fees.
Nevada	Amount due, protest fees 3 times amount of check but not less than $100 nor more than $500.
New Hampshire	Amount due, interest, court costs, reasonable costs of collection and $10 per day after judgment. If check issued to city or town, amount due, $15 fee plus protest, bank and legal fees; if issued to state agency, amount due, $5 fee plus protest and bank fees.
New Mexico	Amount due, costs of suit, protest fees.
North Carolina	Thirty days after written demand, lesser of $500 or 3 times the amount owing on check, but not less than $100.
North Dakota	Amount due, collection fees not to exceed $10, and $100 or 3 times amount of check, whichever is less.
Oregon	When maker fails to tender amount due after written demand made by payee, payee may recover damages in an amount equal to $100 or triple the amount for which the check, draft or order is drawn, whichever is greater, provided the amount is not greater than $500 over the due amount.
South Carolina	In addition to other fines, defendant shall pay all reasonable court costs, not to exceed $20.
Utah	Amount due, interest and costs of collection, court costs, reasonable attorney's fees.
Virginia	Lesser of $100 or 3 times amount of check.
West Virginia	Amount due, service charge not to exceed $10.
Wyoming	Amount due as well as damages equal to the amount so owing but no more than $1,000 plus reasonable attorneys' fees.

Miscellaneous

The Georgia and Virginia Statutes provide that in a civil action for false arrest or malicious prosecution the failure of the plaintiff to make the check good within a specified period of time after presentment or notice is a complete defense.

A Colorado statute makes the drawer of a bad check liable to the payee for his expenses including reasonable attorney's fees incurred in collection. Colorado also provides by statute that a person who passes a bad check knowing that the issuer thereof does not have sufficient funds to cover the check is guilty of a misdemeanor and shall upon conviction be punished by a fine of not less than $50 and not more than $750, or imprisonment in the county jail for not more than six months, or by both fine and imprisonment.

Oregon prohibits the recovery of reasonable attorney's fees to the prevailing party in an attack on a check which has been dishonored for lack of funds unless plaintiff makes written demand for payment of a claim not less than 10 days before the date of commencement of the action.

Tennessee permits any holder of a bad check to prosecute the maker or drawer.

OTHER COMMERCIAL CRIMES

In addition to the laws which have already been discussed with regard to worthless checks, there are many other laws under which fraudulent practices can be made the subject of criminal prosecution, e.g.:
1. Frauds by use of mail, wire, radio and television.
2. False Financial Statements.
3. Bankruptcy (see Chapter 28).
4. Perjury.
5. Misappropriation of Security Interest.
6. Illegal use of a credit card (see Chapter 12).

1. Use of the Mails, Wire, Radio or Television to Defraud

The United States Code, 18 U.S.C. § 1341 (1976), provides that:

> Whoever, having devised or intending to devise any scheme or artifice to defraud, or for obtaining money or property by means of false or fraudulent pretenses, representations, or promises. . . . for the purpose of executing such scheme or artifice or attempting so to do, places in any post office or authorized depository for mail matter, any matter or thing whatever to be sent or delivered by the Postal Service, or takes or receives therefrom, any such matter or thing, or knowingly causes to be delivered by mail according to the direction thereon, or at the place at which it is directed to be delivered by the person to whom it is addressed, any such matter or thing, shall be fined not more than $1,000 or imprisoned not more than five years, or both.

The transmission through the United States mails of a false financial statement, either to a particular individual or corporation, or to a commercial agency, with knowledge of the falsity of the statement and that it will be used to secure the extension of credit to the sender, is an offense under the foregoing statute, and this is true whether or not the sender of the statement is successful in his attempt to defraud.

The elements of the offense are (1) a plan or scheme to defraud, (2) an actual or attempted fraud, and (3) the use of the mails in connection with the execution or attempted execution of the fraud.

Inasmuch as the offense defined by the statute consists of placing, or causing to be placed, any letter, postal card, package, writing, circular, pamphlet or advertisement in any post office or authorized depository for mail matter either

(1) *to be sent,* or (2) *to be delivered* by the post office establishment of the United States, the offense may be prosecuted either at the place of mailing or at the place of delivery.

In order to constitute the offense there must be proof of the following: (1) that the statement is materially false, i.e., the false item or items must have been so misrepresented that, if the true facts had been shown, an ordinarily cautious man would not have extended credit upon the strength of the statement, whereas as falsified such credit would have been extended; (2) that the statement was made or used for the purpose of procuring credit, or the extension of a credit, (3) that it was intended that it should be relied upon, and (4) that it was transmitted through the United States mails.

Of these several elements, the most difficult to prove is that the statement was materially false. If it appears on the face of the statement that it is not a true reflection of financial worth, but is simply an estimate, as for example where round figures are used, it is difficult to obtain a conviction or to interest the prosecuting authorities in prosecuting the offense. An extra burden is placed upon the prosecution if, as frequently happens, a representative of the firm extending the credit fills in the figures and merely procures the maker's signature.

It is essential that there be proof that the statement was mailed by the maker or by the maker's direction. Proof of this fact may be difficult, if the statement be mailed by an agent of the recipient at the direction of the person seeking the credit.

As proof of mailing, the best evidence is the envelope in which the statement was received. It is, therefore, important that the envelope be preserved, attached to the statement by the recipient, and initialed and dated by the person who opened the envelope. Better yet is the use of the self-mailing financial statement form obtainable from the National Association of Credit Management.

The ordinary form of financial statement shows on the asset side the following items: [1]

1. Cash on hand and in the bank.*
2. Accounts receivable.*
3. Notes and acceptances receivable.*
4. Merchandise at market value and at cost.**
5. Machinery, fixtures, and equipment.**
6. Real estate.**
7. Other assets.

On the liability side, the following items usually appear:

1. Owed for merchandise:
    a. on open accounts, notes and acceptances not due, and
    b. on open accounts, notes and acceptances past due.
2. Owed for borrowed money.*
3. Liens or chattel mortgages on merchandise and equipment.*
4. Mortgages on real estate.*
5. Other liabilities.

---

[1] Items marked with * are statements of ascertainable facts, as distinguished from estimates and opinions. Items marked with ** are subject to fluctuations or variations depending upon (a) market conditions, and (b) basis of computation.

Required Proof

The proof which is required for conviction of a crime must be "beyond a reasonable doubt." The problem confronting the prosecuting officer therefore, in determining whether or not he will proceed on an alleged false financial statement, is primarily a question of his ability to convince a court or jury *beyond a reasonable doubt* that the items which are alleged to be false, are in fact false, and that the maker of the statement intentionally and fraudulently misstated them. Consequently, the prosecutor looks for falsity in those items which are susceptible of definite proof *as facts,* as opposed to matters of *opinion and estimation,* and will be found reluctant to proceed with a prosecution which is based on the indefinite items hereinabove referred to.

The following is a breakdown of the various items in relation to the investigation and prosecution of a possible fraud:

Cash: The first item on the assets side of the statement is "Cash in Bank." This item is provable by an investigation of the records of the maker's bank. The next item "Cash on Hand" can be proven only by the maker's own records. If these two items are combined, that is "Cash on Hand and in Bank," it is difficult, if not impossible, to prove the falsity of the item.

Accounts Receivable: "Accounts Receivable Not Due," "Accounts Receivable Past Due" and "Notes and Acceptances Receivable" may be verified from the books of account and records of the maker of the statement.

Inventory: The concern requesting the credit should in every case be required to indicate on what basis the inventory was taken, whether at cost, or cost or market whichever is lower. Seasonal merchandise if allowed to stay in stock is likely to have a small market value as compared with original cost. Unless the maker of the statement preserves his inventory sheets or makes a record of the same in his books, verification of this item is extremely difficult.

Fixed Assets: e.g., land, building, machinery, equipment, etc., should be shown at their depreciated value. However, at best these items represent opinion and, unless so grossly overvalued as to be beyond any reasonable figure, are of little use in establishing fraud.

Other Assets: Assets due from partners and other noncustomers should be carefully scrutinized. In case of bankruptcy or liquidation, it frequently happens that proper entries have not been made on the debtor's books and records. The item is of questionable value as an asset to be relied upon for the extension of credit.

Accounts Payable: This item is important. Generally, the form provides for a separate statement as to "Accounts Payable Past Due" and "Accounts Payable Not Due." These items may best be verified by the books and records of the maker of the statement, but if such records are not available may be verified only by circularization of the creditors.

Other Payables: The item "Acceptances and Notes Payable for Merchandise" is less difficult to prove inasmuch as the notes and acceptances are, or should be, available and bear the signatures of the individual or individuals under investigation.

Taxes, etc.: The item "Taxes, Interest, Rentals, etc." is highly important in these days of high assessments. Tax liabilities are frequently not shown on the financial statement although they may materially affect financial condition. They are easy to verify when the maker of the statement is insolvent as tax authorities invariably file priority claims within the time allowed by law.

Miscellaneous Liabilities: The item "Payable to Partners, Friends, Relatives, etc." is difficult to disprove, and in case of insolvency such items often appear in substantial sums.

Mortgages: The item "Mortgages on Land and Buildings" is usually a matter of public record and, if not correctly set forth in the financial statement, can be proved by official records.

Hypothecated and Collateral Items: The item "Owing to Finance Companies, Banks or Others" may be verified by investigation of the records of finance companies or banks.

In some states a person assigning accounts receivable as collateral security is required to file a statement in a public office showing that he has assigned or intends to assign accounts receivable. Where the statute takes this form, it is not necessary to prove that any property was obtained upon the strength of the statement, but proof that the statement is materially false and *that it was issued for the purpose of procuring credit* is sufficient to make ut a *prima facie* case.

The elements which the prosecutor under such a statute must be prepared to prove are substantially the same as those set forth above with respect to mail frauds, except that it is not necessary to prove that the mails were used for transmission of the statement.

Fictitious Name or Address

18 U.S.C. § 1342 (1976) provides as follows:

Whoever, for the purpose of conducting, promoting, or carrying on by means of the Postal Service, any scheme or device mentioned in section 1341 of this title or any other unlawful business, uses or assumes, or requests to be addressed by, any fictitious, false, or assumed title, name, or address or name other than his own proper name, or takes or receives from any post office or authorized depository of mail matter, any letter, postal card, package, or other mail matter addressed to any such fictitious, false, or assumed title, name, or address, or name other than his own proper name, shall be fined not more than $1,000 or imprisoned not more than five years, or both.

Use of Wire, Radio or Television to Defraud

Section 1343 which was added to Title 18 of the U.S. Code in 1952 in effect extends the provisions of Section 1341 to other means of communication by providing as follows:

Whoever, having devised or intending to devise any scheme or artifice to defraud, or for obtaining money or property by means of false or fraudulent pretenses, representations, or promises, transmits or causes to be transmitted by means of wire, radio, or television communication in interstate or foreign commerce, any writings, signs, signals, pictures, or sounds for the purpose of executing such scheme or artifice, shall be fined not more than $1,000 or imprisoned not more than five years, or both.

2. False Financial Statements

In addition to the federal statute involving the sending of a false financial statement through the mail, (see Use of the Mails to Defraud, *supra*), practically every state has enacted a statute providing for the prosecution of persons obtaining property by means of a false financial statement. Such statutes are generally known as "False Pretense Statutes". A prosecution may be successfully had under such statutes only upon showing that the financial statement was materially false, that the person making the statement knew of its falsity, that it was intended to be relied upon by the person to whom it was sent, and that *money, property or other thing of value was obtained upon the strength thereof.*

In a majority of the "important" commercial states, at the suggestion of the National Association of Credit Management, special statutes have been enacted which provide that:

Any person—

1. Who shall knowingly make or cause to be made, either directly or indirectly, or through any agency whatsoever, any false statement in writing, with intent that it shall be relied upon, respecting the financial condition, or means or ability to pay, of himself, or any other person, firm or corporation, in whom he is interested, or for whom he is acting, for the purpose of procuring in any form whatsoever, either the delivery of personal property, the payment of cash, the making of a loan or credit, the extension of a credit, the discount of an account receivable, the execution, making or delivering by any person, firm, or corporation of any bond or undertaking or the making, acceptance, discount, sale or indorsement, of a bill of exchange or promissory note, for the benefit of either himself or of such person, firm or corporation; or,

2. Who, knowing that a false statement in writing has been made, respecting the financial condition, or means, or ability to pay, of himself, or such person, firm or corporation in which he is interested, or for whom he is acting, procures, upon the faith thereof, for the benefit either of himself or of such person, firm or corporation, either or any of the things of benefit mentioned in subdivision one of this section; or,

3. Who, knowing that a statement in writing has been made, respecting the financial condition, or means, or ability to pay himself or such person, firm or corporation, in which he is interested, or for whom he is acting, represents on a later day, either orally or in writing, that such statement theretofore made, if then again made on said day, would be then true, when in fact said statement if then made would be false, and procures upon the faith thereof, for the benefit either of himself or of such person, firm or corporation, either or any of the things of benefit mentioned in subdivision one of this section:

Shall be guilty of a misdemeanor and punishable by imprisonment for not more than one year or by a fine of not more than one thousand dollars, or both fine and imprisonment.

3. Bankruptcy

See Chapter 28, *infra,* "Bankruptcy Summary of Procedure."

4. Perjury

In addition to perjury statutes relating to bankruptcy, 18 U.S.C. § 1621 (1976) provides as follows regarding perjury in general:

> Whoever— . . . having taken an oath before a competent tribunal, officer, or person, in any case in which a law of the United States authorizes an oath to be administered, that he will testify, declare, depose, or certify truly, or that any written testimony, declaration, deposition, or certificate by him subscribed, is true, willfully and contrary to such oath states or subscribes any material matter which he does not believe to be true . . . is guilty of perjury, and shall, except as otherwise expressly provided by law, be fined not more than $2,000 or imprisoned not more than five years, or both . . .

The various state statutes with regard to the crime of perjury may also be resorted to in an appropriate situation.

5. Misappropriation of Security Interest

Some states have enacted statutes which make it a crime to take or secrete any proceedings of collateral in which there is a security interest. Violation of such statutes is generally a misdemeanor.

6. Illegal Use of a Credit Card

See Chapter 12, *supra*.

CIVIL LIABILITY FOR ISSUING FALSE CREDIT INFORMATION

The case of *Park & Tilford Import Corp. v. Passaic National Bank & Trust Co.*, 129 N.J.L 436, 30 A.2d 24 (1943), decided by the Court of Errors and Appeals of New Jersey, is of great interest and worthy of comment.

The facts were as follows: In October 1938, Park & Tilford wrote a letter to the bank asking for credit information concerning a Mrs. Hanson trading as Broadway Wine & Liquor Shop. The bank replied in a letter reading as follows:

> Olive Mae Hanson, proprietor of the Broadway Wine & Liquor Shop, the subject of your recent inquiry, has carried an account with us since December 1933, balances this year averaging in a moderate three figure amount, and we have extended accommodation up to low four figure amounts, with that amount outstanding today. Our experience with the account has been satisfactory and checkings which we have made in the trade indicate that she has sold in amounts up to $2,300 on regular terms, with payments running from prompt to thirty days slow, although the account was generally classified as satisfactory. Mrs. Hanson's financial statement does not show a large worth but we have been favorably impressed with her and her husband. They operate under light expense and, we believe, have made some progress during the past year, having paid in full a chattel mortgage, which was formerly on the store, during the early part of 1938. They give close attention to the business and cater to a good class of trade.

Park & Tilford had obtained a credit report from a reporting agency regarding Hanson prior to receiving the bank's letter. After receiving the bank's reply to its inquiry, Park & Tilford extended a line of credit to Mrs. Hanson up to $2,500 and sold her merchandise totaling $2,243. In February, 1939, Mrs. Hanson went through bankruptcy and Park & Tilford received a dividend on its claim of $209, leaving an unpaid balance of $2,132.36. Park & Tilford thereafter brought suit against the bank and against Edward H. Roden, its credit manager, charging that the bank's letter was false and fraudulent, that Park & Tilford relied upon the information furnished by the bank to its damage in the sum of $2,132.36.

The case was tried before a jury which returned a verdict for the plaintiff for the full amount sued for. The Court of Errors and Appeals reversed the judgment against the bank and its credit manager, and held:

> The liability of a bank for the representations of its officers as to the credit of third parties is treated in 7 Am. Jur. 198; 9 C.J.S. . . . 415, and seems to require merely good faith in the answer made. The practice of furnishing such information is, however, unwise from the public standpoint. Banks are not chartered to furnish credit ratings for their customers. If liabilities were so created they would not appear upon the books of the bank and would not be observable in audits or examinations. Such reports must, of necessity, be vague since the exact financial condition of a customer is highly confidential.
>
> The evidence in this case at the close of plaintiff's case falls short of the requirements of law.
>
> The plaintiff desired to sell merchandise to the [defendant]. It was dissatisfied with the credit report of Dun & Bradstreet received in the regular course of business. It desired information as to the moral responsibility of Mrs. Hanson. It needed to know nothing further as to her financial responsibility because clearly that was not good. The falsity in the bank's statement is chiefly claimed to be, however, in two particulars: (1) That the average balance was in a moderate three figure amount, when it is said not to have been; and (2) that the bank's experience with the account was satisfactory, when it should not have been so characterized.
>
> The falsity specified as to balance is said to be in this: That an average of $230 shown in the bank's records is not a moderate but low balance. We do not think that the word "moderate" can be used with such exactness. "Moderate" is not a word of exactness. It is quite the contrary. Moderate three figure balances must be understood in the usual sense of the word and cannot have any meaning which the receiver of the letter may ascribe to it. Certainly, there is no reason to suppose that it meant more than $300.
>
> "Moderate" as, in part, defined in Webster's New International Dictionary, is "limited in quantity" and so it is generally understood.
>
> Accounts in banks fluctuate. There are times when very good accounts are very low or overdrawn. In many instances, the bank is satisfied. The bank's letter and the Dun & Bradstreet report indicated bank loans still outstanding. True, the bank did not disclose if it had any information to the effect that Mrs. Hanson had proved a disappointing debtor in her dealings with Bellows & Company and the McKesson Liquor Company. It did state that her business dealings were generally classified as favorable. But the plain-

tiff knew from the Dun & Bradstreet report that she was slow pay, and if they had cared to analyze the report they would have realized that the capital existed, if at all, only so long as the merchandise could be quickly sold at good figures and creditors were not too pressing. The bank was stating its conclusion as to their satisfactory dealings with her. The letter was perhaps somewhat generous but it stated no fact shown to be false within the knowledge of the officer writing the same. Webster's New International Dictionary, in part, defines "satisfactory"—"Sufficient is a satisfactory account."

It does not always follow that because a note is renewed in full that an account is unsatisfactory. The reason given for the renewal may have been perfectly satisfactory to the bank. The point of the whole case is that plaintiff desired to sell its merchandise. Dissatisfied with the credit report received from Dun & Bradstreet, it sought information as to the moral risk in a sale to Mrs. Hanson, and when it received the bank's letter it made the sale.

There is not a word of testimony to indicate that any representations made therein were false. There was nothing in the correspondence between the parties that could have induced any reasonable person to act thereon. The bank was only giving its best judgment of the moral and financial situation of Mrs. Hanson's business. No fact was shown to be false or was there evidence of an intention to deceive, or to induce the plaintiff to make a sale.

Interpretation by the Courts

The law is well settled that one who, knowing that the information will be relied upon in connection with the extension of credit, knowingly furnishes false information, or who, having no knowledge, issues a reckless misstatement or an opinion based on grounds so flimsy as to lead to the conclusion that there was no genuine belief in its truth, is liable for any damage thereby caused. *State Street Trust Co. v. Ernst,* 278 N.Y. 104, 15 N.E.2d 416 (1938). *See also Duro Sportswear, Inc. v. Cogen,* 73 Misc. 534, 131 N.Y.S.2d 20 (Sup. ct. 1954).

An individual, however, is justified in giving his opinion in good faith of the integrity and good standing of a person with whom he has had a business relationship in answer to an inquiry concerning such person. Generally, a response to any such inquiry is deemed a qualified privilege and any such statement if made in good faith and without malice cannot be the basis of any recovery for libel or slander.

Assumed or Fictitious Names

22

The purpose of the state legislatures in enacting statutes requiring the filing of a certificate setting forth the real names of persons transacting business under partnerships or assumed names is well expressed in the case of *Sagel v. Fylar,* 89 Conn. 293, 93 A. 1027 (1915):

> The remedial purpose of the statute manifestly was that the public should have ready means of information as to the personal or financial responsibility behind the assumed name. Its aim was the protection of those who might deal with, or give credit to, the fictitious entity. It obviously was not to provide a means by which persons having received a benefit from another should be enabled to retain it without compensation and to repudiate any agreement for compensation.

93 A. at 1028.

Forms of the Statutes

The forms which these statutes have taken in the several states are substantially similar although there are important differences particularly with respect to the penalty imposed for failure to comply. Summaries of the statutes appear below, and references thereto may be had for specific information. For our present purpose, it is sufficient to state that the law usually requires any person transacting business under a fictitious name or a designation not showing the names of the persons interested as partners in such business, to file in the office of the County Clerk or the Town Clerk, as the case may be, a certificate setting forth the name under which the business is to be conducted and the true or real name or names of the person or persons conducting or transacting such business with the post office address or addresses of such persons.

Statutes Usually Penal

The statutes are usually penal in their nature and provide fines or imprisonment for violation. But in some states, notably California, Colorado, Oklahoma, Oregon and Pennsylvania, no action upon contract can be maintained by an individual or partnership that has failed to comply with the statutes. In Arizona, Michigan, Minnesota, South Dakota, Vermont and Washington, failure to file the required certificate can be cured, providing the certificate is filed prior to the institution of suit, even though the certificate was not on file at the time the cause of action arose.

Effect of Noncompliance on Contracts

There is conflict in the decisions of the different states as to whether these statutes render unenforceable contracts made by persons or partnerships who have failed to comply with their terms, in the absence of specific statutory provision to that effect. The supreme court of Connecticut in *Sagel* held that it was not the intention of the legislature to interfere with the rights and liabilities of the contracting parties, and that the expression of one form of penalty and silence as to any other makes it clear that no further penalty or consequence beyond the possibility of imprisonment was contemplated or intended: "We are of the opinion that the intent of the General Assembly was that the penalty expressed in the statute should be exclusive, and that contracts entered into in the course of a business carried on in disregard of the statute should not be either void or unenforceable." 93 A. at 1028. A contract for the purchase and sale of a commodity not in itself either immoral or otherwise illegal is not, by failure of one of the parties to comply with the assumed name statute, prohibited or made unlawful. Such is the weight of authority although there are decisions to the contrary in some states.

In Case One Partner Retires

If the partnership is conducted under an assumed name, and one of the partners withdraws, the partnership is thereby dissolved, and if the partnership continues to operate under the assumed name, a new certificate must be filed. It is ordinarily the duty of the new partnership to file a new certificate, but in some states, such as Texas, the retiring partner is required by statute to file a certificate witnessing his withdrawal. Failure to file the required certificate is a violation of the statute and is punishable as provided by the law of the state where the business is conducted. As a matter or precaution, the retiring partner should personally notify every customer of the old partnership that he is no longer connected with the firm and is not to be held responsible for firm debts. It is generally accepted that a corporation will do business under the name set forth in its charter and that any change in such name will be effected in accordance with the provisions of the laws of the state of its incorporation. There is case law in some states, however, to the effect that a corporation may legally do business under an assumed name but in most jurisdictions, this is a matter of statute.

Corporations

A number of states permit a corporation to do business using an assumed or fictitious name, i.e., a name other than the one authorized by its certificate of incorporation. Various reasons why corporations would elect to do this include: 1) the unavailability of the name in a state other than that in which it is qualified to do business; 2) the development of a new product line which it wishes to identify separately; 3) preservation of the trade name of a prior corporate entity which has been merged into it.

Set forth in the table below, in addition to the requirements for partnerships, and other business entities, are the statutory requirements of those states that regulate the use of fictitious or assumed names by corporations. The purpose of these statutes is to protect the public that deals with a corporation using an assumed name. The use of an assumed name under most statutes will not give a corporation any rights to that name comparable to the rights it has to its legal corporate name.

ASSUMED OR FICTITIOUS NAMES 22–3

SUMMARY OF STATE LAWS GOVERNING ASSUMED NAMES

ALABAMA

APPLICATION.—Any person or persons carrying on or conducting business under an assumed name, or designation, other than the real name or names of the individual or individuals conducting or transacting business.

WHERE FILED.—Within ten days after written demand by any creditor, such person or persons must file and have recorded in the office of the Judge of Probate in the county or counties where business or businesses are located, a certificate under oath setting forth the name under which such business is conducted and the names of all persons conducting the same, together with post office addresses, and, if any such persons are infants, the age of each infant must be stated.

FILING FEE.—15 cents per 100 words.

PENALTY.—Not more than $500 fine and not more than six months hard labor.

Corporations

The foregoing applies.

ALASKA

APPLICATION.—A person conducting a business may register its name if the name is not the same as, or deceptively similar to the name of a corporation authorized to transact business in the state or to a name that is already registered or reserved.

WHERE FILED.—The owner of a business must file an application for registration with the Commissioner of Commerce. The application must contain his name and address, the name and address of the business and each party having an interest in it, and a statement that he is doing business and the name of the business.

FILING FEE.—To be established by the Department of Commerce, currently $10.

Corporations

No provisions for domestic corporations. When a foreign corporation applying for a certificate of authority, has a name the same as or deceptively similar to that of another registered corporation, it shall: select a name under which it elects to do business in the state, and clearly identify on all advertising, contracts and other legal documents both its corporate name and assumed name.

ARIZONA

APPLICATION.—Any person other than a partnership transacting business in this state under a fictitious name, or a designation not showing the name of the owner of the business or the name of the corporation doing such business. Every partnership transacting business in this state under a fictitious name or designation not showing the names of the persons interested as partners in the business. Except where firm name contains surnames of all partners or one formed for the practice of law or where commercial or banking partnership established and transacting business without this state under a fictitious name, may be used without filing a certificate.

WHERE FILED.—For any person other than a partnership, certificate stating the name and address of the owner of the business and signed by the owner and acknowledged, or if a corporation, the name and address of the corporation signed by the statutory agent and acknowledged. If a partnership, certificate stating names of all members of the partnership and their place of residence signed and acknowledged by all partners. Certificates are to be filed with the recorder of the county where the place of business is situated.

FILING FEE.—$2.

EFFECT ON CONTRACT.—No action upon or on account of any contract made or transaction had can be maintained until certificate has been filed.

Corporations

The foregoing applies.

ARKANSAS

APPLICATION.—All persons other than domestic or foreign corporations conducting or transacting business under any designated name, style, corporate or otherwise, other than the real name of the individual conducting or transacting such business.

WHERE FILED.—Certificate must be filed in office of County Clerk of counties in which such person conducts or transacts such business, or intends to do so, setting forth the name under which such business is, or is to be, conducted or transacted, state of incorporation and location, and a brief statement of the character of the business to be conducted. Certificate must be acknowledged in manner provided for conveyances of real estate. In event of change of ownership, each person disposing of his interest must file certificate similarly acknowledged, setting forth fact of such withdrawal from or disposition of interest in such business.

FILING FEE.—$1.

PENALTY.—Fine not less than $25 or more than $100. Each day of such violation is deemed a separate offense.

Corporations

WHERE FILED.—Domestic corporations file with the Secretary of State and the County Clerk of the county where the corporation's registered office is located, foreign corporations file with the Secretary of State. In both cases, a form is provided by the Secretary of State which form must indicate the fictitious name, the nature of the business to be transacted thereunder, the true corporate name and address of the corporate office registered in Arkansas.

FILING FEE.—$10.

PENALTY.—No action may be brought on any contract, deed, instrument, et al. executed in the fictitious name until the corporation files and pays a civil penalty of $300. In addition, the Attorny General or any affected party may seek an injunction.

CALIFORNIA

APPLICATION.—Every person transacting business under a fictitious name, and every partnership transacting business under a fictitious name, or a designation not showing the names of the persons interested as partners in the business. The fictitious business name statement must be filed within forty days after business is first transacted under the name.

WHERE FILED.—A certificate must be filed with the office of the Clerk of the county in which the principal place of business is situated, stating the name in full and the place of residence of such person or stating the names in full of the members of such partnership and their places of residence. If there is no principal place of business in the state, then filing is made with the office of the clerk in Sacramento.

FILING FEE.—For corporations $10 for the first fictitious business name and $2 for each additional name filed on the same statement and doing business at the same location. For partnerships $10 for filing a fictitious business name statement for one partner and $2 for each additional partner operating under the same fictitious business statement.

PUBLICATION REQUIRED.—Within 30 days after filing the certificate must be published once a week for four consecutive weeks in a newspaper published in county where business is carried on, and if there be none in such county, then in a newspaper in an adjoining county. Affidavit of publication must be filed with County Clerk within thirty days after completion of publication.

EFFECT ON CONTRACT.—No action upon or on account of any contract or contracts made or transactions had under fictitious name, or any partnership name, may be maintained in any court of the state until certificate has been filed and publication made.

DISCONTINUANCE.—A similar certificate may be filed and published upon ceasing to do business under the assumed name.

Corporations

The foregoing applies.

COLORADO

APPLICATION.—Person or persons trading or doing business under any representative name, or using as a part of the name the words "and Company."

WHERE FILED.—County Recorder's office of the county of residence as well as the county where the trade or business is carried on and the office of the Secretary of State.

FILING FEE.—$10 plus fee provided by statute (currently $2) for each county.

PENALTY.—Fine $10 to $300, imprisonment for 10 days to 90 days, and no suit for collection of their debts is permitted.

Corporations

The foregoing applies.

CONNECTICUT

APPLICATION.—Person conducting or transacting business under any assumed name, or any desgnation, name or style, corporate or otherwise, other than the real name or names of the individual or individuals conducting or transacting the business.

WHERE FILED.—Office of Town Clerk of town where business is conducted or contracted.

FILING FEE.—$2 for first 200 words and 50¢ for each additional 200 words.

PENALTY.—Fine not more than $500 or imprisonment of not more than one year.

EFFECT ON CONTRACT.—Does not prevent enforcement of contract.

Corporations

The foregoing applies.

DELAWARE

APPLICATION.—Persons, firms or associations engaged in prosecuting or transacting business by using any trade name or title, which does not disclose the Christian and surnames of such persons, or, in case of a firm or association, the Christian and surname of each and every person comprising said firm or association. Change of membership in partnership or firm must be registered in like manner.

WHERE FILED.—Office of Prothonotary of each county in which business is transacted.

FILING FEE.—$5.

PENALTY.—Fine not more than $100 or imprisonment not exceeding three months or both.

Corporations

Corporations are specifically excluded from the statute.

DISTRICT OF COLUMBIA

No statutory provision.

FLORIDA

APPLICATION.—Person or persons engaged in business under a fictitious name.

WHERE FILED.—Clerk of the Circuit Court of county where principal place of business.

PUBLICATION REQUIRED.—Registration may not be made until the person or persons desiring to engage in business under a fictitious name have advertised his or their intention to register fictitious name at least once a week for four consecutive weeks in some newspaper as defined by law in the county where said registration is to be made, and registration must not be accepted by the Clerk of the Circuit Court except upon receiving proof of such publication.

FILING FEE.—$4 for first page and $2 for each additional page.

PENALTY.—Neither the business nor the members nor those interested in doing such business may defend or maintain suit either as plaintiff or defendant, until law is complied with, and any person violating this law may be charged with a misdemeanor, and upon conviction be fined the sum of $500 or sentenced to jail for 60 days, or both.

Corporations

The foregoing applies.

GEORGIA

APPLICATION.—Every person firm, partnership or corporation, carrying on in the state any trade or business under any trade name or partnership name or other names, which do not disclose the individual or corporation ownership of the trade, business or profession carried on under such name. Does not apply to persons practicing a profession under partnership name, to limited partnership doing business under filed limited partnership name, or to corporations doing business under corporate names.

WHERE FILED.—In the office of the Clerk of the Superior Court of the county where business is chiefly carried on, or, in case of domestic corporation, in county of its legal domicile. Notice of application giving names and addresses of each person, firm, or partnership to engage in business under such trade name or partnership name, must be published in the paper in which the sheriff's advertisements are printed once a week for two weeks. Any person, firm, partnership already registered is required to file a new and amended statement of registration except in the event of a change of ownership.

WHEN FILED.—Before commencing business.

EFFECT ON CONTRACTS.—Statute declares contracts to be valid although provisions are not complied with.

FILING FEE.—$2.

PENALTY.—Punishable as misdemeanor by a fine of $1000 or one year imprisonment or both. For failure to register, court costs will be charged against any such person, firm or corporation doing business under an assumed name, where a party of any action whether on tort or contract but there is no other penalty.

REMARKS.—No partnership may insert in its firm name the name of any person not actually a partner if the same would tend to confuse or mislead the public.

Corporations

The foregoing applies.

HAWAII

APPLICATION.—May be registered by signer proprietor, partnership or corporation.

WHERE FILED.—In the office of the State Treasurer.

FILING FEE.—$10.

IDAHO

APPLICATION.—Any person or persons doing business in the state under any assumed or fictitious name, or under any designation, name or style, partnership or otherwise, other than the true and real names of the person or persons conducting or transacting such business or having an interest therein. Does not apply to corporations or to partnership names which include names of all partners.

WHERE FILED.—Office of Recorder of County or counties in which said business is to be conducted or transacted. New certificate to be filed in case of change in ownership or interest.

FILING FEE.—$2 per page.

EFFECT ON CONTRACT.—Not invalid, but no suit may be maintained in state courts without proof of compliance. Failure to file *prima facie* evidence of fraud in securing credit.

PENALTY.—Misdemeanor punishable by fine of $25 to $200.

Corporations

Corporations are excluded from the statute.

ILLINOIS

APPLICATION.—No person or persons may conduct or transact business in the State under an assumed name, or under any designation, name or style, corporate or otherwise, other than the real name or names of the individual or individuals conducting or transacting such business.

WHERE FILED.—Office of the Clerk of the County Court of the county in which such person or persons conduct or transact or intend to conduct or transact such business, a certificate setting forth the name under which the said business is, or is to be, conducted or transacted, and the true or real full name or names of the person or persons owning, conducting or transacting the same, with the post office address or addresses of said person or persons and every address where the business is to be conducted or transacted in the county. All name and address changes must likewise be recorded.

NOTICE OF THE FILING.—Must be published in a newspaper of general circulation published within the county in which the certificate is filed. Notice must be published once a week for 3 consecutive weeks. The first publication shall be within 10 days after the certificate is filed in the office of the County Clerk. Proof of publication shall be filed with the County Clerk within 50 days from the date of filing the certificate. Upon receiving proof of publication, the Clerk shall issue a receipt to the person filing such certificate but no additional charge shall be assessed by the Clerk for giving such receipt. Unless proof of publication is made to the Clerk, the certificate of registration of the assumed name is void.

FILING FEE.—$2.50

PENALTY.—Any person or persons carrying on, conducting or transacting business who fails to comply with the provisions of this Act, is guilty of a Class C misdemeanor.

Corporations

The foregoing applies.

ASSUMED OR FICTITIOUS NAMES

INDIANA

APPLICATION.—Person or persons conducting or transacting business under any name, designation or title other than the real name or names of the person or persons conducting or transacting such business, whether individually or as a firm or partnership.
WHERE FILED.—Office of Recorder of county in which place or places of business or office or offices are situated; a copy certified by county recorder to be filed with secretary of state.
FILING FEE.—$1.
PENALTY.—Fine not less than $100 nor more than $1,000.
EFFECT ON CONTRACT.—None.

Corporations

The foregoing applies.

IOWA

APPLICATION.—Any person or copartnership conducting business under any trade name or any assumed name of any character other than the true surname of each person or persons holding or having any interest in such business. All name changes must be likewise recorded.
WHERE FILED.—County recorder of county in which business is to be conducted.
FILING FEE.—$3.
PENALTY.—Single misdemeanor.

Corporations

WHERE FILED.—Foreign and domestic corporations must file an application setting forth the trade name with the Secretary of State.
FILING FEE.—$20 plus annual fee of $5.
PENALTY.—A corporation failing to pay the annual fee can lose the right to use the fictitious name.

KANSAS

No statutory provisions.

KENTUCKY

APPLICATION.—All persons carrying on business under an assumed name including corporations and limited partnerships when using assumed name. Excluding instate corporations and partnerships with at least one true name.
WHERE FILED.—Office of Clerk of county or counties in which business is conducted; for corporation, partnership or business trust, certificate of assumed name must also be filed with the Secretary of State.
FILING FEE.—$10 for filing with Secretary of State, add $5 for filing each certificate with county clerk.
PENALTY.—Fine not less than $25 nor more than $100, or imprisonment in county jail for not less than 10 or more than 30 days, or both. Each day business is continued in violation of the statute is deemed a separate offense.
EFFECT ON CONTRACT.—None.

Corporations

The foregoing applies.

LOUISIANA

APPLICATION.—Any person or persons conducting business in Louisiana under an assumed name, or under any designation, name or style, corporate or otherwise, other than the real name or names of the individuals conducting the business.
WHERE FILED.—Office of the Register of Conveyances in New Orleans or in the office of the Clerk of the Court of the parish or parishes in which business is to be conducted.
FILING FEE.—25 cents per copy filed.
PENALTY.—Misdemeanor, subject to fine of not less than $25 or more than $100, or imprisonment of not less than 10 days or more than 60 days, or both. Each day business is conducted in violation of Statute is deemed a separate offense.
EFFECT ON CONTRACT.—None. The contract is not made a nullity, where the only penalty affixed by the statute to its violation is making it a misdemeanor and subjecting the offender to a fine. Fraud having been committed would, of course, be a defense to an action on the contract.

Corporations

Corporations are specifically excluded from the statute.

MAINE

APPLICATION.—Person or persons conducting or transacting business under any name, designation or title other than the real name or names of the person or persons conducting or transacting such business, whether individually or as a firm or partnership. Does not apply to corporations. A corporation desiring to do business under an assumed name shall file with office of the Secretary of State a statement setting forth the corporate name and address of its registered office; that it intends to transact business under an assumed name, and the assumed name which it proposes to use.

WHERE FILED.—Office of City or Town Clerk where business is to be carried on.

FILING FEE.—$2.

PENALTY.—For failure to file certificate, $5 fine for each day in default. False oath to such certificate is perjury. Continued use may be enjoined upon suit by the Attorney General or by any person adversely affected by such use.

REMARKS.—Not permitted in any judicial proceedings to contradict statements in such certificate.

Corporations

WHERE FILED.—Foreign and domestic corporations must file a statement with the Secretary of State. The statement need indicate the corporate name, the registered Maine office, notice of intention to use the assumed name, the assumed name itself and the locations where it is to be used. A separate statement must be filed for each assumed name intended to be used.

FILING FEE.—$5.

PENALTY.—The Attorney General or any affected party may seek an injunction.

MARYLAND

APPLICATION.—Any person or persons engaged in a mercantile, trading or manufacturing business, under a fictitious name.

WHERE FILED.—Office of Clerk of Superior Court, Baltimore City, or Clerk of Circuit Court for county in which business is conducted.

FILING FEE.—$10 plus $1 for each signature on the certificate.

PENALTY.—Any person who owns, operates, or directs an unincorporated organization, firm, association, or other entity which includes in its name the word "corporation," "incorporated," or "limited" or an abbreviation of any of these words or which holds itself out to the public as a corporation is guilty of a misdemeanor and on conviction is subject to a fine not exceeding $500. This does not prohibit a limited partnership from using the term "limited partnership" in its name. Willful execution and filing of false certificate punishable by fine up to $1,000, imprisonment for one year, or both.

EFFECT ON CONTRACT.—None.

REMARKS.—If such certificate has not been filed, the person or persons may be sued in their fictitious name, and process in such a suit may be served upon them, and after judgment the assets of the business conducted in the fictitious name may be seized on execution.

Corporations

No provision.

MASSACHUSETTS

APPLICATION.—Any person or persons conducting business under any title other than the real name of the person conducting the same, or a partnership conducting business under any title not including the true surname of at least one partner, or a corporation conducting business under any other title than its true corporate name.

WHERE FILED.—Office of Clerk of every city or town in which place or places of business or office or offices are located.

FILING FEE.—$1.

PENALTY.—Fine not more than $100 for each month during which violation continues.

EFFECT ON CONTRACT.—Persons may sue and be sued even though they may not have complied with the requirements of the statute.

Corporations

Foregoing applies.

ASSUMED OR FICTITIOUS NAMES

MICHIGAN

APPLICATION.—Any person or persons carrying on, conducting or transacting business under any assumed name or any designation, name or style, other than the real name or names of the individual or individuals owning, conducting or transacting such business.

WHERE FILED.—Office of Clerk of county or counties in which business is owned, conducted or transacted or an office or place of business maintained. Certificate to be filed in duplicate, before business is commenced, on form furnished by County Clerk. Filing is effective for 5 years and is required to be renewed prior to the expiration of each five-year period. County Clerk is authorized to reject any assumed name which is likely to mislead the public, or any assumed name already filed in the county or so nearly similar thereto as to lead to confusion or deception.

FILING FEE.—$6, renewal fee $4.

PENALTY.—Fine not less than $25 nor more than $100, or imprisonment in county jail, not exceeding 30 days, or both. Each day business conducted in violation of law is deemed a separate offense.

EFFECT ON CONTRACT.—Does not void contracts, but any person or persons failing to file a certificate are prohibited from bringing suit in any of the courts of the state in relation to any contracts or other matter made or done by such person or persons under an assumed name until after a full compliance with the statute.

MISCELLANEOUS.—If business location is changed a certificate to that effect must be filed, and if the change is to another county, an assumed name certificate must be filed in the new county. If a concern operating under an assumed name goes out of business, a certificate of discontinuance must be filed wherever the original assumed name certificate was filed. Filing certificate by 2 or more persons is *prima facie* evidence of partnership. Where nonresident files a certificate he must file a consent that suits may be commenced against him by service of process on County Clerk.

Corporations

WHERE FILED.—Domestic of foreign corporations must file a statement indicating both the true name and the fictitious name with the administrator.

FILING FEE.—No provision.

PENALTY.—No provision

MINNESOTA

APPLICATION.—Any person, including corporations, carrying on or conducting a commercial business under any designation, name or style which does not set forth the true name or names of every person interested in such business.

WHERE FILED.—Office of the Secretary of State.

PUBLICATION.—The certificate must be published in a qualified newspaper, in the county in which the person has a principal or registered office, for two successive issues. Filing is generally effective for 10 years, unless renewed within 6 months of expiration of the 10 year period. Duplicity or similarity with a previously filed name is permitted.

PENALTY.—Violation is a misdemeanor punishable by a fine not exceeding $100 and a term in jail not to exceed 60 days.

FILING FEE.—$15, renewal $6.

EFFECT ON CONTRACT.—In any civil action commenced in any court on account of any contract made by, or transaction had, on behalf of such business, defendant may set up as a defense that the certificate has not been filed and the action will thereupon be stayed until the certificate is filed.

Corporations

The foregoing applies.

MISSISSIPPI

No statutory provision.

MISSOURI

APPLICATION.—Persons, partnership, associations or corporations engaging in business under any name other than the true name of such persons, partnership, association or corporation.

WHERE FILED.—Secretary of State within 5 days of beginning of such business.

FILING FEE.—$2.

PENALTY.—Violation is a misdemeanor.

Corporations

The foregoing applies.

MONTANA

APPLICATION.—Every partnership, individual corporation or other association transacting business under a fictitious name or a designation not showing the names of the persons interested as partners in the business and individuals transacting business under a fictitious name, or a designation purporting to be a firm name or corporate name. Secretary of State may not register business, other than corporation or limited partnership, with words "corporation," "company," "incorporated," or "limited" in name.

WHERE FILED.—Office of the Secretary of State. Filing is effective for five years.

FILING FEE.—Registration fee $15. Renewal or amendment of registration $10.

EFFECT ON CONTRACT.—No action can be maintained until certificate is filed and publication made.

Corporations

The foregoing applies.

NEBRASKA

APPLICATION.—Every name under which any person shall do or transact business in this state, other than the true name of such person, is declared to be a "trade name" and it is unlawful for any person to engage in or transact any business in the state under a trade name without first registering the same. Exemption for persons doing business under trade name prior to March 17, 1951.

WHERE REGISTERED.—Trade name must be registered with the Secretary of State on a form supplied by the Secretary. The form must disclose: The name and address of the applicant and, if a corporation, the state of incorporation, the trade name, how long used in the state and the nature of the business.

FILING FEE.—$100, renewal fee is $100.

PENALTY.—Any person not excepted from the application of the law transacting business under a trade name without registration shall be deemed guilty of misdemeanor and fined not less than $10 nor more than $100. Each day of violation a separate offense.

Corporations

The foregoing applies.

NEVADA

APPLICATION.—Persons, corporations, firms, or partnerships (except for limited partnerships) conducting, carrying on or transacting business under an assumed or fictitious name or designation which does not show the real name or names of the person or persons engaged or interested in such business. In addition, every change in membership of a copartnership.

WHERE FILED.—Office of County Clerk of each county in which business is carried on or is intended to be carried on.

FILING FEE.—$10.

PENALTY.—Noncompliance is a misdemeanor.

EFFECT ON CONTRACT.—Persons violating the Act may not maintain or defend any action or proceeding in any court of the State on any contract made, transactions had, liability incurred, or cause of action, arising out of said business unless prior to commencement of suit, he or they filed the certificate required.

Corporations

The foregoing applies.

NEW HAMPSHIRE

APPLICATION.—Every sole proprietor doing business under any name other than his own, and every partnership or association.

WHERE FILED.—Office of Secretary of State.

FILING FEE.—$20.

PENALTY.—Fine $100. No action abated or writ of attachment affected by certificate.

Corporations

The foregoing applies.

ASSUMED OR FICTITIOUS NAMES

NEW JERSEY

APPLICATION.—Persons transacting business using the designation "and Company" or "& Co." as part of name; persons conducting or transacting business under assumed names, corporate or otherwise.

WHERE FILED.—Office of Clerk of county or counties in which business is transacted together with a duplicate for filing in office of the Secretary of State.

FILING FEE.—$5, plus an additional $5 for duplicate sent to Secretary of State.

PENALTY.—Violation is a misdemeanor.

EFFECT ON CONTRACT.—Does not prevent recovery on executed contract by person who should have complied with statute but did not.

Corporations

WHERE FILED.—A corporation need not file if it uses its true name in the transaction in such a manner as not to be deceptive as to its identity or if it has been authorized to do business in New Jersey under the fictitious name. Otherwise, it must register a certificate with the Secretary of State. The certificate must indicate the true name, the jurisdiction and date of incorporation, the fictitious name, the nature of business to be transacted thereunder, the fact that the corporation had never done business under the name in violation of the statute. Filing effective for 5 years, may be renewed for 5 year intervals.

FILING FEE.—To be prescribed by the Secretary of State.

PENALTY.—Validity of contract not impaired but no corporation may maintain an action arising from a transaction conducted under a fictitious name until it has filed. Upon such filing, the corporation shall pay the prescribed fee plus an amount equal to the fee multiplied by the number of years that it had illicitly used the trade name. Failure to file within 60 days of notice of an obligation to do so served by the Secretary of State subjects the corporation to a fine ranging from $200 to $500.

NEW MEXICO

No statutory provision.

NEW YORK

APPLICATION.—No person shall (a) carry on or conduct or transact business under any name or designation other than his real name, or (b) carry on or conduct or transact business as a member of a partnership, unless such person files a certificate setting forth the name or designation under which, and the address within the county at which, such business is conducted or transacted, the full name or names of the person or persons conducting or transacting the same, including the names of all persons, with the residence address of each such person, and the age of any infants. Must also file amended certificate if any changes, and certificate of discontinuance.

WHERE FILED.—Office of Clerk of each county in which such business is done.

FILING FEE.—$25.

PENALTY.—Noncompliance or falsification of the certificate is a misdemeanor punishable by $1000 fine, one year imprisonment, or both. In addition, no action may be maintained on a transaction made under an unregistered fictitious name until the statute has been complied with.

EFFECT ON CONTRACT.—Failure to comply does not void contract.

CERTIFICATE TO BE DISPLAYED AT PREMISES.—A certified copy of the original certificate, or if an amended certificate has been filed, then of the most recent amended certificate filed, shall be displayed on each place the business for which filed is conducted.

Corporations

WHERE FILED.—Corporations must file with the Department of State and furnish the following information: The true name, the fictitious name, the principal place of business in New York, the name of each county where business is to be conducted, the location within each county where business is to be conducted.

FILING FEE.—$25 plus an additional fee for each county filing effected by the Secretary of State. County fee for each county within New York City is $25; for all other counties, the fee is $3.

PENALTY.—Same as above.

NORTH CAROLINA

APPLICATION.—Before any person or partnership (other than a limited partnership) or corporation engages in business in any county of the state under an assumed name, or any name other than the real name of the owner or owners or corporate name, a certificate must be filed setting forth the name under which the business is to be conducted and the name and address of the owner or owners. The certificate must be signed and acknowledged by the individual owner or by each member in partnership or by an appropriate officer of a corporation. Whenever a partner withdraws from or a new partner joins a partnership, a new certificate must be filed. This requirement does not apply to a partnership engaged in the practice of certified public accountancy if it files with the State Board of Certified Public Accountant Examiners a listing of names and addresses of partners and such listing is available to public inspection.

WHERE FILED.—The office of the Register of Deeds of the county in which business is carried on. It is not necessary to file in any county where no place of business is maintained and where the only business done is the sale of goods by sample, by traveling agents or by mail.

FILING FEE.—No fee.

PENALTY.—Failure to file certificate constitutes a misdemeanor punishable by fine of not more than $50, or imprisonment for not more than 30 days. In addition, failure to file certificate within 7 days after demand made by any person gives rise to cause of action in favor of such person for collection of penalty of $50. Failure to comply with statute does not affect rights in any civil action brought in the courts of this state.

Corporations

The foregoing applies.

NORTH DAKOTA

APPLICATION.—Every partnership transacting business under a fictitious name or designation not showing the names of the persons interested as partners therein.

WHERE FILED.—Office of Clerk of District Court of the county or subdivision in which principal place of business is situated.

PUBLICATION.—Certificate must be published once a week for four successive weeks in newspaper published in the county, or if none is published in the county, then in a newspaper published in adjoining county.

FILING FEE.—$20.

EFFECT ON CONTRACT.—Persons failing to comply may not maintain an action on or account of any contracts made or transactions had in the partnership name until complaince but may subsequently file and thereafter an action may be maintained on prior transactions and contracts.

Corporations

No provision.

OHIO

APPLICATION.—Every person, including various business organizations, who does business under a fictitious name must report the fictitious name to the Secretary of State. The person may, if he wishes, register the trade name with the Secretary. The Secretary is not permitted to accept registration of any trade name that might mislead the public or that is not readily distinguished from other trade names. All reports must be filed within 30 days of the first use of the fictitious name.

WHERE FILED.—Secretary of State.

FILING FEE.—$10. Filing is effective for 5 years. Renewal fee is $10.

PENALTY.—The Attorney General shall bring an action for an injunction upon the request of the Secretary of State.

EFFECT ON CONTRACT.—No action can be commenced or maintained on or on account of any contracts made or transactions had in the partnership name until registration or submission of the report.

Corporations

The foregoing applies.

OKLAHOMA

APPLICATION.—Partnership transacting business under a fictitious name except a commercial or banking partnership established and transacting business within the United States.

WHERE FILED.—Clerk of District Court of county or subdivision where principal place of business is situated.

PUBLICATION.—Published once a week for four successive weeks in a newspaper published in the county if there is one, and if there is none, then in a newspaper published in an adjoining county.

FILING FEE.—$125.

ASSUMED OR FICTITIOUS NAMES 22-13

PENALTY.—None.
EFFECT ON CONTRACT.—Persons failing to comply may not maintain action on, or on account of, any contract made, or transactions had, in the partnership name until compliance. May file subsequently and thereafter action may be maintained on prior transactions and contracts.
REMARKS.—New certificate to be filed and new publication had whenever personnel or partnership changes.

Corporations

WHERE FILED.—A report containing the trade name, the true name, the name and address of the corporation's registered agent in Oklahoma, the nature of the business to be conducted, and the address where the business is to be conducted must be filed with the Secretary of State.
FILING FEE.—No provision.
PENALTY.—No action may be brought on a transaction made under an unregistered fictitious name. The Attorney General or an affected party may seek an injunction.

OREGON

APPLICATION.—No person or persons shall carry on, conduct or transact business in this state under any assumed name or under any designation, name or style, other than the real and true name of each person conducting the business or having an interest therein, unless the name suggests the existence of additional owners or unless such persons file a verified application for registration with the Corporation Commissioner.
WHERE FILED.—Application for registration shall be filed with the Corporation Commissioner and contain the name of the business, the real name and address of each person conducting or having an interest in the business, and each county in which the assumed name is intended to be used to carry on business. The Corporation Commissioner sends the County Clerk in each designated county written notice of registration.
FILING FEE.—$5 for each application for registration or renewal and $1.50 for each county designated for registration or renewal. Registration is effective for five years.
EFFECT ON CONTRACT.—No persons carrying on, conducting or transacting business under an assumed name or having an interest therein, are entitled to maintain any suit or action in any of the courts of this state without alleging and proving that they have registered the assumed business name with respect to the county in which the person conducted the business giving rise to such suit or action.
PENALTY.—Fine not exceeding $100.

Corporations

The foregoing applies.

PENNSYLVANIA

APPLICATION.—Individual or individuals carrying on business under any assumed or fictitious name, style or designation. Where all owners of the business reside out of the Commonwealth of Pennsylvania they shall operate such business through an agent, and certificate shall show name and address of agent.
WHERE FILED.—Office of Secretary of the Commonwealth and in the Office of Prothonotary of county of principal place of business.
PUBLICATION.—Proof of publication of a notice of intention to file a certificate once in a newspaper of general circulation in the political subdivision in the county where the principal office or place of business is located or, if none, in the county paper and also in the legal newspaper if any in the county, must be filed with the application. The Secretary and Prothonatary must be notified of change of location of place of business by filing supplemental statements with such officers.
FILING FEE.—$25 for individuals plus local county fee.
PENALTY.—Noncompliance, violations and false statements are misdemeanors punishable by a fine not exceeding $500 or by imprisonment not exceeding one year, or both.
EFFECT ON CONTRACT.—Failure to register does not abrogate contract and suit may be maintained, but no action shall be instituted or recovery had until the provisions of the Act are complied with and a license fee or fine of $25 is paid to the Secretary of the Commonwealth.
DISCONTINUANCE OR WITHDRAWAL FROM BUSINESS.—Where dissolution has taken place and business discontinued or one or more of the principals have withdrawn, original certificate may be cancelled or a notation made on the record showing the withdrawal made by sworn statement. If statement of cancellation is not filed, the Secretary of Commonwealth may determine that assumed name is ceased to be used and may on ten days notice revoke or cancel the certificate. Amended certificate may be filed for purpose of adding or deleting names of parties.

Corporations

APPLICATION.—Under the Fictitious Corporate Name Act, no corporation alone or in combination with any other entity may conduct business in Pennsylvania (after September 1, 1957) under any fictitious name unless such name is registered. Foreign corporation must be authorized to conduct business in Pennsylvania prior to filing application. Application for registration is to be on a form supplied or approved by the Secretary of the Commonwealth and contain the fictitious name, a statement concerning the character of the business to be conducted, the corporate name, state and date of incorporation, address of principal place of business and registered office in Pennsylvania, name and address of any other entity in combination with which the corporation will conduct such business. The document must be signed by the President or Vice President and the Secretary or Treasurer and the corporate seal shall be affixed thereto.

WHERE FILED.—Office of Secretary of the Commonwealth and in office of Prothonotary of county where registered office of the corporation is located.

FILING FEE.—Original application for registration—$30 to Secretary of the Commonwealth, $10 to the Prothonotary, and local county fee.

AMENDMENT FOR PURPOSE OF CHANGE OF ADDRESS.—$10 and $1.50; for other purposes $15 and $3; filing renewal with Secretary of Commonwealth, $10; filing statement of cancellation, $1 to Secretary of Commonwealth and $1 to Prothonotary.

PENALTY.—Civil penalty of $300 for failure to comply with statute. Criminal penalties for filing false documents up to $2,000 or 6 months imprisonment or both.

EFFECT OF CONTRACT.—Failure to register fictitious name does not impair or affect the validity of any contract but corporation cannot resort to the Pennsylvania courts to enforce agreement made by it under fictitious name until after compliance with statute. Affidavit of compliance must be filed with complaint.

RHODE ISLAND

APPLICATION.—Any person or persons who carry on or conduct business in the state under any assumed name, designation or style other than the real name or names of such person or persons.

WHERE FILED.—Office of Town or City Clerk in town or city in which business is conducted or transacted.

FILING FEE.—$2.

PENALTY.—Fine not exceeding $500 or imprisonment not exceeding one year.

Corporations

Corporations (domestic and foreign) lawfully doing business need not comply.

SOUTH CAROLINA

APPLICATION.—All mercantile and industrial establishments, conducting business under a name not showing the name of the individuals, or in the case of a corporation its legally chartered name.

WHERE FILED.—Clerk of County Court in the county of the principal place of business.

FEES.—No provision.

PENALTY.—Misdemeanor and a fine not to exceed $1 for every day of violation or one day in prison for every five days of violation.

Corporations

The foregoing applies.

SOUTH DAKOTA

APPLICATION.—Persons or copartnerships transacting business under a fictitious name or designation not showing names of persons interested in the business.

WHERE FILED.—Officer of the Register of Deeds of each county where the business is maintained.

FILING FEE.—$5, $2 for each renewal.

EFFECT ON CONTRACT.—No action on account of any contract can be maintained until the statute has been complied with. Also, a lease containing clause that premises would not be used for unlawful business or purpose is subject to forfeiture for non-compliance with this statute.

PENALTY.—Class 2 misdemeanor

Corporations

No provision.

ASSUMED OR FICTITIOUS NAMES

TENNESSEE

No statutory provisions.

TEXAS

APPLICATION.—Any individual or partnership that uses a name or names not including the surname, or a name, including a surname, that suggests the additional owners by including words such as "Company," "& Company," "& Son," and the like. Any limited partnership which uses a name other than the name stated in its certificate of limited partnership; any company except an insurance company under Article 1.29 of the Insurance Code, and any corporation using any name other than the name stated in its articles of incorporation. Must also file new certificate if any change in information. Also certificate of discontinuance.

WHERE FILED.—Unincorporated businesses: must file a certificate with the county clerk in each county where a business premises is maintained or where business will be conducted. Certificate must be executed and acknowledged by each individual or agent whose name appears thereon and shall state the assumed name, the name and address of the individual, partners or company, the laws under which organized, the period (not to exceed 10 years) for which the name will be used, and a statement specifying the form of business (e.g. proprietorship, sole practitioner, joint venture, general partnership, etc.) to be conducted. Incorporated businesses: must file a certificate with the Secretary of State and if required to maintain a registered office in this state, in the office of the county clerk in the county in which such office is located and of the county in which its principal office is located if not the same county where the registered office is located. If the corporation is not required to maintain a registered office, with the secretary of state and in the office of the county clerk of the county in which its office is located, and if not incorporated under the laws of this state, in the office of the county clerk of the county in which its principal place of business in this state is located if not the same as its office. Certificate must be executed and acknowledged by an officer, representative, or attorney for the corporation and shall state the assumed name, the name of the corporation as stated in its articles of incorporation, the laws under which organized and address of its registered office in that jurisdiction, the period (not to exceed 10 years) for which the name will be used, and the form of corporation to be conducted. If required to maintain a registered office in this state, the address of such office and the name of its registered agent and the address of its principal office if not the same as that of its registered office in this state. If not required to maintain a registered office in this state, the office address in this state, and if not incorporated under the laws of this state, the address of its business in this state and its office address elsewhere, if any. Certificate for all corporations must include the county or counties where business is to be conducted under the assumed name.

FILING FEES.—$2 for each certificate filed with the county clerk plus a fee of 50 cents for each move to be indexed; $10 for filing with the Secretary of State.

PENALTIES.—Noncompliance does not affect the validity of any contract or prevent the defending of any action, but no action may be maintained by a party not complying with the act until the required certificate is filed. Court may award expenses including attorney's fees incurred in locating and serving process to party bringing suit against noncomplying party. Intentional noncompliance is a misdemeanor punishable by a fine not exceeding $2,000.

Corporations

The foregoing applies.

UTAH

APPLICATION.—Every person or persons conducting or transacting business in this state under an assumed name.

WHERE FILED.—Office of Secretary of State. Certificate must set forth the name of the business, the true name or names of the person or persons owning and the person or persons conducting such business, the location of the principal place of business and the post office address. Certificate shall be filed not later than 30 days after commencing to conduct or transact said business and is effective for 8 years.

FILING FEE.—$10 for filing and indexing each certificate. $5 for amending certificate.

PENALTY.—Noncompliance is a bar to suit.

Corporations

The foregoing applies.

VERMONT

APPLICATION.—Persons doing business under any name other than their own; every copartnership or association of individuals, except corporations doing business under any name which does not contain the surname of all copartners or members thereof without any other descriptive or designating words, excepting the Christian names or initials of such copartners or members; corporations doing business in the state under any name other than that of the corporation.

WHERE RECORD.—Certificate must be recorded in office of Clerk of town or city where principal place of business is located.

FILING FEE.—$20.

PENALTY.—Any person, partnership, association or corporation carrying on business contrary to the statute may, upon complaint of the Commissioner of Taxes, be temporarily and permanently enjoined therefrom by a court of chancery. Failure to register also renders members liable to forfeiture of $10.

EFFECT ON CONTRACT.—No person, copartnership, association or corporation subject to this Act may institute any proceedings for the enforcement of any right or obligation unless they shall, prior to the commencement of the proceeding, have filed the certificate and paid the registration fee required by the statute.

Corporations

The foregoing applies.

VIRGINIA

APPLICATION.—Any person or corporation conducting or transacting business under an assumed or fictitious name.

WHERE FILED.—Office of Clerk of Court where deeds are recorded. Corporation must also file a copy in the office of the Clerk of the State Corporation Commission.

FILING FEE.—$1 for Clerk of Court's office, and $5 for State Corporation Commission (for corporations only).

PENALTY.—Noncompliance is a misdemeanor; fine not exceeding $1,000 or imprisonment not more than one year or both. Failure to file certificate precludes maintaining any cause of action until the certificate is filed.

Corporations

The foregoing applies.

WASHINGTON

APPLICATION.—Any person or persons who carry on or conduct business in the state under any assumed name, designation or style other than the real name of such person or persons.

WHERE FILED.—Department of Licensing.

FILING FEE.—$5.

EFFECT ON CONTRACT.—No suit can be maintained in any of the courts of the state unless party alleges and proves certificate has been filed, and failure to file certificate is *prima facie* evidence of fraud in securing credit. Certificate filed before suit is brought is sufficient, even though not on file when cause of action arose.

Corporations

The statute expressly excludes corporations.

WEST VIRGINIA

APPLICATION.—Person or persons conducting mercantile business under an assumed name or under any designation, name or style other than the true name or names of those persons conducting such business.

WHERE FILED.—Office of Clerk of county or counties in which business is owned, conducted or transacted.

FILING FEE.—$1.

PENALTY.—Noncompliance is a misdemeanor, punishable by fine of not less than $25, or more than $100, or by not more than 30 days in county jail, or both. Each day of violation is a separate offense.

Corporations

The statute expressly excludes corporations.

WISCONSIN

No statutory provisions.

WYOMING

APPLICATION.—Person or persons conducting mercantile or commission business under a name that does not disclose the real name or names of persons engaged in such business if intent of name is to obtain credit.

WHERE FILED.—Office of the Register of Deeds of the county of the principal place of business.

FILING FEE.—$4 for first page, $2 for each additional page.

PENALTY.—Noncompliance is a misdemeanor and is punishable by a fine not to exceed $1,000 or by imprisonment in county jail for not more than one year.

Corporations

The foregoing applies.

Legal Phases of Collections

23

Collection of past due accounts is an important aspect of the activities of a credit executive. This chapter seeks to advise the executive about the legal phases of collection so that he will be warned against leaving undone those things which he should have done and doing those things which should not have been done.

The importance of collections and the methods used will of course vary according to the business in which they are used. In some lines of industry the amounts uncollected after expiration of the "term" dates are but a small fraction of the total monthly accounts receivable. In other lines the "past due" items frequently represent the margin between profit and loss. Within this broad range the liquidation of accounts is accomplished in three ways: by correspondence, by collection bureaus or by law suits. Special phases of these three methods will be discussed in the following pages.

The slogan used for a number of years by the National Association of Credit Management that "Poor Information, not Poor Judgment, Is the Cause of Most Credit Losses," certainly has a direct bearing upon collection operations. A business that sells its merchandise without regard to the credit of the purchaser would soon be in financial difficulty. In these days of close competition and advanced business methods, business realizes that only when accounts receivable are paid may profits be computed. The credit and collection departments of a business should be regarded just as important as the sales and production departments.

COLLECTION METHODS

Before placing an account in the hands of an attorney, a credit manager will usually exhaust the extra-legal possibilities of collection at his disposal: personal contact with the debtor, telephone and telegraph communication, collection letters and, perhaps, the intervention of a collection agency.

Although it is frequently said that any legal means may be used to collect a debt, courts and state legislatures are becoming stricter in their views as to what means may be employed. Many expedients which may appear to be of value in bringing an obstinate debtor into line may also subject the creditor to possible liability for extortion, libel or invasion of the right of privacy.[1] As

---

[1] Twenty-six states have enacted legislation creating a private right of action for debt collection abuses. They are: Alaska, California, Colorado, Connecticut, District of Columbia, Florida, Georgia, Hawaii, Illinois, Iowa, Louisiana, Maine, Maryland, Massachusetts, Michigan, New York, New Hampshire, North Carolina, Ohio, Oregon, Pennsylvania, Texas, Vermont, Washington, West Virginia, and Wisconsin.

was said in *Clark v. Associated Retail Credit Men of Washington, D.C.,* 105 F.2d 62, 67 (1939), "There is a growing tendency to check offensive collection methods." In pursuing these various methods, therefore, discretion should be the watchword. Retention of a collection agency does not necessarily relieve the creditor of liability for wrongful acts of the agent in seeking to make the collection.

Extortion

The term extortion is generally reserved for an attempt by threat to collect money which is not legally due, *La Salle Extension University v. Fogarty,* 126 Neb. 457, 253 N.W. 424 (1934); *City Purchasing Co. v. Clough,* 38 Ga. App. 53, 142 S.E. 469 (1928), and may bring a criminal penalty as well as civil liability. Nevertheless, the attempt to collect money which is legally due by sending a collection letter calculated to harass the debtor and to coerce payment of the claim may be actionable. In *Barnett v. Collection Service Co.,* 214 Iowa 1303, 242 N.W. 25 (1932), a widow who was dunned for a coal bill amounting to about $28 by a series of letters which included threats to expose her to her employer as a delinquent debtor, was allowed damages for the mental anguish which she suffered.

While the threat to do what one has a legal right to do, as to sue if a just debt is not paid, will not ordinarily result in liability, nevertheless, a threat of bankruptcy, of criminal prosecution, or to render an unfavorable credit report to the members of a credit association, intended to coerce payment of the account, may render one liable. In *Clark v. Associated Retail Credit Men,* above, the debtor was allowed to recover for physical injuries resulting from mental stress which the court found had been intentionally inflicted by the creditor when it wrote to the debtor threatening suit and an unfavorable credit rating among the members of its credit association, if the debt was not paid. This case was decided on demurrer in which the plaintiff/debtor's allegations tending to show malice were deemed true. That the same result would have followed after a trial in which this charge was not sustained by the proof seems doubtful, especially in the light of the dissenting opinion by Justice Vinson. The case nevertheless indicates some of the dangers underlying collection methods which depend upon fear to secure payment of the debt.

Examples of Extortion

In New York the sending of a collection letter threatening exposure as a delinquent debtor to the members of a credit group has been held to be punishable under a statute making it an offense to send or deliver a writing with intent to cause annoyance to any person. *People v. Loveless,* 84 N.Y.S. 1114 (App. Div. 1903).

The use of simulated legal process calculated to scare the debtor into paying, although containing no direct threat, is also punishable in most states. In New York such conduct constitutes a misdemeanor, and the use of a collection notice similar to a summons in size, arrangement of details, use of large type and general appearance, containing printed matter in the nature of a mandatory precept directing the payment of money has been held to fall within the section of the Penal Law so providing. *People v. Globe Jewelers, Inc.,* 249 A.D. 122,

291 N.Y.S. 362 (1st Dept. 1936). Aside from such specific statutory provisions it would seem that a practice of this kind would amount to abuse of process and would be punishable accordingly in most states.

Don'ts for Collection Letters

By far the greatest risk which the creditman may run into pursuing various extra-legal collection methods will be that of incurring liability for libel. The publication of matter which will tend to disgrace or degrade the debtor or to hold him up to public hatred, contempt or ridicule or deprive him of public confidence and esteem may bring one afoul of the law of libel.

Publication means the communication of the defamatory matter to some third person. If communicated solely to the person whom it concerns, it is not actionable. On the other hand, a letter, although addressed to the debtor, sent in such a way that it is likely to be opened and read by a third person may result in a publication. The sending of a telegram necessarily results in publication because the telegram cannot be sent without the reading of the communication by some agent or employee of the telegraph company. It has been held that the dictation of libelous matter to a stenographer constitutes a publication thereof. *Gambrill v. Schooley,* 93 Md. 48, 48 A.730 (1901).

In general, matter which falsely imputes a criminal act, moral turpitude or tends to injure the person defamed in his business is regarded as libelous per se and no special showing of damages need be made in order to allow recovery. Thus in *Judevine v. Benzies-Montanye Fuel & Warehouse Co.,* 222 Wis. 512, 269 N.W. 295 (1936), it was held, in an action to recover damages for libel arising out of the distribution of a handbill advertising plaintiff's account for sale, that the offensive matter must relate to one who relies upon credit in the conduct of his business and that the imputation of want of credit must relate to that business. Recovery has been allowed, however, where the libelous communication related to one not so engaged even though no special damages were shown. *Traynor v. Seilaff,* 62 Minn. 420, 64 N.W. 915 (1895); *McDermott v. Union Credit Co.,* 76 Minn. 88, 79 N.W. 673 (1899); *Tuyes v. Chambers,* 144 La. 723, 81 So. 265 (1919).

In *Glenn v. Esco Corp.,* 268 Ore. 278, 520 P.2d 443 (1974), the court imposed punitive damages on a corporation because of threatening collection letters written by one of its employees, a copy of which had been sent to the debtor's employer. The letter was not accurate and the actual existence of the debt was in doubt. The court, therefore, awarded general damages as well as punitive damages.

Prohibited Collection Practices

Although a creditor has the right to demand payment from the debtor, he may not engage in conduct which is illegal or unlawful. Many states have adopted statutes which have proscribed certain practices as illegal and improper. See Chapter 11. In addition, there are numerous judicial decisions based on common law principles which condemn improper collection practices. See, e.g., *Rugg v. McCarty,* 173 Colo. 70, 476 P.2d 753 (1970); *Montgomery Ward v. Larrogoite,* 81 N.H. 383, 467 P.2d 399 (1970).

The Federal Communications Commission has released a public notice (70-

609) reminding creditors that it is a violation of the telephone company's tariff to use the telephone to frighten, torment or harass another. Practices which come within the scope of this prohibition are:
1. Calling debtors at odd hours of the day or night.
2. Repeated calls.
3. Calls to friends, neighbors, relatives and children making threats.
4. Calls asserting falsely that credit ratings will be hurt.
5. Calls stating that legal process is about to be served.
6. Calls demanding payment for amounts not owed.
7. Calls to place of employment.

A creditor who is in this class may be subject to having his telephone service disconnected or may be subject to fine or imprisonment.

Some of the practices condemned by state laws are:
1. Threats of violence or other criminal means to cause harm to the person, property or reputation of the debtor.
2. False accusation of fraud.
3. Threat to sell or assign the claim, resulting in a loss of any defense by the debtor.
4. Threat of arrest.
5. Use of profane or obscene language.
6. Telephone calls without disclosing the identity of the caller.
7. Unreasonable publicity concerning the indebtedness.
8. Use of any fraudulent, deceptive or misleading representations in seeking to collect claims such as that the debt collector represents an official agency.
9. Use of any unfair or unconscionable means to collect claims, including the collection from the consumer of all or any part of the debt collector's fee or charges.

It is a crime under federal law in the collection of private debts or obligations to use or employ in any communication or correspondence the words National, Federal or United States or the initials U.S. in a manner reasonably calculated to convey a false impression that such communication is from a department, agency or bureau or in any manner represents the United States.

Libel Per Se

The distinction between words which will give rise to an action for libel without any showing of special damage and those which are not actionable unless some specific injury is shown to have resulted, depends largely upon whether or not they are such that a court may presume as a matter of law that they will tend to degrade or disgrace or hold one up to public hatred, contempt or ridicule. To charge another with fraud or dishonesty is libelous per se. In *Fogg v. Boston & L.R. Co.,* 148 Mass. 513, 20 N.E. 109 (1889), it was held to be libelous per se to write of another that he was a swindler; likewise, to charge one with knowingly making false representations with intent to deceive another. *Stewart v. Pierce,* 93 Iowa 136, 61 N.W. 388 (1894). A written charge that one is guilty of falsehood, or implying want of veracity, is usually libelous per se. *Morgan v. Andrews,* 107 Mich. 33, 64 N.W. 869 (1895).

In the cases involving publication of credit information in which recovery has been allowed to one not engaged in business without any showing of special

LEGAL PHASES OF COLLECTIONS

damages, it has been on the theory that the publications involved necessarily imputed dishonesty and want of credit depriving the debtor of public confidence and esteem and holding him up to public hatred, contempt and ridicule. Statutes dealing with restrictions on the disclosure of credit information are treated differently by the courts than libel or defamation statutes. A cause of action for defamation or libel is complete upon publication; the victim need not show any damage to his reputation. On the other hand credit information disclosure statutes require a showing that the debtor's reputation was in fact damaged. In a Florida case, *Heard v. Mathis,* 344 So. 2d 651 (Fla. App. 1977) the court denied recovery—under a statute proscribing disclosure of credit information to anyone other than the debtor's family or a business with a legitimate need for the information—unless the debtor could demonstrate that his reputation was in fact adversely affected by the disclosure.

While the truth of the matter published is ordinarily a complete defense to an action for libel, it should be borne in mind that while the words themselves may state no more than the truth the manner of publication may impute insolvency, bankruptcy or want of credit so as to make the whole thereof libelous. It may be said that the resort to unusual collection methods necessarily implies that the debtor is not amenable to the ordinary means of collection and is therefore not worthy of credit. Among the various devices which have brought creditors afoul of the law of libel are the listing of the debtor's name in a list of delinquent accounts, placarding, envelopes and postcards addressed to the debtor on which there appear words or symbols indicating that the addressee is a delinquent debtor and advertising the debt for sale. In *Thompson v. Adelberg & Berman, Inc.,* 181 Ky. 487, 205 S.W. 558 (1918), the posting of collection cards bearing language of a fairly innocuous character, and containing no false statements, in the windows of the debtor's home and on stakes in her yard where they could be viewed by passersby was held to be actionable. In *Zier v. Hoflin,* 33 Minn. 66, 21 N.W. 862 (1885), an advertisement in a newspaper setting forth nothing more than the facts relating to the debt was held to be libelous by reason of the proximity to a similar advertisement containing scurrilous comment on the character of another debtor.

If the publication of a libel appears in a newspaper, magazine or other media of general circulation, there may be no liability on the part of the newspaper, absent malice, based on the constitutional protection of freedom of the press. See *New York Times v. Sullivan,* 376 U.S. 254 (1964).

The United States Supreme Court, however, recently held in *Dunn & Bradstreet, Inc. v. Greenmoss Builders, Inc.* (No. 83-18, June 26, 1985) that Dunn & Bradstreet was liable for punitive damages as a result of issuing an erroneous credit report which stated that the subject of the report had filed in bankruptcy. Under Vermont law, where the case arose, a jury can impose punitive damages absent proof of any malice on the part of the issuer of the false credit report. The qualified privilege which most states recognize and which permits a bona fide error to be made in a credit report issued by a credit reporting agency did not exist in Vermont. The argument that Dunn & Bradstreet was denied its freedom of speech by imposition of punitive damages was rejected by the Supreme Court. The court held that the doctrine of *New York Times v. Sullivan* did not apply to issues of private concern, such as credit reporting, and applied only to issues of public concern.

Postal Laws

In addition to incurring liability for libel, the mailing of postal cards or letters upon the outside cover of which there appears matter tending to reflect upon the character of the addressee may violate the postal laws. In the United States Criminal Code such matter is declared to be nonmailable and to deposit it or to cause it to be deposited for mailing or delivery may subject one to a fine of not more than $1,000 or imprisonment for not more than one year, or both. 18 U.S.C. § 1718 (1976). The Post Office Department has ruled that cards indicating that the addressee is being dunned for an account that is past due were nonmailable under this provision. It has been held that postal cards threatening suit or other legal action such as garnishment and attachment, fall within the ban. Cards bearing respectful requests for the settlement of credit accounts or that give notice when an account will be due do not fall within this prohibition.

Privilege

While the foregoing cases and principles seem to condemn any publication of credit information which may be damaging to a debtor, the interchange of such information among creditmen having mutual interests to protect is deemed to be privileged and hence does not fall within the condemnation of the law. As stated in *Reynolds v. Plumbers' Material Protective Association,* 30 Misc. 709, 63 N.Y.S. 303 (Sup. Ct. 1900): "Merchants have an interest in knowing and have a right to know the character and financial standing of those who deal or propose to deal with them and of those upon whose standing and responsibility they, in the course of their business, have occasion to rely. They may therefore make inquiries of merchants or other persons who may have information as to the character and financial standing of such persons, and, if merchants or other persons in good faith communicate the information which they have, the communication is privileged." 63 N.Y.S. at 305. Many cases establish the rule that the good faith interchange of credit information among persons interested therein and seeking the information as a guide in the conduct of their own affairs is privileged and not actionable.

Invasion of the Right of Privacy

While, as indicated above, the truth of the matter published, if not published in such a manner as to carry with it the imputation of dishonesty, insolvency or want of credit, may be a defense to an action for libel, the same is not true of an action based upon an invasion of the right of privacy, which may be broadly defined as the giving of publicity to the private affairs, including debts, of another. The right to be free from such undue publicity is one of fairly recent recognition and it is not accepted in all of the states.

About thirty-four jurisdictions recognize a right to privacy, and three have statutes on the subject (New York, Utah and Virginia). Four jurisdictions, Nebraska, Rhode Island, Texas and Wisconsin reject the concept entirely.

The right to privacy must be distinguished from other types of litigation which might be brought under the same or similar facts, such as a suit for malicious prosecution, a suit for extortion, libel or slander or a suit for false imprisonment.

Many of the cases which have considered the question have been influenced by such factors as whether the creditor was motivated by malice, whether the debt was due and truly owed and whether the action of the creditor involved a public disclosure of the indebtedness. However, the better view is that if a right to privacy exists, the motive of the party violating it is not of any consequence in establishing liability.

Section 652(A) of the Restatement of Torts, in Section 652(A) proposes to define a violation of the right to privacy as having occurred when there is,

"(a) unreasonable intrusion upon the seclusion of another, . . . (b) appropriation of the other's name or likeness . . . (c) unreasonable publicity given to the other's private life . . . or (d) publicity which unreasonably places the other in a false light before the public."

It is generally recognized in debt collection cases that the mere threat, institution or prosecution of a legal action as a method of debt collection does not constitute an actionable invasion of privacy, at least in the absence of malice.[1] Accordingly, a creditor has the right to pursue his debtor and persuade him to make payment, to threaten legal action to collect the debt and to resort to the courts to force his right at least where such threat or use of legal process is not attended by undue harassment, malice or other oppressive circumstances. See 42 A.L.R.3rd 865, 869.

In *Rugg v. McCarty,* 173 Colo. 70, 476 P.2d 753 (1973), a creditor repeatedly harassed a sick debtor with numerous telephone calls and threats of garnishment proceedings against her notwithstanding the fact that the creditor did not have a judgment against the debtor. In addition the creditor sent a letter to her employer inquiring how many garnishments would be tolerated. Based on these facts the court found that there was a violation of the debtor's right to privacy and gave judgment against the creditor. The court stated:

When unreasonable action in pursuing a debtor is taken, which foreseeably will probably result in extreme mental anguish, embarrassment, humiliation or mental suffering and injury to a person possessed of ordinary sensibilities, under the same or similar circumstances, then such conduct falls within the forbidden area and a claim for invasion of privacy may be asserted.
Id. at 755.

There are numerous cases, however, which support the efforts of a creditor or his representative to seek collection of a debt owed. In *Timperley v. Chase Collection Service,* 272 Cal. App.2d 697, 77 Cal. Rptr. 782 (1969), the court affirmed a judgment of dismissal of an action commenced by a debtor against a plaintiff based on an alleged violation of his right to privacy. In this case a collection agency wrote a letter to the debtor's employer advising the employer that the debtor had not paid his bill and that legal action would be commenced unless payment was made within five days. As a result of this letter the debtor was forced to resign his job. The court concluded however that a creditor informing a debtor's employer of a debt and requesting his aid where such disclosure is not slanderous, libelous or defamatory and not attended by coercion,

---

[1] However, such acts may under certain conditions violate the FTC Guide Against Debt Collection Deceptions or a local law regulating debt collection practices.

harassment or malice is not a violation of the right to privacy. A similar conclusion was reached by the court in *Lewis v. Physicians and Dentists Credit Bureau, Inc.,* 27 Wash.2d 267, 177 P.2d 896 (1947), in which a claim was made for invasion of the right of privacy based on a telephone call from the creditor to the debtor's employer.

State Statutes Penalizing Non-Payment of Debts

Louisiana has adopted a statute which provides that if a person fails to pay an open account within 15 days after receipt of written demand therefor with a copy of the invoice attached, the debtor shall be liable to the claimant for reasonable collection fees for prosecution and collection of the claim, provided a judgment on the claim is first obtained.

Prompt Payment Statutes

The states of Delaware, Maryland, Montana, Nevada, North Dakota, Ohio, Utah and Virginia have adopted prompt payment statutes.

A prompt payment statute requires the state to pay its bills within a certain period of time from the presentation of an invoice. If the state fails to pay within the prescribed time, the creditor may collect interest at the statutory rate. Indiana has enacted a prompt payment statute covering only certain types of contracts. The Oklahoma legislation has directed the Director of the State Finances to establish procedures to expedite payments to vendors. Congress enacted such legislation for federal debts in 1982.

DEBT POOLING PLANS

Often when a debtor is delinquent in the payment of an account because of financial difficulties, there will be numerous other creditors also pressing their respective claims. In order to minimize the harassment by his creditors, the debtor may pay in full or make partial payments to those who press the hardest, as the exigencies of the situation seem to demand. In other cases a more practical solution will be found in making pro rata payments to all the creditors at periodic intervals. This may be done in accordance with an agreement among creditors and the debtor and through the utilization of the services of an attorney or a trade association.

To an individual burdened with debt who is just one step ahead of the bill collector, threatened with repossession of his automobile and other personal property purchased on the instalment plan, or the threat of litigation to recover other obligations, there is now available the services of various companies which offer to relieve his burdens by budgeting his income and satisfying his creditors. These services are operated under various names and offer "debt adjustment," "prorating," "debt lumping," "budget planning" or "debt pooling." Regardless of the name, the usual procedure is to advise the debtor with respect to budgeting his income, making provision for the periodic payment to the agency of amounts which are then distributed to the various creditors after deduction of the agency's servicing charges. In principle, such debt adjustment appears to be unobjectionable and provides a valuable service to both the debtor and creditors.

LEGAL PHASES OF COLLECTIONS

Evils and abuses have arisen, however, including excessive charges for services, failure to make payments to creditors and the offering of legal advice. In numerous cases, the action of unscrupulous agencies has been to increase rather than diminish the burdens and obligations of the debtor. As a result, legislation has been enacted in a number of states outlawing such debt adjustment practices.

Most states have already enacted legislation on the subject and it is likely that similar legislation will be passed in the near future by other states. The statutes have approached the problem in three ways:

1. Engaging in the business of debt adjustment as defined in the statute is prohibited and fines and/or imprisonment are imposed for violation of the statute.

2. Debt adjustment as defined by the statute is held to constitute the practice of law, and unauthorized persons engaging in such activities are subject to the penalties provided for unlawful practice.

3. Provision is made for the licensing of persons conducting a debt adjustment service and statutory restrictions govern the methods of operation.

Debt Pooling and Trade Association Practices

While the debt adjustment legislation serves a useful purpose in curbing the abuses previously noted, it has caused serious concern among trade associations and credit managers. They are fearful that loosely drawn legislation may unintentionally restrict or prohibit procedures which have been legitimately utilized for years in protecting creditors and assisting debtors in temporary financial difficulties. It has been found advantageous to both creditor and debtor in many instances, in order to avoid the expense and consequences of bankruptcy or other insolvency proceedings, to enter into voluntary agreements for the composition or extension of payment of debts. Under such arrangements the services of an individual or of a board of trade or adjustment bureau may be utilized as a trustee, a creditor's committee secretary or as an agency to perform the necessary services in connection with the payment and distribution to creditors. Appropriate compensation must necessarily be paid for such services.

It has not generally been the intention of legislators to interfere with such legitimate business practices which ostensibly appear to be closely related to the debt pooling services previously described, but in practice are substantially dissimilar. The adjustment bureau or trade association acts for the creditor group and is compensated for the services it renders in such capacity, as distinguished from being compensated by the debtor for the solving of his financial problems and staving off his creditors, together with the furnishing of incidental legal services.

While it is not the intention to prohibit or restrict the legitimate activities of trade and credit associations by this type of legislation, it is important that their methods of operation be scrutinized in the light of existing statutes so that they do not inadvertently transgress the letter of the law. It is also important to the credit executive that the anticipated future legislation does not, in its effort to cure the evils of debt adjustment, deprive him of one of his most effective means of protection against credit losses.

The following extracts from the various statutes will indicate that extreme caution must be used in drawing agreements and in the practices of trade associations, which are to be compensated for services rendered in debt adjustments between debtor and creditors. It is important to note that even where it is not specifically stated, attorneys, banks, judicial officers and nonprofit organizations are exempted from the statutory restriction or licensing requirements. Also, many states permit collection agencies to so operate, frequently requiring a license or permit.

Alabama: No person as a service or for a fee shall engage in business of selling, issuing or otherwise dispersing checks or receiving money as agent for obligors for purpose of paying such obligor's bills, accounts, etc., without first obtaining a license and otherwise complying with statute. License fee is $250 and bond is required in a minimum amount of $5,000 for individual and $10,000 for corporation with $50,000 maximum. Violation of the statute is a misdemeanor punishable by a fine from $100-$500 or up to 12 months imprisonment or both.

Alaska: There is no statute prohibiting debt pooling nor any statute regulating the practice.

Arizona: "No person may engage in the business of a debt management company without the license required by this article." Annual license fee is $200. Statute provides specific procedures and regulations with which licensee must comply.

Arkansas: Debt adjusting is a misdemeanor punishable by fine of not less than $500 nor more than $1,000 or by imprisonment of not more than one year or both. Debt adjusting is the practice of acting for a consideration as an intermediary between a debtor and his creditors for the purpose of settling, compounding or otherwise altering the terms of payment of any debt or contracting to collect a certain amount of money from the debtor periodically and distribute among the debtor's creditors. Attorneys, banks, employers, and nonprofit organizations are not debt adjusters even if they perform these services.

California: No person shall engage in the business, for compensation, of receiving money as agent of an obligor for the purpose of paying bills, invoices, or accounts of such obligor, or acting as a prorater, without first obtaining a license. Merchant-owned credit associations and others are exempted. Limits are placed on the charges which may be received by a prorater commencing with 12% on the first $5,000. Other limitations are placed upon the practices and procedures of those engaged in such prorating. Detailed provisions are also made with respect to the form of contract between a prorater and a debtor. A semiannual accounting to the debtor is required.

Colorado: No individual or corporation shall engage in the business of debt management without a license, except attorneys, banks, judicial officers and others who do so in the regular course of their businesses and professions. Debt management is the planning and management of the financial affairs of a debtor for a fee and receiving money for distribution to creditors. Violation of the statute is a misdemeanor punishable by a fine of no more than $1,000 or imprisonment up to 6 months or both.

Connecticut: Debt adjustment is receiving, for a fee, money for the purpose of distributing it among the creditors of the debtor. Engaging in debt adjustment without a license is punishable by a fine of not more than $1,000 or imprisonment for not more than one year or both for each violation. Each day on which a person engages in debt adjustment without a license is a separate violation.

Delaware: Debt adjusting is a Class B misdemeanor. Debt adjusting is making any contract with a debtor whereby the debtor pays a certain amount of money periodically to the person engaged in the debt adjusting business who for a consideration distributes the same among creditors.

Florida: The practice of "budget planning" is prohibited except as practiced by an attorney admitted to the state bar. Violation of the statute is a misdemeanor.

Georgia: It is a misdemeanor to engage in the debt adjustment business except in the case of attorneys. Debt adjustment is defined as "providing services to debtors in the management of their debts and contracting with a debtor for a fee to: (1) effect the adjustment, compromise, or discharge of any account, note, or other indebtedness, of the debtor, or; (2) receive from the debtor and disburse to his creditors any money or other thing of value."

Hawaii: Debt adjusting is engaging for a profit in a business by acting as an intermediary between a debtor and his creditors for the purpose of settling, compromising or in any way altering the terms of payments of any debts and distributing property or making payment to creditors of the debtor. Debt adjusting is a misdemeanor punishable by a fine of not more than $500 or imprisonment of not more than six months or both.

Idaho: The statute does not prohibit debt adjustment or similar practices. It does require the licensing of collection agencies and bureaus and persons engaging in the business of receiving money from debtors for application to, or prorating of, any creditor or creditors of such debtor, for compensation or otherwise. Licensee shall pay an initial examination fee of $20, post a $5,000 bond and pay an annual permit fee of $50.

Operation of a collection agency without a permit, failure to keep separate trust accounts for creditor's funds, and failure to keep the records required constitute a felony, punishable by up to $5,000 fine or 5 years confinement, or both. Equitable relief is available in addition to fine or punishment.

Illinois: The statute does not prohibit debt adjustment or similar practices. It does require the licensing of collection agencies and bureaus and control procedures for debt adjustment. Licensee shall post a bond up to $7,500 running to the state of Illinois for the use of the state and of anyone who may have a cause of action against licensee. Violation of the statute is a Class B misdemeanor and is punishable by a fine up to $500 or or up to 6 months in jail, or both. Any contract of financial planning made by an unlicensed person shall be null and void and of no legal effect. Unlicensed practice of debt adjustment is a public nuisance and may be enjoined by the state in addition to the above penalties. Detailed provisions are also made with respect to the form of contract required, fees and charges and remittance of funds to the creditor.

Illinois also has a statute permitting nonprofit corporations to be organized for the purpose of giving credit advice and accepting wage assignments for the payment of creditors for individuals earning less than $10,000 per year.

Indiana: Statute does not prohibit debt adjustment practices.

Iowa: Debt management is the planning in management of the affairs of a debtor for the purpose of distributing the same to his creditors. Debt managers must obtain licenses and post a bond in the amount of $10,000 which can be raised to $25,000. Engaging in debt management without a license is a misdemeanor. Remittance of funds must be made within 45 days after initial receipt of funds and within 30 days thereafter. Licensee may not act as a collection agent for the same account without disclosure to both debtor and creditor or collect fees from both debtor and creditor.

Kansas: Prior law prohibiting debt adjusting has been repealed.

Kentucky: Debt adjusting is a misdemeanor punishable by a fine of $500 or imprisonment up to 60 days or both. The court has the power to enjoin debt adjusting activities and appoint a receiver. Those exempt from the statute include creditors of the debtor or any person acting without compensation for services rendered in adjusting debts.

Louisiana: Prior law prohibiting debt adjusting has been repealed.

Maine: Prior law prohibiting "budget planning" has been repealed.

Maryland: Debt adjusting is prohibited. Violation of the statute is a misdemeanor punishable by a fine of up to $500 or up to 6 months in jail or both. Among those exempt from the statute are certified public accountants, bona fide trade associations in the course of arranging adjustment of debts with business establishments and nonprofit organizations provided no fee or charge is imposed.

Massachusetts: Debt adjusting practices by those not authorized to practice law in the state is a misdemeanor and is punishable by a fine of up to $500 or imprisonment up to 6 months or both. Nonprofit credit counseling service corporations are exempt.

Michigan: The statute requires licensing of persons engaged in debt management. The statute contains detailed provisions concerning company records and other activities of the licensees. A surety bond in the amount of $5,000 must be furnished with the application for a license. Violation of the statute is a felony punishable by a fine of up to $5,000 or imprisonment up to 2 years or both.

Minnesota: The statute does not prohibit debt adjustment or similar practices. It does require the licensing of collection agencies and bureaus and control procedures for debt adjustment. The licensee is required to actively seek the consent of all creditors to the plan of distribution set forth in the contract with the debtor. A contract made by an unlicensed person renders the contract null and void and the debtor can recover all fees paid including reasonable attorney's fees. In addition to revocation/suspension of license, violation of the statute is punishable by a fine of up to $10,000. Annual license fee is $100 and minimum bond of $5,000 is required. Other detailed provisions are made with respect to contract form, accounting and prohibited acts.

Mississippi: Debt adjustment is prohibited except for the following: lawyers, banks, title insurers, judicial officers, nonprofit religious or charitable organizations in connection with counseling services, certified public accountants, employers for employees, and bona fide trade or mercantile associations in the course of arrangements of debts with business establishments. Debt adjusting is contracting for a fee to provide services of budget management, debt pooling or debt management. Violation of the statute is punishable by a penalty of up to $500 or up to 6 months in jail or both.

Missouri: The practice of debt adjusting is prohibited and violation constitutes a misdemeanor. The circuit court has the power to enjoin such activity and appoint a receiver. Among those exempt from the statute are creditors or agents of the creditors of the debtor whose services in adjusting the debtor's debts are rendered without cost to the debtor, employer of the debtor, and one who arranges for or makes a loan to the debtor, and who with the debtor's authority acts as adjuster of the debtor's debts in the disbursements of the proceeds of the loan, without compensation for such adjusting services rendered.

Montana: Substantially same as Mississippi. Exemptions same as Missouri's.

Nebraska: Debt management is the planning in management of the affairs of a debtor for the purpose of distributing the same to his creditors. A debtor is defined as a wage earner. Remittances to creditor must be made within 15 days after receipt of any funds, 7 days if received in cash. In no case may licensee retain funds for greater than 35 days.

Nevada: The statute requires licensing of persons engaged in debt management. Annual license fee is $200 and bond of $10,000 is required. Remittance must be made to creditors within 10 days of receipt of funds. Detailed provisions are also made with respect to schedule of fees, contract form, prohibited practices and other guidelines which must be complied with. Engaging in the business of debt adjusting without a license is a misdemeanor.

New Hampshire: Under the law a debt adjuster must be licensed and must post a bond of $10,000 or greater depending on the discretion of the Commissioner of Banks. Provisions are also made with respect to separate accounts, recordkeeping, budget analysis and prohibited acts. Violation of the statute is a misdemeanor for an individual and a felony for other persons.

New Jersey: Prior statute prohibiting debt adjusting has been repealed.

New Mexico: Statute is substantially the same as Missouri's.

New York: Budget planning is a misdemeanor punishable by $500 fine and imprisonment for not more than six months. Budget planning is defined as "the making of a contract with a particular debtor whereby the debtor agrees to pay a sum of money periodically to the person engaged in the budget planning, who shall distribute the same among certain specified creditors in accordance with a plan agreed upon, and the debtor further agrees to pay such person any valuable consideration for such services or any other services rendered in connection therewith." Attorneys, however, are permitted to engage in this practice.

North Carolina: The statute prohibits the practice of debt adjusting or the attempt thereof and violation constitutes a misdemeanor punishable in the discretion of the court but in any case no more than $500 or 6 months imprisonment or both. The Solicitor may bring an action in the Superior Court to enjoin any person from acting or attempting to act as a debt adjuster. The exceptions are similar to those in the statute.

North Dakota: Debt adjustment is prohibited except as practiced by those exempted.

Ohio: Statute is substantially the same as Georgia's. Violation is a misdemeanor, unless party licensed under local law, punishable by a fine between $50 and $1,000 and between 30 days and 6 months in jail or both.

Oklahoma: Debt pooling is defined as making a contract with a particular debtor whereby the debtor agrees to pay a sum or sums of money periodically to the person engaged in the debt pooling who shall distribute the same among certain specified creditors in accordance with a plan agreed upon, and the debtor further agrees to pay such person any valuable consideration for such services or for any other services rendered in connection therewith. Penalty for engaging in the debt adjustment business is a fine from $100 to $500, or imprisonment up to 30 days, or both.

Oregon: The statute requires licensing of persons before engaging in the business of debt consolidation. Such persons must pay an annual license fee and post a $5,000 bond. Penalty of $100 fine or 30 days in prison for practicing without a license. Other violations are punishable by $500 fine or 6 months imprisonment or both for individual and $1,000 for corporation in addition to individual penalties.

Other provisions govern maximum fees, records and audits of the company.

Pennsylvania: Prior law prohibiting practice of debt pooling has been repealed.

Rhode Island: The practice of debt pooling is prohibited. This restriction does not apply to attorneys. Penalty is $200 for each offense.

South Carolina: Statute is substantially the same as Virginia's.

Tennessee: Debt adjusting is prohibited. A violation of the law is punishable by a fine of up to $1,000 or imprisonment for up to 11 months and 29 days, or both. Attorneys, banks, title insurers and abstract companies doing escrow businesses, judicial officers, nonprofit organizations rendering services for not over $10 per month per debtor, and employers for their employees are exempt.

Texas: Statute provides that contract whereby a debtor deposits, periodically or otherwise, a specified sum of money with any person, firm, corporation or association for distribution among creditors, for which the debtor pays a valuable consideration, is debt pooling and is void, and persons engaging in the business of debt pooling are guilty of a misdemeanor. Attorneys are exempt. Statute provides for the establishment of nonprofit debt counseling services under the "Consumer Debt Counseling and Education Act."

Utah: Prior law requiring licensing of debt managers has been repealed.

Vermont: Statute is similar to Iowa. A violation of the statute is punishable by a fine of up to $500 and up to 2 years in prison.

Virginia: Statute provides that "the furnishing of advice or services for compensation to a debtor in connection with a debt pooling plan, pursuant to which the debtor deposits funds for the purpose of distributing them among his creditors, shall be deemed to be the practice of law" and is punishable as a misdemeanor. Statute does not apply to attorneys licensed to practice in state.

Washington: Debt adjusting is the managing, counseling, settling, adjusting, prorating, or liquidating the indebtedness of a debtor or receiving funds for the purpose of distributing said funds among creditors. Debt adjustors must obtain licenses and post a bond in the amount of $10,000 which may be raised in the discretion of the director of the Department of Licensing. A violation of the Debt Adjustment Law is a misdemeanor. Disbursement must be made to creditors within 5 days upon demand of debtor and no later than 30 days within receipt of funds. Fees charged may not exceed 15% of total debt. Other provisions are made with respect to contract form, duties to be performed, investigations, accounting and prohibited practices. Violation of the statute constitutes an unfair or deceptive act or practice in the conduct of trade or commerce.

West Virginia: It is unlawful to solicit debt pooling and unlawful to charge (as a service charge or otherwise) greater than 2% of the money deposited. This percentage restriction does not apply to attorneys. Penalty for violation of the statute is a fine of between $100 and $250 or from 30 to 60 days in jail.

Wisconsin: Statute requires licensing of "adjustment service companies" who are in the business of prorating the income of a debtor to his creditor(s), or of assuming the obligations of any debtor by purchasing the accounts he may have with general creditors, in return for which the principal receives a service charge or other consideration. Annual license fees range from $50 to $100 depending on the population of the city in which the business is located and licensee is required to post bond up to $5,000. Violation of the statute is punishable by fine of no more than $500 or up to 10 days in jail or both.

Wyoming: Statute is substantially the same as Georgia's. Misdemeanor punishable by a fine up to $100 and up to 6 months in jail or both.

COLLECTION BY SUIT

When an account is placed in the hands of an attorney for collection, with instructions to commence suit, he should be furnished with copies of the original written orders for merchandise, if any, and with triplicate copies of the original invoices, showing the dates of delivery, terms of sale, nature of merchandise, and the amount to be collected.

Upon receipt of these papers, the attorney will be in a position to commence the action by service upon the debtor of a summons or such other process as may be required by the law of the state in which the action is to be commenced, together with a statement of the claim in the form of a complaint or such other paper as may be required by law. After service of the process upon the debtor, he is allowed by the laws of all states time in which to answer the allegations of the plaintiff's pleading, and may in his answer set up defenses to plaintiff's claim, including a denial of the allegations of the complaint or any special defenses which he may have such as the statute of limitations, the statute of frauds; additionally, the debtor may claim an offset or counterclaim. New matter constituting a defense (that is, anything other than a general denial) may necessitate the filing of a reply by the plaintiff, or under the laws of some jurisdictions may be deemed to be denied without the necessity of any further pleading by the plaintiff.

Security for Costs

It is customary, when a claim is placed in the hands of an attorney for suit, for the attorney to request a payment or deposit for costs and expenses, or security for costs. In most of the states, at the time of commencement of suit it is necessary for the attorney to incur certain expenses or pay into court various fees. Although the nature of these charges and the amounts thereof vary in different states and in the different courts in the several states, the following are some of the items for which advance payment may be requested: Service of process, filing fees, premiums on court bonds, posting security for costs (particularly where plaintiff is a nonresident), trial fees, jury fees and charges for taxation of costs and entry of judgment.

If an action is placed in the hands of an attorney for suit, his request for security for costs or advance for disbursements should be promptly complied with, not only to facilitate prompt proceedings against the debtor, but also because in many states it is improper for the attorney to advance fees or expenses of litigation for his client.

Collection Fees

To avoid any problem it is advisable for a creditor to establish the rates that may be charged by an attorney in a collection matter at the time the matter is referred. The Commercial Law League of America no longer has a recommended rate schedule. Therefore, each attorney and creditor must make his own arrangements. In addition to the attorney's fee there is usually a suit fee for the commencement of litigation.

Need for Full Information

When the pleadings have been completed, the issues, joined by the allegations of the plaintiff, and the allegations of the defendant, constitute the matters to be determined by the judge or jury. The action is then placed on the calendar of the court for trial. Under the laws of most states the parties are entitled to a trial by jury as a matter of right, but trial by jury may be waived in most jurisdictions and the case tried before a judge without a jury.

Where a trial is before a judge and jury, the function of the judge is to pass upon all questions of law and to submit the facts to the jury, which is the sole judge of the issues of fact.

Credit executives are especially warned of the necessity of gathering together all of the information needed either by their Collection Bureau or by the attorney who is instructed to file suit, so that time will not be wasted in writing back and forth to obtain complete data.

It would be a wise plan to begin to collect such data after the account reaches the delinquency stage. Thus there will be no delay in presenting the case to the attorney, once the decision is reached to force collections by a suit. It is important to send the Collection Bureau or attorney all information about the account that would have any bearing on a case in court. Collection attorneys frequently are faced with a counter claim when they go to court to try a collection case—which may be an unpleasant surprise if the credit executive has neglected to send full information.

After the rendition of a decision by the judge, or a verdict by a jury in case of jury trial, judgment is entered in accordance with the decision or verdict, either for the plaintiff or for the defendant.

The judgment becomes part of the permanent records of the court, and upon entry of the judgment it becomes, in most jurisdictions, a lien upon any real estate which the debtor may own and in some jurisdictions the judgment also becomes a lien upon the debtor's personal property. In other jurisdictions the mere entry of a judgment does not constitute a lien against personal property, and the issuance of an "execution" on the judgment to a sheriff, marshal, constable or other officer is necessary before a lien results. The "execution" is a direction to the officer to collect the amount of the judgment from the property of the judgment debtor. The officer proceeds to levy the "execution" by seizing the property of the judgment debtor and making demand upon the judgment debtor for payment. In the event that he finds nothing upon which to levy, he returns the execution to court unsatisfied. In the event that he succeeds in levying upon the debtor's property, and the debtor fails to pay the judgment, the property is offered for sale by the officer at public auction, to satisfy the judgment, and the proceeds, less the officer's charges and expenses, are then paid to the judgment creditor, who, upon receipt of payment in full, must execute and deliver to the judgment debtor an instrument known as a "satisfaction piece."

The mere commencement of an action does not impound or place any lien upon the property of the defendant, and such lien results only after the plaintiff has established his case, and judgment has been entered.

The question frequently arises as to what court an action should be brought in order to force the collection of account. This point should be determined by the attorney selected to handle this phase of the collection operation.

If a contract provides that attorneys fees and costs are to be recovered in any litigation, creditors in an action on the contract can request reimbursement for court costs and attorney's fees.

Confession of Judgment

A practice in some jurisdictions is to obtain a confession of judgment from the debtor upon the sale of merchandise or loan of money. The confession is a security device which assures creditors of an easy means of entering a judgment without the necessity of going to trial. Since a confession of judgment can usually be entered without so advising the debtor, this practice has become subject to criticism as violative of constitutional rights of due process.

In *Swarb v. Lennox*, 314 F. Supp. 1091 (1970), aff'd 405 U.S. 191 (1972) the U.S. Supreme Court held that confessions of judgment in mortgage transaction by those earning under $10,000 are to be unconstitutional as a violation of due process requirements of notice and opportunity to be heard. See also, *Jamerson v. Lennox*, 356 F. Supp. 1164 (1973), aff'd 414 U.S. 802 (1974) (where the court found that the plaintiffs were barred from asserting the general invalidity of confessions of judgments) and *D. H. Overmeyer Co. v. Frick*, 405 U.S. 174 (1972). The Court in *Overmeyer* held that a confession of judgment was valid in a commercial situation provided that the confession had been bargained for between the parties, and had been willingly, knowingly and intelligently made. It would therefore appear that in the usual commercial debtor-creditor situation, a confession of judgment is valid if so willingly, knowingly and intelligently given by the debtor. However, in consumer transactions there is serious question as to the validity of such judgments.

If a confession of judgment is used as a security device in consumer transactions, the creditor should be certain that the execution of the confession meets the requirements of the Truth In Lending Act which requires adequate disclosure to the debtor of the meaning of the document.

Under recent Federal Trade Commission rules, use of a confession of judgment is deemed an unfair consumer practice. See 9-8 above.

The following is a brief summary of the laws of the various states on the question:

STATES' LAWS ON CONFESSIONS OF JUDGMENT

ALABAMA—Invalid before suit; only the provision authorizing a confession of judgment, and not the whole instrument, is void.

ALASKA—Authorized.

ARIZONA—Not recognized unless the authority is executed after promissory note matures.

ARKANSAS—Debtor must appear in court with assent of creditor to confess.

CALIFORNIA—May confess by signed verified statement.[1]

COLORADO—Void in consumer credit transactions.

CONNECTICUT—May offer judgment before trial; invalid in any instalment contract or related separate agreement.

DELAWARE—Recognized under warrant of attorney with procedural limitations.

D.C.—Power of attorney to confess judgment is prohibited and unenforceable in direct instalment loan and consumer credit sales.

FLORIDA—Valid if executed after action.

GEORGIA—Recognized if made after action commenced.

HAWAII—Void in times sales.

IDAHO—Void in consumer credit transactions.

---

[1] Statute held violative of the fourteenth amendment to the United States Constitution. *Isbell v. County of Sonoma*, 145 Cal. Rptr. 368, 577 P.2d 188 (Cal. Sup. Ct. 1978).

ILLINOIS—Void in consumer credit transactions.

INDIANA—Void before action; use is a misdemeanor. Void in consumer credit transactions.

IOWA—Valid for money due or to become due or to secure contingent liability when verified statement given. Void in consumer credit transactions unless executed after default.

KANSAS—Defendant may offer before trial. Void in consumer credit transactions.

KENTUCKY—Void.

LOUISIANA—Valid after maturity of obligation or for purposes of executory process.

MAINE—Void in consumer credit transactions and home repair contracts.

MARYLAND—Recognized except retail instalment sales for less than $5,000.

MASSACHUSETTS—Not recognized.

MICHIGAN—May be valid if in separate instrument. Invalid in retail charge or instalment sale.

MINNESOTA—May confess judgment by verified, signed, separate statement. Power of attorney to confess judgment prohibited in consumer credit sale contract or obligation.

MISSISSIPPI—Void.

MISSOURI—Valid.

MONTANA—May confess by separate signed verified statement.

NEBRASKA—A debtor may personally appear in court and with the creditor's assent confess judgment.

NEVADA—Valid by signed verified statement. May not be taken by licensed thrift company.

NEW HAMPSHIRE—Void in motor vehicle retail instalment sales.

NEW JERSEY—Invalid in retail instalment contract, retail charge account, or home repair contract.

NEW MEXICO—Void.

NEW YORK—Valid upon debtor's affidavit; invalid before default on instalment contracts for $1,500 or less for goods other than for a commercial or business use; power of attorney to confess judgment prohibited in retail instalment contract.

NORTH CAROLINA—Valid by signed verified statement. Void in consumer credit transactions.

NORTH DAKOTA—May be entered on signed verified statement for specific sum; unenforceable if provided in retail instalment contract.

OHIO—Recognized. Warrants to confess invalid and unenforceable on instruments executed in consumer transactions entered on or after January 1, 1974. Invalid on all other instruments executed on or after January 1, 1974. Instruments without conspicuous warning of loss of rights as to notice and defenses are invalid and unenforceable.

OKLAHOMA—May be entered under warrant of attorney if acknowledged and if affidavit filed by debtor. Void in consumer credit transactions.

OREGON—May be entered if plaintiff assents; must be acknowledged; unenforceable in retail instalment contract of motor vehicle.

PENNSYLVANIA—Recognized, except as to class of natural persons with incomes of less than $10,000. May not serve as a basis for levy, execution, or garnishment under retail instalment contract unless original proceeding filed.

RHODE ISLAND—No provision.

SOUTH CAROLINA—May confess by signed, verified statement. Void in consumer credit transactions.

SOUTH DAKOTA—May confess by signed, verified statement.

TENNESSEE—Void before action.

TEXAS—Provision before action invalid. Prohibited in retail instalment contracts, charge agreements, motor vehicle instalment sale contracts and insurance premium finance agreement.

UTAH—May enter judgment by signed, verified statement by defendant. Void in consumer credit transactions.

VERMONT—Valid if made by debtor in writing; void as to contracts by consumers.

VIRGINIA—Recognized, if warrant names attorney and court. Debtor must have notice; may be set aside within 21 days after notice of entry on any valid defense to an action on the note.

WASHINGTON—May confess by signed, verified statement.

WEST VIRGINIA—May be confessed by defendant in suit. Void in consumer credit transactions.

WISCONSIN—Void and unenforceable and basis for penalties in consumer transactions.

WYOMING—Authority exists for confession of judgment but void in consumer credit transactions.

Jurisdiction

Before suit against a defaulting debtor is initiated, a creditor should determine if he can obtain jurisdiction over the debtor.

A debtor who is a domiciliary of a state is subject to the jurisdiction of the courts of such state, no matter where process of service is effectuated, whether within or without the state.[1] The traditional bases for a state court's jurisdiction over a non-domiciliary are in personam, in rem and quasi in rem.

a. *In Personam*

The most obvious form of in personam jurisdiction is "presence" within the state. Such jurisdiction permits entry of a judgment for any amount of money, subject to any limitation inherent in the court's power. If a summons is delivered to a person while he is physically present in a state, even if travelling through the state, he is subject to the jurisdiction of the court of that state. A state court establishes in personam jurisdiction over a partnership if any one partner is domiciled or is personally served while present in the state. Also, the partnership is considered "present," and subject to the jurisdiction of the court of the state, if it is "doing business" in the state. A corporate officer, unlike a partner in a partnership, is not responsible for the debts of the business he works for; therefore, service on a corporate officer does not necessarily result in jurisdiction over the corporation. A court has jurisdiction over a corporation only when the corporation is "doing business" in the state.[2]

In 1945, in the landmark case of *International Shoe Co. v. Washington,* 326 U.S. 310 (1945), the United States Supreme Court stressed that if the claims sued on were connected with activities conducted within the state, the state may exercise in personam jurisdiction over the defendant, no matter where served with process, in a suit on those claims. This came to be known as "long-arm" jurisdiction. It allows a state to exercise extraterritorial jurisdiction over a non-domiciliary based upon contracts he had with the state if the claim arose from those contracts. See discussion concerning long-arm statutes, page 14-14.

b. *In Rem*

In Rem jurisdiction turns on the presence within the state of property of the defendant. Generally, it is exercised when personal jurisdiction is unavailable. Whether real or personal, if property of the debtor, including debts owed him, is in a state the courts can acquire jurisdiction; such jurisdiction will affect only the debtor's interest in the property.

---

[1] *Milliken v. Meyer,* 311 U.S. 457 462-63 (1940).
[2] For a discussion of what activities constitute "doing business" see page 14-7.

c. Quasi In Rem

Finally, if a person seeks a money judgment against an individual over whom in personam jurisdiction cannot be obtained, the doctrine of quasi in rem jurisdiction allows attachment of any property of the non-domiciliary that happens to be in the state for use as a jurisdictional basis. Unlike in rem jurisdiction, the property forming the basis of the quasi in rem jurisdiction need not be the subject of the litigation. In a quasi in rem case, even if the non-domiciliary is served outside the state and defaults, the doctrine assures the individual seeking the money judgment that the resulting judgment will be good at least to the extent of the value of the seized property. This doctrine has been drastically restricted, if not entirely abrogated, by the Supreme Court decision, *Shaffer v. Heitner*, 433 U.S. 186 (1977). (For a detailed discussion of the effect of *Shaffer* on quasi in rem jurisdiction, see page 14-16.)

STEPS IN SUITS

Attachment

Certain provisional remedies pending determination of a law suit are available to a creditor pursuant to which the property of a defendant may be impounded by an officer of the court, and held to await the outcome of the suit. The remedy most frequently available to a creditor for this purpose is an attachment against the debtor's property.

The word "attachment" has been defined as a method whereby a debtor's property, real or personal, or any interest therein, capable of being taken under a levy of execution, is placed in the custody of the law to secure the interests of the creditor, pending the termination of the cause. That is to say, the writ of attachment is a provisional remedy by which a defendant's property is taken out of his control, during the pendency of an action, so that he is thereby prevented from so disposing of it as to place it beyond the reach of the plaintiff in case the plaintiff is successful in the action.

There are some jurisdictions, notably in the New England states, where practically all actions are commenced by attachment and this is true whether the action is for breach of contract or for tort.

In the New England states, for example, when an account is turned over to an attorney for collection, the usual course followed by the attorney is to prepare at once a writ of attachment, which names all of the banks in the town where the debtor is located, and any other persons who may have in their possession property belonging to the debtor, and to deliver the writ to the sheriff, who thereupon serves it on the debtor and the banks and other parties named. The effect of this is to "attach" whatever property of the debtor may be in the hands of the persons named, so that the debtor, unless he releases the attachment by filing a bond, is unable to draw money from the bank or otherwise to dispose of his property. The attaching party is not required to file a bond or give any other security as evidence of good faith, but obtains the writ of attachment as a matter of right. The debtor, on the other hand, may release the attachment by filing a bond, which takes the place of the attached property, and against which a recovery may be had in case the action terminates in favor of the plaintiff. Under such circumstances, it will readily be seen that judgments obtained after attachment are practically certain to be paid, and there is none of the risk attendant upon litigation which exists in jurisdictions where attachment cannot be had as a matter of right, such as those described in the following paragraphs.

In the majority of states, the writ of attachment is auxiliary to certain classes of actions only, and the statutes specify in detail not only the classes of actions in which the writ may be issued, but also the peculiar circumstances and relationships which must exist in such actions before the writ will issue. In these jurisdictions, therefore, attachment proceedings are of a highly technical nature, and the requirements of the law must be strictly complied with or the attachment will be vacated at the instance of the defendant.

An examination of the statutes shows that attachment may issue in most states in actions on contract, express or implied, and in some states in any civil action. The grounds on which a writ of attachment may be obtained are different in practically every state, but the most usual grounds are:

1. The debtor is a nonresident or a foreign corporation.
2. The defendant has absconded from the jurisdiction or conceals or hides himself.
3. The debtor has done so or is about to remove, conceal, assign or dispose of his property to defraud creditors.

In *New York* there is the additional ground that if the defendant is guilty of a fraud in an action on an express or implied contract a writ of attachment may issue. In general then, it will be seen that aside from nonresidence, an element of fraud or concealment or removal from the jurisdiction must usually be proved to sustain the issuance of a writ of attachment.

In these jurisdictions also, it is generally necessary for the attaching creditor to put up a bond for the payment of any damages which his attachment may occasion. The debtor can then usually release the property by filing a counter bond in the same sum.

Garnishment

Where a third person holds property or is indebted to the defendant, proceedings by way of "garnishment" may, in most jurisdictions, be invoked to procure a judgment directly against the third person to reach the property of the defendant.

Garnishment is a proceeding by which the plaintiff in an action seeks to reach the rights and effects of defendant by calling into court some third party who has such effects in his possession or who is indebted to defendant. The highest court of Kansas has referred to garnishment as "a species of seizure by notice," and in Nebraska it has been defined as "notice to the party in actual possession of the goods or choses in action of a debtor when an attachment has been issued against the debtor, and that the debtor's property in the hands of the party receiving the notice is to be held subject to attachment" *Matthews v. Smith,* 13 Neb. 178, 12 N.W. 821 (1882). The purpose of the remedy is to apply a debt due a defendant from a third person to the extinguishment of a judgment or claim against such defendant.

Garnishment exists in one form or another in practically all the states, except South Carolina. In Massachusetts, New Hampshire, Maine and Vermont, the remedy is called a "trustee process," in Montana garnishment is by attachment. In Pennsylvania it is known as "judgment execution."

In all cases the remedy of garnishment is essentially statutory, and the statutes must be consulted to determine under what conditions it can be applied. In many states garnishment proceedings are limited to actions on contract and are not permitted in actions in tort, though in other jurisdictions this distinction is not made and the various actions are specifically stated in the statute.

State Statutes Differ

The procedure, under the garnishment statutes, differs in the several jurisdictions. In some states it is permitted only after an execution against the original debtor has been returned unsatisfied; in other states it serves as an aid to a writ of attachment, and becomes effective by the simple expedient of serving a copy of the writ of attachment upon the person in whose hands the plaintiff believes there is money or property belonging to the defendant. (*Sniadach*, discussed below, restricts the legality of such process.) In several states the garnishment statutes compel the garnishee (i.e., the third person in possession of the defendant's property) to answer upon oath as to the amount of his indebtedness to the principal debtor, and in some jurisdictions to appear in court at the trial of the action to answer to the plaintiff as to the amount of the defendant's property which he possesses. If the property claimed by the plaintiff to be in the possession of the garnishee is an unliquidated or uncertain sum, it usually cannot be subjected to the plaintiff's claim; and in many states there is a strict rule founded upon the phraseology of the statutes that a claim may not be garnished unless the principal debtor could at common law recover upon it against the garnishee in an action of debt or *indebtatus assumpsit*. The reason for this is that the statutes limit the process to "debts."

It will be seen therefore that the terminology of the various statutes is important in determining what claims or demands are or are not so unliquidated or contingent as to be beyond the reach of the process.

Garnishment is open to anyone not expressly denied the remedy by the terms of a statute whether an individual or a corporation. It is founded upon a subsisting right of action by the defendant against the garnishee, and after service of the writ upon the garnishee or trustee, as the case may be, such person can pay his indebtedness to the principal defendant only at his peril. In Illinois and in several other states garnishment will not lie against the person liable to the judgment debtor on a negotiable note which is not yet due.

Wage Garnishments

The term "garnishment" is often applied to legal process by which the employer of a debtor is served with process requiring him to make payment of the debtor's wages, directly to the judgment creditor. This process is known by many names in the various states such as, wage garnishment, income execution, and attachment of wages.

Until July 1, 1970, the matter had been controlled by state law. However, on that date the federal law on wage garnishments became effective (Title III of the Consumer Creditor Protection Law, known as Truth In Lending Law, see Chapter 9, *supra*). Under the federal law, the amount of weekly wages subject to garnishment is limited to the lesser of 25% of the disposable earnings of the debtor, or the amount by which the weekly disposable earnings exceed

LEGAL PHASES OF COLLECTIONS

30 times the hourly wage. However, in the event that a state wage garnishment law is more beneficial to the debtor or is substantially similar to the federal law, then the Secretary of Labor can exempt such state from coverage by the federal law.

In some states, such as New York, a debtor has to be earning a minimum of $85 a week before his salary can be garnished. In Arizona, Delaware, District of Columbia, Michigan, Minnesota, Montana, New Jersey, New York, North Dakota, Oregon, and Vermont it is unlawful for an employer to dismiss his employee because of the issuance of a garnishment process. The Federal Consumer Protection Act and many state statutes also prohibit discharge of an employee because of a single garnishment proceeding against him.[1]

The U.S. Supreme Court in *Sniadach v. Family Finance Corp. of Bay View*, 395 U.S. 337 (1969), held unconstitutional a Wisconsin statute that permitted garnishment of wages prior to the entry of a judgment establishing the debt. The rationale of the opinion was that the property of the judgment debtor, i.e., his wages, was being taken without due process of law since there had been no adjudication that the debt was valid and owing prior to the enforced payment to the creditor by wage garnishment. Prejudgment garnishment proceedings therefore should not be used. The fact that the debtor does not reside within the state in which the creditor has his business does not necessarily mean that judgment cannot be obtained within the creditors' home state. Under the long-arm statutes discussed in Chapter 14, *supra* page 14-14, a court is able to obtain jurisdiction over a debtor by other than personal service of process in the event that the debtor has "transacted business" within the state, committed a tort within the state or owns real property within the state. The *Sniadach* decision has cast into doubt all prejudgment remedies, and many states have revised their legislation to conform to the new requirements of federal law. For example, California, Nevada, New Hampshire, and Rhode Island have amended their prejudgment procedures.

Connecticut, by statute, provides for a new procedure by which an application to the court is required for an order and summons in those cases in which a prejudgment remedy is sought and thereafter a hearing is held on the application. The act applies to consumer as well as commercial transactions except in such commercial transactions in which the debtor has executed a prior waiver as provided for in the statute. It is recommended that in Connecticut as a matter of routine procedure commercial creditors obtain a written waiver for debtors. Similarly, Kansas has recently changed its law relating to garnishment provid-

---

[1] The following states have statutes prohibiting discharging an employee because of a single garnishment proceeding against him:

Alaska, California, Colorado, Georgia, Hawaii, Illinois, Indiana, Iowa, Kansas, Kentucky, Louisiana, Maine, Maryland, Missouri, Nebraska, Ohio, Utah, Virginia, and Wisconsin.

In the following states, discharging an employee because of a garnishment arising out of consumer credit transaction is prohibited:

Idaho, South Carolina, West Virginia and Wyoming.

In Connecticut, discharge, discipline or suspension is prohibited unless more than 7 garnishments in a year.

In Oklahoma, discharge because of garnishment in connection with consumer credit transactions is prohibited unless there are more than 2 garnishments in a year.

In Washington, discharge prohibited unless three garnishments within the year.

ing that garnishment may only be ordered by a judge, not a clerk of the court.

Judgment

A creditor faced with a recalcitrant debtor may have no choice but to commence a civil action against that debtor in order to recover the amount which is allegedly due and owing. If the creditor is successful in such civil action the court will render a "judgment" in the creditor's favor. However, the judgment rendered by the court merely serves to fix the sum of money due the creditor from the debtor. A judgment *per se* does not guarantee that the creditor will be able to recover from the debtor the sum of money which was awarded by the judgment, and indeed a substantial number of judgments recovered remain uncollectible. Thus, where payment of a judgment is not immediately made, the judgment creditor should be acutely aware of its postjudgment collection rights.

A judgment of the courts of any state is the best evidence of indebtedness and can be made the basis of an action in any other state between the same parties. For example, a creditor obtaining a judgment in New York may obtain from the clerk of the court or the county clerk an exemplified copy of the judgment, duly certified by the clerk of the court and by a judge, and with this in hand the creditor may bring an action in any other state setting forth that the judgment was obtained against the defendant and was obtained in the courts of New York. The only defense to such an action would be that the New York court did not have the jurisdiction of the defendant or of the subject matter.

If a judgment be obtained in one county within a given state and it is desired to have an execution issued against property in another county of the same state, it is usually necessary to obtain from the county clerk, the clerk of the court or other appropriate officer of the court or county in which the judgment was filed or docketed, a transcript of judgment. This transcript can usually be filed in any other county within the state and an execution issued thereon exactly as though the judgment had originally been rendered in the latter county.

The United States Constitution provides that judgments of the courts of any state shall be entitled to full faith and credit by the courts of any other state within the United States.

Execution and Levy

The enforcement of judgments by execution and levy is statutory and thus varies from state to state.

An "execution" is an order of the court directing a sheriff or other officer to seize the defendant's property to satisfy a judgment. A "levy" is the process by which the sheriff or other court officer acquires possession and control over the property which is to satisfy the judgment. Generally, a writ of execution is required to be issued by the clerk of the court which rendered the judgment. The issuance of the writ is a ministerial act and thus does not require either a hearing or separate court order in most jurisdictions. Some state statutes provide that specific periods of time must elapse after a judgment is rendered before an execution may issue. These time limits vary greatly among states, and in

LEGAL PHASES OF COLLECTIONS

some instances between different courts of the same state and, therefore, local rules should always be consulted.

The issuance of the execution is generally done at the application of the judgment creditor, but some states, including Minnesota, require the clerk to issue the execution automatically upon the entry of the judgment.

A writ of execution is generally directed to the sheriff or other authorized official of the county within which the debtor's property is situated. The execution directs this official to levy upon the debtor's property described in the writ and to sell same at a public sale after giving the debtor sufficient notice.

It is important to note that just at the time at which the lien status accrues is important in determining the priority to be accorded various competing judgment creditors, it is equally important that execution and levy upon a judgment be made in a timely manner. For example, while the docketing of a judgment in Tennessee creates a judgment lien, if the judgment creditor fails to execute and levy upon the lien within twelve months following the rendition of the judgment, the creditor loses his lien upon the real property of the judgment debtor, and with it his priority over subsequently docketed judgments against the same debtor. As the time for execution and levy varies from state to state a judgment creditor should always consult local statutes for the time limit applicable to the enforcement of its judgment.

Supplementary Proceedings

Where a judgment debtor fails to satisfy a judgment upon demand of the sheriff, marshal or constable, or where the officer has been unable to find property upon which to levy, or the execution has been returned unsatisfied, the judgment creditor may resort to proceedings supplementary to execution in an effort to collect the debt. Supplementary proceedings are governed by statute in all jurisdictions where they are available, and differ in accordance with the statutory provisions. The statutes usually provide that the judgment creditor may, by order or subpoena, direct the judgment debtor or others who may have knowledge of property or assets of the debtor to appear before the court or a referee for examination by the judgment creditor.

The examination in supplementary proceedings is used by attorneys to ferret out fraudulent transfers of the debtor's property and concealed assets.

Judgment Liens

The vast majority of states have enacted legislation which accord to judgments the status of "liens." This lien status provides an otherwise unsecured judgment creditor with a priority over all subsequent judgment lien creditors, as well as any and all unsecured creditors. Therefore, where it becomes necessary to compel the sale of a debtor's property in order to satisfy the claims of his creditors, the proceeds realized by the sale of this property will be applied in satisfaction of the claim of the creditor whose judgment was first to attain the status of a lien. Thus, while a judgment establishes the right of the creditor to a fixed sum of money from the debtor, it is the lien status acquired by or flowing from that judgment which provides the creditor with security and priority over any and all subsequent judgment lien creditors and subsequent and prior consensual lien creditors. Under UCC Section 9-311, a debtor's rights in collateral can be transferred by judgment lien, attachment, levy or garnishment notwithstanding an existing security agreement even if the agreement prohibits such a transfer. Of course, secured creditors' rights cannot be extinguished by any transfer of the debtor.

Since judgment liens are purely creatures of statute, the point in time at which lien status accrues, the scope of the lien, and the means of enforcing the lien vary from state to state.

While the majority view holds that a judgment does not acquire the status of lien with respect to a judgment debtor's real property until it has been duly filed or docketed with the clerk of the county within which the debtor's realty is situated, many state statutes adhere to the view that a judgment becomes a lien upon real property as soon as it is rendered by a court of record. Among the states adhering to the latter view are Arkansas, Delaware, Indiana, Kansas, Maryland, Missouri, New Jersey, and Wyoming. In other jurisdictions such as Colorado, Kentucky, Michigan and Rhode Island, statutes provide that a judgment does not acquire the status of lien, with respect to the judgment debtor's real estate, until execution and levy is actually had against the debtor's property.

As noted earlier, the point in time at which a judgment actually acquires the status of a "lien" is important in determining priority among competing judgment creditors. Therefore, in those states in which the docketing of a judgment creates a lien upon the debtor's realty, the first creditor to docket his judgment is given priority over all subsequently docketed judgments as well as all unsecured creditors. Thus, where several creditors have docketed judgments at various times, the proceeds realized from the sale of the judgment of the creditor who was first to have his judgment docketed. Once this senior judgment lien creditor is satisfied, the proceeds of the sale of the debtor's property may be applied toward the satisfaction of the claims of subsequent judgment lien creditors according to the order in which the judgments were docketed.

In those states which adhere to the rule that a judgment becomes a lien upon the debtor's real property as soon as it is rendered, priority among judgment lien creditors depends upon the order in time in which the judgments were rendered. Thus, the creditor whose judgment was first rendered has priority over all subsequent judgment creditors. In Georgia, however, all judgment liens obtained in damage actions arising from a common disaster or occurrence are equal in rank or priority regardless of the date upon which the judgment was rendered provided the judgment creditor had commenced its action within twelve months from the dates of the common disaster.

Once a judgment acquires the status of a lien upon the judgment debtor's realty, any subsequent transfer of ownership of that real property is subject to the preexisting lien. Thus, where a creditor has obtained a judgment lien upon the debtor's real property any subsequent transfer of ownership of such property is subject to the lien. The creditor, however, may not use its lien status against the proceeds acquired by the debtor as a result of this subsequent sale. Rather, the judgment lien creditor's recourse is solely and exclusively to the land. Thus, even though title to the judgment debtor's property has passed to another, the preexisting judgment lien entitles the creditor to execute and levy against the real property.

LEGAL PHASES OF COLLECTIONS

While the time of the accrual of lien status varies greatly from state to state, there seems to be general agreement among the states with respect to the scope of judgment liens. In almost every state a judgment lien operates only with respect to the debtor's real property. It is only in Alabama, Georgia and Mississippi that judgment liens apply to both real and personal property. The statutes of an overwhelming majority of states provide that a judgment does not become a lien with respect to a judgment debtor's personal property until such time as a writ is issued, or levy is actually made upon the property by the county sheriff or another appropriate official.

Moreover, there seems to be universal agreement among the states that a judgment lien operates as a "general lien," effective upon all of the judgment debtor's real property situated within the county wherein the judgment was rendered or docketed. Thus, the lien acquired by a judgment creditor does not attach to a specific parcel of the debtor's realty, to the exclusion of all other real property holdings.

In order for the judgment creditor to obtain a lien on property in a different county from that within which the judgment was rendered or docketed, generally it is necessary that the creditor file a transcript of the judgment in the county in which the property is located. Such requirements are governed by state law.

Creditors should be aware that all states have homestead and personal property exemption laws that exempt certain real and personal property from levy and execution from judgment creditors. They are discussed below on page 23-50.

Thus, it is apparent that the rendering of a judgment, or even the acquisition of a judgment lien, is by no means the final step in the collection process. It is only through the enforcement of the judgment that the creditor is finally able to satisfy its claim. As with the acquisition of lien status, jurisdictions vary greatly with respect to the proper method of enforcing judgments. Generally, the preferred method of enforcing a judgment is by execution and levy. However, a few states, including West Virginia, allow for the enforcement of a judgment only by way of an action upon the judgment, while several states allow judgment creditors to choose between these two methods of enforcement. These latter states include: Connecticut, Massachusetts, Mississippi, Montana, Nebraska, North Carolina and Wisconsin.

The following table sets forth how a creditor can obtain a judgment lien on real property of the debtor in each of the states:

State	How Lien Status Is Achieved
Alabama	Judgment of court of record acquires lien status with respect to judgment debtor's property once judgment is registered with clerk of the county within which debtor's property is situated. Lien is effective against all of judgment debtor's property, both real and personal. Lien effective for 10 years.
Alaska	Judgment of any court becomes a lien when filed with recorder of the district within which debtor's real property is situated. Lien effects real property owned by judgment debtor when judgment is recorded or thereafter acquired but before lien expires. Lien effective for 10 years.

State	How Lien Status Is Achieved
Arizona	Judgment rendered by court of record becomes lien when abstract of judgment, certified by clerk of the rendering court, is filed and recorded in office of county recorder. A recorded judgment becomes a lien against all the judgment debtor's real property situated within that county except exempt property. Lien effective for 5 years from date of judgment.
Arkansas	Judgments and decrees of Circuit and Chancery courts are liens on real estate of judgment debtors from time judgment or decree is rendered. Lien applies only to debtor's real estate situated within county wherein judgment or decree was rendered. To extend lien to real property in another county, certified copy of judgment or decree must be filed in the office of the circuit clerk of that county. Lien effective for 3 years.
California	Judgment of court of record becomes a lien once abstract of judgment, certified by the clerk of the recording court, is recorded with the county recorder. Once recorded, judgment lien applies to all debtor's real property situated within that county, whether owned by the judgment debtor at that time or acquired thereafter. Lien effective for 10 years.
Colorado	Judgment becomes lien on judgment debtor's real property once a transcript of judgment, certified by the clerk of rendering court, is filed with the office of county recorder. The lien applies to real property situated within the county in which the judgment is so filed. Lien effective for 6 years from entry of judgment.
Connecticut	Mere rendering of judgment does not constitute a lien unless creditor attached debtor's property during course of action. If personal property was attached by creditor, judgment lien effective for 60 days following rendition of final judgment. If real property was attached, lien continues for four months following judgment. Lien may be recorded in town clerk's office in any town where real property situated. Lien effective for 20 years.
Delaware	Judgment of Superior Court constitutes a lien on judgment debtor's real property situated within the county from date of entry of the judgment. Judgments of Common Pleas Court and Justice of the Peace become liens on real property once transcripts of such judgments are filed in Superior Court. Lien effective for 10 years.
District of Columbia	Final judgments or decrees of District Court or Superior Court become liens from date judgment is filed and recorded with office of recorder of deeds. Lien applies to all judgment debtor's freehold and leasehold interests in real property. Lien effective for 12 years.
Florida	Judgment or decree becomes lien on the debtor's real property once certified copy of judgment is recorded in lien record of county wherein debtor's real property is situated. Lien effective for 20 years.
Georgia	Judgment becomes lien once it is entered on the general execution docket. Judgment liens take priority according to date en-

State	How Lien Status Is Achieved
	tered upon said execution docket, and are effective against all of the judgment debtor's property, both real and personal situated within the county wherein judgment is entered upon execution docket. Lien effective for 7 years.
Hawaii	Judgment or decree becomes lien upon real property once copy of judgment, certified by clerk of rendering court, is recorded with the Bureau of Conveyances.
Idaho	Judgment becomes a lien when abstract is recorded with clerk of the county in which property is situated. Once recorded judgment lien applies to all judgment debtor's real property within that county. Lien effective for 5 years.
Illinois	Judgment becomes a lien with respect to real property registered under Land Titles ("Torrens") Act once it is filed with registrar of titles and entered upon register. With respect to land not registered under Torrens Act, judgment becomes a lien when filed with recorder of deeds for county within which property is situated. Lien effective for 7 years; may be extended for additional 7 years.
Indiana	Judgment of court of record becomes a lien on all judgment debtor's real property situated within the county wherein judgment was rendered. Judgment becomes a lien against judgment debtor's real property situated elsewhere only upon filing of transcript with clerk of the appropriate county. Lien effective for 10 years.
Iowa	Judgment of district court becomes a lien from date judgment is entered upon docket and lien index. Lien extends to all judgment debtor's real property situated within the county in which judgment was entered. With respect to real estate located outside such county, judgment becomes a lien once transcript of judgment is filed in the district court of the county within which such real estate is located. Lien effective for 10 years.
Kansas	Upon rendition, a judgment of District Court is a lien on all debtor's real estate situated within the county. Lien effective from time petition stating claim against debtor was filed; however, under no circumstances may the lien take effect more than four months before entry of judgment. Judgment becomes a lien on debtor's real property situated outside the county once attested copy of journal entry of judgment is filed with Clerk of District Court for the county in which debtor's real property is located.
Kentucky	Judgments are not liens against any of judgment debtor's property. In order to obtain a lien judgment creditor must deliver writ of execution to the proper public officer. Once writ is delivered to this officer the creditor has a lien on all of the judgment debtor's property, whether real or personal. In order to preserve lien against subsequent purchasers or lessees of judgment debtor's real property, a memorandum of the lien should be filed

State	How Lien Status Is Achieved
	with the county clerk of the county within which the property is situated.
Louisiana	Judgment is not a lien on debtor's real property until recorded with recorder of mortgages for the parish within which the property is situated. Once recorded, lien becomes effective against all debtor's real estate within that parish. Lien effective for 10 years.
Maine	Judgment is not a lien on debtor's property. In order to obtain a lien, creditor must have attached debtor's property while action was pending. Attachment may proceed only pursuant to court order, and such order may only be entered after a hearing on notice to debtor and upon a finding by the court that creditor is reasonably likely to recover judgment in an amount equal to, or greater than, the value of the property sought to be attached.
Maryland	Judgment of Circuit Court is lien on debtor's real property within the county wherein judgment was rendered. Lien is effective from date of judgment. Judgment may become a lien on debtor's realty located outside of the county by filing certified copy of docket entry with Clerk of the county wherein the realty is situated. Lien effective for 12 years.
Massachusetts	Judgment is not a lien; however, judgment becomes a lien against all of debtor's real property once recorded with registry of deeds. Judgment may be sued on in civil action.
Michigan	Judgment is not a lien on debtor's real property until notice of levy has been recorded in the office of the register of deeds for the county wherein the realty is situated. Thus upon obtaining judgment, creditor should obtain a writ of execution and have same delivered to the appropriate officer for levy. Real property is bound by the lien from the time of levy, but no levy upon real estate is effective against subsequent *bona fide* purchasers unless notice of levy is recorded. Lien effective for 10 years.
Minnesota	Judgment of district or county court becomes a lien once it is entered and docketed by the clerk of that court. Lien is effective upon all debtor's real property within the county, whether owned by the debtor at the time the judgment is docketed or acquired thereafter. Lien effective for 10 years.
Mississippi	Judgment becomes a lien against debtor's real and personal property once recorded in the office of the clerk of the Circuit Court of the county within which the property is situated. Lien effective for 7 years from the entry of the judgment or decree.
Missouri	Judgment is a lien upon the debtor's real property from the day judgment is rendered. Lien applies to all of the debtor's real property within the county in which judgment was rendered. Judgment becomes a lien on real property located elsewhere once a transcript is filed with the circuit clerk of the county wherein property is located. Lien effective for 3 years.

LEGAL PHASES OF COLLECTIONS

State	How Lien Status Is Achieved
Montana	Judgment becomes a lien once it is docketed, and is effective against all debtor's real property within the county. The clerk of the court is required to docket a judgment immediately upon entry thereof. Lien effective for 6 years..
Nebraska	Judgment of district court is lien upon debtor's real property situated within the county from the time it is rendered. Judgment becomes lien on real property located in other counties once transcript is filed in office of the Clerk of the district court of that county. Lien effective for 5 years.
Nevada	Judgment becomes a lien only upon filing of a certified transcript of the original docket, abstract, or copy of judgment with the county recorder for the county within which the debtor's real property is located. Lien is generally effective for 6 years from the date of the original docketing.
New Hampshire	No lien is created by rendition, entry or docketing of a judgment. However, if creditor attached debtor's property when suit commenced, the lien created by that attachment continues from the time judgment is rendered for sixty days upon personal property, and six years upon real property.
New Jersey	Judgments (except district and municipal court judgments) create qualified liens upon debtor's real property from time judgment is entered upon the court's minutes. Entry of judgment creates a lien upon realty which gives creditor priority over subsequent deeds and mortgages. However, subsequent judgment creditor who executes and levies upon real property acquires priority over prior judgment creditors who fail to levy. Lien effective for 20 years.
New Mexico	Judgment is a lien on debtor's real property from date upon which a certified transcript is filed with the county clerk of the county within which the property is located. Lien effective for 14 years.
New York	Judgment becomes a lien upon debtor's real property once it is docketed by the clerk of the county within which the debtor's real property is situated, or from the time of the filing of a notice of levy pursuant to an execution. Once lien is obtained it is effective against real property then owned or thereafter acquired by judgment debtor. Lien effective for 10 years.
North Carolina	Judgment of Superior Court is a lien upon debtor's real property situated within county in which judgment is docketed. Transcript filed with county clerk in any county where debtor has realty will be a lien upon that property. Lien effective for 10 years from entry of judgment.
North Dakota	Judgment becomes a lien once it is docketed by the clerk of the court. Lien is effective upon all debtor's real property except homestead, then owned or thereafter acquired, which is located within the county in which the judgment is docketed. Judgment becomes a lien upon debtor's real property located in another county once a transcript is filed in that county. Lien effective for 10 years.

State	How Lien Status Is Achieved
Ohio	Judgment of court of general jurisdiction is lien upon real property once a certificate of the judgment is filed with the clerk of the Common Pleas Court for the county wherein the land is situated. Judgment does not become a lien against registered land until a certified copy of the judgment is filed with the office of the county recorder. Lien status may also be obtained upon debtor's real property via seizure under execution. Lien effective for 5 years.
Oklahoma	Judgment of court of record becomes a lien on a debtor's real property after a certified copy of judgment is filed with the county clerk of the county wherein the property is situated. However, unless execution is issued and levied upon within one year following the judgment, the creditor's priority is lost as against subsequent judgment creditors. Lien effective for 5 years.
Oregon	Judgments of Circuit or County Courts are liens upon debtor's real property situated within those counties wherein the judgment, or a transcript thereof, is docketed. Lien applies to property then owned or thereafter acquired by the debtor. Lien effective for 10 years.
Pennsylvania	Judgment of court of record is a lien once it is entered and indexed. Lien applies to all debtor's real property located within that judicial district. Lien created by entry and indexing of judgment applies only to real property which is then owned by the debtor. Creditor may obtain lien upon debtor's property acquired thereafter by execution and levy. Lien effective for 5 years.
Rhode Island	Judgment is not a lien upon debtor's property until execution is levied. First creditor to levy upon execution is entitled to have his claim satisfied before all creditors who levy thereafter.
South Carolina	Judgment becomes a lien from the time it is entered. Lien is effective upon all of the debtor's real property located within the county wherein the judgment is entered, or a transcript thereof is filed. Lien effective for 10 years.
South Dakota	Judgment of court of record is a lien once it is docketed, and applies to all of debtor's real property except homestead situated within the county in which the judgment is docketed, or a transcript thereof is filed. Lien effective for 10 years.
Tennessee	Judgment of court of record, general session court or justice of peace over $500, becomes a lien once certified copy of the judgment is registered in the county wherein the debtor's real property is situated. Lien effective for 1 year.
Texas	Lien is created once an abstract of a judgment is recorded with the county clerk of county wherein the debtor's real property is located. Lien extends to real property then owned or thereafter acquired by debtor. Lien effective for 10 years.
Utah	Judgment of district court is a lien once it is docketed. Lien applies to all of the debtor's real property within the county

LEGAL PHASES OF COLLECTIONS

State	How Lien Status Is Acquired
	wherein the judgment is docketed, or a certified transcript has been recorded. Lien effective for 8 years.
Vermont	Judgment does not become a lien until it is recorded in the county wherein the judgment debtor's real property is located. Once recorded, judgment may constitute a lien on any real property of judgment debtor.
Virginia	Judgment becomes a lien once it is recorded on the judgment lien docket in the county clerk's office, and is effective upon all of debtor's real property situated within that county. Lien extends to real property acquired by debtor before or after the judgment is docketed. Lien effective for 20 years.
Washington	Judgment of the Superior Court, and those judgments of District Court which are filed with the Superior Court, are liens upon all debtor's real property situated within the county in which the judgment was rendered. Lien is effective from time judgment is entered. Lien becomes effective upon real property located in another county once a certified transcript of the judgment is filed with the county clerk of that county. Lien effective for 10 years.
West Virginia	Lien is created against the real property of a judgment debtor once a judgment against that debtor is entered. However, this lien is not effective against subsequent *bona fide* purchasers unless docketed by the clerk of the county commission for the county wherein the real property is situated. Lien effective for 10 years.
Wisconsin	Judgment of court of record is a lien on real property from the time the judgment is rendered, provided judgment is properly docketed thereafter. Lien effective for 10 years.
Wyoming	Judgment becomes a lien upon the debtor's real property situated within the county in which the judgment was rendered from the time the judgment is entered. Judgment is not a lien on debtor's real property located in other counties until such property is seized in execution. Lien effective for 5 years.

Enforcement of Foreign and Federal Judgments

Unless a state has adopted the Uniform Enforcement of Foreign Judgments Act, the judgment of one state cannot be automatically enforced in another state despite the constitutional requirement that "full faith and credit" be given to the judgments of sister states; it is necessary that a new suit on the judgment be commenced against the debtor. Although proof of liability will be easier, there still is the attendant expense and delay of a new suit. Under the Uniform Enforcement of Foreign Judgments Act, however, the judgment creditor is only required to file an authenticated copy of the foreign judgment with the clerk of the court of the state in which enforcement is sought, and advise the debtor thereof. The judgment so filed has the same effect as a judgment issuing out of the state of the court in which the judgment has been filed, and all local enforcement proceedings are available to execute the judgment. The Uniform

Act does not apply to judgments of foreign countries. Enforcement of such judgments depends on state law and generally a suit on the judgment is required.

The following states have enacted the Uniform Act: Alaska, Arizona, Arkansas, Colorado, Connecticut, Hawaii, Idaho, Illinois, Iowa, Kansas, Maine, Minnesota, Missouri, Nebraska, Nevada, New York, North Dakota, Ohio, Oklahoma, Oregon, Pennsylvania, South Dakota, Tennessee, Texas, Utah, Washington, Wisconsin and Wyoming.

Under Rule 69(a) of the Federal Rules of Civil Procedure, a federal judgment can be enforced by use of the legal procedures authorized by the state law of the state within which is located the federal court which issued the judgment.

Statutory Repossession (Replevin)

Almost all states have adopted some form of statutory repossession procedures by which personal property wrongfully taken can be recovered. Such procedures are designated in some states as replevin actions. These statutes are in addition to UCC provisions authorizing a secured creditor to respossess collateral. The procedures of each state are different and legal counsel should be consulted before any such proceeding is initiated.

The essence of the remedy of replevin is the recovery of a chattel by one who has a general or a special property interest in the thing taken or detained. Obviously, a plaintiff with no title and with no right to possession has no right to take the property in dispute by replevin from the possession of another, no matter how defective the latter's title may be. To recover in replevin, the plaintiff must show a title or possessory right superior to that of the defendant.

Credit men are most frequently confronted with the problem of replevin in conditional sale and chattel mortgage contracts. Upon completion of a sale of goods in which both title and possession have passed to the buyer, the seller has no right to maintain a replevin action. It is only when the sale is made on conditions which are to be performed by the buyer, the failure of performance of which prevents title passing, that replevin will lie.

In the case of conditional sales and chattel mortgage contracts, the right to possession is ordinarily in the buyer and mortgagor respectively. The usual provision in the contract is that upon default in the performance of the agreement, the right to possession shall vest in the conditional vendor, or mortgagee, subject to rules and regulations which are usually provided in the statutes of the various states. The requirements of these state laws differ. Some permit replevin upon default regardless of the amount of money paid on the contract; others permit replevin without accounting to the buyer or mortgagor only in the event that less than half of the contract price is paid, while, finally, some states prescribe limitation on the right to replevin when more than half of the contract price is paid. These provisions are sometimes derived from the common law and most frequently, from the statutes passed regulating such transactions.

In *Fuentes v. Shevin*, 407 U.S. 67 (1972), the United States Supreme Court, in two companion cases, considered the statutes of Pennsylvania and Florida which permitted a creditor to obtain a writ of replevin to recover property wrongfully detained by a debtor, without any requirement of prior notice to the debtor or of a judicial hearing. Both cases were factually similar in that the debtors had purchased consumer goods from their respective creditors on instalment plans. The documents executed at the time of sale provided that

LEGAL PHASES OF COLLECTIONS

the creditors could recover the property in the event of a default in payment.

The cases arose under similar factual situations. The plaintiffs borrowed relatively small sums of money from banks issuing promissory notes and pledging personal property as security. The security agreement provided that in the event of default the secured party was entitled to take possession of the property. On the occasion of the default by the debtors, the creditors did proceed to recover the property. Repossession was accomplished by the basic remedy of self-help pursuant to UCC 9-503 which provides: "Unless otherwise agreed a security party has on default the right to take possession of the collateral . . . [and] may proceed without judicial process if this can be done without breach of the peace . . . ."

The Court held that both statutes were constitutionally defective in not providing notice and an opportunity to be heard prior to the taking of the debtors' property by the creditors. The fact that a hearing could be held after the property had been recovered was not sufficient to cure the defect, nor was the requirement that a bond be posted an adequate substitute for the prior hearing. The Court saw no meaningful distinction between the household goods in question in the case before it and the matter of wage assignments which it had considered in the *Sniadach* case discussed *supra*, page 23-23.

The court dismissed the contention that the requisite state action was lacking because the actions of the defendants were pursuant to contractual rights rather than to any statute or by act of any state official. It held that the acts of the defendants were pursuant to rights that flowed from the contract, and such rights were predicted on state law and power, namely the Code. Therefore, the acts of repossession were made "under cover of state law." But see to the contrary *Nowlin v. Professional Auto Sales, Inc.*, 496 F.2d 16 (8th Cir. 1974), which represents the opinion in the majority of jurisdictions.

Section 9-503 of the Uniform Commercial Code gives a secured party the right to take possession of the security upon default of the debtor without judicial process if this can be done without a breach of the peace. However, recent judicial decisions place in doubt the validity of these remedies when enforced without prior notice to the debtor.

A California statute which permitted a creditor to repossess goods without a prior hearing was held in violation of the fourteenth amendment to the Federal Constitution. *Adams v. Egley*, 338 F. Supp. 614 (S.D. Calif. 1972).

Mitchell v. W. T. Grant Co., 416 U.S. 600 (1974) is more favorable from the creditor's point of view. The Supreme Court reconsidered the question of a state replevin law. At issue was a Louisiana statute under which a local judge issued a writ of sequestration without any prior notice to the debtor which the court found constitutionally valid. The Court distinguished the facts at issue in *Mitchell* from that in *Fuentes* as follows: (1) the writ of replevin was issued by a judge rather than a clerk; (2) the debtor was entitled to a hearing on the matter of possession thus minimizing the time within which he would be denied his property, and (3) in order for the writ to be issued the creditor had to supply an affidavit containing evidentiary facts as opposed to the mere conclusory statements required by the applicable statutes in *Fuentes*.

It would appear therefore that prior notice is now not an absolute requirement of state law but depends on the particular statute involved; however, the safest course of action for a creditor would be to provide such notice.

In *Fontiane v. Industrial National Bank of Rhode Island*, 111 R.I. 6, 298 A.2d 521 (1973), a court held that despite a provision in the contract that creditor could peacefully repossess property without notice to the debtor such a provision was so unconscionable as to be against public policy.

Satisfactions of Judgments

Almost all states have statutory requirements which provide that a satisfaction must be filed by a creditor if a debtor satisfies the indebtedness, whether voluntarily or through judgment enforcement proceedings.

The requirements vary from state to state. For example, in California and Virginia, a creditor must file a satisfaction of judgment within 30 days of receipt of payment in full while Arkansas and Florida require that a satisfaction be filed within 60 days. Some states, e.g., California and Illinois, require that a satisfaction be filed within a certain amount of time upon written demand by the debtor after payment in full.

The form of the satisfaction may be statutorily prescribed, such as in California, District of Columbia, Florida, Michigan, New Jersey, New Mexico, and North Dakota; or the creditor may be required to merely make an entry of satisfaction upon the judgment record, such as in Alabama and Iowa. Other states, e.g., Ohio, Oklahoma, Oregon, South Dakota, Wisconsin, and Wyoming, provide suggested forms of satisfactions.

Creditors must be certain to check the appropriate law in the state where the original judgment was entered as well as the law in each state where an authenticated copy of the judgment was filed.

LIMITATIONS OF ACTIONS

Statutes of Limitations are concerned with the period of time within which an action may be brought to enforce a legal right. Their purpose is to compel the commencement of litigation within a prescribed time, not only because the law looks with suspicion upon stale claims but also because of the difficulty of proof after passing of time with loss of documents and other evidence, failure of memory, and death or removal of witnesses from the jurisdiction.

The statutes are matters of adjective or evidentiary law and not of a substantive character. The defense that the statutory number of years has elapsed since the particular cause of action accrued must be affirmatively pleaded after the commencement of an action for otherwise the statute is deemed waived and a recovery may be had in spite of the staleness of the claim. On the other hand, the pleading of the statute affords a complete and perfect defense to the action regardless of its merits and the certainty of proof that may be adduced to support it.

The time limitations prescribed in each state vary with the type of action, the longest period being generally that for actions on instruments under seal and the shortest for actions on oral contracts or open accounts. Where difficulty of proof is the greatest, the statutory period is the shortest.

Many statutes provide that the limitations can be tolled or suspended in the event a defendant is out of the state or resides within the state under a false name. In addition, some statutes provide that the statute be extended if during the period of limitations the plaintiff is either an infant or an incompetent or in prison for a term of years. The period of limitations is often also extended in the event that the liable party fraudulently concealed the existence of the cause of action on which the claim is based. Should the claimant die prior to the running of the statute, the limitation often will not terminate, if the claim survives, until a stated time after his death, such as four months in Hawaii.

When Statute Begins to Run

The period of limitation begins to run from the date that a cause of action first accrues which is a matter determined by state law. It is at times difficult, however, to determine at what precise time this occurs. Some examples are set forth as follows:

CONTRACTS IN GENERAL: A cause of action accrues when either party first breaches a term of the contract. Where time of performance under the contract is fixed, the cause will accrue upon the termination of such period. Where no time is specified in the contract, an action for failure to perform may be brought after a reasonable time has elapsed during which performance might have been made. Where either party announces his intention not to comply with his contractual obligation, a cause of action arises for anticipatory breach of contract at that time.

OPEN BOOK ACCOUNTS: Compute time from entry of last item in the account.

CONTRACTS OF SALE: An action for the purchase price accrues at time of delivery unless the parties have agreed upon a different date for payment.

BROKER'S CONTRACT: Compensation is due upon completion of services and statute runs from that date.

FACTOR'S CONTRACT: The weight of authority holds that the statute does not commence running against a consignor until the factor has rendered an account or instructions have been given to remit, or a demand for an account is made and not complied with.

BREACH OF WARRANTY: Ordinarily a warranty relating to a present condition is breached at the date contract is made; but if the warranty relates to a future event, such as production capacity of a particular machine over a period of time, a cause of action does not arise until the event occurs.

GUARANTY CONTRACTS: Where the contract is one of indemnity or guaranty of collection, a cause of action does not accrue against the guarantor until the creditor has exhausted his remedies against the principal debtor. But where the contract is one of absolute guaranty of payment, the cause accrues and statute begins to run from the time the obligation of the principal debtor first becomes due.

SURETIES, INDORSERS AND OTHER ACCOMMODATING PARTIES: May maintain an action against their principal only after full payment of the principal's obligation and the statute runs in favor of the principal from the time of such payment.

BILLS AND NOTES: A cause of action accrues to the holder and the time limitations begins to run from the date that a demand may first be made for payment. If a time note, the demand may not be made until the dates of maturity. If a demand note it may be made at once.

SECURED DEBT: It is a general rule that taking of collateral will not affect the running of the statute on the debt itself.

What Law Governs

Where the parties live in different states, and where the contract sued upon was made in a third, the question arises: Which statute of limitations will control?

(Continued on page 23-41.)

STATES' LAWS ON TOLLING OF STATUTE AND REVIVING OF BARRED DEBT [1]

State	Tolling of Statute — Part Payment	Tolling of Statute — Written Acknowledgment	Tolling of Statute — Written Promise	Reviving of Barred Debt — Part Payment	Reviving of Barred Debt — Written Acknowledgment	Reviving of Barred Debt — Written Promise
Alabama	X					X
Alaska	X	X	X	X	X	X
Arizona		C	C		X	X
Arkansas	C	C	C	X	X	C
California	X	X	X	X	X	X
Colorado	X		X	X		X
Connecticut	C	C	C	C	C	C
Delaware	C	C	C	C	C	C
D.C.	C	X	X	C	X	X
Florida	C	C	C		X	X
Georgia		X	X		X	X
Hawaii	C			C	C	C
Idaho	X	X	X	X	X	X
Illinois	X		X	X		X
Indiana	X	X	X	X	X	X
Iowa		C	C		X	X

23–38

Kansas	X	X	X	X	X
Kentucky	C	C	C		X
Louisiana	X	X	X	X	
Maine	X	X	X	X	
Maryland	X	X	X	X	X
Massachusetts	X	X	X	X	X
Michigan		X	X	C	X
Minnesota	X	X	X	X	X
Mississippi		X	X		X
Missouri	X	X	X		X
Montana	X	X	X	X	X
Nebraska	X	X		X	X
Nevada	X	X	X	X	X
New Hampshire	C	C	C	C	C
New Jersey	X	X	X	X	X
New Mexico	X	X	X	X	X
New York	X	X	X	X	X
North Carolina	X	X	X	X	X
North Dakota	X	X	X	X	X

STATES' LAWS ON TOLLING OF STATUTE AND REVIVING OF BARRED DEBT [1] (Continued)

State	Tolling of Statute				Reviving of Barred Debt		
	Part Payment	Written Acknowledgment	Written Promise		Part Payment	Written Acknowledgment	Written Promise
Ohio	X	X	X		X	X	X
Oklahoma	X	X	X		X	X	X
Oregon	X	X	X		X	X	X
Pennsylvania	C	C	C		C	C	C
Rhode Island	C	C	C		C	C	C
South Carolina	X	X	X		X	X	X
South Dakota	X	X	X		X	X	X
Tennessee		C	C			C	C
Texas		C	C			X	
Utah	X	X	X		X	X	X
Vermont	C	C	C		C	C	C
Virginia		X	X			X	X
Washington	C	C	C		C	C	C
West Virginia		X	X			X	X
Wisconsin	X	X	X		X	X	X
Wyoming	X	X	X		X	X	X

[1] X indicates statutory authority and C indicates authority based on case law.

LEGAL PHASES OF COLLECTIONS

(Continued from page 23-37.)

The place of contracting and domicile of the parties are not determinative and it has been held that an action may be maintained although the statute has run against the claim in the state where the contract was made or where the parties reside. The place where the action is brought will determine whether the claim is timely asserted according to the laws of that jurisdiction. It is provided by statute in some states, however, that an action may not be maintained in such state where the cause of action was barred by the statute of the state where the cause of action arose.

Part Payment, Acknowledgment of Debt and New Promise

In most jurisdictions part payment, acknowledgment of the debt or new promise will toll the running of the statute of limitations or revive a barred debt and the statute will commence to run again from the date of the last payment, the date of acknowledgment of the obligation or promise to pay.

The table on pages 23-38–23-40 summarizes the law on the subject.

Limitations of Actions on Judgments

When an action is brought and judgment is entered against one of the parties to such action the judgment is effective for a period of years ranging from one to twenty depending on the state statutes and the court rendering the judgment, *i.e.,* whether a court of record or not, and whether the judgment is a domestic or foreign judgment. The table of statutes of limitations on pages 23-42–23-45 sets forth these periods of limitations in the various states.

A court of record is generally a court taking and keeping a permanent record. It may be stated generally, however, that courts of the justice of the peace and in some cases municipal courts are not courts of record. Other civil courts in most jurisdictions are courts of record. Most states have a longer statute of limitations for judgments of courts of record than for judgments of courts not of record.

A foreign judgment is a judgment secured in another jurisdiction than the one in which suit thereon is brought. Thus, in the state of New York, every judgment secured in any other state of the United States or foreign country is a foreign judgment. It should be noted that although each of the states is required to give full faith and credit to the judgments of its sister states, the judgment creditor usually may not avail himself of the remedies provided in one state for enforcement of a judgment secured in another without reducing his claim to judgment in the former state. This is done by bringing suit in one state on the judgment secured in the other. A domestic judgment is a judgment secured in the same state in which suit thereon is brought. In many states the statute of limitation for domestic judgments is longer than that for foreign judgments.

Lost Documents in Suits

The loss or destruction of an original document on which a claim is based, or which is necessary for proof of the claim, is not necessarily fatal to the successful prosecution of the suit. *(Continued on page 23-46.)*

LIMITATIONS FOR CIVIL ACTIONS

(Letters indicate footnotes. Figures indicate years.)
O-Oral—W-Written

State	Promissory Notes	Open Accounts	Instruments and Contracts Under Seal	Ordinary Contracts	Domestic Judgments in Courts of Record	Domestic Judgments in Courts not of Record	Foreign Judgments in Courts of Record	Foreign Judgments in Courts not of Record
Ala. ...	6	3(a)	10	6(a)	20	6	20	No prov.
Alaska .	6	6(a)	10	6(a)	10	10	10	10
Ariz. ...	6(b)	3(a)	6(b)	6-W—3-O(a)	5	5	4 or (d)	4 or (d)
Ark. ...	5	3(a)	5	5-W—3-O(a)	10	10*	10	10
Calif. ..	4	4(a)	4	4-W—2-O(a)	10	10	10	10
Colo. ...	6	6(a)	6(a)	6(a)(c)	20	6	6	6
Conn. ..	6	6(a)	6-W—3-O(a)	6-W—3-O(a)	20(ff)	20(ff)	No. prov.	No. prov.
Del.	6	3(a)	No Prov.	3(a)	No. prov.	No. prov.	No. prov.	No. prov.
D.C. ...	3	3(a)	12	3(a)	3	3	(d)	(d)
Fla.	5	4(a)	No Prov.	5-W—4-O(a)	20	5	7	7
Ga.	6	4(a)	20	6-W—4-O(a)	7(e)	7(e)	5	5
Hawaii .	6	6(a)	6(a)	6(a)	10	6	6	4
Idaho ..	5	4(a)	5	5-W—4-O(a)	6	6	6	6
Ill.	10	5(a)	10(f)	10-W—5-O(a)	20	No. prov.	5	5
Ind.	10	6(a)	20	(y)(a)	20	15	20	15

* Can be renewed.

Iowa	10	5(a)	10	10-W—5-O(a)	20(ee)	10	20	10
Kan.	5	3(a)	5	5-W—3-O(a)	Kept alive by execution every five years			No prov.
Ky.	15(h)	5(a)(i)	15	15-W—5-O(a)	15	15	15	15
La.	5	3	10	10	10(dd)	10(dd)	10(dd)	10(dd)
Me.	6(j)	6(a)	20(a)	6(a)	20(v)	6(k)(v)	20	6
Md.	3(a)	3(a)	12	3(a)	12	12	12	12
Mass.	6(l)	6(a)	20	6(a)	20(v)	6	20(v)	9
Mich.	6(a)	6(a)	6(a)	6(a)	10	6	10	6
Minn.	6(a)(cc)	6(a)(cc)	6	6(a)(cc)	10	10	10	10
Miss.	6	3	6	6-W—3-O(a)	7	6	7(m)	6
Mo.	10(a)	5	10(a)	10(a)	10	5	10	5
Mont.	8	5(a)	8	8-W—5-O(a)	10	5	10	5
Neb.	5	4(a)	5	5-W—4-O(a)	Kept alive by execution every five years			5
Nev.	6	4(a)(aa)	6	6-W—4-O(a)	6(aa)	6	6	6
N.H.	6	6(a)	20	6(a)	20	20	20	20
N.J.	6	6(a)	16[1]	6(a)	20	6	20	20(d)
N.M.	6	4(a)	6	6-W—4-O(a)	14	6	14	6
N.Y.	6(a)	6(a)	6(a)	6(a)	20	20(v)	20(v)	20(v)
N.C.	3	3(a)	10	3(a)	10	7	10	7

LIMITATIONS FOR CIVIL ACTIONS (Continued)

(Letters indicate footnotes. Figures indicate years.)
O-Oral—W-Written

State	Promissory Notes	Open Accounts	Instruments and Contracts Under Seal	Ordinary Contracts	Domestic Judgments in Courts of Record	Domestic Judgments in Courts not of Record	Foreign Judgments in Courts of Record	Foreign Judgments in Courts not of Record
N.D.	6(a)	6(a)	6(c)	6(a)	10	10	10	10
Ohio	15	6(a)(t)	15	15-W—6-O(a)	21	21	15	15
Okla.	5	3(a)	5	5-W—3-O(a)	execution every five years		3	3
Ore.	6	6(a)	No limit(u)	6(a)	10	10	10	10
Pa.	6	6(a)	20	6	6	6	6	6
R.I.	10	10	20	10	20	20	20	20
S.C.	6	6(a)	20	6(a)	10	10	10	10
S.D.	6	6(a)	20	6(a)	20	20	10	10
Tenn.	6	6(a)	6(a)	6(a)	10	10	10	10
Texas	4	4(a)	4	4-W—2-O(a)	10	10	10	10
Utah	6	4(a)	6	6-W—4-O(a)	8	8	8	8
Vt.	6(o)	6(a)	8	6(a)	8(bb)	6	8(bb)	6
Va.	5	3(a)	5	5-W—3-O(a)	20	20	10	10
Wash.	6	3(a)	6	6-W—3-O(a)	6	6	6	6
W.Va.	10	5(a)	10	10-W—5-O(a)	10	10	10	10

[1] Note: An action founded upon an instrument under seal by a merchant or bank, finance company or other financial institutions in New Jersey must be commenced within 6 years after the cause of action accrues.

LIMITATIONS FOR CIVIL ACTIONS (Continued)

(Letters indicate footnotes. Figures indicate years.)
O-Oral—W-Written

State	Promissory Notes	Open Accounts	Instruments and Contracts Under Seal	Ordinary Contracts	Domestic Judgments in Courts of Record	Domestic Judgments in Courts not of Record	Foreign Judgments in Courts of Record	Foreign Judgments in Courts not of Record
Wis. . . .	6	6(a)	20(p)	6(a)	20	6	20	6
Wyo. . .	10	8(a)	10	10-W—8-O(a)	5(q)	5(q)	5	5

(a) Uniform Commercial Code §2-725 provides a 4 year statute of limitations as to *sales* contracts. The parties may by original agreement reduce the period of limitation to not less than one year, but they may not extend it.
(b) Instruments executed without the state, 4 years.
(c) Contracts affecting real property, 10 years.
(d) Suit may be brought on a foreign judgment unless statute of limitations has run against it in the jurisdiction where it was entered.
(e) Judgments are dormant 7 years after rendition if no execution, or 7 years after execution or 7 years after written notice of public effort to enforce is filed with the clerk.
(f) Vendor's lien, mortgage, 20 years.
(g) Contract to convey land, 15 years; contract for payment of money, 10 years.
(h) If note has been placed on the footing of a bill of exchange, 5 years.
(i) An action on a merchant's account must be instituted within 5 years from January 1 following the dates or time of delivery of the articles charged in the account.
(j) If attested by witnesses, 20 years.
(k) Judgments of Trial Justices Courts, 20 years.
(l) If note attested by witness and action brought by original payee or executor or administrator, 20 years.
(m) If debtor resided in Mississippi when foreign judgment was rendered, then it is barred in 3 years.
(n) Held by case law to be 20 years.
(o) If note attested by witnesses, 21 years.
(p) If action accrues outside the state, 10 years.
(q) May be revived within 21 years after it becomes dormant.
(r) As provided in state giving judgment.
(s) May be revived once by filing a transcript of the judgment before the limitation expires, action may be brought within 7 years after revival.
(t) 15 years written accounts.
(u) An action on a sealed instrument entered into before August 13, 1965 must be commenced within 10 years.
(v) Presumption of payment arises after 20 years.
(w) Except as provided in Maine UCC Sec. 2-725.
(x) Special limitations apply to counter claims.
(y) 6 years Oral, 10 years Money, 15 years Realty, 20 other than money.
(z) An action on a merchant's account must be commenced within 5 years of the next January 1st succeeding the date of delivery.
(aa) Nevada limitation periods apply unless further limited by UCC.
(bb) If a promissory note was witnessed—21 years.
(cc) Except where Uniform Commercial Code otherwise applies.
(dd) Foreign judgments unenforceable in foreign state are unenforceable in Louisiana.
(ee) No judgment in an action for foreclosure of a real estate mortgage or deed of trust or for rent or judgment of credits assigned by a receiver of a closed bank when assignee is not a trustee for creditors or depositors shall be enforced and no execution thereon given for other than as a set-off or counter-claim after 2 years from the entry thereof. The judgment may not be renewed except by voluntary written stipulation of the parties.
(ff) 10 small claims.

23–45

(Continued from page 23-41.)

The original document is, of course, the best evidence, and no substitute for the original document will be accepted if the document itself can be produced. But if it can be proved that the original document has been lost or destroyed, secondary evidence of the contents of the document is admissible.

Such secondary evidence may be a copy of the missing paper or, if no copy exists, the contents of the instrument may be proven by the oral testimony of witnesses who are familiar with its terms and provisions.

The general rule is that a copy of the missing document must be used if obtainable, and only on proof that neither the original document nor a copy is accessible may oral testimony be admitted. Failure to produce the original document must in all cases be satisfactorily explained.

EXEMPTIONS

So deeply ingrained in the body politic as a natural right is the theory of exemptions, that legislatures are willing to keep on the statute books laws which admittedly do great injustice to creditors, and courts in many cases tend to give a liberal construction to those laws or constitutional provisions if, as is often the case, exemptions are named in the state constitution.

The table shown below pages 23-50–23-60 is presented with realization of the limitations inherent in a summary of laws so arranged. The provisions of nearly every state go into much detail, naming in many instances a long list, mainly household articles, which are exempt. But to have these lists before him is not necessary in order to permit the creditor to act intelligently, for what interests him most is the *amount in dollars* of the exemptions, both homestead and personal. Of course, a creditor should carefully check the applicable law in the state.

In many states, a debtor is required to file for a homestead exemption or take some other action before he is entitled to claim it. Therefore, in the event a creditor is confronted with debtor claimed homestead exemption, the creditor should ascertain whether the debtor has complied with state requirements as to filing the exemption. On pages 23-48–23-49 is a table of states which require a debtor to file a statement claiming exemption.

In some states, before a creditor can proceed to levy against a homestead property with a value in excess of that permitted by law, he must fulfill certain statutory requirements. For instance, in Colorado the creditor must file an affidavit showing the description of the property, the name of the claimant of the homestead, the fair market value of the property, that no previous execution arising out of the same judgment has been levied upon the property and attach the affidavit of a professionally qualified independent appraiser.

The list below indicates how exempt property can be waived in each state. It is important to note that the list does not deal with the situation where an individual attempts to waive his exemption in advance of sale or levy, *i.e.*, by agreement or executory contract. In most states this is void as against public policy. It also violates the rules of the Federal Trade Commission. See 9-9 above. In this list the abbreviation PPE stands for personal property exemption and HE stands for homestead exemption.

WAIVER OF EXEMPTIONS

Alabama—PPE—Waiver must be in writing but cannot waive exemption as to certain cooking utensils, furniture, etc.

LEGAL PHASES OF COLLECTIONS

HE—Waiver must be signed by both husband and wife, and witnessed.

Alaska—PPE—Waiver is not prohibited.

HE—Exemption can only be waived if there is knowledge of the right and the intention to relinquish it.

Arizona—PPE and HE—Waiver of exemption rights is void and unenforceable except process used to enforce security interest or obtain possession of leased property and when done with notice.

Arkansas—PPE and HE can both be waived, but not in advance. Must be executed by both spouses.

California—PPE can be waived and up to one-half of earnings of the 30-day period preceding levy will be waived unless the exemption is specifically claimed. HE may be waived if both husband and wife execute and acknowledge and file for record.

Connecticut—PPE can be waived by presenting property to the levying officer, but only if party had knowledge of the property's exempt status at the time of presentation.

HE—No waiver legislation.

Delaware—PPE may be waived by husband and wife jointly.

HE—No waiver legislation.

D.C.—PPE cannot be waived.

HE—No waiver legislation.

Florida—No general waiver of PPE, but specific liens may be created against which exemption may not be claimed.

HE can be waived only by abandonment or alienation and waiver in promissory note or mortgage is unenforceable.

Georgia—PPE and HE—Waiver effective, but not as to wearing apparel or household furniture and provisions up to $300.00 in value.

Hawaii—No special statute or cases dealing with waiver of exemptions.

Idaho—PPE—Can be waived and exemption of earnings is automatically waived for failing to file claim for exemption.

HE—Can also be waived or released.

Illinois—PPE—Can be waived.

HE—Can be waived but wife is not bound unless she joins therein.

Indiana—PPE—Can be waived.

HE—No waiver legislation.

Iowa—All exemptions can be waived except as to those for unemployment compensation and old age assistance.

Kansas—PPE—Can be waived by chattel mortgage if signed by husband and wife.

HE—Cannot be waived.

Kentucky—PPE—Can be waived, but not in advance.

HE—Waiver must be joined in by both husband and wife and must be in writing.

Louisiana—PPE and HE—Waivers must be in writing and the latter must be signed by the wife if any.

Maine—PPE—Can be waived. HE—May be waived. If married, joinder of husband and wife necessary.

HE—Can be released by deed and joinder of wife.

Maryland—

PPE—Can be waived by a writing entered on the Court docket.

HE—No waiver legislation.

Mass.—PPE and HE—Can be waived, the latter requiring the wife's written joinder

Michigan—PPE—Waiver can be express or implied. HE—No specific statutes, but waiver of exemption is indicated.

Minnesota—All PPE except wages can be waived.

HE—Can't be waived except by writing signed by the husband and wife creating a specific charge on the homestead.

Mississippi—PPE—Can be waived by contract creating a lien thereon and any exemption is waived by failure to claim it. General waivers of exemptions in advance not enforceable.

HE—Cannot be waived except by an instrument which conveys real property.

Missouri—PPE—Is waived unless claimed.

HE—Can be waived and if a wife exists she must sign and acknowledge the waiver.

Montana—PPE—May be waived.

HE—Is permitted if specific and executed by claimant and spouse, if any.

Nebraska—Both PPE and HE permitted to be waived under case law.

Nevada—HE—Can be waived by written abandonment, signed, acknowledged and recorded, or by conveyance or mortgage executed by husband and wife.

PPE—No statutory or case law as to waiver.

N.H.—PPE—May be waived by agreement or by conduct as can HE. The latter must be executed by the husband and wife with the formalities of a land conveyance.

New Jersey—PPE—Can be waived.
HE—No statutory provisions as waiver of exemption.

N.M.—PPE—May be waived as can HE.

New York—Both PPE and HE can be waived by executing and acknowledging a notice of waiver and recording it. As a general rule the exemption cannot be waived by contract.

N.C.—PPE and HE waivers are regarded with disfavor and will usually not be enforced.

N.D.—PPE—May be waived. HE—May be waived by head of family.

Ohio—Here as in many other states the exemption, by statute, cannot be waived in advance, but a waiver upon levy or sale of the property is valid.

Oklahoma—Both PPE and HE can be waived.

Oregon—PPE can be waived. HE—No statutory provision.

Pennsylvania—PPE—May not be waived by express or implied contract.
HE—No waiver legislation.

R.I.—PPE—May be waived.
HE—No exemption.

S.C.—There are no cases or statutes dealing with the waiver of PPE.
HE—Can only be waived if executed by both the husband and wife.

(Continued on page 23-61.)

TABLE OF STATES WHICH REQUIRE DEBTOR TO FILE WRITTEN STATEMENT CLAIMING PERSONAL EXEMPTION AND HOMESTEAD EXEMPTION

State	Personal Property Exemption	Homestead Exemption
Alabama	Yes	Yes
Alaska	No	No
Arizona	No	Yes
Arkansas	Yes	No
California	No	Yes
Colorado	No	No [1]
Connecticut	No	No
Delaware	Yes	No
District of Columbia	Yes	No
Florida	Yes	Yes
Georgia	Yes	Yes
Hawaii	No	No
Idaho	Yes	No
Illinois	Yes	No
Indiana	Yes	Yes
Iowa	No	Yes
Kansas	No	Yes [2]
Kentucky	No	No
Louisiana	No	No
Maine	No	Yes
Maryland	No	No
Massachusetts	No	No
Michigan	No	No
Minnesota	No	No [3]
Mississippi	No	No
Missouri	Yes	No

LEGAL PHASES OF COLLECTIONS   23–49

TABLE OF STATES WHICH REQUIRE DEBTOR TO FILE WRITTEN STATEMENT CLAIMING PERSONAL EXEMPTION AND HOMESTEAD EXEMPTION *(Continued)*

State	Personal Property Exemption	Homestead Exemption
Montana	No	Yes
Nebraska	Yes [4]	No [5]
Nevada	No	Yes
New Hampshire	No [6]	Yes
New Jersey	No	No
New Mexico	Yes	Yes
New York	No	Yes
North Carolina	No	Yes
North Dakota	Yes	Yes [11]
Ohio	No	Yes
Oklahoma	No	Yes
Oregon	No [7]	Yes
Pennsylvania	No	No
Rhode Island	No	No
South Carolina	No	Yes
South Dakota	Yes [8]	No
Tennessee	No	No
Texas	No	No
Utah	No	Yes
Vermont	No	No
Virginia	No	Yes
Washington	No [9]	Yes
West Virginia	No	Yes
Wisconsin	No	No
Wyoming	No [10]	No

[1] Although written claim of valid homestead exemption is not required, better practice dictates filing a claim with clerk of court of record where writ was issued. Filing should be within 10 days after property levied upon or taken into possession by officer (15 Colo. 223).

[2] If homestead not selected or set apart, notice in writing must be sent to court.

[3] If owner removes from homestead for more than six consecutive months, homestead exemption is lost unless within that time he files with registrar of deeds of county in which homestead lies.

[4] If additional personal property exemption is taken in lieu of homestead exemption, debtor must file inventory list under oath.

[5] On levy of execution, debtor must notify officer as to property claimed as homestead. Judgment creditor may file verified petition that the property claimed exceeds the statutory amount of exemption.

[6] In event exempt property is levied upon, exemption must be claimed or it is lost and consent to the levy will be implied from nonaction.

[7] Exempt property must be selected by the debtor or his agent when levy is made or, is thereafter, before sale and as soon as he knows that levy has been made. Otherwise exemptions are waived.

[8] Absolute exemptions are not waived by failure to claim them. Debtor may claim his additional exemptions at any time up to five days after notice of such levy. Such claim is made by service of the claim on creditor and officer and filing the same with the court.

[9] Debtor must deliver verified list of property claimed as exempt to officers making levy.

[10] No general statutory provisions on filing on claim exemptions. However, if wages are garnished, exemption must be claimed in court where wages are garnished.

[11] Bankruptcy Court's finding of homestead exemption is a declaration of homestead and copy of bankrupt's discharge of bankruptcy may be filed to constitute notice.

EXECUTION EXEMPTIONS [1]

STATE	HOMESTEAD AMOUNT	HOMESTEAD WHO MAY CLAIM	PERSONAL PROPERTY AMOUNT	PERSONAL PROPERTY WHO MAY CLAIM	WAGES [2]
Alabama	Area 160 acres. Value $5,000.	Any resident.	Personal property to $3,000 and necessary family clothing, family portraits and books. Personal property is exempt in the custody of a trustee in bankruptcy is exempt to the bankrupt and cannot be garnished. Insurance for benefit of wife and children to extent of premium of $1,000 per year.	Any resident.	Of laborers or employees residents of the State in an amount equal to 75% of wages. On judgments based on consumer transactions greater of 80% of weekly disposable income or amount by which disposable earnings per week exceed 50 times federal minimum hourly wage. "Disposable earnings" means earnings remaining after deductions required by law; periodic payments pursuant to pension, retirement or disability programs are not "disposable earnings."
Alaska	Area 160 acres in country. ¼ acre in town or city, laid off in blocks or lots. Value not in excess of $27,000. For trailer or mobile home the exemption is $12,000.	Any resident who owns and uses same as his actual abode.	$1500 of personal property, clothing and household goods; $300 of pets; $500 of jewelry; $1,400 of tools; $1,500 of automobile, if value does not exceed $10,000.	Any resident.	Income in excess of $175 per week or $275 where debtor's earnings are household's sole support or 25% of individual's disposable income for any week is subject to execution. For periods other than weekly, monthly, or semimonthly, maximum is $700 per month.
Arizona	Residence and land of debtor, equity interest in apartment, not to exceed $50,000 in value, mobile home and land on which it is located not to exceed $50,000 in value. Claim for exemption must be filed in office of County Recorder.	Any person 18 or over married or single who resides in state.	Property must be designated by debtor. Household goods, up to $4,000, $2,500, artisans' tools, professional man's equipment, various farm implements, and miscellaneous articles. Money received by surviving spouse or child upon life of deceased spouse or parent not exceeding $20,000.	Every family.	One-half of earnings for 30 days prior to levy when necessary for use of family. 75% of disposable earnings or 30 times the Federal minimum hourly wage, whichever is greater.
Arkansas	Value $2,500. Nor less than 80 acres regardless of value. In city, not over one acre and improvements. Same value as country, not to be reduced to less than ¼ acre regardless of value.	Resident married or head of family (surviving spouse and dependent minor children).	Not head of family: Specific articles as selected not exceeding value of $200 in addition to wearing apparel. Head of family: Articles to value of $500 besides clothes. Exemption does not apply to debts in payment of articles for which purchase price is claimed.	Resident who is not married or head of family. Married or head of family.	Constitutional exemption: Single person—$200 including personal property other than wearing apparel. Head of Family—$500 including personal property other than wearing apparel. Laborers and Mechanics—Wages for 60 days exempt provided statement is filed that said wages plus personal property holdings are less than constitutional exemption. First $25 a week net wages absolutely exempt. Wages may be garnished for support of children under 18.

[1] Bankruptcy and execution exemptions may differ.
[2] Title III of the Federal Consumer Credit Protection Act exempts from garnishment the greater of 75% of disposable earnings per work week or an amount each week equal to 30 times the Federal minimum hourly wage. The exemption does not apply to support orders or orders of any court of bankruptcy. The statute does not provide that an employee cannot be discharged because his earnings have been subjected to garnishment for *one* indebtedness.

23–50

California	By any head of a family, of not exceeding $30,000 cash value, over and above all liens and encumbrances on the property at time of any levy of execution thereon; by any person 65 or older not exceeding $45,000 in cash value. If a person is 65 years of age or physically or mentally disabled and unable to work, the limit is $55,000. Dwelling includes mobile home. Dwelling can include condominium or can be situated on property leased for a period of thirty years or more. Declaration must be recorded with county recorder. Debtors may claim exemption for a dwelling house which has not been declared a homestead but in which debtor or his family actually resides and which could be selected as a homestead pursuant to law.	Resident head of family. By any other resident.	Numerous necessary articles for their business, trade, calling, profession, etc., up to $2,500 over and above all encumbrances on the property and household furniture and equipment. Motor vehicle to value above encumbrances on the vehicle provided that the value of the vehicle shall not exceed $1,200, or as set forth in Used Car Guide or if not set forth $1,000, house trailer occupied by debtor family to value of $9,500 above all encumbrances on the house trailer. Relocation payments for a period of six months. Residents are entitled to an exemption on proceeds from disability, death, retirement, pension and unemployment insurance plans, and the like whether government sponsored or paid pursuant to private programs. In some instances, the exemption does not apply to court orders for child or spousal support.	Any person. Farmers, mechanics, miners, truckmen, professional men, etc.	Greater of (1) 75% of disposable earnings for workweek; or (2) amount each week equal to 30 times federal minimum hourly wage. No exemption for 50% of judgment debtor's earnings minus wage assignment amount under support order. All paid earnings are exempt if prior to payment to employee, they were subject to an earnings withholding order or wage assignment for support. That portion of debtor's earnings proven necessary for support of himself or family unless debt incurred for personal services, the order is for delinquent support, or the order is for state tax liability.
Colorado	No limitation on area. Homestead occupied as home exempt to $20,000 in excess of any liens or encumbrances. Word "homestead" must be entered on margin of record title.	Householder, head of family	Necessary wearing apparel for each head of family, single person and dependent to the extent of $400 per person; watches, jewelry and articles of adornment of each head of family, single person and dependent $100 per person; library, family pictures and school books of head of family and dependents to the extent of $500, single person to the extent of $200; burial sites; household goods to the extent of $1,000 in value for head of family and $400 for a single person; provisions and fuel on hand for use head of family and dependents to the extent of $300, for a single person $100; every head of family engaged in agriculture, livestock not exceeding $2,000 and horses, mules, carts, machinery not exceeding $1,500, in the case of a single person, $1,000 and $750 respectively; pensions or compensation as a result of service in the Armed Forces; stock in trade, supplies, fixtures, tools of business not exceeding $750; motor vehicle not exceeding $500; library of a professional person not exceeding $750; life insurance policies to the extent of $5,000; house trailer to the extent of $2,500 while occupied as a place of residence by head of the family; aggregate value of all items excepted shall be limited to $12,500.	Single resident or head of family.	70% of earnings due head of family and 35% of earnings due a single person; also subject to UCCC provisions for consumer debts.
Connecticut	No homestead exemption.		Certain specific articles such as apparel, household furniture entirely exempt, and other articles up to designated values. One motor vehicle to $1,500.	Resident.	Wages cannot be garnished.

23–51

EXECUTION EXEMPTIONS (Continued)

STATE	HOMESTEAD — AMOUNT	HOMESTEAD — WHO MAY CLAIM	PERSONAL PROPERTY — AMOUNT	PERSONAL PROPERTY — WHO MAY CLAIM	WAGES[2]
Delaware	No homestead exemption.		Books, pictures, church pew, burial lot, wearing apparel of family, sewing machines, implements of trade not exceeding $75 in New Castle, Sussex counties and $50 in Kent County. General exemption of personal property—New Castle County $200, Kent County $150.	Any resident.	Exemption of 85% of wages. Support orders—75% of net wages exempt on order for support of one child reduced by 5% for each additional child. Wages or salary are exempt from garnishment for 60 days from date of default on a contract or installment account.
District of Columbia	No homestead exemption.		Implements and tools to extent of $200. Household furniture, etc., to value of $300; also certain miscellaneous articles. Wearing apparel.	Any resident being head of a family. Resident head of family or householder. All persons.	Greater of 75% of disposable earnings per week or amount of disposable earnings per week equal to 30 times Federal minimum hourly wage. *Withholding by Garnishee-Employer*—90% of first $200 of gross wages payable in a month, 80% of gross wages payable in a month in excess of $200 and under $500. Calendar month consists of 4⅓ workweeks. *Debtor Principal Support of Family*—$200 each month of earnings other than wages of resident or non-resident earning major portion of livelihood in D.C. exempt for two months preceding issuance of writ. *Debtor Not Principal Support of Family*—$60 each month is exempt. Support judgments 50% of gross wages exempt.
Florida	160 acres in country, ½ acre in city. No limit on value may be claimed by recording declaration of homestead or after levy and before sale by ratifying officer who is to sell, in writing of claim of homestead. Interest in 98-year lease qualifies for Homestead exemption.	Head of family residing in state. Surviving tenant by the entirety or spouse of the owner.	$1,000 of personal property is exempt.	Head of family residing in state.	Entire wages of the head of family when wages are due for personal labor or services of such person. Amount exempt is exclusive of payroll deductions for taxes. Courts may limit exception for alimony or child support.
Georgia	Real estate not to exceed $500 in city or 50 acres in country with improvements, not to exceed $200 plus additional 5 acres for each child under 16. Includes specified personal property. Waiver note or written waiver if given contemporaneously with transaction would hold, but a sale or assignment of homestead has priority to ordinary waiver.	Head of family or aged or infirm person or one having care of dependent minor of any age.	Value $5,000, real or personal or both set apart by petition. Purchase money debt enforceable against. (Either this exemption or homestead exemption may be claimed but not both.)	Head of family or aged or infirm person or one having care of dependent female of any age.	Greater of 75% of disposable earnings per week or amount by which disposable earnings exceed 30 times the federal minimum hourly wage. General exemption ineffective against support orders and alimony decree where notice is given. Where garnishment based on such judgment, a maximum of 50% of disposable earnings subject to garnishment.
Hawaii	An interest in one parcel of property owned by head of family or person 65 years or older may not exceed $30,000 when owned by any other person may not exceed $20,000 as determined by assessed valuation.	Any person.	Various specified articles of personal property. (The exemption does not apply, however, to execution on a judgment recovered for the purchase price of such goods as on a foreclosure of a security agreement or other encumbrancing instrument on the goods.)	Any resident.	One-half of the wages due every laborer or person working for wages is exempt.

23–52

Idaho	$25,000 in excess of mortgage. Exemption is confined to dwelling house and land on which it is situated. Declaration must be executed and recorded.	Family.	Burial plot, necessary health aids, public assistance benefits, health benefits—100% exemption; if necessary for support: income of various types and some assets—100% exemption; necessary furnishings and appliances, personal clothing, books, musical instruments, animals, family portraits, one firearm, and heirlooms—value not to exceed $500; personal jewelry—value not to exceed $250; implements, professional books, tools of the trade—value not to exceed $1,000; 1 motor vehicle—value not to exceed $500; various other types of property.	Actual resident.	Greater of 75% of disposable earnings for workweek or amount each week equal to 30 times federal minimum hourly wage. Married woman's wages are exempt from garnishment for husband's debt. For judgments arising from debt on consumer credit sale, greater of (1) 75% of disposable earnings for workweek; or (2) amount each week equal to forty times federal minimum hourly wage. Support orders: Maximum is 50% if other child or a spouse, 40% if not.
Illinois	$7,500 in land with buildings, owned or leased, occupied as residence.	Householder having a family.	Wearing apparel, Bible, school books, family pictures, military pensions for 1 year. $2,000 in any other property. $1,200 in motor vehicle, $750 in implements, professional books or tools of trade.	Any person. Where married persons maintain and reside in separate residences qualifying as homestead property, each residence shall receive 50% of the total reduction in equalized assessed valuation provided for.	Greater of 85% of gross amount of wages, salary, commission, bonuses and periodic payments pursuant to a retirement or pension plan, or amount of weekly disposable wages not in excess of 30 times federal minimum hourly wage.
Indiana	No homestead statute. Personal or family residence, $7,500; other real estate or tangible personal property $4,000. In no event shall total exemptions exceed $10,000. Wife can claim one-third of any real estate owned by husband.	Resident householder. Where a husband and wife are each conducting a separate and distinct business each may have the full exemption of $1000.	Tangible personal property, along with other nonresidential personal property, not to exceed $4,000. Intangible personal property, including choses in action (but excluding debts owing, and income owing) up to $100.	Debtor residing in state. Where a husband and wife are each conducting a separate and distinct business out of their own individual funds each may claim separate exemption.	UCCC provides exemption for 75% of disposable earnings per week or the amount in excess of 30 times the Federal minimum hourly wage, whichever is greater. The following provisions have not been repealed by the UCCC and appear to be in conflict with it: Householder exemption not exceeding $25. In *Mims v. Consumer Credit Corp.* (Ind. Sup. Ct., March 13, 1974), the court held that statute most beneficial to householder would be enforced. Exemptions are inapplicable to alimony, support orders and wages earned by nonresidents within the state. For support orders: Maximum is 50% if a spouse or other child, 40% if not.
Iowa	If within city or town plot must not exceed one-half acre, otherwise not more than 40 acres, but if in either case value is less than $500, it may be enlarged to reach that amount. Exceptions: Homestead liable for deficiency remaining after exhausting all other nonexempt property where debt is contracted prior to acquisition of homestead; by written contract stipulating that homestead shall be liable; also, for debts incurred for work done or material furnished exclusively for the improvement of homestead; also, if no survivor or issue, for payment of debts to which it might at that time be subject if it had never been held as a homestead.	Resident, head of family, husband or wife.	Wearing apparel, one shotgun, books, pictures or musical instruments, certain livestock food for six months, kitchen furniture not to exceed $1,000 in aggregate or $200 in one item. $2,000 in aggregate in household goods or $200 in one item. $1,200 in one motor vehicle. $5,000 in aggregate in musical instruments. Tools, equipment, books, etc. used in trade or profession, limited number of farm animals. Wearing apparel and trunk to contain same. Proceeds of life insurance.	Resident, head of family. Non-resident or unmarried resident not head of family.	75% of disposable earnings for week or amount by which disposable earnings for week exceed 30 times federal minimum hourly wage, whichever is greater. Except for child support orders, maximum amount that can be garnished in any year is $250 for each creditor. For consumer credit debt, exemption is greater of 75% of disposable weekly earnings, or forty times federal hourly minimum wage. Debtor earning less than $12,000 per year—maximum sum permitted to be executed is $250.

EXECUTION EXEMPTIONS *(Continued)*

STATE	HOMESTEAD AMOUNT	HOMESTEAD WHO MAY CLAIM	PERSONAL PROPERTY AMOUNT	PERSONAL PROPERTY WHO MAY CLAIM	WAGES [2]
Kansas	160 acres, farm; 1 acre in city, occupied as residence. No limitation in value.	Any resident.	Head of household: (1) Furnishing and supplies, including food & clothing for a period of 1 year; (2) one means of conveyance; (3) family burial plot; (4) equipment or other means of production necessary in carrying on a trade, business, occupation or profession not to exceed $5,000; (5) jewelry not exceeding $500 in value.	Any resident.	75% of disposable earnings for week or amount by which disposable earnings exceed 30 times federal minimum hourly wage, whichever is greater. For support orders: 40% of weekly disposable earnings or 50% if debtor is supporting a spouse or child not involved in the support order; exemption is reduced by 5% if garnishment is necessary to enforce a support order issued more than 12 weeks prior to the workweek. Wages earned and payable out of state are fully exempt in absence of personal service on debtor.
Kentucky	$5,000 including improvements, unless liability existed before purchase of land. Mortgage on homestead, release or waiver must be in writing and signed also by wife and recorded.	Householder.	Many articles, household goods, wearing apparel, etc., not to exceed $3,000 in value, mechanic's tools, livestock not to exceed $3,000 in value; one motor vehicle not to exceed $2,500 in value if used by person engaged in farming or who uses vehicle in his employment, library of professional men, etc.	Resident with a family.	Greater of 75% of disposable income per week or 30 times federal minimum hourly wage. Exemptions inapplicable to support orders. Wages earned outside of state are exempt if exempt in that state unless debtor was personally served in Kentucky or was a resident of Kentucky when earlier debt or action arose. Exemptions inapplicable to support orders.
Louisiana	$15,000 not over 160 acres. Exemption may be waived. Claim must be in writing and recorded in parish where homestead is situated.	Resident with family or other dependents.	Certain articles specified in statute, such as clothing, tools of a trade and other articles.	Householder.	75% of disposable earnings for any week, but not less than 30 times the federal minimum hourly wage in effect when the wages are payable. For child support, 50% of disposable earnings. Loans with interest in excess of 10%—lender cannot use garnishment.
Maine	$7,500 if declaration is filed with registry of deeds. The term "homestead" includes a mobile home used by the householder as his principal residence.	Householder.	Motor vehicle $1,200; clothing; furniture, appliances; and similar items, the debtor's interest not to exceed $200 in any particular item that is held for personal, family or household use; jewelry $500; tools not to exceed $1,000; furnaces, stove and fuel not to exceed 10 cords of wood, 5 tons of coal or 1,000 gallons of petroleum products.	Resident.	Greater of 75% of disposable earnings for week or amount by which disposable earnings exceed 30 times federal minimum hourly wage. 75% of weekly disposable earnings of 40 times the hourly wage in consumer transactions. Wages due debtor for wife's or minor child's personal service are exempt. Trustee process—100% of wages exempt. Support orders: Maximum of 50% if another child or a spouse, 40% if not. Exemptions do not apply to court ordered support orders in Chapter 13 bankruptcy cases, state or federal taxes.

23–54

Maryland	None.	Bona fide residents.	$120 multiplied by the number of weeks in which such wages due were earned or 75% of such wages, whichever is greater. Except that in Caroline, Worcester, Kent and Queen Anne counties exemption for any workweek shall be greater of 75% of wages due or 30 times federal minimum hourly wage.
Massachusetts	$50,000 in value of land and buildings. Must be established by deed or declaration and recorded.	Householder, including holder of possessory interest by lease, or otherwise, provided the estate serves as the principal residence of the debtor and the debtor has a family.	$500 in household goods, clothing and other items kept for household, personal, or family use; $3,000 in real or personal property. Many articles. Household furniture not exceeding $3,000 in value. Materials and stock necessary for carrying on trade or business, value of $500. Cash savings or deposits not to exceed $80. An automobile necessary for personal transportation or to secure or maintain employment, not exceeding $700. Up to $125. Trustee Process—Wages for personal labor or services earned but not paid exempted from attachment to amount of $125 per week. Exemption of $75 of personal income which is not otherwise exempt by law.
Michigan	$3,500 in lot, if in city, and not exceeding 40 acres in extent, if in country or 1 lot if in city.	Resident citizen.	As to householders: certain articles, household goods, amounting to $1000. As to businessmen: tools, implements, stock in trade necessary to carry on business, $1,000. Partners' right in specific partnership property is not subject to attachment or execution except on a claim against the partnership. When partnership debt there is no exemption under the laws. No statutory provisions—Federal law controls—75% of earnings or 30 times minimum federal wage, whichever is greater.
Minnesota	80 acres in country, in village or city ½ acre with improvements. No limitation in value.	Resident.	Farm machines and implements and livestock produce and standing crops not exceeding $5,000 in value; tools and stock of a trade or business not exceeding $5,000 in value except that the total of all of the above shall not exceed $5,000; clothes, household furniture, etc., not exceeding $4,500 in value; one motor vehicle to the extent of a value not exceeding $2,000; other specific articles; a mobile home, the earnings of a minor child of any debtor by reason of any liability of any such debtor not contracted for the special benefit of said child. Nothing exempt from execution or attachment in action for balance of purchase price thereof. Greater of 75% of disposable earnings or 40 times the federal minimum hourly wage. Where debtor has been on relief, exemption for a period of 6 months from date of return to private employment.
Mississippi	$30,000 in value and not exceeding 160 acres if outside city, town or village. Homestead can be house or apartment or condominium. Homestead exemption is denied under certain circumstances where portions of property are rented or used for other commercial purposes.	Citizen householder with family. Husband or wife, widow or widower without a family, or not occupying homestead, if over 60 years of age, who has been an exceptionship.	Tools, equipment, etc., used in connection with trade or profession; the books of a student, wearing apparel of every person, libraries of all persons, including books, drawings and paintings, not exceeding $1,200 in value and other specified articles. Specified articles of farm equipment animals and produce, plus household and kitchen, not exceeding in value $1,200 and all family portraits. After a 30-day grace period, the greater of 75% of disposable earnings or the amount equal to 30 times the minimum hourly federal wage law. Exemptions not applicable to taxes, pensions.
Missouri	$5,000 in value in dwelling house and land.	Head of family. Non head of family.	Household furnishings and clothes to $1,000. Jewelry to $500. Any other property to $400. Implements, professional books and tools to $2,000. Motor vehicle to $500. Mobile home used as residence to $1,000. Greatest of (1) 75 percent of disposable weekly earnings, (2) weekly amount equal to 30 times federal minimum hourly wage or (3) 90% of disposable weekly earnings for resident head of family. Exemptions inapplicable to debtor's about to leave the state, support orders, bankruptcy court order under Chapter 13, and alimony.

EXECUTION EXEMPTIONS (Continued)

STATE	HOMESTEAD AMOUNT	HOMESTEAD WHO MAY CLAIM	PERSONAL PROPERTY AMOUNT	PERSONAL PROPERTY WHO MAY CLAIM	WAGES [2]
Montana	Not exceeding $40,000 assessed valuation on 320 acres of agricultural land or ¼ acre in city, and dwelling house or mobile home thereon.	Resident head of family. Resident single person over 60 years.	Special articles, including household goods, and tools to carry on business. One automobile or truck value of $1,000. Proceeds of life insurance purchased with premiums not exceeding $500 per year. Professional libraries. Minor entitled to $1,000. Property of either spouse can be selected for exemption. Only wearing apparel to unmarried person under 60 years. Non resident not entitled to exemption.	Resident head of family. Resident single person over 60 years.	All wages for 45 days preceding garnishment if necessary for support of family. If debt incurred for gasoline or common necessities then only 50% are exempt. Earnings for personal services are exempt only to the extent allowed by federal law.
Nebraska	$6,500, consisting of dwelling in which claimant lives and its appurtenances, not over 160 acres in country; 2 adjoining lots in city.	Head of family.	Personal possessions of debtor and family; necessary wearing apparel of debtor and family; kitchen utensils and household furniture selected by debtor to $1,500; equipment or tools not exceeding $1,500; provisions for debtor and family necessary for 6 months' support; and fuel necessary for 6 months. All articles intended to be exempt shall be chosen by debtor, his agent or legal rep.; pension of soldier and sailor and property purchased therewith $2,000; life insurance on life of insured or his beneficiary in an amount paid for by annual premium not exceeding $500.	Any resident debtor.	Greatest of 75% of disposable earnings or amount equal to 30 times federal minimum hourly wage or 85% of disposable earnings if wage earner is head of family. Exemptions are inapplicable to support orders and bankruptcy court orders.
Nevada	Land with house or mobile home with or without land of value not exceeding $90,000, but does not apply to claim for purchase price, taxes on property or lien of mortgage or deed of trust created by and with the consent of the husband and wife.	Any head of family or husband or wife or single person.	Private libraries over $1,500; family fixtures and keepsakes; necessary household goods, appliances and furniture not over $3,000; farm trucks, farm stocks, farm tools, supplies and seed not over $4,500; professional libraries, office equipment supplies, tools, instruments and materials used to carry on the trade not over $4,500; dwelling of a miner or prospector, cars and appliances necessary to carry on mining operations and mining claim actually worked by debtor not over $4,500; one vehicle not over $1,000 if necessary for occupation or profession of debtor; fire engines, hooks and ladders and apparatus of fire company; all arms, uniforms required by law to be kept by debtor plus one gun selected by debtor; all court houses, jails and property related thereto; all monies growing out of any life insurance if annual premium paid not over $1,000.		The amount by which disposable earnings exceed 75% of disposable earnings for any pay period or 30 times the minimum hourly Federal wage law. Exemption does not apply to support orders and state and federal tax debts.
New Hampshire	$5,000 (not including mobile home or trailer)	Debtor, wife and children of debtor.	Household furniture $2,000, wearing apparel and tools in trade to value of $1,200. Stove, refrigerator, provisions and fuel to value of $400, one automobile to the value of $1,000, jewelry to value of $500. Also miscellaneous property set forth in statute.	Debtor.	Wages to $40 ($50 on loan contract) for labor performed after service of writ; wages for labor performed before service exempt unless action founded on debt on judgment issued by state court. In such case wages equal to 50 times federal minimum hourly wage are exempt. Special exemption for small loan law debts. 50% of disposable earnings subject to child support order for weekly, monthly or other pay period.

23–56

		...sonal property, value $1,000, and wearing apparel.	Head of resident family.	Minimum exemption of $48 per week; 90% exemption if earnings are $7,500 per year or less. If earnings are more than $7,500 reduced exemption percentage by order of court.
New Mexico	$20,000.	Husband and wife or widow or widower living with unmarried daughter or minor son or person supporting himself.	Resident. There are some minor differences for a non-head of household.	Greater of 75% of debtor's disposable earnings or of excess of 40 times federal minimum hourly wage rate. Disposable earnings is that part of debtor's salary remaining after deduction of amounts required to be withheld by law. For child support, 50% of disposable earnings during any pay period.
New York	Lot of land with dwelling, a mobile home, shares of stock in cooperative apartment corporation or condominium owned and occupied as a principal residence not to exceed $10,000 in value above liens and encumbrances. No exemption from judgments recovered for purchase price of homestead or for taxes or assessments. Security deposit for rental of realty used as residence of debtor or his family, and utility services deposits are exempt.	Resident householder or woman, principal residence only.	Wearing apparel, household goods under certain values. Many specified articles. $500 real or personal property exclusive of articles required if debtor has no homestead, unless debt is for necessaries or for manual labor. Resident not having household has additional exemption of $1,000 of personal property. One motor vehicle, clothing, furniture, tools of trade of $1,500. Books and jewelry in amount of $2,500. Personal property used as security under UCC is not exempt. All wearing apparel, household goods, television set, tools, implements to the value of $600. Certain other articles.	Householder or woman. Male person, not householder, has similar exemption ($450) not including household furniture.	Earnings of $85 or less per week are entirely exempt; and 90% of earnings for services within 60 days before and any time after income execution; exemption may be reduced by amount court determines unnecessary for reasonable requirements of debtor and dependents.
North Carolina	Property used as a residence not to exceed $1,000 in value.	Resident.	Articles of personal property not to exceed $500.	Resident.	Earnings for personal services for 60 days preceding levy if necessary for support of family. For support orders, exemptions are inapplicable up to 40% of monthly disposable earnings.
North Dakota	Resident land and dwelling house with improvements not to exceed $80,000 over and above liens.	Resident.	Head of a family, money or personal property $5,000; single person, money or personal property, $2,500. All wearing apparel and clothing of the debtor and his family or one year's provisions and fuel and crops raised by him on an area not to exceed 160 acres occupied as his homestead. Resident in addition to other exemption $7,500; (2) motor vehicle exemption not to exceed $1,200; (3) accrued dividends interest or cash surrender value of life insurance policy not to exceed $4,000; (4) debtor's right to receive (a) payment not to exceed $7,500 on wrongful death actions or (b) on account of personal injury for pecuniary loss $1,000; (c) social security benefits.	Head of a family or single person.	Greater of 75% of debtor's disposable earnings or of excess of 40 times federal minimum hourly wage rate. 100% of earnings for personal services within 60 days can be exempted by judge upon affidavit of need for support of family.
Ohio	$1,000.	Husband and wife living together, a widow or a widower living with an unmarried daughter or unmarried minor son.	Certain specified articles, including wearing apparel to $300, tools and implements for carrying out profession, trade or business to $300. The dollar amounts of these articles are twice as much in the case of a head of a family.	Resident.	Of earnings owed debtor for services rendered within 30 days before attachment, process, judgment or order, the greater of: (1) if paid weekly, 30 times federal minimum hourly wage; if paid bi-weekly, 60 times minimum hourly wage, if paid semi-monthly, 65 times minimum hourly wage; if paid monthly 130 times minimum hourly wage; or (2) 75% of disposable earnings. If creditor notified in writing that debtor has entered into a debt-scheduling agreement unless creditor gives 15 day written notice of objection, creditor may not garnish. Garnishment allowed if debtor more than 45 days overdue on plan or plan terminated.

23–57

EXECUTION EXEMPTIONS (Continued)

STATE	HOMESTEAD AMOUNT	PERSONAL PROPERTY WHO MAY CLAIM	PERSONAL PROPERTY AMOUNT	WHO MAY CLAIM	WAGES [2]
Oklahoma	$5,000, or if homestead is not within any city, town, or village, it shall consist of not more than 160 acres of land, which may be in one or more parcels, to be selected by the owner.	Resident.	Numerous articles, household furniture, books, pictures, wearing apparel, specified animals, tools, etc. Motor vehicle of a value not to exceed $1,500 as well as mobile homes used as residences.	All persons.	75% of all earnings for personal or professional services earned during the 90 days before execution. Garnishment to satisfy child support order may, in certain cases, extend to 33⅓% of debtors wages. Earnings for personal services are 100% exempt from garnishment prior to trial court judgment with statutory exceptions.
Oregon	Not over $15,000 or $20,000 for 2 debtors and not exceeding one block in any town or city laid off into blocks and lots; not exceeding 160 acres elsewhere. In case of mobile home, $13,000 one debtor, $18,000 2 debtors. Proceeds of sale exempt for one year if to be used to purchase another homestead.	Resident householder.	Books, pictures, musical instruments to $300; wearing apparel, jewelry and other personal items to $900; household goods, furniture and radio $1,450; domestic animals to $1,000; tools, library, etc. necessary to carry on trade of profession except for payment of debt, contracted to assist in carrying on trade or profession to $750; vehicle to $1,200; other specific exemptions. No article is exempt from execution on judgment recovered for its purchase price.	Householder.	Greater of 75% of disposable earnings for week or amount by which disposable earnings exceed 40 times the federal minimum hourly wage. Exemptions are inapplicable to any support orders and bankruptcy court orders.
Pennsylvania	None.		$300 in real or personal property, also sewing machines, wearing apparel, other specified articles including retirement funds and accounts and certain leased articles.	Resident.	100% of all wages in hands of employer; does not apply to support orders, board for four weeks or less or student loan obligations.
Rhode Island	Burial lot.		Wearing apparel, household goods to value of $500, tools used in trade to value of $500. Certain personal property of a housekeeper not exceeding $1,000. Certain farm animals.	Resident.	Wages due not exceeding $50, social welfare payments.
South Carolina	$1,000. No limitation in area.	Head of family.	Personal property of head of family to $500; $300 for person not head of family.	Head of family. Persons not head of family.	100% of earnings for personal service earned within 60 days. Garnishment prohibited with respect to debt arising from a consumer credit transaction.
South Dakota	A homestead is absolutely exempt. If the property is sold, then the proceeds up to $30,000 will be exempt for 1 year from receipt thereof, 160 acres in the country or one acre if in town.	Head of family, or in case he fails to claim, any member of the family over 14 years of age.	$1,500 to head of family. $600 to person not head of family in addition to absolute exemptions; i.e., books to $200, wearing apparel, provisions and fuel for one year. Both of the above are in addition to what are known as absolute exemptions.	Debtor, his agent or attorney, head of family or in case of his failure to do so by any member of his family over the age of 14 years.	100% of earnings for personal services within 60 days if necessary for support of family. Federal exemption applies in all other cases.
Tennessee	$5,000. No limitation in area. Property jointly owned by debtors $7,500.	Resident.	Personal property up to $4,000 in aggregate. Residents are entitled to absolute exemption on necessary and proper wearing apparel of debtor and his family, family portraits, Bible and school books.	All persons who are bona fide citizens and permanent residents of Tennessee.	Greater of 75% of disposable earnings per week or amount by which disposable earnings exceed 30 times the federal minimum hourly wage (does not apply to child support orders or to alimony to unmarried spouse); additional $2.50 per week exemption for each resident, dependent child under 16. Does not apply to taxes.

23-58

Texas	Homestead for a family, if not in a city, town or village, not more than 200 acres; single person not in a city, town or village not more than 100 acres; for family or single person in a city, town or village lot or lots not to exceed one acre; burial lot.	Head of family.	Personal property not to exceed an aggregate fair market value of $15,000 for each single adult person and $30,000 for a family which can include the following: furnishings of a home; all the following implements necessary for farming or ranching: tools, equipment, books used in trade or profession, wearing apparel, firearms, athletic and sporting equipment. Any two of the following means of travel: two animals, a saddle and bridle for each: horses, colts, mules, donkeys, bicycle or motorcycle, wagon, cart of dray, automobile, station wagon, truck trailer, camper truck, truck, pick-up truck; livestock and fowl not to exceed the following in number and forage on hand reasonably necessary for their consumption: five cows and their calves, one breeding age bull, 20 hogs, 20 sheep, 20 goats, 50 chickens, 30 turkeys, 30 ducks, 30 geese, 30 guineas; dog, cat and other household pets.	Every family.	100% of current wages.
Utah	$8,000 and $2,000 in addition for wife, also $500 additional for each member of the family. Property not exempt from taxes levied thereon, judgments obtained on debts secured by mortgage on the premises and on debts created for purchase price and debts for failure to provide support or maintenance for dependent children. A creditor may levy against exempt property to enforce a claim for alimony, support or maintenance and state and local taxes.	Head of family.	Specified articles such as furniture up to $500, tools or implements of trade to $1,500 and motor vehicles used in business up to $1,500. In addition a surviving spouse of a domiciled debtor is entitled to $3,500.00 from the estate and household furniture, automobile, furnishings, appliances and personal effects. If no surviving spouse, children entitled to same property. In addition, the surviving spouse and minor children are entitled to allowance from the estate for maintenance during the period of administration.	Head of family.	Garnishment of weekly earnings cannot exceed greater of 75% of weekly earnings or 40 times federal minimum hourly wage for that week.
Vermont	The homestead of a natural person consisting of a dwelling house, outbuildings, and the land used in connection therewith, not exceeding $30,000 in value, and owned and used or kept by such person as a homestead together with the rents, issues, profits and products thereof.	Housekeeper or head of a family.	Specified articles. Specified professional books, clergyman, physician, dentist and lawyer, value $200.	Resident.	75% of disposable earnings for week or excess of 30 times federal minimum hourly wage whichever is greater. Different formula for child support orders. If consumer credit debt, 85% of the debtor's weekly disposable earnings, or 40 times the federal minimum wage, whichever is greater.
Virginia	An estate not in excess of $5,000 comprised of personal and real property of the debtor, to be selected by him. Veterans with at least 40% disability are entitled to extra $2,000 exemption.	Resident householder or head of family.	In addition to the $5,000 estate, enumerated articles such as the family Bible, wedding rings, wearing apparel, furniture, etc.	Resident householder or head of family.	75% of disposable earnings for that week or of excess of 30 times federal minimum hourly wage, whichever is greater. For support orders: 40% of weekly disposable earnings or 50% if debtor is supporting a spouse or dependent child not involved in the support order. Exemption is reduced by 5% if garnishment is necessary to enforce a support order issued more than 12 weeks prior to the beginning of the work week. Exemptions inapplicable to support orders and more than 12 weeks prior to the beginning of the work week. Exemptions inapplicable to support orders and bankruptcy court orders.

EXECUTION EXEMPTIONS *(Continued)*

STATE	HOMESTEAD AMOUNT	HOMESTEAD WHO MAY CLAIM	PERSONAL PROPERTY AMOUNT	PERSONAL PROPERTY WHO MAY CLAIM	WAGES [2]
Washington	Not exceeding $25,000. Consists of dwelling house with pertinent buildings and land or land with improvements purchased with the intention of building a house and residing therein (includes mobile home). May be selected at any time before sale by filing declaration with county auditor. Not exempt from claims of mechanic's, laborer's or materialmen's liens or from mortgages.	Each person or family.	Household furniture and utensils, $1,500. $500 of other goods (no more than $100 in cash), wearing apparel, but not to exceed $750 in value of furs, jewelry and personal items. Motor vehicle to $1,200. Many specially enumerated articles. Pension and life insurance also exempt.	Householder in case of household furniture. Beneficiary in case of pensions and life insurance.	The greater part of 40 times the state hourly minimum wage or of 75% of the disposable earnings of the defendant is exempt from garnishment. Disposable earnings means that part of the earnings remaining after deduction of the amounts required by law to be withheld.
West Virginia	$5,000, including improvements.	Husbands, parents, or infants of deceased or insane parents.	$1,000 for husband, parent residing in state, infant children of deceased parents. Many special articles. $50 worth of tools or implements for mechanics, artisans, and laborers.	Resident and head of family only.	80% of wages due or to become due within one year after issuance of execution or 30 times federal minimum hourly wage. For consumer credit debts, 80% of disposable earnings for week or 30 times federal hourly minimum wage.
Wisconsin	$25,000. Consists of dwelling house and its appurtenances. Not exceeding 40 acres and not less than ¼ acre.	Resident.	Automobiles used and kept for purpose of carrying on debtor's business to value of $1,000. Small tools and implements not exceeding $200 in value, and one tractor worth $1,500. Apparel not to exceed $400 and furniture up to $200.	Resident. Mechanic, artisan or laborer.	Greater of 75% of debtor's disposable earnings or of excess of 30 times federal minimum hourly wage rate. Disposable earnings means that part of earnings after deduction of amounts required by law to be withheld. Employee with dependents—basic exemption of $120 plus $20 per dependent for each 30 day period prior to service of process, maximum exemption 75% of income. Employee without dependents—basic exemption of 60% of income for each 30 day period prior to service of process. Minimum $75, maximum $100. For consumer credit transactions, the greater of (1) 75% of disposable earnings, or (2) $15 per dependent per week plus 40 times the federal minimum hourly wage. Exemptions inapplicable to support orders, bankruptcy court orders.
Wyoming	$10,000. House and lot or lots in city, on farm consisting of any number of acres within the value limitation, or house trailer or movable home. Must be occupied by owner or his family. Creditor may bring proceeding if he believes property worth over $10,000. On sale, if it brings less, creditor liable for expenses.	Householder, being head of family and every resident 60 years or over whether head of family or not. Widow, husband or minor child entitled to homestead on death of owner, subject to debts of deceased.	Bible, pictures, school books, lot in cemetery, furniture, provisions, household articles, value $2,000, clothing value $1,000. Tools, teams, implements, stock in trade to carry on business not over $2,000 and library, instruments and implements, $2,000.	Head of family or person 60 years or over residing in state. Every resident. Professional men.	Judgments on consumer credit sales, home or loan; greater of 75% of disposable earnings or excess over 30 times federal minimum hourly wage. Otherwise, 50% of earnings for personal services within 60 days before levy if necessary for use of resident family. For support orders, 25% of the income.

23–60

LEGAL PHASES OF COLLECTIONS

(Continued from page 23-48.)

S.D.—PPE—Can be waived here in advance. Exemptions not waived by failure to claim.
HE—May be waived in advance, but failure to claim is not a waiver.
Tennessee—PPE—Cannot be waived.
HE—Waiver must be joined by husband and wife.
Texas—PPE—Can be waived. Any personal property exemption is waived by failure to claim it.
HE—Can be waived by alienation or encumbrance. Failure to plead exemption can operate as a waiver.
Utah—Both PPE and HE can be waived if the waiver is joined in by both spouses but may not be waived in advance.
Vermont—PPE—Can be waived by turning property over to levying officer.
HE—Can be waived if both husband and wife join in.
Virginia—All of the PPE except wages and certain household furniture can be waived.
HE—Can be waived by a writing.
Washington—Both exemptions can be waived.
HE—Waiver must be joined in by the wife.
West Virginia—Both the PPE and HE may be waived, but in the latter the wife must join. Waiver may not be made by executory contract.
Wisconsin—Both PPE and HE may be waived and failure to claim the latter may result in a waiver.
Wyoming—No statutory provisions.
HE—Can only be waived by acknowledged instrument specifically releasing homestead.

EXEMPTIONS IN BANKRUPTCY

Under the new Bankruptcy Code a debtor may choose the exemptions given to him under federal law in the Bankruptcy Reform Act *or* the exemptions that he is entitled to under the laws of his state, unless the state passes a law excluding the debtor from taking the federal exemption now provided in the Bankruptcy Act. For a listing of the federal exemption and those states which have superseded it, see page 28-10. A number of states have also special exemption provisions in their statutes which exempt certain property in the event a debtor is in bankrupt. Such states include: Arkansas, Georgia, Iowa, Maine, Maryland, North Dakota and West Virginia. Bankruptcy exemption law may not necessarily be the same as state execution exemption statutes.

EXEMPTIONS ON INSURANCE

In a number of states special provisions of exemption on moneys received from insurance policies have been passed. The following summary shows the main features of these insurance exemptions:

Summary of State Laws Governing Exemptions on Insurance

ALABAMA

Proceeds and avails of life insurance in favor of a person other than himself, exempt as against creditors, except amount of premiums paid with intent to defraud creditors. Benefits from fraternal societies exempt.

ALASKA

Proceeds of life insurance policies in favor of a person other than himself and beneficiaries' certificates are exempt to $5,000. Proceeds of disability insurance are exempt from liability for the debts of the insured and from the debts of the beneficiary.

ARIZONA
Money arising from fire or other insurance upon property exempt from sale on execution. All money received by or payable to surviving wife or child on life of deceased husband or father up to $20,000.

ARKANSAS
Proceeds of life and disability insurance policies, to be paid any beneficiary are exempt.

CALIFORNIA
Proceeds of life, disability or health insurance, if annual premiums do not exceed $500, exempt, and if premiums exceed said sum, a like exemption in the same proportion to the benefits accruing out of insurance, that $500 bears to whole annual premiums paid. But where debts are incurred by a beneficiary of a health or disability policy or by his wife or family for necessaries, benefits to $1,000 are exempt.

COLORADO
Proceeds of life insurance to the extent of $5,000. Proceeds of any claims for personal injuries or loss, destruction or damage of property; also avails of any fire or casualty insurance. Group life insurance exempt. Proceeds of health, accident, or disability 70% exempt for head of family; 35% for single.

CONNECTICUT
Life insurance, when beneficiary is other than the insured, unless secured with intent to defraud creditors. Insurance on property which is itself subject to exemption.

All benefits allowed by any association of persons in this state towards the support of any of its members incapacitated by sickness or infirmity from attending to his usual business shall be exempt and not liable to be taken by foreign attachment or execution; and all moneys due the debtor from any insurance company upon policies issued for insurance upon property, either real or personal, which is exempt from attachment and execution shall, in like manner, be exempt to the same extent as the property so insured.

DELAWARE
Substantially the same as Alabama.

DISTRICT OF COLUMBIA
Proceeds of life insurance and disability insurance are exempt as are proceeds of life insurance except as to premiums paid to defraud creditors.

FLORIDA
Substantially the same as Alabama. No provision with respect to fraternal benefits. Proceeds of disability insurance unless same was taken out for benefit of creditors.

GEORGIA
Substantially the same as Alabama.

HAWAII
All proceeds payable because of the death of the insured and the aggregate net cash value of any and all life and endowment policies and annuity contracts payable to a husband or wife, child, parent or other dependent are exempt from execution, attachment, garnishment or other process for debts or liabilities of the insured. Proceeds from disability insurance are also exempt.

IDAHO
Proceeds of life insurance policies exempt to an amount reasonably necessary for support. Proceeds of group insurance are exempt.

ILLINOIS
Substantially the same as Alabama as well as insurance on homestead if loss occurs.

INDIANA
Substantially the same as Alabama.

LEGAL PHASES OF COLLECTIONS

IOWA
Proceeds of life insurance and accident policies payable to husband, wife or children of the assured are exempt. Proceeds of policies of life insurance and accident insurance payable to surviving widow are exempt from all debts of the beneficiary contracted prior to the death of the assured, but not exceeding $15,000. Fraternal benefits exempt.

KANSAS
Substantially the same as Alabama.

KENTUCKY
Substantially the same as Alabama and in addition includes proceeds of casualty insurance.

LOUISIANA
Proceeds of life, health and accident insurance except debt secured by pledge of the policy. Fraternal benefits exempt.

MAINE
Substantially the same as Alabama.

MARYLAND
Proceeds including cash surrender and loan values, where policy is made for benefit, or assigned to spouse, children, or dependent relative are exempt. Fraternal benefits exempt. Maximum of $500.

MASSACHUSETTS
Life endowment and group annuity contract. Funds of certain relief societies are exempt. Disability insurance benefits liable only for necessities contracted for after accrual of benefits and up to $35 per week.

MICHIGAN
Life insurance contract may exempt proceeds of policy to any creditor of the insured.

MINNESOTA
Moneys arising from fire and other insurance on exempt property, exempt; life insurance proceeds payable to surviving wife or child upon the life of a deceased husband or father exempt, not exceeding $20,000 which shall be increased by $5,000 for each dependent of the surviving spouse or child. When insurance is effected in favor of another, the beneficiary is entitled to proceeds as against creditors and representatives of the person effecting the same. Fraternal benefits exempt.

MISSISSIPPI
Life insurance proceeds exempt not exceeding $50,000. Proceeds of life insurance policy not exceeding $5,000 payable to executor or administrator of insured passes to the heirs or legatees free of all liability for the debts of the decedent except premiums paid on the policy by anyone other than the insured for debts due for expenses of last illness and for burial. If deceased was insured for the benefit of his heirs or legatees and they shall collect the insurance, the sum collected is to be deducted from the $5,000 and the excess of the latter only is exempt; fraternal benefits exempt. Proceeds of insurance on property, real and personal, are exempt as well as income from disability insurance.

MISSOURI
Life insurance payable to the wife of the insured is exempt from the husband's debts, but where premiums were paid out of husband's funds, insurance representing excess of premiums over $500 annually inure to benefit of his creditors. Fraternal benefits exempt.

MONTANA
Life insurance benefits exempt, if annual premiums do not exceed $500. Proceeds of bail insurance exempt. Proceeds of accident insurance exempt. Fraternal benefits exempt.

NEBRASKA
All proceeds of life insurance unless a written assignment to the contrary has been obtained by the claimant. Any loan value in excess of $5,000 of an unmatured life insurance contract is not exempted.

NEVADA

Life insurance exempt to the extent of amount purchased by annual premium of $1,000. If it exceeds $1,000, a like exemption shall exist which shall bear the same proportion to the proceeds accruing that the $1,000 bears to the whole annual premium.

NEW HAMPSHIRE

Benefits of life insurance payable to a married woman are exempt as to her and to her children. Policies of life or endowment insurance effected upon any person upon his own life or life of another, in favor of a third person having insurable interest, is exempt in the hands of the beneficiary against creditors and representatives of the person effecting the same. Fraternal benefits exempt as are insurance proceeds on exempt property.

NEW JERSEY

Substantially the same as Alabama as well as an exemption for disability and health insurance proceeds.

NEW MEXICO

Cash surrender value of life insurance policies is exempt as well as proceeds of health and disability insurance.

The proceeds of a life insurance policy are exempt except by special contract or arrangement, to be made in writing. Fraternal benefits exempt.

NEW YORK

Substantially the same as Alabama. Annuities exempt except as to excess over amount necessary for education and support. Certain accident benefits are also exempt.

NORTH CAROLINA

Proceeds from an insurance policy which insures the life of a husband is exempt if it is for the sole use and benefit of his wife or children or both. Proceeds from group life insurance payable to an employee are exempt.

NORTH DAKOTA

Insurance on exempt property not exceeding the amount of exemption, is exempt. Cash surrender value of life insurance policies payable to wife or children or any relative of insured dependent or liable to be dependent upon him for claims of support, is exempt from creditors of the insured. Avails of a life insurance policy payable by any mutual aid or benevolent society when made payable to the personal representatives of the deceased, his heirs or estate upon the death of a member of such society or of such assured, are not subject to the debts of the decedent except by such contract. Fraternal benefits exempt.

OHIO

Life endowment, insurance or annuity payable to dependent together with their proceeds. Policies of group insurance and proceeds are exempt from claims against employee.

OKLAHOMA

Substantially the same as Alabama.

OREGON

Substantially the same as Alabama.

PENNSYLVANIA

Where the proceeds of a policy of life insurance are retained by the company at maturity or otherwise, pursuant to an agreement, or by the terms of the policy the same may not be alienated or assigned, if prohibited by the terms of the policy or agreement, and if the policy or agreement so provides, no payments on interest or principal shall be subject to the debts, contracts, or engagements of the beneficiary. Any policy or contract of insurance or annuity whereby the insured or the purchaser of the annuity is the beneficiary or annuitant, not exceeding in income thereof $100 per month, is exempt from the claims of creditors. Life insurance, etc., for the benefit of wife or children or dependent relative of the insured, is exempt from the claims of creditors of the insured. Proceeds of accident and disability insurance are exempt. Fraternal benefits exempt.

LEGAL PHASES OF COLLECTIONS

RHODE ISLAND
Substantially the same as Alabama including proceeds of accident and sickness insurance.

SOUTH CAROLINA
Proceeds of life insurance policies for the benefit of any married woman, or heirs and children, or heirs and children of her husband, are exempt from the claims of the husband's creditors and representatives, to the extent of the insurance proceeds not exceeding $25,000. Fraternal benefits exempt.

SOUTH DAKOTA
Proceeds of life insurance to the extent of $10,000 insured to the use of the husband or wife and children of the insured, free and clear of the claims of the insured's creditors, and of the creditors of the surviving husband, wife or children. Proceeds of endowment policies payable to the insured to an amount of $10,000 are exempt. Insurance payable to surviving widow, husband or minor child or children, payable upon insured's death to the order of his assigns, estate, executor or administrator, not exceeding $10,000, insured to the use of the surviving widow, husband, minor child or children are not subject to the debts of the decedent or of the beneficiaries. Fraternal benefits exempt.

TENNESSEE
Proceeds of life, health and disability insurance exempt. Cash surrender value and proceeds of life insurance payable to or for benefit of wife and children are exempt. Net amount payable on life insurance or annuity contract for benefit of, or assigned to, insured's wife, children, or dependent relative is exempt, even if insured could have changed contract beneficiary.

TEXAS
Cash surrender value of any life insurance policy which has been in force more than two years is exempt, provided the beneficiary is a member of the family of the insured. If members of the insured's family are only partially the beneficiaries, the policies are exempt to the extent of their beneficiary interest. Fraternal benefits exempt as are health and accident benefits. Life endowment and group annuity are exempt under certain conditions.

UTAH
Life insurance exempt to the extent reasonably necessary for support. Insurance upon a homestead is exempt. Fraternal benefits exempt. Unmatured life insurance contracts are exempt up to value of $1,500.

VERMONT
Proceeds of life insurance not exceeding $10,000, where right is reserved to charge the beneficiary if payable to householder as head of family. Instalments on health or accident insurance are exempt. The proceeds of fire insurance on exempt property are exempt as are proceeds of health insurance up to $200 per month.

VIRGINIA
Fraternal benefits exempt as well as proceeds of life insurance up to $10,000 and instalment payments on health and accident insurance. Fraternal benefits exempt.

WASHINGTON
Proceeds of life and disability insurance and annuities exempt under certain specified conditions. Proceeds or avails of accident and health insurance exempt from the debts of the assured and any debt of the beneficiary existing at the time the policy is made available for his use. Fire insurance is exempt to extent of exemption of property destroyed.

WEST VIRGINIA
Substantially the same as Alabama.

WISCONSIN
Substantially the same as Alabama except that the exemption attaches only to benefits not exceeding $5,000 where the insured pays the premiums. Proceeds from disability insurance not to exceed $150 per month. Fire insurance upon exempt property including homestead is exempt.

WYOMING

Proceeds of life insurance payable to person other than the insured or person effectuating insurance or executor or administrator of person effecting insurance, are payable to such person free of all claims of creditors.

SOLDIERS' AND SAILORS' CIVIL RELIEF ACT

The Soldiers' and Sailors' Civil Relief Act of 1940, as amended, SO App. U.S.C. §§ 501-591 (1976), continues in effect, and by the terms of the Selective Service Act of 1948, Id. §§ 451-470, its provisions are specifically made applicable to all persons in the armed forces of the United States or thereafter inducted. The various states also have enacted laws suspending the enforcement of certain civil liabilities against such persons. The following summary of the federal act is limited to a consideration of its general effect on the collection of accounts, suits and the enforcement of judgments and other civil remedies against debtors.

The statute applies to all persons in the armed forces of the United States, the Coast Guard and those officers of the Public Health Service who are detailed for duty either with the Army or the Navy. The law is effective in the several states, territories, the District of Columbia, including all territory subject to the jurisdiction of the United States, and applies to proceedings commenced in any court therein.

When under the provisions of the law the right to enforce any obligation or liability against a person primarily liable is suspended by reason of his military service, the protection of the statute may likewise be afforded in the discretion of the court to sureties, guarantors, and indorsers, accommodation makers and others whether primarily or secondarily liable.

Protection Against Default Judgments

In any action or proceeding commenced in any court, if the defendant defaults in appearing, the plaintiff before entering judgment is required to file an affidavit setting forth facts showing that the defendant is not in military service. If such affidavit is not filed, no judgment may be entered without first securing an order of the court directing such entry, and no such order shall be made if the defendant is in service until after the court shall have appointed an attorney to represent the defendant and protect his interest. Unless it appears that the defendant is not in service the court may also require the plaintiff to file a bond to indemnify the defendant, if in military service, against any loss he may suffer by reason of the judgment if thereafter set aside in whole or in part. The making of a false affidavit is punishable by imprisonment not to exceed one year or by fine not to exceed $1,000, or both.

Stay of Proceedings

At any stage of an action or proceeding in which a person in military service is involved either as plaintiff or defendant, during the period of such service or within sixty days thereafter, the court may stay such action or proceeding. The court may also stay the execution of any judgment or order against a person in military service and vacate or stay any attachment or garnishment of property, money or debts in the hands of another, whether before or after judgment. The court may order the stay of such action or the proceedings for

LEGAL PHASES OF COLLECTIONS

the period of military service and three months thereafter, or any part of such period.

The period of time during which a person is engaged in military service shall not be included in computing any period now or hereafter to be limited by any law, regulation or order for the bringing of an action or proceeding in any court, board, bureau, commission or department or other agency of government by or against any person in military service or by or against his heirs, executors, administrators or assigns, whether such cause of action or the right or privilege to institute such action or proceeding shall have accrued prior to or during the period of such service.

No person in military service may be evicted nor his property distrained for the nonpayment of rent during the period of his military service in respect of any premises for which the agreed rent does not exceed $150 per month and which is occupied chiefly for dwelling purposes by the wife, children or other dependents of such person, except upon leave of the court granted upon application therefor.

Stay of Foreclosure of Chattel Mortgages, etc.

Where a proceeding to foreclose a mortgage upon or to resume possession of personal property, or to rescind or terminate a contract for the purchase thereof, has been stayed as provided in the Act, the court may, unless in its opinion an undue hardship would result to the dependents of the person in military service, appoint three disinterested parties to appraise the property and, based upon the report of the appraisers, order such sum, if any, as may be just, paid to the person in military service or his dependent, as the case may be, as a condition of foreclosing the mortgage, resuming possession of the property, or rescinding or terminating the contract.

A person who has entered into an instalment sale contract with a person who thereafter enters the military service, may not exercise any right or option under said contract to rescind or terminate the contract for any breach occuring prior to and during the period of military service.

Miscellaneous Provisions

No contract made by a person who thereafter enters into the military service for interest in excess of 6% per annum is enforceable unless in the opinion of the court the ability of such person in the military service to pay such interest in excess of 6% is not materially affected by reason of military service.

If in any proceeding it appears to the satisfaction of the court that since the date of approval of the Act any contract, property, or interest therein has been transferred or acquired with intent to delay the just enforcement of civil liabilities by taking advantage of this Act, the court may enforce such liabilities without regard to the provisions of the Act.

A certificate as to military service of any individual may be secured from the following: Army—The Adjutant General of the United States Army; Navy—Chief of Naval Personnel; Marine Corps—Commandant, United States Marine Corps. Such certificate signed by any of the officers indicated shall be *prima facie* evidence that the person named therein has not been, or is, or has been, in military service; the time when and place where such person entered military service, his residence at that time, and the rank, branch, and unit of such service that he entered, the dates within which he was in military service, the monthly pay received by such person as the date of issuing the certificate, the time when and place where such person died or was discharged from such service.

It shall be the duty of the foregoing officers to furnish such certificate on application and any such certificate when purporting to be signed by any one of such officers or by any person purporting upon the face of the certificates to have been so authorized shall be *prima facie* evidence of its contents and of the authority of the signer to issue the same.

Where a person in military service has been reported missing he is presumed to continue in the service until accounted for, and no period herein limited which begins or ends with the death of such person shall begin or end until the death of such person is in fact reported to or found by the Department of Defense or Navy, or any court or board thereof, or until such death is found by a court of competent jurisdiction, provided, that no period herein limited which begins or ends with the death of such person shall be extended hereby beyond a period of six months after the time when this Act ceases to be in force.

Dependents of a person in military service are entitled to the benefits accorded to persons in military service with respect to the foreclosure of chattel mortgages and the repossession of personal property, etc., also with respect to the termination of leases, and the stay of foreclosure of liens for the storage of household goods, etc., unless in the opinion of the court the ability of such dependents to comply with the terms of the obligation, contract, lease or bailment has not been materially impaired by reason of the military service of the person upon whom the applicants are dependent.

ENFORCEABILITY OF ARBITRATION CLAUSE

Commercial arbitration agreements today are recognized by statute by the United States Arbitration Act and in all but one state. However, the extent to which these agreements are enforceable differs widely. In overruling the common law, many statutes distinguished between agreements to submit pending disputes to arbitration and agreements to arbitrate unknown disputes which might arise in the future. Most laws provide that all agreements to arbitrate, whether of pending or future controversies, are valid, irrevocable and enforceable. Other laws merely provide that existing and known disputes are arbitrable when the parties agreed by contract to arbitrate them. In existing disputes, however, many statutes require the agreement be made a rule of court before it becomes irrevocable and enforceable.

At this point it is important to note that agreements to submit disputes to arbitration were not void but merely unenforceable in the courts. Some confusion has been caused by commentators' statements that agreements to arbitrate future disputes are void. In most states, such agreements are valid in the sense that it is permissible to enter into such agreements. The only problem that remains is one of enforceability.

As a rule, arbitration clauses do not bind the parties absent an express bilateral agreement. A proposal in contract negotiations to resolve disputes by arbitration has been held under the UCC to constitute a material alteration under UCC 2-207(2) which will only be binding if expressly accepted by the other side. *Marlene Industries Corp. v. Carnac Textiles, Inc.*, 45 N.Y.2d 327, 408 N.Y.S.2d 410, 380 N.E.2d 239 (1978).

Generally, in order for an arbitration award to be enforced it must be confirmed by judicial proceedings in the state in which it was rendered. A problem may arise, however, in connection with enforcement of an arbitrator's award rendered under the laws of a sister state. In most cases, out of state awards can only be enforced by obtaining a confirming judgment in the state in which the award was originally entered. This judgment can then be executed in the desired state by virtue of the full faith and credit provision of the Federal Constitution.

This two-step process can be expensive and time consuming. Two states, Michigan and California, have sought to solve this problem by enacting legislation authorizing confirmation of an out of state arbitration award. In addition, federal district courts have been expressly empowered by title 9 of U.S.C. § 203 to enforce a foreign arbitration award.

It will be convenient, therefore, for purposes of comparison, to divide the state into three groups. The breakdown will be based upon those states which have by statute or judicial law changed the common law rule of revocability which permitted either party to an arbitration agreement to terminate it at will at any time prior to the rendition of an award.

The first group of states to be discussed are those in which there is specific authority by statute or judicial ruling holding an arbitration clause in a commercial contract to be valid, irrevocable and enforceable. The first 36 states listed below, as well as the United States, have statutes that reverse the common law rule of revocability and make written promises to arbitrate specifically enforceable. In some of these states, however, not all aspects of the contract are included within the ambit of the arbitration statute. Those exclusions will be found in the individual description of its state law that follows. In addition, there is a court decision from Colorado that has judicially declared that agreements to arbitrate future disputes are valid and enforceable without the aid of any enabling statute.

The Supreme Court of Colorado held in 1925 that a contract requiring the arbitration of future controversies arising thereunder is binding upon the parties thereto. *Ezell v. Rocky Mountain Bean & Elevator Co.,* 76 Colo. 409, 232 P. 680 (1925). The decision states that the only material difference between statutory arbitration and the common law procedure is that, under the latter, suit must be brought upon the award in order to enforce it, whereas an award under statutory arbitration has the benefit of summary procedures.

The 36 states and federal law in Group I are shown below with brief reference to applicable statutes and court decisions:

GROUP I

1. Alaska. Chap. 232, Laws of Alaska. Effective date: August 6, 1968. Prior to this date, Alaska had no commercial arbitration statute. The previous case law held that neither submission agreements nor agreements to arbitrate future controversies were a bar to a law suit before an award was rendered. Parties were permitted an action for damages in breach of a construction contract. See *Orrick v. Granell,* 14 Alaska 94 (1952). This case should be overruled by the new arbitration statute.

2. Arizona. Rev. Stat. Ann. §12-1501 to 1511. A written arbitration agreement is enforceable and irrevocable. No application to personal injury, tort, or employer-employee disputes or to any insured or beneficiary under insurance or annuity.

3. Arkansas. Stat. Ann. "Uniform Arbitration Act." Act. 1969, No. 260, §23 (34-511 to 34-532). The Arkansas arbitration act was passed in 1969 and it applies only to contracts for construction and/or manufacturing and excludes personal injury or tort matters, labor management disputes and all insurance matters.

4. **California.** Civ. Proc. Code §1281. Written agreement to arbitrate enforceable and irrevocable.

5. **Colorado.** Rule 109, Rules of Civil Proc., Colorado Rev. Stat., *Ezell v. Rocky Mountain Bean & Elev. Co.*, 76 Colo. 409, 232 P.680 (1925). *Sisters of Mercy of Colorado v. Mead & Mount Construction Co.*, 165 Colo. 447, 439 P.2d 733 (Colo. 1968) also involved arbitration in accordance with an agreement to arbitrate future disputes. Award was upheld on grounds that proceedings conformed to Rule 109 of Rules of Civil Procedure.

6. **Connecticut.** Gen. Stat. Rev. §52-408.

7. **Delaware.** Code, Title 10, Ch. 5 §§5701-5728 (1972).

8. **Florida.** Stat. §§682.01-682.22. A written agreement to submit a controversy to arbitration is enforceable and irrevocable except in certain instances as specified in state laws.

9. **Hawaii.** Rev. Laws of Hawaii 1967, Chapter 658-1 et seq. Provision in a written contract to arbitrate is enforceable and irrevocable. Party contesting agreement entitled to jury trial.

10. **Idaho.** Chapter 9 of the Idaho code is amended to include title 7 which permits submission of existing and future controversies to arbitration.

11. **Illinois.** Ann. Stats., Chap. 10, §§101-123.

12. **Indiana.** Burns Indiana Stats, "Uniform Arbitration Act." Acts 1969, Ch. 340, §23, p. 1429 (§3-227-3-248). The Uniform Arbitration Act was passed in 1969 except that it excludes consumer leases, sales and loan contracts. If the parties so stipulate in writing, the agreement may be enforced by designated third parties.

13. **Louisana.** Rev. Stat. Ann. §9:4201. A written agreement to submit a controversy to arbitration is enforceable and irrevocable.

14. **Maine.** In 1967 Maine passed what it termed "an Act adopting the Uniform Arbitration Act" R.S.T. 14, C. 706. However, although most of the provisions of the statute are similar to the Uniform Arbitration Act, §5948 limits its application to construction contracts and collective bargaining agreements.

15. **Maryland.** Chapter 23, Art. 7 effective June 1, 1965. The Maryland law makes all contracts to arbitrate, written on or after June 1, 1965, valid, enforceable and irrevocable. Contracts written prior to this date are still governed by the preceding law authorizing arbitration of causes of action in a pending suit by consent of the parties, Articles 75, §§16 to 21, Annotated Code of Maryland.

16. **Massachusetts.** Ann. Laws Chap. 251, §1. Agreement to submit controversy to arbitration is enforceable and irrevocable.

17. **Michigan.** Stat. Ann. §§27-2483.

18. **Minnesota.** Stat. Ann. §572.08.

19. **Nevada.** Burns Indiana Stats. "Uniform Arb. Act," Nev. Rev. Stats., Title 3. Chap. 38, 38.010–38.240 (1967).

20. **New Hampshire.** Rev. Stat. Ann. §542.1.

21. **New Jersey.** Rev. Stat. §2A-24-1. Arbitration clause does not operate so as to deprive party of ancilliary relief, short of arbitrable matters, by the court unless provision in contract specifically excludes it. *Pyramid Electric Co. v. Staklinski*, 61 N.J. Super. 278, 160 A.2nd 505 (1960).

22. **New Mexico.** Stat. Ann. §22-3-9 to 31. Session of 30th Legislature of State of New Mexico, Uniform Arbitration Act.

23. **New York.** Civil Practice Law and Rules, Art. 75, §§7501-7514.

24. **North Carolina.** General Statutes Article 45A.

25. **Ohio.** Rev. Code Ann. §2711.01. Written agreement to submit controversy to arbitration is enforceable except for certain real estate transactions.

26. **Oklahoma.** Uniform Arbitration Act § 2 (1978).

27. **Oregon.** O.R.S. Title 3, Chap. 33, §33.210. Arbitration award conclusive.

28. **Pennsylvania.** Stat. Ann. Title 5, § 161: Despite the existence of a modern arbitration statute, Pennsylvania courts have held that arbitration proceeds at common law unless the agreement itself provides that the statute governs or a municipal authority is involved. *John A. Robbins Co.*

v. *Airportels, Inc.,* 418 Pa. 257, 210 A.2d 896 (1965), *Wingate Construction Co. v. Schweizer Dipple, Inc.,* 419 Pa. 74, 213 A.2d 275 (1965), *La Vale Plaza Inc. v. R.S. Noonan, Inc.,* 378 F.2d 569 (3rd Cir. 1967).

29. Rhode Island. Gen. Laws Ann. 10-3-2 et seq.: Rhode Island Gen. Laws 37-16-1 et al., known as "The Public Works Arbitration Act," says that any construction contract for a public works project executed in 1962 or thererafter may contain a provision concerning arbitration of disputes and that any such contract executed on or after July 1, 1967, involving a sum of $10,000 or more must contain a clause providing arbitration for disputes and claims arising out of or concerning the performance of interpretation of the contract. School teachers have also been included under this act.

30. South Carolina. Uniform Arbitration Act §1 (1978).

31. South Dakota. Comp. Laws §21-25A-1 to 38 (Supp. 1978).

32. Texas. Vernon's Ann. Civ. Arts. 224-238-6. Although Texas enacted its Modern Arbitration Act effective July 1, 1966, it has excluded from its terms labor agreements, contract of insurance, and construction contracts. Arbitration clauses in Texas must be concluded upon the advice of counsel to both parties as evidenced by counsels' signatures on the agreement.

33. Virginia. Code of Virginia 1952, Chapter 22, §8-503. Parties may submit a controversy to arbitration and agree that submission be entered of record in court. Upon proof of the agreement out of court, or by consent of parties given in court, it must be entered of record and a rule made that parties submit to the resultant award. *Martin v. Winston,* 181 Va. 94, 23 S.E.2d 873 (1943) holds that arbitration is favored and minor defects in the award do not mean that it should be vacated.

Effective July 1, 1968, the Virginia Arbitration Law was amended and §8-503(b) now provides as follows: "Notwithstanding any other provision of law, the parties may enter into an agreement to arbitrate which will be as binding as any other agreement. If, after entry into such agreement, either party refuses to cooperate in the appointment of arbitrator or arbitrators, or if the parties cannot agree upon the arbitrator or arbitrators, then, after 10 days' notice on motion of either party, the court which has jurisdiction of the claim shall act for the party so refusing or failing to agree in the appointment, then the arbitration shall proceed and be as binding as if both parties had cooperated throughout the proceedings. Neither party shall have the right to revoke an agreement to arbitrate except on a ground which would be good for revoking or annulling other agreements."

34. Washington. Rev. Code Ann. §704.010.

35. Wisconsin. Stat. Ann. §298-01. Every contract that is subject to Wisconsin law and does not expressly negate provisions of §298-01 incorporates provisions of that act.

36. Wyoming. Stat. Ann. §1-1048.

37. United States. 9 U.S.C. §§ 1-4. For a discussion of the Federal Arbitration Act see *Bernhardt v. Polygraphic Co. of America,* 350 U.S. 198 (1956) and *Prima Paint Corp. v. Flood & Conklin,* 388 U.S. 395 (1967).

The following 13 states and the District of Columbia, designated Group II, have statutes which provide essentially that agreements to arbitrate *existing* controversies are valid.

The list indicates the many variations in the statutes of these states.

GROUP II

1. Alabama. Code of Alabama, 1958. Title 7, Civil Remedies & Procedure, Chap. 19, §829 et seq. Agreements to arbitrate existing disputes valid; and future disputes as to amount only. *Moss v. W. K. Upchurch,* 278 Ala. 615, 179 So.2d 741 (1965).

2. Georgia. Title 7-101—Common Law Arbitration. Title 7-201—Statutory Arbitration—existing disputes only. Agreements to arbitrate future disputes (American Institute of Arbitrators contract) are void as against public policy. *Wright v. Cecil A. Mason Constr. Co.,* 115 Ga. App. 729, 155 S.E.2d 725 (1967).

3. Iowa. Chap. 679, §§679-1 to 679-18 cover existing disputes. But *Younker Bros. Inc. v. Standard Constr. Co.,* 241 F.Supp. 17 (S.D. Iowa 1965) held where there is substantial interstate transportation and nonresident corporations are involved, the Federal Arbitration Act applies and agreements to arbitrate are enforceable.

4. Kansas. Chapter 5, Article 2, §§5-201 to 5-213 of General Statutes of Kansas, 1949 sanction agreements to arbitrate existing controversies. Court decisions indicate contracts which require arbitration of future disputes are not illegal. *Gillioz v. City of Emporia,* 149 Kan. 539, 88 P.2d 1014 (1939). But failure to appoint an arbitrator constitutes implied revocation of such an agreement. Party revoking is liable for damages for breach of contract. *Thompson v. Phillips Pipeline Co.,* 438 P.2d 146 (Kan. 1968).

5. Kentucky. Existing controversies may by agreement be submitted to arbitration. §§417.010—417.040. Contracts not valid as to future controversies. *Gatliff Coal Co. v. Cox,* 142 F.2d 876 (6th Cir. 1944); *Kentucky River Mills v. Jackson,* 206 F.2d 111 (6th Cir. 1953). Where contract involved interstate commerce, arbitration agreement was enforceable under the United States Arbitration Act.

6. Mississippi. Title 3, Chap. 1. §279 validates arbitration of existing controversies. Either party may revoke an agreement to arbitrate future disputes. *McClendon v. Shutt,* 115 So.2d 740, 237 Miss. 703 (1959).

7. Missouri. Vernon's Ann. Stats. §435.020 authorizes written agreement to arbitrate an existing controversy with agreement for judgment on the award. §435.010 provides such agreement does not bar a suit by any party. §435.259 makes the revoking party liable for costs, expenses, damages including attorney fees in preparing for arbitration. Arbitration agreement voidable at behest of either party before submission to a hearing. *Ewing v. Pugh,* 420 S.W.2d 14 (Kan. Ct. App. 1967). Agreement to arbitrate at the option of either party appears to be valid. *Gillioz v. State Highway Commission,* 348 Mo. 211, 153 S.W.2d 18 (1941). Provision in construction contract for appeal to board of arbitrators was not enforceable, *Thompson v. St. Charles County,* 227 Mo. 220, 126 S.W. 1044 (1910).

8. Montana. Title 93, Chap. 201. Covers existing controversies only. Award rendered by arbitrator pursuant to American Institute of Arbitrators contract was enforceable. *Hopkins v. School District No. 40,* 133 Mont. 534, 327 P.2d 395 (1958).

9. Nebraska. Chap. 25, §25-2103 et seq. cover arbitration of existing controversies. Contracts requiring arbitration of future disputes or as condition precedent to suit are not enforceable. *Havens v. Robertson,* 75 Neb. 205, 106 N.W. 335 (1905).

10. North Dakota. Chap. 32-39 Arbitration. §32.29.01 et seq. authorize arbitration of existing controversies. But see Title 32, Judicial Remedies, §32.04.12 providing that an agreement to submit a controversy to arbitration may not be the subject of an action for specific enforcement. Common law arbitration is not supplanted by the code. *Johnson v. Wineman,* 34 N.D. 116, 157 N.W. 679 (1916).

11. Tennessee. Title 23, Chap. 5, §23, 501 et seq. authorize arbitration of existing controversies whether or not in suit, except certain causes relating to real estate and cases of incompetent persons. As to future controversies contract was not void as ousting courts of jurisdiction where it provided that arbitration should be held under the statute. *R. Lee Tolley Co. v. Marr,* 12 Tenn. App. 505 (1931). Held contrary to public policy when contract precludes as appeal from the award. *Harmon v. Komisar,* 15 Tenn. App. 405 (1932). The arbitration statutes have added to and not abrogated the common law on the subject. *Mierowsky v. Phipps* 432 S.W.2d 885 (Tenn. Sup. Ct. 1968).

12. Utah. Judicial Code, Chapter 31, §78-31-1 covers agreements to arbitrate existing controversies. Contracts to arbitrate future disputes held invalid as ousting courts of jurisdiction. *Johnson v. Brinkerhoff,* 89 Utah 530, 57 P.2d 1132 (1936); *Giannopoulas v. Pappas,* 80 Utah 442, 15 P.2d 353 (1932); *Latter v. Holsum Bread Co.,* 108 Utah 364, 160 P.2d 421 (1945); *Barnhart v. Civil Service Employees Ins. Co.,* 16 Utah 2d 223, 398 P.2d 873 (1965).

13. West Virginia. Chap. 55, Art. 10, §107, Official Code of 1931, covers agreements to arbitrate existing controversies. Although a contract to submit future differences to arbitration is not binding, where a contract for future arbitration of controversies has become executed in respect to any pertinent matter of difference between the parties, the award is binding. *Hughes v. National Fuel Co.,* 121 W.Va. 392, 3 S.E.2d 621 (1939). Statutory procedure is not exclusive but is supplementary to that already existing at common law. *United Fuel Gas Co. v. Columbian Fuel Corp.,* 165 F.2d 746 (4th Cir. 1948).

14. District of Columbia. *John W. Johnson, Inc. v. 2500 Wisconsin Ave., Inc.* 231 F.2d 761 (D.D.C. 1956). Arbitration in the District of Columbia proceeds at common law. Arbitration proceeds according to 9 U.S.C. §1-2 when a transaction "in commerce." Superior Ct. Rule 701 for summary confirmation of awards.

In the third category there is one state which has no statute on commercial arbitration—Vermont. It is probable that Vermont would apply common law principles of arbitration. In such event a suit could be maintained on the award, or the award might be asserted in defense to an action brought by the losing party.

GROUP III

Vermont. For a discussion of the arbitration law of this state, see *Bernhardt v. Polygraphic Co. of America,* 350 U.S. 198 (1956).

Claims Against Decedents' Estates

24

The manner of presentment and payment of claims against a decedent's estate may run the gamut from simplicity to complexity. In many jurisdictions it is the practical and customary procedure for the executor or administrator of a solvent estate, promptly after his qualification, to pay a decedent's debts, funeral and estate administration expenses, without the requirement of a formal claim. Where the estate is insolvent, the claim is disputed or the local procedures demand formal presentment of verified claims, the procedures become more complex and representation by counsel would be advisable.

The summary presented herewith contains a condensed statement of the requirements of the law of the several states with respect to the presentation and filing of claims against the estates of deceased persons. The term "representative" as used in the summary refers to the executor or administrator of the estate. Where a deceased person dies leaving a will, and the same is admitted to probate, "letters testamentary" are issued to the executor named therein; but if the decedent left no will, i.e., died intestate an administrator rather than an executor is appointed and "letters of administration" are issued.

It is the duty of the representative, i.e., the executor or administrator, to take possession of the assets of the decedent, pay the expenses of administration and the claims of creditors, and dispose of the balance of the estate in accordance with the decedent's will, or, if there is no will, in accordance with the statutes governing the distribution of decedent's estates. Unless the decedent's will provided that the executor shall not be required to file a bond, the executor must qualify by filing a bond in a sum as the court may direct; in the case of an administrator, a bond is always required. Under the laws of most states the representative is required either to advertise for claims or to notify creditors to present their claims on or before a specified date. In some states, however, no such notice is required; instead, creditors must file their claims within a time prescribed by law after the appointment of the representative.

SUMMARY OF STATE LAWS GOVERNING CLAIMS AGAINST ESTATES

ALABAMA

1. TIME FOR FILING.—Within six months after grant of letters of administration or letters testamentary are issued or forever barred.
2. WHERE FILED.—Probate Court which issues letters of administration or letters testamentary.
3. MUST CLAIM BE SWORN TO.—Yes.
4. REMARKS.—If estate is insolvent, claim must be filed within six months after declaration of insolvency.

ALASKA

1. TIME FOR PRESENTMENT.—Within four months after date of the first publication of notice to creditors or within three years after decedent's death if notice to creditors has not been published. For claims against decedent's estate which arise at or after the death of the decedent, claims must

be presented within four months after performance of contract by personal representative or four months after claim arises.
2. WHERE PRESENTED.—To representative or to clerk of court.
3. MUST CLAIM BE SWORN TO.—No.

ARIZONA

1. TIME FOR FILING.—Representative must publish a notice to creditors not less than once a week for four weeks. Claims must be presented within four months from first publication. If claimant can show by affidavit he was not within the state and, therefore, had no notice, he may file at any time prior to entry of decree for distribution. If no notice published, claims must be filed within three years of decedent's death.
2. WHERE FILED.—Presented to representative for allowance or rejection. Upon rejection, suit must be commenced within 60 days of mailing of notice of disallowance.
3. MUST CLAIM BE SWORN TO.—No particular form of proof of claim is required.

ARKANSAS

1. TIME FOR FILING.—Within six months from the date of the first publication of the notice or forever barred. If estate is under $1,000 notice may be posted in courthouse.
2. WHERE FILED.—In office of Clerk of Court for Probate or presented to representative.
3. MUST CLAIM BE SWORN TO.—Yes. Affidavit must state nature and amount of claim, that nothing has been paid, that there are no offsets, and that the sum demanded is justly due.

CALIFORNIA

1. TIME FOR FILING.—Within four months after the first publication of the notice to present claims is published by the representative.
2. WHERE FILED.—With a Clerk of the Court, or claim must be exhibited, with the necessary vouchers, to the representative.
3. MUST CLAIM BE SWORN TO.—Yes. Supported by affidavit showing that the amount is justly due, that no payments have been made which are not credited, and that there are no offsets.
4. REMARKS.—If claim is allowed it must be presented to the Judge of the Superior Court for his approval and thirty days thereafter must be filed with the Court. When claim is rejected by either the Court or the representative, the holder must, under penalty of being barred, bring suit within three months if claim is then due, or within two months if claim is not due.

COLORADO

1. TIME FOR FILING.—Within four months after the date of the first publication of notice to creditors or within 1 year after decedent's death if notice has not been published.
2. WHERE FILED.—With court where estate is being administered or with personal representative.
3. MUST CLAIM BE SWORN TO.—No particular form of proof of claim is required.

CONNECTICUT

1. TIME FOR FILING.—Stated in notice published by representative; usually not less than three months or more than twelve months from the time of granting of the order.
2. WHERE FILED.—Exhibited to representative.
3. MUST CLAIM BE SWORN TO.—Yes. Must inform representative of the extent and character of the demand if required by the representative or probate court.
4. REMARKS.—Claim is barred if suit is not brought within four months after notice of disallowance.

DELAWARE

1. TIME FOR FILING.—Within six months from grant of letters testamentary or administration.
2. WHERE FILED.—With representative or with Register of Wills.
3. MUST CLAIM BE SWORN TO.—No; basis of claim must be indicated with name and address of claimant and amount claimed.

DISTRICT OF COLUMBIA

1. TIME FOR FILING.—Claims must be presented within six months after date of first publication of notice of appointment. Suit may be brought to recover amount due, even though no claim is filed, subject to general three-year statute of limitation, provided representative has not distributed estate.
2. WHERE FILED.—Presented to representative and entered upon claims docket of the Register of Wills.

CLAIMS AGAINST DECEDENTS' ESTATES

3. MUST CLAIM BE SWORN TO.—Yes, with statement that the account as stated is true and just, that no part of the claim has been paid, and that all credits have been made.

FLORIDA

1. TIME FOR FILING.—Within three months from the first publication of notice to present claims or within three years after the decedent's death, if notice of administration has not been published, otherwise barred.
2. WHERE FILED.—With the Clerk of Court who serves a copy to the representative.
3. MUST CLAIM BE SWORN TO.—Yes.
4. REMARKS.—Objection to claims may be filed within four months from the first publication of notice to creditors. The court may extend the time for filing objections for good cause shown. If such objection is filed the claimant has 30 days from such service within which to bring suit.

GEORGIA

1. TIME FOR FILING.—Within three months from publication of last notice. If filed thereafter it loses right to equal participation with claims of equal dignity paid before the representative has notice of such unrepresented claims. Representative must give four weeks' notice to present claims.
2. WHERE FILED.—With representative.
3. MUST CLAIM BE SWORN TO.—Verification is not required, but is advisable.
4. REMARKS.—No suit to recover a debt may be commenced against representative until six months after his qualification.

HAWAII

1. TIME FOR FILING.—Claims are barred if not presented by creditors within four months after the first publication of notice by executor or administrator.
2. WHERE FILED.—With representatives.
3. MUST CLAIMS BE SWORN TO.—There is no statutory form of proof of claim. It is advisable that claims are itemized and an affidavit is attached stating that the claim is due and unpaid and that there are no offsets or counterclaims thereto.
4. REMARKS.—Secured creditors may foreclose on security held without filing a claim.

IDAHO

1. TIME FOR FILING.—Within four months after the first publication of notice or forever barred. Where claimant had no notice by reason of being out of state, the court may permit presentation before decree of distribution is entered.
2. WHERE FILED.—With representative.
3. MUST CLAIM BE SWORN TO.—No.
4. REMARKS.—If claim is rejected suit must be brought within three months after date of rejection, if claim is due; if not due, then within two months after becoming due, otherwise claim is barred.

ILLINOIS

1. TIME FOR FILING.—All claims must be presented within six months from date of issuance of letter or are barred as to property inventoried within such period.
2. WHERE FILED.—With Probate Court administering the estate or with representative.
3. MUST CLAIM BE SWORN TO.—Yes. When based on contract, an affidavit must accompany the claim and must state that claim is just, and unpaid, after allowing all credits, deductions and setoffs.
4. REMARKS.—If an additional list of inventory is filed not covering previously inventoried property and clerk of court publishes notice of a new claim date, all claims not filed before such date are barred as to such additional property. All claims filed on or before such date share pro-rata in such additional property according to the classification of the claims.

INDIANA

1. TIME FOR FILING.—Claim should be filed within five months after first published notice to creditors or three months after the court has revoked probate of will if claimant was named as beneficiary in will, whichever is later.
2. WHERE FILED.—In office of clerk where estate proceedings are pending.
3. MUST CLAIM BE SWORN TO.—Affidavit must be attached to claim stating that it is justly due and wholly unpaid, after deducting all credits, setoffs and deductions.

IOWA

1. TIME FOR FILING.—Within six months after the date of publication of notice to creditors, or forever barred.
2. WHERE FILED.—Filed with the Clerk of the District Court of county in which estate is being administered.
3. MUST CLAIM BE SWORN TO.—Yes; if founded on written instrument it must be attached; if upon account, an itemized copy showing the balance should be attached.

KANSAS

1. TIME FOR FILING.—Within six months from the date of first published notice to creditors, or forever barred.
2. WHERE FILED.—With the Probate Court. If under $200, may be allowed by representative without filing with Court.
3. MUST CLAIM BE SWORN TO.—Yes, but if amount exceeds $200 then competent evidence must be produced before the Probate Court to establish claim.

KENTUCKY

1. TIME FOR FILING.—Within one year after appointment of personal representative. If no personal representative is appointed, then three years after decedent's death.
2. WHERE FILED.—With representative.
3. MUST CLAIM BE SWORN TO.—Representative may pay claim without verification when he is satisfied the estate is solvent and that claim is just and owing. Otherwise, claim must be sworn to.
4. REMARKS.—If debt is on a written contract, nothing further than affidavit of claimant required; if upon account, in addition to claimant's affidavit, that of a disinterested person is required.

LOUISIANA

1. TIME FOR FILING.—No particular time specified. Representative must file an account every 12 months. Claims are passed upon and allowed at that time.
2. WHERE FILED.—With representative.
3. MUST CLAIM BE SWORN TO.—Yes.

MAINE

1. TIME FOR FILING.—Within 12 months after grant of administration.
2. WHERE FILED.—With representative or Registry of Probate.
3. MUST CLAIM BE SWORN TO.—Yes, if filed with Registry of Probate.

MARYLAND

1. TIME FOR FILING.—Within six months after publication of notice of appointment of representative. Suit against the estate must be commenced within six months after appointment unless decedent was covered by insurance, in which case the statute of limitations for the particular action governs.
2. WHERE FILED.—With representative or Register of Wills with a copy sent to personal representative.
3. MUST CLAIM BE SWORN TO.—Yes.

MASSACHUSETTS

1. TIME FOR FILING.—No time specified unless estate is insolvent, then within four months from the date of giving bond or the claim will be barred.
2. WHERE FILED.—With representative.
3. MUST CLAIM BE SWORN TO.—No, but preferable practice.

MICHIGAN

1. TIME FOR FILING.—Hearing date is fixed by court after approval of bond of fiduciary, not more than four months nor less than two months from date of first publication of notice to file claims.
2. WHERE FILED.—With fiduciary and with court.
3. MUST CLAIM BE SWORN TO.—Yes. Claim must be in writing, under oath, and contain sufficient detail to inform fiduciary of nature and amount of same. Copy of any writing on which claim is based must be attached.
4. REMARKS.—Creditor may, within 18 months after last date to file claims and before estate

is closed, file application to file claim and application shall be granted not more than one month thereafter, upon payment of costs. After the 18 months, the Court may permit a claim to be filed for special cause.

MINNESOTA

1. TIME FOR FILING.—Within four months after the date of publication of the clerk of court's notice to creditors. If notice is not so published, within three years after the decedent's death.
2. WHERE FILED.—In the Probate Court or sent to the Personal Representative.
3. MUST CLAIM BE SWORN TO.—No, if sent to personal representative. If filed with court see local court rules.

MISSISSIPPI

1. TIME FOR FILING.—Within 90 days from the first publication of notice to creditors. Otherwise barred.
2. WHERE FILED.—With Clerk of the Chancery Court.
3. MUST CLAIM BE SWORN TO.—Yes.
4. REMARKS.—Before Clerk will accept claims, affidavit of claim must be probated and registered. The affidavit of creditor must be attached to the written evidence of the indebtedness. Such affidavit must state that the claim is just, correct and owing from the deceased, that it is not usurious, and that no part of it has been paid.

MISSOURI

1. TIME FOR FILING.—Representative must publish notice requiring creditors to present claims within 6 months after first published notice of letters testamentary or of administration.
2. WHERE FILED.—Probate Court.
3. MUST CLAIM BE SWORN TO.—Yes.
4. REMARKS.—Claim must be served on representative in writing stating the nature and amount of his claim with a copy of the written evidence of indebtedness.

MONTANA

1. TIME FOR FILING.—Within four months from date of first publication of notice to creditors or within three years from date of death if notice has not been published.
2. WHERE FILED.—With representative by mail, return receipt requested, or with the clerk of court.
3. MUST CLAIM BE SWORN TO.—Yes, with statement that the amount is justly due, that no payments have been made thereon, and that there are no offsets. Basis of claim must be indicated with name and address of claimant and amount claimed.

NEBRASKA

1. TIME FOR FILING.—Upon appointment, Representative must publish a notice in a newspaper once a week for three successive weeks. The time for filing claims is two months.
2. WHERE FILED.—Clerk of the Probate Court.
3. MUST CLAIM BE SWORN TO.—Yes.
4. REMARKS.—If claim is not presented within stipulated time, it shall be forever barred unless good cause shown.

NEVADA

1. TIME FOR FILING.—Within 90 days from date of first publication of notice to creditors.
2. WHERE FILED.—Clerk of Court.
3. MUST CLAIM BE SWORN TO.—Yes. If claim is for $250 or more, an affidavit must state that the amount is justly due (or date it will be due), that no payments have been made thereon which are not credited and that there are no offsets to the same.
4. REMARKS.—If claim rejected, suit must be brought within 30 days from date of notice of rejection.

NEW HAMPSHIRE

1. TIME FOR FILING.—Within six months from grant of letters. If estate is insolvent, no presentation is required and notice sent to representative by registered mail stating nature and amount of claim is sufficient.
2. WHERE FILED.—Presented to representative.
3. MUST CLAIM BE SWORN TO.—In discretion of representative.

NEW JERSEY

1. TIME FOR FILING.—Within six months after entry of order of publication to creditors by the Superior Court or surrogate.
2. WHERE FILED.—Presented to representative.
3. MUST CLAIM BE SWORN TO.—Yes, with statement of amount, and particulars of claim.
4. REMARKS.—If claim is not presented in time, claimant may file before distribution of assets and the court may direct payment.

NEW MEXICO

1. TIME FOR FILING.—Within two months of first publication of notice of appointment of executor or administrator or within three years of the decedents death if notice to creditors has not been published.
2. WHERE FILED.—With district court or representative.
3. MUST CLAIM BE SWORN TO.—No.

NEW YORK

1. TIME FOR FILING.—Claims should be presented to fiduciary on or before date fixed in notice to creditors or, if no notice is published, within seven months from the date of the issue of letters.
2. WHERE FILED.—With the representative at the location stated in the notice.
3. MUST CLAIM BE SWORN TO.—Yes, with satisfactory vouchers and affidavit stating the claim is justly due, that no payments have been made thereon, and that there are no offsets against the same to the knowledge of the claimant.
4. REMARKS.—If claim is rejected, creditor must commence suit representative within 60 days after rejection; if claim is not then due, then sue within 60 days after claim becomes due or issue can be tried on a judicial accounting.

NORTH CAROLINA

1. TIME FOR FILING.—Within time specified in general notice to creditors.
2. WHERE FILED.—Exhibited to representative.
3. MUST CLAIM BE SWORN TO.—Within discretion of representative or collector.
4. REMARKS.—Claim must contain name and address of claimant, amount claimed and basis of the claim. Upon failure to file within six months creditor may recover from the representative if he still has funds; if not, he may proceed against the heirs. To the extent that the decedent or the decedent's personal representative is protected by insurance coverage with respect to a claim, that claim is not automatically barred if not presented within six months.

NORTH DAKOTA

1. TIME FOR FILING.—Within three months after the date of the first publication of notice to creditors—provided that claims barred by a nonclaim statute in the state of the decedent's domicile are barred in this state. Within three years after decedent's death if no notice is published.
2. WHERE FILED.—Present to personal representative or file with clerk of court.
3. MUST CLAIM BE SWORN TO.—No if filed with personal representative. If filed with clerk of court consult local court rules.

OHIO

1. TIME FOR FILING.—Within three months after date of appointment of representative. If claim is not filed within four months, claimant may petition for leave to file upon showing lack of notice or other good cause as set forth in statute. If not filed within six months, claim is forever barred.
2. WHERE FILED.—With representative.
3. MUST CLAIM BE SWORN TO.—If representative so requires, affidavit must state that such claim is justly due, that no payments have been made thereon, and that there are no offsets against the same.

OKLAHOMA

1. TIME FOR FILING.—Within two months after publication of first notice to creditors.
2. WHERE FILED.—Presented at place specified in notice.
3. MUST CLAIM BE SWORN TO.—Yes, with necessary vouchers.
4. REMARKS.—Timely claims have preference over late claims.

OREGON

1. TIME FOR FILING.—Claims presented within four months after date of first publication of notice have priority.

CLAIMS AGAINST DECEDENTS' ESTATES

2. WHERE FILED.—Presented to representative.
3. MUST CLAIM BE SWORN TO.—Yes, with necessary vouchers.

PENNSYLVANIA

1. TIME FOR FILING.—Within statute of limitations which continues to run despite death of decedent. If statute would toll within one year after death, however, claim will not be barred until one year after death. Claims may be unenforceable against grantee of real property after one year.
2. WHERE FILED.—With representative.
3. MUST CLAIM BE SWORN TO.—It is not necessary that a claim be verified, but it must be presented and proved in Orphans' Court at audit of account, unless admitted by representative.

RHODE ISLAND

1. TIME FOR FILING.—Within six months from first publication of notice to creditors.
2. WHERE FILED.—In the office of the Probate Court together with affidavit that copy was delivered by hand or registered mail, return receipt requested, to executor or administrator or his attorney.
3. MUST CLAIM BE SWORN TO.—Yes.
4. REMARKS.—For sufficient cause shown the Probate Court may permit a claim to be filed after six months.

SOUTH CAROLINA

1. TIME FOR FILING.—Within five months after publication of notice, or claim will be barred.
2. WHERE FILED.—With representative or Probate Judge.
3. MUST CLAIM BE SWORN TO.—Yes.

SOUTH DAKOTA

1. TIME FOR FILING.—Within two months after publication of notice to creditors.
2. WHERE FILED.—Claims must be filed with Clerk of Court where proceedings are pending, which filing constitutes presentation to executor or administrator.
3. MUST CLAIM BE SWORN TO.—Yes, supported by affidavit stating that the amount is justly due, that no payments have been made thereon which are not credited, and that there are no offsets to the same.
4. REMARKS.—When representative allows claim it must be presented to judge for approval. If rejected by either party, representative must give notice of hearing on rejected claim. If claim is rejected, suit must be brought within 30 days after such rejection, or claim will be barred.

TENNESSEE

1. TIME FOR FILING.—Within 30 days after issuance of letters testamentary or of administration, the executor or administrator must publish notice to creditors or, where estate is less than $1,000, notices must be posted. Claims must be filed within six months after the first publication or posting.
2. WHERE FILED.—Duplicate copies of claim to be filed with clerk of court in which estate is being administered.
3. MUST CLAIM BE SWORN TO.—Claim must be verified by affidavit of creditor stating that the claim is correct, just and valid obligation of the estate and that no payment or security has been received except as indicated therein.

TEXAS

1. TIME FOR FILING.—Those exhibited within six months after the grant of letters are entitled to priority.
2. WHERE FILED.—Exhibited to the representative or Clerk of Court.
3. MUST CLAIM BE SWORN TO.—Yes.

UTAH

1. TIME FOR FILING.—Within three months after the first publication of notice to creditors, or forever barred.
2. WHERE FILED.—Presented to representative.
3. MUST CLAIM BE SWORN TO.—Yes.

VERMONT

1. TIME FOR FILING.—Claims must be filed within four months of first publication of notice; if no notice is published, then within three years.
2. WHERE FILED.—Presented to the commissioners.
3. MUST CLAIM BE SWORN TO.—No.

VIRGINIA

1. TIME FOR FILING.—Within six months of qualification of representative.
2. WHERE FILED.—With personal representative or court-appointed Commissioner of Accounts.
3. MUST CLAIM BE SWORN TO.—No form prescribed but claim should be in writing.

WASHINGTON

1. TIME FOR FILING.—Within four months after the first publication of notice to creditors, but claims against a casualty insurer of decedent can be made within 18 months.
2. WHERE FILED.—Presented to representative who must indorse on claim his allowance or rejection. Claim is then filed with court.
3. MUST CLAIM BE SWORN TO.—Yes, with affidavit stating that the claim is correct, that the amount is justly due, that no payments have been made thereon, and that there are no offsets to the same.
4. REMARKS.—If claim rejected, suit must be brought within 30 days after notice or claim will be barred.

WEST VIRGINIA

1. TIME FOR FILING.—Commissioner appointed by court must publish notice to file which time will not be less than two months nor more than three months after the date of the first publication of notice.
2. WHERE FILED.—At place designated in notice.
3. MUST CLAIM BE SWORN TO.—Yes, accompanied by proper vouchers with statement of character of claim in full detail.

WISCONSIN

1. TIME FOR FILING.—Within three months from first publication of notice to creditors. Creditor who was out of state and proves by affidavit he did not receive notice may be allowed to present his claim up to entry of decree of distribution.
2. WHERE FILED.—In County Court.
3. MUST CLAIM BE SWORN TO.—Yes.
4. REMARKS.—Time to file claims may be extended for good cause, but not beyond two years from date of appointment of executor or administrator.

WYOMING

1. TIME FOR FILING.—Claims must be filed within three months after first publication of notice.
2. WHERE FILED.—In duplicate with Clerk of Court.
3. MUST CLAIM BE SWORN TO.—Yes.

Sales and Use Taxes

Sales and use taxes have been adopted by most all of the states, the District of Columbia, and by various cities including Chicago, Denver, New York, Los Angeles, San Francisco, and New Orleans. State sales and use taxes are the largest single source of state revenue for most states.

With the introduction of the sales tax, the use tax was conceived as a necessary supplement to the successful administration of the retail sales tax. Thus, if for some reason a sale at retail escaped the sales tax, the tangible personal property would be subject to the use tax. The taxing method then became symmetrical and complete.

The decision of the Supreme Court in *Scripto v. Carson,* 362 U.S. 207 (1960), and some prior decisions have opened a broad area for the enforcement of use tax collections by out of state sellers. This subject is considered at length hereinafter under "State Taxation of Interstate Transactions."

Sales Taxes

Sales Office in Taxing State.—There can be no question but that sales made from stocks of goods in the taxing state from a sales office located there are taxable, even though the goods have been manufactured outside the state and delivered to the taxing state after the sale is made. The fact that the seller does not maintain an office in the taxing state will not relieve him from liability for collection of the tax. It is a matter to be given consideration, however, in determining the jurisdiction of the state to enforce collection of the tax by the seller.

Acceptance of Order in Home Office Outside Taxing State.—The common practice of soliciting orders which do not become binding upon the seller until accepted by the home office apparently will not save the seller from the liability for sales tax under many statutes.

Selling Agents.—It has been held by the legal authorities that a seller cannot escape liability for payment of a sales tax by reason of the fact that all of its sales within the taxing jurisdiction were made through an independent exclusive sales agency having an office of its own in the taxing jurisdiction. It seems clear, therefore, that in states which have a tax on sales a seller may not escape liability by dealing through an independent sales agent in the taxing state. It is uncertain, however, whether the same conclusion would be reached in a case where the tax statute was one in the nature of an occupation and privilege tax on the privilege of engaging in the occupation of selling retail in the taxing states. There has been a ruling by the State of Illinois that a seller dealing through an independent sales agency in that state will be subject to payment of the Illinois tax.

F.O.B. Sales.—It is a common practice for sellers to ship merchandise to purchasers F.O.B. point of origin. The general rule is that unless a different intention is expressed, title to the goods sold f.o.b. passes to the buyer on delivery to the carrier or to the point to which the seller agrees to pay freight charges. Thereby delivery and passage of title takes place outside the taxing jurisdiction assuming that the F.O.B. point or the point to which the freight is paid is outside the taxing jurisdiction.

Doing Business in the Taxing State.—There seems to be little question that a seller may be required to collect or pay a sales or use tax imposed by a jurisdiction in which the seller's goods are sold whether or not such seller is "doing business" in the taxing jurisdiction. In *Felt & Tarrant Mfg. Co. v. Gallagher,* 306 U.S. 62 (1939), the Supreme Court held that an Illinois corporation could be compelled by the state of California to collect a use tax on goods sold in California even though the corporation was not doing business in that state. The same result will apparently be reached with respect to collection of sales taxes. Where the seller is not "doing business" in the taxing state, however, the problem of collecting the tax becomes a serious one for the state because of probable inability to secure jurisdiction over the seller to enforce collection of the tax.

Necessity of Interstate Transportation.—Prior to the decision in *McGoldrick v. Berwind-White Coal Mining Co.,* 309 U.S. 33 (1940), it was believed that a provision in a contract calling for transportation of the goods sold across state lines would prohibit taxation by the state to which the goods were destined. The courts had previously made a distinction between taxation of goods which came to rest within the taxing state and those goods which did not. This distinction, however, appears no longer to be of importance.

Use Taxes

Use taxes have been enacted in many jurisdictions as supplements to retail sales taxes. Such taxes are based on the purchase price of merchandise plus the cost of transportation, and are imposed upon the use within the taxing jurisdiction of taxable personal property purchased at retail.

Such taxes are primarily payable by sellers maintaining places of business within the taxing jurisdictions and making sales of property the use of which is taxable, but the ultimate burden of the tax is upon the purchaser. If the seller fails to collect the tax on behalf of the taxing jurisdiction, the tax is payable directly by the purchaser.

State Taxation of Interstate Transactions

States having a use tax require out-of-state sellers to collect the use tax on sales to customers within the state. The power of the states to impose such a requirement has been the subject of considerable litigation, but it is now established that in most cases the state may require collection of the use tax. The question presented in such cases is whether the transaction is strictly interstate in nature or whether the seller has established a sufficient connection or *nexus* with the taxing state to be subject to the state's laws. The following discussion of some of the most significant cases is intended to point out the important factors in such a determination.

In *Felt & Tarrant Mfg. Co. v. Gallagher,* the Supreme Court upheld a California statute which imposed upon an out-of-state seller the obligation to collect use

SALES AND USE TAXES

taxes on interstate sales where the goods were shipped into California. In that case the sales activities in California were carried on by two "general agents" who had specified sales areas allotted to them and were compensated by commissions on orders accepted by the plaintiff outside the state. Two offices were maintained by the agents in California, the leases to which were in the name of the plaintiff.

Nelson v. Sears Roebuck, 312 U.S. 359 (1940), involved an Iowa statute which imposed the duty to collect its use tax on every "retailer maintaining a place of business in this state and making sales of tangible personal property for use in this state." Id. at 361. Sears, Roebuck & Co. did maintain retail stores in Iowa but the use tax in question related to sales through its mail order department completely divorced from its retail stores. The orders were placed by mail by Iowa residents with out-of-state branches and deliveries were made to the customers by mail or common carrier directly from out-of-state. The Supreme Court refused to accede to Sears' contention that the imposition of the obligation to collect the use tax on its separate interstate mail order business was an unconstitutional burden on interstate commerce. *Nelson v. Montgomery Ward & Co.,* 312 U.S. 373 (1940), involved substantially similar facts and the Court reached the same conclusion as in *Sears, Roebuck & Co.* However, one further ground for the decision is noted in *Montgomery Ward:* " '[A]dvertisements have been caused to be printed by the retail stores of the petitioner (Montgomery Ward & Co.) in the State of Iowa, advertising not only retail merchandise, but the ability to complete service through the use of the catalog.' " Id. at 376. This local advertising, the Court held, was not different from the direct solicitation by local agents in the *Felt & Tarrant* case.

Miller Bros. Co. v. State of Maryland, 347 U.S. 340 (1954), appeared for a time to present a bulwark against the tide of decisions sustaining the states' power to tax interstate sales. That 5 to 4 decision, however, has been strictly limited in its subsequent application to its particular facts. Miller Bros. Co. operated a retail store in Wilmington, Delaware. It did not take orders by mail or telephone. A number of residents of nearby Maryland made purchases at the Wilmington store, some taking their goods with them, but in other cases the store made deliveries to their residence in Maryland by common carrier or by the store's own truck. In asserting its right to compel Miller Brothers to collect its use tax on sales to its residents, the state of Maryland pointed out that, (1) the seller's radio advertising from a Delaware station reached Maryland residents, (2) mail circulars were sent to former customers including Maryland residents, (3) it delivered purchases to Maryland by common carrier, and (4) it delivered purchases by its own trucks. The Court held, however, that the limited nature of the Miller Brothers activity within the taxing state was insufficient to afford jurisdiction for the imposition of the tax liability or other obligations of the Maryland use tax. But the Court also made clear that the type of activity described in the *Miller* case was to be distinguished from "invasion of exploitation of the consumer market" or "active and aggressive operation within the taxing state."

One of the most important decisions in this area was made by the United States Supreme Court in 1960 in *Scripto Inc. v. Carson,* which upheld the right of the state to require an out-of-state seller to collect the use tax in situations which had previously been believed to be protected by the interstate commerce clause. As in the case of *Northwestern States Portland Cement Association v.*

State of Minnesota, 358 U.S. 450 (1959), which was decided a year earlier and concerned state income taxes, the Court's decision in *Northwestern* brought a clamor for legislative action by Congress to reverse its effect. Perhaps less conspicuously, but not less determinedly, the cities have followed the efforts of various states to tap the source of additional revenue the Court has opened to them.

The *Scripto* decision, viewed in the light of its factual background, does not appear to be as far-reaching as the implications to be drawn from the Court's opinion and the fact that it is the most recent in a long series of decisions which have gradually whittled away the protection of interstate commerce from state taxation afforded by the Constitution and the earlier interpretation thereof by the Supreme Court.[1]

The Florida statute involved in the *Scripto* case provides (as do most of the other state statutes) that a use tax at the same rate as the sales tax, is payable on the cost price of property used, consumed or distributed or stored for such use or consumption in the state, where at the time of sale the transaction was not subject to the sales tax.[2] The purpose is to reach those sales of property coming into the state which do not take place in the taxing jurisdiction. While the responsibility for collection of the tax is imposed on the seller, the ultimate burden of payment falls upon the purchaser or user and may be collected from him by the state if not otherwise paid. Since collection by the state from individual purchasers constitutes a cumbersome and impractical task, the state statutes and regulations seek to enforce the collection of the tax from the nonresident seller. To accomplish this the Florida statute provides:

> " 'Dealer' also means and includes every person who solicits business either by representatives or by the distribution of catalogs or other advertising matter and by reason thereof receives and accepts orders from consumers in the state, and such dealer shall collect the tax imposed by this chapter from the purchaser and no action either in law or in equity on a sale or transaction as provided by the terms of this chapter may be had in this state by any such dealer unless it be affirmatively shown that the provisions of this chapter have been fully complied with." [3]

Scripto, Inc. was a Georgia corporation engaged in the manufacture of mechanical writing instruments. The Florida sales in question were handled through a division of Scripto known as Adgif Company. The Court noted that in this Adgif operation Scripto "does not (1) own, lease, or maintain any office, distributing house, warehouse or other place of business in Florida, or (2) have any regular employee or agent there. Nor does it own or maintain any bank account or stock of merchandise in the State." 362 U.S. at 209. Orders were solicited by 10 advertising specialty brokers, residents of Florida, who were described by the Supreme Court of Florida as wholesalers or jobbers. Each broker has a specific territory and a written contract providing for payment of commissions on the basis of sales made provided they were accepted by Scripto, and stating that the parties intended "to create the relationship of independent contractor." Orders taken by the brokers were signed as "salesman" and sent directly to

---

[1] *E.g., Brown v. State of Maryland,* 25 U.S. (12 Wheat) 419; *Philadelphia & Reading Ry. Co. v. Commonwealth of Pennsylvania,* 82 U.S. 232 (1873).
[2] Title XIII, Chapt. 212, Florida Statutes of 1949, as amended, Sec. 212.05 (2).
[3] Ibid. Sec. 212.06 (2) (g).

the Atlanta, Georgia, office of Scripto for acceptance. The purchaser made no payments to the salesperson.

The questions presented to the Supreme Court on these facts were (1) whether there was some jurisdictional basis for the imposition of the tax by Florida on a foreign corporation (the question of due process) and (2) whether the effect of the tax was to illegally impose a tax on interstate commerce. The validity of the tax was upheld on both counts with the concurrence of eight members of the Court and a dissent by Mr. Justice Whittaker.

The majority opinion held that the facts of this case indicated a sufficient jurisdictional basis for imposition of the tax, alluding to its decisions in *Miller Bros. Co. v. State of Maryland* where it said there must be found "some definite link, some minimum connection, between a state and the person, property or transaction it seeks to tax." 347 U.S. at 345. The "link" or "minimum connection" found here is described by the Court as follows:

> "First, the tax is a nondiscriminatory exaction levied for the use and enjoyment of property which has been purchased by Florida residents and which has actually entered into and become a part of the mass of property in that State. The burden of the tax is placed on the ultimate purchaser in Florida and it is he who enjoys the use of the property, regardless of its source. We note that the appellant is charged with no tax—save when, as here, he fails or refuses to collect it from the Florida customer. Next, as Florida points out, appellant has 10 wholesalers, jobbers, or "salesmen" conducting continuous local solicitation in Florida and forwarding the resulting orders from that State to Atlanta for shipment of the ordered goods. The only incidence of this sales transaction that is non-local is the acceptance of the order. True, the "salesmen" are not regular employees of appellant devoting full time to its service, but we conclude that such a fine distinction is without constitutional significance. The formal shift in the contractual tagging of the salesman as "independent" neither results in changing his local function of solicitation nor bears upon the effectiveness of local solicitation in securing a substantial flow of goods into Florida."

362 U.S. at 211.

On the second question the Court pointed out: " 'Of course, no state can tax the privilege of doing interstate business. . . . That is within the protection of the Commerce Clause and subject to the power of Congress. On the other hand, the mere fact that property is used for interstate commerce or has come into the owner's possession as a result of interstate commerce does not diminish the protection which he may draw from a State to the upkeep of which he may be asked to bear his fair share.' " Id. at 212 (quoting *General Trading Co. v. State Tax Comm.*, 322 U.S. 335, 338 (1944)).

The Court also found no objection to the fact that the Florida Act required the foreign corporation to act as its tax collector. This is " 'a familiar and sanctioned device,' " 362 U.S. at 212 (quoting *General Trading,* 322 U.S. at 338), it stated, and "moreover, we note that Florida reimburses appellant for its service in this regard." 362 U.S. at 212.

It was expected that further decisions would follow, broadening the areas in which local taxation could affect interstate commerce and income derived therefrom. However, in 1967 the United States Supreme Court decided the case of *National Bellas Hess, Inc. v. Department of Revenue of the State of Illinois,*

386 U.S. 753 (1967), and appeared to have placed a limit on the ability of states to apply the use tax to transactions in interstate commerce. The facts of the case are best set forth by the Court in its decision as follows:

" '[National] does not maintain in Illinois any office, distribution house, sales house, warehouse or any other place of business; it does not have in Illinois any agent, salesman, canvasser, solicitor or other type of representative to sell or take orders, to deliver merchandise, to accept payments, or to service merchandise it sells; it does not own any tangible property, real or personal, in Illinois; it has no telephone listing in Illinois and it has not advertised its merchandise for sale in newspapers, on billboards, or by radio or television in Illinois.' " Id. at 754 (quoting 34 Ill. 2d, 164, 166-167, 214 N.E. 2d, 755, 757). The Court further noted that,

> All of the contacts which National does have with the State are via the United States mail or common carrier. Twice a year catalogues are mailed to the company's active or recent customers throughout the Nation, including Illinois. This mailing is supplemented by advertising "flyers" which are occasionally mailed to past and potential customers. Orders for merchandise are mailed by the customers to National and are accepted at its Missouri plant. The ordered goods are then sent to the customers either by mail or by common carrier.

The Court held that a state may not impose the duty of use tax collection and payment upon a seller whose only connection with customers within the state is by common carrier or the United States mail. However, the Court carefully stated that the decision did not rest on the broad foundation of all that was said in the *Miller Bros.* opinion, because in the *Bellas Hess* case there was neither local advertising nor local household delivery by the seller.

From these and other decisions we may conclude that where appropriate statutes in the taxing state impose an obligation on an out-of-state seller to collect or pay the use tax, such statutes will be enforceable providing one or more of the following conditions are present: (1) The seller maintains a local office in the taxing state, (2) orders are solicited by the out-of-state seller's "salesperson" within the taxing state, (3) a stock of merchandise is maintained within the taxing state from which orders are filled, and (4) the seller has been qualified to do business in the taxing state.

It has also been said that other activities of the seller which constitute an active and aggressive selling campaign or an invasion or exploitation of the consumer market might constitute a sufficient nexus with the taxing state to enable the state to require the collection of use taxes. However, in the *Bellas Hess* case the seller had sales in the state of Illinois in the amount of $2,174,744 for the fifteen months which were in issue in the case. These sales were obtained by twice-a-year catalogue mailings, supplemented by smaller sales books or flyers, which were occasionally mailed in bulk addressed to "occupant."

Bellas Hess also sold on credit; some of these sales were instalment credit sales. However, the facts before the Court did not detail the arrangements within Illinois for credit financing or what the extent of collection activities was within the state of Illinois although it was stated that the seller had never instituted a suit in the state of Illinois.

Although the decision in the *Miller Bros.* case distinguished that situation from a situation in which there was "active and aggressive operation within

SALES AND USE TAXES

the taxing state" or "invasion or exploitation of the consumer market" in the taxing state, it would appear from the more recent *Bellas Hess* case that the activities would have to amount to extremely active operation within the taxing state or would have to involve some physical presence within the state since Bellas Hess was clearly engaged in an active operation in the state of Illinois, and yet was held to be not liable for the collection of use taxes.

This would appear to represent a more formalistic approach by the Supreme Court than has been taken in other recent cases involving the collection of use taxes.

In the *Brown Bros.* case the Court held that occasional incidents of the seller's actual presence in the taxing state were insufficient grounds for requiring collection of the tax absent exploitation or invasion of the consumer market. In the *Scripto* case the Court held that the presence of salesmen in the taxing state created a sufficient connection with the state even though the salesmen were not regular employees but were independent contractors, because "such a fine distinction is without constitutional significance." But in the *Bellas Hess* case the Court hinted that it would have upheld liability for collection of the tax if it had found even the incidental presence which occurred in the *Brown Bros.* case, and yet it did not impose liability despite the fact that the seller regularly and systematically made a large volume of sales to consumers in the taxing state, a situation which the decision in the *Brown Bros.* case indicates would result in liability.

If the Court continues to apply the approach used in the *Bellas Hess* case, the significance to sellers doing an interstate business would be considerable. It would mean that a seller could avoid the obligation to collect the use tax of a given state by carefully refraining from any actual presence in the state and conducting all contact with its customers from without the state. Then, even if the seller had a substantial volume of sales to consumers in the taxing state, it would not have to collect any use tax. On the other hand, if the seller has any activities which bring it into actual contact with the state even though such contact is incidental and sporadic, the seller may be required to collect the tax.

In *Evco v. Jones,* 409 U.S. 91 (1972), the Supreme Court again considered the question of state taxation of interstate activities. At issue was a school tax and gross receipts tax levied by New Mexico on the total proceeds received by a domestic corporation which sold educational services to an out-of-state purchaser, and in addition sold tangible personal property to the purchaser. The Court held that a state could, consistent with the commerce clause of the Federal Constitution, validly tax proceeds from services performed by a taxpayer within the taxing state even though they were sold to purchasers in another state. New Mexico however could not tax gross receipts from the sale of tangible personal property in another state since this constituted an impermissible burden on interstate commerce.

In *National Geographic Society v. California Board of Equalization,* 430 U.S. 551 (1977), National Geographic, a D.C. corporation, maintained two offices in California for the purpose of soliciting advertising for its magazine. It also maintained a mail order business out of D.C., dealing in maps, atlases and books. Although National Geographic had no California office concerned with the mail order business, the Supreme Court upheld California's imposition of a use tax on the business over plaintiff's constitutional objection.

The Court, citing the *Miller Bros.* decision, found that a state could constitutionally tax an out of state seller if some "definite link," some "minimum connection" between the seller and taxing state was shown. It found National Geographic's maintenance of two offices in California for the purpose of soliciting advertising was a sufficient link. It held this link, i.e., advertising with the taxing state did not have to be the same as the activity taxed, i.e., the mail order business. Thus, any concern doing a totally out of state mail order business may be obliged to collect a use tax if it has other minimum contacts with the taxing state, regardless of whether such activities are related to the activity taxed or not.

Federal Legislation Regulating State Taxation of Interstate Commerce

Various legislation has been introduced into Congress which establishes jurisdictional standards to determine when a state may tax interstate commerce activities. The purpose of such bills is to make uniform the application of state taxation of interstate commerce. One of the most recently introduced bills contains three factors to determine whether or not there is a "business location" in the state which would constitute the jurisdictional test for imposition of a corporate income tax. Present sales-and-use-tax jurisdictional standards would generally be preserved by codifying existing law as set out by the Supreme Court. Businesses without a "business location" in the state would be afforded relief from sales tax liability by being allowed to rely on a registration number. To date, however, no such proposed legislation has been adopted.

Most states authorize the enforcement of use tax payment or collection from, or by, out-of-state sellers. There is a definite trend by the states to step up the enforcement of these statutes or to amend the present statutes to reach such sales as come within the scope of the Supreme Court's decisions. It should also be noted that the means are available to the states to enforce such tax collections against nonresident sellers. Most states permit taxing authorities of other states to resort to their courts to collect taxes against their residents. Where a judgment has been procured against a tax debtor, it may be enforced in any state of the Union. In addition, the states may resort to attachment or similar proceedings against any property of the tax debtor within its jurisdiction. In the aforementioned *Miller v. Maryland* case, for example, the state seized the truck which was used in making deliveries in Maryland.

In an effort to solve some of the problems of the interstate taxation of commerce without federal regulation, the Council of State Governments proposed a Multistate Tax Compact which provides for voluntary state action. Twenty-one states are regular members and twelve states are associate members of the Compact. The Compact provides taxpayers with an election to apportion income either under the method provided by local state law or by use of the Uniform Division of Income for Tax Purposes Act which has been substantially adopted by the Compact.

The Compact also provides jurisdictional standards that require tax collection and payment by vendors that directly, or by agent or representative, maintain an office, maintain inventory, solicit orders, and make regular deliveries or engage in any activity in connection with leasing or servicing interstate property. The regulation provides for a Sale and Use Tax Exemption for qualifying sellers. Additionally, the Compact has proposed a model local sales and use law.

SALES AND USE TAXES

This Uniform formula, in use in many states with income tax laws, provides for the apportionment of nonbusiness income based on the location of the income producing property or on the domicile by the taxpayer. Business income is apportioned by the use of a formula which involves three factors: property, payroll and sales. Use of the Uniform formula in one state does not bind the taxpayer to its use in another.

A taxpayer whose activities in the taxing jurisdiction are solely sales in an amount less than $100,000 without any ownership or rental of real estate or tangible personal property, may elect to report and pay any tax due on a percentage of the value of gross sales instead of on net income. Sixteen states have adopted this small taxpayer option, each state setting a rate of tax.

A Multistate Tax Commission was established by the Compact to handle all matters of administration and arbitration. As yet, jurisdictional standards have not been proposed by the Compact.

The United States Supreme Court has held that the Multistate Tax Compact was not violative of the compact clause, the commerce clause or the fourteenth amendment of the Federal Constitution. *United States Steel Corp v. Multistate Tax Commission,* 434 U.S. 452 (1978).

SUMMARY OF STATE STATUTES ON SALES AND USE TAXES

The following summaries cover only sales taxes on sales of goods, wares and merchandise, and taxes on the storage, use and consumption of tangible personal property purchased at retail. The sales and use taxes of most states are also applicable to the sales of services and many specific items in addition to tangible personal property, and exemptions are made in many of the statutes with respect to enumerated classes of transactions. The space available in this volume does not permit of a detailed summary of all the provisions of the Acts or of the exemptions permitted, and reference should be had to the statutes themselves, or to the "All-State Sales Tax Reporter," published by Commerce Clearing House, Inc., or a similar service, for a complete text of the laws, interpretive decisions and the regulations.

ALABAMA

NATURE OF TAX—Gross receipts sales tax and use tax.

IMPOSITION OF TAX—Tax imposed upon every person, firm or corporation selling or leasing tangible personal property at retail, and on the storage, use or other consumption of tangible personal property purchased at retail for storage, use or consumption in the State.

RATE OF TAX—Sales tax: 4% of gross proceeds of sales. Use tax: 4% of sales price. Tax on automobiles, trucks, trailers and semi-trailers at the rate of 1½%. The tax on leases is 4%, except leases of motor vehicles which are 1½%.

WHEN RETURNS DUE—Sales: On or before the 20th of each month. Use: 20th of month following close of each calendar quarter.

LIABILITY FOR PAYMENT—Tax to be collected by seller from purchaser.

LOCAL TAXES—Various counties and cities levy a sales and use tax. A sales and use tax at the rate of 1% is imposed in counties having population of 500,000 or more.

ALASKA

NOTE—As of January 1, 1979, Alaska has no state tax although boroughs and cities may levy 3% sales tax on sales, rents and services and 3% use tax on storage, use or consumption of goods in the locality.

ARIZONA

NATURE OF TAX—Transaction Privilege Tax and Use Tax.

IMPOSITION OF TAX—Every person engaging or continuing in the business of selling tangible personal property at retail, operating a place of amusement or leasing real or personal property, is subject to a tax on the gross proceeds of sale or gross income from business.

RATE OF TAX—Sales tax 5%; Use tax 5%; Occupational Gross Income: varies.

WHEN RETURNS DUE—On or before the 20th of the month after tax accrues.
LIABILITY FOR PAYMENT—Seller liable.

ARKANSAS

NATURE OF TAX—Gross receipts (sales) tax and compensating (use) tax.

IMPOSITION OF TAX—Excise tax upon gross proceeds or gross receipts derived from all sales or rentals of tangible personal property by any person engaged in business in the State, and on the storage, use or consumption of property purchased for use in State.

RATE OF TAX—4% of gross proceeds or gross receipts of sales. Use tax 4% of sales price.

WHEN RETURNS DUE—20th day of each month.

LIABILITY FOR PAYMENT—seller to collect from purchaser.

LOCAL TAXES—Certain major cities authorized to levy a gross receipts tax not to exceed 1%. Counties are authorized to levy a 1% sales and use tax.

CALIFORNIA

NATURE OF TAX—Sales and use.

IMPOSITION OF TAX—Tax imposed upon all retailers for privilege of selling tangible personal property at retail, and upon all persons storing, using or otherwise consuming personal property purchased from a retailer.

RATE OF TAX—Sales tax 6% of gross. Use tax 6%.

WHEN RETURNS DUE—Last day of month after quarter.

LIABILITY FOR PAYMENT—Seller liable.

LOCAL TAXES—All counties and municipalities are empowered to enact a local sales and use tax at the rate of 1¼%. These taxes are administered by the State Tax Agency and returns and payments are made as part of state returns and payments. All 58 counties in California have enacted this local sales and use tax. Counties of Alameda, Contra Costa and San Francisco are authorized to levy an additional 1½% sales and use tax.

COLORADO

NATURE OF TAX—Sales and use.

IMPOSITION OF TAX—Tax is imposed for the privilege of engaging in the business of selling tangible personal property at retail, including installment and credit sales and the exchange of property and upon every person exercising the privilege of storing, using or consuming in the State any articles of tangible personal property purchased at retail.

RATE OF TAX—Sales and use tax—3%. Retailers are allowed to subtract 3⅓% of the tax remitted each month to cover collection expenses.

WHEN RETURNS DUE—Sales: 20th of every month. Use: 20th day of following month.

LIABILITY FOR PAYMENT—Tax to be collected by seller from purchaser.

LOCAL TAXES—Cities and counties have imposed local sales and use taxes of 1%-4%.

CONNECTICUT

NATURE OF TAX—Sales and use.

IMPOSITION OF TAX—Tax imposed upon all retailers for privilege of selling tangible personal property at retail, and upon every person storing, using or otherwise consuming in the State tangible personal property purchased from a retailer.

RATE OF TAX—Sales and use tax—7½%. Taxable services 7½%. No tax on the sale of and the storage, use or other consumption of certain business production machinery and equipment.

WHEN RETURNS DUE—Last day of month after quarter.

LIABILITY FOR PAYMENT—Sales tax to be collected by seller from purchaser; retailer is to collect use tax, but person storing, using or consuming property is liable until tax is paid.

DELAWARE

NATURE OF TAX—Manufacturer's License and Merchants' License. Use tax on leases of tangible personal property other than household furnishing and medical equipment.

IMPOSITION OF TAX—Every individual, copartnership or corporation which manufactures or sells at retail or wholesale is required to obtain a license and pay a tax on proceeds of goods sold for manufacturers and goods purchased for sale by merchants. Tax imposed on leases of real property.

RATE OF TAX—Manufacturer's License—$50 plus ⁴⁄₁₀% of 1% of gross receipts; Wholesaler's License generally $50 plus ⁴⁄₁₀ of 1% of the aggregate purchase price of all goods. Merchant's (Retailer's) License $50 plus ⁷⁵⁄₁₀₀ of 1% of the aggregate purchase price of all goods sold in Delaware. Use tax of 2% on rental of tangible personal property.

SALES AND USE TAXES

WHEN RETURNS DUE—Manufacturers license and merchants license: 20th of each month. Use tax on lease of tangible personal property: quarterly.
LIABILITY FOR PAYMENT—Manufacturer or merchant.

DISTRICT OF COLUMBIA
NATURE OF TAX—Sales and use.
IMPOSITION OF TAX—Tax is imposed on the gross receipts of the vendor from the sale of tangible personal property at retail, and on the use, storage or consumption of tangible personal property and services sold or purchased at retail on which gross sales tax not paid.
RATE OF TAX—Sales tax 6% of gross receipts. Use tax 6% of sales price. Sales and Use taxes on food consumed off retail premises and nonprescription drugs 2%. Rate on restaurant sales, transient accommodations and on-premises alcohol sales, 8%. Parking receipts, 12%.
WHEN RETURNS DUE—20th day of each month.
LIABILITY FOR PAYMENT—Tax to be collected by seller from purchaser.

FLORIDA
NATURE OF TAX—Sales, use, rentals and admissions.
IMPOSITION OF TAX—Applies to gross sales price of tangible personal property sold at retail in the State; to cost price of tangible personal property not sold, but used, consumed, distributed or stored for use or consumption in the State; gross proceeds from lease or rental of tangible personal property; the monthly lease or rental price paid or to be paid by lessee or rentee of tangible personal property.
RATE OF TAX—5%; a discount of 3% of the tax due is allowed as compensation for keeping records and collecting taxes.
WHEN RETURNS DUE—20th day of each month; quarterly if tax for prior quarter not over.
LIABILITY FOR PAYMENT—Sellers required to collect from purchaser, consumer or user.
LOCAL TAXES—Counties chartered before 6/1/76 can levy 1% tax.

GEORGIA
NATURE OF TAX—Sales and use.
IMPOSITION OF TAX—Applies to gross sales price of tangible personal property sold at retail in the State; to cost price of tangible personal property not sold, but used, consumed, distributed or stored for use or consumption in the State; gross proceeds from lease or rental of tangible personal property; the monthly lease or rental price paid or to be paid by lessee or rentee of tangible personal property; and the amount paid or charged for sales of taxable services.
RATE OF TAX—3%.
WHEN RETURNS DUE—20th day of following month.
LIABILITY FOR PAYMENT—Sellers required to collect from purchaser, consumer or user.
LOCAL TAXES—Cities and Counties may impose 1% tax. Designated counties and the city of Atlanta may levy a 1% sales-use tax subject to voter approval.

HAWAII
NATURE OF TAX—General Excise and Use Tax.
IMPOSITION OF TAX—Applies to gross receipts from sales of tangible property, manufacturing and other activities; also to consumption or use of tangible personal property.
RATE OF TAX—General Excise tax rates vary; e.g., retail sales—4%; manufacturers—½ of 1%; general use tax, 4%; use tax on imports for resale, ½ of 1%.
WHEN RETURNS DUE—Last day of following month.
LIABILITY FOR PAYMENT—In case of sales, taxes collected by seller from purchaser.

IDAHO
NATURE OF TAX—Sales and use tax.
IMPOSITION OF TAX—Sales tax on the sale at retail of tangible personal property and use tax on the storage, use or other consumption of tangible personal property.
RATE OF TAX—Sales tax: 4% of sales price. Use tax: 4% of value of property. Recent sales price is presumptive evidence of value.
WHEN RETURNS DUE—By the 20th of every month.
LIABILITY FOR PAYMENT—Seller to collect from purchaser.

ILLINOIS
NATURE OF TAX—Retailer's occupation (sales) tax, use tax, service occupation tax and service use tax.

IMPOSITION OF TAX—Tax is imposed upon gross receipts from sales of tangible personal property at retail by all persons engaging in such business in the State. Use tax is imposed on privilege of using property purchased at retail on which no sales tax was paid.

RATE OF TAX—5%. The cities are authorized to levy sales taxes at a rate not to exceed 1%. Service occupation tax rate 5%, and service use tax 5%. Use tax: 5%. Retailer can deduct 2% of tax due for administrative expenses.

WHEN RETURNS DUE—End of preceding month.

LIABILITY FOR PAYMENT—Sales tax to be paid by seller. Use tax is to be collected by seller from purchaser, but if not so collected, user is liable.

LOCAL TAXES—Cities and counties authorized to levy 1% sales and use tax.

INDIANA

NATURE OF TAX—Sales and use tax.

IMPOSITION OF TAX—Sales tax imposed on the gross income derived from transactions of retail merchants constituting selling at retail as defined in the statute. Use tax imposed on the storage, use or other consumption in this State of tangible personal property purchased at retail.

RATE OF TAX—Sales tax: 5% of gross from retail sales. Use tax: 5% of sales price.

WHEN RETURNS DUE—30th day of following month.

LIABILITY FOR PAYMENT—Seller to collect from purchaser. Retail merchants allowed to deduct specified collection allowance.

IOWA

NATURE OF TAX—Sales and use tax.

IMPOSITION OF TAX—Tax imposed upon the gross receipts from all sales of tangible personal property consisting of goods, wares or merchandise sold at retail and services, and upon all persons using in the State tangible personal property purchased at retail and on the use, consumption and storage of tangible property.

RATE OF TAX—Sales tax: 4% of gross receipts from retail sales. Use tax: 4% of purchase price.

WHEN RETURNS DUE—Last day of month following end of quarter.

LIABILITY FOR PAYMENT—Seller to collect from purchaser.

KANSAS

NATURE OF TAX—Sales and use tax.

IMPOSITION OF TAX—Tax imposed for the privilege of engaging in the business of selling tangible personal property at retail in the State, performing services, and for the privilege of using, storing or consuming within the State articles of tangible personal property purchased at retail.

RATE OF TAX—3%.

WHEN RETURNS DUE—25th of month.

LIABILITY FOR PAYMENT—Seller to collect tax from purchaser, consumer or user, but if not so collected, purchaser or user is liable.

LOCAL TAXES—Counties are authorized to levy a local sales tax at a rate not to exceed 1%. Cities are authorized to levy a local sales tax of .5% or 1% subject to referendum.

KENTUCKY

NATURE OF TAX—Sales and use tax. (Veteran's Bonus Sales and Use Tax).

IMPOSITION OF TAX—Tax on privilege of making "retail sales" or "sales at retail"; excise tax imposed on storage, use or other consumption in the state of tangible personal property.

RATE OF TAX—5%.

WHEN RETURNS DUE—20th day after calendar quarter.

LIABILITY FOR PAYMENT—Sales tax may be collected from consumer by the retailer. Use tax to be collected from consumer but consumer is also liable until tax is paid.

LOCAL TAXES—Mass transit authorities may levy, subject to voter approval, a ½% sales and use tax.

LOUISIANA

NATURE OF TAX—Sales and use tax.

IMPOSITION OF TAX—Imposed on the sale, use, lease or rental of tangible personality. Also, on sales of services.

RATE OF TAX—4%.

WHEN RETURNS DUE—20th day of each month. Quarterly if average liability less than $100 a month.

LIABILITY FOR PAYMENT—Tax to be collected by the seller from the purchaser or consumer.

SALES AND USE TAXES

MAINE
NATURE OF TAX—Sales and use.
IMPOSITION OF TAX—Sales taxes imposed upon all persons selling tangible property at retail within the State. Use tax is imposed on the storage, use or other consumption in the State of tangible, personal property purchased at retail.
RATE OF TAX—Sales tax 5%. Use tax 5%.
WHEN RETURNS DUE—15th day of following month.
LIABILITY FOR PAYMENT—Sales tax to be collected by seller from purchaser. Use tax is payable by the person storing, using or otherwise consuming the property.

MARYLAND
NATURE OF TAX—Sales and use tax.
IMPOSITION OF TAX—Tax on retail sale of tangible personal property and services, storage or use thereof in state, meals, food or drink for human consumption except as sold for consumption by churches, religious organizations, schools, colleges and hospitals, bona fide grocery store or market with no facilities for eating on premises.
RATE OF TAX—Sales tax 5%. Use tax 5%.
WHEN RETURNS DUE—20th day of following month.
LIABILITY FOR PAYMENT—Tax to be collected by the seller from the purchaser.

MASSACHUSETTS
NATURE OF TAX—Sales and use tax.
IMPOSITION OF TAX—Tax imposed on the gross receipts of the sale at retail of tangible personal property and on the storage, use or other consumption of tangible personal property.
RATE OF TAX—5% of sales price of property.
WHEN RETURNS DUE—20th day of following month.
LIABILITY FOR PAYMENT—Seller to collect from purchaser except for motor vehicles, in which case purchaser pays directly to Registrar.

MICHIGAN
NATURE OF TAX—Occupational retail sales and use tax.
IMPOSITION OF TAX—Tax is imposed upon all persons engaged in the business of making sales at retail, for the privilege of engaging in such business, and upon every person storing, using or consuming tangible personal property in the State.
RATE OF TAX—4%.
WHEN RETURNS DUE—15th day of each month.
LIABILITY FOR PAYMENT—Seller to collect from purchaser.

MINNESOTA
NATURE OF TAX—Sales and use tax.
IMPOSITION OF TAX—Tax is on the sale, use, storage or rental of tangible personal property, the sale of meals, admission to places of amusement or athletic events, the furnishing of transit lodging in hotels, motels, etc. and the furnishing of utility services.
RATE OF TAX—6%. Farm machinery 4%. 8.5% on liquor.
WHEN RETURN IS DUE—25th day of following month.
LIABILITY FOR PAYMENT—Retailer to collect tax from purchaser.
LOCAL TAXES—Duluth has imposed a 1% sales and use tax; Minneapolis and Bloomington have a 3% tax on admissions, amusements and transient lodgings; St. Paul has 3% tax on room charges.

MISSISSIPPI
NATURE OF TAX—Sales; salesman's sales, compensating use, compensating wholesale tax.
IMPOSITION OF TAX—Tax is imposed upon the gross proceeds of sales of tangible personal property at wholesale or retail, and for the privilege of use, storage or consumption within the State of tangible personal property purchased, manufactured or rented, and (wholesale compensating tax) for the privilege of engaging in business as a retailer purchasing at wholesale tangible personal property outside the state for sale by retail in the state.
RATE OF TAX—Occupational sales and use taxes are 6% on tangible personal property, with lower rates on certain enumerated items; wholesale rate is 5/8 of 1% on tangible personal property with higher rates on particular items; salesman's tax is 3%.
WHEN RETURNS DUE—20th day of each month.

LIABILITY FOR PAYMENT—Seller.
LOCAL TAXES—Certain cities and counties are authorized to impose specific taxes, e.g., "Convention tax" upon hotels.

MISSOURI

NATURE OF TAX—Sales and use tax.
IMPOSITION OF TAX—Tax imposed upon every retail sale in the State of tangible personal property or services and for the privilege of storing, using, or consuming within the State any article of tangible personal property.
RATE OF TAX—4.225% of retail sales.
WHEN RETURNS DUE—Quarterly on last day of January, April, July and October.
LIABILITY FOR PAYMENT—Seller to collect sales tax from purchaser, but purchaser also personally liable. Use tax to be collected by the seller from the purchaser.
LOCAL TAXES—City and county sales tax authorized.

MONTANA

Only a motor vehicle and cigarette sales tax.

NEBRASKA

NATURE OF TAX—Sales and use.
IMPOSITION OF TAX—Gross receipts from all sales, leases, storage, use, consumption and rentals of tangible personal property, gross receipts of public utilities and the gross receipts from sales admission tickets.
RATE OF TAX—3½%.
WHEN RETURNS DUE—25th of the month.
LIABILITY FOR PAYMENT—Seller to collect tax from purchaser.
LOCAL TAXES—City sales and use taxes authorized.

NEVADA

NATURE OF TAX—Sales and use.
IMPOSITION OF TAX—Tax imposed for the privilege of selling tangible personal property at retail, and for the privilege of using, storing, or consuming tangible personal property purchased at retail.
RATE OF TAX—2% state sales-use tax, plus 2¼% statewide county tax, plus 1½% local school support tax.
WHEN RETURNS DUE—Last day of following month.
LIABILITY FOR PAYMENT—Seller to collect tax from purchaser.
LOCAL TAXES—Counties and Carson City may levy a 5% sales and use tax.

NEW HAMPSHIRE

New Hampshire imposes a tax at a rate of 7% on meals and rooms only.

NEW JERSEY

NATURE OF TAX—Sales and use.
IMPOSITION OF TAX—Sales tax on the retail sale of tangible personal property and service and storage charges. Use tax on the use, storage and consumption of personal property or service not subject to the sales tax.
RATE OF TAX—Sales and use tax 6%.
WHEN RETURNS DUE—Monthly by 20th day if tax exceeds $100 per month, quarterly if tax is less than $100 per month on average.
LIABILITY FOR PAYMENT—Seller to collect from purchaser.
LOCAL TAXES—Localities may impose sales-use tax on incity transactions.

NEW MEXICO

NATURE OF TAX—Gross receipts and compensating tax.
IMPOSITION OF TAX—Tax is a privilege tax imposed upon persons engaging or continuing in business activities in the State, and is imposed upon gross receipts, and an excise tax is imposed on the storage, use or consumption in the State of tangible personal property purchased from a retailer for storage, use or other consumption.
RATE OF TAX—Gross receipts and compensating tax: 3¾%.
WHEN RETURNS DUE—25th day of following month.

SALES AND USE TAXES

LIABILITY FOR PAYMENT—Seller to collect from purchaser.

OCCUPATIONAL LICENSES—A license tax or occupation tax is imposed upon dealers in merchandise other than liquors, the amount of the tax varying with volume of sales. Minimum $5: maximum $150.

LOCAL TAXES—Certain cities and counties authorized to impose a gross receipts tax not to exceed 1%.

NEW YORK

NATURE OF TAX—Sales and use.

IMPOSITION OF TAX—Tax on the retail sale of any tangible personal property not specifically exempted, on sales other than sales for resale of electricity, steam, gas and refrigeration, on the sale of certain services, on the sale of food and drinks to be consumed on the premises including cover charges and entertainment charges and on admission charges in excess of 10¢ to all other amusements not otherwise taxed.

Use tax on the use of tangible personal property purchased at retail, on the use of tangible personal property manufactured or assembled by the user, and on certain services.

RATE OF TAX—4% plus up to 4¼% local tax.

WHEN RETURNS DUE—20th day of the following month if the seller's taxable receipts total $300,000 or more during only one of the four preceding quarters; otherwise 20th day of the following quarter.

LIABILITY FOR PAYMENT—Seller required to collect from purchaser.

LOCAL TAXES—Local county and city sales and use tax may be applicable.

Some cities and counties also have sales and use taxes. The law governing local sales and use taxes is identical to that of the State Tax Law, except that some of the exemptions from the tax vary from those provided in the state law. The maximum combined city and county tax may not exceed 4¼%. New York City imposes an 8¼% tax on the receipts from the service of parking or storing motor vehicles.

RATE OF CITY SALES TAXES—Fulton 3%, Hornell 3%, Kingston 2%, New York City 4¼%, Oswego 3%, Poughkeepsie 3¼%, Saratoga Springs 3%, Troy 3%, Yonkers 4¼%.

RATE OF COUNTY TAXES—Albany 3%, Broome County 3%, Chemung County 3%, Erie County 3%, Jefferson County 3%, Monroe County 3%, Westchester 1¼%.

NORTH CAROLINA

NATURE OF TAX—Sales and use.

IMPOSITION OF TAX—Tax imposed for the privilege of engaging or continuing the business of selling tangible personal property either at wholesale or retail, and on every person storing, using or otherwise consuming in the State tangible personal property purchased or received from a retailer either within or without the State, and on lessors of lodgings for less than 90 continuous days.

RATE OF TAX—Sales tax: Retail sales, 3% of total gross sales. Use tax: 3% of sales price. Lower rates on certain items.

WHEN RETURNS DUE—15th day of each month.

LIABILITY FOR PAYMENT—Seller liable.

LOCAL TAXES—Local county sales or use tax may be applicable in amount of 1%.

NORTH DAKOTA

NATURE OF TAX—Sales and use.

IMPOSITION OF TAX—Gross receipts from all sales, leasing or renting of tangible personal property consisting of goods, wares or merchandise sold at retail and furnishing gas, steam, electricity or communicative services and on admissions to places of amusement and hotel accommodations for periods of less than 30 days, and on the storage, use or consumption in the State of tangible personal property purchased at retail for storage, use or consumption in the State.

RATE OF TAX—Sales and use tax 5% except farm equipment and mobile homes, 3%; alcohol, 5%.

WHEN RETURNS DUE—Last day of month following end of quarter.

LIABILITY FOR PAYMENT—Seller to collect tax from purchaser.

OHIO

NATURE OF TAX—Sales and use.

IMPOSITION OF TAX—Tax is imposed on each retail sale made in the State of tangible personal property, and an excise tax is imposed on the storage, use or other consumption in the State of tangible personal property for storage, use or other consumption in the State, and an additional tax of 4% is imposed for the privilege of engaging in the business of making retail sales within the State.

RATE OF TAX—Sales tax: 5% of gross receipts from retail sales; Use tax: 5% of sales price.

WHEN RETURNS DUE—Sales tax: 23rd day of each month (seller); Use tax: 15th day following end of quarter (purchaser).

LIABILITY FOR PAYMENT—Seller to collect from purchaser for sales tax; purchaser liable for use tax.

LOCAL TAXES—Counties may impose a ½% sales and use tax.

OKLAHOMA

NATURE OF TAX—Sales and use.

IMPOSITION OF TAX—An excise tax is imposed upon the gross proceeds or gross receipts derived from all sales of tangible personal property other than sales for resale, and on every person storing, using or otherwise consuming within the State tangible personal property purchased or brought into the State on the storage, use or other consumption in the State of such property.

RATE OF TAX—Sales tax: 3.25% of gross receipts from retail sales. Use tax: 3% of purchase price.

WHEN RETURNS DUE—Sales tax: 15th day of following month; Use tax: 20th day of following month.

LIABILITY FOR PAYMENT—Seller to collect tax from purchaser.

LOCAL TAXES—Local sales taxes may be levied.

OREGON

No State sales or use tax.

PENNSYLVANIA

NATURE OF TAX—Sales and use.

IMPOSITION OF TAX—Tax on the purchase, use, storage or other consumption of certain tangible personal property and utility services.

RATE OF TAX—6%.

WHEN RETURNS DUE—20th day at end of quarter. Consult Pennsylvania statutes §7217, et seq. for detailed information on filing of returns.

LIABILITY FOR PAYMENT—Seller to collect from purchaser.

LOCAL TAXES—Philadelphia, Pittsburgh and many other cities, townships and school districts levy sales taxes.

RHODE ISLAND

NATURE OF TAX—Sales and use.

IMPOSITION OF TAX—Tax imposed upon gross receipts of retailers from sales and rentals of tangible personal property at retail, including rental of living quarters for 30 days or less, and on the storage, use or other consumption in the State of tangible personal property purchased from any retailer.

RATE OF TAX—Sales tax: 6% of gross receipts of seller. Use tax: 6% of sales price. Special exemption for sales of tools, dies, molds, machinery and equipment.

WHEN RETURNS DUE—20th day of each month. Quarterly reports may be used directly in industry to manufacture goods for sale, permitted.

LIABILITY FOR PAYMENT—Seller to collect tax from purchaser, consumer or user.

SOUTH CAROLINA

NATURE OF TAX—Sales and use.

IMPOSITION OF TAX—Tax levied on the gross proceeds of sales or leases of tangible personal property or gross receipts of any business which the State is not prohibited from taxing under the constitutional laws of the United States or under the Constitution of South Carolina, and on various other specified articles; and on the storage, use or other consumption in the State of tangible personal property purchased at retail for storage, use or other consumption in the State.

RATE OF TAX—5%.

WHEN RETURNS DUE—20th day of following month for sales tax, and 20th day of month after end of calendar quarter for use tax.

LIABILITY FOR PAYMENT—Seller liable.

SOUTH DAKOTA

NATURE OF TAX—Retail sales and use.

IMPOSITION OF TAX—Sales tax imposed upon those engaged in the State in making retail sales

SALES AND USE TAXES 25-17

or furnishing certain designated services. Use tax imposed on the privilege of the use, storage and consumption within the State of tangible personal property purchased for use in State, sale of which not subject to South Dakota Retail Sales Tax.
RATE OF TAX—4%. 3% on farm machinery.
WHEN RETURNS DUE—Bimonthly by last day of month.
LIABILITY FOR PAYMENT—Seller liable.

TENNESSEE
NATURE OF TAX—Sales and use.
IMPOSITION OF TAX—Tax imposed on every person exercising the privilege of engaging in the business of selling tangible personal property at retail in the State, and on every person who exercises the privilege of storing for use or consumption in the State any article of tangible personal property.
RATE OF TAX—5½%.
WHEN RETURNS DUE—On or before 20th day of the next month.
LIABILITY FOR PAYMENT—Seller liable.
LOCAL TAXES—Counties and cities are authorized to levy a tax on the same privileges subject to state sales and use tax. This rate is not to exceed 2¼%.

TEXAS
NATURE OF TAX—Sales and use.
IMPOSITION OF TAX—Tax is imposed on each separate sale of tangible personal property at retail within the State. Excise tax on storage, use or other consumption of tangible personal property purchased, leased or rented after September 1, 1961 and for which sales tax has not been paid.
RATE OF TAX—4.125%.
WHEN RETURNS DUE—On or before the 20th day of the month following the end of each month. If less than $500 owed for month or $1500 for quarter, then due on 20th of month of following quarter.
LIABILITY FOR PAYMENT—Seller to collect from purchaser.
LOCAL TAXES—Cities, towns and villages are permitted to levy a 1% sales and use tax.

UTAH
NATURE OF TAX—Sales and use.
IMPOSITION OF TAX—Excise tax upon gross receipts of sales of tangible personal property at retail, of gas, electricity or other fuel, admission to places of amusement, and certain services, and on the storage, use or other consumption in the State of tangible personal property for storage, use or other consumption in the State.
RATE OF TAX—4⅝% till June 30, 1987, then 4½%.
WHEN RETURNS DUE—30th day following end of quarterly period.
LIABILITY FOR PAYMENT—Seller to collect from purchaser, consumer or user.
LOCAL TAXES—Counties, cities and towns may levy a sales tax of ⅞ of 1%.

VERMONT
NATURE OF TAX—Sales and use.
IMPOSITION OF TAX—Tax on retail sales on all tangible personal property and services or use thereof in state; food consumed off the premises is exempted.
RATE OF TAX—4% for both.
WHEN RETURNS DUE—On 30th day of the following month for sales and use tax, and the 28th of February. Last day of month following quarter for meals and room tax.
LIABILITY—Seller to collect from purchaser.

VIRGINIA
NATURE OF TAX—Sales and use.
IMPOSITION OF TAX—Sales tax on the gross receipts of selling at retail or distributing tangible personal property or renting or furnishing certain things or services. Use tax on the use or consumption of tangible personal property in the State or the storage of such property outside the State for use in the State.
RATE OF TAX—4% (including 1% local tax).
WHEN RETURNS DUE—20th day of following month.
LIABILITY FOR PAYMENT—Tax is paid by the dealer but the dealer shall collect the tax from the purchaser or consumer.
LOCAL TAXES—Cities and counties are authorized to levy a local merchants' license tax and local sales and use tax limited to 1%.

WASHINGTON

NATURE OF TAX—Sales and use.

IMPOSITION OF TAX—Tax levied on each retail sale in the State by persons engaged in business, and for using within the State any article of tangible personal property purchased at retail, or produced or manufactured for commercial use.

RATE OF TAX—6.5%.

WHEN RETURNS DUE—15th day after end of month.

LIABILITY FOR PAYMENT—Seller to collect from purchaser.

BUSINESS TAX—A tax at rate of ⅛ of 1% plus 4% surcharge is imposed on manufacturers, wholesalers and retailers based on value of products manufactured or sales price. Rates applicable to other types of business vary.

LOCAL TAXES—Various cities levy tax based on gross receipts not to exceed 5%.

WEST VIRGINIA

NATURE OF TAX—Sales and use.

IMPOSITION OF TAX—Excise tax upon every sale of tangible personal property and on the use within the State of tangible personal property furnished or delivered within the State to consumers or users within the State.

RATE OF TAX—5%.

WHEN RETURNS DUE—Sales tax: 15th day of each month; Use tax: 15th day of month following end of quarter.

LIABILITY FOR PAYMENT—Seller required to collect tax from purchaser.

WISCONSIN

NATURE OF TAX—Sales and use.

IMPOSITION OF TAX—Sales tax on gross receipts from sale, lease or rental. Use tax on storage, use or consumption, of tangible personal property.

RATE OF TAX—5%.

WHEN RETURNS DUE—Last day of month following end of quarter.

LIABILITY FOR PAYMENT—Seller to collect from purchaser.

LOCAL TAXES—Counties authorized to levy local sales tax at rate ½ of 1%.

WYOMING

NATURE OF TAX—Sales and use.

IMPOSITION OF TAX—Excise tax upon every retail sale of tangible property, and on the storage, use or other consumption in the State of tangible personal property purchased from a retailer for storage, use or other consumption in the State.

RATE OF TAX—3%.

WHEN RETURNS DUE—Last day of following month.

LIABILITY FOR PAYMENT—Seller to collect from purchaser.

LOCAL TAXES—Counties may impose sales tax of ½ of 1% or 1%.

Fraudulent Conveyances— Bulk Transfers

26

The collection of accounts receivable is one of the most serious problems confronting businesses, particularly during times of adverse economic conditions. Debtors since time immemorial have conceived many plans to defraud honest merchants. While the methods employed have been numerous and varied, most have their foundation in the practice of conveying assets of the debtor to a third party in order to render the debtor "judgment proof."

Legislators have realized the difficulties surrounding collection of accounts and from time to time have passed laws in an attempt to frustrate dishonest debtors. The Uniform Fraudulent Conveyance Act, which has been adopted in 25 states,[1] is a codification of the principles of law governing fraudulent conveyances. Unif. Fraudulent Conveyance Act §§ 1-14, 7A U.L.A. 164-366 (1978). The analysis of the Act in the succeeding pages will give the creditor a general understanding of creditors' rights and remedies with respect to fraudulent conveyances.

The Act declares that, "[e]very conveyance made and every obligation incurred by a person who is or will be thereby rendered insolvent is fraudulent as to creditors without regard to his actual intent if the conveyance is made or the obligation is incurred without a fair consideration." Id. § 4, 7A U.L.A. 205.

Insolvency under the Act arises when the present fair salable value of a person's assets is less than the amount that will be required to pay his probable liability on his existing debts as they become due and mature. Id. § 2, 7A U.L.A. 176. It is to be noted that not every conveyance which renders one insolvent is fraudulent as to creditors. If the property is conveyed, or an antecedent debt is satisfied, in good faith, or if a conveyance be made to secure a present advance or antecedent debt in an amount not disproportionately small as compared with the value of the property conveyed, the conveyance is not within the scope of the Act and may not be attacked by creditors. Id. § 3, 7A U.L.A. 181.

Distinction in Intent

A distinction must be drawn between actual intent to defraud and intent as presumed in law. In the former instance, every conveyance is fraudulent as to both present and future creditors. Id. § 7, 7A U.L.A. 242. In the latter instance, the presumption of intent to defraud arises from the facts and circumstances surrounding the transaction. Particular stress is laid on the value of the property conveyed and the consideration received therefor.

Creditors whose claims have matured "may, as against any person except a

---

[1] Arizona, California, Delaware, Idaho, Maryland, Massachusetts, Michigan, Minnesota, Montana, Nebraska, Nevada, New Hampshire, New Jersey, New Mexico, New York, North Dakota, Ohio, Oklahoma, Pennsylvania, South Dakota, Tennessee, Utah, Washington, Wisconsin, and Wyoming.

purchaser for fair consideration without knowledge of the fraud at the time of the purchase, or one who has derived title immediately . . . from such a purchaser, (a) Have the conveyance set aside or obligation annulled to the extent necessary to satisfy his claim, or (b) Disregard the conveyance and attach or levy execution upon the property conveyed." Id. § 9, 7A U.L.A. 304. When a creditor's claim has not matured, he may proceed in a court of competent jurisdiction against any person whom he could have proceeded had his claim matured and pursue the following remedies: (1) Have a receiver appointed to take charge of the property; (2) Restrain the defendant from disposing of his property; (3) Have the conveyance set aside or the obligation annulled; or (4) Obtain any other relief required by the circumstances of the case. Id. § 10, 7A U.L.A. 358.

In those jurisdictions where the Uniform Fraudulent Conveyance Act has not been enacted, the rights of creditors are governed by the common law and statutes, which usually afford remedies similar to those provided for by the Act.

The common law principal of fraudulent conveyance is predicated on the Statute of Elizabeth, adopted in 1570. This statute provides that every conveyance made with the "intent to delay, hinder, or defraud creditors . . . is void." 13 Eliz., ch. 5, § 1. In actuality, however, a conveyance is not void, but only voidable upon application to the courts by creditors of the transferor. The courts regard certain acts known as "badges of fraud" as *prima facie* evidence of intent to defraud. Such badges of fraud include conveyances to family members, transfers by which the debtor retains possession, transfers made while a debtor is involved in litigation or conveyances when one is about to become heavily indebted. The National Conference of Commissioners on Uniform State Laws in 1984 approved the Uniform Fraudulent Transfer Act which supersedes the Uniform Fraudulent Conveyance Act. The Uniform Fraudulent Transfer Act is more complete and comprehensive than the Uniform Fraudulent Conveyance Act. To date it has only been adopted by the states of Hawaii and Oregon.

BULK TRANSFERS

Statutes regulating the sale or transfer of stocks of goods, wares, merchandise and fixtures in bulk have been enacted in every state as part of the Uniform Commercial Code,[1] largely at the instance of the National Association of Credit Management.

These statutes are not designed to prevent a merchant from selling his stock of merchandise and fixtures to another, but only to require that the intention to make such a sale shall be made known in time to give the creditors of the seller an opportunity to protect themselves against possible fraud. In most states, notice of the proposed sale must be given to all creditors personally or by registered mail, but in a few states it is only necessary that notice of the intended transfer be recorded.

The provisions of the Uniform Commercial Code relating to "Bulk Transfers" are to be found in Article 6. The official text of the Code is set forth below with notations made of the major revisions of the various state statutes. The reader is advised to consult the local statute for the more technical variations from the Code.

---

[1] Louisiana also has laws regulating bulk sales.

UNIFORM COMMERCIAL CODE

(Provisions relating to Bulk Transfers)

SECTION 6-101. *Short Title.*—This Article shall be known and may be cited as Uniform Commercial Code—Bulk Transfers.

SECTION 6-102. *"Bulk Transfer"; Transfers of Equipment; Enterprises Subject to This Article; Bulk Transfers Subject to This Article.*—(1) A "bulk transfer" is any transfer in bulk and not in the ordinary course of the transferor's business of a major part of the materials, supplies, merchandise or other inventory (Section 9-109) of an enterprise subject to this Article.[1]

(2) A transfer of a substantial part of the equipment (Section 9-109) of such an enterprise is a bulk transfer [if it is made in connection with a bulk transfer of inventory, but not otherwise].[2]

(3) The enterprises subject to this Article are all those whose principal business is [3] the sale of merchandise from stock, including those who manufacture what they sell.

(4) Except as limited by the following section all bulk transfers of goods located within this state are subject to this Article.[4]

SECTION 6-103. *Transfers Excepted from this Article.*—The following transfers are not subject to this Article:

(1) Those made to give security for the performance of an obligation;

(2) General assignments for the benefit of all the creditors of the transferor, and subsequent transfers by the assignee thereunder;

(3) Transfers in settlement or realization of a lien or other security interests;

(4) Sales by executors, administrators, receivers, trustees in bankruptcy, or any public officer under judicial process;

(5) Sales made in the course of judicial or administrative proceedings for the dissolution or reorganization of a corporation and of which notice is sent to the creditors of the corporation pursuant to order of the court or administrative agency;

(6) Transfers to a person maintaining a known place of business in this State

---

[1] In New York and Oregon, subsec. (1) includes, " 'Bulk transfer' shall also include a transfer out of the ordinary course of business of a major part of the goods, wares and merchandise of a restaurant, or other food dispensing establishment."
In Oklahoma, a bulk transfer also includes a transfer of major part of the services of an enterprise.

[2] Material in brackets is not included in the statute of California. In Washington, subsec. (2) includes bulk transfers "whether or not made in connection with a bulk transfer of inventory, merchandise, materials or supplies."

[3] District of Columbia, Florida, Maryland, Massachusetts, Michigan, Nebraska, Nevada, New Hampshire, New York, North Dakota, Ohio, Oregon, and Washington include food dispensing establishments in subsec. (3). Maryland further includes all sellers of alcoholic beverages.
In California bakers, cafe or restaurant owners, garage owners, and cleaners and dyers and those who manufacture what they sell are covered by subsec. (3).
Idaho includes hotels, restaurants, barber shops and beauty salons to those businesses covered by subsec. (3) while Washington includes restaurants, cafes, beer parlors, taverns, hotels, clubs and gasoline service stations. Wisconsin includes "business by retailers of alcoholic beverages." Delaware includes restaurants within bulk transfer.

[4] California adds a subsec. (5) providing that the word "transfer does not include the creation or modification of a security interest."

who becomes bound to pay the debts of the transferor in full and gives public notice of that fact, and who is solvent after becoming so bound; [1]

(7) A transfer to a new business enterprise organized to take over and continue the business, if public notice of the transaction is given and the new enterprise assumes the debts of the transferor and he receives nothing from the transaction except an interest in the new enterprise junior to the claims of creditors; [2]

(8) Transfers of property which is exempt from execution.[3]

Public notice under subsection (6) or subsection (7) may be given by publishing once a week for two consecutive weeks in a newspaper of general circulation where the transferor had its principal place of business in this state an advertisement including the names and addresses of the transferor and transferee and the effective date of the transfer.[4]

SECTION 6-104. *Schedule of Property, List of Creditors.*—(1) Except as provided with respect to auction sales (Section 6-108), a bulk transfer subject to this Article is ineffective against any creditor of the transferor unless:

(a) The transferree requires the transferor to furnish a list of his existing creditors prepared as stated in this section; and
(b) The parties prepare a schedule of the property transferred sufficient to identify it; and
(c) The transferee preserves the list and schedule for six months next following the transfer and permits inspection of either or both and copying therefrom at all reasonable hours by any creditor of the transferor, or files the list and schedule in (a public office to be here identified).[5]

(2) The list of creditors must be signed and sworn to or affirmed by the transferor or his agent. It must contain the names and business addresses of all creditors of the transferor, with the amounts when known, and also the names of all persons who are known to the transferor to assert claims against him even though such claims are disputed. If the transferor is the obligor of an outstanding issue of bonds, debentures or the like as to which there is an indenture trustee, the list of creditors need include only the name and address of the indenture trustee and the aggregate outstanding principal amount of the issue.

(3) Responsibility for the completeness and accuracy of the list of creditors rests on the transferor, and the transfer is not rendered ineffective by errors or omissions therein unless the transferee is shown to have had knowledge.[6]

---

[1] In California subsec. (6) reads, "Transfers of property which is exempt from enforcement of a money judgment."

[2] California omits subsec. (7) and instead exempts a transfer of goods in a warehouse where a warehouse receipt has been issued and where a copy is kept at the warehouseman's principal place of business and at the warehouse where the goods are being stored.

[3] California exempts those transfers subject to Article 5 of Chapter 6 of Division 9 of the California Business and Professions Code.

[4] This subparagraph has been adopted in Alaska, Georgia, Nebraska, Oklahoma, Oregon, Rhode Island. Georgia adds a subsection similar to this subparagraph providing for public notice.

Washington adds a subsec. (9) exempting sales subject to public auction on lien foreclosures.

[5] See listing, *infra,* p. 27-3, showing place of filing or recording in the respective states.

[6] California omits Section 6-104. Connecticut adds a new section that any bulk transfer involving merchandise of a food dispensing establishment shall be ineffective against claims of an unsecured creditor unless proper notice is given to the unsecured creditor.

SECTION 6-105. *Notice to Creditors.*—In addition to the requirements of the preceding section, any bulk transfer subject to this Article except one made by auction sale (Section 6-108) is ineffective against any creditor of the transferor unless at least ten days before he takes possession of the goods or pays for them, whichever happens first, the transferee gives notice of the transfer in the manner and to the persons hereafter provided (Section 6-107).[1]

SECTION 6-106.[2] *Application of the Proceeds.*—In addition to the requirements of the two preceding Sections:

(1) Upon every bulk transfer subject to this Article for which new consideration becomes payable except those made by sale at auction it is the duty of the transferee to assure that such consideration is applied so far as necessary to pay those debts of the transferor which are either shown on the list furnished by the transferor (Section 6-104) or filed in writing in the place stated in the notice (Section 6-107) within thirty days after the mailing of such notice. This duty of the transferee runs to all the holders of such debts, and may be enforced by any of them for the benefit of all.

(2) If any of said debts are in dispute the necessary sum may be withheld from distribution until the dispute is settled or adjudicated.

(3) If the consideration payable is not enough to pay all of the said debts in full distribution shall be pro rata.[3]

(4) The transferee may within 10 days after he takes possession of the goods pay the consideration into the (specify court) in the county where the transferor had its principal place of business in this state and thereafter may discharge his duty under this section by giving notice by registered or certified mail to all the persons to whom the duty runs that the consideration has been paid into that court and that they should file their claims there. On motion of any interested party, the court may order the distribution of the consideration to the persons entitled to it.[4]

---

[1] In California, notice must be given as provided in Section 6-106(6), where applicable, and Section 6-107. Under Section 6-107, no mailing of notice is required, however, notice must be (a) recorded in office of county recorder at least 12 business days before bulk transfer; (b) published once a week in a newspaper as provided; and (c) delivered or sent by certified or registered mail to the county tax collector.

Connecticut provides that a deposit of not more than 10% on any amount in escrow is not payment within the purview of this section. Washington provides for an additional exemption for sales proceeds impounded in the hands of a bank, licensed escrow agent or attorney.

In Louisiana, notice of proposed sale must be published in official journal of parish.

[2] This section appears only in the Codes of Alaska, Florida, Idaho, Kansas, Kentucky, Maryland, Minnesota, Mississippi, Montana, New Jersey, North Dakota, Oklahoma, Pennsylvania, South Dakota, Tennessee, Texas, Utah, Washington and West Virginia. The numbering of the succeeding sections is accordingly different from that of other states. California imposes similar requirements on transferees (or, if the transaction is handled through an escrow, the escrow's agent), but only to the extent that the consideration consists of any combination of cash and an agreement to pay cash in the future. Moreover, California has enacted §6-101-1 which provides in cases involving an escrow, procedures for application to the escrows agent by creditors seeking satisfaction of their claims.

[3] Minnesota adds after "pro rata" the following: "unless there is an agreement among the creditors to distribute the proceeds on another basis."

[4] This optional subsection has been adopted in New Jersey, Pennsylvania, Tennessee, Utah, Washington, and West Virginia. Florida, Kansas, Maryland, and Minnesota have adopted subsec. (4) with variations.

Georgia omits Section 6-106 and instead enacts a section providing for the definition of public notice. Michigan also omits Section 6-106 and instead enacts a section entitled "Taxing unit as creditor; notice to treasurer."

SECTION 6-107. *The Notice.*—(1) The notice to creditors (Section 6-105) shall state:

   (a) that a bulk transfer is about to be made; and
   (b) the names and business addresses of the transferor and transferee, and all other business names and addresses used by the transferor within three years last past so far as known to the transferee; and
   (c) whether or not all the debts of the transferor are to be paid in full as they fall due as a result of the transaction, and if so, the address to which creditors should send their bills.[1]

(2) If the debts of the transferor are not to be paid in full as they fall due or if the transferee is in doubt on that point then the notice shall state further:

   (a) the location and general description of the property to be transferred and the estimated total of the transferor's debts;
   (b) the address where the schedule of property and list of creditors (Section 6-104) may be inspected;
   (c) whether the the transfer is to pay existing debts and if so the amount of such debts and to whom owing; [2]
   (d) whether the transfer is for new consideration and if so the amount of such consideration and the time and place of payment; [3] and
   (e) if for new consideration the time and place where creditors of the transferor are to file their claims.[4]

(3) The notice in any case shall be delivered personally or sent by registered mail to all the persons shown on the list of creditors furnished by the transferor (Section 6-104) and to all other persons who are known to the transferee to hold or assert claims against the transferor.[5]

SECTION 6-108. *Auction Sales; "Auctioneer."*—(1) A bulk transfer is subject to this Article even though it is by sale at auction, but only in the manner and with the results stated in this section.

(2) The transferor shall furnish a list of his creditors and assist in the preparation of a schedule of the property to be sold, both prepared as before stated (Section 6-104).

(3) The person or persons other than the transferor who direct, control or are responsible for the auction are collectively called the "auctioneer." The auctioneer shall:

---

[1] California omits subsec. (1)(c).

[2] California includes specific provisions about recording, publication and delivery of notice.

[3] Arkansas omits subsec. (2) (d).

[4] Optional subsec. (2) (e) has been adopted in Alaska, Florida, Idaho, Kansas, Kentucky, Maryland, Minnesota, Mississippi, Montana, New Jersey, North Dakota, Oklahoma, Pennsylvania, South Dakota, Tennessee, Texas, Utah, Washington, and West Virginia.

[5] Subsec. (3) has not been adopted in Alaska, California, Indiana, Nebraska, Ohio, Oklahoma, Oregon, Rhode Island, and Wyoming.

Connecticut provides that notice must be filed with the secretary of state while Washington provides that a copy of the notice must be filed in the office of the county auditor of the county in which the property transferred is located.

Florida, Indiana, Nebraska and Washington provide that notice may be delivered personally or by registered or certified mail. Florida also provides that if the transferor resides in a county with a population of over 200,000, notice must be published one time in a daily newspaper.

In New York notice does not have to be given to the holders of bonds, debentures or the like.

(a) receive and retain the list of creditors and prepare and retain the schedule of property for the period stated in this Article (Section 6-104);
(b) give notice of the auction personally or by registered or certified mail at least ten days before it occurs to all persons shown on the list of creditors and to all other persons who are known to him to hold or assert claims against the transferor; [1] and
(c) assure that the net proceeds of the auction are applied as provided in this Article (Section 6-106).[2]

(4) Failure of the auctioneer to perform any of these duties does not affect the validity of the sale or the title of the purchasers, but if the auctioneer knows that the auction constitutes a bulk transfer such failure renders the auctioneer liable to the creditors of the transferor as a class for the sums owing to them from the transferor up to but not exceeding the net proceeds of the auction. If the auctioneer consists of several persons their liability is joint and several.

SECTION 6-109. *What Creditors Protected; [Credit for Payment to Particular Creditors.]*—(1) The creditors of the transferor mentioned in this Article are those holding claims based on transactions or events occurring before the bulk transfer, [3] but creditors who become such after notice to creditors is given (Sections 6-105 and 6-107) are not entitled to notice.[4]

(2) Against the aggregate obligation imposed by the provisions of this Article concerning the application of the proceeds (Section 6-106 and subsection (3) (c) of 6-108) the transferee or auctioneer is entitled to credit for sums paid to particular creditors of the transferor, not exceeding the sums believed in good faith at the time of the payment to be properly payable to such creditors.[5]

SECTION 6-110. *Subsequent Transfers.*—When the title of a transferee to property is subject to a defect by reason of his noncompliance with the requirements of this Article, then:

(1) a purchaser of any of such property from such transferee who pays no value or who takes with notice of such noncompliance takes subject to such defect, but

(2) a purchaser for value in good faith and without such notice takes free of such defect.

---

[1] Subsec. (3) (b) was amended in 1962 to include a reference to certified mail. The 1962 Official Text amendment has not been adopted in Alaska, California, Indiana, Nebraska, Ohio, Oklahoma, Oregon, Rhode Island, and Wyoming.

Connecticut requires that the notice of auction must be filed with the secretary of state at least ten days before the auction occurs.

New York does not require notice to be given to the holders of bonds, debentures or the like.

[2] Optional subsec. (3) (c) has been adopted in Alaska, Florida, Idaho, Kansas, Kentucky, Maryland, Minnesota, Mississippi, Montana, New Jersey, North Dakota, Oklahoma, Pennsylvania, South Dakota, Tennessee, Texas, Utah, Washington, and West Virginia.

[3] But see Section 9-301 (d) (2) which gives priority to the holder of a purchase money security interest over a transferee in bulk in certain situations.

[4] California omits "but creditors who become such after notice to creditors is given (Section 6-105 and 6-107) are not entitled to notice."

Washington specifically defines who are considered creditors of the transferor and are thus entitled to notice.

[5] Optional subsec. (2) has been adopted in Alaska, Florida, Idaho, Kansas, Kentucky, Minnesota, Mississippi, Montana, New Jersey, North Dakota, Oklahoma, South Dakota, Tennessee, Texas, Utah, Washington, and West Virginia.

SECTION 6-111. *Limitation of Actions and Levies.*—No action under this Article shall be brought nor levy made more than six months after the date on which the transferee took possession of the goods unless the transfer has been concealed. If the transfer has been concealed, actions may be brought or levies made within six months after its discovery.[1]

TRANSACTIONS WITHIN THE STATUTES

To be subject to the restrictions of state bulk transfers laws, or the Uniform Commercial Code, the transfer must not only be in bulk but also out of the ordinary course of the transferor's business. It must embrace all, or a major part, or a substantial part of a stock of merchandise or inventory, and under some statutes, including the Commercial Code, materials and supplies as well. Under many statutes restaurants, the sale in bulk of trade fixtures, and inventory of goods, wares and merchandise are within the statute.

Excepted are assignments for the benefit of creditors, sales by executors, administrators, receivers, trustees in bankruptcy, sales under judicial process, and (where the Uniform Commercial Code is in effect) certain additional types of transfers enumerated in Section 6-103.

Sales at public auction are usually not within bulk transfers laws. Some states, however, expressly include such sales, so the laws of those states apply.

Where the transfer is to a corporation or partnership organized to take over the business of the transferor, the transaction is not subject to the provisions of the Uniform Commercial Code Section 6-103(7) but may be expressly covered by a state law independent of the Code.

As between the parties to the transaction, whatever the wording of the statutes, it is uniformly held that transfers in bulk without compliance with statutory requirements may be attacked only by creditors, and that as between the parties themselves the transaction is valid.

EFFECT OF NONCOMPLIANCE

Once the notice has been given in accordance with the statute there is no impediment to the transfer, but, if the notice is not given in accordance with the statute, the sale is declared by the statutes to be "void" or "ineffective" or "presumptively fraudulent and void." In a number of jurisdictions and under an optional provision of the Uniform Commercial Code, the purchaser is obliged, in addition to giving notice, to apply, or see to the application of, the purchase price pro rata to the creditors of the seller. U.C.C. § 6-106.

CREDITORS' REMEDIES

The protection of the statute is available only to creditors whose claims exist at the time of the transfer. Upon receipt of notice that the sale is to take place, the creditor may invoke whatever remedies are available under the general state

---

[1] California, Florida, and Georgia provide for a 1 year period of limitation. In California, if the transfer has been concealed, the period will run from the date of discovery, or the date when discovery should reasonably have been made, whichever occurs first.

law, such as attachment, injunction and the like. In those jurisdictions where the statute requires the purchaser to see that the purchase price is applied to the payment of creditors' claims, creditors are protected to the extent of the consideration for the transfer provided they comply with the statutory provisions with respect to filing their claims.

Under Section 6-106 of the Uniform Commercial Code it is the duty of the transferee to assure that any new consideration which becomes payable upon the transfer of title is applied to pay the debts of the transferor which are either shown on the list furnished by the transferor or filed in writing in the place stated in the notice within 30 days after the mailing of such notice. This duty may be enforced by any creditor. If the consideration payable is not enough to pay all of the debts in full, the distribution shall be pro rata.

The statutes require the purchaser to notify all persons whose names are shown on the list of creditors to be furnished by the transferor, and under the Code and some state statutes, the notice must also be sent to all other persons who are known to the transferee to hold or assert claims against the transferor.

If the name of a creditor is omitted from such list and the transferee has no knowledge of the existence of such creditor's claim, he is fully protected if the statute is complied with to the best of his knowledge, information and belief.

RIGHTS OF SUBSEQUENT PURCHASERS

In the absence of collusion between a transferee in bulk and subsequent purchasers, the creditors of the transferor may not pursue the property into the hands of the subsequent purchasers.

TIME LIMITATION FOR ATTACKING SALE

Under the Uniform Commercial Code, creditors have six months from the date the transferee took possession of the property, or, if the transfer was concealed, they have six months after discovery, to bring a proceeding to set aside the transfer. Some state statutes contain limitations up to as long as one year from the date of maturity of the creditors' claims.

Where no time is especially provided by Bulk Transfers Law, the period of limitation to be applied depends upon the character of the action in which the relief is sought.

REQUIREMENT THAT LIST OF CREDITORS BE PRESERVED

Under the terms of the Uniform Commercial Code and some state statutes, the transferee is required to perserve the list of creditors and the schedule of the property to be transferred for six months following the transfer and to keep the list and schedule open for inspection by any creditor of the transferor. In some states the transferee may, in the alternative file the list and schedule in the office of County Clerk.

PLACE OF FILING OR RECORDING UNDER UNIFORM COMMERCIAL CODE

The place for filing or recording the list of property and schedule of creditors pursuant to Section 6-104 (1) (c) of the Uniform Commercial Code is as follows:

ALABAMA: Secretary of State.
ALASKA: Recorder in district where any part of the goods is located.
ARIZONA: County Recorder in each county where any of the transferred property is located.
ARKANSAS: No provision for filing.
CALIFORNIA: Notice must be recorded in office of County Recorder in county in which property is to be transferred 10 days before transfer, published at least five days before transfer.[1]
COLORADO: Secretary of State.
CONNECTICUT: Secretary of State.
DELAWARE: Secretary of State.
District of COLUMBIA: Recorder of Deeds of the District.
FLORIDA: Clerk of the Circuit Court of the county where the transferor had its principal place of business.
GEORGIA: Clerk of Superior Court of county where seller resides, or, if nonresident individual, corporation or other business entity, with Clerk of Superior Court in county of seller's principal place of business.
HAWAII: Bureau of Conveyances.
IDAHO: Recorder in the county where the property is located.
ILLINOIS: Recorder of any county in which part of the goods is located.
INDIANA: Secretary of State.
IOWA: Recorder in the county or counties where the goods are located.
KANSAS: Clerk of the District Court.
KENTUCKY: County Court Clerk.
MAINE: Secretary of State.
MARYLAND: Clerk of Circuit Court of county where property is located at time of the transfer.
MASSACHUSETTS: State Secretary.
MICHIGAN: Secretary of State.
MINNESOTA: Secretary of State.
MISSISSIPPI: Chancery Clerk of county where the property is located.
MISSOURI: Recorder of Deeds of county where transferor resides.
MONTANA: County Clerk and Recorder of county of transferor's residence and county where property transferred is located at time of transfer.
NEBRASKA: The office in which a security agreement is required to be filed under §9-401 of the U.C.C.
NEVADA: County Recorder in the county where the principal place of the business sold is located.
NEW HAMPSHIRE: Secretary of State.
NEW JERSEY: Secretary of State.
NEW MEXICO: Secretary of State. If debtor has a place of business in only one county of the state, then also with the County Clerk of such county. If

---

[1] Note that California makes recording and publication mandatory; the recording and publication requirements are derived from §3441 (1983) of the Civil Code since California has not adopted §6-104 of the UCC.

the debtor has no place of business in the state but resides in the state, then with the County Clerk of the county in which he resides.

NEW YORK: Department of State.[1]

NORTH CAROLINA: Clerk of the Superior Court of the county where transferor had its principal place of business.

NORTH DAKOTA: Register of Deeds in the county in which the property transferred is situated.

OHIO: County Recorder of county where the goods are located.

OKLAHOMA: County Clerk of county or counties where the goods are located.

OREGON: County Clerk of county where transferor's principal place of business is located.

PENNSYLVANIA: Prothonotary in county where property is located at time of transfer.

RHODE ISLAND: Secretary of State.

SOUTH CAROLINA: Register of Mesne Conveyances or Clerk of the Court in the county where the property was located at time of transfer.

SOUTH DAKOTA: Register of Deeds of county where transaction takes place.

TENNESSEE: Register's Office of county where transferor maintained principal place of business.

TEXAS: County Clerk's office in the county in which the transferor had its principal place of business.

UTAH: County Recorder.

VERMONT: Secretary of State.

VIRGINIA: Clerk's office where deeds are admitted to record for the county or city of the principal place of business of the transferor if an individual or partnership; the registered office of the transferor, if a corporation.

WASHINGTON: County Auditor where property is located. Copy of list must be served on the Department of Revenue.

WEST VIRGINIA: County Clerk of county which transferor's principal place of business is located.

WISCONSIN: Secretary of State.

WYOMING: County Clerk of county where transferor has his principal place of business.

---

[1] New York statute contains special provisions where transferor is obligor on a bond issue. Most states provide that only indenture trustee need be included in list of creditors where there is a bond issue.

Assignments for Benefit of Creditors—Equity Receiverships

An assignment for the benefit of creditors is the "transfer of all or substantially all of debtor's property to another person in trust to collect any money owing to debtor, to sell property, to distribute the proceeds to his creditors and to return the surplus, if any, to debtor." [1] The conveyance is voluntary on the part of the debtor and without compulsion by law and results in the liquidation of the debtor's business. Assignments are regulated by statute in most jurisdictions but also exist at common law.

The assignment is usually made by a written instrument which enumerates the property transferred and the disposition to be made of the property by the assignee designated therein. In most jurisdictions the consent of creditors is not necessary to the validity of the assignment, but such assent is required in some jurisdictions. Only when all creditors have consented to the assignment, however, is the conveyance immune from attack by creditors by the filing of a petition in bankruptcy and the superseding of the assignment by bankruptcy proceedings.

Assignments and Bankruptcy

Many of the states have laws dealing with assignments for the benefit of creditors. It has been held that the states have power to enact such laws, provided they do not impair the obligation of contracts within the meaning of the U.S. Constitution and are not in conflict with the United States Bankruptcy Code. When a debtor has not been proceeded against in bankruptcy and has not himself filed a petition in bankruptcy, an assignment for the benefit of creditors made under a state statute or at common law, which gives no preference to any creditor and does not discharge the debtor without consent of the creditors is not void as in conflict with the Bankruptcy Code. In *Bostwick v. Burnett,* 74 N.Y. 317 (1878), the Court held:

There is nothing in the bankruptcy act which invalidates or affects a voluntary assignment, valid under the laws of the State, where no proceedings in bankruptcy are instituted. . . . [I]f no proceedings in bankruptcy are instituted, and the creditors proceed under the laws of the State for the collection of their debts, those laws must govern and no question under the bankruptcy law can arise.

An assignment for the benefit of creditors constituted an act of bankruptcy under the Bankruptcy Act of 1898. However, the new Bankruptcy Code has eliminated acts of bankruptcy as a requirement to the filing of an involuntary bankruptcy petition. See *supra* pages 28-1–28-2.

The assignment for the benefit of creditors is usually less satisfactory to creditors than administration under the Bankruptcy Code since it does not allow for the recovery of preferences. From the point of view of the debtor it is less advantageous since it does not result in a discharge from debt.

---
[1] Black's Law Dictionary 109 (rev. 5th ed. 1979).

Advantages and Disadvantages of Assignments

The advantage of an assignment as compared to filing a petition in bankruptcy is that it is a relatively inexpensive means for a debtor to liquidate a business in an orderly manner with a minimum amount of publicity. The disadvantage to a debtor is that he is not discharged from his debts.

The disadvantages of the assignment, from the point of view of the creditor, lie in the lack of power to subject the debtor to an examination under oath, the absence of machinery for the recovery of preferential payments, the danger that the proceedings may be wrecked by the filing of a petition in bankruptcy, and the fact that for a debtor an assignment does not permit the discharge of liabilities.

Not infrequently a proposed assignment results in a compromise settlement or merely an extension of time for the payment of the insolvent's debts. Compromise settlements take practically the same form as rehabilitation in bankruptcy. Where the debtor has transferred his assets to a trustee for the benefit of his creditors, whether by assignment or trust mortgage, the unanimous consent of creditors to a proposed composition is necessary in order that the trustee may be protected in surrendering the assets to the debtor.

Common Law versus Statutory Assignments

The distinction between a common law assignment and a statutory assignment often lies solely in the fact that the former is not filed with the courts, and the administration of the estate is conducted under the supervision of a committee of creditors rather than under the supervision of a court. For its validity the common law assignment usually rests upon the consent of creditors. The form of instrument used in the friendly adjustment system, for the purpose of acquiring possession and control of an insolvent debtor's assets, differs according to the statutory and common law of the various states.

As set forth above the most commonly used instrument is an assignment for the benefit of creditors, but in some jurisdictions a security agreement is executed by the debtor to a trustee who thereupon forecloses the same for the benefit of the creditors; in some cases the debtor's affairs are taken care of pursuant to a power of attorney, a declaration of trust, or sometimes merely by means of a bulk sale of the debtor's assets with the purchase price entrusted to a third party for pro rata distribution.

In the case of insolvent corporations various plans are employed to obtain control of the assets for the benefit of creditors, such as a transfer of the corporation's stock in escrow and the election of creditors to the board of directors, or, in some jurisdictions, voluntary dissolution, pursuant to the statutes governing such procedures.

Whatever the form of instrument or procedure, however, the purpose and results are the same, namely, the reduction of the debtor's assets to cash and the distribution of the same among the creditors pro rata in accordance with the amount of their respective claims.

Duties of the Assignee

The duties of the assignee are to collect, preserve and distribute the assets assigned, without preferences, except such as may be prescribed by law or by

ASSIGNMENTS FOR BENEFIT OF CREDITORS

the instrument of assignment. Priorities under the state laws generally correspond to those which obtain in bankruptcy. Notice to creditors of the assignment, and an invitation to file claims on or before a certain date, are frequent statutory requirements; in the absence of statute it is the duty of the assignee to give notice and a reasonable opportunity to file claims.

Under a common law assignment, the powers of the assignee are usually limited by the express terms of the instrument of assignment, and where there is a statute regulating assignments for the benefit of creditors, the powers of the assignee are limited both by the instrument of assignment and by the statute.

The assignee is entitled to such compensation as the instrument of assignment may prescribe except where compensation is fixed by statute, as is usually the case.

At common law an insolvent debtor had the right in making an assignment for the benefit of creditors to give preference to certain creditors or classes of creditors; under some statutes a right to create preferences still exists.

The assignee may be discharged from his trust either by voluntary act of all parties interested in the estate, or he may be compelled to account in appropriate court proceedings, instituted by interested persons.

Summary of Statutory Provisions

There follows a summary of the statutory provisions of those states which provide that assignments be filed and which prescribe the time within which creditors shall file their claims. Such statutory provisions have no application to common law assignments which continue in a state despite the enactment of a statutory assignment procedure.

ALABAMA

FILING—Within 20 days after the assignment is executed, the assignee must file an inventory in the office of the Register of the county in which the most valuable property of the assignor is located.

NOTICE—Notice to creditors must be given by the Register by mail and by publication once a week for three successive weeks and by mail or if there is no newspaper in the county, then by posting a notice on the door of the county courthouse and by mail.

CLAIMS—Claims must be presented to the Register no later than the date specified in the notice. Late claims are paid only after all timely claims have been paid in full.

ALASKA

No statute.

ARIZONA

FILING—A copy of the assignment must be filed by the debtor with the Clerk of the Superior Court of the county where the debtor has his principal place of business.

NOTICE—Within 30 days after the filing of the assignment, assignee must give notice to creditors by mail and by publication in the county where the assignor resides or where his principal business was conducted.

CLAIMS—Creditors must file claims within six months after publication of notice. They must file a consent to the assignment within four months after publication, or, if they receive no actual notice, the consent may be filed any time before the assets are distributed. The debtor's property is distributed to the consenting creditors, whose claims are thereupon discharged.

ARKANSAS

FILING—Assignee must file inventory of assets with the Clerk of the Court having equity jurisdiction within 10 days after date of the assignment.

NOTICE—No provision.
CLAIMS—No provision.

CALIFORNIA

FILING—Debtor must file a sworn inventory in the office of the County Recorder within 20 days after execution of the assignment.

NOTICE—Notice must be given immediately by the sheriff, who calls a meeting of creditors not less than eight nor more than 10 days after the assignment and who also must publish a notice of such meeting.

CLAIMS—Creditors' claims must be presented to the assignee. Thirty days after the first publication, a dividend may be paid to creditors who have already presented their claims. Claims filed thereafter shall be paid in a percentage equal to that already distributed to the early claimants before any future dividends can be paid, if failure to present the claim early was not due to neglect.

COLORADO

FILING—Assignment must be filed with the Clerk of the District Court or the Clerk of the County Court of the county where the assignor resides, or, if he is nonresident, where he has his principal place of business. The assignee must file an inventory within six days thereafter.

NOTICE—Notice is given by publication for four weeks and by mail to each creditor.

CLAIMS—Claims received before the expiration of three months have priority over those presented later unless the creditor can prove he received no notice.

CONNECTICUT

FILING—Assignment and inventory must be filed with the Clerk of the Probate Court having jurisdiction and if the assignment includes real property, with the Town Clerk where the real property is situated.

NOTICE—Public notice must be given within 30 days.

CLAIMS—No provision.

DELAWARE

FILING—Within 30 days after the assignment, the assignee must file an inventory in the office of the Register of Chancery of the county in which the real and personal estate of the assignor is located. The assignee, as soon as inventory is filed, must give a bond at least covering the inventory. It shall inure to benefit of all persons interested upon rendering an account of his trusteeship every year from date of his bond.

NOTICE—Assignee must give notice to all persons in interest as directed by order of the Court of Chancery.

CLAIMS—No provision.

DISTRICT OF COLUMBIA

FILING—Within five days after the date of the assignment the assignee must file same in the land records of the district.

NOTICE—Notice must be given as the court in its discretion directs.

CLAIMS—No provision.

FLORIDA

FILING—Assignment must be filed in the office of the Clerk of the County where the property is located.

NOTICE—Notice must be given personally and by publication once a week for four weeks.

CLAIMS—In-state creditors must present their claims within 60 days, out-of-state creditors within four months.

GEORGIA

FILING—Assignment must be executed and recorded as a deed of real property and an inventory must be filed within 15 days after the assignment is recorded.

NOTICE—Assignee must notify all creditors within 30 days either personally or by mail.

CLAIMS—No provision.

HAWAII

No statute. A trustee or assignee for creditors has the same right, by application to a court of equity, to request and receive instruction or to have his accounts approved or be discharged from his trust, as any other fiduciary according to the usual procedure in equity.

ASSIGNMENTS FOR BENEFIT OF CREDITORS

IDAHO
No statute other than one requiring that the assignee be a resident of the state.

ILLINOIS
No statute.

INDIANA
FILING—Copy of assignment must be filed within 15 days of execution with the Clerk of Circuit Court of the county in which debtor resides. Assignment and an inventory shall be filed by assignee within 10 days of execution with Recorder of the county in which the debtor resides.

NOTICE—By publication for three weeks and by posting in at least five of the most public places in the county where debtor resides.

CLAIMS—Trustee is required to distribute to creditors whenever there are sufficient assets to pay a 10% dividend.

IOWA
FILING—Assignment and inventory must be filed immediately in the office of the Clerk of District Court.

NOTICE—Notice must be given to creditors by publication once a week for six weeks and by mail within three months after the date of the assignment.

CLAIMS—Claims must be filed in the office of the Clerk of the District Court within three months after the first publication. Time for filing may be extended not beyond nine months. Claims filed late do not participate in proceeds of estate until the timely claimants have been paid in full.

KANSAS
No statute.

KENTUCKY
FILING—Within seven days of assignment assignee must file bond and, within 15 days after qualification, file inventory in the Office of County Clerk where debtor resides.

NOTICE—Within two months after the assignment the assignee must give notice by publication and by mail to creditors who reside outside the county. Notice must include the time and place at which he will receive claims.

CLAIMS—Claims must be presented at the time and place specified in the notice or within three months thereafter. Late claims do not participate but the court can order that the same be included any time prior to distribution.

LOUISIANA
FILING—Debtor must petition the court for leave to call a meeting of creditors and surrender his estate to them. Debtor must file a copy of his petition and an inventory in the Office of the Notary.

NOTICE—Creditors residing within the county are to be served personally, and those residing outside the county may be served by mail.

CLAIMS—No provision.

MAINE
No statute.

MARYLAND
No statute.

MASSACHUSETTS
FILING—Assignee must deposit a copy of assignment with the Clerk of City or Town in which principal business of debtor is carried on.

NOTICE—Notice to creditors must be given by mail or otherwise.

CLAIMS—Distributed according to Chapter 216 (Courts of Insolvency).

MICHIGAN
FILING—Assignment must be filed within 10 days of assignment in the office of the Circuit Court where the assignor resides.

NOTICE—Within 10 days after the date of the assignment, the assignor must apply to the court to direct disposition of the assets. Notice must be given to all creditors by mail.

CLAIMS—Claims must be filed within 90 days after notice has been given. Assignee may be ordered by the court to accept late claims if presented within one year from the time the assignment was filed.

REMARKS—An employee who is a householder with a family and who assigns his wages in court for the benefit of creditors is entitled to an exemption of 60% but not less than $15 per week plus $2 for each legal dependent, other than his spouse, who is under 18 years of age.

MINNESOTA

FILING—Assignment must be filed with the Clerk of the District Court of the county where the debtor resides or does business.

NOTICE—Assignee must give notice forthwith to each creditor by mail and by publication for one week; notice of payment must be minimum of one week.

CLAIMS—Proof of claim must be filed with assignee at least 20 days before any payment is made.

MISSISSIPPI

FILING—Where property assigned exceeds $1000, assignee must file a petition within 24 hours after the date of the assignment in the Chancery Court of the county where the assignor resides or has his principal place of business, and within 10 days thereafter must file an inventory.

NOTICE—No provision.

CLAIMS—No provision.

MISSOURI

FILING—Assignee must file an inventory within 15 days after the date of the assignment in the office of the Clerk of the Circuit Court of the county where the assignor resides.

NOTICE—Notice to creditors must be given by mail and by publication for four successive weeks.

CLAIMS—Creditors must appear and may present their claims on the date specified in the notice or within three days thereafter.

MONTANA

FILING—A copy of the assignment and inventory must be filed within 20 days after the assignment with the County Clerk of the county in which the debtor resides.

NOTICE—At least 10 days' notice must be given creditors for presentation of claims. Notice must be by mail and by at least one publication in a newspaper.

CLAIMS—Claims must be presented by date specified in notice by mail and publication.

NEBRASKA

No statute.

NEVADA

No statute.

NEW HAMPSHIRE

FILING—Assignment must be filed in the office of the Town Clerk in the town of the debtor's residence or, if nonresident, with the Clerk of the Town in which the property is situated. If realty is assigned, filing must also be with Registry of Deeds in the county where the realty is located.

NOTICE—As judge shall order.

CLAIMS—No provision.

NEW JERSEY

FILING—Assignment must be recorded and filed in the office of the Register of Deeds in counties having such an officer and in other counties in the office of the County Clerk for the county in which debtor resides and with the Surrogate or Clerk of the Superior Court of such county.

NOTICE—Notice must be given to all creditors by publication for four consecutive weeks and by mail within 30 days after the assignment has been recorded.

CLAIMS—Claim must be presented within three months following date of assignment. Claimants who do not file on time do not participate in any dividends paid prior to the time claim was filed.

ASSIGNMENTS FOR BENEFIT OF CREDITORS

NEW MEXICO

FILING—Assignment must be recorded as a deed to real estate, and within 10 days thereafter an inventory must be filed in the office of the Clerk of the District Court of the county in which the assignor resides.

NOTICE—Notice to creditors must be given by publication for four weeks and by mail four weeks prior to the date specified to adjust claims.

CLAIMS—The assignee adjusts claims for three days as specified in the notice.

NEW YORK

FILING—The assignment and inventory must be filed within 20 days of the assignment in the County Clerk's office of the county where debtor resides or has his business.

NOTICE—Notice must be given by publication and mail 10 days before the date specified for the presentation of claims.

CLAIMS—Claims must be filed with the assignee by the date specified in the notice.

NORTH CAROLINA

FILING—Assignment is effectuated by the execution of a deed of trust for the benefit of creditors, which must be registered to be effective, and a schedule of the debtor's property must be filed within 10 days after the deed of trust is registered with the Clerk of the Superior Court, or the debtor may petition the Superior Court requesting that his estate be assigned for the benefit of creditors.

NOTICE—Notice to the creditors is given by the Clerk of the Court in the form of an order to show cause why the debtor's petition should not be granted which order must be published and posted. Creditors have 30 days to answer the order.

CLAIMS—No provision.

NORTH DAKOTA

In North Dakota the statute provides that an assignment for the benefit of creditors shall be administered under the supervision of the District Court.

When an assignment is made, the Public Administrator of the county in which the greatest part of the debtor's assets is located may be appointed receiver either on his own petition or on the petition of any of the creditors. The assignee may act only if no one petitions the court for the appointment of the Public Administrator as receiver.

Any sale of the debtor's property by either the Administrator or the assignee must be authorized by the District Court of the county in which the property is located.

OHIO

FILING—Assignment must be filed within 10 days in the Probate Court of the county where the assignor resides.

NOTICE—Notice must be given by publication within 30 days after the filing of the assignment. Assignee must give bond in 10 days of assignment, and within 30 days of giving bond must give notice by publication of his appointment.

CLAIMS—Claims must be presented within six months after publication unless further time is granted by the probate court.

OKLAHOMA

FILING—Assignment and inventory must be filed in 20 days of assignment with the Register of Deeds in the county where the assignor resided at date of assignment.
NOTICE—No provision.
CLAIMS—No provision.

OREGON

No statute.

PENNSYLVANIA

FILING—Within five days after its date, the assignment, together with an inventory, a list of creditors, a statement of the cause of insolvency and judgments against the debtor, must be filed in the Court of Common Pleas of the county where the debtor resides or where his business is located.

NOTICE—Notice to creditors to present their claims must be given in writing and by publication

for four successive weeks in weekly newspaper and in such legal periodical, if any, as shall be designated by the court.
CLAIMS—Claims must be submitted within six months from notice.

RHODE ISLAND

FILING—Assignment must be filed in the Registry of Deeds in each town where there is real estate in which the assignor has an interest and in the town in which the assignor resides. Assignment and inventory must also be filed with the Clerk of Superior Court for such town.
NOTICE—Notice to creditors must be given by publication and by mail.
CLAIMS—Dividends may be distributed four months after the assignment on 10 days' notice by mail to the creditors.

SOUTH CAROLINA

FILING—Assignment must be recorded in the Office of Register of Mesne Conveyances or the Clerk of County where the property is located or where assignor resides.
NOTICE—Assignee must call meeting of creditors within 10 days after execution of assignment.
CLAIMS—Creditors have power to direct distribution of assets.

SOUTH DAKOTA

FILING—Assignment and an inventory must be filed within 20 days after the date of the assignment with the Recorder of Deeds in the county where the debtor resides, or in case he is a nonresident, where he has his principal place of business, or if neither, where the principal part of his property is located.
NOTICE—Must be given by publication in legal newspaper selected by the court.
CLAIMS—Must be presented on day specified in notice but such day can not be less than four months from the recordation of the assignment.

TENNESSEE

FILING—Must file bond and affidavit with the County Clerk.
NOTICE—Notice to creditors to present their claims must be given by publication for four consecutive issues and by posting on the courthouse door at least 10 days before the date specified for the presentation of claims.
CLAIMS—Claims must be presented by the date specified in the notice but not less than 12 months from date of notice. Failure to make timely presentation bars participation in the fund to be distributed.

TEXAS

FILING—Assignment must be filed immediately in the county of the assigned's residence and in each county in which real property conveyed to the assignee is located.
NOTICE—Within 30 days of assignment notice must be given by publication for three consecutive weeks and must also be given by mail within an unspecified time.
CLAIMS—Creditors must file consents to the assignment within four months after notice has been given, except that a creditor who has not received notice may file his consent any time before distribution. Proof of claim must be filed within six months after notice is given. Assignment operates as a discharge as to all consenting creditors who received at least one-third of the amount due them.

UTAH

FILING—The assignment and an inventory must be filed in the office of the Clerk of the District Court of the county in which the assignor's property is located.
NOTICE—Notice to creditors must be given by publication at least once a week for six weeks, and by mail.
CLAIMS—Claims must be presented within three months after the first publication, however, the court may extend time to present claims but not beyond nine months after publication.

VERMONT

FILING—The assignment, an inventory and a list of creditors must be filed in the office of the Clerk of the County where the assignor resides and where the property is located.
NOTICE—No provision.
CLAIMS—No provision.

VIRGINIA

FILING—Assignment must be recorded in like manner to a deed of real property.

NOTICE—Before any of the property is sold, 10 days' notice must be given to all creditors by registered mail.

CLAIMS—No provision.

WASHINGTON

FILING—Assignment and inventory must be recorded in the record of deeds of the county where the debtor resides.

NOTICE—Notice to creditors must be given by publication for six weeks and by mail.

CLAIMS—Claims must be presented within three months after notice has been given.

WEST VIRGINIA

FILING—Assignment must be recorded in the office of the Clerk of the County Court of the county where the assignor's principal place of business is located and a certified copy must be recorded in every county where there is real property. An inventory and list of creditors must be filed 10 days thereafter with the Clerk of the County Court of the county where the assignment is recorded.

NOTICE—Notice to creditors must be given by mail and by publication for two successive weeks.

CLAIMS—Claims must be made not less than 30 nor more than 60 days after notice is given. Late claims take only what may be left after payment of timely claims.

WISCONSIN

FILING—Assignment must be filed with the Clerk of the Court in the county where assignor has his residence or principal place of business, and if realty is assigned, the assignment must also be recorded in the office of the Register of Deeds of the county where the land is assigned. Within 10 days of the filing of the assignment an inventory must likewise be filed.

NOTICE—Notice must be given promptly by mail and by publication once a week for three successive weeks.

CLAIMS—Claims must be filed within three months from the date of the filing of the assignment.

WYOMING

No statute.

FEDERAL EQUITY RECEIVERSHIPS

Appointment of a federal equity receiver is an extraordinary remedy that is infrequently used. Receivers are not appointed in bankruptcy cases, but may be appointed to administer assets until a federal civil litigation is resolved. Fed. R. Civ. P., Rule 66. An equity receiver is utilized to prevent a party to a suit from depleting the assets of an entity pending final determination of the litigation.

A receiver can be sought by anyone showing an interest in certain property sufficient to justify conserving the property. For example, secured creditors, judgment creditors, shareholders in a corporation and mortgagees can file a petition which should name the creditor as the plaintiff and the debtor as the defendant. The petition should be filed in the United States District Court where the debtor does a substantial amount of business or where the subject of the receivership is located. However, in order for a federal court to exert its jurisdiction, the petitioner's claim must be for more than $10,000 and he must be a resident of a different state than the debtor, *or* the demand for an equity receiver must be premised on the violation of a federal law (e.g., securities law violation). Any creditor desiring to intervene in the proceeding may do so by filing notice of intervention, after which he is entitled to notice of all subsequent proceedings.

As a rule, the receiver continues the business, often with the cooperation of the creditors or a creditors' committee, and eventually either the business is liquidated or the receivership is terminated and the assets returned to the debtor.

STATE RECEIVERSHIPS

State receivers are appointed to either preserve, manage or dispose of the debtor's property. The procedure to appoint a receiver varies from state to state and the request usually comes from a creditor who can show that the property securing the creditor's interest is in danger of being lost. Temporary receivers are frequently appointed for the purpose of conserving the assets of a corporation pending the determination of litigation. Permanent receivers may be appointed by state courts for solvent or insolvent corporations for various types of proceedings including insolvency and dissolution proceedings.

The fees of the receiver and his attorney are at the discretion of the court, with the result that the amount allowed is frequently in excess of the corresponding fees allowed in bankruptcy.

Receivers in all cases, whether appointed by state or federal courts, are officers of the court and cannot be sued for acts by the creditor without permission of the court.

A creditor, having a claim against a corporation for which a receiver has been appointed, should consult counsel for the purpose of having the claim prepared in proper form for filing, and to assure its filing in time to be allowed and its proper representation and protection.

No discharge of the debtor from debts or liabilities is obtainable in receivership proceedings whether federal or state. The functions of the receiver in liquidation or insolvency proceedings are to conserve, protect and distribute the assets of the corporation. In most jurisdictions creditors are not entitled to any direct participation in the proceedings, either by way of examination of the debtor or selection of the receiver, but the entire matter is handled under the direct supervision of the court by which the receiver was appointed. Before a receiver can be discharged from his trust, however, he must file a final account, at which time creditors and other persons interested may appear by attorney and raise objections to items contained in the receiver's account.

Rhode Island, for example, has adopted a wage-earner receivership statute, R.I. Gen. Laws §§ 10-18-1 to 10-18-21 (1982), which provides for special receivership procedures for wage earners. Wage earners are defined as persons earning $12,000 a year or "an amount which, considering the fluctuations in the general price level, is equivalent to . . . $12,000 per annum in calendar year 1968," whichever is greater. Id. § 10-18-3. Under this statute the debtor files a petition stating that he is unable to meet his current debts as they mature and the court appoints a receiver to whom the debtor delivers a written assignment of all his future wages, salaries and commissions. The receiver prepares a plan of payment of secured and unsecured creditors. The statute is intended to be a flexible and effective means of dealing with the problems of wage earners without the stigma or expense of a bankruptcy proceeding.

Bankruptcy— Summary of Procedure

The Bankruptcy Reform Act of 1978 (the "Code") as amended by the Bankruptcy Amendments and Federal Judgment Act of 1984 establishes bankruptcy law and procedure in the United States. The Bankruptcy Amendments Act was necessitated by the United States Supreme Court decision in *Northern Pipeline Construction Co. v. Marathon Pipeline Co.*, 102 Supreme Ct. 1258 (1982), which held that portions of the Code violated Article III of the United States Constitution.

Bankruptcy in the United States is governed solely by Federal law and no state may enact a bankruptcy statute. The purpose of the bankruptcy process is twofold:

1. As a creditor's remedy it marshalls all of the assets of the debtor and provides for equal distribution to all creditors.

2. As a debtor's remedy it provides the debtor with a fresh start in his economic affairs by discharging his past debts.

Bankruptcy proceedings are highly technical and it is desirable to consult legal counsel before any such proceeding is commenced.

Terminology of Bankruptcy

(a) A *debtor* is a person (natural person, partnership or corporation) against whom a case under the bankruptcy law has been commenced. (The term "bankrupt" has been eliminated.)

(b) A *voluntary* petition is one filed by a person asking for relief under this act.

(c) An *involuntary* petition is one filed against a person by his creditors asking that that person obtain relief under the Code. (An involuntary petition against a partnership can be filed by fewer than all of the general partners of such partnership.)

(d) An *order for relief* is obtained in a voluntary case by the filing of a petition with the bankruptcy court.

(e) The *Court of Bankruptcy* is a unit of the United States District Court for the district in which the petition is filed. The United States Bankruptcy Court will be established in each district as an adjunct to the district court.

(f) *Bankruptcy Judges* are appointed to fourteen (14) year terms by the Court of Appeals for the circuit.

(g) The *United States Trustee* system is a pilot program in the following ten districts or groups of districts: (1) Districts of Maine, New Hampshire, Massachusetts, and Rhode Island; (2) Southern District of New York; (3) Districts of Delaware and New Jersey; (4) Eastern District of Virginia and District of Columbia; (5) Northern District of Alabama; (6) Northern District of Texas; (7) Districts of Minnesota, North Dakota and South Dakota; (8) Northern District of Illinois; (9) Central District of California; (10) Districts of Colorado and Kansas. The United States Trustee assumes the administrative duties of the Bankruptcy Judge. The trustee establishes and supervises panels of private trustees as well as designates a panel member to serve as an interim trustee immediately after an order for relief has been issued. (By September 30, 1986, Congress either will decide to permanently enact the system or the pilot program will then terminate.)

(h) An *Interim Trustee* is a disinterested person appointed to act as trustee promptly after the order of relief is obtained. In pilot districts the interim trustee is selected by the United States Trustee from a panel of private trustees. Where there is no pilot program, the court will appoint the interim trustee. The appointment terminates with the election of a trustee by the creditors. (The Code eliminates *receivers* who were previously appointed by the judge as temporary custodians of the debtor's assets.)

(i) A *Trustee* is the permanent liquidating officer of the estate. Normally, the trustee is elected by the creditors. If the creditors fail to elect a trustee, the interim trustee will then serve as the trustee. The trustee is required to be either (1) an individual competent to perform his duties and who resides or has an office in the judicial district in which he is appointed, or (2) a corporation authorized by its charter or bylaws to act in such capacity and having an office in the judicial district in which it is appointed.

(j) An *Individual with Regular Income* is a person whose income is sufficiently regular and stable to make payments under a debt adjustment plan.

(k) A person is *insolvent* when the sum of his debts is greater than all his assets, exclusive of property exempted or fraudulently transferred, at fair valuation. A partnership is *insolvent* when the sum of its debts is greater than the aggregate, at fair valuation, of all the partnership property, exclusive of property exempted or fraudulently transferred, and the sum of each partner's nonpartnership property, with the same exceptions, over his nonpartnership debts. (This definition of insolvency does not apply when an involuntary petition is being contested. In an involuntary case the equity test of insolvency—the inability to pay debts as they become due—is used.)

(l) An *Examiner* is appointed in a reorganization case where no trustee has been appointed, upon the request of a party and when such appointment is in the best interests of the creditors, or when the debtor's fixed, liquidated, unsecured debts, other than goods, services, taxes, or an insider's debt, exceed $5,000,000. An examiner may investigate the conduct and financial condition of the debtor and the operation of the debtor's business. The examiner must report his examination to the court and send a copy or summary to any entity the court designates.

Petition

Who May File Petitions in Bankruptcy

(a) A *voluntary petition* may be filed by any person except a railroad, insurance or banking corporation, savings and loan association or building and loan association, whether such entity is solvent or insolvent.

(b) An *involuntary petition* may be filed against any person except a wage earner, farmer, railroad, insurance or banking corporation, or a building and loan association. Failure to challenge the petition will result in an order for relief. If challenged, an order for relief will be entered if:

1. The debtor is generally not paying his debts as they mature; or
2. A custodian was appointed or took possession of the debtor's property during the 120 day period preceding the filing of the petition. The requirement that an act of bankruptcy must have been committed by the debtor prior to filing of petition has been eliminated.

(c) Petitions in bankruptcy may be filed in the federal judicial district in which the bankrupt had his or its principal place of business, resided or had his or its domicile for the six months preceding the filing of the petition, or for a longer portion of the preceding 180 days than in any other state. If the bankrupt has not had a principal place of business, resided or had his or its domicile within the United States, but has property within the jurisdiction, or has been adjudged bankrupt by a court outside of the United States and has property in the United States, the petition may be filed in the district in which the property is located.

BY WHOM AND WHEN AN INVOLUNTARY PETITION MAY BE FILED

An involuntary petition may be filed by three creditors having noncontingent or disputed claims against the debtor amounting to $5,000 more than the value of any lien on the property securing such claims, unless the total number of creditors is less than twelve, in which case any one creditor may file. A creditor is not estopped from acting as a petitioning creditor because he participated in a prior matter or judicial proceeding, as, for example, where he consented to a prior equity receivership proceeding, or to a prior assignment for the benefit of creditors, or participated in such proceedings, or accepted dividends therein.

The Code provides for penalties against parties who improperly petition for involuntary proceedings. If the petition is dismissed other than on consent of all petitioners and the debtor, the court may grant the debtor: (a) costs, (b) reasonable attorney's fees, or (c) damages resulting from the taking of the debtor's property. If the court finds that the petition was filed in bad faith (i.e., to harass the debtor) the court may award against the petitioners and to the debtor (a) any damages proximately caused by the filing, or (b) punitive damages.

CONTESTED PETITIONS; SUBPOENA

The debtor or a general partner who did not join in the petition against a partnership may appear and file an answer to an involuntary petition within 20 days from the service of the subpoena upon the alleged debtor. The subpoena is returnable within ten days from the date of its issuance unless the court fixes a longer time. If personal service cannot be made, the court may order the summons and the petition to be served by mailing copies to the last known address, if any, and by at least one publication in such manner as the court may direct.

Automatic Stay

The filing of a petition creates an automatic stay of all judicial proceedings. The purpose of the stay is to protect the debtor from his creditors and to prevent any creditor from obtaining special advantages. The stay stops collection efforts, harassment, and foreclosure actions against the debtor. Judgments ob-

tained against the debtor may not be enforced after the stay takes effect. The stay prevents dismemberment of the estate since all attempts to obtain possession of estate property by third parties are enjoined. No lien may be created or enforced against the estate once the stay takes effect. There are several exceptions to the automatic stay, including:
1. Criminal proceedings against the debtor;
2. Collection of alimony, maintenance or support from property that does not pass to the estate;
3. Police or regulatory actions by governmental units;
4. Issuance of a notice of a tax deficiency.

The stay terminates when the case is closed, dismissed, a discharge is granted or denied, or the property which is the subject of the stay ceases to belong to the estate.

The court will grant relief from the stay, in the form of termination, modification, or placement of conditions on it:
1. For cause, including the lack of adequate protection (discussed below); or
2. With respect to a stay of an act against property, if the debtor has no "equity" interest in the property and the property is not necessary to an effective reorganization. The burden of proof on the issue of "no equity" is on the party requesting relief from the stay; the burden of proof on all other issues is on the trustee or debtor in possession. Thirty days after a party's request for relief from a stay, the stay is automatically terminated with respect to that party, unless the court, after notice and hearing, orders a continuation of the stay. If only a preliminary hearing is held within the 30 days after the request for relief from the stay, the court will continue the stay, pending the outcome of the final hearing, if the trustee or debtor in possession can demonstrate a "reasonable likelihood" that he will prevail at the final hearing. The final hearing must be commenced within 30 days of the preliminary hearing.

Damages including costs and attorneys' fees, and in appropriate cases, punitive damages are recoverable by anyone injured by a willful violation of the automatic stay.

Adequate Protection

Adequate protection is required to protect the value of the creditor's security interest against any loss resulting from the automatic stay, the use, sale or lease of the property subject to the interest, and the obtaining of credit by the trustee. If the party that is affected by the proposed actions of the trustee or debtor in possession objects, the court will determine whether the protection provided is adequate.

The Code suggests three methods of protection. The first two methods rely on the value of the interest of the protected entity in the property involved. The third method is based on the "indubitable equivalent" of the entities interest. How value of the creditor's interest is to be determined is not developed in the Code. These matters are left to a case by case determination. The Code seems to envision wide latitude for the courts in valuation: they will not be restricted to either the going concern value or the liquidation value of the property. The first method of adequate protection suggested involves periodic cash payments by the estate to compensate for decrease in the value of the creditor's interest. The use of periodic payments may be appropriate where, for example, the property in issue is depreciating in value at a relatively fixed rate. In providing adequate protection under this method, the trustee also has the option of making a one-time cash payment in lieu of making periodic cash payments. The second method calls for the estate to provide additional or replacement liens on other property so that any loss in value of the original interest can be realized through the new lien. The third method is a catch-all provision which gives the trustee or debtor in possession discretion to grant any kind of protection—except a priority as an administrative expense—which will result in providing the creditor the "indubitable equivalent" of his security interest.

The trustee has the burden of proof on the issue of adequate protection, except that the party seeking an interest in property has the burden of proof on the issue of the validity, priority and extent of such interest.

Duties of the Debtor

The debtor is required to:
(a) file a list of creditors, and unless the court orders otherwise, a schedule of assets and liabilities, and a statement of his financial affairs and a schedule of current income and expenses;
(b) cooperate with the trustee, if a trustee is serving in the case, as necessary to enable the trustee to perform his duties;
(c) surrender to the trustee, if a trustee is serving in the case, all property of the estate and any recorded information, including books, documents, records, and papers, relating to property of the estate;
(d) attend the hearing on discharge and testify with respect to the issues raised;
(e) attend the meeting of creditors and submit to examination by them;
(f) notify the clerk of court of his intentions with respect to the retention or surrender of property as exempt or otherwise within thirty days after filing petition or by the date of the meeting of creditors, whichever is first; within forty-five days after filing such notice of intent, or within such additional time as the court fixes, debtor must perform his intention.

Interim Trustees

(a) *Appointment:* The appointment of an interim trustee promptly after the order for relief in a voluntary case is mandatory under the Code. If the district in which the case has been commenced is part of the United States Trustee system, the United States Trustee will select an interim trustee from the panel of private trustees that he has established. If none of the panel members is willing to serve, then the United States Trustee serves. The United States Trustee can also select a person who was serving as trustee in the case immediately before the order for relief. In districts that do not have a United States Trustee, the Bankruptcy Court will appoint the interim trustee. The Code provides that the interim trustee will be a disinterested person. The interim trustee has all the powers of a trustee. The interim trustee's function terminates upon the election or designation of a trustee.

In an involuntary case, an interim trustee may be appointed before an order for relief in the case. The court, on the request of a party in interest, and after notice and hearing, will appoint an interim trustee if it feels such appointment is necessary to preserve the property of the estate. The interim trustee may take possession of the estate and operate any business of the debtor. The debtor can regain possession only by posting a sufficient bond.

(b) *Compensation:* The interim trustee has the same limitations on compensation as the trustee. See *infra* page 28-10.

Examination and Immunity of the Debtor

The debtor, the debtor's spouse, and any other person may be examined by order of the court, upon application of any party in interest. The examination may relate to acts by, and the property of, the debtor, or to any matter that may affect the administration of the estate or the debtor's right to a discharge. Hostile witnesses may be examined as if under cross-examination, and the party calling such witnesses is not bound by the witnesses' testimony.

The attendance of any person for examination and the production of documentary evidence may be compelled by the use of a subpoena. A person other than the debtor is not required to attend as a witness unless his lawful mileage and fee for one day's attendance are first given to him. The debtor is entitled to be paid his actual and necessary traveling expenses to attend an examination (except at the meeting of creditors and at the hearing upon his discharge) at a distance in excess of one hundred miles from his place of residence.

The debtor can request immunity so that his testimony could not be used against him at a criminal proceeding. If the immunity is granted, the debtor must testify; if immunity is denied, the debtor can claim the privilege against self-incrimination. If the debtor refuses to answer questions after he has been granted immunity, he will not receive a discharge.

Meeting of Creditors

Within a reasonable time after the order for relief has been entered there shall be a meeting of creditors. At least ten days' notice must be given. The debtor is required to be present and may be examined. The bankruptcy judge cannot attend the meeting of creditors. Generally, the interim trustee or the United States trustee will preside. Where it would be beneficial, the court may order a meeting of equity security holders.

ELECTION OF TRUSTEE

An election of a trustee will occur if creditors holding at least twenty percent of allowed, liquidated, unsecured claims request it. A creditor may vote for a trustee if the creditor: (1) holds an allowed, liquidated, unsecured claim not entitled to priority; (2) does not have a materially adverse interest to the interests of the general unsecured creditors, other than an insubstantial equity interest as a creditor; (3) is not an insider. Creditors are permitted to elect one trustee. A candidate is elected if: (1) creditors holding at least twenty percent in amount of those claims specified above actually vote, and (2) the candidate receives a majority in amount of claims of the votes cast. If a trustee is not elected, then the interim trustee shall continue to serve as the trustee in the case.

CREDITORS' COMMITTEE IN LIQUIDATION PROCEEDINGS

General unsecured creditors may elect a committee of between three and eleven members from among themselves. The committee may consult with the ning the administration of the estate and may make suggestions concerning the performing of his duties. The committee may estions to the court.

The trustee is responsible for the estate created by the commencement of the case. The debtor no longer has any interest in the estate. The estate is comprised of:

(a) All legal or equitable interests of the debtor in property as of the commencement of the case, except interests that the debtor holds in trust for another, and beneficial interests subject to restrictions on transfer;

(b) All interests of the debtor and the debtor's spouse in community property that is under the control of the debtor;

(c) All of the debtor's property in the hands of a custodian, or claims against creditors which exceed debts;

(d) The debtor's interest in transfers of property avoided by the trustee;

(e) Inherited property acquired by the debtor within 180 days after the filing of the petition;

(f) Property received through a property settlement with the debtor's spouse or beneficiary acquired by the debtor within 180 days after the filing of the petition;

(g) Proceeds of a life insurance policy that the debtor acquires within 180 days after the filing of the petition;

(h) The proceeds, rents or profits received from the property of the estate;

(i) Any interest in property acquired by the estate after the proceeding is commenced.

The Trustees: Duties, Powers and Compensation

DUTIES OF TRUSTEE

(a) Collect and reduce to money the property of the estate and close the estate as expeditiously as is compatible with the best interests of parties in interest;

(b) Be accountable for all property received;

(c) Investigate the financial affairs of the debtor;

(d) Examine proofs of claims and object, if necessary to the allowance of any claim that is improper;

(e) If advisable, oppose the discharge of the debtor;

(f) Furnish information concerning the estate as is requested by a party in interest;

(g) If the debtor's business is being continued, file periodic reports with any governmental tax collecting agencies;

(h) Make a final report and file a final account with the court of the administration of the estate;

(i) File a bond with the court in favor of the United States conditioned on the faithful performance of his duties.

(j) Ensure that the debtor commences timely payments for administrative expenses and percentage fees for any private standing Chapter 13 trustee.

(k) Ensure that the debtor makes timely payments to creditors.

Powers of Trustee

Sale, Use, Lease of Property

The trustee has the power to use, sell, or lease the property of the estate, subject to certain restrictions. Also, under the new Code, the trustee has been granted the power to alter the secured debt structure of the estate.

The trustee, when not acting in the ordinary course of business, can use, sell or lease property of the estate only after there has been notice to all interested parties, and a hearing. When acting in the ordinary course of business, notice and hearing are not required unless the trustee is using, selling, or leasing "cash collateral." Cash collateral is defined in the Code as cash, negotiable instruments, documents of title, securities, deposit accounts, or other cash equivalents. Cash collateral may be disposed of by the trustee only if the entity that possesses an interest in it consents or the court, after notice and hearing, authorizes its disposition. The court must act promptly when authority to use, sell or lease property is requested; if the hearing is a preliminary hearing, the court may permit the trustee to proceed if there is a reasonable likelihood that the trustee will prevail at the final hearing. The court shall also prohibit or condition the sale, use, or lease of the property as is necessary to provide adequate protection of the security interest.

The Code permits the trustee to sell estate property free and clear of a lien belonging to any entity other than the estate. The sale is subject to the adequate protection requirement. See *supra* page 28-4. Most often adequate protection will consist of having the lien attach to the proceeds of the sale. The trustee may sell free and clear if applicable nonbankruptcy law permits it, the other entity consents, the interest is a lien, the sale price of the property is greater than the amount secured by the lien, and the interest is a bona fide dispute. The trustee may also sell free and clear if the entity holding the interest could be compelled, in a legal or equitable proceeding, to accept a money satisfaction for his interest.

Obtaining Credit

If the trustee is authorized to operate the business of the debtor he may obtain unsecured credit and incur unsecured debt in the ordinary course of business and treat this as an administrative expense. The court, after notice and a hearing, can grant the same power to obtain credit for debts incurred other than in the ordinary course of business. If the trustee is unable to obtain credit in this fashion he may be authorized after notice and hearing to incur debt:

1) with priority over any and all administrative expenses; or,

2) secured by a lien on property of the estate that is not otherwise subject to a lien; or,

3) secured by a junior lien on property that is subject to a lien.

Finally, if credit cannot be obtained with these incentives, and the trustee is unable to obtain credit in any other way, he may after notice and hearing incur debt secured by a senior or equal lien on property of the estate that is already subject to a lien. The trustee can alter the priority of secured debt in this manner only if he has provided adequate protection to the holders of liens on the property on which the senior or equal liens are to be granted.

Avoidance Powers of Trustee

(1) Status of Lien Creditor. As of the date of the filing of the petition the trustee has the status of a lien creditor. In addition to the powers he has as a lien creditor, the trustee will also have the powers of a creditor with a writ of execution against property of the debtor (which was returned unsatisfied as of the commencement of the case) and the powers of a bona fide purchaser of property of the debtor. With these powers, the trustee may avoid transfers of property since one of these categories of creditors or purchasers could have avoided such transfer if such person actually existed. However, in a case filed by an individual debtor whose debts are primarily consumer debts, a trustee may not avoid a transfer if the aggregate value of all property that is affected by the transfer is less than $600. Further, the trustee is a successor to all the rights and powers of existing unsecured creditors and may avoid transfers that such creditors could have avoided.

(2) Statutory Liens. The trustee may avoid the statutory liens on the property of the debtor to the extent that such liens first become effective: (1) upon commencement of a bankruptcy action; (2) when a custodian is appointed; (3) when a debtor becomes insolvent; (4) when an insolvency proceeding, other than under the Code, is commenced against the debtor; (5) when the debtor's financial condition fails to meet a specified standard; or (6) at the time of an execution on the property of the debtor levied at the instance of an entity other than the statutory lienholder. Additionally, a statutory lien can be avoided if the lien is not perfected or enforceable on the date of filing of the petition against a bona fide purchaser or if the lien is a lien for rent.

(3) Time Limitations. The Code limits the time during which the trustee can exercise its avoidance powers to the earlier of two years after the appointment of the trustee or the time the case is closed or dismissed.

(4) Rejection of Executory Contracts. The trustee, subject to the court's approval, may assume or reject any executory contract or unexpired lease of the debtor. Executory contracts generally include contracts on which performance remains due, to some extent, on both sides. If there has been a default on an executory contract or unexpired lease of the debtor, the trustee may not assume the contract or lease unless he:

(a) cures, or provides adequate assurance that he will promptly cure, such default;

(b) compensates, or provides adequate assurance that he will promptly compensate, a party, other than the debtor, to such contract or lease, for any actual pecuniary loss to such party resulting from the default; *and*

(c) provides adequate assurance of future performance under such contract or lease.

In a liquidation case, if the trustee does not assume or reject an executory contract or unexpired lease of the debtor within sixty days after the order for relief, then such contract or lease is deemed rejected.

The Code invalidates bankruptcy clauses that had been permitted under the old Bankruptcy Act. These clauses automatically terminated the contract or lease in the event of bankruptcy. Such a clause frequently hindered reorganization efforts. The Code also partially invalidates restrictions on assignment of contracts or leases by the trustee to a third party. Before such restrictions may be invalidated, however, the trustee must first assume the contract or lease (subject to all the conditions on assuming a contract on which there has been a default) and provide adequate assurance of future performance to the contracting party. Contractual provisions that permit termination or modification in the event of an assignment are also invalidated against the trustee.

Executory Contracts

The Code permits a trustee subject to court's approval to assume or reject any executory contract or unexpired lease. An executory contract is one in which the only obligation that remains is the payment of money. If the debtor rejects an executory contract, the other party to the contract can file a claim for damages it incurs.

Under Chapter 7, trustee is required to assume or reject an executory contract within sixty (60) days after the order for relief. In Chapter 9, 11 or 13, a trustee can assume or reject an executory contract any time before confirmation of the plan. However, on request of a party to contract or lease, court may order trustee to assume or reject contract within a specified time.

If the trustee desires to assume an executory contract, it must cure all defaults that exist under the contract.

There are special provisions in the Code that deal with rejection of leases, particularly shopping center leases, collective bargaining agreements, and time-sharing agreements.

COMPENSATION

The Court may allow reasonable compensation for the trustee's services, payable after the trustee renders the services. The compensation cannot exceed fifteen percent on the first $1,000, six percent between $1,000 and $3,000, three percent on amounts in excess of $3,000.

Exemptions

Certain property of the debtor is exempted from all pre-petition claims. Under former bankruptcy law, the question of exemptions was left entirely to state law. Under the Code, federal exemptions are provided for and are optional. The debtor may elect his state exemptions; however, the states may provide by legislation not to have the federal exemptions apply to their residents.[1]

The exemptions as set out in the Code are:

1. The debtor's aggregate interest, not to exceed $7,500 in value, in real or personal property, that the debtor uses as a residence. A $3,750 limit is placed on the amount of an unused homestead exemption.[2]

2. The debtor's interest, not to exceed $1,200 in value, in one motor vehicle;

3. The debtor's interest, not to exceed $200 in value, in household furnishings and appliances and other items used primarily for personal, family or household purposes;[3] an aggregate dollar ceiling of $4,000 has been placed on the exemption for household goods and personal effects.

---

[1] The majority of states provide by statute that their state exemptions supersede the federal bankruptcy law. Only Connecticut, District of Columbia, Hawaii, Minnesota, Massachusetts, Michigan, New Jersey, New Mexico, Pennsylvania, Rhode Island, Texas, Vermont, and Wisconsin permit the federal exemptions.

[2] Note that the state exemptions may vary greatly from the federal exemptions. For example, Maryland provides that the debtor may exempt the debtor's aggregate interest, not to exceed $2,500 in value, in real or personal property that the debtor uses as a residence. Md. Court & Judicial Proceedings Code Ann. § 11-504 (1983).

[3] Compare New Mexico's exemption of the debtor's interest of $4,000 in one motor vehicle. N.M. Stat. Ann. § 42-10-1 (1983).

4. $500 in jewelry;
5. $400, plus any unused amount in any property in the first exemption;
6. $750 in any implements, books, or tools of the trade of the debtor;
7. An unmatured life insurance contract;
8. $4,000 in any accrued dividend under any unmatured life insurance contract;
9. Professionally prescribed health aids;
10. All rights to social security benefits, unemployment compensation, veteran's benefits, payments under pension or profit sharing plans;
11. Payments traceable to: awards under crime victim's reparation law, wrongful death of a person of whom the debtor was a dependent, compensation for loss of future earnings, to the extent reasonably necessary for the support of the debtor.

Husbands and wives filing jointly are compelled to elect either state or federal exemptions. This prevents a couple from benefiting from both sets of exemption. If the couple fails to agree on which alternative to elect, the husband and wife are deemed to have elected the federal exemption unless state law prohibits the election thereof.

The debtor is granted the right to avoid certain liens and transfers of exempt property. The Code permits the debtor to avoid a judicial lien or nonpurchase money security interest in consumer products or property held for personal, family or household use or in professional books or tools and in professionally prescribed health aids. In addition, the debtor may claim exemption for property recovered by the trustee if the transfer was not voluntarily made by the debtor, the debtor did not conceal the property, and if the debtor could have avoided such transfer under other provisions of the Code.

Allowance of Claims

A creditor may file a proof of claim or, if the creditor fails to make a timely claim, the debtor or trustee may file a proof of claim. If there is no objection, the claim will be allowed. If a claim is unliquidated or contingent and fixing its value would unduly delay the closing of the case, the claim will be estimated by the court and allowed. If an objection to the claim is made by a party in interest, the court will determine the amount of the claim and will allow the claim, except to the extent that:

1. The claim is unenforceable against the debtor for a reason other than it is contingent or unliquidated;
2. The claim is for unmatured interest;
3. The claim is subject to offset against a debt owed the debtor;
4. The claim is for property tax and exceeds the value of the property;
5. The claim is by an attorney or an insider and the claim exceeds the reasonable value of his services;
6. The claim is for post-petition alimony maintenance or child support;
7. The claim is for damages to a landlord, resulting from the termination of a lease, and the claim exceeds the greater of the rent reserved by the lease or fifteen percent of the remainder due under the lease for a period not to exceed three years;
8. The claim is for damages from the termination of an employment contract, and the claim exceeds the compensation provided by the contract for one year

following the date of the petition or the termination of the contract, whichever is earlier;

9. The claim results from a reduction in a tax credit available to the debtor in connection with an employment tax.

Certain post-petition claims are treated in the same manner as pre-petition claims when determining their allowability. In an involuntary case, a claim which is in the ordinary course of the debtor's business or financial activities and which arises after the commencement of the case, will be allowed or disallowed as if the claim had arisen before the filing of the petition. A creditor's claim based on the trustee's rejection of an executory contract and any claims arising from the trustee's recovery of a setoff or voidable transfer will be treated as pre-petition claims. A priority tax claim arising after the commencement of the case will also be treated as a claim which arose prior to the filing of the petition.

Filing Proof of Claim

Under the Bankruptcy Rules an unsecured creditor or an equity security holder must file a proof of claim in both a Chapter 7 and 13 bankruptcy, within 90 days after the first date set for the meeting of creditors. No proof of claim need be filed if there are no assets in the estate. Should assets be discovered later by the trustee, creditors will be so advised and a claim can then be filed.

In a Chapter 11 reorganization case, the creditor is no longer required to file a claim where the debt is included in the schedule of liabilities filed pursuant to 11 U.S.C. § 521(1), unless the claim is listed as disputed, contingent, or unliquidated. In such case, the creditor must file the proof of claim within the time specified by the court. As a matter of good practice, it is nevertheless advisable for creditors to file claims. Under the Rules, the Court shall fix the time within which proofs of claim or interest may be filed. Usually it is prior to the confirmation of the Plan.

The creditor in Chapter 7 and 13 cases must be certain to file within the time specified or else be precluded from collecting on his claim even if the debt is undisputed by the creditor. In Chapter 7 and 13 cases, unlike Chapter 11, creditor or its agent should file the proof of claim. The listing of the claim by the debtor in the schedule of liabilities is not *prima facie* evidence of the claim. Thus, if the creditor fails to timely file, or a creditor is not granted an extension to file by the Court, or the debtor or trustee fails to file the claim in the name of the creditor, and there is no property left in the estate after distribution, the creditor will lose his right to any proceeds from the estate.

A creditor may purposely choose not to file a claim, in order to avoid being brought within the jurisdiction of the bankruptcy court. If a creditor fails to file a claim due to negligence, however, the result can be serious if the amount owed by the debtor is significant.

Secured Claimholders

Secured claimholders are entitled to payment prior to general claimholders to the extent of their secured interest. (The terms secured creditors and unsecured creditors are not used in the Code; they have been replaced by the terms "secured claims" and "unsecured claims.") A creditor whose claim is greater than the value of the property securing his claim will have that claim broken down into two parts: (1) a secured claim to the extent of the value of his collateral (the value is to be determined by the creditor and the trustee or debtor in possession, and if they cannot agree, by the court) and, (2) an unsecured claim for the balance.

Current case law is codified by a provision which entitles creditors to interest and other reasonable costs and fees (including attorney's fees) provided in the security agreement, but only to the extent that the value of the collateral exceeds the value of the claim. Furthermore, the trustee is permitted to recover the reasonable costs and expenses of preserving or disposing of the property where the property's value exceeds the claims against it. The failure of a secured creditor to file a proof of claims is not grounds for the avoidance of the secured creditor's lien.

Priority Claims

The following claims have priority, in the order listed, over other unsecured claims:

1. All costs of administration, including all necessary expenses of preserving the estate, including wages, salaries, or commissions for services rendered after the commencement of the case; any tax incurred by the estate; the expenses of creditors in recovering property for the benefit of the estate; and reasonable compensation for services of an accountant or attorney;

2. In an involuntary case, unsecured claims arising out of the debtor's business after the commencement of the case but before the appointment of the trustee (such expenses incurred after the appointment of the trustee are entitled to a priority as a cost of administration);

3. Wage claims up to $2,000 for each employee, including vacation, severance and sick leave pay, earned in the ninety days before the earlier of the filing of the petition or the end of the debtor's business;

4. Contributions to employee benefit plans arising from services rendered within 180 days of the filing of the petition or the cessation of the debtor's business, whichever occurs first, to the extent of $2,000 for each employee, less the total amount paid in priority wage claims and payments to other employee benefit plans;

5. Unsecured consumer claims of up to $900 for each individual, for deposits made on family or household goods or services that were not delivered;

6. Income taxes for which a return is due within three years of the commencement of the case, property taxes for one year, unemployment, withholding and excise taxes, custom duties and tax penalties.

Only persons who are subrogated to the rights of those having administrative claims and involuntary gap claims receive the same priority status as the original claimant.

Where a creditor holds a lien on property of the debtor, and the trustee's protection of the creditor's interest proves to be inadequate, then the creditor's claim is given priority as an administrative expense.

Fees

The actual and necessary costs and expenses incurred by officers in the administration of estates must be reported in detail, under oath, and examined and approved by the court.

A custodian, trustee, or their attorney or any other attorney rendering services in a bankrupt proceeding, shall not share, or agree to share, his compensation for such services with any other person or share, or agree to share, in the compensation of any other person rendering services in a bankruptcy proceeding, or in connection with such proceeding. An attorney may share his compensation with a law partner, or with a forwarding attorney and may share in the compensation of a law partner. Additionally, attorneys for petitioning creditors that join in an involuntary petition may share in the compensation awarded.

A custodian, trustee, or their attorney or any other attorney, seeking compensation for services rendered by him in a bankruptcy proceeding, or in connection with such proceeding, must file with the court a petition setting forth the value and extent of the services rendered, the amount requested, and what allowances, if any, have theretofore been made to him. Such petition must be accompanied by his affidavit stating whether an agreement or understanding exists between the petitioner and any other person for a division of compensation, and, if so, the nature and particulars of the agreement. If satisfied that the petitioner has shared, or has agreed to share, his compensation, or in the compensation of any other person, contrary to the provisions of the Code, the court shall withhold all compensation from such petitioner.

Dismissal

In order to eliminate repeated filings by the same debtor, the Code provides the debtor is not eligible for bankruptcy relief if a prior proceeding filed by the debtor was dismissed within 180 days for failure to follow court orders, failure to appear before the court or upon a voluntary motion for dismissal following the filing of request for relief from an automatic stay provision.

A consumer debtor is required to advise the court of his income and expenses by filing the appropriate schedules. The schedules allow the court to evaluate the debtor's ability to pay his debts and permit any challenges lodged based on the schedules. If a bankruptcy judge determines that a debtor has the ability to repay his debts under Chapter 13, the judge has the authority to dismiss a case under Chapter 7 if granting relief under such Chapter would constitute a "substantial abuse of the bankruptcy law." There is, however, a presumption against dismissal and a case may be dismissed for "substantial abuse" only when the court acts on its own initiative.

Discharge

(a) *Eligibility:*
To receive a discharge the debtor must be an individual and must have paid his filing fee of $60 for a liquidation case. An individual may submit a written request for waiver of a discharge which the court may approve.

(b) *Grounds for Denial of Discharge:*
The debtor will be granted a discharge unless he:

1. Transferred, removed, destroyed, mutilated or concealed some of his property, or the estate property, intending to hinder or defraud a creditor or estate officer;

2. Concealed, falsified or destroyed information regarding his financial conditions or business transactions, unless such activity was somehow justified;

3. Knowingly made a false statement, presented a false claim, or withheld information in connection with the case;
4. Failed to satisfactorily explain any loss of assets or deficiency of assets to meet his liabilities;
5. Refused to obey a lawful order of the court or refused to testify after being granted immunity;
6. Committed any of the above acts within a year of commencement of the case, during the case, or in connection with another case concerning a family member, business associate or other insider;
7. Received a discharge under the bankruptcy act in a case commenced within six years of the present case.

(c) *Objections to Discharge:*

The trustee, a creditor, and in pilot districts, the United States Trustee may object to the discharge. Also, upon the request of a party in interest, the court may order the trustee to examine the conduct of the debtor to determine whether a ground exists for the denial of discharge.

The court will fix the time for objecting to the discharge but the time shall not be less than 30 nor more than 90 days after the first date set for the first meeting of creditors. The court may extend the time for filing objections. If no objections are filed in the time set, the debtor has fulfilled his duties to appear and be examined at the first creditors meeting, and has not requested a waiver, then the court will grant a discharge. Within forty-five days of the discharge the court will notify by mail all creditors, the trustee, and the attorneys involved.

At the trial on a complaint objecting to a discharge, the objecting party has the burden of proof on the facts essential to his objection.

REVOCATION OF DISCHARGE

On the request of the trustee or a creditor, and after notice and a hearing, the court shall revoke a discharge if:
1. The discharge was obtained through fraud and the requesting party did not know of such fraud until after the granting of the discharge;
2. The debtor acquired property and knowingly failed to report the acquisition to the trustee; or
3. The debtor refused a lawful court order or refused to testify.

The request for the revocation of the discharge must be within one year of the granting of the discharge if fraud is involved. Where acquired property or refusal to obey a court order is involved, the request must be within one year after the granting of the discharge or the closing date of the case, whichever is later.

SCOPE OF A DISCHARGE

A discharge releases the debtor from all debts that arose before the date of the order for relief and all debts that arose after the order for relief but which were treated as pre-petition debts. Whether proof of the debt had been filed or allowed is irrelevant. This discharge, however, does not release the debtor from the following debts:
1. Taxes in which a required return was not filed or was filed late and after two years before the date of filing of the petition; taxes with respect to which debtor made a fraudulent return or wilfully intended to evade or defeat such

taxes; taxes on gross receipts for a taxable year that ended on or before the date of the filing of the petition if a return was required to be filed and was due within three years, including extensions before the commencement of the case; taxes on income and gross receipts owed at any time within 240 days before the commencement of the case and taxes that were not assessed before but were assessable under applicable law or by agreement after commencement of the case; property taxes assessed before commencement of the case and payable without penalty after one year before filing of the petition; taxes required to be collected or withheld and for which debtor is liable; excise taxes on transactions occurring before the filing of the petition and for which a return is due within three years before date of filing of the petition; certain custom duties arising out of importation of merchandise; tax claims arising in the gap between filing of involuntary petition and entry of order for relief. Taxes referred to can be due federal, state or local governments.

2. Money, property or services obtained by false pretenses or fraud, or by a false financial statement which was reasonably relied on;

3. Debts neither listed nor scheduled by the debtor in time to permit timely action by the creditor to protect his rights, unless the creditor had notice or knowledge of the bankruptcy proceedings;

4. Those incurred by the debtor's fraud or embezzlement while acting in a fiduciary capacity;

5. To the debtor's spouse, a child or a former spouse for alimony, maintenance or support created by a separate agreement or in connection with an order of a court of record unless such debt has been assigned to another entity;

6. For willful injury by the debtor to another entity or the property of another entity;

7. For a fine or tax penalty on a nondischargeable tax incurred less than three years before the filing of the petition, which is not compensation for actual pecuniary loss and is payable to a governmental unit;

8. For an educational loan due to the government or a nonprofit institution unless such loan became due more than five years prior to the filing of the petition or would represent an undue hardship on the debtor;

9. Existing prior to an earlier bankruptcy case in which the debtor waived discharge or was denied a discharge of such debts other than on the basis of the six-year bar.

10. For a debt which has been assigned to a governmental unit.

11. For debts incurred as a result of driving while intoxicated.

12. For debts by a consumer for luxury goods or services aggregating more than $500 incurred within forty days prior to filing in bankruptcy and debts of more than $1,000 arising from cash advances within twenty days of filing.

The discharge voids any judgment concerning the liability of the debtor on any debt discharged, whether or not the discharge is waived. It also prevents any creditor whose claim has been discharged from attempting to collect or offset his claim against the debtor's property or community property acquired after the commencement of the case. The protection of community property does not apply if the debtor's spouse has been a debtor within six years preceding the filing of the petition and was not granted a discharge.

Although a debtor may reaffirm a debt by agreement with a creditor after the discharge has been granted, the new Code creates many barriers to such an agreement. The debtor has thirty days to rescind any reaffirmation. At the discharge hearing the court will inform the debtor that a reaffirmation is not required. If the reaffirmed debt is an unsecured consumer debt not reported by counsel, court approval is required after a determination that the affirmation was made in good faith and is in the best interests of the debtor. Reaffirmation is only permitted if made before the granting of a discharge. A reaffirmation agreement can be rescinded "within 60 days."

The debtor's discharge does not affect the liability of any other party on the debt.

A court may now award attorneys' fees to the debtor in the event a creditor unsuccessfully challenges the dischargeability of a consumer debt. To avoid the award of such fees, a creditor must show that its challenge had a reasonable basis both in law and in fact. The court has discretion to award fees based on equitable considerations.

Criminal Offenses

Title 18 of the United States Code provides that various offenses of bankrupts, officers of the bankruptcy court and others may be prosecuted, as follows:

1. A trustee, marshal, custodian or other officer of the court may be imprisoned not more than five years and/or fined not more than $5,000 for knowingly and fraudulently appropriating to his own use, embezzling, spending or unlawfully transferring any property, or secreting or destroying any documents belonging to a bankrupt estate which came into his charge as such officer.

2. Any person may be punished by imprisonment for not more than five years, or by a fine for not more than $5,000, or both, upon conviction of having knowingly and fraudulently: (a) concealed from the trustee, marshal, custodian or other court officer charged with the control or custody of the property, or from creditors in any proceeding under the Bankruptcy Code, any property belonging to the estate of the debtor; (b) made a false oath or account in, or in relation to, any proceeding under this Code; (c) presented under oath any false claim or proof against the estate of a debtor or used any such claim in a proceeding under the Code, personally, by, or as agent, proxy or attorney; (d) received any material amount of property from a debtor after the filing of the petition with intent to defeat the Code; (e) received or attempted to obtain any money or property, remuneration, compensation, reward, advantage or promise thereof from any person for acting or forbearing to act in any proceeding under the Code; (f) concealed, or transferred without concealment, while acting individually or as an officer or agent of any person or corporation, any property of any person or corporation, in contemplation of a proceeding under the Code, or with intent to defeat the Code; (g) concealed, destroyed, mutilated, falsified or made a false entry in any document affecting or relating to the property or affairs of a debtor, after the filing of a proceeding under the Code, or in contemplation thereof; (h) withheld from the marshal, custodian, trustee, or other officer of the court, any document affecting or relating to the property or affairs of the debtor, the possession of which he is entitled, after the filing of a proceeding under the Code.

3. A custodian, trustee, marshal, or other officer of the court, who knowingly purchased, directly or indirectly, any property of the estate of which he is an officer; or who knowingly refused to give a reasonable opportunity to parties in interest to inspect the documents and accounts relating to the affairs of the

estates in his charge, shall forfeit his office and suffer a fine of not more than $5,000.

It is the duty of the judge, receiver or trustee, if he has grounds for believing that an offense under the Bankruptcy Code has been committed, or if he believes that for any reason an investigation should be had in connection with an alleged offense, to report the matter to the United States Attorney for the district in which it is believed the offense has been committed. It then becomes the duty of the United States Attorney to inquire into the facts reported and, if it appears probable that any offense under the Bankruptcy Code has been committed, to present the matter to the Grand Jury.

Where it appears that the United States mails have been used for the purpose of perpetrating a fraud or in connection with the commission of any crime under the Bankruptcy Code, prosecution may, in a proper case, be had for use of the mails to defraud, and the indictment in such case may be found either at the place of mailing or at the place of the receipt of the letter.

It is important, in connection with mail frauds, to retain the envelope in which the letter was received for use as evidence in the prosecution of the offense. In mail fraud cases and most other noncapital federal offenses the limitation for indictment or the filing of an information is five years.

The Bankruptcy Court System and the Appeals Procedure

Bankruptcy judges may hear, determine, and enter orders and judgments in all case proceedings under the Code and in some cases, proceedings if they are related to a case under the Code. A core proceeding is defined as a proceeding concerning: the allowance or disallowance of claims, exemptions, turnover, preferences, modification of the automatic stay, fraudulent conveyances, the dischargeability of particular debts, objections to discharge, lien priority, confirmation of plans, orders on the use of real property, and so forth. It is the bankruptcy judge who is given the discretion to decide whether or not a proceeding is a "core proceeding" or is otherwise related to a case under the Code. In making the finding of whether a proceeding is a core proceeding, the judge is not allowed to base his findings solely on the basis that its ruling may be affected by state law.

In a related case, which is not a core proceeding, a bankruptcy judge may submit proposed findings of fact and conclusions of law to the district court. The district court will issue a final order of judgment, after reviewing *de novo* any matters to which a party has made a timely and specific objection. Furthermore, with the consent of all parties to a proceeding, the district court may refer a proceeding related to a case under the Code to a bankruptcy judge. The bankruptcy judge may then hear the case and enter the appropriate orders and judgments subject to review as outlined below. Just as the district court has the power to refer a proceeding to a bankruptcy judge, it also has the power to withdraw, in whole or in part, any case before a bankruptcy judge. The district court may make such a withdrawal on its own motion or on any timely motion of any party, for cause shown. Upon timely motion of a party, the district court is required to withdraw a proceeding if the court determines that resolution of the proceeding requires consideration of both the Code and other laws of the United States regulating organizations or activities affecting

BANKRUPTCY—SUMMARY OF PROCEDURE 28–19

interstate commerce. The district court is also required to hear and decide all personal injury tort and wrongful death claims.

The Code provides for a system of appeals in which the district court of the district in which the bankruptcy judge is serving has the jurisdiction to hear appeals from final judgments, orders and decrees of the bankruptcy courts. A district court may also hear, with leave of the bankruptcy court, appeals from interlocutory orders and decrees. Also, the judicial council of the circuit may establish a bankruptcy appellate panel, comprised of three bankruptcy judges from districts within the circuit, to hear and determine, upon the consent of all parties, appeals generally heard by the district court. It is the district judges who may, by a majority vote, authorize the referral of proceedings to a judicial panel. Finally, appeals from the district courts are to be taken to the appropriate court of appeals.

Notices

Creditors are entitled to receive at least ten days' notice of (1) all meetings of creditors; (2) all proposed sales of property unless the time is shortened by the judge, or an immediate sale without notice is ordered; (3) the filing of all accounts of the receiver and trustee for which confirmation is asked, and of the time when they will be examined and passed upon; (4) the proposed compromise of any controversy, in which the amount claimed by either party in money or value exceeds $1,000, unless the court for an explained reason orders notice not to be sent; (5) the proposed dismissal of the proceedings except where the dismissal is for failure to pay the costs of the bankruptcy proceeding; (6) all applications by marshals, trustees and attorneys for compensation from the estate and the amounts for which such applications are made.

In a voluntary case, if the debtor's debts are primarily consumer debts, notice must be given by mail to all creditors within twenty days.

Where a Creditors' Committee has been appointed, however, notices of examinations of the bankrupt, of proposed sales of property, and of the compromise of controversies are to be sent only to such Committee and to creditors who have filed with the court a demand that all notices be mailed to them.

Turnover Proceedings

Anyone, other than a custodian, who holds property of the estate is required to turn this property over to the trustee. No turnover is required if the person has obtained a court order authorizing the retention of the property or if the property is of inconsequential value. However, if the property is of value to the estate even if the monetary value is small, turnover is required. In all cases, an accounting is required. Anyone who owes money to the debtor is required to pay this money to the trustee; however, if the debtor also owes this person money, then the person may setoff the amount owed to the debtor. See *infra* "Setoff," page 28-22.

A custodian appointed prior to the bankruptcy case is required to turn over to the trustee and account for property of the debtor which has come into his possession or control as a custodian. A "custodian" is defined in the Code as a receiver or trustee in a nonbankruptcy case or proceeding, an assignee for the benefit of creditors, or as a trustee, receiver or agent under applicable law or under a contract that is appointed or authorized to take charge of a debtor's property to enforce a lien thereon, or to administer such property for the debtor's creditors. The custodian may not make any disbursements from the property unless it is necessary to the preservation of that property. The court is required to protect any obligations incurred by the custodian, provide for reasonable compensation and expenses to the custodian, and to surcharge the custodian for any excessive or improper disbursements. A custodian that is an assignee for the benefit of creditors appointed in the 120 days prior to the commencement of the case, however, is not subject to the surcharge unless compliance with turnover provisions is necessary to prevent fraud or injustice.

Distribution of Property of the Estate

The trustee is generally required to reduce the estate's property to money as expeditiously as is compatible with the best interest of the parties in interest. The money is then distributed as follows:

1. The payment of priority claims in the order specified earlier. See *supra* page 28-13.

2. Payment of other allowed unsecured claims, filed within 90 days after the first date set for the first meeting of creditors, by a creditor, a guarantor of the creditor, the trustee, or the debtor filing for the creditor. Claims not filed within that 90 day period will be paid if the creditor did not have notice or knowledge of the case in time for timely filing but did file the claim in time to permit payment; the time for filing claims is not fixed by the statute but is determined by the bankruptcy rules.

3. Other claims properly filed.

4. Claims, secured or unsecured, arising from any fine, penalty or forfeiture, or punitive damages, arising before the order for relief or the appointment of a trustee, whichever is earlier, unless such claim is compensation for actual pecuniary loss suffered by the holder of the claim.

5. Interest payments on any of the above claims.

6. To the debtor.

If there are insufficient funds to pay the claimants of a particular class in full, then that class will be paid on a pro rata basis. The only exception to this rule is in the case where a reorganization case, see *infra* page 28-24, or an individual repayment plan case, see *infra* page 28-37, is converted to a liquidation case. When this occurs, liquidation administrative expenses are paid before the reorganization or individual payment plan administrative expenses.

Reclamation Proceedings

A creditor who in the ordinary course of his business, sold goods to the debtor while the debtor was insolvent has a right to reclaim those goods. The seller must demand reclamation of the goods within ten days after receipt of the goods by the debtor, and the demand for reclamation must be in writing. The purpose of this provision is to recognize the validity of Section 2-702 of the Uniform Commercial Code which codifies the rights of sellers to reclaim goods sold to insolvent debtors. The court may refuse to permit reclamation, but if it so refuses it must grant the seller either a priority as an administrative

BANKRUPTCY—SUMMARY OF PROCEDURE

expense for his claim or secure the claim by a lien and adequately protect that lien.

Liens

The bankruptcy law recognizes and gives effect to all lien rights created by state law unless the lien is voidable because obtained through legal proceedings within ninety days before the filing of a petition or before the filing of a reorganization petition, and obtained while the debtor was insolvent, or unless the lien is voidable as a preference or a fraudulent conveyance. A trustee may avoid the fixing of statutory liens that become effective when the debtor is insolvent. Thus, if a lien becomes effective only when a case under the Code, or some insolvency proceeding, is commenced, or when a custodian is appointed, it may be avoided. See "Statutory Liens," *supra* page 28-9. Also, since the trustee has the status of a lien creditor (whether or not one actually exists) as of the date of the filing of the petition, liens perfected before that date that are not filed on that date in accordance with state law are voided. The trustee is subordinated to all actual secured claimholders and may void any liens that they may have avoided.[1]

The trustee may avoid a lien that secures a claim for any fine, penalty or forfeiture, unless the lien is compensation for actual pecuniary loss suffered by the holder of the claim. The Code also provides for distribution of property of the estate that is subject to a tax lien. Such property shall be distributed under the following priority system:

1) to a holder of a claim secured by the lien on the same property and that is senior to the tax lien;
2) to administrative expenses, wage claims and consumer creditors granted priority, but only to the extent of the amount of the allowed tax claim secured by the lien;
3) to the tax claimant to the extent that the above priority claimants did not use up his entire claim;
4) to junior lien holders;
5) to the tax claimant to the extent that he was not paid;
6) to the estate.

Statutory liens that are not perfected or enforceable against a bona fide purchaser, whether or not such purchaser exists, on the date of the petition are voidable.

Liens for rent and liens of distress for rent are also voidable, whether the lien is a statutory or common law lien. The trustee may avoid a transfer of a lien even if the lien has been enforced by sale before the commencement of the case.

The trustee has powers to avoid certain liens or obtain a priority status as a lien creditor or bona fide purchaser under what is commonly known as the "strong arm" provision of the Code. Generally this will place the trustee in a superior position against a creditor who has failed to perfect a security interest

---

[1] The Court of Appeals for the Third Circuit has held that for purposes of lien avoidance, there is no distinction between private and government liens. Thus, a lien or a debtor's property obtained by a public creditor, such as a state welfare department, can be avoided. *Gardner v. Pennsylvania,* 685 F. 2d 106 (1982).

or to comply with various state recording statutes with respect to conveyances or encumbrances of real property.

A mechanic's lien is valid even if the notice of the lien is filed after the filing of a petition in bankruptcy if the lien was filed within the time allowed by state law; liens created by chattel mortgages are valid if filed as required by the state statute. Any property subject to a lien, however, may be ordered sold free and clear of the lien if it appears that the bankrupt had an equity in the property, in which event the lien attaches to the proceeds of the sale.

Setoff

A creditor has the right to offset a debt owed to the debtor against a claim of that creditor against the debtor where both debts arose before commencement of the bankruptcy proceedings. The difference between the amounts owed is then either an asset of the bankrupt estate or a claim against the estate. The right of setoff can only be exercised before the date of the filing of the petition since by filing the petition the automatic stay ends the right of setoff. No right of setoff exists when:

1. The creditor acquires the claim from someone other than the debtor within 90 days of the filing of the petition (The debtor is presumed to be insolvent during the 90 days immediately preceding the date of the filing of the petition.), or

2. The debt was incurred within 90 days of the petition for the purpose of obtaining a right to setoff. Furthermore, a creditor may not improve his position by setoff within the 90 days before the filing of the petition. The trustee may recover from such creditor the amount of offset to the extent that any insufficiency on the date of such setoff is less than the insufficiency on the later of 90 days before the date of the filing of the petition, and the first date during the 90 days preceding the date of the filing on which there was an insufficiency.

The setoff situation arises most frequently in connection with bank deposits where, for example, the debtor has funds on deposit with the bank and is, at the same time indebted to the bank for a loan. The relationship between a bank and its depositor is that of debtor and creditor and the bank may, therefore, before the petition is filed, offset its debt to the bankrupt against the bankrupt's debt to it.

Voidable Preferences

The trustee is authorized to avoid transfers that are preferential in nature. A preferential transfer is a transfer which:

1. Is made for the benefit of a creditor;

2. Is made on account of an antecedent debt owed by the debtor prior to the transfer;

3. Is made while the debtor is insolvent; insolvency is presumed within 90 days of the filing of the petition;

4. Is made within 90 days of the filing of the petition, or between 90 days and one year before the filing of the petition by an insider. The Code defines an insider as one who, because of his close relationship with the debtor, will be "subject to closer scrutiny" than another person dealing with the debtor. If the debtor is an individual, then insiders include relatives of the debtor. If

BANKRUPTCY—SUMMARY OF PROCEDURE

the debtor is a partnership, insiders would include a partner or relative of a partner and if a corporation, then insiders include directors, officers, persons in control, and their relatives;

5. Enables the creditor to receive more than he would have received in a liquidation case or if the transfer had not been made.

The trustee may not avoid a transfer as preferential to the extent that such transfer was:

1. Intended by the debtor and the creditor to be a contemporaneous exchange for new value given to the debtor and was in fact a substantially contemporaneous exchange;

2. In payment of a debt incurred by the debtor in the ordinary course of business of the debtor and the transferee, where payment was made according to ordinary business terms after the debt was incurred;

3. A security interest given by the debtor to enable the debtor to acquire the property which the transferred interest secures;

4. To or for the benefit of a creditor, to the extent that after such transfer the creditor gave new value to the debtor on an unsecured basis;

5. A perfected security interest held by a creditor in inventory or receivables, except to the extent that the creditor improved his position during the ninety day period prior to the filing of the petition;

6. Of a security interest for new value, provided the security interest is perfected on or before 10 days after the debtor receives possession of such property.

7. In a case filed by an individual debtor whose debts are primarily consumer debts, and the aggregate value of all property that constitutes or is affected by such transfer is less than $600.

A transfer of real property is perfected when it is valid against a bona fide purchaser. With respect to personal property, a transfer is perfected when it would be valid against a creditor who obtains a judicial lien after the transfer is perfected. Under the Code, a transfer is made when it takes effect if it is perfected within ten days. Otherwise, it is deemed made when the transfer is perfected, if not within the ten-day period. Thus, a transfer which occurred ninety-five days before the filing of the petition, but was perfected only eighty days before the filing of the petition, is deemed made eighty days before the filing of the petition and therefore is subject to be voided as a preferential transfer if the other conditions are met.

Fraudulent Transfers

A trustee is permitted to avoid transfers by the debtor in fraud of his creditors. A transfer which was made in the year preceding the filing of the petition may be voided if it was made with an intent to hinder, delay or defraud a creditor. Transfers made for less than a reasonably equivalent value can be voided if the debtor was insolvent or became insolvent because of the transfer, was engaged in business with an unreasonably small amount of the capital or if the debtor intended to incur debts which were beyond his ability to pay. A trustee of a partnership debtor may avoid any transfers of partnership property to a partner in the debtor made within one year of the petition if the debtor was insolvent or became insolvent as a result of the transfer.

A transfer is made when it is valid against a subsequent bona fide purchaser.

If a transfer is not perfected before the bankruptcy case is commenced, it is considered made immediately prior to the case.

Final Meeting of Creditors

A final meeting of creditors is held when the estate is ready to be closed. At this meeting the trustee's final account, and all applications for allowances not theretofore passed upon, come before the court for its approval. Creditors are entitled to thirty days' notice and may appear and object to any item in the account or any application for compensation.

REORGANIZATIONS

One of the major changes under the new Bankruptcy Code is the consolidation of Chapters X and XI of the former Bankruptcy Act into a single reorganization chapter—Chapter 11. Chapter X under the Bankruptcy Act was designed for the thorough reorganization of the public company. It contemplated rigid and formalized procedures and the imposition of strict financial rules governing a plan of reorganization. Chapter XI of the old Act was originally designed for use by the nonpublic small business. Chapter XI contained a faster procedure for an arrangement of the debtor's unsecured debt, but the secured debt structure could not be altered. Chapter 11 of the new Code attempts to combine the completeness of Chapter X with the speed and flexibility of Chapter XI.

Proceedings under Chapter 11 are designated reorganizations and are available to all who are eligible for liquidation proceedings as discussed above, except stockbrokers and commodity brokers, and railroads. Reorganization may affect the rights of all creditors, secured or unsecured, as well as stockholders. The purpose of a business reorganization case, unlike a liquidation case, is to restructure the finances of a business so that it may continue to operate, pay creditors and produce a return for its stockholders. The purpose of a reorganization or arrangement case for a debtor is to formulate, and have confirmed, a reorganization plan so that it can continue in business.

Terminology

(a) "Affiliate" includes
1. any entity which is 20% owner of or 20% owned by, either directly or indirectly, the debtor;
2. a person whose business is operated under a lease or operating agreement with the debtor;
3. a person substantially all of whose property is operated under an operating agreement with the debtor;
4. any entity that operates the business or substantially all of the property of the debtor under a lease or operating agreement.

Persons whose property is operated under a lease agreement with the debtor are not affiliates.

(b) "Claim" means all rights to payment, whether or not such right is reduced to judgment, liquidated or unliquidated, contingent, secured or unsecured, and all rights to an equitable remedy for breach of performance if such right gives rise to a right of payment.

BANKRUPTCY—SUMMARY OF PROCEDURE

(c) "Corporation" includes an association having the power or privileges that a private corporation, but not an individual or partnership, possesses; a partnership where only partnership property is responsible for the debts; a joint stock company; and an unincorporated company or association or a business trust. It does not include a limited partnership.

(d) "Creditor" is a holder of any kind of claim against the debtor.

(e) "Debtor" includes any person that can be the debtor in a liquidation or straight bankruptcy case, but does not include a commodity broker or stockholder, and a railroad. A municipality may not be a debtor in a reorganization case.

(f) "Debtor in Possession" means debtor except when a qualified person has been selected to serve as a trustee in the case.

(g) "Debts" includes all liabilities on claims.

(h) "Indenture Trustee" means a trustee under an indenture.

(i) "Party in Interest" includes the debtor, a creditor, a creditors' committee, an equity security holder, and an equity security holders' committee.

(j) "Petition" includes all voluntary, involuntary, and joint petition commencing a case under the Bankruptcy Code.

(k) "Securities" includes notes, stocks, bonds, debentures, voting trust certificates, certificates of deposit, interest of a limited partner and a limited partnership, and other claims or interest commonly known as security.

(l) "Substantial Consummation" means the transfer of all or substantially all of the property proposed by the plan to be transferred, with the debtor, or his successor under the plan, assuming the management of all or substantially all of the property dealt with by the plan and the commencement of a distribution under the plan.

Jurisdiction and Function of the Court

The jurisdiction of the bankruptcy court in a reorganization case is governed by the same rules as in a liquidation case. As with a liquidation case, the filing of the petition acts as an automatic stay on other proceedings against the debtor.

In a reorganization case, the bankruptcy court has the power to:

1. Hold a hearing to determine the need for a trustee to assume control of the debtor's business upon the request of a party in interest, an indenture trustee, or the Securities and Exchange Commission. Upon the court's order, the United States Trustee will appoint a disinterested trustee who is subject to the court's approval. In districts where there is no United States Trustee, the court will appoint the trustee;

2. Terminate the trustee's appointment and restore the debtor to possession of the estate property and management of the business. The court is permitted to exercise this power, upon the request of a party in interest or the United States trustee, after notice and hearing, at any time before plan confirmation.

3. Order the appointment of an examiner, in lieu of a trustee, to investigate the affairs of the debtor. Grounds for such an order include: that it would be in the best interests of the creditors; unsecured, liquidated debts other than for goods, services, or owed to an insider, exceed $5,000; for cause, including fraud, or mismanagement. The method of appointment is the same as for a trustee;

4. Appoint a committee of unsecured creditors, as soon as is practicable after the order for relief in districts without a United States Trustee. Additional committees of creditors or equity security holders may be appointed if necessary to assure that such a class of creditors receives adequate representation. The court is also authorized to change the size or membership of a committee if the membership is not representative of the different kinds of claims or interests of creditors;

5. Convert a reorganization case to a liquidation case, or dismiss the case, whenever to do so would be in the best interest of the creditors of the estate (e.g., inability to effectuate a plan, unreasonable delay by the debtor, etc.);

6. Reduce or increase, for cause, the 120 days allowed for a debtor to file a plan and the 180 days after the order of relief for a plan submitted by the debtor is to be accepted by the creditors;

7. Approve of the written disclosure statement on the plan as containing adequate information to enable the creditors to make an informed judgment about the plan;

8. Confirm the reorganization plan if it meets the requirements established in the Code. (See Confirmation *infra* page 28-32.) The court must hold a hearing on the confirmation;

9. Direct the debtor to perform any act necessary for the consummation of the plan, including the execution or delivery of any instrument necessary to effect a transfer of property called for in the plan.

Jurisdiction of Appellate Courts

The same as in liquidation proceedings.

How Proceedings Are Commenced

(a) *Voluntary proceeding:* A debtor may file a petition to effect a reorganization whether or not a liquidation proceeding is pending, either before or after an order for relief has been entered.

(b) *Involuntary proceeding:* Three or more creditors with claims aggregating $5,000 more than the value of any lien on the property of the debtor may file an involuntary petition to have the debtor reorganized under the same conditions as the debtor itself might institute the proceeding. If there are fewer than twelve creditors, only one creditor with an aggregate claim greater than $5,000 need file. Neither a farmer nor an eleemosynary institution can be subjected to an involuntary petition.

Court in Which Federal Proceedings May Be Commenced

A reorganization petition may be filed with the court in whose territorial jurisdiction the debtor has had its principal place of business or its principal assets for the preceding six months or for a longer portion than in any other jurisdiction. A petition may also be filed in a district court where there is a case pending upon the Bankruptcy Code against the debtor's affiliate, general partner, or partnership.

Filing Fees

$200, unless a railroad is involved, in which case, $500.

Procedure for Filing of Involuntary Petition

The same as in liquidation proceedings.

Order for Relief

The filing of a voluntary petition by the debtor commences the case and constitutes an order for relief. The filing of an involuntary petition, if not challenged by the debtor, will also result in a court order for relief under a reorganization plan. If the involuntary petition is controverted the court shall order relief if the debtor is generally not paying his debts as they become due, or in the 120 days prior to the filing, a custodian was appointed or took possession of some of the debtor's property in order to execute a lien. Adequate notice of any order of relief must be given, including notice to any holder of a community claim.

Conversion or Dismissal

The debtor, if he is a debtor in possession, may convert a voluntary reorganization case to a liquidation case. Upon the request of a party in interest, and if in the best interest of creditors and the estate, the court may dismiss a reorganization case or convert it to a liquidation case. Reasons justifying a dismissal or conversion include, but are not limited to, the following:
1. Continuing loss to the estate without likelihood of rehabilitation;
2. Inability to effectuate a plan of rehabilitation;
3. Delay by the debtor which is prejudicial to creditors;
4. Failure to propose a plan within the time fixed by the court;
5. Denial of confirmation of proposed plan and expiration of time for filing plans;
6. Revocation of a plan and denial of another or modified plan;
7. Inability to consummate confirmed plan;
8. Substantial default by the debtor in some aspect of a confirmed plan;
9. Termination of the plan.

Trustee, Debtor in Possession, or Examiner

The debtor shall remain in possession of the business unless a request is made for the appointment of a trustee. The court will hold a hearing to determine the need for a trustee in any case in which a party in interest, an indenture trustee, or the Securities and Exchange Commission requests appointment of a trustee. The court may order appointment only if the protection afforded by a trustee is needed, and the cost and expenses of a trustee would not be disproportionately higher than the value of the protection afforded. Protection of the estate would be called for, for example, in cases involving fraud, incompetence, dishonesty or gross mismanagement of the affairs of the estate by the debtor.

Mere misconduct would not call for the appointment of a trustee, but rather, for the appointment of an examiner. Where an examiner would serve adequately, the appointment of a trustee would be considered too costly. An examiner may be appointed by the court, on a request of a party in interest, and after notice and hearing, to investigate allegations of misconduct or irregularity in the management of the affairs of the debtor. The court will order the appointment of an examiner if such appointment would be in the best interests of the parties involved, *or* the debtor's fixed, liquidated, unsecured debts, other than debts for goods, services, taxes, or owed to an insider, exceed $5,000.

A trustee in a reorganization case has many of the same duties as a trustee in a liquidation case. As in a liqudation case, the trustee is held accountable for all property he has received. If the debtor has not done so, the trustee is required to file with the court the list of creditors, a schedule of assets and liabilities, and a statement of financial affairs. Unless the court directs otherwise, the trustee must investigate the conduct and financial condition of the debtor, the operation of the debtor's business, the desirability of the continuation of the business, and all other matters relevant to the case or to the formulation of a reorganization plan. The results of these investigations must be reported to the court and a copy transmitted to any creditor's committee or equity security holder's committee, any indenture trustee, and to any other entity the court designates. If the debtor has failed to file an acceptable plan within the time allotted by the court, the trustee is required to file the plan or to report why a plan cannot be formulated, or to recommend conversion to a liquidation or an individual repayment plan case, or to recommend dismissal.

Upon the request of a party in interest, at any time before a plan is confirmed, the trustee's appointment may be terminated by the court and the debtor restored to possession and management of its business; the court shall order a termination of the trustee's role upon receiving new evidence that the debtor can be left in possession of its business and property.

A debtor in possession has the same rights and duties as a trustee, except as to investigative duties. The debtor in possession is also subject to the same limitations as a trustee, and to such other limitations and condition as the court prescribes.

Both the trustee and the debtor in possession are authorized to continue the operation of the debtor's business. The business will cease operating only on the order of the court.

First Hearing

A hearing upon at least ten days' notice to all interested parties, including the Securities and Exchange Commission, is to be held not less than twenty days nor more than forty days after the filing of the petition. Notice of the meeting is to be given by mail or, if mailing is impractical, by publication.

Creditors and Creditors' Committees

As soon as practicable after the order for relief, the court shall appoint a committee of creditors holding unsecured claims. If requested by a party in interest and if the court determines that such committees are necessary to assure adequate representation of creditors or of equity security holders, the court may order the appointment of additional committees of creditors or of equity security holders. The committees will represent the various classes of creditors or equity security holders from which they are selected. Ordinarily, the committees will consist of holders of the seven largest claims of interest to be represented. The seven largest equity shareholders, if willing to serve, will compose the committee of equity security holders. The court may change the size of the committee, upon the request of a party in interest, if the membership is not representative of the different kinds of claims or interest to be represented. After the appointment of a committee, the trustee shall meet with the committee to transact such business as may be necessary.

At a scheduled committee meeting, attended by a majority of the members of the committee, and with the court's approval, the committee may select and authorize the employment of one or more attorneys, accountants, or other agents, to represent and perform services for the committee. A committee may:

1. Consult with the trustee or debtor in possession concerning the administration of the case;
2. Investigate the operation of the debtor's business, the desirability of its continuance, and any other matter relevant to the case or to the formulation of a plan;
3. Participate in the formulation of plan;
4. Request the appointment of a trustee or examiner, if one has not been appointed, if necessary to protect the interest of the class represented;
5. Perform other services that are in the interest of those represented.

The committee is not required to make recommendations as to a plan, but is only required to provide its determinations. The committee may also solicit rejections as well as acceptances of a plan.

Who May Propose and File Reorganization Plan

The debtor in possession has the exclusive right to file a plan for the 120 days following the filing of the petition. Any party in interest, including the debtor, the trustee, a creditor's committee, an equity security holders' committee, a creditor, an equity security holder or any indenture trustee, may file a plan *only if:*

(1) a trustee has been appointed;
(2) the debtor has not filed a plan within 120 days after the filing of the petition; *or*
(3) the debtor has not filed a plan that has been accepted by each class of impaired claims or interests within 180 days after the filing of the petition.

The court may, for cause, reduce or increase the period allowed for the filing or acceptance of a debtor's plan. Cause might include an unusually large or unusually small case, delay by the debtor or recalcitrance among creditors.

Claims and Interest

A claim or interest is deemed filed when it is included in the debtor's or trustee's schedule of liabilities unless it is scheduled as a disputed, contingent, or unliquidated claim. This provision dispenses with the need for every creditor and equity security holder to file a proof of claim or interest in a reorganization case. It is advisable, however, to file a proof of claim to avoid the necessity to search the file especially since there might be a discrepancy in the amount of the claim.

If a secured claimholder's collateral is worth less than the debt owed him by the debtor he is deemed to have a general unsecured claim against the debtor for the amount of deficiency. An exception to this is when the collateral is sold during the Chapter 11 proceeding or pursuant to the plan. In such case, the secured claimholder may not file a claim for the deficiency. In the alternative, the class of such a claimholder may elect, by two-thirds in amount of claims and more than half in number, to have the claim secured to the extent it is allowed.

The plan may place a claim or an interest in a particular class only if the claim or interest is substantially similar to other claims or interest in the class. The one exception to this classification system is that the court may lump together all unsecured claims of less than a specified dollar amount when reasonable and necessary for administrative convenience.

Contents of the Plan

The reorganization plan shall:
1. Designate classes of claims and interest, except administrative claims, unsecured claims arising between the filing of an involuntary petition and the appointment of a trustee, and certain tax claims;
2. Specify classes of claims not impaired under the plan;
3. Specify treatment of any class of claims or interest impaired by the plan;
4. Provide equal treatment for all the claims of a class;
5. Provide for the successful consummation of the plan by such means as:
   (a) retention by the debtor of any of the estate's property,
   (b) satisfaction or modification of any liens,
   (c) merger or consolidation of the debtor with one or more persons,
   (d) transfer of any property of the estate to another entity,
   (e) curing, or waiving any default,
   (f) issuance of securities;
6. Provide for inclusion in the charter of a debtor corporation a provision prohibiting the issuance of nonvoting stock and a provision calling for an appropriate distribution of voting power among the classes of stock.

The plan may propose that certain secured or unsecured claims or interests are impaired or unimpaired. The plan may also provide for the assumption or rejection of executory contracts or unexpired leases not previously rejected or accepted by the trustee. (The same limitations imposed upon a trustee's acceptance of executory contracts in a liquidation case are imposed in a reorganization case.) The plan may also provide for the treatment of claims by the debtor against other entities that are not settled before the confirmation of the plan. The plan may call for the settlement of any claims belonging to the debtor against other entities, or provide for the retention and enforcement of those claims by the debtor or an agent. The sale of all or substantially all of the property of the estate may be proposed in the plan along with the distribution scheme for the proceeds among creditors and equity security holders; this would be a liquidation plan.

A plan proposed by an entity other than the debtor may not provide for the use, sale, or lease of the debtor's exempt property under the Code unless the debtor consents to such use, sale or lease.

Impairment of Claims

There are three ways in which the plan may leave a class of claims or interests unimpaired. First, if the legal, equitable, and contractual rights which the claim or interest creates in the holder are not altered by the plan, then those claims are unimpaired. Second, if the holder of the claim is entitled by contract or applicable law to demand or receive accelerated payment after the occurrence of the default, the plan may reinstate the maturity of such claim or interest as such maturity existed before the default and cure the default. In this context, the holder of the claim must be compensated for any damages incurred as a result of a reasonable reliance on such contractual provision where applicable law entitled him to accelerated payment. Third, claims are considered unimpaired if the plan provides for, on the effective date of the plan, payment in cash equal to the allowed amount of the claim, or with respect to a security interest, the greater of the fixed liquidation preference such interest gives to the holder of the interest, and the fixed price at which the debtor may redeem the security from the holder.

Disclosure of the Plan

Before solicitation of acceptance of the plan of reorganization, information about the plan must be disclosed. The information disclosed must be adequate to give the typical investor of each solicited class an opportunity to make an informed and reasonable judgment about the plan. If "adequate information" is provided to all creditors and stockholders whose rights are to be affected, then they should be able to make an informed judgment which protects their own interest. Both the kind and form of information are left essentially to the discretion of the court. The court may approve of a disclosure statement that does not include a valuation of the debtor or an appraisal of the debtor's assets. The Securities and Exchange Commission or a State Corporation Commissioner may appear and be heard on the issue of whether a disclosure statement contains adequate information, but the agencies and officials are not granted the right of appeal from an adverse determination. The requirements of federal and state securities laws do not pertain to disclosure statements. Thus, disclosure statements may be approved even if the statement does not meet the registration requirement or the proxy provisions of the Securities and Exchange Acts. A person who in good faith solicits acceptance or rejection of the plan by use of an approved disclosure statement is immune from any liability under the regulations governing the offer, issuance, sale, or purchase of securities.

Acceptance of the Reorganization Plan

The holder of a claim or interest is allowed to accept or reject a proposed plan or reorganization. Such acceptance or rejection may be tendered before the commencement of the case if: (1) the solicitation of the pre-commencement acceptance or rejection was in compliance with any applicable nonbankruptcy law, rule or regulation governing the adequacy of disclosure in connection with such solicitations, or (2) the solicitation provides the holder adequate information for that holder to make a reasonable judgment concerning the plan.

A class of creditors has accepted a plan if at least two-thirds in amount and more than one-half in number of the allowed claims of the class that voted are cast in favor of the plan. A class of interests have accepted the plan if at least two-thirds of the outstanding equity securities have voted for the plan. On the request of a party in interest, and after notice and a hearing, the court may determine that an entity's acceptance or rejection was not in good faith, or was not solicited in good faith, and exclude the entity's vote from the computation. An unimpaired class is deemed to have accepted the plan and no solicitation or acceptance is required. A class is deemed to have rejected a plan if the class was denied participation in the reorganized debtor.

Modification of the Plan

A plan's proponent may modify the plan before confirmation. When the modified plan is filed with the court it becomes the plan. After confirmation, but before substantial consummation of the plan, the proponent or the reorganized debtor may modify the plan. The court, after notice and a hearing, will confirm the modified plan if the circumstances warranted the modification. The rules applying to classification of claims and the contents of the plan continue to apply to the plan as modified. Disclosure of adequate information concerning the modified plan is also required. The court shall enter an order that the plan is modified and shall be deemed to have been accepted by any creditor who accepted the plan and who fails to file with the court within the fixed time set by the court a written rejection of the modification. Notice of such order, accompanied by a copy of the proposed modification, shall be given to creditors and other parties in interest at least ten days before the time fixed for filing rejections.

Confirmation of the Plan

After notice is given, the court shall hold a hearing on confirmation of the plan. Any party in interest, including the Securities and Exchange Commission and indentured trustees, may object to the confirmation of the plan.

The court shall confirm a plan only if all of the following requirements are met:

1. The plan meets all the requirements of the Code (for example, the requirements concerning content and classification);

2. The proponent of the plan complied with the provisions of the Code (for example, disclosure);

3. The plan was submitted in good faith;

4. All payments made or promised under the plan for costs incurred in the case, or in connection with the plan, are disclosed in the plan. Payments made before confirmation must be reasonable; payments made after confirmation are subject to court approval as reasonable;

5. The plan discloses the identity and affiliation of any individual who will serve as a director, officer or voting trustee in the debtor, or an affiliate or successor to the debtor, and the selection of the individual is consistent with the interests of the creditors. The plan must also disclose the identity and compensation of an insider retained by the reorganized debtor;

6. Any regulatory committee that will have jurisdiction over the debtor has approved any rate change provided for in the plan, or the rate change is conditioned on such approval;

7. Within each class, each holder of a claim has accepted the plan or will receive property under the plan that is of greater value than the claim holder would have received if the debtor were liquidated. Secured creditors who have elected to have their claims secured to the full extent the claim is allowed, rather than to the extent of the value of the collateral securing the claim, must receive or retain under the plan property of a value not less than the value of the creditor's interest in the property that secures the claim;

8. With respect to each class, such class has accepted the plan or such class is not impaired under the plan;

9. Unless the claimholder has agreed to be treated differently, the plan must provide that holders of claims arising from administrative expenses, or claims in an involuntary case arising between the time of the filing of the petition and the earlier of the appointment of the trustee or the order for relief, will receive cash equal to the allowed amount of that claim on the effective date of the plan. Holders of priority wage claims, consumer claims or contributions to employee benefit claims, as defined in the priority claims section under liquidation, will receive deferred cash payments of a value equal to the allowed amount of such claims, if such class has accepted the plan. If the class has not accepted the plan, the class will receive cash equal to the allowed amount of the claim on the effective date of the plan. Claims arising from priority taxes will receive deferred cash payments over a period not exceeding six years after the date of the assessment of the claim, of a value equal to the allowed amount of the claim;

10. At least one class of claims which is impaired, excluding any claims or interests held by insiders, has accepted the plan;

11. There is little likelihood that following the confirmation of the plan, liquidation, or further financial reorganization, of the debtor other than what is called for in the plan, will be necessary.

Cram-Down

If all of the requirements for confirmation are met, except that one impaired class has rejected the plan, the court may still confirm the plan. Confirmation under these circumstances may take place only upon the request of the proponent of the plan. The plan may be confirmed if the court determines that it does not discriminate unfairly, and provides fair and equitable treatment to the impaired class that rejected the plan. One of the elements of fairness is the absolute priority rule: dissenting classes must be paid in full before any junior class may share under the plan. Treatment of secured creditors is slightly different, however, because they do not fall in the priority ladder. Another central element to the "fair and equitable" treatment doctrine is that no class senior to the dissenting class receive more than 100 percent of the amount of its claims. It must be emphasized that the fair and equitable requirement applies only to dissenting classes. Thus, cooperation is fostered by the fact that, in order to ensure plan acceptance, senior creditors may voluntarily give up value to junior creditors so long as no dissenting intervening class receives less than its full share.

(1) The Code provides three tests for determining fairness and equitability of the plan in relation to a dissenting class of secured claimholders. First, the plan will be confirmed if the secured claimholders will retain their lien

on the debtor's property whether the property is retained by the debtor or transferred. In addition, each claimholder must receive deferred cash payments totaling at least the allowed amount of the claim of a value of not less than the value of the holder's interest in the estate interest in the property. Second, a plan may meet the fairness test if it provides for the sale of the property subject to the lien securing the claims and calls for the lien to attach to the proceeds of the sale. Third, a plan is fair and equitable to secured claimholders if it allows for the realization by such holders of the indubitable equivalent of their claims. The standard of "indubitable equivalence" would be satisfied by such means as abandonment of the collateral to the creditor, or giving the creditor a lien on similar collateral.

(2) The court may confirm over the dissent of a class of unsecured claims, including priority claims, if that class will receive under the plan property of a value equal to the allowed amount of their unsecured claims or if no junior class will share under the plan. Thus, an impaired class of unsecured claimholders must either be paid in full or if paid less than in full, no junior class may receive anything under the plan.

(3) With respect to a class of equity security holders, the court may confirm over the dissent of the members of the class, if the members of that class receive their liquidation preference or redemption rights, or if no junior class shares under the plan. A class of impaired interests may include the interest of general or limited partners in a partnership or the interest of the sole proprietor. If the holders of such interest are entitled to a fixed liquidation preference or fixed redemption price on the account of the interest, then the plan may be confirmed over their dissent so long as it provides them property of a present value equal to the greater of the fixed redemption price or the value of the interest. In the event there is no fixed liquidation or redemption price, the plan may be confirmed if it provides the holder of such interest property of a present value equal to the value of the interest.

The court may confirm only one plan, unless the order of confirmation has been revoked. If more than one plan meets all the above requirements, the court shall consider the preferences of creditors and equity security holders in determining which plan is to be confirmed. A plan which meets all of the above requirements but is intended primarily to avoid taxes or provisions of the securities laws will not be confirmed by the court. Where the plan appears to intend an avoidance of taxes objection to confirmation may be made on that ground by the Secretary of the Treasury.

Effect of Confirmation

The provisions of a confirmed plan are binding on the debtor, any entity issuing securities or acquiring property under the plan, and any creditor, equity security holder, or general partner in the debtor. The confirmation of the plan discharges the debtor from any debt that arose before the date of confirmation unless the plan provides otherwise. The discharge is effective against those claims whether or not proof of a claim is filed, and whether or not the claim is allowed.

The discharge also terminates all rights and interests of equity security holders and general partners provided for by the plan. The claims exempted from discharge are the same as the claims exempted from discharge in a liquidation case. They include priority taxes, custom duties, money obtained by fraud, alimony, and child support payments. The debtor is not discharged by the confirmation of a plan, however, if the plan is a liquidating plan and the debtor would be denied discharge in a liquidation case. In other words, if substantially all of the property of the estate is distributed, if the business does not continue, and if the debtor would be denied a discharge or had committed an act which would have led to a denial of discharge in a liquidation case, then a reorganization discharge is not granted.

Confirmation discharges the debtor from claims arising from the rejection from an executory contract or unexpired lease, and claims for a priority tax that does not arise until after the commencement of the case. The court may approve a written waiver of discharge executed by the debtor after the order for relief.

Execution of the Plan

The court may direct the debtor to perform any act that is necessary for the consummation of a plan. This includes satisfaction of a lien and the delivery of any instrument required to effect a transfer of property under the plan.

When a plan requires presentment, or surrender of a security, or performance of any act as a condition to participate in distribution, such act must be done within five years after confirmation. Failure to perform within five years bars one from participation in the distribution.

Revocation of a Confirmation Order

Within 180 days after the confirmation order, a party in interest may request and a court may enter, after notice and hearing, an order revoking the plan if the plan was procured by fraud. The court's order will contain provisions necessary to protect any entity which acquired rights in good faith reliance on the confirmation; the court's order will also contain a provision for the revocation of the debtor's discharge.

Exemption from Security Laws

The issuance of certain securities in connection with a reorganization case are exempted from the registration requirements of Section 5 of the Securities Act of 1933 as well as any other state or local laws requiring registration for offer or sale of security or registration for an issuer or an underwriter of securities. If the plan calls for the offer or sale of a security of the debtor, an affiliate participating in a joint plan with the debtor, or the successor to the debtor, in exchange for a claim against, or an interest in, a claim arising from the administrative expense against the debtor or the debtor's affiliate, such offer or sale is also exempt under the Securities Laws. Also exempted is the offer or sale of any security that arises from the exercise of a subscription right or from the exercise of a conversion privilege when it was issued under the plan. A narrow exemption also exists for the offer or sale of security of an issuer, other than the debtor or the debtor's affiliate, if the security was owned by the debtor when the petition was filed. This exemption only applies if the security issued is subject to the requirements of periodic reports under Section 13 of the Securities and Exchange Act. For a two year period following the filing of the petition, the exempted sale cannot exceed four percent of the outstanding securities of the class and for the 180 days following this two year period, not more than one percent of the outstanding securities at the beginning of such 180 day period. Within 40 days after the security was first offered to the public, a stock broker, if he has supplied an approved disclosure statement, and if the court orders information supplementing the disclosure statement, may execute a transaction of the security free of the security registration laws.

The Code specifies the standards under which a creditor acquiring securities under the plan may resell them. The Securities Act places limitations on sales by underwriters. Under the Code, an entity is an underwriter, as defined by the Securities Act of 1933, if such entity:

1. Purchases a claim against, interest in, or claim for, an administrative expense in the case concerning the debtor with an intent to distribute any security received in exchange for the claim or interest; 2. offers to the holders of securities offered or sold under the plan to offer or sell their securities; 3. offers to buy securities offered or sold under the plan for the holders of such securities, if such offer to buy is made with an intent to distribute those securities and is made under an agreement under the plan; 4. is an issuer as defined in Section 2(11) of the Securities and Exchange Act of 1933, with respect to such securities.

Any entity that would fall within this definition of underwriter as a result of an agreement that provides only for the matching combination of fractional interests in the covered securities or the purchase or sale of fractional interests, is exempted from the definition of underwriter with respect to those agreements.

The offer or sale of securities under the plan in an exempt transaction is deemed a public offering. This provision prevents characterization of the distribution as a "private placement" which would result in certain restrictions on the resale of the securities under the Securities and Exchange Commission Rules. A creditor who, for example, some years later, becomes an underwriter by reacquiring securities issued under a plan, is not exempted.

Finally, the Code provides that the Trust Indenture Act of 1939 does not apply to a commercial note issued under a plan if that note matures within one year after the effective date of the plan.

Tax Consequences

For the purposes of any state or local income taxes, the taxable period of an individual debtor ends on the date of the order for relief, unless the case was converted from a liquidation case. If the case was converted from a liquidation to a reorganization case, the estate is treated as a separate taxable entity dating from the order for relief in the liquidation proceeding. Termination of the taxable year of the debtor commences the tax period of the estate. If multiple conversion of the case occurs, then the estate is treated as a separate taxable entity as of the date of the order for relief of the *first* proceeding under which the estate became a separate taxable entity.

The trustee shall file a state or local income tax return for the estate of the individual debtor for each taxable period after the order for relief during which the case is pending.

The issuance, transfer, or exchange of a security, or the making or delivering of an instrument of transfer under a confirmed plan, is exempt from any state or local stamp tax.

The proponent of a plan may request a declaratory judgment from a local or state taxing authority regarding the tax effects of the plan; these tax effects are considered questions of law. In the event of a controversy, the court may declare the tax effects of the plan of reorganization after the response of the taxing unit or 270 days after the request by the proponent of the plan, whichever is earlier. Unless appealed, the judgment of the court becomes final and binds any taxing authority where the proponent requested that authority to determine the tax effects of the plan.

In the case of a plan whose principal purpose is tax avoidance, the government has the burden of proving avoidance.

ADJUSTMENT OF DEBTS OF AN INDIVIDUAL WITH REGULAR INCOME—CHAPTER 13

Chapter 13 affords relief to individuals with regular income by allowing for the development of "individual repayment plans." Under prior law, only a wage earner could qualify for such relief, but under the new Code such plans are available to others. For example, small businessmen, whose incomes are sufficiently regular to enable payment under a plan, and who have unsecured debts of less than $100,000 and secured debts of less than $350,000 qualify for Chapter 13 relief.

Chapter 13 is completely voluntary; a debtor can not be forced into a repayment plan by creditors. The benefit of a repayment plan to a debtor is that he retains his property and protects his assets while paying his creditors over a period of time. He need not surrender his nonexempt property as is required in a liquidation case. If the debtor is engaged in business, he is permitted to remain in business unless the court orders otherwise.

The duty of the trustee under a Chapter 13 plan is to see to the disbursement of payments to creditors. The trustee is also accountable for all property received, must investigate the financial affairs of the debtor, and advise and assist the debtor in performance of the plan.

The debtor has the exclusive right to propose a plan. The plan may provide for the payment of creditors out of property other than the future income or earnings of the debtor, and for the payment of creditors over a period of three years; for cause, the court may extend this period to five years.

There are six separate requirements for plan confirmation:

1. The plan must comply with the provisions of Chapter 13 and any other applicable provisions of the Bankruptcy Code;
2. All required fees must be paid;
3. In the event there is objection by the trustee or the holder of an unsecured claim, the value of the property to be distributed under the plan must be equal to or exceed (i) the amount of such claim or (ii) all of the debtor's projected disposable income to be received in the three years beginning when the first payment is due. This standard replaces the good faith test previously used.
4. The value of property distributed under the plan for allowed unsecured claims must be not less than the amount that would have been paid under a liquidation plan;
5. With respect to each allowed unsecured claim: (a) the holder of the claim

must accept the plan, or (b) the holder of the claim must retain his lien or recover the value of his claim, or (c) the debtor must surrender the property securing such claim to the claimholder;

6. The debtor must be able to comply with the plan. Payment under the plan must begin within 30 days after filing the petition.

A Chapter 13 plan may treat cosigned consumer debt claims differently than other unsecured claims since cosignors are usually relatives and such debts would be subject to collection by creditors. A separate payment schedule can apply to such debts.

The court must grant the debtor a discharge as soon as practicable after completion of payments under the plan. Waiver of the discharge, with court approval, is permitted. The court may also grant a "hardship discharge" when the debtor has not completed payment, if:

a. the debtor could not be held accountable for the circumstances precluding his payment;

b. the debtor has paid at least liquidation value; and

c. modification of the plan is not practicable.

Modification of a Chapter 13 plan is now possible only if request is made by the debtor, the trustee or the holder of an allowed unsecured claim.

Under Chapter 7, discharge is prohibited if there has been a discharge granted to the debtor within the previous six years. This provision does not apply to Chapter 13. A Chapter 13 debtor is not prevented from seeking another discharge anytime during the six years after a discharge under a prior liquidation or repayment plan.

International Trade 29

The business transactions of the average exporter and credit manager encompass foreign countries too numerous to be dealt with effectively here. A pertinent reference may be found in the National Association of Credit Management publication, the Digest of Commercial Laws of the World, which discusses the commercial laws of 68 countries and is revised quarterly.

However, there is certain information that does not deal strictly with commercial laws and which the editors of the CREDIT MANUAL OF COMMERCIAL LAWS believe would interest its subscribers. We are, therefore, including in this chapter several topics of general interest to the exporter and credit manager.

Washington Agencies that Help to Finance Foreign Trade

United States Agencies

EXPORT-IMPORT BANK OF THE UNITED STATES
811 Vermont Ave., N.W., Washington, D.C. 20571

The Export-Import Bank of the United States (Eximbank), established in 1934, is an independent, wholly-owned financially self-sustaining, agency of the United States Government. It operates under the provisions of the Export-Import Bank Act of 1945, as amended. Its purposes are to facilitate and finance United States foreign trade.

Eximbank's loans, made in dollars and repayable in dollars, finance purchases of United States goods and service exports and must have reasonable assurance of repayment. The Bank is directed by statute to supplement and encourage private capital, not compete with it. The Bank is prohibited from financing sales of military items to economically less developed countries, sales of any items to a country which is engaged in armed conflict with the United States, or sales to Communist countries unless the President determines that it is in the national interest for Eximbank to engage in operations in such countries. Such determinations have been made with respect to Romania, Yugoslavia, Hungary and China.

In addition to making loans, the Bank guarantees repayment of export loans made by commercial lending institutions against commercial and political risks, and participates with the Foreign Credit Insurance Association (FCIA) in issuing a variety of insurance policies covering the risks of short-term and medium-term export credit transactions.

Eximbank has a capital of $1 billion, on which it may pay dividends to the U.S. Treasury, and it may borrow up to $6 billion from the Treasury, on a revolving basis, on which it pays interest. In addition, as of September 30, 1984, it had built up from earnings a reserve of about $1.5 billion against possible losses and other contingencies. A major source of funds in recent years is through borrowings from the Federal Financing Bank.

From its inception through September, 1984, the Bank authorized loans of $73.6 billion, of which $48.3 billion was disbursed. In addition $107.2 billion of export credit insurance and guaranties have been authorized. Some $44.3 billion of this total of approximately $180.8 billion expired unused, for various reasons, and $15.2 billion that was committed had not yet been used. Of $121.3 billion that has been used, $96.8 billion was repaid, and $1.5 billion sold, leaving some $23.0 billion outstanding. Some $514.3 million of loans are in protracted default. Since inception, Eximbank's total net write-off of loans has been only $25.3 million, or about .06% of cumulative loan disbursements. During this same period, Eximbank's insurance and guaranty programs have shown a total net loss, after recoveries, of only $257.9 million, an insignificant 1.01% of shipments.

Methods of Financing Long-term Direct Capital Loans

From the beginning the Bank has made long-term direct capital loans to public and private entities abroad, the latter being owned by foreign nationals, U.S. concerns, or by both. Although in the past the Bank has financed up to 100 percent of the United States materials and services, it now limits its direct financing to that portion which cannot be financed through the private sector—usually maturities in excess of five years. A cash payment of at least 15 percent is paid by the borrower. Such loans run from more than five years, with an interest rate on recently authorized loans of from 9.85 percent per annum to 12.25 percent, depending on the category of the country to which the export will be shipped and the repayment period of the loan. Their real impact in the United States is on the thousands of subcontractors who furnish United States goods and services to the exporting companies for whom the Bank finances substantial overseas sales each year through its long-term capital lending program. During the fiscal year 1984, these authorizations amounted to $1.1 billion.

Financial Guarantees

Eximbank can extend its financial guarantee to cover credit extended by U.S. or foreign financial institutions for the purchase and export of United States goods and services.[1] Foreign financial institutions include branches of U.S. commercial banks and investment banks in other countries; overseas offices of U.S. trading companies and other U.S. financial institutions; foreign commercial, investment, and development banks either public or private; foreign trading companies and other foreign financial institutions.

Under its financial guarantee authority, Eximbank will guarantee repayment by the borrower of principal up to 100 percent of the credit and interest up to one percent over the U.S. Treasury rate. The guarantee will cover commercial and political risks, as delineated in the guaranty contract. Eximbank charges a commitment fee of ⅛ percent for the financial guarantee and a guarantee fee of 0.5 percent per annum on the outstanding balance of the guaranteed loan.

---

[1] As under the direct loan program, a 15% cash payment is required from the borrower.

Applications for the guarantee must be accompanied or supplemented by information sufficient to enable Eximbank to appraise the quality of the proposed credit and the feasibility, engineering, and economics of the proposed project. The financial guarantee agreement between Eximbank and the financial institution will refer, of course, to a loan agreement between that institution and its borrower.

Programs for Medium-term Sales

Eximbank's exporter credit guarantee and insurance programs are of assistance to U.S. suppliers offering credit terms to their foreign purchasers. The exporter may sell the promissory note of his buyer to a U.S. commercial bank, which will buy the note without recourse on the exporter and then obtain a guarantee of repayment from Eximbank (Commercial Bank Guarantee Program). As an alternative, the supplier may obtain from the Foreign Credit Insurance Association, which works in cooperation with Eximbank, an insurance policy on his note. The supplier may hold his insured note with freedom of risk in his own accounts receivable, or he may sell it or use it as collateral with a commercial bank.

There is a required cash payment of at least 15 percent of the contract price—and there is also generally an exporter commercial risk participation of at least 10 percent of the credit.

Eximbank's Small Business Credit Program enables U.S. commercial banks to extend fixed-rate medium-term export loans by providing standby assurance that the bank can borrow from Eximbank against the outstanding value of a medium-term foreign debt obligation. The program is for exports by small businesses, as defined by guidelines of the Small Business Administration.

The Medium-term Credit Program provides fixed interest rate support for medium-term export sales facing officially supported export credit competition from abroad. The program is similar to the Small Business Credit Program, but evidence of officially supported foreign export credit competition must accompany each request.

Eximbank will guarantee repayment on a medium-term revolving line of credit extended by a U.S. bank to a financial institution in a "nonindustrialized" country. The line of credit would be used by the foreign bank to finance customer purchases of capital goods from the U.S. This facility is known as a Bank-to-Bank Guarantee and generally follows the guidelines of the Bank Guarantee Program.

Short-term Programs

The Foreign Credit Insurance Association also provides export credit insurance policies to cover short-term export sales (up to 180 days). No cash payment is required for short-term sales.

Eximbank's Working Capital Guarantee Program satisfies the requirements of the ETC Act of 1982, which was signed into law by President Reagan in October of 1982. Eximbank's guarantee provides export trading companies and other exporters with access to export related working capital loans that would not be provided without Eximbank's assistance.

U.S. International Development Cooperation Agency,
AGENCY FOR INTERNATIONAL DEVELOPMENT

Washington, D.C. 20523

This organization, familiarly known as AID, was created on November 4, 1961, under provisions of the Foreign Assistance Act of 1961, which terminated the International Cooperation Administration and the Development Loan Fund and transferred their functions to the new agency.

AID functions as an agency of the U.S. International Development Cooperation Agency to provide technical and financial assistance to less developed countries of Africa, Asia, Latin America, and the Near East. The objective of this aid is to help the developing countries achieve self-sustaining economic growth.

Development Loans

Development loans are extended only to overseas borrowers and for the most part only to the governments of those countries. These loans are repayable, both principal and interest thereon, in dollars, and must have a reasonable chance of repayment. Proceeds of the loans generally are spent for United States goods and services, though procurement from low-income developing countries and the borrower country is also permitted.

Loan assistance is concentrated on meeting the fundamental needs of the poor majority of people in the developing countries in the areas of food, nutrition and rural development, health and population, and education and human resources development.

Present loan terms vary and permit amortization over a 20, 25 or 40-year period, beginning with a 10-year grace period, in which the interest rate is two to five percent per annum during the grace period and three to five percent thereafter.

Technical Assistance

AID technical assistance activities stress research in agriculture, health, nutrition, population, education, industrial development, science and technology, and urban problems.

Economic Support Fund Assistance

AID Economic Support Fund assistance is to promote economic or political stability in less developed nations.

Housing Guaranty Program

Under AID's Housing Guaranty Program, U.S. investors (such as private savings and loan associations, Federal Home Loan Banks, insurance companies, commercial banks, pension funds) make private home ownership possible throughout the world by providing financing for private and publicly sponsored lower-income housing in developing countries.

Additional information may be obtained from the Office of Housing, Agency for International Development, Washington, D.C. 20523.

Information Sources

AID's Small Business Office informs U.S. suppliers of trade opportunities under AID-financed programs. This is achieved through publication of information on foreign government buying. These publications will be sent to suppliers with U.S. addresses who complete and submit a Mailing List Application to Small Business Office, Agency for International Development, Washington, D.C. 20523. Telephone: (703) 235-1840.

OVERSEAS PRIVATE INVESTMENT CORPORATION

1129 20th Street, N.W., Washington, D.C. 20527

Congress authorized the creation of OPIC in the 1969 amendments to the Foreign Assistance Act of 1961, to assume operation of the private investment incentive programs then administered by the Agency for International Development. The Act stated that OPIC's overall purpose would be to "mobilize and facilitate the participation of United States private capital and skills in the economic and social development of less developed friendly countries and areas, thereby complementing the development assistance objectives of the United States. . . ."

OPIC's authority to issue insurance, direct loans and loan guaranties was renewed by Congress for three years in 1974, for three years in 1978, and for four years in 1981.

OPIC interprets its basic statutory mandate to be the selective encouragement of those private U.S. investment proposals that are likely to be viable, and that offer mutual benefits to the host developing country and to the United States. Such projects should produce some or all of these benefits: in the host country, increased economic growth, domestic revenues, foreign exchange earnings or savings, and training and employment, in the U.S., expansion of export markets, of supplies of raw materials, of contributions to the balance of payments, and increased employment. Under its 1981 legislation, OPIC is directed to concentrate on increasing the participation of small and medium-sized business in international markets and to give preferential consideration to investment in the least developed nations—those with a per capita GNP per annum of $2,950 or less (in 1979 U.S. dollars).

To accomplish these purposes the Corporation offers a number of programs including:

> INSURANCE of private U.S. investments in less developed countries against the risks of inconvertibility, expropriation, and war, revolution, insurrection and civil strife; and against arbitrary drawings of letters of credit posted as bid, performance or advance payment guaranties as required by many governments, particularly in the Middle East.
>
> GUARANTIES of private U.S. loans to projects in less developed countries (usually from institutional lenders such as insurance companies, pension funds, and commercial banks) against commercial as well as political risks.
>
> DIRECT DOLLAR LOANS from the Corporation's capital, repayable in dollars, or foreign currency loans (in Pakistan), to assist in financing private projects sponsored by smaller businesses defined as companies below the "Fortune 1000" in these countries.

SELECTIVE FINANCIAL PARTICIPATION IN INVESTMENT SURVEYS and feasibility studies to evaluate proposed investment projects.

Investors eligible for insurance as U.S. citizens, corporations substantially beneficially owned by U.S. citizens, or substantially wholly-owned foreign subsidiaries of eligible U.S. firms. Insured investments may take the form of equity, debt, licensing, or such other participation as OPIC may approve.

OPIC is bound to its insurance commitment for up to 20 years and coverage extends to 90 percent of the investment and up to twice that amount for attributable earnings or interest.

Normally insurance may not exceed a 20-year period. OPIC has adopted special policies which limit coverage, however, on particularly large investments, on projects in countries where OPIC's total risk exposure is unusually great, and on investments in sensitive project areas. These will be insured on an individually negotiated basis, taking into account the higher risks involved. Investors, other than institutional lenders to unrelated project borrowers, must assume 10 percent of the risk of an investment insured by OPIC. Fees are generally $3/10$ of one percent of the current insured amount for inconvertibility coverage, $6/10$ of one percent for expropriation coverage, and $6/10$ of one percent for war, revolution, and insurrection coverage (¾ of one percent if civil strife is included); with ¼ of one percent under each coverage for the standby amount (.3 of one percent for standby coverage encompassing civil strife). Insurance is not available without host-government approval of the project, or for investments made prior to registration.

A direct loan or a loan which OPIC guarantees is made at commercial interest rates and on commercial terms to a project in which a U.S. investor with experience in the business has an equity participation and management role. The interest rates on an OPIC loan and the fee on the OPIC guaranty of a loan may vary according to OPIC's initial assessment of the risks involved, the anticipated ultimate profitability of the project, and its developmental impact. Normally a guaranteed loan or a direct loan is made for a term of from 7-12 years. OPIC normally looks to the project's cash flow for repayment, rather than to sponsor or local government guarantees.

OPIC's pre-investment assistance, directed primarily to smaller U.S. firms and to investments in the poorest of the less developed countries (those with less than $2,950 per capita GNP n 1979 U.S. dollars), can consist of up to $100,000, representing up to 75% of the cost of a feasibility survey.

Information Sources

OPIC programs are explained in greater detail in the following publications, distributed without charge:

Annual Report

Investment Insurance Handbook

Investment Financing Handbook

Letters of Credit Handbook

OPIC Country List

TOPICS, a quarterly newsletter

INTERNATIONAL TRADE

COMMODITY CREDIT CORPORATION

Department of Agriculture, Washington, D.C. 20250

CCC Export Credit Guarantee Program (GSM-102)

Under the GSM-102 Program, CCC provides, without distinction, coverage for commercial as well as noncommercial risks to U.S. exporters selling U.S. agricultural commodities abroad.

This commercial export program provides payment guarantees to exporters selling U.S. agricultural commodities on credit terms for up to three years. The transaction must be secured by an irrevocable commercial letter of credit issued by an approved bank requiring payment in U.S. dollars. U.S. exporters may assign the payment guarantee to a U.S. bank or other financial institution providing the export financing.

The GSM-102 Program provides the U.S. exporter or the assignee protection in the event the foreign bank is unable to make payment due to commercial or noncommercial reasons, without distinction.

Generally, CCC's guarantee coverage is for 98 percent of the f.o.b. value of the sale, plus a certain amount of interest coverage as determined by CCC on the guaranteed value.

The Program Development Division, Export Credits, Foreign Agricultural Service, U.S. Department of Agriculture, releases press announcements of GSM-102 guarantee availabilities and accepts applications from the U.S. exporters for payment guarantees covering specified exports of U.S. agricultural commodities to designated countries.

International Agencies

WORLD BANK

1818 H Street, N.W., Washington, D.C. 20433

The International Bank for Reconstruction and Development (World Bank) is owned by 148 countries, each subscribing to its capital stock in accordance with that country's own economic strength. The World Bank makes loans to governments, governmental agencies, and private enterprises (with government guaranty) in member countries, mainly toward helping those countries build the foundations of their economic growth.

The Bank was founded at the Bretton Woods Economic and Financial Conference in 1944, began operations in June, 1946, and as of June 30, 1985, has made 2,602 loans totaling about $113 billion to finance projects in more than 100 countries. The first loans, made in 1947, were for European postwar reconstruction.

In 1948 the Bank turned to development lending, and since then its lending has been directed to the less-developed areas of the world. Approximately 18% of its loans in member countries have been for electric power; another 18% for transport improvement—railways, highways, air, waterways and pipelines; 21% for agricultural and rural development; 8% for industry; and the remainder for education, for communications, for water supply, and for other development purposes.

Loans When Private Capital Is Unavailable

The World Bank lends money when private capital is not available on reasonable terms. If the borrower is not a government, the Bank requires the guaranty of the member government concerned. The Bank never lends the total cost of a project or program. Normally it finances only the foreign exchange costs involved in the purchase of imported goods or services, disbursing the loan over the construction period on presentation of evidence that payments have been made for the agreed purposes of the loan.

The Bank demands efficient procurement of supplies, with competitive bidding on the bulk of the orders its loans finance. Its funds may be spent in any member country or in Switzerland, which is not a member but has a special arrangement with the Bank.

As of June 30, 1985, the total subscribed capital of the World Bank was $59 billion in terms of current U.S. dollars, of which only 10 percent is paid in, partly in gold or dollars and partly in local currencies. The rest is subject to call if required to meet the Bank's obligations.

The capital subscribed by the member governments was never intended to finance all the Bank's operations, and the institution itself has been a borrower; it sells its bonds and notes in the capital markets of the world, and as of June 30, 1985, had about $50.3 billion outstanding. These obligations were denominated in 18 currencies.

World Bank loans typically have a maturity of 15–20 years and grace periods of three to five years. The lending rate is based on the cost of the Bank's borrowings, plus a spread of ½ percent. For the first half of fiscal year 1986, the lending rate was 8.82 percent. Since January 1982, the Bank has charged a front-end fee on its loans which is payable when the loans become effective. For loans negotiated after March 1, 1983, and submitted for approval before January 9, 1985, this fee was ¼ of 1% of the principal amount of the loan. For loans submitted thereafter, no fee is being charged. The Bank also imposes a commitment charge (at present ¾ of 1% per annum) on undisbursed portions of loans. On average, less than 5% of a loan is disbursed in the first year after approval and about 65% in the next four years.

No Losses on Loans

Repayments of principal to the Bank and to participants in Bank loans have amounted to more than $19 billion. The Bank never has suffered a loss on a loan, and payment delays have been insignificant. Furthermore, the Bank follows a policy of not taking part in debt rescheduling agreements.

Private Participation In World Bank's Loans

The World Bank also enlists the direct participation of private investors in its loans and has sold $2,980 million of its loans from the beginning of its operations. The Bank is also a catalyst for cofinancing from governments and their agencies, other multilateral financial institutions, export credit agencies, and private banks. Cofinancing directly associates the World Bank's funds with those provided by other sources in financing specific projects in developing countries. Cofinancing sources provided $4.8 billion in fiscal year 1985.

INTERNATIONAL TRADE

Technical Assistance

The World Bank is also a source of technical assistance and it conducts an economic policy dialogue with its borrowing member countries. This policy dialogue helps determine appropriate economic development strategies and identify structural adjustments in developing country economies. Structural adjustment loans are provided to countries willing to undertake such programs. These loans amount to somewhat less than 10 percent of the Bank's total lending.

INTERNATIONAL DEVELOPMENT ASSOCIATION

1818 H Street, N.W., Washington, D.C. 20433

The International Development Association (IDA) was established in September, 1960, as a World Bank affiliate "to promote economic development, increase productivity and thus raise standards of living in the less-developed areas of the world." All World Bank members are eligible to join IDA, and 133 countries have done so, contributing more than $1 billion in initial subscriptions.

IDA's resources are entirely separate from those of the World Bank, and its assistance is concentrated on the very poor countries—mainly those with an annual per capita Gross National Product (GNP) of $790 or less (in 1983 U.S. dollars). By this criterion, more than 50 countries are eligible. In practice, over 80 percent of IDA lending goes to countries with an annual per capita GNP of less than $580. Although IDA is legally and financially distinct from the International Bank for Reconstruction and Development, it shares the same staff, and the projects it assists have to meet the same criteria as do projects supported by the Bank.

The agency started operations in November, 1960, extended the first development credit in May, 1961, and has now extended 1,645 credits to 85 countries for a total of about $34 billion to finance electric power, road construction, harbor dredging, irrigation, drainage and flood-protection projects, school construction, small private industry, and water supply. Because of the easy terms on which it provides finance, IDA relies primarily on the governments of its 32 richest member countries for its resources, and these countries have contributed the bulk of its usable funds. In addition, the World Bank has made transfers to IDA from its net income. IDA is authorized to accept supplementary contributions and is required to maintain a regular review of the adequacy of its resources.

Formalities covering seven general replenishments of IDA funds were completed as follows: in 1964, $745 million; in 1969, $1.27 billion; in 1972, $2.44 billion; in 1975, $4.5 billion; in 1977, $7.7 billion; in 1981, $12 billion; and in 1984, $9 billion.

While IDA may vary the terms of its credits at its own discretion, those extended so far were each for 50 years, without interest. Repayment is due in a convertible currency. Amortization begins after a 10-year grace period, then 1 percent of the principal is repayable annually for 10 years and 3 percent is repayable annually for the last 30 years. A service charge of ¾ of one percent per annum is payable on amounts withdrawn and outstanding, and ½ of one percent per annum on undisbursed balances of development credits negotiated after January 5, 1982, to meet the agency's administrative costs.

IDA assistance may take the form of development credits combined with Bank loans, or development credits only.

The agency has no separate staff but uses that of the World Bank.

INTERNATIONAL FINANCE CORPORATION

1818 H Street, N.W., Washington, D.C. 20433

The International Finance Corporation (IFC), a World Bank affiliate that invests in private industry in developing member countries, has the following principal objectives:

Provision of equity and loan capital for productive enterprises, in association with private investors and management;

Encouragement of the development of local capital markets;

stimulation of the international flow of private capital.

The corporation was established in July, 1956, and as of June 30, 1985, its paid-in capital, subscribed by 127 member governments, was $546 million, and its accumulated earnings were $258 million.

Authorized to borrow amounts up to a limit of four times its (IFC's) unimpaired subscribed capital and surplus, the corporation invests in a wide variety of industries where private capital is not available on reasonable terms.

Financing and Participations

All IFC's investments are made in association with private business, without the guaranty of any government, and it does not provide more than a portion of the total finance required. IFC expects its financial participation to be approximately 15–25% of the total cost of the project financed.

Financing by IFC is available for foreign exchange and for local currency expenditures. It can be used for fixed assets or for working capital. IFC money is not tied to the purchase of specific equipment or to a specific country.

IFC does not engage in operations that are essentially for purposes of refunding or financing, nor does it finance exports or imports.

IFC's initial commitments for its own account normally range from $1 million to over $50 million.

As of June 30, 1985, IFC had approved investments in over 850 private enterprise projects in 84 countries, for a total investment of more than $7,000 million.

There are no uniform interest rates for IFC loans; the rate for each is governed by relevant considerations, such as the risks involved and the prospective overall return.

IFC charges a commitment fee of 1 percent on undisbursed portions of its loans.

IFC also takes an active role in the identification and promotion of projects, and is authorized to help finance pilot operations organized to develop a specific project.

INTERNATIONAL MONETARY FUND

700 19th Street N.W. Washington, D.C. 20431

The International Monetary Fund, also an outgrowth of the Bretton Woods Conference of 1944, is a sister organization of the World Bank. It was formed to promote international monetary cooperation and a balanced growth of world trade. Membership in the Fund is a prerequisite of World Bank membership.

Financial operations of the International Monetary Fund are in the form of drawings from the Fund by member nations under a number of facilities (standby and extended arrangements, compensatory financing and buffer stock). These operations are carried out only with governments and are designed to correct or forestall short-term balance-of-payment problems. The Fund does not lend for specific projects, but, because it promotes international economic and exchange stability in its member nations, it contributes invaluably to the quality of international investments.

The Fund publishes the statistics on its operations in terms of Special Drawing Rights (SDRs). The SDR is an international reserve asset created by the Fund and allocated to its members as a supplement to existing reserve assets. The Fund has allocated a total of SDR 21.4 billion in six allocations, and holdings of SDRs by member countries were 4 percent of total non-gold reserves at the end of March 1985. Members may use SDRs in transactions and operations with other member countries and other designated holders, and with the General Resources Account of the Fund, which also holds SDRs. The SDR is the Fund's unit of account and, increasingly, commercial transactions and private financial obligations are being denominated in SDRs. Its valuation and interest rate are determined on the basis of a basket of five currencies: the U.S. dollar, Deutsche mark, French franc, yen, and pound sterling.

Members' drawings from the Fund totaled the equivalent of SDR 93.2 billion between the beginning of the Fund's operations in 1947 and April 30, 1985. Standby arrangements effective on that date amounted to SDR 3,925.3 million and the arrangements under the Extended Fund Facility totaled SDR 7.750 million.

The capital resources of the Fund come from SDRs and currencies that the members pay under quotas calculated for them when they join the Fund. Members' quotas in the Fund at present amount to SDR 89.2 billion and are closely related to (1) their subscription to the Fund, (2) their drawing rights on the Fund under both regular and special facilities, (3) their voting power, and (4) their share of any allocation of SDRs. Every Fund member is required to subscribe to the Fund an amount equal to its quota. An amount not exceeding 25 per cent of the quota has to be paid in reserve assests, the balance in the member's own currency. The total assets of the Fund's General Resources Account were SDR 105.3 billion on April 30, 1984.

In addition, an arrangement completed in 1962 enables the Fund to borrow up to the equivalent of about SDR 6.8 billion from 10 of its industrialized member countries and Switzerland to forestall or cope with an impairment of the international monetary system. These General Arrangements to Borrow (GAB) have been extended several times and the most recent five-year renewal was to end in October 1985. In early 1983 agreement was reached to increase the credit arrangements under the GAB to SDR 17 billion; to permit use of GAB resources in transactions with Fund members that are not GAB participants; to authorize Swiss participation; and to permit borrowing arrangements with nonparticipating members to be associated with the GAB. Saudi Arabia and the Fund have entered into such an arrangement under which the Fund will be able to borrow up to SDR 1.5 billion to assist in financing purchases by any member for the same purpose and under the same circumstances as in the GAB. The changes became effective on December 26, 1983. The GAB have been used several times to help finance large drawings by participants, most recently for the United States in 1978. The Fund also has supplemented its resources by borrowing for the oil facility in 1974 and 1975 and for the supplementary financing facility, whose resources, totaling SDR 7,784 million from 13 members or institutions, are now fully committed. The supplementary financing facility became operative in 1979. To finance the enlarged access policy, the Saudi Arabian Monetary Agency has agreed to lend medium-term to the Fund up to a maximum of SDR 4 billion in the first year, rising to SDR 8 billion in May 1982, the second year of a six-year commitment period. For the same purpose, the Fund has agreed on short-term borrowing arrangements with the central banks or official agencies of 18 countries which would make SDR 1.3 billion available over a commitment period of two years. The Fund has also concluded four borrowing agreements for a total of SDR 6 billion with the Saudi Arabian Monetary Agency (SAMA), the Bank for International Settlement (BIS), Japan and the National Bank of Belgium.

Members' drawings from the Fund are normally for a term of up to 5 years or up to 10 years under the extended facility. Standby credits allow a member to make drawings on the Fund usually for a 12-month period, although more recently the standby period has been extended to up to three years. A number of provisions aimed at stabilizing internal and external financial and monetary positions of a drawing country are normally part of the arrangements between the Fund and the member. While there is no provision for direct participation in these credits by commercial banks and other private investors, many governments drawing from the Fund in recent years have negotiated loans concurrently from private sources. Many of these private lenders have predicated their loans on the existence of a satisfactory economic stabilization agreement between the borrowing country and the Fund.

In recent years, the Fund has also studied such questions as the adequacy of international liquidity and its own future role in the functioning of the international payments system. An IMF facility for the allocation of Special Drawing Rights was established in 1969 in order to provide additional international liquidity, as and when the need arises. Participants in the facility may count Special Drawing Rights (SDRs) in their reserves and transfer them to other participants against convertible currencies in the event of payments difficulties or adverse developments in their reserves. Distribution of SDR 9,314.8 million was made in 1970, 1971, and 1972. In 1978, an agreement on the resumption of SDR allocations was reached under which SDR 12 billion were allocated to members in a three-year period. The last allocation (SDR 4,052 million) was made on January 1, 1981.

INTER-AMERICAN DEVELOPMENT BANK

808 Seventeenth Street, N.W., Washington, D.C. 20577

The Inter-American Development Bank (IDB) is a hemispheric version of the World Bank but with a more diversified lending pattern. It was organized in 1959 to promote the individual and collective development of its developing member countries in Latin America. Its organizers were the United States and the following 19 Latin American nations:

INTERNATIONAL TRADE

Argentina	Dominican Republic	Mexico
Bolivia	Ecuador	Nicaragua
Brazil	El Salvador	Panama
Chile	Guatemala	Paraguay
Colombia	Haiti	Peru
Costa Rica	Honduras	Uruguay
		Venezuela

As of December 31, 1984, the membership of the Bank had increased to 43 countries with the admission of seven other Western Hemisphere nations —Barbados, Trinidad and Tobago, Jamaica, Canada, Guyana, Bahamas, Suriname—and of 16 nations from outside the hemisphere—Austria, Belgium, Denmark, Finland, France, Germany, Italy, Israel, the Netherlands, Japan, Portugal, Spain, Sweden, Switzerland, the United Kingdom, and Yugoslavia.

The Bank started operations in 1960 with two separate sources of money, its ordinary capital resources and a Fund for Special Operations. The next year the United States established for IDB administration a third major source of money, the Social Progress Trust Fund, to finance social projects. The original resources of the Social Progress Trust Fund have been completely disbursed and repayments on Trust Fund loans are being rechanneled through the Fund for Special Operations. In 1975, Venezuela established the Venezuelan Trust Fund under Bank administration to be used for Latin America's development.

The Bank's funds are maintained and used separately from one another. From them, IDB had authorized, up to December 31, 1984, 1,562 loans amounting to a total of $27,772 million, net of cancellations and exchange adjustments, for projects in its Latin American member countries, and also provided some $48.5 million in nonreimbursable and contingent repayment technical cooperation to help borrowers prepare and execute projects, strengthen local development institutions, and train personnel.

By sectors, the Inter-American Development Bank's lending during the period of 1961-1984 included the following:

	($ million)	(%)
Energy	7,380	26.6
Agriculture	6,319	22.8
Industry and Mining	4,333	15.6
Transportation and Communications	3,511	12.6
Environmental and Public Health	2,472	8.9
Education Science and Technology	1,288	4.6
Urban Development	1,086	3.9
Export Financing	583	2.1
Preinvestment	355	1.2
Tourism	296	1.1
Other	169	0.6
TOTAL	27,772	100

The Bank's Capital Stock

Since June, 1976, the Bank's capital stock has consisted of two separate sets of resources: the ordinary capital, to which only the regional members have subscribed, and the interregional capital, which was established for the nonregional members although regional members may subscribe all or part of their increased subscriptions to that fund.

The subscribed ordinary resources of IDB as of December 31, 1984, totaled $13.6 billion, of which the equivalent of $1.2 billion has been paid in or is in the process of being paid in, part in gold or dollars and part in domestic currency, and $12.4 billion is subject to call. The latter may be called only when needed to meet the Bank's obligations created by borrowings. The United States subscription quota totals $3.8 billion, of which $361.9 million has been paid or is in the process of being paid in and $3.4 billion is callable. As of December 31, 1984, IDB had borrowings outstanding of $2,497 million in its ordinary capital and $3,635 million in its interregional capital.

With its ordinary capital resources the Bank makes loans, repayable in the currencies lent, to private enterprises and public entities of member nations. Terms for the most part are from 7 to 20 years, including grace periods. The Bank currently assesses a variable interest rate applicable to yearly disbursements and linked to the cost of borrowing funds. Up to December 31, 1984, the Bank had authorized from ordinary capital resources 477 loans totaling $8.7 billion net of cancellations and exchange adjustments, in some of which commercial banks and other financial institutions in the United States, Europe, Canada, and Japan had participated with complimentary financing and other participations totaling $642 million.

The interregional capital is subscribed at $10.9 billion, including $974 million in paid-in shares and $9,953 million in callable shares. This new set of resources broadens the multilateral character of the Bank and facilitates its efforts to raise funds in the world capital markets. As with ordinary lending, interest rates and amortization periods of inter-regional capital loans are set by the Bank's Board of Executive Directors and bear a relationship to the average cost of the borrowed resources, the administrative expenses borne by the interregional operations, and reserve formation provisions. As of December 31, 1984, the Bank had authorized from inter-regional capital stock 139 loans totaling $8.1 billion.

On February 25, 1983, the Board of Governors recommended that the Bank's 43 member countries put into effect an increase of $15.7 billion in the institution's resources to help meet Latin America's development capital requirements during the 1983-86 period. The increase, the sixth replenishment of the Bank's resources, entered into effect on December 12, 1983. It will enable the Bank to lend a projected $13 billion in freely convertible currencies to the region during the period, as well as an additional $1.1 billion in nonconvertible currencies.

The resources increase consists of $15 billion of the Bank's authorized capital stock and $703 million of its Fund for Special Operations.

The measures put into effect included the establishment of an Intermediate Financing Facility to subsidize the interest payable on up to $800 million in loans from the capital resources during the period.

The additional resources will enable the Bank to increase its lending volume for Latin America's development during the four-year period at approximately 14 percent per annum. Projections indicate that the lending rate in convertible currencies will rise from more than $3 billion in 1983 to $3.9 billion in 1986.

The increases will raise the Bank's total resources to approximately $43.8 billion, including $34.5 billion in its capital resources, $8.4 billion in its Fund for Special Operations and $1.2 billion administered for various member countries.

The authorized capital increase is being subscribed and the Fund for Special Operations replenishment is being contributed by members principally in the years 1983 through 1986.

Procurement from ordinary capital (OC) and interregional capital (IC) loans authorized since July 9, 1976, or with contracts signed after that date, is tied to the Bank's regional members and the non-regional countries which recently joined.

Fund For Special Operations

From this Fund the Bank lends on terms and conditions adapted to the special circumstances arising in specific countries or in connection with specific projects. These conditions include possible repayment in the currency of the borrower. Starting with $150 million, the Fund's authorized resources as of December 31, 1984, amounted to $7.7 billion, of which the United States quota was $4.3 billion. The Sixth Replenishment is increasing the resources of the Fund by $703 million to a total of $8.4 billion. The U.S. contribution to the increase is $290 million, increasing its total contribution to the Fund to $4.6 billion.

The Fund's scope of operations has also been expanded to include social projects previously financed with the Social Progress Trust Fund. Interest rates now vary from 2 to 4 percent depending on the nature of the project and the degree of development of the borrowing country. Terms generally range from 20 to 40 years, including grace periods.

Procurement anywhere in the Free World is permitted with the proceeds of loans from the original resources of the Fund for Special Operations; from the dollar proceeds of the subsequent contributions, procurement is permitted only in the regional member countries for loans granted prior to December 15, 1976, and only in regional and nonregional countries for loans granted after that date. Up to December 31, 1984, IDB had made 750 Fund for Special Operations loans for a total of $8.9 billion, net of cancellations and exchange adjustments.

Social Progress Trust Fund

This is a $525 million fund that the Bank administers under an agreement with the United States. Its purpose was to provide loans for settlement and improved use of land, low-income group housing, water supply and sewage facilities, and advanced education and training. The original loans were made in dollars, repayable generally in the borrower's currency, but IDB now uses some local currency repayments to buy participations in appropriate Fund for Special Operations loans. It also extends special technical cooperation with repayment funds. As of December 31, 1984, the Bank had authorized 122 loans totaling $535 million, net of cancellations and exchange adjustments, from this trust fund.

Venezuelan Trust Fund

On February 27, 1975, the Bank and the Venezuelan Investment Fund entered into an agreement under which the Bank will administer a $500 million Venezuelan Trust Fund. The resources of the Fund will help finance projects in economically less developed member countries, those with limited markets and those of intermediate development. As of December 31, 1984, the Bank had authorized 39 loans totaling $643 million from this fund.

Other Resources

The Inter-American Development Bank has also administered smaller funds for Latin America's development through agreements with Argentina, Canada, Germany, Norway, Sweden, Switzerland, the United Kingdom, the Vatican, and the Inter-Governmental Committee for European Migration.

Argentina entered into an agreement with the IDB in 1970 to provide special funds in its own currency to help provide counterpart funds for IDB-financed projects in its sister republics of Bolivia, Paraguay and Uruguay. As of December 31, 1984, total loans approved under the arrangement amounted to $23.1 million.

The Canadian fund, which at the end of 1974 amounted to 74 million Canadian dollars, is helping finance long-term economic, technical, and educational assistance projects in Latin America at highly concessional terms. Under the provisions for the admission of Canada as a member of the Bank, all monies received by the Bank after May 3, 1972, as repayment or interest on loans authorized under the agreement will be transferred to the Fund for Special Operations as a contribution of Canada to that fund. As of December 31, 1984, the Bank had approved 20 loans amounting to $73 million Canadian dollars from these resources, of which 19.4 million Canadian dollars had been contributed to the Fund for Special Operations under the agreement. On March 22, 1974, in a further cooperative measure with the Bank, the Government of Canada established a special fund of 1.5 million Canadian dollars to finance the preparation of development projects in Latin America. Subsequently the Canadian Government provided an additional 4.5 million Canadian dollars to this fund. Through December 31, 1984, the total resources committed from this fund, which includes income earned on investments, amounted to $8 million. Under an agreement signed in 1961, the Federal Republic of Germany has participated with the United States and the Bank in financing a program to rehabilitate Bolivia's national tin mines. As of December 31, 1984, these funds totaled $12.6 million. The IDB signed an agreement in 1970 with the Norwegian Government to administer a $2 million Norwegian Development Fund for Latin America on an untied basis at 2½ percent interest.

In 1966, the IDB entered into an agreement with the government of Sweden to administer a $5 million Swedish Development Fund for Latin America. Loans from this fund, made in conjunction with ordinary capital resource loans, are untied, and the entire $5 million has been lent out.

An agreement between the Bank and the Government of Switzerland signed in 1973 authorized the Bank to administer the Swiss Development Fund for Latin America totaling $4.7 million on an untied basis and on terms and conditions similar to those of the Bank's Fund for Special Operations. On November 21, 1980, the Bank entered into an agreement with the Government of Switzerland to administer a special fund designed to improve the living conditions

INTERNATIONAL TRADE 29–17

and productivity of the lowest income groups of the population of its Latin American member countries. The initial contribution of Switzerland to the fund, which is known as The Technical Cooperation and Small Projects Swiss Fund, consisted of 5 million Swiss francs. In addition, the assets at June 30, 1981, of the existing Swiss Development Fund for Latin America, as well as future recoveries from that fund, will be contributed to the fund. On December 14, 1982, the Government of Switzerland and the Bank signed an agreement by which the former agreed to make an additional 8 million Swiss francs available to the Technical Cooperation and Small Projects Swiss Fund over the July 1, 1982 to June 30, 1984, period. On November 27, 1984, Switzerland agreed to make an additional 12 million Swiss francs available to the fund.

The IDB currently administers two funds for the United Kingdom. Under the terms of agreements signed in 1966 and 1972, the Bank has administered cumulative resources for the United Kingdom totaling the equivalent of $8.9 million, all of which have been committed in loan projects.

In 1969, the IDB entered into an agreement with the Vatican to administer a $1 million development fund designed to benefit low-income groups in Latin America. Known as the *Populorum Progressio Fund,* it was lent interest-free on highly concessional terms in 1970 to finance an agrarian reform program in Colombia.

IDB also has agreements with Canada and the Netherlands which have set aside, respectively, 15 million Canadian dollars and 126 million guilders for parallel or independent financing operations in cooperation with the Bank.

FOREIGN CREDIT INSURANCE ASSOCIATION

40 Rector Street, New York, New York 10006

An Aid to Export Expansion

Government-sponsored export credit insurance systems have existed in the United Kingdom, France, Germany, Canada, and most major trading nations for many years. These facilities are widely used by exporters and their financing institutions in all these countries, to safeguard foreign receivables against nonpayment or prolonged delinquency in payment whether caused by the financial difficulties of individual buyers or by political risks such as long delays in converting buyer's payments in their local currencies and transferring these to the exporter in his own hard currency. The banks in England and in some of the other countries named often require that an export credit be insured as a prerequisite to their financing.

No counterpart of these facilities was available to U.S. exporters until 1962 when the Foreign Credit Insurance Association (FCIA) opened an office in New York and began to insure export credits against both commercial credit and political risks which may lead to nonpayment or long-delayed payment by the foreign buyer.

What Is FCIA

FCIA administers the U.S. export credit insurance program on behalf of, and as a joint enterprise between the U.S. Government and the private insurance industry. It came into being when President Kennedy was made conscious of the fact that U.S. exporters were too often at a disadvantage in competing for desirable export orders because they could not match the credit and financing facilities available to their foreign competitors. In his Balance of Payments message to the Congress in 1961 Mr. Kennedy said that he was directing the President of the Export-Import Bank to devise a system that would put the U.S. export trade on an equal footing with foreign competitors in the vital area of credit and finance. Following a careful study, it was decided that the system best suited to U.S. requirements would be one administered by the private insurance industry but back-stopped by the Government through its wholly owned agency, the Export-Import Bank of the United States (Eximbank). The insurance industry responded by organizing FCIA as a voluntary association of insurance companies. Today 10 stock and mutual companies constitute FCIA's membership, which remains open to other qualified insurers.

Risks Covered

The commercial credit risks are defined as insolvency of the buyer or the buyer's failure to pay within six months from due date. Political risks are more varied and less controllable. These include: inability to convert the buyer's local currency payment to dollars and to transfer the dollars to the United States; war, revolution, expropriation, etc.; imposition of new licensing controls which prevent export or import; added transport or insurance charges caused by interruption or diversion of voyage (due to a war emergency, for example). Coverage is also available for a buyer's unjustified failure or refusal to accept a shipment, also for consignments and sales from consigned stocks held abroad.

The insurance usually becomes effective when a shipment leaves the factory en route to the buyer, but the exporter may elect to have it begin from the date of the sales contract. Policies generally are insured for 90 percent against commercial losses, and for 100 percent against political losses. The exporter retains the uninsured percentage for his own account.

Types of Policies

THE MASTER POLICY

The Master Policy enables U.S. exporters to expand international sales substantially through the use of competitive credit terms. It gives exporters the flexibility they need in financing by allowing them to sell their insured receivables to banks. In short, the Master Policy allows the exporter to enter overseas markets with coverage for all his eligible shipments.

The policy is written for shipments during a one-year period and insures all, or a reasonable spread, of an exporter's eligible sales, both short-term credits up to 180 days and medium-term credits up to five years (and longer under certain circumstances). Actual terms of sale vary by product and are tailored to those customary in international trade.

The policy is subject to limits. The *aggregate limit* represents FCIA's maximum liability. The exporter himself may utilize credit limits up to the amount of a *discretionary credit limit* assigned to the policy. A *special buyer credit limit* is available for larger amounts, upon application to FCIA.

Normally, FCIA insures up to 90 percent of the gross invoice value. The exporter retains the other 10 percent for his own account. There is also a deductible, similar to major medical or automobile insurance. The deductible does *not* apply to political coverage since political risks are normally of the unforeseen type, and losses in this area should not penalize the exporter's full scope of coverage. It applies only to commercial coverage and only to the first dollar losses.

THE BANK DEDUCTIBLE POLICY

A policy covering exports of short term products is also available for commercial banking institutions engaged in financing of such transactions for their customers, either on a supplier or buyer credit arrangement. The short term comprehensive policy covers commercial credit risks up to 90 percent and political risks for up to 100 percent on sales of any type of product on terms up to 180 days.

The bank must maintain a regular lending arrangement with approved exporters or foreign buyers for coverage to be available under the policy. Certain U.S. agricultural commodities may also be insured under the policy, with terms extended up to one year and 98 percent commercial coverage available.

The policy has an aggregate limit, discretionary credit and special buyer credit limit, and deductible, as under the Master Policy.

THE MEDIUM-TERM POLICY

The Medium-Term Policy covers capital and quasi-capital goods of U.S. manufacture sold in international trade on terms from 181 days to five years, and occasionally longer. The policy is written on a case-by-case basis. There is no requirement that the exporter insure all his medium-term transactions. He may insure either a single or repetitive sale to an overseas buyer.

Under the terms of the policy, the foreign buyer must make a cash payment on or before delivery of at least 15 percent of the contract price. The remaining portion must be covered by a specified form of promissory note. The note requires payments in approximately equal installments on a monthly, quarterly, or semi-annual basis, with payments made in dollars at a U.S. bank.

Normally, the policy covers 90 percent of commercial credit risks and 100% of political risks. In certain higher risk markets, however, coverage may be less.

Certain U.S. agricultural commodities may also be insured on a case-by-case basis under the Medium-Term Policy, with 98 percent commercial coverage up to one year, provided the buyer makes a cash payment of at least 15 percent.

Most Medium-Term Policies cover both commercial and political risks. But FCIA will issue a policy covering specified political risks only.

THE COMBINATION POLICY

A combination of short and medium term insurance is available, mainly to protect U.S. exporters in transactions with overseas dealers and distributors. Because there is less day-to-day financial and legal supervision over the individual foreign franchised dealer by the U.S. manufacturer—as compared to the amount of credit control exerted over a domestic dealer—many U.S. firms have been hesitant to offer liberal dealer financing. FCIA is changing this attitude by utilizing a liberal concept in overseas dealer financing. This concept involves applying sophisticated financing techniques toward the establishment of insured dealer credit lines for numerous U.S. manufacturers, which previously sold on very secure terms and, therefore, often sold very little through their overseas dealer network.

The Combination Policy affords protection in three areas:

- Parts and accessories on terms up to 180 days.
- Inventory financing, where the exporter may ship goods under a "floor plan" arrangement. Initial coverage is for up to 270 days with no down payment.
- Receivables financing, with terms ranging up to three years following the minimum cash payment upon resale by the dealer or at the end of the inventory period.

Commercial credit risks on parts, accessories and related shelf items are covered up to 90 percent of the gross invoice value and political risks up to 100 percent. "Floor plan" products are covered on the same basis. Receivable financing is normally 90 percent for commercial credit risks, and 100 percent for political risks.

Services Coverage

In mid-1972, FCIA introduced export credit insurance to cover its overseas sales of services. FCIA developed the program to encourage U.S. service industries to expand their foreign business.

Industries benefiting from the coverage include management consultants, engineering service firms, transportation companies and other firms offering the services of U.S.-based personnel to foreign buyers with repayment being made in U.S. dollars in the United States.

Up to now, the export sale of services has generally been done on a restrictive credit basis. With this coverage, companies now can extend prudent terms to gain a greater share of the overseas services market.

New-To-Export Policy

As a stimulus to small business, FCIA offers a New-To-Export Policy to qualified applicants with Commercial Risk coverage from 90 to 95%. Political risk coverage is standard at 100%.

Applicants may also be given an alternate quotation on a Master Policy basis. However, maximum coverage of 90% commercial would not be increased.

The New-To-Export Policy, when issued, can remain in force for a maximum period of five years before being considered for a standard Master Policy arrangement.

Premium Rates

Premium rates are charged on the basis of premium rate schedules applicable to each policy.

FCIA's average premium for a short-term comprehensive policy is approximately 75 cents for each $100 of invoice value. Because of the longer credit terms involved, medium-term rates are higher.

An Aid to Financing

The proceeds of an FCIA policy are assignable to banks and other financing institutions. This means that, with receivables insured against loss, an exporter usually is able to finance foreign business on more liberal terms than otherwise. Indeed some policy-holders say that their lower financing costs and broader credit lines based on this insurance largely offset their FCIA premium costs.

Commercial banks throughout the nation welcome the availability of this insurance. Almost every bank has clients who are already engaged, or are becoming interested, in developing their world markets. The banker's as well as the exporter's risk is minimized. As a result, more and more bankers are taking advantage of their broadened opportunities for export financing. Besides the added earnings deriving from this source, the bankers realize that, by helping their customers to develop new and expanding markets, they stimulate their growth and the economic progress of their communities.

EXTENSION OF CREDIT IN FOREIGN TRADE

There are basic differences between the extension of credit in domestic versus international trade:

1. The risk of the market, as revealed in the habits, commercial practices, customs, laws, and the political situation of the country.
2. The transfer or the exchange risk, which rests on the supply of dollars available to the importer.
3. The terms of sale, which vary from country to country.
4. Transportation facilities—delays in obtaining shipping space will tie up the exporter's capital.
5. The question of insurance. If for any reason insurance companies refuse a shipment of goods, the action will render the extension of credit difficult, if not impossible.

In other words, when we extend credit to a foreign buyer, we must not only explore the capability of the importer to command credit, but we must also establish the effect that any of the factors previously mentioned might exert on the credit of the buyer.

Collection

There are basically six methods of collection or payment terms extended to the foreign customer. These are in order of increasing risk to the shipper: Cash in Advance; Letter of Credit; Documentary Sight Draft (documents against payment); Documentary Time Draft (documents against acceptance); Open Account; and Consignment.

Collecting payment for goods sold abroad involves essentially the same methods used for domestic sales. The difference is one of emphasis and is largely a result of additional credit consideration peculiar to foreign trade.

Every exporter uses one or more of these methods with their variations and combinations and the choice of methods depends on any number of factors, such as:

Credit-worthiness of the buyer, within the framework of company policy. To what extent does the financial and moral responsibility of the buyer justify the extension of credit?

Exporter's capital position. Is the exporter's working capital adequate to allow the delay in payment involved in credit extension?

Competition. Is the exporter's competition offering more lenient terms?

Conditions in the buyer's country. What are the chances of war, payment moratoria, unfavorable political action? Is the economy essentially sound and is the merchandise an economically reasonable import for the country? Is dollar availability a problem which might delay payment?

Others, including size of orders, importance of market, unusual trade practices, etc.

It is not uncommon for a conflict to arise between the buyer's pressure for more lenient terms and the exporter's interest in self-protection. It is perhaps because of this condition that documentary collection is so popular in foreign trade. It offers a rather effective compromise, since its mechanics allow the exporter to grant some leniency in payment terms without exposing himself to the risks of an open account.

SALES AND CREDIT TERMS IN FOREIGN TRADE

As foreign trade definitions have been issued by organizations in various parts of the world, and as the courts of countries have interpreted these definitions in different ways, it is important that sellers and buyers agree that their contracts are subject to the "Revised American Foreign Trade Definitions—1941" and that the various points outlined are accepted by both parties. Therefore, every exporter/importer should make absolutely certain that he and his foreign trading partners have a clear understanding regarding sales and credit terms and their definitions, and that complete agreement exists on products, prices, packaging, quotas, territories, delivery dates, miscellaneous expenses, and related details.

In addition to the foreign trade terms which follow, there are terms that are at times used, such as Free Harbour; C.I.F. & C. (Cost, Insurance, Freight, and Commission); C.I.F. & I. (Cost, Freight, Insurance, and Interest); C.I.F. Landed (Cost, Insurance, Freight, Landed); and others. None of these should be used unless there has first been a definite understanding as to the exact meaning thereof. It is unwise to attempt to interpret other terms in the light of the terms given herein. Hence, whenever possible, one of the terms defined herein should be used.

Also, it is unwise to use abbreviations in quotations or in contracts which might be subject to misunderstanding.

Unless otherwise agreed upon, all expenses are for the account of the exporter up to the point at which the buyer must handle the subsequent movement of the merchandise.

Terms used in foreign business differ from and are more complicated than those used in domestic business. Some of the more common terms are as follows:

1. EX (point of origin)
2. F.O.B. (Free on Board)
   FOB (named inland carrier at named inland point of departure)

INTERNATIONAL TRADE

    FOB (named inland carrier at named inland point of departure plus freight prepaid to named point of exportation)
    FOB (named inland carrier at named inland point of departure plus freight allowed to named point of exportation)
    FOB (named inland carrier at named point of exportation)
    FOB Vessel (named port of shipment)
    FOB (named inland point in country of importation)
3. F.A.S. (Free Along Side)
    F.A.S. Vessel (named port of shipment)
4. C. & F. (Cost and Freight)
    C. & F. (named point of destination)
5. C.I.F. (Cost, Insurance, Freight)
    C.I.F. (named point of destination)
6. EX DOCK
    Ex Dock (named port of importation)

Note: These terms have been revised by the Vienna Congress of International Chamber of Commerce; they revised various terms used in international sales contracts. These have been combined in the INCOTERMS 1980.

In addition to the terms of sales, each exporter should also clearly indicate his terms of payment (credit terms). The most common ones are:

1. CASH IN ADVANCE

    Under 'cash in advance' terms the buyer abroad prepays the entire shipment or a part of it. This type of arrangement is used infrequently. It is, of course, very advantageous to the U.S. exporter since he faces no risk of remaining unpaid for his goods or for part of them, depending on the arrangement. But it is very disadvantageous to the importer since he puts the entire financial burden on him. As competition in today's world market is very keen, exporters ask for payment in advance only if the risk of nonpayment is large.

2. LETTER OF CREDIT
    a) Irrevocable L/C—Confirmed
    b) Irrevocable L/C—Unconfirmed
    c) Revocable L/C

    In the case of irrevocable letter of credit, the exporter is protected against the 'commercial risk,' i.e. the risk of nonpayment caused by the importer's insolvency and the risk that the buyer will break a contract and attempt to refuse payment after the goods have been shipped or are ready for shipment.

    In the case of confirmed irrevocable letters of credit, the exporter is also protected against the exchange transfer risk, i.e. the risk of the foreign government taking action to block the transfer of foreign exchange to the exporter's country.

    In the case of any irrevocable credit, the exporter is normally able to obtain payment as soon as he has made shipment since he can negotiate his drafts with his bank in the United States.

    However, exporters might find foreign buyers reluctant to finance imports with L/C's. For one thing, the buyer's line of credit with his bank may be tied up during the validity period of the L/C. For another, L/C financing may be too costly for the importer as there might be a commission due to the opening bank. And again, due to the competitive market, a Letter of Credit should only be asked for if there is reason to believe that the merchandise remains unpaid.

3. SIGHT DRAFT (Documents against payment)

The supporting shipping documents (usually commercial invoices, bills of lading, and insurance certificates as a minimum) are attached to the draft and deposited with the bank for collection. Importer receives the documents only after he pays the draft.

4. TIME DRAFT (Documents against acceptance)

A typical time draft is collected in much the same way as a sight draft except that it allows the importer a longer time to make his payment. When the draft is presented to the buyer, he accepts it by writing or stamping the word "accepted" across the draft and adding his signature. By doing this he acknowledges that the draft as drawn is acceptable to him and commits himself to pay the amount of the draft when it falls due. The controlling documents are released to the importer when he accepts the draft, and although the exporter does not receive payment before title is passed, he does receive the acceptance, which is an obligation of the importer.

5. CLEAN DRAFTS

Clean drafts are those which do not have documents attached. They are used most often to collect for goods previously shipped on open account, in an attempt to collect stale items, or to provide a written form of obligation in special circumstances.

6. OPEN ACCOUNT

Selling on an "open account" means selling on credit terms arranged between exporter and importer, but where the exporter has little evidence of the foreign buyer's obligation to pay a certain amount at a certain date. Eventual collection of payment may be difficult if the buyer defaults.

7. CONSIGNMENT

Under a consignment contract, goods are only "consigned," but not sold, to the importer abroad. The exporter (consignor) retains title to the merchandise until the importer (consignee) has sold them to a third party. Normally, exporters make this type of arrangement only with their branches or subsidiaries overseas. If made with an agent or other importers, the risk involved must be thoroughly understood.

INTERNATIONAL CREDIT INFORMATION

Credit information is available on the overseas buyer and his country from many sources. It is not unduly difficult to secure this information, although financial statements are less readily given by overseas customers. Furthermore, financial statements are difficult to evaluate because accounting practices and tax regulations differ widely from those in the United States and differ from country to country. The time required to gather information is greater than in domestic operations and for this reason many overseas credit executives build a comprehensive file of information on prospective overseas customers in order to permit quick decisions when necessary.

The following section will concentrate on major sources, both domestic and

INTERNATIONAL TRADE

international, of information on the overseas buyer. As indicated previously, the risk in an overseas transaction depends not only on the individual account, but on the country involved. Information on this aspect of the overseas credit risk, from comprehensive economic and business data on the buyer's country to details on export and import regulations, is made available here in the United States by governmental agencies, by the international departments of banks and of private trade-promotion organizations, and by publishers and organizations devoted exclusively to fostering overseas commerce.

Sources of Information on the Overseas Buyer

Domestic Sources. Exporter's Bank. The bank through which an American exporter conducts his international business usually has extensive credit information on many overseas houses. This invaluable information is issued to clients, upon request. To obtain such information from the bank, a letter should be addressed to the bank's credit department, giving the full name and address of the overseas customer, his local bank (if known), and the nature of the sale, including terms and amount. These facts can be of great assistance in obtaining a complete reply. In many cases, credit information on a buyer may already be in the bank's file or may be obtainable from other domestic sources, and a reply will be received very quickly. In other cases, it will be necessary for the bank to get the information from its overseas offices or correspondents abroad. This is usually done by air mail or Telex.

Bank information generally includes a history of the overseas firm and its antecedents, and some financial data. A fairly satisfactory picture of a firm's credit standing often may be obtained, but where large credit risks are undertaken by the seller, bank reports should be supplemented by information from other sources.

Commercial Credit Reporting Agencies. Dun & Bradstreet issues reports on overseas buyers which closely follow the pattern established for domestic credit reports. Single reports may be bought or a fixed number of reports contracted for in advance.

For the quick obtaining of current credit information on overseas buyers, airmail, Telex or cable services are offered.

United States Department of Commerce. United States overseas service offices—such as embassies and consulates—operated by the Department of State provide reports on overseas markets, industries, and importers. The information in these reports is relayed to the Department of Commerce, where it is compiled into individual country or industry bulletins and trade lists.

Information on individual buyers is compiled into the World Traders Data Reports. These are business reports prepared by the U.S. Foreign Service Department of State available through the Department of Commerce. These reports give general information on companies as well as general reputation, financial and trade references. The WTDR dates back to 1900, making it the oldest government assistance report in the world. It covers financial situation, company status, company firm development, reports on general reputation and buyability of the buyer. A report costs $45. However, World Traders Data Reports are not credit reports and are generally used as supplementary material. Each report must be signed by an American officer of the Embassy issuing this report in order to be of value.

Resources of the FCIB (an association of executives in finance credit and international business). The only real international credit and finance association is the FCIB-NACM Corporation, the international arm of the National Association of Credit Management. It is a member owned and operated service organization, and has been providing a full range of credit and financial services to its members since 1919.

Some of the services the FCIB offers to its membership is the FCIB International Bulletin, published biweekly, on matters concerning International Finance, Credit, Collections and Exchange regulations and problems; a new FCIB newsletter; an extensive international collection service department; and an international country information service, giving detailed information on financial, economic and political situations on most countries. In addition, the FCIB has regular International Round Table Conferences on problems in international finance, credit and collection. These conferences are held monthly in New York and three times a year in a different capital city in Europe. All members receive the minutes of these various meetings—a verbatim report of the discussions held by leading international traders and bankers on problems submitted by the membership. The FCIB operates many industry export credit groups throughout the United States and Europe. Twice a year it publishes an elaborate credit and collection survey conducted on over 102 countries worldwide.

Furthermore, the FCIB provides for its members Credit Interchange Reports with details from other suppliers on selling terms and how buyers pay (their past payment performance). This information is combined with detailed indications and information from the exporter's overseas agents on importers in various countries. Emphasis is on bank and ledger experiences with the overseas buyer— how he buys from other exporters and how he pays—although historical and financial information is also included, in order to reveal most clearly the buyer's current credit status. Each member tells how he rates the account, how long he has sold to the particular buyer, the highest recent credit allowed, what terms of sale are given, and how the buyer conforms to those terms. A careful coding system protects the confidential nature of the information. The FCIB provides Free Reciprocal Reports to all members who contribute information. These reports appear to be a perfect checkup on existing accounts.

The FCIB provides for its members a free Credit Report Service on overseas customers.

In 1974, the FCIB started the International Credit Executives Group (I.C.E. Seminar). This group takes a closer look at the quality of credit management that the foreign subsidiaries and branches of the multi-national companies are practicing. It has proved that there is the opportunity for standardization in a firm's credit practices abroad. Showing the potential for a better return on investment, preparing the reviewer with pointers on 'international savy' and implementing a specific written credit policy are imperative components of the I.C.E.'s key. This group meets in the United States and Europe.

The FCIB already has members in over 20 countries, mainly in North America and Europe, and is steadily growing.

International Trade Publications. Useful sources of credit information on specific overseas buyers are certain publishers of export papers and magazines, especially those which circulate abroad. They often build up worthwhile files on overseas buyers in particular fields, and make these files available to advertisers in their publications.

Overseas Sources. Buyer. A tactful way of soliciting information from the overseas buyer is for the American manufacturer to initiate an *exchange* of antecedent and financial information. Information supplied by the buyer may range from excellent to worthless. At best, he may volunteer valuable data including financial reports, a detailed biography of the principals, and a history of the business going back over several generations. (Due to differences in accounting methods, financial statements when offered cannot generally be subjected to the type of financial analysis common on domestic statements.) At worst, the buyer will provide no information at all, feeling that such a request reflects upon his integrity.

Buyer's Bank. Like information received from the buyer himself, the value of credit information secured directly from the overseas buyer's bank varies in value. In many instances, this information consists merely of a report that the overseas buyer is a respected member of the community. Only occasionally is fairly complete information reported. International banks vary widely in their cooperation with American requests for information.

Exporter's Overseas Sales Representative. The United States exporter's sales representative abroad is considered one of the most valuable sources of information on the overseas buyer's credit worthiness. The experienced sales agent has known his customers for a long period and, in all probability, has had the opportunity to study their business practices firsthand. He is known in the buyer's trade circle and has access to credit information from local banks and commercial sources. He can therefore offer not only a fair picture of a buyer's financial condition, but also much confidential data which would be difficult to obtain from any other source. He may offer information on the overseas buyer's aggressiveness, on personal problems of the buyer which may affect his business dealings, on his standing in the trade and the community, and on his past record and future prospects. If given an intelligent appreciation of the mutual value of credit data to the sales and credit force alike, the sales agent abroad can train himself to be an excellent observer and reporter.

U.S. DEPARTMENT OF COMMERCE

14th St. between Constitution Ave. & E. Street N.W., Washington, D.C. 20230

How the Department of Commerce Is Set Up to Assist You

The Department of Commerce has domestic business and export-expansion support operations to provide assistance to American companies competing in world markets.

International Trade Administration

In broadest terms, the International Trade Administration is the "commerce" part of the Department of Commerce.

It collects information *from* business and *for* business, and translates that information for practical, profitable application *by* business. It serves American companies both at home and in foreign countries.

Its job is to promote America's foreign commerce, because healthy business creates jobs, strengthens our economy and gives us a better standard of living.

To do this job, ITA administers export expansion programs, develops trade and investment policy and operates a network of overseas and domestic commercial offices. ITA also administers controls on exports of certain commodities for reasons of national security, foreign policy or short supply and investigates charges that imports are being unfairly "dumped" (sold below fair value) in the U.S. market or receiving illegal government subsidies.

Trade Development

The United States needs to export. Expanded export sales can offset America's continuing record trade deficits and keep our economy healthy. For the U.S. supplier, exporting can mean valuable new markets and the profits they generate.

Yet, strangely, simple lack of effort by U.S. industry is one of the chief impediments to export growth in this country. For many, exporting seems too complicated, or too time-consuming, or just too much of an unknown. Out of some 300,000 manufacturing firms in this country, only about 30,000—10 percent—are exporters. Yet it is estimated that at least twice that number could export successfully if they tried.

Under America's free-enterprise system, Government can do much to improve the climate for exporting, but only U.S. private industry can make the sales. What Government can do, what ITA does do, is offer export counseling, market information, and promotional assistance that give American firms the confidence, knowledge, and opportunity to succeed in international trade.

To facilitate this effort, ITA has organized its Trade Development group by broad industrial sectors: Aerospace Industries; Automotive Affairs and Consumer Goods; Basic Industries; Capital Goods and International Construction; Science and Electronics; Service Industries; and Textiles and Apparel.

Each of these sector groups fosters the competitiveness and export growth of its industry by developing advantageous trade policies and providing effective trade promotion programs. Thus, for the first time, each American industry has a single, authoritative point of contact for the entire range of Commerce programs relevant to its trade interests.

Rounding out Trade Development's organization are two units that cover issues cutting across industry lines. Trade Information and Analysis gathers and disseminates international trade and investment data for use in export promotion and policy formulation. Trade Adjustment Assistance provides financial and technical assistance to U.S. companies that have been harmed by strong foreign competition.

Trade Development also promotes industry's awareness of the Export Trading Company Act of 1982, which permits U.S. firms to join forces in exporting or in providing export services for other companies. In conjunction with the U.S. Department of Justice, Trade Development can give U.S. exporters limited immunity from U.S. antitrust laws.

INTERNATIONAL TRADE

International Economic Policy

The International Trade Administration is actively involved in the development of U.S. international trade policy as well as direct assistance to the business community to facilitate trade and investment.

ITA's division of International Economic Policy (IEP) unit works to combine its knowledge of foreign markets and the restrictions on U.S access to those markets, and acts to overcome or eliminate those restrictions. This includes making representations to foreign governments on specific bilateral issues, formulating broad policy initiatives designed to increase foreign access, and undertaking efforts to improve the overall international trading environment.

IEP's Office of Multilateral Affairs ensures that the rules of the trading system as embodied in the General Agreement on Tariffs and Trade (GATT) work to the maximum benefit of American business. The office also works with international organizations to ensure that emerging trade issues—in such areas as investment, services, and high technology—are addressed in order to expand the opportunities for American business.

The major arena for developing international trade rules has been the Multilateral Trade Negotiations (MTN). A major example of these negotiations is the Tokyo Round of the MTN, concluded in 1979 after five years of talks, in which the United States and its principal trading partners reduced tariff barriers to trade and agreed to international codes for reducing non-tariff barriers. In the Tokyo Round, ITA did most of the preliminary work of analyzing tariff rates and non-tariff barriers affecting U.S. trade, and the effect of all MTN offers and counteroffers on our industry and commerce. ITA provided staff support and policy guidance to the U.S. team during the negotiations, and took responsibility for implementing the new trade agreements after they were approved by the U.S. Congress.

Counseling business people on trade opportunities and taking action to increase those opportunities requires an in-depth knowledge of the countries with which trade takes place. ITA's International Economic Policy (IEP) unit is responsibile for international trade on a regional and country-specific basis. It is the only organization in the U.S. government with country specialists whose primary responsibility is to follow commercial and economic developments with each of our trading partners.

The unit serves both business and government policy makers and serves as a source of information for any business person who needs counseling on foreign market conditions, commercial policies, and trade regulations. Through the U.S. and Foreign Commercial Service (USFCS) officers abroad and a range of other sources, country specialists develop information on promising trade opportunities, economic and political conditions, successful marketing strategies, government regulations and tariffs. Where trade complaints or disputes arise, country specialists work closely with the USFCS officers at our embassies to resolve them.

In addition to serving the business community directly, IEP coordinates all country and regional activities of the Commerce Department. These activities cover the full spectrum of U.S. international economic relations. In this capacity, the country specialists provide essential support to the policy makers who are actively shaping these relations.

An important part of this activity involves working with USFCS officers abroad to develop strategies for increasing U.S. exports to all regions of the world. In addition, IEP works closely with other Commerce officials to publicize and promote export opportunities and to determine which U.S. products can best compete in specific country markets.

The Office of Policy Coordination works closely with the desk officers to handle commercial policy issues—such as countertrade—which crosscut the various regions. The office collaborates with the Office of the U.S. Trade Representative, the Treasury and State Departments to ensure that our policies respond fully to the needs of the American business community in individual foreign markets.

Trade Administration

(1) Export Administration

ITA administers controls on exports that may, for reasons of national security, foreign policy, or short supply, have a detrimental effect on our national well-being.

Controls are exercised with the least possible disruption to U.S. industry and its trade potential. Most of the work involves processing export license applications, some of which require extensive technical analysis and interagency coordination.

Besides reviewing and analyzing license applications for approval or denial, the staff prepares statistical and analytical reports, develops and publishes export control questions.

ITA also investigates license violations under the Export Administration Act and conducts other compliance checks. Additional staff works to curtail exports found to contribute to a scarcity of goods in the United States.

In addition, ITA administers foreign boycott regulations which prohibit U.S. persons from complying with unsanctioned foreign boycotts against countries that are friendly to the United States. This work includes enforcing the law, advising and educating the public about the law, and making recommendations to better implement the United States' antiboycott policy.

ITA also must insure that United States industry is fully prepared to meet the industrial requirements of the national defense and to respond to any national emergency. Industrial preparedness responsibilities are supported by industrial resource analysis programs, including industrial mobilization evaluation and stockpile management. As mandated by law, ITA sees that purchases for approved defense and energy programs are given preferential treatment by producers. It also provides assistance to resolve delivery problems, allocates basic materials needed for filling approved defense and energy orders, and issues directives to overcome production bottlenecks.

Further, ITA is responsible for planning to insure the preparedness of government to deal with emergencies.

(2) Import Administration

Under the 1980 reorganization of Federal Government trade functions, ITA took on the responsibilities of administering U.S. antidumping and countervailing duty statutes.

INTERNATIONAL TRADE

The antidumping statute is concerned with situations in which foreign manufacturers export their goods to the United States at prices lower than those in their home or third country markets. The countervailing duty statute is concerned with situations in which foreign goods enter the United States with the benefit of foreign subsidies that give the foreign product an unfair competitive advantage in our market.

The antidumping and countervailing duty statutes are two of the most important U.S. laws designed to protect domestic industries against unfair import practices. ITA is responsible for conducting investigations to determine whether imported products are entering the United States at "dumped" prices or with the benefit of a foreign subsidy. If ITA finds this to be the case, a duty in addition to any regular Customs duty is imposed. The additional duty would be equal to the dumping margin or extent of subsidization found.

ITA is responsible for annual reviews of each of these cases in order to calculate the amount of additional duty to be assessed. The investigations conducted by ITA under these two statutes are initiated as a result of petitions filed with ITA on behalf of the allegedly injured domestic industry.

ITA has statutory responsibility for administering U.S. Foreign-Trade Zones and processing applications for new zones. Foreign-Trade Zones are areas under U.S. Customs supervision into which foreign merchandise may be brought without immediately going through the usual formal Customs entry. The goods may be exhibited, stored, assembled, or used in manufacture within the zone, and duties need not be paid unless and until the goods or their end products enter U.S. Customs territory from the zone.

ITA also administers the duty-free importation of scientific instruments for educational or research facilities, and allocates quotas for duty-free imports of watches assembled in the Virgin Islands, Guam and America Samoa.

The U.S. and Foreign Commercial Service

Exporting companies in the United States range from the small manufacturer to the giant conglomerate. Each has its own special needs, whether it be in entering a foreign market for the first time or in testing international demand for a sophisticated new product.

The Commerce Department's U.S. and Foreign Commercial Service, linked through ITA headquarters in Washington, provides the U.S. export community with a network of trade-assistance services that extends from domestic field offices to Foreign Service posts around the world.

At home, ITA operates a chain of 47 District Offices that make up the U.S. Commercial Service. They bring ITA's vast resources directly to the local business community.

The trade specialists in these offices are particularly concerned with assisting small and medium-sized firms—those most likely to be unfamiliar with the exporting process—and providing them with information on finding and developing markets for their products abroad. They provide export counseling, conduct seminars and conferences on exporting, maintain libraries of trade data, provide information and advice on U.S. and international trade regulations, and offer leads to financing and investment opportunities.

To help American business abroad, Foreign Commercial officers posted in U.S. Embassies and Consulates seek out trade opportunities, provide basic data on foreign markets and firms, supply information on U.S. goods and services to foreign buyers and consult with foreign governments on trade questions. They provide direct support to Commerce export promotion activities overseas.

ITA's commercial services also include publication of *Commerce Business Daily,* which provides the business community with information on Federal Government procurement actions and other types of contract awards and business opportunities. Approximately 350,000 procurement and 150,000 contract awards are published annually. The publication has 50,000 paid subscribers.

CHAMBER OF COMMERCE OF THE UNITED STATES—INTERNATIONAL DIVISION

The Chamber of Commerce of the United States is a federation of businessmen and women, firms and organizations, with a membership of over 200,000 companies, 1,200 trade associations and 2,600 commercial organizations (local, state and regional chambers of commerce throughout the United States and American chambers of commerce abroad).

To respond to the needs and challenges facing this widespread membership, which covers international trade and investment, industry, banking, transportation, communications, insurance, construction, agriculture and all other phases of American business, the Chamber maintains specialized groups dealing with the major business activities of the United States.

Activities of the International Division of the U.S. Chamber are illustrated in the following outline. The International Division:

(1) Provides leadership in the formation of effective business viewpoints on important international trade, investment and services, and economic development issues.

(2) Advocates the international interests of American business before the Congress and Executive Branch of the Government and in public forums at home and abroad.

(3) Analyzes foreign trade, development assistance, and investment and services legislation and government administrative procedures, and develops U.S. Chamber policy in these fields. In this connection, the International Division staffs a system of policy committees, task forces and working groups, including the International Policy Committee, the Export Policy Task Force, the International Investment Task Force, the International Economic Development Policy Task Force, and other task forces and technical working groups.

(4) Assists Chamber members in building foreign business through use of manuals, direct Washington liaison, and systematic communication with U.S. business around the world.

(5) Conducts workshops and conferences that address such issues as barter and countertrade and foreign procurement.

(6) Develops educational materials for use of member organizations and the public in the field of international relations, with specialized research into such areas as "Federal Regulation of International Business," "The Price of Ambiguity—More Than Three Years Under the Foreign Corrupt Practices Act" and "National Export Policy—Recommendations for Expanding U.S. Exports." Various texts which are periodically revised include: *Foreign Commerce Handbook* and *Employment Abroad—Facts and Fallacies.* Their newsletter, *International Business Review,* inform readers of developments in the Congress, federal agencies and international organizations affecting international trade and investment.

(7) Maintains liaison with foreign embassies in the United States and with multinational governmental organizations and enjoys consultative status with the United Nations Economic and Social Council.

(8) Staffs the U.S. sections of 14 bilateral and multilateral business councils, the members of which meet regularly with their foreign counterparts to build consensus on key trade, investment, monetary and economic development issues, and to find solutions to pressing international economic problems.

(9) Maintains close working relationships with other U.S. business organizations and represents U.S. business viewpoints before international business and intergovernmental organizations.

(10) Works closely with American chambers of commerce abroad, now operating in 51 locations, which act as spokesmen and advisers for permanent and transient U.S. business executives, maintain liaison with host governments, and help promote trade and investment with the United States.

DOMESTIC INTERNATIONAL SALES CORPORATION

By Walter H. Diamond,[*] Principal
Murphy, Hauser, O'Connor & Quinn
and
Chairman, Advisory Board
International DISC Executives Association

DISC/FSC

Under Title V of the Revenue Act of 1971, Congress approved an export tax incentive to stimulate the sale of United States goods and related services abroad through the use of a United States corporation entitled Domestic International Sales Corporation, or DISC. There are a number of benefits offered United States exporters operating under a DISC. The principal advantage is in the ability of a DISC to defer the payment of United States taxation on up to 50% of its net earnings from exports until such time that they are distributed to the DISC's shareholders or until disposition of the DISC stock is made to its shareholders. Under the Tax Reform Act of 1976, effective as of taxable years beginning after December 31, 1975, the DISC tax deferral is limited to any excess over 67% of the average exports receipts for the base period 1972, 1973, 1974 and 1975 for any taxable year beginning before 1980. For any taxable year beginning in any calendar year after 1979, the base period is the taxable years beginning in the fourth, fifth, sixth and seventh calendar years preceding the particular taxable year. Military exports are restricted to a ceiling equal to 50% of a company's non-military exports. The original 50% tax deferral applies for DISC's with adjusted taxable income of $100,000 or less for a taxable year. If a DISC has adjusted taxable income of more than $100,000 for a taxable year, the amount taken into account is deemed to equal the excess of an amount which would be taken into account over twice the excess of $150,000 over adjusted taxable income. DISC benefits remain for United States companies paying "bribes" but those businesses making these payments are required to repatriate an amount of earnings equal to the "bribe" and are assessed currently on these profits for tax purposes.

The deferral of income from a DISC is reduced from 50% to 42½% effective

---

[*] Mr. Diamond is author of "Foreign Tax and Trade Briefs," the up-to-date tax service of 104 countries published by Matthew Bender & Co., from which this material is reprinted.

for taxable years of corporate shareholders that began after December 31, 1982. Illegal payments may also generate deemed distributions of a DISC under the Foreign Corrupt Practices Act, as revised in the 1982 Income Tax Act. Under the Reagan Administration's bill now in Congress, which is acceptable to the General Agreement on Tariffs and Trade, with one exception companies would qualify for tax deferral on export income only if they establish foreign corporations to make export sales. The deferral would amount to 17 percent of export sales of the parent corporation and the foreign subsidiary would be known as a Foreign Sales Corporation.

A DISC also benefits from special intercompany pricing rules between it and related United States parties, which in effect, guarantee earnings to a DISC without the possibility of a Section 482 intercompany pricing reallocation from the Internal Revenue Service. In addition, there are rules determining the capital structure of a DISC to protect it from an argument by the Internal Revenue Service that it may be a sham corporation. Moreover, a DISC may make a tax-free producer loan for up to five years to a related or unrelated person engaged in the United States manufacturing, production, growing or extraction of export property if the obligation is evidenced by a note with a stated maturity date and under certain other conditions.

Election of DISC's

Under Title V, a corporation must make its election to be treated as a DISC for a taxable year during the 90-day period preceding the beginning of that taxable year.

If a corporation makes a DISC election, the provisions of the law apply for the taxable year of the corporation and for all succeeding taxable years. The provisions also apply to each person who is a shareholder of the DISC for all periods on or after the first day of the first taxable year of the corporation for which the election is effective. Revenue Procedure 72-12 states that all persons who are shareholders of the corporation as of the beginning of the first taxable year for which the election is effective must consent to the election if it is to be valid. To obtain the DISC advantages, a company must meet the following conditions:

(1) It must be a corporation organized in the United States;
(2) 95 percent or more of its gross receipts must constitute "qualified export receipts";
(3) 95 percent or more of the adjusted bases of all its assets must constitute "qualified export assets";
(4) It must have only one class with a par value of at least $2,500; and
(5) It must elect to be treated as a DISC.

Qualified export receipts include gross receipts from the disposition of export property, from the leasing of export property outside the United States, for services related to any qualified disposition (including lease) of export property; dividends from related foreign export corporations; interest from qualified export assets (including producer's loans); receipts for engineering or architectural services on foreign construction projects; and receipts for managerial services in furtherance of the production of qualified export receipts.

Qualified export assets include export property (i.e., property produced in the United States, held primarily for sale or lease for use outside the United States and having at least a 50% United States content); assets used primarily in connection with export property; receivables arising by reason of export-type transactions; money, bank deposits and temporary investments needed for working capital of the DISC; producer's loans; stock or securities of related foreign export corporations; and certain export-related financing obligations.

A second important DISC ruling released by the Treasury, Revenue Ruling 72-166, and incorporated into Regulations 991 and 992, states that a DISC is required to have its own bank account and separate books and records. However, a DISC need not have substance in order to compute its income under either of the "safe-haven" pricing methods. A DISC is required to have an agreement with the manufacturing parent company but need not solicit the sales on which it is allowed a profit or commission. Neither is it required to have employees on its payroll or maintain inventories. Billings and collections may be handled by the parent company in the name of the DISC and the parent company's employees may act for the DISC in all matters. There is no need for the parent company to charge the DISC for any expenses incurred on its behalf. The agreement between the DISC and its parent company may provide that the DISC will receive net income on any transactions handled in its name equal to the maximum amount permitted under the pricing rules. Under the Tax Reduction Act of 1975, companies deriving income from export of certain agricultural products and mineral or timber resources, as well as items declared in short supply under the Export Administration Act of 1969, may not qualify as DISC's.

INTRODUCTION

Under the Tax Reform Act of 1976, DISC benefits are denied to United States persons found cooperating with international boycotts of countries friendly to the United States and to corporations whose controlled foreign subsidiary or DISC has paid any illegal bribe, kickback or similar payment directly or indirectly to a foreign Government official or agent.

State Treatment of DISC's

At the same time New York State approved a bill providing basically the same tax treatment with respect to the income measure of the franchise tax under Article 9-A of the Tax Law as allowed under the Federal income tax law provisions added by the Federal Revenue Act of 1971. In addition, DISC shareholders are now taxed in a somewhat similar manner as they are treated under the Federal law. Specifically, subdivision 1 of Section 208 of the New York State Tax Law was amended to define a "DISC" and a "former DISC" as any corporation which meets the requirements established for Federal income tax purposes under Section 992(a) of the Internal Revenue Code. A new subdivision 8-A was added to Section 208 to provide that investments in a DISC shall not be treated as either subsidiary capital or investment capital for purposes of the franchise tax under Article 9-A. Subdivision 8-A also provides that deemed distributions from a DISC or a former DISC which are taxable as dividends under Section 995(b) and (c) of the Internal Revenue Code and any actual distribution from a DISC or a former DISC shall be treated as business income except an actual distribution which is treated as made out of "other earnings and profits" under Section 996 of the Internal Revenue Code.

Other states may tax DISC's as ordinary corporations or treat them in similar fashion to Federal law. States allowing Federal treatment of a DISC are Alaska, Colorado, Connecticut, Delaware, Georgia, Idaho, Illinois, Indiana, Iowa, Kansas, Maine, Michigan, New Mexico, Oklahoma, Vermont and West Virginia. Shareholders in those states are taxed on earnings in the same manner as provided by Federal law. Florida, Massachusetts and Montana treat their DISC's the same as the Federal legislation with the exception of special provisions for DISC shareholders. The following states and the District of Columbia tax DISC's on income in the same manner as ordinary business corporations and DISC shareholders are taxed on distributed income only: Alabama, Arizona, Arkansas, California, Hawaii, Louisiana, Maryland, Minnesota, Mississippi, Missouri, Ohio, Pennsylvania, Rhode Island, South Carolina, Tennessee, Texas, Utah and Virginia.

In New Jersey DISC's are treated as ordinary taxpayers and corporate stockholders of a DISC are taxable on DISC dividends in the ordinary manner: 100% is excluded if the DISC is a subsidiary while 50% is otherwise excluded. The amount of DISC dividends included in a stockholder's net income, prior to either the 100% or 50% exclusion, is the same amount included in its gross dividends for Federal income tax purposes, whether or not the dividends are actually received. DISC's must make any appropriate statutory adjustments at lines 29 to 36 of the Corporation Business Tax Return to determine their adjusted entire net income for New Jersey Corporation Business Tax purposes. DISC's do not have to complete lines 1 to 27 of the New Jersey tax return because Federal Form 1120-DISC is completely different in line makeup from the New Jersey form. However, all required schedules of the New Jersey Corporation Business Tax must be filed with the entire Form 1120-DISC.

Kentucky provides that DISC's are treated as ordinary corporations and that individual shareholders of DISC's are subject to income tax on dividends distributed to them. However, corporate shareholders are not taxed since divided income received by corporations on and after January 1, 1970 is excluded from gross income for Kentucky corporation income tax purposes.

Massachusetts has three types of DISC's: (1) Wholly-owned DISC's; (2) Viable DISC's; and (3) DISC's with security investment.

New Hampshire, North Carolina, North Dakota, Washington, and Wisconsin DISC corporate income is taxed in the same manner as income of any ordinary business corporation, although there are special provisions concerning the taxation of DISC shareholders.

In North Carolina, earnings from DISC's are deductible as dividends as though they were from ordinary corporations.

Oregon does not tax nonresident individuals since the income arises from intangible assets which Oregon does not tax. Nevada, South Dakota, Washington, and Wyoming have no income taxes, but have license taxes to do business so that special tax treatment for DISC's is not necessary in these four states.

Texas has no corporate income tax but has a franchise tax, which could be steep for large corporations, so it probably will have to act regarding DISC

INTERNATIONAL TRADE

treatment. Texas now treats DISC's as ordinary corporations, and distributions to surplus and undivided profits under the franchise tax are treated as they are for other corporations.

The Deficit Reduction Act of 1984 replaced the DISC legislation in the 1971 and 1982 laws with new Sections 921–927 of the Internal Revenue Code allowing for the establishing of Foreign Sales Corporations (FSCs) and exclusion of income taxes on the deferral income of a DISC whose taxable year begins before January 1, 1985, and closes on December 31, 1984. The FSC was adopted by Congress in response to criticism of DISCs by the signatories of the General Agreement on Tariffs and Trade (GATT) who contended that DISC deferrals amounted to an illegal export subsidy that violated the GATT rules. In an effort to approve a territorial type system of taxation for United States exports designed to comply with GATT, the FSC was adopted.

The FSC must be incorporated outside the United States, with possessions of the United States, excluding the Commonwealth of Pureto Rico, qualifying for foreign-country status. Under the FSC legislation, the tax-exempt income either will be 32% or 30% of the foreign trade income earned by the FSC at arm's length pricing or 1.83% gross sales up to 23% of the combined taxable income, whichever is greater. If a FSC uses arm's length pricing with its related supplier, 32% of it foreign trade income is exempt from U.S. tax. If special administrative pricing rules are used, 16/23 of the foreign trade income is exempt. In the case of a FSC corporate shareholder, the administrative pricing rules will be applied with respect to a corporation substituting 30% and 15/23, respectively. The law states that no tax may be imposed on foreign trading income by possessions of the United States for two years. FSCs may export goods or services and the foreign trading income is exempt from United States Federal income taxes, moreover, domestic corporation owning the FSC shares benefits from a 100% dividend-received deduction for the dividends distributed by the FSC. In addition, there is no deemed distribution to shareholders as under the DISC system.

In order to qualify as a FSC, a corporation must meet four major requirements: (1) maintain a foreign presence; (2) have economic substance; (3) employ foreign management and economic processes giving use to foreign trading income; and (4) use arm's length pricing methods.

The requirement that the FSC be managed outside the United States will be treated as satisfied for a particular taxable year under the rules set forth in the new Internal Revenue Code provisions if:

(1) All meetings of the board of directors of the corporation and all meetings of the shareholders of the corporation are outside the U.S.;

(2) The principal bank account of the corporation is maintained outside the United States at all times during the taxable year; and

(3) All dividends, legal and accounting fees, and salaries of officers and members of the board of directors of the corporation paid during the taxable year are disbursed out of bank accounts of the corporation outside the United States. The sales requirements will be tested on a transaction by transaction basis. However, this requirement will be considered to have been met with respect to sales to a single customer during any taxable year if:

(1) The export property consists of either fungible products or products which are substantially similar;

(2) The products are sold by the FSC under a single contract;

(3) The contract is a term of one year or less which specifies the material terms of each sale; and

(4) The FSC or its agent performs any one of the three activities once with respect to all such sales.

Under the foreign presence test, an FSC must be a corporation organized under the laws of any foreign country or possession (excluding Puerto Rico), that is either (a) a party to an exchange requirements of Section 927 of the United States Internal Revenue Code, or (b) an income tax treaty partner of the United States if the Secretary of Treasury certifies that the "exchange of information" program with that country is satisfactory. A FSC may have no more than 25 shareholders and may not have any preferred stock outstanding at any time during the taxable year.

In preparation for an onrush of the 16,800 registered DISCs to organize their overseas operations in "exchange of information" agreement or treaty countries, the Governor of the United States Virgin Islands has stated that, after the two-year period has elapsed, the Virgin Islands will collect only 1% on income. Legislation to this effect already has been approved by the Virgin Islands. For companies wishing to incorporate in Europe, United Kingdom organizations with operations managed and controlled from the Channel Islands are considered to be attractive. Both the Virgin Islands and the United Kingdom, which offers 100%-income tax exemption, qualify as seat of incorporation under the FSC law since they have "exchange of information agreements" with the United States under their respective special treaty clauses. Cyprus is another European country that welcomes FSC incorporation since it has a low income tax of only 4.25% on companies managed and controlled locally and its Income Tax Treaty with the United States includes an "exchange of information" clause. Export firms with $5 million of sales or less annually may establish FSCs with little or no presence in a foreign country by joining an export trading company operation. Companies with export sales of $10 million or less may establish a new DISC but must pay interest on the deferred income in order to comply with the rules of the General Agreement on Tariffs and Trade. A number of small export companies are liquidating their present DISCs, accepting Congress' amnesty on paying taxes on the accumulated deferred income, and then are establishing new DISCs under the 1984 legislation. However, the deferred income of "small" DISCs is subject to interest charges.

UNIFORM CUSTOMS AND PRACTICE FOR DOCUMENTARY CREDITS (1983 REVISION), THE INTERNATIONAL CHAMBER OF COMMERCE PUBLICATION NO. 400

The Rules have been drawn up by the Commission on Banking Practice and Technique of the International Chamber of Commerce in consultation with the banking associations of many countries. The ICC acts to promote business interests at international levels, to foster the greater freedom of international trade, and to harmonize and facilitate business and trade practices. Paris based, the Chamber has National Committees in 58 countries and has direct members in 50 more. In the United States, Publication No. 400, a comparative study prepared by Bernard Wheble entitled *Documentary Credits: UCP/1974/1983 Revisions, Compared and Explained*, ICC Publication No. 411, and the revised edition of *Guide to Documentary Credit Operations*, ICC Publication No. 415, may be purchased from The ICC Publishing Corporation, 156 Fifth Avenue, Suite 820, New York, N.Y. 10010 at the price of $6.00, $12.95 and $10.95 per copy respectively. Copyright © 1983 by ICC Publishing S.A. All rights reserved. Reprinted with the permission of The ICC Publishing Corporation.

A. General provisions and definitions

Article 1
These articles apply to all documentary credits, including, to the extent to which they may be applicable, standby letters of credit, and are binding on all parties thereto unless otherwise expressly agreed. They shall be incorporated into each documentary credit by wording in the credit indicating that such credit is issued subject to Uniform Customs and Practice for Documentary Credits, 1983 revision, ICC Publication No. 400.

Article 2
For the purposes of these articles, the expressions "documentary credit(s)" and "standby letter(s) of credit" used herein (hereinafter referred to as "credit(s)") mean any arrangement, however named or described, whereby a bank (the issuing bank), acting at the request and on the instructions of a customer (the applicant for the credit),
i) is to make a payment to or to the order of a third party (the beneficiary), or is to pay or accept bills of exchange (drafts) drawn by the beneficiary,
or
ii) authorizes another bank to effect such payment, or to pay, accept or negotiate such bills of exchange (drafts),
against stipulated documents, provided that the terms and conditions of the credit are complied with.

Article 3
Credits, by their nature, are separate transactions from the sales or other contract(s) on which they may be based and banks are in no way concerned with or bound by such contract(s), even if any reference whatsoever to such contract(s) is included in the credit.

Article 4
In credit operations all parties concerned deal in documents, and not in goods, services and/or other performances to which the documents may relate.

Article 5
Instructions for the issuance of credits, the credits themselves, instructions for any amendments thereto and the amendments themselves must be complete and precise.
In order to guard against confusion and misunderstanding, banks should discourage any attempt to include excessive detail in the credit or in any amendment thereto.

Article 6
A beneficiary can in no case avail himself of the contractual relationships existing between the banks or between the applicant for the credit and the issuing bank.

B. Form and notification of credits

Article 7
a. Credits may be either
   i) revocable, or
   ii) irrevocable.
b. All credits, therefore, should clearly indicate whether they are revocable or irrevocable.
c. In the absence of such indication the credit shall be deemed to be revocable.

Article 8
A credit may be advised to a beneficiary through another bank (the advising bank) without engagement on the part of the advising bank, but that bank shall take reasonable care to check the apparent authenticity of the credit which it advises.

Article 9
a. A revocable credit may be amended or cancelled by the issuing bank at any moment and without prior notice to the beneficiary.
b. However, the issuing bank is bound to:
   i) reimburse a branch or bank with which a revocable credit has been made available for sight

payment, acceptance or negotiation, for any payment, acceptance or negotiation made by such branch or bank prior to receipt by it of notice of amendment or cancellation, against documents which appear on their face to be in accordance with the terms and conditions of the credit.

ii) reimburse a branch or bank with which a revocable credit has been made available for deferred payment, if such branch or bank has, prior to receipt by it of notice of amendment or cancellation, taken up documents which appear on their face to be in accordance with the terms and conditions of the credit.

Article 10

a. An irrevocable credit constitutes a definite undertaking of the issuing bank, provided that the stipulated documents are presented and the terms and conditions of the credit are complied with:
i) if the credit provides for sight payment—to pay, or that payment will be made;
ii) if the credit provides for deferred payment—to pay, or that payment will be made, on the date(s) determinable in accordance with the stipulations of the credit;
iii) if the credit provides for acceptance—to accept drafts drawn by the beneficiary if the credit stipulates that they are to be drawn on the issuing bank, or to be responsible for their acceptance and payment at maturity if the credit stipulates that they are to be drawn on the applicant for the credit or any other drawee stipulated in the credit;
iv) if the credit provides for negotiation—to pay without recourse to drawers and/or bona fide holders, draft(s) drawn by the beneficiary, at sight or at a tenor, on the applicant for the credit or on any other drawee stipulated in the credit other than the issuing bank itself, or to provide for negotiation by another bank and to pay, as above, if such negotiation is not effected.

b. When an issuing bank authorizes or requests another bank to confirm its irrevocable credit and the latter has added its confirmation, such confirmation constitutes a definite undertaking of such bank (the confirming bank), in addition to that of the issuing bank, provided that the stipulated documents are presented and that the terms and conditions of the credit are complied with:
i) if the credit provides for sight payment—to pay, or that payment will be made;
ii) if the credit provides for deferred payment—to pay, or that payment will be made, on the date(s) determinable in accordance with the stipulations of the credit;
iii) if the credit provides for acceptance—to accept drafts drawn by the beneficiary if the credit stipulates that they are to be drawn on the confirming bank, or to be responsible for their acceptance and payment at maturity if the credit stipulates that they are to be drawn on the applicant for the credit or any other drawee stipulated in the credit;
iv) if the credit provides for negotiation—to negotiate without recourse to drawers and/or bona fide holders, draft(s) drawn by the beneficiary, at sight or at a tenor, on the issuing bank or on the applicant for the credit or on any other drawee stipulated in the credit other than the confirming bank itself.

c. If a bank is authorized or requested by the issuing bank to add its confirmation to a credit but is not prepared to do so, it must so inform the issuing bank without delay. Unless the issuing bank specifies otherwise in its confirmation authorization or request, the advising bank will advise the credit to the beneficiary without adding its confirmation.

d. Such undertakings can neither be amended nor cancelled without the agreement of the issuing bank, the confirming bank (if any), and the beneficiary. Partial acceptance of amendments contained in one and the same advice of amendment is not effective without the agreement of all the above named parties.

Article 11

a. All credits must clearly indicate whether they are available by sight payment, by deferred payment, by acceptance or by negotiation.

b. All credits must nominate the bank (nominated bank) which is authorized to pay (paying bank), or to accept drafts (accepting bank), or to negotiate (negotiating bank), unless the credit allows negotiation by any bank (negotiating bank).

c. Unless the nominated bank is the issuing bank or the confirming bank, its nomination by the issuing bank does not constitute any undertaking by the nominated bank to pay, to accept, or to negotiate.

d. By nominating a bank other than itself, or by allowing for negotiation by any bank, or by authorizing or requesting a bank to add its confirmation, the issuing bank authorizes such bank to pay, accept or negotiate, as the case may be, against documents which appear on their face to be in accordance with the terms and conditions of the credit, and undertakes to reimburse such bank in accordance with the provisions of these articles.

Article 12
a. When an issuing bank instructs a bank (advising bank) by any teletransmission to advise a credit or an amendment to a credit, and intends the mail confirmation to be the operative credit instrument, or the operative amendment, the teletransmission must state "full details to follow" (or words of similar effect), or that the mail confirmation will be the operative credit instrument or the operative amendment. The issuing bank must forward the operative credit instrument or the operative amendment to such advising bank without delay.

b. The teletransmission will be deemed to be the operative credit instrument or the operative amendment, and no mail confirmation should be sent, unless the teletransmission states "full details to follow" (or words of similar effect), or states that the mail confirmation is to be the operative credit instrument or the operative amendment.

c. A teletransmission intended by the issuing bank to be the operative credit instrument should clearly indicate that the credit is issued subject to Uniform Customs and Practice for Documentary Credits, 1983 revision, ICC Publication No. 400.

d. If a bank uses the services of another bank or banks (the advising bank) to have the credit advised to the beneficiary, it must also use the services of the same bank(s) for advising any amendments.

e. Banks shall be responsible for any consequences arising from their failure to follow the procedures set out in the preceding paragraphs.

Article 13
When a bank is instructed to issue, confirm or advise a credit similar in terms to one previously issued, confirmed or advised (similar credit) and the previous credit has been the subject of amendment(s), it shall be understood that the similar credit will not include any such amendment(s) unless the instructions specify clearly the amendment(s) which is/are to apply to the similar credit. Banks should discourage instructions to issue, confirm or advise a credit in this manner.

Article 14
If incomplete or unclear instructions are received to issue, confirm, advise or amend a credit, the bank requested to act on such instructions may give preliminary notification to the beneficiary for information only and without responsibility. The credit will be issued, confirmed, advised or amended only when the necessary information has been received and if the bank is then prepared to act on the instructions. Banks should provide the necessary information without delay.

C. Liabilities and responsibilities

Article 15
Banks must examine all documents with reasonable care to ascertain that they appear on their face to be in accordance with the terms and conditions of the credit. Documents which appear on their face to be inconsistent with one another will be considered as not appearing on their face to be in accordance with the terms and conditions of the credit.

Article 16
a. If a bank so authorized effects payment, or incurs a deferred payment undertaking, or accepts, or negotiates against documents which appear on their face to be in accordance with the terms and conditions of a credit, the party giving such authority shall be bound to reimburse the bank which has effected payment, or incurred a deferred payment undertaking, or has accepted, or negotiated, and to take up the documents.

b. If, upon receipt of the documents, the issuing bank considers that they appear on their face not to be in accordance with the terms and conditions of the credit, it must determine, on the basis of the documents alone, whether to take up such documents, or to refuse them and claim that they appear on their face not to be in accordance with the terms and conditions of the credit.

c. The issuing bank shall have a reasonable time in which to examine the documents and to determine as above whether to take up or to refuse the documents.

d. If the issuing bank decides to refuse the documents, it must give notice to that effect without delay by telecommunication or, if that is not possible, by other expeditious means, to the bank from which it received the documents (the remitting bank), or to the beneficiary, if it received the documents directly from him. Such notice must state the discrepancies in respect of which the issuing bank refuses the documents and must also state whether it is holding the documents at the disposal of, or is returning them to, the presenter (remitting bank or the beneficiary, as the case may be). The issuing bank shall then be entitled to claim from the remitting bank refund of any reimbursement which may have been made to that bank.

e. If the issuing bank fails to act in accordance with the provisions of paragraphs (c) and (d) of this article and/or fails to hold the documents at the disposal of, or to return them to, the presenter, the issuing bank shall be precluded from claiming that the documents are not in accordance with the terms and conditions of the credit.

f. If the remitting bank draws the attention of the issuing bank to any discrepancies in the documents or advises the issuing bank that it has paid, incurred a deferred payment undertaking, accepted or negotiated under reserve or against an indemnity in respect of such discrepancies, the issuing bank shall not be thereby relieved from any of its obligations under any provision of this article. Such reserve or indemnity concerns only the relations between the remitting bank and the party towards whom the reserve was made, or from whom, or on whose behalf, the indemnity was obtained.

Article 17

Banks assume no liability or responsibility for the form, sufficiency, accuracy, genuineness, falsification or legal effect of any documents, or for the general and/or particular conditions stipulated in the documents or superimposed thereon; nor do they assume any liability or responsibility for the description, quantity, weight, quality, condition, packing, delivery, value or existence of the goods represented by any documents, or for the good faith or acts and/or omissions, solvency, performance or standing of the consignor, the carriers, or the insurers of the goods, or any other person whomsoever.

Article 18

Banks assume no liability or responsibility for the consequences arising out of delay and/or loss in transit of any messages, letters or documents, or for delay, mutilation or other errors arising in the transmission of any telecommunication. Banks assume no liability or responsibility for errors in translation or interpretation of technical terms, and reserve the right to transmit credit terms without translating them.

Article 19

Banks assume no liability or responsibility for consequences arising out of the interruption of their business by Acts of God, riots, civil commotions, insurrections, wars or any other causes beyond their control, or by any strikes or lockouts. Unless specifically authorized, banks will not, upon resumption of their business, incur a deferred payment undertaking, or effect payment, acceptance or negotiation under credits which expired during such interruption of their business.

Article 20

a. Banks utilizing the services of another bank or other banks for the purpose of giving effect to the instructions of the applicant for the credit do so for the account and at the risk of such applicant.

b. Banks assume no liability or responsibility should the instructions they transmit not be carried out, even if they have themselves taken the initiative in the choice of such other bank(s).

c. The applicant for the credit shall be bound by and liable to indemnify the banks against all obligations and responsibilities imposed by foreign laws and usages.

Article 21

a. If an issuing bank intends that the reimbursement to which a paying, accepting or negotiating bank is entitled shall be obtained by such bank claiming on another branch or office of the issuing bank or on a third bank (all hereinafter referred to as the reimbursing bank) it shall provide such reimbursing bank in good time with the proper instructions or authorization to honour such reimbursement claims and without making it a condition that the bank entitled to claim reimbursement must certify compliance with the terms and conditions of the credit to the reimbursing bank.

INTERNATIONAL TRADE

b. An issuing bank will not be relieved from any of its obligations to provide reimbursement itself if and when reimbursement is not effected by the reimbursing bank.

c. The issuing bank will be responsible to the paying, accepting or negotiating bank for any loss of interest if reimbursement is not provided on first demand made to the reimbursing bank, or as otherwise specified in the credit, or mutually agreed, as the case may be.

D. Documents

Article 22
a. All instructions for the issuance of credits and the credits themselves and, where applicable, all instructions for amendments thereto and the amendments themselves, must state precisely the document(s) against which payment, acceptance or negotiation is to be made.

b. Terms such as "first class," "well known," "qualified," "independent," "official," and the like shall not be used to describe the issuers of any documents to be presented under a credit. If such terms are incorporated in the credit terms, banks will accept the relative documents as presented, provided that they appear on their face to be in accordance with the other terms and conditions of the credit.

c. Unless otherwise stipulated in the credit, banks will accept as originals documents produced or appearing to have been produced:
   by reprographic systems;
   by, or as the result of, automated or computerized systems;
   as carbon copies,
if marked as originals, always provided that, where necessary, such documents appear to have been authenticated.

Article 23
When documents other than transport documents, insurance documents and commercial invoices are called for, the credit should stipulate by whom such documents are to be issued and their wording or data content. If the credit does not so stipulate, banks will accept such documents as presented, provided that their data content makes it possible to relate the goods and/or services referred to therein to those referred to in the commercial invoice(s) presented, or to those referred to in the credit if the credit does not stipulate presentation of a commercial invoice.

Article 24
Unless otherwise stipulated in the credit, banks will accept a document bearing a date of issuance prior to that of the credit, subject to such document being presented within the time limits set out in the credit and in these articles.

D1. Transport documents (documents indicating loading on board or dispatch or taking in charge)

Article 25
Unless a credit calling for a transport document stipulates as such document a marine bill of lading (ocean bill of lading or a bill of lading covering carriage by sea), or a post receipt or certificate of posting:
a. banks will, unless otherwise stipulated in the credit, accept a transport document which:
   i) appears on its face to have been issued by a named carrier, or his agent, and
   ii) indicates dispatch or taking in charge of the goods, or loading on board, as the case may be, and
   iii) consists of the full set of originals issued to the consignor if issued in more than one original, and
   iv) meets all other stipulations of the credit.

b. Subject to the above, and unless otherwise stipulated in the credit, banks will not reject a transport document which:
   i) bears a title such as "Combined transport bill of lading," "Combined transport document," "Combined transport bill of lading or port-to-port bill of lading," or a title or a combination of titles of similar intent and effect, and/or
   ii) indicates some or all of the conditions of carriage by reference to a source or document other than the transport document itself (short form/blank back transport document), and/or
   iii) indicates a place of taking in charge different from the port of loading and/or a place of final destination different from the port of discharge, and/or
   iv) relates to cargoes such as those in containers or on pallets, and the like, and/or

v) contains the indication "intended," or similar qualification, in relation to the vessel or other means of transport, and/or the port of loading and/or the port of discharge.

c. Unless otherwise stipulated in the credit in the case of carriage by sea or by more than one mode of transport but including carriage by sea, banks will reject a transport document which:
   i) indicates that it is subject to a charter party, and/or
   ii) indicates that the carrying vessel is propelled by sail only.

d. Unless otherwise stipulated in the credit, banks will reject a transport document issued by a freight forwarder unless it is the FIATA Combined Transport Bill of Lading approved by the International Chamber of Commerce or otherwise indicates that it is issued by a freight forwarder acting as a carrier or agent of a named carrier.

Article 26

If a credit calling for a transport document stipulates as such document a marine bill of lading:

a. banks will, unless otherwise stipulated in the credit, accept a document which:
   i) appears on its face to have been issued by a named carrier, or his agent, and
   ii) indicates that the goods have been loaded on board or shipped on a named vessel, and
   iii) consists of the full set of originals issued to the consignor if issued in more than one original, and
   iv) meets all other stipulations of the credit.

b. Subject to the above, and unless otherwise stipulated in the credit, banks will not reject a document which:
   i) bears a title such as "Combined transport bill of lading," "Combined transport document," "Combined transport bill of lading or port-to-port bill of lading," or a title or a combination of titles of similar intent and effect, and/or
   ii) indicates some or all of the conditions of carriage by reference to a source or document other than the transport document itself (short form/blank back transport document), and/or
   iii) indicates a place of taking in charge different from the port of loading, and/or a place of final destination different from the port of discharge, and/or
   iv) relates to cargoes such as those in containers or on pallets, and the like.

c. Unless otherwise stipulated in the credit, banks will reject a document which:
   i) indicates that it is subject to a charter party, and/or
   ii) indicates that the carrying vessel is propelled by sail only, and/or
   iii) contains the indication "intended," or similar qualification in relation to
   • the vessel and/or the port of loading—unless such document bears an on board notation in accordance with article 27 (b) and also indicates the actual port of loading, and/or
   • the port of discharge—unless the place of final destination indicated on the document is other than the port of discharge, and/or
   iv) is issued by a freight forwarder, unless it indicates that it is issued by such freight forwarder acting as a carrier, or as the agent of a named carrier.

Article 27

a. Unless a credit specifically calls for an on board transport document, or unless inconsistent with other stipulation(s) in the credit, or with article 26, banks will accept a transport document which indicates that the goods have been taken in charge or received for shipment.

b. Loading on board or shipment on a vessel may be evidenced either by a transport document bearing wording indicating loading on board a named vessel or shipment on a named vessel, or, in the case of a transport document stating "received for shipment," by means of a notation of loading on board on the transport document signed or initialled and dated by the carrier or his agent, and the date of this notation shall be regarded as the date of loading on board the named vessel or shipment on the named vessel.

Article 28

a. In the case of carriage by sea or by more than one mode of transport but including carriage by sea, banks will refuse a transport document stating that the goods are or will be loaded on deck, unless specifically authorized in the credit.

b. Banks will not refuse a transport document which contains a provision that the goods may be carried on deck, provided it does not specifically state that they are or will be loaded on deck.

Article 29

a. For the purpose of this article transhipment means a transfer and reloading during the course of carriage from the port of loading or place of dispatch or taking in charge to the port of discharge or place of destination either from one conveyance or vessel to another conveyance or vessel within the same mode of transport or from one mode of transport to another mode of transport.

b. Unless transhipment is prohibited by the terms of the credit, banks will accept transport documents which indicate that the goods will be transhipped, provided the entire carriage is covered by one and the same transport document.

c. Even if transhipment is prohibited by the terms of the credit, banks will accept transport documents which:
    i) incorporate printed clauses stating that the carrier has the right to tranship, or
    ii) state or indicate that transhipment will or may take place, when the credit stipulates a combined transport document, or indicates carriage from a place of taking in charge to a place of final destination by different modes of transport including a carriage by sea, provided that the entire carriage is covered by one and the same transport document, or
    iii) state or indicate that the goods are in a container(s), trailer(s), "LASH" barge(s), and the like and will be carried from the place of taking in charge to the place of final destination in the same container(s), trailer(s), "LASH barge(s), and the like under one and the same transport document.
    iv) state or indicate the place of receipt and/or of final destination as "C.F.S." (container freight station) or "C.Y." (container yard) at, or associated with, the port of loading and/or the port of destination.

Article 30

If the credit stipulates dispatch of goods by post and calls for a post receipt or certificate of posting, banks will accept such post receipt or certificate of posting if it appears to have been stamped or otherwise authenticated and dated in the place from which the credit stipulates the goods are to be dispatched.

Article 31

a. Unless otherwise stipulated in the credit, or inconsistent with any of the documents presented under the credit, banks will accept transport documents stating that freight or transportation charges (hereinafter referred to as "freight") have still to be paid.

b. If a credit stipulates that the transport document has to indicate that freight has been paid or prepaid, banks will accept a transport document on which words clearly indicating payment or prepayment of freight appear by stamp or otherwise, or on which payment of freight is indicated by other means.

c. The words "freight prepayable" or "freight to be prepaid" or words of similar effect, if appearing on transport documents, will not be accepted as constituting evidence of the payment of freight.

d. Banks will accept transport documents bearing reference by stamp or otherwise to costs additional to the freight charges, such as costs of, or disbursements incurred in connection with, loading, unloading or similar operations, unless the conditions of the credit specifically prohibit such reference.

Article 32

Unless otherwise stipulated in the credit, banks will accept transport documents which bear a clause on the face thereof such as "shipper's load and count" or "said by shipper to contain" or words of similar effect.

Article 33

Unless otherwise stipulated in the credit, banks will accept transport documents indicating as the consignor of the goods a party other than the beneficiary of the credit.

Article 34

a. A clean transport document is one which bears no superimposed clause or notation which expressly declares a defective condition of the goods and/or the packaging.

b. Banks will refuse transport documents bearing such clauses or notations unless the credit expressly stipulates the clauses or notations which may be accepted.

c. Banks will regard a requirement in a credit for a transport document to bear the clause "clean on board" as complied with if such transport document meets the requirements of this article and of article 27 (b).

D2. Insurance documents

Article 35
a. Insurance documents must be as stipulated in the credit, and must be issued and/or signed by insurance companies or underwriters, or their agents.
b. Cover notes issued by brokers will not be accepted, unless specifically authorised by the credit.

Article 36
Unless otherwise stipulated in the credit, or unless it appears from the insurance document(s) that the cover is effective at the latest from the date of loading on board or dispatch or taking in charge of the goods, banks will refuse insurance documents presented which bear a date later than the date of loading on board or dispatch or taking in charge of the goods as indicated by the transport document(s).

Article 37
a. Unless otherwise stipulated in the credit, the insurance document must be expressed in the same currency as the credit.
b. Unless otherwise stipulated in the credit, the minimum amount for which the insurance document must indicate the insurance cover to have been effected is the CIF (cost, insurance and freight . . . "named port of destination") or CIP (freight/carriage and insurance paid to "named point of destination") value of the goods, as the case may be, plus 10%. However, if banks cannot determine the CIF or CIP value, as the case may be, from the documents on their face, they will accept as such minimum amount the amount for which payment, acceptance or negotiation is requested under the credit, or the amount of the commercial invoice, whichever is the greater.

Article 38
a. Credits should stipulate the type of insurance required and, if any, the additional risks which are to be covered. Imprecise terms such as "usual risks" or "customary risks" should not be used; if they are used, banks will accept insurance documents as presented, without responsibility for any risks not being covered.
b. Failing specific stipulations in the credit, banks will accept insurance documents as presented, without responsibility for any risks not being covered.

Article 39
Where a credit stipulates "insurance against all risks," banks will accept an insurance document which contains any "all risks" notation or clause, whether or not bearing the heading "all risks," even if indicating that certain risks are excluded, without responsibility for any risk(s) not being covered.

Article 40
Banks will accept an insurance document which indicates that the cover is subject to a franchise or an excess (deductible), unless it is specifically stipulated in the credit that the insurance must be issued irrespective of percentage.

D3. Commercial invoice

Article 41
a. Unless otherwise stipulated in the credit, commercial invoices must be made out in the name of the applicant for the credit.
b. Unless otherwise stipulated in the credit, banks may refuse commercial invoices issued for amounts in excess of the amount permitted by the credit. Nevertheless, if a bank authorised to pay, incur a deferred payment undertaking, accept, or negotiate under a credit accepts such invoices, its decision will be binding upon all parties, provided such bank has not paid, incurred a deferred payment undertaking, accepted or effected negotiation for an amount in excess of that permitted by the credit.
c. The description of the goods in the commercial invoice must correspond with the description in the credit. In all other documents, the goods may be described in general terms not inconsistent with the description of the goods in the credit.

D4. Other documents

Article 42

If a credit calls for an attestation or certification of weight in the case of transport other than by sea, banks will accept a weight stamp or declaration of weight which appears to have been superimposed on the transport document by the carrier or his agent unless the credit specifically stipulates that the attestation or certification of weight must be by means of a separate document.

E. Miscellaneous provisions

Quality and amount

Article 43

a. The words "about," "circa" or similar expressions used in connection with the amount of the credit or the quantity or the unit price stated in the credit are to be construed as allowing a difference not to exceed 10% more or 10% less than the amount or the quantity or the unit price to which they refer.

b. Unless a credit stipulates that the quantity of the goods specified must not be exceeded or reduced, a tolerance of 5% more or 5% less will be permissible, even if partial shipment are not permitted, always provided that the amount of the drawings does not exceed the amount of the credit. This tolerance does not apply when the credit stipulates the quantity in terms of a stated number of packing units or individual items.

Partial drawings and/or shipments

Article 44

a. Partial drawing and/or shipments are allowed, unless the credit stipulates otherwise.

b. Shipments by sea, or by more than one mode of transport but including carriage by sea, made on the same vessel and for the same voyage, will not be regarded as partial shipments, even if the transport documents indicating loading on board bear different dates of issuance and/or indicate different ports of loading on board.

c. Shipments made by post will not be regarded as partial shipments if the post receipts or certificates of posting appear to have been stamped or otherwise authenticated in the place from which the credit stipulates the goods are to be dispatched, and on the same date.

d. Shipments made by modes of transport other than those referred to in paragraphs (b) and (c) of this article will not be regarded as partial shipments, provided the transport documents are issued by one and the same carrier or his agent and indicate the same date of issuance, the same place of dispatch or taking in charge of the goods, and the same destination.

Drawings and/or shipments by instalments

Article 45

If drawings and/or shipments by instalments within given periods are stipulated in the credit and any instalment is not drawn and/or shipped within the period allowed for that instalment, the credit ceases to be available for that and any subsequent instalments, unless otherwise stipulated in the credit.

Expiry date and presentation

Article 46

a. All credits must stipulate an expiry date for presentation of documents for payment, acceptance or negotiation.

b. Except as provided in Article 48 (a), documents must be presented on or before such expiry date.

c. If an issuing bank states that the credit is to be available "for one month," "for six months" or the like, but does not specify the date from which the time is to run, the date of issuance of the credit by the issuing bank will be deemed to be the first day from which such time is to run. Banks should discourage indication of the expiry date of the credit in this manner.

Article 47

a. In addition to stipulating an expiry date for presentation of documents, every credit which calls for a transport document(s) should also stipulate a specified period of time after the date of issuance of the transport document(s) during which presentation of documents for payment, acceptance or negotiation must be made. If no such period of time is stipulated, banks will refuse documents presented to them later than 21 days after the date of issuance of the transport document(s). In every case, however, documents must be presented not later than the expiry date of the credit.

b. For the purpose of these articles, the date of issuance of a transport document(s) will be deemed to be:

i) in the case of a transport document evidencing dispatch, or taking in charge, or receipt of goods for shipment by a mode of transport other than by air—the date of issuance indicated on the transport document or the date of the reception stamp thereon whichever is the later.

ii) in the case of a transport document evidencing carriage by air—the date of issuance indicated on the transport document or, if the credit stipulates that the transport document shall indicate an actual flight date, the actual flight date as indicated on the transport document.

iii) in the case of a transport document evidencing loading on board a named vessel—the date of issuance of the transport document or, in the case of an on board notation in accordance with article 27 (b), the date of such notation.

iv) in cases to which Article 44 (b) applies, the date determined as above of the latest transport document issued.

Article 48

a. If the expiry date of the credit and/or the last day of the period of time after the date of issuance of the transport document(s) for presentation of documents stipulated by the credit or applicable by virtue of Article 47 falls on a day on which the bank to which presentation has to be made is closed for reasons other than those referred to in Article 19, the stipulated expiry date and/or the last day of the period of time after the date of issuance of the transport document(s) for presentation of documents, as the case may be, shall be extended to the first following business day on which such bank is open.

b. The latest date for loading on board, or dispatch, or taking in charge shall not be extended by reason of the extension of the expiry date and/or the period of time after the date of issuance of the transport document(s) for presentation of document(s) in accordance with this article. If no such latest date for shipment is stipulated in the credit or amendments thereto, banks will reject transport documents indicating a date of issuance later than the expiry date stipulated in the credit or amendments thereto.

c. The bank to which presentation is made on such first following business day must add to the documents its certificate that the documents were presented within the time limits extended in accordance with Article 48 (a) of the Uniform Customs and Practice for Documentary Credits, 1983 revision, ICC Publication No. 400.

Article 49

Banks are under no obligation to accept presentation of documents outside their banking hours.

Loading on board, dispatch and taking in charge (shipment)

Article 50

a. Unless otherwise stipulated in the credit, the expression "shipment" used in stipulating an earliest and/or a latest shipment date will be understood to include the expressions "loading on board," "dispatch" and "taking in charge."

b. The date of issuance of the transport document determined in accordance with Article 47 (b) will be taken to the date of shipment.

c. Expressions such as "prompt," "immediately," "as soon as possible," and the like should not be used. If they are used, banks will interpret them as a stipulation that shipment is to be made within thirty days from the date of issuance of the credit by the issuing bank.

d. If the expression "on or about" and similar expressions are used, banks will interpret them as a stipulation that shipment is to be made during the period from five days before to five days after the specified date, both end days included.

Date terms

Article 51

The words "to," "until," "till," and words of similar import applying to any date term in the credit will be understood to include the date mentioned. The word "after" will be understood to exclude the date mentioned.

Article 52

The terms "first half," "second half" of a month shall be construed respectively as from the 1st to the 15th, and the 16th to the last day of each month, inclusive.

Article 53

The terms "beginning," "middle," or "end" of a month shall be construed respectively as from the 1st to the 10th, the 11th to the 20th, and the 21st to the last day of each month, inclusive.

F. Transfer

Article 54

a. A transferable credit is a credit under which the beneficiary has the right to request the bank called upon to effect payment or acceptance or any bank entitled to effect negotiation to make the credit available in whole or in part to one or more other parties (second beneficiaries).

b. A credit can be transferred only if it is expressly designated as "transferable" by the issuing bank. Terms such as "divisible," "fractionnable," "assignable," and "transmissible" add nothing to the meaning of the term "transferable" and shall not be used.

c. The bank requested to effect the transfer (transferring bank), whether it has confirmed the credit or not, shall be under no obligation to effect such transfer except to the extent and in the manner expressly consented to by such bank.

d. Bank charges in respect of transfers are payable by the first beneficiary unless otherwise specified. The transferring bank shall be under no obligation to effect the transfer until such charges are paid.

e. A transferable credit can be transferred once only. Fractions of a transferable credit (not exceeding in the aggregate the amount of the credit) can be transferred separately, provided partial shipments are not prohibited, and the aggregate of such transfers will be considered as constituting only one transfer of the credit. The credit can be transferred only on the terms and conditions specified in the original credit, with the exception of the amount of the credit, of any unit prices stated therein, of the period of validity, of the last date for presentation of documents in accordance with Article 47 and the period for shipment, any or all of which may be reduced or curtailed, or the percentage for which insurance cover must be effected, which may be increased in such a way as to provide the amount of cover stipulated in the original credit, or these articles. Additionally, the name of the first beneficiary can be substituted for that of the applicant for the credit, but if the name of the applicant for the credit is specifically required by the original credit to appear in any document other than the invoice, such requirement must be fulfilled.

f. The first beneficiary has the right to substitute his own invoices (and drafts if the credit stipulates that drafts are to be drawn on the applicant for the credit) in exchange for those of the second beneficiary, for amounts not in excess of the original amount stipulated in the credit and for the original unit prices if stipulated in the credit, and upon such substitution of invoices (and drafts) the first beneficiary can draw under the credit for the difference, if any, between his invoices and the second beneficiary's invoices. When a credit has been transferred and the first beneficiary is to supply his own invoices (and drafts) in exchange for the second beneficiary's invoices (and drafts) but fails to do so on first demand, the paying, accepting or negotiating bank has the right to deliver to the issuing bank the documents received under the credit, including the second beneficiary's invoices (and drafts) without further responsibility to the first beneficiary.

g. Unless otherwise stipulated in the credit, the first beneficiary of a transferable credit may request that the credit be transferred to a second beneficiary in the same country, or in another country. Further, unless otherwise stipulated in the credit, the first beneficiary shall have the right to request that payment or negotiation be effected to the second beneficiary at the place to which the credit has been transferred, up to and including the expiry date of the original credit, and without prejudice to the first beneficiary's right subsequently to substitute his own invoices and drafts (if any) for those of the second beneficiary and to claim any difference due to him.

Article 55

The fact that a credit is not stated to be transferable shall not affect the beneficiary's right to assign the proceeds to which he may be, or may become, entitled under such credit, in accordance with the provisions of the applicable law.

FOREIGN TRADE DEFINITIONS

Up until 1980, American exporters and importers have been governed by a set of definitions known as the American Foreign Trade Definitions, which were issued in 1919 and revised in 1941. These definitions have been replaced by an amended version of Incoterms, the international rules for the interpretation of trade terms, recognized by the rest of the world.

Incoterms were first published in 1953 by the International Chamber of Commerce; revisions were issued in 1967, 1976 and 1980. The 1980 text may be purchased from The ICC Publishing Company, 156 Fifth Avenue, Suite 820, New York, N.Y. 10010. Telephone: (212) 206-1150. A Guide to Incoterms is also available.

Incoterms is copyrighted by the International Chamber of Commerce and is reprinted below with their permission.

INCOTERMS 1980

INTRODUCTION

Purpose of Incoterms

1. The purpose of "Incoterms" is to provide a set of international rules for the interpretation of the chief terms used in foreign trade contracts, for the optional use of businessmen who prefer the certainty of uniform international rules to the uncertainties of the varied interpretations of the same terms in different countries.

2. Frequently parties to a contract are unaware of the differences of trading practice in their respective countries. The existing diversity of interpretation is a constant source of friction in international trade, leading to misunderstandings, disputes and references to the courts with all the waste of time and money that these entail. It was with the object of making available to traders a means of overcoming the worst causes of this friction that the International Chamber of Commerce first published in 1936 a set of international rules for the interpretation of trade terms. These rules were known as "Incoterms 1936." Amendments and additions were later made in 1953, 1967, 1976 and 1980 in order to provide an up-to-date set of rules broadly in line with the current practice of a majority of the businessmen engaged in international trade.

3. The chief difficulties met with by importers and exporters are of three kinds. First, uncertainty as to the law of what country will be applicable to their contracts, second, difficulties arising from inadequate information and, third, difficulties arising from diversity in interpretation. These handicaps to trade can be much reduced by the use of "Incoterms."

Provision for the Custom of the Particular Trade or Port

4. On some points, it has been found impossible to give an absolutely definite ruling. In that case, the rules have left the matter to be decided by the custom of the particular trade or port. Every endeavor has been made to limit such references to custom to the absolute minimum, but it has been impossible to avoid them altogether.

In order to avoid misunderstandings and disputes, the seller and the buyer would be well advised to keep such general and particular customs in mind when negotiating their contract.

Special Provisions in Individual Contracts

5. Special provisions in the individual contract between the parties will override anything provided in the rules.

6. Parties may adopt "Incoterms" as the general basis of their contract, but may also specify particular variations of them or additions to them, such as may be suited to the particular trade or the circumstances of the time or their individual convenience. For instance, some merchants require a CIF supplier to provide war risk insurance as well as marine insurance. In that case, the purchaser may specify "Incoterms CIF plus war risk insurance." The seller will then quote his price on that basis.

Some abbreviations in common use in domestic trade may not be readily understood in international trade. It is recommended that for the sake of clarity the use of such domestic abbreviations should be avoided.

Variations of C & F and CIF Contracts

7. Merchants should be extremely cautious in using, in their contracts of sale, variations of the terms C & F and CIF such as C & F and CIF Cleared and Customs Duty Paid or similar expressions. The addition of a word or even a letter to C & F and CIF may sometimes have an entirely unforeseen result, and the character of the contract may be changed. Merchants may find that a court will refuse to recognize certain variations as being C & F or CIF contracts at all. It is always safer in such cases explicitly to state in the contracts what obligations and charges each party is meant to assume.

"Incoterms" and the Contract of Carriage

8. Merchants adopting these rules in their contracts should keep clearly in mind the fact that they refer solely to the relationship between seller and buyer, and that none of the provisions affect, either directly or indirectly, the relations of either party with the carrier as defined in the contract of carriage.

However, the law of carriage of goods will determine how the seller should fulfil his obligation to deliver the goods "to the carrier." The terms FOB, C & F and CIF, which have been retained unchanged in the present version of "Incoterms," all conform with the practice of delivering the goods on board the vessel. Nowadays goods are usually delivered by the seller to a carrier before shipment on board takes place. In such cases merchants should use the new and amended terms: Free carrier (named point), Freight/Carriage paid to, or Freight/Carriage and Insurance paid to. A definition of "carrier" has been inserted in a note to the term Free carrier (named point).

"Delivered . . ." Terms

9. Unless there is a clear agreement to the contrary expressed in the contract of sale, it is no part of the duties of the seller to procure a policy of insurance available for the benefit of the buyer.

However, in certain circumstances, such as those contemplated in article A.5 of the rules relating to the sale of good on "Delivered at Frontier" terms, the parties might be well advised jointly to consider what duties, if any, the seller or the buyer should assume in matters pertaining to the insurance of the goods from the point of departure in the country of dispatch to the point of final destination chosen by the buyer.

Unless there is a clear agreement to the contrary expressed in the contract of sale, any document of transport placed by the seller at the disposal of the buyer must be clean.[1]

Unless the context otherwise requires, the following expressions have the meanings hereby assigned to them, that is to say:

"Country of dispatch" means the country from which the seller has to dispatch the goods to the named place of delivery at the frontier, or in the country of importation, as the case may be, whether by public carrier or by his own means of transport.

"Expenses" means any costs, charges and expenses of or incidental to the performance by the parties of their respective duties and which shall be incurred, borne and paid by parties in accordance with the rules applicable.

Definition of Bill of Lading

10. As used in these rules the term "bill of lading" is a shipped bill of lading, issued by or on behalf of the carrier, and is evidence of a contract of carriage as well as proof of delivery of the goods on board the vessel.

11. A bill of lading may be either freight prepaid or freight payable at destination. In the former case the document is usually not obtainable until freight has been paid.

Simplified Documentary Practices

12. In liner trade, bills of lading are frequently replaced by nonnegotiable documents ("sea waybills," "liner waybills," "freight receipts," "combined or multimodal transport documents") and the feasibility of transmitting the relevant information by automatic data processing is presently being investigated. When bills of lading are not used in the relevant trade, the parties should either use the Free carrier (named point) or Freight/Carriage paid to terms or alternatively, stipulate in the FOB, C & F and CIF terms that the seller should provide the buyer with the usual document or other evidence of the delivery of the goods to the carrier.

Merchants wishing to use these rules should specify that their contracts will be governed by the provisions of "Incoterms." If they wish to refer to a term in a previous version they should specifically so state.

Ex Works
... (ex factory, ex mill, ex plantation, ex warehouse, etc.)

"Ex works" means that the seller's only responsibility is to make the goods available at his premises (i.e. works or factory). In particular he is not responsible

---

[1] For the definition of the term "clean shipping document" in banking practice, reference should be made to article 18 of "Uniform Customs and Practice for Documentary Credits" (ICC Publication 290). For the possibility of agreement between the parties to the contract of sale as to what clauses about condition, quality or quantity superimposed by the carrier on the document of transport would be acceptable to the seller and the buyer, attention is invited to Publication 283 "The Problem of Clean Bills of Lading."

INTERNATIONAL TRADE 29-53

for loading the goods on the vehicle provided by the buyer, unless otherwise agreed. The buyer bears the full cost and risk involved in bringing the goods from there to the desired destination. This term thus represents the minimum obligation for the seller.

A. The seller must:

1. Supply the goods in conformity with the contract of sale, together with such evidence of conformity as may be required by the contract.

2. Place the goods at the disposal of the buyer at the time as provided in the contract, at the point of delivery named or which is usual for the delivery of such goods, and for their loading on the conveyance to be provided by the buyer.

3. Provide at his own expense the packing, if any, that is necessary to enable the buyer to take delivery of the goods.

4. Give the buyer reasonable notice as to when the goods will be at his disposal.

5. Bear the cost of checking operations (such as checking quality, measuring, weighing, counting) which are necessary for the purpose of placing the goods at the disposal of the buyer.

6. Bear all risks and expense of the goods until they have been placed at the disposal of the buyer at the time as provided in the contract, provided that the goods have been duly appropriated to the contract, that is to say, clearly set aside or otherwise identified as the contract goods.

7. Render the buyer, at the latter's request, risk and expense, every assistance in obtaining any documents which are issued in the country of delivery and/or of origin and which the buyer may require for the purposes of exportation and/or importation (and, where necessary, for their passage in transit through another country).

B. The buyer must:

1. Take delivery of the goods as soon as they are placed at his disposal at the place and at the time, as provided in the contract, and pay the price as provided in the contract.

2. Bear all charges and risks of the goods from the time when they have been so placed at his disposal, provided that the goods have been duly appropriated to the contract, that is to say, clearly set aside or otherwise identified as the contract goods.

3. Bear any customs duties and taxes that may be levied by reason of exportation.

4. Where he shall have reserved to himself a period within which to take delivery of the goods and/or the right to choose the place of delivery, and should he fail to give instructions in time, bear the additional costs thereby incurred and all risks of the goods from the date of the expiration of the period fixed, provided that the goods shall have been duly appropriated to the contract, that is to say, clearly set aside or otherwise identified as the contract goods.

5. Pay all costs and charges incurred in obtaining the documents mentioned in article A.7, including the cost of certificates of origin, export license and consular fees.

FOR-FOT
Free on Rail/Free on Truck
. . . (named departure point)

FOR and FOT mean "Free on Rail" and "Free on Truck." These terms are synonymous, since the word "Truck" relates to the railway wagons. They should only be used when the goods are to be carried by rail.

A. The seller must:

1. Supply the goods in conformity with the contract of sale, together with such evidence of conformity as may be required by the contract.

2. In the case of goods constituting either a wagonload (carload, truckload) lot or a sufficient weight to obtain quantity rates for wagon loading, order in due time a wagon (car, truck) of suitable type and dimensions, equipped, where necessary, with tarpaulins, and load it at his own expense at the date or within the period fixed, the ordering of the wagon (car, truck) and the loading being carried out in accordance with the regulations of the dispatching station.

3. In the case of a load less than either a wagonload (carload, truckload) or a sufficient weight to obtain quantity rates for wagon loading, deliver the goods into the custody of the railway either at the dispatching station or, where such facilities are included in the rate of freight, into a vehicle provided by the railway, at the date or within the period fixed, unless the regulations of the dispatching station shall require the seller to load the goods on the wagon (car, truck).

Nevertheless, it shall be understood that if there are several stations at the point of departure, the seller may select the station which best suits his purpose, provided it customarily accepts goods for the destination nominated by the buyer, unless the buyer shall have reserved to himself the right to choose the dispatching station.

4. Subject to the provisions of article B.5 below, bear all costs and risks of the goods until such time as the wagon (car, truck) on which they are loaded shall have been delivered into the custody of the railway or, in the case provided for in article A.3, until such time as the goods shall have been delivered into the custody of the railway.

5. Provide at his own expense the customary packing of the goods, unless it is the custom of the trade to dispatch the goods unpacked.

6. Pay the costs of any checking operation (such as checking quality, measuring, weighing, counting) which shall be necessary for the purpose of loading the goods or of delivering them into the custody of the railway.

7. Give notice, without delay, to the buyer that the goods have been loaded or delivered into the custody of the railway.

8. At his own expense, provide the buyer, if customary, with the usual transport document.

9. Provide the buyer, at the latter's request and expense (see B.6), with the certificate of origin.

10. Render the buyer, at the latter's request, risk and expense, every assistance in obtaining the documents issued in the country of dispatch and/or of origin which the buyer may require for purposes of exportation and/or importation (and, where necessary, for their passage in transit through another country).

B. The buyer must:

1. Give the seller in time the necessary instructions for dispatch.
2. Take delivery of the goods from the time when they have been delivered into the custody of the railway and pay the price as provided in the contract.
3. Bear all costs and risks of the goods (including the cost, if any, of hiring tarpaulins) from the time when the wagon (car, truck) on which the goods are loaded shall have been delivered into the custody of the railway or, in the case provided for in article A.3, from the time when the goods shall have been delivered into the custody of the railway.
4. Bear any customs duties and taxes that may be levied by reason of exportation.
5. Where he shall have reserved to himself a period within which to give the seller instructions for dispatch and/or the right to choose the place of loading, and should he fail to give instructions in time, bear the additional costs thereby incurred and all risks of the goods from the time of expiration of the period fixed, provided, however, that the goods shall have been duly appropriated to the contract, that is to say, clearly set aside or otherwise identified as the contract goods.
6. Pay all costs and charges incurred in obtaining the documents mentioned in articles A.9 & 10 above, including the cost of certificates of origin and consular fees.

FAS
Free Alongside Ship
. . . (named port of shipment)

FAS means "Free Alongside Ship." Under this term the seller's obligations are fulfilled when the goods have been placed alongside the ship on the quay or in lighters. This means that the buyer has to bear all costs and risks of loss of or damage to the goods from that moment. It should be noted that, unlike FOB, the present term requires the buyer to clear the goods for export.

A. The seller must:

1. Supply the goods in conformity with the contract of sale, together with such evidence of conformity as may be required by the contract.
2. Deliver the goods alongside the vessel at the loading berth named by the buyer, at the named port of shipment, in the manner customary at the port, at the date or within the period stipulated, and notify the buyer, without delay, that the goods have been delivered alongside the vessel.
3. Render the buyer at the latter's request, risk and expense, every assistance in obtaining any export license or other governmental authorization necessary for the export of the goods.
4. Subject to the provisions of articles B.3 and B.4 below, bear all costs and risks of the goods until such time as they shall have been effectively delivered alongside the vessel at the named port of shipment, including the costs of any formalities which he shall have to fulfil in order to deliver the goods alongside the vessel.

5. Provide at his own expense the customary packing of the goods, unless it is the custom of the trade to ship the goods unpacked.

6. Pay the costs of any checking operations (such as checking quality, measuring, weighing, counting) which shall be necessary for the purpose of delivering the goods alongside the vessel.

7. Provide at his own expense the customary clean document in proof of delivery of the goods alongside the named vessel.

8. Provide the buyer, at the latter's request and expense (see B.5), with the certificate of origin.

9. Render the buyer, at the latter's request, risk and expense, every assistance in obtaining any documents other than that mentioned in article A.8, issued in the country of shipment and/or of origin (excluding a bill of lading and/or consular documents) and which the buyer may require for the importation of the goods into the country of destination (and, where necessary, for their passage in transit through another country).

B. The buyer must:

1. Give the seller due notice of the name, loading berth of and delivery dates to the vessel.

2. Bear all the charges and risks of the goods from the time when they shall have been effectively delivered alongside the vessel at the named port of shipment, at the date or within the period stipulated, and pay the price as provided in the contract.

3. Bear any additional costs incurred because the vessel named by him shall have failed to arrive on time, or shall be unable to take the goods, or shall close for cargo earlier than the stipulated date, and all the risks of the goods from the time when the seller shall place them at the buyer's disposal provided, however, that the goods shall have been duly appropriated to the contract, that is to say, clearly set aside or otherwise identified as the contract goods.

4. Should he fail to name the vessel in time or, if he shall have reserved to himself a period within which to take delivery of the goods and/or the right to choose the port of shipment, should he fail to give detailed instructions in time, bear any additional costs incurred because of such failure and all the risks of the goods from the date of expiration of the period stipulated for delivery, provided, however, that the goods shall have been duly appropriated to the contract, that is to say, clearly set aside or otherwise identified as the contract goods.

5. Pay all costs and charges incurred in obtaining the documents mentioned in articles A.3, A.8 and A.9 above.

FOB
Free on Board
. . . (named port of shipment)

FOB means "Free on Board." The goods are placed on board a ship by the seller at a port of shipment named in the sales contract. The risk of loss of or damage to the goods is transferred from the seller to the buyer when the goods pass the ship's rail.

A. The seller must:

1. Supply the goods in conformity with the contract of sale, together with such evidence of conformity as may be required by the contract.
2. Deliver the goods on board the vessel named by the buyer, at the named port of shipment, in the manner customary at the port, at the date or within the period stipulated, and notify the buyer, without delay, that the goods have been delivered on board.
3. At his own risk and expense obtain any export license or other governmental authorization necessary for the export of the goods.
4. Subject to the provisions of articles B.3 and B.4 below, bear all costs and risks of the goods until such time as they shall have effectively passed the ship's rail at the named port of shipment, including any taxes, fees or charges levied because of exportation, as well as the costs of any formalities which he shall have to fulfil in order to load the goods on board.
5. Provide at his own expense the customary packing of the goods, unless it is the custom of the trade to ship the goods unpacked.
6. Pay the costs of any checking operations (such as checking quality, measuring, weighing, counting) which shall be necessary for the purpose of delivering the goods.
7. Provide at his own expense the customary clean document in proof of delivery of the goods on board the named vessel.
8. Provide the buyer, at the latter's request and expense (see B.6), with the certificate of origin.
9. Render the buyer, at the latter's request, risk and expense, every assistance in obtaining a bill of lading and any documents, other than that mentioned in the previous article, issued in the country of shipment and/or of origin and which the buyer may require for the importation of the goods into the country of destination (and, where necessary, for their passage in transit through another country).

B. The buyer must:

1. At his own expense, charter a vessel or reserve the necessary space on board a vessel and give the seller due notice of the name, loading berth of and delivery dates to the vessel.
2. Bear all costs and risks of the goods from the time when they shall have effectively passed the ship's rail at the named port of shipment, and pay the price as provided in the contract.
3. Bear any additional costs incurred because the vessel named by him shall have failed to arrive on the stipulated date or by the end of the period specified, or shall be unable to take the goods or shall close for cargo earlier than the stipulated date or the end of the period specified and all the risks of the goods from the date of expiration of the period stipulated, provided, however, that the goods shall have been duly appropriated to the contract, that is to say, clearly set aside or otherwise identified as the contract goods.
4. Should he fail to name the vessel in time or, if he shall have reserved to himself a period within which to take delivery of the goods and/or the right to choose the port of shipment, should he fail to give detailed instructions in time, bear any additional costs incurred because of such failure, and all the

risks of the goods from the date of expiration of the period stipulated for delivery, provided, however, that the goods shall have been duly appropriated to the contract, that is to say, clearly set aside or otherwise identified as the contract goods.

5. Pay any costs and charges for obtaining a bill of lading if incurred under article A.9 above.

6. Pay all costs and charges incurred in obtaining the documents mentioned in articles A.8 and A.9 above, including the costs of certificates of origin and consular documents.

C & F
Cost and Freight
... (named port of destination)

C & F means "Cost and Freight." The seller must pay the costs and freight necessary to bring the goods to the named destination but the risk of loss of or damage to the goods, as well as of any cost increases, is transferred from the seller to the buyer when the goods pass the ship's rail in the port of shipment.

A. The seller must:

1. Supply the goods in conformity with the contract of sale, together with such evidence of conformity as may be required by the contract.

2. Contract on usual terms at his own expense for the carriage of the goods to the agreed port of destination by the usual route, in a seagoing vessel (not being a sailing vessel) of the type normally used for the transport of goods of the contract description, and pay freight charges and any charges for unloading at the port of discharge which may be levied by regular shipping lines at the time and port of shipment.

3. At his own risk and expense obtain any export license or other governmental authorization necessary for the export of the goods.

4. Load the goods at his own expense on board the vessel at the port of shipment and at the date or within the period fixed or, if neither date nor time has been stipulated, within a reasonable time, and notify the buyer, without delay, that the goods have been loaded on board the vessel.

5. Subject to the provisions of article B.4 below, bear all risks of the goods until such time as they shall have effectively passed the ship's rail at the port of shipment.

6. At his own expense furnish to the buyer without delay a clean negotiable bill of lading for the agreed port of destination, as well as the invoice of the goods shipped. The bill of lading must cover the contract goods, be dated within the period agreed for shipment, and provide by endorsement or otherwise for delivery to the order of the buyer or buyer's agreed representative. Such bill of lading must be a full set of "on board" or "shipped" bills of lading, or a "received for shipment" bill of lading duly endorsed by the shipping company to the effect that the goods are on board, such endorsement to be dated within the period agreed for shipment. If the bill of lading contains a reference to the charter-party, the seller must also provide a copy of this latter document.

Note: A clean bill of lading is one which bears no superimposed clauses expressly declaring a defective condition of the goods or packaging.

The following clauses do not convert a clean into an unclean bill of lading:

(a) clauses which do not expressly state that the goods or packaging are unsatisfactory, e.g. "second-hand cases," "used drum," etc.; (b) clauses which emphasize carrier's nonliability for risks arising through the nature of the goods or the packaging; (c) clauses which disclaim on the part of the carrier knowledge of contents, weight, measurement, quality, or technical specification of the goods.

7. Provide at his own expense the customary packaging of the goods, unless it is the custom of the trade to ship the goods unpacked.

8. Pay the costs of any checking operations (such as checking quality, measuring, weighing, counting) which shall be necessary for the purpose of loading the goods.

9. Pay any dues and taxes incurred in respect of the goods, up to the time of their loading, including any taxes, fees or charges levied because of exportation, as well as the costs of any formalities which he shall have to fulfil in order to load the goods on board.

10. Provide the buyer, at the latter's request and expense (see B.5), with the certificate of origin and the consular invoice.

11. Render the buyer, at the latter's request, risk and expense, every assistance in obtaining any documents, other than those mentioned in the previous article, issued in the country of shipment and/or of origin and which the buyer may require for the importation of the goods into the country of destination (and, where necessary, for their passage in transit through another country).

B. The buyer must:

1. Accept the documents when tendered by the seller, if they are in conformity with the contract of sale, and pay the price as provided in the contract.

2. Receive the goods at the agreed port of destination and bear, with the exception of the freight, all costs and charges incurred in respect of the goods in the course of their transit by sea until their arrival at the port of destination, as well as unloading costs, including lighterage and wharfage charges, unless such costs and charges shall have been included in the freight or collected by the steamship company at the time freight was paid.

Note: If the goods are sold "C & F landed," unloading costs, including lighterage and wharfage charges, are borne by the seller.

3. Bear all risks of the goods from the time when they shall have effectively passed the ship's rail at the port of shipment.

4. In case he may have reserved to himself a period within which to have the goods shipped and/or the right to choose the port of destination, and he fails to give instructions in time, bear the additional costs thereby incurred and all risks of the goods from the date of the expiration of the period fixed for shipment, provided always that the goods shall have been duly appropriated to the contract, that is to say, clearly set aside or otherwise identified as the contract goods.

5. Pay the costs and charges incurred in obtaining the certificate of origin and consular documents.

6. Pay all costs and charges incurred in obtaining the documents mentioned in article A.11 above.

7. Pay all customs duties as well as any other duties and taxes payable at the time of or by the reason of the importation.

8. Procure and provide at his own risk and expense any import license or permit or the like which he may require for the importation of the goods at destination.

CIF
Cost, Insurance, Freight
. . . (named port of destination)

CIF means "Cost, Insurance and Freight." This term is the same as C & F but with the addition that the seller has to procure marine insurance against the risk of loss of or damage to the goods during the carriage. The seller contracts with the insurer and pays the insurance premium. The buyer should note that under the present term, unlike the term "Freight/Carriage and Insurance paid to," the seller is only required to cover insurance on minimum conditions (so-called FPA conditions).

A. The seller must:

1. Supply the goods in conformity with the contract of sale, together with such evidence of conformity as may be required by the contract.

2. Contract on usual terms at his own expense for the carriage of the goods to the agreed port of destination by the usual route, in a seagoing vessel (not being a sailing vessel) of the type normally used for the transport of goods of the contract description, and pay freight charges and any charges for unloading at the port of discharge which may be levied by regular shipping lines at the time and port of shipment.

3. At his own risk and expense obtain any export license or other governmental authorization necessary for the export of the goods.

4. Load the goods at his own expense on board the vessel at the port of shipment and at the date or within the period fixed or, if neither date nor time has been stipulated, within a reasonable time, and notify the buyer, without delay, that the goods have been loaded on board the vessel.

5. Procure, at his own cost and in a transferable form, a policy of marine insurance against the risks of the carriage involved in the contract. The insurance shall be contracted with underwriters or insurance companies of good repute on FPA terms, and shall cover the CIF price plus ten percent. The insurance shall be provided in the currency of the contract, if procurable.[1]

Unless otherwise agreed, the risks of carriage shall not include special risks that are covered in specific trades or against which the buyer may wish individual protection. Among the special risks that should be considered and agreed upon between seller and buyer are theft, pilferage, leakage, breakage, chipping, sweat, contact with other cargoes and others peculiar to any particular trade.

When required by the buyer, the seller shall provide, at the buyer's expense, war risk insurance in the currency of the contract, if procurable.

---

[1] CIF A. 5 provides for the minimum terms (FPA) and period of insurance (warehouse to warehouse). Whenever the buyer wishes more than the minimum liability to be included in the contract, then he should take care to specify that the basis of the contract is to be "Incoterms" with whatever addition he requires.

6. Subject to the provisions of article B.4 below, bear all risks of the goods until such time as they shall have effectively passed the ship's rail at the port of shipment.

7. At his own expense furnish to the buyer without delay a clean negotiable bill of lading for the agreed port of destination, as well as the invoice of the goods shipped and the insurance policy or, should the insurance policy not be available at the time the documents are tendered, a certificate of insurance issued under the authority of the underwriters and conveying to the bearer the same rights as if he were in possession of the policy and reproducing the essential provisions thereof. The bill of lading must cover the contract goods, be dated within the period agreed for shipment, and provide by endorsement or otherwise for delivery to the order of the buyer or buyer's agreed representative. Such bill of lading must be a full set of "on board" or "shipped" bills of lading, or a "received for shipment" bill of lading duly endorsed by the shipping company to the effect that the goods are on board, such endorsement to be dated within the period agreed for shipment. If the bill of lading contains a reference to the charter-party, the seller must also provide a copy of this latter document.

Note: A clean bill of lading is one which bears no superimposed clauses expressly declaring a defective condition of the goods or packaging.

The following clauses do not convert a clean into an unclean bill of lading:

(a) clauses which do not expressly state that the goods or packaging are unsatisfactory, e.g. "second-hand cases," "used drums," etc. (b) clauses which emphasize the carrier's non-liability for risks arising through the nature of the goods or the packaging; (c) clauses which disclaim on the part of the carrier knowledge of contents, weight, measurement, quality, or technical specification of the goods.

8. Provide at his own expense the customary packing of the goods, unless it is the custom of the trade to ship the goods unpacked.

9. Pay the costs of any checking operations (such as checking quality, measuring, weighing, counting) which shall be necessary for the purpose of loading the goods.

10. Pay any dues and taxes incurred in respect of the goods up to the time of their loading, including any taxes, fees or charges levied because of exportation, as well as the costs of any formalities which he shall have to fulfil in order to load the goods on board.

11. Provide the buyer, at the latter's request and expense (see B.5), with the certificate of origin and the consular invoice.

12. Render the buyer, at the latter's request, risk and expense, every assistance in obtaining any documents, other than those mentioned in the previous article, issued in the country of shipment and/or of origin and which the buyer may require for the importation of the goods into the country of destination (and, where necessary, for their passage in transit through another country).

B. The buyer must:

1. Accept the documents when tendered by the seller, if they are in conformity with the contract of sale, and pay the price as provided in the contract.

2. Receive the goods at the agreed port of destination and bear, with the exception of the freight and marine insurance, all costs and charges incurred

in respect of the goods in the course of their transit by sea until their arrival at the port of destination, as well as unloading costs, including lighterage and wharfage charges, unless such costs and charges shall have been included in the freight or collected by the steamship company at the time freight was paid.

If war insurance is provided, it shall be at the buyer's expense (see A.5).

Note: If the goods are sold "CIF landed," unloading costs, including lighterage and wharfage charges, are borne by the seller.

3. Bear all risks of the goods from the time when they shall have effectively passed the ship's rail at the port of shipment.

4. In case he may have reserved to himself a period within which to have the goods shipped and/or the right to choose the port of destination, and he fails to give instructions in time, bear the additional costs thereby incurred and all risks of the goods from the date of the expiration of the period fixed for shipment, provided always that the goods shall have been duly appropriated to the contract, that is to say, clearly set aside or otherwise identified as the contract goods.

5. Pay the costs and charges incurred in obtaining the certificate of origin and consular documents.

6. Pay all costs and charges incurred in obtaining the documents mentioned in article A.12 above.

7. Pay all customs duties as well as any other duties and taxes payable at the time of or by reason of the importation.

8. Procure and provide at his own risk and expense any import license or permit or the like which he may require for the importation of the goods at destination.

Ex Ship
. . . (named port of destination)

"Ex Ship" means that the seller shall make the goods available to the buyer on board the ship at the destination named in the sales contract. The seller has to bear the full cost and risk involved in bringing the goods there.

A. The seller must:

1. Supply the goods in conformity with the contract of sale, together with such evidence of conformity as may be required by the contract.

2. Place the goods effectively at the disposal of the buyer, at the time as provided in the contract, on board the vessel at the usual unloading point in the named port, in such a way as to enable them to be removed from the vessel by unloading equipment appropriate to the nature of the goods.

3. Bear all risks and expense of the goods until such time as they shall have been effectively placed at the disposal of the buyer in accordance with article A.2, provided, however, that they have been duly appropriated to the contract, that is to say, clearly set aside or otherwise identified as the contract goods.

4. Provide at his own expense the customary packing of the goods, unless it is the custom of the trade to ship the goods unpacked.

5. Pay the costs of any checking operations (such as checking quality, measuring, weighing, counting) which shall be necessary for the purpose of placing the goods at the disposal of the buyer in accordance with article A.2.

INTERNATIONAL TRADE   29–63

6. At his own expense, notify the buyer, without delay, of the expected date of arrival of the named vessel, and provide him in due time with the bill of lading or delivery order and/or any other documents which may be necessary to enable the buyer to take delivery of the goods.

7. Provide the buyer, at the latter's request and expense (see B.3), with the certificate of origin and the consular invoice.

8. Render the buyer, at the latter's request, risk and expense, every assistance in obtaining any documents, other than those mentioned in the previous articles, issued in the country of shipment and/or of origin and which the buyer may require for the importation of the goods into the country of destination (and where necessary, for their passage in transit through another country).

B. The buyer must:

1. Take delivery of the goods as soon as they have been placed at his disposal in accordance with the provisions of article A.2, and pay the price as provided in the contract.

2. Bear all risks and expense of the goods from the time when they shall have been effectively placed at his disposal in accordance with article A.2, provided always that they have been duly appropriated to the contract, that is to say, clearly set aside or otherwise identified as the contract goods.

3. Bear all expenses and charges incurred by the seller in obtaining any of the documents referred to in articles A.7 & 8.

4. At his own risk and expense, procure all licenses or similar documents required for the purpose of unloading and/or importing the goods.

5. Bear all expenses and charges of customs duties and clearance, and all other duties and taxes payable at the time or by reason of the unloading and/or importing of the goods.

Ex Quay
(duty paid) . . . (named port) [1]

"Ex Quay" means that the seller makes the goods available to the buyer on the quay (wharf) at the destination named in the sales contract. The seller has to bear the full cost and risk involved in bringing the goods there.

There are two "Ex Quay" contracts in use, namely Ex Quay "duty paid" and Ex Quay "duties on buyer's account" in which the liability to clear the goods for import is to be met by the buyer instead of by the seller.

Parties are recommended always to use the full descriptions of these terms, namely Ex Quay "duty paid" or Ex Quay "duties on buyer's account," or else there may be uncertainty as to who is to be responsible for the liability to clear the goods for import.

If the parties wish that the seller should clear the goods for import but that some of the costs payable upon the import of the goods should be excluded—

---

[1] Ex Quay (duties on buyer's account). There are two "Ex Quay" contracts in use, namely Ex Quay (duty paid) which has been defined above and Ex Quay (duties on buyer's account) in which the liabilities specified in A.3 above are to be met by the buyer instead of the seller.

Parties are recommended always to use the full descriptions of these terms, namely Ex Quay (duty paid) or Ex Quay (duties on buyer's account), or else there may be uncertainty as to who is to be responsible for the liabilities in A.3.

such as value added tax *(VAT)* and/or other similar taxes—this should be made clear by adding words to this effect (e.g. *"exclusive of VAT and/or taxes"*).

A. The seller must:

1. Supply the goods in conformity with the contract of sale, together with such evidence of conformity as may be required by the contract.
2. Place the goods at the disposal of the buyer on the wharf or quay at the agreed port and at the time, as provided in the contract.
3. At his own risk and expense, provide the import license and bear the cost of any import duties or taxes, including the costs of customs clearance, as well as any other taxes, fees or charges payable at the time or by reason of importation of the goods and their delivery to the buyer.
4. At his own expense, provide for customary conditioning and packing of the goods, regard being had to their nature and to their delivery from the quay.
5. Pay the costs of any checking operations (such as checking quality, measuring, weighing, counting) which shall be necessary for the purpose of placing the goods at the disposal of the buyer in accordance with article A.2.
6. Bear all risks and expense of the goods until such time as they shall have been effectively placed at the disposal of the buyer in accordance with article A.2, provided, however, that they have been duly appropriated to the contract, that is to say, clearly set aside or otherwise identified as the contract goods.
7. At his own expense, provide the delivery order and/or any other documents which the buyer may require in order to take delivery of the goods and to remove them from the quay.

B. The buyer must:

1. Take delivery of the goods as soon as they have been placed at his disposal in accordance with article A.2, and pay the price as provided in the contract.
2. Bear all expense and risks of the goods from the time when they have been effectively placed at his disposal in accordance with article A.2, provided always that they have been duly appropriated to the contract, that is to say, clearly set aside or otherwise identified as the contract goods.

Delivered at Frontier
... (named place of delivery at frontier) [1]

"Delivered at Frontier" means that the seller's obligations are fulfilled when the goods have arrived at the frontier—but before *"the customs border"* of the country named in the sales contract.

The term is primarily intended to be used when goods are to be carried by rail or road but it may be used irrespective of the mode of transport.

Attention should be paid to the special interpretations given under point 9 of the introduction.

---

[1] To avoid misunderstandings, it is recommended that parties contracting according to this trade term should qualify the word "frontier" by indicating the two countries separated by that frontier, and also the named place of delivery. For example: "Delivered at Franco-Italian frontier (Modane)."

INTERNATIONAL TRADE

A. The seller must:

1. Supply the goods in conformity with the contract of sale, together with such evidence of conformity as may be stipulated in the contract of sale.

2. At his own risk and expense:

(a) Put the contract goods at the disposal of the buyer at the named place of delivery at the frontier on the date or within the period stipulated in the contract of sale, and at the same time supply the buyer with a customary document of transport, warehouse warrant, dock warrant, delivery order, or the like, as the case may be, providing by endorsement or otherwise for the delivery of the goods to the buyer or to his order at the frontier, and also with an export license and such other documents, if any, as may be strictly required at that time and place for the purpose of enabling the buyer to take delivery of the goods for their subsequent movement, as provided in articles B.1 and 2.

The goods so put at the disposal of the buyer must be clearly set aside or otherwise identified as the contract goods.

(b) Comply with all formalities he may have to fulfil for these purposes, and pay any Customs fees and charges, internal taxes, excise duties, statistical taxes, and so on, levied in the country of dispatch or elsewhere, which he may have to incur in discharge of his duties up to the time when he puts the goods at the disposal of the buyer in accordance with article A.2 (a).

3. Bear all the risks of the goods up to the time when he has fulfilled his obligations under article A.2 (a).

4. Procure, at his own risk and expense, in addition to the documents contemplated in article A.2 (a), any exchange control authorization or other similar administrative document required for the purpose of clearing the goods for exportation at the named place of delivery at the frontier and any other documents he may require for the purpose of dispatching the goods to that place, passing them in transit through one or more third countries (if need be), and putting them at the disposal of the buyer in accordance with these Rules.

5. Contract on usual terms, at his own risk and expense, for the transport of the goods (including their passage in transit through one or more third countries, if necessary) to the named place of delivery at the frontier, bear and pay the freight or other costs of transport to that place, and also, subject to the provisions of articles A.6 and 7, any other expenses of or incidental to any movement whatsoever of the goods up to the time when they are duly put at the disposal of the buyer at that place.

Nevertheless, the seller shall, subject to the provisions of articles A.6 and 7 and at his own risk and expense, be at liberty to use his own means of transport, provided that in the exercise of such liberty he shall perform all his other duties under these Rules.

If no particular point (station, pier, quay, wharf, warehouse, or as the case may be) at the named place of delivery at the frontier is stipulated in the contract of sale or prescribed by the regulations of the Customs or other competent authority concerned, or by the regulations of the public carrier, the seller may, if there are several points to choose from, select the point which suits him best, provided it offers such Customs and other proper facilities as may be necessary to enable the parties to perform their respective duties under these Rules.[1] The point so chosen by the seller must be notified to the buyer,[2] and thereupon that point shall be deemed for the purposes of these Rules to be the point at the named place of delivery at which the goods shall be put at the disposal of the buyer and the risk of the goods shall pass.

6. Provide the buyer, at the buyer's request and risk, with a thorough document of transport normally procurable in the country of dispatch covering on usual terms the transport of the goods from the point of departure in that country to the point of final destination in the country of importation named by the buyer, provided that in so doing the seller shall not be deemed to assume any duty or to incur any risks or expenses other than those he would normally be called upon to incur, perform, bear and pay under these Rules.

7. If it is necessary or customary for the goods to be unloaded, discharged or landed on their arrival at the named place of delivery at the frontier, bear and pay the expenses of such operations including lightering and handling charges.

If the seller elects to use his own means of transport for sending the goods to the named place of delivery then, in such case, he shall bear and pay all the expenses of or incidental to the necessary of customary operations contemplated in the last preceding paragraph.

8. Notify the buyer at seller's expense that the goods have been dispatched to the named place of delivery at the frontier. Such notice must be given in sufficient time to allow the buyer to take such measures as are normally necessary to enable him to take delivery of the goods.[3]

9. Provide, at his own expense, packaging customary for the transport of goods of the contract description to the named place of delivery, unless it is the usage of the particular trade to dispatch goods of the contract description unpacked.

10. Bear and pay the expenses of or incidental to any checking operations, such as measuring, weighing, counting or analyzing of quality, which may be necessary to enable him to transport the goods to the named place of delivery at the frontier and to put them at the disposal of the buyer at that place.

11. Bear and pay in addition to any expenses to be borne and paid by the seller in accordance with the preceding articles, any other expenses of or incidental to the performance of the seller's duty to put the goods at the disposal of the buyer at the named place of delivery at the frontier.

12. Render to the buyer, at buyer's request, risk and expense, a reasonable amount of assistance in obtaining any documents other than those already men-

---

[1] If at the named place of delivery at the frontier there are two customs-posts of different nationalities, it is recommended that the parties should either stipulate which one has been agreed upon, or leave the choice to the seller.

[2] See article A.8 footnote.

[3] Such notice may be served by the seller upon the buyer by sending it through the post by air mail, and addressed to the buyer at his place of business given in the contract of sale. But if the goods have been dispatched by air, or if the distance between the point of departure of the country of dispatch and the named place of delivery at the frontier is short, or if the business addresses of the seller and the buyer are so far apart as to be likely to cause undue delay in the delivery of notice sent through the mail then, in any such case, the seller shall be bound to give such notice to the buyer by sending the same by cable, telegram or telex.

tioned, which may be obtainable in the country of dispatch or of origin, or in both countries, and which the buyer may require for the purposes contemplated in articles B.2 and 6.

B. The buyer must:

1. Take delivery of the goods as soon as the seller has duly put them at his disposal at the named place of delivery at the frontier, and be responsible for handling all subsequent movements of the goods.

2. Comply at his own expense with any Customs and other formalities that may have to be fulfilled at the named place of delivery at the frontier, or elsewhere, and pay any duties that may be payable at the time or by reason of the entry of the goods into the adjoining country or of any other movement of the goods subsequent to the time when they have been duly put at his disposal.

3. Bear and pay the expenses of or incidental to unloading, discharging or landing the goods on their arrival at the named place of delivery at the frontier, in so far as such expenses are not payable by the seller in accordance with the provisions of article A.7.

4. Bear all the risks of the goods and pay any expenses whatsoever incurred in respect thereof including Customs duties, fees and charges from the time when they have been duly put at his disposal at the named place of delivery at the frontier.

5. If he fails to take delivery of the goods as soon as they have been duly put at his disposal, bear all the risks of the goods and pay any additional expenses incurred, whether by the seller or by the buyer, because of such failure, provided that the goods shall have been clearly set aside or otherwise identified as the contract goods.

6. Procure, at his own risk and expense, any import license, exchange control authorization, permits or other documents issued in the country of importation, or elsewhere, that he may require in connection with any movement of the goods subsequent to the time when they have been duly put at his disposal at the named place of delivery at the frontier.

7. Bear and pay any additional expenses which the seller may have to incur for the purpose of obtaining a through document of transport in accordance with article A.6.

8. At seller's request and at buyer's expense, place such import license, exchange control authorization, permits and other documents, or certified copies thereof, at the disposal of the seller for the limited purpose of obtaining the through document of transport contemplated in article A.6.

9. Supply the seller, at his request, with the address of the final destination of the goods in the country of importation, if the seller requires such information for the purpose of applying for such licenses and other documents as are contemplated in articles A.4 and A.6.

10. Bear and pay the expenses incurred by the seller in providing the buyer with any expert third-party certificate of conformity of the goods stipulated in the contract of sale.

11. Bear and pay any expenses the seller may incur in or about his endeavors to assist the buyer in obtaining any of the documents contemplated in article A.12.

Delivered Duty Paid
. . . (named place of destination in the country of importation)

While the term "Ex Works" signifies the seller's minimum obligation, the term "Delivered Duty Paid," when followed by words naming the buyer's premises, denotes the other extreme—the seller's maximum obligation. The term "Delivered Duty Paid" may be used irrespective of the mode of transport.

If the parties wish that the seller should clear the goods for import but that some of the costs payable upon the import of the goods should be excluded— such as value added tax (VAT) and/or other similar taxes—this should be made clear by adding words to this effect (e.g. "exclusive of VAT and/or taxes").

Attention should be paid to the special interpretations given under point 9 of the introduction.

A. The seller must:

1. Supply the goods in conformity with the contract of sale, together with such evidence of conformity as may be stipulated in the contract of sale.
2. At his own risk and expense:
    (a) Put the contract goods at the disposal of the buyer, duty paid, at the named place of destination in the country of importation on the date or within the period stipulated in the contract of sale, and at the same time supply the buyer with a customary document of transport, warehouse warrant, dock warrant, delivery order, or the like, as the case may be, providing by endorsement or otherwise for the delivery of the goods to the buyer or to his order at the named place of destination in the country of importation and also with such other documents, if any, as may be strictly required at that time and place for the purpose of enabling the buyer to take delivery of the goods, as provided in article B.1.

    The goods so put at the disposal of the buyer must be clearly set aside or otherwise identified as the contract goods.

    (b) Provide the import license or permit and bear the cost of any import duties or taxes, including the cost of Customs clearance, as well as any other taxes, fees or charges payable at the named place of destination at the time of the importation of the goods, so far as such payments are necessary for the purpose of enabling the seller to put the goods duty paid at the disposal of the buyer at that place.

    (c) Comply with all formalities he may have to fulfil for these purposes.
3. Bear all the risks of the goods up to the time when he has fulfilled his obligations under article A.2 (a).
4. Procure at his own risk and expense, in addition to the documents contemplated in article A.2 (a), any export license or permit, exchange control authorization, certificates, consular invoice and other documents issued by the public authorities concerned, which he may require for the purpose of dispatching the goods, exporting them from the country of dispatch, passing them in transit through one or more third countries (if necessary), importing them into the country of the named place of destination, and putting them at the disposal of the buyer at the place.
5. Contract on usual terms, at his own risk and expense, for the transport

of the goods from the point of departure in the country of dispatch to the named place of destination, bear and pay the freight or other costs of transport to that place, and also, subject to the provisions of article A.6, any other expenses of or incidental to any movement whatsoever of the goods up to the time when they are duly put at the disposal of the buyer at the named place of destination.

Nevertheless, the seller shall, at his own risk and expense, be at liberty to use his own means of transport, provided that in the exercise of such liberty he shall perform all his other duties under these Rules.

If no particular point (station, pier, quay, wharf, warehouse, or as the case may be) at the named place of destination in the country of importation is stipulated in the contract of sale or prescribed by the regulations of the Customs or other competent authority concerned, or by the regulations of the public carrier, the seller may, if there are several points to choose from, select the point which suits him best, provided it offers such Customs and other proper facilities as may be necessary to enable the parties to perform their respective duties under these Rules. The point so chosen by the seller must be notified to the buyer,[1] and thereupon that point shall be deemed for the purposes of these Rules to be the point at the named place of destination at which the goods shall be put at the disposal of the buyer and the risks of the goods shall pass.

6. If it is necessary or customary for the goods to be unloaded, discharged or landed on their arrival at the named place of destination for the purpose of putting them duty paid at the disposal of the buyer at that place, bear and pay the expenses of such operations, including any lightering, wharfing, warehousing and handling charges.

7. Notify the buyer, at seller's expense, that the goods have been placed in the custody of the first carrier for dispatch to the named place of destination, or that they have been dispatched to that destination by the seller's own means of transport, as the case may be. Any such notice must be given in sufficient time to allow the buyer to take such measures as are normally necessary for the purpose of enabling him to take delivery of the goods.[2]

8. Provide, at his own expense, packaging customary for transport of goods of the contract description to the named place of destination, unless it is the usage of the particular trade to dispatch goods of the contract description unpacked.

9. Bear and pay the expenses of or incidental to any checking operations, such as measuring, weighing, counting or analyzing of quality, which may be necessary to enable him to transport the goods to the named place of destination and to put them at the disposal of the buyer at that place.

10. Bear and pay, in addition to any expenses to be borne and paid by the seller in accordance with articles A.1 to 9 inclusive, any other expenses of or

---

[1] See article A.7, footnote.
[2] Such notice may be served by the seller upon the buyer by sending it through the post by air mail, and addressed to the buyer at his place of business given in the contract of sale. But if the goods have been dispatched by air, or if the distance between the point of departure in the country of dispatch and the named place of destination is short, or if the business addresses of the seller and the buyer are so far apart as to be likely to cause undue delay in the delivery of notice sent through the mail then, in any such case, the seller shall be bound to give such notice to the buyer by sending the same by cable, telegram or telex.

incidental to the performance of the seller's duty to put the goods at the disposal of the buyer at the named place of destination in accordance with these Rules.

B. The buyer must:

1. Take delivery of the goods as soon as the seller has duly put them at his disposal at the named place of destination, and be responsible for handling all subsequent movement of the goods.

2. Bear and pay the expenses of or incidental to unloading, discharging or landing the goods on their arrival at the named place of destination, in so far as such expenses are not payable by the seller in accordance with the provisions of article A.6.

3. Bear all the risks of the goods and pay any expenses whatsoever incurred in respect thereof from the time when they have been put at his disposal at the named place of destination in accordance with article A.2 (a).

4. If he fails to take delivery of the goods as soon as they have been duly put at his disposal, bear all the risks of the goods and pay any additional expenses incurred, whether by the seller or by the buyer, because of such failure, provided that the goods shall have been clearly set aside or otherwise identified as the contract goods.

5. Supply the seller, at his request, with the address of the final destination of the goods in the country of importation, if the seller requires such information for the purpose of applying for such documents as are contemplated in article A.2. (b).

6. Bear and pay the expenses incurred by the seller in providing the buyer with any expert third-party certificate of conformity of the goods stipulated in the contract of sale.

7. Render to the seller, at seller's request, risk and expense, a reasonable amount of assistance in obtaining any documents which may be issued in the country of importation and which the seller may require for the purpose of putting the goods at the disposal of the buyer in accordance with these Rules.

FOB AIRPORT
. . . (named airport of departure)

The rules set forth hereunder for delivery on FOB terms for carriage of the goods by air have been carefully drafted to reflect the usages usually observed in trade. It will be noted that the expression "FOB"—properly meaning "free on board"—is not, in relation to air transportation, to be taken literally but rather as announcing that the next word constitutes the point where the seller's responsibility is to terminate.

A. The seller must:

1. Supply the goods in conformity with the contract of sale, together with such evidence of conformity as may be required by the contract.

2. Deliver the goods into the charge of the air carrier or his agent or any other person named by the buyer, or, if no air carrier, agent or other person has been so named, of an air carrier or his agent chosen by the seller. Delivery shall be made on the date or within the period agreed for delivery, and at the

named airport of departure in the manner customary at the airport or at such other place as may be designated by the buyer in the contract.

3. Contract at the buyer's expense for the carriage of the goods, unless the buyer or the seller gives prompt notice to the contrary to the other party. When contracting for the carriage as aforesaid, the seller shall do so, subject to the buyer's instructions as provided for under article B.1, on usual terms to the airport of destination named by the buyer, or, if no such airport has been so named, to the nearest airport available for such carriage to the buyer's place of business, by a usual route in an aircraft of a type normally used for the transport of goods of the contract description.

4. At his own risk and expense obtain any export license or other official authorization necessary for the export of the goods.

5. Subject to the provisions of articles B.6 and B.7 below, pay any taxes, fees and charges levied in respect of the goods because of exportation.

6. Subject to the provisions of articles B.6 and B.7 below, bear any further costs payable in respect of the goods until such time as they will have been delivered, in accordance with the provisions of article A.2 above.

7. Subject to the provisions of articles B.6 and B.7 below, bear all risks of the goods until such time as they will have been delivered, in accordance with the provisions of article A.2 above.

8. Provide at his own expense adequate protective packing suitable to dispatch of the goods by air unless it is the custom of the trade to dispatch the goods unpacked.

9. Pay the costs of any checking operations (such as checking quality, measuring, weighing, counting) which shall be necessary for the purpose of delivering the goods.

10. Give the buyer notice of the delivery of the goods without delay by telecommunication channels at his own expense.

11. In the circumstances referred to in articles B.6 and B.7 below, give the buyer prompt notice by telecommunication channels of the occurrence of said circumstances.

12. Provide the buyer with the commercial invoice in proper form so as to facilitate compliance with applicable regulations and, at the buyer's request and expense, with the certificate of origin.

13. Render the buyer, at his request, risk and expense, every assistance in obtaining any document other than those mentioned in article A.12 above issued in the country of departure and/or of origin and which the buyer may require for the importation of the goods into the country of destination (and, where necessary, for their passage in transit through another country).

14. Render the buyer, at his request, risk and expense and subject to the provisions of article B.9 below, every assistance in bringing any claim against the air carrier or his agent in respect of the carriage of the goods.

B. The buyer must:

1. Give the seller due notice of the airport of destination and give him proper instructions (where required) for the carriage of the goods by air from the named airport of departure.

2. If the seller will not contract for the carriage of the goods, arrange at his own expense for said carriage from the named airport of departure and

give the seller due notice of said arrangements, stating the name of the air carrier or his agent or of any other person into whose charge delivery is to be made.

3. Bear all costs payable in respect of the goods from the time when they have been delivered in accordance with the provisions of article A.2 above, except as provided in article A.5 above.

4. Pay the price invoiced as provided in the contract as well as the cost of air freight if paid by or on behalf of the seller.

5. Bear all risks of the goods from the time when they have been delivered, in accordance with the provisions of article A.2 above.

6. Bear any additional costs incurred because the air carrier, his agent or any other person named by the buyer fails to take the goods into his charge when tendered by the seller, and bear all risk of the goods from the time of such tender, provided, however, that the goods will have been duly appropriated to the contract, that is to say, clearly set aside or otherwise identified as the contract goods.

7. Should he fail to provide proper instructions (where required) to the seller for the carriage of the goods, bear any additional costs incurred because of said failure and all risks of the goods from the date agreed for delivery or from the end of the period agreed for delivery, provided, however, that the goods will have been duly appropriated to the contract, that is to say, clearly set aside or otherwise identified as the contract goods.

8. Bear all costs, fees and charges incurred in obtaining the documents mentioned in article A.13 above, including the costs of consular documents as well as the costs of certificates of origin.

9. Bear all costs, fees and charges incurred by the seller in bringing and pursuing any claim against the air carrier or his agent in respect of the carriage of the goods.

Free Carrier
. . . (named point)

This term has been designed to meet the requirements of modern transport, particularly such "multimodal" transport as container or "roll on-roll off" traffic by trailers and ferries.

It is based on the same main principle as FOB except that the seller fulfills his obligations when he delivers the goods into the custody of the carrier at the named point. If no precise point can be mentioned at the time of the contract of sale, the parties should refer to the place or range where the carrier should take the goods into his charge. The risk of loss of or damage to the goods is transferred from seller to buyer at that time and not at the ship's rail.

"Carrier" means any person by whom or in whose name a contract of carriage by road, rail, air, sea or a combination of modes has been made. When the seller has to furnish a bill of lading, waybill or carrier's receipt, he duly fulfills this obligation by presenting such a document issued by a person so defined.

A. The seller must:

1. Supply the goods in conformity with the contract of sale, together with such evidence of conformity as may be required by the contract.

2. Deliver the goods into the charge of the carrier named by the buyer on the date or within the period agreed for delivery at the named point in the manner expressly agreed or customary at such point. If no specific point has been named, and if there are several points available, the seller may select the point at the place of delivery which best suits his purposes.

3. At his own risk and expense obtain any export license or other official authorization necessary for the export of the goods.

4. Subject to the provisions of article B.5 below, pay any taxes, fees and charges levied in respect of the goods because of exportation.

5. Subject to the provisions of article B.5 below, bear all costs payable in respect of the goods until such time as they will have been delivered in accordance with the provisions of article A.2 above.

6. Subject to the provisions of article B.5 below, bear all risks of the goods until such time as they have been delivered in accordance with the provisions of article A.2 above.

7. Provide at his own expense the customary packing of the goods, unless it is the custom of the trade to dispatch the goods unpacked.

8. Pay the cost of any checking operations (such as checking quality, measuring, weighing, counting) which shall be necessary for the purpose of delivering the goods.

9. Give the buyer without delay notice by telecommunication channels of the delivery of the goods.

10. In the circumstances referred to in article B.5 below, give the buyer prompt notice by telecommunication channels of the occurrence of said circumstances.

11. At his own expense, provide the buyer, if customary, with the usual document or other evidence of the delivery of the goods in accordance with the provisions of article A.2 above.

12. Provide the buyer with the commercial invoice in proper form so as to facilitate compliance with applicable regulations and, at the buyer's request and expense, with the certificate of origin.

13. Render the buyer, at his request, risk and expense, every assistance in obtaining any document other than those mentioned in article A.12 above issued in the country of departure and/or of origin and which the buyer may require for the importation of the goods into the country of destination (and, where necessary, for their passage in transit through another country).

B. The buyer must:

1. At his own expense, contract for the carriage or the goods from the named point and give the seller due notice of the name of the carrier and of the time for delivering the goods to him.

2. Bear all costs payable in respect of the goods from the time when they have been delivered in accordance with the provisions of article A.2 above, except as provided in article A.4 above.

3. Pay the price as provided in the contract.

4. Bear all risks of the goods from the time when they have been delivered in accordance with the provisions of article A.2 above.

5. Bear any additional costs incurred because the buyer fails to name the carrier, or the carrier named by him fails to take the goods into his charge,

at the time agreed, and bear all risks of the goods from the date of expiry of the period stipulated for delivery, provided, however, that the goods will have been duly appropriated to the contract, that is to say, clearly set aside or otherwise identified as the contract goods.

6. Bear all costs, fees and charges incurred in obtaining the documents mentioned in article A.13 above, including the cost of consular documents, as well as the costs of certificates of origin.

Freight Carriage Paid to
. . . (named point of destination)

Like C & F, "Freight/Carriage paid to . . ." means that the seller pays the freight for the carriage of the goods to the named destination. However, the risk of loss or damage to the goods, as well as of any cost increases, is transferred from the seller to the buyer when the goods have been delivered into the custody of the first carrier and not at the ship's rail. It can be used for all modes of transport including multi-modal operations and container or "roll on-roll off" traffic by trailers and ferries. When the seller has to furnish a bill of lading, waybill or carrier's receipt, he duly fulfills this obligation by presenting such a document issued by the person with whom he has contracted for carriage to the named destination.

A. The seller must:

1. Supply the goods in conformity with the contract of sale, together with such evidence of conformity as may be required by the contract.

2. Contract at his own expense for the carriage of the goods by a usual route and in a customary manner to the agreed point at the place of destination. If the point is not agreed or is not determined by custom, the seller may select the point at the place of destination which best suits his purpose.

3. Subject to the provisions of article B.3 below, bear all risks of the goods until they shall have been delivered into the custody of the first carrier, at the time as provided in the contract.

4. Give the buyer without delay notice by telecommunication channels that the goods have been delivered into the custody of the first carrier.

5. Provide at his own expense the customary packing of the goods, unless it is the custom of the trade to dispatch the goods unpacked.

6. Pay the costs of any checking operations (such as checking quality, measuring, weighing, counting) which shall be necessary for the purpose of loading the goods or of delivering them into the custody of the first carrier.

7. At his own expense, provide the buyer, if customary, with the usual transport document.

8. At his own risk and expense obtain any export license or other government authorization necessary for the export of the goods, and pay any dues and taxes incurred in respect of the goods in the country of dispatch, including any export duties, as well as the costs of any formalities he shall have to fulfil in order to load the goods.

9. Provide the buyer with the commercial invoice in proper form so as to facilitate compliance with applicable regulations and, at the buyer's request and expense, with the certificate of origin.

10. Render the buyer, at the latter's request, risk and expense, every assistance

in obtaining any documents, other than those mentioned in the previous article, issued in the country of loading and/or of origin and which the buyer may require for the importation of the goods into the country of destination (and, where necessary, for their passage in transit through another country).

B. The buyer must:

1. Receive the goods at the agreed point at the place of destination and pay the price as provided in the contract, and bear, with exception of the freight, all costs and charges incurred in respect of the goods in the course of their transit until their arrival at the point of destination, as well as unloading costs unless such costs and charges shall have been included in the freight or collected by the carrier at the time freight was paid.
2. Bear all risks of the goods from the time when they shall have been delivered into the custody of the first carrier in accordance with article A.3.
3. Where he shall have reserved to himself a period within which to have the goods forwarded to him and/or the right to choose the point of destination, and should he fail to give instructions in time, bear the additional costs thereby incurred and all risks of the goods from the date of expiry of the period fixed, provided always that the goods shall have been duly appropriated to the contract, that is to say, clearly set aside or otherwise identified as the contract goods.
4. Bear all costs and charges incurred in obtaining the documents mentioned in article A.10 above, including the cost of consular documents, as well as the costs of certificates of origin.
5. Pay all customs duties as well as any other duties and taxes payable at the time of or by reason of the importation.

Freight Carriage and Insurance Paid to . . . (named point of destination)

This term is the same as "Freight/Carriage paid to . . ." but with the addition that the seller has to procure transport insurance against the risk of loss or of damage to the goods during the carriage. The seller contracts with the insurer and pays the insurance premium.

A. The seller must:

1. Supply the goods in conformity with the contract of sale, together with such evidence of conformity as may be required by the contract.
2. Contract at his own expense for the carriage of the goods by a usual route and in a customary manner to the agreed point at the place of destination. If the point is not agreed or is not determined by custom, the seller may select the point at the place of destination which best suits his purpose.
3. Subject to the provisions of article B.3 below, bear all risks of the goods until they shall have been delivered into the custody of the first carrier, at the time as provided in the contract.
4. Give the buyer without delay notice by telecommunication channels that the goods have been delivered into the custody of the first carrier.
5. Provide at his own expense the customary packing of the goods, unless it is the custom of the trade to dispatch the goods unpacked.
6. Pay the costs of any checking operations (such as checking quality, measur-

ing, weighing, counting) which shall be necessary for the purpose of loading the goods or of delivering them into the custody of the first carrier.

7. At his own expense, provide the buyer, if customary, with the usual transport document.

8. At his own risk and expense obtain any export license or other governmental authorization necessary for the export of the goods, and pay any dues and taxes incurred in respect of the goods in the country of dispatch, including any export duties, as well as the costs of any formalities he shall have to fulfil in order to load the goods.

9. Provide the buyer with the commercial invoice in proper form so as to facilitate compliance with applicable regulations and, at the buyer's request and expense, with the certificate of origin.

10. Render the buyer, at the latter's request, risk and expense, every assistance in obtaining any documents, other than those mentioned in the previous article, issued in the country of loading and/or of origin and which the buyer may require for the importation of the goods into the country of destination (and, where necessary, for their passage in transit through another country).

11. Procure, at his own cost, transport insurance as agreed in the contract and upon such terms that the buyer, or any other person having an insurable interest in the goods, shall be entitled to claim directly from the insurer, and provide the buyer with the insurance policy or other evidence of insurance cover. The insurance shall be contracted with parties of good repute and, failing express agreement, on such terms as are in the seller's view appropriate having regard to the custom of the trade, the nature of the goods and other circumstances affecting the risk. In this latter case, the seller shall inform the buyer of the extent of the insurance cover so as to enable him to take out any additional insurance that he may consider necessary before the risks of the goods are borne by him in accordance with article B.2.

The insurance shall cover the price provided in the contract plus ten per cent and shall be provided in the currency of the contract, if procurable. When required by the buyer, the seller shall provide, at the buyer's expense, war risk insurance in the currency of the contract, if possible.[1]

B. The buyer must:

1. Receive the goods at the agreed point at the place of destination and pay the price as provided in the contract, and bear, with the exception of the freight and the cost of transport insurance, all costs and charges incurred in respect of the goods in the course of their transit until their arrival at the point of destination, as well as unloading costs, unless such costs and charges shall have been included in the freight or collected by the carrier at the time freight was paid.

2. Bear all risks of the goods from the time when they shall have been delivered into the custody of the first carrier in accordance with article A.3.

3. Where he shall have reserved to himself a period within which to have the goods forwarded to him and/or the right to choose the point of destination, and should he fail to give instructions in time, bear the additional costs thereby

---

[1] It should be observed that the insurance provision under A.11 of the present term differs from that under A.5 of the C.I.F. term.

incurred and all risks of the goods from the date of expiry of the period fixed, provided always that the goods shall have been duly appropriated to the contract, that is to say, clearly set aside or otherwise identified as the contract goods.

4. Bear all costs, fees and charges incurred in obtaining the documents mentioned in article A.10 above, including the cost of consular documents, as well as the costs of certificates of origin.

5. Pay all customs duties as well as any other duties and taxes payable at the time of or by reason of the importation.

INTERNATIONAL CHAMBER OF COMMERCE

Through the network provided by the International Chamber of Commerce, a businessman in any country of the world can initiate an idea or opinion or seek a solution to a problem with the assurance that it will receive attention at all meaningful levels from the gathering of experts in Paris to a debate in the United Nations. He may expect not only interest on the part of other members but also commitment. The Chamber's slogan is "World Peace Through World Trade" and a former President of the Chamber described its task as one requiring "that our coolly realistic business approach be imbued with the fiery zeal essential to any great undertaking."

For more than 50 years, the International Chamber of Commerce has enabled businessmen to cooperate across national borders. It affords them a capacity to standardize important commercial practices, to exchange information and experience and opinion. The Chamber also enables businessmen to express views collectively with maximum impact at both national and international levels. The Chamber was founded with a dual commitment to economic freedom and international cooperation and has a record of consistently supporting measures to expand trade and investment and to promote economic development.

The International Chamber is structured much like a national association. Its component members are national committees who draw their support from more than 7,000 companies and associations. Most of these national committees, including the Chamber's United States Council, have their own professional staffs. Most also have standing committees concerned with international issues such as trade policy, banking techniques, monetary affairs and the like.

The Chamber's headquarters are located in an historic building in Paris, where a staff of more than 50 economists, writers, lawyers, translators and others provide essential secretariat services. The main work of the organization, however, is carried out by international commissions of leading businessmen from the various national committees. Most committees have a professional rapporteur of international standing. Chamber staff members are assigned permanently to the United Nations headquarters in New York and to the international agencies in Geneva.

The Chamber's governing body meets in Paris and every three years an international Congress is held in a different part of the world. This general assembly of members provides a forum for policy determination and for program directions.

The record of the Chamber's accomplishments over the years is wide ranging. Its Uniform Customs and Practice for Documentary Credits serves to harmonize these banking procedures in almost every country of the world. On October 1, 1975, a major revision of these rules and procedures went into effect. Copies of the document are essential to anyone engaged in international business. Samples and advertising matter are able to move freely through customs in many countries as a result of a system of carnets issued and guaranteed by national committees. The Chamber's pioneering work in commercial arbitration is one of its outstanding achievements. On the one hand, the Chamber's Court of Arbitration has provided practical services, while on the other, the Chamber has initiated international action to make arbitral awards binding. The Chamber has also made prosaic but important contributions to the standardization of pallet and container sizes, the markings of dangerous goods and even the organization of trade fairs.

On major policy issues, the Chamber has rallied business support for such important steps forward in international cooperation as the formation of the General Agreement on Tariffs and Trade and the Organization for Economic Cooperation and Development. As a proponent of economic development through private investment, it has evolved a set of guidelines for private investors and governments which it believes will ease tensions among the interested parties. The Chamber's guidelines figured prominently in the negotiation by OECD members of the 1976 "Declaration on International Investment and Multinational Enterprises."

From its earliest years, the Chamber sponsored extensive research and studies as part of its procedures in policy determination. It engaged such distinguished experts as James T. Shotwell, Dag Hammarskjold, and Bertil Ohlin and its reports have provided the basis for international solutions of problems as difficult as World War I reparations. For such work, the Chamber was honored by a nomination for the Nobel Peace Prize. The Chamber has recently conducted a study of the relationship between trade and production and the role of the multinational companies in this process. It is also carrying out extensive discussions with representatives of state-trading nations in search of practical means of expanding trade between these countries and those with market economies. In addition, and clearly reflecting the growing concern within the world of industry and commerce about the environment, the Chamber produced in 1975 international agreement on a set of "Environmental Guidelines for World Industry."

The United States Council for International Business is located at 1212 Avenue of the Americas in New York City. International headquarters are at 38 Cours Albert Ier, Paris. A catalog of ICC publications is available from the ICC Publishing Company, 156 Fifth Avenue, Suite 820, New York, N.Y. 10010.

ARBITRATION BY THE INTERNATIONAL CHAMBER OF COMMERCE

When the International Chamber of Commerce (ICC) was founded in 1919, one of its prime purposes was to provide the international business community with a reliable means for settling commercial disputes by arbitration. In addition to establishing arbitration facilities, the founders of the Chamber began an effort that still continues to make arbitration acceptable and arbitral awards binding throughout the world. The advantages of arbitration have proven to be such that arbitration clauses have come to be standard, particularly in international contracts. In the latter case, the assurance against litigation in foreign courts under unfamiliar laws and procedures is especially welcome.

Among the arbitration facilities available to the businessman today, that of the ICC has a special place. It is completely neutral with respect to nationality. It serves members of the business community without national or territorial restrictions and without limits on the nature and subject of the disputes submitted to it so long as they are of a commercial nature in the broadest sense of that term.

Thus, many contracts between businessmen will provide that a dispute of a specific nature should be resolved through arbitration facilities provided by a trade association, while those of a general nature are assigned to ICC arbitration.

Recourse to the ICC's Court of Arbitration as well as to its conciliation assistance is open to all businessmen including those not affiliated with a national committee of the Chamber. The procedure begins when a standard arbitration clause is inserted into a contract. In addition to this standard clause, parties to the contract may specify the number of arbitrators, the location of proceedings, and the like.

Although most users of the ICC arbitration clause are businessmen, it is also proving valuable in contracts between private firms and public agencies including state trade bodies. Provision for arbitration is common not only in contracts involving exchanges of goods and services, but in investment particularly in the developing countries. The International Chamber is a strong proponent of the concept of economic development through private foreign investment and believes that the use of arbitration for settling disputes can be an invaluable incentive for increasing the flow of such investment.

Despite the widespread use of the ICC arbitration clause, the number of disputes that actually become the subject of arbitration is not large. The Chamber's procedures call for an optional initial effort at conciliation before arbitration, which reduces the number of actual cases, and many authorities believe that the presence of the arbitral clause itself is a deterrent to disputes.

Should the parties to a contract require arbitration, the procedure is quite simple. A letter to the Chamber's Court outlining the case and proof of the existence of an agreement to arbitrate, accompanied by a modest fee initiates the proceedings. The Court is made up of lawyers and businessmen from a number of countries. The Court itself does not hear cases but appoints arbitrators from an international panel of qualified experts.

The Chamber has not been content with merely providing facilities for commercial arbitration. It has worked continuously to gain increased international recognition of the validity of arbitral proceedings and to insure enforcement of awards in all countries. At present there are very few countries where an arbitral award can be successfully contested.

Because of the necessity for preciseness in the matter like arbitration, this brief discussion can only outline ICC facilities. Those wishing full information should request two publications, "Rules for the ICC Court of Arbitration" and the descriptive "Guide Arbitration," from The ICC Publishing Company, 156 Fifth Avenue, Suite 820, New York, N.Y. 10010.

THE AAA AND THE ICC

Recently, the International Chamber of Commerce and the American Arbitration Association have concluded a new agreement of cooperation. Under this agreement, the two organizations have gone far to strengthen their facilities for U.S. business. The secretariat resources of AAA offices throughout the United States are now available for cases under ICC clauses and administration. Similarly, the ICC's international facilities stand ready to provide assistance for AAA cases.

When a case arising out of an International Chamber of Commerce clause is heard in the United States, the ICC Rules will apply, and policy direction with regard to handling the case will be given by the ICC; similarly, when a case arising out of an American Arbitration Association clause is heard abroad, AAA Rules will apply, and policy direction will be given by the AAA.

The AAA and the ICC have furthermore decided to join forces to promote institutional arbitration throughout the world.

Finally, the AAA and the ICC have prepared for the exceptional occasion when the parties to a contract cannot agree on a choice of arbitration systems. A joint arbitration clause is available which empowers a special committee, in case of disputes, to determine the place of arbitration and, thereby, the Rules to be applied.

AMERICAN ARBITRATION ASSOCIATION*

140 West 51st Street, New York, New York 10020

International Commercial Arbitration

No businessman likes to go to court, and this dislike increases in intensity when he has to cross a national boundary to do so. The possibility of misunderstandings and disputes, ever present in domestic relations, is magnified when goods and services travel abroad. When such disputes do arise, one side or the other must appear in a foreign court—unless the parties resort to arbitration.

Private, voluntary arbitration does give the international trader a means of overcoming the differences of law and custom by substituting a procedure specifically designed for the businessman and a tribunal composed of arbitrators chosen by the disputing parties because of their impartiality and special knowledge of the industry involved and of the issues in dispute. For many years, arbitration clauses have been a standard feature of purchase order forms and contracts covering the importation of food products, spices, and other commodities. In recent years, businessmen in many other branches of international commerce have also been adopting arbitration. Most international construction contracts today contain an arbitration clause and so do contracts for short and long term licensing and installation of manufacturing processes involving advanced technical designs.

This trend is based on the fact that importers and exporters are usually interested in quick, practical decisions. In the ordinary course of business affairs, arbitration decisions are usually honored simply because this is the only practical way to do business, and remain in business, when one must deal over and over again with the same firms abroad.

But the growth of international commercial arbitration has made impractical the reliance on good-will alone for the enforcement of awards. There are now

---

* Prepared by the Office of General Counsel, American Arbitration Association

several international conventions to enforce both the agreement to go to arbitration as well as the decision when it is rendered. The 1958 United Nations Convention on the Recognition and Enforcement of Foreign Arbitral Awards is the primary international document for this purpose. The United States is a party to this Convention along with 68 other countries including the major trading countries of the world and most of the Socialist countries. Another recent convention is the Inter-American Convention on International Commercial Arbitration promulgated in Panama in 1975 signed by the United States on June 9, 1978 (subject to Congressional ratification) and ratified by eight Latin American countries.

A dramatic example of arbitration serving the interests of international trade occurred when the U.S. Government and representatives of Socialist countries recommended the use of arbitration in connection with trade agreements negotiated during the Summer and Fall of 1972. As a result a new arrangement was adopted by the American Arbitration Association and the USSR Chamber of Commerce and Industry in conjunction with the Stockholm Chamber of Commerce. The main feature of the new arrangement is a model arbitration clause which corporations in the United States and Soviet Foreign Trade organizations may choose to include in their contracts. Known as the "Optional Clause for Use in Contracts in USA-USSR Trade—1977", it provides for arbitration to take place in Sweden, with the Stockholm Chamber of Commerce having the authority to appoint the presiding arbitrator from a panel which has been jointly established by the American Arbitration Association and the USSR Chamber of Commerce and Industry. The panel members are lawyers and judges from a number of different countries other than the USA or USSR. A similar agreement was made, in September 1984, between the American Arbitration Association and the Hungarian Chamber of Commerce, providing for arbitration in Vienna, Austria. More such agreements are expected with other socialist countries.

Beyond that, Polish and Romanian trade agreements have been concluded with the U.S. In the U.S.-Polish trade agreement, both governments encouraged the adoption of arbitration for the settlement of disputes arising out of international commercial transactions between "natural and legal persons" of their respective countries. They specifically recommended that arbitration agreements between such persons "provide for arbitration" under "the Rules of Arbitration of the International Chamber of Commerce . . . or the Arbitration Rules of the Economic Commission for Europe of January 20, 1966, in which case such agreement should also designate an Appointing Authority in a country other than the United States of America or the Polish People's Republic for the appointment of an arbitrator . . . and . . . specify as the place of arbitration a place in a country other than the United States of America or the Polish People's Republic."

The trade agreements also authorized such persons to "decide upon any other form of arbitration which they mutually prefer or agree best suits their particular needs." In this respect bi-lateral conciliation agreements have been entered into between the U.S. Chamber of Commerce and the corresponding Chambers of Commerce of Poland, Hungary, Romania and Bulgaria. With the naming of panels of conciliators on both sides this mechanism of resolving disputes provides an intermediate step before arbitration. The American Arbitration Association will assist in administering any of these conciliation proceedings.

The latest expression of interest in international dispute settlement is found in the trade agreement between the United States and the People's Republic of China signed in Peking on July 7, 1979. Here, the contracting states encourage the use of friendly consultations, conciliation and arbitration. The agreement with China also permits arbitration in the U.S. or China or a third country and emphasizes the use of arbitration institutions. The AAA is one such institution that can help advise on the preparation of arbitral clauses and provide information on conciliation, arbitration and the enforcement of agreements and awards. At the end of 1983, the American Arbitration Association initiated the establishment of the World Arbitration Institute to encourage the use of international commercial arbitration and to promote New York City, and the U.S.A., as attractive advantageous arbitration sites. The World Arbitration Institute does not administer arbitrations or appoint arbitrators. It provides information and education and publishes a quarterly newsletter.

Businessmen and their attorneys have a wide selection of arbitration rules and procedures by which disputes in international trade may be resolved. The United Nations Commission on International Trade Law (UNCITRAL) has completed in 1976 a new set of arbitration rules to be used on a worldwide basis designed to provide uniformity in international ad hoc arbitrations. On December 14, 1976, the U.N. General Assembly adopted a Resolution recommending the use of UNICTRAL Rules in international commercial arbitration. The use of the UNCITRAL Rules is provided for in the Optional Arbitration Clause in U.S./U.S.S.R. trade and is permitted by the U.S.-China trade agreement. These rules also govern the Iran-U.S. claims tribunal established by the Algerian accords. The AAA will serve either as the appointing authority or full service administrator under these rules.

There are a number of other international arbitration organizations from which to choose, including the Court of Arbitration of the International Chamber of Commerce and the Inter-American Commercial Arbitration Commission for trade with the Western Hemisphere. In recent years, the various arbitration organizations of the world have begun to cooperate with one another. One example is a bilateral agreement between the American Arbitration Association and the Japan Commercial Arbitration Association.

There is today a network of cooperating arbitration institutions throughout the world. American businessmen and attorneys can avail themselves of this network through the American Arbitration Association, which is a charter member of the International Council for Commercial Arbitration (ICCA). This organization functions through international congresses and interim meetings, serving as a worldwide forum on information and knowledge of international trade disputes. Since 1976, ICCA has published ten Yearbooks on Commercial Arbitration describing arbitration laws, rules, court decisions and treaty obligations. Its 1986 International Arbitration Congress will take place in New York City, from May 6 to May 9, 1986, and will be organized by the American Arbitration Association.

Despite the simplicity of arbitration, the businessman who plans to provide for this method of dispute settlement in his international trade contracts would be well advised to consult his attorney on legal problems that should be taken into account in drafting arbitration clauses as well as on physical facilities for arbitration that are available in the countries involved. The American Arbitration Association may be consulted either by the businessman or his attorney.

WEBB-POMERENE ACT

The Webb-Pomerene Act passed by Congress on April 10, 1918, grants exemption from the antitrust laws to a combine or "association" organized for the sole purpose of and solely engaged in export trade from the United States to foreign countries.

The Act defines export trade as "solely trade or commerce in goods, wares, or merchandise exported, or in the course of being exported from the United States or any Territory thereof to any foreign nation," and specifically excludes production, manufacture, or selling for consumption or resale within the United States.

The law grants exemption from the Sherman Act, with the proviso that a Webb-Pomerene association or an agreement made or act done by such association—

> is not in restraint of trade within the United States, and is not in restraint of the export trade of any domestic competitor of such association: *And provided further,* That such association does not, either in the United States or elsewhere, enter into any agreement, understanding, or conspiracy, or do any act which artificially or intentionally enhances or depresses prices within the United States of commodities of the class exported by such association, or which substantially lessens competition within the United States or otherwise restrains trade therein.

This law also grants exemption from section 7 of the Clayton Act as to acquisition or ownership of stock or other capital, in export trade, "unless the effect of such acquisition or ownership may be to restrain trade or substantially lessen competition within the United States."

Bonds on Public Works

30

By CHARLES J. HERMAN, Esq.

- Senior Principal & Director of Insurance Claims and Litigation Support Services, Laventhol & Horwath, CPA's
- Member of the Fidelity & Surety Committee and of the Economics of Law Committee of the American Bar Association
- Member of the Fidelity & Surety Committee of the International Association of Insurance Counsel
- Member of the Insurance Committee of the Maryland Bar Association
- Panel of Arbitrators, American Arbitration Association

ROBERT A. KORN, Esq.
of the Philadelphia Bar

- Member of the firm of Korn, Kline & Kutner
- Member of the Forum committee of the Construction Industry of the American Bar Association
- Member of the Fidelity and Surety Section of the American Bar Association.
- Member of the Construction Law Committee of the American Bar Association
- Chairman of the Committee on Construction Contracts, Real Property Section of the Philadelphia Bar Association
- Panel of Arbitrators, American Arbitration Association

Every state of the Union, as well as the Federal Government, now requires that contractors on certain public work furnish a bond for the protection of labor and materialmen.

The federal statute known as the Heard Act was repealed by the Act of August 24, 1935. The present law (49 Stats. 793, chapter 642), as amended, hereinafter called the Miller Act applies to bonds accompanying contracts awarded pursuant to invitations for bids issued on and after October 25, 1935.

The Miller Act corrected the objections to the Heard Act and adopted the suggestion therein made that, in place of one bond for the benefit of both the United States and unpaid subcontractors, two bonds be required: one a performance bond for the protection of the United States and the other for the payment of labor and material claims.

The standard form of payment bond used by the United States is conditioned that the principal shall promptly make payment to all persons supplying labor and material in the prosecution of the work provided for in said contract and any and all duly authorized modifications of said contract. However, the Supreme Court has construed the bond form to deny recovery to one who has furnished material to a materialman who had contracted directly with the principal contractor. *MacEvoy v. U.S. of America* for the use of *Calvin Tomkins* Co. 322 U.S. 102 (1944).

THE A.I.A. APPROVED DOCUMENT

The A.I.A. Document No. 312, 1984, Performance and Payment Bond issued by the American Institute of Architects, as seen below, serves as a commonly used example. It should be noted; however, that some comparable bonds seen by the writer differ from this A.I.A. approved document.

Performance Bond

(A.I.A. Document No. 312)

THIS DOCUMENT APPROVED AND ISSUED BY THE AMERICAN INSTITUTE OF ARCHITECTS, 1735 NEW YORK AVENUE, N.W., WASHINGTON, D.C. 20006.

Any singular reference to Contractor, Surety, Owner or other party shall be considered plural where applicable.

CONTRACTOR (Name and Address):   SURETY (Name and Principal Place of Business):

OWNER (Name and Address):

CONSTRUCTION CONTRACT
  Date:
  Amount:
  Description (Name and Location):

BOND
  Date (Not earlier than Construction Contract Date):
  Amount:
  Modifications to this Bond: ☐ None   ☐ See Page 00–00

CONTRACTOR AS PRINCIPAL   SURETY
Company: (Corporate Seal) Company: (Corporate Seal)

Signature: _____ Signature: _____
Name and Title: Name and Title:

(Any additional signatures appear on page 00–00)

(*FOR INFORMATION ONLY—Name, Address and Telephone*)
AGENT or BROKER: OWNER'S REPRESENTATIVE (Architect, Engineer or other party):

1 The Contractor and the Surety, jointly and severally, bind themselves, their heirs, executors, administrators, successors and assigns to the Owner for the performance of the Construction Contract, which is incorporated herein by reference.

2 If the Contractor performs the Construction Contract, the Surety and the Contractor shall have no obligation under this Bond, except to participate in conferences as provided in Subparagraph 3.1.

3 If there is no Owner Default, the Surety's obligation under this Bond shall arise after:

  3.1 The Owner has notified the Contractor and the Surety at its address described in Paragraph 10 below that the Owner is considering declaring a Contractor Default and has requested and attempted to arrange a conference with the Contractor and the Surety to be held not later than fifteen days after receipt of such notice to discuss methods of performing the Construction Contract. If the Owner, the Contractor and the Surety agree, the Contractor shall be allowed a reasonable time to perform the Construction Contract, but such an agreement shall not waive the Owner's right, if any, subsequently to declare a Contractor Default; and

3.2 The Owner has declared a Contractor Default and formally terminated the Contractor's right to complete the contract. Such Contractor Default shall not be declared earlier than twenty days after the Contractor and the Surety have received notice as provided in Subparagraph 3.1; and

3.3 The Owner has agreed to pay the Balance of the Contract Price to the Surety in accordance with the terms of the Construction Contract or to a contractor selected to perform the Construction Contract in accordance with the terms of the contract with the Owner.

4 When the Owner has satisfied the conditions of Paragraph 3, the Surety shall promptly and at the Surety's expense take one of the following actions:

4.1 Arrange for the Contractor, with consent of the Owner, to perform and complete the Construction Contract; or

4.2 Undertake to perform and complete the Construction Contract itself, through its agents or through independent contractors; or

4.3 Obtain bids or negotiated proposals from qualified contractors acceptable to the Owner for a contract for performance and completion of the Construction Contract, arrange for a contract to be prepared for execution by the Owner and the contractor selected with the Owner's concurrence, to be secured with performance and payment bonds executed by a qualified surety equivalent to the bonds issued on the Construction Contract, and pay to the Owner the amount of damages as described in Paragraph 6 in excess of the Balance of the Contract Price incurred by the Owner resulting from the Contractor's default; or

4.4 Waive its right to perform and complete, arrange for completion, or obtain a new contractor and with reasonable promptness under the circumstances.

.1 After investigation, determine the amount for which it may be liable to the Owner and, as soon as practicable after the amount is determined, tender payment therefor to the Owner; or

.2 Deny liability in whole or in part and notify the Owner citing reasons therefor.

5 If the Surety does not proceed as provided in Paragraph 4 with reasonable promptness, the Surety shall be deemed to be in default on this Bond fifteen days after receipt of an additional written notice from the Owner to the Surety demanding that the Surety perform its obligations under this Bond, and the Owner shall be entitled to enforce any remedy available to the Owner. If the Surety proceeds as provided in Subparagraph 4.4, and the Owner refuses the payment tendered or the Surety has denied liability, in whole or in part, without further notice the Owner shall be entitled to enforce any remedy available to the Owner.

6 After the Owner has terminated the Contractor's right to complete the Construction Contract, and if the Surety elects to act under Subparagraph 4.1, 4.2, or 4.3 above, then the responsibilities of the Surety to the Owner shall not be greater than those of the Contractor under the Construction Contract, and the responsibilities of the Owner to the Surety shall not be greater than those of the Owner under the Construction Contract. To the limit of the amount of this Bond, but subject to commitment by the Owner of the Balance of the Contract Price to mitigation of costs and damages on the Construction Contract, the Surety is obligated without duplication for:

6.1 The responsibilities of the Contractor for correction of defective work and completion of the Construction Contract;

6.2 Additional legal, design, professional and delay costs resulting from the Contractor's Default, and resulting from the actions or failure to act of the Surety under Paragraph 4; and

6.3 Liquidated damages, or if no liquidated damages are specified in the Construction Contract, actual damages caused by delayed performance or non-performance of the Contractor.

7 The Surety shall not be liable to the Owner or others for obligations of the Contractor that are unrelated to the Construction Contract, and the Balance of the Contract Price shall not be reduced or set off on account of any such unrelated obligations. No right of action shall accrue on this Bond to any person or entity other than the Owner or its heirs, executors, administrators or successors.

8 The Surety hereby waives notice of any change, including changes of time, to the Construction Contract or to related subcontracts, purchase orders and other obligations.

9 Any proceeding, legal or equitable, under this Bond may be instituted in any court of competent jurisdiction in the location in which the work or part of the work is located and shall be instituted within two years after Contractor Default or within two years after the Contractor ceased working

or within two years after the Surety refuses or fails to perform its obligations under this Bond, whichever occurs first. If the provisions of this Paragraph are void or prohibited by law, the minimum period of limitation available to sureties as a defense in the jurisdiction of the suit shall be applicable.

10 Notice to the Surety, the Owner or the Contractor shall be mailed or delivered to the address shown on the signature page.

11 When this Bond has been furnished to comply with a statutory or other legal requirement in the location where the construction was to be performed, any provision in this Bond conflicting with said statutory or legal requirement shall be deemed deleted herefrom and provisions conforming to such statutory or other legal requirement shall be deemed incorporated herein. The intent is that this Bond shall be construed as a statutory bond and not as a common law bond.

12 DEFINITIONS

    12.1 Balance of the Contract Price: The total amount payable by the Owner to the Contractor under the Construction Contract after all proper adjustments have been made, including allowance to the Contractor of any amounts received or to be received by the Owner in settlement of insurance or other claims for damages to which the Contractor is entitled, reduced by all valid and proper payments made to or on behalf of the Contractor under the Construction Contract.

    12.2 Construction Contract: The agreement between the Owner and the Contractor identified on the signature page, including all Contract Documents and changes thereto.

    12.3 Contractor Default: Failure of the Contractor, which has neither been remedied nor waived, to perform or otherwise to comply with the terms of the Construction Contract.

    12.4 Owner Default: Failure of the Owner, which has neither been remedied nor waived, to pay the Contractor as required by the Construction Contract or to perform and complete or comply with the other terms thereof.

MODIFICATIONS TO THIS BOND ARE AS FOLLOWS:

(Space is provided below for additional signatures of added parties, other than those appearing on the cover page.)

CONTRACTOR AS PRINCIPAL		SURETY	
Company:	(Corporate Seal)	Company:	(Corporate Seal)
Signature: _____		Signature: _____	
Name and Title:		Name and Title:	
Address:		Address:	

Payment Bond

(A.I.A. Document No. A312)

THIS DOCUMENT APPROVED AND ISSUED BY THE AMERICAN INSTITUTE OF ARCHITECTS, 1735 NEW YORK AVENUE, N.W., WASHINGTON, D.C. 20006.

Any singular reference to Contractor, Surety, Owner or other pary shall be considered plural where applicable.

BONDS ON PUBLIC WORKS 30–5

CONTRACTOR (Name and Address):   SURETY (Name and Principal Place of Business):

OWNER (Name and Address):

CONSTRUCTION CONTRACT
  Date:
  Amount:
  Description (Name and Location):

BOND
  Date (Not earlier than Construction Contract Date):
  Amount:
  Modifications to this Bond: ☐ None   ☐ See Page 00–00

CONTRACTOR AS PRINCIPAL   SURETY
Company: (Corporate Seal) Company: (Corporate Seal)

Signature: _____ Signature: _____
Name and Title: Name and Title:

(*FOR INFORMATION ONLY—Name, Address and Telephone*)
AGENT or BROKER: OWNER'S REPRESENTATIVE (Architect,
                                   Engineer or other party):

1 The Contractor and the Surety, jointly and severally, bind themselves, their heirs, executors, administrators, successors and assigns to the Owner to pay for labor, materials and equipment furnished for use in the performance of the Construction Contract, which is incorporated herein by reference.
2 With respect to the Owner, this obligation shall be null and void if the Contractor:
  2.1 Promptly makes payment, directly or indirectly, for all sums due Claimants, and
  2.2 Defends, indemnifies and holds harmless the Owner from all claims, demands, liens or suits by any person or entity who furnished labor, materials or equipment for use in the performance of the Construction Contract, provided the Owner has promptly notified the Contractor and the Surety (at the address described in Paragraph 12) of any claims, demands, liens or suits and tendered defense of such claims, demands, liens or suits to the Contractor and the Surety, and provided there is no Owner Default.
3 With respect to Claimants, this obligation shall be null and void if the Contractor promptly makes payment, directly or indirectly, for all sums due.
4 The Surety shall have no obligation to Claimants under this Bond until:
  4.1 Claimants who are employed by or have a direct contract with the Contractor have given notice to the Surety (at the address described in Paragraph 12) and sent a copy, or notice thereof, to the Owner, stating that a claim is being made under this Bond and, with substantial accuracy, the amount of the claim.
  4.2 Claimants who do not have a direct contract with the Contractor:
    .1 Have furnished written notice to the Contractor and sent a copy, or notice thereof, to the Owner, within 90 days after having last performed labor or last furnished materials or equipment included in the claim stating, with substantial accuracy, the amount of the claim and the name of the party to whom the materials were furnished or supplied or for whom the labor was done or performed; and

.2 Have either received a rejection in whole or in part from the Contractor, or not received within 30 days of furnishing the above notice any communication from the Contractor by which the Contractor has indicated the claim will be paid directly or indirectly; and

.3 Not having been paid within the above 30 days, have sent a written notice to the Surety (at the address described in Paragraph 12) and sent a copy, or notice thereof, to the Owner, stating that a claim is being made under this Bond and enclosing a copy of the previous written notice furnished to the Contractor.

5 If a notice required by Paragraph 4 is given by the Owner to the Contractor or to the Surety, that is sufficient compliance.

6 When the Claimant has satisfied the conditions of Paragraph 4, the Surety shall promptly and at the Surety's expense take the following actions:

6.1 Send an answer to the Claimant, with a copy to the Owner, within 45 days after receipt of the claim, stating the amounts that are undisputed and the basis for challenging any amounts that are disputed.

6.2 Pay or arrange for payment of any undisputed amounts.

7 The Surety's total obligation shall not exceed the amount of this Bond, and the amount of this Bond shall be credited for any payments made in good faith by the Surety.

8 Amounts owed by the Owner to the Contractor under the Construction Contract shall be used for the performance of the Construction Contract and to satisfy claims, if any, under any Construction Performance Bond. By the Contractor furnishing and the Owner accepting this Bond, they agree that all funds earned by the Contractor in the performance of the Construction Contract are dedicated to satisfy obligations of the Contractor and the Surety under this Bond, subject to the Owner's priority to use the funds for the completion of the work.

9 The Surety shall not be liable to the Owner, Claimants or others for obligations of the Contractor that are unrelated to the Construction Contract. The Owner shall not be liable for payment of any costs or expenses of any Claimant under this Bond, and shall have under this Bond no obligations to make payments to, give notices on behalf of, or otherwise have obligations to Claimants under this Bond.

10 The Surety hereby waives notice of any change, including changes of time, to the Construction Contract or to related subcontracts, purchase orders and other obligations.

11 No suit or action shall be commenced by a Claimant under this Bond other than in a court of competent jurisdiction in the location in which the work or part of the work is located or after the expiration of one year from the date (1) on which the Claimant gave the notice required by Subparagraph 4.1 or Clause 4.2 (iii), or (2) on which the last labor or service was performed by anyone or the last materials or equipment were furnished by anyone under the Construction Contract, whichever of (1) or (2) first occurs. If the provisions of this Paragraph are void or prohibited by law, the minimum period of limitation available to sureties as a defense in the jurisdiction of the suit shall be applicable.

12 Notice to the Surety, the Owner or the Contractor shall be mailed or delivered to the address shown on the signature page. Actual receipt of notice by Surety, the Owner or the Contractor, however accomplished, shall be sufficient compliance as of the date received at the address shown on the signature page.

13 When this Bond has been furnished to comply with a statutory or other legal requirement in the location where the construction was to be performed, any provision in this Bond conflicting with said statutory or legal requirement shall be deemed deleted herefrom and provisions conforming to such statutory or other legal requirement shall be deemed incorporated herein. The intent is that this Bond shall be construed as a statutory bond and not as a common law bond.

14 Upon request by any person or entity appearing to be a potential beneficiary of this Bond, the Contractor shall promptly furnish a copy of this Bond or shall permit a copy to be made.

15 DEFINITIONS

15.1 Claimant: An individual or entity having a direct contract with the Contractor or with a subcontractor of the Contractor to furnish labor, materials or equipment for use in the performance of the Contract. The intent of this Bond shall be to include without limitation in the terms "labor, materials or equipment" that part of water, gas, power, light, heat, oil, gasoline, telephone service or rental equipment used in the Construction Contract, architectural and engineering services required for performance of the work of the Contractor and the Contractor's subcontractors, and all other items for which a mechanic's lien may be asserted in the jurisdiction where the labor, materials or equipment was furnished.

BONDS ON PUBLIC WORKS

15.2 Construction Contract: The agreement between the Owner and the Contractor identified on the signature page, including all Contract Documents and changes thereto.

15.3 Owner Default: Failure of the Owner, which has neither been remedied nor waived, to pay the Contractor as required by the Construction Contract or to perform and complete or comply with the other terms thereof.

MODIFICATIONS TO THIS BOND ARE AS FOLLOWS:

(Space is provided below for additional signatures of added parties, other than those appearing on the cover page.)

CONTRACTOR AS PRINCIPAL		SURETY	
Company:	(Corporate Seal)	Company:	(Corporate Seal)

Signature: _____
Name and Title:
Address:

Signature: _____
Name and Title:
Address:

SUMMARY OF FEDERAL BOND LAWS

The Miller Act

1. AMOUNT OF BOND.—One-half the contract price where the total amount payable by the terms of the contract is not more than $1,000,000; 40% of the contract price whenever the total amount payable by the terms of the contract is more than $1,000,000 but not more than $5,000,000; whenever the total amount payable by the terms of the contract is more than $5,000,000 the payment bond is in the sum of $2,500,000.

2. LABOR AND MATERIAL COVERED.—Labor or material furnished for the construction, alteration or repair of any public building or public work of the United States. See *MacEvoy v. United tates* 322 U.S. 102 (1944) and see page 794 infra. See generally cases cited.

3. NOTICE REQUIRED.—(a) *to surety*—No special statutory provision with respect to a claim under the payment bond. However, the 1966 Federal Tax Lien Act amended the Miller Act by providing effective June 30, 1967, that in order for the Government to maintain an action under the performance bond for unpaid taxes imposed by the United States which were collected, deducted, or withheld from wages paid by the contractor in carrying out the contract, the United States must give written notice to the surety within 90 days after the date when such contractor files a return for the period involved, except that no such notice shall be given more than 180 days from the date when a return for the period was required to be filed under the Internal Revenue Code of 1964. (b) *to principal contractor*—Note that no notice is required by a person having a contractual relationship, express or implied, with the principal contractor. Any person having a direct contractual relationship with a subcontractor but no contractual relation, express or implied, with the principal contractor must give written notice to the contractor within ninety days from the date on which such person performed the last of the labor or furnished or supplied the last of the material for which the claim is made, stating with substantial accuracy the amount claimed

and the name of the party to whom the material was furnished or supplied or for whom the labor was done or performed. Such notice shall be served by mailing the same by registered mail, postage prepaid, in an envelope addressed to the contractor at any place he maintains an office or conducts his business, or his residence, or in any manner in which the United States marshal of the district in which the public improvement is situated is authorized by law to serve summons. (c) *to municipality*—No special statutory provision. (d) *to creditors*—No special statutory provision.

4. TIME FOR SUIT.—The 1959 amendment to the Miller Act provides that no suit shall be brought by a claimant after the expiration of one year after the day on which the last of the labor was performed or material was supplied by him.

The United States has a period of one year should it elect to sue under the Miller Act performance bond for unpaid taxes due by the contractor.

Every person who has the right to sue under the payment bond may institute a separate action thereon in the United States District Court for any district in which the contract was to be performed and executed and not elsewhere, at any time after the expiration of ninety days after the day on which the last labor was performed or the last material was furnished or supplied by him for which such claim is made, but such suit must be commenced within one year after the date on which the last of the labor was performed or material was supplied by claimant.

5. CONTRACTS EXCLUDED.—$25,000 or less. The contracting officer, however, has authority to require a performance bond or other security in cases other than those specified in the above provisions of the Miller Act.

6. PROCEDURE.—The Comptroller General is authorized and directed to furnish to any person making application therefor, who submits an affidavit that he supplied labor or materials for such public works and that payment therefor has not been made or that he is being sued on such bond, a certified copy of such bond and the contract for which it was given. The Comptroller General makes a charge for such photostat copy of these documents.

7. PENALTY FOR FAILURE TO TAKE BOND.—No special statutory provision.

8. SPECIAL PROVISIONS.—The contracting officer is authorized to waive the requirement of a performance bond and payment bond for so much of the work under the contract as is to be performed in a foreign country if he finds that it is impracticable for the contractor to furnish such bonds.

The performance bond is solely for the protection of the United States and is in such amount as the awarding officer deems adequate. The separate payment bond is for the protection of the laborers and materialmen.

9. DECISIONS UNDER MILLER ACT—Discussion of the question of the payment bond claimant's compliance with the statutory notice requirement of the Miller Act as well as the question of a Miller Act Bond furnished by a party who has no contract directly with the federal government *United States for the use of Hillsdale Rock Co. v. Cortelyou & Cole, Inc.* 400 F.Supp. 20 (N.D. Cal. 1975). Written notice given by a materialman within the 90-day period by ordinary mail, but which was actually received by the contractor within the 90-day period, has been held to comply with the statutory requirements. *United States for the use of Hallenbeck v. Fleisher Engineering & Construction Co.* 107 F.2d 925 (2nd Cir. 1939), aff'd 311 U.S. 15, 61 S. Ct. 81, 85 L. Ed. 12 (1940). Where notice under the Miller Act was not sent by registered mail the claimant must sustain the burden of proving receipt. *United States for the use of Twin County Transit Mix, Inc. v. R. P. McTeague Construction Corp.* 264 F.Supp. 619 (E.D. N.Y. 1967).

The Supreme Court has construed the payment bond form used by the United States, to deny recovery to one who has furnished material to a materialman who had contracted directly with the principal contractor. *Clifford F. MacEvoy Co. v. U.S. of America for the use of Calvin Tomkins Co.*, 322 U.S. 102; 64 S. Ct. 890; 88 L. Ed. 1163 (1944). Some state courts hold otherwise.

Even though plaintiff did not meticulously follow registered mail portions of notice requirements of statute, where all relevant parties received actual notice of subcontractor's defalcation within 90-day time period allowed by statute by regular U.S. mail, notice satisfied requirements of Miller Act. *United States for the use of Hillsdale Rock Co. v. Cortelyou & Cole, Inc.*, 581 F.2d. 239 (9th Cir. 1978).

Timely giving of required notice to the contractor is a condition precedent to successful maintenance of suit under Miller Act. *United States for the use of General Electric Co. v. H. I. Lewis Construction Co.*, 375 F.2d 194 (2d. Cir. 1967).

Claimant was not entitled to recover from the surety because of failure to give requisite written notice of claim to the prime contractor as condition precedent to a claim under the Miller Act payment bond. *United States for the use of Excavation Constr., Inc. v. Glenn-Stewart-Pinckney B & D. Inc.* 388 F.Supp. 289 (D. Del 1975). *United States for the use of Ray Weist Constr. Co. v. St. Paul Fire & Marine Insurance Co.* 513 F.2d 159 (9th Cir. 1975).

BONDS ON PUBLIC WORKS 30-9

A contractor for public work can waive the 90-day notice required prior to action on contractor's bond, especially if he has all information which notice would otherwise give him or deals directly with those who might otherwise be expected to give notice, and if he impliedly assumes subcontractor's contract, directs the work and promises payment to those doing the work if they will continue, his liability becomes fixed and the surety's liability is coextensive with his. *United States ex rel. Korash v. Otis Williams & Co.* 30 F.Supp. 590 (E.D. Idaho 1939).

Invoices which a materialman issued to a subcontractor as materials were being furnished, and which subcontractor in turn gave to the general contractor for use in arriving at estimated payments which government was to make during progress of the work, will not be treated as a sufficient compliance with a requirement for notice under the Miller Act. The mere assertion of a general contractor that nothing was owing to subcontractor does not constitute a waiver of the necessity for furnishing the written notice required by the statue. *United States for the use of American Radiator & Standard Sanitary Corp. v. Northwestern Engineering Co.*, 122 F.2d 600 (8th Cir. 1941).

Where public works contractor not only agreed in writing to pay certain obligations, which subcontractor might incur, but actually did make payments, and where contractor not only knew that certain equipment was used by subcontractor but through invoices and other written documents was apprised of all claims, and took action indicating that contractor interpreted his agreement with subcontractor as a direct obligation to pay, the owner of the equipment was not required before suing on contractor's payment bond to give statutory notice as a condition precedent. *United States ex rel. Hargis v. Maryland Casualty Co.*, 64 F.Supp. 522 (S.D. Cal. 1946).

Where materialman, having no contractual relation to contractor, exhibited to contractor as notice of his claim for sand furnished a subcontractor, a writing showing amount claimed and identity of subcontractor, and contractor examined and discussed and might have taken the writing, written notice of claim was sufficiently served as required by Miller Act, to sustain action on public construction payment bond for use of materialman. *Coffee v. United States* 157 F.2d 968 (5th Cir. 1946); *United States for the use of Trane Co. v. Denton Plumbing & Heating*, 123 F.Supp. 881 (N.D. Tex. 1954), aff'd *Houston Fire & Cas. Ins. Co. v. United States*, 217 F.2d 727 (5th Cir. 1954). However, the rule of the Fifth Circuit as expressed in the two cases last cited was not followed by the Seventh Circuit in *Bowden v. United States* 239 F.2d 572 (9th Cir. 1956) cert. denied, *United States for the use of Malloy v. Bowden*, 353 U.S. 957, 77 S. Ct. 864, 1 L. Ed. 2nd 909 (1957), which latter case holds that the giving of written notice as specified by the Miller Act is a condition precedent to the right of a supplier to sue on the payment bond. The writing must be sent or presented to the prime contractor by or on the authority of the supplier and must inform the prime contractor, expressly or by implication, that the supplier is looking to the contractor for payment. See also *McWaters & Bartlett v. United States* 272 F.2d 291 (10th Cir. 1959) for a liberal interpretation of the provision for notice. *United States for the use of Davison v. York Electric Construction Co.* 184 F.Supp. 520 (D.N.D. 1960).

While materialman had no contractual relationship with general contractor on federal project, the general contractor was liable for the cost of any materials purchased and not paid for by its subcontractors for use on the project. *United States for the use of Westinghouse Electric Corp. v. Sommer Corp.* 580 F.2d 179 (5th Cir. 1978).

On May 28, 1974, the Supreme Court of the United States decided that the successful subcontractor in a Miller Act Bond suit was not entitled to recover attorney's fees as costs even though public policy of the state in which suit was brought authorized such award in a suit brought under a bond given to that state or to a political subdivision thereof. *Cass v. United States*, 417 U.S. 72; 94 S. Ct. 2167; 40 L. Ed.2d 668 (1974).

Where the claimant spoke to the local representative of the contractor within 90 days after last performing labor but left no invoice or written claim in any form with this representative and did not submit written data to the contractor within the prescribed 90-day period held claimant had not complied with the notice requirement of the Miller Act. *United States for the use of Acme Transfer & Trucking Co. v. H. S. Kaiser, Inc.* 270 F.Supp. 215 (E.D. Wis. 1967).

One-year statute of limitation period does not begin to run until all work has ceased under a second subcontract on the same project. *Alaska Helicopters, Inc. v. Whirl-Wide Helicopters.* 406 F.Supp. 1008 (D. Alas. 1976).

Although the Miller Act is remedial in nature and intent, the one-year limitations period which forms an integral part of the statute is jurisdictional in character. *United States for the use of Lank Woodwork Co. v. CSH Contractors*, 452 F.Supp. 922 (D. D.C. 1978).

A subcontractor's Miller Act suit was barred by that statute's one-year limitation period where the only materials supplied by the subcontractor within the year prior to the commencement of the suit were replacement items provided seven months after completion of the subcontract work and four months after the termination of the subcontract by the prime contractor. *United States for the use of Laboratory Furniture Co. v. Reliance Insurance Co.,* 274 F.Supp. 377 (D. Mass. 1967).

Congress intended that notice of claim is necessary unless contractual relations, express or implied, between the prime contractor and the claimant existed with respect to the work out of which the claim sought to be enforced against the prime contractor and his surety arose. *United States for the use of Munroe-Langstroth, Inc. v. Praught,* 270 F.2d 235 (1st Cir. 1959).

Court held in favor of the surety as against a payment bond claimant, applying generally accepted law relating to allocation of payments in Miller Act cases. *United States for the use of Clark-Fontana Paint Co. v. Wibco, Inc.* 396 F.Supp. 1253 (D. D.C. 1975), aff'd 176 App. D.C. 241, 539 F.2d 243 (1976).

Requirement of Miller Act that supplier give written notice to prime contractor of claim under payment bond was not satisfied by letter which was received by prime contractor after statutory 90-day period. *United States v. Glenn-Stewart-Pinckney,* 388 F.Supp. 289 (D. Del. 1975).

The materialman must notify the contractor in writing. A notice from the subcontractor to the contractor verified by the materialman does not meet the statutory requirement. *United States for the use of Old Dominion Iron & Steel Corp. v. Massachusetts Bonding Co.* 272 F.2d 73 (3d Cir. 1959); see also *United States for the use of Charles R. Joyce & Son, Inc. v. F.A. Baehner, Inc.,* 326 F.2d 556, (2d. Cir. 1964).

A letter by a subcontractor authorizing the contractor to pay a materialman a sum due by a subcontractor was held to be insufficient. The letter did not constitute direct notice from the materialman. The amount claimed was not described with substantial accuracy *United States for the use of J. A. Edwards & Co. v. Thompson Construction Corp.* 273 F.2d 873 (2d Cir. 1959), cert. denied, 362 U.S. 951, 80 S. Ct. 864, 4 L. Ed. 2d 869 (1960).

A materialman's notice of claim to the prime contractor disclosed through error that the last delivery had been more than 90 days prior to the receipt of notice. Held this inadvertent assertion did not bar recourse under the Miller Act where the contractor had received timely notice in the form of a letter from the materialman's attorney and it appeared that the last delivery had, in fact, been made within the 90-day period. *United States for the use of A. & J. Friedman Supply Co. v. MSI Corp.,* 246 F.Supp. 337 (D. N.J. 1965).

Even if contractor admits knowledge of facts, including amount due, by making a payment on account, there can be no recovery under the surety bond by a claimant who failed to give written notice within the statutory period. *United States v. York Electric Construction Co.* 184 F.Supp. 520 (D.N.D. 1960).

The 90-days for notice with respect to a claimant who leased steel piling to a subcontractor began to run from the date the pilings and/or incidental equipment became last available to use. *United States for the use of Malpass Constr. Co. v. Scotland Concrete Co.* 294 F.Supp. 1299 (E.D. N.C. 1968).

Where a materialman entered into an agreement with a subcontractor and thereafter the contractor guaranteed payment to that materialman, no written notice of the claim was required to be given by materialman to the contractor. *United States for the use of W. E. Foley & Bro., Inc. v. U.S.F.&G. Co.,* 113 F.2d 888 (2d Cir. 1940). *American Casualty Co. v. Southern Materials Co.,* 261 F.2d. 197 (4th Cir. 1958). The fact that the contractor, who had furnished the payment bond in connection with erection of a hangar at an air force base, had knowledge of the agreement between a materialman and a subcontractor and that the contractor had sent directly to the materialman a copy of letter from contractor to subcontractor concerning the delivery and quality of materials, did not alone create a contractual relationship between contractor and materialman. *Cooley v. Barten & Wood,* 249 F.2d 912. (1st Cir. 1957). *U.S. for the use of J. A. Edwards & Co. v. Thompson Construction Corp.,* 172 F.Supp. 161, (D.C. N.Y. 1959) aff'd 273 F.2d 873 (2d Cir. 1959), cert. denied, 362 U.S. 951, 80 S. Ct. 864, 4 L. Ed. 2d 869 (1960). *United States for the use of Noland Co. v. Skinner & Ruddock,* 164 F.Supp. 616 (E.D.S.C. 1958).

A materialman's original complaint was filed less than 90 days after the last day on which he supplied material so that the action was premature. However, the court sustained a supplemental complaint even though the supplemental complaint was not filed until more than one year after the last material was supplied. *Security Insurance Co. v. United States,* 338 F.2d 444, (9th Cir. 1964). See also *United States for the use of Atkins v. Reiten,* 313 F.2d 673 (9th Cir. 1963).

A suit filed within 90 days after the expiration of work is saved by an allowance of supplemental pleadings. *United States v. C. J. Electrical Contractors, Inc.* 535 F.2d 1326 (1st Cir. 1976).

It is essential that the notice required by the Miller Act state a claim directly against the general contractor and that this claim be stated with some specificity as to amount due. *United States for the use of Jinks Lumber Co. v. Federal Insurance Co.,* 452 F.2d. 485 (5th Cir. 1971).

Written notice and accompanying oral statements must inform the general contractor, expressly or impliedly, that the supplier is looking to general contractor for payment. *United States for the*

BONDS ON PUBLIC WORKS   30-11

use of Kinlau Sheet Metal Works, Inc. v. Great American Insurance Co., 537 F.2d. 222 (5th Cir. 1976).

The failure of subcontractor-supplier to inform the prime contractor that supplier had received from subcontractor a check dishonored by insufficient funds and supplier's continued performance of its agreement, without receiving payment, or notifying a prime contractor of the subcontractor's default, did not estop the supplier from asserting a claim under the Miller Act. *United States for the use of Lincoln Electric Products Co. v. Greene Electrical Service,* 379 F.2d 207 (2d Cir. 1967), aff'g, 252 F.Supp. 324 (2d Cir. 1966).

The words "implied contract" in the Miller Act refer to an actual contract inferred from the circumstances, conduct, acts or relations of the parties, showing a tacit understanding. *United States for the use of Bruce Co. v. Fraser,* 87 F.Supp. 1. (W.D. Ark. 1949).

Time limit for starting litigation under Miller Act is a condition precedent to action by suppliers under Act. *United States for the use of Soda v. Montgomery,* 253 F.2d 509 (3rd Cir. 1958), aff'g, 152 F.Supp. 309 (M.D. Pa 1957. Same case 170 F.Supp. 433 (M.D. Pa 1959). *United States for the use of M. A. Hartnett, Inc. v. Enterprise Engineering & Constr. Co.,* 169 F.Supp. 131 (D. Del. 1958). *United States ex rel. Celanese Coatings Co. V. Gullard,* 504 F.2d 466 (9th Cir. 1974).

The one-year period of limitations provided for in the period of limitations provided for in the Miller Act begins to run on the day after the end of the performance of labor; thus, if last day labor was performed on August 30, 1972, the one-year period for suit to recover for rental commenced to run on August 31, and thus suit filed on August 31, 1973, was timely. *United States for the use of Altman v. Young Lumbar Co.,* 376 F.Supp. 1290 D. S.C. 1974).

A suit in the proper federal court in the United States will be sustained even though the work was to be performed in Labrador. *United States for the use of Bryant Electric Co. v. Aetna,* 297 F.2d 665, (2d Cir. 1962) rev'g 196 F.Supp. 106; *United States for the use of Bailey-Lewis-Williams of Florida, Inc. v. Peter Kiewit Sons,* 195 F.Supp. 752 (D. D.C. 1961). aff'd, 299 F.2d 930 (D. D.C. 1962).

Where a materialman, in accordance with the custom to certify payment for materials furnished to a public works contractor at the end of each month, executed a certificate for a certain month although the subcontractor had merely promised to give the materialman a note for the materials furnished, and the contractor relied on this certificate in making payment to the subcontractor of an amount considerably larger than the amount due it for such materials, the materialman may not recover on the contractor's bond for the materials covered by the certificate, but recovery will be allowed the materialman for the balance of his claim. *United States for the use of Noland Co. v. Maryland Casualty Co.* 38 F.Supp. 479 (D. Md. 1941). To the same effect is *Pittsburgh Steel Co. v. Standard Accident Insurance Co.,* 55 F.Supp. 36 (D. S.C. 1944), also *Crane Co. v. James McHugh,* 108 F.2d 55 (10th Cir. 1939). *Moyer v. United States,* 206 F.2d. 57 (4th Cir. 1953).

Where at time government contractor, a partnership, communicated to material supplier the promise of contractor's surety to pay supplier, surety had assumed control of contractor's business and had employed copartner to complete contracts, employer copartner was surety's agent, acting within scope of his authority, so that there was in fact direct communication between surety and supplier, but even if he were not an agent, surety should reasonably have anticipated that its promise to pay would be repeated to suppliers and surety was estopped from pleading Miller Act limitation when supplier relied upon promise and failed to bring action within limitations period. *United States for the use of Humble Oil & Refining Co. v. Fidelity and Casualty Co.* 402 F.2d 893 (4th Cir. 1968.). See also *United States for the use of Nelson v. Reliance Insurance Co.* 436 F.2d 1366 (10th Cir. 1971).

A supplier of pipe to general contractor through third party was estopped to assert claim against the general contractor and his Miller Act surety for pipe furnished where third party falsely represented itself to general contractor to be the supplier and the supplier knew of and acquiesced in this misrepresentation, the general contractor having paid the third party for the pipe. *United States for the use of Gulfport Piping Co. v. Monaco & Sons, Inc.,* 336 F. 2d 636 (4th Cir. 1964). rev'g 222 F. Supp. 175 (D. Md. 1963).

Where the contractor refused to make payment to a subcontractor who had been unable to post a bond unless the subcontractor endorsed such checks to its supplier, and this supplier without knowledge of the contractor immediately re-endorsed those checks to the subcontractor without applying any proceeds towards the materials account, the supplier was estopped by its conduct upon which the contractor had relied to the contractor's detriment from recovering on the Miller Act payment bond for the balance due for materials furnished the subcontractor. *Graybar Electric Co. v. John A. Volpe Construction Co.,* 387 F. 2d 55 (5th Cir. 1967).

Where, at the supplier's request, the contractor made checks jointly payable to the painting subcontractor and the supplier and the supplier either endorsed these checks over to the subcontractor or paid over to the subcontractor the full proceeds thereof after collecting same and the subcontractor used the proceeds of all these checks to pay job debts, held that the legend on the back of each check did not amount to an express waiver of the supplier's rights to sue on the Miller Act bond and a decision in favor of the contractor on the supplier's Miller Act payment bond claim was reversed. *United States v. Glassman Construction Co.,* 387 F.2d 8 (4th Cir. 1968). rev'g 266 F. Supp. 110. Same case 421 F. 2d 212 (4th Cir. 1970).

Letter agreement between materialman and prime contractor, pursuant to which materialman agreed to supply needed materials to subcontractor and prime contractor agreed to make payments due subcontractor by checks payable to subcontractor and materialman jointly, did not place prime contractor and materialman in contractual relationship sufficient to obviate necessity for written notice as condition to action by materialman under Miller Act on bond. *United States for the use of State Electric Supply Co. v. Hesselden Construction Co.,* 404 F. 2d 774 (10th Cir. 1968).

A subcontractor who entered into an arrangement whereby all funds under a wallboard subcontract would be paid by contractor in progress payment checks issued jointly to contractor and sub subcontractor was not estopped by this joint payment procedure from recovering from the contractor a balance admittedly unpaid for the furnishing of wallboard. *United States for the use of Jinks Lumber Co. v. Federal Insurance Company,* 483 F.2d 153 (5th Cir. 1973).

Where a general contractor did not rely on Waiver of Lien by materialman to subcontractor and the general contractor was aware that the lien waiver did not apply to the Miller Act material in question, the materialman's claim for balance due with respect to furnished materials would not be defeated by asserted defense of estopped. *United States for the use of Material Service Co. v. Wolfson,* 362 F.Supp. 454 (E.D.MD. 1973).

Where there was extensive correspondence between the claimant and the surety's agent and and the agent had assured the subcontractor that all valid invoices would be paid upon completion of investigation, the Surety was estopped from asserting the one year period of limitations as a defense to a Miller Act suit. *United States for the use of Atlas Erection Co. v. Continental Casualty Co.,* 357 F.Supp. 795 (E.D. La. 1973).

A surety is held equitably estopped to assert a statute of limitation defense. *United States for the use of Bagnal Builders Supply Co. v. U.S.F.&G. Co.,* 411 F.Supp. 1333 (D. S.C. 1976).

A subcontract provision that final payment thereunder should not be due until the principal contractor received final payment from the United States government must be so construed as not to deprive a subcontractor, who has fully complied with the terms of his subcontract and who in no way is responsible for the delay of complete final payment by the government, from maintaining a suit on the Miller Act bond. *United States for the use of Bailey v. United Pacific Insurance Co.,* 122 F.Supp. 48 (D. N.M. 1954). Any other construction of the subcontract provision would defeat the intent of the Miller Act to provide an efficient and speedy method whereby those supplying labor and material to a government contractor can in event of proper performance of the contract on their part recover by an action on the payment bond. *United States for the use of Ackerman v. The Holloway Co.,* 126 F.Supp. 347 (D. N.M. 1954).

Under the Miller Act requirement of notice of claim within 90 days after performance of last labor and of suit within one year after same date, test is not substantial performance but whether additional work was performed or material supplied as a part of the original contract or merely for the purpose of correcting defects and making repairs following inspection of the project. *United States for the use of Austin v. Western Electric Co.,* 337 F.2d 568 (9th Cir. 1964).

A Miller Act Bond suit is timely if brought within one year following the date on which the last material was furnished by the claimant even though no claim is made for this material. *General Electric Co. v. Southern Construction Co.,* 383 F.2d 135 (5th Cir. 1967), rev'g, 229 F.Supp. 873 (W.D.La. 1964) and 236 F.Supp. 742 (W.D. La. 1964). See *United States for the use of Harris Paint Co. v. Seabord Surety Co.,* 437 F.2d 37 (5th Cir. 1971), aff'g, 312 F.Supp. 751 (N.D.Fla. 1970).

Materials which were shipped C.O.D. and paid for on delivery were not to be considered in determining time notice must be given under Miller Act bond. Since last of materials for which no payment was made were shipped more than 90 days prior to notice given, surety was not liable except for the price of materials payment for which had been guaranteed by prime contractor. *United States for the use of DuKane Corp. v. U.S.F.&G.* 422 F.2d 597 (4th Cir. 1970).

The year for suit prescribed by the Miller Act was extended by reason of the special circumstances in the following case: The action was instituted for material which had been supplied to a subcontractor on a Government project during the time the materialman was conducting business as a debtor in possession pursuant to Chapter XI of the bankruptcy law. The arrangement petition was filed March 31, 1964. Material was supplied from July through October, 1964. On February 15, 1965 the plaintiff materialman was adjudicated a bankrupt. The Miller Act suit was instituted by the trustee in bankruptcy on April 1, 1966, more than one year after the accrual of the cause of action upon which it was based and more than two years from the date of filing of the Petition for Arrangement but less than two years after the date of adjudication of the bankruptcy of the debtor. The court viewed the debtor in possession as separate and apart from the trustee in bankruptcy and held the suit was timely instituted. *United States for the use of Baruch v. Paul Hardeman, Inc.* 260 F.Supp. 723 (M.D.Fla. 1966).

Where claimant was not a party to agreement to sell electric motors and party who sold the motors ordered them from another corporation without giving notice to claimant, claimant could not ratify the transaction to which it was a stranger and could not make it part of single contract together with earlier transaction involving sale of air conditioning equipment in order to make claim under Miller Act timely. *United States for the use of Trane Co. v. Raymar Contracting Corp.*, 406 F.2d 280 (2d Cir. 1968), aff'g, 295 F.Supp. 234 (S.D.N.Y. 1968).

Where certain materials supplied by materialmen were delivered to replace damaged or lost equipment or for corrective purposes and not for accomplishment of the original contract, these items did not serve to toll the running of the 90-day period for giving notice necessary to maintain an action on a Miller Act Payment Bond. *United States for the use of State Electric Supply Co. v. Hesselden*, 404 F.2d 774 (10th Cir. 1968).

Performance of work, which concerned repair or correction and not the accomplishment of original contract, did not serve to toll running of 90-day period provided by Miller Act for filing of claims against bond. *United States for the use of Greenwald-Supon, Inc. v. Gramercy Contractors*, 433 F.Supp. 156 (S.D.N.Y. 1977).

Only work involving original completion of contract may be relied upon to toll 90-day provision of Miller Act for the giving of notice of claim. *United States for the use of Richardson, Inc. v. E.J.T. Construction Co.*, 453 F.Supp. 435 (D. Del. 1978).

The purchase of 120 barrels of cement for $5.15 does not extend the time for filing a suit under the Miller Act where this purchase was not made in good faith but was with the obvious intent of attempting to extend the time for filing suit under the Miller Act. *United States for the use of First Nat. Bank v. U.S.F.&G.*, 240 F.Supp. 316 (N.D.Okla. 1965).

A dealer's act of having replacement floor panels manufactured for the dealer's account, standing alone and in the absence of any act of delivery of the panels to the job site, etc., did not constitute a furnishing or supplying of material to the public project extending the time for notice under the Miller Act. *United States for the use of Floating Floors, Inc. v. Federal Insurance Co.*, 381 F.2d 361 (9th Cir. 1967).

Work done for the purpose of correcting defects or making repairs following inspection of a project will not toll the 90-day notice provision of a Miller Act bond. *Johnson Services Co. v. Transamerica Insurance Co.*, 349 F.Supp. 1220 (S.D. Tex. 1972), aff'd, 485 F.2d 164 (5th Cir. 1973).

The work of a subcontractor in the nature of repairs is held not to toll the one-year statute of limitation for suit by the subcontractor itself. *United States for the use of H. T. Sweeney & Son v. E.J.T. Construction Co.*, 415 F.Supp. 1328 (D. Del. 1976).

Where a materialman brought suit on a Miller Act bond within one year after the materialman had furnished additional material to the contractor at contractor's request for purpose of correcting application of materials, materialman's claim was not barred by the statute of limitations even though more than one year had passed since materialman last supplied material under the original contract. *United States for the use of Palmer Asphalt Co. v. Debardelahen*, 278 F.Supp. 722 (D. S.C. 1967).

The 90-day period for notice by a supplier of equipment commenced to run the day the subcontract was terminated and is not extended by the fact that the supplier of the equipment permitted same to remain at the job site where the contractor made no subsequent use of the equipment. *Frank Briscoe Co. v. United States*, 396 F.2d 847 (10th Cir. 1968).

The 90-day period for notice runs from the date material was last furnished, even though the government had accepted the work prior thereto. Here two gate valves were missing. It was discovered after final settlement. *United States for the use of Noland Co. v. Andrews*, 406 F.2d 790 (4th Cir. 1969).

Where letter to general contractor by claimant referred to a telephone conversation by which the contractor was informed the claimant's name, the Miller Act requirement for notice was met even though the written notice omitted the roofing sucontractor's name *United States for the use of Kelly-Mohrhusen Co. v. Merle A. Patnode Co.*, 457 F.2d 116 (7th Cir. 1972).

A letter which informed the contractor that the supplier was looking to the contractor for payment of the subcontractor's bill, which closed with the statement "if any further information or explanation is needed, please feel free to give us a call" complied with the notice requirements of the Miller Act. *United States for the use of Bailey v. Freethy,* 469 F.2d 1348 (9th Cir. 1972).

Suit instituted on September 21, 1964, by equipment lessor to recover under oral agreement to furnish machinery and equipment together with operators to subcontractor was timely commenced although no operators for the equipment were furnished by the equipment lessor after September 1, 1963, where return of equipment by subcontractor to lessor was entirely up to subcontractor and the subcontractor had choice of keeping on or dismissing equipment operators, and last material was supplied as of October 4, 1963. *Mike Bradford & Co. v. F. A. Chastain Construction,* 387 F.2d 942 (5th Cir. 1968).

A supplier of cabinets was a material supplier to a subcontractor and not a remote material supplier to materialman within the Miller Act where the party who supplied the cabinets had entered into an agreement with the general contractor whereby such supplier took from the general contractor a specific part of the original contract, namely, the furnishing in accordance with plans and specifications of all kitchen cabinets required under the original contract. *J. W. Cooper Constr. Co. v. Public Housing Administration,* 390 F.2d 175 (10th Cir. 1968).

Contractor had numerous jobs each with separate Miller Act bond at the same Navy Yard. Claimant instituted one suit while under the impression there was but one bond after the expiration of one year from last date of furnishing particular material to certain of said projects. Materialman was not allowed to add to the original complaint claims relating to such other prime contracts and bond. *United States for the use of Flynn's Camden Electric Supply Co. v. Home Indemnity Insurance Co.,* 246 F.Supp. 27 (E.D. Pa. 1965).

A Miller Act suit must be brought in the district where the public work contract was to be performed and the parties by agreement may not nullify this statutory requirement. *United States for the use of Vermont Marble Co. v. Roscoe-Ajax Construction Co.,* 246 F.Supp. 439 (N.D. Ca. 1965).

The Miller Act does not contemplate that the subcontractor would become entitled to a performance bond. That is solely a right running to the United States. The subcontractor may not, under a Miller Act bond, claim that, due to the fault of the principal contractor and the United States, completion was negligently delayed. *United States for the use of Lichter v. Henke Construction Co.,* 35 F.Supp. 388 (D.C. Mo. 1940). The purpose of the Miller Act is to protect subcontractors who have furnished labor or materials to a contractor doing work under contract with the United States, and such Act was not intended to provide a basis for recovery between such subcontractor and a third person. Thus in a suit by a subcontractor on the bond, the District Court has no jurisdiction to consider the contractor's counterclaim for a balance alleged to be due by the United States. The United States was merely a nominal party in the action. *United States for the use of Mutual Metal Mfg. Co. v. Biggs,* 46 F.Supp. 8 (E.D. Ill. 1942).

Miller Act allows a government contractor's "unpaid creditors" to realize the benefits of the bond. *United States ex rel. United Brotherhood of Carpenters & Joiners v. Woerfel Corp.* 545 F.2d 1148 (8th Cir. 1976).

A materialman may recover for materials used in the construction of a library building at Howard University, constructed pursuant to the Act of Congress with federal funds, the Secretary of the Interior having required the bonds prescribed by the Miller Act. *United States ex rel. Noland Co. v. Irwin and Leighton,* 314 U.S. 602, 62 S. Ct. 184, 86 L. Ed. 485 (1942), *United States for the use of Gamerston & Green Lumber Co. v. Phoenix Assurance Co.* 163 F.Supp. 713 (N.D. Ca. 1958).

A low rent housing project owned and administered by a local authority is not a federal project within the meaning of the Miller Act, even though this project is financed by loans and annual contributions from the U.S. Housing Authority. *United States for the use of Hutto Concrete Co. v. Magna Building Corp.,* 305 F.Supp. 1244 (D. Ga. 1969). *United States ex rel. Kelly's Tile & Supply Co. v. Gordon,* 468 F.2d 617 (5th Cir. 1972).

The Miller Act does not apply where the contract was with a state, although for the construction of an interstate highway. The United States was not a party to the contract and the bond was not furnished to the United States and did not run in favor of the United States. The materialman's proper remedy was in the state courts of Kentucky. *United States for the use of Miller v. Mattingly Bridge Co.,* 344 F.Supp. 459 (W.D. Ky. 1972).

While the rental of equipment is covered by a Miller Act bond, where there is an outright sale to the contractor no recovery can be had on the bond for the purchase price. *United States v. S. Birch & Sons,* 43 F.Supp. 726 (D. Mont. 1941).

Recovery was allowed for tires furnished for heavy earth moving equipment. *United States for the use of J. P. Byrne & Co. v. Fire Association of Phila.,* 260 F.2d 541 (2d Cir. 1958).

BONDS ON PUBLIC WORKS 30-15

Bonds under the Miller Act are provided in order to protect U.S. from suits rested upon its equitable duty to ensure that subcontractors and suppliers of materials receive payment. Contractor's payment bond covers equipment rental and repairs due first tier subcontractor. Where contractor's bond provided payment for work performed in construction and payment for repairs on machinery consumed in connection with the construction, machinery did not have to be in continual use to be covered by bone. *United States for the use of Mississippi Road Supply Co. v. H. R. Morgan, Inc.,* 542 F.2d 262 (5th Cir. 1976).

A claimant who supplies labor or material directly to the prime contractor or to a subcontractor (i.e. one who both performs labor and furnishes material provided for in the prime contract) is within the class of persons protected by the Miller Act. However, the Miller Act does not protect materialmen who supply other materialmen who in turn may serve prime or subcontractors on the job. *Clifford F.MacEvoy Co. v. United States,* 322 U.S. 102, 64 S. Ct. 890, 88 L. Ed. 1163 (1944).

The payment bond required of prime contractors performing federal construction contracts does not protect employees of a second-tier subcontractor against a default in payment by their employer. *J. W. Bateson Co. v. United States,* 434 U.S. 586, 98 S. Ct. 873, 55 L. Ed. 2d (1978).

Whether party which has contracted with government contractor was a subcontractor entitled to protection of bond under the Miller Act or was a joint venturer not entitled to such protection had to be determined by federal law. *United States for the use of Woodington Electric Co. v. United Pacific Insurance Co.,* 545 F.2d 1381 (4th Cir. 1976).

A sub-sub-subcontractor furnishing labor and material to a subcontractor on a government project is not entitled to bring suit on the Miller Act payment bond. *United States for the use of Newport News Shipbuilding & Dry Dock Co. v. Blount Bros.* 168 F.Supp. 407 (D.Md. 1958). *United States for the use of Whitmore Oxygen Co. v. Idaho Crane & Rigging Co.,* 193 F.Supp. 802 (D.Idaho 1961). *Elmer v. U.S.F.&G.,* 275 F.2d 89 (5th Cir. 1960), cert. denied, 363 U.S. 843, 80 S. Ct. 1612, 4 L. Ed. 2d 1727 (1960).

A supplier of materials to a materialman to a second tier subcontractor was too remote in order to be entitled to recover against the surety under a Miller Act payment bond. *United States for the use of Hasko Electric Corp. v. Reliance Insurance Co.,* 390 F.Supp. 158 (E.D. N.Y. 1975).

A corporation which contracted to supply hydraulic systems for opening and closing missile launcher roof to be installed at missile site, under construction by general contractor, was a subcontractor and not materialman within the purview of the Miller Act even though it did not perform any work at site. Thus supplier of mechanism needed by such subcontractor was covered by the Miller Act bond. *United States v. MSI Corp.,* 350 F.2d 285 (2d Cir. 1965).

Where the prime contractor for government hospital entered into a contract with a manufacturing company to supply and deliver all millwork for the construction of building, and such company gave to a milling company a written purchase order for doors, which doors were delivered to the building site by the milling company, the manufacturing company was a "subcontractor" within the technical sense of the Miller Act, and the milling company could maintain an action on the prime contractor's bond to recover for materials furnished. *United States for the use of Hardwood Products Corp. v. John A. Johnson & Sons,* 137 F.Supp. 562 (W.D. Pa. 1955).

Where a subcontract with third subcontractor contemplated furnishing of materials and performance of labor and third subcontractor performed on the site an integral part of the main contract, claimant was held to be within the jurisdiction of the Miller Act. *McGregor Architectural Iron Co. v. Merritt-Chapman and Scott Corp.,* 150 F.Supp. 323 (M.D. Pa. 1957). The view of the Court in this case was not followed in *AEtna v. Southern, Waldrip and Harvick,* 198 F.Supp. 505 (N.D. Ca. 1961).

Where a prime contractor subcontracted a large portion of the prime contract including asphalt paving work, and the subcontractor in turn sublet the asphalt paving work to another firm, which in turn hired claimant to do the necessary supervisory and testing work, claimant could not recover under the Miller Act bond. *Elmer v. United States Fidelity & Guaranty Co.,* 275 F.2d 89 (5th Cir. 1960), cert. denied, 363 U.S. 843, 80 S. Ct. 1612, 4 L. Ed. 2d 1727 (1960).

Generally, a third level subcontractor stands in too remote a position from the prime contractor's surety to be able to assert a claim on a Miller Act bond. Here the claimant unsuccessfully attempted to establish that the heating and air conditioning subcontractor and the subcontractor who contracted with the claimant were in law one and the same person seeking to pierce the corporate veil. *United States for the use of Powers Regulator Co. v. Farina Construction Corp.,* 261 F.Supp. 278 (D. Mass. 1966), aff'd 376 F.2d 811 (1st Cir. 1967).

A supplier of sand and gravel to a materialman obligated to furnish the prime contract with concrete which was in no way a customized material may not recover under the prime contractor's

Miller Act bond. The Miller Act does not propose to cope with remote and undeterminable liabilities incurred by an ordinary materialman. *United States for the use of Bryant v. Lembke Constr. Co.,* 370 F.2d 293 (10th Cir. 1966).

Supplier of cabinets fabricated according to plans and specifications is a subcontractor and a supplier to that subcontractor is covered by the Miller Act payment bond. *J. W. Cooper Constr. Co. v. Public Housing Administration,* 390 F.2d 175 (10th Cir. 1968).

Firm engaged by prime contractor to furnish labor, supplies and equipment necessary to comply with contract with the federal government calling for sand and gravel was a "subcontractor." *Basich Bros. Constr. Co. v. United States,* 159 F.2d 182 (9th Cir. 1946).

A steel supplier furnishing material to a second tier subcontractor (a joint venture which had agreed to pay for same along with first tier subcontractor which had also agreed to be directly obligated) was a person having a direct contractual relationship with subcontractor of general contractor within the meaning of the Miller Act. Supplier's claim allowed. *Fluor Corp. v. United States,* 405 F.2d 823 (9th Cir. 1969), cert. denied, 394 U.S. 1014, 89 S. Ct. 1632, 23 L. Ed. 2d 40 (1969).

A company which had close relations with the prime contractor and an agreement to supply, detail and install all mill work at a federal project was a subcontractor, although the plywood was simply ordered from the claimant and delivered to the contractor without further alteration or special selection. *United States for the use of Industrial Lumber Co. v. F. D. Rich Co.,* 473 F.2d 720 (9th Cir. 1973), aff'd in part, rev'd in part, 417 U.S. 116, 94 S. Ct. 2157, 40 L. Ed. 2d 703.

Where government's order for materials used in construction of army camp was confirmed by general contractor and claimant shipped its material shortly after receiving such confirmation, such shipment by claimant established a contractual relationship between claimant and general contractor entitling claimant to recover against contractor's surety bond even though the claimant gave no notice in writing to the general contractor within ninety days after the delivery thereof. *United States for the use of Worthington Pump & Machinery Corp. v. John A. Johnson Contracting Corp.,* 139 F.2d 274 (1943), cert. denied, 321 U.S. 797, 64 S. Ct. 937, 88 L. Ed. 1085 (1944).

Repair parts, appliances and accessories which add materially to value of equipment and render it available for other work are not "labor and materials" within coverage of federal contractor's statutory payment bond. *Continental Casualty Co. v. Clarence L. Boyd Co.,* 140 F.2d 115 (10th Cir. 1944).

The surety is liable under the bond for the fair rental value of equipment supplied by a subcontractor, notwithstanding the fact that the main contractor had breached the subcontract but retained and used the subcontractor's equipment. *United States for the use of Susi Contracting Co. v. Zara Contracting Co.,* 146 F.2d 606 (2d Cir. 1944).

A surety is not liable for rental of subcontractor's equipment during the period when the equipment was idle because the government engineer stopped the work as a result of an unexpected complaint that a continuation of the work would endanger railroad property. *United States for the use of Edward E. Morgan Co. v. Maryland Casualty Co.,* 147 F.2d 423 (5th Cir. 1945), aff'g 54 F.Supp. 290 (W.D. La. 1944). However, recovery was allowed where equipment was available for use. *United States ex rel. Carter-Schneider-Nelson, Inc. v. Campbell,* 293 F.2d 816 (9th Cir. 1961), cert. denied, 368 U.S. 987, 82 S. Ct. 601, 7 L. Ed. 2d 524 (1962).

Rental for equipment used in performance of work provided for in federal contract, necessary parts, equipment and appliances wholly consumed in performance of work and current repairs which compensate only for ordinary wear and tear are "labor and materials" within coverage of federal contractor's statutory payment bond. *Continental Casualty Co. v. Clarence L. Boyd Co.* 140 F.2d 115 (10th Cir. 1944).

The surety is liable for rental of construction equipment, for repairs and parts consumed in the work, but not for repairs to the machinery made after the completion of the work. *United States for the use of Roig v. Castro,* 71 F.Supp. 36 (D.P. R. 1947).

In a suit brought against a Miller Act surety for unpaid rentals, the court found notice to be timely when given within 90 days of date lessee (subcontractor) abandoned the work. The surety argued that the period should commence on the date the material was furnished, but the court rejected this argument. The court also held that the plaintiff was not entitled to recover from the surety the value of the unreturned rented equipment because the surety was not a party to the contract which provided that such equipment would be deemed to have been sold to the lessee. *United States for the use of SGB Universal Builders Supply, Inc. v. Fidelity & Deposit Co. of Maryland,* 475 F.Supp. 672 (E.D. N.Y. 1979).

Seller of tractors to government subcontractor on conditional sales contract on which subcontractor defaulted is not covered by payment bond furnished under the Miller Act and likewise is not

BONDS ON PUBLIC WORKS 30-17

entitled to recover for parts and repairs to the tractor furnished largely after the tractors were repossessed. *United States for the use of Miller & Bentley Equipment Co. v. Kelly,* 192 F.Supp. 274 (D.Alas. 1961). See however *United States v. Campbell,* 293 F.2d 816 (9th Cir. 1961), cert. denied, 368 U.S. 987, 82 S. Ct. 601, 7 L. Ed. 2d 524 (1962).

A corporation which dismantled a steam shovel for a subcontractor, transported the shovel from work site to railroad yard and mounted the shovel parts on freight cars for shipment to another job, came within the protection of the Miller Act payment bond. *United States for the use of Benkart Co. v. John A. Johnson & Sons, Inc.,* 236 F.2d 864 (3rd Cir. 1956). The lessee of equipment was held entitled to recover at the rate to which the contractor had assented, even though that charge were more than the amount which the contractor obtained for the excavation work from the government under the prime contract, there being no written agreement whereby the lessor of the equipment accepted or was bound by the terms of the prime contract with the government and the lessor of the equipment had no dealings with the government. *United States for the use of Soda v. Montgomery,* 253 F.2d 509 (3rd Cir. 1958).

The Miller Act Bond covered the replacement cost of machinery and equipment rented to the prime contractor and lost by the sinking of the vehicle in which it was being carried to the site of the building project. *United States for the use of Llewellyn Machinery Corp. v. National Surety Corp.,* 268 F.2d 610 (5th Cir. 1959), cert. denied, 361 U.S. 914, 80 S. Ct. 259, 4 L. Ed. 2d 184 (1959) citing *United States for the use of Norfolk S. R. Co. v. D. L. Taylor Co.,* 268 F.635, (D.C. N.C. 1920), 644, aff'd. 277 F.945 (4th Cir. 1921).

Where a subcontractor failed to complete his work and the contractor sent its truck to the materialman for the remainder of the material ordered by the subcontractor, and the materialman delivered the same under the same invoice number as his previous shipment to the subcontractor, the materialman may recover under the contractor's bond, even though the delivery to the contractor was the only delivery by the materialman within 90 days prior to sending notice to the contractor. *United States for the use of General Electric Supply Corp. v. Harry Hershon Co.* 52 F.Supp. 832 (S.D. N.Y. 1943). In *John A. Johnson & Sons., Inc. v. United States,* 153 F.2d 534 (4th Cir. 1946), aff'g 65 F.Supp. 514, (1945), a brick company was allowed to recover for brick subsequently condemned and rejected by the project engineer where the evidence was insufficient to establish that the brick when originally delivered did not conform to the contract requirements.

Where truckers engaged in construction of airdrome used oil and gasoline obtained from materialmen on subcontractor's credit for driving necessary to the construction and other purposes not related to the construction, but actually hauled material to the job and cost of the oil and gasoline was deducted from their pay therefor, prime contractor and its bondsman could not avoid liability for price of the supposedly misused oil and gasoline. *United States for the use of Magnolia Petroleum Co. v. Core & Planche,* 58 F.Supp. 607 (W.D. La. 1945).

Where gasoline and oils furnished to subcontractor under contract for the federal government were indispensable to the prosecution of the work, were furnished in good faith at the points designated by subcontractor, and deliveries were made under circumstances which justified the supplier in believing that they were in fact used by subcontractor in the fulfillment of his contract, supplier was entitled to recover on contractor's bond under the Miller Act for material so furnished, whether or not such materials were wholly consumed in the prosecution of the work. Some of the oil and gas had been consumed by the truck drivers in traveling for their pleasure. *Glassell-Taylor Co. v. Magnolia Petroleum Co.,* 153 F.2d 527 (5th Cir. 1946).

A materialman seeking to recover under a Miller Act payment bond was not required to have suspected that the subcontractor was diverting material from the public project because the subcontractor picked up materials at a warehouse located some 400 miles from the project, rather than at a nearby warehouse, where the more distant warehouse was located in an area where the subcontractor resided and the subcontractor commuted between his residence and the government project. *United States for the use of Pomona Tile Mfg. Co. v. Kelley,* 456 F.2d 148 (9th Cir. 1972).

A materialman who furnished materials to a subcontractor in good faith and under reasonable belief that materials were intended for use on a federal project, was not required to show actual delivery to and incorporation on the job site in order to maintain action on the Miller Act payment bond. *United States for the use of I. Burack, Inc. v. Sovereign Construction Co.,* 338 F.Supp. 657 (S.D. N.Y. 1972).

A Miller Act Bond does not cover a workmen's compensation award for injuries to contractor's employee. *United States for the use of Gibson v. Harman,* 192 F.2d 999 (4th Cir. 1951).

While the government has now accepted the conclusion of the various appellated courts that the liability of an employer to pay over to the government amounts deducted and withheld from employees' wages is a tax liability rather than a wage liability, the government was successful in collecting in a case involving a housing authority bond which was broader than the Miller Act payment bond. *United States v. Phoenix Indemnity Co.,* 231 F.2d 573 (4th Cir. 1956).

The surety is not liable under the contractor's payment bond for social security, withholding taxes, etc., which the contractor failed to pay into the Treasury of the United States. *In Re Fago Construction Corp.,* 162 F.Supp. 238 (W.D.N.Y. 1957). *General Casualty Co. v. United States,* 205 F.2d 753 (5th Cir. 1953), *U.S.F.&G. v. United States,* 201 F.2d 118 (10th Cir. 1952).

However, the Miller Act amendment effective June 30, 1967 now gives the government a direct cause of action on the Miller Act performance bond under certain conditions for unpaid taxes, deducted or withheld from wages paid by the contractor. *United States v. Algernon Blair, Inc.,* 441 F.2d 1379 (5th Cir. 1971).

Where no state statute provided for recovery of penalties against a surety and where surety on Miller Act performance bond admitted the government's tax claim, the government was not entitled to set off a penalty against the amount recoverable by the surety which had completed the contract from the unpaid retainages. *United Pacific Insurance Co. v. United States,* 320 F.Supp. 450 (D. Ore. 1970).

The Federal Tax Lien Act of 1966 does not affect the government's right to set off against taxes owed to it by the contractor the unpaid contract balance claimed by the surety under its Miller Act payment bond, even though a Miller Act surety which completes the contract on default of the contractor is entitled to the contract retainages in the hands of the government free from setoffs from taxes owed by the contractor to the extent of the surety's loss as completing surety. *AEtna Insurance Co. v. United States,* 456 F.2d 773 (Ct. Cl. 1972).

The trustee of a health and welfare fund may maintain an action against the general contractor's surety, which had executed a bond under the Miller Act to recover from the surety delinquent health and welfare contributions which the contractor was required to pay into the fund under a collective bargaining agreement entered into between an employers' organization, of which the contractor was a member, and an employees' organization of which laborers employed by the contractor were members. *United States for the use of Sherman v. Carter,* 353 U.S. 210 77 S. Ct. 793, 1 L. Ed. 2d 776 (1957). See also *United States ex rel. Sherman v. Carter,* 301 F.2d 467 (9th Cir. 1962).

A supplier furnishing materials to a government contractor can recover from a government surety even though the materials were not used in the performance of a contract but replaced identical materials taken from a contractor's inventory and used on the job. *Commercial Standard Insurance Co. v. United States,* 213 F.2d 106 (10th Cir. 1954). See also *United States for the use of J. A. Edwards & Co. v. Bregman Construction Corp.,* 156 F.Supp. 784 (E.D.N.Y. 1957). See *National U.S. Radiator v. O. C. Loveys Co.,* 174 F.Supp. 44 (D.C. Mass. 1958), aff'd, 275 F.2d 372 (1st Cir. 1960).

Recovery may be had for paint of a type specified by a government contract especially prepared therefor. *United States ex rel. Purity Paint Products Corp. v. Aetna Casualty & Surety Co.,* 56 F.Supp. 431 (D. Conn. 1944). *United States for the use of Morris Paint & Varnish Co. v. Watson,* 129 F.Supp. 573 (D. Neb. 1955). *United States for the use of Color Craft Corp. v. Dickstein,* 157 F.Supp. 126 (E.D. N.C. 1957). *Montgomery v. Unity Electric Co.,* 155 F.Supp. 179 (D.P.R. 1957). See *United States for the use of Westinghouse Electric Supply Co. v. Endebrock-White Co.,* 275 F.2d 57 (4th Cir. 1960). *Roscoe-Ajax Constr. Co. v. United States,* 351 F.2d 305 (9th Cir. 1965).

A supplier who expressly contracted to supply paper wrapped cable could not substitute latex covered cable and recover a greater price. *United States for the use of Westinghouse Electric Supply Co. v. Ahearn,* 231 F.2d 353 (9th Cir. 1955).

A surety under a Miller Act bond cannot oblige the subcontractor to disregard the fair price fixed by the subcontract and limit his recovery to the actual cost of the labor and material furnished by the subcontractor. *United States for the use of Reichenbach v. Montgomery,* 253 F.2d 427 (3rd Cir. 1958), aff'g 155 F.Supp. 384 (E.D. Pa. 1957). See also *Geis Construction Co. v. United States,* 243 F.2d 568 (6th Cir. 1957).

A surety who has paid claims of supplier of labor and material for work done on the Government's St. Lawrence Seaway project has a prior right to the unpaid contract balance which is less than the amount so expended by the surety, and the surety may recover said fund from the trustee in bankruptcy to whom it was paid. *Pearlman v. Reliance Insurance Co.,* 371 U.S. 132 (1962), aff'g 298 F.2d 655 (2d Cir. 1962) which had affirmed In re *Dutcher Construction Co.,* 197 F.Supp. 441, (W.D. N.Y. 1961). The Court in this case explained that in its prior decision. *United States v. Munsey Trust Co.,* 332 U.S. 234 (1947), it held that the Government could exercise the well established common law right of debtor to offset claims of their own.

Equitable lien of unpaid labor or materialman upon funds in hands of U.S. retained from prime contractor extends only to funds which U.S. has determined are due and payable to prime contractor

BONDS ON PUBLIC WORKS   30-19

under terms of prime contract. Materialman or laborer must pursue surety on the bond provided by Miller Act unless it is insolvent and unable to pay amounts to which plaintiffs are entitled. *United States for the use of Reuter v. McDonald Contruction Co.,* 295 F.Supp. 1363 (E.D. Mo. 1968). See also *United States for the use of Brown Brothers Grading Co. v. F. D. Rich Co.,* 285 F.Supp. 572 (D.S.C. 1968).

The Second Circuit sustained the superior right of the surety to moneys recovered on the above project which arose out of a change order negotiated as a result of a claim by the trustee in bankruptcy for the contractor that the contractor had encountered changed conditions in that the material found at the job site was more difficult to excavate and handle. Held that the trustee in bankruptcy and general creditors had no interest in this fund. *In Re Dutcher Constr. Corp.,* 378 F.2d 866 (2d Cir. 1967).

A prime contractor on a Navy contract is not liable for unpaid claims of subcontractors when the Secretary of the Navy has waived furnishing of payment bonds as provided by the Miller Act. The action of the Secretary of the Navy in so waiving the furnishing of a payment bond is not open to collateral attack. *Harry F. Ortlip Co. v. Alvey Ferguson Co.,* 223 F.Supp. 893 (E.D. Pa. 1963), citing *Gallaher & Speck, Inc. v. Ford Motor Co.,* 226 F.2d 728 (7th Cir. 1955). See also: *United States v. Smith,* 324 F.2d 622 (5th Cir. 1963) which holds that the United States is not liable under the Federal Tort Claims Act to unpaid materialmen for failure of government contracting officers to require the prime contractor to furnish a Miller Act payment bond.

Where supplier was aware that government subcontractor was engaged in several operations and that it was furnishing welding supplies and materials for all the projects, supplier was not in good faith furnishing all the supplies for use on the project covered by payment bond under Miller Act. Under these circumstances supplier could recover only for those materials which related to bonded project. *United States for the use of Chemetron Corp. v. George A. Fuller Co.,* 250 F.Supp. 649 (D. Mont. 1965).

A joint venture contractor may not recover his expenditures under the Miller Act payment bond. *United States for the use of Briggs v. Grubb,* 358 F.2d 508 (9th Cir. 1966).

One who lends money to a contractor has no rights as such lender under a Miller Act payment bond and cannot become an obligee. Even if effect of letter to bank making bank an additional obligee under Miller Act Bond was to create a private contract between bank and obligor, by virtue of which obligor was oabligated to bank as a lender of money to same extent as it was obligated to laborers and materialmen under the Miller Act, the provisions of the Miller Act would have to be read into contract, and plaintiff's claim would be barred by time for suit limitation provided in Miller Act for failure to commence suit prior to expiration of the year. *American Bank and Trust Co. v. Trinity Universal Ins. Co.,* 194 So.2d 164 (1966); aff'd 205 So.2d 35 (1967).

Applying Florida law, the United States Court of Claims decided that an architect who merely prepared plans but who did not actually superintend the performance of any work was neither a materialman nor a laborer and that such an architect can assert a lien against funds retained by the *J. J. Henry Co., Inc. v. United States* 411 F.2d 1246 (Ct. Cl. 1969).

A judgment in the state court of Florida in a suit between a subcontractor and the prime contractor does not bind the surety in the subcontractor's Miller Act suit against it. *United States Fidelity and Guaranty Co. v. Hendry Corp.,* 391 F.2d 13 (5th Cir. 1968), cert. denied, 393 U.S. 978, 89 S. Ct. 446, 21 L. Ed. 2d 439 (1968).

A federal court, in which a subcontractor had commenced an action under Miller Act payment bond against the prime contractor and its surety to recover a balance due on a subcontract, was authorized under the Federal Arbitration Act to stay the Miller Act proceedings pending arbitration as called for by the subcontract, the arbitration agreement being valid and enforceable under applicable local law. *United States for the use of Capolino Sons, Inc. v. Electronic & Missile Facilities, Inc.* 364 F.2d 705 (2nd Cir. 1966); *United States for the use of DeLay & Daniels, Inc. v. American Employers Insurance Co.* 290 F.Supp. 139 (D.S.C. 1968).

Miller Act rights are not waived by an arbitration provision in an underlying subcontract. *United States for the use of Portland Constr. Co. v. Weiss Pollution Control Corp.,* 532 F.2d 1009 (5th Cir. 1976).

Invocation of arbitration proceedings does not dispense with the requirement of institution Miller Act suit within the year. *United States for the use of Wrecking Corp. v. Edward R. Marden Corp.,* 289 F.Supp. 141 (D.Mass. 1968), aff'd, 406 F.2d 525 (1st Cir. 1969).

In *United States for the use of Chicago Bridge & Iron Co. v. ETS-HOKIN CORP.,* 397 F.2d 935 (9th Cir. 1968), aff'g, 284 F.Supp. 471 (N.D.Cal. 1966) the contention that a Miller Act claimant is entitled to a judicial termination of his claim, notwithstanding the fact that the claim arises out of a written contract containing an otherwise valid arbitration clause and that such right to judicial termination cannot be waived by an arbitration clause contained in the written contract out of which the claim arises or be overridden by the policy or provisions of the Federal Arbitration Act, was rejected. The Appellate Court held it was not error for the District Court to deny the subcontractor's motion that the court vacate its previously issued stay pending arbitration. Following arbitration award in favor of the prime contractor the subcontractor moved for vacating the stay and the award. The provision for arbitration contained in the subcontract was held proper and enforceable and the award was properly confirmed in the District Court in and for the district in which it was made.

A contract calling for the removal of certain government property and its sale at a nominal price, on the basis that the property would be restored and placed in condition for its future utilization for the government, is a public contract within the provisions of the Miller Act. *U.S. for the use of Warren v. Kimrey*, 358 F.Supp. 1404 (E.D.Ark. 1973).

There is no provision in the Miller Act for the award of attorney's fees in Miller Act suits. Prior to 1974, the general rule was that the successful Miller Act plaintiff's entitlement to attorney's fees was determined by reference to the prevailing policy of the State in which the suit was heard. *United States for the use of Pritchard Products Corp. v. Fullerton Construction Co.*, 407 F.2d 1002 (4th Cir. 1969). In *F.D. Rich Co. vs. United States*, 417 U.S. 116 94 S. Ct. 2157, 40 L. Ed. 2d 703 (1974), the Supreme Court reaffirmed the "American Rule" governing the award of attorney's fees in Federal Court litigation and held that attorney's fees are not recoverable unless there is a statute or enforceable contract specifically providing for them. A plaintiff's right to interest is still determined by the law of the State in which the contract and bond were performed. *Illinois Surety Co. v. John Davis Co.*, 244 U.S. 376 (1917).

Although equipment rentals provided for recovery of attorney's fees, such fees were not recoverable under general terms of the payment bond, which referred to the supplying of labor and material in prosecution of the work provided for in the contract. *United States for the use of Carter Equipment Co. v. H. R. Morgan, Inc.* 544 F.2d 1271 (5th Cir. 1977). rev'd on rehearing 554 F.2d 164 (5th Cir. 1977).

In the cases of *United States for the use of Mariana v. Piracci Construction Co.* 405 F.Supp. 904 (D. DC. 1975) and *United States for the use of Otis Elevator Co. v. Piracci Construction Co.* 405 F.Supp. 908 (D. DC. 1975), the U.S. District Court for the District of Columbia has allowed a subcontractor to recover delay costs from a prime contractor's surety under the provisions of the Miller Act.

Miller Act surety of a general contractor is bound by the dealings between its principal and a subcontractor, even though the surety was not a privy to those dealings. *United States for the use of Fireman's Fund Ins. Co. v. Frank Briscoe Co.*, 462 F.Supp. 114 (E.D.La. 1978).

General contractor could not recover on its counterclaim for breach of warranty on workmanship and materials if its wrongful conduct caused subcontractor to terminate subcontract, *United States for the use of Cannon Air Corp. v. National Homes Construction Corp.*, 581 F.2d 157 (8th Cir. 1978).

Plaintiff, who might have been supplier of sub, was found to have contractual relationship with prime from date on which parties met and prime told supplier to continue work. At that time there was doubt as to whether supplies met government tests. However, prime told supplier "go ahead," and supplier continued to deliver materials. Thus, notice requirements of Miller Act (40 U.S.C. §270b(a)) were not applicable, but court found proper notice had been given if required. *United States for the use of Keener Gravel Co. v. Thacker Construction Co.*, 478 F.Supp. 299 (E.D. Mo. 1979).

Sub sued prime's Miller Act surety for services performed under three contracts. District court dismissed one claim and granted sub summary judgment as to other two. On appeal, court reversed summary judgment on one claim, affirmed other two holdings, and remanded. *Claim #1.* Surety argued that statute of limitations had run, but uncontradicted evidence showed that subcontractor was performing work within one year prior to filing suit. Summary judgment for subcontractor was affirmed. *Claim #2.* Federal suit was brought more than one year after work was completed, but subcontractor argued that state suit brought within one-year period interrupted statutory period. Court disagreed and affirmed dismissal when subcontractor presented no evidence of estoppel. *Claim #3.* District Court had granted subcontractor summary judgment even though suit had been brought in district other than one where work was to be performed. Court of Appeals reversed. Miller Act venue provision is for benefit of defendants and is to be strictly construed. As to this claim, summary judgment was reversed and case remanded. One judge dissented. *United States for the use of Harvey Gulf International Marine, Inc. v. Maryland Casualty Co.*, 573 F.2d 245 (5th Cir. 1978).

Supplier of subcontractor sued prime contractor and Miller Act surety. Defenses: suit was not brought within one year, nor was proper written notice given within ninety days of supplying of last material. Court treated defenses as motion for summary judgment. Held, for supplier. As for timeliness of suit, court held that last work done by subcontractor was in performance of contract, not repair, measuring time from date work was done by subcontractor from supplier. As to written notice, court held: (1) because prime contractor received notice, absence of registered mail was of no legal significance; (2) fact that prime contractor received notice was sufficient even though notice was received through surety; and (3) for purposes of motion of summary judgment, contents of written notice could not be held as sufficient under Miller Act. *United States for the use of Richardson, Inc. v. E.J.T. Construction Co.,* 453 F.Supp. 435 (D.Del. 1978).

Subcontractor sued prime contractor and Miller Act surety in Eastern District of Louisiana. Prime and surety moved to change venue persuant to subcontract provision placing venue in New Jersey. Court granted motion, and subcontractor moved to recall order. Motion denied. Contractual provision as to venue was valid despite provision of Miller Act laying venue in jurisdiction where contract was to be performed and executed, "and not elsewhere." *In Re Firemen's Fund Insurance Companies, Inc.,* 588 F.2d 93 (5th Cir. 1979). For opinion of district court, see *United States for the use of Fireman's Fund Ins. Co. v. Frank Briscoe Co.,* 462 F.Supp. 114 (E.D.La. 1978).

Supplier of subcontractor sued prime contractor and Miller Act surety. All parties moved for summary judgment, supplier claiming that notice was proper, and surety denying it. Reversing trial court's decision for supplier, court of appeals held that delivery in August, for which payment was made, would not be used to determine whether notice was timely. Last material for which supplier was making claim was delivered during prior April, more than 90 days before notice. Summary judgment was granted prime and surety. One judge dissented. *United States for the use of Olmsted Electric v. Neosho Construction Co.,* 599 F.2d 930 (10th Cir. 1979).

Court held that third-tier subcontractor, who had no contractual relation with primary subcontractor, was too remotely connected with subcontractor to have cause of action under Miller Act. *In Re Garden State Erectors, Inc.,* 599 F.2d 1279 (3rd Cir. 1979).

Other Projects

The Atomic Energy Commission in connection with construction work under prime fixed price construction contracts requires bid, payment and performance bonds in which the agent of the Commission is designated as the obligee, which bonds in all other respects follow the form required by the United States on lump sum construction work. On a cost type prime contract the Atomic Energy Commission does not require such bonds but does require the contractors on such cost type contracts to secure a Miller Act type of bond from subcontractors. *United States v. Harder Industrial Contractors, Inc.* 225 F.Supp. 699 (D.Ore. 1963). See also *Fidelity and Deposit Co. of Maryland v. Harris* 360 F.2d 402 (9 Cir. 1966) which deals with a construction subcontractor payment bond required by the National Aeronautics and Space Administration.

The Army Procurement procedure includes the provision that the penalty of the performance bond required in connection with a construction contract shall be in the amount at least equal to fifty percent of the contract price and that when in connection with a construction contract there is executed a change order in excess of $25,000 or a supplemental agreement providing for any increase in the contract price, an additional performance bond and additional payment bond to cover the increase will be furnished.

The Federal Procurement Regulations generally effective October 1, 1964 provide: Where a payment bond has been provided, the contracting officer may furnish the name and address of the surety or sureties thereon to persons who have furnished, or have been requested to furnish, labor and/or material for use in the prosecution of the work required by the contract in question. In addition, the contracting officer may furnish to persons who satisfy him that they have provided labor and/or material, and have not received payment, additional general information on such matters as the progress of the work, payments and the estimated percentage of completion.

The Small Business Administration requires 100% performance and payment bonds. *von Lusch v. Hoffmaster* 253 F.Supp. 633 (D.Md. 1966).

The United States Department of Housing and Urban Development (HUD), Federal Housing Administration, issued a new FHA performance bond, Form No. 2452 (revised Jan. 1968), which form is in substance the previous FHA Form No. 2452 except that the payment obligation was deleted. Later in 1968, it issued a new FHA payment bond Form No. 2452-a which is in substance the American Institute of Architect's payment bond form set out below in this chapter of the CREDIT MANUAL.

Corporate surety is not required where the estimated cost of construction or rehabilitation is $200,000 or less if a "personal indemnity agreement" is executed by the principal individual or individuals responsible for construction or rehabilitation of the project.

In 1967 FHA revised its regulations to waive bonding for rehabilitation jobs under 11 units, regardless of the total price for which FHA made a commitment to insure the property mortgage.

The schedule of requirements as promulgated Oct. 17, 1968, reads in part:

"(1) For walk-up garden type structures where the estimated cost of construction or rehabilitation is $2,000,000 or less, a 10% performance bond and a 10% payment bond shall be provided;

"(2) For walk-up garden type structures where the estimated cost of construction or rehabilitation exceeds $2,000,000, a 25% performance bond and a 25% payment bond shall be provided;

"(3) For high-rise elevator type structures, a 50% performance bond and a 50% payment bond shall be provided.

"As an exception to the foregoing requirements, a cash deposit or an irrevocable letter of credit equal to one-half of the amount of the indicated performance bond or 10% of the estimated cost of construction or rehabilitation, whichever is the greater, may be accepted in lieu of the performance and payment bonds. The amount of bonds, cash deposits or letters of credit will in each instance be calculated on the FHA estimate of construction or rehabilitation costs."

HUD under date of March 1969 promulgated a new payment bond (FHA Form No. 3452-A). This bond runs only to the lending institution as obligee and is used when the owner and the contractor are more or less interrelated. It is for the use and benefit of claimants as therein defined.

The definition of claimant is the same as appears in the labor and material payment bond (A.I.A. Document No. 311, Paragraph 1) which is set out below in this chapter of the CREDIT MANUAL. The agreement for suit after 90 days is the same as Section 2 of said A.I.A. Form 311. However, there is a difference in Paragraph 3(a) under this FHA payment bond. A claimant other than one having a direct contract with the principal must give written notice to the principal *and* the surety within 90 days after such claimant performed the last of the work or furnished the last of the materials for which the claim is made. The provision for suit within one year following the date on which the principal ceased work on the contract and the provision for placing of suit is the same as Sections 3(b) and 3(c) of the said A.I.A. payment bond Form 311. The FHA performance bond revision of March 1969 is FHA Form 3452.

Excepted from the foregoing are projects within the states of California, Florida, Louisiana and Texas where the bonds must comply with local statutory requirements. Cash deposits or letters of credit will not be accepted in these four states.

The new payment bond form for use in Florida is 2452F.

Necessary to Check on Bonds

As amended in 1955, the Secretary of the Army, or Secretary of the Navy, or Secretary of the Air Force, or the Secretary of the Treasury may waive the provisions of the Miller Act with respect to cost-plus-a-fixed-fee and other cost type contracts for the construction, alteration or repair of any public building or public work of the United States or with respect to contracts for manufacturing, construction, alteration, repair, etc., of vessels, aircraft, munitions, material or supplies of any kind or nature for the Army, Navy, Air Force or Coast Guard. Since 1970, the Secretary of Commerce has the discretionary right to waive Miller Act bonds with respect to vessel programs within his jurisdiction.

Thus, while it may be assumed that the Miller Act bonds have not been waived with respect to lump-sum construction contracts, a potential supplier of labor and material under any government contract to be performed within territorial United States should ascertain whether there has been any change in the practice of the governmental department involved from that indicated above with respect to the salutary requirement which has now existed for over seventy years, which bond requirement should not be waived.

State Bond Laws

By CHARLES J. HERMAN, Esq.

- Senior Principal & Director of Insurance Claims and Litigation Support Services, Laventhol & Horwath, CPA's
- Member of the Fidelity & Surety Committee and of the Economics of Law Committee of the American Bar Association
- Member of the Fidelity & Surety Committee of the International Association of Insurance Counsel
- Member of the Insurance Committee of the Maryland Bar Association
- Panel of Arbitrators, American Arbitration Association

ROBERT A. KORN, Esq.
of the Philadelphia Bar

- Member of the firm of Korn, Kline & Kutner
- Member of the Forum Committee of the Construction Industry of the American Bar Association
- Member of the Fidelity and Surety Section of the American Bar Association
- Member of the Construction Law Committee of the American Bar Association
- Chairman of the Committee on Construction Contracts, Real Property Section of the Philadelphia Bar Association
- Panel of Arbitrators, American Arbitration Association

ALABAMA

1. AMOUNT OF BOND.—In addition to a performance bond in the amount of the contract price, any person entering into a contract with the state or any county, municipal corporation or subdivision thereof for the repair, construction or prosecution of any public building, public work, highway or bridge is required before commencing such work to execute an additional surety bond for the protection of labor and materialmen in an amount not less than 50% of the contract price. (39 Code of Alabama § 1-1)

2. LABOR AND MATERIAL COVERED.—Labor, materials, feedstuffs or supplies used in the construction, repair or prosecution of any public building, public work, highway or bridge.

3. NOTICE REQUIRED.—(a) *To surety*—Written notice to the surety of the amount and nature of the claim must be given 45 days prior to the institution of suit on the additional bond. The giving of said notice by registered mail, postage prepaid, addressed to the surety at any of its places of business or offices constitutes compliance with the statute. (b) *To principal contractor*—No special statutory provision. (c) *To municipality*—See Procedure below. (d) *To creditors*—No special statutory provision.

4. TIME FOR SUIT.—Claimant may institute an action upon the additional bond any time after 45 days after the written notice to the surety but such suit must be commenced not later than one year from the date of final settlement of the contract.

5. CONTRACTS EXCLUDED.—Less than $1,000.

6. PROCEDURE.—Every person having the right to sue on the additional bond, upon written application to the authority under whose direction such work has been prosecuted, setting out that labor, materials, feedstuffs or supplies for such work have been supplied by him and that payment therefor has not been made, shall be promptly furnished with a certified copy of the additional bond and contract and is authorized to bring suit on said bond in the county where the work provided for in the contract is to be performed or in any county where the contractor or his surety does business.

7. PENALTY FOR FAILURE TO TAKE BOND.—No special statutory provision.

8. SPECIAL PROVISIONS.—In the event the surety or the contractor fails to pay a claim in full within 45 days after the mailing of the notice as above required, the claimant shall be entitled to recover in addition to the amount of his claim a reasonable attorney's fee together with interest on such claim from the date of notice to the surety.

Immediately after the completion of the principal contract, the contractor must give notice of said completion by newspaper advertisement within the city or county wherein the work has been performed for a period of four successive weeks and final settlement may not be made upon the contract until the expiration of thirty days after the completion of the work. If there is no newspaper published in the city or county wherein the work has been performed, the above notice may be given by posting at the county court house for a period of thirty days.

County Commission of Dale County is authorized to require a reasonable surety bond to guarantee the actual construction and installation of public streets, public roads, drainage structures, and public utilities before the sale or offering for sale of any lots from such subdivision or addition to the public.

An act approved May 28, 1980 provides that the awarding authority in making progress payments shall not retain more than 5 percent of the estimated amount of work done and the value of materials stored on the site, and after 50 percent completion has been accomplished, no further retainage will be withheld. The retainage above set out shall be held until final completion and acceptance of all work covered by the contract, unless the awarding authority provides for the maintenance of an escrow account at least equal to the retainage amount set forth above.

9. DECISIONS.—Final settlement is the date of the approval of the final estimate by the Governor and the issuance of a voucher by the examiner of accounts. *U.S. Fidelity & Guaranty Co., v. Andalusia Mfg. Co.,* 222 Ala. 637, 134 So. 18 (1931); *Union Indemnity Co. v. Ricks,* 224 Ala. 514, 140 So. 597 (1932); *U. S. F. & G. Co. v. Yielding Brothers Co.,* 225 Ala. 307, 143 So. 176 (1932).

The statute prohibits final settlement until 30 days after the completion of a contract. *Rep. Att'y. General, Quar. Rep.* Oct.-Dec. 1938, pp. 34, 35.

Groceries furnished to contractor for employees on job and consumed in performance are supplies within the bond, although there is no liability for groceries for contractor and his family, even though meals were furnished certain employees on the job. *U.S. Fidelity & Guaranty Co. v. Benson Hardware Co.,* 222 Ala. 429, 132 So. 622 (1931).

A road contractor's bond covers small and incidental repairs resulting from ordinary wear and tear on appliances in performing of contract, but does not cover major repairs on permanent equipment or purchase price of such appliances as wagons, automobiles or trucks, though worn out before completion of job. Small tools, although they may ordinarily outlast the work, are not supplies within the bond. *U.S. Fidelity & Guaranty Co., v. Benson Hardware Co.,* 222 Ala. 429, 132 So. 622 (1931); *Standard Accident Insurance Co. v. Dodd,* 225 Ala. 285, 142 So. 574 (1932).

Materialman may recover on road contractor's bond for pipe, although part was used on road contract overlapping that covered by bond and some of it was thereafter taken up. Recovery may also be held for road fabric furnished for use on the highway project. *U.S. Fidelity & Guaranty Co. v. Benson Hardware Co.,* 222 Ala. 429, 132 So. 622 (1931).

The fact that the contractor advertised that he would not be responsible for debts incurred by subcontractor does not relieve surety of its statutory liability for supplies furnished subcontractor. *Pettus v. State,* 24 Ala. App. 525, 137 So. 466 (1931).

A claim for rental of machinery and equipment is within the coverage of the contractor's bond. *U.S. Fidelity & Guaranty Co. v. Armstrong,* 225 Ala. 276, 142 So. 576 (1932).

Recovery has been allowed for nails, wire, cement, shovels, wheelbarrows and small tools used in construction of a temporary camphouse, the construction of which was necessary in the prosecution of the public work, which temporary structure was abandoned upon completion of the public work; *U.S. Fidelity & Guaranty Co. v. Simmons,* 222 Ala. 669, 133 So. 731 (1931); but recovery has been denied under the bond for piping used temporarily in supplying water, which piping was removed after the completion of the job; *U.S. Fidelity & Guaranty Co. v. Andalusia Manufacturing Co.,* 222 Ala. 637, 134 So. 18 (1931).

The rental of shovel by road construction contractor to move top soil is within obligation of contractor's statutory bond to pay for all material and supplies furnished in performance of work.

A claim for gasoline and oil furnished for operation of trucks and machines used in highway construction, as well as for transportation of laborers to and from work, was held to be within the highway contractor's bond. *Benson Hardware Co. v. Taylor,* 24 Ala. App. 480, 136 So. 863 (1931).

The construction of an electric distribution system for a city was within terms of statute requiring the giving of a bond by contractors for the repair, construction, or prosecution of any public building, or public works. *Universal Electric Construction Co. of Alabama, v. Robbins,* 239 Ala. 105, 194 So. 194 (1940).

Freight charges on materials furnished by materialmen held recoverable from contractor's surety

STATE BOND LAWS   31-3

as part of materials furnished by materialmen to the contractor where prepayment of freight charges was part of the overall transaction. *Columbus Rock Co. v. Alabama General Insurance Co.,* 153 F.Supp. 827 (M.D. Ala. 1957).

A bank which lent money to a contractor for purpose of paying for labor and materials used in carrying out the contract was not protected by a bond which combined the obligation of performance and was further conditioned for the payment of all labor and materials furnished and debts incurred by the prime contractor of his subcontractors in and about the performance of the work contracted for. *Bank of Auburn v. U.S. Fidelity & Guaranty Co.* 295 F.2d 641 (5th Cir. 1961).

Where labor and material bond given by school contractor sought on its face that bond was executed in compliance with statute, court read provisions of the statute into the bond. *American Casualty Co. v. Devine,* 275 Ala. 628, 157 So.2d 661 (1963).

Material supplied on contemplation that it would be used on project did not preclude materialmen from recovery under the contractor's bond. The materialmen who sought recovery under the bond must establish any material was supplied in good faith. *Riley Stabler Construction Co. v. Westinghouse Electric Co.,* 396 F.2d 274 (5th Cir. 1968).

Attorney fees are allowable to claimants under labor and material bonds but not to obligee of a performance bond. *Cincinnati Insurance Co. v. City of Talladega,* 342 So.2d 331 (Ala. 1977).

An owner's liability for failure to require a payment bond as required by statute matures with final payment made to the contractor rather than when work commenced. *W. B. Headley v. Housing Authority of Prattville,* 347 So.2d 532 (Ala. 1977).

Giving of a bond by a subcontractor in itself does not excuse the general contractor from liability for acts and omissions of subcontractor; owner then has both general contractor and subcontractor to look to in event of a breach by subcontractor. *United States Fidelity & Guaranty Co. v. Jacksonville State University,* 357 So.2d 952 (Ala. 1978).

ALASKA

1. AMOUNT OF BOND.—One-half of the contract price where the total amount payable by the terms of the contract is not more than $1,000,000; 40% of the contract price whenever the total amount payable by the terms of the contract is more than $1,000,000 but not more than $5,000,000; whenever the total amount payable by the terms of the contract is more than $5,000,000 the payment bond is in the sum of $2,500,000. (36 Alaska Statutes § 25.010)

2. LABOR AND MATERIAL COVERED.—Labor and material furnished for the construction, alteration or repair of any public building or public work of the state. See Remarks below.

3. NOTICE REQUIRED.—(a) *To surety*—No special statutory provision. (b) *To principal contractor*—No notice is required by a person having a contractual relationship, express or implied with the principal contractor. Any person having a direct contractual relationship with a subcontractor but no contractual relationship, express or implied, with the principal contractor must give written notice to the contractor within ninety days from the date on which such person performed the last of the labor or furnished or supplied the last of the material for which the claim is made, stating with substantial accuracy the amount claimed and the name of the party to whom the material was furnished or for whom the labor was performed. Such notice shall be served by mailing it by registered mail, postage prepaid, in an envelope addressed to the contractor at any place where he maintains an office or conducts his business or his residence, or in any manner in which a peace officer is authorized to serve summons. (c) *To municipality*—No special statutory provision. (d) *To creditors*—No special statutory provision.

4. TIME FOR SUIT.—Every person who has the right to sue under the payment bond may institute an action thereon in the Superior Court of Alaska in the name of the state for the use of the person suing, at any time after the expiration of ninety days after the day on which the last of the labor was performed or material was furnished for which the claim is made, but such suit must be commenced within one year after the date of final settlement of the contract.

5. CONTRACTS EXCLUDED.—Effective June 14, 1982, the threshold of contracts requiring bonds increased from $50,000 to $100,000.

6. REMARKS.—When no payment bond has been furnished, the contracting department shall not approve final payments to the contractor until the contractor files a written certification that all persons who supplied labor or materials in the prosecution of the work provided for in the contract have been paid.

Governor is authorized to waive competitive bidding and contract bond requirements for public contracts under $100,000 in an area designated by proclamation as an area impacted by an economic disaster.

A municipality, by ordinance adopted by its governing body, may exempt contractors from certain bond requirements in the construction or repair of public works projects if the estimated cost of the project does not exceed $400,000 and (1) the contractor is, and for two years immediately preceding the award of the contract has been, a licensed contractor having his or its principal office in the state; (2) the contractor certifies that he has not defaulted on a contract awarded to him during the period of three years preceding the award of a contract for which a bid is submitted; (3) the contractor submits a financial statement, prepared within a period of 9 months preceding the submission of a bid for the contract demonstrating that the contractor has a net worth of not less than 20% of the amount of the contract for which a bid is submitted; and (4) the total amount of all contracts which the contractor anticipates performing during the term of performance of the contract for which a bid is submitted does not exceed the net worth of the contractor reported in the financial statement prepared and submitted under (3).

7. PENALTY FOR FAILURE TO TAKE BOND.—No special statutory provision.

8. DECISIONS.—In Alaska, the District Court in its discretion may allow attorney fees in a Miller Act suit. *U.S. v. Breeden*, 110 F.Supp. 713 (D. Alas. 1953).

The District Court in Alaska also permitted a subcontractor's unpaid materialmen to recover against the surety on a subcontractor's bond. *Anchorage Sand & Gravel Co. v. Alaska Dock & Bridge Builders, Inc.*, 119 F.Supp. 943 (D. Alas. 1954).

Where a surety has satisfied claims of all laborers and materialmen and has completed construction of the contract, the surety is entitled to recover from the owner, a Housing Authority, the amount of a progress payment mistakenly mailed by the Housing Authority disbursing officer to the bank.

When a creditor knows that money paid to him is received from a bonded project, it is his duty to apply the payment against the account for that project. *Palmer Supply Co. v. Walsh & Co.* 575 P.2d 1213 (Alaska 1978).

ARIZONA

Performance bond and payment bond amount equal to the full contract amount.

1. AMOUNT OF BOND.—100% of the contract price solely for the protection of claimants supplying labor or material to the contractor or his subcontractors in the prosecution of the work provided for in contracts for the construction, alteration or repair of the public work. (34 Arizona Revised Statutes § 222) See Section 8 below.

2. LABOR AND MATERIAL COVERED.—Labor or material furnished in the prosecution of the work provided for in such contract.

3. NOTICE REQUIRED.—(a)*To surety*—No statutory provision. (b) *To principal contractor*—By persons having a direct contractual relationship with a subcontractor, who have no contractual relationship, express or implied, with the contractor, within 90 days from the date on which such claimant performed the last of the labor or furnished or but no such suit shall be commenced after the expiration of one year from the date supplied the last of the material for which such claim is made. See Section 6 below. (c) *To municipality*—No statutory provision. (d) *To creditors*—No statutory provision.

4. TIME FOR SUIT.—Must be commenced not later than one year from the date on which the last of the labor was done or performed or materials were furnished or supplied for which claim is made.

5. CONTRACTS EXCLUDED.—No express statutory provision. However, if less than $100,000, a state agency, board or commission shall include an agreement to make use of arbitration in the public works contract.

6. PROCEDURE.—Every such claimant who has not been paid in full before the expiration of a period of 90 days after the date on which the last of the labor was done or performed by him or materials were furnished or supplied by him for which such claim is made, has the right to sue on such payment bond for the amount, or the balance thereof, unpaid at the time of institution of said suit in the name of such claimant together with a reasonable attorney's fee to be fixed by the court, provided, however, that any such claimant having a direct contractual relationship with subcontractor of the contractor furnishing such payment bond but no contractual relationship, express or implied, with such contractor must give the 90-day written notice referred to in section 3(b) above.

This notice is required to state with substantial accuracy the amount claimed and the name of the party to whom the material was furnished or supplied for which the labor was done or performed. "Such notice shall be served by registered or certified mail, postage prepaid, in an envelope addressed to the contractor at any place he maintains an office or conducts his business or at his residence."

The contracting body is required to furnish, to anyone making written application therefor who states that he has supplied labor or material for such work and payment therefor has not been made or that he is being sued on such bond or that it is the surety thereon, a certified copy of such bond and the contract for which it was given, which copy is *prima facie* evidence of the contents, execution and delivery of the original.

7. PENALTY FOR FAILURE TO TAKE BOND.—No statutory provision.

8. SPECIAL PROVISIONS.—Such payment bond is required before any contract is executed for the construction, alteration, or repair of any public building, public work or improvement of the state or any county, city or town, or officer, board or commission thereof, and irrigation, power, electrical, drainage and flood control districts, tax levying public improvement districts, and county or city improvement districts.

Each such bond is required to include a provision allowing the prevailing party in a suit on the bond to recover such reasonable attorney's fees as may be fixed by the court.

Another section provides that it shall be illegal for the invitation for bids, or any person acting or purporting to act on behalf of the contracting body, to require that such bonds be furnished by a particular insurance company, or through a particular agent or broker.

This new article does not apply to contracts awarded pursuant to any invitation for bids issued on or before the effective date of this new article.

No construction contract may be awarded by any political subdivision of the state for new buildings or improvements within a two mile radius of the state capitol building without a request for permission from, and written approval by, the Governor.

An act approved June 6, 1977 provided that the State Board of Education shall adopt rules prescribing uniform and competitive bidding, contracting and purchasing practices for all school districts in the state. Effective July 23, 1982, a cash bond may be provided in lieu of a surety bond as required for any budget units.

Effective April 12, 1983, dealing with contract bonds relating to county improvement contracts (amends section 11-723 of the Revised Statutes) to newly provide that, if that the board of directors finds that the contractor is unable to continue with the work or to perform the work according to the contract, they may hold the contractor in default and make demand on the surety to act in accordance with the contract and terms of the performance bond. If the surety fails to act within sixty days of receiving written notice, the board of directors may order that bids be received from other contractors to complete the work. Work will be awarded to the lowest responsible bidder. If cost to complete work exceeds the monies or bonds available for payment, the board of directors shall make a demand on the defaulting contractor's bondsman for payment of the difference within twenty days of the mailing of the notice. The demand may not exceed the penal sum of the performance bond.

9. DECISIONS.—A bond required in connection with the contractor's license bond statute was construed to cover a claim for rental of equipment leased to a licensed contractor. *Arizona Gunite Builders, Inc. v. Continental Cas Co.*, 105 Ariz. 99, 459 P.2d 724 (1969).

"Subcontractor" contrasted to "materialman" as to remoteness of proper payment bond claimant. *Tiffany Construction Co. v. Hancock & Kelley Construction Co.*, 24 Ariz. App. 504, 539 P.2d 978 (ct. App. 1975).

Absent any direct contractual relationship between general contractor and second crane lessor which furnished crane to first crane lessor for use on contractor's project, second crane lessor had no claim on bond obtained by general contractor pursuant to bonding statutes and was not entitled to recover as supplier of material and labor to general contractor. *Advance Leasing and Crane Co. v. Del E. Webb Corp.*, 117 Ariz. 451, 573 P.2d 525 (1977).

General contractor may be liable to underpaid employees of subcontractor as third-party beneficiaries of contract but does not thereby become liable as employer for statutory treble-damage penalty; liability of surety on payment bond was limited by statute and terms of bond. *Rogers v. Speros Construction Co.*, 119 Ariz. 289, 580 P.2d 750 (1978).

Statute is to be liberally construed to protect those who furnish labor and material. *Norman S. Wright & Co. v. Slaysman*, 124 Ariz. 321, 604 P.2d 252 (1979).

Suit by second-tier subcontractor on high school construction contract, against prime contractor and surety on prime's performance and payment bond. On appeal by plaintiff from adverse judgment, held, reversed and remanded. (1) Violation of statute forbidding subletting of public contract to subcontractor who had not paid Arizona state and county taxes for at least two years did not render subcontract unenforceable. (2) Since parties concede there were no material issues of fact, plaintiff was entitled to judgment. *E & S Insulation Co. of Arizona v. E. L. Jones Construction, Co.*, 121 Ariz. 468, 591 P.2d 560 (Ct. App. 1979).

ARKANSAS

1. AMOUNT OF BOND.—A sum equal to the amount of the contract. (14 Arkansas Statutes Annotated § 604)

2. LABOR AND MATERIAL COVERED.—The bond shall be conditioned upon prompt payment of labor and material furnished in the prosecution of the contract to execute and deliver the contract.

3. NOTICE REQUIRED.—No special statutory provision except in connection with contracts for public works of school districts in excess of $30,000 which require public notice prior to receipt of bids.

4. TIME FOR SUIT.—Until six months from the date final payment is made on the contract.

5. CONTRACTS EXCLUDED.—Contracts under $3,000.

6. PROCEDURE.—No special statutory provision.

7. PENALTY FOR FAILURE TO TAKE BOND.—No special statutory provision.

8. SPECIAL PROVISIONS.—Suit may not be brought outside the State of Arkansas. The provisions of this amendment of 1957 are required to be read into the contractor's bond. Contract actions by a resident subcontractor, supplier or materialman against a prime contractor or subcontractor who is a nonresident of this State or who is a foreign corporation may be brought in the county in which plaintiff resided at the time the cause of action arose. A 1977 law states that when a performance bond is furnished, the contractor shall be entitled to payment of 90% of earned progress payments when due, with the public agency retaining 10% to assure faithful performance of the contract. All sums withheld by the public agency shall be held in escrow and shall be paid to the contractor within 30 days after the contract has been substantially completed. This act does not apply to contracts entered into by the State Highway Commission.

A law approved March 28, 1979 provides that whenever the laws of the State provide for the furnishing of a corporate security or surety bond, to assure financial security, the person, firm or corporation required to provide such bond may, in lieu thereof, provide such bond by furnishing certificates of deposit issued by Arkansas banks and savings and loan associations or direct general obligation securities issued by the State of Arkansas or any agency or instrumentality thereof, by any political subdivision of this State, or by the United States or any of its agencies, in the principal amount of not less than the amount of the bond to be provided.

9. DECISIONS.—Where the bond furnished a private owner by a contractor, executed in Arkansas, is on a form approved by the American Institute of Architects which requires suit to be brought within two years from the date final payment became due under the contract, and such a provision is violative of public policy of South Carolina where the contract was to be performed but was valid in Arkansas where the bond was executed, the Arkansas law was held to govern. *McCrary v. U.S. Fidelity & Guar. Co.,* 110 F. Supp. 545 (W.D. S.C. 1953).

Where there is nothing contained in the language of the bond conditioned for payment of materials furnished in the erection of a schoolhouse to indicate that it was intended to be a statutory bond and the bond provides for suit within a year, suit may be brought within the year notwithstanding the statutory limitation of suit to within six months. *National Surety Co. v. Standard Lumber Co.,* 186 Ark. 664, 54 S.W.2d 988 (1932).

The surety is liable for the price of pipe used in highway construction work, although pipe, after completion of such highways, could be used on other construction work. The pipe was necessary incident for supplying water to the concrete mixer and wetting down the concrete on the road surface after it was laid. *Detroit F. & S. Co. v. Yaffe Iron & Metal Co.,* 184 Ark. 1095, 44 S.W.2d 1085 (1932).

"Final estimate" means conclusion and determination by person having final authority. *Consolidated Indemnity & Insurance Co. v. Fischer Lime & Cement Co.,* 187 Ark. 131, 58 S.W.2d 928 (1933).

Final payment, within statute providing that no action shall be brought on surety bond after six months from date "final payment" is made on the contract, means the last payment. Hence, payment where the contractor received 95% of the contract price with a 5% retainage allegedly to protect owner with respect to minor claims and differences was not final payment within the statute. *Tucker Paving Corp. v. Armco Steel Corp.,* 242 Ark. 49, 411 S.W.2d 888 (1967).

Subcontractor may recover under a bond conditioned for the payment of labor and material claims although not filed in the Circuit Clerk's office. *Benton County Lumber Co. v. National Sur. Co.,* 179 Ark. 941, 18 S.W.2d 1017 (1929).

In suits under the Miller Act allowance of statutory penalty is to be determined by the State law. An Arkansas statute imposes a twelve per cent penalty on an insurer which fails to pay for loss within the time specified in the policy after demand therefor. The purpose of this statute is to reimburse a litigant for expenses incurred in performing a contract. The good faith of an insurer in denying liability is not a valid defense under this statute. However, this statute is highly penal and should be strictly construed. *United States ex rel. Magnolia v. H. R. Henderson,* 126 F.Supp. 626 (W.D. Ark, 1955). Here, an oil company which furnished a subcontractor with oil for use at the project, where the subcontractor and the surety refused to pay for the oil, was held entitled under Arkansas law to recover the twelve per cent penalty and attorney's fees from the surety.

A materialman may not recover on a bond of indemnity even though this bond incorporates by reference the original contract which called for a performance bond. *Employers Liability Assurance Co., Ltd. v. A. W. Johnson,* 234 Ark. 806, 354 S.W.2d 733 (1962).

A manufacturer which sold its material to a distributor who sold material to a subcontractor is not within the coverage of the contractor's statutory payment bond. *B. Sweetser Constr. Co. and U.S. Fidelity & Guar. C. v. Newman Brothers, Inc.,* 236 Ark. 939, 371 S.W.2d 515 (1964).

The surety on a contractor's bond not liable to the seller of tires where only a small fraction of the material required for the job was hauled to the bonded project in a truck owned by the contractor. *Proctor Tire Service Inc. v. National Sur.,* 242 Ark. 695, 415S.W.2d 45 (1967).

Effect of bond period of limitations different than statute of limitations. *City of Hot Springs v. National Sur. Co.,* 258 Ark. 1009, 531 S.W.2d 8 (1975).

Contractor principal held not to be an indispensable party defendant to an action against surety under a public works payment bond. *Jack Wood Constr. Co. v. Ford,* 258 Ark. 47, 522 S.W.2d 408 (1975).

Claimant under a payment bond was not entitled to recover statutory penalties and attorney's fees because the claimant was not entitled to recover the full amount sought against the payment bond surety. *Highlands Ins. Co. v. William Burris Masonry Contractors, Inc.,* 258 Ark. 694, 528 S.W.2d 405 (1975).

CALIFORNIA

The legislation commonly referred to as the "California Public Works Bond Act" will be found in the Government Code. This code incorporates by reference with respect to procedure certain provisions of the California Code of Civil Procedure. Unless otherwise indicated the abstract below refers to the California Public Works Bond Act. From time to time reference will be made to provisions of various codes which are not the same as those found in the California Public Works Bond Act.

1. AMOUNT OF BOND.—Every person to whom is awarded a contract involving an expenditure in excess of $25,000 for the improvement, erection or construction of any building, road, bridge, or other structure, excavating or other mechanical work for the state or any political subdivision or agency of the state is required, before entering upon performance of the work, to file a payment bond executed by either two or more good and sufficient sureties or by a corporate surety, in a sum not less than

  a. one-half of the total amount payable by the term of the contract where the total amount payable does not equal or exceed five million dollars;
  b. one-fourth of the total amount payable by the terms of the contract when the total amount payable is not less than five million dollars and does not exceed ten million dollars;
  c. if the total amount payable by the terms of the contract exceeds ten million dollars a bond in the sum of $2,500,000 is sufficient. (West Ann. Civ. Code § 3248 as amended)

2. LABOR AND MATERIALS COVERED.—The contractor's bond must provide that, if the contractor or his subcontractors fail to pay for any materials, provisions, provender or other supplies, power or teams, used in, upon, for or about the performance of the work contracted to be done, or for any work or labor thereon of any kind, or for amounts due under the Unemployment Insurance Code with respect to work or labor performed under the contract, or for any amounts required to be deducted, withheld, and paid over to the Franchise Tax Board from the wages of employees of the contractor and his subcontractors pursuant to Section 18806 of the Revenue and Taxation Code with respect to such work or labor, that the surety or sureties will pay for the same, in an amount not exceeding the sum specified in the bond, and also, in case suit is brought upon the bond, a reasonable attorney's fee, to be fixed by the court. A 1961 amendment provides that the contractor may require of his subcontractors a bond to indemnify the contractor for any loss sustained by the contractor because of any default by the subcontractor under this provision.

3. NOTICE REQUIRED.

(a) *To surety.* No specific statutory provision.

(b) *To principal contractor.* Within 90 days from the date on which claimant furnished the last of the labor or materials for which such claim is made, state with substantial accuracy the amount claimed and the name of the party to whom the labor or material was furnished. This notice is required by every claimant (other than a person who performs actual labor for wages or is a claimant under an express trust fund established pursuant to a collective bargaining agreement as described in section 3111 of the Civil Code) who has no direct contractual relationship with the contractor furnishing the bond.

This notice is required to be served by mailing the same by registered or certified mail, postage prepaid, in an envelope addressed to the contractor at any place he maintains an office or conducts his business or his residence or by personal service.

(c) *To Public Agency.* A claimant having no contractual relationship with the prime contractor other than a person who performed actual labor for wages or an express trust fund, and who intends to file a stop notice with the public agency concerned, and thereby cause the withholding of payment from the contractor for public work must give written preliminary notice to both the prime contractor and the public agency concerned within twenty days after having first furnished labor, services, equipment or material to the job site. Note, however, that Section 3250 of the Civil Code says, in regards to payment bond for public works: "The filing of a stop notice is not a condition precedent to the maintenance of an action against the surety or sureties on the bond.

4. TIME FOR SUIT ON BOND.—On a public works project, any claimant must file suit not later than six months from the time within he is entitled to file a stop notice. The stop notice must be filed within thirty days of the recordation of the notice of completion or cessation or, if no such notice is filed, within ninety days after actual completion or cessation of work. Section 3184 of the Civil Code.

The surety may waive this limitation as to the time for suit and where the surety has acted in good faith in so doing an indemnitor may not object thereto. *Fidelty & Deposit Co. of Maryland v. Whitson,* 187 Cal. App. 2d 751, 10 Cal. Rptr. 6 (1961).

Claims to the owner (formerly covered in Section 1190.1, Code of Civil Procedure) are now discussed only for private work.

The verified claim filed with the public entity (formerly covered in Section 1192.1, Code of Civil Procedure) has been transferred to the discussion of stop notice for public work in the Civil Code, and restricts filing of the stop notice to (a) within 30 days after the recording of a notice of completion, cessation, or acceptance, where such notice is recorded, and (b) within 90 days after completion or cessation where there is no notice of such.

Sections 3083 and 3086 (Civil Code) give equivalents of completion and define notice of completion, which verified notice must be recorded in the office of the county recorder of the county in which the site is located within ten days after such completion. For public works, the completion of such work shall be deemed to be the date of acceptance, and a cessation of labor on a public work for a continuous period of 30 days shall be a completion thereof, except for contracts awarded under the State Contract Act.

The California Public Works Bond Act provides for reasonable attorney's fees to be fixed by the court. One section requires such a provision to be included in the bond. The other provides that upon the trial of the action the court may award to the prevailing party reasonable attorney's fees to be taxed as costs.

The trial court has wide discretion in fixing attorney's fees and all elements bearing on the particular litigation should be weighed by the court in reaching its conclusions. *Independent Iron Works, Inc. v. Tulcre County,* 207 Cal. App. 2d 164, 24 Cal. Rptr. 361 (1962).

5. CONTRACTS EXCLUDED.—Under $25,000.

6. PENALTY FOR FAILURE TO TAKE BOND.—Unless the contractor's bond is filed and duly approved, no claim in favor of the contractor arising under the contract shall be audited, allowed or paid. Persons who have in good faith performed work upon the contract or supplied material for the execution thereof, shall receive payment of their respective claims in the manner provided by the Code of Civil Procedure upon giving verified notice by filing statements.

7. SPECIAL PROVISIONS.—The contractor's bond is required by its terms to insure to the benefit of any persons named in Section 3181 of the Civil Code so as to give a right of action to such persons or their assigns in any suit brought upon the bond. This statute lists mechanics, materialmen, contractors, subcontractors, lessors of equipment, artisans, architects, registered engineers, licensed land surveyors, machinists, builders, teamsters and draymen, and all persons and laborers of every class performing labor upon or bestowing skill or other necessary services on, or furnishing materials or leasing equipment to be used or consumed in or furnishing appliances, teams or power contributing to a work of improvement except for an original contractor. A discussion of now-repealed Section 1192.1 of the Code of Civil Procedure, which formerly covered this topic, can be found in earlier editions of the manual.

Effective September 2, 1981, a letter of credit may be filed in lieu of the bond as required of subdividers by the city or county. A 1980 declaratory amendment exempts providers of architectural, engineering and land surveying services.

The State Contract Act applies principally to state contracts in excess of $5,000. It provides that every contract within its coverage shall provide for the filing of separate surety performance and payment bonds by the contractor, and that each such bond shall be in a sum equal to at least one-half of the contract price except as otherwise provided in Section 3248 of the Civil Code or the California Toll Bridge Authority Act.

The Toll Bridge Authority Act which is part of the Street and Highway Code provides that the Department of Public Works shall require of each contractor such bonds for the faithful performance of any contract or subcontract entered into pursuant to said chapter and for the payment of any labor, materials, or supplies used in, upon, for or about the performance of the work contracted to be done, fixing such terms and conditions, and in such amounts, as it deems to be for the best interest of the State.

The California Street and Highway Code provides in connection with contracts for removal or relocation of structures or contracts for leasing of tools or equipment for state highway purposes, that such contracts are not subject to the provisions of the State Contract Act (which State Contract Act defines project as including "the erection, construction, alteration, repair or improvement of any state structure, building, road or other state improvement of any kind" which will exceed in cost a total of $25,000).

The California Street and Highway Code provides that the above contracts for removal or relocation of structures or leasing of tools and equipment in excess of $2,500 shall be accompanied by labor and material bonds. The Department may require performance bonds when necessary. The advertisement for each contract shall state whether or not a bond shall be required. Where a performance bond is required, labor and material bonds are required.

This Street and Highway Code also requires a public works contractor's labor and material payment bond substantially similar to the contractor's bond required by the California Public Works Bond Act. It also provides that each person whose claim has not been paid by the contractor, or his subcontractors, shall have a first lien upon and against the assessments and reassessments and any bonds which may be issued to represent any assessment or reassessment, which lien may be enforced by action brought within three months after the date of the filing of the verified statement in the superior court of the county in which such work was done.

Any bond given pursuant to said title will be construed most strongly against the surety and in favor of all persons for whose benefit such bond is given. Under no circumstances shall a surety be released from liability from those for whose benefit such bond has been given by reason of any breach of contract by the owner and original contractor or on the part of any obligee named in such bond.

The Civil Code also provides that the filing of a stop notice is not a condition precedent to the maintenance of an action against the surety or sureties on the payment bond. An action on the payment bond may be maintained separately from and without the filing of an action against the public entity by whom the contract was awarded or any officer thereof.

Section 3267 added to the Civil Code October 29, 1971, applicable prospectively, reads that nothing contained "in this title" shall be construed to give to any person any right of action on any original contractor's private or public work payment bond described in Chapter 6, (private work) or 7 (public work) "of this title, unless the work forming the basis of his claim was performed by such person for the principal on such payment bond, or one of his subcontractors, pursuant to the contract between the original contractor and the owner."

8. REMARKS.—Effective January 1, 1983 Sections 14816 through 14818 of the Government Code, relating to the regulations of the purchase of Electronic Data Processing goods and services by the State, have been transferred to the Public Contract Code.

9. DECISIONS.—Since a decision can depend on the statute in existence at the time when the cause of action arose, and since there are so many California statutes dealing with the subject under consideration, an experienced local attorney should be consulted promptly.

Where suit is not commenced within the statutory period, claim on bond is barred. *Summerbell v. Weller,* 110 Cal. App. 406, 294 P. 414 (1930).

Bucket, elevator, scale, scrapers, pulleys, belts, etc., furnished for and consumed on a highway job were held to be material under public contractor's bond. Equipment which would ordinarily be entirely consumed on particular job for which it is purchased is protected by the bond, but the bond does not cover the purchase price of equipment useful on more than one job. *Young Macky Co. v. Cupps,* 213 Cal. 210, 2 P. 2d 321 (1931).

Charges for hotel equipment, such as dishes, food for operating hotel, and for contractor's equipment, such as small tools and coal, consumed by highway contractor, held recoverable against surety on the bond. In this case, recovery was allowed for supplies to mess-house, although there were transients accommodated their amounting to less than 1% of the operation of the mess-house. *McCormack Saeltzer Co. v. Haidlen,* 119 Cal. App. 96, 6 P.2d 255 (1931).

A person furnishing labor or materials has both a right of action on the surety bond and a right to enforce a lien on the moneys due the contractor. These remedies are not exclusive and one is not waived when the other is exercised. *Sunset Lumber Co. v. Smith,* 95 Cal. App. 307, 272 P. 1068 (1928).

A contractor's agreement with the Government and public works bond did not obligate the contractor or its surety to pay a materialman for materials furnished a subcontractor to be used in mixing concrete which the subcontractor was selling to the contractor at a fixed price. *A. Farnell Blair Co. v. Hollywood State Bank,* 102 Cal. App. 2d 418, 227 P. 2d 529 (1951).

Recovery was allowed plastering subcontractor against general contractor and its surety for extra work done at request of general contractor. *C. F. Bolster Co. v. J. C. Boespflug Co.* 167 C.A.2d 143, 330 P.2d 83 (1958).

The California Department of Public Works may not dispense with payment bonds in connection with toll bridges and their approaches. *S & C Electric Co. vs. Fidelity and Casualty Co. of New York,* 205 F. Supp. 901. (N.D. CAl. 1962)

Supplier who had direct contractual relationship with contractor, engaged in constructing sewer for sanitary district, was not required to give notice to contractor as condition precedent to maintaining direct cause of action on the contractor's payment bond. *The Duncanson-Harrelson Co. vs. Travelers Indemnity Company,* 209 Cal. App. 2d 62, 25 Cal. Rptr. 718 (1962).

A prime contractor has sufficient notice of the claim of a supplier under a subcontract as to permit the supplier to sue on the prime contractor's statutory bond where the supplier's credit manager served on the prime contractor's agent a schedule showing the amount owing by subcontractor for the supplies and the agent forwarded the notice to the prime contractor. *California Electric Supply Co. v. United Pacific Life Insurance Co.* 227 Cal. App. 2d 138, 38 Cal. Rptr. 479 (1964).

The execution by a sub-subcontractor of a lien waiver did not estop this claimant from suing the surety of the prime contractor for amount due and did not constitute a release of the sub-subcontractor's claim against the bond where the waiver did not mention the surety and was given at the request of the prime contractor made through the subcontractor. *Bonded Products Co. v. R. C. Gallyon Construction Co.* 228 Cal. App. 2d 186, 39 Cal. Rptr. 347 (1964).

Where supplier served on prime contractor's agent a schedule showing amount owing by subcontract for the supplies and the agent forwarded that notice to the prime contractor, the prime contractor had sufficient notice of supplier's claim to permit the supplier to sue under the statutory bond prescribed by the Public Works Act. *California Electric Supply Co. v. United Pacific Life Insurance Co.,* 227 Cal. App. 2d 186, 38 Cal. Rptr. 479 (1964).

A supplier of material to a subcontractor on a subcontractor's bond which required "any claimant" to sue within a year may not recover in an action brought over three years after the subcontractor ceased work despite the fact that this supplier did not learn of the existence of the bond until one month before suit. The year limitation was not restricted merely to the contracting parties, it bound third party beneficiary as well. *Sanders v. American Casualty Company of Reading,* 269 Cal. App. 2d 306, 74 Cal. Rptr. 634 (1969).

In a case of local government contracts, limitations as to a suit on the bond and as a claim on stop notice runs from completion of the entire project, rather than from the date of performance of the claimant. *Consolidated Electric Distributors, Inc. v. Kirkham, Chaon & Kirkham, Inc.,* 18 Cal. App. 3d 54, 95 Cal. Rptr. 673 (1971).

Where the bonded contract called for completion of contract within 12 months, and the public body obligee did not grant extensions, cause of action occurred after the expiration of 12 months. It having been more than four years (California's general statute of limitations' prescribed time period) since the expiration of the 12 months, the California Court of Appeals held for the surety, rejecting the public body obligees' argument of surety's continuing obligation. *Los Angeles v. Security Insurance Co.,* 52 Cal. App. 3d 808, 125 Cal. Rptr. 701 (1975).

Where equipment rented by contractor was provided on a 3-month minimum basis, the fee for the three months was awarded despite the equipment's having been unused for one month due to disagreement between contractor and city. *John A. Artukovich Sons v. American Fidelity Fire Insurance Co.,* 72 Cal. App. 3d 940, 140 Cal. Rptr. 434 (1977).

The court has held to a four-year limitation on discovering defects, rather than the ten-years-past-completion limit (valid for the contractor but not the surety) and allowed suit against surety. The statute's notification requirement was met by a sub-subcontractor's timely stop notice to school district and the district's subsequent correspondence with the prime contractor and the surety. *Fidelity Sound Systems v. American Bonding Co.,* 85 Cal. App. 3d Supp. 13, 149 Cal. Rptr. 674 (1978).

Suit by materialman on school construction project, against school district owner, subcontractor who ordered materials, and surety on prime contractor's payment bond. On appeal by owner from judgment against it, held, reversed. (1) Where stop notice had been served by materialman, and prime filed release bond, school district was not liable for releasing funds to prime. Materialman should have proceeded against release bonds, which was substituted for the stopped funds. (2) Fact that materialman's dispute was with subcontractor, and that release bond was furnished by prime contractor and did not name subcontractor as principal, does not change the result. *Cal-Pacific Materials Co. v. Redondo Beach City School Dist.,* 94 Cal. App. 3d 652, 156 Cal. Rptr. 590 (1979).

One who contracts directly with the owner is an "original contractor" within the meaning of the provisions of this statute specifying the time for filing his claim of lien. *Scott, Blake & Wynne v. Summit Ridge Estate, Inc.,* 251 Cal. App. 347, 59 Cal. Rptr. 587 (1967).

Subcontractor's time to file mechanic's lien for improvement of lots or tracts which is subject to acceptance by public or governmental authority, commences on date of acceptance by the authority. *Southwest Paving Co. v. Stone Hills,* 206 Cal. App. 548, 24 Cal. Rptr. 48 (1962).

Where the completion notice was not properly signed and did not disclose the name of the general contractor, the notice was ineffective to reduce the period for recording claim of lien from 90 days to 30 days. A subcontractor who filed prelien notice and recorded his mechanic's lien within 90 days after completion of the project was held entitled to foreclose his lien. *Howell v. Gunderson,* 250 Cal. App. 2d Supp. 961, 58 Cal. Rptr. 553 (Super. Ct. 1967).

A notice of completion filed by an owner before actual completion of the improvement is premature. *Scott, Blake & Wynne v. Summit Ridge Estates, Inc.,* 251 Cal. App. 2d 347, 59 Cal. Rptr. 587 (1967).

COLORADO

The Colorado Code includes a statute which provides that every contractor to whom is awarded a contract for more than $50,000 for the construction, repair of public work for the state or any political subdivision thereof, before entering upon the performance of the work shall execute and deliver a surety bond in a penal sum for not less than one-half of the contract price conditioned for the faithful performance of the contract and payment of labor and material as is hereinafter abstracted. In addition, the Construction Bidding for Public Projects Act of 1981 requires public bidding for contracts over $50,000. A law approved on June 3, 1977 allows a certified or cashier's check or a bank money order made payable to the Treasurer of the State of Colorado or to the treasurer or other officer designated by the governing body of the contracting local government to be accepted in lieu of a bond. In addition a separate provision applicable to counties, cities, towns or school districts requires a payment bond which latter statute will be described under Subdivision 8 hereof, Special Provisions. The statute first above mentioned will now be abstracted.

1. AMOUNT OF BOND.—Not less than one-half of the contract price. (38 Colorado Revised Statutes § 26-105)

2. LABOR AND MATERIAL COVERED.—Labor, materials, team hire, sustenance, provisions, provender, or other supplies used or consumed by contractor or his subcontractor in or about the performance of the public work.

3. NOTICE REQUIRED.—(a) *To surety*—No special statutory provision. (b) *To principal contractor*—No special statutory provision. (c) *To municipality*—Affidavit; see Procedure below. (d) *To creditors*—No special statutory provision.

4. TIME FOR SUIT.—Within six months after the completion of the public work and not afterwards. The Supreme Court of Colorado in *General Electric Company v. Webco Construction Co.,* 164 Colo. 232, 433 P.2d 760 (1967) reviewed the Colorado statutes and concludes that this six months limitation applies to contracts regardless of the amount thereof.

5. CONTRACTS EXCLUDED.—Less than $50,000.

6. PROCEDURE.—Person furnishing labor or material to contractor or subcontractor, at any time up to and including the time of final settlement for the work contracted to be done, which final settlement shall be duly advertised at least ten days prior thereto in the county or counties, where the work was contracted for and wherein such work was performed, may file, with the official awarding the contract, a verified statement of the amount due and unpaid, whereupon such official shall withhold payments from contractor sufficient to insure the payment of such claim, until the same has been paid or the claim has been properly withdrawn. However, such funds shall not be withheld longer than ninety days following the date fixed for final settlement, unless an action is commenced within that time to enforce such unpaid claim and notice thereof is filed with the public body by whom the contract was awarded.

7. PENALTY FOR FAILURE TO TAKE BOND.—No special statutory provision.

8. SPECIAL PROVISIONS.—In addition to the statute abstracted above, a separate code provision requires any person entering into a contract for more than $50,000 with any county, city, town or school district for the construction or repair of any public building or public work, before commencing work, to execute in addition to all bonds that may now or hereafter be required of

them, a penal bond conditioned that such contractor shall at all times promptly make payments of all amounts lawfully due to all persons supplying or furnishing him or his subcontractors with labor or material used or performed in the prosecution of the work provided for in such contract. Such claimants have a right of action directly against the principal and surety on such bond and such action must be brought within six months after the completion of the work and not afterwards.

Notwithstanding the monetary qualification, the governing body of any county, city, town, or school district determining it to be in the best interest of the county, city, town, or school district may require the execution of a penal bond for any contract of $50,000 or less.

The respective code provisions have been clarified in *General Electric Company v. Webco Construction Co.* See subsection 4 above.

No public servant shall, directly or indirectly, require or direct a bidder on any public building or construction contract which is about to be or has been competitively bid, to obtain any surety bond or contract of insurance required in such bid, contract, or by any law, ordinance or regulation, from a particular insurer, agent or broker. A public servant does maintain the right to approve or reject a surety bond or contract of insurance as to form, sufficiency, or the lack of financial capability of an insurer selected by a bidder. This section shall apply only to contracts entered into on or after July 1, 1977.

9. DECISIONS.—Recovery may be had for hay and automobile truck repairs under a bond given in connection with a grading and paving contract. *Stryker v. Toliver & Kinney Mercantile Co.*, 77 Colo. 347, 236 P. 993 (1925).

Recovery may be had for hay and automobile truck repairs under a bond given in connection with a grading and paving contract. *Stryker v. Toliver & Kinney Mercantile Co.*, 77 Colo. 347, 236 P. 993 (1925).

The statute providing that within 90 days after date for final settlement under public improvement contract, one whose claims have not been paid "may" commence action against surety on contractor's bond, is merely "permissive" and not "mandatory," and creates a lien for 90 days on funds held by contracting board without barring action on the bond. *Continental Casualty Co. v. Rio Grande Fuel Co.*, 108 Colo. 472, 119 P. 2d 618 (1941).

A general contractor's items of work, on a small matter requiring completion or correction after inspection of sewage plant and after plant was in operation, was deemed not insubstantial, for purpose of computing limitation on supplier's action on statutory payment bond. *Hensel Phelps Construction Co. v. General Sign Corporation*, 460 F.2d 109 (10th Cir. 1972).

The principal contractor is required to furnish a performance bond where previously a bond for prompt payment of suppliers and materialmen was deemed sufficient. Permits a direct action by a supplier against the principal and the surety. *Fulton v. Coppco, Inc.*, 407 F.2d 611 (10th Cir. 1969).

A bond legally delivered but not signed by the principal is held to be effective against the surety. *Tanco, Inc. v. Houston General Insurance Co.*, 38 Colo. App. 133, 555 P.2d 1164 (1976).

A subcontractor is one contracting with principal contractor or another contractor to perform a substantial, specified portion of a public works contract. Supplier to materialman is not entitled to protections of contractor's bond and payment withholding statutes. *Lovell Clay Products Co. v. Statewide Supply Co.*, 41 Colo. App. 166, 580 P.2d 1278 (1978).

Where surety agreement provides that principal and surety will be directly and severally liable, creditor may, at his option, bring action against both principal and surety or either one alone. *Fountain Sand and Gravel Co. v. Chilton Construction Co.*, 40 Colo. App. 363, 578 P.2d 664 (1978).

CONNECTICUT

1. AMOUNT OF BOND.—In the amount of the contract. (49 C.G.S.A. § 41)

2. LABOR AND MATERIAL COVERED.—Labor and materials in the prosecution of the work provided for in contract for the construction, alteration or repair of any public building or public work of the State or any subdivision thereof. The word "material" includes the rental of equipment used in the prosecution of such work.

3. NOTICE REQUIRED.—(a) *To surety:* No special statutory provision. (b) *To principal contractor:* Any person having direct contractual relationship with a subcontractor but no contractual relationship, express or implied, with the contractor must give written notice to such contractor within ninety days from the date on which such person performed the last of the labor or furnished or supplied the last of the material for which claim is made, stating with substantial accuracy the amount claimed and the name of the party to whom said material was furnished or supplied or for whom said labor was done or performed. Such notice shall be served by mailing the same by registered mail, postage prepaid, in an envelope addressed to the contractor at any place he maintains

STATE BOND LAWS 31-13

an office or conducts his business or at his residence. (c) *To municipality:* No special statutory provision. (d) *To creditors:* No special statutory provision.

4. TIME FOR SUIT.—No suit shall be commenced after the expiration of one year after the day on which the last of the labor was performed or materials were supplied by the claimant.

5. CONTRACTS EXCLUDED—Less than $1,000.

6. PROCEDURE.—Suit must be brought in the Superior Court of the county in which the contract was to be performed, regardless of the amount in controversy. Each agency of the state or of any subdivision thereof, in charge of the construction, alteration or repair of any public building or public work of the state or of any subdivision thereof, shall furnish, to any person making application therefor who submits an affidavit that he has supplied labor or materials for such work and payment therefor has not been made or that he is being sued on such bond, a copy of such bond and the contract for which it was given, certified by the administrative head of such agency, which copy shall be prima facie evidence of the contents, execution and delivery of the original. Applicants shall pay for such certified copies such fees as are provided.

7. PENALTY FOR FAILURE TO TAKE BOND.—No special statutory provision.

8. SPECIAL PROVISIONS.—If the contractor does not pay his subcontractors within 45 days after he is paid by the state or municipality, the subcontractor can send notice of claim by registered or certified mail. The contractor will be obliged, ten days after receipt of the notice, to place the amount claimed plus 1% interest in an escrow account. If the contractor refuses and litigation or arbitrations finds him liable, he will also be responsible for counsel fees and interest. A dispute between the contractor and any of his subcontractors, does not excuse the contractor from withholding payment from other subcontractors.

Effective October 1, 1982, any public works contract which is estimated to cost more than $25,000 must be awarded to the "lowest responsible and qualified bidder."

9. DECISIONS.—A supplier of material to a subcontractor may not maintain an action on the performance bond given by a highway contractor to the State Highway Department of Connecticut, as this performance bond was not written for the benefit of persons who furnished labor or material in the prosecution of the work provided for in the contract. The separate payment bond was plainly intended for the benefit of persons such as the claimant who furnished material or labor used or employed in the execution of the contract. *Long v. Ferris,* 196 Misc. 567, 94 N.Y.S. 2d 493 (Cty. Ct. N.Y. 1949).

The statute which authorizes the Attorney General to furnish to certain persons a certified copy of the contract and the bond for any public work, applies to municipalities, since the Attorney General is in a position to require the officers of any political subdivision to furnish to him copies of contracts and bonds for public works entered into by them in behalf of their municipalities. *City of Norwalk v. Daniele,* 143 Conn. 85, 119 A.2d 732 (1955).

The Little Miller Act of Connecticut has been construed in *International Harvester v. L. G. DeFelice & Son, Inc.,* 151 Conn. 325, 197 A. 2d 638 (1964) Conn. to allow recovery for material substantially consumed or expected to be so consumed within the period of the contract but not for capital equipment.

The similarity between the Miller Act and the Connecticut statutes makes decisions of the federal courts, relative to the Miller Act, helpful in adjudicating the Connecticut statute. *International Harvester Co. v. L. G. DeFelice & Son, Inc.,* 151 Conn. 325, 333, 197 A. 2d 638; *Pittsburgh Plate Glass Co. v. Dahm,* 159 Conn. 563, 271 A. 2d 55 (1970).

The statute relating to surety bonds given in connection with government project must be read into the provisions of such bond, even where the bond's terms differ from the statute. A provision in the subcontract requiring suit to be brought in New York and not elsewhere was held unreasonable. *Johnson Acoustics, Inc. v. P. J. Carlin Construction Co.,* 29 Conn. Supp. 457, 292 A.2d 273 (Super Ct. 1971).

An attempt by materialman to recover against the city, in quantum meruit for materials supplied, where prime contractor furnished surety bond, was disallowed. *Kerite Co. v. City of Norwalk,* 32 Conn. Supp. 168, 344 A.2d 364 (1975).

DELAWARE

On July 16, 1963 Delaware adopted a statute for award of contracts for public works by State agencies. "Agency" is defined to mean any board, department, bureau, commission or officer of the State. This statute is abstracted as follows:

1. AMOUNT OF BOND.—100% of the contract price. (29 Delaware Code Annotated § 6909)

2. LABOR AND MATERIAL COVERED.—The bond is conditioned for the faithful performance of the contract and payment for labor and material. Every person furnishing material or performing labor under the contract may maintain an action thereon for the recovery of such sum as may be

due from the contractor. "Material" is defined to mean materials, equipment, tools, supplies or any other personal property but does not include electric, gas, water, telephone or similar utilities.

3. NOTICE REQUIRED.—No special statutory provision.

4. TIME FOR SUIT.—If the bond so provides, no suit shall be commenced after the expiration of one year following the date on which the successful bidder ceases work on the contract, otherwise suits may be commenced at any time within three years following the date the last work was done on the contract. See Special Provisions pertaining to this new statute.

5. CONTRACTS EXCLUDED.—Effective July 14, 1981, the threshold for bonds on contracts for public works increased from $2,500 to $10,000.

6. PROCEDURE.—The supplier may maintain an action on the bond for his own use in the name of the State in any Court of competent jurisdiction.

7. PENALTY FOR FAILURE TO TAKE BOND.—No special statutory provision.

8. SPECIAL PROVISIONS.—No person or surety in any action brought under this new statute or on the bond required thereby may assert as a defense to such action, the claim that the bond given pursuant to such statute contains a limitation or restriction not provided for by this statute. A 1975 act exempts the Delaware Reclamation Project from the contracting and bond requirements.

9. DECISIONS.—Where the contract expressly required the contractor to pay for all materials, labor, drawings and other items necessary to complete the work, held a subcontractor had a right of action on the contractor's performance bond. *Royal Indemnity Co. v. Alexander Industries, Inc. ex rel. Berger Acoustical Co.,* 58 Del. 548, 211 A.2d 919 (1965).

The labor of transporting materials to be used and actually used by a contractor on public work, regardless of the length of the haul, is labor within the meaning of the statute and a common carrier may recover under the contractor's bond for freight and demurrage incident to the transportation of such material, notwithstanding its common law lien for charges. The statute will be liberally construed. *State, ex. rel. Pennsylvania R. R. v. AEtna Casualty & Surety Co.,* 34 Del. 158, 145 A. 172 (1929).

Unless the form of bond is broader than that required by the statute, it would seem that liability is restricted to the payment of claims due subcontractors. Generally, the bond is conditioned that the contractor and his surety shall promptly pay all lawful claims of subcontractors, materialmen and laborers. Of course, a materialman may recover under such a bond. *Board of Education v. AEtna Casualty & Surety Co.,* 34 Del. 355, 152 A. 600 (1930).

Unless it be shown that lumber used for scaffolding could not have been used again as lumber, whether as scaffolding or otherwise, recovery may not be had for the lumber under a bond conditioned for the payment of labor performed and material furnished in carrying forward, a performing or completing of a public contract. However, recovery may be had for materials which do not become a component part of the physical structure, provided such materials have been actually or practically consumed or used up in connection with the completion of the work. *Board of Education v. AEtna Casualty & Surety Co.,* 35 Del. 100, 159 A. 367 (1932).

Thus, recovery may be had under a bond for fuel, lubricating oil and like supplies which are necessary for the operation of machinery and are consumed in the use thereof, but not for such supplies as wire rope for use in operating gas or steam shovels, ordinary shovels, pick handles and the like; labor performed in the repair of highway equipment or premiums on workmen's compensation insurance. *Warner Company v. Schoonmaker,* 20 Del. Ch. 165, 174 A. 449 (Ch. 1934).

One who furnished and hauled a large quantity of earth for a subcontractor and moved certain contract equipment for a subcontractor, may maintain suit on the bond given by the contractor to a Housing Authority conditioned that the contractor shall pay each person furnishing material or performing labor in and about the prosecution of the work provided for in the contract. *Wilmington Housing Authority, v. Fidelity & Deposit Company of Maryland,* 43 Del. 381, 47 A.2d 524 (1946).

Failure of equipment supplier to file claim on private work performance bond within limitation of one year stated in bond, fatal to claim. *Rumsey Electric Co. v. Burlington Electric Corp.,* 334 A.2d 226 (Del. 1975), aff'd 358 A.2d 712 (Del. Super. Ct. 1976).

Purpose of this bond requirement, in addition to protection for suppliers, etc., is to ensure full compliance with the terms of the contract. *State ex. rel. Christopher v. Planet Ins. Co.,* 321 A. 2d 128 (Del. Super. Ct. 1974).

The University of Delaware has full control of its affairs, including contract matters, as given by special law. Therefore the University follows the general statutory requirements in this section, but in a private capacity. *Rumsey Elec. Co. v. University of Del.,* 334 A. 2d 226 (Del. Super. Ct. 1975).

STATE BOND LAWS

DISTRICT OF COLUMBIA

1. AMOUNT OF BOND.—One-half of the total amount payable by the terms of the contract whenever the total amount payable by the terms of the contract shall be not more than $1,000,000. Whenever the total amount payable by the terms of the contract is more than $1,000,000 and not more than $5,000,000, the payment bond shall be in a sum equal to 40% of the total amount payable by the terms of the contract. Whenever the total amount payable by the terms of the contract shall be more than $5,000,000, the payment bond shall be in the sum of $2,500,000. (1 District of Columbia Code § 1104)

2. LABOR AND MATERIAL COVERED.—Labor or material furnished for the construction, alteration or repair of any public building or public work of the District of Columbia. See: *MacEvoy v. U.S. of America ex rel. Calvin Tomkins Co.,* 322 U.S. 102 88 L. Ed. 1163 (1944).

3. NOTICE REQUIRED.—(a) *To surety*—no special statutory provision. (b) *To principal contractor*—no notice is required by a person having a contractual relationship, express or implied, with the principal contractor. Any person having a direct contractual relationship with a subcontractor, but no contractual relationship, express or implied, with the principal contractor must give written notice to the contractor within ninety days from the date on which such person performed the last of the labor or furnished or supplied the last of the material for which the claim is made, stating with substantial accuracy the amount claimed and the name of the party to whom the material was furnished or supplied or for whom the labor was done or performed. Such notice shall be served by mailing the same by registered mail, postage prepaid, in an envelope addressed to the contractor at any place he maintains an office or conducts his business, or his residence, or in any manner in which the United States marshal for the District of Columbia is authorized by law to serve summons. (c) *To municipality*—no special statutory provision. (d) *To creditors*—no special statutory provision.

4. TIME FOR SUIT.—No suit shall be brought by a claimant after the expiration of one year after the date on which the last of the labor was performed or material was supplied by him.

5. CONTRACTS EXCLUDED.—$25,000 or less. The Commissioners have authority to require a performance bond or other security in addition to the performance and payment bond especially prescribed by the statute. No work capable of execution under a single contract, nor any purchase of material where the total expenditure involved is greater than $25,000, shall be subdivided or lessened for the purpose of reducing the sum of money to be paid therefore to less than that amount.

6. PROCEDURE.—The Commissioners are authorized and directed to furnish to any person making application therefor, who submits an affidavit that he has supplied labor or material for such work and payment therefor has not been made or that he is being sued on any such bond, a certified copy of such bond and the contract for which it was given which copy is prima facie evidence of the contents, execution and delivery of the original.

7. PENALTY FOR FAILURE TO TAKE BOND.—No special statutory provision.

8. PLACE OF SUIT.—United States District Court for the District of Columbia, irrespective of the amount of the controversy in such suit. Every person who has the right to sue under the payment bond may institute a separate action thereon in the name of the District of Columbia for the use of the person suing. The District of Columbia shall not be liable for the payment of any costs or expenses of any such suit.

9. DECISIONS.—Each creditor's rights are independent of those of other creditors. Each is able to control his own limitation period by filing his own suit within one year from the time he furnished the last of his labor or materials to the prime contractor. *Joseph F. Hughes & Co. v. District of Columbia ex rel. Noland Co.,* 413 F.2d 376 (D.C. Cir. 1969).

10. EARLIER DECISIONS.—Final settlement within the former statute is a settlement of the entire contract and all substantial claims arising under it and its performance. Hence mere determination of charges or credits or of amounts earned, without regard to charges or other claims or contingent liabilities, is insufficient. *U.S. Casualty Co. v. D.C. ex rel. North American Cement Corp.,* 107 F.2d 652 (D.C. Cir. 1939).

Where, after default under a contract for highway repair on March 27, 1934, a monthly voucher for work done prior to default was made up and checked, after which the District Commissioner directed retention of payment pending completion of the work, and on March 1, 1935, approved recommendation for return of the matter to the Highway Department for approval of voucher and payment, following which voucher was approved March 6, 1935, by Engineer and Director of Highways and sent to auditor's office, where it was approved March 22, 1935, when a check was drawn which was paid a week later, final settlement of the contract within the above statute was held to take place March 6, 1935. *U.S. Casualty Co. v. D.C. ex. rel. North American Cement Corp.,* 107 F.2d 652, 71 App. D.C. 92 (D.C. Cir. 1939).

Where a claimant had not been aware of pendency of another suit on bond of contractor for public work, and became aware of such fact after the expiration of a year, the District of Columbia Federal District Court had authority, in the exercise of sound discretion, to grant claimant leave to intervene nunc pro tunc, notwithstanding District of Columbia statute prescribing one-year period within which claimant's intervening petition must be filed. *District of Columbia v. American Excavation Co.* 64 F.Supp. 19 (D.D.C. 1946).

Even though under the contract the owners could probably have demanded of the contractor a combined performance and labor and material payment bond, it was held that laborers and materialmen could not recover on the indemnity bond which the owner accepted instead. The surety's obligation was measured by the condition stated in the bond. *Bevard v. New Amsterdam Casualty Company,* 132 A.2d 157 (D.C. 1957).

Where a Virginia contractor furnished a school board a bond conditioned for payment of labor and material claims which bond required a claimant to give written notice to any two of the following: the contractor, the owner or the surety, within ninety days after claimant furnished the last of claimant's labor or material, and no such notice was given by a claimant who had sold and delivered building materials to a subcontractor, judgment in favor of the surety affirmed. *U.S. Plywood Company v. Continental Casualty Co.,* 157 A.2d 286 (D.C. 1960).

The statute is to be liberally construed in favor of those who contribute labor or materials for public work and the bond covers a claimant who furnished piles treated with creosote. *Humphreys & Harding, Inc., vs. District of Columbia ex rel. The Joslyn Company,* 293 F.2d 150, 110 D.C. App. 311 (D.C. 1961).

Final settlement occurred not when the Director of the Department of Buildings and Grounds accepted all work performed under the contract but subsequently when he approved final voucher for payment owing contractor. *District of Columbia for use James McHugh Construction Co. v. B. F. Rodney Co.* 219 F.Supp. 192 (D.D.C. 1963).

Remote subcontractor could not recover on general contractor's labor and material payment bond where bonds limited class of proper claimants to those having direct contract with general contractor or with a subcontractor of general contractor. *Aetna Casualty & Surety Co. v. Kemp Smith Co.,* 208 A.2d 737 (D.C. App. 1965).

Language of letter sent from subcontractor's assignee to general contractor which referred to amount allegedly due subcontractor was too limited and too ambiguous to permit legal conclusion that general contractor's failure to respond to letter constituted not only agreement with figures in letter representing balance due subcontractor but also complete settlement of all claims arising from subcontract. *Wm. F. Klingensmith, Inc. v. District of Columbia ex rel. Reliance Insurance Co.,* 370 A.2d 1341 (D.C. App. 1977).

In respect to construction on the subway line, the demolition subcontract between prime contractor and subcontractor did not incorporate the prime contract disputes clause by reference, since, in the absence of express contractual language, it could not be assumed that the subcontractor intended to forfeit or condition its right to recover on payment bond. *Washington Metropolitan Area Transit Auth. ex rel. Noralo Corp. v. Norair Engineering Corp.,* 553 F.2d 233, 180 D.C. App. 88 (D.C. Cir. 1977).

FLORIDA

1. AMOUNT OF BOND.—In an amount equal to the contract price. (12 Florida Statutes § 255.05)

2. LABOR AND MATERIAL COVERED.—Labor, material and supplies used directly or indirectly in the prosecution of the work by persons defined in Section 713.01: contractors, subcontractors, subsubcontractors, laborers, materialmen and professional lienors.

3. NOTICE REQUIRED.—(a) *To surety*—A claimant who is not in privity with the contractor and who has not received payment for his labor, materials or supplies, shall, within 90 days after performance of the labor or complete delivery of materials and supplies, deliver to the surety written notice of the performance of the labor or delivery of the materials or supplies and of the nonpayment. (b) *To principal contractor*—A claimant, except a laborer, who is not in privity with the contractor and who has not received payment for his labor, materials or supplies shall, within 45 days after beginning to furnish labor, material or supplies for the prosecution of such work, furnish the contractor with a notice that he intends to look to the bond for protection. A claimant who is not in privity with the contractor and who has not received payment for his labor, material, or supplies, shall within 90 days after performance of the labor or after complete delivery of all the materials and supplies, deliver to the contractor written notice of the performance of the labor or delivery of the material and supplies and of the nonpayment. (c) *To municipality*—Application

STATE BOND LAWS 31-17

to governmental entity having charge of the work. (d) *To creditors*—No special statutory provision.

4. TIME FOR SUIT.—No action or suit for labor, materials or supplies used directly or indirectly in the prosecution of the work of any subcontractor may be instituted or prosecuted against the contractor unless both notices referred to in sections 3(a) and 3(b) above have been given. No action or suit shall be instituted or prosecuted against the contractor or against the surety on the bond required by the statute after one year from the performance of the labor or completion of delivery of the materials or supplies. See DECISIONS below.

5. CONTRACTS EXCLUDED.—Effective April 21, 1982, the threshold for exemption from the bond requirement increased from $25,000 to $100,000.

6. PROCEDURE.—A 1977 amendment specifies that the suit on the bond is to be filed in the county in which the construction work is being done.

7. PENALTY FOR FAILURE TO TAKE BOND.—No special statutory provision.

However, a municipality is not liable for its failure to take a bond protecting subcontractors and materialmen. *I. W. Phillips Co. v. Board of Public Instruction of Pasco County,* 98 Fla. 1, 122 So. 793 (1929).

The provision in the statute requiring a bond for the benefit of laborers and materialmen be furnished before the commencement of work imposes a duty on the School Board in connection with the school structure to see that the contractor did not begin work until such bond was executed, posted and duly approved, and such duty gives rise to individual liability to one injured by failure of the board members to perform such a duty.

8. REMARKS.—The statute above abstracted had previously been amended effective July 1, 1971 to clairify that the construction may be for the State of Florida or any county, city, political subdivision or public authority thereof.

A 1980 amendment provides that the payment provisions of all bonds furnished for public work contracts shall, regardless of form, be construed and deemed statutory bond provisions.

For respective rights and defenses of parties under legislation prior to 1963, see: *Delduca v. United States Fidelity & Guaranty Company,* 357 F.2d 204 (5th Cir. 1966). See also: *Aetna Casualty & Surety Company v. Board of Public Instruction,* 195 So.2d 41 (Fla. Dist. Ct. App. 1967). *Mass. Bonding Co. v. Bryant,* 189 So.2d 614 (Fla. 1966).

9. SPECIAL PROVISIONS.—Work on school buildings is covered by a separate statute requiring the contractor to furnish both a performance bond for 100% of the contract price and a payment bond in accordance with the above-abstracted statute. A corporation contracting to do oiling work for a contractor constructing a road was held to be a subcontractor within the highway bond, and not a "joint adventurer," notwithstanding a provision in the contract for sharing of profits. *Tidewater Const. Co. v. Monroe County,* 107 Fla. 648, 146 So. 209 (1933).

10. DECISIONS UNDER FORMER STATUTE.

The statute authorizing recovery of attorney's fees in actions on insurance policies is inapplicable to suits on fidelity or surety bonds. *United Bonding Insurance Company v. International Bank of Miami,* 221 So.2d 20 (Fla. Dist. Ct. App. 1969).

A lessee of digging equipment who used equipment to remove marl from marl pit and delivered marl to road job site some seven or eight miles from marl pit was a "materialman" and not a "subcontractor," and hence, lessor could not recover for rental of equipment on the statutory bond for performance of State road work. *Troup Brothers, Inc. v. State of Florida ex rel. Meadows Southern Construction Co.,* 135 So.2d 755 (Fla. Dist. Ct. App. 1961), followed in *Duval County Hospital Authority v. Daniel,* 254 So.2d 830 (Fla. Dist. Ct. App. 1971).

A common law performance bond issued in connection with the construction of public works, but which was not furnished in accordance with and for the sole purpose of complying with the requirements of the Florida statute governing the bonds of contractors constructing public buildings was not affected by the time limitations for bringing suit as set forth in such statute. A suit by a materialman on such type of bond may be instituted within the five year time limitations prescribed by the Florida Statute of Limitations regarding suits on written contracts, not under seal. *United Bonding Insurance Co. v. City of Holly Hill,* 249 So.2d 720 (Fla. Dist. Ct. App. 1971).

A subcontractor's performance bond conditioned to reimburse the general contractor for all loss and damage general contractor might sustain by reason of default on the part of the subcontractor did not make a materialman, supplying material to the subcontractor a third-party beneficiary under such bond. *State of Florida for use Westinghouse Electric Supply Co. v. Wesley Construction Co.,* 453 F.2d 1366 (5th Cir. 1972) affirming 316 Fed. Supp. 490 (Fla. 1970).

Where a construction contract for a Florida apartment building required the contractor to provide payment and performance bonds, and the surety issued a bond purporting to protect against liens, the bond was construed and applied as a statutory bond on which a subcontractor could sue even though the subcontractor had not perfected a lien and the bond provided that no right of action should accrue for the use of benefit of any person other than the named owner and lender. *Houdaille Industries, Inc. v. United Bonding Insurance Co.,* 453 F.2d 1048 (5th Cir. 1972). The court distinguished *State of Florida for use Westinghouse v. Wesley Construction Co.,* 316 F. Supp. 490 (S.D. Fla. 1972) affirmed 453 F.2d 1366 (1972).

Where the bond given to a housing authority contained provisions more extensive than required by the statute, its terms were held to be sufficiently board, to extend coverage to damages for delay and negligent or intentional interference with subcontractor's performance. *Travelers Indemnity Co. v. Housing Authority of the City of Miami,* 256 So.2d 230 (Fla. Dist. Ct. App. 1972).

Sub-subsubcontractor's materialman was denied protection of prime contractor's bond as being too remote to be covered. *William H. Gulsby, Inc. v. Miller Construction Co.,* 351 So.2d 396 (Fla. Dist. Ct. App. 1977).

The bond statute's provisions of timeliness and required notice were not applicable where the bond furnished, in several ways less strict than the law prescribed, made no mention of the governing statute and did not set up time and notice limitations. *Southwest Florida Water Management District v. Miller Construction,* 355 So.2d 1258 (Fla. Dist. Ct. App. 1978).

In consolidated cases involving mechanic's liens, owners filed proceedings to discharge liens on the basis that a valid contractor's payment bond covered the claims involved. Trial court entered orders discharging five liens. Payment bond surety successfully moved to vacate the orders of discharge, and owners appealed. Held, affirmed as to 2 liens, and reversed as to 3. (1) Legal effect of the bond is to prevent perfection of a mechanic's lien against the owner's property. (2) Owners were entitled to discharge of 3 liens because of disclaimer, failure to answer owner's complaint for discharge, and in one case, establishment of the payment bond defense. (3) As to remaining 2 liens, where payment bond defense was controverted, discharge was improper. *Goldberger v. United Plumbing & Heating, Inc.,* 358 So.2d 860 (Fla. Dist. Ct. App. 1978).

Suit by materialman to subcontractor on shopping center construction project against prime contractor and its surety on payment bond and lien transfer bonds. Trial court dismissed claim on transfer bond and dismissed claim on payment bond for failure to join subcontractor. On appeal by plaintiff, held, reversed and remanded. (1) Existence of payment bond is defense to claim on subsequently furnished transfer bond, but should be raised by answer. Complaint claiming on the payment bond did not show existence of the defense and plaintiff is entitled to make inconsistent claims at pleading stage. (2) Subcontractor is not an indispensable party to claim on prime's payment bond. *Alpha Elec. Supply, Inc. v. F. Feaster, Inc.,* 358 So.2d 892 (Fla. Dist. Ct. App. 1978).

Owner of building sought to hold surety under construction performance bond responsible for alleged latent defects first noticed after statute of limitations for suit under bond. The Circuit Court for Orange County entered summary judgement in favor of surety, and owner appealed. The District Court of Appeal held that surety was not liable for payment, since latent defects complained of were not covered by bond once owner accepted building after architect certified substantial completion and since statute of limitations had run. *Fla. Bd. of Regents v. Fidelity and Deposit Co.* 416 So.2d 30 (Fla. Dist. Ct. App. 1978)

GEORGIA

1. AMOUNT OF BOND.—Total amount payable by the terms of the contract. (13 Official Code of Georgia § 10-1)

2. LABOR AND MATERIAL.—The use and protection of all subcontractors and all persons supplying labor or goods in the completion of the work.

3. NOTICE REQUIRED.—(a) To Surety—no special statutory provision. (b) To Principal Contractor—no special statutory provision. (c) To Municipality—no special statutory provision. (d) Creditors—no special statutory provision.

4. TIME FOR SUIT.—If Claimant is not paid before the expiration of 90 days after the day on which the last of the labor was done or performed by him, or material or equipment or machinery was furnished or supplied by him for which claim is made, he shall have the right to sue on such payment bond to enforce payment of his claim. Suit may not be brought after one year of the completion of the contract and the acceptance of the public building or work by the proper public authorities.

Every suit instituted under this section shall be brought in the name of the claimant without the public body being made a party thereto.

5. CONTRACTS EXCLUDED.—Less than $20,000.

6. PROCEDURES.—Every person entitled to the protection of the new separate payment bond who has not been paid in full for labor or material furnished in the prosecution of the work referred to in said bond before the expiration of a period of ninety days after the day on which

STATE BOND LAWS 31-19

the last of the labor was done or performed by him or material or equipment or machinery was furnished or supplied by him for which such claim is made, or when he has completed his subcontract for which claim is made, shall have the right to sue on such payment bond for the sums due him; provided, however, that any persons having direct contractual relationship with a subcontractor, but no contractual relationship expressed or implied with the contractor furnishing such payment bond, must give written notice to the contractor within ninety days from the day on which such person performed the last of the labor, or furnished the last of the material or machinery or equipment for which such claim is made, stating with substantial accuracy the amount claimed and the name of the party to whom the material was furnished or supplied or for whom the labor was performed or done. Notice may be served by mail or in any manner in which the sheriffs of Georgia are authorized by law to serve summons or process.

The official who has the custody of the bond is authorized and directed to furnish to any proper applicant a copy of the bond and the contract for which it was given, a certified copy thereof to be primary evidence admitted in court without further proof.

7. PENALTY FOR FAILURE TO TAKE BOND.—Title 95 of the Highway Code relating to roads, bridges and ferries was amended and revised and a Code of Public Transportation adopted by a bill approved April 18, 1973. This 1973 statute provides, in connection with the Department of Transportation and counties and municipalities that where the contract price exceeds $20,000, no construction contract shall be valid unless the contractor first shall give the performance and payment bonds required by the Act approved February 27, 1956. If the payment bond is not taken, the county or the municipality shall be liable for loss to subcontractor's laborers and materialmen as provided in Section 1706, Title 23, Code of Georgia of 1933 as amended for loss to them resulting from failure to take such bond.

8. SPECIAL PROVISIONS.—No public contract is valid for any purpose unless the contractor furnishes the bond required by the statute.

The municipality may require the contractor to strengthen his bond or to furnish a new bond, whenever the municipality concludes that the original surety is no longer proper or sufficient, and may determine the contract and complete the work at the expense of the contractor and his surety if such additional bond is not furnished.

A certified copy of the bond is admitted in evidence at trial without further proof.

A school district may maintain an action on a bond as trustee for the use of unpaid subcontractors and materialmen where the bond is conditioned for the payment of labor and material claims. *Union Indemnity Co. v. Riley,* 169 Ga. 229, 150 S.E. 216 (1929).

9. DECISIONS.—In order to recover against the county, the materialman must show that he sustained a loss by reason of the municipality's default. *West Green School Dist. v. People's Planing Mill Co.,* 42 Ga. App. 677, 157 S.E. 343 (1931).

Gas and oil furnished a contractor performing public work are materials for which recovery may be had under the bond. *Sinclair Refining Co. v. Colquitt County,* 42 Ga. App. 718, 157 S.E. 358 (1931).

Recovery may be had for rental of machinery under the statute which requires a bond conditioned "for the use of the obligee and all other persons doing work or furnishing skill, tools or machinery or material under or for the purpose of such contract." *American Surety Co. v. Koehring,* 44 Ga. App. 769, 162 S.E. 840 (1931); *American Surety Co. v. Corr Service Erection Co.,* 47 Ga. App. 295, 170 S.E. 325 (1933).

Bond conditioned for the payment of machinery covers the reasonable rental value thereof or purchase price thereof if such purchase price does not exceed the reasonable rental value of the machinery during the period of time required by the public work. *Moore v. Standard Accident Ins. Co.,* 48 Ga. App. 508, 173 S.E. 481 (1934).

The surety is liable for labor and materials used in incidental repairs to contractor's machinery employed in work, but not for machinery available for other work or major repairs involving a substantial rebuilding of the machinery. *Yancey Bros. v. American Surety Co.,* 43 Ga. App. 740, 160 S.E. 100 (1931). The statute in question not only protects persons doing work for or furnishing materials to the contractor, but also protects subcontractors and employees of subcontractors furnishing work or materials for the purpose of the principal contract. *Western Casualty & Surety Co. v. Fulton Supply Co.,* 60 Ga. App. 710, 4 S.E.2d 690 (1939).

While there may be recovery on a public contractor's bond for material and labor used in incidental and current repairs to the contractor's machinery, the claimant failed to show that all of the items for which claim was made were consumed in the work of construction. *Bremer, Inc. v. United Bonding Insurance Co.* 122 Ga. App. 183, 176 S.E.2d 633 (1970).

The purpose of statute requiring bond to be executed by one contracting to construct or grade a public highway is to protect those who furnish work tools, machinery, skill and materials in the execution of contracts for public works to which the mechanics' and materialmen's lien laws of the state do not apply. *Motor Supply Co. v. St. Paul Mercury Indemnity Co.,* 67 Ga. App. 236, 19 S.E.2d 737 (1942); *Whitley v. Bryant,* 59 Ga. App. 58, 200 S.E. 317 (1939).

Railroad's claim for unpaid freight and demurrage charges for shipments used in construction of state highway project is a claim for "doing work or furnishing skill, tools, machinery or materials" within statute, and contractor's bond given pursuant thereto, and a railroad may recover on such bond, notwithstanding it had a carrier's lien which it could have exercised by withholding delivery. *Sommers Const. Co. v. Atlantic Coast Line R. Co.,* 62 Ga. App. 23, 7 S.E.2d 429 (1940).

Where construction contract and contractor's bond required contractor to attach paid bills and affidavits that material and work had been fully paid for, to drafts drawn by contractor against obligee on bank, and provided that provisions of bond could not be altered without written consent of surety, and drafts drawn by contractor against obligee on bank, without attaching thereto such paid bills and affidavits, were paid, surety not consenting in writing to change in terms of payment was not liable to obligee. *Mauney v. Hartford Accident & Indemnity Co.,* 68 Ga. App. 515, 23 S.E.2d 490 (1942).

Premiums for workmen's compensation, employer's liability and other public liability and property damage insurance is not within the coverage of the public contractors' bond. *Seibels, Bruce & Co. v. National Surety Corporation,* 63 Ga. App. 520, 11 S.E.2d 705 (1940).

The statute providing that no action can be instituted on public contractor's bond after one year from completion of contract and acceptance of work by public authorities should be strictly construed and should not be extended to apply a limitation to a cancelled contract. *National Surety Corporation v. Wright,* 70 Ga. App. 838, 29 S.E.2d 662 (1944).

Although the contractor's bond statute authorizing suit on the bond after giving notice to prime contractor should be liberally construed, condition precedent of notice must be substantially complied with. *Brown v. Seaboard Surety Company,* 107 Ga. App. 820, 131 S.E.2d 776 (1963).

Ivey Construction Co. v. Southwest Steel Products, 111 Ga. App. 527, 142 S.E.2d 394 (1965), construing an A.I.A. form of payment bond given to a County Board of Education, states that the bond was given in compliance with Code 23-1705 without indicating when the bond was executed, holds that the provision in the bond that no action shall be commenced thereon without written notice by the claimant to the principal owner, or surety, was a condition unauthorized by the statute. Claimant sued as a subcontractor. Georgia rejects the notice requirement but holds bond valid. *Home v. Battey Machinery Company,* 109 Ga. App. 322, 136 S.E.2d 193 (1964).

Surety on subcontractor's payment bond which purported to include all persons furnishing labor, services and materials under or for purpose of contract between prime contractor and subcontractor was not liable to person who supplied labor and materials to subcontractor of subcontractor where subcontractor was not liable under contract to such supplier. *West End Tin Shop Inc. v. Broylis and Broylis,* 117 Ga. App. 11, 159 S.E.2d 774 (1968).

Where the last shipment of material to the job site by the materialman claimant was refused by the subcontractor, returned and placed in the materialman's warehouse, this item could not be the basis of a notice of claim. Notice with respect to prior materials was furnished too late. *Downtowner of Atlanta, Inc. v. Dunham-Bush,* 120 Ga. App. 342, 170 S.E.2d 590 (1969).

The prime contractor agreed to issue checks payable jointly to the sub and his materialman but the checks were deposited by the subcontractor without the materialman's endorsement and honored. Held, the arrangement as to the checks and their negotiation did not operate as payment to relieve the public works contractor surety and the materialman was allowed to recover against the contractor and his surety. *Insurance Company of North America v. Atlas Supply Co.,* 121 Ga. App. 1, 172 S.E.2d 632 (1970).

Actual knowledge or notice on the part of a contractor of account owing by subcontractor to a supplier of materials on public project does not dispense with the statutory requirement of written notice. *Porter-Lite Corporation v. Warren Scott Contracting Co.,* 126 Ga. App. 436, 191 S.E.2d 95 (1972).

The provisions in a subcontract which incorporate by reference the general conditions of a prime contract and explicitly provide that the subcontractor assumed towards the prime contractor those obligations which the prime contractor assumed towards the Authority in the prime contract, rendered the subcontractor subject to the provisions in the prime contractor requiring the parties to submit contract disputes to arbitration. The existence of the Miller Act does not call for following the rationale of the Miller Act under the above circumstances. *J.S. & H Construction Co., v. Richmond County Hospital Authority,* 473 F.2d 212 (5th Cir. 1973).

In action brought on a labor and material payment bond for materials furnished by plaintiff to a subcontractor, the language of the bond clearly indicated that the parties intended for those materialmen who supplied materials under contract with the principals "or with a subcontractor of the principal" to have a beneficial interest in the bond. *Robinson Explosives, Inc., v. Dalon Contracting Co., Inc.,* 132 Ga. App. 849, 209 S.E.2d 264 (1974).

Under payment bond restricting coverage to all persons doing work or furnishing skills, tools, machinery, supplies and materials under or for purpose of contract, loans made by a bank to contractor were not covered, and surety could not be held liable under its bond for such loans. *Travelers Indemnity Co. v. West Georgia National Bank,* 387 F. Supp. 1090 (N.D. Ga. 1974).

Ga. Code Ann. § 103-210 allows the obligee on the surety bond to recover in addition to its loss not more than 25% of the liability as a penalty plus all costs and attorney's fees in the event a corporate surety fails to commence performance of a contract of suretyship within sixty days after notice from the obligee.

In the case of *The Travelers Indemnity Co. v. Sasser & Company,* 226 S.E.2d 121, 138 Ga. App. 361 (1976), the Court of Appeals held that the obligee named in the bond is the only person that can recover the penalties and that a "claimant" on a payment and performance bond is not entitled to the same status as the "obligee" and cannot, therefore, recover the penalties provided by the statute.

Where the claimant's attorney gave notice to the bond surety, and the prime contractor, within the stated time limitations, the court proclaimed this sufficient notice. *Amcon, Inc. v. Southern Pipe & Supply Co.,* 134 Ga. App. 655 215 S.E.2d 712 (1975).

In a case where the surety had been declared insolvent, dissolved, and ordered liquidated, the ancillary receiver was not bound by default judgments ordered after the liquidation. *Short v. State,* 235 Ga. 394, 219 S.E.2d 728 (1975).

Rental on pasture land is not covered. *Chapman v. Argonaut Ins. Co.,* 135 Ga. App. 885, 219 S.E.2d 620 (1975).

A supplier whose contract included responsibility to periodically check installed equipment filed a timely claim preceding last required equipment check and within 90 days of last billing, although claim was more than 90 days after last shipment. *Fireman's Fund Insurance Co. v. Fischer & Porter Co.,* 143 Ga. App. 533, 239 S.E.2d 174 (1977).

A subcontractor's failure to be certified by state authority resulted in dismissal of his bond suit. *Metric Steel Co. v. BLI Construction Co.,* 147 Ga. App. 380, 249 S.E.2d 121 (1977).

Where prime contractor ceased work on state project, subcontractor could recover only for work it performed and not for lost profits, since the contract had no provision of lost profits. *Fonda Corp. v. Southern Sprinkler Co., Inc.,* 144 Ga. App. 287, 241 S.E.2d 256 (1977).

Where a city overpaid the contractor, relying on the architect's certificates of progress, surety was held responsible to city for excess payments. *Balboa Insurance Co. v. Fulton Co.,* 148 Ga. App. 328, 251 S.E.2d 123 (1978).

A materialman who supplied electrical goods to a wholesale supplier specifically for use on a bonded construction job was considered a subcontractor and protected by the contractor's payment bond. *Travelers Indemnity Co. v. Cleveland Electric,* 147 Ga. App. 653, 249 S.E.2d 624 (1978).

Where all work under contract with state highway department had been performed and the project had been accepted by the department, subcontractor's action on contractor's bond, filed more than one year thereafter, was barred by statute providing that no action on bond of public works contractor can be brought after one year from completion of contract and acceptance of the work by the public authorities, and this was so even though the state highway department had made final payment to contractor within one year prior to the filing of the action. *American Surety Company of N.Y. v. Ed Smith & Sons, Inc.,* 100 Ga. 658, 112 S.E.2d 211 (1959).

A county is liable to a materialman for loss which the materialman sustained through the county's failure to take the statutory bond from the highway contractor, even though the county gave the materialman notice that the county would not be responsible for the materials which he furnished to the contractor. *Eatanton Oil & Auto Co. v. Greene County,* 53 Ga. App. 145, 185 S.E. 296 (1936).

A materialman who accepts an order by the contractor directing the county to pay the materialman directly and executes a release to the county with respect to such material may thereafter sue the county for material subsequently furnished to the contractor and recover for the county's failure to require the contractor to furnish the statutory bond. *Eatanton Oil & Auto Co. v. Greene County,* 53 Ga. App. 145, 185 S.E. 296 (1936). However, he may not recover for the material furnished prior to the release. *Eatanton Oil & Auto Co. v. Greene County,* 181 Ga. 47, 181 S.E. 758 (1935).

A materialman's claim against a county for failure to exact the bond is barred where suit was not brought prior to the expiration of a year after the contractor's insolvency and the date on which the claim against the contractor originally matured. *Standard Oil Co. v. Jasper County,* 53 Ga. App. 804, 187 S.E. 307 (1936).

HAWAII

1. AMOUNT OF BOND.—Fifty percent of the contract price. If the contract is a price-term, open-end, or requirements contract under which the total amount cannot be estimated, the amount of the bond will be specified in the bid requirements. (9 Hawaii Revised Statutes 103-34)

2. LABOR AND MATERIAL COVERED.—All labor and materials furnished to the contractor and used in the prosecution of the work provided for in such contract.

3. NOTICE REQUIRED.—(a) *To surety:* no special statutory provisions: (b) *To its principal contractor:* no special statutory provision; (c) *To municipality:* no special statutory provision, except as set forth in subdivision 4 hereof; (d) *To creditors:* A creditor instituting a first suit must must give personal notice of the pendency of the suit to all known creditors. In addition thereto, notice by publication for at least three successive weeks is required to be given in some newspaper of general circulation in the State (county) at least once in each of three successive weeks, the last publication to be at least one month before the expiration of the five-month period hereafter referred to.

4. TIME FOR SUIT.—If the State starts suit the claimant must intervene therein. If no action is brought by the State within two months from the completion and final settlement of any contract, the claimant upon applying therefor and furnishing an affidavit to the superintendent of public works or other officer representing the State in the matter of such contract that labor or materials for the prosecution of such work have been furnished by him, and that payment therefor has not been made, will be furnished with a certified copy of the contract and bond upon which he is authorized to bring an action in the name of the State in the Circuit Court of the circuit in which the contract was to be performed and not elsewhere, for his use and benefit. This separate action by the claimant shall not be commenced until after complete performance of the contract and final settlement thereof, but must be commenced within four months after the performance and final settlement and not later.

5. CONTRACTS EXCLUDED.—Bond not required for contracts made pursuant to informal bids under § 103.22 Att. Gen. Op. 72-14.

6. PROCEDURE.—See Time for Suit, in the foregoing. Where an action has been instituted by a claimant, only one action may be brought. Any other creditor may file his claim in this action and be made a party thereto within five months after performance and final settlement, and not later. If the amount of the liability of the surety on the bond is insufficient to pay the full amount of all claims, then, after the State has been paid in full, the claimants who are interveners pro-rate the balance.

7. PENALTY FOR FAILURE TO TAKE BOND.—No special statutory provisions.

8. SPECIAL PROVISIONS.—The surety, after paying the claim of the State, may deposit the balance of the bond penalty in Court for distribution among proper claimants, and upon so doing the surety is relieved from further liability.

The term "final settlement" means the time when the contracting officer of the State shall publish notice that he has determined and certified as to the amount deemed by him to be due to or from the contractor after the work called for by the contract is fully completed (although full payment is not then made and the amount may be subject to change), which notice is required to be published in a newspaper of general circulation in the State printed and published in Honolulu or in the county in which the work was contracted to be performed.

On July 14, 1969, Hawaii enacted a statute which provides that the contractor's license board may require a specialty contractor to put up a surety bond in the penal sum of $2500.00, and may require a general contractor to put up a surety bond in a sum not less than $5,000, such bond to be conditioned upon the payment of wages to the employees of the contractor when due, giving unpaid employees a right of action on the bond in their own names, which wage claim should have priority over other claims and also conferring a right of action to any person injured or damaged by the wrongful act of the licensee.

These statutes apply with equal force and effect to all formal contracts entered into with a county, in which cases, the word "State" shall be construed to mean and include the county.

9. REMARKS.—The State of Hawaii requests that state and county agencies inform any contractor issued a public contract of the laws allowing the substitution of retainage with general obligation bonds and the benefit of doing so. 103-32.2 Hawaii Revised Statutes.

10. DECISIONS.—The bonding company which is surety on a contractor's bond in cases of contracts with the State is not liable on the bond to reimburse the State for payments made by the State to materialmen where the contractor has defaulted, since materialmen are not entitled to liens against public works. Nor can the State amend an action as the sole plaitiff upon such bond for the

recovery of the value of labor or materials supplied to the contractor in the prosecution of the work. *Territory v. Pac. Coast Casualty Co.,* 22 Hawaii 446 (1915).

A provision of contractor's bond that action on bond must be brought within 60 days "from the date on which said contract is completed" does not mean that time runs from substantial completion of the building, when there are defects to be remedied and amount to be paid remains undetermined because of the defects. *Honolulu Roofing Co. v. Felix,* 49 Hawaii 578, 426 P.2d 298 (1967).

IDAHO

Effective Feb. 17, 1965, Idaho adopted the dual bond system substantially similar to the Miller Act. (The former statute was reviewed in the 1968 and prior issues of the Credit Manual.) This new statute may be cited as the Public Contracts Bond Act and is abstracted as follows:

1. AMOUNT OF BOND.—A surety payment or performance bond in an amount to be fixed by the contracting body but in no event less than 50% of the contract amount. (54 Idaho Code 1926)

2. LABOR AND MATERIAL COVERED.—Construction, alteration or repair of any public building or public work or improvement in the State of Idaho or any political subdivision, public authority or public instrumentality thereof. Coverage was extended by an 1980 amendment to the renting or leasing of equipment.

3. NOTICE REQUIRED.—(a) *To surety:* No special statutory requirement. (b) *To principal contractor:* No notice is required by a person having a contractual relationship, express or implied, with the principal contractor. Any person having a direct contractual relationship with a subcontractor but no contractual relationship, express or implied, with the principal contractor must give written notice to the contractor within 90 days from the date on which such claimant performed the last of the labor or furnished or supplied the last of the material or equipment for which such claim is made, stating with substantial accuracy the amount claimed and the name of the person to whom the material was furnished or supplied or for whom the labor was done or performed. Each notice shall be served by mailing the same by registered or certified mail, postage prepaid, in an envelope addressed to the contractor at any place he maintains an office or conducts his business or at his residence. (c) *To municipality:* No special statutory provision. (d) *To creditors:* No special statutory provision.

4. TIME FOR SUIT.—No such suit shall be commenced after the expiration of one year from the date on which claimant performed the last of the labor or furnished or supplied the last of the material or equipment for which such suit is brought except that if the claimant is a subcontractor of the contractor no such suit shall be commenced after the expiration of one year from the date on which final payment under the subcontract became due. See also Subsections 6 and 7 hereof.

5. CONTRACTS EXCLUDED.—No special statutory provision.

6. PROCEDURE.—Every suit insituted on the payment bond must be brought in appropriate court in any county in which the contract was to be performed and not elsewhere, after the expiration of 90 days after the day after claimant furnished the last of the labor or material for which such claim is made.

The contracting body is authorized and directed to furnish to any one making application therefor who submits an affidavit that he has supplied labor or material for such work and payment thereof has not been made or that he is being sued on the bond or that it is the surety thereon, a certified copy of such bond and the contract for which it was given, which copy is prima facie evidence of the contents, execution and delivery of the original.

7. PENALTY FOR FAILURE TO TAKE BOND.—Any public body subject to this statute who fails or neglects to obtain the required payment bond shall, upon demand, itself make prompt payment to all persons who have supplied materials or performed labor in the prosecution of the work under the contract, and if such creditor has a direct right of action upon his account against such public body in any court having jurisdiction in any county in which the contract was to be performed and executed, which action must be commenced within one year after the furnishing of materials or labor.

8. SPECIAL PROVISIONS.—The prevailing party upon each separate cause of action shall recover reasonable attorney's fees to be taxed as costs.

Subcontractors who accept promissory notes from public works contractor and executed affidavits of payment at request of contractor were permitted to show that the notes were accepted as collateral where payment was made of the retained percentage to the prime contractor without receipt of the evidence by the municipality. *Minidoka County v. Krieger,* 88 Idaho 395, 399 P.2d 962 (1964).

The Idaho Housing Agency statute, by amendment effective March 27, 1974 requires the housing sponsor receiving a loan or its contractor to post "labor and materials, construction performance, surety bonds or make other assurances of completion in amounts related to the housing project cost as established by the agency's regulations, and to execute such other assurances and guarantees as the agency may deem necessary."

A law effective July 1, 1979 amends the section of the Public Contracts Bond Act which requires a performance and a payment bond of not less than 50% of the contract amount on contracts for problem works, to additionally provide that public bodies requiring a performance bond or payment bond in excess of 50% of the total contract amount shall not be authorized to withhold from the contractor any amount exceeding 5% of the total amount payable to the contractor as retainage. Further, the public body shall release to the contractor any retainage for those portions of the project accepted by the contracting public body and the contractors as complete within 30 days after such acceptance.

9. DECISIONS.—Recovery on the bond is not limited to labor and materials lienable under the mechanic's lien law in its application to private structures, but extends to all labor or materials that directly or indirectly contribute to the construction of the work, even though such materials do not actually enter into the permanent structure. Incidental repairs to machinery and truck for washing and conveying gravel for highway and construction work are covered by the contractor's bond. Clothing and tools not consumed or destroyed in the construction of the highway held not covered thereby. *People v. Storm,* 49 Idaho 246, 287 P. 689 (1930).

A highway construction contract and contractor's bond, securing payment for labor, materials and supplies, must be liberally construed as covering not merely labor and materials which are lienable under mechanic's lien law in relation to private structures, but all labor or materials directly or indirectly contributing to construction, including repairs, parts, hardware, gas, oil, servicing, labor and other similar items, but not tools or new equipment, unless actually consumed on job. *The State of Idaho,* ex rel *Modern Motor Company, Inc. v. H & K Construction Company, Inc.,* 75 Idaho 492, 274 P.2d 1002 (1954).

Crushing and stockpiling of gravel for some future use does not constitute "construction, alteration, or repair" of a public work within statute requiring a contractor's bond for such construction, alteration, or repair. *Rogers vs. County of Nez Perce,* 83 Idaho 467, 364 P.2d 1049 (1961).

A provision in a payment bond providing that no suit shall be commenced thereunder by any claimant after the expiration of one year following the date the contractor ceased work on said contract was enforceable so as to allow a subcontractor to institute suit on the bond within the above period, notwithstanding the statutory provision that no suit on the payment bond shall be commenced after the expiration of one year from the date on which claimant performed the last labor or furnished the last material, a period which expired prior to the time for suit as sanctioned in the bond. *City of Weippe v. J. R. Yarno,* 94 Idaho 257, 486 P.2d 268 (1971).

Where tire company furnished to public works contractor tires and anti-freeze and where the supply was essential to maintain in operational condition a front end loader used by the contractor on the public works project, the supplies were "materials" within Public Contracts Bond Act. *City of Weippe v. Yarno,* 96 Idaho 319, 528 P.2d 201 (1974).

Where public works contractor ceased work first or second week in November 1968 and suit for value of materials supplied to the contractor was not commenced until February 1970, one-year statute of limitations barred the action, notwithstanding that city did not hold the contractor in default of the contract until July of 1969. *City of Weippe v. Yarno,* 96 Idaho 319, 528 P.2d 201 (1974).

Portion of Public Contracts Bond Act of 1965 requiring a written notice of claim by subcontractor to contractor within 90 days after date the last of materials were supplied was inapplicable to claim by wholesaler which had direct contractual relationship with contractors. I.C. § 54-1927. *Consolidated Supply Co. v. Loyale Babbitt,* 96 Idaho 636, 534 P.2d 466 (1975).

Public works contract bond provision that "No suit or action may be maintained under the bond unless it shall have been instituted within two years from the date on which final payment under the contract falls due" extended time limit under Public Contracts Bond Act provision that action under bond must be brought within one year after date claimants supplied last of materials for which action is brought. I.C. § 54-1927.

Effect of bond period of limitations different than statute of limitation. *Consolidated Supply Co. v. Loyale Babbitt,* 96 Idaho 636, 534 P.2d 466 (1975)

Suit by supplier of concrete to subcontractor on state university construction contract, against subcontractor, prime contractor, and prime's payment bond surety. On appeal by prime contractor and surety from adverse judgment, held, affirmed. (1) Evidence supported trial court's finding that claimant sufficiently notified prime that prime was being looked to for payment. (2) Plaintiff should be granted attorney's fees on appeal. *Consolidated Concrete Co. v. Empire West Constr. Co.,* 100 Idaho 234, 596 P.2d 106 (1979).

STATE BOND LAWS

ILLINOIS

1. AMOUNT OF BOND.—Fixed by the official awarding the contracts. (29 Smith-Hurd Illinois Annotated Statute § 15)
2. PUBLIC WORKS.—Public work of any kind to be performed for the state or a political subdivision thereof.
3. LABOR AND MATERIAL COVERAGE.—Material used in such work and for all labor performed in such work, whether by subcontractor or otherwise.
4. NOTICE REQUIRED.—
   (a) To *surety*—No specific statutory provision.
   (b) To *principal contractor*. See 4(c) below.
   (c) To *municipality*. Every person furnishing material or performing labor, either as an individual or as a subcontractor for any contractor with the State or any political subdivision thereof, has a right to sue on the bond provided, however, that any person having a claim for labor or material as aforesaid shall have no such right of action unless he shall have filed verified notice of claim with the officer, board, bureau or department awarding the contract within 180 days after the date of the last item of work or the furnishing of the last item of materials and files a copy of the notice with the contractor within 10 days after filing the notice with the officer.

The claim shall be verified and shall contain (1) the name and address of the claimant; the business address of the claimant within the State of Illinois and if the claimant be a foreign corporation having no place of business within the State of Illinois, the notice shall state the principal place of business of said corporation, and in the case of a partnership the notice shall state the name and residence of each of the partners; (2) the name of the contractor for the government; (3) the name of the person, firm or corporation by whom the claimant was employed or to whom he or it furnished materials; (4) the amount of the claim; (5) a brief description of public improvement sufficient for identification.

The statute further provides that no defect in the notice shall deprive the claimant of his right of action on the bond, unless it shall affirmatively appear that such defect has prejudiced the rights of an interesting party asserting the same. This statutory provision with respect to defects in the notice of the subcontractor's claim does not excuse failure to file the timely notice.

5. TIME FOR SUIT.—The statute provides that no action shall be brought on the bond until the expiration of 120 days after the date of the last item of work or the furnishing of the last item of materials, except in cases where the final settlement between the public body and the contractor shall have been made prior to the expiration of the 120 day period "in which case action may be taken immediately following such final settlement, nor shall any action of any kind be brought later than six months after the acceptance by the State or political subdivision thereof, or the building project or work."
6. FORM OF SUIT.—The suit on the bond is required to be in the name of the state or the political subdivision thereof entering into the public works contract for claimant's use and benefit.
7. PLACE OF SUIT.—The statute provides such suit shall be brought only in the circuit court of the state in the judicial district in which the contract is to be performed.
8. PROCEDURES.—In the suit the claimant is required to file a copy of the bond, certified by the party or parties in whose charge such bond shall be, which copy shall, unless execution thereof be denied under oath, be prima facie evidence of the execution of the original.
9. PENALTY FOR FAILURE TO TAKE BOND.—No specific statutory provision.

A municipality is not liable to labor or material men for work done or materials furnished because of its failure to obtain the statutory surety bond from contractor conditioned on payment of claims for labor and material furnished for contractor. *Gunther v. O'Brien Bros. Construction Co.*, 369 Ill. 362, 16 N.E. 2d 890 (1938).

10. SPECIAL PROVISIONS.—The lien law of Illinois now gives subcontractors and persons who furnish material, apparatus, fixtures, machinery or labor either to the contractor or a subcontractor for a public improvement of the state or a political subdivision thereof a lien on the unpaid money, bonds or warrants due or to become due the contractor. *Chicago Pump Co. v. Lakeside Engrg. Corp.*, 296 Ill. App. 126, 15 N.E. 2d 929 (1938).

The claimant, before payment or delivery of such unpaid money, bond or warrant is made, must notify the official of the state or political subdivision thereof, whose duty, in the case of state work, is to let such contract, or, in the case of work for a political subdivision, is to pay such contractor, of his claim by written notice, furnishing a copy of such notice to the contractor. In the case of state work, the notice is required to be a sworn statement of the claim, showing with particularity the several items and the amounts claimed to be due.

The person so claiming a lien, within ninety days after filing notice with the proper official, must (1) commence proceedings, (2) notify the proper official of the state or political subdivision thereof of such action, and (3) serve appropriate legal papers on such official. In the case of state work, such suit must be commenced and papers served not less than fifteen days before the date when the appropriation from which such moneys are to be paid will lapse.

It is the duty of the official, after such statement has been filed with him, to withhold payment of a sum sufficient to pay such claim for the period limited for the filing of suit, unless otherwise notified by the claimant. Upon expiration of such period, the funds or other property are released to the contractor, unless suit has been instituted. An official violating the duty imposed upon him by the above statute is liable upon his official bond to the claimant serving such notice for the damages resulting from such violation.

The statute further provides that, for the purpose thereof, the word "contractor" shall include any subcontractor.

11. DECISIONS.—A subcontractor may recover on a bond conditioned that the principal shall promptly make payment to all persons supplying him with labor or material in the prosecution of the work. *Board of Education v. AEtna Indemnity Co.*, 159 Ill. App. 319 (1911). See also *Board of Education to use v. AEtna Casualty and Surety Co.*, 305 Ill. App. 246, 27 N.E. 2d 337 (1940).

Where the surety defends in good faith, interest will not be allowed in suit on bond. *Board of Education, etc., to use Floorcoverings Inc. v. Aetna Cas. & Surety Co.*, 305 Ill. App. 246, 27 N.E. 2d 337 (1940).

Where contract with Board of Education for erection of addition to school building provided that contractor should pay subcontractors, and condition of public construction bond given to board was that contractor should faithfully perform the contract and pay obligee all damages sustained by reason of any default of the contractor, and the principal contract was made part of the bond, a subcontractor was allowed to recover on the bond especially in view of statute requiring public bodies and officials in making contracts for public works to see that bonds are furnished by contractors which will protect materialmen and subcontractors.

The statutory period for suit, etc. commenced on the date of the claimant's last labor or material, rather than on the date of the last labor or material furnished on the entire job. *Board of Education, Northfield Township High School District, etc. v. Pacific National Fire Insurance Co.* 19 Ill. App. 2d 290, 153 N.E. 2d 498 (1958).

Subcontractor's timely letter to surety enclosing claims for material furnished was substantial compliance with statutory notice requirement as prerequisite to suit on contractor's bond. *City of DeKalb ex rel. International Pipe and Ceramics Corp. v. Sornsin*, 32 Ill. 2d 284, 205 N.E. 2d 254 (1965).

Suppliers to subcontractors are covered by the Illinois Payment Bond. *Housing Authority of County of Franklin ex rel. Smith-Alsop Paint & Varnish Co. v. Holtzman*, 120 Ill. App. 2d 226, 256 N.E. 2d 873 (1970).

Despite the broadness of the statute in describing materials covered, equipment rental recovery was denied in a reversal by the Illinois Court of Appeals where the specific bond mentioned only "repairs" on equipment, and not rental. *Board of Local Improvements v. St. Paul Fire & Marine Insurance Co.*, 39 Ill. App. 3d 255, 350 N.E. 2d 36 (1976).

The Illinois Supreme Court, reversing a lower court, upheld the exemption of construction bonds from a statute prohibiting self-indemnification. Surety was held responsible for injuries suffered at a construction site. *Capua v. W. E. O'Neil Construction Co.*, 67 Ill. 2d 255, 367 N.E. 2d 669 (1977).

This requirement of filing a verified notice of the claim is mandatory. *Board of Education, Northfield Twp. High School, Dist. No. 225, Cook County ex rel. of Palumbo v. Pacific Nat. Fire Ins. Co.*, 19 Ill. App. 2d 290, 153 N.E. 2d 498 (1958); *McWane Cast Iron Pipe v. AEtna Casualty & Surety Co.*, 3 Ill. App. 2d 399, 122 N.E. 2d 435 (1954). A subcontractor's timely letter to public works contractor's bonding company enclosing claims for material verified was held substantial compliance with requirements of this section as prerequisite to suit on the contractors' bond. *City of DeKalb for use of International Pipe & Ceramics Corp. v. Sornsin*, 32 Ill. 2d 284, 205 N.E. 2d 254 (1965).

In 1941 the statute requiring the public works contractor to execute the surety bond was amended to provide that each such bond shall be deemed to contain the provision that the contractor and sureties agree to pay all persons having contracts with the contractor, or with subcontractors, all just claims due them for labor performed or material furnished in the performance of the contract, when such claims are not satisfied out of the contract price, after final settlement between the public body and the contractor had been made. The question arose whether this amendment prohibited any suit on the bond until after final settlement had been made, even though the amendment did not in any way refer to the separate section of this statute which deals with the time for suit.

It was subsequently held that the two sections of the statute must be read together in order to get the true intent of the legislature and should be construed liberally in order to effectuate the remedial legislative purpose. *Chicago Housing Authority ex rel. General Bronze Corp. vs. U. S. F & G Co.,* 49 Ill. App. 2d 407, 199 N.E. 2d 217 (1964).

The statute gives a right of action to unpaid subcontractors and material men after final settlement even though they have not availed themselves of the provision permitting right of action on bond prior to final settlement if notice requirements are met. *Board of Education of Northfield Twp. High School Dist. No. 225 Cook County ex rel. Palumbo v. Pacific Nat. Fire Ins. Co.,* 19 Ill. App. 2d 290, 153 N.E.2d 498 (1958). This Northfield case also holds that the 120 day period for suit and the 180 day period for verified notice commenced on date of each claimant's last labor and material, rather than on the date of the last labor and material furnished on the entire job.

Where the contractor's bond provided for prompt payment of person supplying labor and material, the fact that final settlement between the School District and the contractor for work performed by the contractor for school buildings had not been made, did not preclude the plaintiff as supplier of electrical material to the contractor from bringing suit against the surety for the contractor. *Board of Education, Decatur School Dist. No. 61, Macon v. Swam,* 5 Ill. App. 2d 124, 124 N.E. 2d 554 (1955).

In a case construing the statutory provision that action may not be brought on a public works contractors bond later than six months after acceptance, held a resolution of municipality was not required for "acceptance," which occurred on final payment on engineer's certificate of completion and utilization of improvement by the municipality. *United City of the Village of Yorkville, Kendall County, ex rel. of James B. Clow & Sons, Inc. v. W. J. Lewis Construction Co.,* 48 Ill. App. 2d 463, 198 N.E. 2d 863 (1964).

INDIANA

1. AMOUNT OF BOND.—Total contract price, except in case of state highway, road and bridge contracts, where the bond must be in an amount set by the Highway Commission but not less than the total contract price. (5 Burns Indiana Statutes Annotated § 16-5-2)

2. LABOR AND MATERIAL COVERED.—Any labor or services performed or materials furnished or services rendered in the construction, erection, alteration or repair of any public building, work or improvement of any nature or character.

On April 23, 1975, the bond statute pertaining to highway contracts was amended to provide that the combined performance and payment bond should be conditioned upon the payment by the contractor and by all subcontractors for all labor performed or materials furnished or other services rendered in the construction of the highway.

3. NOTICE REQUIRED.—(a) *To surety*—On state highway, road and bridge contracts, a claimant is required, within one year after the acceptance of the improvement by the State Highway Commission, to furnish to the surety a statement of the amount due, and no suit may be instituted on the bond until the expiration of 60 days after furnishing such statement. (b) *To principal contractor*— No special statutory provision. (c) *To municipality*—See Procedure and Remarks. (d) *To creditors*— No special statutory provision.

4. TIME FOR SUIT.—Except in the case of state highway, road and bridge contracts, no suit shall be brought against surety until the expiration of thirty days after the filing of the verified duplicate statement, but action must be commenced within sixty days from the date of the final completion and acceptance of the public building or public work. In the case of state highway, road and bridge contracts, suit may not be brought on the bond until the expiration of sixty days after the furnishing of the statement of the amount due to the surety. Suit on such bond may be instituted at the expiration of such period of sixty days, but the suit must be commenced within eighteen months from the date of the final acceptance of such highway or improvement. See Remarks (Section 9).

5. CONTRACTS EXCLUDED.—No special statutory provisions except in the bond requirements on highway contracts effective April 3, 1975, the State Highway Commission may waive the requirement of the bond on contracts of $100,000 or less (amended 1979); provided, however, in lieu of said bond, the Commission may establish, by rules or regulations, such requirements as in its discretion are necessary to assure payment of subcontractors, suppliers and employees by the contractor.

6. PROCEDURE.—Except in the case of state highway, road and bridge contracts, every person who has furnished labor or material shall file, within sixty days after the completion of such labor or services or within sixty days after the last item of material shall have been furnished by them, with the public body entering into the principal contract a duplicate verified statement of the amount due and owing, and it shall be the duty of such public body to forthwith deliver to the surety or sureties on such bond one of said duplicate statements. The procedure with reference to state highway, road and bridge contracts is set out under Time for Suit above.

7. PENALTY FOR FAILURE TO TAKE BOND.—No special statutory provision.

8. SPECIAL PROVISIONS.—The provisions and conditions of the statute operate as and become a term of any public contract bond.

The failure of the public officer to deliver a copy of the verified statement to the surety shall in no way affect or invalidate the right of subcontractors or materialmen.

Effective July 1, 1980, a state agency, on contracts for public works in excess of $100,000, shall elect to (1) withhold no more than 10% until the work is 50% complete, and nothing thereafter; or (2) withhold no more than 5% until the work is substantially complete. It further provides that upon substantial completion of the work there are any remaining uncompleted minor items, an amount equal to 200% of the value of each item shall be withheld until the item or items are completed.

9. REMARKS.—The statutes of Indiana have been construed by its courts to provide that a claimant on a highway project has a choice of remedies. The claimant may, if he so desires, file his claim with the agents of the public body, the statute providing that it shall be the duty of the public body to withhold final payment to the contractor until such contractor has paid his subcontractors, laborers and materialmen but containing the provision that such supplier of labor and material must file with such public body within sixty days from the last labor performed, last material furnished or last services rendered duplicate verified statements of the amount due and owing. If the claimant exercises the right given him by filing the statements and thus impounds the money due the contractor, the claimant takes such right subject to the provisions of the statute limiting and fixing the time within which the action can be prosecuted against the surety on the bond. However, this right to impound the funds being optional, a claimant may maintain an action under the public works contractor's bond even though the claimant did not file its verified statement of claim with the public body within sixty days from the furnishing of the last labor performed or last services rendered, or proved that within the period of one year from the filing of such claim the claimant instituted the action on the public works contractor's bond. *Concrete Steel Co. v. Metropolitan Casualty Insurance Co.,* 95 Ind. App. 649, 173 N.E. 651 (1932); *Eagle Indemnity Co. v. McGee,* 92 Ind. App. 537, 175 N.E. 663 (1931); *Equitable Surety Co. of St. Louis v. Indiana Fuel Supply Co.,* 70 Ind. App. 75, 123 N.E. 22 (1919); *U.S.F. & G. Co. v. State ex rel Hale,* 71 Ind. App. 648, 125 N.E. 420 (1919).

10. DECISIONS.—A claim for gasoline and oil for trucks used to haul road material to highway project and used in the operation of machinery on road construction work was held within the contractor's bond. *Miller Constr. Co. v. Standard Oil Co.,* 205 Ind. 509, 185 N.E. 639 (1933).

Notice of claim for materials furnished for use in the construction of a state highway may be served on the contractor's surety either before or within a year after the acceptance of the highway by the State Highway Commission. *Fidelity & Casualty Co. v. Sinclair Refining Co.,* 94 Ind. App. 92, 156 N.E. 169 (1927).

A materialman may maintain a suit on a public contractor's bond which requires claims to be filed with the owner within the time and in the manner required by law, notwithstanding the materialman's failure to file such a claim with the public body within sixty days after the last item of labor and material was furnished. Such a claim must be filed with the public body only when the materialman seeks to impound the funds in the hands of the public body due the contractor. *General Asbestos & Supply Co. v. AEtna C. & S. Co.,* 101 Ind. App. 207, 198 N.E. 813 (1935).

Under statute contemplating acceptance of highway prior to payment of subcontractors or materialmen, acceptance on contractor's false affidavit that all claims had been paid did not affect rights of unpaid materialmen, except to commence running of statutory period for proceeding against surety on contractor's bond. *Kosmos Portland Cement Co. v. D. A. Y. Constr. Co.,* 101 F. 2d 893 (7th Cir. 1939).

Recovery may be had under the bond for prepaid freight for which a highway contractor agreed to reimburse a materialman. *Metropolitan Casualty Insurance Co. v. Natural Rock Asphalt Co.,* 103 Ind. App. 687, 6 N.E. 2d 739 (1937).

Where a supply house supplies material directly to a public improvement on order from a dealer and bills the dealer for the material so shipped, and thereafter the subcontractor who purchased said material pays the dealer therefor in full, the supply house may not maintain an action on the bond of the general contractor. *Republic Creosoting Co. v. Foulkes Contracting Co.,* 103 Ind. App. 457, 8 N.E. 2d 416 (1937).

Recovery may be had at the fair hourly rate for the use of truck and operator engaged in hauling material on a state highway project. Liability under the bond is not limited merely to the wages of the operator. *Middle West Roads Co. v. Gradmont Haulage Co.,* 103 Ind. App. 297, 7 N.E. 2d 528 (1937).

Where the bond is broader than that prescribed by the statute, being conditioned for the payment of debts incurred by contractor in the prosecution of the work, the surety is liable thereunder for money used to purchase labor and materials required in the construction of the highway. *Massachusetts Bonding & Insurance Co. v. Bankers Surety Co.,* 96 Ind. App. 250, 179 N.E. 329 (1932).

Where the actual terms of the bond are not so broad as the statute, the statute will be read into the bond. *Indiana Asphalt Paving Co. v. Bergen,* 105 Ind. App. 250, 11 N.E. 2d 68 (1937).

Where school city, pursuant to authority granted by receiver for surety of defaulting contractor for construction of school building, agreed to pay to the one who completed the building for the surety all the balance of funds in its hands except sufficient to pay claims which had matured into liens, the school city had no right to withhold more than enough to pay those liens, and contractor who completed the building was entitled to a lien and to receive all the balance due over and above the amount necessary to pay those liens. *MacDonald v. Calumet Supply Co.,* 215 Ind. 549, 21 N.E.2d 400 (1939).

A materialman may not recover for gasoline and oil, furnished to a subcontractor in an action on statutory bond furnished by general contractor who had contract for highway improvement, unless the materials were furnished on the credit of and with the understanding that they were to be used in carrying forward the contract secured by the bond. *Ohio Oil Company v. Fidelity & Deposit Company of Maryland,* 112 Ind. App. 452, 42 N.E.2d 406 (1942).

A subcontractor is entitled to the benefit of a provision in contractor's bond relating to the payment of attorney's fees, in a suit against the sureties on such bond. *Western & Southern Indemnity Co., et al. v. Cramer,* 104 Ind. App. 219, 10 N.E.2d 440 (1937).

The proper statutory period in a materialman's suit is one year from final settlement with the public works contractor and not 60 days from final acceptance of the project. *AEtna Casualty & Surety Company v. Geo. Mesker Steel Corp.,* 140 Ind. App. 400, 223 N.E.2d 768 (1967).

Where the contractor's payment bond on a private project uses the following broad language, "all indebtedness incurred for all labor and materials," held, a supplier of a subcontractor could recover thereon even though the owner had paid the prime contractor and the prime contractor had paid the subcontractor. *Western Cas. & Sur. Co. v. State ex rel. Southeastern Supply Co.,* 146 Ind. App. 431, 256 N.E.2d 398 (1970).

Where certain rented equipment was never returned and there was evidence that some of the equipment was used by the general contractor after the subcontractor who had leased same had left the site, the surety was liable to the subcontractor for the rent until the equipment was returned. *Lakus v. United Pacific Insurance Co.,* 452 F.2d 207 (7th Cir. 1971).

Since there are no "liens" on public works, a subcontractor's not perfecting a lien on city funds did not free surety from claim, nor did subcontractor's acceptance of a secured note. *American States Insurance Co. v. Floyd I. Staub, Inc.,* 175 Ind. App. 244, 370 N.E. 2d 989 (1977).

IOWA

1. AMOUNT OF BOND.—Not less than 75% of the contract price, excepting that, in contracts where no part of the contract price is paid until after the completion of the public improvement, the amount of the bond may be fixed at not less than 25% of the contract price. (38 Iowa Code § 573.2 as amended)

2. LABOR AND MATERIAL COVERED.—Labor performed or material, services or transportation furnished in the construction of a public improvement under a contract with the principal contractor or with subcontractors. Material embraces feed, provisions and fuel, but not personal expenses or personal purchases of employees for their individual use.

3. NOTICE REQUIRED.—(1) *To surety*—No special statutory provision. (b) *To principal contractor*—No part of the unpaid fund due the contractor shall be retained on claims for material furnished other than material ordered by the general contractor or the authorized agent thereof unless such claims are supported by a certified statement that the general contractor has been notified within thirty days after the materials are furnished, or by itemized invoices rendered to the contractor during the progress of the work, of the amount, kind and value of the material furnished for use upon said public improvement. (c) *To municipality*—Claimant may file with officer charged by law to issue warrants in payment of the public improvement an itemized written statement of his claim. In case of highway improvements for the county, claims shall be filed with the county auditor of the county letting the contract. In case of contracts for improvements on the farm-to-market highway system paid from farm-to-market funds, claims shall be filed with the auditor of the state department of transportation commission. (d) *To creditors*—No special statutory provision.

4. TIME FOR SUIT.—Claims may be filed with the proper officer at any time before the expiration of thirty days immediately following the completion and final acceptance of the improvement, and at any time after said thirty-day period if the public corporation has not paid the full contract

price and no action is pending to adjudicate rights in and to the unpaid portion of the contract price. Court may allow claims to be filed during the pendency of any action, at any time after the expiration of thirty days and not later than sixty days following the completion and final acceptance of the public improvement. The action is in equity and must be instituted in the county where the improvement is located.

5. CONTRACTS EXCLUDED.—Effective July 1, 1982, the threshold of public improvement contracts requiring bonds increased from $5,000 to $25,000. However, bond may be required when the contract price does not equal that amount.

6. PROCEDURE.—No special statutory provision.

7. PENALTY FOR FAILURE TO TAKE BOND.—No special statutory provision.

8. SPECIAL PROVISIONS.—The obligation of the public officer to require and of the contractor to execute and deliver the bond may not be limited or avoided by contract.

Demolition contracts are now considered public improvements. Effective 1985.

Cash or approved securities may be deposited with the municipal corporation in lieu and in place of the bond.

The retained percentage of the contract price shall, in no case, be less than 5%, and constitutes a fund for the payment of claims of labor and materialmen, and shall be retained by the public corporation for a period of thirty days after the completion and final acceptance of the improvement. If, at the end of said thirty-day period, claims are on file, the public corporation shall continue to retain from said unpaid funds a sum not less than double the total amount of all claims on file. Any party in interest may, at any time after thirty days and not less than sixty days following the completion and final acceptance of the public improvement, institute an action in equity in the county where the improvement is located.

Where the retained percentage is insufficient to pay all claims of labor and materialmen, claims prorate, each according to its own class. If, after the retained percentage has been applied to the payment of established claims, there remain unpaid any such claims in whole or in part, judgment shall be entered for the amount thereof on the bond.

Contractor may, upon written demand, require claimants to institute action within thirty days after the completion and final acceptance of the public improvement.

Where a contractor abandons the work on a public improvement or is legally excluded therefrom, the improvement shall be deemed completed for the purpose of filing claims from the date of the official cancellation of the contract. The only fund available for the payment of claims of persons for labor performed or material furnished shall be the amount then due the contractor, if any, and, if the amount be insufficient to satisfy such claims, the claimant shall have the right of action on the bond given for the performance of the contract.

When at least 95% of any contract for the construction of public improvements has been completed to the satisfaction of the public contracting authority and owing to conditions beyond the control of the construction contractor, the remaining work on the contract cannot proceed for a period of more than sixty days, such public contracting authority may make full payment for the completed work and enter into a supplemental contract with the construction contractor involved on the same terms and conditions so far as applicable for the construction of the work remaining to be done, provided that contractor's bondsman consents and agrees that bond shall remain in full force and effect.

9. DECISIONS.—A subcontractor may sue on the bond to enforce payment of his claim, even though he has not perfected a lien against the funds in the hands of the public official. *Streator Clay Mfg. Co. v. Henning Vineyard Co.,* 176 Iowa 297, 155 N.W. 1001 (1916).

A claim for meats and groceries purchased by employees of highway contractor for themselves and families, as well as for materials furnished to employees, was held not to cover "materials within statute." *Coon River Assn. V. McDougall Construction Co.,* 215 Iowa 861, 244 N.W. 847 (1932).

The statute requiring materialmen to bring suit on the bond within six months after final acceptance of the public improvement has no application to a suit by a municipality for claims the municipality paid subcontractors. The municipality's action did not accrue until after judgments against it; as a municipality, the ten year limitation governing actions on written contracts applies. *City of Waukon v. Southern Surety Co.,* 214 Iowa 522, 242 N.W. 632 (1932); *Southern Surety Co. v. Jenner Bros.,* 212 Iowa 1027, 237 N.W. 500 (1931).

A person drilling blasting holes in quarry of seller of crushed rock to county for use in highway, though entitled to personal judgment against seller, is not entitled to lien on funds due seller from county as statute permits lien only when labor or material is furnished under contract with principal contractor or with subcontractor. *Nolan v. Larimer & Shaffer,* 218 Iowa 599, 254 N.W. 45 (1934).

Failure to file a claim with Highway Commission within thirty days after completion and acceptance of construction work did not defeat materialman's right to recover upon contractor's bond. *Cities Service Oil Co. v. Longerbone,* 232 Iowa 850, 6 N.W.2d 325 (1942).

The claimant must file an itemized and sworn statement of his demand but the fact that he claims items which by the statute he is not entitled to, does not nullify his proceeding. *Penn v. Northern Building Co.,* 140 F. 973 (C.C.N.D. Iowa, 1905). *Epeneter v. Montgomery County,* 98 Iowa 159, 67 N.W. 93 (1896).

A school district which under its contract for the construction of a public building reserves the right to retain a named percentage of the contract price until at least sixty days after the completion of the building, and pays out said retained amount prior to the time provided in the contract and statute, with knowledge that subcontractors were furnishing materials for said building, will, in equity, be deemed to have said retained percentage on hand for the discharge of claims duly filed under the statute. *Stukas & Sons v. Miller & Ladehoff,* 197 Iowa 824, 198 N.W. 65 (1924).

A school district may, though not authorized so to do and though protected by a bond, complete its partially erected building when abandoned by the contractor, and may apply the unpaid payments under the contract to the costs of such completion, even though this defeats the materialman in his attempt to establish a lien on the bond. *Ludowici Caladon Company v. Indiana School District,* 169 Iowa 669, 149 N.W. 845 (1914).

While gasoline, oils and greases consumed or used by haulers in hauling other material which actually goes into the physical improvement, constitute material "furnished in the construction" of the public improvement the materialman must show that such material was actually so used. *Rainbo Oil Company v. McCarthy,* 212 Iowa 1186, 236 N.W. 46 (1931).

A materialman is not a "subcontractor" and one taking a contract from a materialman to haul gravel to point where it was to be delivered to paving contractor has no lien on retained percentages withheld by State. *Forsberg v. Koss,* 218 Iowa 818, 252 N.W. 258 (1934).

Under statute relating to effect of abandonment of public works, and providing that only fund available for payment of claims for labor or material shall be the amount then due contractor, and if such amount be insufficient to satisfy claims, claimant shall have right of action on the bond, there is a right of action on contractor's bond if percentage of contract price which the public corporation is required to retain is insufficient to satisfy claims. *Sinclair Refining Co. v. Burch,* 235 Iowa 594, 16 N.W.2d 359 (1944).

In *Bourrett v. W. M. Bride Construction Co.,* 248 Iowa 1080, 84 N.W.2d 4 (1956), a building contractor's bond to indemnify a named owner of lots on which a building was to be constructed against loss or damage because of the contractor's failure was held only to indemnify owner, especially in view of the express condition in the bond that no right of action should accrue thereon for any other person.

It is not necessary that either contract, performance bond or both show on their face that a supplier may sue on the bond. If the contract documents construed together show an obligation on the part of the contractor to pay subcontractor for material and the bond is an appropriate undertaking, the subcontractor may recover thereon. *Westinghouse Electric Corporation vs. Mill & Elevator Co.,* 254 Iowa 874, 118 N.W.2d 528 (1963).

Although State Board of Regents, suing dissolved construction corporation and its construction bond surety for breach of contract arising out of a sewer construction job, contended otherwise, there was not a direct obligation running to Regents from surety which entitled Regents to recover regardless of construction corporation's liability. *State v. Bi-State Construction Co.,* 269 N.W.2d 455 (Iowa 1978).

KANSAS

1. AMOUNT OF BOND.—Not less than the sum total of the contract. (60 K.S.A. § 1111)

2. LABOR AND MATERIAL COVERED.—All indebtedness incurred for supplies, materials or labor furnished, used or consumed in connection with or in or about the construction of said public improvements or in making such public improvements, including gasoline, lubricating oils, fuel oils, greases, coal and similar items used or consumed directly in furtherance of the improvement. A surety performance bond in the amount of the contract is required with respect to all contracts for the erection of any courthouse, jail or other county building, or the construction of a bridge, the cost of which exceeds $10,000.

3. NOTICE REQUIRED.—No special statutory provision, except in connection with the improvement of highways. A claimant for labor, materials or supplies furnished in the construction, improvement, reconstruction and maintenance of a state highway system may not sue on the bond unless, within six months after the completion date of the contract, according to the records of the State Highway Commission, there be filed with the State Highway Commission an itemized statement of the amount

of the indebtedness, which itemized statement must be sworn to and acknowledged before a notary public or other officer authorized to administer oaths.

4. TIME FOR SUIT.—On bonds other than state highway bonds, no action shall be brought on the bond after six months from the completion of the public improvement. On bonds given in connection with the construction, improvement, reconstruction and maintenance of the state highway system, no action may be brought after one year from the completion of the contract.

While a suit on a statutory bond must be brought within six months from the completion of the work, suit may be brought on a bond conditioned for the payment of labor and materialmen contracting directly with the principal contractor at any time within five years after accrual of cause of action, since such a bond is a non-statutory bond. *Rural High School District ex. rel. Berger Mfg. Co. v. American Surety Co.,* 84 S.W.2d 648 (Mo. Ct. App. 1935). (interpreting Kansas statute).

5. CONTRACTS EXCLUDED.—Under $1,000 in connection with state highway construction or maintenance. Other contracts under $10,000.

6. PROCEDURE.—No special statutory provision.

7. PENALTY FOR FAILURE TO TAKE BOND.—No special statutory provision.

8. SPECIAL PROVISIONS.—Bond shall be on file in the office of the Clerk of the District Court of the county in which such public improvement is to be made or erected. When the bond is approved and filed, no lien may be had against the public improvement.

A law approved on May 10, 1978, enacted the Kansas Small Business Procurement Act to establish a set-aside program for small businesses. A general construction business is small if its gross income annually for the preceding three fiscal years did not excess $4 million. The director of purchases shall have the authority to place nonconstruction contracts up to $50,000 and construction contracts up to $100,000 in the state set-aside program for small businesses. The Secretary of Transportation shall have the authority to place highway contracts up to $100,000 in the state set-aside program for small businesses. Surety guarantees shall be required for highway contracts awarded by the Secretary of Transportation and on construction contracts awarded hereunder which are not highway contracts if deemed necessary by the director of purchases.

9. DECISIONS.—The statute is constitutional and covers an indebtedness for gasoline and oil furnished in connection with the construction of a public highway. *Wolfe Tire Corp. v. Stanton,* 133 Kan. 713, 3 P.2d 650 (1931).

Where the surety voluntarily pays claims of materialmen more than six months after the expiration of the limitation period in bond, the surety is a mere volunteer and such payments do not give surety any priority upon funds due contractor retained by the county. *Weber Implement Co. v. Duback,* 132 Kan. 309, 295 P. 979 (1931).

Where a construction contract, which was part of completion bond, required owner and contractor to pay claims for labor and materials used in construction of apartment building, claimants for labor and materials so used were entitled to enforce payment of their claims from surety on the bond, notwithstanding provision of bond that no right of action should accrue thereon for use of anyone other than specified obligees. *Haynes Hardware Co. v. Western Casualty and Surety Co.,* 156 Kan. 356, 133 P.2d 574 (1943).

Where surety bond referred to construction contract and by reference made it a part of the bond, and specifications, which were part of the contract, defined a surety as a party who engages to be responsible for the entire and satisfactory fulfillment of the contract and for payment for all loss or debts incurred in fulfilling the contract, and provided that bond must guarantee payment of all labor, materials, rentals, etc., surety was required to pay claim against contractor for rentals, repairs, and transportation costs of equipment rented to contractor, whether claim was lienable or otherwise. *American Surety Co. of New York v. Brummel,* 184 F.2d 935 (10th Cir. 1950).

The six-month limitation on actions on public contractors' bond commences running on completion of the public improvement according to the plans and specifications irrespective of whether the public officials used a single or separate contract for various parts of the improvement. *Bayer Construction Company, Inc. v. White-Layton Mechanical Contractors, Inc.,* 190 Kan. 535, 376 P.2d 930 (1962).

Hauling company held not entitled to recover on statutory bond required to secure payment to suppliers of labor and material where its charge for equipment and other charges for labor and material were so commingled as to defy separation. *State of Kansas v. Bob Eldridge Construction Co.,* 397 S.W.2d 7 (Mo. Ct. App. 1965).

A completing surety has a right to retained funds dated back to the time of execution of the bond, which is superior to the rights of a bank under a security assignment executed subsequent to the bond. The surety's priority was not lost by its failure to file a financing statement under the Uniform Commercial Code. *United States Fidelity and Guaranty Company v. First State Bank,* 208 Kan. 738, 494 P.2d 1149 (1972).

A performance bond surety has an interest in retained funds in the hands of owner which was superior and prior to the rights of the bank. The surety is not required to file a financial statement under the Uniform Commercial Code to preserve its rights to the contract balances. *U. S. F. & G. Co. v. First State Bank of Salina,* 208 Kan. 738, 494 P.2d 1149 (1972).

KENTUCKY

The Kentucky legislature has in 1978 adopted a Model Procurement Code, which includes provisions mandating bonds on public construction projects, as described below. The law is effective for state contracts on Jan. 1, 1979 and effective for local contracts on Jan. 1, 1980.

1. AMOUNT OF BOND.—A performance bond in the amount of 100% of the contract price, and a payment bond in the same amount. (67A Kentucky Revised Statutes § 740)

2. LABOR AND MATERIAL COVERED.—All persons supplying labor and material to the contractor or his subcontractors for the performance of the work provided for in the contract.

3. NOTICE REQUIRED.—This is not covered in the new statute, but the Kentucky laws dealing with summary proceedings and declaratory judgments (under which provisions bond issues are decided) simply require that notice be served on "party against whom judgment is sought" no less than ten days prior to the actual serving of the motion for summary judgment. The notice must describe the type of proceeding and cause of action and the day on which motion will be made. The service must be performed by an authorized officer on the defendant personally or his authorized representative.

4. TIME FOR SUIT.—This also is not specified in the new statute. Kentucky's general statute of limitations includes civil actions on bonds in the class of procedures which must be initiated within fifteen years after cause of action has accrued. However, the Kentucky courts have allowed the right to specify a shorter period, i.e. one year, in the bond.

5. CONTRACTS EXCLUDED.—Under $25,000.

6. PROCEDURE.—No special provisions.

7. PENALTY FOR FAILURE TO TAKE BOND.—No special provisions.

8. SPECIAL PROVISIONS.—The new statute gives the government (specifically, at the state level, the secretary of the executive department for finance and administration; at the local level, the public agency involved) the right to issue regulations specifying the form of the bonds and to require additional security. For local contracts, this can include payment bonds covering taxes and unemployment insurance premiums.

In 1974, Kentucky passed a statute regulating public improvements performed by urban-county governments. This act includes the following: "Each contract shall be supported by a performance bond for the full amount thereof, with good surety to be approved by the governing body."

9. DECISIONS PRIOR TO NEW STATUTE.—Subcontractors may recover on a bond conditioned for payment of labor and material bills. *Mid-Continent Petroleum Corp. v. Southern Surety Co.,* 225 Ky. 501, 9 S.W.2d 229 (1928).

A subcontractor is within a bond conditioned to pay "each and every person who may furnish . . . labor or material." *Cent. Indem. Co. v. Shunk Mfg. Co.,* 253 Ky. 50, 68 S.W.2d 772 (1934); *Blair & Franse Constr. Co. v. Allen,* 251 Ky. 366, 65 S.W.2d 78 (1933).

Road construction machinery, lost or mislaid equipment, repairs, payment of freight, and damage to equipment because of insufficiency to withstand work are not items for which recovery may be had within a contractor's bond. *Cent. Ind. Co. v. Shunk Mfg. Co.,* 253 Ky. 50, 68 S.W.2d 772 (1934); *Marion Steam Shovel Co. v. Union Indemnity Co.,* 225 Ky. 817, 75 S.W.2d 541 (1934); *Thew Shovel Co. v. Massachusetts Bonding & Ins. Co.,* 261 Ky. 712, 88 S.W.2d 960 (1935).

Claims for improvement contractor's purchase of permanent tools, equipment, boiler, etc., not consumed in constructing improvement, are not allowable against the surety. *Union Indemnity Co. v. Penna. Boiler Wks.,* 246 Ky. 473, 55 S.W.2d 367 (1932).

A materialman may recover from a highway contractor's surety even though that materialman, at contractor's request, had refrained from filing a claim with the highway commissioner at a time when the highway commissioner held sufficient money to pay materialman's claim. A materialman is under no legal duty to file his claim with the highway commissioner or give any notice to surety. *National Union Indemnity Co. v. Standard Oil Co.,* 262 Ky. 392, 90 S.W.2d 375 (1936).

The falsity of a contractor's affidavit as to payment of bills for labor and material incurred by contractor does not relieve the contractor's surety from liability for money expended in discharge of subcontractor's liens, where performance of the contract was guaranteed by the bond. *Fidelity & Casualty Co. v. Board of Regents,* etc., 287 Ky. 439, 152 S.W.2d 581 (1941).

An insurance premium is neither "labor," "material," nor "supplies" as such terms are used in Kentucky statute providing a lien in favor of persons who furnish labor, material or supplies for the construction of a public improvement. In re *Zaepfel & Russell, Inc.,* 49 F. Supp. 709 (W.D. Ky. 1941), *aff'd, Farmers State Bank v. Jones,* 135 F.2d 215 (6th Cir. 1943); *Charles E. Cannel Co. v. D. & D. Millwork Co.,* 288 Ky. 319, 156 S.W.2d 170 (1941).

A materialman who sold to a subcontractor lumber used in making concrete forms, scaffolding, and an elevator hoist was allowed to recover under the bond of a contractor constructing sewer pumping station for City. *Charles E. Cannel Co. v. D. & D. Millwork Co.,* 288 Ky. 319, 156 S.W.2d 170 (1941).

A compensated surety on contractor's labor and material bond given in connection with the construction of a public school in Kentucky was not prejudiced by reason of unpaid supplier's acceptance of contractor's 90-day promissory notes as evidence of indebtedness and was not discharged from liability under the bond. *Crane Supply Company v. American States Insurance Co.,* 310 F.2d 712 (6th Cir. 1962).

See: *Robert Simmons Construction Co. v. Powers Regulator Co.,* 390 S.W.2d 901 (Ky. 1965).

A time limitation in an insurance contract though shorter than the statutory period is not invalid if not unreasonably short. *Simons Construction Company v. American States Ins. Co.,* 426 S.W.2d 441 (Ky. 1968).

There are two distinct lines of decisions in Kentucky:

If a surety bond, when read in connection with a Kentucky public improvement contract, contains a provision obligating the contractor to pay for material, it constitutes a provision inuring to the benefit of materialmen, upon which they are entitled to maintain an action directly against the surety. If the bond, when read in connection with a Kentucky public improvement contract, is one solely to secure performance of a contract, and contains no language from which an express obligation to pay third parties for materials may be derived, action thereon by materialmen may not be maintained. The true basis for determining the liability of a surety must be deduced from the terms of the surety bond, construed liberally to effectuate a purpose for which given. Held lessor of construction equipment may maintain action against surety on performance bond for unpaid rental for equipment leased to contract for performance of Kentucky public improvement contract where the performance bond incorporates the contract by reference and contract provides that contractor will pay for all materials used in performing contract. *Ill-Mo Contractors, Inc. v. Aalcan Demolition and Contracting Co.,* 431 S.W.2d 165 (Mo. 1968).

A prime contractor's performance and payment bond, given in connection with a housing project which provides not only for performance but also that it is for the use of "all persons doing work or furnishing skills, tools, machinery, supplies or material, under or for the purpose of the contract hereinafter referred to" covers a claim by a supplier of material to a subcontractor. *American Radiator and Standard Sanitary Corp. v. Albany Municipal Housing Commission,* 441 S.W.2d 433 (Ky. 1969).

Where material was supplied for an unbonded project and later recovered and reused by the contractor on a bonded project, the bond's protection of supplies furnished "for use" on bonded project was not applicable. In making this judgment, the court relied in part on principles governing the right to assert mechanic's/materialmen's liens. However, where contractor could reasonably assume that his supplies would be used on bonded project, contractor's failure to keep specific track of use of sold materials is not a barrier to claim on bond. *U.S. Fidelity & Guaranty Co. v. Miller,* 549 S.W. 2d 316 (Ky. App. 1977).

A prime contractor who attempted with a letter to deny responsibility for subcontractor's payment, despite initial agreement to contrary with supplier, was held liable to supplier on performance bond. *Henry A. Petter Supply Co. v. Hal Perry Construction,* 563 S.W. 2d 749 (Ky. App. 1978).

LOUISIANA

1. AMOUNT OF BOND.—Not less than 50% of the contract price. See Special Provisions below. (38 L.S.A. § 2216)

2. LABOR AND MATERIAL COVERED.—All labor performed, materials furnished, and transportation or delivery of such materials to site, in the construction, erection, alteration or repair of any public building, road work, or improvement. An amendment of June 22, 1960, excludes claims of persons to whom money is due for the lease or rental of movable property.

3. NOTICE REQUIRED.—(a) *To surety*—No special statutory provision. (b) *To principal contractor*—An amendment approved July 20, 1960 provides that before any person having a direct contractual relationship with a subcontractor but not contractual relationship with a contractor shall have a right of action against the contractor or the surety on the bond furnished by the contractor, he shall record his claim as set forth in subsection (c) hereof or give written notice to said contractor

within 45 days from the recordation of the notice of acceptance by the owner of the work or notice by the owner of default, stating with substantial accuracy the amount claimed and the name of the party to whom the material was furnished or supplied or for whom the labor or service was done or performed. Such notice shall be served by mailing the same by registered or certified mail, postage prepaid, in an envelope addressed to the contractor at any place he maintains an office in the State of Louisiana. See the requirement for notice under the amendment of July 14, 1962, set forth under Section 4 hereof entitled TIME FOR SUIT. (c) *To municipality*—Any person to whom money is due for doing work, performing labor or furnishing materials and supplies for use in machines used in the construction, alteration or repair of any public works, excluding persons to whom money is due for the lease or rental of movable property, may, after the maturity of his claim and within 45 days after the recordation of acceptance of the work by the governing authority or notice of default of the contractor or subcontractor, file a sworn statement of the amount due him with the governing authority having the work done and recorded in the Office of the Recorder of Mortgages for the parish in which the work is done. This is an abstract of a 1960 amendment. Prior provision for filing of sworn statement of amount due appeared in earlier issue of CREDIT MANUAL. (d) *To creditors*—No special statutory provision.

4. TIME FOR SUIT.—Within one year from the registry of acceptance of the work or notice of default of the contractor. Two prescriptive statutes both enacted in 1962 contain different limitation periods. The court concluded that the three-year prescription was inapplicable but that the one-year prescription governed. *Marquette Cement Mfg. Co. v. Normand,* 249 La. 1027, 192 So.2d 552 (1966). A 1982 amendment has changed the three-year limitation to five, applicable to contracts entered into after September 10, 1982.

5. CONTRACTS EXCLUDED.—Effective September 10, 1982, the threshold for bonds on contracts for public works increased to $100,000.

6. PROCEDURE.—No special statutory provision.

7. PENALTY FOR FAILURE TO TAKE BOND.—Where the public authority executing the contract for the public improvement fails to take the bond required by statute, it is liable to claimants who have furnished labor and material to the same extent that a surety on a statutory bond would have been liable. *Police Jury v. Gaspard,* 161 La. 70, 108 So. 128 (1926).

The provision for filing of sworn statement of amount due, referred to in subsection 3(c) above, continues with the following: "After the filing and recordation of claims, any payments made by the governing authority without deducting the amount of the claims, so served on it, shall make the authority liable for the amount of the claims."

8. SPECIAL PROVISIONS.—If at the end of the forty-five day period for filing and recording sworn statements of the amounts due to claimants (see Subdivision 3 above) there remain unpaid any claims which have been duly filed and recorded, the authority having the work done shall file a petition citing such claimants, the contractor, the subcontractor and the surety on the bond. The authority shall assert whatever claims it has against any and all such parties in said petition and shall require the claimants to assert whatever claim they have. Should the public authority have a claim on the bond it shall be paid prior to any other claims. If the authority does not file a petition to start such a proceeding within forty-five days after the default of the contractor or within forty-five days after the acceptance of the work, any claimant may do so.

9. REMARKS.—In 1966 Section 4802 of Title 9 of the Louisiana Revised Statutes was amended to require every contract entered into for the repair, construction or improvement of any work on immovable property by a general contractor or other person undertaking such general contract with an owner to be reduced to writing and duly recorded in the parish wherein such work is to be executed before the date fixed on which the work is to commence or not more than 30 days after the date of said contract.

Such recordation preserves the privileges on the structure and on the land on which it is situate in favor of every contractor, subcontractor, laborer, furnisher of material, machinery or fixtures, etc., as their interest may arise. The owner of such work shall require of every such contractor a surety bond as follows. For all contracts not exceeding $10,000 the amount of the bond shall be the amount of the contract. If the contract is over $10,000 but does not exceed $100,000 the penal sum of the bond must be not less than 50% of the amount of the contract but not less than $10,000 in any event. If the contract is over $100,000 but does not exceed $1,000,000, the bond shall be not less than one-third of the amount of the contract; and if the contract exceeds $1,000,000 the bond shall be not less than one-fourth on the amount of the contract. The bond is required to be attached to and recorded with the contract and the bond is required to be conditioned for the faithful performance of the contract and payment of all subcontractors, laborers and furnishers of material, machinery and fixtures jointly as their interest may appear.

A claimant is required to serve upon the owner a sworn detailed statement of his claim by registered mail or personal service and is required to duly record a sworn statement showing the total amount of his claim in the office of the clerk of court or recorder of mortgages for the parish in which said work has been done not later than 30 days after recordation in said local public office of notice by owner of acceptance of said work or notice by the owner of the default of the contractor. The claim recorded as above set forth preserves the privilege against the property for a period of one year from the date of its recordation and may be enforced by a civil action in the parish in which the land is situated. Such cause of action shall prescribe within one year from the date of the recordation of the claim in the mortgage records.

Notice of filing of suit (giving the name of the court, the title and number of the proceedings and the date of filing, a description of the property and a reference to the recorded contract) on said claim must be recorded within a year from the date of recordation of the inscription of said claim to preserve claimant's rights.

If no objections are made by any claimant to the solvency or sufficiency of the surety bond, the public authority shall obtain, ten days after the service of notice on each claimant having a recorded claim of said proceeding, a certificate to that effect which certificate shall relieve the authority of any personal liability. If objections are made to the solvency or sufficiency of the surety by any claimant and such objections are sustained the public authority is liable to all claimants to the same extent as the surety on the contractor's bond. It is not sufficient that the surety be solvent only at the time the bond of the contractor is signed and approved but such solvency must exist at the time creditors assert their claims against the public authority. *Tyler Co. v. Merrill Engineering Co.*, 181 La. 191, 159 So. 319 (1935); *Bickham v. Womack*, 181 La. 837, 160 So. 431 (1935). The bond is conditioned for the payment by the contractor and by all subcontractors for all material or supplies furnished for use in machines used in the construction, erection, alteration or repair of said public building, road, work or improvement.

Said bond must be recorded with the contract in the office of the Recorder of Mortgages of the parish wherein the work is to be done on the day said work begins and not later than thirty days thereafter.

Any payments made by the public officer after the receipt by said authority of the claimant's sworn statement and the due recording thereof without first deducting the amount of the claims so made make said public authority liable for the amount of the claim.

Nothing in the statute shall be so construed as to deprive any claimant, within the terms of the statute, of his right of action on the bond, which action right shall accrue at any time after the maturity of his claim. Claim of municipality is entitled to preference.

If a claimant shall have made a demand for payment upon the principal and surety and refrained from instituting suit for thirty days thereafter, the successful claimant may be allowed 10% of his claim as attorney's fees.

In case of damage to the State Highway system caused by flood or other disaster requiring immediate attention or for improvement to cost $2,000 or less, the successful bidder is required to furnish satisfactory bond in such amount as may be required by the rules and regulations of the Louisiana Highway Commission.

10. DECISIONS.—Lumber, nails and supplies used by contractor in constructing piledriver or in constructing forms for concrete piers are items for which recovery may be had under payment bond. *Slagle-Johnson Lumber, Inc. v. Landis Construction Co.*, 379 So. 2d 479 (La. 1979).

Recovery may be had for gasoline. *Williams & Gray v. Stewart*, 147 So. 103 (La. App. 1933).

A surety is not liable for labor and material used in repairing contractor's truck. *Rester v. Moody & Stewart*, 172 La. 510, 134 So. 690 (1931).

Claimant merely hiring out teams and equipment is not a subcontractor and may not recover under a highway contractor's bond. *A. L. Mays & Sons v. Rickerson*, 142 So. 183 (La. Ct. App. 1932).

It would appear that recovery may be had for feed supplied either to the principal contractor or to the subcontractor, but not for groceries. *Whittington v. Nelson Bros. Construction Co.*, 141 So. 491 (La. Ct. App. 1932).

A subcontractor may not recover attorney's fees against the surety where he failed to prove that he made a demand upon the surety and its principal for payment thirty days prior to the commencement of suit. *Nelson Mfg. Co. v. Wilkerson*, 152 So. 157 (La. Ct. App. 1934).

Where there is but one unpaid labor and material claim, the claimant may sue the Louisiana Highway Commission directly to enforce the Commission's personal liability where the surety is insolvent. There is no need to invoke a concursus proceeding to determine the liability under the bond. Such a proceeding can be used only where there are two or more claimants. *Albin v. Harvey & Jones*, 162 So. 658 (La. Ct. App. 1935).

Where a materialman failed to file sworn statements of his account with the City, the City is not liable for his claim, even though the City has paid the contractor in full prior to forty-five days after the acceptance of the work. If the claimant had given such notice to the City, then the City would have been liable. *American Creosote Works v. City of Natchitoches,* 182 La. 641, 162 So. 206 (1935).

Where a public work has been completed and accepted and a part of the contract price of the work remains in the hands of the public body or is deposited in the registry of the court, the assertion of a materialman's or laborer's claim to payment by preference out of said fund is timely whether filed of record within or after the lapse of a period of 45 days after the acceptance of the work. *Goldberg v. Banta Bros.,* 183 La. 10, 162 So. 786 (1935).

The effect of recording and serving a sworn statement of the amount due for materials furnished or labor done on any public work is to create a lien upon or to impound, so to speak, any balance due to the contractor by the authority having the work done to the extent of the claim or claims so recorded and served. The contractor, by giving a bond, may release the fund so impounded or so subjected to the recorded claim, if he does not acknowledge owing the claim or claims. *Pittman Bros. Const. Co. v. First Sewerage Dist. of Lake Charles,* 193 La. 307, 190 So. 563 (1939).

Claim by owners arising out of defective and incomplete construction of building by contractor was not prescribed by failure to sue within one year following recordation of acceptance of building, in accordance with statute relating to an action against a surety, since such statute is intended merely to limit period within which materialmen and laborers may bring action against a contractor's surety. *Costanza v. Cannata,* 214 La. 29, 36 So.2d 627 (1948).

A contractor may borrow money from a bank to finance his operations and in good faith apply earned estimates above retained percentages to the satisfaction of loans actually used in paying laborers, materialmen and subcontractors. The retained percentage cannot be diverted by the owner or anyone else to be prejudice of the surety. *American Indemnity Co. v. Webster Parish School Board,* 98 F.Supp. 360 (W.D. La. 1951), citing *Claiborne Parish School Board v. Fidelity & Deposit Co. of Maryland,* 40 F.2d 577 (5th Cir. 1930).

Where subcontractor was in default on plumbing, heating and ventilation subcontract, attorney's fees, costs of photostats, telephone tolls, premium for bond for payment of job creditors' claims against subcontractor obtained by general contractor in order to obtain release of contract funds, etc., were chargeable against subcontractor under provisions of subcontractor's surety bond. *Coburn Supply Co. v. James E. Caldwell Co.,* 231 La. 1026, 93 So.2d 546 (1957).

Any breach of building contract by owner or contractor did not affect rights of action of workmen and materialmen against surety on performance bond for labor and materials used in work under building contract. *Moore Steel, Inc. v. Snow,* 85 So.2d 648 (La. App. 1956).

Under contract where seller agreed to supply structural steel to a general contractor f.o.b. site, seller was a materialman not a subcontractor, and supplier of parts of the steel to the seller may not recover from the contractor or contractor's surety. *Jesse F. Heard & Sons v. Cahaba Steel Co.,* 126 So. 2d 375 (La. App. 1960).

Materials which form a component part of completed structure or are consumed in work are considered covered by the contractor's bond for public works and surety is liable therefor, but instrumentalities forming part of contractor's plant or equipment used in doing work which survived performance and remain property of the owner after completion of contract are not covered by the bond. *B. & G. Crane Service, Inc. v. Anderson Brothers Corp.,* 132 So.2d 681 (La. Ct. App. 1961).

A surety on a highway contractor's bond was not liable for items furnished to the subcontractor for his personal use, for tires, tubes and tools which were furnished for the subcontractor's truck and which survived completion of the work or for the purchase price or for the repair of tools, appliances or instrumentalities forming part of the contractor's plant or equipment which survived performance of the contract and was available for use on other projects. *Waldrip Tire & Supply Co., Inc. vs. Campbell Construction Company,* 158 So.2d 464 (La. App. 1963).

A materialman who furnished plumbing supplies to a subcontractor was not required, in a suit on the contractor's public works bond, to prove that the supplies had been incorporated into the building because the supplies had not been delivered directly to the job site but had been delivered to a warehouse and then transported to the job site.

Lessor of manned equipment was not entitled under statute to recover for rental of equipment and operators. *Mayeaux v. Lamco, Inc.,* 180 So.2d 425 (La. Ct. App. 1965).

In a suit by a subcontractor who sandblasted and recoated pipefittings which were then delivered to and incorporated into a housing project, "work done" is not whether same was performed at the site but whether work went into the project. *Coating Specialists v. Pat Caffey Contractor, Inc.,* 194 So.2d 380 (La. 1976).

Supplier of materials to a materialman on a public works project has no right of action against a general contractor or his surety. *Bailey v. R.E. Heidt Construction Co.,* 205 So.2d 503 (La. App. 1967); *Coating Specialists, Inc. v. Pat Caffey Contr., Inc.,* 194 So. 2d 380 (La. 1967).

Where furnisher of materials sold and delivered goods to subcontractor used in performance of its subcontract with prime contractor, in construction of building, and subcontractor failed to pay for materials and amount sued for was actual indebtedness of subcontractor, prime contractor and his surety under terms of surety bond were liable. *Apex Sales Company, Inc. v. Wilson Abraham,* 201 So. 2d 184 (La. App. 1967).

One who lends money to a contractor has no rights as such lender under a Miller Act payment bond and cannot become an obligee. *American Bank & Trust Co. v. Trinity Universal Ins. Co.,* 194 So. 2d 164 (1966); affirmed 205 So. 2d 35 (1961), 251 La. 445, 194 So. 2d 164 (La. Ct. App. 1966), *aff'd,* 251 La. 445, 205 So.2d 35 (1967).

A bond which was conditioned for payment of claims of materialmen and also for full performance of the contract requiring the principal to pay all claims of furnishers, suppliers and those rendering services was sufficient to be construed a statutory bond within the Louisiana Private Works Act. *Continental Casualty Co. v. Associated Pipe & Supply Co.* 447 F.2d 1041 (5th Cir. 1971).

A surety bond in connection with the construction of a housing complex for a private owner containing a provision for payment of labor and materialmen was held not to cover a claim for rental of machinery and equipment furnished to a subcontractor. *Arrow Construction Co., Inc. v. American Employers Insurance Co.,* 273 So.2d 582 (La. App. 1973).

There are no rights of action on private works performance bond other than those reposed in the obligees named in the bond.

In determining whether claimant supplied materials to another materialman and therefore not entitled to lien under public works contracts law or supplied materials to a subcontractor and therefore entitled to lien, test is whether person furnishing materials thereafter performed any labor in attaching or incorporating materials into building or improvements involved in case. *Thurman v. Star Electric Supply, Inc.,* 307 So.2d 283 (La. 1975).

Where the claimant could prove neither that he furnished services to prime contractor or subcontractor, nor privity of contract with the prime contractor, he was not allowed to recover for engineering services. *Richard & Gaudet v. Housing Authority,* 323 So.2d 168 (La. Ct. App. 1975).

Fee for towing service was held recoverable. *Canal Towing v. Gulf South Dredging,* 345 So.2d 567 (La. Ct. App. 1977).

Surety was obliged to reimburse contractor for the subcontractor's workmen's compensation insurance fees paid by contractor, where subcontractor required such fees and subcontractor made arrangements with contractor to cover them in emergency and ultimately defaulted on them. Surety's claim that it was not aware that contractor was making payments for sub (since subcontractor's insurer was not qualified to do business in Louisiana) was rejected by appellate court since bond specified that "changes or alterations of the contract" do not alter surety's responsibility. *Pittman Construction Co. v. Meadows,* 337 So.2d 892, 894 (La. Ct. App. 1976).

Even where there was no binding contract between subcontractor and prime, clear evidence that the prime was unjustly enriched by subcontractor's work mandates recovery. *Sam Capitano, Jr. v. Huber, Hunt & Nichols, Inc.,* 359 So.2d 308 (La. App. 1978).

Where a subcontractor completed work on which earlier subcontractor defaulted, materialman could not apply payments to first (defaulting) subcontractor to claim of completing subcontractor. *Paul M. Davison v. L. T. Brown, Contractor, Inc.,* 356 So.2d 572 (La. Ct. App. 1978), AMD 364 So.2d 583 (La. 1978).

Materials which were not part of final structure (plywood, lumber and nails used in pouring concrete) were not covered by bond.

Suit by materialman to subcontractor on state university football stadium project, against contractor and its payment bond surety. Reversing the Court of Appeal, the Supreme Court, holding in favor of plaintiff, materialmen said that plywood, lumber and nails, used to make forms for concrete, were consumed in construction and thus covered by the payment bond.

MAINE

On March 5, 1971, Maine adopted a separate performance and payment bond statute effective 91 days after adjournment of the legislature. This new statute is abstracted as follows:

1. AMOUNT OF BOND.—100% of the contract price.
2. LABOR AND MATERIAL COVERED.—Labor or material supplied to the contractor or his subcontractor in the prosecution of the work provided for in the contract for the construction, alteration or repair of any public building or other public improvement or public work including highways awarded to any person by the state or by any political subdivision or quasi municipal corporation or by any public authority. The term "material" includes rental of equipment.

STATE BOND LAWS

3. NOTICE REQUIRED.
(a) *To surety*—no special statutory provision;
(b) *To principal contractor*—no notice is required by a claimant having a contractual relationship, express or implied, with the principal contractor. Claimants who have no contractual relationship, express or implied, with such contractor must give written notice within 90 days. See subsection 5 and 7 below.
(c) *To municipality*—no special statutory provision.
(d) *To creditors*—no special statutory provision.

4. TIME FOR SUIT.—No suit shall be commenced prior to 90 days from the date on which claimant furnished the last of the labor or material for which such claim is made and no "such action may be commenced after the expiration of one year from the date on which the last of the labor was performed or material was supplied for the payment of which such action is brought. Provided that in the case of a material supplier where the amount of the claim is not ascertainable due to the unavailability of final quantity estimates such action may be commenced before the expiration of one year from the date on which the final quantity estimates are determined. However, the notice of claim from the material supplier to the contractor furnishing the payment bond shall be filed before the expiration of 90 days following the determination by the contracting authority of the final quantity estimate."

5. PLACE OF SUIT.—The county in which the principal or surety has its principal place of business.

6. CONTRACTS EXCLUDED.—Contracts under $25,000.

7. PROCEDURE.—A claimant having a direct contractual relationship with a subcontractor of the contractor but no contractural relationship, express or implied, with such contractor shall not have the right of action upon such payment bond unless he shall have given written notice to such contractor within 90 days from the date on which such claimant performed the last of the labor or furnished or supplied the last of the material for which such claim is made, stating with substantial accuracy the amount claimed and the name of the party to whom the material was furnished or supplied or for whom the labor was done or performed. Such notice shall be served by registered or certified mail, postage prepaid, in an envelope addressed to the contractor at any place he maintains an office or conducts his business or at his residence.

8. PENALTY FOR FAILURE TO TAKE BOND.—No special statutory provision.

9. SPECIAL PROVISIONS.—The contracting body and the agent in charge of its office shall furnish to anyone making written application therefor who states that he has supplied labor or materials for such work, and payment therefor has not been made, or that he is being sued on any such bond, or that he is the surety thereon, a certified copy of such bond and the contract for which it was given, which copy shall be prima facie evidence of the contents, execution and delivery of the original. Applicants shall pay for such certified copies such reasonable fees as the contracting body or the agent in charge of its office fixes to cover the actual cost of preparation thereof.

In any contract awarded by the Department of Transportation for the construction and maintenance of public highways, bridges and other structures, the department may withhold up to 5% of the money due the contractor until the project under the contract has been accepted by or for the department. When the contract has been substantially completed, the department may, upon request, further reduce the amounts withheld if it deems it desirable and prudent. The reduction shall not reduce the amount withheld to an amount less than the amount of any pending claim against the contractor filed by a subcontractor. The contractor may withdraw the whole or any portion of the retainage upon depositing certain securities with the State Treasurer.

10. DECISIONS.—The Highway Department has the right to require such bonds as an incident to its authority to enter into contracts for the construction of highways. *Foster v. Kerr & Houston*, 133 Me. 389, 179 A. 297 (1935).

Where, pursuant to the statute conferring upon the State Highway Commission full power relating to the furnishing of bonds by the successful bidders, a bond is required conditioned that the contractor shall faithfully perform the contract and pay all bills for labor, material and equipment and for all other things contracted for and used by him in connection with the work, a surety is obligated to pay claims for items such as tires, tubes, vulcanizing and re-treading services rendered to the contractor only when substantial consumption of said items occurs in the construction of the particular highway project. *Carpenter v. Susi*, 152 Me. 1, 121 A.2d 336 (1956).

One of main requirements of a contractor's bond dealing with construction of highways is to guarantee payment of bills for labor, material and equipment as well as faithful performance of contract. A bank does not by mere act of loaning money to a contractor for the purpose of paying labor become subrogated to rights of the laborer for purpose of suing surety on contractor's bond. *Newport Trust Co. v. Susi*, 153 Me. 51, 134 A.2d 543 (1957).

Suit may be maintained by the obligee on a bond conditioned for payment of certain labor and material claims for the benefit of a supplier of material furnished a subcontractor and required in the completion of a federal project. *Verrier v. American Fidelity Co.*, 163 F. Supp. 919 (D. Me. 1958).

MARYLAND

1. AMOUNT OF BOND.—50% of the total amount payable by the terms of the contract. A separate statute for highway work requires a bond in the full amount of the contract; bridge contracts require a bond double the amount of the contract. (Art. 21 Annotated Code of Maryland § 3-501)

2. LABOR AND MATERIAL COVERED.—For the protection of all persons supplying labor and material to the contractor or his subcontractor in the prosecution of the work provided for in the contract.

The recodification effective July 1, 1974 adds to the above coverage "including lessors of equipment to the extent of the fair rental value thereof."

3. NOTICE REQUIRED.—

a. *To surety.*—No special statutory provision.

b. *To principal contractor.*—Any person having direct contractual relationship with a subcontractor of the contractor, or with any sub-subcontractor of the contractor, but no contractual relationship, express or implied, with the contractor furnishing said payment bond, must give written notice to the contractor within ninety (90) days from the date on which said person did, or performed, the last of the labor or furnished or supplied the last of the material for which such claim is made, stating with substantial accuracy the amount claimed and the name of the party to whom the material was furnished or supplied, or for whom the labor was done or performed. Such notice shall be served by mailing the same by registered or certified mail, postage prepaid, in an envelope directed to the contractor at any place he maintains an office or conducts his business, or his residence. A notice complied with the statutes when it was mailed within 90 days of claimant's last work although not received by the contractor until after this 90-day period had expired. *Montgomery County Board of Education ex rel. Carrier Corp. v. Glassman Constr. Co.*, 245 Md. 192, 225 A.2d 448 (1967).

Where the contractor was given notice by regular mail and it was admitted that the notice was received, following Miller Act precedents, the court held such notice to be sufficient under the Maryland statute. *State Roads Comm'n ex rel. Mobil Oil Corp. v. Contee Sand & Gravel Co.*, 308 F. Supp. 650 (D. Md. 1970).

c. *To municipality.*—No special statutory provision.

d. *To creditors.*—No special statutory provision.

4. TIME FOR SUIT.—Every person who has the right to sue under the payment bond must institute suit in the appropriate Court of the political subdivision in which the contractor had his principal place of business and not elsewhere, at any time after the expiration of ninety (90) days after the day on which the last labor was performed or the last material was furnished or supplied by him for which said claim is made, but no such suit shall be commenced after the term of one year after the date of final acceptance of the work performed under the contract.

5. CONTRACTS EXCLUDED.—$25,000 or less, except in the case of highways, where there are no exclusions, bond must not be less than the contract price. The public body may require a performance bond or other security in addition to the surety performance bond in such amount as shall be adequate for the protection of the public body and the above described payment bond, also in cases other than those specified in the section of the statute requiring such bonds with respect to contracts exceeding $25,000 in amount for the construction, alteration or repair of any public building or public work or improvement of the State of Maryland or any political subdivision thereof. Cash or other security, satisfactory to the contracting officer, may be furnished in lieu of a bond.

6. PROCEDURE.—The State Comptroller or the officer in charge of the office wherein the aforesaid bonds are required to be filed is authorized and directed to furnish, to any person making application therefor who submits an affidavit that he has supplied the labor, or material, for such work and payment therefor has not been made, or that he is being sued on any such bond, a certified copy of the bond which copy shall be prima facie evidence of the contents, execution and delivery of the original. The applicant shall pay for such certified copy such reasonable fees as the appropriate public official shall fix to cover the cost of preparation thereof.

7. PENALTY FOR FAILURE TO TAKE BOND.—No special statutory provision, except in the Transportation Code: The contractor who fails to promptly execute the bond forfeits the contract and the bid bond, and the surety will be liable for the damage caused by this failure which is sustained by the Maryland Transportation Authority.

STATE BOND LAWS

8. SPECIAL PROVISIONS.—Bonds payable to the State of Maryland shall be filed in the office of the State Comptroller. Any other bonds shall be filed in the office of the public body concerned.

The 1963 amendment broadened the provision for place of suit under the payment bond to permit such suits "in the political subdivision in which the contract was to be performed and executed or in the political subdivision where the contractor has his principal place of business and not elsewhere." And the 1974 act continues this provision. Any contractor covered by such (payment bond) shall not be required to furnish a waiver of mechanics liens to the State.

A recodification of the laws relating to payment and performance bonds, mechanics liens, etc. effective July 1, 1974 broadens the coverage under the payment bond and also provides that "Any contractor prior to receiving a progress or final payment under a contract covered hereunder shall certify in writing that he has made payment from proceeds of prior payments, and that he will make timely payments from the proceeds of the progress or final payment then due him, to his subcontractors and suppliers in accordance with his contractual arrangements with them." There are several changes in 1978, due to the enaction of a new Transposition Code.

9. DECISIONS.—A bond of a contractor given in connection with state work does not cover rent or depreciation of a steam shovel leased to a subcontractor as part of his regular business equipment or the cost of its redelivery to the owner. *State v. National Surety Co.,* 148 Md. 221, 128 A. 916 (1925).

Hauling and trucking of sand, gravel, etc., is labor and material within the statute and a bond executed thereunder. *London, etc., Indemnity Co. v. State,* 153 Md. 308, 138 A. 231 (1927).

A corporation which furnishes steel girders to a subcontractor, which subcontractor erected said girders and was paid in full therefor by the general contractor, may not maintain a right of action in the bond given by said general contractor to the Mayor and City Council of Baltimore in connection with the erection of a public school building in that city, which bond is conditioned for the performance of the contract and further that the contractor shall promptly pay all claims made against the contractor by any person for the nonpayment of labor performed in and about the erection of the structure or the work to be done under the contract for which the contractor is liable and for all materials incorporated in the work for which the said contractor is liable. *Mayor and City Council of Baltimore ex rel. Lehigh Structural Steel Co. v. Maryland Casualty Co.,* 171 Md. 667, 190 A. 250 (1937).

A municipal contractor's bond providing for payment of claims for all "material" furnished, installed, erected and incorporated in structure covered a claim for lumber used in building concrete forms and scaffolding. *Fidelity & Deposit Co. of Md. v. Mattingly Lumber Co.,* 176 Md. 217, 4 A.2d 447 (1939).

In the construction of a schoolhouse, a county board of education was not an "agency of the State" within statute relating to performance bonds given to State or any of its agencies and limiting actions thereon to one year from completion of work and acceptance thereof. Action on performance bond given county board of education in connection with contract for construction of schoolhouse was subject to twelve years limitation period. *Board of Education of Cecil County, et al. v. Phillip Lange, et al.,* 182 Md. 132, 32 A.2d 693 (1943). Recovery for the claimant who furnished and installed electrical equipment for this project under an agreement with the subcontractor was upheld. *Lange et al. v. Board of Education of Cecil County,* 183 Md. 255, 37 A.2d 317 (1944).

Where the undertaking stated in the payment bond was to "make payment to all persons supplying labor and materials in prosecution of work provided for in said contract," the language of the bond was broad enough to establish liability of the general contractor and surety for supplies furnished to subcontractor. *Board of Education of Montgomery County v. Victor N. Judson, Inc.,* 211 Md. 188, 126 A.2d 615 (1956).

Suit by materialman filed more than one year from date of final acceptance of the contractor's work was barred by the statute of limitations. *Frisco v. Aetna Insurance Company,* 235 Md. 472, 201 A.2d 781 (1964).

Final acceptance to start the running of the limitation under the statute must be unqualified, unconditional and for complete performance of the contract. A suit instituted after the Board of Education took actual possession of the premises and accepted the project contingently but prior to the time when the architect issued his final certificate was instituted within the statutory period. *U.S.F.&G. v. Hamilton & Spiegel, Inc.,* 241 Md. 133, 215 A.2d 735 (1966).

Where there remained services for contractor to perform, and city was withholding payment of balance of construction contract price, dates when conditional acceptance was given to ice rink and conditional acceptance was given to remainder of structure were not dates of "final acceptance" within statute prohibiting filing of materialman's suit more than one year after date of final acceptance of work performed under contract. *Joseph J. Hock, Inc. v. Baltimore Contractors, Inc.,* 252 Md. 61, 249 A.2d 135 (1969).

Where the contract documents called for installation of equipment the equipment was not installed until in workable condition, hence recovery was allowed for the cost of repairs to the equipment damaged, after installed, by mud and water in flood.

Where a supplier and a general contractor entered into an agreement that the general contractor would make payment to the joint order of the supplier and subcontractor monthly for all materials supplied by the subcontractor, acceptance of checks in a greater amount than presently due without so informing the contractor did not estop the supplier from claiming under the payment bond when the supplier turned over the excess of the payment to the subcontractor. There was no obligation or authorization on the part of the supplier to retain proceeds from any check in excess of cost of materials. *N. S. Stavrou Inc. v. Beacon Elec. Supply Co.,* 249 Md. 451, 240 A.2d 278 (1968).

Under a general contractor's payment bond protecting those supplying material or labor used or reasonably required for use in the performance of the contract, a supplier who in good faith delivered material ordered by the subcontractor to the building site is protected by the bond even though the order received by the supplier was for twice the material required. *The Ruberroid Co. v. Glassman Construction Co.,* 248 Md. 97, 234 A.2d 875 (1967).

Under a dual obligation payment bond executed in favor of the owner of an apartment project and a lender bank which protected suppliers of material "used or reasonably required for use," subcontractor's tender of goods which conformed to contract was the equivalent of delivery and fixed general contractor's duty to pay for them, and hence subcontractor could recover from surety even though the goods were never delivered because subcontractor never received requested delivery instructions from general contractor. *Aetna Insurance Co. v. Maryland Cast Stone Co. Inc.,* 254 Md. 109, 253 A.2d 872 (1969).

Maryland does not follow the Federal Court decision with respect to allowing recovery for equipment rental under a payment bond furnished under Maryland's "Little Miller Act." *Williams Construction Co. Inc. v. Construction Equipment Co.,* 253 Md. 60, 251 A.2d 864 (1969).

$32 worth of labor and material to change a floor mount to a ceiling mount of a heating and cooling unit, which had been sold for approximately $44,000, when unit did not fit into the space indicated by the drawings was such a modification as to allow the claimant to recover where the required notice was given within 90 days from the date the modification was made. *R. T. Woodfield, Inc. v. Montgomery Co. Bd. of Education,* 252 Md. 33, 248 A.2d 895 (1969).

Subrogation rights of the surety relate back to the date of the contract, since that is the date on which the surety's obligation is made binding. *Finance Co. of America v. U.S. Fidelity & Guar. Co.,* 277 Md. 177, 353 A.2d 249 (1976).

A performance bond that specified that the contractor must carry $1,000,000 worth of insurance for protection of third persons was held not to cover the state's cost for cleaning up damage resulting from faulty waste disposal on highway construction project, although the state agency was allowed to recover from the contractor. *State Highway Administration v. Transamerica Insurance Co.,* 278 Md. 690, 367 A.2d 509 (1976).

Where a contractor on a city project furnished a single surety bond and then defaulted, leading to action on the bond by both the city and the subcontractor, bond was held to cover both performance and payment requirements. The court decided that the statute implies first protection to laborers and materialmen rather than to the city, and the bond's clause giving the city primacy of claim is to be disregarded. *Baltimore v. Fidelity & Deposit Co. of Maryland,* 282 Md. 431, 386 A.2d 749 (1978).

Statute required two bonds for all public work in excess of $5,000; one was to be performance bond in amount deemed adequate by public body; other was to be payment bond in amount not less than 50 percent of contract price. Surety issued one bond in amount of contract price. Surety sought declaratory judgment as to bond coverage. Court determined that bond was to be construed under terms of statute and held: (1) if suppliers and laborers have claims in excess of 50% of contract price, those claims are protected by bond, up to penal sum of bond, and public is protected by balance; and (2) if suppliers and laborers have claims less than 50% of bond, those claims are protected by bond, and public is protected up to 50% of bond. *Baltimore v. Fidelity & Deposit Co. of Maryland,* 282 Md. 431, 386 A.2d 749 (1978).

MASSACHUSETTS

1. AMOUNT OF BOND.—The total contract price. (149 Massachusetts General Laws § 44E)

2. LABOR AND MATERIAL COVERED.—An amendment approved August 19, 1957, extended the coverage as follows: Contracts executed by the Commonwealth, and by counties, cities and towns; labor performed or furnished or materials used or employed in such construction or repair, including lumber so employed which is not incorporated in the construction or repair work and is not wholly

or necessarily consumed or made as worthless as to lose its identity, but only to the extent of its purchase price less its fair salvage value, and including also any material specially fabricated at the order of the contractor or subcontractor for use as a component part of said public building or other public work so as to be unsuitable for use elsewhere, even though such material has not been delivered and incorporated into the public building or public work, but only to the extent of its purchase price less its fair salvage value and only to the extent that such specially fabricated material is in conformity with the contract, plans and specifications or any changes therein duly made, rental or hire of vehicles, steam shovels or rollers propelled by steam or other power, concrete mixers, tools and other appliances and equipment employed in such construction, reconstruction, alteration, remodeling, repair or demolition; and for payment by such contractor and subcontractors of any sums due trustees or other persons authorized to collect such payments from the contractor or subcontractors, based upon the labor performed or furnished as aforesaid, for health and welfare plans and other fringe benefits which are payable in cash and provided for in collective bargaining agreements between organized labor and the contractor or subcontractors; provided, that any such trustees or other persons authorized to collect such payments for health and welfare plans and other fringe benefits shall, subject to the following provisions, be entitled to the benefit of the security only in an amount based upon labor performed or furnished as aforesaid for a maximum of two hundred and forty consecutive calendar days.

The foregoing amendment of 1957 was further amended July 18, 1962, to extend the coverage to include "payment of transportation charges for materials used or employed" in such public work "which are consigned to the contractor or to a subcontractor who has a direct contractual relationship with the contractor" and also "for payment of transportation charges directly related to such rental or hire."

3. NOTICE REQUIRED.—

(a) *To surety*—No special statutory provision.

(b) *To contractor*—An amendment approved July 17, 1972, effective after October 16, 1972, provides that a claimant having a contractual relationship with a subcontractor, but not with the general contractor, must give notice of a claim in writing to the general contractor within sixty-five days after the day on which the claimant last performed labor or furnished labor, materials, equipment, appliances or transportation, stating with substantial accuracy the amount claimed, the name of the party for whom such labor was performed or such labor, materials, equipment, appliances or transportation was furnished.

A claimant shall have the right to enforce any part of a claim covering specially fabricated material included in the paragraph (1) coverage only if such claimant has given the contractor principal written notice of the placement of the order and the amount thereof not later than twenty days after receiving the final approval in writing for the use of the material. The notices provided for in this paragraph (3) shall be served by mailing a sworn statement by registered or certified mail postage prepaid in an envelope addressed to the contractor principal at any place at which the contractor principal maintains an office or conducts his business, or at the contractor principal's residence, or in any manner in which civil process may be served."

(c) *To municipality*—No special statutory requirements. 149 MGLA § 29.

(d) To creditors—No special statutory provision.

4. TIME FOR SUIT.—A claimant who has not been paid in full within sixty-five days after the due date for the labor, materials, equipment, appliances or transportation furnished by such claimant has the right to enforce any such claim by filing a petition in equity within one year after the day such claimant last performed the labor or furnished the labor, materials, equipment, appliances or transportation included in his claim, and by prosecuting the claim thereunder by trial in the superior court to final adjudication.

5. CONTRACTS EXCLUDED.—Statute requires that bond must be furnished where the amount of the contract is more than $5,000 in the case of the Commonwealth and more than $2,000 in the case of a contract with a county, city, town, district or other political subdivision.

6. PROCEDURE.—After the filing of a petition the parties may move for a speedy trial. However, the court may examine all claims that may arise under the statute which have been duly filed in accordance therewith and determine the respective amounts due such claimants and their right to participate in the security and apply the security to the claimants held entitled hereto.

7. PENALTY FOR FAILURE TO TAKE BOND.—No special statutory provision.

8. SPECIAL PROVISIONS.—The 1972 amendment reads: The court shall not dismiss any petition on the ground that it was filed before the sixty-fifth day after the day the claimant last performed the labor or furnished the labor, materials, equipment, appliances or transportation included in the claim, nor shall the court dismiss any petition on the ground that a claim involves more than one contract with the same party and that the one year period has elapsed as to any one contract;

provided, that the court shall not enter a decree upon any claim or part thereof prior to the seventieth day after the day the claimant last performed the labor or furnished the labor, materials, equipment, appliances or transportation included in the claim.

A decree in favor of any claimant under this section shall include reasonable legal fees based upon the time spent and the results accomplished as approved by the court and such legal fees shall not in any event be less than published rate of any recommended fee schedule of a statewide bar association or of a bar association in which the office of counsel for claimant is located, whichever is higher.

9. REMARKS.—The amendment approved July 19, 1972, effective after October 16, 1972, clarifies the rights of both subcontractors and general contractors for payment by the awarding authority under public works contracts, requires such contracts to contain specific provisions pertaining to payment and also provides for judicial relief with respect to disputed amounts.

This 1972 amendment also provides: "Any assignment by a subcontractor of the rights under this section to a surety company furnishing a bond under the provisions of section twenty-nine of chapter one hundred forty-nine shall be invalid. The assignment and subrogation rights of the surety to amounts included in a demand for direct payment which are in the possession of the awarding authority or which are on deposit pursuant to subparagraph (f) of paragraph (1) shall be subordinate to the rights of all subcontractors who are entitled to be paid under this section and who have not been paid in full."

Statutes of 1959, 1960, and 1962 abstracted in the 1972 and prior issues of the Credit Manual are not reproduced. They may be applicable to contracts to which the amendment of 1972 does not apply.

10. DECISIONS.—Prior to the 1972 amendment a claimant who failed to file a sworn statement of claim or petition in equity as required by the statute may not recover on the statutory payment bond as a common law bond by reasons of provisions going beyond the statute. The bond must be enforced solely as a statutory bond. *Martin Fireproofing Corp. vs. AEtna Insurance Co.,* 346 Mass. 498, 194 N.E.2d 101 (1963).

Although a surety which had completed performance after default by contractor had not filed a financing statement under the Uniform Commercial Code, the surety was subrogated to the government's right to hold the unpaid progress payment and final retainage and had a superior right to these funds as against a bank which had loaned the contractor money, taken an assignment and duly filed a financing statement covering the assignment. *National Shawmutt Bank of Boston v. New Amsterdam Casualty Company, Inc.,* 290 F. Supp. 664 (D. Mass. 1968), aff'd, 411 F.2d 843 (1st Cir. 1969), followed: *Framingham Trust Co. v. Gould Nat'l Batteries, Inc.,* 427 F.2d 856 (1st Cir. 1970); *Canter v. Schlager,* 358 Mass. 789, 267 N.E.2d 492 (1971).

The statute is applicable to housing authorities and the filing of sworn statements of claim is a prerequisite to recovery. *Philip Carey Co. v. Peerless Casualty Co.,* 330 Mass. 319, 113 N.E.2d 226 (1953).

A subcontractor supplying school house equipment must strictly comply with the statute requiring the filing of a statement of claim and petition with the town clerk. *Town of Hopkinton v. Sturtevant Co.,* 285 Mass. 272, 189 N.E. 107 (1934).

Recovery may be had for gasoline, motor oil, grease and coal consumed in the operation of highway equipment, as well as for lead-in wire used to transmit electric current and consumed in the work. *American Casting Co., v. Commonwealth,* 274 Mass. 1, 174 N.E. 174 (1931).

Premiums due upon liability insurance policy issued to public works contractor are not covered by the bond. *Bay State Dredging Co., v. Ellis & Son Co.,* 235 Mass, 263, 126 N.E. 468 (1920).

Under the old statute which required that a materialman must file a sworn statement of claim prior to the expiration of 90 days after he ceased to furnish the material, the 90 days begins to run from the last date on which the materials were received from the consignee, rather than the date when the materials were shipped by the materialman. *Mosaic Tile Co. v. Rusco Products of Massachusetts, Inc.,* 350 Mass. 433, 215 N.E.2d 171 (1966).

The statutory requirement of notice of the placement of an order for specially fabricated material to be given to the prime contractor within 20 days after such placement should be construed as requiring such notice only where the specially fabricated material has been ordered by a subcontractor but not used or employed. Where the specially fabricated materials have been incorporated into the structure, no notice of such placement is required. *Lawrence Plate & Window Glass Co. v. Varrasso Bros., Inc.,* 353 Mass. 631, 233 N.E.2d 897 (1968).

A wholesale and retail dealer in electrical supplies, furnishing supplies to subcontractor installing electrical equipment in school building pursuant to a contract relating to dealer's own stock and pursuant to a different contract relating to materials specially fabricated for such school job by manufacturer, could not reach security furnished by principal contractor's labor and material bond for the specially fabricated material, the last delivery of which occurred after the statutory period for filing of dealer's sworn statement. *Massachusetts Gas & Electric Light Supply Co. v. Rugo Construction Co., Inc.,* 321 Mass. 433, 71 N.E.2d 408 (1947).

A wood mill operator who prepared and furnished a special interior trim for a city hall, in accordance with plans of general contractor, even though he performed no labor on the building, was not a "materialman" but a "subcontractor" within the statute securing claims for labor and material furnished to contractors and "subcontractors" on public works, and the city was properly ordered to pay a claim for lumber sold to and so used by the mill operator out of moneys held by it. *Holt & Bugbee Co. v. City of Melrose,* 424 Mass. 311, 41 N.E.2d 562 (1942).

Where items such as those furnished by a supplier to a subcontractor were in common use and with little or no adaptation the cost could be completely recovered, these items were not unsuitable for use elsewhere and did not come within the provision of the statute relative to notice for specially fabricated material. *Westinghouse Electric Corp. v. J. J. Grace & Son, Inc.,* 349 Mass. 664, 212 N.E.2d 213 (1965).

Where a supplier furnished to a subcontractor, for use in a construction project, a number of items, supplied at different times, not under a single contract but by filling a continuing series of orders relating to the bonded project, a single statement of claim may be filed covering all the items. *Westinghouse Electric Corp. v. J. J. Grace & Son, Inc.,* 349 Mass. 664, 212 N.E.2d 213 (1965).

Where a supplier acting in good faith and in fulfilment of its contract with a subcontractor shipped materials to the subcontractor which the subcontractor claimed were not included in a prior shipment, although they were billed and may have been shipped although not received at the earlier time, the date of shipment of the replacement parts, even though no additional charge was made by the supplier, could be used to extend the time for the filing of a notice of claim by the supplier. The supplying of the replacement parts was not a voluntary gratuitous act but constituted an effort by the supplier to complete contract. *International Tel. & Tel. Co. v. Hartford Accident & Indemnity Co.,* 357 Mass. 282, 257 N.E.2d 787 (1970).

Where a supplier supplied materials to an original subcontractor who went into bankruptcy before finishing its work, and the materials were incorporated into the public building by another subcontractor who finished the work, the supplier was entitled to payment from the general contractor's bond even though the second subcontractor, before incorporating the materials in the building, had purchased the materials from the original subcontractor's trustee in bankruptcy. *American Air Filter Co. v. Innamorati Bros., Inc.,* 358 Mass. 146, 260 N.E.2d 718 (1970).

Under contract for construction of section of state highway, both sums retained and surety bond constitute security for payment of claims of laborers and materialmen. The retained sums were held by the Commonwealth in the nature of a trust for the benefit of those described in the statute. *J. J. Struzziery Co. v. Taurasi Co.,* 340 Mass. 481, 165 N.E.2d 120 (1960).

The legislature, in providing that no claim for transportation charges is valid unless written notice of the amount is given to the contractor principal on the bond within twenty days after delivery of materials, appliances or equipment, intended this twenty-day notice provision to refer only to separate transportation charges and not to a situation in which a transportation charge is included in the cost of the material. *Mavrofrides v. Blanchard Co.,* 361 Mass. 540, 281 N.E.2d 270 (1972).

The Massachusetts bond statute does not prohibit a laborer or materialman from voluntarily substituting the procedure of arbitration for his right to litigate and a suit on the bond will be stayed pending arbitration.

Seller of blasting supplies, which were used by buyer in quarrying stone furnished to general contractor for airport runway extension, was not entitled to protection of general contractor's statutory payment bond since the buyer was a material supplier rather than a subcontractor; in any event, the materials supplied by the buyer were not "specifically fabricated * * * so as to be unsuitable for use elsewhere," within meaning of statute requiring a payment bond of a government contractor. *James D. Shea Co., v. Perini Corporation,* 2 Mass. App. Ct. 912, 321 N.E.2d 831 (1975).

The fact that furnished material was not actually put in use by subcontractor does not change the right of the supplier to recover the cost of the material after filing a timely notice well within required 90 days after equipment was shipped. *International Heating & Air Conditioning Corp. v. Rich Construction Co.,* 372 Mass. 134, 360 N.E.2d 636 (1977).

Court found that contractor refused to return specially manufactured goods. When contractor did not pay for such goods, supplier sued contractor and its payment bond surety. Surety argued that it had no liability for conversions. However, court found otherwise and affirmed judgment for goods' value. *C.C.&T. Constr. Co. v. Coleman Bros. Corp.,* 391 N.E.2d 1256, 8 Mass. App. 133 (1979).

Prime contractor subcontracted portion of work to subcontractor who, in turn, subcontracted to HEMCO. HEMCO failed to pay vacation, insurance, and pension funds to union trustee under collective bargaining agreement. Trustees sued prime's payment bond surety. Surety defended on basis of 1972 amendment to bond statutes, claiming amendment limited laborers to those of first-tier subcontractors. Court disagreed, analyzing statute as notice requirement for suit on bond. *Peters v. Hartford Accident & Indem. Co.,* 389 N.E.2d 63, 377 Mass. 863 (1979).

MICHIGAN

1. AMOUNT OF BOND.—In an amount fixed by government unit to not less than 25 percent of the contract price. (129 M.C.L.A. 202)

2. LABOR AND MATERIAL COVERED.—Labor, material, or both used or reasonably required for use in the performance of the contract, including that part of water, gas, power, light, heat, oil, gasoline, telephone service or rental of equipment directly applicable to the contract.

3. NOTICE REQUIRED.—(a) *To surety*—No special statutory provision.

(b) *To principal contractor*—No notice is required by a claimant having a contractual relationship with the principal contractor. A claimant not having a direct contractual relationship with the principal contractor does not have a right of action upon the payment bond unless:

(I) Claimant has within 30 days after furnishing the first of such material or performing the first of such labor served on the principal contractor a written notice which shall inform the principal of the nature of the materials being furnished or to be furnished or labor being performed or to be performed and identifying the party contracting for such labor or material and the site for the performance of such work or the delivery of such materials; and

(II) Claimant has given written notice to the contractor and the governmental unit involved within 90 days from the date on which the claimant performed the last of the labor or furnished or supplied the last of the material for which the claim was made, stating with substantial accuracy the amount claimed and the name of the party to whom the material was furnished or supplied or for whom the labor was done or performed.

The statute reads: "Each notice shall be served by mailing the same by certified mail, postage prepaid, in an envelope addressed to the principal contractor, the governmental unit involved, at any place at which said parties maintain a business or residence."

(c) *To municipality*—See Subdivision 3 (b) II above.

(d) *To creditors*—No special statutory provision.

4. TIME FOR SUIT.—One year from time on which final payment was made to the principal contractor.

5. CONTRACTS EXCLUDED.—Less than $50,000.

6. PROCEDURE.—Performance and payment bonds are required to be filed in the office of the governmental unit awarding the contract. The agent in charge of the office of the governmental unit is required to furnish to an applicant who submits an affidavit that he has supplied labor or material for the work and payment therefor has not been made, or that he is being sued on such bond or that it is the surety thereon, a certified copy of the bond and the contract for which it was given. These copies constitute prima facie evidence of the contents, execution and delivery of the original.

The statute reads: "An action instituted on the payment bond shall be brought only in the appropriate court in the political subdivision in which the contract was to be performed."

7. PENALTY FOR FAILURE TO TAKE BOND.—No special statutory provision.

8. SPECIAL PROVISIONS.—The statute reads: "The principal contractor shall not be required to make payment to a subcontractor of sums due from the subcontractor to parties performing labor or furnishing materials or supplies, except upon the receipt of the written orders of such parties to pay to the subcontractor the sums due such parties." In addition, "Neither the invitation for bids, nor any person acting, or purporting to act, on behalf of the governmental unit shall require that the bonds be furnished by a particular surety company, or through a particular agent or broker, or through a company, agent or broker in any particular locality."

While this 1963 statute requires a performance and payment bond before contract for construction, alteration, or repair of any public building or public work or improvement of the state or a county, city, village, township, school district, public educational institution, other political subdivision, public authority or public agency is awarded, it expressly excludes the State Highway Department for bond coverage. With respect to contracts awarded pursuant to an invitation for bids issued on or before the effective date of the 1963 law, and all state highway projects, the old law applies.

Effective July 23, 1981, the Department of Transportation may establish specifications relating to retainage on highway contracts. Effective February 17, 1982, the contractor may provide an irrevocable letter of credit instead of the bonds if the principal contractor is a railroad.

9. DECISIONS.—Where materialman had failed to give 30-day notice that material was being furnished or to be furnished, materialman, as such, could not recover on performance bond. *Hub Electric Co., Inc. v. Aetna Casualty & Surety co.*, 400 F. Supp 77 (E.D. Mich. 1975), *aff'd*, 585 F.2d 183 (6th Cir. 1978), *cert. denied*, 440 U.S. 936 (1979).

Subcontractor's failure to serve principal contractor with notice of its claim within 30 days of commencing work as required precluded subcontractor's right of action on payment bond, despite subcontractor's contention that it substantially complied with notice requirement. *Charles W. Anderson Co. v. Argonaut Insurance Co.*, 62 Mich. App. 650, 233 N.W.2d 691 (1975).

While Michigan law allows a retainage fee to be set aside from payments, it does not mandate it, so failure to retain funds does not absolve surety from responsibility. *Chris Nelson & Son, Inc. v. Michigan Corp.*, 84 Mich. App. 29, 269 N.W.2d 295 (1978).

Where a written agreement was not signed by all participating parties, their intent to enter contract was sufficient to hold prime contractor responsible on performance bond, for breach of contract. *Earl Dubey & Son, Inc. v. Macomb Concrete Corp.*, 81 Mich. App. 662, 266 N.W.2d 152 (1978), *cert. denied*, 441 U.S. 944 (1979).

A surety may, by its bonding contract, agree to accept a greater liability than that required under Michigan Public Works Bonding Act although, for reasons of public policy, it may not contract for less. M.C.L.A. §§ 129.206, 129.207. *Hub Electric Co. v. Gust Construction Co.*, 585 F.2d 183 (6th Cir. 1978), *cert. denied*, 440 U.S. 936 (1979).

Suit by subcontractor on prime contractor's payment bond. On appeal by surety from judgment for plaintiff, held, reversed and remanded. (1) One-year limitation on suits on bond was unambiguous, not prohibited by law, and was enforceable. (2) Fact that plaintiff was a third-party beneficiary of the bond did not render limitation inapplicable. *Camelot Excavating Co. v. St. Paul Fire & Marine Ins. Co.*, 89 Mich. App. 219, 280 N.W.2d 491 (1979).

MINNESOTA

1. AMOUNT OF BOND.—Not less than the contract price, provided that, in contracts made by the State Board of Control or the Highway Department on behalf of the state, the penalty on the bond shall be not less than three-fourths of the contract price. (25 Minnesota Statutes Annotated § 429.06)

2. LABOR AND MATERIAL COVERED.—Claims of all persons doing work or furnishing skill, tools, machinery or materials, or insurance premiums, or sales or wage tax, or equipment or supplies for any camp maintained for the feeding or keeping of men and animals engaged under or for the purpose of such contract.

3. NOTICE REQUIRED.—(a) *To surety*—The official with whom the claimant files written notice of his claim, upon receipt of such notice, shall mail one copy thereof by registered mail to each of the sureties on the bond, at their last known address. See notice to municipality and special provisions below. (b) *To principal contractor*—The official with whom the claimant files written notice of his claim, upon receipt of such notice, shall mail one copy thereof by registered mail to the principal contractor, at his last known address. See notice to municipality and special provisions below. (c) *To municipality*—No action shall be maintained on the bond unless, within 120 days after the completion of the contract and the acceptance thereof by the proper public authority, the claimant shall file a written notice specifying the nature and amount of his claim and the date of furnishing the last item thereof in the office of the Commissioner of Insurance, in case the contract is for the performance of work for the state or any department thereof, or in the office of the County Auditor, in case the contract is let by any county, municipal corporation or other public board or body, of the county in which such municipal corporation, public board or body is situate, and, if situate in two or more counties, then such notice shall be filed in the office of the County Auditor of each of the counties. (d) *To creditors*—No special statutory provision.

4. TIME FOR SUIT.—No action shall be maintained unless the 120 day notice to the principal and surety is given, nor unless the action is begun within one year after the service of such notice.

5. CONTRACTS EXCLUDED.—Bonds are no longer required with respect to negotiated contracts for public work at a state owned institution or installation not in excess of $5,000; however, where the contractor in such circumstances elects to forgo the bond, a 1975 amendment prescribes a deposit, in the form of a certified or cashier's check, with the state treasurer. The deposit must be in the amount in which a bond would otherwise be required. To bring action on the deposit, a claimant must notify the commissioner of administration and the state treasurer of the amount and nature of his claim, and the name of the depositor. This action must be brought within 90 days of completion of the contract, but judgment will not be entered for at least 30 days after such claim is instituted, during which time the state or other parties entitled to a share of the deposit may join the suit.

6. PROCEDURE.—No special statutory provision.

7. PENALTY FOR FAILURE TO TAKE BOND.—If the bond is not taken, the corporation or body for which work is done under the contract shall be liable to all persons furnishing labor, skill or material to the contractor, and for any loss resulting to them from such failure.

8. SPECIAL PROVISIONS.—No public contract is valid for any purpose unless the contractor shall have given the bond for the protection of labor and materialmen.

If, after the giving of the bond, the contract price should, for any reason, be increased, an additional bond may be required, the penalty of which shall be not less than the amount of such increase, and, if such additional bond be not furnished within ten days after such demand, the work on such contract shall cease until an additional bond is furnished.

If the amount realized on the bond be insufficient to discharge all claims in full, the parties pro-rate.

Whenever any of the sureties on the bond have become insolvent, or, for any cause, are no longer proper or sufficient securities, the municipal corporation may require the contractor to furnish a new or additional bond within ten days and thereupon, if so ordered by the municipal corporation, all work on such contracts shall cease until new or additional bond is furnished. If the bond is not furnished within such time, the municipal corporation may, at its option, determine the contract and complete the same as the agent and at the expense of the contractor and the sureties.

The claimant, at the time he furnishes the written notice, must furnish at least two copies thereof. The official with whom said notice is filed is entitled to charge a fee for filing said notice and mailing the copies. The failure of the Commissioner of Insurance or the County Auditor with whom such notice is filed to mail said copies as provided by the statute shall in no way affect the validity of the claim or the right of the claimant to maintain an action thereof.

Judgment in the suit cannot be entered prior to 30 days after notice is given.

A 1977 act directs officials to partially indemnify bonding companies who provide performance bonds on state contracts awarded to small businesses and small businesses owned by the economically and socially disadvantaged.

A public contracting agency may reserve as retainage from any progress payment on a public contract for a public improvement an amount not to exceed five percent of the payment. A public agency may reduce the amount of the retainage and may eliminate retainage on any monthly contract payment if, in the agency's opinion, the work is progressing satisfactorily.

In lieu of cash retainage, the contractor may deposit bonds or securities with the public contracting agency or in any bank or trust company. Interest on the securities shall be payable to the contractor as it accrues.

Whenever the construction or improvement of any county state-aid highway, municipal state-aid street, and local improvement is to be done by contract, and the construction or improvement is not financed in whole or in part by federal aid highway money, the governing body shall agree in the contract to pay the contractor on account an amount not to exceed 95% of the value of the work until 95% or more of the work is completed.

9. REMARKS.—The statute pertaining to bonds covers every municipality or other public board or body in the state, any provision in any general or specific act or charter to the contrary notwithstanding. It is not necessary to obtain leave of court to bring any action against any principal or surety on any such bond. A 1977 statute adds the construction work performed under contract for the Metropolitan Sports Facilities Commission to those projects requiring the bonds described above.

10. DECISIONS.—The requirement of written notice within ninety days after the completion of the contract and acceptance thereof to the County Auditor is a condition precedent which must be performed before the right to bring action on the bond accrues. *Ceco Steel Products Corp. v. Tapager,* 208 Minn. 367, 294 N.W. 210 (1940); *State of Minnesota Dept. Highways v. Cornelius,* 289 Minn. 521, 184 N.W.2d 779 (1971).

It has been decided prior bond legislation had no application to St. Paul, which has a home-rule charter which became effective in 1914. While legislation may supersede the provisions of home-rule charters, this Act was not intended to have that effect. *Guaranteed Concrete Brick Co. v. Garrick Bros.,* 185 Minn. 454, 241 N.W. 588 (1932). Notice required by the old statute does not apply to bonds given by those who enter into contracts with the city of Duluth for public work. *Rand Kardex Service Corp. v. Forrestal,* 174 Minn. 579, 219 N.W. 943 (1928).

Notice mailed to the surety at its home office in another state constitutes compliance with the statute. *Benson v. Barrett,* 171 Minn. 305, 214 N.W. 47 (1927).

A claimant who fails to bring a suit within a year after the filing of the required notice with the Commissioner of Insurance may not maintain an action on the bond even though the suit was brought within a year after completion and acceptance of the highway by the State Highway

STATE BOND LAWS

Commissioner. The notice in this case was given some months prior to the acceptance of the highway by the Highway Commissioner. *Shandorf v. Standard Surety & Casualty Co.,* 198 Minn. 96, 268 N.W. 843 (1936).

The charter of Duluth gives the city council power to enact ordinances regulating the letting of contracts for public work and prescribing surety bonds. *Rand Dardex Service Corp. v. Forrestal,* 174 Minn. 579, 219 N.W. 943 (1928).

Although denominated a lease, a conditional sales contract transferring powers to a highway subcontractor does not impose on principal contractor or his surety obligation for reasonable rental. *Motor Power Equipment Co. v. Park Transfer Co.,* 188 Minn. 370, 247 N.W. 244 (1933).

Premiums for public liability, collision, and property damage insurance procured by highway subcontractor are not included within term "insurance" as used in bond statute. "Insurance" within the meaning of the statute is restricted to workmen's compensation insurance. *Kunz Ins. Agency v. Phillips,* 191 Minn. 626, 255 N.W. 90 (1934).

The cost of repairs to a fleet of trucks used by a subcontractor in highway work is covered under a bond conditioned to pay all claims for work, tools, machinery, skill, materials, insurance premiums, equipment and supplies; and, a mechanic employed by a highway subcontractor to keep such motor vehicles in working condition is an employee within the purview of the statute. *General Motors Truck Co. v. Phillips,* 191 Minn. 467, 254 N.W. 580 (1934).

While there may be recovery for material and labor used in incidental repairs of contractor's machinery, *Miller v. American Bonding Co.,* 158 N.W. 432, 133 Minn. 336 (1916), there can be none for major repairs involving replacement of old with new parts in absence of proof that the parts were consumed in the work. *Clifton v. Norden,* 178 Minn. 288, 226 N.W. 940 (1929).

The cost of equipment required by trucks while in use on highway projects is not covered by the bond. *Mack International Motor Truck Co. v. Western Surety Co.,* 194 Minn. 484, 260 N.W. 869 (1935).

Substantial completion of the project does not constitute "completion of the contract" within the meaning of the bond statute. *Guaranteed Gravel & Sand Co. v. AEtna Casualty & Surety Co.,* 174 Minn. 366, 219 N.W. 546 (1928).

A school building is not "accepted" within the purview of the statute when the school district because of a shortage in school buildings makes use of the building before it is fully completed and there is nothing to show that the school district regarded the work as completed. *Guaranteed Gravel & Sand Co. v. AEtna Casualty & Surety Co.,* 174 Minn. 366, 219 N.W. 546 (1928).

Where city required contractor, who had contract for construction of street improvements, to furnish statutory performance bond for protection of laborers and materialmen, the city discharged its full duty and its officers were not trustees for purpose of enforcing liability accruing to them through delinquency of the contractor. *Farmers State Bank of Madelia, Inc. v. Burns,* 212 Minn. 455, 4 N.W.2d 330 (1942).

Under statute providing that no action shall be maintained on public contractor's bond unless, within 90 days after acceptance of contract by proper public authorities, claimant shall file a written notice, etc., highway contract was accepted by proper public authorities when commissioner of highways approved the voucher for final payment and hence a materialman's notice filed with Commissioner of Insurance within 90 days thereafter was timely. *Wheeler Lumber Bridge & Supply Co. v. Seaboard Surety Co.,* 218 Minn. 443, 16 N.W.2d 519 (1944).

The statute relating to public contractor's bond requires not only that the work must be completed but that the contract must be accepted by the proper authorities before the 90 day period for filing notice of claim under such bond commences. *Elk River Concrete Products Co. vs. American Casualty Co. of Reading,* 262 Minn. 310, 114 N.W.2d 655 (1962).

Giving of statutory notice of claim filed with county auditor of county in which municipal corporation, public board, or body is situated is a condition precedent to an action on a general contractor's bond by a materialman in regard to a construction contract with a municipality. *Grazzini Bros. & Company v. Builders Clinic, Inc.,* 280 Minn. 540, 160 N.W.2d 259 (1968).

A claimant who fabricated doors for a subcontractor, which doors were especially made and built with a variety of materials and designs, was a subcontractor and entitled to recover on the prime contractor's bond. *Weyerhaeuser Company v. Twin City Millwork Co.,* 291 Minn. 293, 191 N.W.2d 401 (1971).

A surety who after the contractor defaulted completed performance and paid claims of laborers and materialmen in an amount which exceeded the balance of the contract price retained by the owner, has a superior right to this contract balance and is not required to file under the Minnesota Uniform Commercial Code. *In Re J. V. Gleason, Inc. v. AEtna Casualty & Surety Co.,* 452 F.2d 1219 (8th Cir., Minn. 1971).

Where the bond contained a section providing for an extension of the time within which suit had to be filed beyond that specified in the bond statute, the bond's language governed. *Nelson Roofing Contracting Inc. v. C. W. Moore Co.*, 310 Minn. 140, 245 N.W.2d 866 (1976).

A subcontractor's claim against prime contractor and surety was denied by surety on grounds of timeliness but court ruled that a settlement agreement which backdated the contract completion date was invalid. *A.J. Chromy Construction Co. v. Commercial Mechanical Services, Inc.*, 260 N.W. 2d 579 (Minn. 1977).

MISSISSIPPI

1. AMOUNT OF BOND.—Both the performance bond and payment bond not less than the contract price. (19 Mississippi Code Annotated § 13-9)

2. LABOR AND MATERIAL COVERED.—All persons supplying labor or material used in the prosecution of the work.

3. NOTICE REQUIRED.—(a) *To surety*—No special statutory provision. (b) *To principal contractor*—Persons having a direct contractual relationship with a subcontractor but not the contractor must give written notice to the contractor within a 90 day period after the date on which the last of the labor was performed by him or the last of the materials was furnished by him. (c) *To municipality*—No special statutory provision. (d) *To creditors*—Notice of the pendency of suit shall be made by publication in some newspaper of general circulation published in the county or town where the contract is being performed if there be such paper; otherwise, in a paper having a general circulation therein, for at least three weeks, the last publication to be at least one week before the trial of the suit.

4. TIME FOR SUIT.—If the municipal corporation starts suit, subcontractors and materialmen intervene therein. If no suit is brought by the municipality within six months from the completion and final settlement of the contract, claimant may start suit. All suits must be brought within one year after the performance and final settlement of the contract or within one year after abandonment by the contractor. The period does not begin to run, however, until the obligee publishes a notice in a newspaper published in a county in which the contract or some part thereof was performed, or in a newspaper having a general circulation in such a county.

Suit by subcontractors and materialmen may not be instituted until after (1) complete performance of the contract, (2) final settlement thereof, (3) the public body has published notice thereof in some newspaper published in the county or, if there be none, then in some newspaper having a general circulation therein.

Suit must be commenced within one year after performance and final settlement of the contract and not later, provided that, if the contractor quits or abandons the contract before its completion, suit may be instituted by any such claimant on said bond and shall be commenced within one year after such abandonment and not later.

An amendment of May 15, 1962, sanctions intervention by other claimants where suit has been instituted under the contract bond. However, such intervention must occur within the time limited for such persons to bring an original action. It also permits the surety to require all known claimants under the bond to be joined as parties in any action thereunder.

5. CONTRACTS EXCLUDED.—$1,000 or less, State Highway work. Emergency contracts exceeding $1,000 may be made without rules and regulations set forth in cases of flood or other emergencies where public interest requires no delay.

Effective March 16, 1982, whenever a contract is less than $25,000, the owners may elect to make a lump sum payment at the end of the job. In such cases, a performance bond is not required.

6. PROCEDURE.—If municipal corporation institutes suit, claimants intervene therein, and all claims are subject to the prior rights of the municipal corporation. If no suit is brought by the municipal corporation within six months after the completion and final settlement of the contract, claimant shall furnish affidavit to the municipal corporation. Claimant is then furnished with a certified copy of the bond. Only one action may be brought upon the bond. Other creditors intervene in the suit first brought. Creditors prorate if the bond is inadequate to pay the amount due all creditors.

7. PENALTY FOR FAILURE TO TAKE BOND.—No special statutory provision. See Remarks.

8. SPECIAL PROVISIONS.—Full and final payment of all sums due contractors under all public construction contracts shall be made within forty-five (45) days after the date the work has been completed in full compliance with all the terms and provisions of the contract. Final payment due the contractor shall not be made until the consent of the contractor's surety has been obtained in writing and delivered to the proper contracting authority. The time for the institution of suit shall not begin to run until the municipal corporation has made final settlement or determined the abandonment and published notice thereof in some newspaper in the county where the public improvement is situated or, if there be none, then in some newspaper having a general circulation therein.

STATE BOND LAWS

9. REMARKS.—The surety bond required by the State Highway Commission is for construction, reconstruction or other public work except maintenance where the amount of the contract exceeds $1,000. The 1970 statute contains the following: "the word 'equipment', in addition to all equipment incorporated into or fully consumed in connection with such projects shall include the reasonable value of the use of all equipment of every kind and character and all accessories and attachments thereto which are reasonably necessary to be used and which are used in carrying out the performance of the contract, and the reasonable value of the use thereof, during the period of time the same are used in carrying out the performance of the contract, shall be the amount as agreed upon by the persons furnishing the equipment and those using the same to be paid therefor, which amount, however, shall not be in excess of the maximum current rates and charges allowable for leasing or renting as specified in Section 1, Chapter 260, Laws of 1962, being Section 8330, Mississippi Code of 1942. The word 'labor' shall include all work performed in repairing equipment used in carrying out the performance of the contract, which repair labor is reasonably necessary to the efficient operation of said equipment; and the words 'materials' and 'supplies' shall include all repair parts installed in or on equipment used in carrying out the performance of the contract, which repair parts are reasonably necessary to the efficient operation of said equipment."

10. DECISIONS.—Surety is not liable for groceries and merchandise furnished a commissary operated for profit. *Pidgeon Thomas Iron Co. v. LeFlore County,* 135 Miss. 155, 99 So. 677 (1924).

The failure of the Board of Supervisors to take the bond does not render the members thereof individually liable to the unpaid subcontractors. *Pidgeon Thomas Iron Co. v. LeFlore County,* 135 Miss. 155, 99 So. 677 (1924).

The bond does not cover items required to maintain a camp for workmen, but does cover food and supplies if the commissary is not operated for profit. *McElrath & Rogers v. Kimmons & Sons,* 146 Miss. 775, 112 So. 164 (1927).

Where, after the contract had been completed, the city commissioners approved an estimate of the balance due the contractor and ordered payment thereof, there was a "final settlement" of the contract within the meaning of the bond statute, even though actual payment of the balance was not made until some time later. *Dixie Minerals Corp. v. Dixie Asphalt Paving Co.,* 172 Miss. 218, 159 So. 562 (1935).

Where a materialman furnished material indiscriminately to a contractor then engaged in the construction of three separate projects, each bonded by the same corporate surety, he may maintain a suit against the contractor and the surety to ascertain the place where the various items of material so furnished by the materialman were used. *U. S. F. & G. Co. v. Plumbing Wholesale Co.,* 175 Miss. 675, 166 So. 529 (1936).

Provision of bond given by state highway contractor guaranteeing payment of expense, costs and attorney's fees that might be incurred in enforcement of contract or obligations of the bond inures to the benefit of laborers and materialmen. *Day et al. v. Royce Kershaw Inc.,* 185 Miss. 207, 187 So. 221 (1939).

Recovery was allowed against the surety upon a performance bond of a subcontractor for premiums on policies of liability insurance. *Hartford Accident and Indemnity Co. v. Hewes,* 193 Miss. 850, 11 So.2d 309 (1943).

Bond of contractor under statute relating to bonds of contractors constructing or repairing public buildings requires that all laborers and materialmen be paid for labor and materials that go into construction of public buildings, regardless of whether they are remote materialmen or have furnished materials directly to principal contractor. *Western Cas. & Sur. Co. v. Stevens,* 218 Miss. 627, 67 So.2d 510 (1953).

A suit against surety on the performance bond of a construction company under a contract with a municipality was premature where the contract had not been completely performed at the time of the institution of the original suit and six months had not elapsed within which the municipality had the first right to sue the surety on the bond. *Walker Construction Company v. Construction Machinery Corporation,* 223 Miss. 145, 77 So.2d 712 (1955).

Where the contractor executed a bond to a realty company, which had obtained a defense housing contract, conditioned on faithful performance of the contractor's obligation to supply labor, supervision, tools and equipment for performance of the contract, fuel and necessary repairs supplied by a service station operator to the contractor's vehicles on the project were within full contemplation of both contractor and its surety and were covered by the bond. *Seaboard Surety Company v. Bosarge,* 226 Miss. 482, 84 So.2d 517 (1956). See also, *H. F. Vann Nieuwenhuyze & Sons Construction Co. v. Irby,* 232 Miss. 474, 99 So.2d 651 (1958).

Recovery allowed for ditching work performed by machine rather than by hand for a subcontractor is within the purview of the general contractor's surety combination performance and payment bond, which provides that it is for the benefit of the housing authority and all persons doing work or furnishing skill, tools, machinery or material under or for the purpose of the contract.

The Court held this was not a suit to recover for material and equipment furnished in performance of a contract, but for labor done with a machine. *H. F. Vann Nieuwenhuyze & Sons Construction Company v. Irby,* 232 Miss. 474, 99 So.2d 651 (1958).

The statute making laborers and materialmen third party beneficiaries under contractor's bond does not include lessors of equipment in its protection. *Great American Insurance Company v. A. L. Busby,* 247 Miss. 39, 150 So.2d 131 (1963).

A steel company which under contract with school construction contractor was obligated to furnish specific materials, fabricate them and finally erect them into school building at point distant from company's own plant, in accordance with the plans and specifications was a subcontractor and not a materialman. Claimant who supplied specific steel items to the steel company could recover from construction contractor and his payment bond surety. *O'Neal Steel Company v. Leon C. Miles, Inc.,* 187 So.2d 19 (Miss. 1966).

Highway construction contract payment bond did not cover rental or depreciation on tractor and five scrapers furnished to contractor under rental purchase agreement. These items were not substantially consumed on bonded project but constituted long life expensive additions to contractor's capital plant. *Transamerica Ins. Co. v. Carter Equip. Co.,* 206 So.2d 632 (Miss. 1968).

Under contractor's bond whereby surety and principal agreed that every claimant (defined as a person having direct contract with principal or subcontractor of principal who had not been paid within 90 days after date of claimant's last work or furnishing of materials) might sue on bond, supplier to subcontractor, which had given notice provided for by bond to principal, the bonding company and owner, was entitled to recover on bond for materials furnished subcontractor which was allegedly paid in full by principal before receipt of timely notice. Surety under highway bond was not liable for amount due from contractor under rate-purchase agreement calculated to induce purchase of equipment which was not substantially consumed by the project and had life expectancy greatly in excess of the particular contract. Under statute requiring surety on highway bond to guarantee payment to persons furnishing contractor with labor, materials, equipment and supplies, the bonded project is covered and not long lived equipment reasonably anticipated to be necessary for fulfillment of road contract at hand but capable with its life expectancy of many other similar projects. *Graybar Elec. Co. v. St. Paul Fire and Marine Ins. Co.,* 195 So.2d 82 (Miss. 1967).

A retailer of steel to general contractor is not a subcontractor merely because it performed some cutting and prefabrication of steel. Supplier of steel to retailer was a materialman of a materialman and his claim was not covered by the bond. *Frazier v. O'Neal Steel, Inc.,* 223 So.2d 661 (Miss. 1969).

A surety's right to subrogation is unaffected by the filing requirements of the Uniform Commercial Code. *Travelers Indemnity Co. v. Clark,* 254 So.2d 741 (Miss. 1971).

Erroneous transposition of figures from a worksheet to a bid form by a contractor's representative relieves contractor of bond forfeiture. *Mississippi State Building Commission v. Becknell Construction, Inc.,* 329 So.2d 57 (Miss. 1976).

Where contractor agreed to supply subcontractor with tractor to use on project, but took tractor back from subcontractor before project was completed, contractor could not charge subcontractor for rental of replacement tractor used to complete project. *O. J. Stanton & Co. v. Dennis,* 360 So.2d 669 (Miss. 1978).

Buyer was not entitled to judgment against surety on performance and payment bond executed on contract for public works project where supplier failed to either plead or prove publication of notice of pendency of suit as required by notice provisions of statute governing public works contracts, notwithstanding that surety made no challenge to lack of publication at trial level. *Travelers Indemnity Co. v. Munro Oil and Paint Co.,* 364 So.2d 667 (Miss. 1978).

The municipality is required to publish notice of final settlement or abandonment of the contract by the contractor. A suit brought more than one year after final settlement is not barred where the municipality failed to publish such notice of final settlement. *Marquette Cement Mfg. Co. v. Fidelity & Deposit Co.,* 173 Miss. 164, 158 So. 924 (1935); *Dixie Minerals Corp. v. Dixie Asphalt Paving Co.,* 172 Miss. 218, 159 So. 562 (1935).

The fact that a suit was brought by a materialman on the contractor's bond within one year after the abandonment of the contract, but prior to the time when the municipality published notice of such abandonment, does not bar a subsequent suit by another materialman instituted within a year after publication of notice of such abandonment. *U. S. F. & G. Co. v. Plumbing Wholesale Co.,* 175 Miss. 675, 166 So. 529 (1936).

Publication of notice of abandonment or of final settlement is as essential to the commencement of the period of time for suit as is the fact of such abandonment or final settlement. *U. S. F. & G. Co. v. Plumbing Wholesale Co.,* 175 Miss. 675, 166 So. 529 (1936).

A suit on a highway contractor's bond is premature when instituted prior to publication of notice of final settlement, even though suit was not started until after final settlement had taken place. *Royce Kershaw Inc. v. State to use of Day,* 176 Miss. 757, 169 So. 690 (1936).

A fourth tier supplier to a third tier subcontractor was allowed to recover under a State Highway Bond for supplies, labor, and material, used in the performance of the prime contract, the court distinguishing the pending claim from one where a materialman furnished material to another materialman. *Mississippi Road and Suppply Co. v. Western Casualty and Surety Company,* 246 Miss. 510, 150 So.2d 847 (1963).

Recovery was denied a claimant on a bond of indemnity furnished by a sub-subcontractor to a subcontractor for equipment rental, repairs, and repair parts, small tools and other supplies furnished by the claimant to the sub-subcontractor. *Great American Insurance Company v. A. L. Busby,* 247 Miss. 39, 150 So.2d 131 (1963).

MISSOURI

1. AMOUNT OF BOND.—No special statutory provision, except in the case of county building contracts which is 110% of the amount to be given for erecting the building. (See generally Chapter 107, Vernon's Annotated Missouri Statutes.)

2. LABOR AND MATERIAL COVERED.—Material, lubricants, oil, gasoline, grain, hay, feed, coal and coke, repairs to machinery, groceries and food-stuffs, equipment and tools, consumed or used in connection with the construction of the public improvement and all insurance premiums, both compensation and all other kinds of insurance, on said work and for labor performed in such work, whether by subcontractor or otherwise. Bonds for road work for special road contracts and with respect to certain street improvements and municipal public works are required for the performance of the contract and the payment of all labor and material used or employed in the performance of such contract. In connection with road and bridge contracts over $500, bonds are required to be conditioned for the performance of the contract and also that the contractor will promptly pay for material and labor used and equipment rented in the performance of the contract.

3. NOTICE REQUIRED.—No special statutory provision.

4. TIME FOR SUIT.—No special statutory provision except in St. Louis. See Remarks.

5. CONTRACTS EXCLUDED.—No special statutory provision.

6. PROCEDURE.—Less than $10,000.

7. PENALTY FOR FAILURE TO TAKE BOND.—No special statutory provision. Public officials who fail to require a bond are personally liable to materialmen for material sold to insolvent contractor. *Burton Machy. Co. v. Ruth,* 194 Mo. App. 194, 186 S.W. 737 (1916), later App. 196 Mo. App. 459, 194 S.W. 526.

8. SPECIAL PROVISIONS.—None.

9. REMARKS.—The Revised Code of General Ordinances for St. Louis contains a section providing that no suit shall be instituted on the bond after the expiration of 90 days from the completion of the public contract. This provision of the St. Louis Code was held not arbitrary or unreasonable. *City of St. Louis ex rel. Glasco Elec. Co. v. Dunham Constr. Co.,* 138 S.W.2d 707 (Mo. Ct. App. 1940).

In August of 1959 Missouri enacted a new bond statute making it the duty of all officials of the State and of any political subdivision thereof in making contracts for public works of any kind to require the contractor's bond as above abstracted. We have been advised that these provisions have appeared for years in bond forms prepared by the State of Missouri, especially the State Highway Department, but that in some instances bonds as prepared for certain political subdivisions of the State did not always follow the State form. The new statute provides that all bonds executed and furnished thereunder shall be deemed to contain the requirements and conditions as set out in the statute, regardless of whether the same be set forth in said bond or of any terms or provisions of said bond to the contrary notwithstanding.

In 1963 Missouri adopted a statute pertaining to construction of work on state highways which requires the successful bidder to furnish a surety performance bond in a sum equal to the contract price.

10. DECISIONS.—*Forgarty v. Davis,* 305 Mo. 288, 264 S.W. 879 (1924), holds that an officer's neglect of a ministerial duty imposed by statute for the benefit of individuals is actionable; that a failure to incorporate in a writing the provision which a statute specifically requires an officer to incorporate therein is a neglect of an official duty, but that such public officials are not individually liable to a subcontractor for failure to execute a bond in the form required by the statute from the contractor if the bond taken by the board is sufficient to support an action thereon by the subcontractor. In this case, the provisions of the statute were read into the bond taken and it was decided that subcontractors could recover thereunder. See also *Camdenton Cons'd School District v. N.Y. Casualty Co.,* 340 Mo. 1070, 104 S.W.2d 319 (1937).

Recovery may be had by a subcontractor for labor necessary for the fulfillment of a contract whether personally performed by the subcontractor or performed by his employees. *City of St. Louis ex rel. Sears v. Southern Surety Co.,* 333 Mo. 180, 62 S.W.2d 432 (1933), overruling an earlier decision to the contrary.

Laborer, under the statute, means one who labors with his physical powers in the service and under the direction of another for fixed wages. *Missouri State Highway Comm. v. Coopers Constr. Co.,* 268 S.W. 701 (Mo. Ct. App. 1925).

Gasoline, oil, etc., used in tractor on highway job is covered by the contractor's bond. *State ex rel. Penn Lubric Oil Co. v. Lyle,* 222 Mo. App. 676, 5 S.W.2d 453 (1928).

Recovery may not be had under highway construction bond for groceries furnished men on highway construction job. *State v. Gillioz,* 60 S.W.2d 696 (Mo. Ct. App. 1933).

A materialman may recover the fair value of material sold and delivered to the contractor, even though the bond as written fails to comply with the form of the statute and is merely conditioned that the contractor shall indemnify the School District against loss or damage directly arising by reason of the failure of the contractor to faithfully perform the contract. *Camdenton Cons'd School District v. New York Casualty Co.,* 340 Mo. 1070, 104 S.W.2d 319 (1937).

A surety is not liable to reimburse a subcontractor for his attorney's fees under a statute which provides that, in any action against an insurance company, if it appears that the company had vexatiously refused to pay such loss, the court or jury may allow the plaintiff certain damages and a reasonable attorney's fee, especially where the litigation is not without reasonable cause or excuse. *Camdenton Cons'd School District v. New York Casualty Co.,* 340 Mo. 1070, 104 S.W.2d 319 (1937).

A person who furnished bricks to a materialman who in turn furnished such bricks to subcontractor for use in a city hospital was held not to have a right under the bond. *City of St. Louis ex rel. Stone Creek Brick Co. v. Kaplan-McGowan Co.,* 233 Mo. App. 789, 108 S.W.2d 987 (1937).

The 10-year statute of limitations was held applicable in an action upon a guardian's bond. *Title Guaranty & Surety Co. v. State of Missouri,* 105 F.2d 496 (8th Cir. 1939).

The purpose of the statute requiring a public works contract bond is to provide persons furnishing labor and material the bond security in lieu of mechanics' liens which are inapplicable to public property. *State of Missouri vs. AEtna Casualty & Surety Co.,* 350 S.W.2d 418 (Mo. Ct. App. 1961).

City code provision and clause in bond limiting suits to 90 days from completion of the contract is not in conflict with the statutory requirement which contains no limitation of time of suit. *City of St. Louis ex rel. Atlas Plumbing Supply Co. v. AEtna Cas. & Sur. Co.,* 444 S.W.2d 513 (Mo. App. 1969).

A provision in a payment bond requiring the claimant to give written notice within ninety days after furnishing the last of the materials for which claim is made is valid. This provision is reasonable and does not thwart the purpose or intent of the statute. *Reorganized School District v. Compton Construction Co.,* 483 S.W.2d 674 (Mo. App. 1972).

Surety is not liable for wrongful interference in requesting owner to withhold payment of contract funds for a Missouri public works project. *Gerstner Electric, Inc. v. American Insurance Co.,* 520 F.2d 790 (8th Cir. 1975).

In action brought by city against general contractor and its surety to recover monies due subcontractor under contract, judgment against contractor was determinative of extent of liability of its surety under bond and for interest to date on which verdict was returned. *City of St. Louis v. Tru-Bounce, Inc.,* 562 S.W.2d 158 (Mo. App. 1978).

Suit was brought by materialman on Illinois university construction project, against surety on contractor's performance and payment bond, in Missouri court. Surety sought prohibition to prevent court from proceeding. Held, writ of prohibition made absolute. (1) Illinois statute limiting suit to Illinois court in district where contract was to be performed was valid, and rendered action on bond local, rather than transitory. (2) Statute forms part of contract, and contract to limit suit to Illinois court was valid and binding on claimant. *State ex rel. U.S. Fidelity & Guar. v. Mehan,* 581 S.W.2d 837 (Mo. App. 1979).

MONTANA

1. AMOUNT OF BOND.—Full contract price, unless the amount thereof is fixed by the general ordinance. In no event shall the penal sum be less than 25% of the contract price. (Section 18-2-203, Montana Code Annotated.)

In 1979, Montana amended its statute to increase the amount of the bid security which may be required on public contracts to 10 percent of the proposal.

2. LABOR AND MATERIAL COVERED.—Provender, materials, supplies, provisions or goods supplied and performed or labor furnished in the prosecution of the public work.

3. NOTICE REQUIRED.—(a) *To surety*—No special statutory provision. (b) *To principal contrac-*

STATE BOND LAWS 31–55

tor—Not later than thirty days after the date of the first delivery of the provender, material, supplies or provisions to any subcontractor or agent of any person, firm or corporation having a subcontract with respect to the prosecution of said public work, delivered or sent by registered mail to the contractor. This notice must contain the name of the subcontractor or agent ordering or to whom the same was furnished and state that such contractor or his bond will be held for the same. No suit or action shall be maintained in any court against the contractor or his bond to recover for such provender, provisions, material or supplies or any part thereof unless such notice shall have been given. This is section 6-402. Under section 6-404 as amended in 1957, notice is required to be given to the municipality within ninety days from and after the completion of the contract, as is set forth in subdivision (c) hereof. (c) *To municipality*—No right of action shall be had on the bond unless within ninety days from and after the completion of the contract and the acceptance of the work by the public officials the claimant shall present to and file with the public body a notice in writing substantially in the form as required by the statute.

4. TIME FOR SUIT.—No special statutory provision.
5. CONTRACTS EXCLUDED.—No special statutory provision.
6. PROCEDURE.—No special statutory provision.
7. PENALTY FOR FAILURE TO TAKE BOND.—The municipal corporation is liable to the persons intended to be protected by the bond to the full extent and for the full amount of all the debts so contracted by any subcontractor as well as the contractor.
8. SPECIAL PROVISIONS.—Statute does not apply to any money loaned or advanced to any contractor, subcontractor or any other persons in performance of the work.

No action shall be maintained against the contractor or his bond to recover for provender, provisions, material or supplies, unless the above notice has been given.

Any city or town may impose such conditions and obligations in the bond as may be deemed necessary for its proper protection in fulfillment of the terms of the contract secured thereby and not in conflict with the statute.

Montana requires any contractor who contracts with another to do any work or perform any services for the other except personal services of the contractor not involving work of hired employees, to furnish a surety bond or other form of security in an amount equal to the contractor's average monthly payroll as estimated by the Commissioner for the purpose of insuring the wages and fringe benefits of all workers employed by the contractor for the contract work. This statute effective July 1, 1975 exempts resident contractors who present to the Commissioner a financial statement duly certified attesting to a net worth of the contractor in excess of $50,000.

Montana amended its statute to provide that bids on state construction contracts no longer need be accompanied by a certified check for five percent of the amount bid, but rather, bids must be accompanied by bid security in the amount of ten percent of the bid, such security to consist of cash, cashier's check, certified check, bank money order, or bank draft, drawn and issued by a national banking association located in the state or by any banking corporation incorporated under the laws of the state, or a bid bond or bonds executed by an authorized surety corporation.

Effective July 1, 1981, Sections 18-2-201 and 18-2-202 MCA were amended to require that contractors awarded public works jobs must be bonded by two or more sureties acceptable to the governmental body letting the contract or with a surety company licensed in Montana. Bonding is not required when the governmental entity permits the deposit with the contracting governmental entity or agency of acceptable security equal to the contract sum to guarantee faithful performance of the contract and payment of all laborers, suppliers, materialmen, mechanics and subcontractors. Acceptable surety includes lawful money of the United States or a cashier's check, certified check, bank money order or bank draft drawn or issued by any banking corporation incorporated under the laws of the State of Montana or by a national banking association located in Montana. Also acceptable are Certificates of Deposit or money market certificates issued by any bank or Savings and Loan Association licensed to do business in Montana.

9. DECISIONS.—The acceptance by the state highway engineer on behalf of the State Highway Commission of a public improvement is not such acceptance by the Commission as is required under the statute. Therefore a claimant who failed, after the completion of the contract and the acceptance of the work by the state engineer, to file with the appropriate public officials the notice required by the statute would not lose his right to sue on the bond. *Kirkpatrick v. AEtna Casualty & Surety Co.,* 104 Mont. 212, 65 P.2d 1169 (1937).

The notice to municipality required as above may be given prior to the acceptance of the improvement by the required public officials. *Kirkpatrick v. AEtna Casualty & Surety Co.,* 104 Mont. 212, 65 P.2d 1169 (1937).

Where a highway contract filed with the Highway Commission provides that the contractor shall not transfer any part thereof without the consent in writing of the Commission, and that any subcontractor shall be considered the agent of the contractor and the contractor shall be responsible for any indebtedness incurred by such agent, where the Highway Commission did not consent to a subletting, the seven-day notice required by the statute need not be given by a claimant who furnished the subcontractor with petroleum products for carrying on its work on the highway. *H. Earl Clack Co. v. Staunton,* 105 Mont. 375, 72 P.2d 1022 (1937).

Where the contract goes beyond the requirements of the statute and evinces a purpose to protect laborers and those who furnished supplies to subcontractors, the liability of the contractor is extended thereby. *H. Earl Clack Co. v. Staunton,* 105 Mont. 375, 72 P.2d 1022 (1937).

The Montana courts have heretofore followed the construction placed by the Supreme Court of Washington, the Montana statute having been modeled on the Washington statute. *H. Earl Clack Co. v. Staunton,* 105 Mont. 375, 72 P.2d 1022 (1937).

The prevailing use plaintiff is entitled to recover as compensation for attorneys' fees such sum as the court deems reasonable for instituting and prosecuting the claim against the surety. *United States v. Reliance Ins. Co. of Philadelphia,* 227 F. Supp. 939 (D.Mont. 1964).

Where a surety has paid three suppliers who have not given a 10-day notice of claim as provided in the bond it may not urge this notice provision against a similar claim against another supplier. *C. Weissman & Sons v. St. Paul Fire & Marine Ins. Co.,* 152 Mont. 291, 448 P.2d 740 (1968).

A claimant who failed to follow the procedures of the Miller Act may still pursue an action against the general contractor and the surety on the subcontractor's performance bond where the surety took over for subcontractor upon its default and completed the contract. *Mountain Construction, Inc. v. Crick Co.,* 158 Mont. 345, 491 P.2d 1224 (1971).

General Contractor held to have waived right to notice from materialman where he knew from beginning of project that materialman was supplying masonry materials to subcontractor for job and consented thereto. *Treasure State Industries, Inc. v. Leigland,* 151 Mont. 288, 443 P.2d 22 (1968).

Subcontractor's nonresident surety was subject to suit in any county which the plaintiff-general contractor designated, and the principal on the bond was not a necessary party in order for suit to be maintained. *Morgen and Oswood Construction Co., Inc. v. United States Fidelity and Guarantee Company,* 167 Mont. 64, 535 P.2d 170 (1975).

Where a prime contractor's bond guaranteed completion of the project to the university and indemnity for claims for labor and materials, plaintiff's subcontractor was considered not to be a third-party beneficiary of the bond, and a claim solely for the expense of delay allegedly caused by the prime contractor and one of the prime contractor's other subcontractors against the surety was dismissed. *J. Louis Crum Corp. v. Alfred Lindgren, Inc.,* 564 S.W.2d 544 (Mo. App. 1978).

NEBRASKA

1. AMOUNT OF BOND.—On January 1, 1982 the Nebraska Construction Lien Act became effective, in part providing that if an owner or prime contractor has procured a surety bond no mechanic's lien can attach. The bond of the surety company must obligate it, to the extent of the extent of the penal sum of the bond, to pay all sums owing to construction lien claimants other than the prime contractor for services and material. If a contract is less than $1,000,000, then the penal sum must not be less than 50% of the contract price. For contracts in excess of $1,000,000 the penal sum must not be less than 40% of the contract price and for contracts in excess of $5,000,000, not less than $2,500,000. Under the Act, no lien attaches to real estate owned by the government. (Revised Statutes of Nebraska, § 52-132, § 52-141.) The amount of the bond on a public structure or improvement to which the mechanics' lien laws do not apply shall be not less than the contract price. (Reissue Revised Statutes of Nebraska, 1943 § 52-118.)

2. LABOR AND MATERIAL COVERED.—Labor performed, materials furnished and rental of equipment actually used in the erecting, furnishing or repairing of public building, bridge, highway or other public structures or improvements for the State of Nebraska or any political subdivision thereof.

3. NOTICE REQUIRED.—Any person having direct contractual relationship with a subcontractor, but no contractual relationship, express or implied, with the contractor furnishing said bond, shall have a right of action upon the bond upon giving written notice to the contractor within ninety days from the date on which such person did or performed the last of the labor or furnished or supplied the last of the material for which such claim is made, stating with substantial accuracy the amount claimed and the name of the party to whom the material was furnished or supplied or for whom the labor was done or performed. Such notice shall be served by registered or certified mail, postage prepaid, in an envelope directed to the contractor at any place where he maintains

an office or conducts his business, or his residence or in any other manner in which a notice may be served.

4. TIME FOR SUIT.—A suit may be instituted on the bond ninety days after the date on which the last of the labor was done and performed by claimant or materials furnished or supplied by him. No suit may be instituted against the surety more than one year after the date of completion of claimant's performance.

5. CONTRACTS EXCLUDED.—The above bond statute is applicable to contracts to which the general provisions of the mechanic's lien laws do not apply and where the mechanics and laborers have no lien to secure the payment of their wages and where materialmen who furnish material or who lease equipment for such work have no lien to secure payment therefor.

In 1979, whenever any public school district expends public funds in excess of $40,000 for the construction, remodeling or repair of any school-owned building or for site improvements, the Board of Education is required to advertise for bids in the regular manner established by the Board and accept or reject bids pursuant to the Revised Statutes relating to the letting of public contracts.

6. PROCEDURE.—The action shall be brought in the name of the party claiming the benefits thereof.

7. PENALTY FOR FAILURE TO TAKE BOND.—Public authorities are not liable individually to one furnishing material or labor on public work for failure to require the statutory bond. *Paxton & Vierling Iron Works v. Village of Naponee,* 107 Neb. 784, 186 N.W. 976 (1922).

8. SPECIAL PROVISIONS.—No contract shall be entered into by the public officials until the bond has been filed and approved.

The statute creating public power and irrigation districts provides that the laws with reference to contractors' bonds shall be applicable to contracts of the public power and irrigation districts, provided that, in the event of sudden or unexpected damage, hazard or emergency, or where delay might result in damage, injury or impairment of the plant, works, system or to the property belonging to the district, the board of directors may, in its discretion, declare an emergency and proceed with the necessary repairs or other work without first complying with certain other provisions of the statute, such as advertising the project, awarding the contract to the lowest possible bidder, etc.

9. DECISIONS.—A contractor's bond conditioned for the payment of claims for labor, equipment, gas, oils, materials or supplies used or employed on the contract includes labor and materials required in making minor repairs to trucks, gas and oil consumed in the operation of the trucks, as well as groceries and supplies for a cook-shack. However, recovery may not be had under such a bond for the purchase price of trucks purchased for the job or such major repairs as the installation of a new radiator in a truck. *West v. Detroit Fidelity & Surety Co.,* 118 Neb. 544, 225 N.W. 673 (1929).

Recovery may be had on a contractor's bond broader than the statute for rental of equipment, transportation of the equipment to and from the job, and for supervisory services rendered by claimant to the contractor after the contractor encountered difficulties with the Highway Commission. *Peter Kiewit Sons Co. v. Nat'l Casualty Co.,* 142 Neb. 835, 8 N.W.2d 192 (1943).

Labor and material used in a public work project, whether furnished directly to a contractor or subcontractor, is within the bond. *Iddings Co. v. Lincoln Constr. Co.,* 104 Neb. 124, 175 N.W. 643 (1919). In this case recovery was allowed for coal used as fuel for hoisting engine.

No suit on public contractor's bond may be commenced after expiration of one year after final settlement of the principal contract. Final settlement precedes final payment and denotes proper administrative determination with respect to amount due. *Westinghouse Electric Supply Co. vs. Brookley,* 176 Neb. 807, 127 N.W.2d 465 (1964).

Rental for use of tractors furnished in connection with surfacing work on state highway was covered under statute requiring public works contract bond to be executed. This case also holds that a party which contracted with general contractor to deliver gravel at site of highway project and to furnish it on a daily basis to keep the project moving was a "subcontractor" so that general contractor was liable on its public works contract bond for tractor rentals accrued by the party in the course of the highway project. *McElhose v. Universal Surety Co.,* 182 Neb. 847, 158 N.W.2d 228 (1968).

Final settlement was made with respect to amount due following completion of the project which was accepted by the owner and action was barred one year thereafter. *Boyd v. Benkelman Public Housing Authority,* 188 Neb. 69, 195 N.W.2d 230 (1972).

Statute limiting actions on bond to one year after "final settlement of principal contract" refers to determination by proper authority that contract has been completed, that final payment is due, and of amount due and that where architect's last certificate was only one certifying full completion, suit was timely if brought within one year of that certificate. *Zimmerman's Elec., Inc. v. Fidelity & Deposit Co. of Md.,* 194 Neb. 248, 231 N.W.2d 342 (1975).

In suit against principal and bonding company where issue of liability of surety was not presented to jury and judgment was against principal only, attorney's fee was not recoverable. *Ritzau v. Wiebe Const. Co.,* 191 Neb. 92, 214 N.W.2d 244 (1974).

A school district's suit seeking recovery for a defective roof against the contractor, the contractor's performance bond surety, the architect and the roofing supplier was held to be time barred, the record showing that all claims for defects in the roof were discoverable and discovered in such time that claims against the defendants were either barred by the four year period of limitation or the two year limitation if a date of discovery rule was applied. *Grand Island School District v. Celotex Corp.,* 203 Neb. 559, 279 N.W.2d 603 (1979).

NEVADA

March 25, 1963 Nevada adopted a separate performance and payment bond statute applicable to public projects other than contracts subject to the State Highway and Roads Act. This new statute is abstracted as follows:

1. AMOUNT OF BOND.—The payment bond shall be not less than 50% of the contract price. (Nevada Revised Statutes, Chapter 339-025)

2. LABOR AND MATERIAL COVERED.—Labor performed or materials furnished in the prosecution of the work.

3. NOTICE REQUIRED.—

(a) *To surety*—No special statutory provision.

(b) *To principal contractor*—No notice is required by a claimant having a contractual relationship, expressed or implied, with the principal contractor. Any claimant who has a direct contractual relationship with any subcontractor of the contractor who gave such payment bond, but no contractual relationship, expressed or implied, with such contractor, may bring an action on the payment bond, only

(I) If he has, within 30 days after furnishing the first of such materials or performing the first of such labor, served on the contractor a written notice which shall inform the latter of the nature of the materials being furnished or to be furnished, or the labor performed or to be performed, and identifying the person contracting for such labor or materials and the site for the performance of such labor or materials; and

(II) After giving written notice to such contractor within 90 days from the date on which the claimant performed the last of the labor or furnished the last of the materials for which he claims payment.

The statute reads: "Each written notice shall state with substantial accuracy the amount claimed and the name of the person for whom the work was performed or the material supplied, and shall be served by being sent by registered mail, postage prepaid, in an envelope addressed to such contractor at any place in which he maintains an office or conducts business, or at his residence."

(c) *To municipality*—No special statutory provision.

(d) *To creditors*—No special statutory provision.

4. TIME FOR SUIT.—A period commencing 90 days after the date on which claimant performed the last of the labor or furnished the last of the material for which he claims payment but no such action may be commenced after the expiration of one year from the date on which the claimant performed the last of the labor or furnished the last of the material for the payment of which such action is brought.

5. CONTRACTS EXCLUDED.—Under $5,000.

6. PROCEDURE.—The performance and payment bonds are required to be filed in the office of the contracting body which awarded the contract for which such bonds were given. The contracting body is required to furnish a certified copy of any payment bond and the contract for which such bond was given to any person who makes an application for such copy and who submits an affidavit stating that: "He has supplied labor or material for the completion of the work provided for in the contract, and that he has not been fully paid for such labor or material; or he is the defendant in an action brought on a payment bond; or he is surety in a payment bond on which an action has been brought." These certified copies constitute prima facie evidence of the contents, execution and delivery of the original.

The statute requires: "Every action on a payment bond as provided in section 4 of this Act shall be brought in the appropriate court of the political subdivision where the contract for which the bond was given was to be performed."

STATE BOND LAWS

7. PENALTY FOR FAILURE TO TAKE BOND.—No statutory provision under the 1963 law. See, however, Section 7 under old law below.

8. SPECIAL PROVISIONS.—The statute reads: "It is unlawful for any representative of a contracting body, in issuing an invitation for bids, to require that any bond specified in section 3 of this Act be furnished by a particular surety company or through a particular agent or broker."

While this 1963 statute requires a performance bond and a payment bond with respect to contracts for the construction, alteration or repair of any public building or other public work or public improvement, it defines the contracting body as follows:

" 'Contracting body' means any officer, employee, board, bureau, commission, department, agency or institution of the State of Nevada, or of any county, city, district, municipal corporation, quasi-municipal corporation, political subdivision, school district, educational institution or other public instrumentality, which has authority to contract for the construction, alteration or repair of any public building or other public work or public improvement."

It expressly excludes contracts subject to the provisions of Chapter 408 of Nevada Revised Statutes, the Highway and Roads Act.

Effective April 18, 1975, an Elko City-County Civic Authority was established, the statute providing that any construction contract may be let on a lump sum or on a unit basis, the bidder being required to give an undertaking with a sufficient surety or sureties approved by the Board of Commissioners of the Authority in an amount fixed by it for the faithful performance of the contract and for payment of labor and materials.

9. REMARKS.—Effective July 1, 1965, the statute relating to Bonds and Cash Deposits of Contractors was amended to provide that the amount of each bond or cash deposit shall be not less than $5,000 nor more than $20,000; that after a licensee has acted in the capacity of a licensed contractor in the State of Nevada for not less than two consecutive years the board might release the obligee from the requirement of bond or cash deposit if evidence supporting such relief is presented to the board; that the bond or deposit should be for the benefit of the owner of the property to be improved, an employee of the contractor performing labor on or about the site of the construction project or any person who is injured by an unlawful act or omission of the contractor in performance of the contract. No action may be commenced on the bond or deposit after the expiration of two years following the date of the act on which the action is based. A claim of any employee of the contractor for labor is preferred. Laborer claimants, if necessary, must pro rate. If the surety makes a payment without awaiting court action the amount of the bond is reduced to the extent of any payment made by the surety in good faith.

10. DECISIONS.—A supplier who has not given notice to the general contractor within 30 days after first furnishing material but has given 90-days notice after last furnishing material may not recover on the bond in view of the express statutory requirement for such earlier notice. Mere knowledge on the part of the general contractor that the supplier was on the job or had supplier material does not avoid the necessity for such 30-days preliminary notice. *Garff v. Bradley,* 84 Nev. 79, 436 P.2d 428 (1968).

Nevada amended its statute to read that if the labor commissioner has reason to believe that an employee has a valid and enforceable claim for wages against a contractor, he may require the public body to withhold from any payment due the contractor under this section and pay the labor commissioner instead, an amount equal to the amount claimed by the employee. This amount shall be paid to the employee if the claim is resolved in his favor, otherwise it shall be returned to the public body for payment to the contractor.

Old Statute

1. AMOUNT OF BOND.—The bond required of a contractor under the Nevada Highway and Roads Law is the total amount of the contract price, but the statute provides that such bond or bonds "shall be performance bonds or labor and material bonds or bond." Thus, by the terms of the statute, strictly speaking, the bond could be limited to performance of the contract. The prior law provided that one-third of the total bond should be a payment bond and our information is that the old form is being continued. The Nevada Revised Statutes pertaining to the general contractor's bond require a sum equal to at least twenty-five per cent of the contract price.

2. LABOR AND MATERIAL COVERED.—All just debts contracted by the contractor for labor performed and materials furnished for the work of erection, construction, alteration or repair of any public building or structure. The Highway and Road Law of 1957 provides that the labor and material bond shall (a) secure payment of state and local taxes relating to the contract, premiums under the Nevada Industrial Insurance Act, contributions under the Unemployment Compensation Law, and payment of claims for labor, materials, provision, implements, machinery, means of transportation or supplies furnished upon or used for the performance of the contract; and (b)

provide that if the contractor or his or its subcontractor or subcontractors, assign or assigns, fail duly to pay for such taxes, premiums, contributions, labor and materials required of, and used or consumed by, such contractor or his or its subcontractors, the surety shall pay the same in an amount not exceeding the total sum specified in the bond together with interest at a rate of 8 per cent per annum.

A statute approved March 22, 1961 provides for a surety bond in an amount equal to the contract price, conditioned for the performance of the contract and payment for all just debts contracted by the contractor for labor performed upon and materials furnished for the work provided to be done by the contract.

3. NOTICE REQUIRED.—(a) *To surety*—No special statutory provision except in the case of highway projects for which see Section 4 below. (b) *To principal contractor*—No special statutory provision except in the case of highway projects for which see Section 4 below. (c) *To municipality*—Claimants under highway bonds must file a verified claim with the Department of Highways. See 4 hereinafter.

The Statute approved March 22, 1961 provides that no action may be brought upon the surety payment bond unless the party who performed the labor upon or furnished materials for the work required to be done gave written notice to: (a) the principal; (b) the obligee, and (c) the sureties within ninety days after such party performed the last of the work or labor or furnished the last of the materials for which such claim is made. Said notice must state with substantial accuracy the amount claimed and the name of the party to whom the materials were furnished or for whom the work or labor was done. Said notice must be served upon each of the above parties at any place where they regularly maintain an office for the transaction of business in Nevada, or by mailing such notice by registered or certified mail, postage prepaid, to such office address.

4. TIME FOR SUIT.—With respect to bonds given for the work of erection, construction, alteration or repair of any public building or structure, suit must be commenced within ninety days after the completion and acceptance of such public building or structure, and no such action may be tried or judgment rendered thereon until the expiration of such ninety day period.

In the case of highway bonds, any person who has furnished labor, materials, provisions, implements, machinery, means of transportation, supplies used or consumed by the contractor or his or its subcontractor or subcontractors whose claim has not been paid and who desires to be protected under the bond, shall file with the Department a claim in triplicate within thirty days from the date of final acceptance of the contract, which claim must be executed and verified before a notary public and contain a statement that the same has not been paid. "One copy shall be filed in the office of the department and the remaining copies shall be forwarded to the contractor and surety."

Any such person so filing a claim may at any time within six months thereafter commence an action against the surety or sureties on the bond for the recovery of the amount of the claim and the filing of such claim shall not constitute a claim against the Department. Failure so to sue within said six month period bars any right of action against the surety.

The statute of March 22, 1961 authorizes a claimant if not paid in full before the expiration of ninety days after the date on which the last of claimant's work or labor was done or performed or materials were furnished to sue upon said statutory bond for the amount of claimant's just debts for such labor and material. Such suit must be commenced within one year following the date on which the principal ceased work on the contract.

5. CONTRACTS EXCLUDED.—$500 or under.

6. PROCEDURE.—No special statutory provision.

7. PENALTY FOR FAILURE TO TAKE BOND.—If the party letting the contract shall fail to exact and take the bond, or shall knowingly accept insufficient sureties thereon, such party and the individual officers and agents thereof, by whom such contract was authorized, shall be jointly and severally liable to all who have performed labor or material for the public work provided to be done by such contract, to an amount not exceeding 25% of the contract price, but wherever the party itself shall pay, upon default of the contractor, any liability hereby created, it shall have a right of action, jointly and severally, against the individual officers and agents thereof, by which said contract was authorized, and against their bondsmen, if any, for any amount or amounts so paid.

Where the unpaid claims of labor and materialmen are more than the amount of the bond, the claimants prorate and to this end the District Court may consolidate all actions.

No bonds shall be invalid by reason of any defect or form, or qualifications of sureties, or for a failure of the sureties to qualify, and no such bond need be signed by the contractor.

8. SPECIAL PROVISIONS.—The State Highway Engineer, before making final payment on any highway contract, is required to publish, for a period of at least two weeks in a newspaper of general circulation in the county wherein the work was contracted for and performed and for a

STATE BOND LAWS

period of at least ten days in a newspaper of general circulation throughout the State, a notice of final acceptance of the contract. No final settlement of such contract may be had until thirty days after such acceptance of the contract.

9. REMARKS.—Whenever the Highway Department has cause to believe that the contractor's surety or sureties have become insufficient, it may demand in writing of the contractor such further bonds or additional sureties, in a total sum not exceeding that originally required, as is necessary, considering the extent of the work remaining to be done. Thereafter no payment shall be made upon such contract to the contractor or any assignee of the contractor until such further bonds or additional sureties have been furnished.

10. DECISIONS.—A person furnishing labor and material who has a right to sue under the contractor's bond, in that one-third of the penal sum of such bond is additional protection for such labor and materialmen, does not have an equitable lien on the retained percentage payable to the contractor without regard to claims which subcontractors and materialmen may have filed with the department. *Union Indemnity Co. v. Drumm,* 57 Nev. 242, 62 P.2d 698 (1936).

Surety was held liable to labor and materialmen as third part beneficiaries regardless of the wording of the bond. *Acoustics, Inc. v. American Surety Company of New York,* 74 Nev. 6, 320 P.2d 626 (1958).

Brochure given by sub-subcontractor to subcontractor who forwarded it to contractor was insufficient to satisfy the 30-day notice requirement of statute relating to claims on payment bond where brochure did not set forth the amount claimed and was not sent directly to contractor by registered mail as specified by statute. *Capriotti, Lemon and Associates, Inc. et al v. Johnson Service Company,* 84 Nev. 318, 440 P.2d 386 (1968).

NEW HAMPSHIRE

1. AMOUNT OF BOND.—At least 100 per cent of the contract price or of the estimated cost of the work if no aggregate price is agreed upon. (New Hampshire Revised Statutes Annotated § 447:16.)

2. LABOR AND MATERIAL COVERED.—The bond is conditioned upon the payment by the contractor and subcontractors for all labor performed or furnished, all equipment hired including trucks, all material used, fuels, lubricants, power, tools, hardware and supplies purchased by the principal contractor and used in carrying out said contract, and for labor and parts furnished upon the order of the contractor for the repair of equipment used in carrying out said contract.

3. NOTICE REQUIRED.—(a) *To surety.* See subdivision (c) below. (b) *To principal contractor.* No special statutory provision. (c) *To municipality.* In order to obtain the benefit of such bond any person, firm or corporation having any claim for labor performed, materials, machinery, tools, or equipment furnished as aforesaid, shall within ninety days after the completion and acceptance of the project by the contracting party, file in the office of the Secretary of State, if the state is a contracting party, or with the Department of Public Works and Highways, if the state is a party to said contract by or through said department, or in the office of the Clerk of the Superior Court for the county within which the contract shall be principally performed, if any political subdivision of the state is a contracting party, a statement of the claim; a copy of which shall forthwith be sent by mail by the office where it is filed to the principal and surety.

4. TIME FOR SUIT.—One year after filing of claim as above.

5. CONTRACTS EXCLUDED.—Generally those under $25,000.

6. PROCEDURE.—The court examines all claims filed in accordance with the statute, fixes a date for hearing with notice to all creditors, the contractor and the sureties, and finds the respective amounts due the claimants.

7. DECISIONS.—If a city sees fit to provide a bond which fails to secure a benefit for unpaid subcontractors, such a subcontractor, not being a party to the principal contract, cannot complain. *Mason v. Portland Constr. Co.,* 85 N.H. 487, 160 A. 477 (1932).

Failure by a subcontractor to take the required steps to preserve a lien on any moneys due or to become due the contractor by the public authorities does not bar the subcontractor from maintaining an action on the public works bond required by a statute. *Guard Rail Erectors v. Standard Surety & Casualty Co. of N.Y.,* 86 N.H. 349, 168 A. 903 (1933).

The fact that the principal contractor has been fully paid by the state is not a defense in an action by a materialman against the surety on the contractor's bond. *American Bridge Co. v. United States Fidelity & Guaranty Co.,* 87 N.H. 62, 174 A. 57 (1934).

Statute providing that a subcontractor having claim for labor and materials furnished to contractor engaged to construct public works must file claim with Secretary of State within 90 days after materials and labor have been furnished, constitutes a condition precedent to obligation of contractor's surety. *Therrien et al. v. Maryland Casualty Company,* 97 N.H. 180, 84 A.2d 179 (1951).

The statute relating to the obtaining of surety bonds by persons who contract in behalf of political subdivision of state for construction of public buildings, and providing procedure for enforcement of claims of creditors of principal, does not abolish common-law liability. Petition of *Leon Keyser, Inc.,* 97 N.H. 404, 89 A.2d 917 (1952).

The statute relating to obtaining of surety bonds by persons who contract in behalf of political subdivision of state for construction of public buildings, and providing procedure for enforcement of claims of creditors of principal, does not prohibit incorporation in bond of conditions which are additional to conditions required to be contained in bonds under the statute. Petition of *Leon Keyser, Inc.,* 97 N.H. 404, 89 A.2d 917 (1952).

The statute will be read into the bond to afford protection to all classes of persons contemplated by the statute. Petition of *Leon Keyser, Inc.,* 97 N.H. 404, 89 A.2d 917 (1952).

A garage and office building which contractor agreed to construct for city waterworks constitutes a "public building" within the statute relating to obtaining of surety bonds by persons who contract in behalf of political subdivision of state for the construction of public buildings. Petition of *Leon Keyser, Inc.,* 97 N.H. 404, 89 A.2d 917 (1952).

New Hamsphire statute relating to obtaining of surety bonds for public construction projects does not abolish common law liability, nor does it prohibit incorporation in bonds of conditions which are additional to conditions required to be contained therein by the statute. *Robinson Clay Products Co. v. Beacon Construction Co. of Mass.,* 339 Mass. 406, 159 N.E.2d 530 (1959).

The fact that a public works surety bond furnished pursuant to statute contained extrastatutory obligations did not excuse claimant from complying with notice provision and time for suit provision of statute as a condition precedent to maintaining a suit. *American Fidelity Co. v. Cray,* 105 N.H. 132, 194 A.2d 763 (1963).

Addendum to indemnity bond agreeing that bond should guarantee performance of contract by general contractor in compliance with the contract changed the bond into one which expressly bound the contractor to pay all subcontractors for labor and materials and, upon general contractor's default, surety was obligated to pay the subcontractors. *Rivier College vs. St. Paul Fire & Marine Insurance Co.,* 104 N.H. 398, 187 A.2d 799 (1963).

Supplier of fuel and lubricants to contractor engaged on highway project was bound by the statutory requirements that a statement of claim shall be filed with the designated party within 90 days after claimant ceases to perform the labor and material and that the claimant shall within one year after filing such claim file his petition to enforce his claim. These periods are not extended by insolvency or breach of contract. *American Fidelity Company v. Cray,* 105 N.H. 132, 194 A.2d 763 (1963).

The fact that notice was filed before completion and not within ninety days thereafter did not preclude enforcement of claim under the bond. *General Electric Co. v. Dole Company,* 105 N.H. 477, 202 A. 2d 486 (1964).

NEW JERSEY

1. AMOUNT OF BOND.—At least 100% of the contract price. (N.J.S.A. 2A:44-144.)

2. LABOR AND MATERIAL COVERED.—All labor performed or materials, provisions, provender or other supplies, or teams, fuels, oils, implements or machinery used or consumed in, upon, for or about the construction, alteration or repair of any public building or other public work or improvement.

3. NOTICE REQUIRED.—(a) *To surety*—At any time before the acceptance of the public improvement or within 80 days thereafter. See Procedure below. (b) *To principal contractor*—No special statutory provision. (c) *To municipality*—No special statutory provision. (d) *To creditors*—No special statutory provision.

4. TIME FOR SUITS.—No suit shall be brought against the sureties on said bond until the expiration of 80 days after the acceptance of the public improvement by the duly authorized board or officer, but suit must be commenced within one year from the date of such acceptance of the building, work or improvement.

5. CONTRACTS EXCLUDED.—As of February 8, 1980, a public body may waive the bond requirements on contracts for public works not in excess of $20,000.

6. PROCEDURE.—Claimant, at any time before the acceptance of the public improvement by the duly authorized board or officer or within 80 days thereafter, shall furnish the sureties on the bond a statement of the amount due to claimant. No suit shall be brought against any such sureties on said bond until the expiration of 80 days after the acceptance of the public improvement by the duly authorized board or officer. If said indebtedness shall not be paid in full at the expiration of said 80 days, claimant may bring an action in his own name upon the bond.

7. PENALTY FOR FAILURE TO TAKE BOND.—No special statutory provision.

8. SPECIAL PROVISION.—Recovery by any claimant under the bond is subject to the conditions and provisions of the statute to the same extent as if such conditions and provisions were fully incorporated in the bond form.

The Municipal Mechanics' Lien Act provides only for a lien on the contract price. Any person furnishing labor or material required under the terms of any contract for any public improvement, including the furnishing of oils, gasoline and lubricants and vehicles used toward the performance or completion of any such contract, has a lien for the value of such labor, etc., upon the moneys due or growing due under the contract and in the control of the public agency, provided such claimant, at any time before the whole work to be performed by the contractor for the public agency is either completed or accepted by resolution of the public agency, or within 60 days thereafter, files with the chairman, secretary or clerk of the public agency a notice of such lien claim, verified by oath in the form required by the statute.

The funds to which a lien has attached by such procedure may be released and paid to the contractor by his filing a bond in double the sum of all claims so filed. Where notice of lien claim has been so filed with the public agency, it may serve notice upon the contractor that such claim has been filed and require the contractor to show cause, within 5 days from the service of such notice, why the claim should not be paid. If the contractor shall fail to file with the financial officer of the public agency, within said 5-day period, a statement, duly verified, that the lien claim is unfounded and untrue, the public agency may pay, without the order of any court, the claim out of the funds in its possession upon which the claimant has a lien.

No such lien shall be binding on the funds of the public agency unless a suit to enforce the lien claim is brought within 60 days from the date the work to be performed by the contractor is either completed or accepted by resolution of the public agency, but, if any suit is brought by any claimant, the lien of any other claimant may be preserved and enforced by filing an answer setting up his claim in such suit within the time provided for by the practice of the court or such time as may be allowed him by the court in such suit.

The local public contracts law (C. 40A:11-1, et seq.) was amended effective March 28, 1980 to provide that a contract or agreement involving construction and reconstruction, alteration, repair or maintenance of any building, structure, facility or other improvement to real property, the total price of which exceeds $100,000 shall provide for partial payments at least one each month as the work progresses. Two percent of the amount due on each partial payment shall be withheld by the contracting unit pending completion of the contract or agreement. The contract or agreement may also provide for partial payments at least once in each month on all materials placed along or upon the site, or stored at secured locations, which are suitable for the use and execution of the contract or agreement, if the person providing the materials furnishes releases of liens for the materials at the time each estimate of work is submitted for payment. The total of all the partial payments shall not exceed the cost of the materials.

The Municipal Mechanics' Lien Act, the Contractors' Public Works Bond law and the Trust Fund Act are in pari materia and in attempting construction thereof must be read together. *Wilson v. Robert A. Stretch, Inc.*, 44 N.J. Super. 52, 129 A.2d 599 (1957).

9. REMARKS.—The bond must be conditioned for the payment by the contractor and by all subcontractors or his or its subcontractor of all indebtedness which may accrue to any person, firm or corporation for the labor or material covered as indicated in subdivision 2 hereof.

10. DECISIONS.—The statute contemplates a final, complete and unconditional acceptance of the building or improvement which is the subject matter of the contract. *Yale & Towne Mfg. Co. v. AEtna Casualty & Surety Co.*, 110 N.J.L. 592, 166 A. 473 (1933); *John P. Callaghan, Inc. v. Continental Casualty Co.*, 110 N.J.L. 390, 166 A. 83 (1933). *Williamsport Planing Mill Co. v. Maryland Casualty Co.*, 129 N.J.L. 333, 29 A.2d 731 (1943). See *Williamsport Planing Mill Co. v. Board of Education of City of Paterson*, 130 N.J.L. 321, 32 A.2d 591 (1943).

Where the resolution adopted by the public body is not a final, complete and unconditional acceptance and shows that the work which was the subject matter of the contract was not then completed in several substantial parts the resolution is not an "acceptance" within the meaning of the statute. The resolution in this case qualified the acceptance to a future time, namely, when the items specified in the report of the architect were completed. *Johnson Service Co. v. American Employers' Insurance Co.*, 113 N.J.L. 494, 174 A. 756 (1934).

The approval by a school board of a recommendation by its Committee of School Properties that work of a contractor be accepted subject to counsel's approval of any guarantees that may be required, and of the Committee's recommendation that final certificate be paid subject to the receipt and approval of certain releases and the payment of lien claims, does not constitute the final, complete and unconditional acceptance of the work or improvement as contemplated by the statute. *Paul H. Jaehnig, Inc. v. Standard Acc. Ins. Co.*, 18 N.J. 536, 87 A.2d 558 (1952).

Public work cannot be accepted as of an earlier date prior to the date on which the acceptance was actually made. If back-dating were allowed, claimants under the bond might be excluded by back-dating for a period of time longer than that in which notice is to be filed. *Johnson Service Co. v. Seaboard Surety Co.,* 112 N.J.L. 493, 171 A. 828 (1934).

The fact that final payment on the contract was inadvertently made prior to the actual completion of the building does not prejudice a materialman who gave the required notice within eighty days after the work which was the subject matter of the contract was finished and accepted. *Johnson Service Co. v. American Employers' Insurance Co.,* 113 N.J.L. 494, 174 A. 756 (1934).

A subcontractor, furnishing materials for the construction of school building under contract awarded by city board of education, may not maintain an action on contractor's bond for the price of such materials instituted before acceptance of the building by resolution of board. *Williamsport Planing Mill Co. v. Board of Education of City of Paterson,* 130 N.J.L. 321, 32 A.2d 591 (1943).

Action by school board in taking possession of premises and in reletting contract on default of original contractor is not acceptance of the work within the meaning of the statute. *Newman v. Maryland Casualty Co.,* 112 N.J.L. 122, 170 A. 46 (1934).

Where the right of recovery on a surety bond depends on certain preliminaries, among which is that a statement must be filed a certain length of time after acceptance, and there are two different dates of acceptance of the work, a materialman is not obliged to choose one of the conflicting dates, but may properly maintain two separate actions which will be consolidated by the court. *Igoe Bros. v. National Surety Co.,* 112 N.J.L. 243, 169 A. 841 (1934).

A surety is not liable for damages caused by breach of a building contract. *Schaeffer Iron Wks. v. Standard Accident Insurance Co.,* 2 F. Supp. 764 (D.N.J. 1933).

A material supply house which sold granite to a subcontractor, which granite went into the public improvement, may recover under the contractor's bond. *First Mechanics National Bank of Trenton v. N.J. Brick & Supply Co.,* 112 N.J.L. 218, 171 A. 176 (1934).

A person who furnishes labor and material under a subcontractor will not be denied recovery under the bond of the general contractor. The amount claimed was $1,700 but a verdict is rendered in his favor for only $670.70. The claim as filed was held not to constitute a wilful and fraudulent misstatement. *Monahan v. Seaboard Surety Co.,* 126 N.J.L. 148, 18 A.2d 40 (1941).

Interest on the claim of a person who furnishes trucking services, lath material and nails to a subcontractor will be allowed in a suit on a subcontractor's bond from a period commencing eighty days after the acceptance of the building, notwithstanding that the amount recovered is less than the amount claimed. *Monahan v. Seaboard Surety Co.,* 126 N.J.L. 148, 18 A.2d 40 (1941); *J. Jacob Shannon & Co. v. Continental Casualty Co.,* 106 N.J.L. 200, 148 A. 738 (1930).

When a building contract provided that a part of the payment due should be retained till completion of the work, a release executed by a subcontractor, in order to secure final payment, releases the surety on a public work bond as completely as it would release the public body responsible for payment otherwise. *Brooks-Wright, Inc. v. Maryland Casualty Company,* 135 N.J.Eq. 510, 39 A.2d 446 (1944), reversing *Brooks-Wright Inc. v. Maryland Casualty Co.,* 29 A.2d 882, 133 N.J.Eq. 15 (1943). *John N. Price & Sons v. Maryland Casualty Co.,* 146 F.2d 807 (3d Cir. 1945), reversing 50 cert. denied, 325 U.S. 859, 65 S. Ct. 1197, 89 L. Ed. 1978 (1945).

Money paid by a public body to a public contractor constitutes a trust fund for laborers and materialmen, and where a contractor's surety has paid a materialman he may proceed against the fund paid to the contractor. *Graybar Electric Co. v. Manufacturers Casualty Co.,* 37 N.J. Super. 284, 117 A.2d 196 (1955), *aff'd,* 21 N.J. 517, 122 A.2d 624 (1956). For other cases dealing with the trust fund theory, see *National Surety Co. v. Barth,* 11 N.J. 506, 95 A.2d 145 (1953).

Bailor of front end loader, together with bucket, blade, grease gun and volume gun, for use by subcontractors on municipal drain project, would be entitled in a properly instituted case under the Bond Act to recourse on bond filed by the principal contractor. *Wilson v. Robert A. Stretch, Inc.,* 44 N.J. Super. 52, 129 A.2d 599 (1957).

The public works contractor's bond is required primarily for the benefit of the public agency or body for which the work is being done, and only secondarily for the benefit of the materialmen, subcontractors and others, whose labor and material go into the performance of the contract. The purpose of the statutory prohibition of institution of any action on any such bond by subcontractors or materialmen, until after the acceptance of the project, is to protect the security of the public body in the bond from depletion or impairment by prior action against the surety before it is known whether the contractor has faithfully performed his contract with the public board or body, and, if not, what loss has consequently been sustained by the public body. *Samuel Braen's Sons v. Fondo,* 52 N.J. Super. 188, 145 A.2d 145 (1958).

Loan of money which was used to make payroll and for purchase of materials was not covered by statutory bond. *Board of Ed. of City of Bayonne v. Kolman,* 111 N.J. Super. 585, 270 A.2d 64 (1970).

A materialman under a materialman may not recover under the Municipal Mechanics Lien Act. *Morris County Industrial Park vs. Thomas Nicol Co.,* 35 N.J. 522, 173 A.2d 414 (1961).

Under Trust Fund Act, where prime contractor's payee is a subcontractor owing a materialman for goods used in the work, he ought, in good conscience, use enough of the payment to satisfy that charge and the material-recipient, with knowledge of the source, should be bound to allocate it accordingly. *Hiller & Skoglund, Inc. v. Atlantic Creosoting Co.,* 40 N.J. 6, 190 A.2d 380 (1963).

Supplier of bankrupt subcontractor held entitled to recover on contractors bond conditioned for payment to persons supplying material even though claimant did not have a mechanic's lien or anything enforceable against the owner. *Schlanger v. Federal Insurance Company,* 44 N.J. 17, 206 A.2d 874 (1965).

Where prime contract required prime contractor to pay all claims for labor and material, prime contractor's bond conditioned on prime contractor's faithful performance of prime contract benefited subcontractor, although there was no express provision in bond for payment of unpaid claims. *Amelco Window Corp. v. Federal Ins. Co.,* 127 N.J. Super. 342, 317 A.2d 398 (1974).

Upon a showing that the improvements have been made, municipality may assign its rights under subdivision bond where assignment is for purpose of obtaining performance guaranteed by the bond. *Clearwater Associates, Inc. v. F. H. Bridge and Son Contractors,* 144 N.J. Super 233, 365 A.2d 200 (1976).

A public body obligee was not entitled to recover damages from a subdivision bond surety when the public body had been required to pay third parties by reason of the negligent installation of a storm sewer, the court concluding that the bond only guaranteed completion of the stipulated improvements. *Township of Wyckoff v. Sarna,* 136 N.J. Super. 512, 347 A.2d 16 (1975).

The provision in the statute that no suit can be brought on a bond until 80 days after "acceptance of the building, work or improvement by the duly authorized board or officer" precluded a claimant from instituting suit 80 days after the claimant finished work. *Maurice Keating, Inc. v. Township of Southampton,* 149 N.J. Super. 118, 373 A.2d 421 (1977).

Court held that a $102,000 deficiency in a bid bond was waivable by a public authority where the notice to bidders allowed authority to waive minor defects; the bidder filed a proper bond within 24 hours and the waiver did not adversely affect competitive bidding. *Marvec Allstate, Inc. v. Gray & Fear, Inc.,* 148 N.J. Super. 481, 372 A.2d 1156 (1977).

The construction of moderate income housing which was sponsored by private parties was considered private work even though the project was partially financed by the New Jersey Housing Finance Agency. *V. Petrillo & Son, Inc. v. American Construction Co.,* 148 N.J. Super. 1, 371 A.2d 799 (1977).

In a suit on a performance bond by a county alleging defective work some 20 years prior to suit, it was held that the suit against the prime contractor and the surety was barred by the ten year statute of limitation even though the defect was latent and not discoverable until approximately one year prior to suit. The existence of a debt of its principal is essential to an obligation of the surety. *County of Hudson v. Terminal Construction Corp.,* 154 N.J. Super. 264, 381 A.2d 355 (1977).

The Trust Fund Act does not extend benefits to materialmen of a subcontractor, said Act only applies to those who furnish labor or material to the prime contractor. The procedural time requirements of the Public Works Bond Act does not apply to the Trust Fund Act. *Universal Supply Co. v. Martell Constr. Co., Inc.,* 156 N.J. Super. 327, 383 A.2d 1163 (1978).

Having paid owner for the loss caused by a fire, the owner's insurance carrier was subrogated the owner's right to sue multiple prime contractors and their performance bond sureties under the terms of the performance bonds in question *Hartford Fire Insurance Co. v. Riefolo Constr. Co.,* 161 N.J. Super. 99, 390 A.2d 1210 (1978), *aff'd,* 81 N.J. 514, 410 A.2d 658 (1980).

The requirement that a bid bond surety be licensed to do business within the state is a material condition and cannot be waived. *George Harms Constr. Co. v. Ocean County Sewage Auth.,* 163 N.J. Super. 107, 394 A.2d 360 (1978).

Language of surety bond requiring payment of "all cost and damage" suffered by reason of failure to complete structure was not broad enough to allow an award of counsel fees to a municipality that instituted suit against the property owner and surety to recover reasonable cost of boarding up structure and cleaning debris when the construction of such structure was not completed. However, the fact that the obligee had not completed its remedial work did not preclude it from a recovery on the bond. *Middletown Township v. Colen,* 164 N.J. Super. 193, 395 A.2d 928 (1978).

NEW MEXICO

1. AMOUNT OF BOND.—50% of the contract price. If personal surety be accepted, the amount of the bond shall be the full contract price and the surety shall justify under oath in amounts above liabilities and exemptions aggregating double the amount of the bond. (New Mexico Statutes 1978 Annotated, Cpt. 13-4-18.)

2. LABOR AND MATERIAL COVERED.—All just claims for labor performed, and materials and supplies furnished, upon or for the work of construction, alteration, improvement or repair of any public buildings, structure or highway or for any public work, furnished under the original contract or under any subcontract. See Remarks below.

3. NOTICE REQUIRED.—(a) *To surety*—No special statutory provision. (b) *To principal contractor*—Any person having a direct contractual relationship with a subcontractor but no contractual relation, express or implied, with the principal contractor, must give written notice to the contractor within ninety days from the date on which such person performed the last of the labor or furnished or supplied the last of the material for which the claim is made, stating with substantial accuracy the amount claimed and the name of the party to whom the material was furnished or supplied or for whom the labor was done or performed. Such notice shall be served by mailing the same by registered mail, postage prepaid, in an envelope addressed to the contractor at any place he maintains an office or conducts his business, or his residence, or in any manner in which the service of summons in civil process is authorized by law. (c) *To municipality*—Claimant in such suit shall notify the public body of the beginning of the action, stating the amount claimed and no judgment shall be entered in such action within thirty days after giving such notice. (d) *To creditors*—No special statutory provision. See Remarks below.

4. TIME FOR SUIT.—After the expiration of ninety days after the day on which the last of the labor was done or performed, or materials were furnished, for which such claim is made. Under the amendment of 1953 no suit on the bond may be commenced after the expiration of one year from the date of final settlement of the contract. The date of final settlement is the date set by the public body in the final closing and settlement of payment, if any be due the contractor.

5. CONTRACTS EXCLUDED.—$500 or under.

6. PROCEDURE.—No claim shall be entered in any suit within thirty days after the claimant has notified the municipality of the beginning of the action, stating the amount claimed.

7. PENALTY FOR FAILURE TO TAKE BOND.—No special statutory provision. A state is immune from suit and hence a citizen cannot sue an agency of the state for failure to take a bond. *Dougherty v. Vidal,* 37 N.M. 256, 21 P.2d 90 (1933). Sovereign immunity in New Mexico was abolished by *Hicks v. State,* 88 N.M. 588, 544 P.2d 1153 (1975). By legislation promulgated in 1976, sovereign immunity was reinstated except in eight classes of activities. Thus, the holding in *Dougherty* can be challenged.

8. SPECIAL PROVISIONS.—Whenever the surety is insolvent or becomes insufficient the municipality may require the contractor to furnish a new or additional security within ten days; and thereupon if the municipality shall so order, all work on the contract shall cease until such new or additional bond is furnished. If not furnished within said time the municipality may at its option take over and complete the work as the agent and at the expense of the contractor and his sureties and shall be entitled to use any equipment, material and supplies of the delinquent contractor in completing the work.

9. REMARKS.—Under the amendment of 1953 the obligee named in the bond and any person having a cause of action on the bond may be admitted on motion as a party to the claimant's action and the court shall determine the rights of all parties thereto. If the amount realized on such bond be insufficient to discharge all claims in full, such amount shall be distributed among the parties entitled thereto pro rata.

The public body is required to furnish a claimant who submits an affidavit that he has supplied labor or material for the work and payment therefor has not been made, and that he or it is being sued on any such bond, a certified copy of the bond and contract, and, in case final settlement of the contract has been had, a certified statement of the date of such settlement which is conclusive.

By statute approved April 2, 1965, every person licensed under the provisions of the Contractor's License Law and every applicant for contractor's license is required to file a surety bond acceptable to the Contractors License Board, which bond shall be subject to payment of judgments resulting from: (a) the failure of the licensee or applicant to substantially perform any undertaking pursuant to the provisions of the Contractors' License Law or comply with the Uniform Building Code; (b) the failure of the licensee or applicant to pay any moneys when due for materials, labor or supplies rendered in connection with such licensee or applicant's operations as a contractor.

A new section to the New Mexico Statute was enacted in 1967 to provide that unpaid premiums

STATE BOND LAWS

or charges for the furnishing of workmen's compensation insurance furnished to any contractor or subcontractor, required by the terms of his contract or by law to obtain or carry such insurance, are defined to be material furnished to the contractor or subcontractor for use in the performance of the contract, and the person, firm or corporation so furnishing the same has the same right and remedies against any performance bond given in connection with such contract as if the workmen's compensation insurance so furnished was physical property and as though a lien had been filed against the improved premises but shall not have a lien against the "improved premises."

An amendment approved April 9, 1975 requires the performance bond furnished by a contractor who does not have its principal place of business in New Mexico, to cover taxes owed the state arising out of the construction services rendered under the original contract.

This amendment also requires such nonresident contractor to furnish the commissioner or his delegate with a surety bond, or other acceptable security, in a sum prescribed by the statute, to secure payment of the tax imposed on the gross receipts from the contract.

10. DECISIONS.—A letter directed to the resident agent of the surety, sent 13 days after the last work was done, by the attorney for a claimant which had furnished labor and services in the construction of four state highways under a single contract (which letter stated that there was a balance due claimant for labor and services performed on said highways and enclosed a copy of a letter to the contractor reciting that the time for filing a claim within thirty days after the date of last delivery would shortly expire and requested the contractor to pay the claim before a day stated), complies substantially with the statutory requirement. The two letters, construed together, identify the contract and the bond given to secure its performance, state definitely that the claim is for labor and services, not material and supplies, and set forth the amount due. While these letters do not accurately state the date on which the last labor was furnished, they do so by indirection in that they say in effect that thirty days since the last services had not yet expired but would soon expire. *American Surety Co. v. Gilmore Oil Co.,* 83 F.2d 249 (10th Cir. 1936).

The statute does not contemplate identical notices to the principal, the surety and the obligee. Substance in identity is the yardstick by which to measure compliance with the statute. *American Surety Co. v. Gilmore Oil Co.,* 83 F.2d 249 (10th Cir. 1936).

While compliance with the statute is a condition precedent to the maintenance of an action on the bond, the statute is remedial and should be liberally construed. Substantial compliance with its requirements is sufficient. *Silver v. Fidelity Deposit Co.,* 40 N.M. 33, 53 P.2d 459 (1935). In this case, the only notice sent to the surety was a copy of a letter addressed by the State Highway Department to the principal contractor, stating that the Department was in receipt of a claim against the contractor for materials and supplies. This notice was held insufficient because it referred only to materials and supplies, whereas the claim included labor, and because the notice failed to set forth the date such labor was last furnished.

Premiums on workmen's compensation and public liability insurance, both of which were required under building contractor's contract with board of education for construction of school building, were not "supplies" within meaning of contractor's performance bond providing for payment of just claims for labor performed and materials and supplies furnished upon or for work under contract, so as to render the contractor's surety liable therefor. *Anderson v. United States Fidelity & Guaranty Co.,* 44 N.M. 483, 104 P.2d 906 (1940). See 1967 Statute review under Remarks above.

A surety which issued its conventional bond in reliance upon a promise that funds would be advanced for construction and sustained a loss to unpaid materialmen because moneys were not advanced was held to be a third party beneficiary who could sue upon the contract to make the advances even though it was not designated as such therein. *Hamill v. Maryland Casualty Co.,* 209 F.2d 338 (10th Cir. 1954).

Where a notice is not sent to the proper party, a materialman may not maintain an action on the bond. *Taylor v. Via,* 284 P. 2d 211, N.Mex. (1955). 59 N.Mex. 320.

A supplier of materials to a subcontractor may not maintain a suit on the contractor's surety bond where the materialman failed to give the statutory 90-day written notice of the subcontractor's failure to pay. *State for use Komac Paint & Wallpaper Store v. McBride,* 74 N.M. 233, 392 P.2d 577 (1964).

NEW YORK

Effective September 1, 1964, New York amended Section 137 of the State Finance Law relating to the payment bond required on state public improvement contracts to eliminate the provision which required labor and material claimants to file and enforce a mechanic's lien as a condition to enforcement of the payment bond and to provide for recovery as follows:

1. AMOUNT OF BOND.—No special statutory provision. (New York Consolidated Laws Service, Vol. 31A Sec. 137 generally)

2. LABOR AND MATERIAL COVERED.—Labor or material furnished to the contractor or his subcontractors in the prosecution of the work provided for in a contract for the prosecution of a public improvement for the State of New York. See Special Provisions below.

3. NOTICE REQUIRED.—(a) *To surety:* No special statutory provision. (b) *To principal contractor:* No notice is required by a person having a direct contractual relationship with the principal contractor. Any person having a direct contractual relationship with a subcontractor of the contractor furnishing the payment bond but no contractual relationship, express or implied, with the principal contractor, must give written notice to the contractor within 120 days from the date on which the last of the labor was performed or the last of the material was furnished for which his claim was made, stating with substantial accuracy the amount claimed and the name of the party to whom the material was furnished or for whom the labor was performed. The notice shall be served by delivering the same personally to the contractor or by mailing the same by registered mail, postage prepaid, in an envelope addressed to the contractor at any place where he maintains an office or conducts his business or at his residence, provided, however, that where such notice is actually received by the contractor by other means, such notice shall be deemed sufficient. (c) *To municipality:* No special statutory provision. (d) *To creditors:* No special statutory provision.

In June of 1980, the above law was amended to require notice within one hundred twenty days for those persons who do not have a contractual relationship express or implied with the prime contractor.

4. TIME FOR SUIT.—No action on a payment bond shall be commenced after the expiration of one year from the date on which final payment under the claimant's subcontract became due.

Effective June 23, 1980, the limitation of suit provision was amended to require suits on payment bonds no later than the expiration of one year from the date on which final payment under the claimant's subcontract became due.

Every person who has the right to sue under the payment bond may institute an action thereon in his own name for the amount, or the balance thereof, unpaid at the time of commencement of his action, at any time after the expiration of a period of ninety days after the day after which the last of the labor was performed or materials were furnished by him for which the claim is made.

5. SPECIAL PROVISIONS.—A copy of such payment bond shall be kept in the office of the head of the department or bureau having charge of the public improvement in connection with which the bond was given and a copy shall also be kept in the office of the Comptroller; such copies shall be open to public inspection.

A payment bond required pursuant to this new statute may provide that the place of trial of an action on a bond shall be in the county in which the contract of the contractor who furnished the bond was to be performed or, if such contract was to be performed in more than one county, then in any such county, and not elsewhere.

The expression "furnished material" or other similar expressions whenever used in this section shall be deemed to include the reasonable rental value for the period of actual use of machinery, tools or equipment, and the value of compressed gases furnished for welding or cutting, and the value of fuel and lubricants consumed by machinery operating on the improvement, or by motor vehicles owned, operated or controlled by the contractor or his subcontractors while engaged exclusively in the transportation of materials to or from the improvement for the purposes thereof.

The expression "moneys due to persons furnishing labor to the contractor or his subcontractors" includes all sums payable to or on behalf of persons furnishing labor to the contractor or his subcontractors, for wages, health, welfare, nonoccupational disability, retirement, vacation benefits, holiday pay, life insurance or other benefits, payment of which is required pursuant to the labor law or by the contract in connection with which the bond is furnished or by a collective bargaining agreement between organized labor and the contractor or subcontractors, and which are computed upon labor performed in the prosecution of the contract. A trustee or other person authorized to collect such payments has the right to sue on the payment bond in his own name and subject to the same conditions as if he were the person performing the labor upon which such sums are computed.

Effective June 30, 1980, in any action on a payment bond furnished pursuant to this section, any judgment in favor of a subcontractor or material supplier may include provision for the payment of interest upon the amount recovered from the date when demand for payment was made pursuant to the labor and material payment bond and provided further that the court may determine and award reasonable attorney's fees to either party to such action when, upon reviewing the entire record, it appears that either the original claim or the defense interposed to such claim is without substantial basis in fact or law.

Subsection 5-322.3 to the General Obligations Law, effective July 9, 1981, requires the filing of

STATE BOND LAWS

a copy of any payment bond executed in connection with a contract for the improvement of real property other than one for a public improvement, within thirty days of execution by the owner of the improvement in the Office of the County Clerk in the County in which the improvement is to be undertaken. Filing is required only with a contract for the improvement of real property in excess of $100,000. Failure of the owner to file the payment bond will result in a successful claimant being awarded reasonable attorney's fees by the Court.

6. PENALTY FOR FAILURE TO TAKE BONDS.—No special statutory provision.

Effective July of 1976, New York amended Section 163-a of the State Finance Law by establishing a procedure for the granting of preferences in the letting of state contracts to resident bidders who do not happen to be the lowest responsible bidder.

Effective September 1, 1976, New York amended, revised and renumbered subdivision six and subdivision seven of section thirty-eight of the Highway Law, relating to bond requirements and retainages on highway contracts. Unless the bond is dispensed with, before entering into a contract for such construction, the contractor shall execute a bond guaranteeing that he will perform the work in accordance with the terms of the contract and the plans and specifications, and that he will commence and complete the work within the time prescribed in the contract. The bond shall also provide against any direct or indirect damage that shall be suffered or claimed on account of such construction or improvement until such time as the highway is accepted.

In the case where a performance bond is dispensed with, the contract shall provide for partial payments with 20 percent being retained from each progress payment until the entire contract work has been completed and accepted, at which time, the commissioner of transportation shall, pending the payment of the final estimate, pay not to exceed 75 percent of the amount of the retained percentage.

In cases where there is a performance bond, five percent shall be retained from each progress payment until the entire contract work has been completed, at which time the commissioner shall, pending payment of the final estimate, pay not to exceed 70 percent of the amount of the retained percentage.

Whenever a contract shall in the judgment of the commissioner of transportation be substantially complete and in his judgment the withholding of the retained percentage would be an injustice to the contractor, the commissioner of transportation may, provided the regional director certifies that the essential items in the contract have been completed, direct the regional director to include in the final account such uncompleted items and pay therefore at the item prices in the contract upon the contractor depositing with the commissioner of transportation a certified check drawn upon a legally incorporated bank or trust company equal to at least double the value of such uncompleted work. This deposit may be used by the commissioner of transportation to complete the uncompleted portion of the contract and shall be returned to the contractor if he completes the uncompleted portion within a specified number of working days after he has been notified to proceed with the work.

No certificate approving or authorizing a partial or final payment shall be made by the commissioner of transportation until he is satisfied that all laborers employed in the work have been paid for their services for the last payroll period preceeding the said partial or final payment.

Final payment is due within 90 days after acceptance of the project and if not paid within this time period, shall bear interest at the rate of four percent provided the failure to make such payment is not a result of any fault of the contractor.

No certificate authorizing the first partial payment or final payment shall be made to a foreign contractor unless such contractor furnishes proof that all New York state taxes have been paid.

7. REMARKS.—Materialman under subcontractor may have benefit of payment bond without general contractor of surety having the right to set off against the materialman any claim against subcontractor. *Certified Industries, Inc. v. Royal Indemnity Co.*, 43 Misc.2d 761, 252 N.Y.S.2d 345 (Sup. Ct. 1964).

Under a payment bond whereby the general contractor and its surety agreed that the bond should be for the benefit of any materialman having just claim and that materialmen should have direct right of action against general contractor and surety, a materialman was one of the class intended to be protected and the general contractor and surety did not have the right to set off against the materialman any claim against the subcontractor. *Certified Industries, Inc. v. Royal Indemnity Co.*, 43 Misc.2d 761, 252 N.Y.S.2d 345 (Sup. Ct. 1964).

A completing surety was held to have priority over the assignee of accounts receivable with respect to funds held by a Board of Education. The surety was not required to comply with Article 9 of the Uniform Commercial Code. *AEtna Casualty Surety Co. v. Perrotta*, 62 Misc.2d 252, 308 N.Y.S.2d 613 (Sup. Ct. 1970).

A substantial reduction in retainage by obligee, without consent of the surety, was held to discharge the surety. *Schooley Enterprises, Inc., v. Paso Contracting Corp.,* 33 App. Div. 2d 981, 307 N.Y.S.2d 388 (1970).

Where a claimant waived a right to file a mechanic's lien, held, he could not maintain suit on the payment bond. *New Rochelle Roofing, Cornice & Skylight Works, Inc. v. Gevyn Constr. Corp.,* 33 App. Div. 2d 774, 306 N.Y.S.2d 729 (1969).

Service of notice of claim by supplier of materials to a subcontractor on public project was insufficient where the notice was sent by ordinary mail, since the statute expressly requires same to be sent by registered mail, regardless of the fact that this notice was actually received by the contractor. *Ulster Electric Supply Co. and Maryland Casualty Co.,* 35 App. Div. 2d 309, 316 N.Y.S.2d 159 (1970), *aff'd,* 30 N.Y.2d 712, 332 N.Y.S.2d 648 (1972).

In 1953 the Department of Public Works of the City of New York restored the requirement of a performance bond and now also requires a payment bond conditioned that the contractor and subcontractors to whom work under the contract is sublet shall pay or shall cause to be paid all lawful claims for labor, and for materials and supplies, whether incorporated in the permanent structure or not, as well as for teams, fuels, oils, implements or machinery furnished, used, or consumed by the contractor or any subcontractor at or in the vicinity of the site of the project in the prosecution of the work.

The Board of Education of the City of New York on April 27, 1950 adopted a resolution restoring bond requirements on construction contracts and contracts for "furniture and equipment where labor and installation is involved." By and large, the forms used are an adaptation of those now in use by the New York City Housing Authority, except that the labor and material coverage appears in the separate payment bond. The penal sum of each of the performance and payment bonds is fixed at one hundred per cent of the contract price.

Certain public or quasi-public bodies in New York sometimes waive the requirement of a bond.

8. DECISIONS.—While materialmen do not have the right to sue in their own names upon a bond given to a municipal corporation conditioned that the contractor shall faithfully perform his contract and pay the debts due labor and materialmen, nevertheless, the municipality may sue in equity for the enforcement of the promise to pay labor and materialmen, although the fund, when collected, will be held for the benefit of laborers and materialmen. *Johnson Service Co. v. E. H. Monin, Inc.,* 253 N.Y. 417, 171 N.E. 692 (1930).

However, an unpaid subcontractor may not compel the municipality to so proceed. *Van Clief v. City of New York,* 141 Misc. 216 (1931).

From the fact that a general contractor required a subcontractor to give both a performance bond and a payment bond and that the latter was conditioned only on the subcontractor promptly making payment to all persons supplying labor and material in the prosecution of the work provided for in the subcontract, it is to be inferred that suppliers of labor and material to the subcontractor were intended to be benefited and have a right against the surety on the subcontractor's separate labor and materialmen's bond. *Daniel-Morris Co. v. Glens Falls Indemnity Co.,* 308 N.Y. 464, 126 N.E.2d 750, 128 N.Y.S.2d 760 (1955); *Neill Supply Co. Inc. v. Fidelity and Deposit Company of Maryland,* 152 N.Y.S.2d 157 (Sup. Ct. 1956).

Where an additional bond shows the intention to confer a direct benefit upon third parties as a class, a member of that class may sue upon the bond. *McClare v. Massachusetts Bonding & Insurance Co.,* 266 N.Y. 371, 195 N.E. 15 (1935).

The divergent rules depending on the form of the bond, the existence or absence of a statute requiring same, and other technical aspects are briefly reviewed in *Daniel Morris Co. Inc. v. Glens Falls Indemnity Company,* 101 N.Y.S.2d 535 (Sup. Ct. 1950), modified, 283 App. Div. 504, 128 N.Y.S.2d 760 (1954) *aff'd,* 308 N.Y. 464, 126 N.E.2d 750 (1955).

The City of Buffalo requires every contractor entering into a contract with the city for the construction of any public improvement to give a bond with sureties approved by the head of the department executing the contract in an amount to be specified in the contract. Any person or corporation furnishing material or rendering labor in the execution of the contract may sue the surety on the bond for the payment of his or its claim. Such suit must be brought within one year after the claim against the contractor has accrued. Notice of the commencement of the suit and of subsequent proceedings must be given to the Corporation Counsel of the city. This notice need not be given before the suit is brought and a notice given any time before final judgment is entered is sufficient. *Eddy v. Fidelity & Deposit Co.,* 256 N.Y. 276, 192 N.E. 410 (1934).

The Buffalo Sewer Authority Act of 1935 requires the contractor on a construction contract exceeding $2,000 in cost to give a bond upon which persons furnishing labor and materials may sue within one year after the accrual of their respective claims against the contractor. This Buffalo Sewer Authority Act has been declared constitutional in a case which does not discuss the bond proviso thereof. *Robertson v. Zimmerman,* 268 N.Y. 52, 196 N.E. 740 (1935).

STATE BOND LAWS								31-71

Under a bond given pursuant to the charter of the City of Buffalo to the City, which provides that any subcontractor, materialman, laborer and third person having just claims arising out of or in connection with the execution of the contract may maintain an action on the bond, an insurance company is entitled to recover the sum due it for premiums on compensation and liability insurance furnished the contractor. *Merchants Mutual Casualty Co. v. U. S. F. & G. Co.,* 253 App. Div. 151, 2 N.Y.S.2d 370 (1938).

Where the bond of a public improvement contractor to a Water District obligated the contractor and surety to pay all persons for labor and materials, and gave all persons furnishing labor or materials a direct right of action on the bond, the surety was liable to all claimants proving claims for furnishing labor or materials in connection with the construction contract, notwithstanding such claimants were not entitled to share in fund remaining in the hands of municipal officials. *American Surety Co. v. Wells Water District,* 253 App. Div. 19, 1 N.Y.S.2d 614 (1938), *aff'd,* 280 N.Y. 528, 19 N.E.2d 926 (1939).

The statute relating to sums received by a contractor for a public improvement does not bar a banker from applying these construction funds if deposited in the contractor's account with the Bank, without inquiry, upon the contractor's indebtedness to the Bank. *Raymond Concrete Pile Co. v. Federation Bk. & Tr. Co.,* 288 N.Y. 452, 43 N.E.2d 486 (1942) adhered to, 290 N.Y. 611, 48 N.E.2d 709 (1943); *New York Trap Rock Corp. v. National Bank of Far Rockaway,* 285 N.Y. 825, 35 N.E.2d 498 (1941).

Where suit is instituted in New York on a bond given in connection with an R.E.A. project in Tennessee, New York will follow the decision of the highest court in Tennessee to the effect that the statutory provision for notice and time for suit will prevail over the provisions in the bond fixing different time limitations. *Graybar Electric Company v. New Amsterdam Casualty Company,* 292 N.Y. 246, 54 N.E.2d 811 (1944), rehearing denied, 292 N.Y. 643, 55 N.E.2d 512 (1944), cert. denied, 323 U.S. 715, 65 S. Ct. 42, 89 L. Ed. 575 (1944).

A materialman's right to recover against the surety under the labor and material bond posted under State construction contract, is not dependent upon the State owing money to contractor at the time notices of lien were filed. However, where the State has declared a construction contract void under provisions for termination upon contractor's default, a strict forfeiture of retained percentages which results in depriving lienors of possible satisfaction seems contrary to public policy, and whether unexpended balance in State's hands constituted a fund to which liens might attach was dependent on whether state suffered damage due to contractor's default. *Hartford Accident & Indemnity Co. v. First National Bank & Trust Co. of Paterson,* 281 App. Div. 607, 121 N.Y.S.2d 308 (1953), appeal dismissed, 307 N.Y. 634, 120 N.E.2d 833 (1954), rehearing denied, 307 N.Y. 879, 122 N.E.2d 755 (1954).

The provision in the bond with respect to private work, that no suit shall be commenced in a State Court other than in and for the county in which the project is situated, pertains to remedy only and is not a defense to an action instituted in another county. *Graziano Co. v. Indemnity Insurance Company of North America,* 286 App. Div. 867, 142 N.Y.S.2d 44 (1955), *aff'd,* 1 N.Y.2d 817, 135 N.E.2d 604 (1956).

Where a performance bond executed by a general contractor, besides protecting owner from all loss and damage which he might sustain by reason of default on part of contractor, referred to the general contract and made it a part thereof, and the contract, among other things, stated that general contractor agreed to furnish a bond to cover payment of materials, bond although not covering work performed by subcontractors would be deemed to have provided for payment of materials no matter who furnished the materials, whether a subcontractor or a materialman only, and therefore surety was liable under such bond to those who furnished materials, even though owner, after contractor's default, completed the contract for less than the original contract price. *Schmidt v. Duggan,* 15 Misc.2d 108, 180 N.Y.S.2d 679 (Sup. Ct. 1958), *aff'd,* 10 App. Div. 2d 797, 198 N.Y.S.2d 98 (1960).

Service of a written notice written 90 days after furnishing last item of material or work is required to support a claim for payment on an A.I.A. Payment Bond. *Triangle Erectors, Inc. v. James King & Sons,* 41 Misc.2d 12, 244 N.Y.S.2d 433 (Sup. Ct. 1963).

A surety who has posted performance and labor and material payment bonds for a public improvement is not required to file a financing statement under the Uniform Commercial Code. Here, the surety who completed the project after the contractor had defaulted was held entitled to the construction funds held by the Board of Education as against the contractor's accounts receivable assignee. *Aetna Casualty & Surety Co. v. Perrotta,* 62 Misc. 252, 308 N.Y.S.2d 613 (Sup. Ct. 1970).

An action against a subcontractor's surety, begun nearly six years after the subcontractor abandoned the work and more than two years after final payment was allegedly due, was not barred by a provision in the bond that suit must be instituted within two years after the date on which final payment falls due, since due to failure to complete the work final payment never became due. *Stanley R. Benjamin, Inc. v. Fidelity & Casualty Co. of N.Y.,* 72 Misc.2d 742, 340 N.Y.S.2d 578 (Sup. Ct. 1972).

Materialman who supplied backstops for rehabilitation contract was not entitled to recover from surety when backstops were not used by contractor. *Hartford Accident & Indemnity Co. v. Dovel-Martin Pipe Fabricators, Inc.,* 82 Misc.2d 714, 371 N.Y.S.2d 577 (Sup. Ct. 1975).

Prime plumbing contractor could not recover for delay damages against the Performance and Payment bond executed by general contractor's surety. *Novak and Co., Inc. v. Travelers Indemnity Co.,* 85 Misc.2d 957, 381 N.Y.S.2d 646 (Sup. Ct. 1976), *aff'd,* 56 App. Div. 2d 418, 392 N.Y.S.2d 901 (1977).

Supplier's timely service of notice of mechanics' lien on account of public improvement on parties to whom notice was to be given pursuant to the terms of bond was held to be requisite notice under the bond entitling recovery, despite the fact that the supplier failed to indicate he was making a claim on the bond, but rather, only indicated he was claiming a lien against funds payable to the general contractor. The court refused to read into the bond the provisions of the State Finance Law. *Sullivan Products Corp. v. Edward L. Nezelek, Inc.,* 52 App. Div. 2d 986, 383 N.Y.S.2d 463 (1976).

Remote subcontractor was not protected by prime contractor's surety bond which defined claimant as "one having a direct contract with principal or with a subcontractor of principal." *American Industrial Contracting Co. v. Travelers Indemnity Co.,* 54 App. Div. 2d 679, 387 N.Y.S.2d 260 (1976), *aff'd,* 42 N.Y.2d 1041, 399 N.Y.S.2d 206, 369 N.E.2d 762 (1977).

Where electrical subcontractor had fully performed all obligations required and expected of it, claim of subcontractor was justly due within meaning of the payment bond, and the fact that the general contractor had not received payment from the owner did not preclude liability of the surety. *Schuler-Haas Electric Co. v. Aetna Casualty & Surety Co.,* 40 N.Y.2d 883, 357 N.E.2d 1003, 389 N.Y.S.2d 348 (1976).

A per diem liquidated damage clause which was intended to cover the owner's damages for delay did not preclude the owner from suing the general contractor and its surety under a clause indemnifying the owner for neglectful acts of the general contractor causing damages to another contractor. *M. Eisenberg & Bros., Inc. v. White Plains Housing Authority,* 55 App. Div. 2d 599, 389 N.Y.S.2d 390 (1976).

A subcontractor's suit against the prime contractor and the prime contractor's surety was held barred because the subcontractor failed to give timely statutory notice of its claim. The court also dismissed the subcontractor's claim against the owner which sounded in quasi-contract because the owner had not received unjust enrichment, but rather extra work is held to be for the benefit of the prime contractor. *Schuler-Haas Elec. Corp. v. Wager Constr. Corp.,* 57 App. Div. 2d 707, 395 N.Y.S.2d 272 (1977).

A subcontractor whose work was completed was allowed to recover its retainage against the payment bond surety despite language in the subcontract that retainage was not payable until work was completed and approved by the relevant public agencies. Said subcontract language was construed not to be a condition precedent to payment. *Public Service Improvements, Inc. v. Jack Parker Constr. Corp.,* 59 App. Div. 2d 671, 398 N.Y.S. 2d 427 (1977).

A materialman to a materialman is not protected by the Public Works Payment Bond. *Neo-Ray Products, Inc. v. Boro Elec. Installation, Inc.,* 65 App. Div. 2d 687, 409 N.Y.S. 2d 729 (1978), *aff'd,* 48 N.Y.2d 781, 423 N.Y.S.2d 922, 399 N.E.2d 952 (1979).

Claimant was not liable for escalation costs when the statute granting 15 percent escalation to contractors and materialmen on certain projects was enacted after the surety executed its bond. Claimant's suit was barred by claimant's failure to institute its action within one from the date it delivered its materials. *Buffalo Slag Co. v. H&D Constr. Co.,* 94 Misc.2d 212, 404 N.Y.S.2d 292 (Sup. Ct. 1978).

Although building owner's conduct in changing terms under a general contract might have the effect of releasing the sureties from liability to it, such changes, if not authorized or participated in by a subcontractor, will not defeat a subcontractor's recovery on the payment bond. Hence, the subcontractor could not have suffered any injury by the owner's actions and, therefore, had no basis to assert a claim against the owner. *Area Masonry, Ltd. v. Dormitory Authority of the State of New York,* 64 App. Div. 2d 810, 407 N.Y.S.2d 279 (1978).

A subcontractor's cause of action was dismissed as being time barred inasmuch as suit was not commenced within one year from the date of final payment. However, the subcontractor's claim for extra work has held within the terms of the bond, and a trial was ordered to determine the amount of such claim. *Concrete Constr. Corp. v. Commercial Union Ins. Co. of New York,* 68 App. Div. 2d 866, 414 N.Y.S.2d 703 (1979).

A finding that the prime contractor was justified in abandoning the work was supported by the evidence and, accordingly, contractor had a right to terminate its performance because of breaches by the owner. Because there was no default, the surety of the contractor had no liability. *Farrell Heating, Plumbing, Airconditioning Contractors, Inc. v. Facilities Dev. and Improvement Corp.,* 68 App. Div. 2d 958, 414 N.Y.S.2d 767 (1979).

NORTH CAROLINA

Effective September 1, 1974 Chapter 44A is amended by inserting a new article 44A-24, abstracted as follows:

1. AMOUNT OF BOND.—100% of contract price conditioned upon the prompt payment for all labor or materials for which a contractor or subcontractor is liable. (General Statutes of North Carolina, Sec. 44A-26.)

2. LABOR AND MATERIAL COVERED.—All materials furnished or labor performed in the prosecution of the public work, whether or not the labor or materials enter into or become a component part of the public improvement, including gas, power, light, heat, oil, gasoline, telephone services and rental of equipment or the reasonable value of the use of equipment directly utilized in the performance of the public work.

3. NOTICE REQUIRED.—(a) *To surety*—no special statutory provision. (b) *To principal contractor*—Any claimant who has a direct contractual relationship with any subcontractor but has no contractual relationship, express or implied, with the contractor must give written notice to the contractor within 90 days from the date on which the claimant performed the last of the labor or furnished the last of the materials for which he claims payment stating with substantial accuracy the amount claimed and the name of the person for whom the work was performed or to whom the material was furnished. This notice is required to be served by registered or certified mail, postage prepaid, in an envelope addressed to such contractor at any place where his office is regularly maintained for the transaction of business or served in any manner provided by law for the service of summons. (c) *To municipality*—No special statutory provision. (d) *To creditors*—No special statutory provision.

4. TIME FOR SUIT.—At any time after the expiration of 90 days after claimant performed the last of the labor or furnished the last of the material for which he claims payment, but no such suit may be commenced after the expiration of the "longer period of one year from the day on which the last of the labor was performed or material was furnished by the claimant, or one year from the day on which final settlement was made with the contractor."

5. CONTRACTS EXCLUDED.—Generally $30,000 or less.

In 1977, North Carolina amended its statute to increase the threshold of public building contracts requiring separate letting for subdivisions of mechanical trades from $20,000 to $50,000.

In 1979, North Carolina amended its statute to increase the threshold of public building contracts requiring bid bonds and competitive bidding from $10,000 to $30,000.

Effective March 13, 1981, the county of Mecklenburg and the city of Charlotte increased the threshold of contracts requiring bonds and competitive bidding for the purchase of apparatus, supplies, material and equipment from $5,000 to $30,000. Orange County increased the threshold on the latter contracts from $5,000 to $10,000.

6. PROCEDURE.—Any person entitled to bring an action or any defendant in an action on a payment bond may require the contracting body to certify and furnish a copy of the payment bond and of the construction contract covered by the payment bond, upon 10 days notice and payment of reasonable cost. These certified copies constitute prima facie evidence of the contents, execution and delivery.

7. PENALTY FOR FAILURE TO TAKE BOND.—Designated official who fails to require the bonds guilty of a misdemeanor.

8. SPECIAL PROVISIONS.—Contracting body "means any department, agency, or political subdivision of the State of North Carolina which has authority to enter into construction contracts."

Highway work is included.

No act of or agreement between a contracting body, a contractor or a surety shall reduce the period of time for giving notice or commencing action or otherwise reduce or limit the liability of the contractor or the surety on the payment bond.

The contractor must either furnish the required performance and payment bonds or deposit moneys or government securities for the full amount of the contract to secure its faithful performance and payment of all sums due for labor and materials.

The following applies to contracts awarded prior to September 1, 1974:

1. AMOUNT OF BOND.—Equal to the contract price up to $2,000; when the contract price is

between $2,000 and $10,000, the amount of the bond shall be $2,000 plus 35% of the excess of the contract price over $2,000; when the contract price is over $10,000, the amount of the bond shall be $2,000 plus 25% of the excess of the contract price over $2,000. Amount of bonds under Highway Commission contracts is fixed by regulations of the Commission.

2. LABOR AND MATERIAL COVERED.—All labor and all materials and supplies furnished for public work under a contract or agreement made directly with the principal contractor or subcontractor.

3. NOTICE REQUIRED.—(a) *To surety*—No special statutory provision in section 2445 of the Code of 1927 as amended. However, the statute pertaining to bonds given by any contractor to the Highway Commission requires claimant to file a statement of the claim with the contractor and the surety, and, in event the surety is a corporation, with the general agent of such corporation within the State of North Carolina, within 12 months from the completion of the contract. Prior to the amendment of 1969, this statement of claim was required to be filed within six months from the completion of the contract. (b) *To principal contractor*—See notice of surety above. (c) *To municipality*—No special statutory provision. (d) *To Creditors*—Instituting creditor or creditors shall give notice to all persons informing them of the pendency of the suit, the names of the parties, with a brief recital of the purposes of the action, which notice shall be published at least once a week for four successive weeks in a newspaper published and circulated in the county in which the action is brought, and, if there be no newspaper, then by posting at the courthouse door and three other public places in such county for thirty days. Proof of such service shall be made by affidavit as provided in case of the service of summons by publication.

4. TIME OF SUIT.—It has been decided under a State Highway Bond that suit may be brought within three years after the completion of the work by the principal contractor. *Chappell v. National Surety Co.,* 191 N.C. 703, 133 S.E. 21 (1926). See Remarks.

5. CONTRACTS EXCLUDED.—$500 or less, State Highway $5,000.

6. PROCEDURE.—Suit must be instituted in a North Carolina court having jurisdiction of the amount of said bond and any number of labor and materialmen whose claims are unpaid have the right to join in one suit. Only one action or suit may be brought upon the bond, which said suit shall be brought in the county in which the building, road or street is located, and not elsewhere. Creditors may intervene in any pending suit within six months from the bringing of the action and not later. Creditors prorate where recovery on the bond is inadequate to pay the amount due all in full. See Remarks below.

7. PENALTY FOR FAILURE TO TAKE BOND.—Official whose duty it is to take the bond is guilty of a misdemeanor if he fails to require the said bond. However, such public officials may not be held individually liable, either in their official or individual capacities. *Warner v. Hallyburton,* 187 N.C. 414, 121 S.E. 756 (1924); *Hunter v. Allman,* 192 N.C. 483, 135 S.E. 291 (1926); *Noland Co. v. Board,* 190 N.C. 250, 129 S.E. 577 (1925).

8. SPECIAL PROVISIONS.—Statute conclusively presumed to have been written into every bond. No action shall be brought upon any bond given by any contractor of the Highway Commission until after the completion of the work contracted to be done by the contractor.

Any person entitled to bring an action has the right to require the State Highway Commission to furnish information as to when the contract is completed. Any claim of the State Highway Commission against the bond and the surety thereon shall be preferred as against any cause of action in favor of any laborer, materialman or other person, and constitutes a first lien or claim against the said bond and the surety thereon.

In 1977, North Carolina amended its law relating to bid bonds required on public building contracts, to delete the condition of the bond that requires the surety to pay double the amount of the bond if the surety fails to make prompt payment.

Also in 1977, North Carolina passed a bid mistake statute which permits the withdrawal of bids on contracts for public works due to an unintentional clerical error (as opposed to a judgmental error) and/or an unintentional omission.

9. DECISIONS.—Labor and materialmen are protected whether or not the condition for their benefit is written into the bond. *Standard Electric Time Co. v. Fidelity & Deposit Co. of Maryland,* 191 N.C. 653, 132 S.E. 808 (1926).

If the materials are furnished for a particular public improvement, the person furnishing the same may recover on the bond whether or not the materials were actually incorporated into the public improvement. *Standard Sand Co. v. McClay,* 191 N.C. 313, 131 S.E. 754 (1926); *Moore v. Builders Material Co.,* 192 N.C. 418, 135 S.E. 113 (1926).

There is nothing in the statute which prohibits the parties to the bond from agreeing upon a reasonable time for bringing suit and barring any suit thereafter instituted. Such a reasonable provision will be sustained. *Horne Wilson Co. v. National Surety Co.,* 202 N.C. 73, 161 S.E. 726 (1932).

Where the trustees of a school district failed to retain the 15% of amount due contractor, as provided by contract, the school district was held liable to the surety for the surety's loss on labor and material claims. *Sanford Sash & Blind Co. v. Mooney,* 202 N.C. 830, 162 S.E. 556 (1932); *Fidelity & Deposit Co. of Maryland, v. Board of Education,* 204 N.C. 607, 169 S.E. 926 (1933).

A subcontractor may not sue on a bond given to the trustees of a teachers' college, conditioned for payment of labor and material claims. Such an entity is not a municipal corporation. *Hunt Mfg. Co. v. Hudson,* 200 N.C. 541, 157 S.E. 799 (1931).

Roofing, beds and bedding used in operation of boarding house for employees not covered by highway contractor's bond in the absence of evidence that such boarding was necessary under the circumstances or part of the contract of hiring. *Jenkins Hardware Co. v. Globe Indemnity Co.,* 205 N.C. 185, 170 S.E. 643 (1933).

The fact that a contractor's performance bond granted laborers and materialmen the right to maintain action against the surety did not change surety's status to that of a principal debtor. To entitle materialmen to recover from surety on a contractor's performance bond, materialmen must allege and prove a debt due by the contractor for material furnished him for use in performance of the contract with the owner. *Carolina Builders Corp. v. New Amsterdam Cas. Co.,* 236 N.C. 513, 73 S.E.2d 155 (1952).

Where prime contractor who entered into a North Carolina State Highway contract is bound to pay for materials used on project whether furnished by himself or subcontractor, failure of subcontractor to pay for materials furnished him is in the same category as failure of contractor to pay for labor or materials giving rise to lien, and, generally, loss resulting from such failure is covered by performance bond whether or not payment for labor or materials is expressly required by bond or contract. *Saint Paul Mercury Ind. Co. v. Wright Contracting Co.,* 250 F.2d 758 (4th Cir. 1958).

Where bond is given to assure payment of labor and material entering into the construction of a state highway, the institution of an action thereon must await completion of the contract and a claimant must file a statement of his claim with the contractor and the surety within 6 months from completion of the contract. *American Bridge Division, United States Steel Corp. vs. Brinkley,* 255 N.C. 162, 120 S.E.2d 529 (1961).

Where the statute prescribed six months after the last furnishing of labor and material, a provision in a payment bond requiring notice of claim to be given to the contractor and the surety within 90 days of last furnishing of material was held to be invalid. *Amarr Co. v. J. M. Dixon, Inc.,* 5 N.C. App. 479, 168 S.E.2d 475 (1969).

Subcontractors and materialmen who had not given notices of claim before payment to a general contractor for the construction of private projects, could not recover on the general contractor's bonds which were not required by construction contracts and which provided that they were given solely for the protection of owners, even though one contract required the contractor to pay for all labor, materials and equipment. *West Durham Lumber Co. v. AEtna Casualty and Surety Co.,* 12 N.C. App. 641, 184 S.E.2d 399 (1971); cert. denied, 280 N.C. 180, 185 S.E.2d 704 (1972).

Supplier of materials to general contractor could not sue general contractor's surety on project overseen by Housing Authority because Housing Authority was considered a municipal corporation and supplier had not intervened in previous action which had been brought on the bond. Suit was allowed, however, against the contractor. This case construes the prior North Carolina public works statute. *S. C. M. Corp., Glidden-Durkee Division v. Federal Construction Co.,* 29 N.C. App. 592, 225 S.E.2d 162 (1976).

Suit by equipment renter against highway construction subcontractor and its surety on payment bond. Summary judgment in favor of the surety was affirmed, the court holding that all parties considered the bond given by the subcontractor to be a private bond, and not one required by statute; that a private bond conditioned to pay for all labor and materials does not cover a claim for rental of equipment which is a component of the contractor's plant. In addition, claims for replacement of tires and repairs were not covered by the bond. The tire replacements added value to the equipment and made it available for other work. The repairs which were made were made after the return of equipment and were not needed to keep the equipment operating during the construction work. *Bullard v. North Carolina National Bank,* 31 N.C. App. 312, 229 S.E.2d 245 (1976).

The claim of a lessor of machines to a subcontractor is covered by the subcontractor's payment bond, the claimant was entitled to recover for repairs in excess of the ordinary wear and tear and for abnormal tire wear as provided in the lease. Since services charges on outstanding balances were not provided for in the lease, they could not be recovered under the bond, but the claimant could recover interest at the legal rate from the due date on such balance. *Interstate Equip. Co. v. Smith,* 292 N.C. 592, 234 S.E.2d 599 (1977).

A contractor was held entitled to repudiate its contract when the contract failed to comply with a North Carolina statute which requires contracts with a county to be in writing and to include a clause stating that provision for payment of the monies has been duly made by an appropriation or by authorized bonds or notes. Hence, the contractor's surety was also released from its bond liability. *Rochingham County v. L.A. Reynolds Co.,* 31 N.C. App. 151, 228 S.E.2d 652 (1976).

NORTH DAKOTA

1. AMOUNT OF BOND.—Equal to contract price. (North Dakota Century Code, Title 48, Chpt. 48-01, Sec. 48-01-01.)

2. LABOR AND MATERIAL COVERED.—All materials or labor or supplies used for machinery and motor power equipment in connection with contracts for the erection, repair or alteration of any public building or other public improvement except municipal improvements made under special assessment statutes.

Every nonresident public works contractor is required by an amendment approved March 9, 1961 to include in the surety performance bond further added provisions to insure the payment of contributions due to the unemployment compensation division and to the North Dakota workmen's compensation fund of all premiums to become due on wages paid for labor performed in such work or project. Such contractor also shall include in such bond provisions to insure the payment to the State of North Dakota of the State income tax upon income derived from such work or project and upon income to become due from such work or project.

3. NOTICE REQUIRED.—

(a) *To surety*—No special statutory provision.

(b) *To principal contractor*—An amendment approved March 21, 1973, provides that any person having a direct contractual relationship with a subcontractor but no contractual relationship with the contractor furnishing the bond shall not have a right of action against the bond unless he has given written notice to the contractor within ninety days from the date on which the person completed his contribution, stating with substantial accuracy the amount claimed and the name of the person for whom the contribution was performed. Each notice shall be served by registered or certified mail, postage prepaid, in an envelope addressed to the contractor at any place he maintains an office, conducts his business or has a residence.

(c) *To municipality*—No special statutory provision.

(d) *To creditors*—See Special Provisions below.

4. TIME FOR SUIT.—Within six months after the first publication of notice to file claims given by contractor or surety (under old statute).

The amendment approved March 21, 1973, provides that a claimant who has not been paid in full within ninety days after completion of his contribution of labor or material shall have the right to sue on such bond for the amount unpaid at the time of institution of suit. Such suit must be commenced within one year after completion of the claimant's contribution of labor, material or supplies. This section of the statute, prior to the above amendment, required suit to be brought within six months after the first publication of notice to file claims was given by the contractor or surety. Any person who has furnished labor, materials or supplies on a highway contract performance bond must commence suit within one year of final acceptance. Proper notice of the claim must be given within 90 days after completion of the work. N.D. Senate Bill 2285 Regular Session 1983.

5. CONTRACT EXCLUDED.—Effective July 1, 1981, Section 11-11-28 of the Century Code, relating to the bid bond required on public works contracts, was amended to provide that where the bid is $10,000 or less, the bidder may, in lieu of a bond, accompany the bid with a separate envelope containing a certified or cashier's check equal to 5% of the full amount of the bid. When a bidder's bond is required it shall be in the sum equal to 5% of the full amount of the bid, executed by the bidder as principal and by a surety company authorized to do business in the State.

6. PROCEDURE.—No special statutory provision.

7. PENALTY FOR FAILURE TO TAKE BOND.—Any officer and the members of any board who shall fail to take a bond before entering into such a public contract shall be personally liable for all such bills, claims and demands which are not paid within thirty days after the completion of the work. *Crane & Ordway Co. v. Sykeston School District,* 36 N.D. 254 (1917), 162 N. W. 413.

8. SPECIAL PROVISIONS.—The old act provides that at any time after the completion of the

public improvement, the principal contractor or his surety may publish a notice in the official newspaper printed and published in the county where such improvement is completed, and if such improvement shall extend to more than one county, then at least in one such newspaper in each county, stating that the said improvement has been completed and that all persons who furnished labor, material or supplies to any subcontractor, naming them, for the making of such improvement must file their claims with the contractor or his surety within six months after the first publication of the notice.

This notice shall specify the name and address of the commission or agency of the State, county, township, school district or municipality which caused the improvement to be made and the name and address of the contractor or surety, and claims shall be filed at both addresses so specified, provided that if the contractor be a non-resident of the State of North Dakota he shall designate a place in said State where claims may be filed, the notice to be published once each week for four successive weeks in the said official newspaper.

The law relating to the organization of irrigation districts merely requires the contractor to furnish a performance bond.

The amendment approved March 21, 1973, provides that the contracting body and the agent in charge of its office are authorized and directed to furnish a certified copy of the bond and the contract for which it was given to anyone making an application therefor who submits an affidavit that either he has supplied labor or materials for such work or improvement and that payment has not been made, or that he is being sued on any such bond. Applicants shall pay the actual cost of the preparation of the certified copy of the bond and the contract. The certified copy of the bond shall be prima facie evidence of the contents, execution, and delivery of the original.

In March of 1977, the North Dakota Code was amended as follows: In case of a default on the part of the bidder or contractor in the performance of the work as provided in his contract, the sum named in the bond shall be taken and held to cover the amount necessary to compensate the municipality for the correction, repair or replacement caused by such default, and that the full amount thereof may be recovered from said bidder and his sureties in an action by the municipality against them on said bond only in the event of a complete failure of performance on the part of the contractor. Nothing herein shall be construed to prevent the municipality from receiving the amount, not in excesss of the amount of the bond, necessary to compensate the municipality for correction, repair or replacement caused by default of the contractor which does not constitute complete failure of performance by the contractor.

9. DECISIONS.—An electric company which merely sold electrical supplies and equipment to a contractor was not a subcontractor but was a materialman. A manufacturer who sold and billed supplies to such materialman delivered to the site, was held not to be within the coverage of a contractor's public works bond. When such materialman was paid, the obligation of the bond was fulfilled. The materialman's failure to pay the manufacturer did not result in a claim under the payment bond. *Kinney Electric Manufacturing Co. v. Modern Electric Co.,* 149 N.W.2d 69 (N.D. 1967).

City recovered judgment against sewer and water contractor and its performance bond surety for $518,000 damage for failure of contractor to compact soil under payment. Subsequently, contractor and surety moved for relief from judgment on grounds that soil had stablized making fewer repairs necessary, and that city had made only half of needed repairs for a cost of only $40,000. City took position that restoration to condition called for by contract would cost one million dollars. Court refused to modify judgment holding that the newly discovered evidence of facts did not justify relief from the judgment; that the city was not required to repair property in order to collect and retain damages for breach of contract; effect of judgment on economic condition of contractor was not grounds for setting aside judgment; and nothing presented was sufficiently extraordinary to justify the reopening of the judgment. *City of Wahpeton v. Drake-Henne, Inc.,* 228 N.W.2d 324 (N.D. 1975).

OHIO

1. AMOUNT OF BOND.—Contract price. (Ohio Revised Code, Section 153.54. See Section 153.571 of Ohio Revised Code for combination bid and performance/payment bond form.)

2. LABOR AND MATERIAL COVERED.—All labor performed or materials furnished in carrying forward, performing or completing a contract for the construction, demolition, alteration, repair or reconstruction of any public improvement.

3. NOTICE REQUIRED.—(a) *To surety*—At any time after furnishing labor or material, but not later than ninety days after the acceptance of the public improvement by the duly authorized board or officer, claimant shall furnish surety a statement of the amount due. No suit shall be

brought against the surety on said bond until after sixty days after the furnishing of said statement. (b) *To principal contractor*—No special statutory provision. (c) *To municipality*—No special statutory provision. (d) *To creditors*—No special statutory provision.

4. TIME FOR SUIT.—No suit shall be brought against the surety until after sixty days after the furnishing of the statement, but suit must be commenced not later than one year from date of acceptance of the public improvement.

5. PROCEDURE.—If such indebtedness is not paid in full at the expiration of said sixty days, claimant may bring an action in his own name upon the bond. See Remarks.

6. PENALTY FOR FAILURE TO TAKE BOND.—Officer who violates statute shall be fined a sum not exceeding $1,000.

7. SPECIAL PROVISIONS.—Recovery by any claimant under the statutory form of bond is subject to the conditions and provisions of the statute to the same extent as if such conditions and provisions were fully incorporated in the bond form.

8. REMARKS.—The Ohio statute pertaining to contracts made by the Director of Transportation provides that the Director shall require a performance bond and a separate payment bond, each in an amount equal to 100% of the estimated cost of the work; the payment bond to be conditioned for the payment by the contractor and all subcontractors for labor performed or materials furnished in connection with the work, improvement or project involved. (Ohio Revised Code, Section 5525.16.)

Effective September 30, 1963 the statute of Ohio relative to notice requirements for mechanics' liens has been amended to read: Any subcontractor, materialman, laborer or mechanic who has performed labor or furnished material, fuel, or machinery or who is performing labor or furnishing material, fuel, or machinery for the construction, alteration, removal or repair of any property, appurtenance, or structure described in the statute conferring a lien for erecting a house, mill, bridge, etc. (§1311.02) and in the statute conferring a lien upon streets, roads, sidewalks, etc. (§1311.03) or for the construction, improvement, or repair of any turnpike, road improvement, sewer, street, or other public days thereafter must file a copy of his notice with the County Recorder of the county or counties where the property is situated.

The proper filing of such notice gives the claimant a preference as to payments subsequently due from the public body over such of the other claimants who have failed prior to the date any such payment is due to file the statement of claim and to record the same. Such lien claimants have no priority among themselves, but payment thereon shall be made to them in amounts prorated according to the amount of the then existing valid claim of each. The failure of any claimant to file a copy of his statement with the County Recorder or Recorders does not affect the validity of his lien with respect to persons other than such of his fellow claimants who have filed copies of their statements with the County Recorder or Recorders. Such lien claimants who have failed to make such filing with the improvement or public building under a public works contract and under an agreement between such a subcontractor or materialman and a principal contractor or subcontractor at any time, not to exceed 4 months from the performance of the labor or the delivery of the machinery, fuel or material, may file with the public body a sworn and itemized statement of the amount and value of such labor performed, and material, fuel, or machinery furnished, stating when the last of such labor was performed and when the last of such material, fuel, or machinery was furnished, containing a description of any promissory notes that have been given to the lien claimant on account, setting forth all credits and setoffs and stating the post office address of the claimant. Proof that such sworn and itemized statement was mailed by registered mail to the address of the public body is prima facie evidence of the filing thereof.

Upon receipt of such notice the public body or its representative is required to detain from the principal contractor all subsequent payments as do not in the aggregate exceed such claim or claims.

The claimant filing his statement as above in order to notify other claimants within 10 County Recorder or Recorders have no priority among themselves, but, after all claims having preference over theirs have been paid, payment shall be made to them in amounts prorated according to the amount of the then existing valid claim of each.

Effective August 27, 1976, Ohio amended, revised and consolidated various sections of the Code relating to retainage on public improvement contracts made by the state or any county, township, municipal corporation, school district or other political subdivision so that progress payments would be made to contractors at the rate of 92 percent of the estimates prepared by the contractor and approved by the architect or engineer. All labor performed after the job is 50 percent completed is to be paid for at the rate of 100 percent of the estimate submitted by the contractor and approved by the engineer. Thereafter, from the date the contract is 50 percent complete, all funds retained under the contract are required to be deposited in an escrow account. When the major portions of the project are substantially completed and occupied, or in use, or otherwise accepted, and there exists no reason to withhold retainage, the retained percentage held in connection with such portion is required to be released from the escrow and paid to the contractor, the owner only withholding that amount necessary to assure completion. This statute also provides for the payment of interest at the prime rate if retainages are not properly paid.

In June of 1980, school districts were excluded from coverage under the state's uniform building contracting procedures. In addition, only school district contracts exceeding $15,000 are subject to the bid security law.

In 1975 Ohio amended its Code and now requires that when a surety bond is accepted from a surety company by the Director of Transportation on a contract, it shall not be for more than 10 percent of the Company's capital and surplus, unless the amount in excess of 10 percent is fully reinsured. In addition, if the original contractor is placed in default, the surety is required to enter upon the project and complete the work which it bonded. If the surety fails to so complete, then any additional cost reasonably incurred by the Director of Transportation as a result of such failure or refusal shall be computed by the Director and become the liability of the surety, which liability is not limited by the amount of the contract performance bond.

9. DECISIONS.—The provisions of Sections 2365-1 and 2365-4 and the provisions of the statute pertaining to road work are not inconsistent, but can be and are to be read and construed together, so as to give effect to both, and a road improvement bond must be in a sum equal to one-half the estimated cost of the work, but not less than one-half of the contract price. *Southern Surety Co. v. Standard Slag Co.,* 117 Ohio St. 512, 159 N.E. 559 (1927).

Materialmen and subcontractors may avail themselves of the security of the bond, even though they are not expressly named therein, and even though the statutory provision for payment for labor and materials is entirely omitted. *Southern Surety Co. v. Chambers,* 115 Ohio St. 434, 154 N.E. 786 (1926); *American Guaranty Co. v. Cliff Wood Coal & Supply Co.,* 115 Ohio St. 524, 155 N.E. 127 (1926).

The security of the bond is available to a party furnishing to a materialman material, cut according to the specifications of the contract, and which goes directly, substantially without further fabrication, into the construction. *American Guaranty Co. v. Cincinnati Iron & Steel Co.,* 115 Ohio St. 626, 155 N.E. 389 (1927).

Where the work was discontinued after the public body and the surety company arrived at a new contract under which the surety finished the work, the court allowed the claimant to maintain an action on the bond, stating that acceptance of the work under the original contract, upon which the claimant was relying, never occurred. *National Surety Co. v. Mansfield Lumber Co.,* 32 Ohio App. 146, 167 N.E. 691 (1928).

If the loss sustained by the municipality exceeds the penal sum named in the bond, the municipality is entitled to apply the full penal sum named in the bond to reduce its loss and the subcontractors, laborers and materialmen, in such event, have no right of recovery under the bond. *Cleveland, etc., Co. v. Garfield Heights,* 116 Ohio St. 338, 156 N.E. 209 (1927).

The statement required by the statute to be furnished to the surety need not be prepared with the particularity of detail required in a statement of account. It is sufficient if the statement advises the surety of the amount due and that it is for labor performed or material furnished in the construction of the improvement for which the bond was given. *Southern Surety Co. v. Schmidt,* 117 Ohio St. 28, 158 N.E. 1 (1927).

The statement must be furnished to the surety by the claimant or his attorney or agent; forwarding the statement to the clerk of a school board, or other public authority for whom the improvement is being constructed, is not sufficient, even though the surety knows its contents. *Globe Indemnity Co. v. Wassman,* 120 Ohio St. 72, 165 N.E. 579 (1929).

The furnishing of the statement is jurisdictional, and without it no action can be maintained on the bond by a subcontractor, materialman or laborer. *Atkinson v. Orr-Ault Construction Co.,* 124 Ohio St. 100, 177 N.E. 40 (1931).

When the authorized agent of a surety represents to claimants that their claims are correct and will be paid, and that they need do nothing further in respect to their claims, and the claimants rely upon such representations to their prejudice, the surety is estopped from thereafter asserting its right to compliance by the claimants with the statute. *Globe Indemnity Co. v. Wassman,* 120 Ohio St. 72, 165 N.E. 579 (1929).

The failure to furnish the surety a statement of the amount due the claimant is a bar to maintaining an action on the bond. *Atkinson v. Orr-Ault Constr. Co.,* 124 Ohio St. 100, 177 N.E. 40 (1931).

A subcontractor who properly files a statement can maintain suit against the Secretary of Highways to prevent payment to the principal contractor, notwithstanding the rule which precludes suit against the state. *State ex rel. Nixon v. Merrell,* 126 Ohio St. 239, 185 N.E. 56 (1933).

A Kentucky company seeking to recover under an Ohio statute from an Ohio highway contractor's surety for balance due on materials furnished to the contractor for the construction of culverts in Ohio, was required to show compliance to the Ohio statute requiring a statement to the surety of the amount due from the contractor within 90 days from the completion of the work. *Maryland Casualty Co. v. Newport Culvert Co.,* 277 Ky. 320, 126 S.W.2d 468 (1939). The fact that laborers and materialmen had not perfected statutory liens was immaterial in determining the surety's right to recover from the county an amount equal to judgments against the surety in favor of unpaid materialmen and laborers after the commissioners paid retained percentages to the contractor without the surety's consent. *Hochevar v. Maryland Casualty Co.,* 114 F.2d 948 (6th Cir. 1940).

Materialmen in alleging that statement of amount due was furnished to surety on bond of public improvement contractor within 90 days after acceptance of the work could not recover on the bond. *General Electric Supply Corp. v. Wiley Electric Co.,* 47 Ohio App. 196, 191 N.E. 706 (1933).

A subcontractor who first perfects a lien on a portion of the contract price deposited by the public body with a local official for the protection of labor and materialmen and then, without the knowledge of the surety, voluntarily releases his lien on said fund, thereby releases the surety on the contractor's bond to the extent of the security so released, but not for the balance of his claim. *Boyd v. Royal Indemnity Co.,* 126 Ohio St. 322, 185 N.E. 422 (1933).

Coal furnished to a road contractor to be used by him for the purpose of heating asphalt for spreading on the highway top surface is "material furnished" within the meaning of the bond statue. *Lingler v. Andrews,* 56 Ohio App. 487, 10 N.E.2d 1021 (1936).

Materialmen and laborers, who fail to perfect statutory lien on the sum due the contractor under a state highway construction contract by filing their claims with the Director of Highways, have no lien against such fund. *In re: Gilmore,* 28 F.Supp. 1010 (S.D. Ohio 1933).

An "acceptance" within statute requiring subcontractors to furnish contractor's surety with statement of amount due within ninety days after acceptance of public improvement must be an administrative determination of actual completion of work in accordance with terms of contract and in compliance with plans and specifications, and this must be fixed by public record and readily ascertained. An informal acceptance by the board members over the telephone is inadequate. *Nesbitt, Inc. v. Massachusetts Bonding & Insurance Co. of Boston,* 49 N.E.2d 765 (Ct. App. 1942).

A statute providing that, from date of completion or acceptance by municipality, 4% of the contract price should be retained, as security for faithful performance of the contract, did not preclude final acceptance of work until payment of final retainage by city. There is nothing in this statute which postpones the date of "acceptance" to the date of the payment of the final retainage. A subcontractor who furnished statement of amount due to the surety on the contractor's bond more than 90 days after acceptance of the work and who sued the surety therefor more than one year after acceptance failed to comply with the statutory requirements and hence was precluded from recovering from the public works contractor's surety. *Ben Tom Corporation v. Buckeye Union Casualty Co.,* 2 Ohio Miss. 125, 207 N.E.2d 582 (1964).

There must be an administrative ruling of actual completion of the work set forth in a public record to constitute the final acceptance. *Southern Surety Co. v. Schmidt,* 117 Ohio St. 28, 158 N.E. 1 (1927).

Word "subcontractor" as used in statutes dealing with bonds required by contractors and subcontractors in connection with construction of public buildings, will be given its ordinary meaning so that it includes one who, under contract with general contractor, merely furnishes material for use in performance of general contract and so that it excludes a subcontractor of a subcontractor of the general contractor. *Weybrecht's Sons Co. v. Hartford Accident & Indemnity Co.,* 161 Ohio St. 436, 119 N.E.2d 836 (1954).

Surveying services constitute labor within the purview of the contractor's bond statute and bond conditioned for payment by highway contractor of claims for labor performed by the completing contractor. *Kline v. Federal Insurance Co.,* 6 Ohio Op. 2d 445, 152 N.E.2d 911 (1958).

Statute prohibiting any suit against surety until sixty days after furnishing of statement creates condition precedent which must be complied with. *Whitaker Merrell Co. v. Claude A. Janes, Inc.,* 173 N.E.2d 402 (Ct. Cm. Pl. 1961).

A subcontractor who furnished statement of amount due to surety on subcontractor's bond more than 90 days after acceptance of the work and sued surety therefor more than one year after such acceptance, had not complied with the statute and was precluded from recovery on such bond. *Ben-Tom Corporation v. Buckeye Union Casualty Company,* 2 Ohio Misc. 125, 207 N.E.2d 582 (1964).

A supplier of repair parts to equipment used by a general contractor for the repair by the contractor of heavy construction equipment used in the performance of road construction with the state is covered by the bond. *Mountaineer Euclid, Inc. v. Western Casualty & Surety Co.*, 19 Ohio App. 2d 185, 250 N.E.2d 768 (1969).

OKLAHOMA

The Act which took effect March 25, 1968 provides:
1. AMOUNT OF BOND.—Not less than the contract amount. (61 Okl. St. Ann. § 1)
2. LABOR AND MATERIAL COVERED.—All indebtedness by contractor or his subcontractors for labor and materials and repairs to and parts for equipment used and consumed in the performance of said contract.
3. NOTICE REQUIRED.—(a) *To surety*—Any person having direct contractual relationship with a subcontractor performing work on said contract but no contractual relationship expressed or implied with contractor furnishing said payment bond must give written notice to the contractor *and* surety on said payment bond within 90 days from the date on which said person did or performed the last of the labor or furnished or supplied the last of the material or parts for which such claim is made stating with substantial accuracy the amount claimed and the names of the parties to whom the material or parts were supplied or for whom the labor was done or performed. Such notice is required to be served by registered or certified mail, postage prepaid in an envelope addressed to the contractor at any place he maintains an office or conducts his business together with a copy thereof to the surety or sureties on said payment bond. (b) *To principal contractor*—No notice is required by a person having a contractual relationship expressed or implied with a principal contractor but every person having a direct contractual relationship with a subcontractor must give both to the contractor and to the surety 90 days notice reviewed under subsection (a) above. (c) *To municipality*—No special statutory provision. (d) *To creditors*—No special statutory provision.
4. TIME FOR SUIT.—No action shall be brought on said payment bond after one year from the date on which the last of the labor was performed or materials or parts furnished for which such claim is made.
5. CONTRACTS EXCLUDED.—$7,500 or less (affidavit required).
6. PROCEDURE.—A bond is required to be filed in the office of the agency, municipality or government instrumentality that is authorized by law and does enter into the contract for the construction of the public improvements or building or repair to same. The officer with whom the bond is filed is required to furnish a copy thereof to any person claiming rights thereunder.
7. SPECIAL PROVISIONS.—A June 5, 1975 amendment provides that no work shall be commenced until all required bonds have been provided by the contractor to the awarding public agency.

In June of 1980, there was enacted a requirement that each bidder shall accompany his bid with a sworn statement that he has not been a party to any collusive agreement which restricts the competitive bidding process.
8. PENALTY FOR FAILURE TO TAKE BOND.—No special statutory provisions.
9. SPECIAL PROVISONS.—A statute approved April 1, 1970, provides that any person furnishing labor or material for a public work who has not been paid therefor, may file at any time prior to the expiration of 20 days following the completion of the contract for public work a stop notice with the public agency concerned. Any such person having contractual relationship with the contractor, other than a person who performed actual labor for wages, may file such a notice but no payment shall be withheld from any such contractor after the expiration of said 20 days unless the party making a claim shall have served the public agency with proof that he has instituted a legal action within such time to effectuate collection. Upon filing a legal action, the public agency usually withholds the amount claimed within the action and pays the balance to the contractor. Statutory guaranties are required by the claimant.

In October of 1977, Oklahoma amended its statute relating to public buildings and public works with respect to contracts exceeding $2,500 to provide that at any time the contractor has completed in excess of 50 percent of the total contract, the 10 percent retainage shall be reduced to 5 percent, provided the owner has determined satisfactory progress is being made, and upon approval by the surety. The contractor is given the right to withdraw any part or the whole of the amount which has been retained by depositing with the public agency appropriate security in the form of United States Treasury bonds, notes or bills; general obligation bonds of the State of Oklahoma; or certificates of deposit from a state or national bank having its principal office in the State of Oklahoma.

The amendment provides that the awarding public agency shall pay to the contractor interest at the rate of three-fourth percent (¾%) per month of the final payment due the contractor. For the lump sum contracts the interest shall commence thirty (30) days after the work under the contract has been completed and accepted and all required material certifications and other documentation required by the contract have been furnished the awarding public agency by the contractor, and shall run until the date when the final payment or estimate is tendered to the contractor.

For contracts bid by unit prices the interest shall commence sixty (60) days after the above conditions are satisfied. When contract quantities or the final payment amount is in dispute, the interest-bearing period shall be suspended until the conclusion of arbitration and settlement of the dispute.

10. DECISIONS.—Where a fabricator entered into a contract with a prime contractor to fabricate steel to be installed in a municipal project covered by a statutory bond, the fabricator was a "subcontractor" and indebted to the supplier of the steel. The prime contractor's statutory bond covered the supplier's claim. *City of Purcell v. Merco Manufacturing, Inc.* 324 F.Supp. 210 (W.D. Okla. 1971).

Liability under a payment bond for materials furnished on public works project does not attach to any material not consumed in the construction of the project. *Mid-Continent Casualty Co. v. P & H Supply, Inc.* 490 P.2d 1358 (Okla. 1971).

The term "completion," as used in statute providing that no action shall be brought on performance bond filed by contractor engaged in construction of a public building after six months from completion of said public building, means actual completion of the building as contracted for without regard to the stipulated performance by the parties. *L.E. Smith v. Minneapolis-Honeywell Regulator Co.,* 236 F.2d 573 (10th Cir. 1956).

Statutes relating to bonds to be filed by contractors are designed for protection of creditors, and one is not entitled to relief thereunder unless he has performed labor or rendered services for which there is a debt due him. *Porter v. Mid-American Paving Co.,* 301 P.2d 1005 (Okla. 1956).

Spraying of timber and brush by helicopter is not a lienable item. *Browning vs. Allied Helicopter, Inc.,* 309 F.2d 712 (10th Cir. 1962).

Sections 1 and 2 of the former 1961 statute created no rights, liability or cause of action in derogation of the common law. The six months liability provision contained therein was held to be an ordinary statute of limitations, not an extinguishment of the rights, liability and cause of action. *Phillips Petroleum Co. v. U.S. Fidelity & Guaranty Co.,* 442 P.2d 303 (Okla. 1968).

The surety bond is liable for health and welfare payments which contractor was obliged, pursuant to agreements with industry benefit fund, to pay to the fund for each hour worked by the contractor's employees. *Pipeline Industry Benefit Fund v. AEtna Casualty & Surety Insurance Co.,* 503 P.2d 1286 (Okla. 1972).

Subrogation rights of surety have priority over rights of assignee bank who loaned money to contractor. *Mid-Continent Casualty Co. v. First National Bank & Trust Co. of Chickasho,* 531 P.2d 1370 (Okla. 1975).

Supplier of subcontractor who failed to give the required 90 day notice to contractor could not recover on prime contractor's performance bond as the prime contract did not provide for payment of such claims by the prime contractor, and did call for the "statutory" bond which would have protected the supplier but for his failure to give the proper notice. *G. A. Mosites Co. of Ft. Worth, Inc. v. AEtna Casualty & Surety Co.,* 545 P.2d 746 (1976).

OREGON

1. AMOUNT OF BOND.—Public contracts, unless exempted, are based upon competitive bidding. A surety bond, cashier's check or certified check of the bidder must be attached to all bids as security. Approved security shall not exceed 10% of the amount bid. If contract awarded, bond shall be equal to contract price. (See Oregon Revised Statutes, Vol. 2, Chpt. 279.027, 279.029.)

2. LABOR AND MATERIAL COVERED.—The State and the political subdivisions thereof are required to procure a public contractor's bond to the effect that

(a) The obligations of a contract shall be faithfully performed;

(b) Payment shall promptly be made to all persons supplying labor or materials to the contractor or his subcontractor for prosecution of the work provided in the contract;

(c) All contributions due the State Industrial Accident Fund and the State Unemployment Compensation Fund from the contractor or his subcontractor, in connection with the performance of the contract, shall promptly be made;

(d) All sums required to be deducted from the wages of employees of the contractor and his subcontractor pursuant to the Oregon Revised Statutes shall be paid over to the State Tax Commission. See Special Provisions.

3. NOTICE REQUIRED.—Any person claiming to have supplied labor or material, including any person having a direct relationship with a subcontractor or an assignee of such person or a person claiming monies due the State Compensation Department, the State Department of Employment

Trust Fund or the State Tax Commission in connection with the performance of the contract has a right of action on the bond, cashier's check or certified check if he or his assignee has presented and filed a Notice of Claim before the expiration of six (6) months immediately following the acceptance of work by the affirmative action of the public body which let the contract.

If the claimant has a direct contractual relationship with a subcontractor but no direct contractual relationship with the contractor furnishing the bond, cashier's check or certified check, such claimant shall have a right of action if he gives written notice to the contractor prior to the acceptance of work by the affirmative action of the public body which lets the contract.

Such notice must be in writing addressed to the appropriate public body and setting forth information such as the name of the claimant; a brief description of the labor or material performed or furnished and the name of the person who performed or furnished labor or material; if the claim is for other than labor or materials, a brief description of the claim; the amount of the claim and the name of the principal and surety or sureties upon the bond and a brief description of the work involved for which the bond was issued.

A person who has made such claim, or his assignee, may institute an action on the contractor's bond.

4. TIME FOR SUIT.—A claimant who has filed notice of claim with the municipality as above required, or his assignee, may institute an action on the contractor's bond in the Circuit Court of the State or the Federal District Court of said district not later than two years after the acceptance of the work.

5. CONTRACTS EXCLUDED.—The Public Contract Review Board or the local contract review board may exempt certain contracts. (Oregon Revised Statutes, Vol. 2, chpt. 279.033.)

6. SPECIAL PROVISIONS.—A person furnishing or providing medical, surgical, or hospital care or other needed care and attention, incident to sickness or injury, to the employees of a contractor or his subcontractor, is deemed to have performed labor for the work.

7. PENALTY FOR FAILURE TO TAKE BOND.—The State of Oregon and the officers authorizing the contract are jointly liable for the labor and material used in the prosecution of any work under the contract, and for claims due the State Industrial Accident Fund, the State Unemployment Compensation Trust Fund and the State Tax Commission, if the contract was entered into with the State of Oregon. The public body and the officers authorizing the contract are jointly liable if the contract was entered into on behalf of a public body other than the State.

8. REMARKS.—In 1941, Oregon adopted a statute covering the construction of airports and another for the construction of a bridge over the Columbia River. Both these statutes require a bond for the protection of labor and material claimants, but neither sets out any terms or limitations with respect to recovery.

A statute approved Feb. 26, 1965, requires every public contract to contain a condition that the contractor shall make payment promptly as to all persons supplying to such contractor labor or material for the prosecution of the work provided for in such contract and that the contractor shall pay all contributions or amounts due the State Industrial Accident Fund from any contractor or subcontractor incurred in the performance of a contract. Further that the contractor shall not permit any lien or claim to be filed or prosecuted against the public body on account of any labor or material furnished and also pay the State Tax Commission sums withheld from employees pursuant to the pertinent Oregon statute.

For every public works contract for which a surety bond is required, the bond shall provide that the above conditions shall be faithfully performed and also shall be conditioned to make prompt payment to all persons supplying labor or material to the contractor or his subcontractor for prosecution of the public work.

Effective January 1, 1976, Oregon Chapter 279 was revised and amended. The new act creates a Public Contract Review Board. This Board may exempt certain contracts from the requirement of furnishing performance and/or payment bonds. Unless such an exemption is granted, upon being awarded a contract, the bidder must execute and deliver to the contracting agency a good and sufficient bond in a sum equal to the contract price for the faithful performance of the contract. In lieu of a surety bond, the successful bidder may submit a cashier's check or certified check if approved by the Board.

A person claiming to have supplied labor or materials for the prosecution of the work provided for in the contract, including any person having direct contractual relationship with a subcontractor, has a right of action on the contractor's bond, cashier's check or certified check provided he has presented and filed a notice of claim prior to the expiration of six months immediately following the acceptance of the work by the affirmative action of the public body which let the contract.

Any person having a direct contractual relationship with the subcontractor but no direct contractual relationship with the contractor furnishing the bond, cashier's check or certified check shall have a right of action on the security only if that person gives written notice to the contractor prior to the acceptance of the work by the affirmative action of the public body which lets the contract.

The notice of claim required shall be presented to and filed with the Secretary of State or the clerk or auditor of the public body which let the contract. This notice must be in writing.

The person who has filed and served the notice of claim may institute an action on the contractor's bond, cashier's check or certified check in the Circuit Court of the state or the Federal District Court of the district.

The action shall be on the relation of the claimant, or his assignee, as the case may be, and shall be in the name of the public body which let the contract. It may be prosecuted to final judgment and execution may be had for the use and benefit of the claimant, or his assignee.

The action must be instituted no later than two years after the acceptance of the work by the affirmative action of the public body which let the contract.

If the contract is one for which a bond, cashier's check or certified check is required and the contractor fails to pay for labor or materials or to pay claims due the State Industrial Accident Fund, the State Unemployment Compensation Trust Fund, or the Department of Revenue, and the officers of the public body which let the contract fail or neglect to require the person entering into the contract to execute the bond, cashier's or certified check, then and in that event the State of Oregon and the officers authorizing the contract are jointly liable for these charges.

Oregon Statute 279.575 is amended to allow for the withholding from progress payments of an amount not more than five percent of the price of the work completed. A contracting agency may also reduce the amount of retainage to less than five percent if the contractor deposits bonds and/or securities with the contracting agency to be held in lieu of retainage.

The contracting agency is required to pay to the contractor interest at the rate of one percent per month on the final payment due the contractor, interest to commence thirty days after the work under the contract has been completed and accepted and to run until the date when the final payment is tendered to the contractor.

9. DECISIONS.—Unloading, dismantling and hauling a steam shovel ninety miles and assembling it was held "labor for prosecution of contract work" within the highway contractor's bond. *State of Oregon for the use of Jones v. Feak*, 141 Or. 481, 18 P.2d 203 (1933).

The bond covers incidental repairs reasonably necessary to keep the contractor's equipment in operation at the job, but does not cover substantial repairs. *State of Oregon for the use of Stater Motor Co. v. Metropolitan Casualty Ins. Co.*, 145 Or. 367, 26 P.2d 1094 (1933).

Plaintiff's notice of claim on public works bond which named the contractor and also the subcontractor to whom the labor and materials were furnished was sufficient although the notice did not name the surety and was not filed with the clerk of the school district, who however received and filed the notice. *School District No. 1 v. A. G. Rushlight & Co.*, 232 Or. 341, 375 P.2d 411 (1962).

Conditional acceptance does not meet requirements of statute providing that action against prime contractor and his surety must be instituted within two years after acceptance of work by affirmative action of public body which let the contract. *State ex rel. Union Iron Works v. P. S. Lord Mechanical Contractors*, 250 Or. 508, 443 P.2d 638 (1968).

The statute requiring notice to a general contractor within ninety days after delivery did not apply to deliveries before the effective date of the contract, but did apply to deliveries after that date. *State of Oregon ex rel. Town Concrete Pipe Inc. v. H.A. Andersen*, 264 Or. 565, 505 P.2d 1162 (1973).

Notice by materialman sent the general contractor by regular mail sufficiently complied with the statute, which statute provided that the notice was to be served on the contractor personally or by certified or registered mail, where the contractor admitted receipt of the notice. *State of Oregon ex rel. Town Concrete Pipe, Inc., v. H.A. Andersen*, 264 Or. 565, 505 P.2d 1162 (1973).

Claim of subcontractor against surety denied where penal sum of bond is exhausted and the only theory of liability is that by obtaining an assignment of progress payments then due and payable surety has taken over the project, making it directly liable to subcontractor plaintiff. *Copeland Sand and Gravel, Inc. v. Insurance Company of North America*, 288 Or. 325, 607 P.2d 718 (1980).

Subcontractor was entitled to a *quantum meruit* recovery against prime contractor and its surety when prime improperly terminated the subcontract. In addition, subcontractor was entitled to prejudgment interest from the date the subcontract was terminated. *City of Portland v. Hoffman Constr. Co.*, 286 Or. 789, 596 P.2d 1305 (1979).

PENNSYLVANIA

The Pennsylvania Public Works Contractor Bond Law of 1967, which took effect January 20, 1968, is abstracted as follows:

STATE BOND LAWS 31–85

1. AMOUNT OF BOND.—100% of the contract price for contracts exceeding $5,000.00. (8 P.S. § 193)

2. LABOR AND MATERIAL COVERED.—All labor or materials supplied to the prime contractor to whom the contract was awarded or to any of his subcontractors in the prosecution of the work provided for in such contract whether or not the material furnished or labor performed enters into and becomes a component part of the public building or other public work or public improvement including highway work. "Labor or materials" includes public utility services and reasonable rental of equipment but only for the periods when equipment rented is actually used at the site.

3. NOTICE REQUIRED.—(a) *To surety*—No statutory provisions. (b) *To principal contractor*— By persons who have no contractual relationship with the contractor, within 90 days, see subsection 7 below. (c) *To municipality*—No statutory provision. See REMARKS below. (d) *To creditors*—No statutory provision. See REMARKS below.

4. TIME FOR SUIT.—A claimant who has performed labor or furnished material in the prosecution of the work provided for in any contract for which a payment bond has been given and who has not been paid in full therefor before the expiration of ninety days after the day on which the claimant performed the last of the labor or furnished the last of the materials for which he claims payments, may bring an action on the payment bond in his own name, in assumpsit, to recover any amount due.

A claimant who has a direct contractual relationship with any subcontractor of the prime contractor who gave a payment bond but has no contractual relationship, with such prime contractor may bring an action on the payment bond only if he has given written notice to such contractor within ninety days from the date on which the claimant performed the last of the labor or furnished the last of the materials for which he claims payment, stating with substantial accuracy the amount claimed and the name of the person for whom the work was performed or to whom the material was furnished.

Notice shall be served by registered or certified mail, postage prepaid, in an envelope addressed to the contractor at any place where his office is regularly maintained for the transaction of business or served in any manner in which legal process may be served.

An action upon any payment or performance bond must be commenced within one year.

5. CONTRACTS EXCLUDED.—Contracts under $5,000.

6. PENALTY FOR FAILURE TO TAKE BOND.—No statutory provisions. See subsection 7 under prior statute (below).

7. SPECIAL PROVISIONS.—"Contracting body" means any officer, employee, authority, board, bureau, commission, department, agency or institution of the Commonwealth of Pennsylvania or any State-aided institution, or any county, city, district, municipal corporation, municipality, municipal authority, political subdivision, school district, educational institution, borough, incorporated town, township, poor district, county institution district, other incorporated district or other public instrumentality, which has authority to contract for the construction, reconstruction, alteration or repair of any public building or other public work or public improvement, including highway work.

"State-aided institution" shall mean and include any institution which receives State funds directly or indirectly for the construction, reconstruction, alteration or repair of its buildings, works or improvements, including highway work.

A new section provides that it shall be unlawful for any representative of a contracting body in issuing an invitation for bids to require that any bond specified by the statute be furnished by a particular surety company or through a particular broker or agent, prescribing penalties.

Effective January 1, 1977, any action on a payment of performance bond must be commenced within one year pursuant to 42 Pa. Statt. Ann §5523(4).

8. A public utility is not a public instrumentality and therefore not required to take a bond. *Southwest Alloy Supply Co. v. Pennsylvania Power & Light Co.*, 66 Pa. D.&C.2d 3 (1974).

Damage caused to tractor is not recoverable under bond. *Kuhn v. Torr Construction Co.*, 64 Pa. D.&C.2d 332 (1974).

Surety sued indemnitors for losses incurred on performance and payment bonds. The indemnitors defended on the grounds that the surety failed to properly file its financing statement on the receivable of the principal and therefore the security interest was invalidated in the bankruptcy proceeding of the principal. It was held that the indemnity agreement providing for release of indemnity did not affect the liability of the indemnitors, which was considered an unconditional guarantee, and the failure to perfect its security interest did not amount to a *pro-tanto* release of the indemnitors. *Fireman's Fund Insurance Co. v. Joseph Biafore, Inc.*, 385 F. Supp. 616 (E. D. Pa. 1974), *aff'd*, 526 F.2d 170 (3rd Cir. 1975).

The Department of General Services (successor to the Pennsylvania G. S. A.) has the right to elect to sue a surety on a contractor's performance bond either in the Commonwealth Court, in the county where the contract was to be performed, or in the county where the principal had his principal of business at the time of execution of the bond. *General State Authority v. Pacific Indemnity Co.,* 24 Pa. Commw. Ct. 82, 354 A.2d 56 (1976).

Prior Law:

PENALTY FOR FAILURE TO TAKE BOND.—No special statutory provision. However, a public body which fails to take such a bond is not guilty of negligence for the breach of such public duty. *Szilyagi v. City of Bethlehem,* 312 Pa. 260, 167 A. 782 (1933).

Where a municipality fails to require a contractor employed in or about a public improvement to secure an additional bond as required by law for the payment of labor and material and machinery, the courts will compel the performance of this public duty by mandamus. *Szilagyi v. City of Bethlehem,* 312 Pa. 260, 167 A. 782 (1933).

DECISIONS.—In 1931 and 1933, a series of bills was passed, clarifying and making uniform the requirement that the contractor furnish an additional bond for the protection of labor and materialmen. The constitutionality of this legislation has been sustained. *Commonwealth, v. Great American Indemnity Co.,* 312 Pa. 183, 167 A. 793 (1933).

Where the aggregate of all claims is less than the penal sum named in the bond, interest may be recovered from the surety in like manner as interest is payable by the contractor. *Commonwealth v. Great American Indemnity Co.,* 312 Pa. 183, 167 A. 793 (1933); *Commonwealth of Pennsylvania for the use of Fort Pitt Bridge Works v. Continental Casualty Co.,* 429 Pa. 366, 240 A.2d 493 (1968).

A surety is liable under a bond voluntarily executed even though the coverage is broader than that of the statute or ordinance. For illustration, recovery may be had for the construction of walks, curbs, gutters, etc., *Easton School District, v. Continental Casualty Co.,* 304 Pa. 67, 155 A. 93 (1931), for hauling fill to the area required in the grading of a public street, *Philadelphia v. Stange,* 306 Pa. 178, 159 A. 7 (1932), and for sewer pipe laid in the city street, *Philadelphia v. Jafolla,* 311 Pa. 575, 167 A. 569 (1933).

Recovery is allowed for oil and gasoline consumed in the operation of the highway equipment. *Commonwealth v. Ciccone,* 316 Pa. 111, 173 A. 642 (1934).

Tires and related products are covered by a state highway contractor's payment bond if a reasonable man would believe they would be substantially used up on the job. *Commonwealth ex rel. Walters Tire Service, Inc. v. National Union Fire Insurance Co.,* 434 Pa. 235, 252 A.2d 593 (1969).

A public works contractor's surety is not required to file financing statements in accordance with the provisions of the Uniform Commercial Code. *Jacobs v. Northeastern Corporation,* 416 Pa. 417, 206 A.2d 49 (1965), followed, as to progress payments in the assignment, *National Shawmut Bank of Boston v. New Amsterdam Casualty Company, Inc.,* 290 F. Supp. 664 (D. Mass.), aff'd, 411 F.2d 843 (1st Cir. 1969). To the same effect are the following recent decisions: *AEtna Cas. & Surety Co. v. Perrotta,* 308 N.Y.S.2d 613, 62 Misc.2d 252 (1970); *Compania General DeSeguros, S.A. v. First Nat'l City Bank,* 306 F. Supp. 1360 (D.C.Z. 1969). *In Re J. V. Gleason & Co. v. AEtna Casualty & Surety Co.,* 452 F.2d 1219 (8th Cir. 1971); *Reliance Insurance Companies v. Alaska State Housing Authority,* 323 F. Supp. 1370 (D. Alaska 1971); *Travelers Indemnity Co. v. Clark,* 254 So.2d 741 (Miss. 1971); *U. S. Fidelity & Guaranty Co. v. First State Bank,* 208 Kan. 738, 494 P.2d 1149 (1972); *Midcontinent Casualty Co. v. First National Bank and Trust Company,* 531 P.2d 1370 (Okla. 1975).

A materialman was denied a right of action under a performance bond given by a subcontractor to a contractor in connection with a PWA project. *Fleck-Atlantic Co. v. Indemnity Insurance Co. of North America,* 326 Pa. 15, 191 A. 51 (1937). See also *Peter J. Mascaro Co. v. Milonas,* 401 Pa. 632, 166 A.2d 15 (1960).

Telephone service is not within the coverage of a Pennsylvania school bond. *U. S. Fidelity & Guaranty Co. ex rel. Reedy v. American Surety Co.,* 25 F. Supp. 280 (M.D. Pa. 1938).

An additional bond given to a school district conditioned, among other things, that the contractor should "likewise pay for all machinery employed on or about such work or improvement," does not cover a claim for ladders, trestles and extension steps, scaffolding, jacks and other equipment sold to a painting subcontractor. Such apparatus and equipment sold and delivered by a claimant to the contractor and used by the contractor for painting school auditoriums is not material furnished in the prosecution of the work within the contemplation and intendment of the contracts or of the bonds given to secure their performance. *Philadelphia School District ex rel. v. B. A. Shrages Co., Inc.,* 134 Pa. Super. Ct. 533, 4 A.2d 558 (1939), aff'd, 336 Pa. 433, 9 A.2d 900 (1939).

In *Harris v. American Surety Co.*, 372 Ill. 361, 24 N.E.2d 42 (1939), it was held, construing a bond given in connection with the construction of a freight elevator in Pennsylvania, that a subcontractor could maintain suit on a bond conditioned that the principal contractor should complete the building in accordance with the specifications and satisfy all claims and demands incurred therein. Interest at six per cent from the date when the money sued for became due was awarded. *Otis Elevator Co. v. American Surety Co. of New York,* 314 Ill. App. 479, 41 N.E.2d 987 (1942).

Where a building contract entered into between an owner and the contractor provides that the contractor shall provide and pay for all materials and labor necessary to complete the work, and a bond executed by the contractor and a corporate surety company and delivered to the owner incorporates the building contract and is conditioned upon performance by the contractor of all the matters in the building contract and payment by the contractor of all loss or damages which the owner might sustain by reason of default on the part of the contractor, the bond inures to the benefit of a materialman. Having undertaken to insure the performance of all of the obligations of the contractor, if the surety intended to avoid contingent liability for the payment of materialmen, it should have incorporated that exception in its bond. *Pennsylvania Supply Co. v. National Casualty Co.,* 152 Pa. Super. Ct. 217, 31 A.2d 453 (1943). See, however, *Dravo-Doyle Co. v. Royal Indemnity Co.,* 372 Pa. 64, 92 A.2d 554 (1952).

Recovery may not be had for unpaid premiums on a policy of workmen's compensation insurance under a highway contractor's bond which provides that the contractor shall in all respects comply with and perform the terms and conditions of his contract, or under the labor and materialmen's bond given pursuant to the Highway Code. *Commonwealth for the use of Penna. Mfrs'. Ass'n. v. Fidelity & Deposit Company of Maryland,* 355 Pa. 434, 50 A.2d 211 (1947).

The owner of a tractor used by a subcontractor, in the course of its work under the subcontract, damaged while in use, is not a third party beneficiary under a contract between the contractor and the Commonwealth of Pennsylvania, which agreement requires the contractor to maintain such public liability and property damage insurance as will protect him and any subcontractor performing work covered by the contract from claims for damages for personal injury and property damage, the language of the contract in the case leading to the conclusion that the insurance proviso therein was not intended to be for the benefit of those who might be injured in their person or their property. *Mowrer v. Poirier & McLane Corp.,* 382 Pa. 2, 114 A.2d 88 (1955).

The provisions failed to support a claim for repairs to machinery or for tires furnished by subcontractor. *Barnyak vs. Headwaters Construction Co.,* 411 Pa. 350, 192 A.2d 342 (1963).

The right of action given subcontractor under a labor and material payment bond to sue in the state where the general contract was performed was contracted away by the subcontractor in *Central Contracting Co. v. Maryland Casualty Co.,* 242 F. Supp. 858 (W.D. Pa. 1965).

Where there is no express statutory provision on the bond, a requirement for notice added in the bond (or a limitation as to the time of suit on the bond), if reasonable, will be sustained. *Barati v. M.S.I. Corporation,* 212 Pa. Super. Ct. 536, 243 A.2d 170 (1968); *Scranton School District v. Casualty & Surety Company of Hartford,* 98 Pa. Super. Ct. 599 (1930).

Where an employee of the principal was hired to develop and control all electrical work in a particular area and was to receive one-half of the profits of all electrical jobs secured in the area in addition to a weekly salary, the surety on the labor and material payment bond was bound to pay the employee one-half of the profits for work entered into or done prior to execution of the surety agreement. *Miller v. Commercial Electric Construction, Inc.,* 223 Pa. Super. Ct., 216, 297 A.2d 487 (1972).

A payment bond surety was held not liable for lost profits or delay damage costs. *Lite-Air Products, Inc. v. Fidelity & Deposit Co. of Maryland,* 437 F. Supp. 801 (E.D. Pa. 1977).

A television equipment subcontractor delivered, installed and demonstrated its equipment in December 1974. The subcontractor returned to the public work site in January 1975, to adjust the unit and conduct a second demonstration. The subcontractor instituted suit in January of 1976 and the surety company moved for summary judgment on the basis of a one year statute of limitation from the date of furnishing last labor and material. It was held that the affidavits submitted by the subcontractor should be read in a manner most favorable to the subcontractor and, consequently, summary judgment should not have been granted in favor of the payment bond surety. *Lehigh Elec. Products Co. v. Pennsylvania National Mutual Casualty Insurance Co.,* 257 Pa. Super. Ct. 198, 390 A.2d 781 (1978).

Subcontractor's argument that the one year statute of limitations did not begin to run against a surety until the subcontractor realized that the prime contractor could not pay was rejected, and surety was granted summary judgment. In addition, court granted summary judgment in favor of owner holding that a suit on the bond was the subcontractor's exclusive remedy. *Visor Builders, Inc. v. Devone Tranter, Inc.,* 470 F.Supp. 911 (M.D.Pa. 1978).

Surety's preliminary objections to suit on a performance bond were overruled when it was not clear whether the liquidated damage provision in the contract was the exclusive remedy for the recovery of damages. *Pennsylvania Department of Environmental Resources v. Hartford Accident & Indemnity Co.,* 40 Pa. Cmwlth. Ct. 133, 396 A.2d 885 (1979).

PUERTO RICO

1. AMOUNT OF BOND.—The Commonwealth of Puerto Rico requires a payment bond for not less than ½ the contract amount. The penal sum of the payment bond required by various Authorities in Puerto Rico varies in amount. (T.22 L.P.R.A. § 48)

2. LABOR AND MATERIAL COVERED.—The payment bond required by the Commonwealth of Puerto Rico from every contractor who is awarded a contract for the construction, reconstruction, enlargement, alteration, or preparation of any public work covers

(I) The payment to the workers and employees for the contractor, of the salaries and wages earned by them in their work, and

(II) The payment, to the persons selling, supplying or delivering equipment, tools and material for the work, of the price or value of the materials, equipment, and tools supplied, sold or delivered.

The conditions of the separate payment bond required by various authorities differ somewhat. Same will be reviewed under Remarks below. The combined Performance and Payment Bond required by the Puerto Rico Urban Renewal and Housing Corporation is conditioned under performance and also that the contractor shall promptly make payment to all persons supplying labor and material in the prosecution of the work provided for in the contract.

In addition, the Commonwealth of Puerto Rico requires a special labor payment bond in favor of the Secretary of Labor, which is equal to 10% of the total project. On a prescribed Spanish form.

3. NOTICE REQUIRED.—(a) *To surety*—No special statutory provision;

(b) *To principal contractor*—The law of Puerto Rico applicable to bonds taken by the Commonwealth of Puerto Rico first reads that every person who has worked as a worker or employee on or who has supplied, sold or delivered materials, equipment and tools for work and who has not been paid, in whole or in part, his salaries or wages or the price of the materials, equipment and tools sold, delivered or supplied for the work shall have the right to file suit on the bond without necessity for previous notice for recovery of any amount, which may for such reason be owing him.

It also reads: "Any person or persons who have a direct contractual relationship with a subcontractor on the work and who have or do not have an expressed or implied contractual relationship with the contractor on the work, who has posted the bond, may institute action against the contractor, the bond of the contractor, the bondsmen of the contractor, or against any of said bondsmen, for the recovery of any part of:

"(1) any amount which may be owed them by the subcontractor for salaries or wages they have earned as employees or workers of the subcontractor on the work; and

"(2) any amount which may be owed them by reason of their having supplied, sold or delivered materials, equipment and tools for the subcontractor on the work.

"Suppliers or sellers of materials, equipment and tools to the subcontractor shall be obligated, before instituting action against the contractor, his bond, or his bondsmen, to notify the contractor, by registered mail, of their claim. At the expiration of thirty days from the mailing of said notice they may institute the action herein authorized.

"Workers and employees of the subcontractor may institute action at any time without previous notice to the contractor of their claim."

(c) *To municipality*—No special statutory provision.

(d) *To creditors*—No special statutory provision.

4. TIME FOR SUIT.—Suppliers or sellers of materials, equipment and tools to the subcontractor is required to wait thirty days from the date of mailing of notice to the contractor before instituting suit on the contractor's public work bonds. Suit must instituted by all claimants within six months after final acceptance of the work by the Commonwealth of Puerto Rico.

5. CONTRACTS EXCLUDED.—No special statutory provision.

6. PROCEDURE.—Suit must be instituted in the name of the interested party or parties in the part of the Superior Court having jurisdiction for the area within which the work is located or in which the complainant, or, if more than one, any of them resides.

With regard to the same work all claims for salaries and wages may be joined in one single complaint, and all claims for materials, equipment and tools supplied, sold or delivered may be joined in another single complaint.

7. FAILURE TO TAKE BOND.—No special statutory provision.

STATE BOND LAWS

8. SPECIAL PROVISIONS.—The statute pertaining to bonds required by the Commonwealth of Puerto Rico above reviewed requires the payment bond to be posted "in behalf of The People of Puerto Rico." The People of Puerto Rico "comprise The People of Puerto Rico, the departments, agencies, and instrumentalities thereof, the municipal governments, and the Government of the Capital."

Subcontractor is defined in the statute as follows: "Any person or persons who, as independent contractors, do any part of the work awarded to the contractor."

"Work" and "Public Work" are defined in the statute as follows: "Any construction, reconstruction, alteration, extensions, or improvements, made under a contract awarded to a contractor by The People of Puerto Rico."

The contractor is "under obligation to pay the salaries and wages of the employees and workers on the work for periods not longer than one week; and to pay punctually, as they fall due, the bills and invoices presented to him by any natural or artificial persons who have supplied, sold, or delivered materials, equipment and tools for the work."

It is the duty of the inspector of the work to make sure that the contractor is in the same manner paying the wages and salaries earned by the workers and employees on the work. If this is not done, the inspector is required to notify the Secretary of Public Works and the latter, the Secretary of Labor. The Commissioner of the Interior (now Secretary of Public Works, is defined to "comprise the Commissioner of the Interior of Puerto Rico, but it shall be understood that the obligations imposed upon him by this Act shall be equally applicable to the mayors, the municipal directors of public works, and the chiefs of departments, divisions, agencies, or instrumentalities of The People of Puerto Rico, under whose direction or supervision, or under contract with whom, a public work is executed."

9. REMARKS.—The Puerto Rico Urban Renewal and Housing Corporation form of combined Performance and Payment Bond does not specifically incorporate or refer to any of the provisions of the laws of Puerto Rico above analyzed. Nor do the separate performance or payment bonds of the Commonwealth of Puerto Rico nor the performance or payment bonds of the following Puerto Rico authorities:

Aqueduct and Sewer Authority, Industrial Development Company, Ports Authority, Water Resources Authority.

These Authorities require separate Performance and Payment Bonds (except the Puerto Rico Aqueduct and Sewer Authority), which are substantially the same with respect to Performance and Payment Bonds required by the Miller Act with respect to public work of the United States performed in Puerto Rico or elsewhere in the United States.

The Payment Bond of the Puerto Rico Aqueduct and Sewer Authority is conditioned that the contractor and all subcontractors to whom any portion of the work provided for in the contract is sublet shall pay all lawful claims of subcontractors and materialmen for labor performed and materials furnished in the carrying forward, performing or completing of said contract. . . . and shall promptly make payment to all persons who perform labor or render services in the prosecution of the work provided for in said contract. All persons who have performed labor or rendered services as aforesaid are given by this bond form a direct right of action against the principal and surety which right of action is required to be asserted in proceedings instituted in Puerto Rico. Insofar as permitted by the laws of Puerto Rico such rights of action are required to be asserted in a proceeding instituted in the name of the obligee to the use and benefit of the respective claimants who have a right to be made a party to such proceedings but not later than 12 months after complete performance of the contract and final settlement thereof.

The term "Person" as used in the bond refers to any person engaged in the prosecution of the work provided for by the contract, who is an agent, servant or employee of the contractor or of any subcontractor, or of any assignee of said contractor or of any subcontractor, and also anyone so engaged who performs the work of a laborer or a mechanic regardless of any contractual relationship between the principal, or any assignee of any said subcontractor, and such laborer or mechanic but does not include office employees not regularly stationed at the site of the work.

Effective May 1976, Puerto Rico amended its bond law so that any surety bond that guarantees contract fulfillment, whether it be a civil or criminal bond or guarantee of any type of obligation shall be binding severally upon the insurer and the principal, but subject to the terms of prescription or forfeiture.

The surety insurer that is bound pursuant to the above paragraph is required to satisfy the debt of the principal upon demand of the creditor, after verifying within a term of 90 days the existence, liquidity, and eligibility of the claim. If within this term, the insurer does not satisfy the claim for just cause, he shall be in violation of the Code.

10. DECISIONS.—A surety on a prime contractor's bond is bound only by the contract it made.

Hence where it is clear that the party intended to limit the surety's liability to persons who have contracts, directly with the principal for labor and material furnished, a supplier to a subcontractor has no right of action on such bond. *American Radiator and Standard Corp. v. Maryland Casualty Co.,* 374 F.2d 839 (1st Cir. 1967).

The controlling date for the term of six months established by the time for suit provisions of the Act to guarantee the payment of salaries and material supplied within which a supplier may bring an action for the recovery of money for materials supplied against the surety of a contract of a public works begins to run from the date the work was finally accepted by the Commonwealth, and not from the date on which said work was finished. *Commonwealth P. R. Gases Corp. v. Pagan Const., Inc.,* 99 P.R.R. 338 (1970).

A supplier to a subcontractor of a public works has no cause of action against the general contractor because of it failed to notify the contractor of the amount owed by the subcontractor 30 days before filing of its complaint. *Arzuaga and Santana, Inc. v. Rivera,* 100 P.R.R. 122 (1971).

RHODE ISLAND

1. AMOUNT OF BOND.—Not less than 50% and not more than 100% of the contract price. (General Laws of Rhode Island, Title 37 § 37-12-1)

2. LABOR AND MATERIAL COVERED.—All labor performed or materials and equipment furnished. Recovery as to equipment means payment of the reasonable rental value as determined by the respective department during the period of its use.

3. NOTICE REQUIRED.—

(a) *To surety*—None.

(b) *To principal contractor*—an amendment of modified amendment of 1973 and May 20, 1975 provides that any person having direct contractual relationship with a subcontractor, but no contractual relationship express or implied with a contractor furnishing a payment bond shall have right of action upon said payment bond giving written notice to said contractor within ninety days from the date of which such person did or performed the last of the labor or furnished or supplied the last of the material or equipment for which such claim is made, stating with substantial accuracy the amount claimed and the name of the party to whom the material or equipment was furnished or supplied or for whom the labor was done or performed. Such notice shall be served by mailing the same by certified mail, postage prepaid, in an envelope addressed to the contractor at any place he maintains an office or conducts his business, or his residence.

(c) *To municipality*—Under the statute prior to the amendment approved May 15, 1973, within sixty days after the date of final settlement, a claimant was required to file a written claim in form prescribed by the respective department verified by affidavit, which shall set forth clearly the items of labor performed or furnished or of materials or equipment furnished and not paid for to the claimant, when and for whom said items were performed or furnished and for the performance of what contract with the respective department, the charges made therefor respectively and how much remains unpaid of such charges and the name and address of the claimant.

An amendment approved June 12, 1961 provides that notice required by the claimant in the case of a contract with the State be filed with the particular department or other political subdivision that entered into the original contract and in the case of a city such notice shall be filed with the City Treasurer and in the case of a town such notice shall be filed with the Town Treasurer regardless of the department or political subdivision of the city or town that entered into the original contract.

4. TIME FOR SUIT.—Under the amendment effective May 15, 1973 suit is required to be commenced prior to the expiration of one year after the date on which the last of the labor was performed or the material was supplied by any person claiming under said section. Every such person who has not been paid in full for the labor or material furnished before the expiration of ninety days after the date on which the last of the labor was done or performed by him or materials were furnished or supplied by him, has the right to sue on the payment bond for the amount or the balance thereof at the time of institution of such suit.

Under the May 20, 1975 amendment no suit shall be commenced after the expiration of two years, or under the maximum time limit as contained within the labor or material payment bond, whichever period is longer, after the day on which the last of the labor was furnished or material or equipment supplied by claimant.

5. CONTRACTS EXCLUDED.—State, city, town, etc., contracts of $1,000 or less. Bridge contracts under $500.

6. PROCEDURE.—Under old Act where a suit has been brought on the bond, any other person claiming to be a creditor under the bond and having filed a claim with the respective department may, within the aforesaid period of nine months or within thirty days after the bringing of such

STATE BOND LAWS

suit, and not later, intervene and become a party in the first suit thus brought, and, by so intervening, may have the rights of such other person adjudicated in such suit. If two or more such suits are filed in said court on the same day the one in which the larger sum is claimed is regarded as the earlier suit.

The 1969 Act gives the State a priority over other claimants under the bond and the 1973 amendment allows labor and materialmen to intervene in a suit brought by the State.

The amendment effective May 15, 1973, changed the provision for intervention to read as follows: "When a suit has been so brought on the bond by a person claiming to be a creditor under the bond and is pending, any other person claiming to be a creditor under the bond may intervene and become a party in the first suit thus brought and pending and by so intervening may have the rights of such other person adjudicated in suit. If two or more of such suits be filed in said court on the same day, the one in which the larger sum shall be claimed shall be regarded as the earlier suit. All suits brought upon the bond as provided in this chapter shall be consolidated together by the court and heard as one suit."

7. PENALTY FOR FAILURE TO TAKE BOND.—No express statutory provision.

8. SPECIAL PROVISIONS.—The surety may pay into the registry of the court the penal sum named in the bond, less any amount which the surety may have paid to the state in satisfaction of liability to the state under the bond, and, by so doing, be discharged from all further liability under the bond.

9. REMARKS.—The date of final settlement, for the purposes of the Act providing for bonds in connection with state public roads, bridges and public buildings, is the date on which the work covered by the contract shall have been completely performed by the contractor and accepted by the respective departments or shall have been abandoned by the contractor before its completion or shall have been taken away from the contractor by action of the respective department by reason of a breach of the contract by the contractor and said respective department shall have determined the final amount which is due the contractor for the complete performance of said work or which would be due the contractor if all the creditors under the bond had been paid in full.

Effective June 1, 1976, Rhode Island amended General Law Section 27-29-4(9) to provide that a contractor or subcontractor who is required to procure a surety bond or policy of insurance with respect to any building or construction contract shall have free right of choice of an agent and insurer, provided that the owner or contractor shall have the right (1) to require evidence at a reasonable time prior to commencement on renewal of risk, that such insurance has been obtained in an amount equal to the amount required by the builder, creditor, lender or seller; (2) to require insurance in an authorized insurer having a licensed resident agent; and (3) to refuse to accept insurance in a particular insurer on reasonable grounds related to solvency.

In 1979, Rhode Island amended its laws relating to contractor's bonds, to provide that upon substantial completion of the work required by a contract with any municipality, or any agency or political subdivision thereof, for the construction, reconstruction, alteration, remodeling, repair of improvement of sewers and water mains, the awarding authority may deduct from its payment a retention to secure satisfactory performance of the contractual work not exceeding five percent of the contract price unless otherwise agreed to by the parties. In the case of periodic payments, the awarding authority may deduct from its payment a retention to secure satisfactory performance of the contractual work not exceeding five percent of the approved amount of any periodic payment unless otherwise agreed to by the parties.

Where materialman when furnishing to subcontractor materials used in construction of town hall was unaware of existence of contractor's bond given to the town, and contractor paid subcontractor in full without knowledge that materials had been acquired from the materialman, who was not paid by subcontractor, said materialman could not recover on bond requiring contractor to pay for materials furnished in prosecution of the work, which stated that the bond was made for benefit of all persons furnishing material on account of the contract. *Providence Pipe & Sprinkler Co. v. AEtna Casualty and Surety Co.,* 69 R.I. 51, 31 A.2d 1 (1943).

Where surety on bond for faithful performance of building contract, being notified of breaches of contract by contractors, advised owners that the differences might be settled without intervention of surety, surety thereby waived any claim that owners were precluded from recovering on bond by failure to comply with contract or that surety was discharged by material alteration in contract. *Sormanti v. Deacutis,* 79 R.I. 361, 89 A.2d 191 (1952).

A claimant who failed to give the required statutory notice may not recover on the payment bond. *Worthington Air Conditioning Co. v. Lincoln & Lane Co.,* 106 R.I. 575, 261 A.2d 853 (1970).

Supplier of subcontractor sued prime contractor and prime's surety. Surety defended on grounds that it failed to receive timely notice pursuant to the requirements of statute. It was held that the statute relied upon by the surety was not applicable, but that the statute dealing with remedies when the government is the owner of the land was applicable. *Providence Electric Co. v. Donatelli Building Co.,* 116 R.I. 340, 356 A.2d 483 (1976).

An action in a state court by subcontractors on a surety bond was removed by the surety on grounds of diversity of citizenship. On a motion by surety to dismiss on the ground that the clause in the bond limited suit to Massachusetts courts, it was held that where the surety bond on which the plaintiff-subcontractors were suing provided that suit could be brought only in the county where construction of the project was situated or in the United States District Court for the district in which project was situated, and the construction project was located in Massachusetts, plaintiff had no right under the bond. *Rossi Sheet Metal Works v. American Employers Insurance Co.,* 439 F.Supp. 895 (D.R.I. 1977).

It was held that the six year statute of limitation did not apply to an action on a payment bond, but rather the claimant was required to bring suit within one year after the prime contractor ceased work on the project. Hence, claimant's suit was time barred. *Vaudreuil v. Nelson Engineering & Construction Co.,* 399 A.2d 1220 (R.I. 1979).

SOUTH CAROLINA

June 7, 1963 South Carolina adopted the two bond system for public highway construction contracts. This new statute is abstracted as follows:

1. AMOUNT OF BOND.—The payment bond shall not be less than double the contract price.

Note: A contractor performing public highway construction contracts over $10,000 must furnish a performance and indemnity bond in the full amount of the contract but no less than $10,000 which shall be for the benefit and protection of the Highway Department, County or Road District and (2) a payment bond in an amount not less than 50% of the contract for the protection of all persons supplying labor and material under the contract. (Code of Laws of South Carolina, 1976 Annotated § 57-17-660.)

2. LABOR AND MATERIAL COVERED.—Labor and material supplied in the prosecution of the highway work.

3. NOTICE REQUIRED.—(a) *To surety*—No special statutory provision.

(b) *To principal contractor*—No notice is required by a claimant having a contractual relationship, expressed or implied, with the principal contractor. However, any claimant having a direct contractual relationship with a subcontractor but no contractual relationship, expressed or implied, with the contractor must give written notice to contractor within 90 days from the date on which claimant did or performed the last of the labor or furnished or supplied the last of the material for which the claim is made stating with substantial accuracy the amount claimed and the name of the party to whom material was furnished or supplied or for whom labor was done or performed.

Where a materialman's claim on the public work contractor's bond for monies alleged to be due by a subcontractor failed to aver compliance with the statutory requirement for notice, the materialman was denied recovery on the bond claim. *Metal Serv. Corp. v. Industrial Elec. Co.,* 253 S.C. 507, 171 S.E.2d 703 (1970).

(c) *To municipality*—No special statutory provision.

(d) *To creditors*—No special statutory provision.

4. TIME FOR SUIT.—Laymen having a contractual relationship with a subcontractor not with the contract or has a right of action on the bond providing he gave notice to the contractor within 90 days of performance of his services. Every person, who has provided labor and materials and who has not been paid within 90 days of the date on which the labor or material was supplied, may sue on the bond. In no event, may suit be commenced more than one year after the final settlement of the contract.

5. CONTRACTS EXCLUDED.—Under $10,000.

Effective May 1976, South Carolina requires that public works contracts exceeding $30,000 be let pursuant to competitive bidding.

6. PENALTY FOR FAILURE TO TAKE BOND.—No special statutory provision.

7. SPECIAL PROVISIONS.—On July 30, 1981 South Carolina enacted the Consolidated Procurement Code patterned after the American Bar Association's model procurement code.

8. DECISIONS PRIOR TO 1963 STATUTE.—Abstract below.

A claimant who had supplied material to a subcontractor could maintain an action against the surety on the subcontractor's bond, even though claimant had not previously given notice to the prime contractor within the 90-day period for notice prescribed by the Miller Act, or commenced the action on the Miller Act payment bond within the statutory year. *United States for the use of Wheeling-Pittsburgh Steel Corp. v. Algernon Blair, Inc.* 329 F. Supp. 1360 (D.S.C. 1971).

To extent that proceeds from bank loans made to contractor were used by it in completing contractor's construction of low rent housing project before contractor defaulted, loans represented debts incurred by contractor in or about performance of work contracted for within meaning of performance and payment bond executed by contractor's performance surety, and surety was therefore liable to bank for amount of loans which remained unpaid. *First National Bank of South Carolina v. U.S. Fidelity & Guaranty Co.,* 373 F. Supp. 235 (D.S.C. 1974).

Old Statute

A highway contractor's surety agreeing to be responsible for payment of "all debts pertaining to the work" is liable for the purchase price of a small movable gasoline pump with accessories. It was not necessary that the supplies be totally used or consumed in the work. The bond in this case was much broader in scope and more comprehensive in terms than most bonds. *American Hardware Co. v. Detroit Fidelity & Surety Co.,* 159 S.C. 263, 156 S.E. 770 (1931).

Horse and mule feed are "materials and supplies" within the purview of a highway bond. *Molony v. Pennell,* 169 S.C. 462, 169 S.E. 283 (1933).

Where the bond covers materials furnished to a subcontractor, the contractor may not avoid liability by notifying materialmen that contractor would not pay for supplies furnished subcontractor. *Molony v. Pennell,* 169 S.C. 462, 169 S.E. 283 (1933).

Where the state highway department required the contractor to pay all "debts" and the contractors' bonds required performance of the contract in conformity with the department's requirements, a worker injured in the construction of the road was permitted to recover damages for his injuries from the surety on the bond. *Cantey v. Newell Contracting Co.,* 175 S.C. 74, 178 S.E. 342 (1935).

Tools, machinery and appliances used in performances of a construction contract, although worn out in the progress of the work, are not such labor and materials as are ordinarily contemplated by contractor's bonds. *Kline v. McMeekin Construction Co.,* 220 S.C.L. 281, 67 S.E.2d 304 (1951). Steel beams furnished to bridge subcontractor which were essential part of a derrick used to raise other steel beams to be fastened in place within superstructure of bridge were not "materials" and "supplies" within purview of contractor's bond and no recovery for beams could be had on the bond. *Kline v. McMeekin Construction Co.,* 220 S.C.L. 281, 67 S.E.2d 304 (1951).

Under the A.I.A. form of labor and material payment bond, South Carolina has held that tools, machinery and appliances used by the contractor although worn out in the process of the work are not such labor and materials as are ordinarily contemplated by the contractor's bond but that scaffolding equipment while necessary to the prosecution of the contractor's work must be classified as a part of tools, appliances and equipment used by the contractor whether purchased or leased. The surety conceded liability for an item of $92.70 for rental on the equipment. The court concluded that the surety was not liable for the loss of the equipment. *South Carolina Supply & Equipment Co. v. James Stewart & Co.,* 238 S.C.L. 106, 119 S.E.2d 517 (CD.S.C. 1961).

Where the contractor furnished a private owner a bond, executed in Arkansas, on a form approved by the American Institute of Architects which requires suit to be brought within two years from the date final payment became due under the contract, and such a provision is violative of public policy of South Carolina where the contract was to be performed but was valid in Arkansas where the bond was executed, the Arkansas law was held to govern. *McCrary v. U.S. Fidelity & Guaranty Co.,* 110 F. Supp. 545 (D.S.C. 1953).

In a suit on the contractor's bond for material furnished by a claimant to a subcontractor and used in the construction of a school building, held that interest was properly allowed where the amount due was definite or definitely ascertainable. *Crane Co. v. Continental Casualty Co.,* 234 S.C. 44, 106 S.E.2d 674 (1959).

A rentor of heavy construction equipment was not permitted recovery on the payment bond of a state highway contractor, the court holding that coverage on a payment bond depends on the nature of equipment and that bulldozers, tractors, graders and trucks were the sort of equipment that would not be consumed in one contract and, therefore, would become part of the contractor's "plant"; and were not covered by the bond. *Rish v. Theo Brothers Construction Co.,* 269 S.C. 226, 237 S.E.2d 61 (1977).

State Department of Mental Health's claim of sovereign immunity was rejected in a suit brought by a completing surety, the court holding that by authorizing the Department to enter into a construction contract, the state impliedly waived its immunity from suit to the extent of its contractual obligations. *Kinsey Construction Co. v. South Carolina Department of Mental Health,* 272 S.C. 168, 249 S.E.2d 900 (1978).

SOUTH DAKOTA

1. AMOUNT OF BOND.—Not less than contract price. (Volume 2 S.D.C.L. § 5-21-1.)

2. LABOR AND MATERIAL COVERED.—Labor and material used in the prosecution of the work provided for in the public contract.

An amendment approved March 18, 1957, provides that where the contractor or subcontractor furnishes surety bonds for faithful performance of the public work contract, there is imposed an additional obligation upon the surety to the State of South Dakota that said contractor or subcontractor shall promptly pay all taxes which may accrue to the State of South Dakota under the provisions of the "Use Tax Act of 1939." Such liability on the part of the surety is limited to two per cent of the amount of the contract price.

3. NOTICE REQUIRED.—(a) *To surety*—No special statutory provision. (b) *To principal contractor*—anytime after the completion of any work or improvement for any public body the contractor may issue notice stating that the improvement has been completed and that all subcontractors or persons furnishing any item of labor, service, skill, material, shipment or supplies for any subcontractor must file their claims with the contractor within 120 days after the first publication of such notice. Assuming that the labor is proper (there are specific requirements concerning notice), the claim by any subcontractor or any other person will be barred as a claim or lien against the public body and contractor if such claim is not filed within 120 days from the date of first publication. If notice is not timely, all claims, setoffs or counterclaims will be barred as to the public body or contractor or surety. (c) *To municipality*—No special statutory provision. (d) *To creditors*—Personal notice of the pendency of such suit must be given to all known creditors and, in addition thereto, notice shall be given by publication in some newspaper of general circulation published in the county where the contract is being performed for at least three successive weeks, the last publication to be at least three months before the time limited for suit.

4. TIME FOR SUIT.—If no suit is brought by the public corporation within 6 months of the completion and final settlement of the contract, any person furnishing the contractor with labor or material shall, on proper application therefor, be provided with a certified copy of the contract and surety. Such person shall be permitted to bring suit in the name of the public corporation for his use and benefit against the contractor and surety from whom he has not received payment. If suit is instituted against the surety of the contractor, it may not be commenced until 6 months after the complete performance of the contract and final settlement thereof. Any suit commenced more than one year thereafter shall be barred.

5. CONTRACTS EXCLUDED.—Effective July 1, 1982, Section 5-23-11.1 of the Code was amended to authorize the Bureau of Administration to waive the requirement of a bid bond, certified check, cash or other security and the requirement of a performance bond or surety when the bid submitted or the contract awarded does not exceed $25,000. Prior thereto, the threshold amount was $2,000.

6. PROCEDURE.—If municipality institutes suit, claimants intervene therein and their claims are subject to the prior rights of the municipality. If no suit is brought by municipality within six months from the completion and final settlement of such contract, claimant shall furnish affidavit to municipality that labor or material for the prosecution of the public work has been supplied by him and payment for the same has not been made. Claimant is then furnished with a certified copy of the contract and bond, upon which he may sue in the name of the municipality in the Circuit Court of the county in which said contract was performed, and not elsewhere, for his use and benefit. Only one action may be brought on the bond. Other creditors intervene in the suit first brought. Creditors prorate if the bond is inadequate to pay the amount due all creditors.

7. PENALTY FOR FAILURE TO TAKE BOND.—Corporation shall be liable to pay all persons who have performed labor or furnished material that entered into the public building the value of the work or material, and an action may be maintained therefor, provided same is commenced within ninety days from the acceptance of the work for which the same is claimed.

8. SPECIAL PROVISION.—In 1971 a statute was adopted for the registration of nonresident contractors with the Commissioner of Revenue which requires such nonresident contractor, before entering into the performance of any contract in South Dakota, to provide bond or other form of assurance conditioned that all taxes including contributions under the Unemployment Compensation Law which may accrue to the State of South Dakota or to a political division thereof on account of the performance of such contract will be paid when due. It further provides for the withholding of sufficient monies due on any subcontract to guarantee payment of such taxes, etc.

9. DECISIONS.—Rental of equipment used in the construction of a highway is within the provisions of a contractor's bond conditioned for payment of all just claims for materials, supplies, food, tools, appliances, labor and all other just claims incurred by contractor. *Western Material Co. v. Deltener,* 64 S.D. 62, 264 N.W. 207 (1936).

Where, by reason of the contractor's failure to furnish a bond in compliance with the Code of South Dakota, the school district was compelled to pay for materials on the contractor's failure to do so, the school district was permitted to recover the amount it had expended in payment of such claims from the principal contractor's surety, the principal contract to furnish materials being construed to mean without expense to the school district other than the contract price. *Anderson Lumber Co. v. Miner Township School District,* 56 S.D. 586, 230 N.W. 23 (1929).

The payments for repairs on tires furnished for trucks used in hauling crushed rock in construction of highway were within provisions of highway contract bond securing claims for "materials, supplies, tools, appliances, and labor" in carrying out provisions of highway construction contract. Generally an item is within the coverage of such a bond if it is such that cost accountants would charge it as a direct expense item to a particular job and not to plant and equipment. *Margulies v. Ogdie,* 69 S.D. 352, 10 N.W.2d 513 (1943).

10. SPECIAL PROVISIONS.—The remedy under the bond is the exclusive remedy to a person furnishing labor or material in the prosecution of a highway contract.

Gas and oil furnished and used in prosecution of highway construction contract constituted "materials" within coverage of contractor's bonds, even though materials so furnished were not incorporated into contract work.

This case also held if contractor's performance bond is sufficiently definite and precise to impose liability to pay claims of third parties, the bond furnished to the state or a public agency is an enforceable obligation irrespective of minimum requirements of statute and affords right of action to person furnishing labor or materials. *State of South Dakota for the use of J. D. Evans Equipment Co. v. Johnson,* 83 S.D. 444, 160 N.W.2d. 637 (1948).

Gas and oil furnished and used in prosecution of highway construction contract constituted "materials" within coverage of contractor's combined performance and labor and material payment bond, even though materials so furnished were not incorporated into contract work. *South Dakota ex rel. J. D. Evans Equipment Company v. Jewett Johnson,* 83 S.D. 444, 160 N.W.2d 637 (1948).

TENNESSEE

1. AMOUNT OF BOND.—Bond shall be 25% of the contract price on all contracts in excess of $10,000. (Tennessee Code Annotated Vol. 3A § 12-4-201.)

As amended in April, 1985, the governing statute provides that in lieu of the required bond, certain securities or cash may be substituted at the percentage rate required for the bond. The securities include United States treasury bonds, notes and bills, Tennessee general obligation bonds and certain certificates of deposit and letters of credit.

2. LABOR AND MATERIAL COVERED.—Labor or material furnished to a contractor or to any immediate or remote subcontractor under him.

3. NOTICE REQUIRED.—90 days after completion of work, notice by personal delivery or registered mail to the contractor who executed the bond or the public official letting the contract.

4. TIME FOR SUIT.—Several persons entitled may join in one suit on bond or one may file a bill in equity on behalf of all such who may, upon execution of a bond for costs, by petition assert their rights in the proceedings, provided that action shall be brought or claims so filed within six months following the completion of such public work or the furnishing of such labor or materials.

Under the Highway Code as amended, effective July 1, 1967, all actions on bonds furnished under the Highway Code shall name the Commissioner of Highways as a party defendant and may be instituted in any court of competent jurisdiction in the State of Tennessee but no such action shall be commenced after the expiration of one year following the date of the first publication of the notice required to be published in some newspaper in the county where the work was done, etc.; that settlement is about to be made, notifying all claimants to file notice of their claims with the department. See Special Provisions below.

5. CONTRACTS EXCLUDED.—$10,000 or less.

6. PROCEDURE.—The person furnishing labor and/or material shall, after such labor or material is furnished, within ninety days after the completion of such public work, give written notice to either the contractor or the public official who had charge of the letting of the contract, by return-receipt registered mail or by personal delivery, such written notice to set forth the nature and itemized account of the material furnished or labor done, balance due therefor and a description of the property improved; provided that, in the case of public work undertaken by a municipality, the required notice or statements so mailed or delivered to the mayor thereof shall be deemed sufficient; in the case of public work by any county, the required notice or statements so mailed or delivered to the Chairman of the County Court of such county shall be deemed sufficient; in

the case of public work by the state, the required notice so mailed or delivered to the governor shall be deemed sufficient.

7. PENALTY FOR FAILURE TO TAKE BOND.—Public officer who fails to obtain the bond is guilty of a misdemeanor. No similar counterpart in Highway Code.

8. SPECIAL PROVISIONS.—The statute pertaining to public works contracts (other than highway projects) provides that in the event the contractor who has executed the bond gives notice in writing by return receipt, registered mail, to any laborer furnishing material or to any such immediate or remote subcontractor that he will not be responsible therefor, then such person who thereafter furnishes such material or labor shall not secure advantage of the provisions of this statute for materials furnished or labor done after the receipt of such notice.

The statute pertaining to highways provides that the performance of a highway contract shall not be finally accepted until the general contractor has satisfied the Highway Department that all materials "used by him, his subcontractors or his agents" have been paid for and until "laborers and other employees working for him, his subcontractors or his agents" have been paid. The Highway Department is required to take the initiative and advertise in the county where the work was done thirty days prior to final settlement. Such advertisement must state the date of the proposed final settlement and notify claimants to file notice with the Department not less than thirty days after the last published notice.

The Highway Commissioner is required to withhold, for a period of sixty days after the date of the last advertisement, sufficient funds to pay all claims so filed. If a claimant brings suit against the contractor within such sixty-day period, the Highway Department pays such retained fund into court, otherwise to the contractor.

This sixty-day limitation does not apply to an action against a surety on a contractor's bond to recover the balance due for materials furnished the contractor after crediting the amount paid the materialmen by the commissioner from the sum so withheld. *Atlantic Refining Co. v. Standard Accident Insurance Co.,* 174 Tenn. 11, 120 S.W.2d 687 (1938).

The Highway Code requires, before final settlement, thirty days' notice in a newspaper published in the county where the work is done, or, if no newspaper is published in that county, in a newspaper in an adjoining county, that settlement is about to be made, and notifying all claimants to file notice of their claims, verified by affidavits, with the Department, the period for filing such notice to be not less than thirty days after the last published notice. The Highway Commissioner must withhold a sufficient sum from the contract price to pay all claims of which notice is filed with him for a period of sixty days from the date of the last advertisement, to allow claimants to sue and prove their claims against the contractor in some court of competent jurisdiction. In the event suit is brought against the contractor within sixty days from the date of the last advertising, the Department is required to pay the amount of the claim into court unless the contractor deposits a satisfactory refunding bond. Where suit is not brought within the sixty day period, the Commissioner is authorized to pay the sum so withheld to the contractor. A suit against a refunding bond substituted for the retainance must be brought within the same sixty day period. It is too late to institute such suit approximately three years after the advertisement for the filing of claims was made. *Hurst v. Dawson Brothers & Beaver,* 167 Tenn. 572, 72 S.W.2d 767 (1934).

On October 1, 1981 legislation was promulgated, applicable only to Greene County, requiring a private contractor to either post a cash bond or be bonded by a bonding or insurance company in an amount equal to the estimated cost of any damage to a public road before proceeding with construction and excavation in rights of way of public roads. A person violating the provision of this Act is guilty of a misdemeanor and subject to a fine of not less than $25 nor more than $50.

9. DECISIONS.—Labor and materialmen, to bring themselves within the protection of the bond of a contractor who has abandoned the contract, must file their claims within thirty days after the abandonment of the contract by the contractor. *Bristol v. Bostwick,* 139 Tenn. 304 202 S.W. 61 (1917). However, a mere temporary cessation of, or interference with, the work not acquiesced in by the contractor will not work a forfeiture, for only the existence of legal cause will terminate his rights under the contract. When the work is taken over by the municipality for sufficient legal cause, the time for the thirty-day period commences to run. *Bristol v. Bostwick,* 146 Tenn. 205, 240 S.W. 774 (1922).

In *Cass v. Smith,* 146 Tenn. 218, 240 S.W. 778 (1922), the court fixed the time when the contract was abandoned as the date when receivers for the contractor were appointed.

Notice given by materialmen within thirty days after the abandonment of the work by the contractor was held binding as against the surety, although the surety took over and completed the contract. *Kimball v. Parks,* 151 Tenn. 103, 268 S.W. 117 (1925).

It has been held that a highway contractor and its surety are not liable for work done by the subcontractors of a subcontractor. *Southern Construction Co. v. Halliburton,* 149 Tenn. 319, 258

STATE BOND LAWS   31-97

S.W. 409 (1923); *Pan American Petroleum Corp. v. McQuarry,* 164 Tenn. 646, 51 S.W.2d 854 (1932).

A surety on a State highway contractor's bond is liable only for materials consumed in use or intended to be consumed. *Nicks v. Baird,* 165 Tenn. 89, 52 S.W.2d 147 (1932).

The surety of a state highway contractor is liable for rental of a steam shovel under the statutory bond for payment of labor and materials. *Nicks v. Baird,* 165 Tenn. 89, 52 S.W.2d 147 (1932).

In *Hurst v. Dawson Brothers & Beaver,* 167 Tenn. 572, 72 S.W.2d 767 (1934), the suit was instituted not only against the surety on the bond given in order to procure the release of the retained percentage, but also against the surety on the original performance bond, which was conditioned for the payment of labor and material claims. The court held that the surety on this latter bond was also relieved from liability by reason of the three years' delay in starting suit. See the limitation for suit in the current code abstracted in subdivision 4 above.

Where, in response to a letter from a materialman, the contractor answered by ordinary mail that the contractor would not be responsible for materialman's invoices, the materialman may maintain an action on the bond, because the Tennessee statute requires such repudiation to be in writing and sent by return-receipt registered mail. Notice by ordinary mail was deemed to be insufficient, the court holding that, where a specified method of giving notice is prescribed by a statute, that method is exclusive. *Hibbler-Barnes Co. v. Mark K. Wilson Co.,* Tenn. Ct. of Appeals (1940).

The statutory provision for notice and limitation of action was held to prevail over provisions of the bond fixing different time limits. *City of Knoxville v. Burgess,* 180 Tenn. 412, 175 S.W.2d 548 (1943). Decision followed in *Graybar Electric Co. Inc. v. New Amsterdam Casualty Co.,* 292 N.Y. 246, 54 N.E.2d 811 (1944), rehearing denied, 292 N.Y. 693, 55 N.E.2d 512 (1944), cert. denied, 323 U.S. 715, 65 S. Ct. 42, 89 L. Ed. 575 (1944), reversing 33 N.Y.S. (2d) 435 and 42 N.Y.S. (2d) 919. *Thompson & Green Machinery Co. v. M. P. Smith Construction Co.,* 44 Tenn. App. 26, 311 S.W.2d 614 (1957). More recently, a labor and material payment bond which gave rights beyond those provided by the public works statute by eliminating notice as a prerequisite to action and by allowing one year instead of six months upon completion of work to sue, permitted material supplier to sue on bond and within the year. *National Surety Corporation v. Fischer Steel Corp.,* 213 Tenn. 396, 374 S.W.2d 372 (1964).

A performance and payment bond obligating a general contractor surety to pay all just claims for work, skill, tools, materials and debts incurred by contractor or any immediate or remote subcontractor and providing that the bond for the use of the housing authority and all persons doing work or furnishing skills, tools, machinery or materials did not entitle the Commissioner of Department of Employment Security to recover unpaid employment compensation taxes due by a subcontractor. *Scott v. Travelers Indemnity Co.,* 215 Tenn. 173, 384 S.W.2d 38 (1964).

Where the statute with respect to public contracts incorporated by reference into the bond contained a six-months limitation for suit and the statute with respect to highways is silent as to the time for suit, the six-months limitation was held to apply to the state highway contract payment bond. *Thompson & Green Mach. Co. v. Travelers Indem. Co.,* 57 Tenn. App. 592, 421 S.W.2d 643 (1967). (Time changed by 1967 Amendment. See Sec. 4 above.)

Where the payment bond covered material "used by the principal or any immediate or remote subcontractor or furnisher of material under him," recovery was allowed a manufacturer who sold hardware to materialman who thereafter delivered it to the job and then this material was incorporated into the project. *J. A. Jones Constr. Co. v. Lawrence Bros. Inc.,* 57 Tenn. App. 415, 419 S.W.2d 186 (1966).

The fact that a supplier of materials to a company which installed air conditioning system in a county building had no knowledge of the bond executed by the contractor in whose name the air conditioning company bid for the job, and that the supplier did not materially change its position in reliance thereon and extended credit to the air conditioning company on open account, did not bar the supplier's action against the surety company on the bond. *Air Temperature, Inc. v. Morris,* 63 Tenn. App. 90, 469 S.W.2d 495 (1970).

A payment and performance bond which was issued by the surety in connection with the contractor's work on a housing authority project and which limited the liability of the surety in accordance with the terms of the statute and did not broaden the liability beyond such terms was a statutory rather than a common-law bond; thus, a subcontractor who had not complied with the terms of applicable statutes could not maintain a suit as the surety on the bond. *Heglar v. McAdoo Contractors, Inc.,* 487 S.W.2d 312 (Tenn. Ct. App. 1972).

Failure of commissioner of Employment Security to comply with 90 day notice requirements and six months time limitation for suit mandated dismissal of suit. *Griggs v. Peerless Ins. Co.,* 528 S.W.2d 182 (Tenn. 1975).

Cashing by supplier of check marked "account in full" did not constitute accord and satisfaction, where person with whom supplier had dealt as issuer—contractor's agent marked through the words prior to cashing. Failure of surety on the bond to deny that timely notice of the claim was given and that suit was brought within six months after completion of the project in its answer denied it the right to rely on those defenses. *Sawner v. M. P. Smith Construction Co.*, 526 S.W.2d 492 (Tenn. Ct. App. 1975).

The claims of the state, counties, municipalities, and political subdivisions thereof are placed in the same category as those of materialmen and laborers and are subject to the same restrictions and requirements as all others for whose benefit the bond was required. *Griggs v. Peerless Insurance Co.*, 528 S.W.2d 182 (Tenn. 1975).

If the statute of limitations is a bar to suit on behalf of the contractor, the surety is likewise discharged *Hill v. City of Chattanooga*, 533 S.W.2d 311 (Tenn. Ct. App. 1975).

Suit by a remote subcontractor on municipal construction project against prime contractor and prime's payment bond surety was held to be timely where the bond was conditioned to protect all laborers and materialmen as required by Public Works Act, and also independently of said statutes, the general six-year statute of limitation applied rather than the six-month special limitation of Public Works Act. Therefore, a suit brought more than six months but within the six years after the claim arose was not time barred. *Varner Constr. Co. v. Mid-South Specialties*, 547 S.W.2d 569 (Tenn. 1977).

The evidence presented supported the determination that the contracts were for use of equipment and therefore were leases and not conditional sales. Hence, the claim for rental was within the bond coverage. The statute governing highway contractor's bonds did not require notice by a claimant to the surety before bringing suit. *United States Fidelity & Guaranty Co. v. Thompson & Greenmach Co.*, 568 S.W.2d 821 (Tenn. 1978).

Dismissal of a suit brought by the State University Board of Regents because of the statute of limitation was held to be error inasmuch as the statute was not applicable to suits brought by the state. *Dunn v. W. F. Jameson & Sons, Inc.*, 569 S.W.2d 799 (Tenn. 1978).

TEXAS

In 1959, Texas enacted a new Public Works Bond statute known as the MacGregor Act. It reflects an intention of the Legislature to change the public policy of the State as previously declared by Supreme Court decisions under the former statute. Section "B" of this MacGregor Act was amended as of June 2, 1969, to allow a proper claimant to recover reasonable attorney fees. This statute was supplemented by an act effective August 28, 1967, to include notice and bonding requirements for nonresident construction contractors. Texas courts have stated that the intention of the 1959 Legislature was to provide a simple, direct method of giving notice and preventing claims of laborers, materialmen and subcontractors. *United Benefit Fire Insurance Co. v. Metropolitan Plumbing Co.*, 363 S.W.2d, 843 (Ct. App. 1962); *U. S. Fidelity & Guaranty Co. v. Parker Brothers & Company*, 437 S.W.2d, 880 (Ct. App. 1969).

1. AMOUNT OF BOND.—The amount of the contract. (Vernon's Ann. Civ. St. Art. 2368a Sec. 2)

2. LABOR AND MATERIAL COVERED.—(a) All labor used in direct prosecution of the work.

(b) Material is construed to mean any part or all of the following:

(1) Material incorporated in the work, or consumed in the direct prosecution of the work, or ordered or delivered for such incorporation or such consumption.

(2) Material specially fabricated on the order of the prime contractor or of a subcontractor for use as a component part of said public project, so as to be reasonably unsuitable for use elsewhere, even though such material has not been delivered or incorporated into the public project, but in such event only to the extent of its reasonable costs, less its fair salvage value, and only to the extent that such specially fabricated material is in conformity and compliance with the contract documents.

(3) Rent at a reasonable rate and actual running repairs at a reasonable rate for construction equipment, used in the direct prosecution of the work at the project site, or reasonably required and delivered for such use.

(4) Power, water, fuel and lubricants, when such items have been consumed or ordered and delivered for consumption, in the direct prosecution of the work.

3. NOTICE REQUIRED.—The detailed statutory provisions for notice involve:

(a) All claimants having a direct contractual relationship with the prime contractor.

(b) Claimants who do not have a direct contractual relationship with the prime contractor.

(c) Notices with respect to unpaid retainages.

STATE BOND LAWS

(d) Notices required for unpaid bills other than notices solely for retainages.

The MacGregor Act of 1959 requires every person entering into a formal contract in excess of $2,000 with the State or any political subdivision thereof for the construction, alteration or repair of any public building or in the prosecution or completion of any public work, before commencing such work, to execute two statutory corporate surety bonds, one thereof a performance bond conditioned for the faithful performance of the work, solely for the protection of the public body; the second, a payment bond solely for the protection of claimants supplying labor and material as defined in the statute.

An amendment effective July 11, 1973, excludes contracts under $3,000 from the bond requirement by any city or county or subdivision of any county. There is also a provision where such contracts are under $50,000, the municipality may in lieu of the bond requirement provide that no money will be paid to the contractor until completion and acceptance of the work by the city or the county.

Every claimant who has furnished labor or material in the prosecution of the work provided for in such contract, who has not been paid in full therefor, has the right of action on the bond within the time hereinafter set forth, provided,

(a) Notice required for unpaid bills other than notices solely for retainages.

Such claimant shall have given within 90 days after the 10th day of the month next following each month in which the labor or material was furnished in whole or in part, for which such claim is made, written notice of the claim by certified or registered mail, addressed to the prime contractor at his last known business address or his residence, *and* to the surety or sureties. Such notice must be accompanied by a sworn statement of account, stating in substance that the amount claimed is just and correct and that all just and lawful offsets, payments and credits known to the affiant have been allowed. Such statement of account must include therein the amount of any retainages applicable to the account that have not become due by virtue of the terms of the contract between the claimant and the prime contractor or between the claimant and a subcontractor. When the claim is based on a written agreement, the claimant has the option to enclose with the sworn statement of account, as such notice, a true copy of such agreement and advising completion or value of partial completion of same.

(1) When no written agreement exists between the claimant and the prime contractor or between the claimant and a subcontractor (except as provided in the next paragraph hereof, which is subparagraph (b) (a) (2) of the statute, such notice must state the name of the party for whom the labor was done or performed, or to whom the material was delivered, the approximate dates of performance and delivery, describing the labor or material or both in such a manner so as to reasonably identify the same and the amount due therefor. The claimant shall generally itemize his claim and shall accompany same with true copies of documents, invoices or orders sufficient to reasonably identify the labor performed or material delivered for which claim is being made. Such documents and copies thereof must have thereon a reasonable identification or description of the job and destination of delivery.

(2) When the claim is for multiple items of labor or material or both, to be paid on a lump sum basis, such notice must state the name of the party for whom the labor was done or performed or to whom the material was delivered, the amount of the contract and whether written or oral, the amount claimed and the approximate date or dates of performance or delivery or both, describing the labor or materials or both, in such a manner so as to reasonably identify the same.

(3) Where a claimant who is a subcontractor or materialman to the prime contractor or to a subcontractor has a written unit price agreement completed or partially completed, such notice shall be sufficient, if such claimant attaches to his sworn statement of account a list of units and unit prices as fixed by his contract and a statement of such units completed and partially completed.

(b) Claimants who do not have a direct contractual relationship with the prime contractor unless an individual mechanic or laborer is claiming for wages, must also comply with the following additional requirements which are applicable to the claim:

(1) If any agreements exist between the claimant and any subcontractors by which payments are not to be made in full therefor in the month next following each month in which the labor was performed or material was delivered or both, such claimant must give written notice by certified or registered mail, addressed to the *prime contractor* at his last known business address or his residence, within 36 days after the tenth day of the month next following the commencement of the delivery of the materials or the performance of the labor, that there has been agreed upon between the claimant and such subcontractors such retention of funds. Such notice must indicate generally the nature of such retainage.

(2) Such claimant who has no direct contractual relationship with the prime contractor must

give written notice by certified or registered mail within 36 days after the 10th of the month next following each month in which the labor was done or performed in whole or in part or materials delivered in whole or in part, that payment therefor has not been received. A copy of the statement sent to the subcontractor suffices as such notice to the prime contractor.

(3) If the basis of the claim by such claimant who does not have a direct contractual relationship with the prime contractor is an undelivered specially fabricated item or is material specially fabricated on the order of the prime contractor or of a subcontractor for use as a component part of said public project, as has been described in subdivision (2), subsection (b) (2) of this analysis, such claimant must give written notice by certified or registered mail as prescribed in the preceding subparagraph (1) of which this is subparagraph (3), to the prime contractor, within 45 days after the receipt and acceptance of an order for such specially fabricated material, that such an order has been received and accepted.

(c) Notices of retained percentages. Retainage as referred to in the McGregor Act is defined as any amount representing any part of the contract payments which is not required to be paid to the claimant within the month next following the month in which the labor was done or materials furnished or both.

Where the contract between the prime contractor and the claimant or between the subcontractor and the claimant provides for retainages as above defined, such claimant must give, on or before 90 days after final completion of the contract between the prime contractor and the public body, an additional notice, viz., written notices of the claim for such retainage by certified or registered mail to the *prime contractor* at his last known business or home address, *and to the surety or sureties.* Such notices shall consist of a statement showing the amount of the contract, the amount paid, if any, and the balance outstanding. No claim for such retainage contained in such notice shall be valid to an extent greater than the amount specified in the contract between the prime contractor or the subcontractor and the claimant to be retained, and in no event greater than 10% of such contract. Such additional notice with respect to retained percentages is not required if the amount claimed is part of a prior claim which has been made as heretofore described.

4. TIME FOR SUIT.—Suit may not be filed prior to the expiration of 60 days after the filing of the claim. No suit may be brought on the payment bond after the expiration of one year after the date on which suit may be first brought thereon under this statute.

5. CONTRACTS EXCLUDED.—Effective in 1975, $15,000 or less.

In June of 1977, contracts excluded are those less than $25,000.

6. PROCEDURE.—All suits instituted under the McGregor Act shall be brought in a court of competent jurisdiction in the county in which the project or work or any part thereof is situate.

7. PENALTY FOR FAILURE TO TAKE BOND.—No special statutory provision.

8. SPECIAL PROVISIONS.—Any bond furnished by any prime contractor in an attempted compliance with the McGregor Act shall be treated and construed as in conformity with the requirements of said Act as to rights created, limitations thereon and remedies provided.

Any person who shall willfully file a false and fraudulent claim under the statute shall be subject to the penalties for false swearing. In the event any contractor who shall have furnished the bonds provided by this statute shall abandon performance of his contract or the awarding authority shall lawfully terminate his right to proceed with performance thereof, because of a default or defaults on his part, no further proceeds of the contract shall be payable to him unless and until all costs of completion of the work shall have been paid by him. Any balance remaining shall be payable to him or his surety as their interest may appear.

The contracting authority is authorized and directed to furnish to any person making application therefor, who submits an affidavit that he has supplied labor, rented equipment or materials for such work, or that he has entered into a contract for specially fabricated material, and payment therefor has not been made, or that he is being sued on any such bond, a certified copy of such payment bond and the contract for which it was given, which copy shall be prima facie evidence of the contents, execution and delivery of the original. Applicants shall pay for such certified copies such reasonable fees as the contracting authority may fix.

In Spring of 1975, by two separate Acts, there was created a Farwell Hospital District and a Lavaca Hospital District by the terms of which all contracts for construction involving an expenditure of more than $10,000 may be made only after due advertising. The provisions of the McGregor Act relating to performance and payment bonds applies to these construction contracts.

In June of 1975, three separate Acts were passed with respect to the Teague Hospital District, Moulton Hospital District and the Valverde County Hospital District requiring all contracts for construction involving an expenditure of more than $2,000 be made only after due advertising, and that the provisions of the McGregor Act relating to performance and payment bonds apply to these construction contracts.

In 1975, legislation was passed with respect to the Nueces River Authority requiring contracts for construction involving an expenditure of more than $10,000 be made only after due advertising, and that the provisions of the McGregor Act relating to performance and payment bonds apply to its construction contracts.

In June of 1977, effective 90 days after adjournment, the Texas legislature amended its water code to provide that contractor shall execute corporate surety bonds as required by the general law for public works to guarantee the completion of the contract and the payment of laborers, subcontractors, materialmen and suppliers.

In 1977, legislation was passed with respect to the Midland County Hospital District, Shackelford County Hospital District, Reagan Hospital District and Refugio County Memorial Hospital District requiring contracts for construction involving an expenditure of more than $10,000 be made only after due advertising, and that the provisions of the McGregor Act relating to performance and payment bonds apply to these construction contracts.

In 1983, legislation was passed with respect to the Foard County Hospital District, the Mason County Hospital District and the Sutton County Hospital District, requiring contracts for construction involving an expenditure of more than $10,000 be made only after competitive bidding as provided by Article 2368a.3, Vernon's Texas Civil Statutes. The McGregor Act, as it relates to performance and payment bonds, applies to these construction contracts.

In 1983, legislation was passed which provided for the regulation of "contractors" who contract with the state to operate an "auxiliary enterprise" or perform an "auxiliary enterprise" service at a state agency or at a state-supported institution of higher education. House Bill No. 2363 provided that each contractor shall execute a bond issued by an authorized surety company in an amount determined by the agency or institution, not to exceed the contract price, payable to the state, and conditioned on the faithful performance of the obligations, agreements, and covenants of the contract. An "auxiliary enterprise" is defined as a business activity conducted at a state agency or at a state-supported institution of higher education that provides a service to the agency or institution but is not funded through appropriated money.

9. RIGHT OF LIEN AGAINST SUCH CONSTRUCTION FUND.—A supplier of labor, material, apparatus, fixtures, machinery to any contractor under a prime contract, where such prime contract does not exceed $2,000 for any public improvements in Texas, is given a lien on the moneys, bonds or warrants due or to become due such contractor for such improvements, provided such claimant shall, before any payment is made to such contractor, notify in writing the public officials whose duty it is to pay such contractor of his claim. Such written notice is required to be given by certified or registered mail with a copy to the contractor at his last known address or his residence, and must be given within 30 days after the 10th day of the month next following *each month* in which labor, materials, apparatus, fixtures or machinery were furnished, for which such lien is claimed.

Such notice, whether based on a written or oral agreement, must state the amount claimed, the name of the party to whom such was delivered or for whom it was performed, with date and place of delivery or performance and describing the same in such manner as to reasonably identify said material, apparatus, fixtures, machinery, or labor and the amount due therefor, identify the project where material was delivered or labor performed.

Such notice shall be accompanied by a statement under oath stating that the amount claimed is just and correct and that all payments, lawful offsets, and credits known to the affiant have been allowed.

10. DECISION UNDER MCGREGOR ACT.—*United Benefit Fire Insurance Co. v. Metropolitan Plumbing Co.*, 363 S.W.2d 843 (Tex. Ct. App. 1962), construes liberally the notice requirements which are set forth in detail therein. See also: *Standard Concrete Pipe Sales Corp. v. Ed Johansson Construction Co.*, 382 S.W.2d 754 (Tex. 1964).

A delivery of a platform lift to a building site in September was such a delivery that fixed the beginning of the 90-day period within which to give the original contractor's surety notice of materialman's claim for its purchase price, although the lift was not usable until the November delivery of a transformer. *Fidelity & Deposit Co. of Maryland v. Industrial Handling Engineers, Inc.* 474 S.W.2d 584 (Tex. Ct. App. 1971).

The notice requirements of the statute are to be liberally construed and substantial compliance is all that is required. *General Electric Supply Co. v. Epco Constructors, Inc.*, 332 F. Supp. 112 (S.D. Tex. 1971).

However, the requirement of notice to the surety within ninety days is not a mere statute of limitation but is a substantive condition precedent to the cause of action. *Bunch Electric Co. v. Tex-Craft Builders, Inc.*, 480 S.W.2d 42 (Tex. Ct. App. 1972).

The notice a materialman is required to give the prior contractor under the McGregor Act is given when mailed by the materialman rather than when received by the contractor. *Buckner v. Anderson-Dunham, Inc.,* 482 S.W.2d 350 (Tex. Ct. App. 1972).

Where subcontractor furnished general contractor a surety with copy of contract and advised both that work under such agreement had been completed, notice was not defective because of failure to itemize labor and material furnished. *Lesikar Construction Co. v. Acoustex, Inc.,* 509 S.W.2d 877 (Tex. Ct. App. 1974). But see *Texcraft Builders, Inc. v. Allied Constructors of Houston,* 465 S.W.2d 786 (Tex. Ct. App. 1971) where insuror to bill or invoice and telephone conversations with surety was held to be insufficient notice.

A bond conditioned to pay "any and all other expense incurred in the performance or attempted performance" of the contract was held liable for premiums on compensation insurance where the contract expressly provided that the contractor carry such insurance. *Davis Co. v. Callaghan Construction Co.,* 298 S.W. 273 (Tex. Ct. App. 1927), reversing and remanding *Southern Surety Co. v. Callaghan Constr. Co.,* 283 S.W. 1098 (Tex. Ct. App. 1926), which held that recovery may be had for lumber used to construct forms, which lumber, after such use, was worthless.

An assignment by the contractor to his surety is not an abandonment. *Massachusetts Bonding & Insurance Co. v. Steele,* 293 S.W. 647 (Tex. Ct. App. 1927).

A surety is not entitled to have the funds prorated between materialmen who have established a lien and those who have established a claim under the bond. *Metropolitan Cas. Ins. Co. v. Cheany,* 32 S.W.2d 691 (Tex. Ct. App. 1930), *aff'd,* 55 S.W.2d 554 (Tex. Ct. App. 1932).

Unpaid laborers and materialmen may establish a lien on the money, bonds or warrants due or to become due to the contractor by giving a written notice of the indebtedness to the officers of the state or municipality whose duty it is to pay the contractor. Such written notice can be given before the last or any instalment remains to be paid the contractor *Texas Co. v. Schriewer,* 38 S.W.2d 141 (Tex. Ct. App. 1931), Mod. 53 S.W.2d 774 (1934). When the proper officer is so notified, he is required to retain sufficient money, bonds or warrants to pay such claim.

Such a lien may be released by the filing of a surety bond payable to the claimants in double the amount of the claim. Such a bond must be filed with the officer in charge of paying the contractor and must be approved by him. Such officer is required to forward, by registered mail, to each claimant an exact copy of the bond. The filing and approval of the bond releases and discharges all liens on the fund. One bond may be made payable to all claimants. Suit may be brought at any time within six months after filing the bond. Each claimant may maintain a separate claim thereon.

Where a surety is obligated to pay subcontractor's claim, subcontractor is entitled to have said claim paid in full out of funds impounded by the filing of a notice with state highway department. Bonding company may not thereafter buy up claims against contractor, for payment of which it was liable, and, by filing same with state highway commission, share ratably with other creditors, whose claims it ws obligated to pay, in the distribution of the imported funds. *McClintic-Marshall Corp. v. Maryland Casualty Co.,* 100 S.W.2d 438 (Tex. Ct. App. 1936).

Materialmen and laborers, who had valid liens against funds due from city for construction of public works, should not have been precluded from participating in the distribution of such funds, merely because they also had filed their claims against contractor's surety on the contractor's bond pursuant to statute. *Mass. Bonding & Insurance Co. v. Farmers & Merchants State Bank,* 139 Tex. 310, 162 S.W.2d 657 (Tex. 1942).

Generally, a subcontractor's bond for performance of all terms and conditions of his contract and payment of all claims for labor performed and materials furnished is one of indemnity for protection of original contractor and not for benefit of laborers and materialmen. *Employers Liability Assurance Corp. Ltd. v. Trane Co.,* 139 Tex. 388, 163 S.W.2d 398 (1942).

Although the language in a bond for faithful performance of a public works contract is broader than that required to be imposed by statute, the statute provides the procedure and remedy for presenting a claim for labor and material against a contractor's bond, and where the claimant did not comply with the statutory requirement that the claim by itemized and sworn to and duly filed with the County Clerk, the claimant will be denied recovery. *Fidelity & Deposit Co. v. Big Three Welding Equipment Co., Inc.,* 151 Tex. 278, 249 S.W.2d 183 (1952).

The surety on building contractor's bond, covering indebtedness for labor and material, is not liable for workmen's compensation or liability insurance premiums, in absence of express assumption of, or statute expressly imposing, such liability. *Knox v. Ball,* 144 Tex. 402, 191 S.W.2d 17 (1945).

Materialmen and laborers seeking to recover amounts due them from public works contractor in suit against surety on contractor's performance bond must establish by sworn itemized accounts, filed with County Clerk, that materials were furnished and labor performed within 90 days after delivery of materials and performance of work, as required by statute, and are not entitled to benefits thereof, in absence of such showing. *Pacific Indemnity Co. v. Bowles & Edens Supply Co.,* 290 S.W.2d 353 (Tex. Ct. App. 1956).

STATE BOND LAWS

Tires, tubes and tire repairs sold to subcontractor are not within the bond statute which provides that anyone who furnishes material . . . machinery or labor to any contractor for any public improvement shall have a lien on the moneys due or to become due such contractor for such improvements. *Pelphrey v. Walker,* 323 S.W.2d 266 (Tex. Ct. App. 1959).

Where general contractor for construction of city fire station executed a performance bond and a labor and material payment bond which provided that furnishers of labor and material could sue on bond for indebtedness due upon giving notice to any two of the principal, owner, or surety within 90 days after labor or materials were furnished, and materialman complied with requirements of bond itself but he did not comply with statute concerning filing of claims for labor and materials furnished to any contractor with County Clerk, materialman was not entitled to recover from surety following general contractor's default on contract. *Elliot Shiels Planing Mill Co. v. American Automobile Insurance Co.,* 331 S.W.2d 383 (Tex. Ct. App. 1960).

Road machinery leased to subcontractor for use of highway project is not "material supplied" within the public contractors' bond statute. *Trinity Road & Bridge Co., v. Watson,* 341 S.W.2d 956 (Tex. Ct. App. 1960).

Breach damages such as loss of anticipated profits on unperformed work resulting from termination of contract were not allowable against surety, but overhead, supervision and profit on work performed were proper items of damage under bond. *Citodel Construction Co. v. Smith,* 483 S.W.2d 283 (Tex. Ct. App. 1972).

Surety may waive compliance by subcontractor by letter acknowledging receipt of subcontractor's claim which state surety would pay all valid and verified claims. *General Insurance Company v. Smith & Wardroup,* 388 S.W.2d 262 (Tex. 1965).

The Texas Hardeman Act's ban on additional suits against owners did not cover an action against additional nonstatutory security or preclude the claimant from recovering on the labor and material payment bond furnished to the United States by the owner in connection with the construction and subsequent leaseback to the United States of a Post Office Building. *Johnson Service Co., v. Trans America Insurance Co.,* 485 F.2d 164 (5th Cir. 1973).

Where prime contractor was controlled by owner of apartment building, notice to such owner of sum due for paint supplied by materialman to subcontractor was also notice to prime contractor. *Da-Col Paint Manufacturing Co. v. American Indemnity Company,* 517 S.W.2d 270 (Tex. 1974).

Where materials furnished to subcontractor were actually used in performance of work covered by subcontracts, surety on performance and payment bonds issued on subcontractor's behalf was liable to materialmen for cost of such materials even if such materials were furnished prior to execution of bond. *Parliament Insurance Co. v. L. B. Foster Co.,* 533 S.W.2d 43 (Tex. Ct. App. 1975).

Requirement of notice to surety within 90 days with respect to claim under payment bond on public contract is not a mere statute of limitation but is a substantive condition precedent to the existence of the cause of action. *Bunch Elec. Co. v. Tex-Craft Builders, Inc.,* 480 S.W.2d 42 (Tex. Ct. App. 1972).

Notice which a subcontractor is required to give surety under Subdivision B (a) of the McGregor Act is given when mailed by the subcontractor rather than when received by the surety; accordingly, when subcontractor gave notice on the 89th day of the 90 day period, and the notice was sent registered mail, it was timely notwithstanding the fact that the letter was not received until the 91st day. *Johnson Service Co. v. Climate Control Contractors, Inc.,* 478 S.W.2d 643 (Tex. Ct. App. 1972).

Claims of municipal contractor's materialmen and subcontractors who did not perfect claims against contractor's surety and who were not third party beneficiaries, were subordinate to secured claim of bank, which lent money to contractor and perfected security interest in contract rights assigned it, as to rights in funds retained by city. *Corpus Christi Bank and Trust v. Smith,* 525 S.W.2d 501 (Tex. 1975).

Contractor's surety whose funds were required to complete project had a priority over the claim of a bank to whom contractor had assigned contract balances. *First Hutchings-Sealy Nat. Bank v. Aetna Casualty & Surety Co.,* 532 S.W.2d 114 (Tex. Ct. App. 1975).

Where contractor on a municipal project agreed to correct any defects appearing within one year from the date of final acceptance by the municipal district, the district, in respect to the statute barring suit on a performance bond after the expiration of one year from the date of final completion of the contract, had a full year to file suit after the one year "remedy" period had elapsed. *Bayshore Constructors v. Southern Montgomery County Municipal Utility District,* 543 S.W.2d 898 (Tex. Ct. App. 1976).

The statute allowing suit in the county where the project was situated was held to come within the general provision requiring controverting affidavits to be filed to sustain venue in any county other than that urged in a plea of privilege. Plaintiff subcontractor's failure to file a controverting affidavit to the prime contractors and its surety's plea of privilege to have the case transferred to their counties of residence resulted in said plea of privilege being sustained. *Dahlstrom Corp. v. Asphalt Equip., Inc.,* 543 S.W.2d 183 (Tex. Ct. App. 1976).

A prime contractor brought suit against the state of Texas and filed third-party complaints against numerous subcontractors working on the project. Thereafter, the state sued the prime contractor in another action, and along with six performance bond sureties for costs caused by delayed performance. The court held that the initial suit instituted by the prime contractor would cause the state's suit to abate as a prior pending action. Since the sureties were only secondarily liable, their absence from the first suit did not prevent the application of Texas' abatement rule. *State v. T. C. Bateson Constr. Co.,* 562 S.W.2d 538 (Tex. Ct. App. 1978).

It was held that a claimant's notice to the prime contractor and its surety met the statutory requirements as to the description of labor performed and material furnished, that the stipulation between the claimant and the first-tier subcontractor as to the amount due, made in court was binding on the prime contractor and its surety. *Sims v. William S. Baker, Inc.,* 568 S.W.2d 725 (Tex. Ct. App. 1978).

It was held that since the surety was not a party to the transaction between the subcontractor and the insurance agent who was seeking to recover workmen's compensation premiums, the surety's failure to file a sworn denial to plaintiff's claim would not furnish a basis for granting summary judgment against the surety. *Trinity Universal Ins. Co. v. Patterson,* 570 S.W.2d 475 (Tex. Ct. App. 1978).

Plaintiff subcontractor's evidence was insufficient for plaintiff to recover against prime contractor and its surety on payment bond. *Phoenix Mechanical Plumbing Co. v. Ponderosa Constr. Co.,* 566 S.W.2d 323 (Tex. Ct. App. 1978).

When the plaintiff's complaint affirmatively showed that plaintiff had not given the required statutory notice of claim, defendant surety was entitled to summary judgment. *Trucker's, Inc. v. South Texas Constr. Co.,* 561 S.W.2d 855 (Tex. Ct. App. 1977).

When the performance bond referred to a contract which barred the contractor to successors of the named owner, and the bond did not prohibit transfer of title, the successor/owner of school property was entitled to benefits of the bond and, therefore, could sue thereon. *Balboa Ins. Co. v. Snyder Consol. Independent Dist.,* 574 S.W.2d 879 (Tex. Ct. App. 1977).

A payment bond surety is entitled to all offsets to which its principal is entitled without the necessity of the surety seeking such relief by motion. *Robberson Steel, Inc. v. J. D. Abrams, Inc.,* 582 S.W.2d 558 (Tex. Ct. App. 1979).

Subcontractor was held to be entitled to recover its attorney's fees under state law, when its suit based on diversity of citizenship was consolidated with its suit which was pending under the Federal Miller Act. *United States for the use of A. C. Garrett v. Midwest Constr. Co.,* 619 F.2d 349 (5th Cir. 1980).

UTAH

March 22, 1963 Utah adopted a separate performance and payment bond statute with respect to contracts for public buildings and public works.

1. AMOUNT OF BOND.—A payment and performance bond in an amount equal to 100% of the contract amount. (Utah Code Annotated § 63-56-38, Vol. 7A)

2. LABOR AND MATERIAL COVERED.—Labor and material supplied to the contractor or his subcontractors in the prosecution of the public work.

3. NOTICE REQUIRED.—(a) *To principal contractor or surety*—No notice is required by a claimant having a contractual relationship expressed or implied with the principal contractor. Any claimant who has a direct contractual relationship with a subcontractor but no contractual relationship expressed or implied with the contractor furnishing such payment bond must give written notice to the contractor and surety company within 90 days from the date on which such claimant performed the last of the labor or supplied the last of the material for which such claim is made noting with substantial accuracy the amount claimed and the name of the person to whom the material was supplied or for whom the labor was performed. The statute provides that this notice shall be served on the contractor and surety company at any place the contractor or surety company maintains an office or conducts business by mailing the same by registered or certified mail, postage prepaid.

(b) *To municipality*—No special statutory provision.

(c) *To creditors*—No special statutory provision.

4. TIME FOR SUIT.—A period commencing 90 days after the date on which claimant performed the last of the labor or furnished the last of the material for which he claims payment, but no

STATE BOND LAWS

suit may be commenced by a claimant under § 63-56-38 more than 180 days after a surety finally denies that claimant's claim.

5. CONTRACTS EXCLUDED.—No special statutory provision except as is set forth in subdivision 8, Special Provisions, below.

6. PROCEDURE.—The performance and payment bonds are required to be filed in the office of the department, board, commission, institution, agency, or other contracting body awarding the contract. The contracting body and the agent in charge of its office are authorized and directed to furnish, to anyone making application therefor who submits an affidavit that he has supplied labor, or materials for such work and payment therefor has not been made or that he is being sued on any such bond, or that it is the surety thereon, a certified copy of such bond and the contract for which it was given, which copy shall be prima facie evidence of the contents, execution, and delivery of the original. Every suit instituted on the aforesaid payment bond shall be brought in the appropriate court in the political subdivision in which the contract was to be performed and not elsewhere.

7. PENALTY FOR FAILURE TO TAKE BOND.—Any public body subject to this Act which shall fail or neglect to obtain the delivery of the payment bond as required by this Act, shall, upon demand, itself promptly make payment to all persons who have supplied materials or performed labor in the prosecution of the work under the contract, and any such creditor shall have a direct right of action upon his account against such public body in any court having jurisdiction in the county in which the contract was to be performed and executed which action shall be commenced within one year after the furnishings of materials or labor.

8. SPECIAL PROVISIONS.—In any action brought upon either of the bonds provided herein, or against the public body failing to obtain the delivery of the payment bond, the prevailing party, upon each separate cause of action, shall recover a reasonable attorney's fee to be taxed as costs.

The statute reads: "It shall be illegal for the invitation for bids, or any person acting or purporting to act, on behalf of the contracting body to require that such bonds be furnished by a particular surety company, or through a particular agent or broker."

In 1979, Utah amended its Code to increase the threshold for bonds on contracts let by irrigation districts from $3,000 to $30,000.

9. DECISIONS.—The right of contractor who paid labor and material bills incurred by subcontractor under surety bond of subcontractor considered in *Utah State Building Board v. Walsh Plumbing Company*, 16 Utah 2d 249, 399 P.2d 141 (1965).

10. RECOVERY FOR FAILURE TO REQUIRE BOND.—Utah also has a statute allowing recovery by a materialman against an owner who failed to require a bond from the contractor. *Day & Night Heating Co., v. C. M. Ruff*, 19 Utah 412, 432 P.2d 43 (1967).

11. REMARKS.—Claim for groceries and supplies furnished for boarding house conducted by a highway subcontractor was held chargeable to the surety under the bond. There were no other boarding house accommodations within twenty-two miles. Claims for labor and repairs and for sundry small parts and accessories for automobiles and trucks used by highway subcontractor were held chargeable against the surety under the bond. Claim for gas, lubricating oil and grease, as well as for hauling the same, used in subcontractor's machinery employed in construction of highway, held chargeable against the surety under the bond. *J. F. Tolton Inv. Co. v. Maryland Cas. Co.*, 77 Utah 226, 293 P. 611 (1930).

Statute providing that it shall be unlawful for any person to engage in the capacity of contractor without having a license therefor did not bar an unlicensed subcontractor from suing on a contractor's bond or from suing directly a homeowner who failed to require a bond from his general contractor. *Whipple v. Fuller*, 5 Utah 2d 211, 299 P.2d 837 (1956).

Although a six-month contractual limitation period in a subcontractor's payment bond for filing suit was in violation of an Insurance Code provision that no such limitation shall be for a period of less than one year, the entire limitation provision in the bond was not void, but would be construed and applied as if it had specified one year. An action filed more than four years after the principal completed performance of the contract was barred. *Lister v. Great American Insurance Co.* 26 Utah 2d 10, 484 P.2d 156 (1971).

Where a subcontractor violated its agreement with the prime contractor not to sublet any work without the permission of the prime contractor, the contract price agreed upon by said contractor and subcontractor would not be binding upon the contractor or the surety on the public works bond. The recovery by the sub-subcontractor on the bond should be limited to the reasonable value of the work done and material furnished, not exceeding the sub-subcontract price. *Steel Components, Inc. v. U.S. Fidelity & Guaranty Co.*, 28 Utah 2d 25, 497 P.2d 646 (1972).

Date on which last materials were furnished was not extended by subsequent substitution of new and different controls to correct supplier's error. *A.A. Maycock, Inc. v. General Insurance Co. of America*, 24 Utah 2d 369, 472 P.2d 424 (1970).

An amendment approved March 6, 1973, increases the minimum amount for which competitive bidding is required from $2,000 to $12,000 in counties of the first and second class, and from $1,000 to $10,000 in counties of the third and fourth class, and from $5,000 to $8,000 in counties of the remaining classes, and provides that the person to whom any such contract is awarded shall be required to execute a bond for the faithful performance of the contract.

Failure to give ninety days notice precludes recovery under bond. *American Oil Co. v. General Contracting Corp.*, 17 Utah 2d 330, 411 P.2d 486 (1966).

Subcontractor's suit for retainage was timely when filed within one year of prime contractor's receipt of payment on final estimate since prime contractor was not obligated to pay subcontractor for work performed prior to the time prime contractor received payment from owner. *Foss Lewis & Sons Construction Co. v. General Insurance Co. of America*, 30 Utah 2d 290, 517 P.2d 539 (1973).

The one-year Public Works Bond Statute of Limitations was not applicable to suit on a subcontractor's payment bond, but rather, the general six-year statute of limitation applied. *Arnold Machinery Co. v. Prince*, 550 P.2d 193 (Utah 1976).

A claim by an unlicensed subcontractor against the payment bond of the prime contractor and its surety would not be dismissed on a motion for summary judgment inasmuch as the unlicensed subcontractor was dealing with a licensed prime contractor and much as the unlicensed subcontractor was dealing with a licensed prime contractor and the entire project was under the supervision of the licensed project engineer. *Fillmore Prods., Inc. v. Western States Paving, Inc.*, 561 P. 2d 687 (Utah 1977).

VERMONT

1. AMOUNT OF BOND.—The penal sum of the additional bond is to be in such an amount as the Highway Board shall direct. (Title 19 U.S.A. § 4)

2. LABOR AND MATERIALS COVERED.—The additional bond is conditioned for the payment, settlement, liquidation and discharge of claims of all creditors of the contractor for materials, merchandise, labor, rent or hire of vehicles, power shovels, rollers, concrete-mixers, tools and other appliances, professional services, premiums and other services used or employed in carrying on the work, and is further conditioned for the payment of taxes, both state and municipal, and contributions to the state unemployment compensation commission accruing during the term of performance of said contract.

Recovery for professional services, premiums and other services was added by the amendment approved May 31, 1961.

3. NOTICE REQUIRED.—(a) *To surety:* No special statutory provision; see 4 below. (b) *To principal contractor:* No special statutory provision; see 4 below. (c) *To municipality:* The amendment approved May 31, 1961 reads that in order to obtain the benefit of such bond the claimant must file with the highway commissioner a sworn statement of his claim within 90 days after the final acceptance of the project by the State of Vermont or within 90 days from the time such taxes or contributions to the Vermont Employment Security Board are due and payable.

Prior to this amendment, the sworn statement was required to be filed within 90 days after claimant ceased to furnish the labor and material or equipment for which claim was made, or within 90 days from the time such taxes or contributions to the State unemployment compensation fund became due and payable.

4. TIME FOR SUIT.—Within one year after filing his claim with the Commissioner of Highways, claimant must institute suit on the bond, with notice and summons to the contractor, the surety and the Commissioner of Highways, to enforce such claim, or must intervene in a suit theretofore instituted. Such suit must be brought in the county where the creditor resides or, if he is a non-resident, in the county of Washington. Petitions to intervene shall be brought in any county where the prior suit is pending.

5. CONTRACTS EXCLUDED.—No special statutory provision.

6. PROCEDURE.—See 4 above. Where suit has been instituted, any other person who has filed a claim with the Commissioner of Highways may intervene therein by applying to the court in which such suit is instituted. The court in such case, before making final disposition of such petition, shall examine all claims which have arisen under the bond and which have been duly filed with the Commissioner of Highways and, after notice to all creditors who have filed claims, shall determine the respective amounts due such parties claimant and their rights to participate in the security, and shall apply said security to the claimants entitled thereto.

7. PENALTY FOR FAILURE TO TAKE BOND.—No special statutory provision.

8. REMARKS.—An amendment effective February 21, 1953 provides that no final payment shall be made under any public works contract until the contractor shall have duly filed in the appropriate public office a sworn statement setting forth that all claims for material and labor performed under the contract have been and are paid for the entire period of time for which the final payment is to be made. Disputed claims are to be so designated. Whereupon, the amount claimed to be due the laborer shall be deducted from the final payment and retained by the public body until the determination of the dispute and then paid by the public body to the person or persons found entitled thereto.

9. DECISIONS.—While there is no statute requiring a public works bond, where a public body requires the contractor to furnish a bond conditioned for the completion of the work and the payment of labor and material claims, the municipality may maintain an action in its name for the benefit of unpaid labor and materialmen. *Maryland Casualty Co. v. Portland Construction Co.,* 71 F.2d 658 (2d Cir. 1934).

Where an indemnity bond furnished for performance of contract to construct school buildings was conditioned in part on payment by contractor of all claims for material, and on subcontractors making payments for all labor performed and "services rendered" for them, material furnished to subcontractor was not within the quoted words and was not covered by the bond. *Town of Windsor for the use of Samson Plaster Board Co. v. Standard Accident Insurance Co.,* 112 Vt. 426, 26 A.2d 83 (1942).

A subcontractor is entitled to recover from the general contractor's performance bond surety the fair and reasonable value to the surety of the work performed and the materials furnished by the subcontractor prior to the contractor's default on the contract and the surety's undertaking of completion. However, the surety was entitled to withhold payment to the subcontractor's suppliers pending determination of the controversies between them and such withholding did not constitute tortious interference in the subcontractor's business relations with its suppliers. *Lev Spear Construction Co. v. Fidelity & Casualty Co.,* 446 F.2d 439 (2d Cir. 1971).

It was held that the fact that the Federal Department of Health, Education and Welfare made an annual grant to a state agency to partially fund the interest due on bonds to construct a college performing arts center, did not place the project within the Miller Act with the result that jurisdiction was not vested exclusively in the applicable Federal District Court. *Westinghouse Electric Supply Company, v. B. L. Allen, Inc.,* 135 Vt. 488, 380 A.2d 62 (1977).

VIRGINIA

The Virginia Public Procurement Act, § 11-35 et seq. of the Code of Virginia, which became effective on January 1, 1983, contains specific provisions dealing with bid bonds, performance bonds and payment bonds. The following introductory background reviews the law as it existed prior to the enactment of the Virginia Public Procurement Act.

Virginia has a separate performance and payment bond statute with respect to contracts for public works. In addition, the Virginia statute provides that no contractor, as a lowest responsible bidder to an authority, county, city, town school district or agency thereof shall subcontract any work required for the contract except under the following conditions:

Each subcontractor shall furnish, and the contractor shall require as a part of the agreement between the subcontractor and the contractor, a payment bond with surety thereon in the amount of fifty percent of the work sublet to the subcontractor which shall be conditioned upon the payment to all persons who have, and fulfill, contracts which are directly with the subcontractor for performing labor and furnishing materials in the prosecution of the work provided for in the subcontract. Every such bond shall be construed, regardless of its language, as incorporating, within its provisions, the obligation to pay those persons who furnish labor or materials, provided, however, that subcontracts between the contractor and a manufacturer or a fabricator shall be exempt from the provision requiring a payment bond and provided further that subcontracts for less than two thousand five hundred dollars each are also exempt. Provision for said payment bonds shall be made a part of each agreement between the owner and the contractor. In the event a contractor fails to require from a subcontractor the bond so provided for, any person who has and fulfills contracts directly with such subcontractor for performing labor and furnishing materials in the prosecution of the work provided for in the subcontract shall have a direct right of action against the obligors and sureties on the payment bond required of the contractor.

Persons who have, and fulfill, contracts which are directly with the contractor for performing labor and furnishing materials in the prosecution of construction work shall have a direct right of action against the obligors and sureties on the payment bond required of the contractor. Persons who have, and fulfill, contracts which are directly with subcontractors for performing labor and furnishing materials in the prosecution of the work provided for in the subcontract shall have a direct right of action against the obligors and sureties on the bond required of the subcontractors.

Effective June 1976, Virginia amended Section 11-23 of its Code, relating to the performance and payment bond required of contractors and the payment bond required of subcontractors on public work contracts with any authority, county, city, town, school board or any agency thereof, to include contracts for the construction, improvement or repair of water mains.

1. AMOUNT OF BOND.—The contract amount. (Code of Virginia, § 11-58.)
2. LABOR AND MATERIAL COVERED.—Labor performed and material furnished in the prosecution of the work.
3. NOTICE REQUIRED.—
   (a) *To surety*—No special statutory provision.
   (b) *To principal contractor*—No special statutory provision.
   (c) *To municipality*—No special statutory provision.
4. TIME FOR SUIT.—Any action on a payment bond must be brought within one year after the day on which the person bringing such action last performed labor or last furnished or supplied materials. (Code of Virginia, § 11-60.) Every such action shall be brought in a Virginia court of competent jurisdiction in and for the county or other political subdivision of the Commonwealth of Virginia in which the project, or any part thereof, is situated, or in the United States District Court for the district in which the project, or any part thereof, is situated, and not elsewhere.

In 1977 Virginia amended its Public Works Act to provide that suit shall be brought in a Virginia court of competent jurisdiction and the venue therefor shall be as specified in subdivision 6, of §8.01-261, or in the United States District Court for the district in which the project, or any part thereof, is situated, and not elsewhere.

5. CONTRACTS EXCLUDED.—Contracts of $100,000 or less, unless required by a public body. (Code of Virginia, § 11-58.)
6. REMARKS.—The Virginia highway code which required suit to be brought against the Department of Highways within one year after completion of the work on the project to the satisfaction of the chief engineer, Department of Highways, was amended in 1969 to include an additional provision which reads:

> "No suit or action shall be brought against the contractor or surety on any such contract or claim unless the same shall be brought within five years after the completion of the work on the project to the satisfaction of the chief engineer, Department of Highways."

Effective June 1976, Virginia amended and revised Title 33.1 of its Code, relating to limitation of suits and adjustment of claims on state highway contracts executed after June 30, 1976 to provide that no suit or action shall be brought against the contractor or surety on any such contract or claim unless the same shall be brought within five years after the completion of the work on the project to the satisfaction of the chief engineer, Department of Highways and Transportation.

7. DECISIONS.—Where a Virginia contractor furnished a school board a bond conditioned for payment of labor and material claims which bond required a claimant to give written notice to any two of the following: the contractor, the owner or the surety, within ninety days after claimant furnished the last of claimant's labor or material, and no such notice was given by a claimant who had sold and delivered building materials to a subcontractor, judgment in favor of the surety affirmed. *U. S. Plywood Corp. v. Continental Casualty Co.,* 157 A.2d 286 (D.C. 1960).

Materialman may recover against surety notwithstanding dispute between owner and contractor. *Phoenix Insurance Company v. Lester Brothers,* 203 Va. 802, 127 S.E.2d 432 (1962).

It is no defense to a claim by a supplier to a subcontractor under an A.I.A. form of payment bond that the contractor paid subcontractors under their respective subcontracts an aggregate amount greater than the penal sum of the payment bond. Neither the contractor nor the surety in this case presented evidence to show that the sums paid subcontractors were made as a result of claims presented under and against the payment bond. *Noland Company v. West End Realty Corporation,* 206 Va. 938, 147 S.E.2d 105 (1966).

Where the general contractor failed to require the statutory bond from a subcontractor, this subcontractor's supplier had a right of action against the general contractor and its surety even though the general contractor had paid the subcontractor. To be a subcontractor under the Virginia bond statute, it is not necessary that the person furnish both labor and material. *Vulcan Materials Company v. Betts,* 315 F. Supp. 1049 (W.D. Va. 1970), *aff'd.,* 451 F.2d 597 (4th Cir. 1971).

A subcontractor's materialman may recover under the general contractor's labor and materials payment bond containing coverage broader than that required by the statute, even though there was no evidence that the general contractor had failed to obtain a payment bond from the subcontractor. *Reliance Insurance Co. v. Trane Co.,* 212 Va. 394, 184 S.E.2d 817 (1971).

A statutory provision as to the time for suit is prohibitory of any other limitation. *Joseph R. Hughes & Co., Inc. v. George H. Robinson Corp.,* 211 Va. 4, 175 S.E.2d 413 (1970).

Where the general contractor on a public project failed to require a payment bond from a subcontractor and the subcontractor failed to pay the supplier, supplier's cause of action against the general contractor and its surety accrued when the supplier's work was completed and the subcontractor failed to pay, not when the contract between subcontractor and supplier was executed. *Johnson Service Co. v. Glaubke Construction Co., Inc.,* 213 Va. 466, 193 S.E.2d 655 (1973).

The intent of this section is to protect persons furnishing supplies, material and labor in and about the construction of the public improvement mentioned in the statute whether they be furnished to the principal contractor or to a subcontractor, and the statute will be liberally construed. *Thomas Somerville Co. v. Broyhill,* 200 Va. 358, 105 S.E.2d 824 (1958).

Prime contractor failed to require its subcontractor to furnish a bond. Material supplier rented subcontractor steel sheet pilings which were used in the project, some of which subcontractor failed to return. It was held that the unpaid rental charges and the missing materials which subcontractor did not return were within the statutory definition of "furnishing materials" thereby making prime contractor and its surety liable. *R. C. Stanhope, Inc. v. Roanoke Construction Co.,* 539 F.2d 992 (4th Cir. 1976).

Supplier of materials to subcontractor was not required to trace his material into the project in order to be projected by general contractor's bond. *Solite Masonry Units v. Piland Construction Co.,* 217 Va. 727, 232 S.E.2d 759 (1977).

Proceeding by a prime contractor on a state highway construction contract against its railing subcontractor and its performance bond surety in which the subcontractor counterclaimed for damages. On appeal it was held that the evidence showed that the prime contractor's delays prevented the performance by the subcontractor and, therefore, the subcontractor was entitled to damages for lost profits, prime contractor's claim being dismissed. *R. G. Pope Construction Co. v. Guard Rail of Roanoke,* 219 Va. 111, 244 S.E.2d 774 (1978).

Owner of land adjacent to site of state highway contract was held not to be a third party beneficiary of the performance bond issued by the general contractor with the result that the surety was held not to be liable for damages done by contractor to the adjoining land. *Richmond Shopping Center, Inc. v. Wiley N. Jackson Co.,* 220 Va. 135, 255 S.E.2d 518 (1979).

It was held that a school board could not recover its attorney's fees in establishing its basic claim of breach of contract or in proving the elements of damages for such breach against the defaulting contractor and its performance bond surety. It was further held that the contractor and its surety were given due credit for the reasonable usable value of materials on hand when the contract was terminated and the owner informed bidders that it could use the materials which the defaulted contractor had left on the site. Contractor and surety were held not to be entitled to a credit for state sales taxes paid by completing contractor. Court further held that the contractor and its surety were not liable for the estimated value of a one year warranty and that liquidated damages was the proper measure of delay damages. *Ranger Construction Co. v. Prince William County,* 605 F.2d 1298 (4th Cir. 1979).

WASHINGTON

1. AMOUNT OF BOND.—Full contractor price, except in cases of cities and towns, in which case the municipality may, by general ordinance, fix and determine the amount of the bond, provided same shall not be less than 25% of contract price. See Remarks (Section 9). (Revised Code of Washington Annotated 39.08.030)

2. LABOR AND MATERIAL COVERED.—The bond is conditioned for the payment of laborers, mechanics, subcontractors and materialmen, and all persons who shall supply such person or persons with provisions or supplies for the carrying on, prosecution or doing of any public work.

An amendment approved March 21, 1967 provides that the statutory provision shall not apply to any money loaned or advanced to any such contractor.

3. NOTICE REQUIRED.—(a) *To surety*—No special statutory provision. (b) *To principal contractor*—Every person, firm or corporation furnishing materials, supplies or provisions shall, not later than ten days after the date of the first delivery of such materials, supplies or provisions to any subcontractor or agent of any person, firm or corporation having a subcontract for the construction, performance, carrying on, prosecution or doing of such work, deliver or mail to the contractor a notice in writing, stating, in substance and effect, that such person, firm or corporation has commenced to deliver materials, supplies or provisions for use thereon, with the name of the subcontractor or agent ordering or to whom the same is furnished, and that such contractor and his bond will be held for the payment of the same. No suit may be maintained in any court against the contractor

or his bond to recover for such material, supplies or provisions or any part thereof unless this notice has been given. (c) *To municipality*—Credit shall not have any right of action on the bond unless, within thirty days from and after the completion of the contract with an acceptance of the work by the executive action of the municipal officers, the creditor shall present to and file with such public official a notice in writing in substance of claim. This notice must be signed by the person or corporation making the claim or giving the notice, and, after being presented and filed, the notice becomes a public record. (d) *To creditors*—No special statutory provision.

4. TIME FOR SUIT.—No special statutory provision.
5. CONTRACT EXCLUDED.—Under $25,000.
6. PROCEDURE.—Notice must be given to the proper municipal officers within thirty days from and after the completion of the contract. See Notice to Municipality above.
7. PENALTY FOR FAILURE TO TAKE BOND.—Municipality is liable to all persons authorized to sue on the bond to the full extent and for the full amount of all debts due them by the contractor.
8. SPECIAL PROVISIONS.—Bond is filed with County Auditor of the county where such work is performed or improvement made, except in cases of cities or towns. In such cases, the bond is filed with the Clerk or Comptroller thereof.

Statute has no application to any money loaned or advanced to any such laborers or materialmen.

The municipality is required to retain a sum not to exceed 5% of the contract price as a trust fund for the protection and payment of materialmen. This fund is retained for a period of thirty days following final acceptance of the work, and every person performing labor or furnishing supplies toward the completion of said improvement or work has a lien upon the fund, provided due notice of the lien of such claimant is given, as provided under notice to municipality above. Where, in any improvement, the contract price exceeds $100,000, but 5% shall be reserved on estimates in excess of said sum.

After the expiration of thirty days following the final acceptance of the improvement and the expiration of the time for filing lien claims, said reserve or all amount thereof in excess of a sufficient sum to meet and discharge the claims of materialmen and laborers who have filed proper claims, with a sum sufficient to defray the cost of such action and attorneys' fees, shall be paid to the contractor. Persons filing a lien claim against said reserve fund have four months from the time of filing claims against the said fund in which to bring an action for the foreclosure of such lien. If the lien claimant fails to bring an action within the said four months, the reserve fund is discharged from the lien of said claimant and the moneys so held are required to be forthwith paid to the contractor. However, the limitation of four months is not a limitation upon the right to sue the contractor or his surety where no right of foreclosure against the fund is sought.

In 1977, Washington amended its Code relating to the retainage on public works contracts to provide that the state, county, municipality or other public body, 30 days after completion and acceptance of all contract work other than landscaping, may release and pay in full the amounts retained during the performance of the contract (other than continuing retention of five percent of the monies earned for landscaping) subject to the other provision of the Code relating to the payment to contractors of amounts in excess of any liens.

In order to participate in such preferred fund, the creditor must qualify as a lien claimant by giving the statutory notice of claim of lien. *Denham v. Pioneer Sand & Gravel Co.*, 104 Wash. 357, 176 P. 333 (1918).

A materialman who admits he is not endeavoring to enforce any statutory liability against the surety has no rights against a trust fund established by the contractor, his sureties and a bank for the payment of labor and material bills and loans made in connection with the project. *Fuller & Co. v. Sheble Construction Co.*, 198 Wash. 84, 87 P.2d 287 (1939).

9. REMARKS.—An Act approved March 26, 1963 provides with respect to contracts for public improvements or work by the state or any political subdivision thereof for a reserve from moneys earned by the contractor on progress estimates, a sum equal to 10% of such estimate which sum is to be retained by the public body as a trust fund for the protection and payment of persons who shall perform labor upon such contract and who shall supply such persons or subcontractors with provisions and supplies for the carrying on of such work and for the benefit of the state with respect to taxes imposed pursuant to Title 82 which may be due from such contractor. This percentage was decreased to a maximum of five in 1982. Said funds shall be retained for a period of 30 days following the final acceptance of the work and every person performing labor or furnishing supplies toward the completion of such work, is given a lien on the fund so reserved provided that notice of lien of such claimant shall have been given as required by Washington statutes, now existing or hereinafter amended.

After 50% satisfactory completion, the contractor may request that retainage be reduced to 100% of the value of the work remaining on the project.

The Flood Control Act of 1935 requires any person except the State of Washington or the United States to whom a contract may have been awarded by a Flood Control District for construction purposes to enter a bond to the State of Washington with good and sufficient surety for at least seventy-five per cent of the contract price, conditioned for the faithful performance of said contract and with such further provisions as are required by law.

On March 21, 1967 an amendment was adopted providing that the respective public entity might in lieu of the bond retain 100% of the contract amount for a period of 30 days after date of final acceptance or until receipt of all necessary releases from the tax commission and the department of labor and industries.

Effective June 10, 1982, at the option of the contractor, the public entity may in lieu of the bond retain 50% (instead of 100%) of the contract amount for the 30 day period.

In 1979, Washington amended its statute to increase the threshold of contracts let by sewer districts and water districts requiring bonds from $5,000 to $12,500.

10. DECISIONS.—The fact that some work was done after acceptance of a building as completed does not show fraud on the part of the Port Commission in accepting the work by a resolution which was made a public record, so that the filing of a claim against the contractor's bond thirty-one days thereafter was too late. *Pearson v. Puget Sound Machinery Depot*, 99 Wash. 596, 169 P. 961 (1918).

Acceptance of work done under a county highway construction contract by resolution of the board of county commissioners after partial completion of the project starts the running of the thirty-day period for filing notice in writing of the claim with the proper municipal authorities. *Hazard v. C. E. O'Neill Co.*, 6 Wash. 2d 667, 108 P.2d 660 (1940).

Under the statute providing that claims by laborers, mechanics, and others on bond executed by person contracting with public bodies must be filed within thirty days after acceptance of work by affirmative action of governmental body, the statutory period starts running after date of acceptance, absolute and final in its terms, even though a small amount of work remains to be done on contract. *National Blower & Sheet Metal Co. v. American Surety Co. of New York*, 41 Wash. 2d 260, 248 P.2d 547 (1952).

Where acceptance by school board was conditional upon performance by contractor of certain enumerated work called for by contract, it was not "acceptance" within statute providing that laborers, mechanics, and others must file claim with governmental body within thirty days after acceptance of work by affirmative action of governmental body in order to have right of action on bond executed by contractor. *National Blower & Sheet Metal Co. v. American Surety Co. of New York*, 41 Wash. 2d 260, 248 P.2d 547 (1952).

Where a contract is not completed by the contractor, the claimant is required to file this notice with the municipal officers within a reasonable time after the work was discontinued. *Puget Sound Bridge & Dredging Co. v. Jahn & Bressi*, 148 Wash. 37, 268 P. 169 (1928).

A claim filed a year and a half after the beginning of adjustment between the county and the contractor should not be allowed, even though the job was not completed by the contractor, as the claim was not filed within a reasonable time after discontinuance of the work. *Hazard v. C. E. O'Neill Co.*, 6 Wash. 667, 108 P.2d 660 (1940).

A subcontractor's claim against statutory bond given for performance of construction contract with school district should have been filed with the school district, and hence only letters from subcontractor to school district could be considered in determining whether the statute requiring notice had been complied with so as to give subcontractor a cause of action on the bond. *Fidelity & Deposit Co. of Maryland v. Conway, Inc.*, 14 Wash. 551, 128 P.2d 764 (1942).

Actual notice to the surety of claim against performance bond cannot take the place of the written notice required by statute to be filed with the body to whom bond was given in order to entitle claimant to sue on the bond. *Fidelity & Deposit Co. of Maryland v. Conway, Inc.*, 14 Wash. 2d 551, 128 P.2d 764 (1942).

A claim for first-aid equipment furnished to a subcontractor and for maintenance of a first-aid station equipped with X-ray, medicine, physicians, etc., is unenforceable as a claim for labor, provisions or supplies. *Western Clinic & Hospital Assn. v. Gabriel Construction Co.*, 168 Wash. 411, 12 P.2d 417 (1932).

A highway contractor's improper use of blasting powder would not absolve the surety on his bond from liability for the cost of powder purchased. *Randanite Co. v. Smith*, 172 Wash. 390, 20 P.2d 33 (1933).

A notice sent to a public official is an insufficient basis for recovery against the contractor's surety where the notice contained no indication that the claimant looked to the surety. *U. S. Fidelity & Guaranty Co. v. Port of Seattle*, 169 Wash. 19, 13 P.2d 33 (1932).

A surety is not estopped from denying a tardy claim for material furnished because it has joint control of the contractor's bank account and has countersigned certain checks. *U. S. Fidelity & Guaranty Co. v. Port of Seattle,* 169 Wash. 19, 13 P.2d 33 (1932).

A materialman has a lien against the retained percentage in addition to his right upon the bond. His right under the bond is not lost by his failure to bring an action within four months to foreclose his lien on the retained percentage. *U. S. Fidelity & Guaranty Co. v. Montesano,* 160 Wash. 565, 295 P. 934 (1931).

An irrigation district is a municipal corporation within the meaning of the bond statute. *Brown Bros. v. Columbia Irrigation District,* 82 Wash. 274, 144 P. 74 (1914).

Recovery may be had for fuel for steamshovels used in excavating, for services performed by teams with drivers furnished to the contractor, and for hay and grain to feed the horses. *National Surety Co. v. Bratnober Lumber Co.,* 67 Wash. 601, 122 P. 337 (1912).

The bond covers a claim for provisions supplied to a contractor for his boarding camp where the camp was necessarily operated by the contractor because of the inaccessible location of the project. *McDonald Bros. & Metcalfe v. Maryland Casualty Co.,* 150 Wash. 386, 273 P. 192 (1928).

However, room and board furnished to laborers of highway contractor are not provisions and supplies for the carrying on of the work covered by the bond where the project was not located in a distant or inaccessible place and rooms and boarding from persons other than the contractor were available. *Rogers v. Rowland,* 168 Wash. 148, 10 P.2d 988 (1932).

A subcontract to haul all the sand, gravel and cement used in county road improvement is an agreement to furnish labor and it is not necessary to give notice within ten days as is required of persons supplying material. *Bishop v. Ryan Construction Co.,* 106 Wash. 254, 180 P. 126 (1919).

The reserve fund retained from the contract price is a trust fund for the benefit of materialmen, laborers and the surety. Failure by materialman paid by surety to file a lien against such trust fund does not defeat the surety's right to recover the amount of such payments from the fund. *U. S. Fidelity & Guaranty Co. v. Montesano,* 160 Wash. 565, 295 P. 934 (1931).

Damage to the surety from wrongful payment of fund reserved from contract price is the amount of the fund wrongfully paid the contractor, and the surety may sue the city as a result of such payment of these trust funds. *U. S. Fidelity & Guaranty Co. v. Montesano,* 160 Wash. 565, 295 P. 934 (1931).

One who merely supplies gravel to a contractor is a materialman and not a subcontractor within the meaning of the bond statute, and persons supplying such materialmen with labor or material have no right to recover under the principal contractor's bond. *Northwest Roads Co. v. Clyde Equipment Co.,* 79 F.2d 771 (9th Cir. 1935). In this case, a claim was denied for rental of machinery used by such materialman in furnishing crushed rock needed in the performance of a road construction project.

Under the ordinary statutory bond, recovery is limited to such materials as were consumed in or became part of the work. However, where the bond incorporates by reference the building contract, which gives the term "materials" a broader definition, recovery will be allowed for tires and tubes used on the job though not consumed, as well as for lanterns, wire brush, pipe dies and generator. *Western Steel Casting Co. v. Edland,* 187 Wash. 666, 61 P.2d 155 (1936).

A provision in a contract prohibiting assignments without the written consent of the public body does not in any way affect the right of a materialman to recover on the bond for material furnished to a subcontractor. The award of a subcontract is not an assignment within the meaning of the clause prohibiting assignments. *Crane Co. v. Musgrave & Blake,* 102 Wash. 59, 172 P. 866 (1918).

Where the original contractor fails to file his subcontracts as required by law, he thereby waives the right to notice within ten days after the first delivery of materials from persons who furnish material to a subcontractor, and a materialman who did not give such notice but who did, after completion of the work and within thirty days after acceptance thereof by the board of county commissioners, file claims against the bond and the fund to be paid by the county to the original contractor, has a right to payment out of said fund and under said bond. *Cascade Construction Co. v. Snohomish County,* 105 Wash. 484, 178 P. 470 (1919).

Under a statute requiring contractors for public work to give a bond to pay for labor, provisions and supplies, rent for machinery leased to state highway contractor was "provisions and supplies." *U. S. Fidelity & Guaranty Co. v. Feenaughty Machinery Co.,* 197 Wash. 569, 85 P.2d 1085 (1938).

The test of whether a given thing constitutes a "supply" or "equipment" within statutes relating to public contractors' bonds and materialmen's liens is whether the article forms a part of the finished structure; and in addition if, although such things do not become a physical part of the finished product, structure or improvement, they are entirely consumed in the course of the construction, they are "supplies" and not "equipment." *U. S. Fidelity & Guaranty Co. v. Feenaughty Machinery Co.,* 197 Wash. 569, 85 P.2d 1085 (1938).

Where the construction contract with the city authorized subcontracts to which the city should give its consent, a partnership hired by the contractor to do all the general work was a subcontractor and not the contractor's general agent. Hence persons furnishing material to the partnership and not giving the ten-day notice that they were commencing to deliver material were not entitled to relief against the contractor and the surety on the contractor's bond. Nevertheless, such persons who had not given the contractor said ten-day notice could participate in the percentage retained by the city and deposited in court under the contract with the principal contractor where the statute relating to retained percentages did not require such notice. *Maryland Casualty Co. v. City of Tacoma,* 199 Wash. 72, 90 P.2d 226 (1939).

The requirement for notice under the statute is not complied with by the mailing of a letter to the public officials inclosing a statement of the account due the claimant without any mention of the surety or the filing of a formal notice as required by said section. *Standard Accident Insurance Co. v. Interlocking File Corp.,* 166 Wash. 260, 6 P.2d 383 (1932).

Where contractors and city prior to completion of work on sewage disposal plant entered into supplemental contract stating that existing contract should be terminated but that supplemental contract did not alter contractors' obligation under existing contract which had been accepted as completed on preceding day, there was no "completion of the contract" so as to require *filing of notice* of claim with City Clerk within 30 days by subcontractors who had previously furnished supplies to contractors. *U. S. Pipe & Foundry Co. v. Goerig,* 31 Wash. 2d 22, 195 P.2d 91 (1948).

The purpose of the statutory requirement that a materialman of subcontractor on municipal construction project notify prime contractor in writing within 10 days that he has commenced to deliver material is to enable prime contractor to protect himself against obligations of the subcontractor. Where the materialman has failed to give the statutory notice, the materialman has been denied recovery under the public works contractor's bond. While such a statutory requirement may be waived by the prime contractor the burden is on the materialman to show facts constituting the waiver. *Austin v. Wilder Co.,* 65 Wash. 2d 456, 397 P.2d 1019 (1965).

A sub-subcontractor has no right of action on a surety bond furnished by the subcontractor to the prime contractor which provides for the payment to all persons supplying labor and material and other obligations incurred by the subcontractor which bond of the subcontractor expressed no intention that persons in claimant's position should have a right to sue thereon. A third party supplier of labor or material has no right of action against a common law bond in private construction unless the terms of the bond expressly give that right. *Brower Co. v. Noise Control of Seattle, Inc.,* 66 Wash. 2d 204, 401 P.2d 860 (1965).

Notice construed to constitute substantial compliance with statutory requirement. *Foremost-McKesson Systems, etc. v. Nevis,* 8 Wash. App. 300, 505 P.2d 1284 (1973).

Where the sum tendered by the contractor on a public improvement to a supplier did not include accrued costs, the supplier was not prevented from recovering attorney's fees, interest and costs under a statute allowing attorney's fees. *C-Star Concrete Corp. v. Hawaiian Insurance Co.,* 8 Wash. App. 872, 509 P.2d 758 (1973).

Under the statute which requires notices of claims against the bonds of contractors for public work projects to substantially comply with the form contained therein, a notice is sufficient if it is directed to the proper body, if it is filed within 30 days from the completion of the contract and the acceptance of the work, if it identifies the bond, surety and the work involved, and if it gives some notice of an intent to claim against the bond. *Foremost-McKesson Systems Division of Foremost-McKesson, Inc. v. Nevis,* 8 Wash. App. 300, 505 P.2d 1284 (1973).

Subcontractor's unpaid union fringe benefits were recoverable under statutory payment bond, upon the ground that the union trustee claimants stood in the shoes of the laborers of the insolvent subcontractor in question. *James Crabtree v. LeNay Lewis,* 86 Wash. 2d 282, 544 P.2d 10 (1975).

Where the City's purported acceptance of a bid changed the time of performance in a material manner not implied in the original offer, no enforceable contract was created and, therefore, the bidder's refusal to perform did not constitute a breach. *City of Roslyn v. Paul E. Hughes Construction Co.,* 19 Wash. App. 59, 573 P.2d 385 (1978).

Supplier of pumps to a contractor on a county sewer project was permitted to recover the price of pumps; the contractor was entitled to an offset for failure of the supplier to make warranty repairs and performance tests, and statutory attorney's fees were denied as the surety had no such adverse interest in the case as would justify an award. *Lakeside Pump & Equipment, Inc., v. Austin Construction Co.,* 89 Wash. 2d 839, 576 P.2d 392 (1978).

A delayed payment clause in a contract between the general contractor and its subcontractor would be construed to mean that payment to the subcontractor will only be postponed for a reasonable time. Hence, where a prime's contract had been canceled, and the question of the prime's default was still in litigation some years after cancellation, a finding that a reasonable time had expired was proper, and that the provision making the prime liable for reasonable value of the subcontractor's work on cancellation based liability on *quantum meruit* rather than a fraction of the subcontract price, an allowance of profit to the subcontractor was within the range of evidence of reasonable profit. *Amelco Electric v. Donald M. Drake Co.,* 20 Wash. App. 899, 583 P.2d 648 (1978).

The record supported the trial court's determination that a bidder acted in good faith, without gross negligence, gave prompt notice of discovery of error in bid; and that bidder would suffer substantial loss unless relieved of its bid error, whereas the town, when informed of the error, had not greatly changed its position and could have avoided damage. Hence, the bidder was relieved of his bid. *Town of LaConner v. American Construction Co.,* 21 Wash. App. 336, 585 P.2d 162 (1978).

WEST VIRGINIA

1. AMOUNT OF BOND.—In contracts for the construction, alteration or repair of public buildings other than school edifices, penal sum equal at least to the reasonable cost of the materials, machinery, equipment and labor required for the completion of said contract. In the case of highway work, in such penal sum as the State Road Commissioner shall require, but not to exceed the contract price. A bond in double the amount of the contract price is required in connection with contracts for the building or repair of school property. (West Virginia Code § 18-5-12, § 17-4-20, § 38-2-39.)

2. LABOR AND MATERIAL COVERED.—All materials, machinery, equipment and labor delivered to the contractor for use in the erection, construction, improvement, alteration or repair of any public building used or to be used for public purposes. All material, gas, oil, repairs, supplies, equipment and labor used in and about the performance of a highway contract. Effective May 27, 1971, the statute with respect to highway contractors' bonds was amended to cover claims for "all material, gas, oil, repairs, supplies, tires, equipment, rental charges for equipment and charges for the use of equipment, and labor used by him in and about the performance of such contract, or which reasonably appeared, at the time of delivery or performance, would be substantially consumed in and about the performance of such contract." See Section 8, Special Provisions below.

3. NOTICE REQUIRED.—No special statutory provision.

4. TIME FOR SUIT.—No special statutory provision.

5. CONTRACTS EXCLUDED.—No special statutory provision, except that no bond is required with contracts for the building or repairing of school property where the contract price does not exceed $100.

6. PROCEDURE.—No special statutory provision.

7. PENALTY FOR FAILURE TO TAKE BOND.—No special statutory provision. A county court was held not to be liable at the suit of an assignee of a Mechanic's Lien creditor for acceptance of a contract without a bond. *Moss Iron Works v. Jackson County Court,* 89 W.Va. 367, 109 S.E. 343 (1921).

8. SPECIAL PROVISIONS.—The statutes above abstracted deal with public works. As a general rule public property is not subject to Mechanic's Liens, such encumbrances being contrary to public policy.

The separate Mechanic's Lien Law dealing with private projects provides that any owner may limit his ability with respect to such Mechanic's Liens by recording his agreement with the general contractor in the office of the Clerk of the County Court wherein such building is situate prior to the beginning of construction thereof and by requiring to be given by his general contractor and by recording with such general contract a surety bond in a penalty equal to the contract price, conditioned that in the event any laborer, materialman or other person having perfected his lien be deprived by the recordation of the owner's contract from receiving from such owner the amount of his lien (out of the unpaid portion of the contract price), then such surety bond shall be responsible to such lienor for the amount not collected by such lienor from the owner or from the property.

Where the contract and bond were recorded under the provisions of this section a person furnishing materials to a subcontractor cannot recover therefor on the bond without complying with the Mechanic's Lien Law. *Atlas Powder Co. v. Nelson,* 124 W.Va. 298, 20 S.E.2d 890 (1942).

Where the claimant has failed to comply with the statutes requiring him to give notice of his lien to the owner, claimant is not entitled to recover under the contractor's bond even though the bond was broader than required by the statute. *Fireproof Products Co. v. Logan,* 113 W.Va. 703, 169 S.E. 400 (1933). *Williams Company v. Bailey,* 68 W.Va. 681, 70 S.E. 696 (1911).

Although the language of this section is broad, it is not applicable to state agencies or public buildings. *Moss Iron Works v. Jackson County Court,* 89 W.Va. 367, 109 S.E. 343 (1921).

This section does not require a bond to be given for the payment of all mechanics' and materialmen's liens. The statutory form is so worded but the courts look to the requirement of the statute itself and not to such form. *Bluefield Supply Co. v. Smith Construction Co.,* 115 W.Va. 537, 177 S.E. 296 (1934).

9. DECISIONS.—Recovery may not be had for foodstuffs furnished to employees of road contractor upon latter's order under the bond securing payment of wages due or materials furnished, where it does not appear that there were circumstances of necessity or a contractual undertaking which required contractor to furnish groceries for his employees. *Bowling v. Julian Const. Co.,* 110 W.Va. 275, 158 S.E. 165 (1931).

Recovery may be had for repairs incidental to the use of subcontractors' regular equipment while employed in construction of road. *National Equipment Corp. v. Pinnell,* 114 W.Va. 558, 172 S.E. 790 (1933).

The State Road Commission is a "legal body" required by statute to obtain a public improvement bond. *Rhoades v. Riley,* 113 W.Va. 679, 169 S.E. 525 (1933).

A surety is not liable for either the purchase price or rental of a tractor which should be part of a highway contractor's regular equipment. *Rhoades v. Riley,* 113 W.Va. 679, 169 S.E. 525 (1933). *National Equipment Corp. v. Pinnell,* 114 W.Va. 558, 172 S.E. 790 (1933).

A person furnishing material to a subcontractor may maintain an action on a surety performance bond given by the subcontractor to the principal contractor where such bond provided that the subcontractor would pay the claims of "all and every person furnishing material or performing labor in and about the construction" of the project. *Standard Oil Co. of New Jersey v. Smith,* 116 W.Va. 16, 178 S.E. 281 (1935).

A principal contractor and his surety are not liable to a person who did not furnish labor or material either to the general contractor or to a subcontractor. Claimant in this case was a person who had furnished labor and material to another surety company which had bonded a defaulting subcontractor, which later surety undertook to complete its principal's subcontract. *Rosenbaum v. Price Constr. Co.,* 117 W.Va. 160, 184 S.E. 261 (1936).

One who furnishes labor and material to a person who in turn furnishes stone to a general contractor may not recover under the bond of the general contractor. Recovery may not be had under the bond of the general contractor for material furnished to or work performed for a materialman, even though that materialman contracts directly with the principal contractor. *Marsh v. Rothey,* 117 W.Va. 94, 183 S.E. 914 (1936).

West Virginia Code does not require claimant to give notice to or to make claim against funds retained by the state prior to asserting claim on bond. *Ben-Tom Supply Co. v. V.N. Green & Co.,* 338 F. Supp. 59 (S.D.W.V. 1971).

Although a statutory bond given by a highway contractor to secure the payment of "all repairs" will be liberally construed, the surety's obligation will not be extended to cover repairs to equipment which are of a major nature adding substantially to the value of the equipment which are of a major nature adding substantially to the value of the equipment unless the repairs either are reasonably expected to be substantially consumed in and about the performance, of the contract, or were in fact substantially consumed in and about the performance of the contract for which the bond was given. *Cecil I. Walker Machinery Co. v. Stauben, Inc.,* 230 S.E.2d 818 (W.Va. 1976).

WISCONSIN

1. AMOUNT OF BOND.—Not less than contract price. (Wisconsin Statutes Annotated § 779.14)

2. LABOR AND MATERIAL COVERED.—All labor or material furnished, used or consumed in making a public improvement or performing a public work, including fuel, lumber, building materials, machinery, vehicles, tractors, equipment, fixtures, apparatus, tools, appliances, supplies, electric energy, gasoline and other motor oil, lubricating oils and greases, and premiums for workmen's compensation insurance, and the contributions for unemployment compensation.

3. NOTICE REQUIRED.—No special statutory provision.

4. TIME FOR SUIT.—No later than one year after the completion of the work under the contract. This period of limitation began to run against a contractor from the date of completion of the work under the principal contract, not from the earlier completion of the work under the subcontract. *Honeywell, Inc. v. Aetna Casualy & Surety Co.,* 52 Wis. 2d 425, 190 N.W.2d 499 (1971).

5. CONTRACTS EXCLUDED.—All contracts with state for amount less than $2,500 and all other contracts involving less than $500. On state contracts, Department of Administration may waive bond requirement if there are adequate guarantees.

6. PROCEDURE.—Any party in interest may, within one year after the completion and acceptance of the contract, maintain an action in his own name against the contractor and the sureties upon

the bond. If the amount realized on the bond is insufficient to satisfy all of the claims in full of the parties in interest, the parties prorate.

7. PENALTY FOR FAILURE TO TAKE BOND.—No special statutory provision. However, in *Cowin & Co. v. Merrill,* 202 Wisc. 614, 233 N.W. 561 (1930), it is decided that the bond required by the statute is mandatory and that a municipality entering into a contract without requiring the contractor to give bond for the payment of materialmen is liable to the materialmen not paid by the contractor.

8. SPECIAL PROVISIONS.—Any person furnishing any material, as defined in subdivision 2 above, to any contractor for public improvements in this state, except in cities of the first class, however organized, may have a lien on the money, bonds or warrants due or to become due to the contractor for such improvement, provided such person shall, before payment is made to the contractor, notify the public officials whose duty it is to pay such contractor of his claim by written notice. It is the duty of such official so notified to withhold a sufficient amount to pay such claims until the same are established and thereafter to pay the amount thereof to the claimant. Any officer violating this duty is liable on his official bond to the persons serving such notice for the damages resulting from such violation. Persons serving such notice will be paid pro rata in proportion to the amounts due under their respective contracts.

As of June 1, 1974 the statute relating to construction lien rights given a payment bond was amended to provide that in any case where the prime contractor, pursuant to agreement with the owner, has furnished a payment bond, all liens except those of any prime contractor do not exist. The statute pertaining to the elimination of lien rights where the contractor has furnished a surety bond conditioned for the payment of labor and material claims, was also amended as of June 1, 1974.

In 1975, Wisconsin amended its statute with respect to contracts for which a performance bond is required to require that all such contracts contain a provision authorizing the Board, in case the work under any contract is defaulted or not completed within the time required, to take charge or authorize the surety to take charge of the work and to finish it at the expense of the contractor and the sureties, and to apply the amounts retained from estimates to the completion of the work.

Effective June 1976, Wisconsin amended its statute with respect to public work contracts of "municipalities" to require that contracts exceeding $1,000 be awarded to the lowest responsible bidder. Said amendment also states that the retainage on such contracts shall be ten percent until fifty percent of the work has been completed. After fifty percent completion, no additional amounts may be retained unless the architect or engineer certifies that the job is not proceeding satisfactorily. Upon substantial completion of the work, an amount retained may be paid to the contractor. When the work has been substantially completed except for work which cannot be completed because of excusable conditions, the municipality may make additional payments, retaining at all times an amount sufficient to cover the estimated cost of the work still to be completed, or in the alternative, may pay out the entire amount retained and receive from the contractor guarantees in the form of a bond or other collateral sufficient to insure completion of the job.

It is further provided that the term, municipality, shall mean the State, except the Department of Transportation, and any town, city, village, county, school district, vocational, technical and adult education district, board of school directors, sewer district, drainage district, or any other public or quasi-public corporation, officer, board or other public body.

9. DECISIONS.—A public works contractor is not liable to a subcontractor's subcontractor for labor and material furnished in the construction of a state bridge. In Wisconsin, recovery is denied remote furnishers of material, whose participation in the matter is unknown to the principal contractor. *Gilson Bros. Co. v. Worden-Allen Co.,* 220 Wis. 347, 265 N.W. 217 (1936).

The term "claim," as used in statutes dealing with "claims" against moneys due highway contractors from the state, is more comprehensive than "lien" and includes non-lienable items so long as they are germane to performing contracts on public work. *Morris F. Fox & Co. v. State,* 229 Wis. 44, 281 N.W. 666 (1938).

Recovery may be had for machinery, fuel or lumber used in whole or in part in making a public improvement, as well as for the reasonable rental value or use value of machinery required in the construction of the public improvement. However, such material or machinery must be furnished for employment or use upon the public improvement with respect to which the bond was given or with respect to which a lien is claimed on the contractor's funds. Recovery under the bond may not be had, neither may a lien be maintained on funds due or to become due the contractor, for the purchase price of machinery. *Osgood Co. v. Peterson Construction Co.,* 231 Wis. 541, 286 N.W. 54 (1939).

A contract to furnish sand and gravel to city, by which the surety guaranteed performance by the contractor and agreed to pay all claims for work or labor performed and material furnished

STATE BOND LAWS   31-117

in and about such contract, was enforceable in an action of law by a third party beneficiary able to bring himself within its terms. *Knuth v. Fidelity & Casualty Co. of New York,* 275 Wis. 603, 83 N.W.2d 126 (1957).

Subcontractor's cause of action to recover directly from town for materials supplied to principal contractor who had not been required by town to give bond to protect subcontractor as required by statute was barred because of failure of subcontractor to file notice of claim against town as required by statute. *Smith v. Town of Pershing,* 10 Wis.2d 352, 102 N.W.2d 765 (1960).

The Wisconsin Building Corporation was held not to be a "public board or body" and university dormitory construction not to be a "public improvement." *Blaser & Kammer vs. Don Ganser and Associates, Inc.,* 19 Wis. 2d 403, 120 N.W.2d, 629 (1963) 4 F.S.N., §151, 4 F.S.N., §143 and §149.

Even though a supplier of the subcontractor or of the contractor on a high school construction project was not entitled to statutory lien, nevertheless in view of the labor and material payment bond's broader definition of claimant as one having a direct contract with the principal or with a subcontractor of the principal for labor or material used in performance of the contract, the supplier of the subcontractor was a "claimant" and could recover under the bond. *Peabody Seating Co., Inc. v. Jim Cullen, Inc.,* 56 Wis. 2d 119, 201 N.W.2d 546 (1972).

Where the labor material payment bond defined a claimant as one having a direct contract with the principal or with a subcontractor of the principal, a supplier to a subcontractor was deemed to be a claimant who could recover under the bond. *Peabody Seating Co. v. Jim Cullen, Inc.,* 56 Wis. 2d 119, 201 N.W.2d 546 (1972).

Sewage Commission was not entitled to damages against sewer contractor and its performance bond surety for failure to complete project when records showed that the contractor was entitled to relief under the changed conditions' clause of the contract, and the Commission failed to negotiate an adjustment when the contractor's costs were so greatly increased by the changed condition that he could not continue without financial assistance or an adjustment. *Metropolitan Sewerage Commission v. R. W. Construction, Inc.,* 72 Wis. 2d 365, 241 N.W.2d 371 (1976).

Where bank knew that the funds it was receiving from general contractor were proceeds of a public improvement contract, the bank had an obligation to inquire regarding the claims of unpaid suppliers and to hold the funds for the benefit of unpaid workers or materialmen. *Schneider Fuel and Supply Co. v. West Allis State Bank,* 70 Wis. 2d 1041, 236 N.W.2d 266 (1975).

Was held that the Wisconsin statute which allows relief from bid mistakes only applies when the mistake of the contractor was "free from carelessness, negligence or inexcusable neglect." Bidders claim of an error in the amount of $378,000 was rejected. *Nelson, Inc. v. Sewerage Commission,* 72 Wis. 2d 400, 241 N.W.2d 390 (1976).

WYOMING

1. AMOUNT OF BONDS.—Not less than one-half of the contract price, except where such price exceeds $100,000 in which case the bond shall be in such amount as the officer awarding the contract deems sufficient. (Wyoming Statutes Annotated, Vol. 5 § 16-6-112)

2. LABOR AND MATERIAL COVERED.—In February of 1963 the Code was amended to allow recovery for goods of any kind which were totally or partially used or expended in the execution of the contract. The coverage prior to this amendment read as follows:

Under an amendment effective April 1, 1957, whenever any contract is entered into by the State or any political subdivision thereof for public buildings or public work, where the contract price exceeds the sum of $500 the contractors are required before beginning the work to execute a bond for the use of the public body "for all taxes, excises, licenses, assessments, contributions, penalties and interest thereon" when, and if, the same may be lawfully due the State or any of said political subdivisions or instrumentalities, and also for the use and benefit of all persons who may perform any work or labor or furnish any material in the execution of the contract, conditioned for the performance and completion of the contract, and to pay as they become due all just claims for work or labor performed and materials furnished and taxes, excises, licenses, assessments, contributions and penalties and interest accrued in the execution of such contract.

3. NOTICE REQUIRED.—(a) *To surety*—No special statutory provision. (b) *To principal contractor*—No special statutory provision. (c) *To municipality*—Claimant must notify the municipality of the beginning of his suit, giving the name of the parties, describing the bond sued upon and stating the amount and nature of his claim. (d) *To creditors*—No special statutory provision.

4. TIME FOR SUIT.—Suit must be brought within one year after the date of the first publication of notice of final payment of the contract.

5. CONTRACTS EXCLUDED.—$500 or under.

6. PROCEDURE.—Claimant must notify the municipality (see Notice to Municipality above). No

judgment may be taken in such action within thirty days after the giving of such notice. The municipality may intervene in the suit and the court determines the rights of all parties thereto. If the amount realized on such bond is insufficient to discharge all such claims in full, the creditors prorate.

The public officials under whose contract the public work is being carried on and conducted, and upon whose approval final estimates for the construction of the work are paid, must, forty days before such final estimate shall be paid, cause to be published in a newspaper of general circulation published nearest the point at which such work is being carried on once a week for three successive weeks, and also post in three conspicuous places on such work a notice setting forth in substance that the work has been accepted as completed and that the contractor is entitled to final settlement therefor and that upon a specified day (the 41st day after the first publication of the notice) the contractor will be paid the full amount due him under the contract.

7. PENALTY FOR FAILURE TO TAKE BOND.—No.

8. SPECIAL PROVISIONS.—Wherever any surety becomes insolvent or, for any cause, is no longer proper or sufficient, the municipality may require the contractor to furnish new or additional bond within ten days, and thereupon, if so ordered by such municipality, all work on such contract shall cease until the new or additional bond is furnished. If such bond be not furnished within such time, the municipality may, at its option, determine the contract and complete the same as the agent and at the expense of the contractor and his surety. No instalment or final payment may be made under any formal municipal contract for the construction or repair of public works until the contractor shall have filed with the public official who executed the contract a sworn statement setting forth that all claims for work and labor performed under the contract have been and are paid for the entire period of time for which the instalment or final payment is to be made. If any such claim shall be disputed, the sworn statement shall so state and the amount claimed to be due the laborer shall be deducted from the moneys otherwise payable to the contractor and held by the public body until the determination of the dispute.

The provisions of the amendment of April 1, 1957, are deemed to be included in all bonds executed after that date, whether or not expressly written into such bond.

Nothing in the statute requiring notice of intention to make final settlement with the contractor shall be construed as relieving the contractor or the surety on its bond from any claim or claims for work or labor done or materials or supplies furnished on contract.

Effective May 20, 1981 persons desiring to bid on state construction projects are permitted to combine their bonding capacity in any way so as to meet the bonding requirements of the Department of Administration and Fiscal Control.

9. DECISIONS.—Service of notice of claim to surety by registered mail is sufficient. *Shoshoni Lumber Co. v. Fidelity & Deposit Co. of Maryland,* 46 Wyo. 241, 24 P.2d 690 (1933).

The surety is liable for the cost of lumber used for forms less salvage value of the lumber, as well as for coal used in blacksmith's shop incident to bridge construction, and also for groceries essential to the maintenance of a construction camp. *Shoshoni Lumber Co. v. Fidelity & Deposit Co. of Maryland,* 46 Wyo. 241, 24 P.2d 690 (1933).

When machinery is actually on job and repairs become necessary to keep it in operating condition to the end that the job might be completed, the bond in such a case ought to cover the repairs. *Colorado Builder's Supply Co. v. National Fire Insurance Co.,* 423 P.2d 79 (Wyo. 1967).

Where contractor and creditor agreed as to application of payments made by contractor, surety could not force a different application after creditor made claim for amounts covered by bond. *National Union Fire Insurance Co. v. Studer Tractor and Equip. Co.,* 527 P.2d 820 (Wyo. 1974).

United States District Courts

32

Set forth below is a list by state of the United States District Courts as authorized by Congress 28 U.S.C. §§ 81-131. Correspondence with any court should set forth the names of the district, the city, and the state within which the court is situated.

ALABAMA

Alabama is divided into three judicial districts known as the Northern, Middle, and Southern Districts of Alabama.

NORTHERN DISTRICT

(a) The Northern District comprises seven divisions.
 (1) The Northwestern Division comprises the counties of Colbert, Franklin, and Lauderdale.
 Court for the Northwestern Division is held at Florence.
 (2) The Northeastern Division comprises the counties of Cullman, Jackson, Lawrence, Limestone, Madison, and Morgan.
 Court for the Northeastern Division is held at Huntsville and Decatur.
 (3) The Southern Division comprises the counties of Blount, Jefferson, and Shelby.
 Court for the Southern Division is held at Birmingham.
 (4) The Eastern Division comprises the counties of Calhoun, Clay, Cleburne, and Talladega.
 Court for the Eastern Division is held at Anniston.
 (5) The Western Division comprises the counties of Bibb, Greene, Pickens, Sumter, and Tuscaloosa.
 Court for the Western Division is held at Tuscaloosa.
 (6) The Middle Division comprises the counties of Cherokee, De Kalb, Etowah, Marshall, and Saint Clair.
 Court for the Middle Division is held at Gadsden.
 (7) The Jasper Division comprises the counties of Fayette, Lamar, Marion, Walker, and Winston.
 Court for the Jasper Division is held at Jasper.

MIDDLE DISTRICT

(b) The Middle District comprises three divisions.
 (1) The Northern Division comprises the counties of Autauga, Barbour, Bullock, Butler, Chilton, Coosa, Covington, Crenshaw, Elmore, Lowndes, Montgomery, and Pike.
 Court for the Northern Division is held at Montgomery.
 (2) The Southern Division comprises the counties of Coffee, Dale, Geneva, Henry, and Houston.
 Court for the Southern Division is held at Dothan.
 (3) The Eastern Division comprises the counties of Chambers, Lee, Macon, Randolph, Russell, and Tallapoosa.
 Court for the Eastern Division is held at Opelika.

SOUTHERN DISTRICT

(c) The Southern District comprises two divisions.
 (1) The Northern Division comprises the counties of Dallas, Hale, Marengo, Perry, and Wilcox.
 Court for the Northern Division is held at Selma.
 (2) The Southern Division comprises the counties of Baldwin, Choctaw, Clarke, Conecuh, Escambia, Mobile, Monroe, and Washington.
 Court for the Southern Division is held at Mobile.

ALASKA

Alaska constitutes one judicial district.
Court is held at Anchorage, Fairbanks, Juneau, Ketchikan, and Nome.

ARIZONA

Arizona constitutes one judicial district.
Court is held at Globe, Phoenix, Prescott, and Tucson.

ARKANSAS

Arkansas is divided into two judicial districts known as the Eastern and Western Districts of Arkansas.

Eastern District

(a) The Eastern District comprises five divisions.
(1) The Eastern Division comprises the counties of Cross, Lee, Monroe, Phillips, Saint Francis, and Woodruff.
Court for the Eastern Division is held at Helena.
(2) The Western Division comprises the counties of Conway, Faulkner, Lonoke, Perry, Pope, Prairie, Pulaski, Saline, Van Buren, White, and Yell.
Court for the Western Division is held at Little Rock.
(3) The Pine Bluff Division comprises the counties of Arkansas, Chicot, Cleveland, Dallas, Desha, Drew, Grant, Jefferson, and Lincoln.
Court for the Pine Bluff Division is held at Pine Bluff.
(4) The Northern Division comprises the counties of Cleburne, Fulton, Independence, Izard, Jackson, Sharp, and Stone.
Court for the Northern Division is held at Batesville.
(5) The Jonesboro Division comprises the counties of Clay, Craighead, Crittenden, Greene, Lawrence, Mississippi, Poinsett, and Randolph.
Court for the Jonesboro Division is held at Jonesboro.

Western Division

(b) The Western District comprises six divisions.
(1) The Texarkana Division comprises the counties of Hempstead, Howard, Lafayette, Little River, Miller, Nevada, and Sevier.
Court for the Texarkana Division is held at Texarkana.
(2) The El Dorado Division comprises the counties of Ashley, Bradley, Calhoun, Columbia, Ouachita, and Union.
Court for the El Dorado Division is held at El Dorado.
(3) The Fort Smith Division comprises the counties of Crawford, Franklin, Johnson, Logan, Polk, Scott, and Sebastian.
Court for the Fort Smith Division is held at Fort Smith.
(4) The Harrison Division comprises the counties of Baxter, Boone, Carroll, Marion, Newton, and Searcy.
Court for the Harrison Division is held at Harrison.
(5) The Fayetteville Division comprises the counties of Benton, Madison, and Washington.
Court for the Fayetteville Division is held at Fayetteville.
(6) The Hot Springs Division comprises the counties of Clark, Garland, Hot Springs, Montgomery, and Pike.
Court for the Hot Springs Division is held at Hot Springs.

CALIFORNIA

California is divided into four judicial districts known as the Northern, Eastern, Central, and Southern Districts of California.

Northern District

(a) The Northern District comprises the counties of Alameda, Contra Costa, Del Norte, Humboldt, Lake, Marin, Mendocino, Monterey, Napa, San Benito, Santa Clara, Santa Cruz, San Francisco, San Mateo, and Sonoma.
Court for the Northern District is held at Eureka, Oakland, San Francisco, and San Jose.

UNITED STATES DISTRICT COURTS

EASTERN DISTRICT

(b) The Eastern District comprises the counties of Alpine, Amador, Butte, Calaveras, Colusa, El Dorado, Fresno, Glenn, Inyo, Kern, Kings, Lassen, Madera, Mariposa, Merced, Modoc, Mono, Nevada, Placer, Plumas, Sacramento, San Joaquin, Shasta, Sierra, Siskiyou, Solano, Stanislaus, Sutter, Tehama, Trinity, Tulare, Tuolumne, Yolo, and Yuba.

Court for the Eastern District is held at Fresno, Redding, and Sacramento.

CENTRAL DISTRICT

(c) The Central District comprises the counties of Los Angeles, Orange, Riverside, San Bernardino, San Luis Obispo, Santa Barbara, and Ventura.

Court for the Central District shall be held at Los Angeles and Santa Ana.

SOUTHERN DISTRICT

(d) The Southern District comprises the counties of Imperial and San Diego.

Court for the Southern District is held at San Diego.

COLORADO

Colorado constitutes one judicial district.

Court is held at Boulder, Denver, Durango, Grand Junction, Montrose, Pueblo, and Sterling.

CONNECTICUT

Colorado constitutes one judicial district.

Court is held at Bridgeport, Hartford, New Haven, New London, and Waterbury.

DELAWARE

Delaware constitutes one judicial district.

Court is held at Wilmington.

DISTRICT OF COLUMBIA

The District of Columbia constitutes one judicial district.

Court is held at Washington.

FLORIDA

Florida is divided into three judicial districts known as the Northern, Middle, and Southern Districts of Florida.

NORTHERN DISTRICT

(a) The Northern District comprises the counties of Alachua, Bay, Calhoun, Dixie, Escambia, Franklin, Gadsden, Gilchrist, Gulf, Holmes, Jackson, Jefferson, Lafayette, Leon, Levy, Liberty, Madison, Okaloosa, Santa Rosa, Taylor, Wakulla, Walton, and Washington.

Court for the Northern District is held at Gainesville, Marianna, Panama City, Pensacola, and Tallahassee.

MIDDLE DISTRICT

(b) The Middle District comprises the counties of Baker, Bradford, Brevard, Charlotte, Citrus, Clay, Columbia, De Soto, Duval, Flagler, Hamilton, Hardee, Hernando, Hillsborough, Lake, Lee, Manatee, Marion, Nassau, Orange, Osceola, Pasco, Pinellas, Polk, Putnam, Saint Johns, Sarasota, Seminole, Sumter, Suwannee, Union, and Volusia.

Court for the Middle District is held at Fernandina, Fort Myers, Jacksonville, Live Oak, Ocala, Orlando, Saint Petersburg, and Tampa.

SOUTHERN DISTRICT

(c) The Southern District comprises the counties of Broward, Collier, Dade, Glades, Hendry, Highlands, Indian River, Martin, Monroe, Okeechobee, Palm Beach, and Saint Lucie.

Court for the Southern District is held at Fort Lauderdale, Fort Pierce, Key West, Miami, and West Palm Beach.

GEORGIA

Georgia is divided into three judicial districts known as the Northern, Middle, and Southern Districts of Georgia.

NORTHERN DISTRICT

(a) The Northern District comprises four divisions.

(1) The Gainesville Division comprises the counties of Banks, Barrow, Dawson, Fannin, Forsyth, Gilmer, Habersham, Hall, Jackson, Lumpkin, Pickens, Rabun, Stephens, Towns, Union, and White.

Court for the Gainesville Division is held at Gainesville.

(2) The Atlanta Division comprises the counties of Cherokee, Clayton, Cobb, De Kalb, Douglas, Fulton, Gwinnett, Henry, Newton, and Rockdale.

Court for the Atlanta Division is held at Atlanta.

(3) The Rome Division comprises the counties of Bartow, Catoosa, Chattooga, Dade, Floyd, Gordon, Murray, Paulding, Polk, Walker, and Whitfiled.

Court for the Rome Division is held at Rome.

(4) The Newnan Division comprises the counties of Carroll, Coweta, Fayette, Haralson, Heard, Meriwether, Pike, Spalding, and Troup.

Court for the Newnan Division is held at Newnan.

MIDDLE DISTRICT

(b) The Middle District comprises seven divisions.

(1) The Athens Division comprises the counties of Clarke, Elbert, Franklin, Greene, Hart, Madison, Morgan, Oconee, Oglethorpe, and Walton.

Court for the Athens Division is held at Athens.

(2) The Macon Division comprises the counties of Baldwin, Bibb, Bleckley, Butts, Crawford, Hancock, Houston, Jasper, Jones, Lamar, Monroe, Peach, Pulaski, Putnam, Twiggs, Upson, Washington, and Wilkinson.

Court for the Macon Division is held at Macon.

(3) The Columbus Division comprises the counties of Chattahoochee, Clay, Harris, Marion, Muscogee, Quitman, Randolph, Stewart, Talbot, and Taylor.

Court for the Columbus Division is held at Columbus.

(4) The Americus Division comprises the counties of Ben Hill, Crisp, Dooly, Lee, Macon, Schley, Sumter, Terrell, Webster, and Wilcox.

Court for the Americus Division is held at Americus.

(5) The Albany Division comprises the counties of Baker, Calhoun, Dougherty, Early, Miller, Mitchell, Turner, and Worth.

Court for the Albany Division is held at Albany.

(6) The Valdosta Division comprises the counties of Berrien, Clinch, Cook, Echols, Irwin, Lanier, Lowndes, and Tift.

Court for the Valdosta Division is held at Valdosta.

(7) The Thomasville Division comprises the counties of Brooks, Colquitt, Decatur, Grady, Seminole, and Thomas.

Court for the Thomasville Division is held at Thomasville.

SOUTHERN DISTRICT

(c) The Southern District comprises six divisions.

(1) The Augusta Division comprises the counties of Burke, Columbia, Glascock, Lincoln, McDuffie, Richmond, Taliaferro, Warren, and Wilkes.

Court for the Augusta Division is held at Augusta.

(2) The Dublin Division comprises the counties of Dodge, Johnson, Laurens, Montgomery, Telfair, Treutlen, and Wheeler.

Court for the Dublin Division is held at Dublin.

(3) The Savannah Division comprises the counties of Bryan, Chatham, Effingham, Evans, Liberty, Screven, and Tattnall.

Court for the Savannah Division is held at Savannah.

(4) The Waycross Division comprises the counties of Atkinson, Bacon, Brantley, Charlton, Coffee, Pierce, and Ware.

Court for the Waycross Division is held at Waycross.

UNITED STATES DISTRICT COURTS   32-5

(5) The Brunswick Division comprises the counties of Appling, Camden, Glynn, Jeff Davis, Long, McIntosh, and Wayne.
Court for the Brunswick Division is held at Brunswick.
(6) The Statesboro Division comprises the counties of Bulloch, Candler, Emanual, Jefferson, Jenkins, and Toombs.
Court for the Statesboro Division is held at Statesboro.

HAWAII
Hawaii constitutes one judicial district which includes the Midway Islands, Wake Island, Johnston Island, Sand Island, Kingman Reef, Palmyra Island, Baker Island, Howland Island, Jarvis Island, Canton Island, and Enderbury Island: *Provided,* That the inclusion of Canton and Enderbury Islands in such judicial district shall in no way be construed to be prejudicial to the claims of the United Kingdom to said Islands in accordance with the agreement of April 6, 1939, between the Governments of the United States and of the United Kingdom to set up a regime for their use in common.
Court is held at Honolulu.

IDAHO
Idaho, exclusive of Yellowstone National Park, constitutes one judicial district.
Court is held at Boise, Coeur d'Alene, Moscow and Pocatello.

ILLINOIS
Illinois is divided into three judicial districts known as the Northern, Central, and Southern Districts of Illinois.

NORTHERN DISTRICT
(a) The Northern District comprises two divisions.
(1) The Eastern Division comprises the counties of Cook, Du Page, Grundy, Kane, Kendall, Lake, La Salle, McHenry, and Will.
Court for the Eastern Division is held at Chicago.
(2) The Western Division comprises the counties of Boone, Carroll, DeKalb, Jo Daviess, Lee, McHenry, Ogle, Stephenson, Whiteside, and Winnebago.
Court for the Western Division is held at Freeport and Rockford.

CENTRAL DISTRICT
(b) The Central District comprises the counties of Adams, Brown, Bureau, Cass, Champaign, Christian, Coles, De Witt, Douglas, Edgar, Ford, Fulton, Greene, Hancock, Henderson, Henry, Iroquois, Kankakee, Knox, Livingston, Logan, McDonough, McLean, Macoupin, Macon, Marshall, Mason, Menard, Mercer, Montgomery, Morgan, Moultrie, Peoria, Piatt, Pike, Putnam, Rock Island, Sangamon, Schuyler, Scott, Shelby, Stark, Tazewell, Vermilion, Warren, and Woodford.
Court for the Central District is held at Champaign/Urbana, Danville, Peoria, Quincy, Rock Island, and Springfield.

SOUTHERN DISTRICT
(c) The Southern District of Illinois comprises the counties of Alexander, Bond, Calhoun, Clark, Clay, Clinton, Crawford, Cumberland, Edwards, Effingham, Fayette, Franklin, Gallatin, Hamilton, Hardin, Jackson, Jasper, Jefferson, Jersey, Johnson, Lawrence, Madison, Marion, Massac, Monroe, Perry, Pope, Pulaski, Randolph, Richland, St. Clair, Saline, Union, Wabash, Washington, Wayne, White, and Williamson.
Court for the Southern District is held at Alton, Benton, Cairo, and East Saint Louis.

INDIANA
Indiana is divided into two judicial districts known as the Northern and Southern Districts of Indiana.

NORTHERN DISTRICT
(a) The Northern District comprises three divisions.
(1) The Fort Wayne Division comprises the counties of Adams, Allen, Blackford, De Kalb, Grant, Huntington, Jay, Lagrange, Noble, Steuben, Wells, and Whitley.
Court for the Fort Wayne Division is held at Fort Wayne.

(2) The South Bend Division comprises the counties of Cass, Elkhart, Fulton, Kosciusko, La Porte, Marshall, Miami, Pulaski, St. Joseph, Starke, and Wabash.
Court for the South Bend Division is held at South Bend.
(3) The Hammond Division comprises the counties of Benton, Carroll, Jasper, Lake, Newton, Porter, Tippecanoe, Warren, and White.
Court for the Hammond Division is held at Hammond and Lafayette.

Southern District

(b) The Southern District comprises four divisions.
(1) The Indianapolis Division comprises the counties of Bartholomew, Boone, Brown, Clinton, Decatur, Delaware, Fayette, Fountain, Franklin, Hamilton, Hancock, Hendricks, Henry, Howard, Johnson, Madison, Marion, Monroe, Montgomery, Morgan, Randolph, Rush, Shelby, Tipton, Union, and Wayne.
Court for the Indianapolis Division is held at Indianapolis and Richmond.
(2) The Terre Haute Division comprises the counties of Clay, Greene, Knox, Owen, Parke, Putnam, Sullivan, Vermilion, and Vigo.
Court for the Terre Haute Division is held at Terre Haute.
(3) The Evansville Division comprises the counties of Davies, Dubois, Gibson, Martin, Perry, Pike, Posey, Spencer, Vanderburgh, and Warrick.
Court for the Evansville Division is held at Evansville.
(4) The New Albany Division comprises the counties of Clark, Crawford, Dearborn, Floyd, Harrison, Jackson, Jefferson, Jennings, Lawrence, Ohio, Orange, Ripley, Scott, Switzerland, and Washington.
Court for the New Albany Division is held at New Albany.

IOWA

Iowa is divided into two judicial districts known as the Northern and Southern Districts of Iowa.

Northern District

(a) The Northern District comprises four divisions.
(1) The Cedar Rapids Division comprises the counties of Benton, Cedar, Grundy, Hardin, Iowa, Jones, Linn, and Tama.
Court for the Cedar Rapids Division is held at Cedar Rapids.
(2) The Eastern Division comprises the counties of Allamakee, Black Hawk, Bremer, Buchanan, Chickasaw, Clayton, Delaware, Dubuque, Fayette, Floyd, Howard, Jackson, Mitchell, and Winneshiek.
Court for the Eastern Division is held at Dubuque and Waterloo.
(3) The Western Division comprises the counties of Buena Vista, Cherokee, Clay, Crawford, Dickinson, Ida, Lyon, Monona, O'Brien, Osceola, Plymouth, Sac, Sioux, and Woodbury.
Court for the Western Division is held at Sioux City.
(4) The Central Division comprises the counties of Butler, Calhoun, Carroll, Cerro Gordo, Emmet, Franklin, Hamilton, Hancock, Humboldt, Kossuth, Palo Alto, Pocahontas, Webster, Winnebago, Worth, and Wright.
Court for the Central Division is held at Ford Dodge and Mason City.

Southern District

(b) The Southern District comprises six divisions.
(1) The Central Division comprises the counties of Boone, Dallas, Greene, Guthrie, Jasper, Madison, Marion, Marshall, Polk, Poweshiek, Story, and Warren.
Court for the Central Division is held at Des Moines.
(2) The Eastern Division comprises the counties of Des Moines, Henry, Lee, Louisa, and Van Buren.
Court for the Eastern Division is held at Keokuk.
(3) The Western Division comprises the counties of Audubon, Cass, Fremont, Harrison, Mills, Montgomery, Page, Pottawattamie, and Shelby.
Court for the Western Division is held at Council Bluffs.

UNITED STATES DISTRICT COURTS

(4) The Southern Division comprises the counties of Adair, Adams, Clarke, Decatur, Lucas, Ringgold, Taylor, Union, and Wayne.
Court for the Southern Division is held at Creston.
(5) The Davenport Division comprises the counties of Clinton, Johnson, Muscatine, Scott, and Washington.
Court for the Davenport Division is held at Davenport.
(6) The Ottumwa Division comprises the counties of Appanoose, Davis, Jefferson, Keokuk, Mahaska, Monroe, and Wapello.
Court for the Ottumwa Division is held at Ottumwa.

KANSAS

Kansas constitutes one judicial district.
Court is held at Kansas City, Leavenworth, Salina, Topeka, Hutchinson, Wichita, Dodge City, and Fort Scott.

KENTUCKY

Kentucky is divided into two judicial districts known as the Eastern and Western Districts of Kentucky.

Eastern District

(a) The Eastern District comprises the counties of Anderson, Bath, Bell, Boone, Burbon, Boyd, Boyle, Bracken, Breathitt, Campbell, Carroll, Carter, Clark, Clay, Elliott, Estill, Fayette, Fleming, Floyd, Franklin, Gallatin, Garrard, Grant, Greenup, Harlan, Harrison, Henry, Jackson, Jessamine, Johnson, Kenton, Knott, Knox, Laurel, Lawrence, Lee, Leslie, Letcher, Lewis, Lincoln, McCreary, Madison, Magoffin, Martin, Mason, Menifee, Mercer, Montgomery, Morgan, Nicholas, Owen, Owsley, Pendleton, Perry, Pike, Powell, Pulaski, Robertson, Rockcastle, Rowan, Scott, Shelby, Trimble, Wayne, Whitley, Wolfe, and Woodford.
Court for the Eastern District is held at Ashland, Catlettsburg, Covington, Frankfort, Jackson, Lexington, London, Pikeville, and Richmond.

Western District

(b) The Western District comprises the counties of Adair, Allen, Ballard, Barren, Breckenridge, Bullitt, Butler, Caldwell, Calloway, Carlisle, Casey, Christian, Clinton, Crittenden, Cumberland, Daviess, Edmonson, Fulton, Graves, Grayson, Green, Hancock, Hardin, Hart, Henderson, Hickman, Hopkins, Jefferson, Larue, Livingston, Logan, Lyon, McCracken, McLean, Marion, Marshall, Meade, Metcalfe, Monroe, Muhlenberg, Nelson, Ohio, Oldham, Russell, Simpson, Spencer, Taylor, Todd, Trigg, Union, Warren, Washington, and Webster.
Court for the Western District is held at Bowling Green, Louisville, Owensboro, and Paducah.

LOUISIANA

Louisiana is divided into three judicial districts known as the Eastern, Middle, and Western Districts of Louisiana.

Eastern District

(a) The Eastern District comprises the parishes of Assumption, Jefferson, Lafourche, Orleans, Plaquemines, Saint Bernard, Saint Charles, Saint James, Saint John the Baptist, Saint Tammany, Tangipahoa, Terrebonne, and Washington.
Court for the Eastern District is held at New Orleans and Houma.

Middle District

(b) The Middle District comprises the parishes of Ascension, East Baton Rouge, East Feliciana, Iberville, Livingston, Pointe Coupee, Saint Helena, West Baton Rouge, and West Feliciana.
Court for the Middle District is held at Baton Rouge.

Western District

(c) The Western District comprises the parishes of Acadia, Allen, Avoyelles, Beauregard, Bienville, Bossier, Caddo, Calcasieu, Caldwell, Cameron, Catahoula, Claiborne, Concordia, Jefferson, Davis,

De Soto, East Carroll, Evangeline, Franklin, Grant, Iberia, Jackson, Lafayette, La Salle, Lincoln, Madison, Morehouse, Natchitoches, Ouachita, Rapides, Red River, Richland, Sabine, Saint Landry, Saint Martin, Saint Mary, Tensas, Union, Vermilion, Vernon, Webster, West Carroll, and Winn.
  Court for the Western District is held at Alexandria, Lafayette, Lake Charles, Monroe, Opelousas, and Shreveport.

MAINE
  Maine constitutes one judicial district.
  Court is held at Bangor and Portland.

MARYLAND
  Maryland constitutes one judicial district.
  Court is held at Baltimore, Cumberland, and Denton and at a suitable site in Prince Georges County not more than five miles from the boundary of Montgomery and Prince Georges Counties.

MASSACHUSETTS
  Massachusetts constitutes one judicial district.
  Court is held at Boston, New Bedford, Springfield, and Worcester.

MICHIGAN
  Michigan is divided into two judicial districts known as the Eastern and Western Districts of Michigan.

EASTERN DISTRICT

(a) The Eastern District comprises two divisions.
  (1) The Southern Division comprises the counties of Genesee, Jackson, Lapeer, Lenawee, Livingston, Macomb, Monroe, Oakland, Saint Clair, Sanilac, Shiawassee, Washtenaw, and Wayne.
  Court for the Southern Division is held at Ann Arbor, Detroit, Flint, and Port Huron.
  (2) The Northern Division comprises the counties of Alcona, Alpena, Arenac, Bay, Cheboygan, Clare, Crawford, Gladwin, Gratiot, Huron, Iosco, Isabella, Midland, Montmorency, Ogemaw, Oscoda, Otsego, Presque Isle, Roscommon, Saginaw, and Tuscola.
  Court for the Northern Division is held at Bay City.

WESTERN DISTRICT

(b) The Western District comprises two divisions.
  (1) The Southern Division comprises the counties of Allegan, Antrim, Barry, Benzie, Berrien, Branch, Calhoun, Cass, Charlevoix, Clinton, Eaton, Emmet, Grand Traverse, Hillsdale, Ingham, Ionia, Kalamazoo, Kalkaska, Kent, Lake, Leelanau, Manistee, Mason, Mecosta, Missaukee, Montcalm, Muskegon, Newaygo, Oceana, Osceola, Ottawa, Saint Joseph, Van Buren, and Wexford.
  Court for the Southern Division is held at Grand Rapids, Kalamazoo, Lansing, and Traverse City.
  (2) The Northern Division comprises the counties of Alger, Baraga, Chippewa, Delta, Dickinson, Gogebic, Houghton, Iron, Keweenaw, Luce, Mackinac, Marquette, Menominee, Ontonagon, and Schoolcraft.
  Court for the Northern Division is held at Marquette and Sault Sainte Marie.

MINNESOTA
  Minnesota constitutes one judicial district comprising six divisions.
  (1) The First Division comprises the counties of Dodge, Fillmore, Houston, Mower, Olmsted, Steele, Wabasha, and Winona.
  Court for the First Division is held at Winona.
  (2) The Second Division comprises the counties of Blue Earth, Brown, Cottonwood, Faribault, Freeborn, Jackson, Lac qui Parle, Le Sueur, Lincoln, Lyon, Martin, Murray, Nicollet, Nobles, Pipestone, Redwood, Rock, Sibley, Waseca, Watonwan, and Yellow Medicine.
  Court for the Second Division is held at Mankato.

(3) The Third Division comprises the counties of Chisago, Dakota, Goodhue, Ramsey, Rice, Scott, and Washington.
Court for the Third Division is held at Saint Paul.
(4) The Fourth Division comprises the counties of Anoka, Carver, Chippewa, Hennepin, Isanti, Kandiyohi, McLeod, Meeker, Renville, Sherburne, Swift, and Wright.
Court for the Fourth Division is held at Minneapolis.
(5) The Fifth Division comprises the counties of Aitkin, Benton, Carlton, Cass, Cook, Crow Wing, Itasca, Kanabec, Koochiching, Lake, Mille Lacs, Morrison, Pine, and Saint Louis.
Court for the Fifth Division is held at Duluth.
(6) The Sixth Division comprises the counties of Becker, Beltrami, Big Stone, Clay, Clearwater, Douglas, Grant, Hubbard, Kittson, Lake of the Woods, Mahnomen, Marshall, Norman, Otter Tail, Pennington, Polk, Pope, Red Lake, Roseau, Stearns, Stevens, Todd, Traverse, Wadena, and Wilkin.
Court for the Sixth Division is held at Fergus Falls.

MISSISSIPPI

Mississippi is divided into two judicial districts known as the Northern and Southern Districts of Mississippi.

Northern District

(a) The Northern District comprises four divisions.
(1) Eastern Division comprises the counties of Alcorn, Attala, Chickasaw, Choctaw, Clay, Itawamba, Lee, Lowndes, Monroe, Oktibbeha, Prentiss, Tishomingo, and Winston.
Court for the Eastern Division is held at Aberdeen, Ackerman and Corinth.
(2) The Western Division comprises the counties of Benton, Calhoun, Grenada, Lafayette, Marshall, Montgomery, Pontotoc, Tippah, Union, Webster, and Yalobusha.
Court for the Western Division is held at Oxford.
(3) The Delta Division comprises the counties of Bolivar, Coahoma, De Sota, Panola, Quitman, Tallahatchie, Tate, and Tunica.
Court for the Delta Division is held at Clarksdale.
(4) The Greenville Division comprises the counties of Carroll, Humphreys, Leflore, Sunflower, and Washington.
Court for the Greenville Division is held at Greenville.

Southern District

(b) The Southern District comprises five divisions.
(1) The Jackson Division comprises the counties of Amite, Copiah, Franklin, Hinds, Holmes, Leake, Lincoln, Madison, Pike, Rankin, Scott, Simpson, and Smith.
Court for the Jackson Division is held at Jackson.
(2) The Eastern Division comprises the counties of Clarke, Jasper, Kemper, Lauderdale, Neshoba, Newton, Noxubee, and Wayne.
Court for the Eastern Division is held at Meridian.
(3) The Western Division comprises the counties of Adams, Claiborne, Issaquena, Jefferson, Sharkey, Warren, Wilkinson, and Yazoo.
Court for the Western Division is held at Natchez and Vicksburg: *Provided,* That court shall be held at Natchez if suitable quarters and accommodations are furnished at no cost to the United States.
(4) The Southern Division comprises the counties of George, Hancock, Harrison, Jackson, Pearl River, and Stone.
Court for the Southern Division is held at Biloxi and Gulfport.
(5) The Hattiesburg Division comprises the counties of Covington, Forrest, Greene, Jefferson Davis, Jones, Lamar, Lawrence, Marion, Perry, and Walthall.
Court for the Hattiesburg Division is held at Hattiesburg.

MISSOURI

Missouri is divided into two judicial districts known as the Eastern and Western Districts of Missouri.

Eastern District

(a) The Eastern District comprises three divisions.

(1) The Eastern Division comprises the counties of Crawford, Dent, Franklin, Gasconade, Iron, Jefferson, Lincoln, Maries, Phelps, Saint Charles, Saint Francois, Saint Genevieve, Saint Louis, Warren, and Washington, and the city of Saint Louis.

Court for the Eastern Division is held at Saint Louis.

(2) The Northern Division comprises the counties of Adair, Audrain, Chariton, Clark, Knox, Lewis, Linn, Macon, Marion, Monroe, Montgomery, Pike, Ralls, Randolph, Schuyler, Scotland, and Shelby.

Court for the Northern Division is held at Hannibal.

(3) The Southeastern Division comprises the counties of Bollinger, Butler, Cape Girardeau, Carter, Dunklin, Madison, Mississippi, New Madrid, Pemiscot, Perry, Reynolds, Ripley, Scott, Shannon, Stoddard, and Wayne.

Court for the Southeastern Division is held at Cape Girardeau.

Western District

(b) The Western District comprises five divisions.

(1) The Western Division comprises the counties of Bates, Carroll, Cass, Clay, Henry, Jackson, Johnson, Lafayette, Ray, Saint Clair, and Saline.

Court for the Western Division is held at Kansas City.

(2) The Southwestern Division comprises the counties of Barton, Barry, Jasper, Lawrence, McDonald, Newton, Stone, and Vernon.

Court for the Southwestern Division is held at Joplin.

(3) The Saint Joseph Division comprises the counties of Andrew, Atchison, Buchanan, Caldwell, Clinton, Daviess, De Kalb, Gentry, Grundy, Harrison, Holt, Livingston, Mercer, Nodaway, Platte, Putnam, Sullivan, and Worth.

Court for the Saint Joseph Division is held at Saint Joseph.

(4) The Central Division comprises the counties of Benton, Boone, Callaway, Camden, Cole, Cooper, Hickory, Howard, Miller, Moniteau, Morgan, Osage, and Pettis.

Court for the Central Division is held at Jefferson City.

(5) The Southern Division comprises the counties of Cedar, Christian, Dade, Dallas, Douglas, Greene, Howell, Laclede, Oregon, Ozark, Polk, Pulaski Taney, Texas, Webster, and Wright.

Court for the Southern Division is held at Springfield.

MONTANA

Montana, exclusive of Yellowstone National Park, constitutes one judicial district.

Court is held at Billings, Butte, Glasgow, Great Falls, Havre, Helena, Kalispell, Lewistown, Livingston, Miles City, and Missoula.

NEBRASKA

Nebraska constitutes one judicial district.

Court is held at Lincoln, North Platte, and Omaha.

NEVADA

Nevada constitutes one judicial district.

Court is held at Carson City, Elko, Las Vegas, and Reno.

NEW HAMPSHIRE

New Hampsire constitutes one judicial district.

Court is held at Concord and Littleton.

NEW JERSEY

New Jersey constitutes one judicial district.

Court is held at Camden, Newark, and Trenton.

NEW MEXICO

New Mexico constitutes one judicial district.

Court is held at Albuquerque, Las Cruces, Las Vegas, Roswell, Santa Fe, and Silver City.

UNITED STATES DISTRICT COURTS　　　　　　　　　　32-11

NEW YORK

New York is divided into four judicial districts known as the Northern, Southern, Eastern, and Western Districts of New York.

Northern District

(a) The Northern District comprises the counties of Albany, Broome, Cayuga, Chenango, Clinton, Columbia, Cortland, Delaware, Essex, Franklin, Fulton, Greene, Hamilton, Herkimer, Jefferson, Lewis, Madison, Montgomery, Oneida, Onondaga, Oswego, Otsego, Rensselaer, Saint Lawrence, Saratoga, Schenectady, Schoharie, Tioga, Tompkins, Ulster, Warren, and Washington.

Court for the Northern District is held at Albany, Auburn, Binghamton, Malone, Syracuse, and Utica.

Southern District

(b) The Southern District comprises the counties of Bronx, Dutchess, New York, Orange, Putnam, Rockland, Sullivan, and Westchester, and concurrently with the Eastern District, the waters within the Eastern District.

Court for the Southern District is held at New York and White Plains.

Eastern District

(c) The Eastern District comprises the counties of Kings, Nassau, Queens, Richmond, and Suffolk and concurrently with the Southern District, the waters within the counties of Bronx and New York.

Court for the Eastern District is held at Brooklyn and Hempstead (including the village of Uniondale).

Western District

(d) The Western District comprises the counties of Allegany, Cattaraugus, Chautauqua, Chemung, Erie, Genesee, Livingston, Monroe, Niagara, Ontario, Orleans, Schuyler, Seneca, Steuben, Wayne, Wyoming, and Yates.

Court for the Western District is held at Buffalo, Canandaigua, Elmira, Jamestown, and Rochester.

NORTH CAROLINA

North Carolina is divided into three judicial districts known as the Eastern, Middle, and Western Districts of North Carolina.

Eastern District

(a) The Eastern District comprises the counties of Beaufort, Bartie, Bladen, Brunswick, Camden, Carteret, Chowan, Columbus, Craven, Cumberland, Currituck, Dare, Duplin, Edgecombe, Franklin, Gates, Granville, Greene, Halifax, Harnett, Hertford, Hyde, Johnston, Jones, Lenoir, Martin, Nash, New Hanover, Northampton, Onslow, Pamlico, Pasquotank, Pender, Perquimans, Pitt, Robeson, Sampson, Tyrrell, Vance, Wake, Warren, Washington, Wayne, and Wilson and that portion of Durham County encompassing the Federal Correctional Institution, Butner, North Carolina.

Court for the Eastern District is held at Clinton, Elizabeth City, Fayetteville, New Bern, Raleigh, Washington, Wilmington, and Wilson.

Middle District

(b) The Middle District comprises the counties of Alamance, Cabarrus, Caswell, Chatham, Davidson, Davie, Durham (excluding that portion of Durham County encompassing the Federal Correctional Institution, Butner, North Carolina), Forsythe, Guilford, Hoke, Lee, Montgomery, Moore, Orange, Person, Randolph, Richmond, Rockingham, Rowan, Scotland, Stanly, Stokes, Surry, and Yadkin.

Court for the Middle District is held at Durham, Greensboro, and Winston-Salem.

Western District

(c) The Western District comprises the counties of Alexander, Alleghany, Anson, Ashe, Avery, Buncombe, Burke, Caldwell, Catawba, Cherokee, Clay, Cleveland, Gaston, Graham, Haywood,

Henderson, Iredell, Jackson, Lincoln, McDowell, Macon, Madison, Mecklenburg, Mitchell, Polk, Rutherford, Swain, Transylvania, Union, Watauga, Wilkes, and Yancey.
Court for the Western District is held at Asheville, Bryson City, Charlotte, Shelby, and Statesville.

NORTH DAKOTA

North Dakota constitutes one judicial district comprising four divisions.

(1) The Southwestern Division comprises the counties of Adams, Billings, Bowman, Burleigh, Dunn, Emmons, Golden Valley, Grant, Hettinger, Kidder, Logan, McIntosh, McLean, Mercer, Morton, Oliver, Sioux, Slope, and Stark.
Court for the Southwestern Division is held at Bismarck.

(2) The Southeastern Division comprises the counties of Barnes, Cass, Dickey, Eddy, Foster, Griggs, La Moure, Ransom, Richland, Sargent, Steele, and Stutsman.
Court for the Southeastern Division is held at Fargo.

(3) The Northeastern Division comprises the counties of Benson, Cavalier, Grand Forks, Nelson, Pembina, Ramsey, Rolette, Towner, Traill, and Walsh.
Court for the Northeastern Division is held at Grand Forks.

(4) The Northwestern Division comprises the counties of Bottineau, Burke, Divide, McHenry, McKenzie, Mountrail, Pierce, Renville, Sheridan, Ward, Wells, and Williams.
Court for the Northwestern Division is held at Minot.

OHIO

Ohio is divided into two judicial districts known as the Northern and Southern Districts of Ohio.

NORTHERN DISTRICT

(a) The Northern District comprises two divisions.

(1) The Eastern Division comprises the counties of Ashland, Ashtabula, Carroll, Columbiana, Crawford, Cuyahoga, Geauga, Holmes, Lake, Lorain, Mahoning, Medina, Portage, Richland, Stark, Summit, Trumbull, Tuscarawas, and Wayne.
Court for the Eastern Division is held at Cleveland, Youngstown, and Akron.

(2) The Western Division comprises the counties of Allen, Auglaize, Defiance, Erie, Fulton, Hancock, Hardin, Henry, Huron, Lucas, Marion, Mercer, Ottawa, Paulding, Putnam, Sandusky, Seneca, Van Wert, Williams, Woods, and Wyandot.
Court for the Western Division is held at Lima and Toledo.

SOUTHERN DISTRICT

(b) The Southern District comprises two divisions.

(1) The Western Division comprises the counties of Adams, Brown, Butler, Champaign, Clark, Clermont, Clinton, Darke, Greene, Hamilton, Highland, Lawrence, Miami, Montgomery, Preble, Scioto, Shelby, and Warren.
Court for the Western Division is held at Cincinnati and Dayton.

(2) The Eastern Division comprises the counties of Athens, Belmont, Coshocton, Delaware, Fairfield, Fayette, Franklin, Gallia, Guernsey, Harrison, Hocking, Jackson, Jefferson, Knox, Licking, Logan, Madison, Meigs, Monroe, Morgan, Morrow, Muskingum, Noble, Perry, Pickaway, Pike, Ross, Union, Vinton, and Washington.
Court for the Eastern Division is held at Columbus and Steubenville.

OKLAHOMA

Oklahoma is divided into three judicial districts known as the Northern, Eastern, and Western Districts of Oklahoma.

NORTHERN DISTRICT

(a) The Northern District comprises the counties of Craig, Creek, Delaware, Mayes, Nowata, Osage, Ottawa, Pawnee, Rogers, Tulsa, and Washington.
Court for the Northern District is held at Bartlesville, Miami, Pawhuska, Tulsa, and Vinita.

UNITED STATES DISTRICT COURTS

EASTERN DISTRICT

(b) The Eastern District comprises the counties of Adair, Atoka, Bryan, Carter, Cherokee, Choctaw, Coal, Haskell, Hughes, Johnston, Latimer, Le Flore, Love, McCurtain, McIntosh, Marshall, Murray, Muskogee, Okfuskee, Okmulgee, Pittsburg, Pontotoc, Pushmataha, Seminole, Sequoyah, and Wagoner.

Court for the Eastern District is held at Ada, Ardmore, Durant, Hugo, Muskogee, Okmulgee, Poteau, and S. McAlester.

WESTERN DISTRICT

(c) The Western District comprises the counties of Alfalfa, Beaver, Beckham, Blaine, Caddo, Canadian, Cimarron, Cleveland, Comanche, Cotton, Custer, Dewey, Ellis, Garfield, Garvin, Grady, Grant, Greer, Harmon, Harper, Jackson, Jefferson, Kay, Kingfisher, Kiowa, Lincoln, Logan, McClain, Major, Noble, Oklahoma, Payne, Pottawatomie, Roger Mills, Stephens, Texas, Tillman, Washita, Woods, and Woodward.

Court for the Western District is held at Chickasha, Enid, Guthrie, Lawton, Mangum, Oklahoma City, Pauls Valley, Ponca City, Shawnee, and Woodward.

OREGON

Oregon constitutes one judicial district.
Court is held at Coquille, Eugene, Klamath Falls, Medford, Pendleton, and Portland.

PENNSYLVANIA

Pennsylvania is divided into three judicial districts known as the Eastern, Middle, and Western Districts of Pennsylvania.

EASTERN DISTRICT

(a) The Eastern District comprises the counties of Berks, Bucks, Chester, Delaware, Lancaster, Lehigh, Montgomery, Northampton, Philadelphia, and Schuylkill.
Court for Eastern District is held at Allentown, Easton, Reading, and Philadelphia.

MIDDLE DISTRICT

(b) The Middle District comprises the counties of Adams, Bradford, Cameron, Carbon, Centre, Clinton, Columbia, Cumberland, Dauphin, Franklin, Fulton, Huntingdon, Juniata, Lackawanna, Lebanon, Luzerne, Lycoming, Mifflin, Monroe, Montour, Northumberland, Perry, Pike, Potter, Snyder, Sullivan, Susquehanna, Tioga, Union, Wayne, Wyoming, and York.
Court for the Middle District is held at Harrisburg, Lewisburg, Scranton, Wilkes-Barre, and Williamsport.

WESTERN DISTRICT

(c) The Western District comprises the counties of Allegheny, Armstrong, Beaver, Bedford, Blair, Butler, Cambria, Clarion, Clearfield, Crawford, Elk, Erie, Fayette, Forest, Greene, Indiana, Jefferson, Lawrence, McKean, Mercer, Somerset, Venango, Warren, Washington, and Westmoreland.
Court for the Western District is held at Erie, Johnstown and Pittsburgh.

PUERTO RICO

Puerto Rico constitutes one judicial district.
Court is held at Mayaguez, Ponce, and San Juan.

RHODE ISLAND

Rholde Island constitutes one judicial district.
Court is held at Providence.

SOUTH CAROLINA

South Carolina constitutes one judicial district comprising ten divisons.
(1) The Charleston Division comprises the counties of Beaufort, Berkeley, Charleston, Clarendon, Colleton, Dorchester, Georgetown, and Jasper.

Court for the Charleston Division is held at Charleston.
(2) The Columbia Division comprises the counties of Kershaw, Lee, Lexington, Richland, and Sumter.
Court for the Columbia Division is held at Columbia.
(3) The Florence Division comprises the counties of Chesterfield, Darlington, Dillon, Florence, Horry, Marion, Marlboro, and Williamsburg.
Court for the Florence Division is held at Florence.
(4) The Aiken Division comprises the counties of Aiken, Allendale, Barnwell, and Hampton.
Court for the Aiken Division is held at Aiken.
(5) The Orangeburg Division comprises the counties of Bamberg, Calhoun, and Orangeburg.
Court for the Orangeburg Division is held at Orangeburg.
(6) The Greenville Division comprises the counties of Greenville and Laurens.
Court for the Greenville Division is held at Greenville.
(7) The Rock Hill Division comprises the counties of Chester, Fairfield, Lancaster, and York.
Court for the Rock Hill Division is held at Rock Hill.
(8) The Greenwood Division comprises the counties of Abbeville, Edgefield, Greenwood, McCormick, Newberry, and Saluda.
Court for the Greenwood Division is held at Greenwood.
(9) The Anderson Division comprises the counties of Anderson, Oconee, and Pickens.
Court for the Anderson Division is held at Anderson.
(10) The Spartanburg Division comprises the counties of Cherokee, Spartanburg, and Union.
Court for the Spartanburg Division is held at Spartanburg.

SOUTH DAKOTA

South Dakota constitutes one judicial district comprising four divisions.
(1) The Northern Division comprises the counties of Brown, Campbell, Clark, Codington, Corson, Day, Deuel, Edmonds, Grant, Hamlin, McPherson, Marshall, Roberts, Spink, and Walworth.
Court for the Northern Division is held at Aberdeen.
(2) The Southern Division comprises the counties of Aurora, Beadle, Bone Homme, Brookings, Brule, Charles Mix, Clay, Davison, Douglas, Hanson, Hutchinson, Kingsbury, Lake, Lincoln, McCook, Miner, Minnehaha, Moody, Sanborn, Turner, Union, and Yankton.
Court for the Southern Division is held at Sioux Falls.
(3) The Central Division comprises the counties of Buffalo, Dewey, Faulk, Gregory, Haakon, Hand, Hughes, Hyde, Jackson, Jerauld, Jones, Lyman, Mellette, Potter, Stanley, Sully, Todd, Tripp, and Ziebach.
Court for the Central Division is held at Pierre.
(4) The Western Division comprises the counties of Bennett, Butte, Custer, Fall River, Harding, Lawrence, Meade, Pennington, Perkins, Shannon, Washabaugh, and Washington.
Court for the Western Division is held at Deadwood and Rapid City.

TENNESSEE

Tennessee is divided into three judicial districts known as the Eastern, Middle, and Western Districts of Tennessee.

Eastern District

(a) The Eastern District comprises four divisions.
(1) The Northern Division comprises the counties of Anderson, Blount, Campbell, Claiborne, Grainger, Jefferson, Knox, Loudon, Monroe, Morgan, Roane, Scott, Sevier, and Union.
Court for the Northern Division is held at Knoxville.
(2) The Northeastern Division comprises the counties of Carter, Cocke, Greene, Hamblen, Hancock, Hawkins, Johnson, Sullivan, Unicoi, and Washington.
Court for the Northeastern Division is held at Greenville.
(3) The Southern Division comprises the counties of Bledsoe, Bradley, Hamilton, McMinn, Marion, Meigs, Polk, Rhea, and Sequatchie.
Court for the Southern Division is held at Chattanooga.
(4) The Winchester Division comprises the counties of Bedford, Coffee, Franklin, Grundy, Lincoln, Moore, Van Buren, and Warren.
Court for the Winchester Division is held at Winchester.

UNITED STATES DISTRICT COURTS

MIDDLE DISTRICT

(b) The Middle District comprises three divisions.

(1) The Nashville Division comprises the counties of Cannon, Cheatham, Davidson, Dickson, Houston, Humphreys, Montgomery, Robertson, Rutherford, Stewart, Sumner, Trousdale, Williamson, and Wilson.

Court for the Nashville Division is held at Nashville.

(2) The Northeastern Division comprises the counties of Clay, Cumberland, De Kalb, Fentress, Jackson, Macon, Overton, Pickett, Putnam, Smith, and White.

Court for the Northeastern Division is held at Cookeville.

(3) The Columbia Division comprises the counties of Giles, Hickman, Lawrence, Lewis, Marshall, Maury, and Wayne.

Court for the Columbia Division is held at Columbia.

WESTERN DISTRICT

(c) The Western District comprises two divisions.

(1) The Eastern Division comprises the counties of Benton, Carroll, Chester, Crockett, Decatur, Gibson, Hardeman, Hardin, Haywood, Henderson, Henry, Lake, McNairy, Madison, Obion, Perry, and Weakley.

The Eastern Division also includes the waters of Tennessee River to low-water mark on the eastern shore wherever such river forms the boundary between the western and middle districts from the north line of Alabama north to the point in Henry County, Tennessee, where the south boundary of Kentucky strikes the east bank of the river.

Court for the Eastern Division is held at Jackson.

(2) The Western Division comprises the counties of Dyer, Fayette, Lauderdale, Shelby, and Tipton.

Court for the Western Division is held at Memphis and Dyersburg.

The district judge for the Eastern District in office on November 27, 1940, shall hold court in the Northern and Northeastern Divisions. The other judge of that district shall hold the terms of court in the Southern and Winchester Divisions. Each may appoint and remove all officers and employees of the court whose official headquarters are located in the divisions within which he holds court and whose appointments are vested by law in a district judge or chief judge of a district.

TEXAS

Texas is divided into four judicial districts known as the Northern, Southern, Eastern, and Western Districts of Texas.

NORTHERN DISTRICT

(a) The Northern District comprises seven divisions.

(1) The Dallas Division comprises the counties of Dallas, Ellis, Hunt, Johnson, Kaufman, Navarro, and Rockwall.

Court for the Dallas Division is held at Dallas.

(2) The Fort Worth Division comprises the counties of Comanche, Erath, Hood, Jack, Palo Pinto, Parker, Tarrant, and Wise.

Court for the Fort Worth Division is held at Fort Worth.

(3) The Abilene Division comprises the counties of Callahan, Eastland, Fisher, Haskell, Howard, Jones, Mitchell, Nolan, Shackleford, Stephens, Stonewall, Taylor, and Throckmorton.

Court for the Abilene Division is held at Abilene.

(4) The San Angelo Division comprises the counties of Brown, Coke, Coleman, Concho, Crockett, Glasscock, Irion, Menard, Mills, Reagan, Runnels, Schleicher, Sterling, Sutton, and Tom Green.

Court for the San Angelo Division is held at San Angelo.

(5) The Amarillo Division comprises the counties of Armstrong, Brisco, Carson, Castro, Childress, Collingsworth, Dallam, Deaf Smith, Donley, Gray, Hall, Hansford, Hartley, Hemphill, Hutchinson, Lipscomb, Moore, Ochiltree, Oldham, Parmer, Potter, Randall, Roberts, Sherman, Swisher, and Wheeler.

Court for the Amarillo Division is held at Amarillo.

(6) The Wichita Falls Division comprises the counties of Archer, Baylor, Clay, Cottle, Foard, Hardeman, King, Knox, Montague, Wichita, Wilbarger, and Young.

Court for the Wichita Falls Division is held at Wichita Falls.

(7) The Lubbock Division comprises the counties of Bailey, Borden, Cochran, Crosby, Dawson, Dickens, Floyd, Gaines, Garza, Hale, Hockley, Kent, Lamb, Lubbock, Lynn, Motley, Scurry, Terry, and Yoakum.
Court for the Lubbock Division is held at Lubbock.

SOUTHERN DISTRICT

(b) The Southern District comprises six divisions.
(1) The Galveston Division comprises the counties of Brazoria, Chambers, Galveston, and Matagorda.
Court for the Galveston Division is held at Galveston.
(2) The Houston Division comprises the counties of Austin, Brazos, Colorado, Fayette, Fort Bend, Grimes, Harris, Madison, Montgomery, San Jacinto, Walker, Waller, and Wharton.
Court for the Houston Division is held at Houston.
(3) The Laredo Division comprises the counties of Jim Hogg, La Salle, McMullen, Webb, and Zapata.
Court for the Laredo Division is held at Laredo.
(4) The Brownsville Division comprises the counties of Cameron and Willacy.
Court for the Brownsville Division is held at Brownsville.
(5) The Victoria Division comprises the counties of Calhoun, DeWitt, Goliad, Jackson, Lavaca, Refugio, and Victoria.
Court for the Victoria Division is held at Victoria.
(6) The Corpus Christi Division comprises the counties of Aransas, Bee, Brooks, Duval, Jim Wells, Kenedy, Kleberg, Live Oak, Nueces, and San Patricio.
Court for the Corpus Christi Division is held at Corpus Christi.
(7) The McAllen Division comprises the counties of Hidalgo and Starr.
Court for the McAllen Division shall be held at McAllen.

EASTERN DISTRICT

(c) The Eastern District comprises seven divisions.
(1) The Tyler Division comprises the counties of Anderson, Cherokee, Gregg, Henderson, Panola, Rains, Rusk, Smith, Van Zandt, and Wood.
Court for the Tyler Division is held at Tyler.
(2) The Beaumont Division comprises the counties of Hardin, Jasper, Jefferson, Liberty, Newton, and Orange.
Court for the Beaumont Division is to be held at Beaumont.
(3) The Sherman Division comprises the counties of Collin, Cook, Denton, and Grayson.
Court for the Sherman Division is held at Sherman.
(4) The Paris Division comprises the counties of Delta, Fannin, Hopkins, Lamar, and Red River.
Court for the Paris Division is held at Paris.
(5) The Marshall Division comprises the counties of Camp, Cass, Harrison, Marion, Morris, and Upshur.
Court for the Marshall Division is held at Marshall.
(6) The Texarkana Division comprises the counties of Bowie, Franklin, and Titus.
Court for the Texarkana Division is held at Texarkana.
(7) The Lufkin Division comprises the counties of Angelina, Houston, Nacogdoches, Polk, Sabine, San Augustine, Shelby, Trinity, and Tyler.
Court for the Lufkin Division is held at Lufkin.

WESTERN DISTRICT

(d) The Western District comprises seven divisions.
(1) The Austin Division comprises the counties of Bastrop, Blanco, Burleson, Burnet, Caldwell, Gillespie, Hays, Kimble, Lampasas, Lee, Llano, Mason, McCulloch, San Saba, Travis, Washington, and Williamson.
Court for the Austin Division is held at Austin.
(2) The Waco Division comprises the counties of Bell, Bosque, Coryell, Falls, Freestone, Hamilton, Hill, Leon, Limestone, McLennan, Milam, Robertson, and Somervell.
Court for the Waco Division is held at Waco.
(3) The El Paso Division comprises the county of El Paso.
Court for the El Paso Division is held at El Paso.

UNITED STATES DISTRICT COURTS

(4) The San Antonio Division comprises the counties of Atascosa, Bandera, Bexar, Comal, Dimmit, Frio, Gonzales, Guadalupe, Karnes, Kendall, Kerr, Medina, Real, and Wilson.
Court for the San Antonio Division is held at San Antonio.
(5) The Del Rio Division comprises the counties of Edwards, Kinney, Maverick, Terrell, Uvalde, Val Verde, and Zavalla.
Court for the Del Rio Division is held at Del Rio.
(6) The Pecos Division comprises the counties of Brewster, Culberson, Jeff Davis, Hudspeth, Loving, Pecos, Presidio, Reeves, Ward, and Winkler.
Court for the Pecos Division is held at Pecos.
(7) The Midland-Odessa Division comprises the counties of Andrews, Crane, Ector, Martin, Midland, and Upton.
Court for the Midland-Odessa Division is held at Midland. Court may be held, in the discretion of the court, in Odessa, when courtroom facilities are made available at no expense to the Government.

UTAH

Utah constitutes one judicial district comprising two divisions.
(1) The Northern Division comprises the counties of Box Elder, Cache, Davis, Morgan, Rich, and Weber.
Court for the Northern Division is held at Ogden.
(2) The Central Division comprises the counties of Beaver, Carbon, Daggett, Duchesne, Emery, Garfield, Grand, Iron, Juab, Kane, Millard, Piute, Salt Lake, San Juan, Sanpete, Sevier, Summit, Tooele, Uintah, Utah, Wasatch, Washington, and Wayne.
Court for the Central Division is held at Salt Lake City.

VERMONT

Vermont constitutes one judicial district.
Court is held at Bennington, Brattleboro, Burlington, Montpelier, Rutland, Saint Johnsbury, and Windsor.

VIRGINIA

Virginia is divided into two judicial districts known as the Eastern and Western Districts of Virginia.

EASTERN DISTRICT

(a) The Eastern District comprises the counties of Accomac, Amelia, Arlington, Brunswick, Caroline, Charles City, Chesterfield, Culpeper, Dinwiddie, Elizabeth City, Essex, Fairfax, Fauquier, Gloucester, Goochland, Greensville, Hanover, Henrico, Isle of Wight, James City, King and Queen, King George, King William, Lancaster, Loudoun, Louisa, Lunenburg, Mathews, Mecklenburg, Middlesex, Nansemond, New Kent, Norfolk, Northampton, Northumberland, Nottoway, Orange, Powhatan, Prince Edward, Prince George, Prince William, Princess Anne, Richmond, Southampton, Spotsylvania, Stafford, Surry, Sussex, Warwick, Westmoreland, and York.
Court for the Eastern District is held at Alexandria, Newport News, Norfolk, and Richmond.

WESTERN DISTRICT

(b) The Western District comprises the counties of Albermarle, Alleghany, Amherst, Appomattox, Augusta, Bath, Bedford, Bland, Botetourt, Buchanan, Buckingham, Campbell, Carroll, Charlotte, Clarke, Craig, Cumberland, Dickenson, Floyd, Fluvanna, Franklin, Frederick, Giles, Grayson, Greene, Halifax, Henry, Highland, Lee, Madison, Montgomery, Nelson, Page, Patrick, Pittsylvania, Pulaski, Rappahannock, Roanoke, Rockbridge, Rockingham, Russell, Scott, Shenandoah, Smyth, Tazewell, Warren, Washington, Wise, and Wythe.
Court for the Western District is held at Abingdon, Big Stone Gap, Charlottesville, Danville, Harrisonburg, Lynchburg, and Roanoke.

(c) Cities and incorporated towns are included in that district in which are included the counties within the exterior boundaries of which such cities and incorporated towns are geographically located or out of the territory of which they have been incorporated.

WASHINGTON

Washington is divided into two judicial districts known as the Eastern and Western Districts of Washington.

Eastern District

(a) The Eastern District comprises the counties of Adams, Asotin, Benton, Chelan, Columbia, Douglas, Ferry, Franklin, Garfield, Grant, Kittitas, Klickitat, Lincoln, Okanogan, Pend Oreille, Spokane, Stevens, Walla Walla, Whitman, and Yakima.

Court for the Eastern District shall be held at Spokane, Yakima, Walla Walla, and Richland.

Western District

(b) The Western District comprises the counties of Clallam, Clark, Cowlitz, Grays Harbor, Island, Jefferson, King, Kitsap, Lewis, Mason, Pacific, Pierce, San Juan, Skagit, Skamania, Snohomish, Thurston, Wahkiakum and Whatcom.

Court for the Western District shall be held at Bellingham, Seattle, and Tacoma.

WEST VIRGINIA

West Virginia is divided into two judicial districts known as the Northern and Southern Districts of West Virginia.

Northern District

(a) The Northern District comprises the counties of Barbour, Berkeley, Braxton, Brooke, Calhoun, Doddridge, Gilmer, Grant, Hampshire, Hancock, Hardy, Harrison, Jefferson, Lewis, Marion, Marshall, Mineral, Monongalia, Morgan, Ohio, Pendleton, Pleasants, Pocahontas, Preston, Randolph, Ritchie, Taylor, Tucker, Tyler, Upshur, Webster, and Wetzel.

Court for the Northern District is held at Clarksburg, Elkins, Fairmont, Martinsburg, and Wheeling.

Southern District

(b) The Southern District comprises the counties of Boone, Cabell, Clay, Fayette, Greenbrier, Jackson, Kanawha, Lincoln, Logan, McDowell, Mason, Mercer, Mingo, Monroe, Nicholas, Putnam, Raleigh, Roane, Summers, Wayne, Wirt, Wood, and Wyoming.

Court for the Southern District is held at Beckley, Bluefield, Charleston, Huntington, Lewisburg, and Parkersburg.

WISCONSIN

Wisconsin is divided into two judicial districts known as the Eastern and Western districts of Wisconsin.

Eastern District

(a) The Eastern District comprises the counties of Brown, Calumet, Dodge, Door, Florence, Fond du Lac, Forest, Green Lake, Kenosha, Kewaunee, Langlade, Manitowoc, Marinette, Marquette, Menominee, Milwaukee, Oconto, Outagamie, Ozaukee, Racine, Shawano, Sheboygan, Walworth, Washington, Waukesha, Waupaca, Waushara, and Winnebago.

Court for the Eastern District is held at Green Bay, Milwaukee, and Oshkosh.

Western District

(b) The Western District comprises the counties of Adams, Ashland, Barron, Bayfield, Buffalo, Burnett, Chippewa, Clark, Columbia, Crawford, Dane, Douglas, Dunn, Eau Claire, Grant, Green, Iowa, Iron, Jackson, Jefferson, Juneau, La Crosse, Lafayette, Lincoln, Marathon, Monroe, Oneida, Pepin, Pierce, Polk, Portage, Price, Richland, Rock, Rusk, Saint Croix, Sauk, Sawyer, Taylor, Trempealeau, Vernon, Vilas, Washburn, and Wood.

Court for the Western District is held at Eau Claire, La Crosse, Madison, Superior, and Wausau.

WYOMING

Wyoming and those portions of Yellowstone National Park situated in Montana and Idaho constitute one judicial district.

Court is held at Casper, Cheyenne, Evanston, Lander, and Sheridan.

Specimen Credit and Other Instruments

33

The Use of Forms

In setting forth specimen forms in this section of the Credit Manual our purpose is to familiarize the credit executive with the various types of contracts and instruments which are the subject of discussion in previous chapters of the book. These forms should not be used as a substitute for competent professional advice.

In some cases a simple form may satisfy the requirements of the situation in which it is used. In many cases, however, the wrong form, or the failure to properly adapt the form to the needs of the parties, may have disastrous results. Most of the states have statutory forms for specific purposes, or impose requirements about matters which must be set forth in certain types of instruments. In some states, by legislative or judicial decree, a particular form of instrument, such as a judgment note, may be invalid or unenforceable. With competent legal advice, however, an instrument may be drawn which will accomplish the intent of the parties without violating statutory restrictions.

In addition to the forms set forth below, there have been reproduced, throughout the textual material in the various chapters, forms pertinent to the subject matter covered. It is recommended that reference be made to the text material in preceding chapters before the use of any forms in this chapter.

Specimen Forms of Acknowledgment as Prescribed by the Uniform Acknowledgment Act

(1) For an individual acting in his own right:

State of _____
County of _____
   The foregoing instrument was acknowledged before me this (date) by (name of person acknowledged).
       (Signature of person taking acknowledgment)
       (Title or rank)
       (Serial number, if any)

(2) For a corporation:

State of _____
County of _____
   The foregoing instrument was acknowledged before me this (date) by (name of officer or agent, title of officer or agent) of (name of corporation acknowledging) a (state or place of incorporation) corporation, on behalf of the corporation.
       (Signature of person taking acknowledgment)
       (Title or rank)
       (Serial number, if any)

(3) For a partnership:
   State of _____
   County of _____
      The foregoing instrument was acknowledged before me this (date) by (name of acknowledging partner or agent), partner (or agent) on behalf of (name of partnership), a partnership.
   (Signature of person taking acknowledgment)
   (Title or rank)
   (Serial number, if any)

(4) For an individual acting as principal by an attorney in fact:
   State of _____
   County of _____
      The foregoing instrument was acknowledged before me this (date) by (name of attorney in fact) as attorney in fact on behalf of (name of principal).
   (Signature of person taking acknowledgment)
   (Title or rank)
   (Serial number, if any)

(5) By any public officer, trustee, or personal representative:
   State of _____
   County of _____
      The foregoing instrument was acknowledged before me this (date) by (name and title of position).
   (Signature of person taking acknowledgment)
   (Title or rank)
   (Serial number, if any)

Affidavit

STATE OF _____
COUNTY OF _____

_____ (name of deponent), being duly sworn, deposes and says:

                                                 Name

Sworn to before me
this _____ day of _____.

_____
        Notary Public

Indorsement on Check Constituting Accord and Satisfaction

This check is in full payment and settlement of the following items: (Insert items); Indorsement will constitute acceptance in full settlement of (all) (the following) claims against the undersigned.

Arbitration Clause for Domestic Trade Contracts

Any controversy or claim arising out of or relating to this contract, or the breach thereof, shall be settled by arbitration, in accordance with the rules, then obtaining, of the American Arbitration Association, and judgment upon the award rendered may be entered in the highest court of the forum, state or federal, having jurisdiction.

Arbitration Clause for Foreign Trade Contracts

Any controversy or claim arising out of or relating to this contract, or the breach thereof, shall be settled by arbitration, in accordance with the rules, then obtaining, of the American Arbitration

Association. This agreement shall be enforceable and judgment upon any reward rendered by all or a majority of the arbitrators may be entered in any court having jurisdiction. The arbitration shall be held in _____ or where jurisdiction may be obtained over the parties. Three arbitrators shall be selected. Unless the parties have agreed upon qualified persons, one arbitrator shall be appointed by each party and the two so chosen shall designate the third. If either party fails or neglects, within a period of fourteen days after written notice by the other, to select an arbitrator upon its part, or if the two selected by the parties cannot agree upon a third within seven days after they have been chosen, the Arbitration Committee of the American Arbitration Association, upon the request of either party, shall appoint such arbitrator or arbitrators from its National Panel within a period of fourteen days.

(Address inquiries regarding clauses and rules of procedure to the American Arbitration Association, 140 W 51 Street, New York, N.Y. 10019.)

Assignment of an Account

I, ..., of ...., in consideration of the sum of .... dollars paid to me by ...... of ...., the receipt whereof is hereby acknowledged, do hereby sell, assign, and transfer to said ...., all and whatsoever sum or sums of money now due and becoming due to me from .... of ....; to have and to hold the same to the said ...., with power to collect the same in my name and as my attorney thereunto duly authorized, to his own use.

It is expressly understood, however, that I shall forever be kept and saved harmless by the said .... from all cost or charge hereafter for and from the expense of the collection of the sum and sums hereby sold and assigned.

In witness, etc.

....L.S.

Assignment of Wages Due and to Become Due

I, ..., of ...., in the county of ...., in consideration of ...... dollars to me paid by .... of ...., the receipt whereof I do hereby acknowledge, do hereby assign and transfer to said .... all claims and demands which I now have, and all which at any time between the date hereof and the .... day of .... next I may have against .... of ...., for all sums of money due, and for all sums of money and demands which, at any time between the date hereof and the said .... day of .... next, may and shall become due to me for services as a ....; to hold the same to the said ...., his executors, administrators, and assigns, forever. And I do hereby constitute and appoint the said .... to be my attorney irrevocable in the premises, to perform all acts, matters, and things touching the premises in like manner to all intents and purposes as I could if personally present.

In witness, etc.

....L.S.

Notice by Assignee to Debtor of Assignment of a Debt

To: ....

I hereby give you notice that by an agreement in writing, dated the .... day of ...., 19..., and made between .... of ...., of the one part, and myself of the other part, the debt of .... dollars owing by you to the said ...... has been absolutely assigned to me, my executors, administrators, and assigns; and further take notice that you are hereby required to pay to me, or such person as I may appoint, the said debt of .... dollars on or before the .... day of .... next, and in default thereof I shall pursue such remedies as are allowed by law for recovery of the said debt.

Dated this ... day of ..., 19...

....L.S.

Notice to Debtor by His Creditor of the Assignment of a Debt

Sir: I have this day assigned the debt of .... dollars now due from you to me to .... of .... and I hereby request you to pay the said sum to him forthwith, and I declare that his receipt for the same shall be a sufficient discharge to you from said debt.

Yours, etc.,

....L.S.

Financing Statement

See §4 of Chapter 7, *supra.*

Assignment by a Corporation

The .... company of ...., a corporation organized and existing, under and by virtue of the laws of the state of ...., and having its principal office at ...., in said state, pursuant to a resolution of the board of directors, passed on the .... day of ...., 19...., in consideration of .... dollars, the receipt whereof is hereby acknowledged, does hereby sell, assign, transfer, and set over unto .... of ...., all that (here name property assigned) in the hands of (name persons holding the property of company for sale). For a more complete description of the property hereby conveyed reference is made to inventory of said property bearing date of .... day of ...., 19...., and contained in the inventory book of said company.

Said company has caused this instrument to be signed in its name, by its president, and sealed with its corporate seal, attested by its secretary, this ..... day of ......, 19...

.... Company
By ....
President.
Attest: (Corporate Seal)
....
Secretary,
(Corporate form of acknowledgment)

Agreement for Account Stated

(Set forth account as it appears upon the books of the creditor or as agreed upon by the parties.) An account stated has been given me and I admit that it is true and correct and that I owe to .... the amount stated therein in the sum of ....
Dated ...., 19....

(Signature of Debtor)

Agreement to Revive a Debt Discharged by Bankruptcy

Agreement made this ..... day of ....., between .... of .... hereinafter called the debtor, and ...... of .... hereinafter called the creditor.

On the .... day of ...., 19...., the debtor, being then indebted to the creditor in the sum of .... dollars, was adjudged a bankrupt, and under such bankruptcy his creditors have been paid a dividend of .... per cent on their claims, and he has been fully discharged from all liability for the residue of said debts. Nevertheless, the debtor considers himself morally bound to pay the creditor the residue of said debt, and desires to pay the same in full.

In consideration of the facts before recited, also of the agreement on the part of the creditor hereinafter contained, and for the purpose of rendering himself legally liable to said creditor for the payment of the remainder of said debt from which he was discharged in bankruptcy, amounting to the sum of .... dollars, the said debtor hereby expressly acknowledges that he is justly indebted to the said creditor in said sum of .... dollars, and agrees to pay said sum within .... months from the date hereof, together with interest thereon at the rate of .... percent per annum.

The creditor, in consideration of the agreement, hereby agrees that he will not sue for, or require payment of, the debt, unless and until default shall be made in payment thereof at the time hereinbefore appointed. In witness, etc.*

---

* The new Bankruptcy Code has placed severe restrictions on reaffirmation, especially in the area of consumer debt. See Chapter 28, *supra* p. 28-1.

Agreement to Pay a Debt Contracted During Infancy

This agreement, made, etc. (parties as in preceding form).

On the .... day of ...., 19...., the debtor, being then a minor, purchased of the creditor .... for the sum of .... dollars, and having now attained his majority and being desirous of ratifying the purchase, to give full effect to this liability for the payment of such debt, proposes to enter into the following agreement: In consideration of the purchase and delivery of .... to him, and of the agreement on the part of the creditor hereinafter contained, he, the debtor, expressly acknowledges the said debt to be justly due to the said .... and agrees to pay the same within .... months from the date hereof, together with interest at the rate of .... percent per annum.

And the said creditor, in consideration of the promise and agreement hereinbefore contained, hereby agrees that he will not sue for or require payment of the said debt unless and until default shall be made in payment thereof at the time hereinbefore appointed.

In witness, etc.

Agreement to Revive a Debt Barred by Statute of Limitations

This agreement, made, etc. (parties as in preceding form).

On the .... day of ...., 19..., the debtor purchased of the creditor an .... for the sum of .... dollars.......... Years have passed and the purchase is unpaid and barred by the statute of limitations. The debtor, desirous to renew the indebtedness to give full effect to his liability for payment of such debt, enters into the following agreement:

In consideration of said purchase and the delivery of said .... to him and the forbearance of said creditor to sue for said purchase price before recovery was barred by operation of law, the debtor hereby acknowledges the debt to be justly due, and agrees to pay the same within .... years from the date hereof, together with interest thereon at the rate of .... percent per annum.

The creditor, in consideration of the agreement hereinbefore contained, hereby agrees not to sue for or require the payment of said debt unless and until default shall be made in the payment at the time herein appointed.

In witness, etc.

Proof of Claim with Power of Attorney

(Not to be used in bankruptcy cases)

County of .... } ss:
State of ....

On this .... day of ...., 19..., personally appeared .... the subscriber, and made oath that the account hereto annexed is just and proper and that he has not directly or indirectly, to his knowledge, received any part of the money charged as due by such account, nor any security or satisfaction for the same, nor any promissory note or other negotiable instrument for the said debt, other than that which is annexed hereto. The subscriber hereby appoints .... or his representatives, and each of them, attorneys in fact authorizing them and each of them to receive and collect the aforesaid debt, or any payments of dividends thereon, with power to compromise, settle or adjust the claim upon such terms as the attorney may deem best, as fully as the subscriber could do if personally present. ....

Subscribed and sworn to before me this .... day of .... 19....

....
Notary Public

General Form of Bill of Sale

I .... of .... in the County of .... and State of .... in consideration of the sum of $....... to me in hand paid by .... of .... the receipt of which is hereby acknowledged have granted, bargained, sold, conveyed, transferred and delivered and by this instrument do bargain, sell, grant, convey, transfer and deliver unto the said .... the following goods and chattels:

TO HAVE AND TO HOLD the same unto the said ...., his executors, administrators and assigns forever;

And I do for myself, my executors, administrators and assigns covenant and agree to and with the said .... to warrant and defend the said .... goods and chattels hereby sold to the said .... his executors, administrators and assigns against all and every person and persons whomsoever.

IN WITNESS WHEREOF, I have hereunto set my hand and seal the ...... day of ...., 19....

Signed, sealed and delivered in presence of

..........................(L.S.)

(Acknowledgment)

STATE OF ....⎫
CITY OF ....⎬ ss:
COUNTY OF ....⎭

being duly sworn, deposes and says, that .... resides at ....
........................, in the City of ....

That .... is the person who executed the within bill of sale.

That .... is the sole owner .. of the property described in the bill of sale, and has full right to see and transfer the same.

That the property is free and clear of any liens, mortgages, debts or other encumbrances of whatsoever kind or nature except, ...

That .... is not indebted to anyone and has no creditors.

That no judgments exist against ...., in any court, nor are there any replevins, attachments or executions issued against .... now in force; nor has any petition in bankruptcy been filed by or against h .....

That this affidavit is made to induce .... to purchase the property described in said bill of sale, knowing that .... will rely thereon and pay a good and valuable consideration therefor.

Sworn to before me this ....

.... day of .... 19..........

(add acknowledgment of subscriber)

General Form of Compromise Agreement

AGREEMENT made this ...... day of .... 19..., between .... with an address at No. ......, ... Street, ..., hereinafter called the Debtor, and .... with an address at No. ...... Street, ..., hereinafter called the Creditor, WITNESSETH:

WHEREAS, a dispute has arisen between the Debtor and Creditor with reference to a claim made by the Creditor against the Debtor for .... in the amount of ....

WHEREAS, the parties hereto are desirous of compromising and settling the said dispute,

NOW, THEREFORE, it is agreed that in consideration of the mutual covenants and agreements herein set forth, the Debtor shall pay to the Creditor in full settlement of the claim made against him as hereinbefore stated the sum of $......

The Creditor shall accept the said amount of $....... in full settlement of all claims which he may have against the Debtor and shall upon receiving full payment of such amount execute and deliver to the Debtor a release in due form of law, of all such claims.

IN WITNESS WHEREOF, the parties have signed this document the date first above written.

(Signatures, seals and acknowledgments of parties)

Guaranty of Past and Future Indebtedness

(The following form specifically limits the liability of the guarantor and has the advantage of specifically permitting the creditor to extend the time of payment to the principal debtor without notice to the guarantor and without releasing the guarantor's liability.)

To ....

Gentlemen:

For and in consideration of *(recite actual consideration)*, the receipt of which is hereby acknowledged, I guarantee unconditionally, at all times, unto you, the payment of any indebtedness or balance of indebtedness of .... of .... State of .... hereinafter called debtor, to you, to an amount not exceeding .... dollars, whether such indebtedness now exists, or is incurred hereafter, and in whatever form it may be evidenced.

I waive notice of acceptance of the guaranty, and all notice of the goods and merchandise sold by you to the debtor, and all notice of defaults by the debtor, and I consent to any extension or extensions of the time or times of payment of the indebtedness, or any portion thereof, and to any change in form, or renewal at any time, of such indebtedness, or any part thereof, or to any evidence thereof taken at any time by you.

This is to be a continuing guaranty, and the extension of the time of payment or the acceptance of any sum or sums on account, or the acceptance of notes, drafts or any security from this debtor, shall in no way weaken the validity of this guaranty. Should any purchase heretofore or hereafter made by the debtor, of you, be not paid at maturity, you shall have the right to proceed against me therefor at any time, without any notice and without any proceeding or action against the said debtor, and I waive any demand for payment.

This guaranty shall continue at all times to the amount of .... dollars regardless of the amounts paid by the debtor and shall not be revoked by death of the guarantor but shall remain in full force until the undersigned or the executor or administrator of the undersigned shall have given notice in writing to make no further advances on the security of this guaranty and until such written notice shall be received by you from the undersigned or his executor or administrator. A registry return receipt for said letter shall be conclusive evidence of receipt of notice or revocation.

This guaranty shall not be abrogated by any change in the firm or status of the debtor, whether caused by death, by the admission of any new member or members or by the withdrawal of any member or members, or by any change from any cause.

It is further understood that nothing herein contained shall prevent you from extending credit to the debtor, to an amount exceeding the sum above stated, being the amount guaranteed hereunder, at any time, and such action on your part shall not affect this guaranty.

Should you extend credit to the debtor, in a sum or sums exceeding the amount of this guaranty, then you shall have the right to make such application of any payment or payments on account, as you may see fit.

Should the said debtor, at any time, become bankrupt or insolvent, then in that event you shall have the right, at your option, without demand or notice whatsoever, to prove and file your entire claim in any court of competent jurisdiction, whether such claim exceeds the amount of this guaranty or not, and to collect any dividends that may be realized on the entire claim; and in that event you shall have the right, at your option, without any notice or demand, to proceed against me at any time, for the difference between the amount of said entire claim due you by the said debtor, and the amount of such dividend or dividends thereon, up to and including the sum above stated, being the amount guaranteed hereunder; if such difference should exceed the sum above stated I shall not be liable for such excess, but for any difference between said entire indebtedness and said dividends thereon, up to and including the sum above stated, being the amount guaranteed hereunder, you shall have the right to proceed against me, at any time, without any demand or notice whatsoever.

The guarantor hereby waives the benefit of all Homestead Exemption laws.

I have hereunto set my hand and seal at .... State of ...... this ...... day of .... 19.....

Corporate Guarantee of Payment of Future Debts

The .... (corporation), organized under the Laws of the State of ...., (address), in consideration of $ ...... (or for good and valuable consideration) the receipt of which is hereby acknowledged, does hereby guarantee full payment of any debts that may be incurred by .... during the period ...., such amounts to be paid in full not later than the .... day of ...., 19 ....

(Corporation)

By:_____

Lease of Personal Property

Agreement of Lease dated .... 19 ...., between .... CORPORATION, having its principal place of business at No. .... Street, ..., herein called "Lessor", and .... residing at No. .... Street, ..., herein called "Lessee".

Lessor hereby leases to Lessee the following personal property which property together with all replacement parts, additions, repairs and accessories heretofore or hereafter incorporated therein or affixed thereto are herein called "equipment";
Make .... Model ....·.... Serial No.(Set forth in complete detail)
1. Term. The term of this lease commences upon ....
....

2. Rent. As rent for said equipment, Lessee shall pay Lessor, at the address above, the sum of .... Dollars ($......) which Lessee hereby promises to pay to Lessor in .... instalments commencing on .... 19 ..., as follows:
$ ...... on the ...... day of ...., 19 ...,
(In same manner set forth other amounts and dates)

3. Location. The equipment shall be located at .... and shall not be removed therefrom without Lessor's prior written consent.

4. Use. Lessor shall comply with all laws relating to the use, operation or maintenance of the equipment. If Lessor supplies Lessee with labels stating that the equipment is owned by Lessor, Lessee shall affix and keep the same upon a prominent place on the equipment.

5. Acceptance. Lessee acknowledges that he has fully inspected and accepted said equipment in good condition and repair.

6. Inspection. At all times during business hours, Lessor shall have the right to inspect the equipment or observe its use.

7. Alterations. Without the prior written consent of Lessor, Lessee shall not make any alterations, additions or improvements to the equipment. All additions and improvements of whatsoever kind or nature made to the equipment shall belong to and become the property of Lessor upon the expiration, or earlier termination of this lease.

8. Repairs. Lessee, at its own cost and expense, shall keep the equipment in good repair, condition and working order and shall furnish any and all parts, mechanisms and devices required to keep the equipment in good mechanical and working order.

9. Loss and Damage. Lessee hereby assumes and shall bear the entire risk of loss and damage to the equipment from any and every cause whatsoever. No loss or damage to the equipment or any part thereof shall impair any obligation of Lessee under this lease which shall continue in full force and effect. In the event of loss or damage of any kind whatever to any item of equipment, Lessee at the option of Lessor shall: (a) place the same in good repair, condition and working order; or (b) replace the same with like equipment in good repair, condition and working order.

10. Insurance. Lessee agrees to take out insurance against risks of fire, malicious mischief and theft in the equipment which names the Lessor as an insured, and to send copies of such policy or certificates thereof to Lessor.

11. Surrender. Upon the expiration or earlier termination of this lease, Lessee shall return the equipment to Lessor in good repair, condition and working order, ordinary wear and tear resulting from proper use thereof alone excepted.

12. Taxes. Lessee shall keep the equipment free and clear of all levies, liens and encumbrances and shall pay all license fees, assessments, charges and taxes (municipal, state and federal) which may now or hereafter be imposed upon the ownership, leasing, renting, sale, possession or use of the equipment. If Lessee fails to pay any said fees, assessments, charges or taxes, Lessor shall have the right, but shall not be obligated, to pay the same. In such event, the cost thereof shall be repayable to Lessor with the next installment of rent, and failure to repay the same shall carry with it the same consequence, including interest at ... percent (..%) per annum, as failure to pay any installment of rent.

13. Indemnity. Lessee shall indemnify Lessor against, and hold Lessor harmless from, any and all claims, actions, suits, proceedings, costs, expenses, damages and liabilities, including attorney's fees, arising out of, connected with, or resulting from the equipment, including without limitation the manufacture, selection, delivery, possession, use, operation or return of the equipment.

14. Default. If Lessee with regard to any item or items of equipment fails to pay any rent or other amount herein provided within ten (10) days after the same is due and payable, or if Lessee with regard to any item or items of equipment fails to observe, keep or perform any other provision of this lease required to be observed, kept or performed by Lessee, Lessor shall have the right to exercise any one or more of the following remedies:

(a) To declare the entire amount of rent hereunder immediately due and payable as to any or all items of equipment, without notice or demand to Lessee.

(b) To sue for and recover all rents, and other payments, then accrued or thereafter accruing, with respect to any or all items of equipment.

(c) To take possession of any or all items of equipment without demand or notice, wherever same may be located, without any court order or other process of law. Lessee hereby waives any and all damages occasioned by such taking of possession. Any said taking of possession shall not constitute a termination of this lease as to any or all items of equipment unless Lessor expressly so notifies Lessee in writing.

(d) To terminate this lease as to any or all items of equipment.

(e) To pursue any other remedy at law or in equity. Notwithstanding any said repossession, or any other action which Lessor may take, Lessee shall be and remain liable for the full performance of all obligations on the part of Lessee to be performed under this lease.

All such remedies are cumulative, and may be exercised concurrently or separately.

15. Bankruptcy. Neither this lease nor any interest therein is assignable or transferable by operation of law. If any proceeding under the Bankruptcy Code, as amended, is commenced by or against the Lessee, or if the Lessee is adjudged insolvent, or if the Lessee makes any assignment for the benefit of his creditors, or if a writ of attachment or execution is levied on any item or items of the equipment and is not released or satisfied within ten (10) days thereafter, or if a receiver is appointed in any proceeding or action to which the Lessee is a party with authority to take possession or control of any item or items of the equipment, Lessor shall have and may exercise any one or more of the remedies set forth in paragraph 14 hereof; and this lease shall, at the option of lessor, without notice, immediately terminate and shall not be treated as an asset of Lessee after the exercise of said option.

16. Lessor's Expenses. Lessee shall pay Lessor all costs and expenses, including attorney's fees, incurred by Lessor in exercising any of its rights or remedies hereunder or enforcing any of the terms, conditions, or provisions hereof.

17. Assignment. Without the prior written consent of Lessor, Lessee shall not (a) assign, transfer, pledge or hypothecate this lease, the equipment or any part thereof, or any interest therein or (b) sublet or lend the equipment or any part thereof, or permit the equipment or any part thereof to be used by anyone other than Lessee or Lessee's employees. Consent to any of the foregoing prohibited acts applies only in the given instance; and is not a consent to any subsequent like act by Lessee or any other person. Subject always to the foregoing, this lease inures to the benefit of, and is binding upon, the heirs, legatees, personal representatives, successors and assigns of the parties hereto.

18. Lessor's Assignment. It is understood that Lessor contemplates assigning this lease and/or mortgaging the equipment, and that said assignee may assign the same. All rights of Lessor in the equipment and hereunder may be assigned, pledged, mortgaged, transferred, or otherwise disposed of, either in whole or in part, without notice to Lessee. The assignee's rights shall be free from all defenses, setoffs or counterclaims which Lessee may be entitled to assert against Lessor. No such assignee shall be obligated to perform any duty, covenant or condition required to be performed by Lessor under the terms of this lease.

19. Ownership. The equipment is, and shall at all times be and remain, the sole and exclusive personal property of Lessor; and the Lessee shall have no right, title or interest therein or thereto except as expressly set forth in this lease.

20. Interest. Should Lessee fail to pay any part of the rent herein reserved or any other sum required by Lessee to be paid to Lessor, within ten (10) days after the due date thereof, Lessee shall pay unto the Lessor interest on such delinquent payment from the expiration of said ten (10) days until paid at the rate of ... percent (..%) per annum.

21. Notices. Service of all notices under this agreement shall be sufficient if given personally or mailed to the party involved at its respective address hereinafter set forth, or at such address as such party may provide in writing from time to time. Any such notice mailed to such address shall be effective when deposited in the United States mail, duly addressed and with postage prepaid.

22. Gender; Number. Whenever the context of this lease requires, the masculine gender includes the feminine or neuter, and the singular number includes the plural; and whenever the word "lessor" is used herein shall include all assignees of lessor. If there is more than one lessee named in this lease, the liability of each shall be joint and several.

IN WITNESS WHEREOF the parties hereto have executed these presents this ...... day of ...., 19 ....

(Signatures, seals and acknowledgments of parties)

....
....

Release of Lease of Personal Property

I, ..., of ...., do hereby certify that a certain lease of personal property dated .... day of ...., 19. ...., and filed in the office of the county clerk of ....

county ...., the .... day of ...., 19. ..., No. ......, for the lease of property therein described by the undersigned, as lessor, to ...., as lessee, to secure the payment of $........, has been satisfied, paid and discharged in full, and the county clerk of said county is hereby authorized to satisfy and cancel the same of record.

Dated: .... 19...
Witnesses:

....
(Signature of lessor)

(If the person executing this release does not personally appear before the clerk, the release must be acknowledged.)

Power of Attorney

Short Form

I, ..., of the town of .... in the county of .... and state of ...., do hereby make, constitute and appoint ...., of the town of ...., in the county of ...., and state of ...., my true, sufficient and lawful attorney, for me and in my name to (here state subject matter of power); and to do and perform all necessary acts in the execution and prosecution of the aforesaid business in as full and ample a manner as I might do if I were personally present.

In Witness Whereof, I have hereunto set my hand and seal the .... day of ...., in the year one thousand nine hundred and ....

.... L.S.

Signed, sealed and delivered in presence of
....

General Release

I, ... for and in consideration of the sum of $........ in hand paid by .... have remised, released, and forever discharged and by these presents for .... heirs, executors and administrators remise, release and forever discharge the said .... heirs, executors and administrators of and from any and all matter of action and actions, cause and causes of action, suits, debts, dues, sums of money, accounts, reckonings, bonds, bills, specialties, covenants, contracts, controversies, agreements, premises, variances, trespasses, damages, judgments, extents, executions, claims and demands whatsoever, in law or in equity which against .... ever had, now have, or which .... heirs, executors or administrators hereafter can, shall or may have, for, upon or by reason of any matter, cause or thing whatsoever, from the beginning of the world to the day of the date of these Presents.

In Witness Whereof, ... have hereunto set hand and seal the .... day of .... one thousand nine hundred and ....

Sealed and delivered in the presence of
....

....
(Acknowledgment.)

Waiver of Right to File Mechanic's Lien

Whereas the undersigned ...., residing (or, ... with principal place of business) at .... Street, ..., ..., is about to furnish certain materials and to perform certain labor (or, ... is furnishing materials and performing labor; or, ... has furnished certain materials and performed certain labor) in the matter of improvement of certain real property owned by .... of .... Street, ..., ..., which real property is designated and known as (give brief description of realty).

Now, therefore, in consideration of the sum of One (1.00) Dollar and other valuable considerations received by the undersigned, he hereby covenants and agrees that he shall not in any claim or file a mechanic's or other lien against the aforesaid premises or any part thereof of any of the materials heretofore or hereafter furnished by him or for any work or labor heretofore or hereafter

SPECIMEN CREDIT AND OTHER INSTRUMENTS 33-11

performed or furnished by him in connection with the improvement of said premises aforesaid by the erection thereon of a two-story dwelling house and garage and the undersigned hereby formally and irrevocably releases and waives in writing any and every lien, charge or claim of any nature whatsoever that he has or may at any time be entitled to have against said premises in connection with the said improvement: (excepting and reserving, however, to the undersigned all right that he has to receive and enforce payment of said account by ....).

In witness whereof, this instrument has been executed and delivered the .... day of ...., 19....

....
(Acknowledgment.)

Satisfaction of Mechanic's Lien

I, ..., do hereby certify, that a certain mechanic's lien, filed in the office of the clerk of the county of ...., the .... day of .... 19..., at ...... o'clock in the .... noon, in favor of .... claimant, against the building and lot situated on the .... street, in .... between .... and .... streets, and known as No. .... in said street, ... owner and contractor, is discharged.

Letter of Credit

Sir:

We hereby agree to accept and pay at maturity any draft or drafts on us at _____days sight, issued by _____located at _____to the extent of $_____ and negotiated through your bank.

Any draft drawn under this letter must state that it is drawn under Letter of Credit issued by _____No. _____Date _____

This Letter of Credit shall be valid to and until the _____ day of _____, 19___

Very truly yours,

....

Negotiable Promissory Note

$1,000.00   City, State,.................. 19...

Sixty days after date, (or, on the .... day of ...., 19... or, on demand), I promise (or, we promise—or, we jointly and severally promise) to pay to A. B., or order (or, to A. B. or bearer), one thousand dollars (with interest), for value received.

....
(Signature.)

Signed, sealed and delivered in the presence of
....

Instalment Note

$..........   ...., 19...

.... after date I .... promise to pay to the order of ...., ... dollars with interest at the rate of ... per cent, per annum, in .... equal instalments as follows:

    On ...., 19..., ... Dollars
    On ...., 19..., ... Dollars
    On ...., 19..., ... Dollars

It is hereby expressly agreed that upon default in payment of any one of said instalments, which default shall extend over a period of more than .... (...) days, then all subsequent instalments on this note, with interest, shall at once become due and payable at the option of the legal holder thereof without demand or notice, demand and notice being hereby expressly waived. The makers, endorsers and all guarantors of this note severally waive demand, protest and presentation for payment and notice of nonpayment and protest, and also waive any and all defenses on the ground of any extensions or partial payment which may be granted or accepted by the holder before or after the maturity of this note or any part thereof.

We also agree that if proceedings are commenced to collect this note by process of law ... percent. (10%) shall be allowed and included in the judgment thereon as attorney's fees. Value received.

....
(Signature.)

Signed, sealed and delivered in the presence of
....

Notes Series with Default Clauses

$.......... ...., 19...
.... after date I .... promise to pay to the order of
.... Dollars, payable at .... Value received.
This note is No. .... of a series of .... notes for .... each due as follows: .... It is hereby specifically agreed that in case of the nonpayment at maturity of this note or any of the notes of this series, then all of the said notes shall immediately become due and payable at the option of the legal holder thereof.

....
(Signature)

No................................ Date ....
Signed, sealed and delivered in the presence of
....

(Note: A series of notes which do not contain a default clause are separate instruments and non-payment of one such note gives the holder of the others no right of action prior to maturity thereof.)

Judgment Note [1]

$.......... ...., 19...
.... after date for value received I .... promise to pay to the order of .... dollars, at .... with interest at .... percent, per annum, from and after date, until paid. And to further secure the payment of said sum, ... authorize, irrevocably, any attorney of any court of record to appear for .... in said court, and confess judgment without process in favor of the holder of this note for such amount as may appear to be unpaid thereon, hereby expressly waiving all benefit under the exemption laws of .... with costs and ... per cent, attorney's fees, and to waive all errors in any such proceedings, and to consent to immediate execution upon such judgment, hereby ratifying and confirming all that ... said attorney may do by virtue hereof.

Signed ....

Security Agreement Under Article 9 of the Uniform Commercial Code [2]

LENDER hereby agrees to lend to BORROWER such amounts as may from time to time be agreed upon. To secure its obligation to repay such indebtedness in accordance with the schedule hereinafter set forth, BORROWER hereby creates in favor of LENDER a security interest in all of BORROWER'S present and future accounts chattel paper, contract rights, documents of title, equipment inventory and general intangibles. BORROWER shall be free to process, use and sell or otherwise dispose of any of the collateral hereunder but the security interest hereby created

---

[1] Check Local Law to determine if permissible. See table in Chapter 18, *supra*. Some states do not permit recovery of attorney's fees in a fixed percentage of the debt, but will only allow reasonable attorney's fees.

[2] See Chapter 7, *supra*.

shall continue in the proceeds [1] and products of any such collateral and in any other personal property hereafter acquired whether as replacements or substitutes for such collateral or otherwise.

Signature and address of Lender
Borrower

....
....

Date: .... 19...
Accepted:
Signature [2] and address of Lender
....
....

A Form of Subordination Agreement

In order to induce (name of bank or other lender), hereinafter referred to as "Bank," to make and renew loans and extend credit to (name of borrower) .... hereinafter called "Borrower," in such manner and amounts and upon such terms and conditions as the Borrower may from time to time request or agree to, and in consideration of any such loan, renewal or extension of credit which the Bank may make, (name of creditor or creditors)... hereinafter called "Creditor," hereby agrees, forthwith upon the making of any such loan, renewal or extension of credit, to subordinate and does hereby wholly subordinate, as herein provided, any and all claims which the Creditor may now or hereafter have against the Borrower to any and all claims which the Bank may now or hereafter have against the Borrower.

Until payment in full with interest of all of said claims of the Bank, the Creditor agrees not to accept any payment or satisfaction of any kind of, or any security for, and not to surrender or release, any of said claims hereby subordinated. If the Creditor should so receive any such payment, satisfaction or security, the Creditor agrees forthwith to deliver the same to the Bank in the form received, endorsed or assigned as may be appropriate, for application on account of, or as security for, said claims of the Bank and until so delivered agrees to hold the same in trust for the Bank. At any time and insofar as any of said claims hereby subordinated may be evidenced by any instrument in writing the Creditor agrees to affix to every such instrument, in form and manner satisfactory to the Bank, a statement to the effect that the same is subject to this agreement and, upon request, agrees to assign or endorse and deliver any such instrument to the Bank.

The Creditor hereby assigns, transfers and sets over to the Bank all of said claims hereby subordinated, effective at the option of the Bank in event of default by the Creditor or the Borrower with respect to any obligation to or agreement with the Bank or in event of the commencement of any liquidation, bankruptcy, insolvency, reorganization or dissolution proceedings by or against the Creditor or the Borrower or of the death of either thereof or of any partner of either thereof. In any such event all of said claims of the Bank and all of said claims hereby subordinated shall, at the option of the Bank, forthwith become due and payable, without demand or notice, and the Bank may, in its absolute discretion, in its own name or the name of the Creditor or otherwise, take any action for the collection of said claims hereby subordinated by process of law, by proof of debt in any proceedings or otherwise, may receive the proceeds thereof and give acquittance therefor and, after deducting the costs and expenses of any action taken, including reasonable counsel fees, may apply the proceeds on account of said claims of the Bank and shall account to the Creditor for any balance remaining.

The Bank shall not be under any duty to take any action in connection with any of said instruments delivered or claims assigned to it and shall not be responsible in any respect in connection therewith, whether for action it may take or refrain from taking or otherwise, except for willful alfeasance.

The Creditor agrees from time to time, upon request, to make, execute and deliver any endorsements, assignments, proofs of claim, affidavits, consents, agreements or other instruments which the Bank may, in its absolute discretion, deem necessary or desirable in order to effectuate the purposes of this agreement in accordance with its true intent and meaning and the Creditor hereby

---

[1] In those states which have adopted the 1972 code, a security interest extends to proceeds of the collateral by operation of law. Therefore, it is not necessary in those states that the security agreement specifically mention proceeds. See U.C.C. §9-306.

[2] Under the 1962 code, the secured party's signature is only required when the agreement is to be filed as a financing statement. Since the 1972 code eliminates the necessity of the secured party's signature on a financing statement, the secured party's signature is unnecessary on a security agreement in those states which have adopted the revisions.

irrevocably constitutes and appoints the Bank and any of its present or future officers severally attorneys in fact for and on behalf of the Creditor, with full power of substitution and revocation, in its own name or in the name of the Creditor or otherwise, so to do, in the exercise of which discretion and power the decision of the Bank or the decision of any of its said officers shall be conclusive as to all persons and for all purposes.

Without notice of the Creditor and without in any way impairing or affecting this agreement, the Bank may from time to time, in its absolute discretion, for value or without value, renew or extend the time of payment of any said claims of the Bank, modify in any manner or release in whole or in part any security therefor or the obligations of any endorsers, sureties or guarantors thereof or release from the terms of this or of any other subordination agreement any claims subordinated.

The Borrower, for the consideration hereinabove stated, authorizes and approves any act or thing which may be done in accordance herewith and agrees not to make any payment of or on account of, give any security for, or accept any surrender or release in whole or in part of, any of said claims hereby subordinated.

The Creditor and the Borrower agree to make and maintain in their books of account notations satisfactory to the Bank of the rights and priorities of the Bank hereunder and from time to time on request, to furnish the Bank with sworn financial statements. The Bank may inspect the books of account and any records of the Creditor or the Borrower at any time during business hours. The Creditor and the Borrower waive notice of acceptance hereof and all other notice or demand whatever. No waiver by the Bank of any right hereunder shall be valid unless in writing and no waiver of any right shall be deemed a waiver of any other right. Nothing herein shall limit or affect in any manner any right the Bank may have by virtue of any other instrument or agreement. The words "Creditor" and "Borrower" as herein used shall include the plural as well as the singular and if "Creditor" or "Borrower" includes two or more they shall be jointly and severally bound hereby. The word "claims" as herein used shall mean all liabilities without limitation, whether due or not due, direct or contingent, determined or undetermined in amount, however acquired, evidenced or arising and any part thereof.

This agreement shall inure to the benefit of the Bank, its successors and assigns, and shall be binding upon the Creditor and the Borrower and their respective legal representatives, successors and assigns. It shall be a continuing agreement and shall be irrevocable and shall remain in full force and effect until all of said claims of the Bank shall have been paid in full and until the Bank shall have received notice in writing of election to terminate it as to future loans or extensions of credit but, notwithstanding such notice or any other notice or the death or incompetency of any party hereto, this agreement shall continue to remain in full force and effect as to all said claims of the Bank then outstanding and any renewals or extensions thereof theretofore or thereafter made.

In witness whereof, this agreement has been duly executed this . . . . day of . . . . 19 . . . .
Creditor: . . . .
Borrower: . . . .
(Acknowledgments.)

Security Agreement for Accounts Receivable

AGREEMENT made this . . . . . . day of . . . . 19. . . , by and between . . . . , a corporation duly organized to do business in the State of . . . . with its principal place of business at . . . . hereinafter called the "Secured Party," and . . . . with its principal place of business at . . . . hereinafter called the "Debtor."

I. *Creation of Security Interest*

Debtor hereby grants a personal security interest in and assigns to the Secured Party the collateral described in paragraph II below to secure payment and performance of all debts, liabilities and obligations of Debtor of any kind whenever and however incurred to Secured Party.

II. *Collateral*

The collateral of this security agreement is all of the accounts receivable presently existing and hereafter arising of the Debtor, and all personal property in which the Debtor has an interest now or hereafter in the control or possession of the Secured Party and the proceeds [1] of the above described collateral.

III. *Obligations of Debtor*

A. Debtor shall pay to, turn over to and deposit with the Secured Party all proceeds in the

---

[1] *See supra* p. 33-13, note 1.

SPECIMEN CREDIT AND OTHER INSTRUMENTS

form of cash and negotiable instruments for the payment of money received by Debtor from an Account Debtor in payment of or on Account and the Secured Party shall have the exclusive right in accordance with this Security Agreement to the proceeds paid, turned over or deposited by Debtor.

B. Debtor shall pay immediately without notice and irrespective of any credit term in any instrument or writing evidencing indebtedness, if Secured Party so elects, any or all indebtedness, of Debtor to Secured Party upon Debtor's default under this Security Agreement or if Secured Party deems itself insecure.

C. Debtor shall pay on demand all expenses and expenditures of Secured Party, including reasonable attorneys' fees and legal expenses incurred or paid by Secured Party in protecting, enforcing or exercising its interests, rights or remedies created by, connected with or provided in this Security Agreement or performance pursuant to this Security Agreement.

D. Debtor shall pay to Secured Party upon demand, any balance due to Secured Party in the event that the account debtors fail to pay on the due date, the respective accounts in satisfaction of Debtor's obligation to the Secured Party.

E. Debtor shall not voluntarily or involuntarily subject the collateral or its proceeds or allow the collateral or its proceeds to be subjected to any interest of any transferee, buyer, secured party, encumbrancer or other third person, shall not modify the contracts with the Account Debtors or diminish any security for any Account, and shall not bring suit to enforce payment of an Account without giving Secured Party notice in advance in writing and without first receiving written consent from Secured Party.

F. Debtor shall, at its expense, do, make, procure, execute and deliver all acts, things, writings and assurances as Secured Party may at any time require to protect, assure or enforce its interests, rights and remedies created by, provided in or emanating from this Security Agreement.

G. Until deposit in accordance with this Security Agreement, Debtor shall hold all proceeds received in payment of or on an Account, and shall hold all other collateral of this Security Agreement for or on behalf of Secured Party separate and apart from and shall not commingle the proceeds or collateral with any of Debtor's funds or property.

IV. *Debtor represents and warrants that:* (A) its principal place of business is in the .... (B) the accounts that form the basis of this Security Agreement represent goods sold or services performed as follows: .... and (C) the account is not subject to any prior or subsequent assignment, claim, lien or security interest other than that of the Secured Party, nor is the claim subject to setoff or counterclaim, defense, allowance or judgment.

V. *Default.*

1. Debtor shall be in default under this Security Agreement if any one of the following occurs:

A. When there is misstatement or false statement in connection with, noncompliance with, or non-performance of any of the Debtor's obligations, agreements or affirmations under or emanating from this Security Agreement.

B. Upon death, dissolution, termination of existence, insolvency, business failure, appointment of a receiver of the Debtor or any surety of Debtor, making of an assignment for the benefit of creditors by Debtor, the calling of a meeting of creditors of, or the commencement of any proceeding under any bankruptcy or insolvency laws by or against Debtor or any surety for Debtor, or the termination by a surety for Debtor's obligations of its contract of suretyship.

VI. *Secured Party's Rights and Remedies*

A. Rights and Remedies Exclusive of Default. Secured Party or its nominee or agent may

(1) Upon written notice to Debtor notify or require Debtor to notify Account Debtors obligated on any or all of Debtor's Accounts to make payment directly to Secured Party, and may take possession of all proceeds of any Accounts in Debtor's possession.

(2) Take any steps which Secured Party deems necessary or advisable to collect discharge or extend the whole or any part of the Accounts or other collateral or proceeds, and to apply the proceeds to Debtor's indebtedness to Secured Party in accordance with the provisions of this Security Agreement.

(3) Call at Debtor's place or places of business at intervals to be determined by Secured Party and, without hindrance or delay, inspect, audit, check and make extracts from the books, records, journals, orders, receipts, correspondence and other data relating to the collateral or to any transaction between Debtor and Secured Party.

(4) Subrogate to all of Debtor's interests, rights and remedies in respect to any Account,

including the right to stop delivery and upon notice from Debtor that the Account Debtor has returned, rejected, revoked acceptance of or failed to return the goods or that the goods have been re-consigned or diverted, the right to take possession of and to sell or dispose of the goods, unless Secured Party fails to advise Debtor of its intended exercise of such rights within five business days after receipt of notice.

B. Upon Debtor's Default, Secured Party shall have all of the rights and remedies provided in this Security Agreement and in the Uniform Commercial Code in force in .... at the date of this Security Agreement.

VII. *Debtor's Rights and Remedies.*

Debtor shall have the right to collect and enforce at its own expense as agent for Secured Party all Accounts until Debtor is in default hereunder or until Secured Party notifies Debtor that it will collect any or all Accounts pursuant to this Security Agreement.

VIII. *Additional Agreements and Affirmations.*

A. Debtor's Agreements and affirmations. Debtor agrees and affirms

(1) That its only places of business are those appearing beneath his signature below and that he will promptly notify Secured Party of any change of location of any place of business or of the addition of any new place of business.

(2) That at the time Secured Party's security interest attaches to any of the collateral or its proceeds, Debtor is the lawful owner with the right to transfer any interest therein, that the collateral and its proceeds are not and will not be the subject of any financing statement on file or subject to the interest of any person except under this Security Agreement and that Debtor will defend the collateral and its proceeds against the lawful claims and demands of all persons.

IX. *Mutual Agreements.*

A. "Secured Party" and "Debtor" as used in this Security Agreement shall include the heirs, executors, administrators, successors, representatives, receivers, trustees and assigns of those parties.

B. The laws of .... shall govern the construction of and the rights and duties of the parties to this Security Agreement.

C. This Security Agreement includes all amendments and supplements thereto, and all assignments, instruments, documents, Accounts and other writings submitted by Debtor to Secured Party pursuant to this Security Agreement, but neither Debtor nor Secured Party shall be bound by an undertaking not expressed in writing.

D. If any of the provisions of this Security Agreement shall contravene or be held invalid under the laws of any jurisdiction, the Security Agreement shall be construed as if not containing such provisions and the rights and obligations of the parties shall be construed and enforced accordingly.

This Agreement is executed this .... day of .... 19. ...

By [1] _____

Security Agreement for Equipment

This agreement made this ...... day of ...., by and between .... with an address at .... hereinafter called the "Secured Party" and .... with an address at .... hereinafter called the "Debtor."

I. *Creation of Security Interest.*

Debtor hereby grants a personal security interest in and assigns to the Secured Party the Collateral described in paragraph II below to secure payment and performance of all debts, liabilities and obligations of Debtor of any kind whenever and however incurred to Secured Party.

II. *Collateral.*

....
....
....
....
....
....

---

[1] *See supra* p. 13-13, note 1.

III. *Debtor's Obligations.*
   A. Debtor shall pay to Secured Party the sum or sums evidenced by the promissory note or notes executed pursuant to this security agreement in accord with the terms of such note or notes.
   B. The Collateral will not be misused or abused, wasted or allowed to deteriorate, except for the ordinary wear and tear of its intended primary use.
   C. The Collateral will be insured until this security agreement is terminated against all expected risks to which it is exposed and those which Secured Party may designate, with policies acceptable to Secured Party and payable to both Secured Party and Debtor as their interests appear, and with duplicate policies deposited with the Secured Party.
   D. The Collateral will be kept at the Debtor's place of business, aforementioned, where Secured Party may inspect it at any time.
   E. The Collateral will not be sold, transferred or disposed, or subject to any paid charge, including taxes of any subsequent interest of a third party created or suffered by Debtor, voluntary or involuntary, unless Secured Party consents in writing to such charge, transfer or disposition.
   F. Debtor will sign and execute any financing statement or other document or procure any document and pay all connected costs necessary to protect the security agreement against the rights of interests of a third person.
   G. Debtor will reimburse Secured Party for any action to remedy a default under this agreement.
IV. *Secured Party's Obligations.*
Secured Party hereby sells the Collateral and shall transfer possession thereof to Debtor on ....·19....
V. *Default.*
Misrepresentation or misstatement in connection with, noncompliance with or nonperformance of any of Debtor's obligations or agreements under paragraphs III and VIII shall constitute default under this Security Agreement. In addition, Debtor shall be in default if bankruptcy or insolvency proceedings are instituted by or against the Debtor or if Debtor makes any assignment for the benefit of creditors.
VI. *Secured Party's Rights and Remedies.*
   A. Secured Party may assign this security agreement, and ....
   (1) If Secured Party does assign this security agreement, the assignee shall be entitled, upon notifying the Debtor, to performance of all of Debtor's obligations and agreements under paragraphs III and VIII, and assignee shall be entitled to all of the rights and remedies of Secured Party under this paragraph VI, and
   (2) Debtor will assert no claims or defenses he may have against Secured Party or against its assignee except those granted in this security agreement, and .... B. Upon Debtor's default, Secured Party may exercise his rights of enforcement under the Uniform Commercial Code in force in the State of .... at the date of this security agreement and, in conjunction with, addition to or substitution for those rights, at Secured Party's discretion, may
   (1) Enter upon Debtor's premises to take possession of, assemble and collect the Collateral or to render it unusable, and
   (2) Require Debtor to assemble the Collateral and make it available at a place Secured Party designates which is mutually convenient, to allow Secured Party to take possessions or dispose of the Collateral, and
   (3) Waive any default or remedy any default in any reasonable manner without any or all Accounts or other collateral or proceeds, or to sell, transfer, compromise, waiving the default remedied and without waiving any other prior or subsequent default.
VII. *Rights and Remedies of Debtor.*
Debtor shall have all of the rights and remedies before or after default provided in Article 9 of the Uniform Commercial Code in force in the State of .... at the date of this security agreement.
VIII. *Additional Agreements and Affirmations.*
   A. Debtor Agrees and Affirms
   (1) That information supplied and statements made by him in any financial or credit statement or application for credit prior to this security agreement are true and correct, and
   (2) That no financing statement covering the Collateral or its proceeds is on file in any public office and that, except for the security interest granted in this security agreement, there is no adverse lien, security interest or encumbrance in or on the Collateral, and
   (3) That the addresses of Debtor's residence and place or places of business, if any, are those appearing below his signature, and
   (4) That if Debtor is also buyer of the Collateral, there are no express warranties unless they appear in writing signed by the seller and there are no implied warranties of merchantability or fitness for a particular purpose in connection with the sale of the Collateral.

B. Mutual Agreements.

(1) "Debtor" and "Secured Party" as used in this security agreement include the heirs, executors or administrators, successors or assigns of those parties.

(2) The law governing this secured transaction shall be that of the State of .... in force at the date of this security agreement.

(3) If more than one Debtor executes the security agreement; their obligations hereunder shall be joint and several.

Executed in triplicate this ...... day of ...., 19....

By _____
    Secured Party [1]

By _____
    Debtor

_____
Address

_____
Debtor's Residence

_____
Address of Chief Place of Business

Addresses of other places of business

_____

_____

---

[1] *See supra* p. 13-12, note 2.

SPECIMEN CREDIT AND OTHER INSTRUMENTS 33–19

Disclosure Statement as Required by Federal Law for Instalment Loan *

BORROWER'S NAME AND ADDRESS

1. This is an instalment loan payable in consecutive monthly instalments on the day of each month beginning on ....
2. The amount of each payment due is as follows:
   (a) First: ....
   (b) Others: ....
   (c) Final: ....
3. The amount of the loan and finance charges is as follows:
   (a) Amount Financed ....
   (b) FINANCE CHARGE ....
   (c) Total of Payments (a + b) ....
   (d) ANNUAL PERCENTAGE RATE ....
   (e) Official Fees (Explain) ....
   (f) Total ....
   ....
4. A late charge in the amount of $.......... of the delinquent instalment will be levied if the scheduled payment is not received within ten (10) days after the due date.
5. If the loan is prepaid in full before the final installment date, the borrower shall receive a rebate of unearned interest. Any unpaid late charges will be deducted from this rebate. Where the earned portion of the Finance Charge is $10 or less, only that portion of the Finance Charge in excess of $10 will be returned.
6. The loan is secured by a Security Agreement covering: ....
   ....
   ....

   I acknowledge receipt of this statement.

   ....
   Signature of Borrower

---

* Regulation Z of the Truth-in-Lending Act, 12 C.F.R. § 226.17(a) (1983), requires that the disclosure be clear and conspicuous. Note that Regulation M, which governs consumer leasing, requires that disclosures be printed in not less than the equivalent of 10-point type, .075 inch computer type, elite size typewritten numerals, or in legible handwriting. 12 C.F.R. § 213.4 (1983). The terms "FINANCE CHARGE" and "ANNUAL PERCENTAGE RATE" are required to be used and must be printed more conspicuously than the balance of the numbers.

RETAIL INSTALMENT CONTRACT
(Conditional Sale Contract)

Date ...., 19 ..... Buyer's Name ....
To .... (Please Print)
          (Seller)   Buyer's
....   Address ....
          (Place of Business)   (Number)
                                          .... (Street)
                                                           (City)
                                          Installation Address,
                                          if different .... (State)

I/we (meaning the undersigned buyer or buyers) buy from you and you sell, the following goods:

(Adequate description of goods or services, including the make and model, if any, in the case of goods customarily sold by make and model.)

                                    (Note 1)

NOTICE TO THE BUYER

1. Do not sign this agreement before you read it.
2. If it contains any blank space you are entitled to a completely filled in copy of this agreement.
3. Under the law, you have the right to pay off in advance the full amount due and under certain conditions to obtain a partial refund of the credit service charge.

1. (A) Cash sale price .... $ ....
   (B) Cash sale price of any accessories and/or services
       not included in (A) .... $ ....
       (separately itemized)
2. Sales tax (if any) .... $ ....
3. Excise tax (if any) .... $ ....
4. Total items (1), (2) and (3) .... $ ....
5. Down payment:
   (A) Cash .... $ ....
   (B) Trade-in Allowance (description of goods)
6. Item (4) minus item (5) .... $ ....
7. Insurance premiums (if any) .... $ ....
8. Official fees (if any) .... $ ....
9. Principal balance (sum of Items (6), (7) and (8)) . $ ....
10. Credit Service Charge .... $ ....
11. Time balance (sum of Items (9) and (10)) .... $ ....
12. Time sale price (sum of Items (5) and (11)) ..... $ ....

```
        Insurance Coverage
        Type           Cost
        ...............................
        ...............................
        Insurance, if any; to be procured
```

Note:
(2)
by ....

33–20

RETAIL INSTALMENT CONTRACT *(Continued)*

(3) which * (including any balance payable under prior contracts) * I/we, jointly and severally, agree to pay in .... instalments of $.......... each .... commencing one month from date or on ...., 19...., and a final instalment of $........... at ....* or such other address as .... commencing one month from date or on

(5) I/we are notified in writing, on the .... day of each .... *
............, 19.... *

(6) * Should I/we default in payment of any instalment and such default continue for a period of ten days, I/we agree to pay a delinquency charge of five per cent (5%) of the amount of each instalment in default or the sum of Five Dollars ($5.00) whichever is less and to make such payment not later than one month after such default. In event of this Contract becoming due and payable and being referred to an attorney for collection, I/we shall pay, in addition to the amount then remaining to be paid hereunder, a further amount equal to twenty per cent (20%) thereof.*

(7) * Acceptance of payments in lesser amounts or after they are due shall not be a waiver of any of your rights under this contract.*

(8) * If you consolidate this purchase with my/our prior balance such balance may be inserted later. The maximum credit service charge on the consolidated total shall not exceed $10.00 per $100.00 per annum by a sum in excess of $12.00 and, either the amount of and the period between the instalments to be paid by me/us shall be the same as in that contract, included in the consolidated total, which provides for the highest rate of repayment, or the due date of the last instalment to be paid by me/us and the period between the instalments shall be the same as in that contract, included in the consolidated total, which is the last to mature.*

(9) Title to the goods purchased under this *and prior* contract(s) shall be retained by you until all amounts due shall have been paid, subject to allocation of payments and release of security as provided by law. I/we shall *pay all taxes on the goods,*

(11) keep the goods safely and will not sell, remove or encumber them. If I/we should default in the payment of any sum payable under this Contract *or in the performance of any of the other terms and provisions hereof,* any and all amounts then remaining unpaid hereunder, shall, at the option of the seller, become due and payable forthwith.#

(13)* You may assign this contract. If you do so my/our claims against you shall not be affected. Unless I/we notify the assignee within ten (10) days after notice of assignment has been mailed to me/us, I/we shall not assert such claims against the assignee.*

(14) Identifying numbers or marks of the goods and the due date of the first instalment may be inserted later.

(16) This is our entire agreement and cannot be changed orally. (15)

* Accepted:
Seller's Name .... *
By .... *
* Witness: .... *

Suggested Form No. 21 7-57 *See Reference*
New York Conference on Instalment Selling *Notes next page*

* **THIS IS A RETAIL INSTALMENT CONTRACT, THE RECEIPT BY THE BUYER OF AN EXECUTED COPY OF WHICH IS HEREBY ACKNOWLEDGED.***

Buyer's Signature ....
Co-Buyer's Signature ....
Co-Buyer's Address ....

33–21

Retail Instalment Contract

(Reproduced herewith on two preceding pages is a suggested form of retail instalment contract under the New York State Retail Instalment Sales Act. N.Y. Pers. Prop. §§ 401-422 (McKinney 1976 & Supp. 1983). This form is a conditional sale contract which conforms to the statutory requirements. A number of states have enacted retail instalment sales laws which require contracts to adhere rigidly to statutory requirements regarding form. It is recommended that counsel be consulted in connection with the preparation of appropriate forms for use in the various states.)

REFERENCE NOTES TO RETAIL INSTALMENT CONTRACT FORM

Marginal notes, * * and # are inserted in text as references to notes. They should be deleted from text for final use.

(1) Inapplicable captions in the tabulations may be omitted; for instance: cost and description of insurance where no separate charge is made; taxes or other charges where there are none. Additional items may be included to explain the computations in determining the amount to be paid by the buyer. Sellers who collect sales tax at time of sale and furnish customer a separate invoice showing sales tax and comply with other requirements of law may word the first caption "Cash sale price including any taxes." Items 9, 11 and 12 of the text are requirements of the law but may be in a revised order if more in conformity with the seller's routine. Sellers who prefer may revise captions under "Down Payment" to provide separate spaces for "Cash Deposit .... $ ...." and "Cash on or before delivery............. $ ...." The line numbers may be revised or deleted from text when printed.
(2) This provision for insurance coverage is necessary only if a separate charge is made to the buyer for such insurance. In that event the contract must state whether the insurance is to be procured by the buyer or the seller, and if procured by the seller he must within 30 days after delivery of the goods or furnishing of the services, deliver or mail to the buyer at the address contained in the contract a notice thereof or a copy of the policy or policies or a certificate or certificates of the insurance so procured.
(3) Text between * * may be omitted by Sellers not desiring to consolidate balance under prior contracts with balance under this contract.
(4) If any instalment substantially exceeds in amount any prior instalment other than the down payment, you must comply with Section 402(3)(b)(2) of the Act relative to "Balloon Payments."
(5) Text between * * may be omitted by Sellers who carry their paper or do not require this clause. Sellers who do not carry their own paper should insert a clause to provide for assignment of the contract. They should confer with their financing agency with respect to the form and content of the contract.
(6) Text between * * may be omitted by Sellers not desiring to collect a delinquency and collection charge or attorney's fees.
(7) * * Sellers who desire may omit this clause.
(8) Sellers who use this clause in their contract must be certain the credit service charge does not exceed that permitted by the Act.
(9) Text between * * may be omitted by Sellers not desiring add-on provision.
(10) Text between * * may be omitted where goods are not subject to any tax.
(11) Text between * * may be omitted by Sellers who do not wish to avail themselves of the right to accelerate default for any reason other than non-payment.
(12) Sellers who desire may insert the following clause: "To avoid delay and expense, it is mutually agreed that all parties waive the right to a trial by jury."
(13) See Note 5 above.
(14) Sellers who do not desire to collect sales tax separately or with down payment, should add the following sentence in text of agreement, "If the cash sale price includes a sales tax, I/we agree that any payment of a deposit or instalment includes only that proportionate part of the sales tax which is applicable to such payment." Appropriate modification may be required for other future taxes.
(15) The Act requires any acknowledgment of delivery of a copy to be printed in ten point bold type, directly above the space reserved for the buyer's signature in the contract. (See forms for example of 10 point bold type.)
(16) The text between * * including the signature may be omitted by Sellers not desiring to reserve the right to make the effectiveness of the agreement conditioned upon their "acceptance." Such Sellers may insert at the end of the present text of the contract: "This contract to become effective only upon approval of credit risk by seller." The purpose of this insertion is to enable the Seller to deliver a copy of the contract immediately but nevertheless have the opportunity of verifying the acceptability of the buyer's credit and availability of the goods.
(17) Sellers who desire may omit provision for witness to the execution of contract by the buyer.

Glossary of Legal Terms

ACCELERATION CLAUSE: A clause in contracts of debt which makes the entire amount due upon the debtor's default.

ACCEPTANCE (With respect to commercial paper): The drawee's engagement to honor the draft as presented.

ACCOMMODATION INDORSER: One who places his indorsement without compensation on a note, in effect acting as a guarantee of payment.

ACCORD AND SATISFACTION: A settlement agreement by which a claim is satisfied and discharged.

ACKNOWLEDGMENT (With respect to an instrument): The statement of a competent officer, usually a notary public, that the person who has executed an instrument has appeared before him and sworn to the facts of its execution.

ACTION: A suit at law or in equity.

ACTIONABLE: Affording grounds for a legal action.

ADMINISTRATOR: One appointed to manage and distribute an estate where the decedent has not left a will, or where for some reason an executor has not been appointed or qualified under the will.

AFFIDAVIT: A statement sworn to or affirmed before an official who is authorized to administer oaths—usually a notary public.

AFTER-ACQUIRED PROPERTY: Property which a debtor acquires after the execution of a mortgage or other form of indebtedness and which secures such indebtedness.

AGENT: A person authorized by another, i.e., the principal, to act for him.

AMICUS CURIAE: "Friend of the court." A term frequently used to designate one not a party to the proceeding but who has filed a brief regarding the issue or principle of law to be decided.

ARBITRATION: The determination of a dispute by a disinterested third person, or persons, selected by the disputants.

ASSIGNMENT: The transfer of property rights by one person, known as the assignor, to another, known as the assignee.

ASSIGNMENT FOR BENEFIT OF CREDITORS: A transfer of all of a debtor's property to another person in trust to collect any money owed to the debtor, to sell property, to distribute proceeds and to return any surplus to debtor.

ASSUMPSIT: A form of action for the recovery of damages for the nonperformance of a contract.

ATTACHMENT: Taking property into custody of the court, either to satisfy a judgment ultimately to be rendered or as a method of acquiring jurisdiction.

ATTESTATION: The act of witnessing the execution of an instrument.

ATTORNEY-IN-FACT: A person who is authorized by power of attorney to act for another.

BAILMENT: The delivery of property by one, known as the bailor, to another, known as the bailee, to be held in custody for certain purposes.

BEQUEST: A gift of personal property by will.

BILL OF EXCHANGE: A written order, which may be negotiable or nonnegotiable, directing one party to pay a certain sum of money to the drawer or to a third person.

BILL OF LADING: Receipt and contract issued by a common carrier for the shipment of goods.

BILL OF SALE: A written instrument by which one transfers his rights or interest in chattels and goods to another.

BLANK INDORSEMENT: Indorsement which consists only of the signature of the indorser and does not state in whose favor it is made.

BLUE SKY LAWS: State legislation which regulates the issuance and sale of corporate securities.

BONA FIDE: In good faith.

BONA FIDE PURCHASER: One who buys property without knowledge or notice of any defects in the title of the seller.

BULK TRANSFER: The transfer of inventory or trade fixtures or a major portion thereof not in the ordinary course of business.

CAVEAT EMPTOR: "Let the buyer beware." In the absence of a warranty a buyer purchases goods at his own risk, unless the seller is guilty of fraud.

CERTIORARI: A writ of a higher court issued to a lower court directing the lower court to transmit its proceedings for review. In most cases the United States Supreme Court requires an application for certiorari to be made to it before it will hear an appeal from a lower court.

CHATTEL: Any type of personal property as distinguished from real property.

CHATTEL MORTGAGE: Security interest taken by the mortgagee in personal property of the mortgagor. A pre-Uniform Commercial Code device.

CHOSE: A thing; personal property. *Chose in action:* property not in possession but a right of action exists for such possession. A claim or right to recover a debt or damages.

COLLATERAL SECURITY: A separate obligation which is given to secure the performance of the primary obligation in a contract.

COMMON CARRIER: One whose business it is to transport passengers or freight for the public.

GLOSSARY OF LEGAL TERMS

CONDITIONAL SALE: An instalment sale in which the goods are delivered to the buyer, but title remains with the seller until payment is made for the goods.

CONSIDERATION: The required element in all contracts by which a legal right or promise is exchanged for the act or promise of another party. The inducement to a contract.

CONSIGNMENT: The shipment of goods or chattels by means of a common carrier from one party known as the consignor to another known as the consignee; also, the transfer of property to another for sale by him.

CONVEYANCE: The transfer of an interest in realty; a deed. Sometimes includes leases and mortgages.

COPYRIGHT: The exclusive right granted by common law or the Federal Government to publish and reproduce copies of writings and drawings.

COUNTERCLAIM: A claim asserted by the defendant in opposition to or deduction from the claim of the plaintiff.

COVENANT: A promise made by one person to another.

DEBIT CARD: Device similar to a credit card allowing the account of the cardholder with a bank or other person to be charged even though no credit is thereby extended.

DEVISE: The gift of real property in a will. Also *(verb)*, to give real property by will.

DISHONOR: The nonpayment of a negotiable instrument on its due date.

DRAFT: A bill of exchange.

DRAWEE: The person on whom a bill of exchange or a draft is drawn.

DRAWER: The person who draws a bill or draft.

EASEMENT: The right of one person to use the land, or a portion of the land, of another for a specific purpose without obtaining possession thereof.

EMINENT DOMAIN: The power of the sovereign government to take private property for public purposes.

EQUITY OF REDEMPTION: The right of a mortgagor to redeem his property after the mortgage is past due.

ESCROW: The delivery by a grantor of a deed or of personal property to a third person for delivery to the grantee upon the happening of certain conditions.

ESTOPPEL: A rule of law which precludes a person from denying certain facts because of previous inconsistent conduct or statements.

FACTOR: One who has received goods or merchandise for sale on behalf of another.

FEE SIMPLE: Absolute ownership of real property.

FIXTURE: A chattel which has been permanently affixed to real estate and may or may not be severable therefrom without injury to the property.

FORECLOSURE: The legal act by which the owner of a mortgage cuts off the rights or interest of the mortgagor in the mortgaged property.

FRANCHISE: A license, privilege or right granted by a government or the owner of a trademark or tradename permitting another to sell the product under that name or mark.

GARNISHMENT: The legal process by which property due to a debtor and in the hands of a third person is attached.

GUARANTEE: To assume the liability for such debts of another in the event of his default.

GUARANTY: A contract by which one undertakes to be liable for the debt of another person in the event of his default.

HOLDER IN DUE COURSE: A bona fide holder who takes an instrument for value without notice of it being overdue or of possible defenses.

INCHOATE: Not yet completed or finished. Used in reference to rights which have not become absolute, such as a wife's inchoate right of dower during the lifetime of her husband.

INDEMNITY: Compensation paid for damage or loss sustained or anticipated.

INDORSEMENT: The signature of the person transferring a negotiable instrument.

INFANT: A person who has not reached legal maturity; a minor.

INSOLVENCY: Condition of a person who is unable to pay his debts as they fall due. The general term is to be distinguished from a person who is bankrupt and whose liabilities exceed assets.

INSURABLE INTEREST: A substantial interest in the subject of the insurance which will entitle a person to obtain insurance.

INTESTATE: A person who dies without a will.

JOINT LIABILITY: Liability imposed upon two or more persons.

JOINT TENANCY: The ownership of property by two or more persons with the survivor taking the interest of the deceased.

JOINT VENTURE: A legal entity consisting of several persons jointly undertaking a commercial enterprise for profit. The joint venture does not entail a continuing relationship among the parties, but rather covers one particular transaction.

LACHES: An unreasonable delay. Notwithstanding the provisions of statutes of limitation, a court of equity may deny relief because a party neglects to assert a right.

LETTER OF CREDIT: A promise by a debtor's bank to pay the creditor upon presentation of specified documents.

GLOSSARY OF LEGAL TERMS

Lien: The right to satisfy a debt out of certain property owned by the debtor.

Liquidated Damages: The amount expressly stipulated by the parties as the amount of damages to be recovered in the event of a breach of contract.

Lis Pendens: A pending suit. An instrument filed or recorded in a court or registry office which affords public notice of the pendency of an action, such as a proceeding to foreclose a mortgage.

L.S. *(Locus Sigilli):* An abbreviation following a signature to take the place of a seal.

Minor: A person who has not reached legal maturity; an infant.

Mortgage: An interest in land created by a written instrument providing security for a debt.

Negligence: The failure by a reasonable person to use sufficient care, diligence and skill which he is required to use for the protection of others from injury or damage.

Negotiable: That species of property which can be transferred by endorsement and delivery.

Nisi Prius: A term used to denote courts or terms of court held for the trial of civil actions with a jury.

Nominal Damages: The award of a minimal sum where no serious loss or damage has been sustained.

Notary Public: A public officer empowered to administer oaths and take acknowledgments.

Per Capita: By the head. In the law of descent and distribution, this term is used to indicate the right of descendants to take shares equally as members of a class who have the same relationship with one another.

Per Curiam: By the court. A term generally used to denote the opinion or decision of the court as a whole rather than that of a single judge.

Perfection: The proper recording or filing of an instrument, thereby giving notice to the world; usually applied to the perfecting of a security interest under the Uniform Commercial Code.

Perjury: A false statement made under oath.

Personal Property Right: All rights and interest owned in goods or chattels as distinguished from an interest in real property.

Per Stirpes: By roots or stock. In the law of descent and distribution, this term is used to indicate the right of descendants to take shares by representation of a deceased parent.

Pledge: Bailment of personal property to secure a debt.

Preference: Paying or securing to one or more creditors, by an insolvent debtor, of all or a part of a claim to the exclusion of other creditors. Also a right acquired by a creditor by statute or legal proceeding to have his claim satisfied out of the debtor's assets before other creditors.

PRESENTMENT: The production of a negotiable instrument to the drawer or acceptor for payment.

PRIMA FACIE: Evidence sufficient in law to establish a fact unless rebutted.

PRIVITY: A mutual or successive relationship between parties as to a particular transaction.

PROBATE: The act or process of proving a will or other instrument valid or invalid.

PROTEST: A formal document declaring the dishonor of a negotiable instrument.

RATIFICATION: The confirmation of a previous act of oneself or of another taken on one's behalf.

REAL PROPERTY: Land and everything that is permanently affixed to it.

RECEIVER: A person appointed by the court to take custody over property in litigation or insolvency.

RECLAMATION: A term used in bankruptcy to denote a right or proceeding on the part of a person having title to property to recover the same when it is in possession of the bankrupt, debtor, receiver or trustee.

REHABILITATION (of a Debtor): A wage earner's plan; a type of partial bankruptcy where a debtor keeps property and pays a court-established proportion of a debt.

REORGANIZATON (under the Bankruptcy Act): Debtor reorganizes, rather than liquidates, and creditors claim future earnings of the bankrupt, rather than property presently held.

REPLEVIN: An action to recover the possession of personal property taken or withheld from the owner unlawfully.

RESCISSION: The annulment of a contract as a result of which both parties are returned to their former positions.

RES JUDICATA: A matter which has been decided. This is a legal doctrine to the effect that once an issue has been finally decided between the parties by a court of competent jurisdiction, it cannot thereafter be litigated by those parties in a new proceeding before the same or any other court.

SATISFACTION: The discharge of an obligation by paying a party what is due.

SEAL: Originally a wax impression, but today consists of any written figure or form.

SECURITY INTEREST: Any interest in property acquired by contract for the purpose of securing payment or performance of an obligation.

SETOFF: A counter claim that a defendant has against a plaintiff and which arises out of a different transaction.

STATUTE OF FRAUDS: A term applied to a statute which requires agreements to be in writing in order to maintain a suit or action thereon.

STATUTE OF LIMITATIONS: A law which limits the length of time within which a suit must be commenced before the right to sue is lost.

SUBROGATION: The substitution of one person in place of a creditor whose rights he acquires.

SUMMONS: A writ or notice requiring a person to appear before a court to answer a complaint.

SURETY: A person who agrees to be liable for the debt or contractual obligations of another.

TENANCY BY THE ENTIRETY: The joint ownership of property by a husband and wife with right of survivorship.

TENANCY IN COMMON: The common and undivided ownership of property with no right of survivorship.

TESTATOR: A person who makes a will.

TORT: A private or civil wrong exclusive of a breach of contract.

TORTIOUS: Wrongful; having the quality or nature of a tort.

TURNOVER PROCEEDING: A summary proceeding authorized under the provisions of the Bankruptcy Act requiring a bankrupt to turn over property to a receiver or trustee for administration. It may also be used in connection with property belonging to the bankrupt held by a third person.

ULTRA VIRES: The unauthorized acts of a corporation in violation of its certificate or charter of incorporation.

UNDERWRITER: A person who guarantees to furnish money by a definite date to a business or government in return for an issue of bonds or stock.

USURY: The charge of illegal interest.

VENUE: Used to indicate the county, district or other place where a case is or will be tried. In many cases the law specifies the venue with particularity, such as the county of residence of one of the parties. The venue may be changed for the convenience of witnesses or other reasons.

WAIVER: The relinquishment or refusal to accept some right or benefit. A waiver may result from an express agreement, by the act of a party or by failure to take appropriate action when required.

WARRANTY: The representation that an article has certain properties, the breach of which subjects one to financial liability.

WRIT: An order issued from a court in the name of the sovereign or state directing the person named to comply with the directions contained therein. Under the common law all actions were instituted by the issuance of a specific form of writ and no cause could be instituted unless a recognized form of writ was executed therefor.

Index by Subjects and States

	PAGE
ACCEPTANCE Bank and Trade	18-14
Accommodation Paper	18-45
ACCEPTANCE OF OFFERS	2-1, 2-3, 2-6
ACCORD AND SATISFACTION	3-6
ACCOUNTS RECEIVABLE	
Assignment of	6-9
Summary: Louisiana	6-10
ACKNOWLEDGING OFFERS	2-4
ACKNOWLEDGMENTS	
Contracts Generally	4-17
AGENTS	16-1
Signature by	4-16
For Undisclosed Principal	16-2
Duties of Agents	16-2
AGREEMENTS	
To Discharge Contract	3-2
Statute of Frauds	4-1
Statutory Requirements	4-2
For Sale of Land	4-3
Not to Be Performed Within a Year	4-3
Promise by Executor or Administrator	4-3
Debt of Third Person	4-4
Consideration of Marriage	4-4
Sales of Goods or Personalty	4-4
Uniform Commercial Code Provisions	4-5
Representations as to Credit	4-5
Promises to Pay Infancy Debt	4-6
Agreement Not to Be Performed During Life of Promisor	4-6
Assignment of Wages	4-6
Sale of Vessels	4-6
Chattel Mortgages	4-7
California Special Statutes	4-7
Louisiana's Special Statutes	4-7
Forms	33-12–33-18
ALABAMA	
Assignment for Benefit of Creditors	27-3
Assumed Name Laws	22-3
Bad Check Laws	21-3, 21-6
Bonds on Improvements	31-1
Bulk Transfer	26-10
Claims Against Estates	24-1
Collection Agency Requirements	11-3
Exemptions	23-46
Exemptions on Insurance	23-61
Financing Statements (Code)	7-5, 7-34
Judgment Notes	18-10
Landlord's Liens	20-30
Leasing of Personal Property	10-2
Limitations for Civil Actions	23-42
Mechanics' Liens	19-6
Personal Property Liens	20-1

	PAGE
Retail Instalment Sales	8-8
Taxes—Sales and Use	25-9
ALASKA	
Assignment for Benefit of Creditors	27-3
Assumed Name Laws	22-3
Bad Check Laws	21-3, 21-6
Bonds on Improvements	31-3
Bulk Transfers	26-10
Claims Against Estates	24-1
Collection Agency Requirements	11-4
Exemptions	23-50
Exemptions on Insurance	23-61
Financing Statements (Code)	7-5, 7-34
Judgment Notes	18-10
Landlord's Liens	20-30
Leasing of Personal Property	10-2
Limitations for Civil Actions	23-42
Mechanics' Liens	19-7
Personal Property Liens	20-2
Retail Instalment Sales	8-1, 8-8
Taxes—Sales and Use	25-9
ANTITRUST AND TRADE REGULATION LAWS	13-1
Sherman Act	13-1
Clayton Act	13-4
Robinson-Patman Act	13-5
Federal Trade Commission Act	13-12
Antitrust Procedures Act	13-13
1976 Antitrust Act	13-14
State Antitrust Laws	13-14
Fair Trade Acts	13-15
Exchange of Credit Information	13-16
Court Decisions	13-18
Membership in Credit Groups	13-21
ARBITRATION, COMMERCIAL	23-68
Arbitration Clauses (Forms)	33-2
Enforceability	23-68
ARIZONA	
Assignment for Benefit of Creditors	27-3
Assumed Name Laws	22-3
Bad Check Laws	21-3, 21-6
Bonds on Improvements	31-4
Bulk Transfers	26-10
Civil Penalties for Bad Check	21-13
Claims Against Estates	24-2
Collection Agency Requirements	11-4
Exemptions	23-51
Exemptions on Insurance	23-62
Financing Statements (Code)	7-5, 7-35
Judgment Notes	18-10
Landlords' Liens	20-30
Leasing of Personal Property	10-2
Limitations for Civil Actions	23-42
Mechanics' Liens	19-8
Personal Property Liens	20-3

INDEX-2

	PAGE		PAGE
Retail Instalment Sales	8-8	Washington . 27-9 Wisconsin ..	27-9
Taxes—Sales and Use	25-9	West Virginia 27-9 Wyoming ...	27-9

ARKANSAS

Assignment for Benefit of Creditors	27-3	Federal Equity Receiverships	27-10
Assumed Name Laws	22-3	ASSIGNMENTS (Forms for)	
Bad Check Laws	21-3, 21-6	Of an Account	33-3
Bonds on Improvements	31-5	Notice by Assignee	33-3
Bulk Transfers	26-10	Of Wages Due and to Become Due	33-3
Claims Against Estates	24-2	Notice by Creditor	33-3
Collection Agency Requirements	11-5	By a Corporation	33-4
Exemptions	23-50	**ASSUMED NAME LAWS**	
Exemptions on Insurance	23-62	Purpose of the Statutes	22-1
Financing Statements (Code)	7-5, 7-36	Forms of the Statutes	22-1
Judgment Notes	18-10	Statutes Usually Penal	22-1
Landlords' Liens	20-30	Effect of Noncompliance	22-1
Leasing of Personal Property	10-3	In Case One Partner Retires	22-2
Limitations for Civil Actions	23-42	Summary of State Laws	22-3
Mechanics' Liens	19-9	Alabama ... 22-3 Nevada.....	22-10
Personal Property Liens	20-4	Alaska ..... 22-3 New	
Retail Instalment Sales Laws .	8-1, 8-8	Arizona .... 22-3 Hampshire	22-10
Taxes—Sales and Use	25-10	Arkansas ... 22-3 New Jersey .	22-11
		California... 22-4 New Mexico	22-11
ARRANGEMENTS, Procedure under		Colorado ... 22-4 New York ..	22-11
Chapter XI (Bankruptcy Act)		Connecticut . 22-5 North	
See under BANKRUPTCY—PROCE-		Delaware ... 22-5 Carolina ..	22-11
DURE		District of North	
ASSIGNMENT OF ACCOUNTS		Columbia . 22-5 Dakota ...	22-12
RECEIVABLE	6-9	Florida ..... 22-5 Ohio	22-12
Louisiana Law Summary	6-10	Georgia .... 22-5 Oklahoma .	22-12
		Hawaii ..... 22-6 Oregon	22-13
ASSIGNMENT FOR BENEFIT OF		Idaho ...... 22-6 Pennsylvania	22-13
CREDITORS	27-1	Illinois ..... 22-6 Rhode Island	22-14
Summary of State Laws	27-3	Indiana..... 22-7 South	
Alabama ... 27-3 Montana ...	27-6	Iowa .... 22-7 Carolina ..	22-14
Alaska ..... 27-3 Nebraska ...	27-6	Kansas ..... 22-7 South	
Arizona .... 27-3 Nevada.....	27-6	Kentucky... 22-7 Dakota ...	22-14
Arkansas ... 27-3 New		Louisiana ... 22-7 Tennessee...	22-15
California... 27-4 Hampshire	27-6	Maine ...... 22-8 Texas	22-15
Colorado ... 27-4 New Jersey .	27-6	Maryland ... 22-8 Utah	22-15
Connecticut . 27-4 New Mexico	27-7	Massachusetts 22-8 Vermont....	22-16
Delaware ... 27-4 New York ..	27-7	Michigan ... 22-9 Virginia	22-16
District of North		Minnesota .. 22-9 Washington .	22-16
Columbia . 27-4 Carolina ..	27-7	Mississippi .. 22-9 West Virginia	22-16
Florida ..... 27-4 North		Missouri.... 22-9 Wisconsin ..	22-17
Georgia .... 27-4 Dakota ...	27-7	Montana ... 22-10 Wyoming ...	22-17
Hawaii ..... 27-4 Ohio	27-7	Nebraska ... 22-10	
Idaho ...... 27-5 Oklahoma .	27-7	**ATTACHMENT**	23-20
Illinois ..... 27-5 Oregon	27-7	**ATTORNEY**, Power of (Form)	33-10
Indiana..... 27-5 Pennsylvania	27-7	**ATTORNEY'S FEES**, Stipulation	18-7
Iowa .... 27-5 Rhode Island	27-8	**BAD CHECK LAWS**	21-1
Kansas ..... 27-5 South		State Laws	21-3
Kentucky... 27-5 Carolina ..	27-8	Alabama 21-3, 21-6 Connecticut	
Louisiana ... 27-5 South		Alaska .. 21-3, 21-6	21-3, 21-7
Maine ...... 27-5 Dakota ...	27-8	Arizona . 21-3, 21-6 Delaware	
Maryland ... 27-5 Tennessee...	27-8	Arkansas 21-3, 21-6	21-3, 21-7
Massachusetts 27-5 Texas	27-8	Califor- Dist. of Co-	
Michigan ... 27-5 Utah	27-8	nia ... 21-3, 21-6 lumbia	21-3, 21-7
Minnesota .. 27-6 Vermont....	27-8	Colorado 21-3, 21-7 Florida .	21-3, 21-7
Mississippi .. 27-6 Virginia ...	27-9		
Missouri.... 27-6			

INDEX-3

	PAGE		PAGE
Georgia . 21-3, 21-7		Jurisdiction of Court	28-25
Hawaii . 21-3, 21-8	No. Carolina	Jurisdiction of Appellate Courts .	28-26
Idaho . . . 21-3, 21-8	. . . 21-3, 21-10	How Proceedings Are Commenced	28-26
Illinois . . 21-3, 21-8	No. Dakota	Court in Which Proceedings May Be	
Indiana . 21-3, 21-8	. . . 21-3, 21-10	Commenced	28-26
Iowa . . . 21-3, 21-8	Ohio . 21-3, 21-10	Filing Fees	28-27
Kansas . 21-3, 21-8	Oklahoma	Procedure for Filing of Involuntary	
Kentucky	. . . 21-3, 21-10	Petition	28-27
. . . . . 21-3, 21-8	Oregon 21-3, 21-10	Filing of the Petition	28-27
Louisiana	Penn. . 21-3, 21-10	Conversion or Dismissal	28-27
. . . . . 21-3, 21-8	Rhode Is.	Trustee or Debtor in Possession .	28-27
Maine . . 21-3, 21-8	. . . 21-3, 21-10	First Hearing	28-28
Maryland . . 21-3, 21-8	So. Carolina	Creditors' Committee	28-28
	. . . 21-3, 21-10	Who May Propose Plan	28-29
Massachusetts . . 21-3, 21-9	South Dakota	Contents of the Plan	28-30
	. . . 21-3, 21-10	Impairment of Claims	28-31
Michigan 21-3, 21-9	Tennessee	Disclosure of Plan	28-31
Minnesota	. . . 21-3, 21-11	Acceptance of Plan	28-31
. . . . . 21-3, 21-9	Texas . 21-3, 21-11	Confirmation of Plan	28-32
Mississippi	Utah . 21-3, 21-11	Cram-Down	28-33
. . . . . 21-3, 21-9	Vermont	Exemption from Security Laws . .	28-35
Missouri 21-3, 21-9	. . . 21-3, 21-11	Tax Consequences	28-36
Montana 21-3, 21-9	Virginia	Adjustment of Debts of Individual	
Nebraska 21-3, 21-9	. . . 21-3, 21-11	with Regular Income	28-37
Nevada . 21-3, 21-9	Washington		
New Hampshire . 21-3, 21-9	. . . 21-3, 21-11	BILATERAL OFFERS	2-4
	W. Virginia		
New Jersey	. . . 21-3, 21-11	BILL OF SALE, FORM FOR	33-5
. . . . . 21-3, 21-9	Wisconsin		
New Mexico	. . . 21-3, 21-11	BILLS OF SALE	
. . . . . 21-3, 21-9	Wyoming	See Documents of Title, this index.	
New York	. . . 21-3, 21-11		
. . . 21-3, 21-10		BONDS ON PUBLIC WORKS	30-1
		Heard Act	30-1
CIVIL PENALTIES IN SOME STATES	21-13	Miller Act	30-1, 30-7
		Labor and Material Payment Bond	
BAILMENTS	6-1	(Form)	30-2
		Performance Bond (Form)	30-2
BANK ACCEPTANCES	18-14	Summary of Federal Bond Laws . . .	30-2
BANKRUPTCY—PROCEDURE		BONDS (State Laws)	
GENERAL	28-1	Alabama . . . 31-1	Maryland . . . 31-40
Terminology	28-1	Alaska 31-3	Massachusetts
Automatic Stay	28-3	Arizona 31-4	 31-42
Adequate Protection	28-4	Arkansas . . . 31-5	Michigan . . . 31-46
Interim Trustees	28-5	California . . . 31-7	Minnesota . . 31-47
Meeting of Creditors	28-6	Colorado . . . 31-11	Mississippi . . 31-50
Creditors' Committee	28-6	Connecticut . 31-12	Missouri 31-53
Trustee	28-7	Delaware . . . 31-13	Montana . . . 31-54
Sale, Use, or Lease of Property . .	28-8	District of Co.	Nebraska . . . 31-56
Allowance of Claims	28-11	 31-15	Nevada 31-58
Secured Claimholders	28-12	Florida 31-16	New
Priority Claims	28-13	Georgia 31-18	Hampshire 31-61
Discharge	28-14	Hawaii 31-22	New Jersey . 31-62
Bankruptcy Court & Appeals . . .	28-18	Idaho 31-23	New Mexico 31-66
Turnover	28-19	Illinois 31-25	New York . . . 31-67
Distribution of Estate Property . .	28-20	Indiana 31-27	North
Reclamation	28-20	Iowa 31-29	Carolina . . 31-73
Setoff	28-22	Kansas 31-31	North Dakota
Voidable Preferences	28-22	Kentucky . . . 31-33	 31-76
REORGANIZATIONS		Louisiana . . . 31-35	Ohio 31-77
Terminology	28-24	Maine 31-38	Oklahoma . . 31-81

INDEX-4

	PAGE		PAGE
Oregon 31-82	Texas 31-98	CLAIMS AGAINST ESTATES	24-1
Pennsylvania 31-84	Utah 31-104	State Statutes	24-1
Puerto Rico . 31-88	Vermont ... 31-106	Alabama ... 24-1	Nevada 24-5
Rhode Island	Virginia ... 31-107	Alaska 24-1	New
.... 31-90	Washington 31-109	Arizona 24-2	Hampshire 24-5
South	West Virginia	Arkansas ... 24-2	New Jersey . 24-6
Carolina .. 31-92	 31-114	California ... 24-2	New Mexico 24-6
South Dakota	Wisconsin . 31-115	Colorado ... 24-2	New York .. 24-6
.... 31-94	Wyoming .. 31-117	Connecticut . 24-2	North
Tennessee ... 31-95		Delaware ... 24-2	Carolina .. 24-6
		District of	North
BULK TRANSFERS	26-2	Columbia . 24-2	Dakota ... 24-6
General	26-2	Florida 24-3	Ohio 24-6
Uniform Commercial Code Provisions	26-3	Georgia 24-3	Oklahoma .. 24-6
Transactions within Statutes	26-8	Hawaii 24-3	Oregon 24-6
Effect of Noncompliance	26-8	Idaho 24-3	Pennsylvania 24-7
Creditors' Remedies	26-8	Illinois 24-3	Rhode Island
Rights of Subsequent Purchasers ...	26-9	Indiana 24-3	 24-7
Place of Filing or Recording in States	26-10	Iowa 24-4	South
		Kansas 24-4	Carolina .. 24-7
CALIFORNIA		Kentucky ... 24-4	South
Assignment for Benefit of Creditors	27-4	Louisiana ... 24-4	Dakota ... 24-7
Assumed Name Laws	22-4	Maine 24-4	Tennessee ... 24-7
Bad Check Laws 21-3,	21-6	Maryland ... 24-4	Texas 24-7
Bonds on Improvements	31-7	Massachusetts 24-4	Utah 24-7
Bulk Transfers	26-10	Michigan ... 24-4	Vermont 24-8
Claims Against Estates	24-2	Minnesota .. 24-5	Virginia 24-8
Collection Agency Requirements ...	11-6	Mississippi .. 24-5	Washington . 24-8
Exemptions	23-51	Missouri 24-5	West Virginia 24-8
Exemptions on Insurance	23-62	Montana ... 24-5	Wisconsin .. 24-8
Financing Statements (Code) . 7-5, 7-36		Nebraska ... 24-5	Wyoming ... 24-8
Judgment Notes	18-10		
Landlords' Liens	20-30	CLAYTON ACT	13-4
Leasing of Personal Property	10-3		
Limitations for Civil Actions	23-42	CODE (Uniform Commercial)	1-1
Mechanics' Liens	19-10		
Personal Property Liens	20-4	COLLECTION AGENCY LAWS ...	11-1
Retail Instalment Sales 8-1,	8-8		
Special Statutory Provisions in Contract	4-7	FAIR DEBT COLLECTION PRACTICE ACT	11-1
Taxes—Sales and Use	25-10	Alabama ... 11-3	Maryland ... 11-14
Truth in Lending	9-9	Alaska 11-4	Massachusetts 11-14
		Arizona 11-4	Michigan ... 11-15
CASH DISCOUNTS 5-3-5-6		Arkansas ... 11-5	Minnesota .. 11-16
		California ... 11-6	Mississippi .. 11-16
"CASH ON DELIVERY"	5-1	Colorado ... 11-6	Missouri 11-17
		Connecticut . 11-7	Montana ... 11-17
CHATTEL MORTGAGES	6-7	Delaware ... 11-8	Nebraska ... 11-17
Form of Contract	6-8	District of	Nevada 11-18
Louisiana Law Summary	6-8	Columbia . 11-8	New
Rule Under Statute of Frauds	4-1	Florida 11-8	Hampshire 11-18
		Georgia 11-9	New Jersey . 11-19
CHECKS		Hawaii 11-9	New Mexico 11-19
For Less Than $1	18-21	Idaho 11-10	New York .. 11-20
Marked "In Full of Account"	18-21	Illinois 11-11	North
Stopping Payment	18-22	Indiana 11-11	Carolina .. 11-20
Time Limitations by States	21-3	Iowa 11-12	North Dakota
Postdated	21-4	Kansas 11-12	 11-21
Table of Bad Check Laws 21-6-21-11		Kentucky ... 11-12	Ohio 11-21
Civil Penalties in Various States ...	21-13	Louisiana ... 11-13	Oklahoma .. 11-22
		Maine 11-13	Oregon 11-22

INDEX—5

	PAGE		PAGE
Pennsylvania 11-23		Mechanics' Liens	19-12
Rhode Island		Personal Property Liens	20-4
.... 11-23		Retail Instalment Sales	8-1, 8-8
South		Taxes—Sales and Use	25-10
Carolina .. 11-23		Truth in Lending	9-9
South Dakota			
.... 11-24		**COMMERCIAL CRIMES**	
Tennessee ... 11-24		BAD CHECK LAWS	21-1
Texas 11-24		Nature of the Crime	21-1
Utah 11-25		Constitutionality	21-1
Vermont 11-25		Time Within Which Checks May Be	
Virginia 11-25		Made Good	21-2
Washington . 11-26		Table of Time Limits (by States)	21-3
West Virginia		Checks for Preexisting Debts	21-3
.... 11-26		Postdated Checks	21-4
Wisconsin .. 11-27		Stopping Payment	21-4
Wyoming ... 11-27		Necessity of Damage	21-12
COLLECTIONS, Legal Phases	23-1	Table of Bad Check Laws ..	21-6–21-11
Methods	23-1	Notice of Nonpayment	21-12
Threats, Extortion	23-2	Rules of Evidence	21-12
Prohibited Practices	23-3	To Whom Statutes Apply	21-13
Libel	23-4	OTHER COMMERCIAL CRIMES	21-15
Postal Regulations	23-6	Use of Mails, Wire, Radio or Televi-	
Privilege	23-6	sion to Defraud	21-15
Invasion of Privacy	23-6	False Financial Statements	21-19
Non-Payment of Debts	23-8	Bankruptcy	21-19
Prompt Payment Statutes	23-8	Perjury	21-20
Debt Pooling Plans	23-8	Civil Liability for Issuing False	
Trade Association Practices	23-8	Credit Information	21-20
State Laws	23-9	**COMMON LAW OR MASSACHU-**	
Collection by Suit	23-15	**SETTS TRUSTS**	14-19
Confession of Judgment	23-17		
State Laws	23-17	**COMMUNICATION OF OFFER** ...	2-2
Steps in Suits	23-20	**COMMUNICATION OF ACCEP-**	
Attachment	23-20	**TANCE**	2-6
Garnishment	23-21		
State Statutes Differ	23-22	**COMMUNITY PROPERTY**	17-1
Judgment	23-24	States Having Such Laws	17-1
Execution and Levy	23-24	Property on 50-50 Basis	17-1
Replevin	23-34	Property Presumed to Belong to Com-	
Statutes of Limitations	23-36	munity	17-3
State Laws on Tolling of Statute	23-38	Husband's Dominion over Property	17-3
Limitations for Civil Actions (by		Effects of Death of a Spouse	17-4
States)	23-42	Pitfalls for Creditors	17-5
Waiver of Exemptions (by States)	23-46	**COMPETENCY**	2-7
States Requiring Written Statements		Infants	2-7
for Exemptions	23-49	Table on Competency of Infants	2-8–2-9
Table of Exemptions by States	23-50	Married Women	2-11
Exemptions on Insurance	23-61	Insane Persons	2-11
Soldiers' and Sailors' Civil Relief Act	23-66	Corporations	2-11
Commercial Arbitration	23-68	Agents	2-12
COLORADO		**COMPOSITION OF CREDITORS** ..	2-14
Assignment for Benefit of Creditors	27-4	**CONDITIONAL SALES**	6-5
Assumed Name Laws	22-4	Fixtures	6-6
Bad Check Laws	21-3, 21-7	Goods for Resale	6-7
Bonds on Improvements	31-11		
Bulk Transfers	25-10	**CONFESSIONS OF JUDGMENT** ...	23-16
Civil Penalties for Bad Check	21-13	**CONNECTICUT**	
Claims Against Estates	24-2	Assignment for Benefit of Creditors	27-4
Collection Agency Requirements	11-6		
Exemptions	23-51		
Exemptions on Insurance	23-62		
Financing Statements (Code)	7-5, 7-37		
Judgment Notes	18-10		
Landlords' Liens	20-30		
Leasing of Personal Property	10-3		
Limitations for Civil Actions	23-42		

INDEX-6

	PAGE
Assumed Name Laws	22-5
Bad Check Laws	21-3, 21-7
Bonds on Improvements	31-12
Bulk Transfers	26-10
Civil Penalties for Bad Checks	21-13
Claims Against Estates	24-2
Collection Agency Requirements	11-7
Exemptions	23-51
Exemptions on Insurance	23-62
Financing Statements (Code)	7-5, 7-37
Judgment Notes	18-10
Landlord's Liens	20-30
Leasing of Personal Property	10-4
Limitations for Civil Actions	23-42
Mechanics Liens	19-14
Personal Property Liens	20-5
Retail Instalment Sales	8-1, 8-9
Taxes—Sales and Use	25-10
Truth in Lending	9-9

CONSIDERATION (See Contracts) . 2-12
  Mutuality 2-13
  Inadequacy 2-13
  Composition of Creditors 2-14
  Statutes Affecting Consideration ... 2-14

CONSIGNMENTS 6-2

CONSUMER CREDIT PROTECTION
ACT 9-1

CONSUMER PRODUCTS SAFETY
ACT 9-7

CONSUMER PROTECTION 9-1

CONTRACTS 2-1, 4-1
  Classification of 4-1
  Offer and Acceptance 2-1
  Competency of Parties 2-7
  Consideration 2-12
  Signature 4-15
  Acknowledgments on 4-17
  Performance of 3-1
  Under Seal 4-18
  Mistakes 3-5
  Fraudulent 3-5
  Consent, Reality of 3-5
  Interpretation of 3-1
  Assignments of 3-6
  Discharge of 3-2
    By Performance 3-2
    By Breach 3-2
    By Agreement 3-2
    Accord and Satisfaction 3-6
    By Operation of Law 3-3
  Tender of Performance 3-3
  Enforcement of 3-6
  Limitations for Suit 3-6
  Necessity of Writing 4-1
  STATUTORY REQUIREMENTS 4-2
    Sale of Lands 4-3

	PAGE
Not to Be Performed within a Year	4-3
Promise by Executor or Administrator	4-3
Debt of Third Person	4-4
Consideration of Marriage	4-4
Sale of Goods or Personality	4-4
Representation as to Credit	4-5
Promises to Pay Debts Contracted in Infancy	4-6
Not to Be Performed During Life of Promisor	4-6
Assignment of Wages	4-6
Sales of Vessels	4-6
Chattel Mortgages	4-7
California Statute	4-7
Louisiana Statute	4-7
Agents	4-16
Title Retention	5-2
Sales under UCC	1-4, 1-28

CONVEYANCES, Fraudulent 26-1

CORPORATE REORGANIZATIONS
See under BANKRUPTCY—PROCEDURE

CORPORATIONS 14-1
  Advantages of Incorporation 14-1
  Constitutional Provisions 14-1
  Director Liability 14-2
  DOMESTIC CORPORATIONS 14-3
  FOREIGN CORPORATIONS 14-3
    Constitutional Restrictions 14-5
    Licensing Procedure 14-5
    Penalties for Interstate Violations 14-6
  INTERSTATE BUSINESS 14-7
    By Traveling Salesmen or Mail .. 14-9
    Isolated Transactions 14-9
    Institution of Suit 14-10
    Sales by Samples 14-10
    Installations and Construction .. 14-10
    When Interstate Business 14-11
    When Not Interstate Business .. 14-11

CREDIT CARD 12-1
  Forms of Plans 12-1
  Obligations of Parties 12-2
  Lost, Stolen, Misused Card 12-3
  Criminal Liability for Misuse 12-6
  State Statutes 12-7
  Federal Criminal Statutes 12-9

CREDITORS
  Composition of 2-14
  Meetings 28-6, 28-24

CRIMES
See COMMERCIAL CRIMES

DEBT COLLECTION. *Guide Against
Debt Collection Deceptions* 11-1

DEBT POOLING 23-8
  States' Statutes 23-9

INDEX–7

	PAGE		PAGE
DECENTS' ESTATES	24-1	ESTATES—CLAIMS AGAINST	24-1
		Summary of State Laws	24-1

DELAWARE
Assignment for Benefit of Creditors	27-5
Assumed Name Laws	22-5
Bad Check Laws	21-3, 21-7
Bonds on Improvements	31-13
Bulk Transfers	26-10
Civil Penalties for Bad Check	21-13
Claims Against Estates	24-2
Collection Agency Requirements	11-8
Exemptions	23-52
Exemptions on Insurance	23-62
Financing Statements (Code)	7-5, 7-38
Judgment Notes	18-10
Landlords' Liens	20-30
Leasing of Personal Property	10-4
Limitations for Civil Actions	23-42
Mechanics' Liens	19-15
Personal Property Liens	20-5
Retail Instalment Sales	8-9
Taxes—Sales and Use	25-10
Truth in Lending	9-10

DIRECTOR LIABILITY	14-2

DISCOUNT, Terms of	5-3, 5-4

DISTRICT OF COLUMBIA
Assignment for Benefit of Creditors	27-5
Assumed Name Laws	22-5
Bad Check Laws	21-3, 21-7
Bonds on Improvements	31-15
Bulk Transfers	26-10
Civil Penalties for Bad Check	21-14
Claims Against Estates	24-2
Collection Agency Requirements	11-6
Exemptions	23-52
Exemptions on Insurance	23-62
Financing Statements (Code)	7-5, 7-38
Judgment Notes	18-10
Landlords' Liens	20-30
Leasing of Personal Property	10-4
Limitations for Civil Actions	23-42
Mechanics' Liens	19-15
Personal Property Liens	20-5
Retail Instalment Sales	8-9
Taxes—Sales and Use	25-11
Truth in Lending	9-10

DOCUMENTS OF TITLE
Generally	1-70
Warehouse Receipts: Special Provisions	1-71
Bills of Lading: Special Provisions	1-73
Warehouse Receipts and Bills of Lading: Negotiations and Transfer	1-74

EQUAL CREDIT OPPORTUNITY ACT	9-7

EQUITY RECEIVERSHIPS	27-1

EXCHANGE OF CREDIT INFORMATION	13-16

EXEMPTIONS	23-46
State Statutes	23-50
Alabama	23-50
Alaska	23-50
Arizona	23-50
Arkansas	23-50
California	23-51
Colorado	23-51
Connecticut	23-51
Delaware	23-52
Dist. of Col.	23-52
Florida	23-52
Georgia	23-52
Hawaii	23-52
Idaho	23-53
Illinois	23-53
Indiana	23-53
Iowa	23-53
Kansas	23-54
Kentucky	23-54
Louisiana	23-54
Maine	23-54
Maryland	23-55
Massachusetts	23-55
Michigan	23-55
Minnesota	23-55
Mississippi	23-55
Missouri	23-55
Montana	23-56
Nebraska	23-56
Nevada	23-56
New Hampshire	23-56
New Jersey	23-57
New Mexico	23-57
New York	23-57
North Carolina	23-57
North Dakota	23-57
Ohio	23-57
Oklahoma	23-58
Oregon	23-58
Pennsylvania	23-58
Rhode Island	23-58
South Carolina	23-58
South Dakota	23-58
Tennessee	23-58
Texas	23-59
Utah	23-59
Vermont	23-59
Virginia	23-59
Washington	23-60
West Virginia	23-60
Wisconsin	23-60
Wyoming	23-60

EXEMPTIONS ON INSURANCE
State Statutes	23-61
Alabama	23-61
Alaska	23-61
Arizona	23-62
Arkansas	23-62
California	23-62
Colorado	23-62
Connecticut	23-62
Delaware	23-62
Dist. of Col.	23-62
Florida	23-62
Georgia	23-62
Hawaii	23-62
Idaho	23-62
Illinois	23-62
Indiana	23-62
Iowa	23-63
Kansas	23-63
Kentucky	23-63
Louisiana	23-63
Maine	23-63
Maryland	23-63
Massachusetts	23-63
Michigan	23-63
Minnesota	23-63
Mississippi	23-63
Missouri	23-63
Montana	23-63
Nebraska	23-63
Nevada	23-64
New Hampshire	23-64
New Jersey	23-64
New Mexico	23-64
New York	23-64
North Carolina	23-64
North Dakota	23-64
Ohio	23-64
Oklahoma	23-64
Oregon	23-64
Pennsylvania	23-64

INDEX-8

	PAGE		PAGE
Rhode Island 23-65		Utah 23-65	
		Vermont 23-65	
South Carolina .. 23-65		Virginia 23-65	
		Washington . 23-65	
South Dakota 23-65		West Virginia 23-65	
Tennessee... 23-65		Wisconsin .. 23-65	
Texas 23-65		Wyoming ... 23-66	

	PAGE
EXTORTION	23-2
FACTORS' LIENS	6-10
FAIR CREDIT REPORTING ACT .	9-4
FALSE CREDIT INFORMATION .	21-20
Civil Liability for	21-20
FALSE FINANCIAL STATEMENTS	21-19
FEDERAL BOND LAWS	30-1
FEDERAL TAX LIEN LAW	19-1
FEDERAL TRADE COMMISSION ACT	13-12
FILING OR RECORDING FEES (by States)	7-30
FILING REQUIREMENTS (by States)	7-33
FINANCE CHARGES	18-43
FINANCING STATEMENT FORMS (Under Uniform Commercial Code)	7-5, 7-6, 7-7
FLORIDA	
Assignment for Benefit of Creditors	27-5
Assumed Name Laws	22-5
Bad Check Laws	21-3, 21-7
Bonds on Improvements	31-16
Bulk Transfers	26-10
Civil Penalties for Bad Check	21-14
Claims Against Estates	24-3
Collection Agency Requirements ...	11-8
Exemptions	23-52
Exemptions on Insurance	23-62
Financing Statements (Code) .	7-5, 7-38
Judgment Notes	18-10
Landlords' Liens	20-30
Leasing of Personal Property	10-4
Limitations for Civil Actions	23-42
Mechanics' Liens	19-16
Personal Property Liens	20-5
Retail Instalment Sales	8-1, 8-9
Taxes—Sales and Use	25-11
Truth in Lending	9-10
FOREIGN CORPORATIONS	
Rights to Contract	14-3
Constitutional Restrictions	14-5
Licensing Procedure	14-5

	PAGE
Interstate Business, What Constitutes	14-7
Sales by Traveling Salesmen or by Mail	14-9
Isolated Transactions	14-9
Institution of Suit	14-10
Sales by Samples	14-10
Installations, Construction Work ...	14-10
Sale of Goods Stored in State as Interstate Business	14-12
Consignment Sales	14-12
Office in Foreign State	14-13
Salesroom in Foreign State	14-13
Guarantees by Corporations	14-17
When Guaranty Is Authorized	14-17
Corporations as Guarantors	14-18
FOREIGN TRADE DEFINITIONS .	29-48
FORMS:	
Acknowledgment	33-1
Financing Statement under Code	7-5, 7-6, 7-7, 33-4
Labor and Material Payment Bond	30-2
Performance Bond	30-3
Arbitration Clauses	33-2
Indorsement on Check	33-2
Assignment of an Account	33-3
Assignment of Wages Due and to Become Due	33-3
Notice by Assignee to Debtor	33-3
Notice to Debtor by His Creditor ..	33-3
Assignment by a Corporation	33-4
Agreement to Revive a Debt Discharged by Bankruptcy	33-4
Agreement to Pay a Debt Contracted during Infancy	33-5
Agreement to Revive a Debt Barred by the Statute of Limitations	33-5
Proof of Claim with Power of Attorney	33-5
Bill of Sale	33-5
Compromise Agreement	33-6
Guaranty of Past and Future Indebtedness	33-6
Lease of Personal Property	33-7
Release of Lease of Personal Property	33-9
Power of Attorney	33-10
General Release	33-10
Waiver of Right to File Mechanic's Lien	33-10
Satisfaction of Mechanics' Lien	33-11
Letter of Credit	33-11
Negotiable Promissory Note	33-11
Instalment Note	33-11
Notes in Series with Default Clauses	33-12
Judgment Note	33-12
Security Agreement, Article 9 of Code	33-12
Security Agreements	33-14, 33-16
A Form of Subordination Agreement	33-13

INDEX–9

	PAGE		PAGE
Disclosure Statement	33-19	HEARD ACT	30-1
Retail Instalment Contract	33-20–33-22	HUSBAND AND WIFE	
FRAUDS, Statute of (See Statute of Frauds)	4-1	Partnership between	15-8
		IDAHO	
FRAUDULENT CONVEYANCES	26-1	Assignment for Benefit of Creditors	27-5
Distinction in Intent	26-1	Assumed Name Laws	22-6
Bulk Transfers—Uniform Commercial Code Provisions	26-2	Bad Check Laws	21-3, 21-8
Transactions within the Statutes	26-8	Bonds on Improvements	31-23
Effect of Noncompliance	26-8	Bulk Transfers	26-10
Remedies of Creditors	26-8	Civil Penalties for Bad Check	21-14
Rights of Subsequent Purchasers	26-9	Claims Against Estates	24-3
Attacking Sales	26-9	Collection Agency Requirements	11-10
List of Creditors	26-9	Exemptions	23-53
Place of Filing or Recording in States	26-9	Exemptions on Insurance	23-62
		Financing Statements (Code)	7-5, 7-40
GARNISHMENT	23-20	Judgment Notes	18-11
GEORGIA		Landlords' Liens	20-30
Assignment for Benefit of Creditors	27-4	Leasing of Personal Property	10-5
Assumed Name Laws	22-5	Limitations for Civil Actions	23-42
Bad Check Laws	21-3, 21-7	Mechanics' Liens	19-20
Bonds on Improvements	31-18	Personal Property Liens	20-6
Bulk Transfers	26-10	Retail Instalment Sales	8-10
Claims Against Estates	24-3	Taxes—Sales and Use	25-11
Collection Agency Requirements	11-9	Truth in Lending	9-11
Exemptions	23-52	ILLINOIS	
Exemptions on Insurance	23-62	Assignment for Benefit of Creditors	27-5
Financing Statements (Code)	7-5, 7-39	Assumed Name Laws	22-6
Judgment Notes	18-11	Bad Check Laws	21-3, 21-8
Landlords' Liens	20-30	Bonds on Improvements	31-25
Leasing of Personal Property	10-4	Bulk Transfers	26-10
Limitations for Civil Actions	23-42	Claims Against Estates	24-3
Mechanics' Liens	19-17	Collection Agency Requirements	11-11
Personal Property Liens	20-6	Exemptions	23-53
Retail Instalment Sales	8-1, 8-9	Exemptions on Insurance	23-62
Taxes—Sales and Use	25-11	Financing Statements (Code)	7-5, 7-40
GLOSSARY OF LEGAL TERMS	34-1	Judgment Notes	18-11
HAWAII		Landlords' Liens	20-31
Assignment for Benefit of Creditors	27-4	Leasing of Personal Property	10-5
Assumed Name Laws	22-6	Limitations for Civil Actions	23-42
Bad Check Laws	21-3, 21-8	Mechanics' Liens	19-20
Bonds on Improvements	31-20	Personal Property Liens	20-7
Bulk Transfers	26-10	Retail Instalment Sales	8-1, 8-10
Civil Penalties for Bad Check	21-14	Taxes—Sales and Use	25-11
Claims Against Estates	24-3	Truth in Lending	9-11
Collection Agency Requirements	11-9	INDEX TO SECURED TRANSACTIONS UNDER CODE	7-1
Exemptions	23-52		
Exemptions on Insurance	23-62	INDIANA	
Financing Statements (Code)	7-5, 7-39	Assignment for Benefit of Creditors	27-5
Judgment Notes	18-11	Assumed Name Laws	22-7
Landlords' Liens	20-30	Bad Check Laws	21-3, 21-8
Leasing of Personal Property	10-5	Bonds on Improvements	31-27
Limitations for Civil Actions	23-42	Bulk Transfers	26-10
Mechanics' Liens	19-18	Civil Penalties for Bad Check	21-14
Personal Property Liens	20-6	Claims Against Estates	24-3
Retail Instalment Sales	8-1, 8-9	Collection Agency Requirements	11-11
Taxes—Sales and Use	25-11	Exemptions	23-53
Truth in Lending	9-10	Exemptions on Insurance	23-62

	PAGE		PAGE
Financing Statements (Code)	7-7, 7-41	JUDGMENT NOTES (By States)	18-10
Judgment Notes	18-11	Validity of Stipulation for Attorney's	
Landlords' Liens	20-31	Fee	18-10
Leasing of Personal Property	10-5	Form	35-12
Limitations for Civil Actions	23-42	JURISDICTION	23-19
Mechanics' Liens	19-22	In Personam	23-19
Personal Property Liens	20-7	In Rem	23-19
Retail Instalment Sales	8-1, 8-10	Quasi In Rem	23-20
Taxes—Sales and Use	25-12		
Truth in Lending	9-11	KANSAS	
INFANTS (Competency of)	2-8	Assignment for Benefit of Creditors	27-5
		Assumed Name Laws	22-7
INSANE PERSONS		Bad Check Laws	21-3, 21-8
Competency of	2-11	Bonds on Improvements	31-31
INSOLVENCY (see also under Bank-		Bulk Transfers	26-10
ruptcy)	1-24, 1-46, 1-56	Claims Against Estates	24-4
		Collection Agency Requirements	11-12
INSTALMENT NOTE (Retail), Form		Exemptions	23-54
for	33-20–33-22	Exemptions on Insurance	23-63
INTENT TO DEFRAUD	21-1	Financing Statements (Code)	7-5, 7-42
		Judgment Notes	18-11
INTEREST AND USURY	18-23	Landlords' Liens	20-31
Interest on Credit Sales	18-43	Leasing of Personal Property	10-6
Interest on Past Due Accounts	18-39	Limitations for Civil Actions	23-43
Legal Rates of Interest (States)	18-26	Mechanics' Liens	19-23
INTERNATIONAL TRADE	29-1	Personal Property Liens	20-9
United States Agencies	29-1	Retail Instalment Sales	8-10
International Agencies	29-7	Taxes—Sales and Use	25-12
		Truth in Lending	9-12
INTERSTATE AND INTRASTATE			
BUSINESS	14-11	KENTUCKY	
IOWA		Assignment for Benefit of Creditors	27-5
Assignment for Benefit of Creditors	27-5	Assumed Name Laws	22-7
Assumed Name Laws	22-7	Bad Check Laws	21-3, 21-8
Bad Check Laws	21-3, 21-8	Bonds on Improvements	31-33
Bonds on Improvements	31-29	Bulk Transfers	26-10
Bulk Transfers	26-10	Claims Against Estates	24-4
Civil Penalties for Bad Check	21-14	Collection Agency Requirements	11-12
Claims Against Estates	24-4	Exemptions	23-54
Collection Agency Requirements	11-12	Exemptions on Insurance	23-63
Exemptions	23-53	Financing Statements (Code)	7-7, 7-42
Exemptions on Insurance	23-63	Judgment Notes	18-11
Financing Statements (Code)	7-5, 7-41	Landlords' Liens	20-31
Judgment Notes	18-11	Leasing of Personal Property	10-6
Landlords' Liens	20-31	Limitations for Civil Actions	23-43
Leasing of Personal Property	10-5	Mechanics' Liens	19-24
Limitations for Civil Actions	23-43	Personal Property Liens	20-9
Mechanics' Liens	19-22	Retail Instalment Sales	8-1, 8-10
Personal Property Liens	20-8	Taxes—Sales and Use	25-12
Retail Instalment Sales	8-1, 8-10	Truth in Lending	9-12
Taxes—Sales and Use	25-12		
Truth in Lending	9-12	LABOR AND MATERIAL PAY-	
JOINT VENTURES	15-1	MENT BONDS (Form)	30-2
Similar to Partnerships	15-2	LANDLORDS' LIENS	20-29
Different Features	15-2	State Statutes	20-30
		Alabama ... 20-30 Colorado ... 20-30	
JUDGMENT	23-24	Alaska ..... 20-30 Delaware ... 20-30	
		Arizona .... 20-30 District of	
EXECUTION AND LEVY	23-24	Arkansas ... 20-30 Columbia . 20-30	
		California ... 20-30 Florida 20-30	

INDEX—11

	PAGE		PAGE
Georgia 20-30		North	
Hawaii 20-30		Carolina .. 20-32	
Idaho 20-30		North	
Illinois 20-31		Dakota ... 20-32	
Indiana 20-31		Ohio 20-32	
Iowa 20-31		Oklahoma .. 20-32	
Kansas 20-31		Oregon 20-32	
Kentucky ... 20-31		Pennsylvania 20-33	
Louisiana ... 20-31		Rhode Island	
Maine 20-31		 20-33	
Maryland ... 20-31		South	
Massachusetts 20-31		Carolina .. 20-33	
Michigan ... 20-31		South Dakota	
Minnesota .. 20-31		 20-33	
Mississippi .. 20-31		Tennessee... 20-33	
Missouri 20-32		Texas 20-33	
Montana ... 20-32		Utah 20-33	
Nebraska ... 20-32		Vermont 20-33	
Nevada 20-32		Virginia ... 20-33	
New		Washington . 20-33	
Hampshire 20-32		West Virginia	
New Jersey . 20-32		 20-33	
New Mexico 20-32		Wisconsin .. 20-33	
New York .. 20-32		Wyoming ... 20-33	

Mechanics'		19-2
Landlords'		20-29
Personal Property		20-1

LIMITATION FOR CIVIL ACTIONS 23-41

Alabama ... 23-42	Nevada 23-43
Alaska 23-42	New
Arizona 23-42	Hampshire 23-43
Arkansas ... 23-42	New Jersey . 23-43
California ... 23-42	New Mexico 23-43
Colorado ... 23-42	New York .. 23-43
Connecticut . 23-42	North
Delaware ... 23-42	Carolina .. 23-43
District of	North Dakota
Columbia . 23-42	 23-44
Florida 23-42	Ohio 23-44
Georgia 23-42	Oklahoma .. 23-44
Hawaii 23-42	Oregon 23-44
Idaho 23-42	Pennsylvania 23-44
Illinois 23-42	Rhode Island 23-44
Indiana 23-42	South
Iowa 23-43	Carolina .. 23-44
Kansas 23-43	South Dakota
Kentucky ... 23-43	 23-44
Louisiana ... 23-43	Tennessee... 23-44
Maine 23-43	Texas 23-44
Maryland ... 23-43	Utah 23-44
Massachusetts 23-43	Vermont 23-44
Michigan ... 23-43	Virginia 23-44
Minnesota .. 23-43	Washington . 23-44
Mississippi .. 23-43	West Virginia
Missouri 23-43	 23-44
Montana ... 23-43	Wisconsin .. 23-45
Nebraska ... 23-43	Wyoming ... 23-45

LAWS OF AGENCY		16-1
LAWS OF CONTRACTS		2-1
LEASE OF PERSONAL PROPERTY		
Secured Transactions		10-1
Federal and State Laws		10-1, 10-2
Form for Security Agreement under		
Article 9 of Code		33-12
LEGAL CAPACITY (Contracts)		2-7
LEGAL PHASES OF COLLECTIONS		23-1
Collection Methods		23-1
Debt Pooling Plans		23-8
Collection by Suit		23-15
Steps in Suit		23-20
Limitations for Civil Actions		23-41
What Law Governs		23-37
Part Payment		23-41
Acknowledgment of Debt		23-41
Exemptions		23-46
Exemptions on Insurance		23-61
Soldiers' and Sailors' Relief Act ...		23-66
Arbitration		23-68
LEGAL TERMS—GLOSSARY		34-1
LEGALITY OF SUBJECT MATTER		2-12
LETTERS OF CREDIT		1-63
Specimen		18-20
LIBEL		23-4
Postal Laws		23-6
LIENS		
Factors' Liens		6-10
Priority of Certain Liens		7-19

LIMITATIONS FOR SUIT: CON-		
TRACTS		3-6
LIMITED PARTNERSHIPS		15-6
How Formed		15-7
Relationship to Third Persons		15-7
Insolvency of		15-8
LOUISIANA		
Assignment of Receivables		6-10
Assignment for Benefit of Creditors		27-5
Assumed Name Laws		22-7
Bad Check Laws		21-3, 21-8
Bonds on Improvements		31-36
Chattel Mortgages		6-8
Claims Against Estates		24-4
Collection Agency Requirements ...		11-13
Exemptions		23-54
Exemptions on Insurance		23-63
Factors' Liens		6-10
Financing Statement		7-7
Frauds Statute		4-1, 4-7
Judgment Notes		18-12
Landlords' Liens		20-31
Leasing of Personal Property		10-6
Limitations for Civil Actions		23-43
Mechanics' Liens		19-25

INDEX-12

	PAGE
Personal Property Liens	20-10
Retail Instalment Sales	8-1, 8-10
Special Statutory Provisions in Contracts	4-7
Taxes—Sales and Use	25-12

MAIL OR TELEGRAPH, OFFER AND ACCEPTANCE 2-6

MAINE
Assignment for Benefit of Creditors	27-5
Assumed Name Laws	22-8
Bad Check Laws	21-3, 21-8
Bonds on Improvements	31-38
Bulk Transfers	26-10
Civil Penalties for Bad Check	21-14
Claims Against Estates	24-4
Collection Agency Requirements	11-13
Exemptions	23-54
Exemptions on Insurance	23-63
Financing Statements (Code)	7-5, 7-43
Judgment Notes	18-12
Landlords' Liens	20-31
Leasing of Personal Property	10-6
Limitations for Civil Actions	23-43
Mechanics' Liens	19-26
Personal Property Liens	20-10
Retail Instalment Sales	8-1, 8-10
Taxes—Sales and Use	25-13
Truth in Lending	9-13

MARRIED WOMEN 2-11, 15-8

MARYLAND
Assignment for Benefit of Creditors	27-5
Assumed Name Laws	22-8
Bad Check Laws	21-3, 21-8
Bonds on Improvements	31-41
Bulk Transfers	26-10
Civil Penalties for Bad Check	21-14
Collection Agency Requirements	11-14
Claims Against Estates	24-4
Exemptions	23-55
Exemptions on Insurance	23-63
Financing Statements (Code)	7-5, 7-44
Judgment Notes	18-12
Landlords' Liens	20-31
Leasing of Personal Property	10-6
Limitations for Civil Actions	23-43
Mechanics' Liens	19-27
Personal Property Liens	20-11
Retail Instalment Sales	8-1, 8-11
Taxes—Sales and Use	25-13
Truth in Lending	9-13

MASSACHUSETTS
Assignment for Benefit of Creditors	27-5
Assumed Name Laws	22-8
Bad Check Laws	21-3, 21-9
Bonds on Improvements	31-42
Bulk Transfers	26-10
Civil Penalties for Bad Check	21-14

	PAGE
Claims Against Estates	24-4
Collection Agency Requirements	11-14
Exemptions	23-55
Exemptions on Insurance	23-63
Financing Statements (Code)	7-6, 7-44
Judgment Notes	18-12
Landlords' Liens	20-31
Leasing of Personal Property	10-7
Limitations for Civil Actions	23-43
Mechanics' Liens	19-28
Personal Property Liens	20-11
Retail Instalment Sales	8-1, 8-11
Taxes—Sales and Use	25-13
Truth in Lending	9-14

MASSACHUSETTS OR COMMON LAW TRUSTS 14-19

MECHANICS' LIENS 19-2
Satisfaction of (Form)	33-11
State Statutes	19-6
Alabama	19-6
Alaska	19-7
Arizona	19-8
Arkansas	19-9
California	19-10
Colorado	19-12
Connecticut	19-14
Delaware	19-15
District of Columbia	19-15
Florida	19-16
Georgia	19-17
Hawaii	19-18
Idaho	19-20
Illinois	19-20
Indiana	19-22
Iowa	19-22
Kansas	19-23
Kentucky	19-24
Louisiana	19-25
Maine	19-26
Maryland	19-27
Massachusetts	19-28
Michigan	19-29
Minnesota	19-30
Mississippi	19-32
Missouri	19-33
Montana	19-34
Nebraska	19-35
Nevada	19-36
New Hampshire	19-37
New Jersey	19-37
New Mexico	19-40
New York	19-41
North Carolina	19-45
North Dakota	19-46
Ohio	19-47
Oklahoma	19-49
Oregon	19-50
Pennsylvania	19-52
Rhode Island	19-53
South Carolina	19-54
South Dakota	19-54
Tennessee	19-55
Texas	19-56
Utah	19-58
Vermont	19-59
Virginia	19-59
Washington	19-61
West Virginia	19-62
Wisconsin	19-62
Wyoming	19-64

MEMBERSHIP IN CREDIT GROUPS 13-21

MICHIGAN
Assignment for Benefit of Creditors	27-5
Assumed Name Laws	22-9
Bad Check Laws	21-3, 21-9
Bonds on Improvements	31-46
Bulk Transfers	26-10
Claims Against Estates	24-4
Collection Agency Requirements	11-15

INDEX-13

	PAGE
Exemptions	23-55
Exemptions on Insurance	23-63
Financing Statements (Code)	7-5, 7-45
Judgment Notes	18-12
Landlords' Liens	20-31
Leasing of Personal Property	10-7
Limitations for Civil Actions	23-43
Mechanics' Liens	19-29
Personal Property Liens	20-12
Retail Instalment Sales	8-1, 8-11
Taxes—Sales and Use	25-13
Truth in Lending	9-15

MILLER ACT 30-1, 30-3

MINNESOTA
Assignment for Benefit of Creditors	27-6
Assumed Name Laws	22-9
Bad Check Laws	21-3, 21-9
Bonds on Improvements	31-47
Bulk Transfers	26-10
Civil Penalties for Bad Check	21-14
Claims Against Estates	24-5
Collection Agency Requirements	11-16
Exemptions	23-55
Exemptions on Insurance	23-63
Financing Statements (Code)	7-5, 7-46
Judgment Notes	18-12
Landlords' Liens	20-31
Leasing of Personal Property	10-7
Limitations for Civil Actions	23-43
Mechanics' Liens	19-30
Personal Property Liens	20-12
Retail Instalment Sales	8-1, 8-11
Taxes—Sales and Use	25-13
Truth in Lending	9-15

MISSISSIPPI
Assignment for Benefit of Creditors	27-6
Assumed Name Laws	22-9
Bad Check Laws	21-3, 21-9
Bonds on Improvements	31-50
Bulk Transfers	26-10
Civil Penalties for Bad Check	21-14
Claims Against Estates	24-5
Collection Agency Requirements	11-16
Exemptions	23-55
Exemptions on Insurance	23-63
Financing Statements (Code)	7-5, 7-46
Judgment Notes	18-12
Landlords' Liens	20-31
Leasing of Personal Property	10-7
Limitations for Civil Actions	23-43
Mechanics' Liens	19-32
Personal Property Liens	20-13
Retail Instalment Sales	8-11
Taxes—Sales and Use	25-13

MISSOURI
Assignment for Benefit of Creditors	27-6
Assumed Name Laws	22-9
Bad Check Laws	21-3, 21-9

	PAGE
Bonds on Improvements	31-53
Bulk Transfers	26-10
Civil Penalties for Bad Check	21-14
Claims Against Estates	24-5
Collection Agency Requirements	11-17
Exemptions	23-55
Exemptions on Insurance	23-63
Financing Statements (Code)	7-7, 7-47
Judgment Notes	18-12
Landlords' Liens	20-32
Leasing of Personal Property	10-7
Limitations for Civil Actions	23-43
Mechanics' Liens	19-33
Personal Property Liens	20-13
Retail Instalment Sales	8-1, 8-11
Taxes—Sales and Use	25-14

MISTAKES
In Contracts	3-5

MONTANA
Assignment for Benefit of Creditors	27-6
Assumed Name Laws	22-10
Bad Check Laws	21-3, 21-9
Bonds on Improvements	31-54
Bulk Transfers	26-10
Claims Against Estates	24-5
Collection Agency Requirements	11-17
Exemptions	23-56
Exemptions on Insurance	23-63
Financing Statements (Code)	7-5, 7-47
Judgment Notes	18-12
Landlords' Liens	20-32
Leasing of Personal Property	10-7
Limitations for Civil Actions	23-43
Mechanics' Liens	19-34
Personal Property Liens	20-13
Retail Instalment Sales	8-1, 8-11
Taxes—Sales and Use	25-14

MUTUALITY OF CONSIDERATION 2-13

NEBRASKA
Assignment for Benefit of Creditors	27-6
Assumed Name Laws	22-10
Bad Check Laws	21-3, 21-9
Bonds on Improvements	31-58
Bulk Transfers	26-10
Civil Penalties for Bad Check	21-14
Claims Against Estates	24-5
Collection Agency Requirements	11-17
Exemptions	23-56
Exemptions on Insurance	23-63
Financing Statements (Code)	7-5, 7-48
Judgment Notes	18-12
Landlords' Liens	20-32
Leasing of Personal Property	10-8
Limitations for Civil Actions	23-43
Mechanics' Liens	19-35

INDEX-14

	PAGE
Personal Property Liens	20-14
Retail Instalment Sales	8-11
Taxes—Sales and Use	25-14
NEGOTIABLE INSTRUMENTS	18-1
Uniform Commercial Code Governs	18-1
What Instruments Negotiable	18-1
Rules of Construction	18-2
Persons Liable	18-2
Who May Execute	18-2
Indorser before Delivery	18-2
Consideration	18-2
Acceptance	18-2
Accommodation Party	18-2
Bearer Instrument	18-2
Liability of Indorsers	18-3
Negotiation	18-4
Warranties	18-4
Holder in Due Course	18-4
Collection	18-4
Presentation and Demand	18-4
Protest	18-5
Time of Payment	18-5
Discharge	18-5
Negotiable	18-6
Demand Before Suing	18-6
Defenses	18-6
Checks	18-7
VALIDITY OF STIPULATION FOR ATTORNEYS' FEES	18-7
Effect Upon Instrument	18-7
Effect Upon Negotiability	18-7
Validity and Enforceability	18-7
Interpretation by the Courts	18-8
What Law Governs	18-8
JUDGMENT NOTES	18-9
Table by States	18-10
Form	33-12
"TRADE" AND "BANK" ACCEPTANCES	18-14
Legal Nature and Incidents of Trade Acceptances	18-16
Negotiability	18-17
Right of Bank to Charge	18-17
Alternatives under Code	18-18
Necessity for Protest	18-19
Stopping Payment	18-19
Effect on Mechanics' Lien	18-19
CHECKS	18-21
Checks for Less Than One Dollar	18-21
Checks Marked "In Full of Account"	18-21
Stopping Payment	18-22
INTEREST AND USURY	18-23
Interest Table by States	18-26
CORPORATE USURY DEFENSE—BY STATES	18-37
INTEREST ON PAST DUE ACCOUNTS	18-39
INTEREST ON CREDIT SALES	18-43
FINANCE OR SERVICE CHARGES	18-43

	PAGE
CALCULATION OF INTEREST	18-44
Accommodation Paper	18-45
NEVADA	
Assignment for Benefit of Creditors	27-6
Assumed Name Laws	22-10
Bad Check Laws	21-3, 21-9
Bonds on Improvements	31-58
Bulk Transfers	26-10
Civil Penalties for Bad Check	21-14
Claims Against Estates	24-5
Collection Agency Requirements	11-18
Exemptions	23-56
Exemptions on Insurance	23-64
Financing Statements (Code)	7-5, 7-48
Judgment Notes	18-12
Landlords' Liens	20-32
Leasing of Personal Property	10-8
Limitations for Civil Actions	23-43
Mechanics' Liens	19-36
Personal Property Liens	20-15
Retail Instalment Sales	8-1, 8-12
Taxes—Sales and Use	25-14
NEW HAMPSHIRE	
Assignment for Benefit of Creditors	27-6
Assumed Name Laws	22-10
Bad Check Laws	21-3, 21-9
Bonds on Improvements	31-61
Bulk Transfers	26-10
Civil Penalties for Bad Check	21-14
Claims Against Estates	24-5
Collection Agency Requirements	11-18
Exemptions	23-56
Exemptions on Insurance	23-64
Financing Statements (Code)	7-6, 7-49
Judgment Notes	18-12
Landlords' Liens	20-32
Leasing of Personal Property	10-8
Limitations for Civil Actions	23-43
Mechanics' Liens	19-37
Personal Property Liens	20-15
Retail Instalment Sales	8-12
Taxes—Sales and Use	25-14
Uniform Commercial Code	1-2
NEW JERSEY	
Assignment for Benefit of Creditors	27-6
Assumed Name Laws	22-11
Bad Check Laws	21-3, 21-9
Bonds on Improvements	31-62
Bulk Transfers	26-10
Claims Against Estates	24-6
Collection Agency Requirements	11-19
Exemptions	23-57
Exemptions on Insurance	23-64
Financing Statements (Code)	7-6, 7-50
Judgment Notes	18-12
Landlords' Liens	20-32
Leasing of Personal Property	10-8
Limitations for Civil Actions	23-43

INDEX-15

	PAGE
Mechanics' Liens	19-37
Personal Property Liens	20-16
Retail Instalment Sales	8-1, 8-12
Taxes—Sales and Use	25-14
Truth in Lending	9-15

NEW MEXICO

Assignment for Benefit of Creditors	27-7
Assumed Name Laws	22-11
Bad Check Laws	21-3, 21-9
Bonds on Improvements	31-66
Bulk Transfers	26-10
Civil Penalties for Bad Check	21-14
Claims Against Estates	24-6
Collection Agency Requirements	11-19
Exemptions	23-57
Exemptions on Insurance	23-64
Financing Statement (Code)	7-7, 7-50
Judgment Notes	18-13
Landlords' Liens	20-32
Leasing of Personal Property	10-8
Limitations for Civil Actions	23-43
Mechanics' Liens	19-40
Personal Property Liens	20-17
Retail Instalment Sales	8-1, 8-12
Taxes—Sales and Use	25-14
Truth in Lending	9-15

NEW YORK

Assignment for Benefit of Creditors	27-7
Assumed Name Laws	22-11
Bad Check Laws	21-3, 21-10
Bonds on Improvements	31-67
Bulk Transfers	26-11
Claims Against Estates	24-6
Collection Agency Requirements	11-20
Exemptions	23-57
Exemptions on Insurance	23-64
Financing Statements (Code)	7-5, 7-51
Judgment Notes	18-13
Landlords' Liens	20-32
Leasing of Personal Property	10-8
Limitations for Civil Actions	23-43
Mechanics' Liens	19-41
Personal Property Liens	20-18
Retail Instalment Sales	8-1, 8-12
Taxes—Sales and Use	25-15
Truth in Lending	9-16

NORTH CAROLINA

Assignment for Benefit of Creditors	27-7
Assumed Name Laws	22-11
Bad Check Laws	21-3, 21-10
Bonds on Improvements	31-73
Bulk Transfers	26-11
Civil Penalties for Bad Checks	21-14
Claims Against Estates	24-6
Collection Agency Requirements	11-20
Exemptions	23-57
Exemptions on Insurance	23-64
Financing Statements (Code)	7-5, 7-51

	PAGE
Judgment Notes	18-13
Landlords' Liens	20-32
Leasing of Personal Property	10-9
Limitations for Civil Actions	23-43
Mechanics' Liens	19-45
Personal Property Liens	20-19
Retail Instalment Sales	8-1, 8-12
Taxes—Sales and Use	25-15

NORTH DAKOTA

Assignment for Benefit of Creditors	27-7
Assumed Name Laws	22-12
Bad Check Laws	21-3, 21-10
Bonds on Improvements	31-76
Bulk Transfers	26-11
Civil Penalties for Bad Check	21-14
Claims Against Estates	24-6
Collection Agency Requirements	11-21
Exemptions	23-57
Exemptions on Insurance	23-64
Financing Statements (Code)	7-5, 7-52
Judgment Notes	18-13
Landlords' Liens	20-32
Leasing of Personal Property	10-9
Limitations for Civil Actions	23-44
Mechanics' Liens	19-46
Personal Property Liens	20-19
Retail Instalment Sales	8-1, 8-13
Taxes—Sales and Use	25-15
Truth in Lending	9-16

OFFER (Contracts)

OFFER (Contracts)	2-1
Communication of	2-2
Termination of Offer	2-3
Acceptance of	2-3
Unilateral Offers	2-4
Bilateral Offers	2-4
Orders Solicited by Salesmen	2-4
Rejection of Offer	2-5
Counteroffer	2-5
Communication of Acceptance	2-6
Acceptance by Telegraph	2-6
Silence as Acceptance	2-7

OHIO

Assignment for Benefit of Creditors	27-7
Assumed Name Laws	22-12
Bad Check Laws	21-3, 21-10
Bonds on Improvements	31-77
Bulk Transfers	26-11
Claims Against Estates	24-6
Collection Agency Requirements	11-21
Exemptions	23-57
Exemptions on Insurance	23-64
Financing Statements (Code)	7-5, 7-53
Judgment Notes	18-13
Landlords' Liens	20-32
Leasing of Personal Property	10-9
Limitations for Civil Actions	23-44
Mechanics' Liens	19-47
Personal Property Liens	20-20

INDEX-16

	PAGE
Retail Instalment Sales	8-1, 8-13
Taxes—Sales and Use	25-15

OKLAHOMA
Assignment for Benefit of Creditors	27-7
Assumed Name Laws	22-12
Bad Check Laws	21-3, 21-10
Bonds on Improvements	31-81
Bulk Transfers	26-11
Claims Against Estates	24-6
Collection Agency Requirements	11-22
Exemptions	23-58
Exemptions on Insurance	23-64
Financing Statements (Code)	7-5, 7-53
Judgment Notes	18-13
Landlords' Liens	20-32
Leasing of Personal Property	10-9
Limitations for Civil Actions	23-44
Mechanics' Liens	19-49
Personal Property Liens	20-20
Retail Instalment Sales	8-1, 8-13
Taxes—Sales and Use	25-16
Truth in Lending	9-16

OREGON
Assignment for Benefit of Creditors	27-7
Assumed Name Laws	22-13
Bad Check Laws	21-3, 21-10
Bonds on Improvements	31-82
Bulk Transfers	26-11
Civil Penalties for Bad Check	21-14
Claims Against Estates	24-6
Collection Agency Requirements	11-22
Exemptions	23-58
Exemptions on Insurance	23-64
Financing Statements (Code)	7-5, 7-54
Judgment Notes	18-13
Landlords' Liens	20-32
Leasing of Personal Property	10-9
Limitations for Civil Actions	23-44
Mechanics' Liens	19-50
Personal Property Liens	20-21
Retail Instalment Sales	8-13
Taxes—Sales and Use	25-16
Truth in Lending	9-17

OUTLINE OF MECHANICS OF SECURED TRANSACTIONS
	7-2

PARTNERSHIPS
	15-1
Uniform Partnership Acts	15-2
State Statutes Apply	15-2
Partnership Contract	15-3
Dissolution of	15-4
LIMITED PARTNERSHIPS	15-6

PENNSYLVANIA
Assignment for Benefit of Creditors	27-7
Assumed Name Laws	22-13
Bad Check Laws	21-3, 21-10
Bonds on Improvements	31-84
Bulk Transfers	26-11

	PAGE
Claims Against Estates	24-7
Collection Agency Requirements	11-23
Exemptions	23-58
Exemptions on Insurance	23-64
Financing Statements (Code)	7-5, 7-54
Judgment Notes	18-13
Landlords' Liens	20-33
Leasing of Personal Property	16-10
Limitations for Civil Actions	23-44
Mechanics' Liens	19-52
Personal Property Liens	20-22
Retail Instalment Sales	8-13
Taxes—Sales and Use	25-16

PERFORMANCE BOND
	30-3

PERSONAL PROPERTY LIENS
	20-1

POSTAL LAWS (See Libel)
	23-6

POSTDATED CHECKS
	21-4

POWER OF ATTORNEY (form)
	33-10

PRINCIPAL AND AGENT
	16-1
How Agents Are Appointed	16-1
Liability of Agents	16-2

PROCEDURE IN BANKRUPTCY
	28-1

PROMISSORY NOTES (form)
	33-11

PROOF OF CLAIM (form)
	33-5

PUERTO RICO
Bond Law	31-88

REJECTION OF OFFER
	2-5

RELEASE
Of Lease of Personal Property (form)	33-9
General (form)	33-10

REPLEVIN
	23-34

REPRESENTATIONS (Credit)
	4-5

RETAIL INSTALMENT SALES
	8-1
Contract Requirements	8-1
Licensing Provisions	8-3
Insurance Provisions	8-4
Refinancing, Extensions, Rescheduling	8-5
Remedies of Seller	8-5
Penalties	8-7
Filing and Recording	8-7

RETURN OF GOODS
	6-3

RHODE ISLAND
Assignment for Benefit of Creditors	27-8
Assumed Name Laws	22-14
Bad Check Laws	21-3, 21-10
Bonds on Improvements	31-90
Bulk Transfers	26-11
Claims Against Estates	24-7
Collection Agency Requirements	11-23
Exemptions	23-58

INDEX-17

	PAGE
Exemptions on Insurance	23-65
Financing Statements (Code)	7-5, 7-55
Judgment Notes	18-13
Landlords' Liens	20-33
Leasing of Personal Property	10-10
Limitations for Civil Actions	23-44
Mechanics' Liens	19-53
Personal Property Liens	20-22
Retail Instalment Sales	8-1, 8-13
Taxes—Sales and Use	25-16

RIGHTS OF MARRIED WOMEN 2-11, 15-8

ROBINSON-PATMAN ACT 13-5

SALES, Chattel Mortgages	6-7
Sales Contracts, Conditional	6-5

SALES AND USE TAXES
General	25-1
Sales Taxes	25-1
Use Taxes	25-2
State Taxation of Interstate Transactions	25-2
Court Decisions	25-2
Federal Legislation	25-8
State Statutes	25-9
Alabama	25-9
Alaska	25-9
Arizona	25-9
Arkansas	25-10
California	25-10
Colorado	25-10
Connecticut	25-10
Delaware	25-10
Dist. of Col.	25-11
Florida	25-11
Georgia	25-11
Hawaii	25-11
Idaho	25-11
Illinois	25-11
Indiana	25-12
Iowa	25-12
Kansas	25-12
Kentucky	25-12
Louisiana	25-12
Maine	25-13
Maryland	25-13
Mass.	25-13
Michigan	25-13
Minnesota	25-13
Mississippi	25-13
Missouri	25-14
Montana	25-14
Nebraska	25-14
Nevada	25-14
New Hampshire	25-14
New Jersey	25-14
New Mexico	25-14
New York	25-15
North Carolina	25-15
North Dakota	25-15
Ohio	25-15
Oklahoma	25-16
Oregon	25-16
Pennsylvania	25-16
Rhode Island	25-16
South Carolina	25-16
South Dakota	25-16
Tennessee	25-17
Texas	25-17
Utah	25-17
Vermont	25-17
Virginia	25-17
Washington	25-18
West Virginia	25-18
Wisconsin	25-18
Wyoming	25-18

SALES UNDER CODE 1-3, 1-28
General Provisions	1-28
Form, Formation, Readjustment	1-6, 1-30
General Obligation, Construction	1-33
Title, Creditors, Purchasers	1-43

	PAGE
Performance	1-46
Breach, Repudiation, Excuse	1-51
Remedies	1-56

SALES CONTRACTS 1-28

SALES IN BULK (See Bulk Transfers) 26-1

SALES ON SECURITY 6-1
Bailments	6-1
Consignments	6-2
Leases	6-4
Trust Receipts	6-5
Conditional Sales Contracts	6-5
Chattel Mortgages	6-7
Assignment of Accounts Receivable	6-9
Factors' Liens Laws	6-10
Secured Transactions Under Art.	7-1

SALESMEN 14-9

SATISFACTION OF MECHANICS'
LIEN (form) 33-11

SECURED TRANSACTIONS SUPERSEDED BY UCC ARTICLE 9 .. 6-1

SECURED TRANSACTIONS UNDER CODE ARTICLE 9 7-1
Outline of Mechanics	7-2
Creating the Security Interest	7-2
Perfecting the Security Interest	7-2
Financing Statement Form	7-5
Financing Statement (Form) (Massachusetts, etc.)	7-6
Financing Statement (Form) (Indiana, etc.)	7-7
When Filing Is Required	7-7
Instruments or Documents	7-8
Place of Filing, Fees	7-9, 7-30–7-33
Formal Requisites of Financing Statements	7-10
Formal Requisites of Amendments	7-10
Duration of Filing; Lapse	7-12
Continuation Statements	7-12
Termination	7-13
Assignment of Security Interest	7-14
Release of Collateral	7-14
What Law Governs	7-15
Property Brought into State	7-15
Rights of Third Parties	7-17
Rights of Buyer of Goods	7-18
Rights of Purchaser of Chattel Paper and Nonnegotiable Instruments	7-18
Rights of Purchasers of Instruments and Documents	7-19
Priority of Certain Liens	7-19
Priority Among Conflicting Security Interests in Same Collateral	7-19
Priority of Security Interest in Fixtures	7-20
Priority when Goods Are Affixed to Other Goods	7-22

INDEX-18

	PAGE		PAGE
Priority when Goods Are Commingled or Processed	7-22	SOUTH DAKOTA	
		Assignment for Benefit of Creditors	27-8
Priority Subject to Subordination	7-23	Assumed Name Laws	22-14
Secured Party Not Obligated on Contract of Debtor	7-23	Bad Check Laws	21-3, 21-10
		Bonds on Improvements	31-94
Defenses Against Assignee: Modification of Contract After Notification of Assignment; Term Prohibiting Assignment Ineffective; Identification and Proof of Assignment	7-23	Bulk Transfers	26-11
		Claims Against Estates	24-7
		Collection Agency Requirements	11-24
		Exemptions	23-58
		Exemptions on Insurance	23-65
		Financing Statements (Code)	7-51, 7-56
When Security Interest Attaches; After-Acquired Property; Future Advances	7-25	Judgment Notes	18-13
		Landlords' Liens	20-33
		Leasing of Personal Property	10-10
Use or Disposition of Collateral Without Accounting Permissible	7-25	Limitations for Civil Actions	23-44
		Mechanics' Liens	19-54
Agreement Not to Assert Defenses Against Assignee; Modification of Sale Warranties	7-25	Personal Property Liens	20-23
		Retail Instalment Sales	8-14
		Taxes—Sales and Use	25-16
Rights and Duties When Collateral Is in Secured Party's Possession	7-25	SPECIMEN INSTRUMENTS	33-1
Request for Statement of Account or List of Collateral	7-26	STATE ANTITRUST LAWS	13-14
		STATE BOND LAWS	31-1
Secured Party's Right upon Default	7-27	STATE CONSUMER PROTECTION	9-20–9-23
INFORMATION BY FILING OFFICER	7-30		
FEES PAYABLE TO FILING OFFICER (by States)	7-30	STATE LAWS ON COLLECTION AGENCIES	11-3
FILING REQUIREMENTS ON FINANCING STATEMENTS (by States)	7-33	STATE TAXATION OF INTERSTATE COMMERCE	25-2
1972 REVISIONS	7-27		
		SUBAGENTS	16-2
SHERMAN ACT	13-1	SUBORDINATION (Form)	33-13
SIGNATURES	4-15	SUIT, Collection by	23-15
SOLDIERS' AND SAILORS' CIVIL RELIEF ACT	23-66	TAXES, Sales and Use	25-1
		TENNESSEE	
SOUTH CAROLINA		Assignment for Benefit of Creditors	27-8
Assignment for Benefit of Creditors	27-8	Assumed Name Laws	22-15
Assumed Name Laws	22-14	Bad Check Laws	21-3, 21-11
Bad Check Laws	21-3, 21-10	Bonds on Improvements	31-95
Bonds on Improvements	31-92	Bulk Transfers	26-11
Bulk Transfers	26-11	Claims Against Estates	24-7
Civil Penalties for Bad Check	21-14	Collection Agency Requirements	11-24
Claims Against Estates	24-7	Exemptions	23-58
Collection Agency Requirements	11-23	Exemptions on Insurance	23-65
Exemptions	23-58	Financing Statements (Code)	7-7, 7-56
Exemptions on Insurance	23-65	Judgment Notes	18-13
Financing Statements (Code)	7-9, 7-55	Landlords' Liens	20-33
Judgment Notes	18-13	Leasing of Personal Property	10-10
Landlords' Liens	20-33	Limitations for Civil Actions	23-44
Leasing of Personal Property	10-10	Mechanics' Liens	19-55
Limitations for Civil Actions	23-44	Personal Property Liens	20-24
Mechanics' Liens	19-54	Retail Instalment Sales	8-1, 8-14
Personal Property Liens	20-22	Taxes—Sales and Use	25-17
Retail Instalment Sales	8-13	Truth in Lending	9-17
Taxes—Sales and Use	25-16		
Truth in Lending	9-17	TERMS OF PAYMENT	5-3

INDEX-19

TEXAS
Assignment for Benefit of Creditors	27-8
Assumed Name Laws	22-15
Bad Check Laws	21-3, 21-11
Bonds on Improvements	31-98
Bulk Transfers	26-11
Claims Against Estates	24-7
Collection Agency Requirements	11-24
Exemptions	23-59
Exemptions on Insurance	23-65
Financing Statements (Code)	7-5, 7-57
Judgment Notes	18-14
Landlords' Liens	20-33
Leasing of Personal Property	10-10
Limitations for Civil Actions	23-44
Mechanics' Liens	19-56
Personal Property Liens	20-24
Retail Instalment Sales	8-1, 8-14
Taxes—Sales and Use	25-17
Time Price Doctrine	18-43
Truth in Lending	9-17

TOLLING OF STATUTES
23-38–23-40

TRADE ACCEPTANCES
18-16

TRADE REGULATION LAWS
	13-1
Objects of Antitrust Laws	13-1
Sherman Act	13-1
Clayton Act	13-4
Robinson-Patman Act	13-5
Federal Trade Commission Act	13-12
1976 Antitrust Act	13-14
State Antitrust Laws	13-14
Fair Trade Acts	13-15
Antitrust Laws and Exchange of Credit Information	13-16
Court Decisions	13-18
Membership in Credit Groups	13-21

TRUST RECEIPTS
6-5

TRUTH IN LENDING
9-8–9-17

UNIFORM COMMERCIAL CODE
	1-1
Article 1: General Provisions	1-2, 1-21
Article 2: Sales	1-3, 1-28
Article 3: Commercial Paper	1-7, 1-62
Article 4: Bank Deposits and Collections	1-9, 1-62
Article 5: Letters of Credit	1-12, 1-63
Article 6: Bulk Transfers	1-12, 1-69
Article 7: Warehouse Receipts, Bill of Lading, Other Documents	1-13, 1-69
Article 8: Investment Securities	1-14, 1-76
Article 9: Secured Transactions	1-15, 1-76
1972 Revision	7-27
Article 10: Effective Date	1-76
Article 11: Effective Date and Transition Provisions	1-76

UNIFORM CONSUMER CREDIT CODE
9-24

UNIFORM STATE LAWS; UNIFORM SALES ACT
1-1

U.S. DISTRICT COURTS
32-1

USE TAXES
25-1

USURY AND INTEREST
	18-23
Corporate Usury Defense	18-37

UTAH
Assignment for Benefit of Creditors	27-8
Assumed Name Laws	22-15
Bad Check Laws	21-3, 21-11
Bonds on Improvements	31-104
Bulk Transfers	26-11
Civil Penalties for Bad Check	21-14
Claims Against Estates	24-7
Collection Agency Requirements	11-25
Exemptions	23-59
Exemptions on Insurance	23-65
Financing Statements (Code)	7-5, 7-58
Judgment Notes	18-14
Landlords' Liens	20-33
Leasing of Personal Property	10-10
Limitations for Civil Actions	23-44
Mechanics' Liens	19-58
Personal Property Liens	20-24
Retail Instalment Sales	8-1, 8-14
Taxes—Sales and Use	25-17
Truth in Lending	9-17

VERMONT
Assignment for Benefit of Creditors	27-8
Assumed Name Laws	22-16
Bad Check Laws	21-3, 21-11
Bonds on Improvements	31-106
Bulk Transfers	26-11
Claims Against Estates	24-8
Collection Agency Requirements	11-25
Exemptions	23-59
Exemptions on Insurance	23-65
Financing Statements (Code)	7-7, 7-58
Judgment Notes	18-14
Landlords' Liens	20-33
Leasing of Personal Property	10-10
Limitations for Civil Actions	23-44
Mechanics' Liens	19-59
Personal Property Liens	20-25
Retail Instalment Sales	8-1, 8-14
Taxes—Sales and Use	25-17

VIRGINIA
Assignment for Benefit of Creditors	27-9
Assumed Name Laws	22-16
Bad Check Laws	21-3, 21-11
Bonds on Improvements	31-107
Bulk Transfers	26-11
Civil Penalties for Bad Check	21-14
Claims Against Estates	24-8
Collection Agency Requirements	11-25
Exemptions	23-59

INDEX-20

	PAGE
Exemptions on Insurance	23-65
Financing Statements (Code)	7-5, 7-59
Judgment Notes	18-14
Landlords' Liens	20-33
Leasing of Personal Property	10-11
Limitations for Civil Actions	23-44
Mechanics' Liens	19-59
Personal Property Liens	20-25
Retail Instalment Sales	8-1, 8-14
Taxes—Sales and Use	25-17

WAGES
Assignment (Form)	33-3
Assignment, Gen. Discussion	4-6
Assignment, Table of State Laws	4-8–4-14
Wage Earners' Exemptions	23-46
Waiver of Exemptions	23-46

WASHINGTON AGENCIES
That Finance Foreign Trade	29-1

WASHINGTON STATE
Assignment for Benefit of Creditors	27-10
Assumed Name Laws	22-16
Bad Check Laws	21-3, 21-11
Bonds on Improvements	31-109
Bulk Transfers	26-11
Claims Against Estates	24-8
Collection Agency Requirements	11-26
Exemptions	23-60
Exemptions on Insurance	23-65
Financing Statements (Code)	7-5, 7-59
Judgment Notes	18-14
Landlords' Liens	20-33
Leasing of Personal Property	10-11
Limitations for Civil Actions	23-44
Mechanics' Liens	19-61
Personal Property Liens	20-25
Retail Instalment Sales	8-1, 8-15
Taxes—Sales and Use	25-18
Truth in Lending	9-17

WEST VIRGINIA
Assignment for Benefit of Creditors	27-9
Assumed Name Laws	22-16
Bad Check Laws	21-3, 21-11
Bonds on Improvements	31-114
Bulk Transfers	26-11
Civil Penalties for Bad Check	21-14
Claims Against Estates	24-8
Collection Agency Requirements	11-26
Exemptions	23-60
Exemptions on Insurance	23-65

	PAGE
Financing Statements (Code)	7-5, 7-60
Judgment Notes	18-14
Landlords' Liens	20-33
Leasing of Personal Property	10-11
Limitations for Civil Actions	23-44
Mechanics' Liens	19-62
Personal Property Liens	20-27
Retail Instalment Sales	8-1, 8-15
Taxes—Sales and Use	25-18

WISCONSIN
Assignment for Benefit of Creditors	27-9
Assumed Name Laws	22-17
Bad Check Laws	21-3, 21-11
Bonds on Improvements	31-115
Bulk Transfers	26-11
Claims Against Estates	24-8
Collection Agency Requirements	11-27
Exemptions	23-60
Exemptions on Insurance	23-65
Financing Statements (Code)	7-5, 7-60
Judgment Notes	18-14
Landlords' Liens	20-33
Leasing of Personal Property	10-11
Limitations for Civil Actions	23-45
Mechanics' Liens	19-62
Personal Property Liens	20-27
Retail Instalment Sales	8-1, 8-15
Taxes—Sales and Use	25-18
Truth in Lending	9-18

WYOMING
Assignment for Benefit of Creditors	27-9
Assumed Name Laws	22-17
Bad Check Laws	21-3, 21-11
Bonds on Improvements	31-117
Bulk Transfers	26-11
Civil Penalties for Bad Check	21-14
Claims Against Estates	24-8
Collection Agency Requirements	11-27
Exemptions	23-60
Exemptions on Insurance	23-66
Financing Statements (Code)	7-5, 7-61
Judgment Notes	18-14
Landlords' Liens	20-33
Leasing of Personal Property	10-11
Limitations for Civil Actions	23-45
Mechanics' Liens	19-64
Personal Property Liens	20-28
Retail Instalment Sales	8-15
Taxes—Sales and Use	25-18
Truth in Lending	9-18